THE DEVIATION

AND

RESTORATION

OF THE

HUMAN RACE

BY:
THEODORE VERHEVEN

The Expulsion from Eden

The Prodigal Son

First Edition   2006
Second Edition   2011
Third Edition   2016
Printed in the United States of America

Edited and typed by J.J. Rodgers
Cover design by author

Library of Congress Control No: 2006927824

International Standard Book Number
ISBN - 10: 0-9786612-4-9
ISBN - 13: 978-0-9786612-4-3

Biblical quotations are from the
Revised Standard Version, Copyrighted ©
1946, 1952, 1971, 1973, and used by permission of
the Division of Christian Education of the
National Council of the Churches of Christ
in the United States of America.

This Book is Dedicated

To

God the Creator

Our

Eternal Parents

Who Will Always Love Us

Without their continual inspiration,
encouragement, and Guidance, this
book could not have been written.

TABLE OF CONTENTS

vi

viii

Foreword

The main purpose of writing this book is that the reader will understand him/herself better and is no longer confused about religious beliefs and opinions, to do away with much of the misunderstanding of Bible interpretation and theology, and to put it in a language everyone can understand. Also, to fill the void between the rapid development of science, from which people profit without accepting the ethical consequences, and religion which concerns itself with the moral and spiritual development of the people. Because the education system follows mainly materialistic sciences, that is, the development and training of the mental faculties, young people are being taught to seek and look for information and instructions outside themselves. They, therefore, do not know that they should also cultivate their more inner faculties and open their "eyes and ears" to the unmanifested Source of all life. Being continually distracted by technology, they are held adrift from their divine center and God. To conceal their inner emptiness, anxiety, hopelessness, despair, and insecurity, they drink (or) take drugs, etc., which is nothing else but a substitute for the "high" of spiritual life.

This manuscript is also written with those in mind who do not have the time to go deep within to seek for the meaning and purpose of their lives, for those whom are disappointed in religion, and also those who want to understand the deeper meaning of their religion and philosophies as being good and divine. Many religions are alike in essence, while different in forms. Judaism, Islam, and nominal Christianity are non-mystical religions, in which the sacred is encountered by the individual outside rather than within themselves. We find esotericism in many systems of belief: Kabbalism and Hassidism in Judaism, Sufism in Islam, Mystics and Saints in Christianity, and many mystics are also found in Hinduism, Buddhism, and other esoteric groups. Many of them believe that the way shower is the Christ Spirit who lives within humans and who appears in the form of our highest ideal, and for many, that is the Universal Christ. Others may look for a bodily avatar, and for them, one will be provided. This writing clarifies and fulfills much of the teaching of Christianity and other non-Christian religions and reaches beyond Christianity to a more universal Christ. It not only attempts to explain the inner meanings of symbols and parables but also integrates the teachings of the Bible with concepts of other religions, philosophies, and with a branch of psychology called the "transpersonal". In the latter, God is often called the Universal Self, and the Soul or Divine Spirit the transpersonal Self.

NOTE: We can consider ourselves truly educated when we are not only intellectually developed but also spiritually.

This work gives an overview of the stages of growth of the personality or ego mainly in its fallen state. After it has become developed and purified, it becomes the dwelling of the newly generated Soul or divine center of our being. The Soul or Spirit of Christ also grows through the stages of growth toward maturity as the first step in its eternal development. This paper does not make the mistake of disregarding the old base of morality and spirituality but function on that foundation, thus, not spirituality without ethics or moral standards. The origin and nature of evil should not be dismissed or passed over but must be dealt with if the human race is to progress. Thus, the inherited evil which is deeply embedded in the human spirit or psyche should be completely rooted out; otherwise, it will grow again when committing the same sin. The first step to remove it from our being is to know how it originated and what its nature is. Thus, the personality needs to be purified, not only by good behavior but also by right emotion, desires, and thought, thus clearing the channel between the lower self (ego) and the budding Higher Self or Soul.

We may ask, "If humans have a deep desire to be one with God and be good, why are they also living an evil life separate from God?" How did evil, which is the cause of moral laxity and spiritual emptiness, have so much power over our lives, and how can I distinguish between good and evil forces? How is God, since the beginning, restoring the fallen world of God's creation? What is the ideal world like, and how can I help our Eternal Parents to implement Their most important Divine Plan?

The earth personality consists of the physical, emotional, and mental selves or mind complex and is formed of what one feels, thinks, and believes, which is reflected in the root, the stem, and the leaves of the plant, while the flower represents one's Higher Self or Divine Spirit. Through centuries of unchecked evolvement, the unrestored good/evil personality and its sensibility has become overdeveloped, especially after the Renaissance in Western Society. This development was in particular emphasized in the nineteenth century, when human progress was measured by the rational and material life and less so in its ethical, moral, and spiritual development. Today, to live for sensory pleasures and sensuality has become most important. They are taught directly and indirectly to measure success in life not by personal meaning but by fortune, power, fame, and images. This is all for greater ego gratification and inflation. Individuals whom have not known divine life and backsliders may experience "being in love", which makes them happy but attaches them to the person they love. At a lower level, humans "fall in love" instead of growing in love, and many do not know the difference between authentic love and the lower desire or the lust of the eye, and the lust of the flesh. Thousands of couples are living together out of wedlock and sneer at the God-ordained institution of marriage, and sexual perversion is at an all-time high.

REMARK: Of all the people living at that time, Adam and Eve were the first pair which had the potential to attain spiritual perfection. However, by "eating" the symbolic fruit before they were mature, they became like the symbolic "Tree of the Knowledge of Good and Evil" instead of the "Tree of Life".

Many sections of the book are used to explain the life of the good and good/evil personality, of which the latter lives according to the "spirit of the world", with its predominant evil way of life. This is contrary to divine life, the life of a superman/woman who is in control of and uses the personality as its vehicle. Unlike the lower selves which live more or less the lives of separation (as an island), the Higher Selves are completely united with each other (below the surface), as they are firmly connected with the "rock-bottom of universality". They no longer commit harmful and wicked acts and are certainly capable of loving others as themselves because "we are them and they are us, and hurting another is hurting yourself". For them, the law of karma, which is a most effective criminal justice system, is no longer operative as it is for those whom are living the life of the personality and whom see themselves as separate.

God , who has His dwelling place in the Divine Spirit, which latter lives within the inner personality or human spirit, is not ready to favor any human being (no respecter of persons), because He/She lives within everyone, even as a Spirit Particle. When God helps someone, the Spirits also assist anybody and anything at the same time. The Creator, who is in essence male and female, perfectly unified, consists of Spirit and body (universe) and resides within all of creation and is manifested to its fullest degree in restored humans. It is assumed here that God (who designed and created everything from simple to complex) exists and no attempt is made to prove it. Intellectual understanding may present information about God, but spiritual understanding knows God. To know God who is continually expanding and reproducing is not only knowing the Truth but especially knowing their living Spirits (the Spirit of the Father and Holy Spirit) personally by everyday experiences.

NOTE: From the above, we may conclude that humans have been given a choice, to either accept the life of the personality or divine life ,that of the shining moon or the radiating sun. In the latter case, the exploration of deep inner space, or the dimension of the divine world, has begun.

We may ask," How can I know the God of Love, Intelligence, and Will and get close to Him?" Why does He as a self-sustaining Being create human beings and the universe in His image? What is my relationship with God and the universe? Could He be not only a divine Master or Father but also a Mother to me as well, who needs us as we need them as their precious children?

Truth is the real nature of the Divine Spirit or Soul, when the dormant spark of divinity is first awakened and is then virgin born as a Christ child. It is loved and fed with the pure Word of God or Truth. This Truth body or Soul lives forever and is truly the fountain of eternal youth.

This discourse is also written for the increasing number of individuals whom wants to know more definitely about immortality than a mere promise of heaven. They want to know what happens to them when they die, the trip everyone is going to make. Do I see my deceased loved ones again? Do my inner personality and memory survive the death of the body? Where do I go when passing away from the earth dimension, and what is life after death like in this undiscovered country? Is there a heaven or a hell? While living on earth, how do I communicate with the dead, or rather, the living, without any adverse effects, and is it right to do so? Is it possible to communicate with spirits in a sleep state when my spirit separates more or less from my body? How do I deal with earthbound spirits and evil spirits? Throughout the book, many of those questions and many more have been answered and almost all psychic phenomena in the Bible have been explained. It also makes plain how to open and vitalize our dormant psychic and divine senses so that a greater part of the environment becomes known. It also answers the big question: How did Jesus come back after His crucifixion?

REMARK: As the Soul assimilates only what is pure, the human spirit or psyche is fed intellectual food, which can be right or wrong, and the body takes in physical food. Each body has its own set of senses and also has its teachers and healers.

As parapsychology has investigated much of psychic phenomena, material scientists are beginning to show interest in the more dense or etheric dimension of life, which ether is found throughout the macrocosmic universe and is formed in a human being when taking its first breath. It is the inner constitution of a plant and is beside the psychic constituent, the more dense body of an animal. Let us explore inner space or the etheric and the psychic dimension of life.

The truth found in this book is not the whole truth because the flow of truth is never ending. However, Truth itself is unchanging, and a new revelation and expression of a deeper truth is given at times when the people in their understanding and awakening are ready to receive it. But it is always on the foundation of an older expression, fulfilling and expanding the latter. Intellectual theory, for example, may exist for a long time but fade away when a new theory comes into existence. Religious beliefs may continue for a thousand years but will eventually lose its unfading luster because relative truth cannot endure when a new expression of truth arises. Religion should, therefore, not make of the truth they have a closed system, with no open door to accept a higher truth.

To understand the Bible interpretation and spiritual philosophy, the reader is asked to have an open inquiring mind and a desire to explore new dimensions. It is only when you are continually and freely observing, inquiring, and learning that truth is found. Become a seeker of Truth, and be independent of any human authority. Be a more powerful and unique person instead of an imitation of someone else, and God loves you more as a select individual to join God's family as valuable co-creators and co-operators of His Divine Plan.

Through many life experiences, older people know that there is no freedom without the law, and the more developed a person is, the freer he/she has become, not only physically but also psychologically and spiritually. They also know that the acquisition obtained by dishonesty and cheating are unsustainable gains and will soon be taken away or become lost. It is not possible to avoid this because each time an individual misbehaves in action, emotion, and thought, the karmic consequences of one's misconduct become attached to the person and carries with him or her. However, a few older persons who identify with their physical bodies and grow old without maturing are often depressed and think that life will soon be all over. Other elders whom are more developed tell the unhappy few, "If the outer personality is growing older, the inner personality is becoming ever beautiful and wiser." They are all digesting their life experiences so that they will be absorbed and assimilated in their human spirits and Souls. The wise ones also know that life on earth is a workshop, a boot camp, or training ground. Humans grow faster on earth as in the afterlife because there are more challenges, changes, and problems to overcome, such as the struggle for survival, unfolding creative abilities and talents by competing. When doing right, they develop virtues, gaining valuable qualities, building character, and ultimately becoming mature sons and daughters of God.

NOTE: The author hopes that this writing articulates and rings true for you and resonate and reverberate what is already within you, that I have put myself out of the way (my personality) so that the Universal Christ will become more real to you.

As the opening pages recount the creation and fall of humans, the successive pages (with intervention of related subjects – see Table of Contents) tell of the steps God has taken to recover from that fall. The author has described in detail why humans could never reach their potential and is, therefore, always been seeking for completion and integration of their alienated parts. The writer also gives many examples of how the evil nature of humans is being expressed and exposed in daily living while explaining many related Bible verses. He also believes that evil forces within and without humans will do everything they can to keep you from benefiting from this book. They will distract you and detour you and will arrange interruptions. This book is a declaration of independence from all evil forces which are continually conspiring against God and His plan of salvation. They have used the human race to do their bidding and have enslaved them at all levels. All humans are in great need to be delivered from bondage.

We now declare war against all evil forces. Come! Let us enlist in the army of God.

REMARK: The last chapter "Why We Should Pray and Read the Bible" is very important in building a strong relationship with God and standing strong in our fight against the evil in the world.

Theodore Verheven
December 25, 2010

The Fall of Lucifer, Eve and Adam

After having served God for a long period of time, [#1]Lucifer the archangel began to resent obeying God's laws (Ezek. 28:14,15), especially at the time of the [#2]creation of Adam and Eve. During that period he came to know that Adam as a child of God, upon perfection, would rule over him (1 Cor. 6:3). Lucifer became the adversary, or satan, when he rebelled against the sovereignty and principle of God, wanting to dominate Adam and Eve as he did over the angelic world (Isa. 14:12-14; Rev. 12:9).

The story began when the serpent (symbol of satan) "deceived Eve by his cunning" (2 Cor. 11:3; 1 Tim. 2:14) not to believe in the Word of God but in his words, by distorting the truth of God. By saying; "Did God say, 'You shall not eat of any tree of the garden?'" (Gen. 3:1), he put doubts in Eve's mind and confused her about God's command to eat of all the trees, except one. Lucifer further implied that God does not love her, by not allowing her to do what she wanted, and He can therefore not be trusted. In this way satan attempted to take over the place of God and become her god (2 Cor. 4:4), which is the sin of [#3]pride, and "goes before a fall" (Proverbs 16:18). It is also the beginning of the worship of false gods or creatures (Rom. 1:22-25). He also persuaded immature Eve, by appealing to her emotion, to decide for herself –while she was still a teenager– what is good and evil. This would enable her to pass moral judgment on others; to choose self rule over God's rule, doing her own will instead of God's Will, and thus becoming [#4]self-reliant and independent of God's direction. Impressed by his personality, position, prestige, influence, and power, Eve began to respond to his persuasion and "possessive love".

Instead of feeling a respectful love for Eve, as a teacher has for a student, the relationship between Lucifer and Eve evolved in a mutual and consenting one. Lucifer then completely won her over, by seducing her human spirit (psyche) to join with his "spirit" in an unlawful [#5]sexual union (Matt. 5:28). She then received his evil psychic elements and became like him in character. Later, in a similar fashion, the "sons of God" – fallen angels – took wives of the "daugh-

---

[#1] to [#5] See Appendix.

ters of men" (Gen. 6:1-4), whom forsook or "left their proper dwelling" place (Jude 6). Those demons and human spirits whom had intercourse with [#6]earthly women were generally called incubuses in the Middle Ages.

Thereafter, Eve gave some of [#7]"the fruit" to Adam, whose life was mainly ruled by his [#8]personality or ego, by first seducing the pure human spirit or psyche of Adam. Acting on her feelings, she "pulled him down" to her level. Adam looked on Eve as the only source of his love or rather the object and source of his sensation, and began to see himself as separate from God. The emotional energy between each other developed in an intense desire and passion, which overwhelmed and blinded their reason. They, as teenagers, fell in love, or rather lust, and committed [#9]fornication without God's blessing because their act was initiated by satan, and their [#10]Divine Spirit or Soul was undeveloped. Both their personalities became contaminated with the evil qualities of satan, or original sin, and were no longer pure.

"Then the eyes of both were opened, and they knew that they were naked" (Gen. 3:7), by becoming sexually aware in the sense of wrongfulness or having carnal knowledge. No longer innocent, Adam and Eve felt [#11]ashamed of what they had done and covered the lower parts of their bodies with "fig leaves" and [#12]"hid themselves" from the Lord God.

Being created in "God's image", but also in the "image of satan", by accepting "his knowledge", they became good as well as evil and became "men of double mind" (James 4:8). Thus, [#13]their personalities not only inherited good qualities of God, but, in addition, acquired evil qualities of satan. When they and their descendants choose to do the Will of God, He becomes their Father; but when they at one time or another, do the will of satan, he becomes their father (John 8:44).

By dominating the lives of Eve and Adam and through them all their descendants, satan became "the god of this world" (2 Cor. 4:4), the rul-

---

[#6] to [#13] See Appendix.

er of this world" (John 12:31), owner of the world (Matt. 4:9-9), which came under his power (1 John 5:19), and spiritual death came to the Adamic race (Gen. 2:17).

We may compare the relationship of Adam and Eve as that which existed and went wrong between [a]Romeo and Juliet, which play was immortalized by Shakespeare, and the medieval legend of [b]Tristan and Isolde, whom were all in their teens. They, like Adam and Eve, rushed in a sexual union while immature and without the blessing of their elders.

The descendants of Adam and Eve, as couples, acted in a similar fashion by seeing each other, that is, their personalities, as the source of love and not the Spirit of God; which should have been expressed through their Divine Spirit or Original Nature. They became, however, addicted to the wrong kind of love, which is not true love but selfish desire, and became dependent on the other in an unwholesome way. This resulted that they became emotionally attached to each other and were afraid to lose one another. In extreme cases they would rather kill each other if they cannot "have each other". Thus, instead of allowing themselves to grow, they indulge in their partner for their physical gratification. By loving, or rather desiring each other too much, they soon start fighting each other, because they become obsessed with their relationship, which becomes more and more destructive. Their [#14]"love" (lust or intense passion) for one another is therefore excessive, possessive, and selfish, whereby they separate themselves, not only from the Light of God within people, but also from their own inner Illumination.

This could not have happened to Adam, Eve, and their posterity when they would have been blessed by God after reaching maturity. Thus, not only of their pure and innocent personalities or egos, but also of their Divine Spirits, as it is animated individually with the active Spirit of God (Rev. 21:3). When God's Spirit rules their life, He becomes the Source of their love and life, and their love for each other is not only personal, but also universal. Not intense, concentrated, and selfish as that between Romeo and Juliet, but higher, spiritual uplifting,

---

[a] Many other known lovers, such as Anthony and Cleopatra, Lancelot and Guinevere of Camelot, Paris and Helen, Dante and Beatrice, victims of Greek tragedy, and many others, were greatly disappointed or found a tragic death.

[b] Their story was later played and sung in Richard Wagner's opera, in the 19th century and in operas of today.

[#14] See Appendix.

spread out to other people and all forms of creation. This impersonal [15]form of love unites all people at the divine, or "level of God", whom become their heavenly Parents.

Are Marriages Sanctified by God?

Because of the fall of the primal pair, ideal marriages have never been realized on this earth. God has never truly blessed couples in divine marriages. That is why Jesus praised those "who have made themselves [16]eunuchs for the sake of the kingdom of heaven" (Matt. 19:12). Apostle Paul could therefore say, "So that he who marries his betrothed does well; and he who refrains from marriage will do better" (1 Cor. 7:38). The Apostle also said, "If they cannot exercise self-control, they should marry. For it is better to marry than to be aflame with passion" (1 Cor. 7:9). In other words, it is better to live a married life than to think continually about sexual gratification, and to suffer from a burning desire. Further, Paul said in 1 Cor. 7:28, "It is no sin" to marry, but the couple will be *pleasing each other more than the Lord, and will thus be more "anxious about worldly affairs" (1 Cor. 7:33,34). Thus, instead of living a divine life, they are more inclined to live the life of the personality, which is the reflection of [17]"the world" which is good and evil.

From Paul's writing we may draw the conclusion that the highest way of life is to be chaste in thought and behavior. That sex within the strict confines of [18]marriage is tolerated, but that the couples become more "worldly". That they as husbands and wives become more like fallen Adam and Eve in nature, and thus come more under the influence and power of satan.

Although Jesus and Paul set the highest standard, most Christians accepted later the lower standard as set forth in the writings of an "other Paul" in Tim. 5:14, that "younger widows marry" and "bear children", and in Heb. 13:4, that "marriage be held in honor among all, and let the marriage bed be undefiled".

Because the unmarried status, especially celibacy, was valid higher than the married position in the early Christian church, marriages were not blessed by the church. However, couples were often required to enter in a legal contract, according to the law and custom of the land. [19]Sex in marriages –how and when– was strictly controlled by the

---

[16] to [19] See Appendix.
* It is recognized by Bible writers that married couples will have problems as the result of human imperfection.

church, especially during the [20]Middle Ages. It was not until the eleventh century that marriages were executed before the door of the church, with a priest as witness. However, in the thirteenth century, marriages were performed by a priest in the church.

It was not so much the act of procreation what the clergy at that time worried about, but the sexual action between a married couple was often accompanied by lustful desires. This resulted that they suffered of a spiritual decline every time they satisfied those evil desires. Some of those couples asked the church for help in the spiritual problems they were having. The clergy advised them to limit their sexual relations as much as possible and not "love" each other too much. In other words, they should not have intense (lustful) desires for each other; otherwise those desires would be the same as those between Adam and Eve, which were centered on satan. The evil within their human nature or human spirit would also be strengthened. The final result would be that the couples become more lustful, selfish, and prideful. Thus, they will have a tendency to become less obedient to God and His Laws, and do not respect His authority and that of His true representatives. They may even experience, at times, in their feeling and thinking, antagonism towards God, and are not much inspired to do His Will. They may also become weak willed and lazy with regard to the things of God. The evil impulses or sinful tendencies in their human nature may become so strong that they start to curse the same God they loved before, and thus condemn themselves "outside the Garden of Eden".

The church became more mature during the time of the [21]Protest(ant) Reformation, which began in 1517 A.D. with Martin Luther (1483-1546). He said that before God, all believers (the spiritual born) are equal; God and scripture are their only authorities and that they, through Christ, can directly communicate with God without a (Catholic) priest as mediator (priesthood of all believers). He also said that the (Holy) Spirit speaks to the Heart (Divine Spirit) of all believers, interprets the Bible, and guides His "elect" in their daily life (John 16:13).

[22]Jean Calvin (1509-1564), the French reformer, agreed with Luther –who was married– that a man needed a wife as a companion and for support, and that the main purpose of marriage was not only procrea-

---

[20] to [22] See Appendix.

tion. They probably could say this because the love between the couples of believers has become more spiritual and divine, that is more pure and virtuous and thus less sensual and erotic. This purification already began on a small scale in the twelfth century when the *wandering troubadours in Southern Europe began to emphasize divine love or true romantic love between men and women. Thereafter, marriages became more accepted by the church, and became eventually a sacrament.

At the time of the Renaissance, and the following centuries, the intellect of the people became more developed and stronger. This acted as "a brake", to check and control "the endless" lower sensual and sexual desires, which to [23]Buddhist belief is the cause of suffering and dissatisfaction.

Calvin also said that humans were originally made in "God's image" as pure beings, but they fell and became corrupted, although part of God's image still remains in them. Thus their personalities became good as well as evil.

Today we find expressions of Calvinism in the Reformed and Presbyterian churches, and it is also strongly rooted in the Baptists of today and Puritans of (New) England in the past, including the pilgrim fathers.

---

* Women in general have been severely treated by the Greek and Roman civilizations and as the "Gateway to Hell" by many Christians that a reaction surely was to occur. The troubadours discovered in many women the divine feminine and expressions of the Divine Mother which they adored and sang to.
[23] See Appendix.

Causes and Consequences of Sexual Misconduct

The unspiritual (natural) couples whom are living the life of the good and evil personality and thus "are still of the flesh" (1 Cor. 3:3), will have a difficult time overcoming carnal desires. This embraces [24]many people whom are still living according to the moral laws of the Old Testament, including the faithful Mohammedans. For them, the practices such as fornication, adultery, homosexuality, and bestiality are forbidden, but not unlimited and uncontrollable sexual relations between husband and wives. It is therefore easy for them to backslide to immoral pagan practices and live without moral laws, to the *second level or stage. Strict laws and severe punishment are, for that reason, necessary as a preventive measure.

When the evil self or false self of the personality is in charge of one's life, so is selfish desire, which seeks sexual pleasure in the relationship. The lack of it is seen today by many counselors as a psychological problem, because they are "seeing" those problems from the lower level of their being. When satisfaction of the feeling of lust, by "making love", becomes the most important goal, then true love is not present. The couples become slaves to the sexual instinct of their (lower) human psychic – or astral bodies (1 Cor. 7:9). It is often said by the male population, which is at the level of ordinary awareness or consciousness, "You can't live with them, but you can't live without them."

Wanting to have sex occupies [25]the minds of most [26]men and women whom are living the life of the good and evil personality. They continually dream and fantasize about it, and spend much of their free time and money on the pursuit of sexual conquests. This seems, for many of them, the most important value system, instead of seeking for mental and spiritual values.

Furthermore, they are daily [27]stimulated by sexual images from the media, advertisements, magazines, etc., and scantily clad [28]women appeal to the easily aroused sexual instinct of men. By wearing short skirts and other alluring practices, many women capitalize on the strong

---

[24] to [28]See Appendix.
* See Seven Stages of Development.

sexual urge of men, and often use them for their own interest and advancement.

Dwelling upon those images can trigger responses in the body by releasing hormones to prepare it for sexual activity, just as anger can prepare the body to fight by releasing its particular hormones. When seeking for the pleasures of sex becomes their most important lifestyle, they start living "below the belt" at the [a]second level. It motivates them to become more successful and powerful –like Lucifer–, in order to attract more women whom are in a hurry –like fallen Eve–, to make themselves more attractive and sexy to those men. Those seductive women easily lure and drag the weak men to their level of consciousness (Prov. Chapters 5-7). By stunting the men and themselves in their moral and spiritual development, who in turn induce others to become like them, the erotic women have to pay a heavy karmic price. Besides, they cannot be really happy with what they are doing, because they, as human spirits, are no longer in touch with their budding Divine Spirits or True Selves and the god Selves of other people. The result is that they are out of harmony with the universe and its forces, and the better ones may even feel [#29]guilty. Thus, they no longer have the feeling that "everything is going my way".

Another consequence of the promiscuous behavior of men and women is that their consciousness gets stuck in or near the [b] "second level" of their personality, and they become – are called – and appear like animals – "horny and cloven hoofed". This can be observed by the (dirty) language they speak, the (low-rated) movies they like to see, the (sexually implicit) music they like to hear, the books (pornographic literature and obscene romance) they like to read, and the friends they like to have, to impress them with gossip and sex stories. The final result is that they become more selfish, sensual, insecure, greedy, indulgent, pessimistic, materialistic, atheistic, in pursuit of the pleasures of life and having a "good time" for themselves. Living this kind of life will also create in them desires to get something without laboring for it. This also includes the many forms of [#30]gambling, which much of society permits. Those people eventually become a great burden to the same society.

Those frequent and unnecessary indulgences in the pleasures of sex

---

[a],[b] See Seven Stages of Development.
[#29] to [#30]See Appendix.

are a [31]waste of physical vigor and vital energy of the [a]etheric body. People eventually become slaves to their lower desires and passions and are always craving for more. One of the results of these indulgences is that the compositions of their spirit bodies become coarser after every indulgence. They will attract undesirable entities – with or without bodies – of lower vibrations, because it can only respond to them.

The focusing mind of the spiritual men and women whom are backsliding (1 Cor. 2:15), becomes an instrument of the lower self or personality, which is good and evil, instead of the Higher Self (Divine Spirit) which is always good and pure. Because the mind is in league with the selfish and sensual lower nature, it is no longer possible for the Higher Self to control the body. The divine flow is obstructed and the Divine Spirit becomes imprisoned and eventually dies of lack of nourishment from its host or personality.

Spiritual Love Exceeds Human Love

Spiritual people know and understand that sensual enjoyment is only a passing sensation, and is merely a shadow of the peace, joy, and bliss of the higher spiritual life.

The joy of the union of the personality with the Real Self or Higher Self surpasses many times the pleasures of the physical union. What is experienced in a sexual relation is only a trickle of the experience of enlightenment, when the male (Self) and the female (self) within the being of a human come into an eternal union.

To have a "love affair with the divine" is so much greater than the happiness of romantic involvement or sentimental affection, which is also called love. Earthly love is only a reflection of the love experienced in the higher planes of life. This love is not only personal but also encompasses all of humanity.

As human love can be polluted, by becoming selfish, possessive, and counterfeit, Christ love is always pure; it cannot be pretended or be touched by human conditions. Christ's love is infinite, while human love is limited.

---

[31] See Appendix.
[a] See "The Etheric Body".

The bliss of spiritual love far exceeds physical passions, as the sun outshines the flame of a flickering candle. The light and warmth of the sun is like the Love and Truth of God, which always shines with the same strength on the good and the bad.

To have been touched by God's Love can never be forgotten, and the memory of that experience will always be treasured as a priceless possession. No one can take it away or erase it, and those whom have been loved even so briefly are always seeking for another encounter with His or Her Love.

Apostle Paul expressed this Love in Rom. 8:38-39:

> For I am sure that neither death, nor life, nor angels,
> nor principalities, nor things present, nor things to
> come, nor powers, nor height, nor depth, nor anything
> else in all creation, will be able to separate us from
> the love of God in Christ Jesus our Lord.

[a]Why Homosexuality Is Wrong

The pursuit of the pleasures of sex may even degenerate to homosexuality, whose main purpose is the gratification of lust, while bonding on the lowest level of the personality, which is selfish and evil in nature.

Homosexuals are usually [b]much more promiscuous as married heterosexual couples, and in order to get more sexually stimulated or "turned on", they may easily fall into more deviant and destructive behavior. This conduct will only strengthen their inherited fallen nature of Lucifer the archangel, who became satan (Isa. 14:12; Rev. 12:9), and come more under his power and control, and all of his cohorts. They will attract other people like themselves, with or without bodies, but also the most evil entities, such as fallen angels or demons. As Jude 6-7 put it:

> And the angels that did not keep their own position but left their proper dwelling have been kept by him in eternal chains in the nether gloom until the judgment of the great day; just as Sodom and Gomorrah and the surrounding cities, which likewise acted immorally and indulged in [c]unnatural lust, serve as an example by undergoing a punishment of eternal fire.

Sexual intercourse between two men or two women is not an act of creation but an abuse of the energy of creation, for personal pleasure. No good thing will come from it on the physical, emotional, and mental levels of their personalities. By acting out on those levels their promiscuity, they strengthen the evil part or satanic nature of their good/evil personality, and are, at those times, truly satan's children (John 8:44).

The abuse at the physical level results in diseases of the colon, liver, and many other ailments and infections, because the homosexual lifestyle is not appropriate to the organism. However, the moderate

---

[a] See, for a more extended explanation, the booklet "Why Homosexuality is Wrong", written by same author.

[b] Most gay men tend to have hundreds of impersonal sexual partners a year, while lesbians are more personal and emotional in their relationships, and are committed to one partner for a longer period of time.

[c] This verse suggests that homosexuality originated with Lucifer and the fallen angels.

monogamous heterosexual way of life is free of sexual diseases. As Paul said in Romans 1:26-27:

> God gave them up to dishonorable passions. Their
> women exchanged natural relations for unnatural, and the
> men likewise gave up natural relations with women and were
> consumed with passion for one another, men committing
> shameless acts with men and receiving in their own per-
> sons the due penalty for their error.

As age-old venereal diseases such as syphilis and gonorrhea were no longer a serious health threat because they were curable, it helped along the sexual revolution of the 1960s, with its free-swinging sexual lifestyles. During the 1970s, a new kind of venereal disease "genital herpes" came along, and caused an epidemic. Many people at that time became more cautious about their sexual behavior because it was not curable. Consequently, it was not fatal and symptoms could be treated, and therefore most people continued with their promiscuous way of living.

Because America and the world did not heed this warning, they were suddenly confronted in the early 1980s with a most horrible disease, which was first discovered among male homosexuals. This new sexually transmitted disease was called "AIDS", and is always fatal because it destroys the immune system of the body. As of today, no cure has been found, and over 25 million people worldwide have died.

For many people the sexual revolution is over, but unfortunately for many others, including the homosexual community, stubbornly continue in their wrong lifestyle. They do not seem to understand that disregard for God's laws on sex and moral conduct threatens not only the health of millions, but also their moral and spiritual lives. When those people, especially homosexuals, do not listen to "God's Voice", they will degenerate and destroy families and generations to come, and will cause the downfall of civilization(s).

The abuse at the emotional level results in intense hatred and destructive jealousy between homosexuals, more so than between "love- sick" heterosexuals, which may even result in murder. Because their possessive relationship is based mainly on lust (intense desire), they see the other (personality), especially the more masculine as the sole source of happiness, instead of the budding Divine Selves of their mates. Thus, if one party shows a dislike for the other, the [a]feelings of the other individual are hurt. They become moody, suffer from anxiety and stress, become depressed and even suicidal. Because they are attached and want to possess each other, they continually worry about losing each other, and are thus very insecure of what they have. The desire and craving for each other, which is recognized in Buddhism as the cause of emotional distress and misery, makes them very selfish and therefore do not care much about other people.

The abuse at the mental level results in being [b]dishonest and deceptive to each other. Homosexuals are often unreasonable, narrow-minded, and critical. They have a tendency to blame and accuse the other of things they have done, and are therefore suspicious of the other's intentions. Some of them have certain beliefs, which the other doubts and cannot accept. One party may be opinionated, rigid, and quick to judge the other, which results in quarrels. They complain a lot, because they think that the other is trying to betray them. The final result is that they live together, but do not trust themselves and the other party.

When some of them insist and continue their relationship with the same sex, the receptive males eventually become more feminine in their attitudes. Thus, not only their inner personality or human spirit changes but also their outer personality or body. This happens when male testosterone levels decrease and the female hormone estrogen increases. These hormonal changes are also strongly influenced by the thoughts, fantasies, and desires of homosexuals. Some lesbians have high testosterone levels, and are therefore more aggressive than the women with the passive roles, whom have more estrogen. When they have progressed that far, it will be very difficult to change their addiction, not only their thought patterns and desires, but hormones as well.

It is relatively easy for humans beings, whom are good and evil, and are not influenced or controlled by their (newly-born or developed) Divine Spirits or Souls, to deviate and rebel against God's design or nature. This is what the fallen angels and our pagan forebears did in primitive societies.

---

[a] Feelings cannot be hurt by someone who lives a divine life.

[b] By being dishonest and deceptive, one becomes split in his personality, creating a double image of what one believes to be true and the expression of a different truth, thus losing their integrity.

One of the psychological causes of homosexuality in a boy's life may be a possessive and overprotective mother who may discourage the development of his budding masculinity. This development is even more stunted when the boy's father is not around physically or psychologically, whom he can imitate as his role model, and be accepted as a man among men. Girls (also boys) may turn to a homosexual lifestyle when they have been physically and psychically abused by men whom they trusted, and therefore do not want to be ruled by them. Some of the girls do not respect their mother and her role in life, while others are afraid of pregnancy.

Boys and girls may have homosexual experiences while they are young, and would like to fantasize about them, thus strengthening their sexual orientation.

Some men are more masculine in a physical sense, while others are built less manly. The first would better fit the more feminine women, while the latter would be compatible with the more masculine women. This does not mean that the latter are feminine oriented. Many of them are sensitive, spiritually inclined, and have artistic inclinations.

However, if some of those men and others (including women) choose to entertain in their mind, or much worse to act out homosexual tendencies, they will morally decline and degenerate quickly. When thoughts and emotions express themselves through corresponding actions, fundamental changes will happen in their lives, which will have a permanent impact on the development of character. According to the same principle, the most effective way to overcome a bad habit is by simply not doing it.

Many of the self-righteous same sex individuals are even trying to force God and society to accept their unprincipled, rebellious, and perverse lifestyle. However, they conveniently forget that they also have to live according to the laws of God which strictly forbid such relationships (John 14:15; 1 John 2:4). Before any deep and intimate relationship with God is possible, they first have to abide by the mandates and warnings, as given in:

> Genesis 19:1-29, which describes the wicked people of
> Sodom and Gomorrah and its destruction, with Judges
> 19 as a description of a similar story.
> Leviticus 20:13 clearly says, "If a man lies with a male
> as with a woman, both of them have committed an

abomination; they shall be put to death, their blood is
upon them." See also Leviticus 18:22.
In the New Testament we find important passages
against male and female homosexuality in Romans 1:26-28;
1 Corinthians 6:9-10 and 1 Timothy 1:9-10

Those laws and ordinances were given to people whom are at a low level of moral development. They are still true for many people today, even when they are more knowledgeable. Those people are still under the moral law, which demands the full penalty, and not under grace (Rom. 6:4) as the redeemed are (Gal. 4:5) whom live by the life of the indwelling Christ (Gal. 2:20). Those rules and principles of conduct are designed and laid down because they are good and necessary. They protect the people externally and internally against themselves and from others, as a fence would protect little children.

Jesus said about 2000 years ago in Mark 10:6-8:

> But from the beginning of creation, "God made them male
> and female" (Gen. 1:27). "For this reason a man shall
> leave his father and mother and be joined to his wife, and
> the two shall become one flesh" (Gen. 2:24).

As it is obvious to everyone, the male and female bodies are of different structures and function in a different way in order to bring forth children. They should be raised in a family of a father who is a male and a mother who is a female.

After physical death the human spirits live on, and their psychic structures or bodies are less male and female, because they have no organs to produce children. When they enter the higher realms of the spirit world they are neither male nor female.

> For when they rise from the dead, (spiritual) they neither
> marry nor are given in marriage, but are like the angels
> in heaven (Mark 12:25).

For in Christ "there is neither male nor female" (Gal. 3:28).

The newly-formed Christ or Divine Spirit (Gal. 4:19) is neither male nor female, but androgyne, male (andro) and female (gyne), completely one, but in a highly developed form. It is recognized by Jungian analysts as an archetype.

Androgyne, however, is not meant here the state or condition of hermaphroditism, in which both sexes simultaneously exist, which for humans is an abnormality. It is also not a psychological relationship between human spirits, wherein the male psyche at times acts out the female role and the female psyche the role of the male. It cannot be bisexuality, which is a physical relation between partners of the same and different genders. The latter are often confused about masculine and feminine roles, especially when they act out like transvestites. They may also be –more or less– influenced by male or female spirits, particularly when they are sensitive and (or) believe in reincarnation. In the latter case the believers are strongly affected and even identify with the influencing spirits, who impress the believers in the life experiences of the spirits. Reincarnationalists may then believe that those impressed and implanted thoughts are their own. They say that they have memories of past lives, whose lives are of nobody else, but of those spirits. Besides, spiritualists whom make contacts with spirits always find family members in the "spirit world". They never have to say to the family of the loved ones "that the spirit of Uncle Teddy cannot be contacted because he has taken another body, and lives somewhere on earth as a male or female".

Androgyne should also not be identified with certain behaviors, where men wear foppish clothes or women appear like boys. It is also not an external or innate homosexual behavior. Androgynous relations take place at the deepest level of the human psyche, between Divine Spirits or Original Selves, and create genuine "brotherhood" among all people.

In Genesis 1:26, God said to the angels (psychic beings), who are neither male nor female and have not been differentiated, "Let us make man in our image; after our likeness" (Gen. 1:26) --- "So God created man in His own image, in the image of God He created him; (neither male nor female) male and female He created them" (Gen. 1:27). Thus, "God created man", --- "in the likeness of God" (Gen. 5:1), Who is male in His calling and male and female in their invisible attributes, which exist externally in [a]perfect union and harmony. "Man" as a potential being was first differentiated (Gen. 2:21-23) or separated into male and female, whom first develop on all levels of their being as separate entities and then are united physically, psychologically, and spiritually as a new and developed united being.

---

[a] God does not exist of two beings who occasionally unite. There is therefore no separate Father or Mother God (goddess). When we pray in the name of the Father, we mean Abba or God as the whole or perfect United Being.

God, who is neither male nor female, but androgynous in its essentiality, contains all the pairs of opposites in potentiality, such as positive and negative, male and female, but not yet differentiated. When the "cosmic egg finally was broken", and energy released, creation began, in dual forms. The universe (macrocosm), including the earth, with its minerals, plants, and animals was created first, while humans as the microcosm and prototype were created last. Thus God created everything in the universe in [b]pairs, so that His maleness and femaleness can be expressed and energy created between the [c]polarities. He thus created humans to expand and multiply and to gather experience and grow thereby.

The more human beings are like male and female in their body characteristics, the more immature they are. When their inner personalities grow through education, they become more involved in the mental realm and less involved in the physical domain. Thus, they become more in harmony with the male and female aspects of their beings. This is also true when they become older and wiser. Humans become less male and female when they participate in laws and customs of certain societies. They become also more like the other gender when couples of the opposite sex are living in a close relationship with each other.

However, when people are spiritually born (born of God), their personalities become much less of the stereotype male or female, because they are –more or less– guided by their Divine Spirits or Souls. This is the case of great spiritual leaders, such as Jesus Christ, Krishna, Buddha, and many others, such as some monks and priests, whom may even look like they are neither male nor female. This is so because the Divine Spirit or Christ Body is born of God and is androgynous in nature. The Gospel according to Thomas says:

---

[b] A human being created in the image of God consists of male and female (yang and yin), while the earth, which is under the dominion of human entities, is dual in nature, with its animals (male and female), plants (stamen and pistil), molecules and atoms with their positive and negative substances and charges. In addition, each entity consists of an internal nature, which is like the external form. Humans, for example, are made up of spirit body (psyche) and physical body; animals of psychic body (astral body) and physical body; plants of vital body and dense body; and molecules, atoms, and subatomic particles of internal natures and external forms.

[c] All forms of energy, like psychic energy and electricity, can only flow between positive and negative poles. However, in the higher spiritual realm(s), another principle applies: that of like attracts like and not opposites attract, as in the human, animal, and mineral worlds. The law of polarity is only applicable in the physical and lower spheres.

> When you make the inner as the outer and the outer as the inner and the above as the below, and when you make the male and the female into a single one, so that the male will not be male and the female (not) be female – then you shall enter the kingdom.

The new androgyne is aware of his or her sexual identity, and expresses a natural, unforced male or female sexuality. However, some creative people whom have more originality and individuality, and are in close touch with their Divine Spirits or Beings, misinterpret the male/female feeling of their androgynous Selves. They should ascend above the duality and not degenerate to the lowest level, by physically and emotionally expressing their desires for the same sex. Otherwise, they will fall from their high state to the level of their lower selves, which is good and evil, or even lower at the level of the fallen angels, whom are only evil and are known as demons. The above may explain the reason that homosexuality prevails when humankind is entering a new level of spiritual growth.

How to Overcome Homosexuality

To break the habit of wrong sexual desires is, first of all, to stop all sexual activities with homosexual partner(s), and not make any contact with them (1 Cor. 5:9-13) because it is very easy to be contaminated with their psychic vibration. Secondly, to cease desiring and [a]fantasizing about those partners, whereby one will attract their spirits, especially during sleep, when spirits are able to roam freely. Thirdly, to stop thinking about them, so that thought transfer (telepathy) or communication does not occur between them.

(1) Further, it would also be helpful to eat more [b]high vibration foods, such as fruits and vegetables in order to make the body less coarse, and thus more susceptible to higher desires and thoughts. It is also important to clean the physical and [c]etheric bodies as often as possible because they are in close contact (via energy centers) with the emotional and mental components of the (human) spirit body, as water in a sponge and air in water. Therefore, one part of the human psyche affects the other. When, for example, the vibration of the human spirit is high, so is the vibration of the physical body – thus experiencing less sexual problems. It is also recommendable to spend time in natural settings, admiring its beauty, and walking (dancing) in harmony with nature's rhythm.

(2) Be joyful and make people happy, and try to love them unconditionally and receive their appreciation and love. Sing uplifting songs, appreciate noble art, and seek for its beauty, truth, and harmony. Listen to and play high vibration music to awaken the Divine Spark within, such as classical music and others that do not descend to the level of the personality. However, they should certainly not become involved with music and songs that awaken their sexuality, such as rock music and sensual songs of low character.

---

[a] Sexual fantasy and imaginations towards another person may be light, half-hearted, and unconscious, but they may become more real when entities begin to focus on each other (phone sex). This may be called psychic seduction because the other party may not always know what is going on. When their relation becomes very intense and vivid, they may engage in a sexual relation in the psychic realm, by having psychic or astral sex with their disengaged spirits.

[b] Meat coarsens, makes dense, and lowers the vibration of the physical body, and also creates animal passion. It therefore affects the emotional and mental parts which, in turn, becomes a less effective vehicle of the Soul.

[c] See "The Etheric Body".

(3) See good movies, read inspiring poetry and books, and try to understand the hidden meanings. Seek for Truth and Beauty within and without yourselves, and try to connect with your Divine Spark or Self and those Selves of the people you meet, as the Buddhists and many others do. However, your reading should be selective; otherwise, it is easy to pollute your mind and human spirit.

Finally, visualize yourself leading a life you want to live, in harmony with natural laws and principles.

By persisting in the new activities of the personality, the emotional and mental components of the human spirit will not only be in harmony, but also the composition of those parts will gradually change to a [a]higher vibration, [b]purifying the whole personality. This, in turn, changes the emotional part by replacing lower (sensual) desires with higher ones, and negative emotions (hatred-resentment-depression-etc.) with positive ones (love-joy-peace-etc.). The emotional self is then no longer dull (as in brownish-red, gray, or sludge-green) and muddy (as a dirty window), or agitated by worry and anxiety, and becomes clearer. We change the mental part by substituting evil and lower thoughts with pure and higher forms of thinking. In addition, we may at times try to still the mind as in meditation. Thus, through the exercises of the [c]physical, emotional, and mental parts of our being, the personality or lower self becomes more receptive and transparent, so that the "sun" of the budding Higher Self is able to guide and shine through and illuminate the physical consciousness. Then we can say with Christ that the "pure in [d]heart" will see God (Matt. 5:8).

By disciplining the mind or inner self and controlling the body, you will learn valuable lessons of self-control. You will develop the qualities of persistence, perseverance, courage, self-respect, and honor, thus strengthening your character and overcoming temptation. Living in this manner will create a base to attract high thought vibrations, spiritual entities, and newly-found physical friends. You should, of course, live in an environment (neighborhood) where the psychic at-

---

[a] Because the mental and emotional elements exist in every cell of the physical body, higher thought and emotions change the cellular consciousness and, thus, the chemistry of the body, raising the vibration of the atoms.

[b] Through this process of purification, psychological blocks are removed, which obstruct the Divine flow.

[c] Physical exercises also include the control of the appetites, urges of the body, and bad habits.

[d] Heart here means the inner personality or self (emotional-mental-subconscious) from which comes evil (Matt. 15:19; Mk. 7:21). See also Concordance of the Bible.

mosphere is high and compatible with your new lifestyle. Contacting people whom also want to change or have changed might be very helpful because there is strength in a group, from which you can draw, which will lighten your psychological burden.

However, it would be much easier to change when you believe in God the Creator, who is always willing to help as soon as humans make the [a]required condition, by asking for His help (John 16:23-24). By consistent prayer and meditation, you may make a breakthrough or [b]widen the channel between the personality and the budding Divine Self, so that God can guide you directly through your Divine Spirit and pure conscience. If it needs to be, God as Divine Parents may guide you to a particular religious community.

Joining a high religious organization can be very helpful wherein you usually can count on people whom are willing to help, and may even [c]share your heavy burden. By listening and accepting their teachings, especially the pure Word(s) of God, "the soil" of your personality is being prepared. The sowed Divine Seed(s) (Matt. 13:1-23) is able to grow and eventually [d]become a Divine Spirit, by assimilating the Words of God in your Divine Being, who is, unlike the personality, always pure and noble. By experiencing the Love of God through your teacher(s) or adopted spiritual parent(s), the inner core of your personality or Original Self is growing and will receive the Holy Spirit in the innermost core of the personality, as soon as it is ready to receive it (Acts 2:4). Thus, by accepting the Universal Christ as your Savior, your Divine Self or Fetus is formed and grows in the womb of the personality and is born as a baby Divine Spirit or Soul (1 Pet. 2:2). The Spirit of God will then find its permanent dwelling place (Rev. 21:3) within the temple of the growing Divine Spirit or your individual Christ Spirit (1 John 2:12-14).

---

[a] Unrestored humans should ask God every day and every time, to let Him know, that you are still on His side.

[b] Some exercises one can do to remove psychic blocks and to broaden this link, are to forgive others and to think about their spiritual well-being, to read inspired Words, witness to the Divine Truth, meditate and pray a lot, and thank our Creator for what we are and have become. It is only through the Divine Spirit or Self within our personality that we really have direct access to God, our Father and Mother, at all times and in all places.

[c] Some people, especially the ones whom have compassion and are good listeners, have the ability to absorb negative psychic elements from you, and are even willing to take your karmic burdens on themselves.

[d] See "The Birth and Evolution of the Divine Spirit or Soul".

ᵃThis conversion or initiation experience is the best that can happen to you or anyone, when the whole (good and evil) personality is cleansed and purified by the Holy Spirit, without much effort on your part. As Apostle Paul expressed it in a letter to the Ephesians:

> Put off your old nature which belongs to your former
> manner of life and is corrupt through deceitful lusts,
> and be renewed in the spirit of your minds, and put on
> the new nature, created after the likeness of God in
> true righteousness and holiness (Eph. 4:22-24).
> See also (Col. 3:9-10).

Thereafter, the budding Divine Spirit ("Christ be formed in you" (Gal. 4:19)), in close association with the Holy Spirit of God, will lead your divine life, and you will overcome all obstacles and temptations. We are then able to say with Paul, "It is no longer I (personality-ego) who lives, but Christ who lives in me" (Gal. 2:20).

However, you not only get close to God by knowing the Truth, but by knowing Them personally as Divine Parents, through everyday experiences of Their Presence. They will lead, guide, and talk to you, and you will eventually trust them and know that they truly love you. You will accept them as your Parents whom will never let you down or forsake you. They have become for you, not only the God of the universe, but also of "my Heart".

When you become a "new creation" (II Cor. 5:17), you will understand spiritual things (1 Cor. 2:14), and you are also able to distinguish good from evil by using your newly awakened faculty of †higher intuition. You will then think with total comprehension and arrive at Truth without recourse to your faculty of thinking. You also begin to express the fruit of your Divine Spirit or divine qualities, such as: love, joy, peace, patience, kindness, goodness, etc. (Gal. 5:22).

ᵃ Complete conversion guarantees a likely change from an abnormal to a normal lifestyle. When, after a period of struggle, one's Divine Spirit is in control of one's (purified) personality, one comes in control of one's life (Gal. 5:23). However, before this can happen, one may backslide (a few times) and may temporarily lose control through temptation. But, with the help of fellow believers and through prayer, fasting, and exorcism, one may finally recover.

† As higher intuition is perceived through the upper energy centers, such as the third eye, lower intuition is perceived through the lower energy centers such as the solar plexus. Lower intuition is usually more developed in women than in men, and is often spoken of as instinct or gut feeling.

When the budding Divine Spirit begins to rule the personality, your intellect starts to become illuminated and your emotions begin to become radiant with true love and compassion. There will be a new light in your eyes, which radiates through your expanding aura and creates a strong magnetism and spiritual charisma. There is a broader love in your heart, and you have a deeper capacity to understand things. You have become kind, considerate, unselfish, and wise. You are no "longer under law but under grace" (Rom. 6:15), and "love is the fulfilling of the law" (Rom. 13:10), which Jesus came "to fulfill" (Matt. 5:17). By living according to this new lifestyle, you will not make any moral debt (karma) to your fellow humans, and thus have no need to make amendments. You are no longer a servant (or enemy) of God as, for example, some people of the lower religions and primitives are, whom usually expect material blessing as reward for their good behavior. You, however, are becoming a child of God, whom you may call Father or Mother or simply Parents, and spiritual blessing is more important to you. They usually appear to us in the form of our highest ideal, which we love the most, which, for many of us is the Universal Christ and the Holy Spirit. Thus, by losing self-consciousness and gaining God consciousness, you are discovering a New World of Love and Light.

You are not only perceiving the material world with its life force, but to a certain extent also the penetrating psychic world through your more developed psychic senses and the divine world, which permeates both world, through your budding divine or spiritual senses. This greater world is more alive and enchanted with all kinds of beings whom you never knew existed. You are "seeing" God everywhere, because their Mind and Consciousness pervades the universe, which is their body, when it was created by them out of chaos (Gen. 1:2).

Being in harmony with the universe and its forces, "everything will be going your way" and your life will be a song.

And finally, to quote Apostle Paul in 1 Corinthians 6:9-11:

> Do you not know that the unrighteous will not inherit
> the kingdom of God? Do not be deceived; neither the
> immoral, nor idolaters, nor adulterers, nor sexual perverts,
> nor thieves, nor the greedy, nor drunkards, nor revilers,
> nor robbers will inherit the kingdom of God. And such

were some of you. But you were washed, you were sanctified, you were justified in the name of the Lord Jesus Christ and in the Spirit of our God.

Unification of Male and Female in God's Image

A man resembles the masculinity of God and the male or yang aspects of creation, while the woman resembles the femininity of God and the kingdoms of nature in its female or yin expressions. Neither is complete and fulfilled without the other. When they are united in body, spirit, and Soul, they truly represent God as their Parents and are a [a]microcosm of the universe(s) in their physical and non-physical aspects.

A "decent" of power occurs as soon as a couple of opposite polarities are united. The quantity and quality of that force depends on the [b]level of development they have achieved. This may explain the experience of happiness, joy, and bliss between the partners, especially when the relationship is more spiritual than emotional. The man and woman are blended in complete oneness of will and purpose or vibrate in tune with each other and become "one flesh" (Gen. 2:24). Together, they create a synergism, which is greater than both.

Having found and united with the other half, the world is expanded, becomes more comprehensive, and responds with more beauty and harmony, because "heaven", which is more the domain of man and "earth", which is more like the character of a woman, are more united and whole for them.

True and Selfish Love Between Couples

When a couple is "in love", whose true nature is universal and unconditional rather than personal and selfish, it connects them to the giver of all life. This love is all embracing, and includes and empowers all forms of life. It seeks to unite all that is separate and divided, serve and give comfort to the helpless, and is in continual pursuit of the whole. The expressions and qualities of this love whose main tenet is spiritual are "joy, peace, patience, kindness, goodness, faithfulness, gentleness, self-control", which are "the fruit of the Spirit" (Gal. 5:22). We may add to those expressions the attributes of: compassion, con-

[a] The human spirits (as vehicles of their developed Divine Spirits) of the male and female, is the microcosm of the lower and higher spirit worlds, and their physical bodies (as vehicles of the spirits) are the microcosm of the physical world.

[b] The level of development in a savage is mostly physical and emotional. In a more civilized human, the mental part is included, while a more developed human being is at an intuition level, which includes the physical, emotional, mental, and spiritual quadrants.

cern, forgiveness, tolerance, devotion, generosity, reverence, honor, nobility, wisdom, understanding, perfection, courage, creativity, truthfulness, faithfulness, honesty, gratitude, dignity, etc. By expressing those spiritual and pure human values, we are taking care of and take full responsibility for the growth of others at all levels of their beings.

However, different qualities are expressed by the good and evil personalities of the couple such as ego love, which is often egotistic, selfish, possessive, envious, distrustful, and lustful. The good and evil personality has also a strong tendency to be occupied with the negative emotions and thinking of: pessimism, worry, anxiety, self-pity, self-doubt, self-seeking, insecurity, frustration, and they rationalize and complain a lot. They are also doubtful, fearful, resentful, argumentative, reactive, defensive, critical, etc.

The *evil part of the personality, fallen or satanic nature, imposter, liar, and Antichrist, expresses itself in hatred of God and condemning Him and His servants, and accusing the latter of crimes they have not committed. Those evil people are cold, lifeless, ruthless, cruel, deceitful, and unforgiving. They are also arrogant, prideful, tyrannical, and lustful for sex and power. Evil beings despise, ridicule, scoff, and mock those who do God's Will and try to frustrate God's plan to establish the Kingdom of God, while maintaining their pseudo kingdom. They are unconcerned for the welfare of others, and do not, or rather, cannot truly love the people, themselves, or their mates and are condemned (unless they change) to live in this state of being or being in hell. Many of the "good people", however, whom are good and evil, often cooperate with the evil people and demons (fallen angels) because they do not know what they do (Luk. 23:34).

However, the energy of pure love between the couple transforms and empowers the beloved, so that he or she can perform any tasks with much energy and ease. The loved ones appear better to behold and they find talents and excellence in each other, which was not seen before. They are happy and in harmony with each other and the world, which they express freely for everyone to see in the life they live, which has become like a song and dance.

---

* This evil part within the human spirit is also named evil self, false self, or inner devil. In the Bible, it is called "old nature" (Eph. 4:22); "the flesh" (Gal. 5:16-17; Rom. 8:5-8); "old self" or "old man" (Rom. 6:6). For the expression of this satanic nature see Mark 7:21-23; Rom. 1:29-31; Gal. 5:19-21; 2 Tim. 3:2-5.

What he sees in her and what she sees in him is not so much their personalities and their faults, but their *Divine Sparks or the budding Divine Spirits within their human selves. Having developed compassion (not passion), they are looking much deeper into each other than other people, who do not seem to understand what this particular couple sees in each other. Once the pair has seen a glimpse of divine reality in the other and its potential divine qualities, they can never forget. They may even identify and (or) bestow expressions on the other person's external self with imaginary divine qualities and virtues. As a flower opens to the heat and light of the sun, or the seed under the ground germinates to the first warmth of spring, so the strong affection of the lover tends to call the hidden Divine Sparks and the latent divine qualities into manifestation. By giving and receiving love from their budding Divine Spirits, the couple becomes spiritually alive and the God Self of the lover recognizes and seeks out the God self within the beloved. Because the relationship of the pair is based on the divine within each other and not on their external personalities or egos, they can be true to the other and thus do not have to wear masks of pretense. The other person is seen as unique and special, and they are engaged on the physical, emotional, mental, and spiritual levels. They are truly in love and will become complete as one soul in two bodies by losing oneself in and becoming like the other person, and thus "become one flesh" (Gen. 2:24).

NOTE: As soon as the pair starts looking at each other in a lustful way, their consciousness will fall or sink, especially when they express this feeling in a sexual relationship because the divine relationship is no longer there. The satanic nature or the evil part of the personality takes the place of the divine nature or Self as an impostor, and they start living the life of the evil personality and satan becomes their lord and master.

Comparing the Relations of Adam and Eve with Couples Today

The ideal love between the couples is comparable to what Adam and Eve felt for each other, while they were growing as brother and sister to maturity. Because the personalities of Adam and Eve were only good, the love between them was pure and innocent. This love is also matched, to some degree, by some people today, whose personalities are, for the most part, noble and good. Although this relationship may

---

* The Divine Spark, the Consciousness of God, dwells in all human beings and in all aspects of creation.

not last long when they are no longer "in love" but "fall in love", especially when they have also an unlawful physical relationship.

As described in the third chapter of Genesis, in symbolic terms, Adam and Eve fell into ordinary human consciousness. This happened to them while they were, as teenagers, in the process of developing their personalities and Divine Spirits. As a result, they did not die physically as some people believe (because it is natural), but spiritually (see Gen. 2:17) because they, as personalities, lost their relationships with their Divine Spirits and were thus no longer able to communicate with the God of their Divine Beings. Their pure personalities or egos became [32]good and evil or tainted with original sin. Having inherited this sin from their ancestors, most people are usually not aware that they are expressing in their daily life the good as well as the evil qualities of their personalities. They are often confused of what is good and evil, and are therefore easily persuaded by others to do evil while they think that they are doing good.

Adam and Eve and Their Descendants Lost Lordship Over Creation

Because of the fall of the first authentic pair, they and their ancestors never became true Lords of the creation and therefore Apostle Paul could say in Romans 8:19-21:

> For the creation waits with eager longing for the revealing
> of the sons of God; for the creation was subjected to futility,
> not of its own will but by the will of him who subjected it
> in hope; because the creation itself will be set free from its
> bondage to decay and obtain the glorious liberty of the
> children of God.

Although the primitive people whom lived before Adam and Eve were undeveloped (not evil), their behavior was ethical and orderly, and much in tune with the natural and universal laws. They, therefore, were in harmony and in close touch with all aspects of creation and took care of it as well as they could. The primitives did not misuse or squander nature and its resources as most descendants of Adam and Eve did. The latter, as members of the fallen adamic race, were inclined towards evil, and came under the influence of evil forces.

---

[32] See Appendix.

Adamic descendants *lost the intrinsic sense of appreciation and beauty of nature and therefore could not truly love and value it.

Thus, due to the fall, the creation lost their qualified Lords (Gen. 2:19-20), and therefore "the whole creation has been groaning in travail" (Rom. 8:22). The created objects became infused and permeated with energy of the evil and lower planes, which were created by human beings. The mineral kingdom does not respond well to the low human vibration. Plants of their particular domain do not grow to their full potential and animals become fearful and antagonistic toward the people and among themselves. By not receiving true and mature love from their "caretakers", the creation has never been fully alive psychically and a mutual hostility came to exist between humans and nature.

The creation, however, will become restored by the perfected sons and daughters of God, whom will become its stewards and co-creators with God, thus fulfilling the prophecy in Isaiah 11:6-7:

> The wolf shall dwell with the lamb, and the leopard
> shall lie down with the kid, and the calf and the
> lion and the fatling together and a little child shall
> lead them. The cow and the bear shall feed; their
> young shall lie down together; and the lion shall eat
> straw like the ox.

The Suffering Heart of God

The Lord God was stricken with grief when Adam and Eve separated themselves from Him and united with satan. Because their consciousness became far removed from God's Consciousness, He "called to the man and said to him, 'Where are you?'" (Gen. 3:9)

For millions of years God prepared the earth and its evolving people for the final arrival (by birth) of their most precious beings whom, as their true children, would become completely like them, created in their image and likeness (Gen. 1:26). While Adam and Eve were growing up, they were a great joy to God, the angels, and their physical parents whom guided them in their daily life. However, they were thrown off the path of growth by rebellious angel(s), at the time they were entering from the stage of personality – to spiritual development

---

* This is especially true for western society, who increasingly, after the Renaissance, began to live a life independent of nature and lost much of its touch with it.

with the birth of their Soul. The Creator, who had given them free will, could only warn, but could not help them to prevent the fall. God, their spiritual Parents, had to watch with *"tears in their eyes", how their most lovely children deviated from the principles of growth. The fallen Adam and Eve and their descendants began to live outside the garden of God's domain (Gen. 3:23-24), according to the non and pseudo principles of satan.

Seeing the wicked posterity of Adam and Eve, they became a source of great distress and sorrow for God, as expressed in Genesis 6:6, "And the Lord was sorry that he had made man on the earth, and it grieved him to his heart." Because of one good man Noah, he did not destroy all people. Later, at the time of Moses, God gave them simple laws (10 Commandments), as the first step in living according to God's principles.

When the people thereafter became rebellious again in the course of their restoration or salvation, God their Creator expressed His grieving and broken Heart through Isaiah the prophet:

> Hear, O heavens, and give ear, O earth; for the Lord
> has spoken: 'Sons have I reared and brought up,
> but they have rebelled against me. The ox knows its
> owner, and the ass its master's crib; but Israel does not
> know, my people do not understand' (Isa. 1:2-3).

Hosea writes: "When Israel was a child, I (the Lord) loved him, and out of Egypt I called my son. The more I called them, the more they went from me; they kept sacrificing to the Ba'als, and burning incense to idols. Yet it was I who taught Ephraim to walk, I took them up in my arms; but they did not know that I healed them" (Hosea 11:1-3).

When in the time of Jesus more advanced principles were given, God as parents spoke through Jesus as recorded in Matt. 23:37-38:

> 'O Jerusalem, Jerusalem, killing the prophets and
> stoning those who are sent to you! How often
> would I have gathered your children together as a

---

* God, like humans, have feelings as expressed in the Bible, as loving (John 3:16), pitying (Ps. 103:13), compassionate (Ex. 22:27), weary (Is. 1:14), angry (Ex. 4:14), jealous (Ex. 20:5). God is not a distant, impersonal being, but is directly involved in human affairs, and when humans suffer they also suffer as heart-broken Parents for their lonely and lost children, whom are seeking for their Parents.

hen gathers her brood under her wings, and you
would not! Behold, your house is forsaken and
desolate.'

In the story of the prodigal son, in Luke Chapter 15; God became
known as a true and loving Father, who is easy to forgive our sins, and
accept us the way we are, as soon as we are willing to return to Him.
By doing so, we recognize the Lord as our Father and reject [33]satan as
our evil father (Acts 26:18; John 8:44), and our satan-oriented lifestyle.

The above Bible verses give some indication as to the suffering and
sorrow of God, since the fall of their most precious children. They
could not completely reveal or share their Heart with their little
struggling children because they would not understand. For them, God
is almighty, all knowing, and powerful, and is not capable of any
suffering. Besides, the little ones do not even know the purpose of
creation and God's plan of restoration.

Because of the fall, our relationship with God, who is the source of
love, power, and joy was greatly impaired and thus also the relationship
between our Divine Spirits (god Selves) and our personalities and the
god Selves of others. This resulted that no real "brotherhood" among
people and nations has ever been established. Instead, they continue in
their self-destructive behavior, by hatred, hostility, alienation, and
endless warfare.

A direct relationship between God and humans, for almost all of the
people of the Western world before the advent of Jesus Christ (and for
most people today), was not possible because their Divine Spirits or
Souls remained unborn. The people were thus dependent, for their
communication and guidance, on God's chosen few, such as prophets,
priests, and others. Thus, the unregenerated could only believe in a
God who remains distant, aloof, and outside themselves. Because of
this separation the people have been suffering from spiritual hunger and
thirst, restlessness, and loneliness, as it was movingly expressed in
psalms 42:1-2:

As a heart longs for flowing streams, so longs my soul
for thee, O God. My soul thirsts for God, for the living
God. When shall I come and behold the face of God?
My tears have been my food day and night.

---

[33] See Appendix.

[a]A Short Overview of the History of Restoration

After the fall, Adam and Eve began to live the life of the good and evil personalities, outside "the garden of Eden" (Gen. 3:23); because living a spiritual or divine life and becoming the symbolic tree of life (Gen. 2:9) was no longer possible (Gen. 3:22-24). The adamic race had to hope and wait for the coming of the Savior, who will "bruise" the head of satan (Gen. 3:15).

After Adam and Eve died spiritually, God immediately began to carry out His restoration plan, to reinstate Adam's family. He did this by means of Adam's sons, Cain and Abel whom were placed in the positions of Lucifer and Adam. As Lucifer the elder did not want to be ruled by Adam, but killed him spiritually; Cain (who represented Lucifer on the [b]evil side), likewise did not want to unite with Abel, (who represented Adam on the good side), and slew him. It was revealed through this act that the fallen nature or evil qualities of satan were strongly embedded in Adam's family. This nature could therefore not be removed by reversing the process of the fall, and the restoration was delayed, until Noah's family was chosen ten generations later.

The descendants of Adam's family became like the animals in the field, where the strong preyed upon the weak, and the law of "survival of the fittest" was the only law they respected. Human life had little value, and they, unlike the [c]animals (whom act by instinct) mutilate and kill each other (consciously) for no other purpose than to feel pleasure in the degrading and suffering of their victims. They were even worse than the Chaldeans (see Habakkuk 1) whom were like hardened criminals and thirsty for blood. In that lawless society where "might is right", [*]any ruler could arbitrarily impose at the people his own laws.

---

[a] For a more detailed explanation – See the Divine Principles by Young Oon Kim. Third Edition 1963. – Published by the Holy Spirit Association for the Unification of World Christianity.

[b] Cain the first son was not all evil, but the evil part of his personality was stronger than the good part, while the good part of Abel, the second son, was stronger than the evil part. For many people today, who are living the life of the personality (which is good and evil) may at one time express the evil side and at another time the good side of their personality. The Cain and Abel situation was later made right by Esau the first born, who united with Jacob in Isaac's family.

[c] Some animals whom are or have been strongly influenced by evil people do also kill members of their own species.

[*] There was no freedom in that society. There is little freedom by living under the Law of God, but complete freedom when living a spiritual or divine life (2 Cor. 3:17; John 8:32).

The sovereign or ruling party could punish the people as much as they want, without any regard to [34]natural or moral laws.

In Genesis Chapter 6, verses 5 and 6 it is written:

> The Lord saw that the wickedness of man was great
> in the earth, and that every imagination of the thoughts
> of his heart was only evil continually. And the Lord
> was sorry that He had made man on the earth, and it
> grieved Him to His heart.

God did not only lose His precious children, but their descendants were in continual rebellion against His Will. However, the Lord did not abandon them, but continued with the restoration process to reinstall Noah's family as a substitute for Adam's family.

As Adam's family consisted of eight members, Noah's family was also made up of the same number. Because Ham and his brothers failed to unite with Noah, who represented God, Shem the first born and Ham the second son were not given the opportunity to play and overcome the roles of Cain and Abel. Thus, the restoration was again delayed for ten generations, until Abraham was chosen as the central figure to carry out God's restoration plan.

The first step in the restoration process was finally made in Abraham's family, when Esau the first born of Isaac (son of Abraham and Rebekah) united with his younger brother [a]Jacob (Gen. 33:4) who was in the Abel position. The original blessing given to Adam to "be [b]fruitful and multiply" and "have dominion" over the creation (Gen. 1:28), was given instead to Noah (Gen. 9:7), and finally passed to Abraham and his family (Gen. 12:2-3). God thereafter called Himself "the God of Abraham, the God of Isaac, and the God of Jacob" (Gen. 3:15). Thus, the restoration at the foundation level was finally accomplished in Abraham's family.

---

[34] See Appendix.

[a] After Jacob wrestled and overcame the angel he received a new name – "Israel" (Gen. 32:28). Thereafter his descendants were called Israelites.

[b] To be fruitful is not only to be mature in one's integrated personality (physical-emotional-mental) but also in one's Divine Spirit, wherein the Spirit of God abides (1 Cor. 3:16; Rev. 21:3).

Communication with the Invisible World Is Being Restored

Since the fall, the descendants of Adam and Eve began increasingly to live with the awareness of the physical aspect of life. They were seeking for material values, instead of the spiritual values of e.g. truth, beauty, and goodness. As a result, their personalities became coarser (in vibration) and their [35]psychic senses of their human spirits began to atrophy. The result is that most of them lost much of their sensitivity towards the psychic world and were no longer able to communicate with spirit beings. They no longer had a viable relationship with their own human spirits or psychic selves, and were only vaguely conscious of a multi-dimensional existence. The materialists may encounter in their daily life "strange feelings and experiences", especially when they go to sleep, when their spirit bodies –more or less– separate from their physical bodies. Some of the most uninformed whom believe that thoughts and emotions are produced by the brain, have become so antagonistic that they ridicule anyone who believes in the survival of physically dead.

The belief in life after death before the advent of Christ, was mostly that of unbelief because the human spirits whom "pass on" were not much developed. Although their appearances were shadow and ghost-like, they nevertheless will become more alive (Isa. 26:19; Dan. 12:2); when their Divine Spirits are resurrected or restored (from being dead to being born through God's Love and His Words through Christ (John 11:25,26)), at the time of the appearance of God's Savior. During the life of Jesus Christ, who spoke with Moses and Elijah (Luk. 9:30), and after His death, all kinds of communications were happening between the departed, regenerated Christians, and their brethren on earth (not Christians in name (Rev. 3:1)). The personalities of the Christians, whom were born of God, experience the sense of eternity because they were closely associated with their Divine Spirits, which are like God, eternal and fully alive. They therefore had no problem in the belief of a life after death. Paul spoke of the physical and spiritual bodies (1 Cor. 15:44) and someone who was "caught up to the third heaven – whether in the body or out of the body" (11 Cor. 12:2).

Some humans whom were still able to communicate with the dead, called mediums in (Deut. 18:11), could only make contact with lower human beings and demons, because they were like them. This ability

---

[35] See Appendix.

to contact spirits suggests that the dead (spirits) do exist and are able to communicate. The Bible said that the ones whom died were "gathered to his people" (Gen. 25:8,17). Moreover, it said that we should protect ourselves against the "spiritual hosts of wickedness" (Eph. 6:12), and to "test the spirits to see whether they are of God" (1 John 4:1). The ones whom are in a spiritual tomb are in the lower spiritual realm (not physical tomb with its judgment – which is an old Jewish belief) and are living with Abraham (Luke 16:22). But the rich man in the story of Luke is living in the much lower realm from which he cannot escape, because of the spiritual barrier created by the low vibration of his spirit body. However, the thief on the right side of Jesus, who was crucified with Jesus, defended the Lord and was told to be in Paradise with Jesus (Luke 23:43). Paradise was a much higher spiritual realm than the place where Abraham was, which appeared like a tomb (John 5:28,29).

The above-said mediums had little control over their lower psychic facilities, which was instinctual and based in their solar plexus or guts, as that in higher animals. The Israelites were warned in Deut. 18:9-14, not to become, and heed to sorcerers, soothsayers, mediums, and others. (See also Lev. 19:31, 20:27). They were thus not to communicate with the dead through them. Besides, most of the dead were spirits of those people through which the Lord God wanted to separate His people from. This warning was certainly also for those Israelites, whom in their fascination with the unseen world may heed to the defiled mediums or channelers, instead of listening to the *prophets or messengers (consecrated mediums) sent by Him (Isaiah 8:18,19).

NOTE: Paranormal powers are often shunned by sages because it may become a great temptation to misuse those powers for one's own aggrandizement, and thus strengthen the false self of their ego, who always is seeking to manipulate people and control its environment.

A demonstration of a higher power (using God forces) and lower forces (using evil powers) was given at the court of Pharaoh, where Moses' serpent swallowed the serpents of the sorcerers (Exodus 7:8-13). Another demonstration between the spirits of the Lord and evil spirits was given at Mount Carmel, when Elijah alone was victorious over the 450 false prophets of Baal (1 King 18:17-46). See also Deut. 13:1-5, and other confrontations in Acts 8:9-12, 13:6-12. Jesus warned

---

* The prophets, by using their higher psychic faculties, knew that they were inspired by God. They often said: "Thus says God" (2 Chron. 24:2), or "Thus says the Lord" (2 Sam. 7:5).

against false prophets in Matt. 7:15, 24:11,24; and Jeremiah 27:9 against lying prophets.

The confrontation was between the higher and lower psychic realm or mediumship, whereby the latter was in service of the evil part of one's personality or the deceiver and Antichrist. It was also a confrontation between white and black magic.

Continuation of the History of Restoration

The Tabernacle: Symbol of Humans

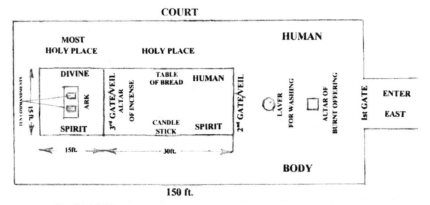

Ex. 26:15-25
30 cubits long, 10 cubits wide, 10 cubits high (1 cubit=+/-1.5 ft.)
see also 1 Kings 6:2 which temple is twice as big

Another important step in the restoration was undertaken by Moses and his people on a tribal, and later on a national level, when they occupied the land of Canaan. They received at Mount Sinai, instructions for the [36a]tabernacle, wherein God "may dwell in their midst" (Ex. 25:8). The people wanted to worship a visible representation, until they were ready to worship an invisible God and His Commandments. Within the Most Holy Place (Ex. 26:34) or Holy of Holies (Heb. 9:3) is located the Ark of the Covenant (Ex. 25:10, 40:3), wherein the "two tables of the testimony" (Ex. 31:18) found their place (Deut. 9:9-11, 10:1-5), wherein God could speak to the people (Ex. 25:22) above the golden mercy seat (Lev. 16:2) of the Ark, between two golden cherubim. The Ark also contained a golden urn with manna (Ex. 16:32-35; Heb. 9:4) which probably represented pure spiritual nourishment and New Truth (Rev. 2:17), and "Aaron's rod that budded" (Num. Ch. 17; Heb. 9:4). The rods of the leaders of the other tribes remain lifeless; only the rod of Aaron of the tribe of Levi had budded and brought forth blossoms and yielded almonds.

The rod of Aaron may be a symbol of the Divine Spirit (Word of God) and used by the life giving Spirit of God for Judgment (Isa. 11:1-4; Rev. 19:15), division in good and evil (Luke 12:51), guidance from the evil to the ideal world (Ex. 14:16), support, strength, and defense

---

[36a] See Appendix.

(Eph. 6:17). It is also a symbol of fully awakened Christians whom constantly generate new life (buds), raise their spiritual children (blossom them), and lead them to maturity (bears fruit).

The tabernacle, which is 45 feet long, 15 feet wide, and 15 feet high, truly represents a human being, and the manner to restore humans to the original intention of their Creator. God was therefore very particular in planning it, and the Israelites in constructing it. Every detail holds great significance about ourselves, humanity, the lessons we have not learned, and, above all, of the Designer, whose tabernacle is the microcosm and pattern of the universe.

The Holy Place could be likened to the human spirit or psyche and the Most Holy Place to the Divine Spirit or Soul. The Ark can be likened as the representation of the Divine Presence within the Soul, or as an individualized Spirit of God (Rev. 21:3).

As the brain of a human being is located in the upper part of the torso, which body is likened to the court, the essence of the Divine Spirit will find its abode in the upper part of the human spirit (which is its body) and direct the purified human mind and spirit, so that they all become one being. The physical body is the vehicle of the human spirit, which in turn will become the vehicle of the Divine Spirit, who is always one with the indwelling Spirit of God.

The furniture of the Holy Place consisted of the incense altar, the golden lamp stand or candlestick, which is the only source of visible light. On the north side of the Holy Place can be seen the table of shewbread containing twelve loaves of bread, representing the twelve tribes of Israel whom were encamped around the tabernacle.

How more one moves towards the "throne of God", how more precious the metal. Gold, for example, was used abundantly in the Holy of Holies, and can be likened to the quality of the Divine Spirit, which is pure, incorruptible, and will not become dull (tarnish). Forty-eight boards of acacia wood covered with gold rested in silver sockets, which is the foundation of the tabernacle. Silver and the precious wood can be likened to the human spirit, which has not been corrupted. The altar of burnt offering, the laver and sockets of the court pillars were made of brass, which metal is like the physical constitution of human beings.

There was only one way to approach the "throne of God" and that was through the three gates. The first gate was the 30-foot court gate, through which everybody may pass, whom wanted to make an offering at the brazen altar. As Heb. 9:22 has it "under the law almost everything is purified with blood, and without the shedding of blood there is no forgiveness of sin".

The second gate at the entrance of the tabernacle was narrower and higher. Through this veil, only the God appointed *priests, chosen from the Levites, were allowed to enter in order to perform their service in the Holy Place. Through the very narrow third gate or veil, which curtain (of blue, purple, scarlet) was embroidered with cherubim, only the high priest could enter the Most Holy Place. He did so once a year, at the Day of Atonement, with animal blood, which he offered for himself and for the errors of the people.

The way modern men and women can "approach God" or grow spiritually, is much the same as that of the Israelites by entering from "outside", through the "first gate of repentance". As there was a barrier between the wilderness and the tabernacle, so there is also a separation between "the world" (John 15:18) and the church or temple grounds, wherein people are living a moral and spiritual life. As the first gate was wide and easy to find; so it is not difficult for "sinners" to find a church, through which they can find – and believe in God and worship Him. After they have repented for their sins, they may, as the Israelites before them, atone for their sins, and pay a ᵃlesser indemnity condition, for their wrongdoing.

As the Old Testament priests had to clean themselves every day in the brazen laver before they were allowed access to the Holy Place, believers in Christ should purify and raise the vibration of their bodies continually by eating the right kinds of food in moderation and abstaining from alcohol, tobacco, drugs, and other harmful substances. In addition, they should follow moral laws, and should be cleansed of their wrongdoing every time they commit those harmful acts by repentance, reconciliation, and penance (Matt. 5:23-24).

---

* In Hinduism, priests were chosen from the Brahman caste. They were, as the Levite priests, not allowed to marry outside their clan, in order to keep their lineage pure.

ᵃ When the people accept the crucified Lord as their Savior, they pay a lesser amount to restore their relationship with God and His people. Thus, no longer the same amount as "An eye for an eye and a tooth for a tooth" (Matt. 5:38), as it was relevant in the Old Testament era.

Having been morally purified in their [b]personality by following the Ten Commandments as the priests in the Old Testament did, believers may enter through the second gate. By passing through this veil, the dormant psychic senses or faculties begin to open, so that they are able to communicate with the [c]good spirits or entities of the invisible spirit world. Then they participate fully in one of the seven churches, which should be united as one. This is symbolized by the candlestick or lamp stand (Rev. 1:12,20), with their shaft and six branches which shall be "one piece of hammered work of pure gold" (Ex. 25:36). According to Ex. 25:33,34, each of the six branches had three sets of buds, flowers, and almonds, while the central shaft had four sets. This candlestick can be compared to the basic spiritual family, based on the physical families of Adam and Noah, with their three sons and daughters. As the growth of the almond tree goes through three stages: buds, flowers, and fruit, the spiritual development of an individual is likened to the stages of little children (babies), young men, and fathers in Christ (1 John 1:12-14). The lamp stand also represents the seven lamps or torches of fire burning before the throne, "which are the seven spirits of God" (Rev. 4:5). The seven lamps on top of the shaft and branches should be well supplied with *oil, so that it always will burn, to keep the believers spiritually awake, and always be ready for the Spirit of Christ (Matt. 25:3), who walks in the midst of the lamp stands (Rev. 1:13).

By studying and assimilating the Word of God in their beings, which is symbolized by the bread on the table, believers in Christ are being cleansed and purified (Eph. 5:26; John 15:3) of lower desires and evil thoughts, and Christ is being formed in them (Gal. 4:19). As the manna in the Ark and the loaves of bread remind the people that Yahweh provides for the physical needs, He also provides for the spiritual needs of all believers. As it is written in Matt. 4:4, "man shall not live by bread alone, but by every word that proceeds from the mouth of God". See also John 6:32-58.

As the Israelites were guided by the "pillar of cloud by day and the pillar of fire by night" (Ex. 13:21,22) to reach the Promised Land;

---

[b] In other parts of the world, different philosophies, such as Confucianism came about, whose task also was to restore the human personality (humanism).

[c] Those whom do not lead a moral life should not communicate with the unseen world because they will only attract evil spirits and demons, according to the law of attraction.

* Oil was used for food, for light, and anointing with the Spirit of God (Zech. 4:1-6). Kings and prophets in the Bible were anointed with oil (2 Sam. 2:4; 1 Kings 19:16). Messiah means the "Anointed One", dedicated – consecrated to God.

believers will likewise be guided by the Spirit of the Universal Christ (who died in Adam but became alive in Jesus Christ (Rev. 1:17-18)) and the Holy Spirit as True Parents, to reach spiritual maturity and live in the Kingdom of God.

After a period of prayer and contemplation, symbolized by the altar of incense (Ps. 141:2; Rev. 8:3-4) before the "seat of God", they accept Christ as their Savior and receive the Holy Spirit and are spiritually born. They are then qualified to "enter the Most Holy Place" and communicate with God "face to face". There is no "darkness" in this place because it is well lit with the spiritual light of the "Shekenah glory" of the Presence of God. "And the city has no need of sun or moon to shine upon it, for the glory of God is its light, and its lamp is the Lamb" (Rev. 21:23, 22:5).

By following the example of the priests, by implementing the [36b]Ten Commandments, the people in the time of Moses would eventually become servants in their relationship with God and thus were allowed to enter the Holy Place. They are then no longer in need to sacrifice vegetables and animals (Heb. 9:11-14) "without blemish" (Num. Ch. 29), but are then expected to obey the Ten Commandments, which is an external voice but will become part of their inner being. As Jeremiah 31:33 instructed, "I will put my law within them, and I will write it upon their hearts" (Psalms 40:8) or "minds" (Heb. 10:16). By obeying the laws of God, the conscience of the Israelites became clearer, and the "Voice of God" stronger, so that they could be more receptive and agreeable with the *prophets and others, when God spoke through them.

Purifying or stripping the personalities of the evil qualities of satan (original sin) and bringing the Israelites back to the point where Adam and Eve came in their development, was accomplished to some degree in the Old Testament dispensation, by obeying God and His laws.

Here, the people are waiting, with great anticipation, for the advent of Christ (as predicted in Isaiah 9,11, and 60), to lead "them back" to the [37]lost "garden of Eden", whose entrance, and the way to the Tree of Life, has been blocked by the "cherubim and a flaming sword" (Gen. 3:24)

[36b] See Appendix.

* Previous to the advent of Christ the path of initiation was not open – only for a chosen few – such as high priests, prophets, and kings.

[37] See Appendix.

As Apostle Paul has it, in 1 Cor. 15:45,47, "The first man Adam became a living being; the last Adam became a life-giving spirit --- The first man was from the earth, a man of dust (living the life of the personality); the second man is from heaven" (living a divine life, that is the individualized Spirit of God via the Divine Spirit is in charge of the personality)". "As in Adam all die (spiritual death caused by the fall of Adam and Eve), so also in Christ shall all be made alive" (spiritually alive – birth and growth of Divine Spirit (1 Cor. 15:22)).

Christ's mission is to restore spiritual life to all humanity (Rom. 5:12-21). His mission was thus to abolish angel-type world of master and servant, and to establish adamic-type world of Father and son, Mother and daughter.

The Mission and Nature of Christ

When the long-awaited Messiah finally came, the New Testament dispensation began, with His birth in the city of David called Bethlehem. Thereafter, His personality and Divine Spark "increased in wisdom and stature" (Luk. 2:52). The Christ or Divine Spirit was born, when He (like Adam and Eve) was a teenager, within His pure personality, which was [38]born without original sin. Jesus was therefore a true human being, and was called the "Son of Man", but was also called the "Son of God". At the time of His baptism he was filled with the Holy Spirit (Luk. 3:22, 4:1), and, in addition, after His struggle with satan (Matt. 4:1-11), was given Sonship or Lord over heaven and earth (Matt. 11:27, 28:18). This unique and only Son position was endowed to Adam, but because of the fall, left Adam and came back through the ministry of Jesus Christ as the *last Adam (1 Cor. 15:45).

> I am the first and the last, and the living one;
> I died and behold I am alive for evermore (Rev. 1:18).

Throughout His ministry, Jesus was overshadowed and became one with the Son or Universal Christ. The Son, together with Jesus Christ, was the Savior and Redeemer, and "in Christ God was reconciling the world to Himself" (1 Cor. 5:19). The Son was portrayed as the Christ of faith in the Gospel of John and in the "I am" sayings of the same

---

[38] See Appendix.

* As the last Adam position was being fulfilled by the Son or Christ Consciousness of God, the last Eve position was being realized by the Holy Spirit of God, until a suitable Bride has been found (Rev. 19:7).

Gospel. He was the one who guided Christians throughout history, while they were also being comforted by the Holy Spirit.

After a short mission, Jesus "was despised and rejected by men; a man of sorrows, and acquainted with grief, and as one from whom men hide their faces" (Isaiah 53:3).

The moment Jesus died on the cross "the curtain (Ex. 26:33) of the temple was torn in two, from top to bottom, and the earth shook, and the rocks were split; the tombs (lower spiritual realm) also were opened, and many bodies of the saints who had fallen asleep were raised" (spiritually) – (Matt. 27:51-52).

The inner sanctuary or the Holy of Holies, could in the past only be entered through the curtain or veil by the high priest (Heb. 9:7-8) who was allowed to communicate with God directly. Because the tabernacle of Moses is the symbol of every individual, the barrier or veil between the god Self (Divine Spirit) and the human self (personality) within the believer was likewise broken (Heb. 10:19-20). Thus, the door to God's Presence was finally open to all followers of Christ. Thereafter, at the day of Pentecost, 120 people were filled with the Holy Spirit (Acts 2:1-4). They will "have the right to the Tree of Life" (Rev. 22:14), "eat of the Tree of Life" (Rev. 2:7), and become the Tree of Life, after they have washed "their robes" of their personalities (physical-etheric-emotional-mental sheaths). Then they "enter the city (Garden of Eden) by the gates" (each one according to his or her exotic beliefs).

> And I heard a loud voice from the throne saying,
> 'Behold, the dwelling of God is with men. He will
> dwell with them, and they shall be His people, and
> God Himself will be with them; He will wipe away
> every tear from their eyes, and death shall be no more,
> neither shall there be mourning nor crying nor pain
> anymore, for the former things have passed away'
> (Rev. 21:3-4).

As the Words of the Gospel have become part of the believer's most inner Being, the Spirit of God now speaks instead of the voice of Conscience, and the Kingdom of God is no longer without but within (Luk. 17:21). They are therefore no longer "under law but under grace" (Rom. 6:14).

Those people whom were born again (born of God) or initiated in divine life, were for the first time called or nicknamed Christians (little Christs) in the early church at Antioch (Acts 11:26). They were like Jesus Christ, in their expressions of their Divine or Christ Spirit, which was formed and shaped by the teachings of Jesus. Because their Souls were governing the personalities of true Christians, Apostle Paul could say, "It is no longer I (personality) who lives, but Christ (Divine Spirit) who lives in me" (Gal. 2:20) or "until Christ be formed in you" (Gal 4:19).

The Battle between Good and Evil

Because the original sin (evil qualities of satan) is still present to some degree in one's ªgood/evil personality, depending on one's ancestors and life lived, it needs to be rooted out completely when growing to perfection or spiritual maturity. Therefore, it is not possible to grow unless one removes the inherited satanic nature such as: pride, rebellion, lust, greed, [39]etc., which is deeply embedded in one's personality. This has become more difficult because the ᵇevil part of the personality or fallen nature, has taken the vacant place of the Divine Spirit. It acts as an imposter and will do anything in its power to preserve its identity and uphold its domain.

That is why there is such a [40]great struggle within oneself, when the awakened and emerging Divine Spirit begins the great battle with the fallen or satanic nature. This evil nature, in some of Paul's writings, is also called "the flesh", which creates the impulse to do evil. "For the desires of the flesh are against the Spirit, and the desires of the Spirit are against the flesh" (Gal. 5:17; Rom. 8:6).

This fallen nature or inborn evil desire is also called "old nature" or "old man"; "put off your old nature which belongs to your former manner of life --- and put on the new nature" (Eph. 4:22,24). It is a fight for the spiritual life and death of the born-again individual, and as Peter advised us: "Abstain from the passions of the flesh that wage war against your soul" (1 Pet. 2:11). The divine and evil natures are always warring against each other; that is why the young Paul lamented in Romans 7:19-23:

> For I do not do the good I want, but the evil I do
> not want is what I do. Now if I do what I do not
> want, it is no longer I that do it, but sin which dwells
> within me. So I find it to be a law that when I want
> to do right, evil lies close at hand. For I delight in
> the law of God, in my innermost self (Divine Spirit)

ª When one no longer fears God and does not want to defend Him and is ashamed to talk about Him, and does not like to live according to His laws, his or her life is being swayed to the evil side of the personality.

ᵇ In psychology it is called the shadow side of the human personality. This evil part is no longer able to obey the Will of God. It loves to hear about and see evil, and encourages others to do evil.

[39] - [40] See Appendix.

but I see in my members (physical, emotional, and
mental parts of the personality) another law at war
with the law of my mind and making me captive to
the law of sin which dwells in my members.

There is thus not only a conflict between the good and evil within
the personality of good people, but a [a]fierce battle is being waged
between the Divine Spirit and the [b]evil part of the ego or satanic nature
of generated believers. As the first battle, guided by one's conscience,
is weak and easily lost, the second battle can be won with the help of
the Holy Spirit.

The fight between good and evil inwardly and outwardly has been
going on for ages. It all began in a more visible way when Michael and
his angels fought against Lucifer and his angels (Rev. 12:7,8). The
Essenes (a Jewish sect at the time of Jesus) expressed it, as the fight
between "the sons of light and the sons of darkness".

When the Divine Spirits of individuals are not much developed, and
when the born-again Christians do not have much spiritual support,
they will easily backslide to their former good/evil lifestyle. The
backsliders or carnal Christians, need to be addressed again as Paul did
in 1 Cor. 3:3 and Heb. 5:12. Some of them are killed spiritually by evil
people or demons whose father is satan, who "was a murderer from the
beginning" (John 8:44), because he killed Adam and Eve spiritually
(Gen. 2:17, 3:6). Satan also inspired Herod to kill the baby Jesus,
which is an indication that satan and his cohorts like to kill vulnerable
physical and spiritual babies. However, when the aspirant on the
spiritual path survives the onslaught and temptations, the old sin nature
becomes progressively lessened in the psyche of the individual. It will
eventually lose its savor, and to do evil is of no joy anymore. Those
individuals will be pure in heart (Matt. 5:8) or in their psyche, and evil
things will no longer rise up out of their hearts (Mark 7:20-23). Satan
and evil spirits with or without bodies are no longer able to influence
those individuals and become powerless and bound (Rev. 20:2).

---

[a] For more detail of this battle see the "The Birth and Evolution of the Divine Spirit or
Soul".

[b] This satanic nature is not satan himself, as some people say, but his inherited nature
or characteristic. Jesus and His Disciples, whom were truly doing God's Will, were
daily confronted with satan and evil spirits – as indicated in Matt. 16:23 and Luke 22:3.
They surely believed in the reality of satan.

How to Subdue the Evil Nature

First of all, we should not let our mind be used by our false self, but only by our Divine Spirit or True Self. Secondly, we should stop feeding the evil part of our personality with evil deeds, attitudes, and desires. In this way we do not inflate it, but "starve it to death". Thus we do not yield to the prompting of our "old nature", which is antagonistic to God, but only to the inspiration of our "new nature" (Eph. 4:24; 2 Pet. 1:4; 2 Cor. 5:17), which we can verify with our higher or divine nature.

We should be able to overcome all temptations, by the power of the written Word (Matt. 4:1-10) and the Holy Spirit. However, if we get tempted, it is good to listen to Paul's wise counsel as it is written in 1 Cor. 10:13:

> No temptation has overtaken you that is not common
> to man. God is faithful, and He will not let you be
> tempted beyond your strength, but with the temptation
> will also provide the way of escape, that you may be
> able to endure it.

Dealing with Immature Marriages

The ones whom have overcome the evil within their human selves and have reached maturity of their human personality and Divine Spirit will be blessed by God in marriage, and bring forth talented and creative children, without original sin.

However, good people do not have to wait to get married until they reach full maturity or perfection (Matt. 5:48) because this is, for most people at this time, an unattainable goal. They therefore can marry when they have at least grown to physical maturity, and have attained an elevated degree of psychological and moral development and a measure of spiritual growth. This marriage may be called a conditional marriage. The couples may then seal their marriage after they have grown to perfection. *This is the best that most people in their present state of evolution can do.

Because of imperfection, the good/evil human personality is not pure, and often resists to be ruled by the budding, but pure Divine Spirit or Higher Self, of one's being, which has not yet gained enough strength to control the personality. The result is that lust and selfishness can still be found in the relationship of the couple, instead of respect, mutual love, and a longing to have immaculate children.

If the people belong to a religious organization, they should firmly abide by the marriage laws and customs of their faiths. The couples should also participate in the available – physical, psychological, spiritual – support systems of their faiths, so that it will be easier to

---

* Below we find some wit and wisdom of immature marriages:

"One was never married, and that is his hell, another is, and that is his plague" – Robert Burton.
"There are good marriages, but practically no delightful ones" – La Rochefoucauld.
"Marriage, to tell the truth, is an evil, but it is a necessary evil" – Menander.
"It (marriage) is like a cage; one sees the birds outside desperate to get in, and those inside desperate to get out" – Montaigne.
"The marriage state is the most complete image of heaven and hell we are capable of receiving in this life" – Richard Steele.
"Marriage is popular because it combines the maximum of temptation with the maximum of opportunity" – George Bernard Shaw.
"The world has grown suspicious of anything that looks like a happy married life" (Oscar Wilde).

keep their marriage *vow. Others should remind themselves that God is the Source of their love and not their lovers. Atheists may believe that this universal love is expressed through the inner core or Self of their personality which is also called Higher Self (in contrast with the lower self or ego) and Buddha nature. It is also good to invoke a divine blessing on one's marriage, either by themselves or a representative of an organization(s), which can be of great psychological and spiritual support for the union of the couple.

A worthy conditional marriage would occur if the man and woman have well-integrated and mature personalities, wherein their minds are well developed and in charge of their instincts and feelings of their bodies. Thus, they should have reasonable control over their emotions, and not be enslaved by passions or uncontrollable lust.

In addition, they should be entering, or be in the †fourth stage of life, when the newborn Divine Spirits (spiritual man (1 Cor. 2:15)) are becoming more and more in charge of their personalities, especially in the higher stages. The love between a man and a woman will be more pure and spiritual and less sensual and erotic. They will then have a stronger tendency to harmonize the act of creation, with the purpose and forces of creation. When they become mature spiritually, their Divine Spirits or Souls, aided by the Holy Spirit, are better able to lead and regulate sexual relations, and fight against the evil still lingering in their human selves. "For the desires of the flesh are against the Spirit, and the desires of the Spirit are against the flesh" (Gal. 5:17).

They will bring forth children whom are increasingly reflecting the characteristics or qualities of God, as "the fruit of the Spirit" (Gal. 5:22-23) or Soul qualities, such as: "love, joy, peace, patience, kindness, goodness, faithfulness, gentleness, self-control". In addition, we may add a few more treasures of the Divine Spirit, and of the virtuous integrated human psyche or spirit such as affection, happiness, caring, mercifulness, fortitude, duty, boldness, integrity, trustfulness, wonder, inventiveness humbleness, wholeness, respect, sympathy, optimism, goodwill, consideration, strong will and strength, beauty and harmony, [41]etc. as it is expressed through the purified emotion and mental clarity of the personality.

---

* A typical marriage vow is: "For better for worse, for richer for poorer, in sickness and in health, to love and to cherish, till death do us part."

† Those people abide by the principles of higher religions. See Seven Stages of Development.

[41] See List of positive and its opposite negative qualities, evil words, and attributes created by humanity after the fall.

Those qualities can be developed more effectively on the earth plane, where there is more hardship and thus greater obstacles to overcome, than in the spirit world where life is much easier. This development, however, is not always gained for those whom are rich in earthly possessions. They therefore do not have to deal with economic conditions, which are more difficult, because everyone is still living in and dealing with the fallen world. #42It certainly is not easy for those whom have to serve others in order to survive – which was originally intended in a less harsh way – gain valuable experience, growth, and accumulate goodness in their being.

It is, however, not recommended to get married when the personalities of the couple are immature and more evil than good. As Paul exhorted in 1 Thess. 4:3-5:

> For this is the Will of God, your sanctification: that you
> abstain from unchastity; that each one of you know how
> to take a wife for himself in holiness and honor, not in
> the passion of lust like heathen who do not know God.

Paul is not addressing here "wordly people" whom are living the life of the good and evil personalities – such as most Greeks and Romans of his time – but to regenerated believers whom are trying to live a divine life, thus to those whom have made spiritual progress. As soon as a couple starts lusting after each other, they backslide to ordinary human consciousness from the height of spiritual consciousness. They become "wordly" again by pleasing each other more than the Lord, that is their external selves, instead of their inner Selves (1 Cor. 7:32-35).

Some ministries say that couples can do what they want in the confines of their marriage, and many are eager to take their advice, and thus are *using their marriage certificate as a license for unlimited sex. They can, however, not hide behind this certificate and be exempt from the consequences of sexual indulgence which causes a decline in their moral and spiritual lives (unless they are already fallen) and may produce children whom are born in lust.

#42 See Appendix.

* Geert Groote (d 1384), a Dutch theologian (see *21) who echoed the voice of great church fathers and saints, said that the married state was not only less perfect (than celibacy) but can be dangerous, a trap or a great obstacle to a human's way to heaven. Matrimony does not give a remedy against lustful desires, unless one continues to fight against those desires.

Others go so far as to use pornographic videos to keep their so-called "love life" going. Paul, however, advises couples whom experience difficulties in their marriage to abstain from each other "for a season" and devote themselves to prayer (1 Cor. 7:5). This allows the purifying love of God to flow through themselves and to each other, and to conceive a child in love (immaculately) without passion.

A man and a woman should not marry because of physical attraction and sex appeal because they will disappear. This may happen at any time and will most likely happen when the couple gets [43]older and the physical beauty is no longer there, and the inner beauty – radiating from their Divine Spirits – is not or is little developed. Sex and sexual desire alone cannot keep the relationship going, when true affection and spiritual love are not present. Thus, instead of the sentimental love of the personality, which is emotional in character, couples should try to love each other in an unselfish way, that is, with their most inner beings.

Let me give here two examples of the relationships of the couple with and without the involvement of their most inner beings.

A mutual physical attraction between a man and woman occurs when psychic energy is flowing between them (as all forms of energy flow between polarities) and they *begin to like each other. They may get to know the other or get acquainted with their inner personality by talking to the opposite party. By understanding each other, which results in mutual trust, more energy is exchanged and they long for the other, especially when they remember their happy encounters. When, however, in addition to being psychically involved, the couple is also spiritually oriented, they experience higher energy exchange which makes them more elated and in love. The pair is grateful, experiences joy, and has concern for each other. They also appreciate and adore the other, and because they are in love, they see only beauty and the universe in the other person.

Other men and women whom are living the life of the personality may meet and are attracted to each other physically and emotionally,

---

[43] See Appendix.

* It happens sometimes that the man and woman "fall in love" at first sight. They not only match (in their polarities) and identify with each other (having same traits), but are also sensitive to the auric wavelength or vibration of the other, which has blended with their own, in the emotional, mental, and spiritual aspects of their being.

53

which soon develops into a sexual desire for each other, with the result that they no longer be and grow in love, but ^a"fall in love". Because they are operating from a lower level of their being, their emotional expression or so-called love is ^bonly restricted to one person, and are therefore not in oneness with the universal forces. This romantic attachment easily results in that the male and female start to enjoy themselves through the use of the other, which is nothing else but mutual lust. They might be living for a long time together, but do not really know each other. Because they are deprived of true love, the couple is blaming each other for being unhappy, which causes a marital hatred to set in, which may result in divorce.

They should also not rush into a union or wedding when they are madly "in love" with each other, because this is not true love, but only an emotional "high" (infatuation) or "adolescent love". It is also called by some, romantic love (as portrayed by romans and movies), which eventually wears itself out under the tension of daily life. Some experience this kind of love as a tingling sensation, especially when the auras of the pair are in close proximity to each other, and emotional energies are flowing. If the strong emotional involvement in each other does not work out, the frustration and disappointment they experience can also be strong and may easily lead to divorce or breakup. Therefore, a productive and satisfying relationship requires more of a commitment, responsibility, and maturity than just the "emotional high" of being in love. Besides, this "high", because of its intensity, cannot last long.

NOTE: A couple may fall in love physically by beauty and lust, emotionally by infatuation, and ascend in love spiritually by seeing the divine in the other.

They should not engage, if one party seeks self-indulgence, when their satanic nature or Antichrist is ruling his or her life and the other party to live a spiritual life, when their Divine Spirit or Christ Spirit is ruling her or his spiritual life. However, there are exceptions (1 Cor. 7:12-16).

They all should ask God to [44]find the right spouse for them (Mr. and Mrs. Right) so that they will be happy in their marriage and enjoy

---

^a Because the consciousness of the couple has fallen to a lower level of their being, they are more interested in satisfying the lust for each other, and care less about other people.

^b This restricted love is later extended to family and society, whereby they want to live isolated from other people.

[44] See Appendix.

their children whom are holy (1 Cor. 7:14) and of their own reflection of goodness.

What Does the Bible Say about Marriage and Divorce?

Marriage is a divine institution, which is described before the fall in Genesis 2:18, "Then the Lord God said, 'It is not good that the man should be alone; I will make him a helper fit for him.'" "Therefore a man leaves his father and his mother and cleaves to his wife and they become one flesh" (Gen. 2:24). They were to "be fruitful (become mature) and multiply, (bring forth children) and fill the earth and subdue it" (have dominion) (Gen. 1:28).

Jesus said in Mark 10:6-9, "but from the beginning of creation, 'God made them male and female.' 'For this reason a man shall leave his father and mother and be joined to his wife, and the two shall become one flesh'. So they are no longer two but one flesh. What therefore God has joined together, let no man put asunder." In Luke 16:18, Jesus said, "Everyone who divorces his wife and marries another commits adultery, and he who marries a woman divorced from her husband commits adultery" (see also Mark 10:11-12). A lower standard was used in Matt. 5:32, "Everyone who divorces his wife, except on the grounds of unchastity, makes her an adulteress" (see also Matt. 19:9). This, however, does not mean that the innocent party has to press for divorce, even if it is permissible. They can reconcile and rebuild their marriage.

In the Old Testament era, a man was allowed to divorce his wife after having "found some indecency in her" (Deut. 24:1-4), although they should not divorce their wives in order to marry younger women. "For I hate divorce, says the Lord" (Mal. 2:13-16). Jesus commented in Matt. 19:8, "For your hardness of heart Moses allowed you to divorce your wives, but from the beginning it was not so." By saying this, Jesus set up the norm of people's behavior, as it was to be before the fall of the first human couple.

Apostle Paul said in 1 Cor. 7:2, "Because of temptation to immorality, each man should have his own wife and each woman her own husband." "To the married I give charge, not I but the Lord, that the wife should not separate from her husband and that the husband should not divorce his wife" (1 Cor. 7:10-11). "The law is binding on a person only during his life? Thus a married woman is bound by law to her husband as long as he lives; but if her husband dies she is discharged from the law concerning the husband" (Rom. 7:1-2). Paul, like Jesus, used the highest standard, although a lower standard was used in 1 Tim. 5:14 and Heb. 13:4, concerning marriages.

As God is perfect, He cannot but establish anything less than a perfect standard concerning relationships and marriage. Because people are far from perfection, it is not always possible to impose a perfect law on imperfect or immature people. Churches of different denominations have made some concessions because they all recognize that sexual abstinence after divorce is not possible for most of the faithful, and therefore should allow them to *remarry.

Problems in Marriage

Problems may occur in a marriage when one or both parties are immature. They want their spouses to be perfect in every way, and to continually give them whatever they want. If one party can no longer give what the other party wants their relation will not last long and they soon look for someone else. This breakup is hastened when some persons may think that there is nothing wrong with them, and that all the faults lie with the other half.

The romantic stage or honeymoon will soon be over when the pair discovers that marriage is also about commitment, responsibility, and sacrifice. This is especially true when children are born of them, whom they have to take care of. However, by raising their children, parents learn unconditional love, which is closely related to God's love (if it is not abusive and not too possessive), which surely speeds up their growth and development.

While they saw, in the beginning of their marriage, only good qualities in the other, they are later rudely awakened to the fact that their spouses not only have bad habits and psychological problems, but also discover the evil or shadow sides of their personalities. When the shadow personality emerges in one party it will be in conflict consciously and (or) unconsciously with the good personality of the other party. Therefore, in order to stay together, it is good to pray to-

---

* In the Catholic tradition, marriage is a sacred covenant and can only be broken through a special annulment. In many other Christian traditions and Judaism, divorce and subsequent remarrying is allowed in the case of infidelity, physical abuse, mistreatment of children, addictions, etc.

gether, thus raising their consciousness to a higher level.

Individuals whom are living a divine or spiritual life should be in control of their lives and limit their sexual embraces; otherwise they may easily backslide to ordinary human consciousness. This is especially true when the couple, at times, is so much enslaved by uncontrollable passion that they become overly jealous and try to possess and dominate each other. This will surely give a serious blow to their relationship and might break up their marriage.

A relationship is short lived when the pair continually thinks about sexual relationships. Their consciousness will fall and get stuck in the *second level of their beings and thus begin to live a life "below the belt". When he or she lust after each other in marriage, they will also lust after other men and women. They may then search for ultimate sexual excitement and fulfillment in new partners by practicing ªwife swapping or swinging. Because when sexual passion does not let itself be controlled by mental or spiritual power, it starts to have a life of its own and becomes easily perverted. It may soon degenerate to abusive behavior and aggression of the male partner and emotional reactivity and aggression of the female partner. As many people know, aggression and sexual behavior are closely linked. Other ᵇperversions, such as masochism (receiving pain), sadism (inflicting pain), homosexuality (sodomy and lesbianism), pederasty, bestiality, etc. are also the result of the isolation of sexuality from spirituality. By practicing sexual perversion, the male becomes like his master satan and the female like Eve after the fall.

Exchanges of Energy and Fluids

Every person we meet affects us in some way and changes us to some degree, through the exchange of ideas, thoughts, emotions, words, etc., depending on the duration, receptivity, and intensity of the

---

* See Seven Stages of Development.

ª Our culture, as expressed in some women and men magazines, recommend to their readers to have extra-marital affairs to practice a healthy alternative lifestyle in order to bring "life back" into their marriages, thereby ignoring the Old Testament injunction (for people whom are living the life of the good/evil personality) that adulterers are put to death (Lev. 20:10); and the admonition in the New Testament (for people whom are living a spiritual life) not to commit adultery.

ᵇ Because of excessive use, the sexual sensibilities become dulled or jaded. This is one important reason that some people get only sexually stimulated or "turned on" by practicing perversions.

communication. Thus, the ones with whom we frequently are in contact with, at our work and place we live, influence us profoundly through the vibrations of their etheric, psychic, and spiritual bodies, and the radiation – projecting wavelengths – of their auras. [a]Apostle Paul warned believers not to have fellowship with sinners (1 Cor. 5:11,13) "not to associate with anyone who bears the name of brother if he is guilty of immorality or greed", --- "not even to eat with such a one". So strong is Paul's warning against fellowship with them that he commands that they be driven from their midst. As the Dutch saying goes, "Die slapen onder het zelfde deken, krygen dezelfde streken" [b](The ones whom are sleeping under the same blanket will acquire the same tricks.)

When married lovers exchange deep kisses, an exchange of bodily fluids takes place, which may even affect their blood quality. When they have sexual intercourse, an exchange of special fluids takes place, which is actually a transmuted form of blood. Through this act they not only procreate but also incorporate, by becoming one blood or "one flesh". However, not only an interchange of fluids occurs between the pair, but also an intense form of energy (electrical and magnetic) exchange, at different levels of their being. This is especially true in [c]orgasm or climax, when the auras of the couples for a moment become one, and the partners are transformed to a state of universal awareness, creating a unity of all opposites. Through this act, they exchange or take away from each other a small part of the energy field. Because partners are not always at the same level of growth, one may feel charged and the other drained through this encounter.

By opening the energy fields to one another, they may absorb each other's positive and negative elements such as: love or hate, happiness or sadness, peace or anxiety, faith or fear, trust and doubt, hope or dis-

---

[a] Paul is speaking to baby Christians whom are weak and vulnerable. See "The Birth and Evolution of the Divine Spirit or Soul".

[b] By touching each other, there is not only a sensation of touch, but also a bio-magnetic exchange takes place, and an intermingling of their auras which can be in harmony or disharmony. High caste Hindus do not allow themselves to be touched or shake hands in order to avoid psychic contamination, especially not with low caste people, the so-called untouchables.

[c] Besides a discharge of sexual fluid (a carrier of etheric force), orgasm is also a discharge of accumulated sexual energy which is derived mainly from one's life force and is also called libido in psychological terms.

appointment, etc., as well as the basic natures of every social evil such as: pride, lust (passionate sexual desire), *greed (excessive desire to possess things), and license (selfish freedom without responsibility). However, they may also absorb from each other the good qualities they are lacking and acquire some of their characteristics, and may, after a length of time, resemble each other in their main aspects! Thus, the men become more yin (domestic), while the women become more yang (outgoing).

Sexual intercourse thus entails a momentary fusion, which may be superficial and passing or deep and lasting. It depends on the emotional, mental, and spiritual rapport of the couple and the length of involvement. When this relationship is lasting, it may take as much as seven years or longer to entangle their energies or magnetic tie, and become free from each other.

Apostle Paul said in 1 Cor. 6:16:

> Do you not know that he who joins himself to a prostitute,
> becomes one body with her? For, as it is written, "The
> two shall become one flesh."

By having sex with many partners the promiscuous, especially prostitutes, absorb some of the substances of the others, including karmic burdens. They become psychically confused and often do not know who they really are. By starting to mingle with one sexual partner, who absorbs a psychic part of you and, in turn, may pass his and your part onto others. In this way you will affect and become affected by the other sexual partners, and are uncertain of your identity.

NOTE: If someone has fallen in love, or worse, had sexual relations with the other party (also in marriage), he or she can more easily influence, tempt, and drag down the other psychically and spiritually, even after they are no longer together.

---

* Someone who is greedy has an insatiable desire or craving to acquire something, beyond what one needs or deserves. It is an unscrupulous eagerness for gain, ignoring the needs of others whom they manipulate into poverty.

Expression through Energy Centers

In a relationship, the human and Divine Spirit is able to express itself through the body by means of [a]energy centers (vortices of energy) which are located in the [b]etheric body and in higher bodies. [c]There are seven main centers; they may be completely or partially open or atrophied. In a highly advanced spiritual person all the centers are fully open, while in a materialistic person only the lower three centers are fully developed or open. Thus the higher centers of the people who are living the life of the personality are sluggish and dormant. The first energy center (chakra in Hindu teaching) is located at the base of the spine and receives (from surrounding and other centers) and distributes power and vitality to the nervous system. It is the abode of self-preservation. The second energy center or sacral chakra is located at the groin and receives (from surrounding and other centers) and distributes power, thus energizing the sexual nature. The third energy center is located at the solar plexus or guts and receives (mainly from the lower spiritual or astral plane) and distributes power for expressing emotions and desires. The fourth energy center is located at the heart area, while the fifth is found at the throat area, the sixth at the brow, and the seventh at the top of the head. The last four energy centers are mainly connected with the higher spiritual or divine planes.

Through the energy vortices, different aspects of the human spirit and Soul are able to express themselves through the physical body. Couples who engage in a sexual relationship should do so face to face, so that through the alignment of their chakras the greatest amount of energy will be exchanged. Some of these centers may be only partially opened of one party and fully opened in the other party. This may cause disharmony, which results that the unmatched part of one's being seeks unconsciously for a balance. If they cannot find this equilibrium in their mate they may look for someone else, unless, through strong compassion between couples, the closed centers are being opened. Because of imperfection of the mates, the consummation cannot be completed on all the seven planes; there will always be a yearning for complete union and balance of the energy centers.

---

[a] Butterflies in our stomach, pounding in our heart, frogs in our throat, orgasm are manifestations of the presence of energy centers in our being.

[b] See "The Etheric Body".

[c] See Seven Stages of Development.

Most people love from the *solar plexus, which is the center of possessive, addictive, and selfish love. They love conditionally with attachment and might say, "I love you – provided..." and may think, if you give me what I want. They have a tendency to control, own, and manipulate others, by using love or rather the emotional force and attraction as the means of barter. This love causes much excitement and disappointment and is also known as a bad imitation of true romantic love.

When you say to someone, "I love you", from which level of your being do you experience the feeling? From the first, security and survival; from the second, sex and sensual gratification; from the third, to have power and possession; or in the heart, where spiritual or divine life begins. In this fourth center you will experience true love, which is not identified with the emotion, but is expressed through the emotion. Through this center you love freely, purely, openly, without any condition, and, in turn, are accepted as the person you are, without qualification, demands, or ownership. This spiritual love or Heart communication is unconditional, everlasting, and is like the love Apostle Paul explained in 1 Cor. 13:4-7:

> Love is patient and kind; love is not jealous or boastful;
> it is not arrogant or rude. Love does not insist on its own
> way; it is not irritable or resentful; it does not rejoice at
> wrong, but rejoices in the right. Love bears all things,
> believes all things, hopes all things, endures all things.

Psychical Relationships of Couples

Some lovers are so sensitive that they are able to communicate their emotions and thoughts without speaking, even from a distance. Because of their intimate relationship, they are attuned closely to each other's psychic vibration. The lovers, therefore, make not only contact through their external voice (e.g. telephone), but also psychically through their human spirits, which is called thought transfer or telepathy. While the spirits of the pair are, at times, through mental projection and day dreaming united, they can be together for longer periods, when both are sleeping. When they fall asleep the couple becomes unconscious, because their spirits separate (more or less) from

* When two lovers experience a tingling sensation in their solar plexus, they should understand that this is a clear indication that they love each other from the level of their personalities (the lower three) and not from the height of their Divine Spirits, which is elating, uplifting, blissful, and universal.

their bodies and much of their consciousness is transferred temporarily to the spirit body or psyche. Freed from their bodies, the spirits of the lovers can roam freely in a different dimension, and there is a possibility that they can meet each other. However, through practice, they may consciously separate from their bodies, meet and explore together the other world in full awareness and control. This is called astral travel. At this plane or dimension they can fully experience each other by literally *blending or merging with each other, much more than in the physical dimension. Thus, the pair has not only the opportunity to be physically together but also psychically while their bodies are sleeping. Having grown spiritually they will unite their purified astral or lower spirit body with their growing Divine Spirits or Souls. The Eternal Soul will then use the mortal spirit as a vehicle to travel to the lower and higher dimensions of the spirit world(s). The couple will then become what God intended them to be from the "beginning", a pair wherein the individualized Spirit of God will dwell forever "and they shall be His people" (Rev. 21:3).

Spiritual Relationships of Couples

In the higher realms or kingdoms (John 14:2), a spiritual or mystical marriage may take place, when the human spirit or psyche integrates or unites with one's own Divine Spirit or Soul. Thus, the human spirit as female, marries or unites with its own Divine Spirit or Spirit of Christ within as male. The most important sacrament in Gnosticism took place in the bridal chamber, wherein the feminine spirit of the practioner united with their developing masculine Spirit or Soul. Nuns to this day are called "Brides of Christ", while spiritual brothers experience a divine closeness which develops into a love relationship. Here the inner marriage was thus achieved in place of outer marriage, after the human spirit has been prepared to receive the heavenly bridegroom, which is like Jesus Christ in character.

The spiritual or divine relationships between men and women are much deeper and stronger than the human relation between their personalities, even when the latter are married. As spiritual brothers and sisters they love each other with their Souls, and there is also a deep love between same sex adults. It has been said that David's love for Jonathan exceeded his love for women. "For he (Jonathan) loved him as he love his own soul" (1 Sam. 20:17). There was also a deep

---

* It is also called melding. Spirits are able, with little resistance, to walk through each other when they are in harmony.

love between Ruth and Naomi (see the Book of Ruth), Jesus and "the beloved disciple" and Paul with his close disciples.

NOTE: There are a small number of spiritual people whom experience in their life sexual problems, especially those whose animal nature is still strong, because of their abnormal sex life. This also includes those whom have complete control of their physical life, but let thoughts about sex play a very important role in their life. Some of them are stimulated in the wrong way by having sexual thoughts about Christ and goddess(es). Although mystics are usually successful in drawing higher energies from divine sources, however, if they occupy themselves with sex too much, those abundant energies will be transformed or transmuted in the lower creative centers instead of the higher ones. This results that they are even more stimulated by sexual forces than before. This is why many spiritual leaders fall or may become monsters of lust. As the saying goes: "The greater the sinner, the greater the saint."

Children of Noble and Less Noble Birth

Most children are born with more or less original sin, depending on the moral and spiritual development (level of consciousness) of their parents and their ancestors and *how and in which state the creation act was performed. Jesus of Nazareth, for example, was conceived in obedience to the plan of the Creator. His parents were virginal or pure in thought word and deed, backed up by a long line of ancestors of forty-two generations (Matt. 1), whom, under the guidance of God, made compensations so that Jesus could be born without original sin, from a passionless or virgin body.

Although many children are born with original sin, they appear innocent and react in a truthful way. They are (unlike the hypocrites) on the inside the same as on the outside. This is why Jesus liked them so much, as recorded in Matt. 19:13-15. He said in Mark 10:15, "Truly I say to you, whoever does not receive the Kingdom of God like a child shall not enter it." The people He addressed should have the characteristics or qualities of childlike trust, obedience, and dependency on Him and His teaching. They should also express the childlike traits of humility, simplicity, purity, candor, and be easily taught and guided.

Although children usually are honest and tell the truth, they need to be protected continually because they are impressionable and thus easi-

---

* Highly developed married initiates have made the creation act a sacrifice and have achieved the immaculate conception, without being carried away by passion and evil desire, but instead by being strongly motivated by intention and purpose.

ly influenced and molded by good but also evil forces. This is especially true of little children, whose conscience is not much developed, so that they are not able to discern between good and evil. The original sin or the dormant evil within the children may easily be awakened, when it is stimulated by the environment and society where they live. This is why they can be, at times, cruel to each other and rebellious towards their parents. They should therefore be disciplined as Proverbs advises. See Prov. 13:24, 22:6, 23:13.

When some of the older children are continually reprimanded for the evil words they say and the evil deeds they do, those children eventually learn to put on "a mask". In this manner they show a good face and hide their real intentions, thus becoming hypocritical, like so many people in society, and are no longer true to themselves. Like so many adults, they have become very clever, shrewd, and cunning to suppress, hide, and *cover up the evil impulses within them (Mark 7:21), in order to hold on to the external image they have created of themselves for others. By living the life of the good/evil personality, it is very important what others think about them. They also learn from evil people how to deceive and manipulate others, so that they will be Number One in the pecking order.

The Importance of the Sexual Act

A couple should have †no sex before marriage in order to be as pure in character as possible, for the most important and significant act of human creation. They should therefore prepare themselves for parenthood by moral and spiritual discipline. At the time of the creation of a child, they ought to be at their very best, in their physical, mental, and spiritual attitude. They should not only join each other at the physical/emotional level as the savages, but more at the physical/emotional/mental levels as civilized people or even better by

---

* The violent way some people react to criticism can be an indication of how much they protect the false part of their ego, instead of letting their real self stand the light of day.

† The Bible teaches that a man and woman should have no sex before marriage or commit fornication. (See 1 Cor. 6:13,18; 1 Thess. 4:3-8; Eph. 5:1-7.) This also means that they should not touch those parts that incite them to lust after each other. To have premarital sexual experimentation with many men or women, according to modern argument, in order to have more joy in marital sex later, is completely absurd and foolish. By exchanging physical and psychic elements with others, a psychological bond is created and will interfere with the virgin relationship of one's marriage for many years to come, which may lead to divorce.

including the spiritual quadrant as well, as highly evolved people do. Through meditation or contemplation the couple integrates their body, emotion, and mind and connects them with their Divine Spark or Spirit. Then they invoke the forces of good and align themselves with the creative forces of the universe, so that the creation act is one with the forces and the purpose of creation.

Through the sexual act, the two bodies of the pair unite and create a new composite body, when the sperm and the egg converge. The separate energy fields of the couple also merge into one, to create a new and stronger field, which is greater than the sum of the energies of the individuals, when they would act independently. Depending on the level of consciousness the pair has achieved, the unadulterated energy of creation is, however, modified to some degree and will decide the nature of what they create. He and she should, during their embrace, strongly visualize wanting a healthy and superior child, especially at the moment of fusion. The highest ideal is to conceive and rear saintly children whom will fulfill the plan of the Creator in the restoration or salvation of the world. The children, in turn, will always be grateful to their parents whom always love them, and provide the best education for them. Those children live with ease and everything comes their way.

Children Conceived Through Passion

However, the lack of sexual control has brought into the world millions of unwanted children whom are not planned by the parents. They are the result of an "accident" and strong desire for sexual satisfaction, which is instigated by their good/evil ego, which seeks only pleasure in the relationship. Being undeveloped, the unqualified see the sex act as recreation, instead of creation, desiring the embrace, but not the fruits and the responsibility. The children are conceived through lustful passion instead of through the chaste and controlled will of the Divine Spirit, whose principal aspiration is the love and joy of creation instead of the short-lived pleasure of sex. The ones whom are legally married have a tendency to indulge themselves, instead of practicing self-control as they did before marriage. Those couples whom have unlimited sex after the child is conceived should not be surprised that passion rules the child from the moment it is born.

The children whom are conceived through passion instead of compassion carry with them an unconscious feeling that they are not really wanted and have become a burden instead of a blessing. They, therefore, rebel against their parents (2 Tim. 3:2; Rom. 1:30) and all authority of society where they live, and also experience difficulties in accepting a God who is all love. Unlike the children whom are conceived of God's love – expressed through humans – the original sin is strong in the children whom are conceived of lust or satanic love. The latter are more likely to be born with a body that is prone to disease and weak; a mind that is uncreative and feeble; the emotions, which easily react in anger and are resentful; and the will, which is easily persuaded and powerless. Because they are living the life of the good/evil personality, whereby the evil within them is stronger than the good, they are more inclined to become criminals than the ones whom act out the good in their moral life. Some of the potential criminals may degenerate to a level where they have to be locked up in prisons and insane asylums with other undesirables at the expense of the taxpayer.

REMARK: It is ironic that many people spend lots of time and effort in the science of animal breeding, but do not care much about the improvement of their own species: the physical, mental, and, above all, the spiritual qualities, which is the science of euthenics.

Words to Teenagers

Many teenagers of today are idealistic and wonder about the meaning of life, because they sense that there is something wrong with society, to whose rules and regulations they have to conform. Being at a critical turning point in their life, they have to make an important decision: either to continue living the life of the personality and become part of "the world" (John 8:23; Rom. 12:2) which is good and evil, or start [a]living a spiritual life or divine lifestyle in a higher and different world, which is only good and divine (John 18:36).

As Adam and Eve were still teenagers when they were tempted to eat of the symbolic fruit, teenagers of today will likewise be tempted to have a sexual relation before they are ready to be married. Like Adam and Eve who ate from the Tree of the Knowledge of Good and Evil, teenagers may likewise, when they give in to temptation, get stuck in the good and evil lifestyle. They, like Adam and Eve, will be living outside the Garden of Eden or in [b]"the world" and it would become more difficult to begin living a divine life.

From about the ages of 13 to 19 the teenager or youth passes through a crucial time in her or his bodily development. It is the period of growth between childhood/puberty to physical maturity. With the onset of puberty, hormonal changes take place in the bodies of the boys and girls whereby they become more masculine and feminine and are capable of reproduction. At that time, every adolescent girl or boy begins to discover [c]sexual attractions, feelings, and desires, and begin to notice the opposite sex. They may, at times, experience infatuation or become possessed by a foolish and unreasoning love or passion, or puppy or calf love. However, this is not mature love, which is sacrificial and giving; it is only an emotional excitement. They therefore still need to grow or rise in love instead of falling in love. This feeling of desire or passion is often mistaken as true love, and when it leads to sexual experimentation, it is nothing more than lust.

---

[a] Teenagers of every generation have to make the same choice as Adam and Eve when they become mature in their personality: to live a human or divine life.

[b] For a more detailed explanation of "the world" see "The Birth and Evolution of the Divine Spirit or Soul".

[c] Physical attractions are caused by the activity of the positive and negative poles of the etheric bodies. At that time boys and girls should no longer be intimate and play together.

67

In order to prepare the teens for adult life they need to know about sexual matters and how to behave themselves with the opposite sex. However, sex education, as it is taught in most schools today, is little more than "safe" sex training. It does not free them of the sexual problems and desires, but only increases it. Many teachers, whom are thinking and acting like fallen Lucifer and Eve, say that teenagers should be allowed to express themselves sexually, which result has become obvious in this sex ridden society. Other teachers are worried that the teens may die of sexual diseases and thus hand them condoms, telling them in such way that sexual relations before marriage are all right. They excuse themselves by saying that young people will have sex anyway. Thus, instead of teaching birth control, which gives rise to promiscuity, they should teach sex control first. Apostle Paul said to Timothy, who faced a young man's temptation, "Shun youthful passions and aim at righteousness, faith, love, and peace, along with these who call upon the Lord with a pure heart" (2 Tim. 2:22). When sex ᵈeducation is given, it is very important to teach also moral laws and principles and the psychological and spiritual aspects of sex, so that sex and love can be integrated.

During those trying years in the formation of character, the emotional aspect of the personality of the youth is in the process of development, while the mental aspect or the mind is not mature and strong enough to properly control the emotions. The emotions can therefore easily be influenced by music, which is emotional in character. When the music is low in vibration, such as for example jazz and rock, the emotional vibration bodies or sheaths of the teenagers eventually come to have the same rate of frequencies. This shows itself by their negativity and changes in dark moods, which also influence their thinking, because their emotional aspect is closely aligned with the thinking facility. This continual onslaught of rhythm is especially disastrous for those whom are trying to live a moral and (or) divine life. On the other hand, high vibration music such as, for example, classical, religious music, new age, and natural sounds, and others have been known to have positive effects on many people. It has been said that the music of Beethoven and Handel was to awaken the Divine Spark within the people. Western music descended later, from the higher or divine, to the lower level of human personality. Much of Western mu-

---

ᵈ The educational system, through which they have gone, is of such a nature that they have been taught to look outward for information and instructions, ignoring the cultivation of inner communication.

sic today is sexual in character. It not only stimulates and *excites the emotions and plays on the lower desires, but also has an effect on the movement of the bodies. This is especially true of jazz, which had its roots in Africa. By following its rhythm and beat, the dancers awaken their sexuality and become very sensual in their movements. Some of the lower types of music have inspired people to do "the twist", which is the movements of their lower bodies, which is similar to that of a snake.

NOTE: Different types of music influence different energy centers. The low vibration, such as drums, activate the first center, while much of today's popular music awakens the lower energy centers. True love songs stimulate the heart or fourth center, while the organs, harps, violins, and others may open the higher centers.

In order for teenagers to ªovercome sexual desires, the love towards God must be sufficiently developed and must supercede the love for their partner(s). In order to reach this level of growth they should be ᵇborn spiritually or come to realize their True Self or Divine Spirit in which God is hidden. Their budding Divine Spirits, which have a strong will of its own, will then, together with the individualized Spirit of God, rule the life of the personality, so that they easily overcome all temptations. They then have entered the Garden of Eden, through their particular gate, after purifying "their robes" (physical, emotional, mental sheaths) and earned the right to the Tree of Life, and live forever (Rev. 22:14).

> Then I saw a new heaven and a new earth; for the first heaven and the first earth had passed away, and the sea was no more. And I saw the holy city, New Jerusalem, coming down out of heaven from God, prepared as a bride adorned for her husband; and I heard a loud voice from the throne saying, "Behold, the dwelling of God is with men.

---

* The use of drugs and alcohol usually concur when playing profane music, which is loud and destructive to the psyche. Music with sexually seductive lyrics and profanity was also known in Bible times. See Ex. 32:17-19; Isaiah 23:16; Psalms 69:12.

ª By living a spiritual or divine life, sublimation and transmutation of sexual energy happen without much conscious effort on your part (see also Appendix 25), thus not by depleting oneself of physical energy by strenuous exercises.

ᵇ It will be more difficult to be spiritually born when one's ego is overdeveloped or inflated. They therefore should unite with their budding Divine Spirit or Higher Self as soon as they have reached maturity in their personality. In the New Age or Kingdom of Heaven, there is no longer a need to go through a special process of restoration, such as "being born again" because children are without sin, and will grow up in a normal way. See "The Birth and Evolution of the Divine Spirit or Soul".

He will dwell with them, and they shall be His people, and God Himself will be with them; He will wipe away every tear from their eyes, and death (spiritual) shall be no more, neither shall there be mourning nor crying nor pain anymore, for the former things have passed away." (Revelation 21:1-4)

THE

APPENDIX

The Appendix

#1 The Archangel Lucifer

The name [a]Lucifer is mentioned in Isaiah 14:12 of the King James Version as: "How art thou fallen from heaven, o Lucifer, son of the morning!" He and his angels were not only servants and messengers of God (Rev. 22:9; Luk. 1:31), but also servants to His children, whom are to become Lords of creation. Lucifer and the angels could only reach a certain level of development, comparable to the growth of personalities or egos of the human species; but could never become Divine Beings as Adam and Eve or become the Tree of Life (Gen. 3:24; Rev. 22:14).

#2 The Creation of Adam and Eve

[b]Adam and Eve were the first human pair, whom had the potential to become divine or God-like in their nature. Many other people were living at that time, because Cain found himself a wife in the land of Nod (Gen. 4:16-17). Those other people were not mentioned in the Bible because they were not directly involved in God's dispensation of restoration. Although those people were endowed with a Divine Spark as part of God's essence, their human spirits (emotion-intellect-will) had to grow for a long period of time before their personalities would be ready to house Divine Spirits or Souls. Eventually, Adam and Eve were born of those parents whose personalities were sufficiently grown. They would become mature in their personalities, be born of God, and grow to perfection in their newly acquired Souls.

---

[a] The king of Babylon was like the fallen archangel Lucifer in character (Isa. 14). Lucifer could never become like God; that is another reason why he wanted it.
[b] He was called Adam because his body was made from the ground –Adamah– (Gen. 2:7).

#3 Different Forms of Pride

This is not the pride of being, accomplishment, or belonging, but the false pride of exalting and overestimating one's self or ego. Many people (like satan) are puffed up with pride (1 Tim. 3:6), or have an inflated or overdeveloped ego. By magnifying their importance, they become arrogant and boastful. Of some people, it is said that they have a big ego, which is being fed by worship and flattery. They are "full of air" and vainglorious. One is also prideful when he or she is trying to rule someone who is spiritually higher or take his or her position, including one's own Divine Spirit or Self.

At the non-religious or personality level, prideful or arrogant persons look down upon others and are indifferent to them, which causes separation and division among people. In order to preserve the illusion of superiority and beef up their feeling of insecurity, they put others down while boasting and bragging continually about themselves and their achievements, without giving credit to anyone. The proud and the haughty are self-seeking, looking for personal glory and craving for attention and admiration. Their egos expand or inflate when they are praised or flattered and contract when they are criticized.

On the other hand, humble and modest persons recognize that they are not isolated beings, and that all their achievements were only possible with the cooperation of fellow human beings. They are certainly not contemptuous of the poor and needy. The meek and unassuming are educable, teachable, can take criticism, and readily admit that they are and have been wrong. They also recognize that their successes can be more dangerous than their failures, especially when they start to compare their "greatness" with the smallness of "inferior persons".

People can also be *prideful in a religious sense when they do not acknowledge God as the Creator, who bestows the endowments and the talents they possess, and by taking personal credit and unreasonable acclaim for their achievements. Thus, the arrogant do not show any humility by appreciating all of one's abilities and talents as gifts of God, and to use them to carry out His Will and purpose. The proud, the

---

* Pride is regarded by traditional Christian teaching as the first of the seven deadly sins and is considered by many theologians, especially St. Augustine and Martin Luther, as the very essence or root of sin. It is the refusal to submit and be dependent upon God, by seeking to be one's own God while living the life of the good/evil personality.

high and mighty, do not want to accept themselves as creatures of God (Rom. 1) and do not want to listen to the voice of God, spoken through inspired human beings. The persons who see themselves as very important think that they can manage without God and refuse to submit to His laws. This is especially true for the rich and famous who are tempted to see themselves as self-sufficient, trusting in their wealth and popularity instead of God. Many try to live a separate selfhood apart from God and refuse to repent and live a divine life and be born of God. The proud, who are often identified as those who have their nose in the air with curling lips, may even degenerate to the lowest level and become like their father satan by attempting to be God. They are not only indifferent but also hostile to God, and want to take His place (Isaiah 14:12-14).

Within themselves, the evil or false part of the good/evil ego has taken over the vacant place of the unborn Divine Spirit or Christ Spirit (Gal. 4:19) and starts ruling their life. These persons whom are ruled by their imposter, deceiver, or Antichrist, are full of pride and falsity and have overgrown and swollen egos which need to be continually fed by their attitudes and the veneration, adoration, and praising of others.

One can also be prideful spiritually by having an "holier than thou" attitude. Religious people whom are young in their faith often display an air of smug superiority or "arrogant humility" over the people they are teaching. They are more interested in impressing the people of their newfound truth than the spiritual well being of the people. When the young ones are made spiritual leaders too soon and are recognized and accepted by the community, the leaders may then think that they can get away with everything. Having public support, they communicate less with God and begin to do more their own than God's Will (1 Tim. 3:6).

Many religious workers are motivated by pride and self-interest and are reluctant to take jobs no one wants. They are often lacking in humility by thinking that it is their work instead of that of Christ. They are guilty of spiritual pride when they, like the Pharisees of old (see Matt. 23), display a subtle sense of superiority over the people. They are, however, completely wrong when the workers, in true Luciferian fashion, compete with each other for position, power, and prestige. This happened to James and John who wanted to sit on the left and right hand of Jesus in His glory (Mark 10:37). Peter later wrote, "Likewise you that are younger be subject to the elders. Clothe yourselves, all of you, with humility towards one another, for God opposes the proud, but gives grace to the humble" (1 Peter 5:5). "You boast in your arrogance", but "humble yourselves before the Lord and He will exalt you" (James 4:16,10). (See also Luk. 18:14).

God always chooses the humble ones for a mission and not the proud who are like the fallen archangel Lucifer. It is said in Numbers 12:3, that Moses was the humblest man on earth, and Gideon said that he was the least in his family (Judges 6:11-15). Apostle Paul was modest and called himself "the least of the apostles" (1 Cor. 15:9, 9:16). He was a fellow worker and not a master (2 Cor. 1:24), and he did not solicit praise or exploit the admiration of fellow believers (Matt. 6:2-4). If praise is given, we should not think highly of ourselves (Rom. 12:3) but give it immediately to God, who made all our work possible, so that our righteousness does not end up in self-righteousness.

Finally, Jesus said in Matt. 5:5: "Blessed are the meek, for they shall inherit the earth."

#4 Living A Life Separate from God

Self-reliant here means not to rely on one's immature personality or self to make important decisions, but relying instead on one's Divine Self. Individuals should also aim for: Self-esteem instead of self-esteem of the personality; Self-praise instead of self-praise; Self-confidence instead of self-confidence; Self-determination instead of self-determination of the good/evil personality; Self-righteousness (deeds) of the Divine Selves – which is like fine linen (Rev. 19:8) – instead of the self-righteousness (deeds) of the evil selves – which is like filthy rags (Isa. 64:6) – ; and Selfhood (which seeks not its own at the expense of others) instead of the little selfhood or selfishness of the psychological ego (which seeks gain regardless of others). The latter wants immediate gratification and is the one who inquires if God has forbidden them to eat of the Tree of the Knowledge of Good and Evil. Individuals should also aim for Self-centeredness instead of the self-centeredness of the lower self, which seeks fulfillment of lower desires, and Self-consciousness instead of being self-conscious. The latter individuals are usually shy because they center too much on their personalities, which are usually timid, reserved, bashful, and frightened. This quality seems to be prevalent more in women than in men. Unlike people whom are living a divine life, which is outgoing, expressive, and giving, the ones whom are living the life of the personality show restraint, inhibition, and selfishness. The latter tries to substitute their shortcomings in social interaction by consuming alcohol and drugs or acting in foolish ways.

Finally, instead of living according to God's direction, Eve and Adam (and their descendants) began to live a life as independent and separate beings from God. They made their own rules of moral conduct and judged things with their lower selves or personalities, which became good and evil. By living a life of separation, they are condemned to live the life of a human being instead of a divine being and also acquire a satanic nature. The result of this lifestyle is that their Divine Spirits or Souls cannot be born of God. They therefore cannot live a higher or divine life, wherein the individualized Spirit of God can dwell, and through which it can inspire themselves and others. Thus, instead of accepting God as the Creator and Sustainer, they want to live without God, seeking to be their own god as self-generated and self-sustaining individuals, and desire to adore the creature(s) instead of the Creator (Rom. 1). Thus a beginning was made in the worshipping of false gods, which is forbidden. See the 1st, 2nd, and 3rd Commandments.

#5 Influenced by Satan to Bond with Eve

Some people believe that it was not the spirit of satan who seduced Eve, but a physical man who was strongly influenced or obsessed by satan to have a sexual relationship with her, physically as well as psychically.

#6 Women Are Sensitive to Temptation of Non-physical Forces

It was Eve who was persuaded by Lucifer (who, as an angel, was neither male nor female), to take from the fruit of the Tree of the Knowledge of Good and Evil against God's advice, or had a psychosexual relationship with Lucifer. This inherited tendency to succumb to psychical temptation is deeply embedded in the psyche of women and may awaken when opportunities arise.

Women in general are more impressionable, sensitive, and more feeling oriented than men and can, therefore, be easily influenced by disembodied spirits. That is why they were much more than men accused in the [a]Middle Ages of willingly having sex with their psychic or spirit bodies with low human spirits, demons (fallen angels), and other invisible beings. Some of them were more or less materialized through the use of [b]etheric energy, drawn mainly from the air (also from the earth). As expressed not quite correctly in the Malleus Maleficarum Part II, Chapter IV:

The devils make themselves an "aereal body" which is not wholly earthly or psychical (but etherical) and animate them. It assumes an earthly property through "condensation", which they can effect "by means of gross vapors raised from the earth". "For in the beginning it is just air, but in the end it is inspissated air", or air which has thickened or condensed (p. 109). Through this materialized body, the succubus (female spirit-angel) and incubus (male spirit-angel) are able to copulate physically with a man or a woman.

When people became later more materialistic and thus less psychical or sensitive, their relationship with evil or good spirits also lessened, and the persecution of the witches and warlocks faded away.

#7 Meaning of the Fruit

The meaning of this symbol is, when a fruit is taken of the tree when it is not ripe, it cannot realize its potential value at that time. A sexual affair before maturity results also in a regression of beings involved, toward perfection. It is therefore not wise to partake of the forbidden fruit, which represents sexual intercourse, and to become like the symbolic tree, good and evil. When [c]Adam and Eve would have become mature, they would have "eaten" from the Tree of Life or from the mystical body of Christ (John 6:53-58), and would have become one with the Universal Christ who is described in Revelation 1:12-18.

---

[a] See the Malleus Maleficarum (The Witch Hammer) by Heinrich Kramer and James Sprenger (+/- 1486 – Dover Edition 1971). This was the most important book and guide used in the inquisition. From page 41 and on, read how the writers thought about women of those times, who might have been influenced by pagan spirits.

[b] For a correct explanation, see "The Etheric Body".

[c] To the Jewish philosopher Aristobulus, Adam and Eve signified reason and sensuality, while the serpent represented sexual desire.

#8 The Constitution of the Human Personality

The human or whole personality, which consists of the outer and the inner, is composed of the physical, emotional, and mental matter or mind complex. The outer or earthly personality is called the physical self, physical body, and external self; while the inner personality is called the spirit self, spirit body, psyche, soul, [d]heart, human spirit, and internal self. It feels, perceives, thinks, reasons, and wills. As the spirit self further consists of the spirit body and spirit mind, the physical self, as its reflection, consists of the physical body and physical mind or brain.

The thinking mind may be outbound, dealing with everyday physical life, and (or) inbound by dealing with the inner life.

The substance of the inner and outer personality can be quite coarse in undeveloped people, but more refined in people whom are more mature, especially when their personality is ruled by their Divine Spirit or Soul.

The personality or ego dismantled of its physical body is the human spirit, which consists of a spiritual mind and body and can be separated from the physical body. According to the supposition of *psycho-synthesis, the personal or lower self (human spirit undraped of its emotional and intellectual content) is the "I" or self-consciousness, which gives one a sense of being and permanence, and is an observer of external processes. (We may call it the spirit mind and its evolving Divine Spark.)

People often identify themselves with their body, emotion, or intellect. For example, they say, "I am sick", but I am (the human spirit) cannot be physically sick. To disidentify, they should say, "I have a body, but I am not my body." They also say, "I am irritated", but I am (inner core of being) is not irritated, but its emotion are. To attain self-awareness, they should say, "I have an emotional life, but I am not my emotions"; "I have an intellect, but I am not my intellect."

---

[d] "For out of the heart (good/evil-human spirit-psyche) comes evil---" (Mark 7:21). "The heart is deceitful above all things" (Jer. 17:9). It therefore needs to be purified (Ps. 51:10, 24:4). Should not commit adultery with her in his heart (Matt. 5:28). "For your hardness of heart Moses allowed you to divorce your wives" (Matt. 19:8). "God has sent the Spirit of His Son into our hearts" (Gal. 4:6) and "that Christ may dwell in your heart" (Eph. 3:17).

* Psycho-synthesis by Roberto Assagioli – an Ensalen book. Above content modified by author.

The intellect is an organ of knowledge of the outer world as well as the inner. "It is not my whole being but an instrument of myself." Thus, we should not identify ourselves with our intellect and certainly not with our thoughts, which are constantly changing.

A. ᵃThe Order of Creation

We get to know God not only by reading Scriptures and through personal communication, but also by observing the creation (Rom. 1:20) because He/She cannot but create what they are.

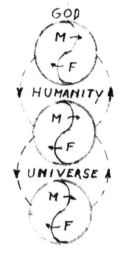

God created man in His own image, in the image of God He created him; male and female He created them (Gen. 1:27).

Humankind created in the image of God is male and female.

The universe created in the image of humans also exists of positive and negative polarities.

M = male	F =female
yang	yin
positive	negative

The human being as the microcosm contains in its inner and outer being the sum of all the essences of the elements, structures, qualities, and characters of the universe, which are called the macrocosm.

NOTE: As Eastern thought believed in the body of God or universe, which is dual in nature – yang and yin – Western philosophy believes in the Spirit of God; a Being of Love, Intellect, and Will, who is not only a Father but also a Mother in essential nature.

The three kingdoms of animal, plant, and mineral have outer and inner features corresponding to the human body and spirit. For example:

ᵃ Main ideas have been taken from "The Divine Principles" by Young Oon Kim. Content has been modified, improved, and more has been added by author.

The elements, structures, qualities, and internal characters of the animals are like that of humans. The psychic or astral bodies of [b]animals resemble that of human spirits. They both participate in and communicate with the invisible planes, which empower their psychic bodies, who in turn –via their etheric bodies– empower the physical bodies. Finally, humans are in possession of many of the psychological qualities of different animals, whereby one or more may be predominant.

NOTE: Some of the differences are: As the spine of animals is horizontal, and they (of the same species) act alike, humans walk upright and everyone is a different individual.

The elements, structures, and internal characteristics of plants correspond to humans as they both have [c]vital or etheric bodies. As the leaves of plants absorb carbon dioxide from the atmosphere, the lungs of humans perform a similar function by breathing air and assimilating vital energy for the growth and functioning of their physical and etheric bodies. The stems (trunk), branches of plants function like the human circulatory system, which distributes nourishment to the plant and human bodies. As the stomach and intestines of humans are like the root of plants in their function of absorbing nutrients, the human circulatory system, the arteries and veins correspond to the xylem and phloem of plants.

As the earth personality of a human consists of a physical, emotional, and mental level, the plant, as a symbol of a human, consists of the root, the stem, and the leaves. The root represents the physical body of the individual because it is closely connected to the earth. The stem represents the emotional component of the individual because it conveys plant juices, whose watery content is the symbol of emotions. The *leaves represent the mental component of the individual because it receives the energy of the Sun and interacts with the air (through photosynthesis) which is the symbol of the mind. The flower, which is the most prominent and beautiful part, accumulates the best elements of the plant, which represents the Divine Spirit or Soul of an evolved individual. In addition, the plants and trees represent the different individuals in character and growth.

---

[b] Animals have only "the breath of life" (Gen. 1:30), but humans are given the breath of God "and man became a living being" (Gen. 2:7).

[c] See "The Etheric Body".

* Leaves of trees are most beautiful in the autumn when they are falling. The different colors truly represent the older people whom have (or supposed to be) become more beautiful and mature in the autumn of their life.

NOTE: Some of the differences are: a human is an inverted plant. As a plant absorbs its food through its lower part (root), a human takes his/her food through the higher part (head). As the plant turns and extends its generative or floral organs towards the Sun, the human reproductive organs are pointed towards the earth. As the plant survives by inhaling carbon dioxide exhaled by humans, it exhales life-giving oxygen, which keeps humans alive.

The elements and characteristics of minerals are made of the same chemical elements and atoms as the physical bodies of humans. The Bible says, "The Lord God formed man of dust from the ground" (Gen. 2:7). The elements even have internal natures or life. It is able to build in matter crystal forms, according to geometrical design. It is a well-known fact that humans of different personalities are attracted to certain stones, which they like, and are harmonious with their external and internal beings.

The plants extract their nourishment from the earth, animals feed upon the plant, and humans take their food from the plant and animal kingdoms. Thus, everything is made of the same chemical ingredients as the soil or earth.

†**NOTE**: The tree-like human being signifies the link between heaven and earth.

We may even compare the structure of the earth to that of the human body. The molten core, surrounded by solid rocks, is like the marrow tissue within human bones. Above the rock mantle and below the crust, we find underground waterways that correspond to blood vessels within the musculature. The crust of the earth, which can be hard or soft, covered with plants and trees or almost bare, high or lowlands, continents or islands, can be likened to the hairy or less hairy skin of a male or female.

Because two-thirds of the earth's surface is covered with water, while the rest of the surface is often saturated with the same; and as water is a symbol of emotion, we can say that the people of planet earth are for the greater part emotionally oriented. As the rocks of the oceans can be likened to the physical body of humans, the layer of muddy and clear water (mixed with air) to the lower and higher emotions, the foggy and clear air to the lower (concrete) and higher (abstract thinking) intellect. Above the stratum of air we find limitless space,

---

† More extensive explanations of the mineral, plant, animal, and human kingdom we can find on pages 320 and 321.

which is represented by the intuition of the Divine Spirit. Far above we find the sun, which is like God, who shines from within the individual through all the layers of intuition, intellect, and emotion to the physical self.

Thus, a human being is a highly evolved animal, the most intelligent and sophisticated animal on earth. It is made up of chemical elements (like minerals), has an etheric body (sheath) (like plants), an emotional body (sheath) like animals, and a mental body (sheath). The mind gives purpose to action; the desire body gives incentive to action, while the vital body gives power to action. Sense impressions of the physical body are changed into sensations, which in turn become feelings and, in a more complex form, emotions. The emotional body (with its lower and higher desires, passion and compassion) is a bridge between the mental and the physical bodies. This human being may become a super human being, when the developed Divine Spirit is guiding the person's life.

NOTE: It took God millions of years to prepare the earth for the final arrival of their most precious children – whom were created last – so that they will enjoy the beautiful world, with its variety of minerals, plants, and animals.

#9 Adam and Eve "Knew" Each Other

The second century church fathers Irenaeus and Clement believed that Adam and Eve were only teenagers when they *"knew" (Gen. 4:1) or united with each other in a sexual union and became "one flesh" (Gen. 2:24), or "one body" (1 Cor. 6:16) without God's blessing.

#10 The Three-fold Nature of Human Beings

Divine Spirit or Soul is also called Higher Self in contrast with the lower self or personality. It is also known as Original Self, True Self, Transpersonal Self, Divine Essence, Truth Body, Inner Light, Word of God, and Inner Spirit of Christ (Gal. 4:19) etc. The people, whose Divine Spirit was ruling their life, were called by Apostle Paul the "spiritual men" (1 Cor. 3:1) compared with the undeveloped "natural"

---

* Throughout the Bible the term "to know"(ledge) is used in the sense of carnal knowledge. "Cain 'knew' his wife, and she conceived and bore Enoch" (Gen. 4:17). Rebecca was described in Gen. 24:16 as "fair to look upon, a virgin, whom no man had known". When King David was old and stricken in years, a maiden was given to comfort him: "But the king knew her not" (1 Kings 1-4). Mary's question, "How shall I conceive seeing that I knew not a man" (Luk. 1:34).

or "unspiritual man" (1 Cor. 2:14) whose good/evil personality was ruling their life.

According to the Bible and some belief systems, a complete human being consists of three main parts: "spirit" (Divine Spirit or Soul), "soul" (human spirit-psyche-mind), and "body" (1 Thess 5:23; Heb. 4:12).

Origin, Christian theologian of the second century, taught that the threefold meaning in scripture corresponds in general to the threefold division in every individual. This division was accepted by the early Christian church until the year 869 A.D. at the 4th council of Constantinople, when the majority of church leaders accepted the idea that human beings are made up of only Soul (Spirit) and body. The latter are called dichotomists. They see humans possessing two parts – Spirit and psyche (soul) – with the soul or human spirit as part of, and the most important portion or function of the body.

[a]Plato gave human beings a tripartite nature – Soul (mind), (human) spirit, and body. According to the psychoanalytical theory of Siegmund Freud the whole personality consists of id (instincts, baser drives, conditional reflexes), ego, and superego.

Thus trichotomists maintain that a human being is tripartite in nature, having three parts – Soul, human spirit, and body. Trichotomists can say, "I am not my personality (having self-consciousness), with its body, emotion, intellect, and will, but I am a Soul (having God-consciousness), own a spirit, and live in a body.

Jews and some Christians believe that a human spirit (soul) is the inner and outer aspect of the same reality, or to put it in Aristotle's terms, [b]the spirit is the "form" of the body, which dies with the body. This theory is also the conviction of Thomas Aquinas (d. 1274) the most influential Catholic theologian. They, therefore, believe in the resurrection of the body.

---

[a] The Soul in Plato's writings is not expressed in clear terms, while the superego of Freud is a mental construct.

[b] In Aristotle, the soul (human spirit) is the vital principle, the formal cause, essence, or entelechy (vital body) of a natural body. It is, however, true that the vital or etheric body is part and parcel of the physical body and dies with the physical, but the human spirit, which is not the vital body, survives physical death. See "The Etheric Body".

Plato, on the other hand, believed in the separation of the spirit and the body. In other words, he believed, unlike Aristotle, in the immortality of the human spirit (soul). This was also the main tenet of the first Christians.

#11 Becoming Shameful

After their sexual relation, and no longer innocent and pure, Adam and Eve covered their lower parts because they had been used in a lustful way and without God's blessing. Originally, sex was to be the most holy creative act, but it became a shameful thing carried on in secret. People, especially men, feel shame when they look at a partly or naked body of a woman (man) and feel a lustful desire welling within them. Because their secret thoughts and fantasies are not pure and holy, their eyes can therefore not endure the sight without generating lust within themselves (Matt. 5:28; 1 John 2:16). They are also ashamed to uncover their inner self, knowing that it is sinful by nature (Matt. 15:19) and therefore continually hide and cover up their real intentions.

Apostle Paul said in Titus 1:15, "To the pure all things are pure, but to the corrupt and unbelieving nothing is pure." When people are pure and virtuous within their being, it is no longer obscene, repulsive, or offensive to see the natural functions of any part of the male or female bodies and to have intimate relations with the opposite sex. On the other hand, people whose minds are not in tune with their higher nature (Rom. 8:5-8) see the world as their own reflection. For them nothing is pure because their lower nature (personality) (with its emotions, desires, and thoughts) are not pure.

However, to feel ashamed and the knowledge that we have an evil nature, is not a mental disorder, as some psychologists claim. It is an indication that we have done something wrong and have some knowledge of good and evil. There are people whom have completely lost their sense of shame because corruption has become their way of life. As Paul has it: "men committing shameless acts with men and receiving in their own person the due penalty for their error" (Rom. 1:27). They, and people like them, such as prostitutes and hardened criminals, are no longer living the good/evil lifestyle as ordinary people do, because the evil part of the personality has taken over their life.

NOTE: Some people are ashamed to talk about and defend the naked God.

#12 Insecurity Caused by Separation

The moment Adam and Eve gave up their personal relationship with the Creator by refusing to live according to His plan or principles of creation, they became "afraid" (Gen. 3:10), because they lost the feeling of security, and fear of living came about. By uniting with satan and living according to His plan (to establish a pseudo-kingdom), they became distant to God and hid themselves from Him. The people after them inherited the spirit of rebellion and hostility toward God (Rom. 8:7) and began to swear, thus condemning themselves outside the Garden of Eden.

NOTE: A similar situation as that of Adam and Eve may develop in people whom have been living a divine life, but "cave in" through temptation and begin living the life of the good/evil personality, or worsen to an evil life. Life for those backsliders has become a toilsome burden and a living hell on earth.

#13 Diagrams of Divine Spirit, Good/Evil and Evil Personalities

God Directed Life
(Rev. 21:3)
Human nature, good and pure,
governed by Divine Spirit

Physical
Human
(Mental)
Divine
(G)
Spirit
(Emot.)
Spirit
Body

Tree of (spiritual) Life
Gen. 2:9; Rev. 22:14

When (good and evil) humans feel, think, and act like God, they are on His side and He becomes their Lord and Father, strengthening their good nature and expanding His kingdom

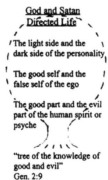

God and Satan
Directed Life

The light side and the dark side of the personality

The good self and the false self of the ego

The good part and the evil part of the human spirit or psyche

"tree of the knowledge of good and evil"
Gen. 2:9

Satan Directed Life
(John 12:31)
"Human nature depraved and corrupt ruled by evil imposter

Physical
Human
(Mental)
Evil
(S)
Nature
(Emot.)
Spirit
Body

Tree of (spiritual) death

When (good and evil) humans feel, think, and act like satan, (Mk. 7:21-23), they are on his side and he becomes their master and father (Jn. 8:44), strengthening their evil nature and expanding his pseudo kingdom.

#14 Lust and Its Consequences

According to the Merriam Webster Dictionary, lust is an intense and unrestrained sexual desire. The Random House College Dictionary says that lust is an uncontrolled, passionate sexual desire. The Webster New World Dictionary asserts that lust is an excessive sexual desire, seeking unrestrained gratification. The Readers Digest Great Encyclopedia Dictionary affirms that lust is a strong overwhelming desire, which seeks for immediate or ruthless satisfaction. A Basic Catholic Dictionary declares that lust is one of the capital or "deadly sins", and is the disordered and unrestrained seeking of sexual pleasure.

The encyclopedia of religion uses the old English word concupiscence (con = intensive, cupio = desire) to describe a fallen human's excessive sexual and general desires. Concupiscence has its Biblical foundation in Rom. 7:8; 1 Thess. 4:5; Gal. 5:16; 1 Jn. 2:16, and is the consequence of original sin. It is therefore:

An inborn evil desire, which becomes lustful
An inborn evil impulse and imagination
Sinful tendencies of fallen human nature
A sin seated in the flesh and human spirit
Overwhelming powerful desire or lust
A tendency to act like satan.

This evil tendency is antagonistic (in feeling and thinking) towards God, rejects His authority, and does not want to obey Him. The individual who harbors this hostility becomes slothful or spiritually lazy to the things of God.

Lust can be divided in six categories – simple fornication – adultery, incest, seduction, rape, and unnatural sins.

The gravest sin against human nature is that of bestiality, because it does not include the same species. After that sodomy is the worst because the same sex is involved. Together with masturbation it prevents procreation. The other sins that incite procreation but are against the order of creation and humanity are incest, adultery, rape, fornication, and lechery, which involve inordinate indulgence between consenting parties. Thus, if one uses his wife inordinately, this sin is that of lechery and lewdness (2 Cor. 12:21).

Sexual love is invested with desire (Lat. libido), pleasure (lat. amor), and lust (Gr. epithymia). Lust is the prostitution of love and is the isolation of sex from love. It is an inordinate or obsessive love of the pleasures of the flesh, and it produces slavery more quickly than any other passion. The person who is a slave to lust is unfit to serve God as a clergy, whether he or she is married or unmarried. Lust does not accept and recognize a person as a "thou", but instead sees the other only as an "object" for the gratification of pleasure, an "it" to be dominated and exploited. The animal man (or woman) who wants to have sex with someone for his or her own physical pleasure (or for money) usually prefers sexual encounters with many persons, and would not like to commit to and have an experience of depth or quality with only one person. Undeveloped persons are therefore not much interested in the other person, and do not care about the unique needs of the other, and are easy to go from one body to the next. Thus, a person having lust in his "heart" looks, therefore, at every man or woman as an object of sex. Lust is an unlawful sexual craving by arousing or inciting sexual desires. One can be lecherous by exciting lustful desires as, for example, an indecent old man or lecher and others that usually express themselves in lewd or obscene language. Lewdness also pertains to those various acts such as caressing and kissing, which incite lustful passions. In the Bible (1 John 2:16-17), it speaks about "the lust of the flesh and the lust of the eyes". (See also Matt. 5:28). Human beings whom are growing up should have learned, after many trials and errors, to distinguish between love and lust. They should master the Luciferian urge, and not allow the power of lust to lead their lives.

In a sexual relationship of married couples, both parties can enjoy themselves by appreciating and valuing each other as unique and special in a loving encounter. However, when they enjoy themselves "through each other", that is mutual lust. Those persons do not really care about each other and are not able to meet with their inner selves. They are merely using the other partner as an instrument or object to satisfy their sexual cravings.

They usually rationalize their addiction to sex by saying that random sexual encounters are expressions of love for each other and are therefore desirable.

One who allows himself/herself to be obsessed by lustful desires may commit acts, which they usually regret when their desires have subsided and as they recover their reason, realizing that it is not worth the price they have to pay.

When humans misuse the God-given power of creation for selfish purposes, they violate natural laws and have to suffer the results. The consequences for promiscuous acts of intercourse for physical pleasure result in: deterioration of physical, emotional, mental, and spiritual capacities; in disease, poverty, and death; and in frustration, anxiety, unrest, and disappointment. Mental genius and power are displaced by mediocrity and mental sloth. By abusing each other, they alienate more from God and the inner beings of other people, which result in abandonment, loneliness, hostility, despair, depression, and suicide, which in turn promote an excessive use of alcohol and drugs. Besides, being occupied continually with sex – being enslaved with lust and fantasies – is an enormous drain of physical, emotional, and mental energy.

Those people whom are living the life of the personality will morally decline when they lust after each other, because the evil selves of their personalities take charge of their lives. The people whom are living divine lives will rapidly decline spiritually because their Divine Spirits are no longer able to take charge of their personalities, and will wither away. They backslide and become carnal again (1 Cor. 3:2-3; Heb. 5:12). The result is that the evil parts within themselves (Matt. 15:19) become stronger and they come also more under the influence and power of evil forces which they attract. When they act wrongly in a sexual way, they also lust for power and domination of people, and in the illegal acquisition of possessions.

Thus, as pure and true love unites couples at a higher level, in tune with the universal forces, lust or selfish love divides a couple at a lower level, in tune with the local evil forces.

NOTE: The final result of promiscuity is that in order to 'turn on', they have to become more wicked – to molest a child or commit sodomy.

A. Love Is A Bittersweet Madness

Greek and Roman poets looked upon this selfish and all-consuming love as a sickness and frenzy which causes a lot of pain. It has been sung in great operas that this love is a "bittersweet madness" and that it is paid by weeping and sorrow. It has also been said that love is death seeking and that an ounce of sexual pleasure delivers a pound of misery.

#15 Explanation of Human and Divine Love

A. Introduction

English speaking people in general use only one word "love" to cover all forms or types of love. "Charity", the Christian love for God and humanity, is seldom used, except in the King James Version of the Bible (1 Cor. 13). Other languages, such as Greek, use three words to describe these types of love, such as <u>Agape</u>, a spiritual or divine love also called benevolence. Agape also includes altruistic love, an unselfish interest and compassion in the welfare of others and good will towards all people. It is the love of God [a]operating in the human heart. <u>Philia</u> – delphia, a friendly or "brotherly" love, includes love of family, community, country, and love of all humankind (philantropia). It is humanistic and social in its character and organization. <u>Eros</u>, erotic or sexual love, includes desire (Lat. libido), pleasure, and lust. It is romantic love imbued with possessive desire and passion. These three words are called in the Latin language <u>Caritas</u>, <u>Delicto</u>, and <u>Amor</u>. People in general also speak of [b]platonic love, whereby they mean a non-sexual bond between the opposite sexes, without any sensual passion. Platonic love includes, in its highest stages, the love of the form so that those whom are in love see only beauty and perceive it as truth.

NOTE: Sexual activity is the physical side of love, desire is the emotional side of love, and altruism is the spiritual side of love.

B. Different Levels of Love

We can make a distinction between the different levels of love. Love in the lowest type of human beings manifests itself as animal passion. When humans evolve, this love shows as a higher type between two people whom are paired and sharing. When they become parents, their love expands and includes their children. In the family, the parents become more unselfish and learn to give unconditional love to their children, which is a purer form of love than they ordinarily have between each other. The children, in return, respond to parental

---

[a] The Spirit can be expressed to the extent that individuals purify their spirit bodies; that is, their thinking, feeling, and willing free from egotism.
[b] Platonic love in the "Phaedo" and "Symposium" dialogues, is not a love devoid of sexual feelings. In the Symposium, this love works sometimes through the flesh, but in its exalted and noblest form is an aspiration toward Truth, Beauty, and Goodness.

love usually in an innocent and virtuous way. Although parents, whom are good and evil, do their best to love their children, they are, however, not entirely free of being selfish and possessive of their offspring. Jesus said in Matthew 10:36-37 that "a man's foes will be those of his own household. He who loves father or mother more than me is not worthy of me; and he who loves son or daughter more than me is not worthy of me". This saying indicates that love relationships among family members are far from perfect.

The next level of love would be the love for one's community, village, or city. By caring for the people, even when almost nobody knows about your concern, prayer, and activity, you nevertheless become the most loved person of that society. Invisible forces will then push you to be in charge of that community, even when you are unwilling or reluctant to take that position, because the one who truly loves the people the most should be in charge, or be counselor of that community.

A still higher level of love is the love for one's nation or devotion to one's country called patriotism. The combined psyche of the people creates a powerful bond and a national spirit, which may become so strong that one is willing to die for his or her country. President John F. Kennedy of America, who was the embodiment of the national spirit in the early 1960s, said during his presidency, "Ask not what the country can do for you, but what you can do for your country." He thus tried to bring the people to a higher level of love, the love for one's own nation.

However, people should not only have a strong love for the people whom are like them. They should also love all the different races of the world(s) because loving the cosmos (which is a macrocosm) means loving yourself (a microcosm). This also includes races that are living in other parts of the galaxy and beyond, such as non-human and human spirits that are living in the many spheres of the invisible etheric, spirit, and divine worlds.

NOTE: You will be able to check how much you love by the amount of sacrifice you are willing to make. The things you are willing to do for that person, family, community, country, world, and cosmos, which are really difficult for you to do, will determine the love you have. It is an easy guide.

C. What is Love?

Love is a cosmic principle, working on all levels of existence. In its most basic form, it is like a divine mortar that cements or holds the positive and negative elements together, in a continual desire and pursuit of the whole. In other words, it is an all encompassing cohesive power or energy, which brings everything and everyone, that is their *polarities, together and keep it together.

The planets are held in their proper positions through cohesive forces while revolving around the sun. The atom (the micro solar system) – with its positive (nucleus) and negative charges (electrons) are drawn towards each other by electromagnetic forces – is held in unity and harmony by the cohesive energies.

In the molecular or chemical world, we see its working when one substance has a tendency to enter in combination with another substance. The result of this affinity or mutual attraction is bonding by forming a perfect connection. Thus, each has something the other wants and needs. It is the attraction of opposites seeking to balance themselves, which is similar to human bonding, although the latter is more complex.

Thus, love holds the particles of the atoms, molecules, and bodies of planets together, through the force of attraction. It is the cohesive energy, which holds not only the universe together but helps bind or connect all people to each other, linking them with the universe.

The power of love at the human level never ceases seeking for the other half in order to live in unity with their beloved at all levels of their being. However, in cases of rape or prostitution, the persons involved may be united bodily in the lower levels of their beings, but separate themselves from each other in the higher levels, especially the divine levels. Because the low emotion of passion pursuits the other for selfish ends, it therefore separates, while compassion unites the two in a complete whole.

D. Attributes of Love

As white light can be dispersed – through prisms or drops of water – in rays or rainbows of different colors, love likewise can be expressed – through human beings – in different qualities or attributes. Love con-

---

* As explained on page 78, everything in the universe is made up of polarities.

tains all the purified qualities of the Divine Spirit or Soul, even as white light contains all the colors of the spectrum.

Love is often expressed through the emotions of peace, joy, harmony, mercy, compassion, and so forth. However, love is not necessarily emotional. It depends on the medium through which it is expressed. If this universal energy finds expression through the emotional part or component of humans, it is experienced as a strong feeling. If it finds expression solely through the intellectual and will component or sheath, then it will cause humans to seek for the truth and break all barriers to know the object by the force of their will. By the same token, one's love and faith in Christ can be expressed through the emotion and (or) by the will. Thus, love is a spiritual quality and can be expressed through the emotions, but also through other aspects of the personality, including the *mind.

Love is also an energy, which can be passed on to that which one loves. The degree of love determines the amount of energy conveyed. A person with a loving nature will send out strong energy vibrations for a great distance without much effort. A self-centered, selfish personality will not be noticed, even when they are a few feet away. Thus, every person creates his/her own field of energy vibration, whose frequency and distance depend upon the quality of his/her feelings and thoughts.

NOTE: We see in today's preaching how the emotions are stirred by an intense and magnetic speech, by a charismatic personality, but without much attainment of spirituality.

---

* God is love is the main tenet of Christianity – other schools of thought say that the main tenet of God is Mind and (or) energy. Hindus and others stress the path of Raja Yoga by using the mind and the will to unite (yoga) with their Divine Essence or Soul, attaining Self-realization, moksha or nirvana. This union can also be realized through "knowledge" (Jnana Yoga) or Bhakti Yoga, through love and devotion (Salvation by faith) or through Karma Yoga, (Salvation by works). The human race, in general, has developed mainly the love aspect of their being (earth is covered 2/3 with water, which represents emotion), while other races (in the galaxy) chiefly developed their mental and will aspects. This makes the people of planet earth very unique, to love God and other creatures, is most sublime. However, they may become entrapped in negative emotions, and this emotive love can also be easily misused.

NOTE: See also the personalities of Mr. Spock in Star Trek and Mr. Tubak in Voyager (in television science fiction) whom have developed their mental ability and very little emotional capacity.

Love is wisdom and strength, purity and virtue, devotion and constancy. Love always loves goodness, and goodness always wills love. Beauty and love are connected. You are beautiful when you are in love. It is the union of truth, beauty, and goodness. There is no such thing as wisdom without love, for love is the essence of wisdom. Thus, true wisdom cannot be wisdom without love. As intellectual expressions or *reason without love can become unloving and cold, so love acting alone may become impulsive. It should therefore be guided by wisdom.

Love is the combination of all the attributes of love, such as: respect, concern, consideration, faithfulness, forgiveness, patience, friendliness, gentleness, kindness, compassion, goodness, acceptance, tolerance, courtesy, understanding, trust, generosity, humility, unselfishness, sincerity, etc.

E. Divine Dimension of Love

While the human dimension of love is centered on the human personalities, the divine dimension of love revolves around the Souls or Divine Spirits, which is much deeper and sacrificial. For example, the spiritual brother and sister relationship between St. Francis of Assisi with St. Clare, St. John of the Cross with St. Teresa, and that between Abelard and Heloise, whose latter relationship went wrong. Early Christians often came together to celebrate a "love feast", or common meals whereby they enjoyed each other through selfless love which shone through their personalities when they were united with their Christ or Divine Spirits.

On a different level, the Soul may become the bride of the individualized Spirit of God, and the people as a group may become the bride of the Universal Christ, their bridegroom. As the Lord was wed to Israel (Ezekiel 16:6-14), who became adulterous by worshipping false gods, the Christian church, as the new Israel, is presented as the bride of Christ (2 Cor. 11:2) and will make itself ready as the New Jerusalem (Rev. 19:6-9, 21:1-2). The Universal Christ was likened by the church fathers as "the bridegroom" (Matt. 9:15, 25:6) and "head of the church" (Eph. 5:23). Those divine relationships were expressed, as many spiritual people say, in the "Song of Solomon".

---

* As feeling becomes love and knowledge evolves into wisdom, reason should expand into intuition.

F. What Does the Bible Say about Divine Love?

"God is love, and he who abides in love abides in God, and God abides in him" (1 John 4:16).

Jesus said, "By this all men will know that you are my disciples, if you have love for one another" (John 13:35).

"If anyone says, 'I love God', and hates his brother, he is a liar; for he who does not love his brother whom he has seen, cannot love God whom he has not seen" (1 John 4:20).

"Love is of God, and he who loves is born of God" (1 John 4:7).

"No one born of God commits sin; for God's nature (Soul) abides in him --- by this it may be seen who are the children of God, and who are the children of the devil" --- when he "does not love his brother" (1 John 3:9,10).

"We know that we have passed out of (spiritual) death into life, because we love the brethren. He who does not love abides in death" (1 John 3:14). Thus God's love is the source of spiritual life and gives life to the people (2 Cor. 3:6).

"You have heard that it was said, 'you shall love your neighbor and hate your enemy'. But I say to you, love your enemies and pray for those who persecute you" (Matt. 5:43-44). "Do good to those who hate you, bless those who curse you, pray for those who abuse you" --- "If you love those who love you, what credit is that to you? For even sinners love those who love them. And if you do good to those who do good to you, what credit is that to you? For even sinners do the same" (Luke 6:27-28, 32-33). "And if you salute only your brethren, what more are you doing than others? Do not even the Gentiles do the same?" (Matt. 5:47)

"Greater love has no man than this, that a man lay down his life for his friends" (John 15:13).

NOTE: When God gives to someone or something, it is not only good for that particular individual, group, or cause, etc., but also good for other people whom are part of the whole.

"You shall love the Lord your God with all you heart, and with all your soul, and with all your mind" --- You shall *love your neighbor as yourself" (Matt. 22:37,39).

If you can love yourself (Divine Spirit), you can also love the Divine or Christ Spirit of your neighbor. If you love people whom are born of God, you will also love God who resides within the people. Those people are closely connected to each other like the nervous system of the human body, and can "feel" each other's happiness and distress as their own. This is the Kingdom of God or Heaven.

When we become perfect (Matt. 5:48), we truly love God with all our heart. Everything that belongs to God also belongs to us. The very being of God is love; therefore divine love in action is God. When the Spirit of Love came over the first Christians, they became one heart and soul, and greeted each other with a holy kiss (1 Pet. 5:14).

A saying which is often expressed in our society says, "Love in your heart is not put there to stay – love is not love until you give it away."

NOTE: When water in a creek is stagnated and does not flow, it becomes dirty, which is also true of love and money.

Apostle Paul in 1 Cor. 13:4-7 provides a vivid description of the divine qualities of love. This is a new kind of love, which was introduced by Jesus Christ. It is the love of God expressed by the Divine Spirit (Soul) of a regenerated individual, and transcends the affections between family members and human passions. The person who is born of God has a new nature or Soul which cannot sin (1 John 3:9), and it is the kind that loves enemies, returns good for evil, and has the capacity of self-giving regardless of the cost.

"Love is patient and kind." It knows that it will bear fruit, and it is always kind because it cannot be unfriendly and cold-hearted.

"Love is not jealous." It is happy that a brother or sister has come into good fortune and achievements, by exercising his/her God-given talents.

"Love is not boastful." It knows that without God and cooperation of others, almost nothing can be accomplished.

---

* We should be able to love ourselves the same as the other, because we are they and they are we. I (Christ Spirit) love your Christ Spirit. We also love the world as ourselves, because as a fully integrated person, we are a microcosm and the world is basically the same, a macrocosm.

"It is not arrogant." Love only flourishes in humility because it is not an intensity of feeling but purity. It certainly does not trumpet what one has done.

"It is not rude." Love will not allow us to act in a vulgar or in a disrespectful way and will always be considerate of others. It acts with courtesy and is always polite.

"Love does not insist on its own way." A loving person does not manipulate others in order to get his/her way, but seeks the other's interest instead of their own. It knows that true happiness is only in giving and serving others.

"It is not irritable or resentful." It is only normal for good/evil personalities to become agitated or provoked or to feel a certain measure of wrath when someone offends them. However, persons whom are living a divine life do not harbor prolonged resentment, but easily forgive and forget.

"It does not rejoice at wrong, but rejoices in the right." Only the evil in one's personality rejoices in the wrong, the Divine Spirit, which is always good and pure and one with God, can only rejoice in the right.

"Love bears all things." Divine love is willing to suffer for righteousness sake, and also has the capacity to heal the negative emotions of grief, self-pity, worry, hatred, greed, lust, fear, resentment, etc.

Love "believes all things, hopes all things". It is innocent, imputes no wrong motives, and sees only the bright side. It has complete trust in God and His Will and also wants to believe in the sincerity of the people.

Love "endures all things". It is able to put up with trial-like condition(s) for long period(s) of time.

Paul said in 1 Cor. 13:8-9 that prophecies will pass away because once it is fulfilled, it is no longer of use, and "tongues they will cease" as many languages have vanished. "Knowledge it will pass away" as the knowledge of the ancient and the Greeks have been improved.

In 1 Cor. 13:1, Paul contrasts love with eloquence of speech. In those days many speakers tried to impress and move the hearers by the art of rhetoric and emotional passions, but Paul said that they were "a noisy gong or a clanging cymbal", without truly loving the people with God's love. He also contrasted love with faith, because to love God is more important than to have faith, which only connects the individual to God. Finally, it is more impressive to show the people his or her divine character than their words or to give their bodies to be burned.

People in the Old Testament era were judged by others upon how good they were in obeying the "Law" or the Ten Commandments (and the additional rules and regulations). Jesus Christ told them that the most important commandment is to love God and neighbor. "On these two commandments depend all the law and the prophets" (Matt. 22:36-40). Later, Apostle Paul said, "Love is the fulfilling of the law" (Rom. 13:10). For example: When we love God, we cannot love other gods and graven images, thus fulfilling the 1st and 2nd Commandments. We certainly would not take His name in vain, and will always remember the Sabbath day to keep it holy, because we love Him – fulfilling the 3rd and 4th Commandments. When we truly love our neighbor, we will always honor our father and mother, and it would be impossible to kill our neighbor(s), thus fulfilling the 5th and 6th Commandments. How could we betray our spouse by committing adultery and steal from those whom we love (6th and 7th Commandments)? It certainly is impossible to bear false witness to those whom we respect and honor and we would not covet or desire enviously anything that belongs to our neighbor(s) whom we love.

G. The Love of the Masters

It might be a good idea for people whom believe that God is an external force (and whom have not yet recognized the God within themselves) to follow – for a while – a true master or teacher, whom is like their unborn or undeveloped Divine Spirits or Souls. In this person, the Individualized Spirit of God is able to express through him or her (Rev. 21:3). The modified wisdom and love of God, as expressed by the teacher(s), is usually eagerly received by receptive students.

As God is not always able to love people directly, male and female masters dedicate themselves to raise and open up the spiritual portion of the students, as flowers grow and open up to the warmth of the sun.

The masters are always creative and constructive in everything they do, which is always good for the betterment of everybody, from whom they bring out the best. Just by their presence, the latent divine qualities or germs of wisdom, love, goodness, etc., which are in everyone, begin to awaken and develop; just as the germs within the seed, through the first warmth of spring, germinate and grow. They attract people to them to be "spiritually fed" from their being and words they speak. They teach mainly by example and attainment and open up the higher energy centers of the people they contact and teach.

NOTE: By interacting with people, they may pull us up or down through the vibration of their bodies (physical-psychological-spiritual) and their higher or lower energy centers.

H. True and Selfish Love Compared

The one kind of love is turned outward to the community; the other is turned inward to the ego. The one looks for the good of all; the other looks only for the good of self.

Love is always away from self (the giving way); lust and greed are toward self (the getting way).

Real love is the willingness to put someone else's welfare and happiness ahead of your own desires – maybe you are not in love. It is not that narrow, limited, calculating, possessive love.

True love frees, it does not bind. Our (misnamed) love for them does not give us the right to possess, dominate, and criticize.

Divine love is often quiet and sincere, and not a gushing sort of emotionalism.

Love does not set limits because it is limitless love.

One is called love of benevolence or goodwill, the other of greed or selfish will. It is also called spiritual or sacred love, contrasting it with carnal or profane love.

It is a universal, unconditioned, impersonal healing force from God rather than a local, conditioned, personal, non-healing force from the good/evil ego.

It was divinely beautiful to notice this selfless, spiritualized kind of love, and to contrast it with the intoxicated play of the senses.

We should become familiar with the love of the Divine Spirit, or Divine Being instead of the sentimental love of the personality.

NOTE: Love is like fire; it is bright, beautiful, alive, growing, and gives heat. However, if fire gets out of control, it becomes destructive. Love can also be likened to pure clean water that flows throughout the universe. By flowing through different entities it may emerge murky, distorted, and be misused to trap, seduce, to harm or to destroy another.

True love is beyond human emotion. It is more than our individual attachments, although we like to believe that those feelings of attachment are love. Divine love is unconditional and [a]nonjudgmental. It is not that warm, cozy feeling you get when you are around someone.

Divine love sacrifices the self on the altar of the whole because it sees the whole before the individual, while the romantic or sexual love is centered on the individual without much regard to the whole.

The love of the Divine Spirit or [b]Self-love does not seek its own, but wants to share its abundance with others. Selfish love seeks to possess, holding people, things, and opinions in their own reserved domain.

Examples of Selfish Love

People speak about love, but what they really mean is desire.

Much of human love is self-serving and egocentric, causing pain and resentment and making union as well as division.

Human love is often conditional. "I'll help you if" --- "You should appreciate it and love me."

When love becomes selfish or satanic, God's love is being blocked and is not able to shine through the personality.

Love that is only emotional rocks just as a boat on the sea.

Someone who is attached to his/her lover and sees that person as the only source of love will be devastated when that person leaves or dies. The heartbroken individual might say, "I depended so much on him (her) and when he (she) died, I thought I lost everything."

NOTE: Our happiness does not come from outside – the source of the joy we are looking for is deep within ourselves and can also be found within the Souls of others.

---

[a] An example of nonjudgmental love is the sun, which shines on the good as well as on the bad.

[b] One of the Buddhist disciplines is to transmute self-love into Self-love, which is love of others.

#16 Explaining Eunuchs and Celibates

[c]Eunuchs are males and, to a certain extent, also females whom are emasculated and thus have lost the physical organs to have sex and much of the physical drive. They were usually employed in harems, especially in Muslim courts.

The word eunuch in the Bible does not always mean a castrated individual. The verse in Matthew 19:12 says: "There are eunuchs whom have been made eunuchs by men, and there are eunuchs whom have made themselves eunuchs [d]for the sake of the Kingdom of Heaven." The latter has to do with renouncing the married state, which is also mentioned in the writings of Paul (see 1 Cor. 7:8). However, "not all men can receive this saying, but only those to whom it is given" (Matt. 19:11). Those whom are called by God to lead a [e]celibate life (1 Cor. 7:17); the ones "whom it is given" understand why they should not marry. They "have undivided devotion to the Lord" (1 Cor. 7:35) and are thus free to love all people with God's Love, which is pure and everlasting. They are the first to be redeemed, learn a new song (higher truth and life), and love others through their Divine or Christ Spirits, as it is expressed through their higher energy centers at the time of the return of Christ (Revelation 14:1-5).

However, for those whom are living the life of the personality, it is very difficult to be celibate or live without a mate. They have a lot of vital energy (if they do not masturbate), burn with desire, and are likely to be angry and nasty at other people. It is often said of them "what they need is a woman or a man". If they change to a spiritual or divine life, they are more agreeable to live with and do not tempt every woman or man they see and meet, and (or) fantasize to have sex with them.

The preservation of sexual energy creates a vigorous, powerful, and

---

[c] Eunuchs whom have lost the sexual organs or clitoris may still harbor a psychic sexual desire, like the celibates whom are not always pure in mind, especially when they are not regenerated. They both pay penance (indemnity) in that way, particularly for the people in their care, so that the community has less sexual and other problems to overcome. Living the sacrificial lifestyle – as they did in monasteries – they also balance the karma of the people so that it will be easier for the people to accept Christ.

[d] God does not deny anything to those whom sacrifice sex and other sensual pleasures for the sake of His Kingdom.

[e] Celibates in western religion have a tendency to repress sexuality – instead of sublimating it – they therefore also suppress their life force. That is why they do not always look physically alive.

radiant personality, which is attractive and irresistible to the opposite sex – which can be a blessing or a curse. Those whom live a chaste life enjoy improved physical health, increased mental power, and unfolding of the innate and latent psychic and spiritual (divine) faculties.

NOTE: The celibate's dedication to Christ is a kind of spiritual or mystical marriage (Luk. 20:35), whereby the human psyche (spirit) as female unites with Christ (Divine Spirit) as the divine male within one's greater Self.

#17 The World and Its Meaning

World here does not mean the earth or cosmos, but rather a class of people, which does not want to submit to the rule of God, and therefore are inclined to place themselves knowingly or unknowingly under the rule of satan. Peter referred to the "ungodly men" in 2 Pet. 3:7, which will be destroyed, but not the earth, and humankind as was so at the time of Noah when only the wicked people died.

True followers of Christ are no part of the world (Jn. 17:16), "but I chose you out of the world, therefore the world hates you" (Jn. 15:19). "I have overcome the world" (Jn. 16:33) and "my kingship is not of this world" (Jn. 18:36). "He who hears the word, but the cares of the world and the delight in riches choke the word, and it proves unfruitful" (Matt. 13:22).

James exhorted "that friendship with the world is enmity with God" (Jas. 4:4). They should resist "the spirit of the world" (1 Cor. 2:12) or the mental attitude that dominates satan's world, and not follow the "course of this world, following the prince of the ªpower of the air, the spirit that is now at work in the sons of disobedience" (Eph. 2:1-3). This rebellious spirit is not only fostered by peer pressure from the people of the earth, but also through the influence of unseen forces (e.g. evil spirits), which ᵇmay work through them.

The spirit of the world manifests itself by: excessive use of drugs and alcohol (which is a mode of self-annihilation); immoral living (lying, cheating, and committing crimes against society); flippant, sarcastic, and unclean speech (which are forms of verbal abuse); pre-

---

[a] As water permeates a sponge, so the spirit or psychic world penetrates the physical atmosphere, wherein human spirits and angels are able to live and influence humans on earth. Those spirits and their thoughts (like the air around us) are, thus, everywhere.

[b] Low and evil spirits are able to work through the people when they feel, think, and act like them, when they live according to the spirit of the world, with its predominant evil way of thinking.

occupation with material possessions (1 Tim. 6:8-10); and sexually seductive music, dirty dancing (Exodus 32:17-19; Isaiah 23:16), and wild parties (Gal. 5:19-21; Rom. 13:13).

1 John 2:15-16 says, "Do not love the world or the things in the world. If anyone loves the world, love for the Father is not in him. For all that is in the world, the lust of the flesh and the lust of the eyes and the pride of life, is not of the Father but is of the world."

As the Bible presents it, the church became a religious harlot with whom "the kings of the earth (as being part of the world) committed fornication". It was called "Babylon the great, mother of harlots" --- and was "drunk with the blood of the saints" (Rev. 17:1-6). The patriarchs of the Orthodox Church and leaders of other religious faiths in Russia and its satellite states were chosen by communist leaders at the time when the official religion was atheism.

In order to raise their own life above the world, mystics of all ages had to reject their false selves, which are formed according to worldly custom and tradition and accept their True Self or Spirit of Christ, who can only live in the divine world. The Christ force works to individualize humans and to separate (stand apart or be holy) them from the group or crowd. They are therefore less affected by peer pressure, mob influence, and what people of the world think about them, and are thus less likely to conform to society's rules and convention.

Rousseau J. (d. 1778) believed that public morals and character become corrupted by the progress of knowledge and living in an organized society, and that virtue could only be found in simplicity when humans live close to nature. He contributed to individualism and democratic thought by elevating the individual above society.

#18 The Function, Purpose, and Blessing in Marriage

A. The Function of the Man and Woman in Marriage

But I want you to understand that the head of every
man is Christ, the head of a woman is her husband,
and the head of Christ is God (1 Cor. 11:3).
Wives, be subject to your husbands, as to the Lord.
For the husband is the head of the wife as Christ is
the head of the church --- Husbands, love your wives,

as Christ loved the church --- let each one of you love his wife as himself, and let the wife see that she respects her husband (Eph. 5:22,23,25,33). Wives be subject to your husbands, as is fitting in the Lord. Husbands, love your wives, and do not be harsh with them (Col. 3:18-19). Husbands, live considerately with your wives, bestowing honor on the woman as the weaker sex, since you are joint heirs of the grace of life, in order that your prayers may not be hindered (1 Pet. 3:7).

The husband who is the head of the household (not in himself but in Christ (1 Cor. 11:3)), ought to show unselfish love and consideration to his wife, and his sexual needs are not put above those of his spouse (1 Cor. 7:3, 4). The wife should respect her husband, knowing that he has to answer to Christ, for the way he functions in his headship, while both should be living in Christ (2 Cor. 5:17) or a divine life.

Man and Woman as Representative of God

Because "God created man in His own image", as "male and female" (Gen. 1:27), it suggests that the man and the woman are the visible manifestation of the invisible God, in whom the dual characteristics of maleness and femaleness are perfectly integrated. The woman should therefore look for the image of the heavenly Father in her husband, who is His representative on earth, while the husband should see in his beloved wife the divine Mother whom he ought to love, contemplate, and cherish. The couple, who has attained perfect union, is not only the true representative of God, but also in their functions as Lord of creation, help to join or link the dual characteristics of masculinity and femininity in the creation in a perfect bond.

B. The Purpose of Marriage

The most important purpose in marriage is to beget or bring forth offspring (Gen. 1:28), and secondly, to bond with each other in order to raise the young. This bonding consists of the fostering of mutual affection, communication, appreciation, encouragement, care, support, mutual trust, companionship, sharing of pain and anxiety, stimulating each other in intellectual, moral, and spiritual development, and discovering the innermost being of themselves and the other. When

103

they have come close to God by finding the growing Divine Spirit in each other, they no longer think that they must have sex in order to overcome loneliness.

C. The Divine Blessing

Marriage of two people has its beginning when someone is attracted to another of a different polarity, which may develop into a rapport with the other. By strengthening this relation, they begin to harmonize with the other's innermost being, which results that a united field is created between the partners, resulting in a complete union. They have become engaged.

By invoking the power and love of God on their union at every level of their being, they will grow in that Love, which binds them to God and each other. When they are one with our Creator's will and purpose they will receive a divine blessing, and when the couple consummates their relationship, their marriage becomes complete. The power of God can also be invoked in a *church ceremony by a priest, minister, or other who stands as a representative of God and their institution. When the couple is bonded to Christ, they not only promise fidelity to God but also to the marriage laws and customs of the organization. Thus, not only the couple takes responsibility for the marriage union, but also the holy institution.

NOTE: Sexuality is the interaction, union, and balancing of opposites, of the positive and negative polarities in all the kingdoms.

#19 Short History of Marriage in the Catholic Tradition

It was not required in Judaism or in early Christianity for a marriage to have any religious rite for its celebration. Saint Augustine in the fifth century formulated, for the first time, a theology of marriage. He taught that marriage is not solely for the procreation of children, but is also for friendship between the spouses. He said that sexual intercourse between spouses is good, but it can be used in a sinful way. Augustine believed that genital pleasure between spouses, even in the act of procreation, is sinful. Saint Gregory I, also called Gregory the Great – pope – from 590-604, agreed with Augustine, and he banned from the church or "holy place" those couples which had recently experienced pleasurable intercourse (lustful sexual desires).

---

* The marriage ceremony alone will not change immoral men and women into persons of purity.

REMARK: Unbelievers of all ages whom are living the lower life of the good/evil personality, whom are "devoid of the Spirit", and are called by Jude 19 "worldly people", "will be scoffers". They will mock those whom are trying to live a divine life, according to the directions of Gregory the Great.

Saint Thomas Aquinas (1225-1274), the most influential Catholic theologian, also conceded with Augustine that the most important function in marriage is the procreation and education of children, and that bonding of the spouses through mutual love was of secondary importance. However, he introduced a new meaning, in which Christian marriage is understood as the symbol of the union between Christ and the church. Marriage was not only a "sign" but also a "cause" of grace, and became one of the seven sacraments of the church. Thereafter, the Council of Florence (1439) degreed that "separation between couples is permissible; in the case of adultery, remarriage is not, for the bond of marriage is perpetual". The church theologians later agreed that consent between a man and a woman initiates marriage; and subsequent sexual intercourse consummates it and makes it indissoluble. This is still the law of the Catholic Church today. In the sixteenth century, the Council of Trent issued a degree (in order to end secret marriages) which established that a marriage would be valid and sacramental only if it was celebrated publicly and witnessed by a priest and two others, which is still the law today in Catholic communities. The 1951 acceptance by Pius XII of the rhythm method of birth control implied that intercourse and procreation were two separate functions and that procreation was no longer the most important aspect of marital intercourse. The Second Vatican Council in the 1960s rejected the traditional formulation of procreation as the primary end of marriage. The final conclusion was that marriage "is ordered to the well-being of the spouses and for the procreation and upbringing of children". In this formulation, neither the procreation nor the mutual love and support of the spouses is specified as primary or secondary.

#20 Medieval Church Followed Doctrine of Augustine

Augustine, who represented the majority of the people at the time of the sack of Rome by the Visigoths in 410 A.D. was also their main teacher. His teaching became eventually church doctrine for the medieval church, which consisted mostly of barbarians, whose personalities and expressions were more evil than good. Augustine said that human nature is totally corrupt, and humans are therefore not able to choose between good and evil. Pelagius the Irish monk, who represented a minority of Greek thinking Christian people, believed that human nature is neither wholly corrupt nor wholly perfect, and that everyone has the freedom to choose.

Augustine's classical book "The City of God" speaks about the church as the Kingdom of God and the city of man as representing the kingdom of satan. Charlemagne, who was crowned emperor in 800 A.D., tried to realize the heavenly city in the Holy Roman Empire.

REMARK: Because humans are good as well as evil, there should also be a third city.

#21 The Preventing and Preparation for the Reformation

Before the Reformation took place, God tried to reform the Catholic Church through signs, revelations, and people, especially through the "Brethren of the Common Life", which was established in 1380 A.D. by Gerard Groote (1340-1384) and by his follower Florentius Radewyns in the city of Deventer, Netherlands. The group consisted of men and women of all walks of life and lived in thirty and more dwellings in the Netherlands and Germany. This movement flourished from the latter part of the 14th century, until the time of the Protestant Reformation in 1517 A.D.

Geert Groote, whom led a successful but unsatisfying worldly life, was attracted by the ideas of the mystic Jan van Ruysbroeck. After a serious illness, he was strongly influenced by a Carthusian monk to become a devout Christian. In about 1374, he began his renewed spiritual life by publicly attacking clerical immorality and abuse of the official church. As a result, he was severely persecuted.

To the pupils of the Common Life belonged Thomas a Kempis, who wrote down the spiritual experiences of his brothers and sisters in the well-known book "The Imitation of Christ". Other members of the community were: Gerard van Zutphen, Hendriekus Mande, Johann Wessel, Adrian VI, pope from 1522, and the young Erasmus (1466-1536). Erasmus was a humanistic Christian who tried to reform the church through education and the correct interpretation of the teachings of Christ. Many people believe that he, with other Dutch theologians, were the forerunners of Martin Luther. It is said of them that they "laid the egg that Luther hatched".

A. The Reformation

In the time of the Reformation, four major church bodies emerged: the Church of England, the Lutherans, the Reformed churches, and the Anabaptists. From the latter came forth the Mennonites, Amish, Baptists, Hutterites, and others. Unlike other churches which believe in infant baptism, the Anabaptists (baptized again) accepted only people in their faith whom were spiritually born and are baptized by them (believers' baptism). As a "communion of the saints" they also believe in the separation of church and state. Soon after their establishment in 1525, the state churches began to persecute them severely and many of them were burned or killed by the sword. Out of this persecuted group the Mennonites emerged, under the leadership of Menno Simons, a Dutch reformer. They say that the function of the state, with its secular leader, is the maintenance of law and order by force, while the purpose of the church, whose head is Christ, is the salvation of the world, through the Word and Love of God. The Mennonites established communities in many parts of the world and also in Lancaster County, Pennsylvania, where they have on display a life-size reproduction of the Tabernacle of Moses.

After the event of the Reformation by Martin Luther, the Protestants aligned more with the Father aspect of God, whom they call Jesus, and the Catholics became inclined to worship the Mother aspect of God whom they call Mary. Preaching the Word of God became important to the Protestants, while feeding and taking care of the downtrodden and poor became most important for the Catholics.

#22 Influence of Calvinism in the World

A. The Story of the Pilgrim Fathers and Democracy

Calvin was the founder in Geneva, Switzerland of a theocracy, which was morally very strict, and adherents to his beliefs were known in France as the Huguenots. From France and from Holland (Netherlands), Calvinism also spread to England and Scotland, and was the basic doctrine of the Reformed churches. It was very influential in forming a new doctrine for the Church of England, which was breaking away from Roman authority. Calvinism also later became the basic doctrine of Puritanism, which wanted to purify the Church of England of all the Catholic doctrines and rituals. From the Puritans emerged a non-conformist group that wanted to completely separate from the Church of England and were severely *persecuted by King James I, and had to flee to Holland. The separatists lived in Amsterdam one year and in Leiden from 1608 until 1620, under the leadership of Pastor John Robinson. Many of them left Holland and sailed on the Mayflower across the Atlantic Ocean, which was like a desert, to the promised land of America, where they landed on Plymouth Rock, in Plymouth, Massachusetts on and about December 21, 1620. Before disembarking, they signed the "Mayflower Compact" in order to govern themselves. They were later known as the Pilgrim Fathers and Robinson, like Moses, never entered the Promised Land.

Following the Pilgrim Fathers, the Puritans came to "New England" in great numbers, and they sent in a petition for the rights of individuals, which became the foundation of Democracy. The American colonies became a refuge for the Puritans and New Amsterdam (New York) a heaven for the Huguenots, whom were severely persecuted by Catholic France.

As a governing body, Calvinism was usually successful, and was the theological system of the Reformed Church, which was of great support and consolidation to the people of Holland, who fought against the invading army of Catholic Spain for eighty years. Except for the Twelve Year Truce, when the Pilgrim Fathers sojourned in Holland. It

---

* King James wanted to fully exercise the "Divine Right of Kings", the medieval idea that the king was chosen by God to rule and was the sole interpreter of His Will. James not only wanted to rule the secular kingdom of the state, but also the spiritual kingdom of the church. However, his authority was threatened by the growing belief that anyone who was in touch with God was capable of sharing in the responsibilities of the government. Therefore, the voice of the people (may become) is the voice of God.

also played an important role as an established church during the 1600s, when Holland was blessed with the "Golden Age" and became a major power, thus establishing not only colonies all over the world, but bringing to the people of many continents the Gospel of Jesus Christ.

The Plymouth colony, from the beginning, had self-government based on "the consent of the governed", with all citizens looking to God for leadership, laws, and protection. It was thus a God-directed government, which looked to God as their Supreme Judge, where the people could only enjoy [a]true freedom under God when they submit to His Principles. This freedom was for the colonists (whom were imbued with a "sense of destiny") so precious that their outcry echoed throughout the land: "Give me freedom or give me death". The kings of England were for them tyrants whom were no longer guided by God. The kings did not want to give up their power over the people, and as long as the people obeyed, paid respect and homage to them, they had that [b]psychic power.

James Madison (d. 1836), 4th President of the United States and called the father of the Constitution, said: "The essence of government is power – power lodged as it must be in human hands will ever be liable to abuse." Because most people are living the life of the personality (which is good and evil) and only a few live a divine life, which is only good, it is to be expected that many of them misuse this power, especially when the evil self is in charge of their life. This evil part of the personality or satanic nature wants to control and have power over others, and uses various and devious means to gain and keep that power.

---

[a] True freedom can only exist within the confines or boundary of God's law. For example, the freedom we enjoy in society exists only as long as we abide by the laws of the nation. When we become outlaws, our freedom is taken away from us by society. Thus, when we are no longer living according to the moral and spiritual laws of God but follow other laws and principles – as the young Paul was inclined to do (Rom. 7:14-24) – we become enslaved to sin and true freedom is lost. Thus, if men and women refuse to be governed by God, their freedom will be taken away from them and they will become subject to a foreign government or be exiled, as it happened to the nation of Israel (as recorded in the Old Testament). However, a time will come when the people do not have to follow laws or principles because they will have God's laws inscribed in their hearts and minds (Heb. 8:10-12). Thus, the inner being becomes the law or principle of itself and in itself.

[b] The ones whose Divine Spirit is in charge of their personality, or those whom are living a divine life, cannot and will not obey the king(s) because their life is governed by God. The kings, being separated from God, have little divine power over them, only psychic power, and only then their personalities (separated from their Divine Spirit) obey the king(s).

Calvinists have always believed that a government in which power is lodged or vested in the hands of a few (oligarchy), or in one ruler with absolute power and authority (despotism), usually leads to oppression or tyranny because of the sinful nature of humans. However, they are convinced that democracy under Law is the best political organization for freedom and liberty, provided that the citizens are men and women of noble character and obedient to God.

#23 A Short Overview of Buddhism

A. Introduction

Buddhism is a religious faith of eastern Asia, founded in Northern India by Gautama Buddha in the sixth century B.C. He came and spoke to the multitude and taught that they not only could ease their misery, sorrow, and discontent, but also reach enlightenment.

Buddha was a great man and appeared as a prophet and messenger of God to his people, but he unfortunately lost sight of the [a]true God (among the many gods) and his movement lost, therefore, much of the spiritual driving force.

Buddha told the people that he was "awake", and that each one of them could overcome the sleep of ordinary consciousness. The discovery, the making real in their lives of their true spiritual self [b](enlightenment) or self-transcendence, is achieved by human effort alone. Thus, everyone is his or her own savior and is responsible for his or her happiness. By not invoking the God forces, the realization of the Self or budding Divine Spirit (Spark), which resides in everyone, became a long and strenuous effort.

Buddhism is a system of thought which does not include a personal concept of God and refuses to pray and sacrifice to any deity or supernatural being.

Buddha taught that the cause of suffering is the belief in an enduring and [c]permanent ego or personality (self), which he called an illusion or [d]maya. This also includes, according to Buddha, the wrong belief that the individual self or human spirit continues to live after death as an independent being. He further taught that the cause of rebirth and suffering is attachment to the personality. Thus, in order to obtain de-

---

[a] After many centuries, the concept of God evolved in Buddhism and was called Amida Buddha.

[b] It is also called in different religions salvation or liberation, Nirvana in Buddhism, Moksha in Hinduism, Satori in Zen Buddhism, and Fana in Sufism.

[c] Buddhists say that the personality or ego is made up of 5 skandas (physical qualities-feeling-perception-will/attention-intellect) or attributes, the tendencies and qualities which distinguish one personality from another. They believe that all of the skandas are impermanent, and that humans wrongfully identify them (whole or part) with himself/herself.

[d] Maya does not mean that a thing does not exist, but what we (as imperfect beings) think or interpret it to be –which may not be what it is in reality– is an illusion.

liverance or become enlightened, the self should become extinct. When the self is non-existent, so are egotism, desire, lust, etc. However, upon death and liberation, an individual life or consciousness (which is forever becoming) does leave the body and merges with the ultimate as a wave with the ocean.

NOTE: As Buddhism and Taoism in China were more concerned about the innermost life of humans, Confucianism in China was more concerned about the development of the inner and outer personality.

Buddhism is a human centered ideology, and they like to explain the origins and workings of the universe in terms of natural laws. They also believe that all people have the potential to develop into a Buddha. There is, for them, no separate "immortal soul" which survives death. When the Buddhists become enlightened or awakened, they become part of the whole or spiritual universe. When aspirants have not been liberated, they have to come back to be *reincarnated and start life on earth and suffering all over again. Buddhist candidates would rather go to the divine world or pure land of ultimate bliss than go through the endless cycles of birth and rebirth, or wheel of birth and death, from which they like to escape by attaining nirvana.

REMARK: The surviving human spirits of the people whom have died (die only once (Heb. 9:27)) will try to possess newborn babies, people, and even animals, especially those individuals whom believe in reincarnation. This belief seems real for those people living on earth whom are influenced, obsessed, or even possessed by human spirits whom (continually) impress them with their experiences of their life on earth. The karmic debt, however, can be paid by the human spirits, not by assuming a new body but by influencing those people on earth to do good deeds so that they both will receive karmic benefits.

---

* The natural law of karma or cause and effect governs everything in the universe. It is a Buddhist (and Hindu) belief that the law of karma requires believers, time after time, to be born on earth in order to balance their karmic account. Thus, if it is not balanced in the course of one's life, they have to reincarnate or re-embody. This return, however, is no longer applicable for those candidates whom have become enlightened or have reached the state of nirvana. They are in perfect harmony with the law of cause and effect, and thus do not make any negative karma.

B. Comparing the Mission of Buddha with Jesus Christ

Our great brother Buddha, the Light of Asia, prepared many people for the mysteries of rebirth or initiation by [a]purifying the personality or ego and contacting the Universal Mind through the [b]void, and developing the indwelling [c]Divine Spark into the process of incubation. About 600 years later Jesus Christ, the radiant Light of the World, came and carried the teaching of Buddha forward to the next stage to a multitude of people. He showed us the manner and ways of spiritual birth of one's Divine Spirit or Soul and its development, and the cooperation of the Universal Christ and the Holy Spirit, which are the male and female expressions of God.

Buddha expounded the main principles of practice, the four noble truths, whereby his disciples could become aware of their budding inner Self or Reality, while Jesus gave the Sermon on the Mount so that His disciples could recognize the Christ without by listening to the Christ within (Matt. 16:15-17).

Buddha and his disciples "enter the Divine stream" but did not enter the next level where the Spirit of God resides (Rev. 21:3), and thus could not experience and believe in God as Jesus and His disciples, whom believed and experienced a God who was personal to them.

Buddha had, through his intuition, contact with the Universal Mind and received, through the illumination of his conscious mind, a certain amount of wisdom; while Jesus was fully aware of and one with God,

---

[a] Before the advent of Christ, the development and purification of the personality was also accomplished (to a certain extent) by the Hebrews in the era of the Old Testament (and thereafter) and by Confucius and many others. In later times, Mohammedans likewise prepare the people in the world to receive the Cosmic Christ. They believe in One God and try to live a moral life (like the Jewish people) while being guided by the angels and become, in their growth, at the same level as their teachers or angels, whom are their mediators between God and them.

[b] The void is the emptiness resulting from the dissolution or death of the personality. Ego death is the absence of the personality or the extinction of the ego. It is thus the nonexistence of self, having no personality or self-image. However, ego death should not be the total elimination of the ego, but only the evil part of the personality, not the good part. What thus needs to die is the inherited evil nature, which wants to be a separate being and does not want to be controlled by the pure Essence or Divine Spirit. The great ensuing struggle is called, in Christianity, the "dark night of the soul". Thereafter, the emerging new personality, after a brief encounter and change, becomes an instrument of the Divine Spirit.

[c] There resides in everyone and everything a Spark of divinity (Stoic belief in Greek philosophy), which should become a flame and fire.

and became the pure channel through which God the Father could pour out His love, wisdom, and power. Buddhism makes no clear distinction between the life of the personality and divine life, while Christianity separates those two in the ego thought system, with its inherent "good and evil" way of thinking, and a thought system based on divine love and wisdom.

People become Buddhists the moment they accept the Buddha as their teacher and guide; they become Christian the moment they accept Jesus Christ as their Savior. Depending upon the level of understanding of the audience, Buddha taught on the [a]enlightened as well as on the mundane levels; Jesus always taught on those two levels. He spoke to His disciples of "the secret of the Kingdom of God" but "for those outside, everything is in parables" (Mark 4:11,34).

As Buddhism developed and especially after the [b]event of Christ, many advanced Buddhists became more and more aware of the nature of reality, which they call original nature or Buddha nature (Dharmakaya), and began to compare it with the Christ nature or Divine Spirit. Some of them could no longer believe in the necessity of complete dissolution of the personality and they began to call the voice of God who speaks to them [c]Dhyani or Amida Buddha. They became more universal and also realized that the Buddha nature is without any duality – neither male nor female (Gal. 3:28). Advanced Buddhists also believe that the experience of the void (shunyata) or ego death comes before the [d]realization of the Self, Buddha, or Christ nature (when developed), and that the void is a necessary transition to the life of Essence or Self.

However, for many conservative Buddhists, the void, the nonexistence of self, is the deepest nature of reality and is the main focus, while the presence and existence of Essence is denied.

---

[a] The ancient Greeks before the time of Jesus Christ taught on the exoteric level the "Less Mysteries" and on the esoteric level the "Greater Mysteries".

[b] Mahayana Buddhism became an established movement in the 1st century A.D.

[c] This living Buddha is called, in Hinduism, Iswara and Immanent Christ in Christianity.

[d] What is called Self-realization in the East, Christians call it "to know Christ" or to be "born again" – that is the birth of the Divine Spirit or Soul or the full awakening of one's Buddha nature. Many transpersonal psychologists speak of realizing the Self, while the goal of the Yogis in India is to realize the Atman. An Indian Brahman, Gnostic, and baptized (of the Spirit) Christian is usually a "reborn" individual. This also includes the Anabaptists, whom believe that no one is a Christian until they are "born again".

Many Buddhists are awaiting the appearance of the future Buddha, the Maitreya.

C. The Four Noble Truths and the Eight-fold Path

They become awakened and enter [a]nirvana by following the four noble truths, which are the foundation of Buddha's teaching. This body of Buddha's teaching is called "Dharmakaya" or the "body of the [b]dharma".

1. Life is full of suffering and dissatisfaction.

Suffering is universal. Humans experience it from birth to death in the basic four sufferings of birth, sickness, old age, and death. All religions acknowledge that the present human condition is not satisfactory. People endure not only physical suffering, such as: injury, starvation, pain, and impermanence, but also psychological suffering, such as: loneliness, separation, insecurity, unhappiness, hopelessness, despair, etc. Thus, a change in behavior and attitude is needed to improve the human situation.

2. Desire and craving are the causes of human suffering.

Humans have a great desire or greed to possess worldly things, which create attachments to those things. They harbor selfish desire for wealth, power, worldly pleasures, and by living to indulge in those desires, it causes them to suffer. The constant discontent that humans have and their continual longing for more and more are also causes of suffering. They should instead strive for what they need and not for what they want. Thus, the selfish desire, thirst, wanting, and cravings are the sources of suffering, which bind humans to the cycle of existence (samsara).

---

[a] Buddha fulfilled life's goal, the realization of nirvana, which means to blow out or to extinguish worldly illusions and passions. It is a final freeing of all that enslaves the human spirit, such as: craving, desire, hatred, egotism, selfishness, delusion, etc. (the extinction of the lower principles in humans). The one who realizes the status of nirvana interrupts the chain of samsara and eliminates rebirth in any of the 5 existences: human world, ashura world, animal world, the Hindu ghost world, and hell. There is no longer a need for the human spirit to be purified and is thus free from future rebirth, sickness, old age, and death, and the end of all suffering.

[b] Dharma means doctrine-teaching-law-justice-righteousness or natural law. Dharmakaya also means the glorious eternal Buddha who is always expounding the dharma.

3. By eliminating selfish desires, suffering will end.

Suffering can be overcome and happiness achieved when humans give up their useless craving for things and learn to live happily with what they have, instead of continually being dissatisfied of what they do not have. They will then be happy and free and no longer obsessed with satisfying their selfish wants, but instead find time to help others with their needs. Otherwise, selfish desires will lead them to rebirth and thus to a continuous desire and suffering.

4. This is possible by following the eight-fold path.

The way to eliminate desire or craving is by practicing the noble eight-fold path, which leads to the end of suffering. When this path of liberation, peace, and happiness becomes a way of life, the practitioners will escape from samsara or the wheel of rebirth. To put it in physical terms, the Buddha (the physician) discovered disease (suffering) and found that its cause was desire. The medicine he gave to his patients to cure the disease was the eight-fold path. As some religions, in their moral development of their people, follow the Ten Commandments, Buddhists follow the eight-fold path to purify the good/evil personality of its evilness, so that the ego will only express good thoughts, words and deeds, and prepare it for nirvana and liberation.

The eight-fold path is known as the middle way, a life of calm detachment, through which a wise person avoids extremes of self-indulgence and austerity, the golden mean or middle path between two extremes.

The eight-fold path covers every aspect of life: the economic, social, ethical, psychological, intellectual, etc., and thus contain all the elements to develop into a wholesome human being.

1. To have right views – without superstition or delusion.

To have right view, knowledge, belief, perception, and understanding of life, one must see life in the world as they really are, without any misconception, false impression, or deception. To have right views is a path of wisdom, a search for the truth, to consider human existence, and to distinguish between good and bad thoughts and deeds. It is also knowledge of the four noble truths and an understanding that all things are without a *self or permanent ego.

2. To have right aspiration – and resolution.

Right aspiration is to have a strong desire or ambition to achieve something noble and to have high and sincere goals. The result of right view is that our understanding of life becomes clearer, and we begin to analyze and try to find answers to many questions such as: "How can I improve my life?"; "What do I want out of this life?"; and the great question: "What is the purpose of living?"

3. To have right speech – truthful and with kindness.

How we express ourselves in language is a sign of our character, and when it is spoken with the wrong or malicious intent, it can do not only a lot of psychological damage, but also result in wrong actions by, for example, breaking up friendships and stirring up fights. We should use speech that brings happiness to others and not use language that is hurtful, such as abusive and harsh expressions, and we ought to always tell the truth. We should also not use speech that injures the reputation of others, or put someone down such as slander or gossip. We should refrain from useless and idle talk and be modest in referring to oneself, and refrain from self-exaltation.

4. To have right conduct – which is peaceful and untainted.

Buddha gave five commandments or precepts of good behavior:
1) Do not harm and kill sentient life, that is those living creatures, which are capable of feeling.
2) Do not steal the property of another or take what has not been given to him or her.
3) Do not indulge in improper or immoral sexual relations. Anyone should live a pure and restrained life, and adultery is strictly forbidden.

---

* Most Western psychologists believe that a strong ego is needed to be successful in life. Thus, their therapy is designed to build up the ego, while that of Buddhism is to minimize it. The purpose of the ego is to organize and consolidate new learning gained through mental, emotional, and sensory awareness. Besides, an individual must first cultivate a self or ego before he or she can really become unselfish. What the Buddhists should actually refer to when they speak of ridding oneself of the ego is to strip oneself of that part of the personality or ego, which is formed by worldly customs and tradition. Thus, the evil part of the ego or the false ego should die, but not the pure and real ego.

4) Do not utter an untruth or lie and deceive others.

5) Do not drink alcohol or take illegal drugs.

Thus, we can use our body for selfish, harmful, or destructive purposes or use our bodies to serve others and to create well being for ourselves and others. Happiness is the outcome of performing good conduct and deeds, which does not cause suffering to anyone.

5. To have right livelihood – which harms no other person.

We should earn our living in a honest way without trickery or deceit so that we do not hurt or exploit others at all levels of their beings. Thus, we should not obtain our happiness at the expense of someone's happiness. Thus, right livelihood is to avoid occupations or trades that result in suffering of other beings and thus violate moral law, such as: manufacture and trade in weapons, prostitution, drug peddling, bartending, killing animals, and destroying the environment. They should have instead a career or lifestyle that promotes moral virtue and spiritual welfare. Right view leads to right aspiration. After having acquired right aspiration, we understand how to express ourselves in speech and how to conduct and have right livelihood. But, to properly exercise the above five ways is to have a well-trained mind. Thus, the last three steps of the eight-fold path is to cultivate our mind – by right effort – right mindfulness and right concentration.

6. To have right effort – to gain control of the self.

Only through effort can something be achieved. It takes effort or the use of mental energy to overcome all manners of temptations and to prevent evil forces from leading our lives. We thus need to have a strong and clear mind to remove harmful negativity from our selves. It also takes effort to become a good person, and it takes a lot of exertion and strength to remain good. It is therefore easy to quickly backslide after having gained, through long periods of trial and error, a measure of moral and spiritual development.

7. To have right mindfulness – to be alert and active.

Right attention is to cultivate an alertness of mind and keep the mind centered or focused on what we are doing. Thus, we should concentrate on the goal and give heed to our problems and to practice right attention while we are sitting, eating, talking, walking, working, etc. By living in the moment, we should constantly be vigilant or watchful of our thoughts, speech, and actions because it is easy to do wrong when we are careless and thoughtless, and thus do not know what we are saying or doing. This happens when our mind is not cleared but cluttered. Our thoughts should be pure, free from lust, greed, desire, hatred, ill will, cruelty, unkindness, revenge, etc. Because thinking is an action of the mind, it can and will cause bad karma to the doer when it is harmful.

8. To have right concentration – to achieve understanding and union with the infinite by meditation and receiving wisdom from the impersonal Universal Mind.

The last and most important state of the eight-fold path is the culmination of right effort and right mindfulness. Cultivating the former two, right concentration comes about. This means the ability not only to focus our attention (as in seven), but also direct our mind to look closely so that we can penetrate more deeply, to find answers to life's questions, existence, and inner and outer reality.

By meditating on the Buddha and his teachings, we may have experiences of our inner reality, which may lead to enlightenment. This will open our inner gate or channel to the flow of insight, wisdom, and understanding. It will give us wonderful bliss and contentment, and all our thoughts, words, and deeds have become enlightened in our path. They have become clearer, pure, refined, enriched, and caring, and are filled with peace.

The ones whom have completed their voyage do not receive mere knowledge but universal wisdom by contacting the Universal Mind through the faculty of intuition (buddhi). They are then better able to discriminate between good and evil and "know" directly, without recourse to reasoning with their lower or concrete mind.

Accordingly, those whom have followed the eight-fold path diligently will break the chain of karma and samsara and eliminate rebirth and *a life of suffering by living on this earth. By practicing the above teaching or dharma, the individuals are placing themselves in harmony with nature and with natural law. Living in accordance with

---

* Human life at that time was short and full of suffering. By living according to the dharma (like Old Testament), life becomes better because the people are more living in accordance with the universal laws. Life becomes at its best when they are no longer living the life of the personality but a divine life. That is when the Divine Spirit of the human constitution is in charge of the personality. They are living in the kingdom of heaven on earth, or what some Buddhists call "living in the pure and blessed land".

this law will result in health, contentment, tranquility, and peace of mind.

D. The Meaning of Desires

Buddhists in general believe that the cause of suffering is fulfilling the lower selfish desires of the personality, the craving or repeated attachments to objects of desire. However, desire in itself is not wrong and should not be with the ego (which causes desires) [a]rooted out because it gives [b]incentive to actions and is thus the driving force of the ego. Life becomes otherwise for ordinary human beings lifeless, boring, empty, dull (without color), and thus not much to live and work for.

In the early stages of growth only unlawful or [c]evil desires should be eliminated from our personality or ego. When humans develop, they should replace lower selfish desires (which holds one and its [d]mind in bondage to one's lower being) with higher desires. Eventually, the [e]"spiritual will" becomes the driving force of people whom are living a divine life, the ones whom have become enlightened. They are those whom have become impersonal or universal and are thus no longer controlled by personal [f]desires.

One of the wondrous results of the above process of clearing the emotions or "washing the windows" of lower desires is that the spiritual light can easily shine through the pure and clear emotional self (as unpolluted water), whereby one's whole being becomes bright, calm, and peaceful. The emotional self becomes still, transparent, stable, steady, and serene and does not easily yield to vibration of fear, worry, and other harmful desires.

---

[a] Conservative Buddhists believe when the ego is rooted out or extinct, selfishness, desires, lust, hatred, discrimination, etc. are also diminished. Buddhists therefore like to behave as if they have no ego.

[b] The vital body gives power to action, the desire incentive, and the mind purpose.

[c] We can make a distinction between good desires, which can be low and selfish, and higher desires. There are, however, also evil desires, which many people have inherited. When, for example, sexual desires are influenced by evil desires, it becomes impure and lustful. When desires for possessions are influenced by evil desires, it becomes greed.

[d] The focusing mind which should be the ally of the True Self or Divine Spirit is separated by and in alliance with the lower being and is also enslaved by desire.

[e] Spiritual Will (faculty of Divine Spirit) is not affected or attached by surrounding objects.

[f] Desire is a debased form of spiritual will, lower in quality and value.

NOTE: An oriental maxim says – kill out desire – resulting in indolence.

REMARK: Many conservative Buddhists believe that the deepest nature of reality is the nonexistence of self (the void), the [a]extinction of the personality or ego death. However, what should be extinct (rooted out) is the false personality, the inflated ego or the false sense of self, by which most people identify with. This we can do by stripping the good/evil ego from its evil or satanic elements – which all people of the Adamic race have inherited from the archangel Lucifer – so that it will become pure (Matt. 5:8) and not tainted (Mark 7:20-23). The evil part of the personality is called in Paul's writing "old nature" (Eph. 4:22) or "old self" (Rom. 6:6). As long as the evil or satanic nature is in charge of the personality, the ego is false. The false or inflated ego (old or evil nature) will do anything in its power to preserve its identity and uphold its domain. The personality is called false because its evil nature is attempting to take the place of Essence or the True Self or Soul (Nature or Reality) through which realization we become enlightened.

E. Final Thought about Jesus and Buddha

The Buddha taught that the only way to deliver from suffering was the suppression of desire and to abstain from every kind of passion and emotion.

Jesus Christ, on the other hand, taught to control and overcome all desires, which he clearly demonstrated.

Buddha also instructed his disciples to retreat from the world in order to avoid [b]temptation.

Jesus mastered his lower nature instead of fearing it and showed by His life and His teachings that it is possible to live in the world but not be part of the world.

Because Buddha suppressed the emotional side of his personality, he was not able to express love as well as Jesus was able to do.

---

[a] Buddhists should not throw out the good ego (baby) with the evil nature of the ego (with the bath water), but only get rid of the evil part.

[b] It is not easy to live in this good/evil world. But, by running away from responsibility, suffering, and temptation, one does not develop valuable "soul qualities". By overcoming stressful circumstances, challenges, and trials, one may develop useful "soul qualities" such as: strength, perseverance, courage, self-control, patience, integrity, goodness, humility, forgiveness, wisdom, and compassion.

Because Buddha directed his followers toward self-mastery, they were most of the time immersed in themselves, concerned about the welfare or spiritual advancement of their own souls so that they did not have much time to help other people. Jesus told His disciples that the Spirit of God will inspire and help them when they bring salvation to all the people of the world.

As the Pratyeka Buddha achieves Buddha-hood for himself, the ideal of the Bodhisattva – which developed after the event of Christ in Mahayana Buddhism – is not to enter the bliss of nirvana but to return and help all the unfortunate ones of the world to receive Buddha-hood. Those whom sacrifice themselves in order to help humanity become Buddhas of compassion and their love has become true, beneficial, and universal.

#24 Jews and Mohammedans Are Bound Together

Abraham is the father of the Jewish and Mohammedan religion because he had two sons representing those religions. One (Isaac) was born through promise of "a free woman" and the other (Ishmael) according to the flesh by "a slave" (Gal. 4:22-23). Both religions believe in One God who lives without. The people of those exoteric religions are in position of servants to God who does not and cannot deal with them directly, except with a chosen few. He therefore sent His angels to lead and guide them (Gen. 18,19). However, members of the mystical factions of those religions found a closer relation with the divine, whom they discover lives within the deepest core of their being. Thus in the esoteric religions, the sacred is encountered within, rather than outside themselves as in exoteric religions. [a]Thus the more religions grow toward the pinnacle of the "mountain of God", the more they are united in oneness and purpose.

Judaism, Islam, Confucianism, Aristotelianism, Human psychology, etc. are non-mystical religions and organizations, while Jewish mysticism (cabalism), Moslem mysticism (sufism), Taoism, Platonism, Transpersonal psychology, etc. are mystical religions and groupings.

Christianity, as originally taught by Jesus Christ, was esoteric in nature and was to deal mainly with the level of the Divine Spirit, but became a religion which dealt more often with the human than with the divine division. Of the latter, we may include here people whom professed to be Christians, but are not true Christians. Apostle Paul called them "men of the flesh" (1 Cor. 3-1). These carnal Christians are not under [b]grace (Rom. 6:14) but are still under moral law (Gal. 3:24), like the Jewish people. The Christians whom are still living outside the Law – 10 Commandments – (1 Cor. 9:21) are still in need of the law, and their conscience needs to be formed again by living under the law (Heb. 8:10). They should and can learn a lot of the Jewish and Mohammedan religions, how to live according to the laws of God.

---

[a] This idea is not a new one.

[b] They are living under higher Principles and are guided by God directly in their daily life.

#25 How the Mind Can Direct and Overcome Sexual Desires

Humans are endowed with mental facilities through which they have imaginations and memory and by which they call forth life-like images, which can be, unlike acts, easily and continually reproduced. As the mind can direct the flow of vital and other energies through the body, passionate thoughts can draw those energies to the lower second energetic center and may create sexual arousal or increase the force of sexuality. Thus, the [a]mental part of humans can therefore arouse desires easily in the feeling or emotional part (sheath) of individuals. Because energy follows thought wherever the attention goes, that is where energy is directed. This may become a problem for people whom have [b]high energy levels. This is especially true for advanced Souls whom in addition also receive more energy from the higher planes, which is transmuted whenever it passes through their lower vehicles. However, if the attention is directed toward unselfish affection, higher mental power, and spirituality, then the lower creative energy will be transmuted and [c]sublimated to the higher levels.

The mental facilities of animals are dormant, or only little developed, so that thought hardly affects their behavior. Their sexual urges (in the form of heat or rut) are only aroused by physical stimulus and earthly forces, which occur only in season or periodical cycles. Thus, unlike the human species whom have free will and have intercourse when and with whom they desire, animals follow their instinct and have only sex when reproduction of their species is desired. And, in accordance with the law of their evolution, which is the law of the body, they select only those whom are the most fit to survive.

Considering the above, we can readily understand that undeveloped humans can become worse than animals when they are in relentless pursuit of gratifying lustful desires. They may eventually become perverse, depraved, and cruel and more dangerous than wild animals (Rom. 1:26-32).

A. What is Sublimation?

Sublimation is the process of transmuting sexual energy (libido) consciously or unconsciously into higher forms of energy, such as, for

---

[a] Sex is neither impure nor pure. When, however, the mind gives it the most important place, then it becomes a problem.

[b] See also **NOTE** on p.62.

[c] See explanation next page.

example, water turning into vapor. Thus, instead of going downwards to the generative organs, the sexual creative energy is [a]deflected upwards and used for higher creative aspects of life. Creative people have therefore less [b]sexual urge than the more "earthbound" people. They are usually more interested in the shaping of the world (which is still in the process of restoration) than in the making of the human species. Thus, more vital energy is available for physical exercises, such as sports; more emotional energy for exercises in personal love and love for humanity; more mental energy for intellectual activities in pursuit of personal benefit and interest for all people; and more spiritual energy for the growth of one's Soul and that of his or her neighbors, country, and world. Instead of the pleasure of biological creation, there is the joy of discovery, invention, and science (physical); arts, poetry, music (emotional); literature, philosophy, psychology (mental); etc., and the welfare of human society. In addition, there is the pursuit and attainment of psychic and spiritual goals and power. This sublimation and transmutation can be gained consciously by loving people of all walks of life and to pour all of one's creative energy into a work of creation. To visualize the highest type of an ideal man and/or womanhood such as the Christ and Madonna and have a divine relation with them.

[b]A person who has become conscious of the surging of sexual impulses can usually find liberation by increasing the quantity and quality of creative output. Thus, instead of seeking physical and (or) psychic gratification, it is worthwhile to focus one's imagination and thought upon something to create. In that case, one's particular creative energy – having its own quality of vibration – goes into a painting and becomes alive and part of the painting, song, writing, poem, music composition, business venture, etc. Physical exercises may be of help by "burning" physical and vital energy, but when it is coupled with creative thought it will be more effective. The most effective way to raise the unused sex energy is to be totally absorbed in creative thinking or work. This is especially true when one devotes his or her attention to spiritual efforts and thoughts by, for example, Holy Scripture reading, meditation, and especially in witnessing.

---

[a] In the beginning it may take long and determined effort to deflect this energy. However, it can be done by consistently refusing to yield to one's lower nature. The rising energy will eventually increase and may even be seen as pouring out from the top of one's head. It is seen as a flame in the statue of Buddha and other great saints.
[b] See b.

Thus, anytime you are absorbed in a creative work the desire for carnal relations disappears. When humans becomes thus more creative, the population of male and female prostitutes will surely diminish. However, it is not wrong to have strong sexual desires as long as it is turned in the right direction because it can be as much a power for good as a power for evil. Someone may be good because the person cannot summon up sufficient energy to be bad. He or she is then so good that they are good for nothing. They are "neither hot nor cold" (wishy-washy), as the people of the seventh church in Laodicea were (Revelation 3:15-16).

NOTE: A particular strong thought or conviction – with its own rate of vibration – affects the mental part of a human temporarily or permanently, when in the latter, the thought is continually repeated. This may affect the whole personality because it also alters, to some degree, the vibration and constitution (as the wind moves the water) of the more dense emotional vehicle "below" and the quality of the divine vehicle "above". For example, if a person thinks evil (or good) of another person, it will be much easier to do it again and this trend will be difficult to change because the mental body is used to that kind of vibration. Those thoughts, in turn, will stir up one's emotions and he or she will also begin to hate the other. Because thoughts also produce waves inthe surrounding psychic atmosphere (which can be of a different nature, like sound creates waves in the air), they will affect the mental bodies or vehicles of people moving in that environment. Their effectiveness depends upon the strength, clearness, distance, and receptivity, provided they are thinking along the same lines and are not occupied with other thoughts. In the emotional realm, when a person sends out a wave of love or anger, it tends to arouse a similar vibration or passion in the emotional body or sheath of another by intensifying it or stirring up the latent germ of good and evil.The other, in turn, radiates love or hate vibrations to an unsuspected third party, who will send out to others until everyone is affected.

B. To Overcome Sexual Problems

As religious disapproval and prohibitions against promiscuous behavior had a considerable impact on people's behavior in the past, the force and influence of this reprehension has been diminishing in the last decades because of the eroding authority of traditional religions. However, the outcry – voiced or not voiced – against immoral behavior is necessary for those whom are living the life of the good/evil personality, and whose sexual appetites and desires are overdeveloped and too much excited. The society, as their reflection, which is guided by the good/evil thought system, continually stimulates those appetites and desires while the influence of biblical teaching on the subject has been diminishing.

As conscious repression of sexual desires may be helpful, it also may lodge as unfulfilled desire in the subconscious mind. Those desires, according to psychoanalysts, may surface to physical consciousness at times and may cause psychological problems.

Uncontrolled gratification of all desires, on the other hand, is much worse than suppression, and it certainly is not the solution to deal with sexual craving because it is not in harmony with the laws of the universe. It therefore causes diseases, disappointments, exhaustion, and deterioration on all levels, moral degeneration, and inner conflicts.

A better option, especially for those whom are living a mundane life, is the transmutation or sublimation of sexual passions. This can be done by transmuting excess sexual energies into creative activities, such as in artistic and *intellectual pursuits; by expressing unselfish love, creating spiritual ideas, concepts, and life, and by the contemplation of the mystical Christ and other divine images and symbols.

However, the natural and ideal way to overcome sexual desires for adults is just to live a divine life, that is when one's Divine Spirit (with its will) is in charge of the personality and its desires. This should happen normally (in the restored world) at the time when children become teenagers, when the sexual desires are awakened, and they start to discover the opposite sex.

C. The Creative Force

The creative force or cosmic energy is a power that pervades the universe and work through receptive and active channels. Whenever humans start creating, they draw pure creative energy from the cosmos, which is used and modified by imperfect people. Thus, the creative force is [a]the source of all human creativity and the generation of life.

The creative force should flow through us continually and let us create on all levels of our being. For most people, much of the energy

---

* …for example, by creating new ideas or putting more power into old ideas.

[a] Siegmund Freud came into contact with many people on his "psychoanalytical coach", whom had sexual problems. By analyzing those people, he came incorrectly to the conclusion that the life force (libido) was only created in the body – was sexual in nature – and that it was the only source of all creative and religious expressions.

of creation centers or rather is arrested at the [b]base of the spine. This accumulated energy is called by the Yogis of the East "Kundalini". They also speak of the awakening and (or) rising of the Kundalini or "coiled serpent", by stimulating and opening up the higher energy or creative centers (chakras) by special techniques. When creative energy flows in its downward rush through a sexual outlet or sex function it may be called sexual energy, and when it flows upwards, spiritual energy.

It is perfectly all right to use creative force for childbearing, but it is very wrong to use it for self-gratification and lustful pleasures. The latter is not only a [c]waste of energy – as it can be used in creating with our minds and unfolding higher powers – but the wrongdoers also have to suffer the consequences, by misusing God's creative energy. This results in the deterioration of physical, mental, and spiritual abilities. Thus, instead of becoming a superhuman or genius, having God Consciousness, they rise no further, and get stuck at the level of ordinary human consciousness, or fall back to less than mediocrity.

The use of creative power for parenthood, to bring to birth a living being, is a most sacred privilege and duty bestowed on human beings, as co-creators of God. Of all the other creatures in the kingdoms, humans alone are self-conscious and self-directing in the exercise of the function of reproduction. This places human beings in a position of grave responsibility in the use and misuse of creative power. Unfortunately, almost all people throughout the ages have used the creative force carelessly and even abused God's creative power.

D. What is Creativity?

When God created the heavens and the earth, the plant, animal, and human kingdoms, He "saw everything that He had made, and behold it

---

[b] When the energy at the base of the spine or root (chakra) is not allowed higher expression, it will result in degeneration at every level of one's being. When sex becomes the sole outlet for life energy or kundalini and the center of one's life, then it becomes destructive. It should therefore rise out of the lower chakras towards the heart, where energy is experienced as love, and towards the throat chakra, which is important in the distribution of creative energy, and is active in true artists. From there, it will culminate in the "third eye" area of the brain, opening it up to receive illumination.

[c] Physical and vital (etheric) energy is not only wasted in the physical gratification, but also psychic energy in the accompanied psychological gratification of sexual imagination and fantasies.

was very good" (Gen. 1:31). Everything God made was original, and He created everything in potentiality, and let human beings as co-creators do the most rewarding work; not only create things out of raw material but also to create human beings, and create themselves at all levels of their beings.

True or essential creativity is a function of the Spark of God within each individual, which becomes more expressive when the Spark develops into a Higher Self or Divine Spirit. The creative force within us is the power of God, which strives to express itself through the human personality in the physical, psychic, emotional, and mental levels. Thus, the manifestation of creativity increases as individuals are more in tune with the God forces, or move closer to God. True creativity is always original, limitless, uplifting, and it always brings humans out of their psychological confinement. *The creative person knows that its inspiration comes from a higher plane of existence, which is not bound by space and time. The power to create is the most precious divine attribute and gift, which God has bestowed upon humans; it gives great joy to life. Thus, each individual who is in tune with his or her Divine Self makes their evolution differ from their brother or sister, and is original in their creation. Their creative ability is that of a genius, who as a co-creator uses the same power as God created the universe.

The human personality itself is not able to create; it "makes" instead of creates. The human ego, without inspiration, can only imitate the ideas and thoughts of others. Most people, by denying their Divine Self, are imitators and try to follow or be like somebody else, instead of being themselves. They are camp followers or conformists and the best they can do is to give form and expression to creativity of someone else.

NOTE: Creativity and intuition are both inspired by the Higher Self and God. Intuition is more passive and receptive, while creativity is more active and inventive. A genius is known to have a mental power far beyond explanation (divine consciousness), manifesting by exceptional originality. They also have a special gift or talent for some specialized activity. A gift is an innate quality that manifests itself without ability. A talent is a natural ability in a specialized field. This faculty may be inborn or acquired. Ability, competence, capacity, aptitude, and skill are based on inheritance, past experience, training, so that the task at hand can be easily performed.

---

* See next page.

E. Profiles and Insights of Creative Persons

Creative individuals are not necessarily intelligent as it is measured by intelligence tests; it is therefore quite possible to be highly creative but of average intelligence. Highly creative people have a tendency to withdraw and be an observer of mundane life. They like solitude more than uncreative people and do not want to give much time to what they regard as unimportant matters of everyday life. They tend to be strongly intuitive and more interested in the inner causes and meaning of the [a]world than in the way it appears to the senses. Creative people seem to be free from conventional restraints, are little influenced by the opinions of others, but rather trust in their own judgments, especially concerning inner matters.

As ordinary people use the logical thinking process to find solutions to problems, highly creative people use the non-logical or creative thinking process to find a fresh, non-repeating or novel solution to a problem. However, some people whom are capable of original thought continue with their conventional way of thinking to find an answer because of their fear of losing social approval, or an unwillingness to put their trust in their intuitive way of thinking.

The creative idea or answer usually comes at a time when the individual is not concentrating on the problem, when the thinking faculty is not engaged, so that the information flow from the subconscious mind (which is the conscious mind of the human spirit – etheric and physical brain –) is not interrupted. It may also be deeper, that the [b]divine flow from the Divine Spirit or Soul is not obstructed. When the individual is in a quiet receptive mood (such as in periods of relaxation, contemplation, walking in nature, journeys to far-away places, taking a bath, or being in a trance-like state, as in day or waking dreams, drowsiness, etc.), the subconscious and the intuitive facilities

---

[a] Many of them sense not only the physical world, but also within the outer world the psychic or spirit world, which latter contains the divine or intuitive world, wherein God has His dwelling. Those three worlds, which interpenetrate each other, are populated with physical and etheric beings, human spirits and angels, and Divine Spirits or saints of all religions. This world is teeming with life and very interesting and revealing of those whom not only sense the existence of the three worlds but also sense God everywhere in all of His creation.

[b] Socrates referred to those insights and flashes of inspiration coming from his "daimon" (not demon) or "genius". This inspirational spirit is called a guardian angel or manifestation of the Holy Spirit in Christian expressions, Higher Self or Soul in esoteric parlance, and Self in psychological language.

send messages directly to the brain. Those premonitions and revelations may also come from other people, with or without bodies, which come as ideas of inventions, insights, or conveyed by dreams from the lower and higher beings and as inspiration from God our Heavenly Father and Mother.

In order to keep the creativity flowing, we should not block the channel or obstruct the divine flow between our Higher Self (Divine Spirit) and lower self (personality), by physical, emotional, and mental abuse; beating/cruelty, worry, hatred, resentment, craving, annoyance, bitterness, egotism, deception, lying, cunning, hypocrisy, and unforgiving. In this way, we come closer to satan in our feelings and thinking, especially when we are prideful, sexually seductive, greedy, and do not want to accept God as our Creator and Sustainer, and refuse to live according to His laws and principles.

At a larger scale, when people are closer to God in their feeling and thinking, we see a time of creative flowering in all endeavors of life. Great artists, writers, scientists, and inventors, came forth, and business enterprises and other unique creations crop up, such as in the golden age of Holland in the seventeenth century, and of the Mohammedans and other societies and nations in the Middle Ages and later. The Shakers and other groups in eighteenth century America displayed great energy and creativity through their many inventions. This was also true during the reign of Queen Victoria in the nineteenth century in England, when they *spread the Gospel of Jesus Christ and their way of life (their laws and how to govern) throughout their colonies. As they were imbued with a sense of destiny, so was America, especially in the nineteenth and twentieth centuries, whom were likewise proclaiming the Gospel throughout the world and their democratic ideas and rights of individuals.

---

* However, in their enthusiasm to spread the pure Gospel of Christ, they also tried to promote their own culture to people whom were already in possession of their unique culture, which the proclaimers could not see through their thick culture glasses.

#26 Sexual Involvement of Men and Women Is Not the Same

Men are much more than women (twelve percent of women according to Kinsley report) to become sexually aroused by visual images and pornographic material. However, when women for a long period of time harbor and (or) are involved in an imagined and psychic sexual relationship, they may become even more aggressive than men, of wanting a physical relationship because their whole being, physical and psychical, is involved.

As most men are more interested in sex, the majority of women want to be involved in romance first because they also like to participate emotionally. That is why they like to read romantic novels or watch plays, wanting to become part of the story. For many ordinary women, *emotional infidelity (falling in love) is, therefore, worse than sexual infidelity of their partners.

---

* Some wives, whom are living the life of the personality, would prefer that her husband went to a prostitute rather than fall in love with another woman because love, unlike prostitution, demands an involvement. For the same reasons, some religious institutions would rather have that their clergy visit a prostitute than to fall in love. In the first case, they will come back to the organization. In the latter they may not return.

#27 What Is Pornography?

Webster's Dictionary tells us that pornography is the depiction of erotic behavior designed primarily to cause sexual excitement. Its intent is thus to arouse, incite, and intensify sexual or erotic lust in the hearts (psyche) and minds of the people, mostly in men. It is usually the external beginning of sexual [a]fantasy or imagination, *harassment, psychic seduction, masturbation, fornication, adultery, [b]rape, and other sexual abuses. The "prostitutes of writing" are no longer disgusted and become addicted to the obscene literature. After having become insensitive, and to arouse sexual excitement, they start watching more kinky activities and may even start acting them out.

Jesus Christ warned against sexual lust in Matt. 5:28: "But I say to you that everyone who looks at a woman lustfully has already committed adultery with her in his heart." 2 Peter 2:14 spoke of wicked people whom "have eyes full of adultery, insatiable for sin", and 1 John 16 of "the lust of the flesh and the lust of the eyes" of worldly people.

By looking at a woman lustfully, especially when having eye contact, it may stir up lustful thoughts in her, which may result in a psychic sexual relationship. It all begins when men (also women), by looking at pornographic pictures, start to fantasize about the women or men they see, which creates in them sexual arousal. They either repress those thoughts or they look at women or men they meet with a roving eye and seductive look. This eventually creates an insatiable lustful desire, when simple sexual intercourse with one spouse is no longer satisfactory. They are looking instead for sexual gratification with many women whom they also like to dominate, degrade, and humiliate.

---

[a] See page #133 for explanation of fantasy.

* Harassment is bothering and offending someone in a sexual manner (although some like it), and it comes in many shapes and forms (Gen. 39:7; Ruth 2:8, 9, 15). It can be physical, such as touching someone in a sexual way; verbal, in sexual proposition, comments, compliments, and jokes (Eph. 5:3-4); and nonverbal, in a flirtatious stare. In Tim. 5:2, young men are commanded to "treat younger women like sisters, in all purity". Albeit, young women may send mixed messages, when they reject sexual advances while wearing clothes that attract attention to their body. Young men should remember that they can want a woman for her body but they can only love her for her character.

[b] See page #134 for explanation of rape.

Pornography, therefore, encourages rape and sexual assault. Women are seen as sex objects, to be used and abused to satisfy one's pleasures. Because the relationship is only superficial, it does not see the other person as a valuable human being with a unique character. Many men therefore say: "Love 'em and leave 'em." The message of pornography is to follow your impulses and desires and not to worry about how your behavior affects others, while morality, marriage, true love, and procreation are not important. Their slogan is, "When it feels good, do it." It exploits and dehumanizes sex, so that human beings are treated as things, or as "an 'it' instead of a 'thou'". It cheapens, debases, and pollutes sex. Wherever it is found, it is a sure sign of the decadence of society.

A. Fantasies and Imagination – Controlling the Mind

Some people say that pornography is harmless because it is only a fantasy, like horror films, science fiction, and dreams. There is, however, no harm in merely seeing and thinking about porn in an objective or in a nonattached way; that is, without any emotional and mental involvement and thus without stirring up any sexual desires and thoughts. On the other hand, when individuals begin to fantasize and imagine themselves of wanting to have sex and allow their desires and thoughts – which are creative – to strengthen their imaginations or fantasies, then the [a]imaginations will become very powerful. The result is that the buildup of psychic energy seeks to express itself and yearns to become a reality in the physical dimension.

Sexual fantasy will also become a psychic and physical reality, not only by looking at porn images, but when the viewer starts to have a psychic relationship with spirits of humans portrayed in those images. Pornographic prostitutes may also seek a sexual psychic relation with someone they know or they are being contacted by spirit beings from the lower psychic realm, which are often earthbound.

Thus, in order not to become an easy prey of lower beings – with or without bodies – and evil forces, we should learn to discipline our unruly emotions and careless play of [b]thoughts. We should therefore

---

[a] When the imagination becomes extremely vivid, it becomes like activities in the spirit world.

[b] As thought is capable of arousing sexual desires, individuals should not be fighting those desires because the mind will then dwell on it and thus feed and strengthen those desires. They should elude it by thinking of something else.

learn to give due respect to our emotions and thoughts and to understand what they are and how they operate.

As the physical body (flesh and bones) consists of what we eat, the human spirit (emotional and mental energy) is made up of what we feel, think, and believe, while the Divine Spirit (divine energy) is composed of the kind of spiritual truth we absorb and assimilate. The physical body feeds of the body of the earth (its staple food) and becomes part of the earth. The human spirit feeds of the body of humanity (intellectual food) and becomes in unity with it, while the Divine Spirit ͨfeeds of the Body of God (Word of God) and becomes one with the whole. We create in the same way in the spirit world as in the physical dimension. There is first the will to create, the imagination comes about, and the idea (abstract thought) is formed. When the abstract thought is being clothed with mind stuff, a more solid thought form is created, which becomes a solid creative object in the spirit world. This thought form in the physical world becomes a plan, which materializes in the slow process of physical action and creation. Thus in the spirit world, the creation is accomplished by the operation of the mind, which is based on the law that energy follows thought, which is a much faster process, and works instantaneously in the higher spirit world.

From the above we can readily see and understand that it is not only important to control and discipline our thoughts while living on earth, but especially when conscious living (or visiting) in the psychic dimension. Thought in the spirit world is real and concrete (as the spirit body is made of psychic energy) can create and build our surroundings and it is also a means of communication and transportation.

B. Rape: Its Effects and Judgment

As the rapist is directly responsible for rape, women whom want the attention of men also invite or risk being raped by wearing a short skirt and (or) a neckline too low. In addition, many rapists are also strongly influenced by pornographic material, which not only increases their desire for sex with anyone, but it also tells them that women like to be violated and used as sex objects. Rapists are usually poorly educated, suffer of hopelessness and despair, have complete disregard for others, and have a strong inclination towards evil. They seek for sexual satis-

---

ͨ For a more elaborate explanation of spiritual food, see "The Birth and Evolution of the Divine Spirit or Soul".

faction by overpowering and hurting their victims. Rape can, however, also occur in a marriage, which has become more and more lustful. The dark or evil side of the man may emerge, which is often accompanied by sadistic beating or battery, which may be received by the woman with great displeasure or she becomes more attached to her husband. The individuals whom are acting out sexual perversions may also attract undesirable psychic entities and create other harmful forces. When rapists are charged for their crimes in court, they often blame the woman for her misbehavior, and that they have learned everything from porn.

The effects of rape can be very traumatic for women whom have grown morally, while living the life of the personality, but will be devastating for those whom have also grown spiritually by living a divine life. The more undeveloped and evil the rapist is, the more women will fall in consciousness or backslide, with the exception of those whom are already fallen or are at the same or even lower level as the rapist.

The experiences of violated women are: "I just hate myself" – "I feel so dirty" – "I feel alienated from people" – "I feel hopelessness and despair" – "I want to die". They feel isolated, guilty somehow, and responsible. In the case of rape in an adulterous relationship, there is disappointment, mutual accusation, and loneliness, whereby the woman experience, in addition, exploitation and defilement, which is also the experience of the majority of women, whom have been raped in a married relationship. In some cultures, unmarried women are cast out by families because they believe that she has been defiled, have become a used item, and are no longer fit for marriage.

Rapists have to pay a heavy toll for their wrongdoing, especially for raping the women whom were living a divine life. If they are not caught and punished by the criminal justice system, the universal law will be against them and relentlessly pursue them in every step they take. It is able to incite the criminals to make "stupid mistakes" or to cause other "unlucky" things to happen, so that they sooner or later are caught by the criminal justice system. They cannot find a place to hide because they carry the karmic imbalance and debt within themselves. If they do not get caught right away by outside authority, the law of karma will relentlessly pursue them by other means or by taking something from them, or forcing the rapists to make amends until the karmic price is paid.

C. Stimulated by Sexual Images

Many people, especially in the Western world (since the sexual revolution or "liberation" of the 1960s), have become obsessed with sex. However, what have been liberated are the perversions of human sexuality and the destruction of wholesome human relationships. It is therefore a false liberation, based on the selfish pursuit of the good/evil personality for sensual pleasure, without any responsibility, and thus enslaving themselves to the desires of the flesh (Gal. 5:13; 1 Pet. 2:16; 2 Pet. 2:19; John 8:34).

Besides getting too little moral teaching, people in general have been increasingly and relentlessly bombarded by sexual images, sounds, and overt and subliminal suggestions from the entertainment, advertisement, and media industries. Being exposed daily, consciously as well as subconsciously, to those images of magazines, newspapers, books, plays, television, motion pictures, videos, internet, and pseudo art, ordinary human beings have become desensitized and find it no longer repulsive and shocking. In other words, the evil part within themselves has been growing and has gotten a stronger hold on the life of their personalities.

Commercials are no longer innocent, but have become more and more pornographic, which is an exaggerated, unnatural, or artificial stimulation of the sex drive. In order to sell products, services, or clinch a deal, businesses use "commercial love-making" or appealing to the sex instinct, as a means to lure customers. This "love-making" is put in an attractive package, that sex for fun is not only a good thing to do, but is also progressive, which is eagerly bought by the young generation. Those enterprises, especially the television networks, continually dangle before the people's eyes that the goal of the relationship between the sexes is to fall in love and stay madly in love. This form of romance is only an "emotional high" or foolish passion and cannot endure the stress of everyday life. Those whom are looking for this immature and shallow love as the perfect love in their mates are disappointed again and again, as their mates do not or rather cannot fulfill those ideal expectations.

As sex sells, it provides huge profits for those enterprises, especially for publishers of pornography and their distributors. Those industries that entice the people to live "below the belt" so that the population becomes more selfish, materialistic, greedy, prideful, deceitful, and depressive, and so forth, have to pay a heavy karmic price. They and the many individuals employed in those enterprises and many other people are the cause of the downfall of civilizations, and the service men who fought to protect their nations and its high principles will have died in vain. Are those sexual perpetrators not the real enemies of the people?

Societies almost everywhere have become sex-ridden to such an extent that most intellectuals and even many clergymen of all faiths, whom are supposed to be the leaders of the people (1 Tim. 3), do hardly oppose sexual misconduct of their parishioners. A great number of clergy has engaged in inappropriate sexual conduct with parishioners or employees and have also become slaves to lustful desires. Therefore, they should be disqualified from practicing the profession of ministry because they no longer belong to Christ (Gal. 5:24). Nevertheless, they continue to preach a false Christ who panders to their desires (2 Tim. 3:5-9). They have become spiritually weak and unsure of what is good and evil and are therefore no longer willing or able to coerce the people under their care to "straighten" out their life, because they have lost moral authority and the power of conviction (Isaiah 59:2). Clerical immorality and abuse has been the greatest cause of the failures of churches and religious organizations and resulted also in the Protestant Reformation.

As long as Israel was under God's protection, Balaam could not curse Israel. The Moabites then set out to lure Israel into committing idolatry and sexual immorality. This tactic succeeded, and Israel lost God's protection (Num. 22; 24:10; 25:1-9; Rev. 2:14). There was a time in the history of Europe that France, who could not conquer England by force, planned to send over 100 prostitutes to demoralize English people, first, so that they lose the will to fight and second, defeat them in battle. In another period of time, the behavior of English soldiers whom occupied France was so immoral that they were easily beaten by the French soldiers, under the leadership of Joan of Arc (1412-1431), the "maid of Orleans". At the urging of Joan of Arc, French soldiers purified themselves morally so that they not only became more energetic, but also that the God forces were able to work through and with them to bring them victory.

Sexual experience without regard to procreation has been more and more accepted and has become a recreation instead of a creation. The result of sexual promiscuity has become very obvious to anyone: millions of abortions, the widespread of sexually transmitted diseases which have become epidemics, the increase of teen pregnancy and suicide, the erosion of family life, and the young generation which has become more violent and addicted to drugs and alcohol. We are also confronted with many people whom are depressed and complain of loneliness, meaninglessness, and of a spiritual emptiness, which they try to fill unsuccessfully with parties and sexual relationships.

#28 A Chapter Dedicated to Women

A. The Sins of Adam and Eve

As it was recorded in Genesis, chapter three, Adam did not live up to his responsibility, and Eve used her femininity in a seductive way to entice Adam to join her in disobeying God by "eating" of the "tree of the knowledge of good and evil" (Gen. 3:6). By allowing himself to do what he knew was wrong, Adam failed to display true masculinity and earn the respect as the strong and reliable future head of a woman (1 Cor. 11:3). He weakly chose to accept the false words of deceived Eve and *allowed himself to be tempted by her, rejecting the Word of God not to "eat", and thus becoming like the symbolic tree, in the life of his personality. Thereafter, he did not like her anymore, and coldly referred to her as "The woman whom thou gavest to be with me" (Gen. 3:12), and began to dominate her.

B. How Women Have Been Treated

Throughout history, women have been treated more as possessions than as companions.

According to the Law of Moses, a woman is her husband's legal property. Exodus 20:17, the tenth commandment, degreed, "You shall not covet your neighbor's house; you shall not covet your neighbor's wife, or his manservant, or his maidservant, or his ox, or his ass, or anything that is your neighbor's."

However, despite the low legal status of Hebrew women during Old Testament times, their social prestige was better than that of women of the surrounding tribes and other races of a different ethnic origin. Many of them at those times were sold in slavery and used as temple prostitutes. Women were severely treated in Hinduism and were expected to be burned alive, together with the corpse of her husband. Women in Buddhism were not allowed to do anything without her Lord's permission, and her only hope of heaven was to be reborn as a man. In Taoism, girl babies are not welcome, and they allow foot binding of all females. The whole of China, as influenced by Confucian thinking, believes that women have no soul, and that killing a woman is no crime.

---

* Adam did not attempt to separate from Eve, but left together with her the "Garden of Eden" or the realm of the Divine Spirit, the Kingdom of God.

C. Description of the Middle Age Church and the Bible about Evil and Good Women

As people in general are good and evil, some women have a tendency to be either extremely good or extremely evil. They either love or hate. According to the Malleus Maleficarum – first part, question VI, (see also Appendix #6), an elaborate textbook for the examination and *extermination of witches; women know no moderation in goodness or vice. When they are governed by good spirits, they are mostly excellent in virtue. However, when they are ruled by evil spirits, they indulge in the worst possible vices because those women are more impressionable, carnal, weak-willed, and feeble-minded than men, and are more ready to receive the influence of disembodied spirits. The aim of the devil and his cohorts to corrupt faith will first be accomplished through the women, whom in turn will deceive and tempt men to become like them and satan.

The inquisitors of the Roman Catholic Church of the Middle Ages said of those evil women that "all wickedness is but little to the wickedness of a woman. What else is a woman but a foe to friendship, an inescapable punishment, a necessary evil, a natural temptation, a desirable calamity, a domestic danger, a delectable detriment, an evil of nature, painted with fair colors."

NOTE: Most forms of witchcraft are a revival and influence of paganism, which existed everywhere in Europe before they were Christianized. They were living the life of the good and evil personality, while Christians are attempting to live a divine life. Most witchcraft covens appoint or elect a woman as a high priestess. Is that so because they are sensitive and impressionable to spirits?

Proverbs chapters 5 and 7 warn about the ways of evil women. Ecclesiastes 7:26 said, "And I found more bitter than death the woman whose heart is snares and nets, and whose hands are fetters; he who pleases God escapes her, but the sinner is taken by her." Ecclesiasticus 25:23 in The Jerusalem Bible states: "I would sooner keep house with a lion or a dragon than keep house with a spiteful wife." Proverbs 21:9, "It is better to live in a corner of the housetop than in a house shared with a contentious woman."

---

* This extermination was based on Exodus 22:18: "Thou shalt not suffer a witch to live" or "You shall not permit a sorceress to live." Martin Luther was quoted to say, "I would burn them all," while John Wesley, his theological opponent and founder of Methodism, was also opposed to all forms of witchcraft.

Many kingdoms have been destroyed by evil women, such as the kingdom of the Jews, which suffered much misfortune through Jezebel and her daughter Athaliah, queen of Judah. The queen caused her son's sons to be killed so that she will reign (2 Kings 11:1-20). The Egyptian kingdom and Romans endured much wickedness through Cleopatra, queen of Egypt. The mother of Nero got her power by killing her husband Claudius I, who was emperor of the Roman Empire (41-54 A.D.) and put her son on the throne.

On the other hand, good women deserve much praise; they have saved nations and kingdoms. For example, Clotilda, who was married in 493 A.D. to Clovis, king of the Salian Franks, won her husband and many of his subjects over to the Christian faith. Gisela, daughter of Emperor Henry II, who married in 995 A.D. Stephen, king of Hungary, was untiring in spreading the faith in their kingdom. The judge and prophetess Deborah did much to save Israel of destruction (Judges 4 and 5) after Israel committed evil "and the Lord sold them into the hand of Jabin, king of Canaan" (took away His protection). Queen Esther saved the Jewish race from annihilation, while they were in exile in Babylon.

The last chapter of Proverbs (31:10-31) speaks very highly about a good wife, whom is called "blessed" by her children and much praised by her husband. "Strength and dignity are her clothing" (31:25). Ecclesiasticus 26:1,14 in The Jerusalem Bible says, "Happy the husband of a really good wife; the number of his days will be doubled." "A silent wife is a gift from the Lord, no price can be put on a well-trained character" and Proverbs 12:4 reminds that "a good wife is the crown of her husband".

Christianity gives a woman her rightful place. The Bible teaches that as a sinner she needs salvation, as a woman she deserves respect; as a relative she merits love.

The unbelieving husband is sanctified by the believing wife (1 Cor. 7:14), who stands on a social equality with her husband. She is the queen of the home. "Husbands, love your wives as Christ loves the church and gave himself up for her, that he might sanctify her" (Eph. 5:25-26).

D. A Short History of Women and Sex

Since the fall of Eve and Adam, women have become more sexually desirous than men. Fathers of the early Christian church often regarded unregenerated women as "the gates of hell". In the Middle Ages, evil women are still the instigators of sex, but albeit in a less sinister sense; while the men were sexually more restrained. In the sixteenth century when the witch trials were in full swing and thereafter, women did not dare to expose any part of their bodies or show any sexual desire and pleasure from sex without fearing for her reputation or life. This view of sex and women became deeply embedded in the psyche of the people of Europe and lasted for a long time. It is not until we approach the nineteenth century (after a sexual permissive interlude of the late 18th century), that the moral landscape changes, women became more innocent and pure, while the men became more aggressive in pursuing them. At those times, the old Christian tradition that the initiative belongs to the male was more emphasized and the good women was to be subservient to the male. It is only in the 1960s that women wanted to be "liberated" and rebelled against religious and civil authority, by wearing clothes that allowed certain body parts to be revealed in a sexually provocative manner. They were also allowed by society to express an open desire and enjoyment of sex. This was the beginning of the sexual revolution, which has been interrupted, but still continues in a less offensive way.

E. How Women Should Behave, Dress, and Adorn Themselves

For women to take their rightful position and be obedient to the man, whose head is Christ (1 Cor. 11:3), they should "learn in silence with all submissiveness. I permit no woman to teach or to have authority over men; she is to keep silent. For Adam was formed first, then Eve, and Adam was not deceived, but the woman was deceived and became a transgressor" (1 Tim. 2:11-14). They should therefore be "submissive to their husbands, as Sarah obeyed (supported) Abraham, calling him Lord" (1 Pet. 3:5,6), and as Esther like Sarah was beautiful and a woman of faith with a gentle and mild spirit (Heb. 11:11; Esther 2:15-17).

"Women should adorn themselves modestly and sensibly in seemly apparel, not with braided hair or gold or pearls or costly attire but by good deeds, as befits women whom profess religion" (1 Tim. 2:9,10). As Peter instructed, "Let not yours be the outward adorning with braiding of hair, decoration of gold, and wearing of fine clothing, but let it be the hidden person of the heart with the imperishable jewel of a gentle and quiet spirit, which in God's sight is very precious" (1 Pet. 3:3,4).

The Bible provides no detailed rules to regulate dress, grooming, or the use of cosmetics. It offers the people broad guidelines so that they can choose wisely from whatever their culture and local customs provide, and also consider their personal taste. Albeit, the women should not wear men's clothing (Deut. 22:5), and they should *veil themselves in church.

Dress and grooming should be modest and extreme styles should be avoided, which would offend others and draw too much attention to their physical appearances. It focuses the attention to the outer person and not to the beauty of the innermost person because when those persons are witnessing, it distracts the people from the Spirit of God who tries to express itself through the witnesser. Although real femininity and masculinity are based on spiritual qualities, the clothes you wear do make a statement about yourself to most people, especially to those whom are materialistic. It is therefore not advisable to appear ugly, with worn out, ragged clothes because you want to "appear spiritually".

Many women whom are living the life of the good/evil personality use a great deal of [a]cosmetics to make themselves more attractive and be noticed by men they like. They also feel more valuable when they possess such charms. Albeit, as it is often the case, their beauty is only as deep as the layers of skin creams they put on, while underneath, their emotions are selfish and do not express true love. Their minds are narrow and petty, and their spiritual or divine lives hardly exist.

Dressing to attract attention of the opposite sex seems to be the primary function of the attire of Western culture. When women are immodestly dressed in a sexually provocative way, they do not enhance true femininity and it certainly does not honor God. As God holds a

---

* See 1 Cor. 11:2-16. These verses explain why women should cover their heads when they pray and prophecy during worship.

[a] We may ask the question, "Do cosmetics and lipstick enhance the beauty of women or make them more seductive?" Those women that use makeup to seduce and "pull down" men, are they not acting like psychological or psychic prostitutes? The difference between a spiritual and materialistic woman can, in most cases, be easily spotted by the amount of makeup and fragrances they use. There are women whom protest when they are regarded as sex objects. However, they are spending much of their time in fashion shops, beauty parlors, cosmetic bars, and in front of their mirrors.

man accountable for his lustful thoughts (Matt. 5:28), He will certainly hold the woman accountable for the way she [b]dresses in public places, even if she does not realize what she is doing. They are tempting and arousing the men not only consciously but also subconsciously. When the married men begin to imagine and fantasize about having sex with them, they become unfaithful to their wives psychically and care less about his children. They not only influence other people with waves of lustful thoughts, but they also "awaken" in them the easily aroused sexual desires, so that the people in their environment may soon feel and think as they do. Besides, they also pollute the air around them and even [c]permeate and contaminate the furniture and other things they use with those low thought vibrations. Although the spreading of those low radiations may be done unconsciously, the perpetrators are karmically responsible for what they have done by inciting others to live out of harmony with the universe and its forces and going against the stream of evolution of those people and humanity as a whole.

There are women whom are expressing more the evil part of their good and evil personalities than their good part. They dress immodestly with high heels, low cut dresses, and short skirts in order to get and keep their jobs and to gain approval of the males whom are acting as true sons of satan. The evil part of their being enjoys the evil attention they are getting and those women may experience it as a psychological thrill. Some of them, as true daughters of fallen Eve, may even use immodest gestures to make themselves sexually more alluring in order to get what they want. By teasing and manipulating those indecent and weak men whom are responding as true sons of fallen Adam, the women get even more than they bargained for.

There is, however, another part within the women that is repressed, resentful, and angry because they feel that in order to be accepted by "the world", they have to prostitute their image and beliefs as daughters of God. Some of them are getting organized and are striking out because they do not want to be exploited and pushed around anymore. They surely have the support of women whom are trying to live a divine life, as restored Eve's. They certainly do not dress indecently

---

[b] Much moral and spiritual damage is done by girls whom are working with short skirts in restaurants and other public places. Some of the men seeing the sparingly clad women begin to fantasize about them, and through imagination, sexual desires are aroused, which they project to those and other women.

[c] The science of psychometry deals with the ways human and other vibrations influence the vibrations of material objects. By holding or touching an object that an individual possessed, information of a person's character and surroundings can be perceived by the impressions received by the psychometrist.

and radiate sexual vibrations to the male population, whom might be attracted more to their spiritual beauty.

Women are usually very sensitive to the onslaught of sexual vibrations of men and are especially vulnerable to the "lust of the eye" (1 John 2:16; 2 Pet. 2:14). The eyes are like etheric portals through which the projected energy of the man may enter the woman's etheric body and thus influence her spirit body. Men are known to have a flirtatious eye and a seductive look and often "undress them with their eyes". On the other hand, innocent men have been warned not to fix their eyes upon certain kinds of women, whom in turn will usually not bother someone who wears a robe or a collar. This "spiritual protection" is also used by nuns of the Christian church, many Mohammedan women, and others whom are dressed and veiled in such a way that they are protected against unwanted male advances and sexual vibrations. They certainly do not want to tempt the men.

F. Physical and Spiritual Beauty of Women

We live in a world that is obsessed with physical appearances, and there are available many artificial ways to enhance physical beauty. Great amounts of money are spent on treatments to improve looks, and many would have us believe that improving their "image" is the road to happiness. They are obsessed because the psychic senses of their human spirit is still dormant, so that they hardly believe in life after death, and their Divine Spirit is little or not developed, which should radiate spiritual beauty to their physical bodies. Many people may be attracted to those people whom exhibit great charm and physical charisma only to discover that behind the appealing mask is often hidden deceit and manipulation.

Physical or sensual beauty can be a woman's "weapon" or a curse, when in the latter case, they are chased and dominated by a male who is still much identified with his animal body. Therefore, physical ugliness is not as bad and can be a protector of women. Besides, the unseemly may radiate spiritual beauty to such a degree that most people and men like them much better than women whom are physically beautiful but ugly within. The latter are like empty shells, devoid of higher intellectual and spiritual life.

Women should nevertheless be attractive, physically as well as spiritually by making themselves youthful and desirable. They should, however, not be seductive by buying sexy clothes in order to look sexy, and to become a threat to their own and male salvation.

When someone is still young and undeveloped, it is a valuable asset to be physically young, beautiful, and attractive. But, if they are developing morally and spiritually, their human spirit and Soul, which are always youthful, will shine through their older growing physical body. The human spirit and physical body will then more and more reflect the beauty of the Divine Spirit or Soul, such as inner grace, compassion, kindness, cheerfulness, contentment, wisdom, forgiveness, nobility, etc.

Thus, when one is getting older outside, he or she becomes more beautiful inside; or when physical beauty wanes, spiritual beauty gains or takes its place. Unfortunately, for too many people this is usually not the case. They are getting older physically, and even after having developed mentally to a high degree, they feel no spiritual life "ticking" within themselves. They feel frustrated, useless, a burden, and rejected by society. When they also are not developed morally, he may become a "dirty old man" (Rom. 6:6) and she may become an evil looking old woman, whom is known as a witch or hag, and does not cease nagging.

Women can however awaken their Divine Spark and develop their Divine Spirit or enhance their spiritual beauty, which will grow and endure forever, when they study and assimilate divine Truth. By cultivating the fruitage of their Souls, such as: love, joy, peace, patience, kindness, goodness, faithfulness, gentleness, self-control (Gal. 5:22,23), it will enhance their femininity and they become women whom are easy to love. Those women show loving kindness, pleasantness, modesty, and a mild and clean tongue (Eph. 5:4). Women whom participate in the "life" saving mission become exceptionally beautiful and irresistible. By witnessing to the people about Christ and His Word, they are aglow with the Spirit of the Divine Mother, which radiates from their face and is shining through their eyes.

The people whom have been inspired by them will, in turn, value their inner beauty much more than their physical beauty, which will eventually fade away. Besides, people do not create deep and fulfilling relationships with their figures, measurements, and hair, but with the essence of whom they are. They will discover that the real value of life is not the body, clothes, and jewelry, but their eternally beautiful Divine Spirit, which is connected and empowered by the Source of all Life.

NOTE: When you are in the presence of a true master (male or female), it is not so much the master you love, but the pure energy of love flowing through that being from the Source of all Love, Truth, Beauty, and Life. This energy will touch you in the innermost part of your being, and which will inspire you to seek the Truth, Love people, and sacrifice for others.

G. Women Whom Get Power Over Men

Eve, who was supposed to be under the dominion of Adam, dominated him instead through sexual temptation. To keep themselves in power over men, evil women accuse the good men of past crimes (Rev. 12:10) because as true daughters of satan, they do not want to be ruled by them.

Some women do anything to undermine the God-given position of their husbands. They act and dress in such a way that the man will give up his position and power as head of the household and potential son of God. These kinds of women, whom are charged with a great deal of sex appeal or animal magnetism, are especially powerful over those men, whom are sexually interested in them in an excessive and possessive way. They control those men by depriving them of sex and let them beg for it. They let the men kneel before them, whereby she becomes the source of his love, happiness, wisdom, and inspiration instead of God, who no longer takes the most important place in the lives of the deceived men. Those *evil women are so seductive and alluring that the strongest and most powerful men, whom have succeeded on the battlefields of the world, are conquered and destroyed by them. This is why men say of those tempting women that "she is a knockout" or "she makes me lose my mind and inflates my senses". They therefore regard them with fearful fascination or awe, and ignorant mistrust and suspicion and even contempt. She is desired and feared, pursued and shunned, and for undeveloped materialistic men, the source of his greatest pleasure. Those women may become lust incarnate and sexually insatiable, which they can only gratify by acting as a paid or unpaid prostitute.

---

* The most dangerous women are those whom are promiscuous and single. They make themselves attractive to those men whom have power and resources, which they want to take away. Those women project consciously and radiate subconsciously a magnetic – attractive energy to those men, which is sexual in nature and by which the men become easily entangled and powerless to resist.

Because Eve preceded Adam in evil, we see in this fallen world that the women still precede and are treated as number one. She goes through the door first, is served first, and likes to be spoken to in meetings as "Ladies and Gentlemen".

However, after a woman learned that the lust, which is in most men, is not in her man, she will stop bossing him. When he starts living a divine life, she even wants to serve and support him and be truly his "helper fit for him" (Gen. 2:18).

H. Differences between Men and Women

In the beginning "When God created man, He made him in the likeness of God. Male and female He created them, and He blessed them and named them Man when they were created" (Gen. 5:1-2).

Thus, the man was first created as a blending of male and female in one person, and thereafter differentiated as male and female.

After having created Adam, the Lord God said, "It is not good that the man should be alone; I will make him a helper fit for him" (Gen. 2:18). "Then the man said, 'This at last is bone of my bones and flesh of my flesh; she shall be called Woman, because she was taken out of Man'" (Gen. 2:23,24).

Adam's role was to be the head of his household (Eph. 5:21-24), and the role for Eve was to cooperate with Adam in accomplishing the main purpose of creation, that is: "to be fruitful (perfection), multiply, and have dominion over the creation" (Gen. 1:28).

Because of the fall of Adam and Eve, they and their descendants were not able to model after the divine image, which is a perfect union of opposites. They never attained the intended wholeness, and have ever since been seeking for completion and integration of their alienated opposites, physically, psychically, and spiritually.

Humans are usually divided into males and females, although this is not always true for all sentient beings. Although man and woman differ from each other physically because of shape and form, they also differ chemically, whereby the man produces and possesses more male hormones than female hormones, and a woman secretes more female than male hormones. In addition, they are also apart when, according to the Jungian school of psychology, the man has within his psyche a female element, which is called anima, and the woman has a male element animus. Thus, no male is wholly male, and no female is wholly female. A feminine nature is found latent in men and a masculine nature latent in women.

NOTE: Some students of the esoteric school maintain that the vital and emotional self of the man is female or negative and that of a woman male and positive.

Men and women not only compliment and attract each other physically but also balance and gravitate toward each other through the stronger and weaker masculine and feminine qualities they possess within their psyche. The psychological complementation of the psyche, however, is not set but more flexible and interchangeable. There are in different degrees assertive and aggressive men whom would fit the quiet nurturing women, and the introspective gentlemen, which balance the ambitious dynamic women. A male, for example, may be more effeminate in his characteristics in order to fit or complement a more aggressive and active woman, and vice versa. Thus, a woman may assume the man's role as a thinker and decision-maker, etc., while the man may, at times, be more receptive, emotional, and intuitive.

They also differ from each other in behavior, desires and interest, from which some of them might be culturally conditioned. As the male is projective, thinks logically, and should be spiritual, the female is receptive, has an emotive mentality, and is inclined to follow her well-developed (gut) feelings or lower intuition. Being more earthly oriented, she takes good care of the body and personality of her child(ren), her day as a mother – "mother's day" – is much celebrated; while the father who should be more responsible for the well-being of his child(ren) in its moral and spiritual development is less celebrated.

The stereotypical male is usually active, goal oriented, individualistic, etc., more intellectual, while the typical female is passive, drawn in, relating, etc., but more emotional in her expression. There is usually not much difference in gender and sex of a couple during their childbearing years. They usually show the typical male qualities such as: aggressiveness, dominance, competitiveness, and hardness; while the females include: passiveness, compliance, cooperation, and tenderness.

NOTE: Because of the woman's physiological experiences, such as menstruation and conception, she is more sensitive and responsive to the phases of the moon and its recurring monthly cycles than the man. She is also more imaginative than the man, who represents the will, which is more allied to the sun forces. The woman is usually more involved in the life of the personality, and is therefore more down-to-earth and practical, and represents the inner, darker, negative, and hidden side of life.

However, those sex differences, by which the male and female identify themselves and which is mainly determined biologically, can be transcended to a certain extent by the more or less evolved human spirit, as in older people. Thus, the more the individual grows through experiences of life, the less they are identified with their bodies, while the less evolved shows typical male and female traits. In the next stage of evolution, the lives of the males and females will be dominated by their evolving Divine Spirits or Souls, which is neither male nor female (Matt. 22:30; Gal. 3:28).

NOTE: The surviving human spirit, after physical death, still looks like a male or female, but is no longer capable of physical reproduction, which can only happen on the earth plane.

I. Imperfect Men and Women of This World – with Its Inherent Good and Evil Way of Thinking – in Search for Their Other Half, Their Psychological and Sexual Preferences and Differences

➤ Men have greater hormonal flow than women and thus have a stronger sex drive.
➤ Men seek for more physical satisfaction in sex, while women seek for more emotional fulfillment.
➤ As the goal of men is "to conquer" the woman of their dreams, the women are more interested in romance (and its stories) in which the men rescue them and "takes her away to his mansion and showers her with diamonds and furs".
➤ As men are more inclined to causal commitment, women want a more lasting relationship.
➤ Female persons have a stronger desire to settle down than men, whom like to roam around more.
➤ Women fall in love and then are aroused, while the men are aroused and then fall in love.
➤ Women seldom pay for sex; men often do.
➤ As the sexual act for females is more precious and lasting, for the males it is a quick release of tension and not long remembered.
➤ Women are not as much aroused by the look and shape of the bodies of men than men are by the bodies of women.
➤ As the men are "turned on" by visual stimuli, women can be swayed by sweet talk and touch.

- ➢ Sex may result in intimacy for men, and intimacy may end in sex for women.
- ➢ As a woman may find erotic satisfaction in romantic involvement, a man finds it mostly in sexual involvement.
- ➢ While men compete by defeating each other, women compete by making themselves more attractive and desirable.
- ➢ As men are able to separate their sexual lives from their feelings, women embrace their feelings and are much more involved.
- ➢ Most men do not like their woman to have physical sex with other men; many women do not like their men to fall in love with other women.
- ➢ As men want to brag about their status, power, learning, and resources, women make themselves more appealing by being youthful, beautiful, and (or) seductive.
- ➢ A woman who has been sleeping with many men is thought of as a slut, whereas a man who has been promiscuous is seen as a stud.
- ➢ For men, the act of sexual intercourse is the most important act of love, and they therefore say, "Let us make love"; but for women, making love also means to be emotionally involved by talk and receiving love in a romantic setting.
- ➢ Almost everywhere, men want sex more than women and are quickly aroused; women want sex less often and their response is much slower, as more of their body is involved.
- ➢ Men want women to respect and admire them, while women want to be noticed and loved by them.
- ➢ The woman is positive and dominant on the emotional level, while the man is positive and subject on the mental level.

Women in general identify more with their emotions than men and long for emotional intimacy. They need to be loved more in order to sustain and heal their emotional selves. When women smile and laugh, more of their being is involved than that of men, and they appear to be happier. They are able to give out more emotional energy, which is attractive in nature, and can be a vehicle of divine love. However, when the emotions of women become negative, they will also complain and nag more than men and may also get deeply involved in a wrong relationship.

In conclusion, the sexual act should not only be mainly physical as the men experience it, or chiefly emotional as the women feel it, but the relationship should also be spiritual.

#29 Guilt – Conscience – Forgiveness

A. What is Guilt?

According to the Readers Digest Dictionary, 1) "the fact or condition of having committed an offense, especially a willful violation of a legal or moral code"; 2) "a feeling of remorse arising from a real or imagined commission of an offense". Guilt is deserving of blame for some offense (culpable).

The basic Catholic dictionary by D.L. owery; "a state or condition of mind and soul that follows upon a personal, free, deliberate transgression of God's law; awareness that one has done wrong gives rise to what are often referred to as 'guilt feelings', that is, feelings of spiritual unrest and discomfort that seek relief. Guilt feelings, in turn, urge the sinful person to repent and to seek reconciliation, and thus once again to experience inner peace. In contrast to true guilt, which follows upon actual sin, false or neurotic guilt seems to arise from a general lack of self worth or a scrupulous conviction that one is always in sin."

Guilt is a psychological pain or unpleasant tension, which is an indication that there is something wrong. It should not be remedied by a "pain killer" but by acknowledgement, making amends or paying penance (indemnity), so that the block – the error – the guilt can be removed between the psyche (subconscious) and Divine Spirit (super-conscious). Thus, to feel guilt is a healthy sign, a warning sign that there is something wrong. However, there are individuals who never experience the anguish and agony of guilt after committing a crime. This is an unhealthy sign, an indication that they do not know that what they have done is wrong. They never develop a conscience, or a concept of right and wrong, and are like *hardened criminals whom commit antisocial acts without any remorse. Those criminals have no sense of guilt, no shame, no love of people, and do not understand in others the pangs of conscience, regret, unselfish love, and embarrassment. They are morally dead, appear cold, lifeless, cruel, and frighten almost anyone they encounter; and are able to spot and draw out the potential swindler, the thief, the liar, and the phony in the people they meet, as a hooker can easily find those whom have a carnal problem.

---

* The fact that many criminals have a conscience and a sense of guilt means that they are not as bad as the hardened criminals. Some of them were caught because they were acting guilty, while others believe that they deserve punishment.

NOTE: When someone is guilty of having wronged another, the guilt is felt and registered within the psyche of the person, and the individual knows that he or she has wronged someone and has a need to repay the debt. When the individual puts forth an effort to repay it, the karmic debt diminishes, as well as the guilt. The penal infliction meted out by the criminal justice system should be proportionate to the offense, or the moral guilt of the wrongdoer. Those whom are guilty often become like lambs going to the slaughter because the good self of their personality, or their Divine Spirit or Higher Self, is not cooperating to liberate them from the punishment which is due in order to restore their disturbed equilibrium (see #34 Karma). We should not harbor resentful thoughts toward individuals that have mistreated us because the law of karma will bring whatever retribution is needed to the abuser.

REMARK: One may be morally guilty and legally innocent, and vice versa. Some of the most vicious and malicious things people do are within the law of the land, and one who acts in obedience to his conscience may break the law but incurs no moral blame or guilt.

B.   The Purpose and Function of Conscience

Guilt is a tool of the conscience, which is in alignment with the superego of the personality, which latter is under the guidance of one's Divine Spirit or Soul (when developed), and whose faculty of intuition (pure conscience) is always one with God's Will. The superego judges the personality or ego and approves or disapproves of its behavior. It blows at times the whistle to mete out punishment in the form of guilt, which is an uncomfortable and nagging feeling and an indication that the person is doing something wrong, a warning not to do it again.

Conscience is a faculty, power, or principle that causes us to feel guilty and guides us in the right way. It is molded primarily by parents and teachers and moral laws such as, for example, the Ten Commandments (Ex. 20; Deut. 5), and other important principles and values. It has become part of the makeup of the personality: "I will put my law within them" (Jer. 31:33; Isa. 51:7). This "law was our custodian until Christ came" (Gal. 3:24), but "you are not under law but under grace" (Rom. 6:14). The faculty of intuition of the newly born pure Divine or Christ Spirit (1 John 3:9; Gal. 4:19) is more developed as the conscience, and is thus better able to distinguish between good and evil as the true voice of God.

Healthy guilt is necessary, especially for young children, because it leads to the development of conscience, which will help them to live in a proper manner. Examining our conscience will help us to discern if our lives are in agreement with the Holy Scriptures. When we do something wrong as, for example, shoplifting and other crimes, our conscience – if it is still intact – declares us guilty, which is experienced as an uncomfortable feeling because our action violated a moral law. However, some people, in the world we are living today, are trying to convince us that we should not feel bad or guilty about anything in life. This attitude not only damages our conscience but also leads to lives without moral direction and value, which results that they are no longer accountable for their actions and are driven by unlimited and uncontrolled freedom without responsibility (license). As Paul expressed it in 1 Tim. 4:1-2: "Now the Spirit expressly says that in the later times some will depart from the faith by giving heed to deceitful spirits and doctrines of demons, through the pretension of liars whose consciences are *seared."

NOTE: Moral degradation usually starts with a single evil thought or desire, which in itself is not evil as long as we reject it. But if we harbor those thoughts or pursue them by, for example, holding a grudge, feeling envy and hatred, or wallowing in pornographic material, those feelings and thoughts may take root and may lead to words, which in turn lead to deeds. "Then desire when it has conceived gives birth to sin; and sin when it is full-grown brings forth spiritual death" (James 1:15).

C. Constructive and Destructive Guilt

Healthy constructive guilt leads to psychological and spiritual growth because it compels us to reconcile infractions or balance karma and to avoid situations that lead to guilt. Thus, the feeling of guilt is a warning sign that we have done something wrong and that reparation or atonement should be made for the damage we have caused to others. True or moral guilt also leads to insight into ourselves and thus makes us aware of shortcomings in our personalities that needs correcting. True guilt is a feeling that we have done something against the will of God and His people, and which motivates us to come back into right relationship with Him. Thus, true guilt or "godly grief produces a repentance that leads to salvation" but false guilt or "worldly grief produces (spiritual) death" (2 Cor. 7:10).

False or destructive guilt is the belief that we have done something wrong when we actually have not. It is often the result of insecurities and frustration and it does not reflect reality. Parents may, for example,

---

* This conscience is unable to function, it is seared, made callous, is withered and hardened, and insensible to distinguish between right and wrong.

say when children fail in their expectations: "Where did we fail as parents?" We should not carry guilt with us or dwell on guilt because it becomes like barriers for the expression of the Divine Spirit or Soul, obstructing the divine flow and thus blocking the channel between the Soul and the personality. Once guilt has served its purpose by sounding the alarm that something is wrong, we shut it off and start to correct the problem. Thus, we should not wallow in guilt feelings, create feelings of inferiority, or punish ourselves needlessly while doing nothing constructive or creative.

NOTE: Guilt, which is imposed on us by our consciences, is not the same as the accusation of satan, his demons, and the evil mind of humans and our own, in order to cast doubt about our spiritual progress and salvation. This accusation creates a false guilt and separates humans from God. When they are burdened by the consciousness of guilt, he or she feels unworthy to talk with his or her God or to seek His aid. (See also #33.) Some people use guilt or lay guilt trips on others so that they can judge, control, and extract obligations from them. To make others feel guilty because they do not do what we want them to do is to show them no respect or consideration, and this was certainly not the idea of Jesus Christ. See John 8:16.

REMARK: Robert Schuller, pastor of the Crystal Cathedral in greater Los Angeles and disciple of Norman Vincent Peale (who wrote the book "The Power of Positive Thinking" and was pastor of the Reformed Church in New York), said: "Authentic guilt is the negative emotions experienced by a conscience mind that passed a personal moral judgment on itself."

D. Psychology and Guilt

As healthy guilt is the remorse we feel over our mistakes, unhealthy guilt is to continually blame ourselves, which can lead to physical and psychological distress. Many psychologists are trained to deal with false or neurotic guilt and a *sense of guilt, which is out of proportion with the actual guilt.

Unfortunately, there are also many therapists and counselors today whom believe that all guilt, positive and negative, is of no use and unhealthy. Their patients like them because by going through psychoanalysis, they can shed guilt without being responsible for their guilt and the need to make amends. However, in this process they are not admitting to any sins and can thus not be forgiven or be reconciled

---

* However, we can always find people who are enjoying the sense of guilt and even try to cultivate it.

to God. Those therapists whom are using this method are probably influenced by Sigmund Freud (1856-1939) who believed that guilt was something we could and should do without, which helped along the spreading of moral relativism. In Freud's theory, the sinner becomes a patient because blame and guilt, as part of the unconscious mind, is irrational, causes psychological pain, and should be removed or killed.

Fortunately, there are also psychologists whom are beginning to believe and think that "guilt is a guardian of our goodness", which keeps us human. When individuals have done something wrong, guilt compels them to fix the problem and thus repair relationships. Thus, feeling guilt can be good because it shows that we are aware of standards of goodness, and that we have a conscience that is in good working order. "They show that what the law requires is written on their hearts (subconscious), while their conscience also bears witness" (Rom. 2:15). But those with defiled or deadened consciences have difficulty seeing the difference or discriminating between right and wrong. "To the pure all things are pure, but to the corrupt and unbelieving, nothing is pure; their very minds and consciences are corrupted" (Titus 1:15).

NOTE: Adam and Eve immediately knew they had disobeyed because guilt and shame welled up in them. Their conscience was not dulled or seared and they did not lose the sense of sin. Many people today have lost, to a great extent, the sense of sin and need to regain it. "If we say we have no sin, we deceive ourselves and the truth is not in us" (1 John 1:8).

E. The Bible and Guilt

In the Old Testament (Lev. 5:17-19), a person who sins unknowingly (unwittingly) will be forgiven when he brings a "guilt offering" to the priest. In the New Testament, those who do not know are forgiven: "Father, forgive them; for they know not what they do" (Luk. 23:34). See also Luk. 12:47, 48; Acts 17:30.

As long as the sinner or wrongdoer acknowledges his or her guilt, there is a chance that they may repent which, in turn, becomes a cleansing and healing process. A guilty conscience should move them to confession and be forgiven. They are then purged of guilt and are able to live with a clear conscience. "Your guilt is taken away, and your sin forgiven" (Isaiah 6:7). Guilt is thus removed most readily by confession and cleansing. "If we confess our sins, he is faithful and just, and will forgive our sins and cleanse us from all unrighteousness"

(1 John 1:9). Love and forgive others, so that the Father can forgive you (Mark 11:25), and thus remove the blockage of the feelings of guilt and resentment, so that the Love of God can flow through our whole being. Those who have truly repented of their sins and asked God for forgiveness will never forget the miraculous way in which they were instantaneously freed from the guilt complex, and felt the peace and the harmony they never experienced before.

F. Forgiveness

The sacrament of Penance as it evolved in the Catholic tradition consists of four parts: contrition-confession-absolution-satisfaction. As the Protestants emphasize more the gratuity of grace (by faith) in their spiritual healing process, the Catholics are more inclined to stress more that "of work", which is the ritual of Penance.

Contrition is a heartfelt sorrow or repentance (remorse-regret) for what one has done (or failed to do) and a sincere desire of never doing it again. The first stirrings of unrest and regret are often caused by the Holy Spirit (Mother Spirit of God) to let us see our sinful condition (Rom. 8:27) and turn to God for forgiveness so that our sinful nature (Rom. 6:6) will die and has no claim upon us.

It has become a custom that Catholics [1]confess their sins to a priest, while Protestants may confess to their minister or elder or simply "lay the matter at the feet of the Lord". Individuals may also confess their sins to each other (James 5:16). By having compassion, a sympathetic listener often takes on the burden and problems of the other, who then feel relieved and uplifted.

Absolution is given by a priest to believers for the remission of sins, to become free of the consequences of sin. This complete forgiveness of sin is effective as soon as the penitent performs the act of penance or satisfaction, as [2]given by the priest. The receiving person is free from

---

[1] Confession is an admission of guilt and reconciliation with God. Those who do not want to admit that they have been wrong, by not admitting or repressing moral guilt, do not want to face who they really are, and are stunted in their moral and spiritual growth. Besides, unacknowledged guilt will torment them, causing increased insecurity, doubt, self-hatred, and other psychological problems.

[2] The priest usually has no difficulty absolving sins because he can also draw from the accumulated merits of his church organization and other merits built up by monasteries.

the consequences of guilt and all accusation and feels a new freedom, self-respect, and peace.

However, when the sin(s) is/are serious, the priest may refuse absolution, unless the culprit promises for a surety that he or she will make restitution (compensation-atonement-amends-indemnity) or right the injury done to another (Matt. 5:23-26). To restore the relationship to the other or [3]society, ask for forgiveness and give compensation, pray, fast, give to the needy or do charity for your neighbor. Do good works, donate your time and energy to a worthy organization, tithe to your church above your share, sacrifice something that is very dear to you, and live the rest of your life in a constructive manner.

Thus, true repentance brings God's forgiveness, which will dissolve the emotional force of distortion of resentment, ill-will, hate, and revenge, so that the person is ready to make amends to ordinary people he or she has wronged whom are not able or ready to forgive. Being cleansed of the guilt of sin or of a sinful past, the sinner still needs to atone for the consequences of sin.

Born-again (born of God) Christians can be more easily forgiven (Eph. 1:6-7) because they are more likely to do the work of the Lord, by living a divine or God-like lifestyle and are usually active in witnessing. They usually do not commit repeatedly the same sin as the unregenerated, who we can find very often in the "confession booths" of their choice. The regenerated true Christians who are being remorseful for their sin often receive forgiveness through grace from God, higher spiritual beings, and ancestors through their merits. They may then experience a down pouring of cleansing power and an increased control of the Cosmic Christ and the Holy Spirit (Rev. 22:17).

Before doing any spiritual work, it is important for the aspirants that they have forgiven all people, including themselves (Mark 11:25). A lack of forgiveness builds up guilt and other psychic blocks in the subconscious and, thus, in the channel between their pure Divine Spirit and their conscious mind, thus hindering the divine flow. By praying for the people they have witnessed to, the spiritual workers are taking their distress, guilt, and sins upon themselves while pleading to God to free the people under their care from bondage. Thus, the workers are doing

---

[3] There is also collective guilt, which can be at the level of family, society, nation, and world.

vicariously for the people what the latter are as yet not able to do for themselves.

In conclusion, I would like to say, when the people have become enlightened and are living in the Kingdom of God, there will be no sense of good and evil and with it, no feeling of guilt, shame, or sinfulness.

#30 The Negative Side of Gambling

A. Introduction

Along with the sexual revolution and the moral decline of the nineteen sixties came the first state-sponsored lottery in New Hampshire, which was soon followed by New York and other states. *Up until 1978 casino gambling was only legal in the state of Nevada; that year it was made legal in Atlantic City, New Jersey, followed by a few other states. But legal gambling really took off when the United States Congress passed the Indian Gaming Act in 1988, allowing gambling on Indian Reservations, especially in the state of Minnesota.

Because of a shift in moral values, many Americans are no longer opposed to gambling and do not feel bad about it when they buy lotteries or go to state approved casinos. They think that lotteries are harmless and that they do not hurt anybody. Besides, it has been accepted by society as a thing to do. This trend has been followed by many private companies that are stuffing peoples' mailboxes with their valueless junk mail.

Legalized gambling, in spite of its rules and regulations, has not really eliminated corruption. It has instead removed the stigma against gambling and inspired more people in betting not only in legal but also in illegal games, which still demand a stiff penalty when caught.

Gambling is wrong not only for economic reasons, but also for criminal, social, moral, and religious reasons. Let us investigate here what this means.

B. Economical Reasons

The reason why many states have and want an official state lottery is to collect additional "painless or voluntary" taxes to finance different projects. However, it is not an efficient way to raise revenues because it is known that the state spends only +/-5 cents to collect a tax dollar, but at least 60 cents to acquire a lottery dollar. This means that the public has to pay two and half times as much money for the lottery ticket as it would have to pay if the Government used extra taxation. The voluntary tax is expensive because it is raised through heavy and

---

* Long before that time many people participated in the so-called charitable games, mainly bingo, which was run by churches, fraternal groups, and many other organizations.

aggressive promotion, which costs about 20% for administration and advertisement, while +/-40% is paid out as prize money. It is unfortunate that this money is raised from the poor and uneducated, those whom can at least afford to lose it.

In order for the state lotteries to be successful and to get as many people betting against unfavorable odds of winning, they emphasize the importance of wealth and living in luxury and that this can all be easily obtained, implying that the road to success is not hard work but fate, luck, and chance. This promotion certainly does not encourage people to self-invest in education, acquire skills, or be productive, which is the "brick road" to attainment. Unlike business ventures whereby both parties gain, gambling is non-productive whereby one class of people gain (lose) or the other lose (gain). By promoting economic immorality, the Government is helping to produce the kind of people who want to get rich without labor. Is that not the attitude of many young people today? Are they not becoming more selfish? This promotion of getting something for nothing is helped along by the news media who made of those whom have won big heroes, and do not mention the many thousands whom have lost many times and are losing all hope. Being persuaded by the media, they believe that they will try one more time to become the great and daring winner.

NOTE: Success in any venture depends upon perseverance, skill, know-how, and wisdom, and not on chance. Businesses and other enterprises (unlike lotteries) are productive in offering goods and services, which will certainly benefit the government by providing jobs and taxes. They would then pay less for welfare, unemployment benefits, and other expenses. Generally speaking, charity and welfare are likely to do more harm than good for those people whom are able to work because it destroys their needs to take initiative and, more importantly, his or her need to look to God for direction, who is always willing to help (Gen. 3:21). This guidance will take them off the freeloader list and give back to them their self-respect.

A different tactic to get people to gamble is used by the casinos, which try to lure as many people as possible to their places by giving them all kinds of incentives. The industry caters especially to older people, whom they transport right to the casino's doorstep. The seniors have to walk deep inside the building to pick up a roll of free quarters, with which they are supposed to gamble and much more of their own money. Once they are trapped inside the main gambling room, without windows and time clocks and seeing flashing lights all around them, they soon catch gambling fever. By hearing the jingling sound of the slot machines or the "one-armed bandits", as well as the tingling sound of money falling, they are hooked forever. The people are so busy wasting their precious time and money in this pseudo kingdom hall that nobody has time to talk to each other or go outside and enjoy God's creation. When the seniors go home in the evening on the same bus, they look disappointed and miserable and believe that they have been taken for a ride.

C. Criminal Reason

The Government body that allowed casinos to come into operation in their State in order to improve economic conditions does not really know or want to know into what kind of a mess they are getting. Casinos attract all kinds of people, but also those of low character, in order to fatten themselves on the many suckers whom are easy to find. The criminals who swarm to gambling communities are gangsters, racketeers, con-men, pimps, prostitutes, dope peddlers, loan sharks, bookmakers, and opportunists who bring with them such legal and illegal businesses as sex shops, liquor stores, off-track betting, pawn shops, and others. Law-abiding citizens whom have lost heavily are tempted to pass bad checks and even try to steal from their fellow citizen. Even public officials and the police, if they work long enough in the gambling *environment may eventually be influenced and corrupted by the low character and makeup of the gambling society. Because the crime rate in the gambling state is about twice the national average, this brings with it much higher police, court, and penitentiary costs for the investigation, prosecution, and punishment of those crimes.

D. Social Reasons

State-sponsored lotteries and casinos are responsible for the explosive increase of compulsive gamblers' organizations (Gamblers' Anonymous and others) all across America. Social organizations estimate that there is between 3 to 5 percent of the adult population that is compulsive and many more have become problem gamblers. Much of the welfare budget of the cities goes to family problems, which are

---

* The psychic environment, which is created through the feeling and thinking of the people, changes considerably and becomes more hell-like. This is shown in the fact that the people feel more insecure than they were before, are more materialistic, and not as nice to their neighbor, whom they feel like cheating. The gambling environment is made much worse by evil spirits and demons whom are already attached to the criminals, and also by those evil beings whom are attracted to and like to come to this low environment from the lowest realm of the spirit world.

related to gambling. Because of the high cost of social and psychological welfare, this certainly is not helping the community prosper.

The struggling wage earner, which does not seem to get ahead, is tempted by the lure of easy money, and to gamble as much as he/she can, in order to be on "easy street" someday or to "make a killing". The result is that fathers (and mothers) of the household often gamble away their whole pay check, especially when they are compulsive, or have an irresistible impulse to gamble. The gamblers whom can no longer sustain their losses start to borrow from relatives and friends or from banks and credit card companies, and eventually wind up on the doorstep of the pawnshop, or even worse fall in the hands of the loan sharks. After they keep losing more money, they are driven to get money illegally by embezzlement, robbery, and other crimes to cover their bad losses. The result of all of this is that they start to drink heavily, lose their jobs, and eventually are contemplating or commit *suicide. Needless to say, the effect of compulsive gambling has a devastating effect on the family, which is dependent upon the father as caretaker. But instead, the wives and the children are not only abused and neglected physically but also are emotional and mentally damaged for a very long time to come. We may conclude here that all form of gambling is a social and psychological disease.

E. Moral Reasons

The State has not only an economical but also an ethical responsibility, especially for those people whom are living the life of the good and evil personality, whom always need encouragement to live the good life. They should not listen or cave in to the loud voice of the relative evil minority, which appears as the majority, by shouting that there is nothing wrong with gambling because everybody is doing it. One of the important tasks of the Government (our big brother) is to educate the people in the evil of gambling. If they cannot maintain the moral and ethical standard of the people in their charge, or even worse become like "the beast" of Revelation 11:7, working under the authority of the dragon (satan) (Rev. 13:4); the Government body is no longer fit to rule the people; that is those whom are relatively good.

---

* The suicide rate in the state of Nevada, the gambling capital of the nation, is about three times as high as that of the national average.

Thinking and moral people know that gambling is based mainly on greed and *coveting, or trying to get what another has. Thus, the very basis of gambling is the notion of getting something for nothing, of desiring material gain at the expense of other people. Gambling corrupts and undermines character because it appeals to human weakness. It awakens and stimulates the evil or shadow side of the personality (ego), which is extremely greedy and selfish. This evil part of the ego or "old nature" (Eph. 4:22) which includes greed and covetousness, is being strengthened or fed by serious and continual gambling, and may eventually rule one's life in an irresistible or compulsive way. Those persons become reckless, callous, and desire enviously what belongs to another, for whom they care less.

As with all evil things people do it always starts out very small and then, without realizing it, the evil impulse becomes stronger, until it overtakes them. As weak as imperfect humans are, they should not even attempt to gamble, not even for fun or recreation, because it is not harmless. They only become more greedy and miserable as can be witnessed by many people in the casinos whom gamble a lot, and never seem to be satisfied.

The moral and psychological impact for the man or woman who loses is that of deep anger, resentment, and bitterness towards their fate and the hatred of the ruined for those people who have taken his or her money. However, the moral effect on the man or woman who won is just as bad or even worse as the ones whom have lost. The winners are usually gloating and assume that their success was due to their own wit, wisdom, and ability, which may encourage them to gamble all of what they have. When the winner does win big in a short time, he or she does not really value the money because they did not really earn it, and therefore have a tendency to waste it (Prov. 13:11). We hear sometimes in the news media that some people who have won big are using the "blood money" of the people who have lost. The money then becomes a curse and bad things will happen to the winners. Because they gained the money from people who became miserable, they also become miserable. And, as is reported in the news of the day, accidents occasionally happen to those who have won a fortune.

---

* Coveting is the grasping selfishness of the false ego, and is a strong desire to have what belongs to another. It is the Tenth Commandment. See Exodus 20:17; Deut. 5:21; Luk. 12:15; Rom. 7:7; Eph. 5:5.

REMARK: It is not wrong to have money, as long as you give something back in the form of your labor, time, energy, talent, skill, etc., but it is certainly wrong to want something for nothing.

It is a *universal principle that anyone must give forth energy in order to receive energy in return, and the energy that is given is that which influences the energy that will be returned. Thus, the cosmic principle works in the following manner: if you give energy of yourself, you create a vacuum, which must be filled. Thus, in order to receive, you must give something of yourself to the universe. By the same principle, if you have not given anything, you cannot expect anything in return.

REMARK: Selfishness or any kind of wrongdoing can be profitable only if chance rules our life, instead of justice.

F. Religious Reasons

For those whom are living the divine life (or the regenerated persons), gambling is completely wrong and is contrary to faith because God is the supplier of all their needs – not greeds – ;(Philippians 4:19; 2 Cor. 9:10). They should therefore not worship the false god of luck and chance (Isa. 65:11) because "you cannot serve (two masters), God and money" (Matt. 6:24). "For the love of money is the root of all evils; it is through this craving that some have wandered away from the faith and pierced their hearts with many pangs" –griefs– (1 Tim. 6:10).

As God is the Creator, humans are co-creators, to build, construct, and produce. They should therefore not get involved in an activity, wherein no services are rendered and no improvement in the condition of living is achieved. The gambling industry is an enterprise that has no life and is only a corpse in the business world, without any productive activity and has therefore no future, and will eventually disappear. Besides, it does not believe in the principle "it is more blessed to give than to receive" (Acts 20:35), because it always takes more than it gives, and is therefore nothing else but a leech, by sucking and sapping the life, strength, and vigor out of society.

If we truly love our neighbor as ourselves (Matt. 22:39), how can we take from them what does not belong to us? Gambling is therefore a threat to the welfare of our fellow human beings, because any gain we make is at the expense of our neighbors.

---

* See Appendix #34.

When we are driven by greed, it can lead to a separation from God and expulsion from His direct domain or Kingdom (1 Cor. 6:9-10). "He who is greedy for unjust gain makes trouble for his household" (Proverbs 15:27). "He who hastens to be rich will not go unpunished" (Prov. 28:20). "A misery man hastens after wealth, and does not know that want will come upon him" (Prov. 28:22). "If any one will not work, let him not eat" (2 Thess. 3:10).

The Bible encourages honest work as a key to success and to become men and women of character and integrity: "He who tills his land will have plenty of bread" (Prov. 28:19), and they should "do their work in quietness and to earn their own living" (2 Thess. 3:12).

Finally, "let each of you look not only to his own interests, but also to the interests of others", and to have the mind of Christ living within us (Phil. 2:4-5), so that we can overcome all addictions and compulsions.

#31 Waste of Physical Vigor and Vital Energy

The lassitude that follows orgasm is valid proof that it depletes the male and [1]female of vital or etheric energy, and the man also suffers the loss of precious fluid through ejaculation. Thereafter, they are [2]exhausted and usually want to eat food, which replenishes the physical and vital energies of their bodies and sleep a long time, in order to fully recuperate.

It is believed that an ounce of seminal fluid or semen, which is the carrier of the sperm, has a high concentration of the most valuable chemicals from which about the same amount can be found in about sixty ounces of blood. It is therefore said that it is "the cream of the milk of blood". Much of the same chemicals can also be found in the brain. To make up for the loss of too much semen, it is extracted from the cerebrospinal fluid of the brain. To produce one single discharge of this seminal fluid, it takes the body about thirty days. Considering the above, it is easy to understand that an excessive discharge of this fluid causes deterioration of brain cells and thus loss of memory. This fact was already recognized by the Greek philosopher Pythagoras in the

---

[1] The woman releases vitally magnetized fluid into her womb, which mixes with the electrochemical substance of the man.

[2] Plants are stunted in their growth when they bloom too prolifically. The gardener therefore prunes the buds so that the strength may go into growth.

sixth century B.C. The male also loses the ability to function sexually (impotency), and it may also weaken the prostate. When the sex organs are abused for a long period of time, it may cause senility, the disease which affects older people. The above also explains why men, on average, live shorter than women by about six to seven years. Besides, women unlike men do not always experience orgasm, and therefore do not lose a small portion of their life force.

NOTE: The Chinese cultural tradition maintains that the manufacture of sperm requires a great deal of physical and vital energy or chi (see "The Etheric Body"), and wasting it through reckless sex and masturbation is a serious threat to the health of the individual.

It is therefore not advisable to waste this precious fluid by using normal sex indiscriminately and abnormally by mutual masturbation (oral and anal intercourse) and to satisfy lustful desires without a partner. In the latter case, when self-satisfaction (manipulation of genital organs) or auto-erotic gratification is practiced in excess, it is known to cause different ailments, such as pimples, blotchy skin, poor memory, blindness, and even insanity. The psychological and moral result of this immoral behavior is that the self-abuser becomes more selfish, suffers from fear, shame, and guilt, feels insecure and inferior, has self-doubt, and hates himself/herself. In this solitary act the perpetrator separates from genuine relationship, and when it becomes habitual, the person may become more locked up in his or her corporeality. The result is that they become more lonely and isolated, and also intensify feelings of frustration, dissatisfaction, and futility.

The Encyclopedia of Catholicism says that "to pursue sexual pleasure or orgasm in a manner not associated with marital intercourse that is love-giving and open to the creation of new life violates the will of God and is immoral".

Auto sexuality should certainly not be used for biological pleasure and to relieve stress and tension as some misguided parents, doctors, educators, and even some ministers say. The latter justify themselves by asserting that masturbation is God's relief valve, for built-up sexual drive. Those religious leaders experience sexual problems because they think too much about sex, which goes against the saying of Jesus in Matt. 5:28. Every time lustful desires succeed over spiritual desires, they are taking a step backwards in spiritual growth.

As children grow into young adults, their sexual desires increase, and when they do not have developed a divine life, they are more tempted to seek sexual gratification by abusing themselves. They should never start because it does not decrease sexual tension and desires; it only increases them, and will lead to habit and bondage. By overcoming this temptation, the teens will experience the wonderful feeling of self-control, freedom, and peace, which are divine qualities or the fruit of the Spirit (Gal. 5:22-24).

> "Blessed is the man who endures trial, for when he has
> stood the test he will receive the crown of life which God
> has promised to those who love him" (James 1:12).

Auto-erotism becomes more evil when human images of pornographic material are involved, which they can make more concrete by creating thought forms. They may actually make contact with those images by psychic projection, or more real when they call forth those images as genuine spirit beings and have a relationship with them, or others they are acquainted with. This may result in psychic rape. Besides, he and she drag themselves and their victims to a lower psychic realm because their spirit bodies have become coarser and thus lower in vibration. Being involved with lustful sexual imagination and fantasy on the psychic plane, they are also creating negative karma on that plane.

The masturbators may not stop with psychic relationships alone, but also want to have a physical relationship with their psychic victims, willingly or unwillingly.

The abusers through their actions attract many evil and earthbound spirits of the lower realm. In that case, masturbation becomes an obsession when those spirits attach to those persons and demand sexual gratification (1 Cor. 7:5), which the individuals experience as an intensive increase of passion and lust. When this happens at night, the individuals may experience it as a wet dream.

To break free of this habit or addiction, hopelessness, and despair, they need to stop it at once or are in need of deliverance by a strong spiritual person. If that is not possible, the uncontrollable sexual passion should be given to God, whom is always willing to remove it (James 4:7-8).

NOTE: For human spirits and their activities to materialize for a short while, they need etheric or vital energy, which they are able to draw from human beings, especially from those whom are yielding great amounts of this bio-magnetic energy. For example, from young people in puberty whom emanate lots of sexual energy and from a persistent masturbator who reaches his or her climax and others. They are usually the center of poltergeist (noisy spirit) activities.

Through a conservative lifestyle, a man may reabsorb his semen and utilize these precious chemicals to nourish and invigorate his brain and other organs, improve overall health, and increase longevity, instead of continually producing it. This is especially true for older people, whom should be more spiritually oriented. Thus, by conserving the semen for (long) periods of time, the individual gains self-control and becomes physically more alive, mentally more alert, and spiritually more receptive. It makes the skin glow, brightens the eyes, sharpens the senses, and activates psychic faculties. Thus, the person has more physical stamina, more vital or life force, more mental, psychic, or spiritual energy (power) coming from the lower and higher planes of life.

People of today are not only materialistic but think too much about sex. The result is that their mind is too much preoccupied about their lower self or personality (physical-emotional-mental), whose five energy centers or chakras (psycho-energetic centers) have only 48 petals or spokes, in the makeup of their etheric or vital bodies. Mature adults should, however, be more spiritual in their thinking because the highest two energy centers of their etheric bodies, which are closely connected to their Divine Spirit or Higher Self, have more than 1000 spokes.

Because energy follows thought, it is directed wherever the attention goes. Sexual energy can therefore be directed downward for physical creation or be *guided upwards to be used for creativity and regeneration on the mental and spiritual levels. However, when the sexual organs are misused, the person not only wastes precious fluid, but also vital or etheric energy. The result is that there is less energy to maintain health by strengthening the etheric body. Because there is less energy available for transmutation, there is thus less intellectual power, creativity, affection, and spiritual progress. Besides, one's consciousness is pulled downward and holds the individual in bondage and earthbound.

---

* The yogi's of India claim that sexual fluid (retas) invigorates one's psycho-mental life through the means of (ojas), which is a subtle energy that rises from the sexual center to the brain – when the semen are preserved – through the process of transmutation. Women can also preserve their sexual charge and transmute it for higher purposes. The yogi's further say that the transmuted energy may break open the door between the ego personality (lower self) and the Higher Self (atman).

#32 The Good and Evil Personalities of Dr. Jekyll and Mr. Hyde

A. Introduction

Their personalities inherited the good qualities of God (as that of Dr. Jekyll) but in addition acquired the evil qualities of satan (that of Mr. Hyde) – as described in the classic novel by R.L. Stevenson.

Jekyll noted another side of his personality, which was at variance with this persona, "a certain impatient gaiety of disposition". This led him to seek certain pleasure in life which he found hard to reconcile with his "imperious desire" to carry his head high. Hence Jekyll noted, he adopted a "more than commonly grave countenance before the public". In other words, the grave countenance Jekyll publicly struck was a mask to shield from others another side to his personality that Jekyll did not want anyone to see and which he regarded with a "morbid sense of shame". As a consequence, Jekyll wrote, "I concealed my pleasure and stood already committed to a profound duplicity of life."

The evil or shadow side of the personality (Mr. Hyde) has desires and thoughts we would never openly admit we have, and certainly would not want to express them. Otherwise, that would destroy the "good" image we have created of ourselves as respectable and "mature" adults (although some people have become very clever to imitate perfect behavior). When the evil nature does crop up, so now and then, we quickly hide it from others because we do not want to be rejected by them. Knowing what we are, we cannot always trust others to be good. A thief, for example, suspects other people to be stealing from him or her, while an adulterous husband suspects his wife of infidelity. Thus, those who are looking for certain faults in others are unconsciously revealing their own. We should therefore not judge so that we are not being judged (Matt. 7:1). As a Dutch saying goes: "zo als de waard is vertrouwd hy zyn gasten" – so as the inn keeper is, trust he his guests. From this we may also come to the conclusion that those whom accuse others of sins are guilty of the same sins they try to hide from others.

Another predominant characteristic of the behavior of the evil person is that they do not think of themselves as evil. They will react violently to criticism and will lash out at anyone who discredits them in order to protect their evil self. Since they must deny their own badness, they must perceive others as bad. Their goodness is a lie and is not as much to deceive others as it is to deceive themselves.

NOTE: However, we may deceive people by flattery or win their good favor by being liberal about evil. This only intensifies the evil self, so that we become more devious and egotistical and thus more difficult for our good self to shine through to our physical self.

B. Behavior of People When the Evil Self Is In Charge of Their Personalities

Dwelling within every human personality, we find two I's, the good part of the personality, created in the image of God and the evil part (old self – Rom. 6:6) created in the image of satan, your false sense of self or the carnal human nature.

Below we find a description of the behavior of humans, when the evil part or shadow side is in charge of the personality, which is expressed as the false personality, ego, I, and self.

The false personality thrives on self-interest, deceit, and justification of anything, as long as it is for its own benefit. It is emerged in spiritual darkness and fear, while pursuing a purposeless and fruitless mundane life, in the midst of hopelessness and despair.

The false ego knows how to pass the buck and to cover up and hide his/her real motive and intention. It goes through life by fooling many people in his or her cunning way and manipulates people while they are trying to stay as inconspicuous as possible.

The false I, in his/her indulgence and self-preservation, knows how to take more than it gives, and vehemently rants and raves to get what it wants. It has not only destroyed many relationships, but also to fulfill its own needs and gratification, it is ravishing the beautiful earth.

The false self is always looking for revenge. They easily forget about their own mistakes while condemning the faults of others. He or she does not want to forget and forgive others for similar mistakes and are making mountains out of molehills for offenses. Thus, we blame little faults in others and excuse great offenses in ourselves – we see the speck in our neighbor's eye and not the beam in our own (Matt. 7:4).

The false personalities in their self-seeking know how to rationalize and justify, and along with false pride allow themselves to wallow in self-pity. They are always there to prey on the weak and abuse others for their self-glorification, self-interest, and self-love. They know how to flatten others in order to get what they want, while their sense of selfhood is dependent upon the praise of others.

The false and inflated egos have managed through conceit to magnify their importance above all others and have been able with vain assertion to exalt themselves, believing that they, as mortal beings, have the right to judge others and to tell them how to live. They also like to pass on some worldly wisdom they have gathered (James 3:15), such as:

You are not your brother's keeper.
Leave him alone; he will get over it.
You made your bed; now lie in it.
I would if I could, but I can't.
That is over and above the call of duty.
Why stick your neck out?
You give an inch; they take a foot.
The more you give, the more they want.
You cannot always follow your conscience.
It is too late for "I am sorry".
A leopard never changes his spots.
He is down-to-earth.
Seeing is believing.
It is a dog-eat-dog world.
It is survival of the fittest.
Every man for himself.
Business is business.
Money talks.
Might makes right.
Better in your pocket than his.

Nobody gives you something for nothing.
Everyone steps on a few toes.
It is all who you know.
Take care of number one first.
What he does not know won't hurt him.
You will do for me and I will do for you.
You scratch my back and I will scratch yours.
One hand washes the other.
It is better to join them than to fight them.
The end justifies the means.
Boys will be boys.
All is fair in love and war.
She is over the hill.
Love 'em and leave 'em.
He is a nobody.
He never amounted to anything.
You are good for nothing.
He is a somebody.
Do as I say, not as I do.
That is the way the ball bounces.

B. Differences between the False Ego, In Which the Evil Elements Predominate and the Pure Ego Without Original Sin

The false ego is made in the image and likeness of the spirit of the world (John 8:23; 1 Jn. 2:15), while the pure ego is made in the image of God.

The false ego is a conformist to the world (Rom. 12:2), while the good ego is not part of the world (Jas. 1:27), with its evil way of thinking.

The false ego is always self-centered (even after physical maturity), while the true ego is always concerned about others (Jas. 1:8).

The false personality wants the country to serve him or her, while the loyal personality likes to serve the country.

The false personality does not like moral truth because it would ruin itself, while the virtuous personality always searches for truth.

The false personality likes to define freedom as license, while the righteous personality understands freedom as responsibility.

The false "I" likes to interpret liberty as doing whatever one pleases, while the moral "I" considers its civil obligation.

The false "I' wants to love people and creation with satanic love, while the innocent "I" wants to love everybody and everything with God-centered love.

The false "I" wants to be the determinant of truth, goodness, and morality, while the faithful "I" sees God as the originator of all values.

The false self does not love God, for it wants to be its own God, while the devout self wants to obey God and His laws.

The false self lives a life of fear and insecurity and believes that it will perish, while the real self believes that it will live forever.

The false self practices the self-centered way of life, such as vanity, lust, greed, and is unconcerned for the welfare of others, while the noble self strives to practice the God-centered way of life, such as humility, love, sharing, and has an outgoing concern for others.

REMARK: The ego or personality is made pure by stripping it of its evil elements with the help of God and our own efforts. This removal of the false covering can also happen on a greater level, in families, tribes, and nations. Then the Divine Spirit or individual Christ Spirit can be born in the purified personality (Gal. 4:19), and at the national level the Messiah or the Universal Christ can be received (come) bodily in that particular purified (chosen) country. The above persons or nation may resist this preparation or stripping, but when it is accomplished or executed, they feel liberated and free.

In order for the personality to become mature and wholesome, we need to purify our body by caring for it, eating the proper kind of food, and exercising right behavior. The emotions should be cleansed of their fear, bitterness, resentment, or grudge, hostility or hatred, suspicion, depression, or despair, and other negative afflictions. The mind should be purified of doubt and disbelief, ignorance, judgments, prejudices, irrelevant thoughts, false ideas and misconception, distrust, pride, narrow-mindedness, and intolerance. For its development, the mind should also take in and absorb or assimilate the right kind of mental food, and the will should be purged of lower desires. The personality as a whole becomes transparent and clear so that the indwelling individual Spirit of God within the Divine Spirit will shine through the emotional and mental layers of the personality to the human physical consciousness, and express itself more fully.

C. Behavior of People Who Are Wearing Masks of Pretension

People tend to hold on to the exterior image or *mask they have painted of themselves for others, so that they will be accepted by "the world" or society by wearing its approved dress and behavior. However, they do not appear as living beings but more as a false front or façade, a pattern of behavior or mannerisms such as, for example, a snob. In order to get along in this good/evil society, they admit to erroneous truth and appear to honest people as phonies and hypocrites, while the latter will lash out on anyone who is trying to expose them in order to "save face" or their mask.

---

* Mask or persona (Latin), is worn by some actors to indicate the part he or she is playing, and is also used by Indians as a dancing mask and by the people in Bali (Indonesia) by playing "wajang". The latter say that we are not the real players of life but only a shadow. It also means a character or role as being played by an actor, and in esoteric parlance, the mask or personality the Higher Self is using to express itself on the earth plane through the lower self (personality) as a vehicle.

The wearers of masks are repressing who they really are by smiling when they do not feel or when their inner being is not smiling, such as a typical salesman or lady. It is not the whole-hearted laugh, but the counterfeit or fake laugh or smile of people who are depending on someone of a high position, which they also like to win over by flattery or by insincere or excessive praise. Albeit, by doing all of this they will only strengthen their artificial, synthetic, or false selves.

Young children whom are not completely formed culturally according to the world and also those who confess their sins appear more sincere, as adults described above, and do not as yet wear a mask. Jesus Christ, who identified with them, liked them very much (Matt. 19:14), but compared the scribes and Pharisees with "whitewashed tombs, which outwardly appear beautiful, but within they are full of dead men's bones and all uncleanness" (corruption) (Matt. 23:27) – like the false or evil self.

NOTE: Shakespeare in his plays looked behind the mask and human pretension and stripped, peeled, or scratched his characters of conventional disguises or false coverings in which they tried to hide. He held the mirror up to all of us, and we (good and evil egos) identify with his characters, which become transparent to our understanding. Shakespeare finally said that we should be true to ourselves.

The Inner You

#33 The Existence and Working of Satan

A. Introduction

There is no religion or folklore in the world which does not have its *evil human spirits and demons (fallen angels), while some of them also believe in a distinct, separate personality that is the ruler of those evil forces.

The ancient Persians call this independent (psychic) angelic being angra mainyu or ahriman, the Buddhists mara the tempter, the Greeks prometheus the titan, and the religion of Islam eblis. The Essenes, a Jewish community and sect at the time of Jesus Christ, called this evil being satan, beelzebul, belial, mastema, azazel, and prince of darkness, commanding the sons of darkness to fight against the Sons of Light.

Most of the Jewish people call him satan, which means adversary opponent, enemy, and obstructer. Christians call him satan or devil, which latter word is derived from the Greek term "diabolus" (which also means slanderer and accuser), and is translated from the Hebrew satan (sathanas).

In the Old Testament books of the Bible, the name satan appears only in three passages – 1 Chronicles 21:1; Job chapters 1 and 2; and Zechariah 3:1-2.

In the New Testament, the devil or satan is also known as:

"The prince of demons" and "beelzebul" in Matt. 9:34; 12:24-27; Luk. 11:15-22; Mk. 3:22.
"The prince of the power of the air" (Eph. 2:2).
"The ruler of this world" (John 12:31; 1 John 5:19) and owner (Matt. 4:8-9).
"The enemy" in Matt. 13:39; Luk. 10:19.
"The evil one" (Matt. 6:13; 13:19; 1 John 2:14; Eph. 6:16).
He is a "father" of those who hate Christ and "was a murderer from the beginning" and "a liar and the father of lies" (John 8:44).
"The god of this world" (2 Cor. 4:4) and "Belial" (2 Cor. 6:15).
"Your adversary" and "roaring lion" (1 Pet. 5:8).

---

* Evil spirits are here also called demons.

"The great (red) dragon" (Rev. 12:3), the "ancient serpent", the "deceiver of the whole world", and the "accuser of our brethren" (Rev. 12:9-10; 12:3; 13:4; 16:13; 20:2).
"Abaddon" or "Apollyon" the destroyer (Rev. 9:11).

Jesus Christ called satan by name in Matt. 4:10; 16:23; Mark 3:26; 4:15; Luk. 10:18; 22:31 and devil in other places of the Gospels as did all of His disciples. Satan is hostile to the men of God and also wants to destroy the work of God (Job 1:9-11; Mark 4:15). He appeared to Eve in the Garden of Eden (Gen. 3:1-5; II Cor. 11:3; Rev. 12:9) and entered into Judas to betray the Lord (Luk. 22:3; John 13:27). He goes forth with "great wrath" (Rev. 12:12) and makes war on those whom are on God's side (Rev. 12:17).

Some scholars have interpreted the passage in Isaiah 14:12-17 as referring to the fall of satan (who is like the King of Babylon and other evil rulers of the earth) and compared it with Luke 10:18: "I saw Satan fall like lightning from heaven." In Revelation chapter nine, a star fell from heaven and became apollyon, the angel of the bottomless pit.

The angel Lucifer (light bearer – bright and shining one), the name before his fall (see Isaiah 14:12, King James Version), was used in the Latin vulgate Bible to translate the term "morning star" or the planet Venus at dawn (day-star). Thus, Lucifer means light bearer, from the Latin lux "light" and ferre "to bear or bring".

B. The Meaning of the Serpent

The serpent of Genesis (chapter 3) who tempted Eve is identified with satan in Revelation 12:9 "and the great dragon was thrown down that ancient serpent, who is called the Devil and Satan". See also Rev. 20:2. The serpent or snake is also identified as satan in the inter-testament or apocalyptic literature. Observe "Wisdom of Solomon" (verse 2:24).

Snakes are cold-blooded, crawl on their bellies, do not respond well to petting or affection, are psychically sensitive, have a forked tongue, are most active (in feeding) at night, and are so inconspicuous that they may go unnoticed even if they are common in an area. Some species are very poisonous, shed their skins, and "sneak up on you", attacking all of a sudden without warning. They are almost universally feared and have caused the deaths of many people. The serpent symbolizes together with the "great red dragon" (Rev. 12:3) the instinctive primitive forces and the uncontrolled lower desires of sentient beings. The dragon is a ravenous, frightful, powerful, fire-breathing monster. It has wings, indicating that it also has a psychic dimension.

However, the serpent in Moses' hand swallowed the serpents of the Pharaoh (Ex. 7:12), and the Israelites were saved later from the bite of serpents by looking up to the bronze serpent of Moses (Numbers 21:6-9; John 3:14). Jesus said in Matthew 10:16 to "be wise as serpents and innocent as doves", which is also the belief of many people in the East, for whom the serpent is a symbol of wisdom. The awakened upraised serpent (kundalini) within humans is for them also a sign of illumination.

C. Description and Belief in Satan

As satan is portrayed as a serpent in Genesis, *he is also seen in symbolic form as half human/half bestial, and for many people in the Middle Ages, to have literally the body of a man and goat combined. They believed that satan was like the Greek god Pan, who was worshipped by the pagans, complete with the beard of a goat, horned, tailed, hairy, and cloven hoofed. The goat, however, is a symbol of materialism, greed, and a lack of spiritual perception and is associated with feelings of sexuality and power, while satan's pitchfork is the symbol of power over the earth and the sea. Jesus said in Matthew 25:31-33: "When the Son of man comes", --- he will separate the sheep (relative good people) from the goats (relative evil people).

Modern liberal Christians whom confused the symbol of satan (as seen occasionally in visions and dreams) with his reality could no longer believe in his existence, and he, along with demons, were dismissed by almost all theologians as superstitious relics of the past or fantasy figures. They minimize or reject them because they are out of fashion in the modern age of science and technology. Because they are usually not fully active in witnessing, they do not experience as much the reality of satan and evil spirits as an opposing force, as Jesus and His disciples did. See 2 Cor. 4:8-9; 6:4-5; 11:23-29; 12:10.

---

* Angels were created neither male nor female (Mark 12:25) and are thus beyond sex. Following Lucifer, whom had a sexual relationship with Eve, "the sons of God (watcher angels) came in to the daughters of men" (Gen. 6:1-4) and became thus more male-oriented. Wanting to take over the position of Adam to be the Lord over the creation, satan did his utmost to develop the characteristics of a male human being.

Jesus Christ personally encountered the devil and defeated him (Luk. 4:1-13). He certainly believed that satan was a real psychic being (Luk. 10:17-20) by saying to him after His temptation: "Be gone, Satan!" (Matt. 4:10) and of His remark to the scribes, whom also believed in satan. "How can Satan cast out Satan?" (Mark 3:23). The early apostles, who built and led the Christian church in its crucial years, constantly talked about the temptation and opposition they experienced from satan and his demons (2 Cor. 4:7-9), and so did all the saints thereafter (read life of the saints).

The devil was to Martin Luther a real, living, and powerful personality who had the capability to materialize and often disturb and interrupt Luther in his work of translating the Bible. At one time, as the story goes, Martin got so mad at the devil's continual interference that he hurled, with all his force (physical-mental-spiritual), a heavy inkpot at him, and satan instantly disappeared.

Thus, all those who do really well in advancing the Kingdom of God and/or are attempting to live a spiritual or divine life, will be persecuted by satan and his angels, evil human beings with or without physical bodies, and humans whose evil part (nature) of their good and evil personality is temporarily in charge of their lives. The persecutors may also include those whom are known as good people and Christians in name.

Those whom are living the life of the personality (good/evil), satan and his demons leave them alone, especially the unbelievers (unregenerated (2 Cor. 4:4)), because they already belong more or less to his kingdom and are doing his will occasionally through the exercise of their evil nature. Besides, they can easily be influenced by evil forces to do satan's bidding, especially when they have a *common base (feel and think like satan). Their evil nature or impulse (inherent predisposition to evil) is then being strengthened by the influence of evil spirits.

All those whom are living close to God and are open psychically, like Jesus Christ, are very much aware of evil in and around people and have, of course, no difficulty believing in evil forces.

---

* Whenever people give in to their evil inclinations and take pleasure when evil is done by other persons, they create a common base with evil spirits or acquire a corresponding disposition. They then unknowingly cooperate with evil beings and become vulnerable to them.

REMARK: People whom do not believe in evil forces should try to witness for Christ for a period of time; they will then be convinced when they encounter opposing forces that are trying to stop them. There are also many people whom are not directly confronted with evil forces; nevertheless, they believe in them. They say that all the evil in the world cannot be blamed on humans alone. Some immature Christians might take advantage of the belief in satan, whom do not want to take any responsibility for their wrong actions by saying, "The devil made me do it."

NOTE: The people in the Middle Ages, whom were obsessed with the idea of satan, built him up or made him more powerful, not only with each new wrongdoing and evil thought, but also by constantly thinking about him and his demons, thus attracting their attention. The more energy they direct to a certain image of satan, the more they strengthen the newly-created thought form of satan, giving him additional power. By the same principle, individuals whom in the past have begun worshipping the gods of their imagination build up the collective thought forms (accumulated energy) of those gods, until they start acquiring a life and power of their own. They may, in turn, influence the people who believe in them.

D. Possessed by Evil Spirits

When Jesus spoke about the devil and his demons, whom he frequently cast out (Matt. 12:28; Mark 1:34; Luk. 11:20), He was not simply repeating superstitions carried over from Babylonian mythology, or saw it only as a case of neurosis or psychosis, as psychiatrists of today like to call it. Not only demons and evil spirits, but satan himself strongly influenced Peter (Matt. 16:23; Mark 8:33) and even momentarily possessed him by seizing control of his personality. Judas, who was completely controlled by satan (Luk. 22:3; John 13:27), came as the betrayer to help arrest Jesus (Matt. 26:46), or as John 14:30 has it: "The ruler of this world is coming", whom was possessing Judas Iscariot. After satan left him, Judas realized what he had done, repented, and hung himself (Matt. 27:3-5).

---

[1] Not only the outer devil grows with each wrongdoing or by hating each other, but also the inner devil (evil part of the personality).

[2] Romans hated the Christians for not believing in their gods. They feared the wrath of their gods on their communities because of the "atheism" of the Christians.

[3] In the language of psychiatry, spirit possession is also called manic depression, hysteria, schizophrenia, multiple personality disorder, etc., which in some cases may also have physiological and psychological causes. The Gospel makes a distinction between the healing of physical and mental ailments and that of possession (Matt. 4:24). In the latter case, Christ always recognized the possessing entity as a person. See Mark 1:23-26; 5:1-15; 9:17-27).

NOTE: Today, it is not uncommon to hear that those people whom are possessed by spirits (having a multiple personality) usually take on the character and personality of the possessing entity, which may be earthbound or a spirit of the evil realm. The latter tries to lure the person in committing evil acts. However, we may also be prompted to commit an evil deed by our own carnal or evil nature (Eph. 4:22; Col. 3:9), or by an influencing, obsessive, or possessive entity. We usually can tell when evil forces are in charge when we experience unexplained impulses and urges to say or do things which are harmful to ourselves and others, of which we are later ashamed of. Evil promotes disease, selfishness, greed, conflicts, misery, etc.

When we feel great fear, heaviness, spiritual cold and darkness, or overwhelming depression and do not feel like praying and witnessing and want to leave the faith or isolate from others in faith, we usually are in the presence of evil spirit(s). They try to tempt us into committing things we usually are not likely to do. It is experienced as "something that came over me", in the form of a strong impulse to do evil. The impulse could be a nagging temptation, extreme discouragement, undiagnosed ailments, destructive jealousy, unfounded irritation, inflaming of lustful passion, flaring anger, intense hatred, bitterness, resentment, criticism, revenge, becoming unusually deceptive and cunning, extreme selfishness and pride, excessive cruelty, irresistible thoughts of destroying things, and an overwhelming desire to commit suicide. While fanning up our inborn evil desires, they also criticize, accuse, and exaggerate the evil in God-chosen religious leaders, thus corrupting our faith in the goodness of God.

The church fathers believed that the devil was not only the symbol of the evil in humans but an evil, malicious, and independent personality. In the Roman Catholic teaching, the devil is much more than the personification of the evil in the world. He is an intelligible figure (he deceived the whole world – Rev. 12:9) and is also capable of emotional expressions (Rev. 12:12).

Both Milton and Dante accepted and did not question the existence of an independent and self-reliant spirit of evil. Milton's "Paradise Lost" speaks about an angel who revolted and was thrown out of heaven. Milton's poetic devil is a heroic and daring rebel (like Prometheus) who did not want to follow any rules and stubbornly refused to live by the Principles of God. Dante's Lucifer in "Inferno" is quite different from the skeptical and separatist figure of Milton. He is made repulsive and ludicrously and is against the divine plan for the evolution of human beings. Dostoevsky's devil of the "Brothers Karamazov" is, however, not an exterior but an interior being (inner devil). It is the inherited evil part or "old nature" (Eph. 4:22; Col. 2:9) of human beings and is portrayed in his writings as mean, sordid, and nasty.

E. Satan Lives Within and Among Us as an Active Force

The source of evil is within human beings (Mark 7:20-23), and he or she can also be persuaded or led into evil through a force independent of them.the force can be evil spirits and (or) humans of this earth as soon as they relate with them in their feeling and thinking. The Antichrist is thus not only an external evil intelligence but also the internal evil or false ego, which thinks itself apart from God and is always struggling with the Spirit of Christ or Divine Spirit within humans whom are living a divine life. In order to liberate from all influences of evil, people thus have to fight the evil forces on two fronts.

NOTE: Because the false ego can be thought of as existing in one's conscious and subconscious, it may sometimes masquerade as the Higher Self, Real Self, or Divine Spirit, and would like to take the place of the Divine Spirit or Soul as an impostor. As long as humans identify themselves with and are attached to the ego (whom they see as their separate self) and that they are nothing but the ego, the false ego maintains its position as the center of their life. The dawning of the Light of Truth in the consciousness of humans is very disturbing and life threatening for the impostor and it will therefore do anything to uphold its position and domain.

Evil began as an external temptation (Gen. 3). Thereafter, the evil impulse or power became deeply embedded in one's psyche or heart (Gen.6:5; 8:21). Clement of Alexandria, in the second century, wrote that satan exists both inside and outside the human mind.

It is said in the Bible that satan can disguise himself as an angel of light (II Cor. 11:14). He may thus [1]appear in a beautiful or most ugly form. He is able to strongly influence or even possess human beings whom have important and powerful positions in the church hierarchy and national governments (Eph. 6:12). He and his demons are also able to possess animals (Mark 5:1-20) or may occasionally become like werewolves, as recorded in medieval folklore.

The devil does not want the people of this earth to know that he and his cohorts work through and among human beings. He, therefore, likes that people do not believe in him so that they will not be on guard

---

[1] Angels and human spirits are able, by their power of thought, to change their lower spirit body (astral body) in many shapes or forms. They can also pretend to be someone else by making a thought form of a person someone is seeking or give a message to. Evil spirits, however, can be easily detected by individuals whom are living a divine life.

or watchful for him and his followers, their invasion and control, and thus not oppose their plan and work. Jesus Christ, however, said, "Watch and pray that you may not enter into temptation" (Mark 14:38). See also 1 Cor. 16:13; 1 Pet. 5:8; and Matt. 13:24:30. The more ridiculous he is believed to be, the better and undetected he and his disciples can do their evil work. Besides, evil beings are like criminals whom do not want anyone to know who they are and what they have done. They assume different names, live under the cover of darkness, and hide themselves from law abiding citizens and spiritual people who sense their evilness and expose them by shining the "Light of Truth" on them.

Satan and the fallen angels or demons (one third whom were [2]thrown down from heaven to the earth – Revelation 12 –) whom are completely evil, in cooperation with the lowest earthbound human spirits, try to do their evil work by attempting to topple people whom are very successful in doing the Will of God. They never say to ordinary people that are good and evil, "I want you to do something that is against the Will of God." The evil ones usually come in disguise as defenders of freedom, so that the mentally and spiritually immature people can disregard the Law of God (like Adam and Eve) and [3]do what they like to do (1 Tim. 4:1-2). A favorite lie they like to tell humans is that they are in possession of an independent self or ego apart from God, thus setting aside the necessity of regeneration or spiritual birth. Immature individuals like to believe this lie because it puts them in the role of a hero operating on his/her own.

---

[2] See also the story of the fall of the angels in the book of Enoch, an apocryphal book, written about 200 B.C.

NOTE: Satan and evil spirits can only live at a certain place in the spirit world, which is the lowest sphere, far away from the people whom live in heaven. But on earth, they can easily mix in with people whom are good and evil and are not easily detected because the people are not aware or sensitive of their presence. Besides, people generally do not believe that satan and demons exist and also do not notice them because they are blinded by their evilness. However, others whom are not obstructed by sinfulness detect evil through the intuition of their Divine Spirit.

[3] They soon start doing what their evil nature wants them to do by indulging in materialism, seeking worldly prestige, and exposing themselves to sensuality by watching movies that inflict a visual (what the eyes see, the mind and ego will follow) and verbal assault on their senses. This stirs their carnality, misdirects their mind, and opens the door to the influence of evil spirits whom project thoughts into the mind, moods into the emotion, and impulses into the will. The result is that they become less sensitive to vulgarity and violence, thus losing the sense of sin and their ability to distinguish between good and evil. This will, in turn, strengthen their evil nature.

The mass of unsaved humanity, whom are living the life of the good/evil personality and are unregenerated (not born of God), do not understand and are not conscious of their status and relationship to God and satan (Eph. 4:18; 1 Cor. 2:14; 2 Cor. 4:3-4). They live more or less independent of God and do not completely belong to God or satan. They, therefore, do not impose a serious threat to satan and his host and can easily be manipulated by them. This also includes some people whom have positions of power such as [1]government officials, employers and their bosses, and parents (Luk. 12:51-53; Matt. 10:34-36; Luk. 21:16), whom can make the life of believers (the ones whom are regenerated or saved) very miserable because they are a great hindrance to satan.

Satan, in his disguise, likes to appear as a friend of the unsaved people, whom he likes to win for his cause. He is known to start great humanitarian works for the reformation of individuals. However, the final result is that those groups become more and more evil. He began World War I to conquer the world with kaiser (emperor) Wilhelm, the physical man, as his representative, but was defeated. He tried again the same feat by using Hitler, the emotional man, but was again conquered by the forces of good. The allied forces also defeated communism in satan's third attempt to establish his pseudo kingdom according to his principles (which is an imitation of the universal brotherhood or the Kingdom of God) by using as his best man Stalin, the intellectual man. Those counterfeit governments seem to be so real that the Book of Revelation says that "the whole earth followed the beast with wonder" and worshipped it (Rev. 13:3-4). Because satan always tries to imitate God (Isa. 14:14), he is therefore called "the ape of God".

Satan is constantly working in human governments at the national and local levels, and his representatives are everywhere to rule nations, cities, religions, institutions, etc. He also works through powerful personalities. Daniel 10:13, 20 shows that satan has special angels or satanic princes assigned to the nations of the earth. They are able to live not only on the earth but also around the earth in another dimension.

---

[1] Christian churches, such as the Congregationalists and Presbyterians, believed that since all men are corrupted by original sin, the less power the official has, the less sin he can commit against the people. We may add here that they can also be corrupted by outside forces. That is why the ultimate power of the state should not repose in any man or body of men, but in a body of laws called the constitution.

Before the age of enlightenment (18th century), it was considered normal and natural to believe that the atmosphere surrounding the physical world was inhabited by good and evil spirits because the people at that time could sense them. Because they were less materialistic and more psychically oriented, evil spirits, witches, and warlocks could become a threat to them as they still are to materialistic people today in a less obvious way.

Apostle Paul said in 1 Thess. 4:17 that we shall "meet the Lord in the air", and in Eph. 2:2, he instructed that we should not follow "the prince of the power of the air", which is a lower spiritual level or vibration, as wherein the Lord can reside. They both reside, however, in the same space (of air). Today, people are becoming increasingly more open to psychic influences, and they again are starting to believe that the surrounding atmosphere is alive with non-physical beings, clouds of emotion and thought energy, and other "strange influences", creating a high or lower psychic atmosphere.

In conclusion, we can say that satan likes to be God by saying to Eve, "You will be like God" (Gen. 3:5), wants to be worshipped as God (Luk. 4:7), and proclaims himself to be God (2 Thess. 2:4). He is also leading the people in the last days to live his lifestyle (2 Tim. 3:1-9). However, in the time of Judgment, by the Word of God or Truth spoken by divine beings, the wheat (children of God) will be separated from the weed (children of the wicked one), whom were thriving in the established and visible church of God (Matt. 13:24-30).

As shown in Isaiah 14:13-14, the character of satan is his preoccupation with himself by saying in his heart:
"I will ascend to heaven"
"I will set my throne on high"
"I will sit on the mount"
"I will ascend above the heights"
"I will make myself like the Most High"

F. God Is Only Good and Cannot Be Evil

It was generally believed by olden civilizations that everything, good and bad (evil), is sent by their Creator and ruler of the universe, and that their gods were responsible for both good and evil. The deities in Hinduism and other religions, as manifestation of the supreme Creator, exercise the powers of creation and destruction, while the gods of ancient Greece and other nations (whom usually were like good/evil humans) were capable and held responsible for the good and evil and other bad things that have fallen on the people. The early Hebrews in pre-exilic times more or less adapted this view and believed that Yahweh or Jehovah – J.H.V.H. – (the God of the Hebrews) is directly or, through His angels, the cause of all the evil and bad events, such as disasters, calamities, judgment, punishment, suffering, etc. For instance:

"Does evil (disaster) befall a city unless the Lord has done it?" (Amos 3:6)

"I form light and create darkness, I make weal and create woe" (Isaiah 45:7).

"Now the Spirit of the Lord departed from Saul, and an evil spirit from the Lord (from His court) tormented him" (1 Sam. 16:14). See also 1 Kings 22:19-23.

The opposite of good as mentioned above is not only *"evil", but also divine judgment, caused by the evil actions of the Israelites. The punishment is meted out by the law of karma (see #34) and is always in complete agreement with God's Will (Jer. 44:2).

In 2 Sam. 24:1 we read: "The anger of the Lord was kindled against Israel, and he incited David against them saying 'go number Israel and Judah'". The same event is later mentioned in 1 Chron. 21:1: "Satan stood up against Israel and incited David to number Israel".

Bible writers whom believed at first that God is good and evil slowly changed their minds when they and the Israelites developed a bigger concept of God and also unfolded more the good side of their personality. They began to understand that their God is not capable of moral evil and thus could no longer accept their Creator as a being of good and evil. There must be a separate source of evil. They found this disconnected source in the Zoroastrian religion when the Israelites were living in exile in Babylonia. This being was an independent evil

---

* The word "evil" is used in the Bible as moral evil and unfortunate occurrences. We like to say here that evil is only created by satan and has, therefore, a separate existence.

REMARK: Considering the above, we should keep in mind that the final version of the Old Testament was written after the Babylonian exile in c. 500 B.C. As it is written in Genesis chapter 1, "God created the world as good."

spirit (god) and was called Ahra Mainyu or Ahriman and was involved in a seemingly continual battle with the holy spirit (god) of – Ahura Mazda, the supreme God – called Spenta Mainyu. The people were thus offered an opportunity to side with the good or evil forces of the universe.

G. How Humans Are Tested by Satan

In the Book of Job, God tries to win satan for His cause, to respect human beings whom, after they are restored, are destined to become Lords over the creation, which also includes the angelic world (1 Cor. 6:3). Because of the fall of Eve and Adam, which was caused by satan, Adam and Eve and their descendants never became true or God-centered rulers, but instead, the world came under the rule of satan (1 John 5:19; Matt. 4:9).

It is reported in the extra-biblical or apocalyptic writing of the life of Adam and Eve that after God had created Adam, He wanted all the angels to bow down to His new creation. Michael the Archangel obeyed, but Lucifer (satan) refused, saying:

> "Why do you press me? I will not worship one who is
> younger than I am, and inferior. I am older than he is;
> he ought to worship me! (Vita Adae et Evae 14:3)

In the Mohammedan Koran, we find a similar story wherein iblis (satan) refused to bow down before Adam as Allah (God) had commanded him.

> "Now there was a day when the sons of God came to
> present themselves before the Lord, and Satan also
> came among them" (Job 1:6). "And the Lord said to
> Satan, 'Have you considered my servant Job, that there
> is none like him on the earth, a blameless and upright man,
> who fears God and turns away from evil'" (Job 1:8).

Satan, being cynical about human goodness, challenged God, saying:

> "Put forth thy hand now, and touch (destroy) all that he
> has, and he will curse thee to thy face. And the Lord
> said to Satan, 'Behold, all that he has is in your power;
> only upon himself do not put forth your hand'" (Job 1:11-12).

After Job overcame all temptation and adversities and proved to satan and God that he was an upright man, "the Lord gave Job twice as much as he had before" (Job 42:10).

NOTE: We may learn from the Book of Job that satan cannot kill a child of God without the Lord's permission. That demons can cause physical affliction, they can make people dumb (Matt. 9:32), blind (Matt. 12:22), crippled (Luk. 13:12), and demons can torment people (Matt. 15:22), driving them to commit suicide (Matt. 17:15). The trials in life are important ways God uses to let us grow and to build our faith. Satan may also use trials and suffering to bring out the worst in us. However, God may occasionally permit this so that we bring out the best in us.

Humans are again confronted in chapter three of the Book of Zechariah. Here, satan acts as an accuser of the high priest Joshua, as a representation of a nation that has done something wrong in the past but has been forgiven by God. Satan is standing on the right side of Joshua as a persecutor and the angel of the Lord as the defender before the throne of God. "And the Lord said to Satan, 'The Lord rebuke you, O Satan! The Lord who has chosen Jerusalem rebukes you!'" (Zech. 3:2).

NOTE: When active Christians have done something wrong, they should confess immediately and receive forgiveness (1 John 1-9). Otherwise, it will lead to excessive guilt, depression, despair, and defeat, obstructing His divine flow, and are therefore no longer able to serve God with power and blessing. They also give their inner devil reason to accuse, rendering them completely worthless.

In the Apocryphal books or extra canonical literature of the second and first century B.C. (which may have been influenced by Babylonian sources), satan developed into an independent principle of evil. On the other hand, the Book of Enoch of c. 200 B.C. gives a vivid description of the story of the fall of the angels and how satan was cast out of heaven.

H. Temptation and Working of Satan in the Life of Christ

At the time of Christ, almost all the Pharisees, Scribes, and people of all levels of society, believed that they were surrounded by good and evil spirits and that satan was the ruler of the evil ones (Mark 3:22-27).

Satan may have triumphed over the first Adam, and become "the god" (1 Cor. 4:4), "the ruler" (John 12:31), and owner (Matt. 4:9) of this world, but God promised a long time ago that the seed of the woman (Christ and true believers) will be hostile to the seed of satan (his followers), and that "he (Christ) shall bruise your head (inner self) and you (satan) shall bruise his heel (outer self)". See Gen. 3:15.

Jesus as "the last Adam" (1 Cor. 15:45) came not only to restore the lost position of the first Adam but also to take away satan's power over the world, and restore him to his original position of servant to God and to His precious human children. As a result, "all hell broke loose".

Satan took direct and offensive action against the promised seed, and there was also an increasing activity of satan's host, whom tried to influence and invade the people around Jesus, especially those whom were against his mission. From the beginning to the end of His ministry, Jesus was confronted daily and was under continual assault from all evil forces satan could muster to destroy the True Son of God.

As reported in the Gospels, satan already appeared at the beginning of Jesus' ministry to overpower Him through temptation.

After His baptism and the descent of the Holy Spirit, Jesus went into the wilderness to be *tempted by satan. Only after He overcame the satanic temptation of misusing His divine power for personal possession (greed), vanity (fame), and selfish ambition (power) did Jesus say, "The time is fulfilled, and the Kingdom of God is at hand" (Mark 1:15).

As it is written in the Gospel of Matthew, chapter 4, "and the devil took him (Jesus) to a very high mountain and showed him all the kingdoms of the world and the glory of them, and he said to him, 'All these I will give you, if you will fall down and worship me'". Satan, who took away the Lordship over the world from the first Adam, offered the kingdoms to the last Adam, provided that satan receive – like the most high – submissive adoration and worship from the Son of God.

---

* In the Gospel of John, it is the people (the inner devil – the evil part of their personality) who play the role of a tempter. They asked Jesus to exhibit His divine authority and powers in public – (Matt. 4:3-6; Jn. 6:30-31; 7:1-5), to make Him king (Matt. 4:8-9; Jn. 6:15), and overcoming His fleshly temptation (Jn. 6:32). In order to take over the position of the first Adam, Jesus Christ (like Adam) had to be tempted, but He had to overcome the first (physical), second (desire), and third (power) temptations. Every follower of Christ who wants to leave the kingdom of satan and false ego is usually tempted while growing to maturity, at the point where Adam and Eve fell, by outer and inner forces of evil.

After satan was defeated in these first attempts to subvert Jesus, "he departed from him until an opportune time" (Luk. 4:13). From the moment Jesus left the wilderness and returned to society, the powers of evil challenged him at every turn, as reported in the Gospel of Mark. After Jesus sent out seventy disciples to preach the Gospel, he "saw Satan fall like lightning from heaven" (Luk. 10:18; John 12:31). As the forces of good increased, the forces of evil became more aggressive and could easily work through the Herodians and Pharisees, whom conspired to kill Jesus (Mark 3:6), which was accomplished after Judas Iscariot betrayed him (Luk 22:3).

Through Jesus' sacrifice on the cross, he had broken the power of the evil one. Satan's head was bruised, and he was severely wounded, but not completely disarmed and destroyed. He is still seen by Gospel writers as having authority over this world.

However, satan and all evil beings and forces can be completely banished. They lose all their authority, influence, and power when the people, with the help of their Spiritual Parents – the Cosmic Christ (Rev. 1:8) and the Holy Spirit, remove their inherited evil or satanic nature and grow to spiritual maturity. Their children will be born without original sin and live in the Kingdom of God on earth as in heaven.

I. The Battle between Good and Evil in the Life of Christians

As satan is hardly mentioned in the Old Testament, he is repeatedly mentioned by the apostles, especially by St. Paul and very often in the Revelation of St. John. "Be sober, be watchful. Your adversary the devil prowls around like a roaring lion" (1 Peter 5:8). "For we are not contending against flesh and blood, but against the principalities, against the powers, against the world rulers of this present darkness, against the spiritual hosts of wickedness in the heavenly places" (Eph. 6:12). "For the devil has come down to you in great wrath because he knows that his time is short!" (Rev. 12:12)

The conflict between good and evil that began in all earnest with Jesus is being continued in the lives of Christians. The earth has become a battlefield where the armies of satan (fallen angels and wicked humans with or without bodies) war against the children of light.

Some individuals discover that the closer they come to Christ, the more they are harassed by evil forces. Anyone who poses a serious threat to evil powers will be targeted and will counter fierce opposition, especially those whom are winning many souls for Christ, as well as those with a future potential. However, people whom are not attacked or tempted by demonic forces are those whom are not doing the Will of God, or even worse, already belong to satan and do satan's will unknowingly.

The Christian churches have always believed that the most saintly people are the ones whom are the most attacked by outside evil forces and also wage a war against the force of evil within themselves. That is the fight between their emerging Christ or Divine Spirit (Gal. 4:19) and their inherited evil nature, fallen nature or old self (Rom. 6:6), or old nature (Eph. 4:22). *This battle can be very fierce for the grown Christian and others because the evil self or Antichrist will do anything in its power to keep its domain over the thought life of the individuals.

REMARK: An evil angelic being with a black face appeared to the author in a vision at the time of writing this paper. Shortly thereafter, the author has been tempted many times, and he is being watchful and prayerful at all times.

Like the Disciples of Christ, the early Christians and the church fathers strongly believed in the existence of evil forces with which they were confronted daily in their lives. This is especially true to those whom were like Jesus Christ, very active in establishing the Kingdom of Heaven. Many of them were like Christ, "slain for the Word of God and for the witness they had born" (Rev. 6:9) and because they "would not worship the image of the beast" (Rev. 13:15). But "thy blood did ransom (purchased) men for God" (Rev. 5:9), or as the saying goes, "the blood of martyrs is the seed of the church", multiplying believers.

Because this Kingdom was not like the Roman Empire (the beast), many Romans could not get along with their Christian neighbors. However, when some Romans, especially those in power, began to persecute the Christians, they made a common base to attract evil spirits whom want to †destroy the followers of Christ. Those persecutions escalated and became so evil that thinking Romans could not understand why they hated Christians so much. Origen (d. . 254),

---

* See "The Birth and Evolution of the Divine Spirit or Soul".

† Those followers of Christ were so strong in their faith that evil beings whom could not kill their Souls sought to kill their bodies by throwing them before the wild beasts (1 Pet. 5:8).

Christian father and theologian, says in his writing "Contra Celsum" "that the souls of those who condemn Christians and those who betray them and enjoy persecuting them are filled with evil and are driven by demons".

J.   Working of Satan in Medieval Times and Modern Europe

Because of the weakening of Christianity, which resulted in the revival of [1]paganism and the belief in witchcraft, the devil and his host came to have a more prominent place among the people of Medieval Europe.   This evil communication began in the ninth century by witches and warlocks and reached its greatest activity in the thirteenth and fourteenth centuries.   Contracts were made with the devil in which men surrendered their souls for his services and they (unlike Jesus (see Matt. 4:9)) began to worship the devil.   This was later highlighted in the famous story of Faust, the philosopher, who made a pact and sold This soul to a devil called Mephistopheless for knowledge and power. When the [2]people of the Middle Ages (whom almost lost sight of the distinction between the spiritual and the secular) became more fearful and obsessed with thoughts of satan and his demons, Pope Innocent VIII declared, in his 1484 papal bull, that Western Europe was infected with demons and witches.   Thereafter, the horrors of the witch-hunt began in earnest and became more intense than before.   Not only the guilty but also many innocent people were tortured and burned alive. The persecution of "sorcerers and wizards" ([3]those whom are doing the works of evil spirits – Ex. 22:18; Lev. 20:27; Deut. 18:10-12; Rev. 18:23 –) and the killing of [4]heretics (which began in the thirteenth century) continued by superstitious and self-righteous Catholics and

---

[1] Pagans are people whom are living the life of the good and evil personality and are unlike true Christians whom are living a divine life. The former will attract and communicate with spirits at their level, which may be deceased pagans or evil spirits, while the latter attract and communicate with spirits at their level, which may be deceased fellow Christians or Saints.

[2] People of the Middle Ages were enchanted and fascinated by the world wherein they were living. Living close to nature, they perceive it to be alive and saw not only its outer beauty but, like an artist, also perceived its inner beauty. Being sensitive, they perceived the world around them, not as materialistic dull and gloomy, but vivid, bright, radiant, and populated with all kinds of psychic and spiritual beings with whom they try to communicate.

[3] This does not include evolved mediums or channelers, whom are in contact with spirits and saints of the higher spirit world.

[4] Heretics are those who hold beliefs or opinions contrary to the established doctrines of their religion. The Dominicans began the persecution of heretics called the Holy Inquisition in 1233 A.D. For them wrong belief (against their dogma) causes spiritual death and is, therefore, worse than physical death.

religious Reformers alike to well in the seventeenth century, while the fanatic Catholics and Protestants persecuted each other just as cruelly.

It was therefore of no surprise that by the end of the seventeenth century a reaction came about, and many people shifted to the other extreme by rejecting almost any thought and belief about the devil. At the time of the Enlightenment, most people began to put more of their faith in reason and science instead of dogma (established assertion of truth), and the eighteenth century became known as the Age of Reason. They became more materialistic in their thinking, which resulted that their psychic senses began to atrophy, and were thus hardly aware of any evil or good spirits. This led to a vanishing belief in the devil, while the persecution of witches greatly diminished and came later to an end. Because most people did no longer believe in the devil as their enemy, they were no longer on guard against satan and his followers. This resulted not only in complacency and spiritual sloth (Matt. 13:24-30), but they could also be easily used or manipulated by those evil forces. Being more insensitive to psychic and spiritual phenomena, many individuals and intellectuals also began to doubt the existence of God and were thus not likely to ask for His help to fight against the evil within them and in the world. Original sin was rarely mentioned by theologians because the majority of intellectuals believed that humans are capable of reaching perfection without any knowledge about evil and a need of a God to redeem themselves. The result was the nineteenth century, wherein the belief in satan was ridiculed or laughed at, and God was "finally" proclaimed "dead" by the German philosopher Friedrich [1]Nietzsche (1844-1900), which was reaffirmed by the "death of God" theologians in the 1960s. Nevertheless, as this movement towards destruction was somewhat delayed by Christian revivals and the revitalization of [2]spiritualism, many people no longer believed that they would become divine beings or the sons and daughters of God. Instead, they became more and more convinced that

---

[1] Nietzsche believed in the will to power and in the "superman", the personality in which the evil element is dominant and the divine quadrant is totally missing. The idea of this satanic personality was later more or less adopted by Fascist movements. National Socialism, under the dictatorship of Adolf Hitler (from 1933-1945) in Germany, came out of the Nazi party – the National German Workers Party established in 1919 and the movement in Italy founded in 1919 by Mussolini. Those started the Second World War and wanted to rule the world under satanic principles. United with Japan, they tried to take over the whole world and establish the kingdom of satan.

[2] Modern spiritualism began in 1848 in Hydesville, Rochester, New York when the Fox sisters heard percussive sounds or rapping from a murdered peddler buried in their house.

they are not only physically but also mentally and spiritually descended from apes, and that they are not much better than they are. The evilness of [3]capitalism, which was based on greed, and the rise of atheistic [4]communism and other human centered ideologies resulted in the horrors of the first, second, and third (cold) world wars and many other atrocities of the twentieth century.

Having learned from the past, people of the twenty-first century should not make or repeat the same mistakes our forebears made. It is, first of all, important to know that God exists, and they as Parents care about their fallen human children (Gen. 3:21), whom have a very hard time living in this satanic world (Gen. 3:16-19) and growing to physical, mental, and spiritual maturity.

In order to avoid suspicion and fear, people of today should have adequate and correct knowledge about life after death. They should be on guard and know how to distinguish between good and evil spirits, so that religious people would no longer put innocent people to death because they heard "voices" from deceased good people and saints. This is well documented in the story of Jeanne D'Arc (1412-1431), the maid of Orleans, France, who was burned alive.

K. The Goal and Activities of Evil Forces

The goal of satanic forces is to undermine our trust in the goodness of God. This already happened in the story of the fall of Adam and Eve in the Garden of Eden (Gen. 3:1-5), when satan, in a very subtle way, made God the evil and him the good one in the eyes of Eve. By disobeying God's command "not to eat of the fruit of the tree" or "touch it, lest you die", Eve succumbed to temptation because she wanted to be "like God, knowing good and evil", become like the Creator instead of the creature (Rom. 1:25), and become independent of God's Will. Having been seduced psychically by satan, Eve, in turn,

---

[3] In the "Wealth of Nations" Adam Smith (1723-1790) wrote that self-interest leads each person to seek his or her own economic advantage, thus contributing to the general welfare, which is not part of his intention. This seems to be the best possible world the good/evil people have come up with while anticipating the establishment of the Kingdom of God.

[4] Communism began in 1848 with the Communist Manifesto – principle of modern communism – published by Karl Marx (German philosopher and Socialist) and Friedrich Engels.

seduced [1]Adam psychically. They then touched each other in a lustful way and then united physically without God's blessing, while they were still teenagers. Thereafter, spiritually immature Adam resented being dependent upon God and wanted to be his own master, which resulted that they both put themselves out of the Garden of God's domain or separated themselves from God and were no longer living according to His laws and principles. The Divine Spark within themselves that had been growing into a Divine Spirit or Soul could not [2]blossom because of the lack of spiritual care and nourishment of their heavenly Parents, and they died spiritually.

Adam and Eve and their descendants became like the fallen archangel Lucifer or satan who became their god, ruler, and father (2 Cor. 4:4; John 12:31; 8:44). Satan does not like to be a servant but wants to be served and worshipped. He is a liar, deceiver, impostor, pretender, accuser, oppressor, murderer, and destroyer without pity. He is arrogant, greedy, lawless, vainglorious, likes to have power over the people (1 John 5:19), and wants to [3]judge and dominate them. He is motivated by pride, immorality, and selfishness, which prompted his rebellion. He is full of hatred, holds a grudge, is suspicious, envious, and wants revenge. As an intellectual, he is skilled in deception, is crafty, cunning, shrewd, double-faced, and crooked.

Satan likes to work through unregenerated or unsaved people (those whom are not born of God) (Eph. 2:1-3) but can also work through the *just saved or little (spiritual) children, whom have not yet overcome the evil one (1 John 2:12-14). He blinds the mind of "unbelievers (unborn) to keep them from seeing the light of the Gospel of the glory of Christ" (2 Cor. 4:4). The (evil) "spirit that is now at work in the sons of disobedience" (Eph. 2:2), for whom "the gifts of the Spirit of God", --- "are folly to him" (1 Cor. 2:14).

---

[1] Adam could have left Eve after she united with satan, but having fallen in love with Eve, he left the Garden with her to face a fearful and insecure future. Eve later admitted that satan deceived her in Gen. 3:13, while Adam tried to blame God for his misfortune by saying, "the woman whom thou gavest to be with me, she gave me the fruit of the tree, and I ate" (Gen. 3:12).

[2] Because they did not mature, they also did not grow out of their selfishness, which became more intense by also becoming evil-minded.

[3] Unlike Jesus Christ (John 8:16), satan and his evil henchmen like to judge and condemn people.

* See "The Birth and Evolution of the Divine Spirit or Soul".

Satan, his host, and the inherited evil or old nature (Eph. 4:22) within humans will do anything to keep you from understanding the Word of God and "snatches away what is sown in his heart" (Matt. 13:19). *This Divine Seed or Word will become a Divine Spirit or Spirit of Christ (Gal. 4:19), and when it is strong enough, it will destroy the impostor, old nature, or "flesh" within human beings (Gal. 5:17) and, thus, weaken satan's power. Evil forces will distract, detour, interrupt, confuse, and even make you critical, using unbelievers, through whom they can easily work, because they are more or less satan's children (1 John 3:8, 10). The unsaved, whom are living the life of the good and evil personality, may ask themselves thereafter, "Why was I so mad at him or her (or them); what has come over me?" Being reasonably good people, they try to make up by serving those they treated so badly or, in cases of the past, worshipping the saints they have killed.

When satan and his sons cannot deceive your mind (as a serpent), they will then try (as a lion) to destroy your body.

Because satan has limited power, one of his strategies is to undermine God-centered values. He and his demonic army promote God-less ideologies and ¹man-centered humanism, so that the people are completely ignorant of a higher divine dimension, wherein they become true sons and daughters of God. In that capacity, they will rule over the angelic world (1 Cor. 6:3). In order to keep the people blind of that fact and stuck in the life of the ²personality (instead of divine life), satan, his demons, and evil people (with or without bodies) promote moral decay, pollute the mind, and pervert the will of anyone they are able to influence.

Satan and his legion (Luk. 8:30) may put thoughts in our minds about things we already desire and strengthen those desires. Satanic suggestions, which cater to sinful desires, are easily accepted, especially by unsaved people, because sinful men like sin. Even those

---

* See "The Birth and Evolution of the Divine Spirit or Soul".

¹ How is it possible for humanistic leaders, whom are good and evil, to tell people how to live the right way? They do not have any wisdom, only some knowledge, appearing as servants of righteousness (2 Cor. 11:12-15; Isaiah 45:24; 64:6; James 3:15).

² Personality is the psyche or human spirit (the reasoning, emotive, and volitional) and body. The doctor may say, "You are what you eat" and the psychologist may say, "You are what you think." The full-grown human being, however, is a Spiritual, psycho and somatic being. A spiritual caretaker or pastor may say, "You are what you believe, accept, and assimilate as Truth", thus becoming a Truth Body, Divine Spirit or Soul.

whom are trying to live a divine life are struggling to overcome those temptations because evilness is deeply embedded within their psyche or heart (Mark 7:21-23).

Being born of original sin, everyone has an evil nature which may be strong or of a lesser intensity. In order to resist satanic forces, we should examine ourselves if we have any specific weaknesses that could be exploited.

Is it pride and selfishness to unscrupulously use others so that a person will always be Number One in the pecking order? Is it lust and self-indulgence to fulfill lustful desires and cravings? Is it greed and possessiveness to grasp desire for one's own wealth, disregarding the needs of others? Is it envy to desire what belongs to another, which is the 10th Commandment?

Do you have thoughts of doing something violent or plans to indulge in sinful behavior? Evil spirits can reinforce those thoughts. Do you have uncontrollable emotional outbursts, such as hatred, rage, intolerance, desires for revenge, which may be strengthened by evil beings and may result in criminal activities? (Eph. 4:26-27)

Evil entities may also kindle our memory of the evil we have done in the past and convey it to our conscious awareness, whereby we are tempted to [1]imagine and fantasize about it, and then they try to persuade us to commit the same deed. This may mean for the disappointed or doubtful believer that he or she will be tempted to be worldly and materialistic again.

Satan and his cohorts usually make contact with the believer and unbeliever through their old nature or old self, which is of the same nature as they are. We have inherited this satanic nature from our ancestors, and it may become better or worse through our individual behavior. This evil nature can be found in our heart or psyche (human spirit); "for out of the heart come evil thoughts, murder, adultery, fornication, theft, false witness, slander" (Matt. 15:19). Evil beings can stir up this evil within ourselves and bring it to the surface of our con-

---

[1] If this sin is of a sexual nature, we should not dwell, think, or fight it because desires will only be nourished by those thoughts. It is better to evade it by turning our minds to something else.

sciousness. This can more easily happen in our [2]sleep when our physical consciousness, with its will, is less in control of the psyche or spirit body.

Invisible enemies that surround us in another dimension will try to attack regenerated believers when their guard is down and when they do not watch over their worst weakness, in which they have indulged most often. Evil entities do not let go easily of someone they have influenced for a long time. They usually hang around for a long time because they know that human beings can be weak, and then try to entrap their victims in the same sin again. This, however, is not true for the spiritually grown whom "have overcome the evil one" (1 John 2:14). They have a spirit of forgiveness (2 Cor. 2:11, 12), free of resentment and revenge, and they "resist the devil" (James 4:7) by being strict in their feeling and thinking and making no concession.

L. How to Overcome the Powers of Evil

Apostle Paul speaks in 2 Cor. 10:3-5, that regenerated believers are engaged in full-scale warfare.

"For though we live in the world we are not carrying on a worldly war, for the weapons of our warfare are not worldly, but have divine power to destroy strongholds" (see also Mk. 3:27; Lk. 11:22).

"Be strong in the Lord and in the strength of his might" (Eph. 6:10).

"He may grant you to be strengthened with might (power) through His Spirit in the inner man" (Eph. 3:16) and to "be filled with the Spirit" (Eph. 5:18), or with the presence of the indwelling Spirit of God (Rev. 21:3), "who strengthens me" (Phil. 4:13), to take a stand against the lure and enticements of evil forces.

"Put on the whole armor of God, that you may be able to stand against the wiles of the devil." For we are fighting "principalities" – strongholds of owners, rulers, employers and their bosses, executives, chiefs, heads, etc., and are struggling against their "powers" (Eph.

---

[2] After physical death, the consciousness of the outer personality will be completely transferred to the spirit body or human spirit, and the latter will be in full control. Before this can happen, the spirit body is more vulnerable to evil forces and less protected. It is therefore advisable, before one goes to sleep (when the spirit body separates from the physical body), that our thoughts are positive or God-centered because they give direction to the subconscious mind and, thus, to the movement of the spirit body in the higher or lower realms. This also has an impact on our life that day when we wake up.

6:12), schemes, deception, cunning, craftiness, wiles, strategy, and all the other psychological devices they have learned in their education to trick people in giving up their hard earned money and to have power over them.

"Therefore, take the whole armor of God, that you may be able to withstand in the evil day, and having done all, to stand" (Eph. 6:13). The whole armor consists of the spiritual weapons of Truth, Righteousness, Gospel of Peace, Faith, Salvation, Word of God, and Prayer (Eph. 6:14-18). The first five fulfill a more defensive role, while the latter two are also used in an offensive way.

Description of the whole armor of God to win spiritual battles against the forces of darkness:

1) "Having girded your loins with truth" (Eph. 6:14).
People at the time of Paul wore girdles to bind and hold together their garments, while the Roman soldier wore a thick leather belt. The girdle or belt of truth, as part of the function of the innermost Truth body, Soul or Christ Spirit and which is formed by the Word of God (Gal. 4:19), should firmly hold together or govern one's outermost members: the physical, emotional, and mental sheaths or robes (Rev. 22:14). Being committed to the truth of God's Word in our inner being, we should also live the truth with our outer being in word and deed. Thus, we are clothed with truth, so that evil forces cannot keep us ignorant and influence and control us with their lies, because they are exposed by the truth of what they are.

2) "Put on the breastplate of righteousness" (Eph. 6:14; 1 Thess. 5:8; Isa. 59:17).
This piece of armor covers the upper front of the soldier's body and protects its vital organs. The breastplate is put in place when we become righteous (and express other divine qualities – Gal. 5:22) in the sight of God by accepting Christ as our Savior, repenting of all our sins, and becoming free of guilt. Satan and his demons can no longer accuse us (Rev. 12:10) and make us feel that we are failures, worthless beings, and not qualified to work for the cause of Christ. However, after our conversion, we are no longer self-righteous, which is like "polluted garment" – filthy rags – (Isa. 64:6; Rom. 3:9-18). Instead, we acquire "the righteousness of God" (2 Cor. 5:21; Eph. 4:24) and put on the rich garment or robes of the personality (Zech. 3:4), which give us confidence and courage to defeat all the evil forces.

3) "Having shod your feet with the equipment (preparation) of the gospel of peace" (Eph. 6:15; Rom. 10:15; Ps. 119:105).

The shoes are important for a Roman warrior because it gives him sure footing, stability, mobility, and a readiness to fight. Our duty is to stand our ground and be alert, watchful, and on guard for satanic invasion (Mk. 14:32-42). We must always be ready to go and do the work of God, not reluctantly but willingly, to spread the gospel of peace. By prayer, we prepare ourselves to walk in the shoes of peace, and by witnessing, we experience the Love and concern of God for the people we meet and talk to. We give to them the good news and leave them with the Love and "Peace of God, which passes all understanding" (Phil. 4:7).

NOTE: True Christians feel a need to protect themselves against the hostile atmosphere of satan's kingdom. They call on saints and guardian angels, sprinkle holy water, use incense, say the Lord's prayer and other Bible verses, chant the name of God and that of Jesus Christ, make the sign of the cross, and say the rosary of the Virgin Mary. Many of them also immerse themselves in spiritual music and devotional songs, whereby the aura of their Inner Being will become bigger, stronger, and brighter. As a result, the aura will not be pierced and open to psychic invasion (as the skin is to bacterial infection) by negative emotions such as fear, hostility, hatred, discord sound, and excessive use of drugs and alcohol. When their aura is filled with love, the sword of hate is barred entrance and will return to the sender, and their love will eventually dispel the force of hate. Esoteric groups and Eastern religion factions are more inclined to shield their god-selves, or put on their psychological and spiritual armor by affirmation of truth, statement of trust, reading inspired words, positive thoughts, meditation, visualizing, and chanting the name of their God and master. Thus, they take a stand against the invasion of unwanted energies and psychic entities. This also includes the negative feelings and thoughts of their own self, the personalities they meet, and those whom are trying to drain them of their vital energy (psychic vampirism) which makes them depleted, exhausted, depressed, and ill. They may further protect their precious Selves by meditation and visualizing a shell, bubble, or tube of white light (drawn from God's omnipresence) around their Higher Self, Soul, or Inner Being. Some people also say or chant mantras (sacred sounds), which act as a barrier against evil forces, while they also evoke and chant the name of their spiritual master with which they have a deep affinity.

4) "Taking the shield of faith, with which you can quench all the flaming (fiery) darts of the evil one" (of the wicked) (Eph. 6:16).

The shield served as a moveable protection for the soldier of the Roman Empire from the (burning) arrow shot by the enemy. We should have a steadfast faith in God and the truth of His Word, "for we walk by faith, not by sight" (2 Cor. 5:7). "He is a shield to those who take refuge in him" (Prov. 30:5). See also Ps. 5:12; Zech. 2:5. The Lord will protect us and ward off the flaming attacks of fear, doubt, disbelief, distrust, confusion, and discouragement and prevent them from starting a fire or growing within our inner self or psyche by dwelling on it, which also causes our Soul to wither by cutting its lifeline.

5) And put on the "helmet of salvation" (Eph. 6:17; Isa. 59:17).

As the helmet served as a physical protection for the head of the Roman fighter, it served as a spiritual protection for the spiritual warrior, for the onslaught of evil thoughts, which may influence our thinking and, in turn, damage the whole of our moral and spiritual life. Paul preached that the helmet is "the hope of salvation" (1 Thess. 5:8), and that we are "abound in hope" through the "power of the Holy Spirit" (Rom. 15:13); the assurance we have to be saved and to belong to the Kingdom of God. Having this helmet firmly in place, the dedicated believer will no longer be swayed by the incursion of deception (2 Cor. 11:3), hopelessness, and despair.

6) Take "the sword of the Spirit which is the Word of God" (Eph. 6:17; Matt. 10:34).

As the physical sword is handled by the Roman soldier to conquer the enemy, the spiritual sword is used by the spiritual worker to subdue the invisible enemy. The sword of the Spirit is used in a defensive way by using scripture to counteract disbelief, mistrust, and temptation and, in an offensive way, by using the Word of God to change people's lives from a satan-centered way of living to a God-centered way. Jesus Christ "the living word" used the sword most effectively when He was confronted with satan in the wilderness (Matt. 4:1-11). He defeated satan's three temptations by replying after every temptation, "It is written", quoting from Deuteronomy verses 8:3; 6:16; 6:13, tying up satan, and taking his possessions (Matt. 12:29). Hebrew 4:12 says that the Word of God is most effective, living, active, and sharp (Rev. 1:16), when its potential life and power are wielded by those whom are filled with the Spirit of God (2 Cor. 3:6). The Word of God, or the vessel of Life, is able to penetrate, cleanse, and change the life of believers, thus separating and liberating them from the power and grip of satan and all of his cohorts.

7) "Pray at all times in the Spirit, with all prayer and supplication (earnest prayer or entreaty to God). To that end keep alert with all perseverance, making supplication for all the saints" (Eph. 6:18).

In order to win the war, all soldiers have to be obedient to their commanders and should also live a moral life. The Christ(ian) warrior should likewise be obedient to the Spirits – the Universal Christ and the Holy Spirit united with the last Adam (Dan. 7:9-10; Rev. 1:12-18; John 1:1) and the last Eve (the Lamb and His Bride – Rev. 21:9). The overshadowing Spirit of the last Adam (1 Cor. 15:45) died in the first Adam but became alive in Jesus Christ (Rev. 1:18). The Spirits and restored Adam and Eve are the expressive aspects of God (whose bodies or universes consist of male and female elements), which function as True Parents of humankind and as masters to the angelic world.

Because prayer is the heart or most important aspect of spiritual warfare, Paul advises us that we should pray "in the Spirit" (see also Jude 20) so that the Universal Christ (expressed through Jesus Christ and others) and the Holy Spirit (expressed through Mary and others) can guide, direct, and empower us to pray for particular needs. Those requirements are always in harmony with God's Will and the Truth of His Word, and those prayers are usually answered in an amazing and surprising way. We may wake up during the night and be prompted by the Spirit(s) to pray for certain people, situations, or other urgencies until we experience that the burden is lifted. Thus, the Spirit(s), with our willing permission, not only tell us what we should pray about; they empower us, illuminate our understanding of the Word, and even intercede for us (Rom. 8:26; 8:34). The Universal Christ, united in one body with Jesus, the only Son, and the Holy Spirit and their female expressions, are responsible for restoring the position of Adam and Eve and all their descendants (2 Cor. 5:19).

NOTE: When we (good/evil beings) pray, we acknowledge God as our Creator, sustainer, and ruler of the universe (not satan) and try to establish communication with Him/Her. When we continue to pray, we widen the channel between God (who lives within our Soul-Divine Spirit) and our physical self and becomes more real to us. We should pray in the morning (after waking) to empower our spirit and to fully align with our physical consciousness. We should also pray before falling asleep in the evening so that our spirit self or psyche (which separates more or less from our physical self) may roam around in the higher spirit world. Praying during the day becomes necessary, especially when we associate with people who are negative and also evil in a low spiritual environment. After the encounter with evil forces, it would be good for us to recharge in a church, prayer room, or shrine in our home.

As spiritually mature individuals, we pray for others who are in need of our help because they are not yet able to make contact with God directly. We take their psychological and spiritual burden upon ourselves and channel the Love and Truth of God to them. By praying daily for our spiritual children, we create a link or lifeline with them and other people we pray for. By continually working for the Lord, our countenance becomes brighter (Luk. 9:29), and our prayer may produce great effects (James 5:16).

Many mystics of Western and Eastern religions try to make contact with their Higher Self (Soul) and God by meditating for long periods of time and by using certain methods, such as quieting their mind and others. Through the continuous use of their special techniques, they eventually may succeed in aligning their Higher Self and the lower self (personality) and integrating them. (See "How to Meditate".)

Paul further counseled us to pray "with all prayer and supplication", which involves different kinds of prayer such as adoration and worship, thanksgiving, confession of sin, and other prayers which not only fulfill the need of the spiritual children but also that of their Heavenly Parents.

"Keep alert with all perseverance." As the Roman soldier cannot afford to close his eyes to the enemy, we should also keep our spiritual senses fully open when confronting evil forces in our prayers. "Continue steadfastly in prayer, being watchful in it" (Col. 4:2). We should always pray (Luk. 18:1) "constantly" (1 Thess. 5:17; Rom. 12:12). Praying without ceasing means that we should acknowledge the Creator in everything we do. In our vocal prayer, we should be insistent in our request (Phil. 4:6), and to ward off evil forces, we should pray with all our might and perseverance, calling on all those whom are able to help us. Finally, we should also pray for others, especially for those that are proclaiming the gospel. As Paul has it "that utterance may be given me in opening my mouth boldly to proclaim the mystery of the gospel" (Eph. 5:19). See also Col. 1:9; James 5:14, 16. See "Why Do We Need to Pray".

In our fight with evil forces, we should keep in mind what Paul said in 1 Cor. 10:13: "No temptation has overtaken you that is not common to man. God is faithful, and he will not let you be tempted beyond your strength, but with the temptation will also provide the way of escape, that you may be able to endure it."

Jesus Christ said to all of us, "Lo, I am with you always, to the close of the age" (Matt. 28:20).

God said, "Be strong and of good courage, do not fear or be in dread of them: for it is the Lord your God who goes with you; He will not fail you or forsake you" (Deut. 31:6; Hebr. 13:6).

#34 The Law of Karma

A. Introduction

The fundamental law of the universe is the law of karma, which works on the physical, emotional, and mental planes of life and must be worked out or returned on the plane they were sown. This law is, in some measure, expressed in physics as: "For every action there is an opposite and equal reaction" and philosophically: every action, word, emotion, and thought produces, in time, a reaction of like quality. Karma – a Sanskrit word meaning deed or action – is also known as the law of consequences or compensation. Applied to the moral sphere, it means: If we do good, good is returned; if we do evil, evil is returned.

Karma is simply the effect of the causes we have set in motion, positive or negative, returning to the doer. The law of karma is not only the law of retribution and punishment but, above all, it teaches, corrects, regulates, balances, and compensates on any level of the multidimensional universe. It seeks to be constructive and beneficial, and it functions as an ideal cosmic police force. This law is impersonal, neither good nor bad, and lets humans learn valuable lessons of life. Those lessons may return again and again in certain cyclic life patterns and will repeat themselves until we have learned them. Through the law of karma, God gives us opportunities to learn from our mistakes and live in harmony with the karmic law. God, however, does not and cannot interfere or suspend His law but leaves humans alone to make their own decisions on how they should act, so that they will grow quickly and wholesome to maturity. In addition, the law teaches individuals restraint, self-control, responsibility, self-reliance, patience, unselfishness, compassion, and forgiveness.

REMARK: It is very important that the people, especially in the Western world, understand that everyday life is governed by justice and not by chance. This will convince them that it is foolish and to their disadvantage to live a life of selfishness and wrongdoing because they can never escape the effects of their harmful and evil deeds.

---

[1] The Spanish-born philosopher Santayama (1863-1952) said that if people do not learn, they are condemned to repeat it.

[2] In order for us to grow even faster, God may at times send us trials and tribulations and let us overcome them. He does this for the sake of testing us, to prepare us for a mission, and to help us grow in character and personality. God may also put us in a situation where we must love and train a person we do not like in order to help us develop our love for all people.

This law should especially be taught to those whom, through ignorance, do harm to others and are then surprised that life is not treating them very well. They should be pitied, not hated or cursed, because they do not know what they are doing. Those people should learn to understand that good deeds and thoughts produce beneficial reactions, such as: gifts, opportunities, growth, etc., while bad deeds and thoughts produce unpleasant reactions, such as: deprivation, missing opportunities, backsliding, etc.

The law of karma corrects wrongdoers in a more accurate way than the criminal justice system is able to do. It is unerring, just, and its "punishment always fits the crime". The criminals not only carry the effects of their misdeed(s) with them in their degraded character but also convey the cause of the imbalance of the universe within them. In order to readjust equilibrium, criminals sooner or later get caught by the foolish mistakes they make or through other circumstances beyond their control. In many cases, the officers of the law are the channels for this correction. When someone is punished for the crime (according to the man-made laws of the land), the punishment meted out may be greater or lesser than the law of karma would permit. The sentence the criminal receives may depend on the laws, former cases, the jury, character of the judge, the persecutor, and defense lawyers. If the criminal gets away with a lesser sentence, he or she still has *to balance the remaining debt, and when the punishment is more than what is deserved, the universal law and other forces will work to reduce the sentence. The debts they have made to society can be paid off quicker when they serve others when confined, write to their victims, ask for forgiveness, pray and fast for them, and most importantly, read the Bible and other books for their physical, emotional, mental, and spiritual development. By doing so, they purify their personality, are reborn spiritually, and start living a divine life.

Capital punishment was usually carried out by those people whom were living under the mosaic dispensation because it was not possible for them, at that time, to restore themselves or receive rehabilitation from others. Therefore, they paid the ultimate price. In the New Testament dispensation, the ones whom have no regret of what they have done by taking the life of another should expect that their life likewise be taken. However, those whom feel deep regret and heartfelt

---

* "Truly, I say to you, you will never get out till you have paid the last penny" (Matt. 5:26).

sorrow (contrition) for what they have done and seek for ways to atone for their sins (especially those whom are living a divine life whom "are not under law but under grace" – Rom. 6:14 –) should not have to give up their life. Having been *forgiven by God, the criminals should be given a chance to redeem themselves, with the help of God-chosen individuals. The latter are mature, willing to sacrifice, and have an abundance of accumulated merit.

REMARK: The laws for the civic and moral conduct do not regulate the feeling and thinking of individuals, as the law of karma is able to do.

The law of return is universally understood as: "What goes around comes around"; "By doing good you will meet good"; "He got what was coming to him"; "You get what you deserve." People often say, "What did I do to deserve this?" or "Why did this happen to me?" Further, they say, "You brought it upon yourself" and "I deserve what I get." As the Dutch saying goes, "The one who digs a hole for another falls in that same hole"; "The one who throws a stone to heaven gets it back on his/her own head."

B. What Does the Bible Say about the Law of Karma?

"Whoever sheds the blood of man, by man shall his blood be shed" (Gen. 9:6).

"If my people who are called by my name humble themselves, and pray and seek my face and turn from their wicked ways, then I will hear from heaven, and will forgive their sin and heal their land" (2 Chronicles 7:14).

"Those who plow iniquity and sow trouble reap the same" (Job 4:8). See also Hosea 10:12-13.

Because "The eyes of the Lord are in every place" (Proverbs 15:3), "He who conceals his transgression will not prosper" (Proverbs 28:13).

"Cast your bread upon the waters, for you will find it after many days" (Ecclesiastes 11:1).

"If a thief steals money or goods, he/she pays double" (Exodus 22:7).

---

* Forgiveness is not meant here "to grant freedom from penalties or consequences of action" but "freedom from accusation, guilt, blame, and resentment".

"Tell the righteous that it shall be well with them, for they shall eat the fruit of their deeds. Woe to the wicked! It shall be ill with him, for what his hands have done shall be done to him" (Isaiah 3:10-11).

"Bring the full titles into the storehouse, that there may be food in my house; and thereby put me to the test, says the Lord of hosts, if I will not open the windows of heaven for you and pour down for you an overflowing blessing" (Malachi 3:10). See also the story of the widow of Zarephath and her son, and how they were miraculously fed (1 Kings 17:8-16) by giving all that they had to Elijah, the chosen servant of God. Compare with a similar story in Mark 12:42-44 of a widow who gave "everything she had" and the lad who gave "five barley loaves and two fish" (John 6:9).

The law of karma in Jesus' discourses is called sowing and reaping and is also known as the law of the harvest. It is expressed in Luke 6:37-38: "Judge not, and you will not be judged; condemn not, and you will not be condemned" (see also Matt. 7:1-2 and Rom. 2:1); "give, and it will be given to you; good measure, pressed down, shaken together, running over, will be put into your lap. For the measure you give will be the measure you get back."

"For all who take the sword will perish by the sword" (Matt. 26:52; Rev. 13:10).

The golden rule, which is in harmony with the law of sowing and reaping, is expressed in Matt. 7:12: "Whatever you wish that men would do to you, do so to them", or as it is usually worded, "Do unto others as you would have others do unto you."

Apostle Paul said in Gal. 6:7, 9, "Do not be deceived; God is not mocked, for whatever a man sows, that he will also reap." --- "And let us not grow weary in well-doing, for in due season [1]we shall reap, if we do not lose heart." In 2 Cor. 9:6-7, Paul said with full conviction, "he who sows sparingly will also reap sparingly, and he who sows bountifully will also reap bountifully. Each one must do as he has made up his mind, not reluctantly or under compulsion, for God loves a cheerful giver". In Romans 1:26, 27 it is recorded that the men and women whom committed dishonorable passion with their own gender received "in their own persons the due penalty for their error".

---

[1] "For we must all appear before the judgment seat of Christ, so that each one may receive good or evil, according to what he has done in the body" (2 Cor. 5:10).

Paul also elaborated in 1 Cor. 9:11, 14 "If we have sown spiritually good among you, is it too much if we reap your material benefit?" --- "Those who proclaim the gospel should get their living by the gospel" (see also Matt. 10:10; Luke 10:7-8). God will "lay it on their heart" to give to those who help humanity and especially the Divine Spirits or Souls of people to grow in any spiritual community. The importance of this growth is emphasized by Jesus Christ in Matt. 6:33, to "seek first his kingdom and his righteousness, and all these things (food-shelter-clothes) shall be yours as well". Thus, when we serve God, then God will look after all our material needs (not greed).

When we [2]leave the earth plane, we cannot take material things with us, not even our bodies. The only real gain we make in this life on earth is receiving spiritual treasures or riches, not earthly treasures (Matt. 6:19-21).

By receiving, understanding, assimilating, and becoming the Truth, our human spirit and our Divine Spirit (Soul) will come into its own by expressing pure human qualities and Soul qualities or the fruits (treasures) of our Divine Spirit (Gal. 5:22). Our surviving human spirit, united with one's Soul, has become substantial and no longer shadow-like or ghost-like. Thus the Soul, with its attributes or qualities, always lives in heaven, even when our physical body is still roaming this earth.

C. Practical Considerations of the Law of Karma

Paul said in Acts 20:35, "It is more blessed to give than to receive." It has also been said, "The gift you give to others is the gift you give to yourself." "For that ye give, that alone you have – that ye lose ye never had." For what you give away to others: your love, time, money (accumulated energy), labor, knowledge, power, etc., is what is really your own. Only when water was poured for others, became it wine (John 2:8-9).

---

[2] Etheric pictures are sometimes flashed before a dying person, which show the lessons learned and not learned, as well as achievements and failures of the life just lived. This "movie" of your life is being transferred from your dying physical and etheric bodies to your surviving spirit body.

REMARK: While living on earth in a physical body, we should first build up our spirit body so that it can house our Divine Spirit. The latter should also be developed and completely integrated, with the spirit body as its object.

When we help another, we help ourselves, but when we harm our neighbor, we harm ourselves. If we give out love, love comes back to us; if we hate someone, hate will be returned to us. If we defraud others, we shall become the victims of fraud and lose everything we have gained by fraud. When we cheat others, we find that we are cheated in the same way. If we steal from others, something of value will be stolen from us. If we grab the opportunities of others, our own will turn bitter. When we are treating our fellow workers badly in order to be promoted, we will be treated in a similar fashion. An attempt to find happiness at the expense of other people starts a chain of bad or "unlucky" occurrences in our lives.

By going through the "same" suffering and bitter experiences we have caused to others, we will eventually learn valuable lessons not to do harm to others or find out the *hard way that crime does not pay. We will then become convinced that any kind of wrongdoing can never be to our advantage because the bad effects of such actions will always return to us in the course of time.

It is exploitation when someone tries to steal another person's job, drive a competitor out of business, and take away the romantic affection of someone whom is already engaged to another person. The gains acquired through intimidation, domination, or control and by dishonesty are gains that cannot last long. Those persons feel insecure of what they have and are always afraid that they will lose what they control and possess, or that someone will take it away from them.

Some individuals prefer to live a life as a parasite or freeloader and excuse or justify themselves by saying that the world owes them a living. If they work at all, they try to steal as much time and things from their employer as they can. According to the law of karma, or to the principle of sowing and reaping, nothing in this life is handed to anyone who is able to work. The Bible says, "if anyone will not work, let him not eat" (2 Thess. 3:10). They should not think snugly that they could get anything for nothing. The persons either pay their debt to society now or they have to pay much later in ways and forms not of their liking, including ill-health. By not giving anything to society, the universe cooperates perfectly by not returning anything to them.

---

* Some people only seem to learn the hard way and do not want to learn by object lessons. As a Dutch saying goes, "The ones whom do not want to hear have to feel" (the consequences) – "Wie niet horen wil, moet voelen."

In the universe of law and justice, there are no free gifts; each person has just what he or she has earned. There is therefore no such thing as luck or chance. Many people whom experience a number of mishaps in their life usually attribute those calamities to "bad luck". When, thereafter, the karma has expanded its force, they become aware that they are back in a period of "good luck". The persons go through life being alternately thrust in "good or bad luck". They do not seem to realize that all that happens to them is the result of their own doing, because they have set in motion the causes of their "good or bad fortune". When they are in a bad period of their life, they may believe that of no fault of their own they are being punished or have fallen on hard times or "ill-luck".

The individuals whom believe that the universe might be run by chance are likely to say, "How I wish that my bad luck would end and that lady luck would bring me more good fortune in life". "Some guys get all the luck"; "You bring me good luck"; "I wish you luck"; "Wish me luck"; "Good luck"; "He /she just ran out of luck."

To paraphrase Emmet Fox, the 19th century American metaphysician: There is no such thing as luck. Nothing ever happens by chance. Everything good or bad that comes into our life is there as the result of an inescapable law, and we are the only operators of that law. Consciously or unconsciously, we have produced the desirable or undesirable conditions in our life, which we have ordered and are being delivered. However, when we think rightfully instead of wrongfully, conditions will improve at once, and all ill-health, poverty, and disharmony must disappear. Life need not be a battle; it can and should be a glorious mystical adventure.

D. The Law of Sowing and Reaping

A farmer who cultivates the soil and sows a particular kind of seed expects to harvest, in due time, the multiplied yield of what was planted. The farmer has complete trust in the law of the harvest and knows that he will reap, in the same field, the same kind of crop as that of the nature of the seed. In other words, if he has planted corn, he does not expect wheat (James 3:12). "For no good tree bears bad fruit, nor again does a bad tree bear good fruit" --- the good man produces good, and the evil man produces evil (Luke 6:43-45).

We reap in the same field, or our actions are worked out or balanced at the same plane (physical-emotional-mental) where we have sown. As expressed in karmic law: for every emotion felt (loving or hateful), for every idea or thought (positive or negative), for every word spoken (good or bad), and for every act committed (creative or constructive), the law adjusts, balances, and compensates. The result goes back to the feeler, thinker, speaker, and doer. Thus, each type of force works on its own plane, in the working out of its action and reaction. For instance, one person may give alms to a beggar wholeheartedly with sympathy, consideration, and a kind word, while another person gives his share in order to get rid of the beggar as a nuisance. Both persons have performed a good act on the physical plane, but the latter person did not earn any karma for the emotional and mental aspects of his/her being and, thus, is not rewarded from those planes.

From this it follows that by indulging in sexual fantasy or having lustful thoughts, the people are creating karma emotionally and mentally.

NOTE: Matt 6:4 says that we should give our alms in secret, "and your Father who sees in secret will reward you". As God's consciousness pervades the spiritual and physical universe, He knows what is going on at all times and all places, while His laws will reward and adjust. This reward will not only be good for one person or group but also for everyone else because He and His laws do not favor one over another. When God works to help one person, it is also good for another person.

Much of the accumulated karma, especially the psychological kind, may be discharged while one is living permanently on the inner planes. In order to wipe out the karma made on the physical outer plane, the surviving human spirit has to inspire the spirit of a suitable person living on earth to do good deeds with his/her physical body. This is not an easy task because the inspired earthly person does not always respond very well. In that case, the descendants of the diseased person of the inner plane have to fulfill this task while they are living on earth.

By inspiring others to do good deeds, the inspirer and the doer receive positive karma. Someone living on earth can likewise inspire or influence others to do good or bad. The positive or negative invisible result of the deed will then go back to the initiator and doer. By the same token, a dictator has the tendency to claim all accomplishments as his own when the people blindly obey him.

When the seed is sown, it may take some time to fully blossom. For example, the good seed the Pilgrim Fathers sowed is being reaped today in a greater measure than in the past. This multiplying effect can also be seen of famous pieces of art, music, and literature, which were created a long time ago.

As a farmer expects a manifold return of the seed he has planted, we likewise can and should expect (Mark 11:24) an abundant return of the seed money we have planted (Matt. 13:31-32) by giving to needy individuals and worthy organizations.

Our contribution to life may be compared to capital deposited in a bank. It is like a great cosmic reservoir of energy, wherein all our giving, services, offerings, prayers, and sacrifices are deposited.

We easily deplete our account when we continually ask for blessings without replenishing by serving and tithing. When we are spiritually bankrupt, we should not expect that God readily answer our prayer. Life is not treating us so generously as before; instead we are experiencing reverses or misfortunes. This is an indication that our "cash balance" is gone and that we must deposit "new capital" if we want to draw more benefits. When we have accumulated a considerable quantity of merit, we may receive some credit or desert when we have done something wrong so that the punishment is limited.

Finally, when we are really convinced that we shall reap what we sow, we should no longer consider ourselves smart by taking from others or seeking to gain by wrongdoing. Only a person lacking common sense and intelligence would try to get something for nothing and go against the universal law of karma, which is part of the body of God.

E. The Law of the Old and New Dispensation

The law of karma or natural law is especially relevant to people whom are living the life of the personality and to people whom are still living according to the Old Testament laws and traditions, which demand equal payment for the wrong done to you or to others. *This

---

* Parents who love their children should teach them consistently what is right or wrong. They should not tell them that a particular act is right today and wrong tomorrow. Otherwise, the children become confused and would give up efforts to improve themselves. The same is true for the developing human race, which would become confused when chance is ruling its life and not the law and perfect justice.

moral law and its Ten Commandments is known as the law of "life for life, eye for eye, tooth for tooth, hand for hand" (Exodus 21:24; Matt. 5:38). This law was in complete agreement with the many actions the Lord God of the Old Testament was indirectly responsible for in guiding His people. For example, in the time of and before Abraham, God was far removed from the consciousness of the people, and they identified their god(s) with the forces of nature they greatly feared. In the time of and before Moses, the people believed in one God, who sometimes appeared as a wrathful and ethical ruler they obeyed and feared. This was the operation of the karmic law, sometimes exercised by angels and directed to people whom had no direct relationship with God. Thus, the Israelites were often confronted with the harsh and severe law of karma.

> Hebrews 9:22 says: "Indeed, under the law almost everything is purified with blood, and without the shedding of blood there is no forgiveness of sin."

In the New Testament dispensation, Jesus Christ opened an opportunity through His work and sacrifice, that anyone whom accepted Christ as their Savior is no longer "under law but under grace" (Rom. 6:14). God is no longer a master to be feared. They are no longer servants of God, as in the Old Testament dispensation, but become His children, whom can relate to Him directly and accept Him as their Heavenly Parents. Thus, those in whom Christ is formed (Gal. 4:19) have become a "new creation" in Christ (2 Cor. 5:17), and the personality "I" or ego is no longer leading their life but their budding Christ or Divine Spirit (Gal. 2:20). Thus, the only sacrifice the people have to make in order to be accepted by God and re-enter the "Garden of Eden" is to accept Jesus Christ as their personal Savior, who overcame the sin of the first Adam by being obedient to God and by overcoming all temptations. However, the sins of karma, which the individual has made in his/her earthly life, and the sins of their immediate ancestors should also be absolved before it is possible of entering the Garden or commencing a clear Divine Life. This [1]clearing, or taking on the other's karma, is often done by saints of all times and religions, the people who brought them to Christ, or they may clear their own. The more karma the person(s) has accumulated, the more

---

[1] This clearing or suffering for sins (paying off a karmic burden) can be done by making sacrifices such as fasting, donating time and money, gifts, good works, long walks, praying to blot out sins, taking on another's burden, and the ultimate sacrifice: martyrdom. The blood of martyrs is known to be the seed of the church. Those sacrifices are also called: restitution, indemnity, penance, reparation, amends, atonement, redemption, and taking on another's karma.

215

they are under the domination of evil forces, who will do everything in their power to keep from having their subjects leave their "evil camp" and entering the Kingdom of God. For candidates to be completely liberated from their evil masters, they have to pay off their own karma, including (through sacrifices or indemnity) the ransom price (which is much less because of Christ's suffering and victory over satan) so that the evil masters no longer have any claim on them.

Living a divine life as Christ-like individuals or Divine Spirits, they no longer accumulate any karma and are able to forgive [2]sins (John 20:23) to those whom are sincerely sorry for what they have done. Although the latter persons – including backsliders – have repented and are forgiven by God, they still need to pay penance or indemnity when they have sinned in order to balance their karma until their Divine Spirit is in [3]complete control of their purified personality. These persons will accumulate much positive karma or merit by praying, witnessing, teaching, and continually serving the people. These individuals not only are able to forgive sins but also absolve all or part of it by taking confession and feeling much compassion for the sinner(s), while praying for them continually.

F. Family, Group, National, and Race Karma

As every cell is responsible for the proper working of the organs and parts of the whole body, each human being is responsible not only for individual karma but also for the ethical, moral, and spiritual conduct of the family, group, community, state, nation, race, world, and its karmic consequences. When one becomes a member of or associate with an organization, religion, or country, he or she is partaking, to some extent, in the collective karma of the relationships above.

The misery (or happiness) of any nation or race is the direct result of the thoughts and acts of individuals who make up the nation or race. [4]If they acted wickedly in the past, they will be treated severely in order to

---

[2] The violation of creeds and theological dogma is not always a sin, when this belief is not based upon the law of cause and effect. This law should be more feared than the fear of hell because it determines our life now and then.

[3] See "The Birth and Evolution of the Divine Spirit or Soul".

[4] Some people whom have no karmic liability have been gone "accidentally" somewhere else or are called away from a catastrophic event, miss the train, ship, or airplane. Yet other people are hurried to the disaster area or become involved in the karmic accidents.

restore harmony, such as conquest, [1]war, disease, plague, sterility (of women), etc., and some natural disasters such as earthquakes, volcanic eruptions, floods, crop failures, droughts, cyclones, hurricanes, tidal waves, etc.

For instance, ancient American people, the Egyptians, the Hawaiians, and others died out, while the Red Skins, Australians, Polynesians, and other unique people are in the process of dying out (through the force of evolution) unless they unite with a more advanced race. Classic Greece and the Roman empires were extinguished as a nation because the leaders were more interested in their own well being than the welfare of the people. Spain and Portugal lost their splendid position of power by committing national crimes against the conquered people, while Holland and England lost their colonies. They all came to conquer and wanted the oppressed people to serve them instead of guiding and serving the people according to the principles of Christ. During the reigns of Louis XIV and XV of France, the well to do acted with selfishness and indifference to the poor and uneducated, which also happened in the reign of the latest Czar of Russia. The result was the French and Communist Revolution. It was easy for Alexander the Great to conquer Persia in his "war of revenge" because the latter had conquered Macedonia in Greece 150 years earlier. The Jewish race, which was most cruelly treated by the Antichrist nation of Germany, acted in a passive meek manner as lambs going to the slaughter. As many white slaves were physically and spiritually liberated in the Roman Empire through the Gospel of Christ, so were many black people liberated when they came at age, especially when they accepted Christ as their Lord and Savior. They expressed themselves as little children of God in those times in the Americas by spiritual song and dance.

REMARK: Many people whom are working for employers still feel that they are slaves, especially when they are humiliated by those bosses who enjoy ruling over their subordinates with evil power.

G. How Does Karma Work?

In order to believe in the law of karma, I shall attempt here to give a reasonable explanation for those individuals whom cannot be convinced of the working of the law by psychic and intuitive appeal alone.

---

[1] Hitler had the armistice signed in the same railroad car and in the same forest as that in which defeated Germany had signed the armistice ending World War I.

A stone, when thrown into a pond (a deed done), disturbs the still water (create disharmony) and causes wavelets to flow around and outward (and send karmic ripples or vibration outbound). This activates all the water particles on its way (effecting different levels of aether) to the bank surrounding the pond. Thus, by impacting upon the surrounding boundary, it brings forth an instantaneous or delayed rebound – depending on the power and nature of the impact – to the initiator of the action, which can be physical, emotional, or mental.

The result of the good and evil deeds, feelings, and thoughts goes to the doer of the action, according to the cyclic law, which is independent of time. Thus, the law of karma always works because all action, desire, and thought disturbs, to some degree, the equilibrium of the universe, and such disturbances always seek to return to the state of balance.

A stone thrown in the air is acted upon by its boundary or gravitation, and the result is that the stone falls back to the earth with an impact and time depending on the initial power.

It reacts and returns to the source of its origin like an echo.

The universe as the body of God is like the human body. It consists of many organisms, which are interdependent of each other. As the pain of a finger is felt by all the parts of the human body, so any negative action is felt throughout the cosmic organism. Did not the Bible say that the Father knows when a sparrow is falling to the ground (Matt. 10:29)? Since everything is inter-linked and interacts with every other being, no entity can live separate from others. All beings are affected by the causes that are set in motion by other entities, which reacts to the performer or the thinker in the degree of the force used.

Everything we think, say, or do becomes part of an energy or force that we send out into the universe and also produces its own vibrations in the various wrappings or auras of our human spirits. Every experience is engraved in our spirit and is always with us as if it were adhered or stuck to our being. We may carry it with us as a dark and heavy burden if this experience resulted in suffering and distress to another being, and it also hinders our moral development. Thus, each time we misbehave, the karmic consequences of our action become attached to us. For example, when we steal, the effect of the deed infuses into our human spirit and remains there. On the other hand, positive emotions, thoughts, and acts result in positive vibrations, which also enter in the makeup at different levels of our existence.

If we take and do not give back, we create imbalance or bad karma, which registers in our subconscious, and we take it with us wherever we go. This negative action also creates imbalance in the universe as a whole, and it will do anything in its power to restore its balance of harmony by making us give back what we have taken. For instance, the debt will be extracted from us when we are and have acted in a selfish and greedy way.

When humans, unlike nature, use their free will to act for their own selfish ends at the expense of the whole, they become ugly, repulsive, distorted, and create harmful karma, which is a disturbance of the harmonious energy of the universe. The mineral, plant, and animal kingdoms (when left alone) create harmony in nature and appear beautiful because they are in tune with the plan of our Creator.

The way the law of karma responds to our actions is proof that we have done the right thing because after we have paid our obligation, we feel that we no longer owe somebody, group, or society anything anymore. Thus, the feeling of debt and guilt is no longer with us. By the same token, when we have given a lot, we feel an assurance that the universe will take care of us.

The activities, moods, or attitudes of a person set up vibratory patterns – harmony or disharmony – within his or her life and begin to influence the individual. Those patterns cannot be prevented or forced to operate contrary to the causes set in motion and, thus, have to work themselves out on the different planes.

Thus, there is no way to escape or cheat the law of karma, and our thoughts, words, and works are recorded in the "Book of Life" by none other than yourself (Rev. 20:12; Phil. 4:3). Besides, the motives of everything we have ever done are known not only to God but also to those who see with the eye of the Spirit.

The action of karma proceeds under the cyclic law, which is independent of time. The effect may be experienced instantly or it can be delayed. In the material realm, action and reaction can be *instantaneous and have the same impact on the objects. In the moral

---

* In chemistry, if the chemical equilibrium is disturbed, it takes some time to neutralize the disturbance.

sphere, it may take much longer, and the action is not always the same as the reaction. When our feeling or thought is selfish, the energy it creates moves in a close curve and returns and expends itself upon its own level. However, when the thought or feeling is unselfish and spiritual, it moves in an open curve, touching the higher realms and bringing back great rewards.

H. The Truth about Reincarnation

Reincarnation – (Latin *re-in* = again, *carnis* = flesh). To come again in a human body as a human spirit or soul. It should not be confused with transmigration or metempsychosis, which is re-embodiment in other kinds of living beings, such as plants and animals, whom were often worshipped. Today, transmigration has generally been accepted as an act of regression.

Reincarnation and karma, as an interwoven system, are the cardinal principles of the Hindu, Buddhist, Jain, Parsee, and Sikh religions and are rejected by Judaism, Christianity, and Islam. We also find reincarnation or rebirth among certain early Greek philosophers, such as Pythagoras, Empedocles, and Plato, and it has been accepted by some segments of the Western mystery tradition. It has been said that Pythagoras (d. 500 B.C.) and the Greeks learned the ideas of reincarnation from their contacts with the culture and religions of India.

Reincarnation, together with its sister law of karma, is an ancient belief that can be traced to early Hindu teaching after early vedic times. At some point or period, the doctrine was probably developed in order to make sense of (the more evil than good-oriented) human life, which was full of suffering, and to give them security and hope for a better future life. This was also the goal of Buddhists and *Middle Age nominal Christians whom were looking with great anticipation for the good life in the nirvana state or in the heavenly state of being, which those Christians thought could only be realized in the afterlife or heaven.

Adherents of the theory of reincarnation believe that the Bible proves the idea of re-embodiment by saying that John the Baptist was

---

* Many people of that time also believed in eternal punishment of hell when they seriously violated God's law and (or) the teaching of the church. This, of course, cannot be true because that would be a great injustice, whereby the effect is all out of proportion with the cause.

the reincarnation of Elijah, the Old Testament prophet. Howbeit, John was fulfilling the same mission as that of Elijah to prepare the way for the Lord (Malachi 4:5; Luke 1:17). Besides, Elijah's reappearance is not a case of reincarnation because he had not died in a normal way but had, instead, been carried in a bodily form into heaven by a chariot of fire (2 Kings 2:1-11). Furthermore, Hebrews 9:27 disproves the idea of rebirth by saying, "it is appointed for men to die once".

Reincarnation is the belief that the soul or the real person not only survives physical death but is also born in a succession of different physical bodies and, thus, many lives on earth. The doctrine further states that the law of karma requires that humans be born again and again if the karmic accounts are not balanced in the course of one life. This belief also allows human beings more than one span of life in which to learn the [1]many experiences and lessons of life and to achieve harmony with cosmic laws. Further, reincarnation is caused by karma settled in former lives but is also the means by which karma can be worked off or balanced. When humans, for example, in previous embodiments have done much evil and harm or have been guilty of little, they will be born and grow up in unfavorable or favorable circumstances. Thus a child, for instance, may have a sickly body, a weak character, a dull mind, a sullen disposition, and other complexes and shortcomings, whereas the other child may have a healthy body, a strong character, intelligent mind, pleasant disposition, and other natural abilities and talents. The doctrine of reincarnation seems to solve the apparent [2]inequalities in people's lives and the [3]problem of evil and injustice by having created, in former lives, the causes of the reward or punishment, which are meted out in this life.

---

[1] In the ideal world of the future, people will live much longer by having a stronger immune system and will not have to cling to only one profession or occupation for economic reasons. They have more free time to pursue all kinds of hobbies and have more opportunities for object learning.

[2] To be born in wealthy circumstances is not always a true blessing. The rich, especially in the world of good/evil, are apt to become selfish by not serving others, have less compassion for the ones who suffer, and are less resourceful, inventive, and persevering than those whom have to make a living. The latter individuals, especially in the world which is in the process of restoration, understand that life on earth is a workshop, a boot camp, a training ground, or schoolroom. They develop valuable soul qualities such as: courage, self-respect, initiative, determination, strength, creativity, patience, confidence, honesty, depth, duty, honor, and forgiveness. Thus, the rich whom have no problems must be a problem to God, for they are not learning about life nor love and do not grow much in their mental and spiritual development.

[3] The problem of evil deals with the question, "If God is all-powerful and good, why does He allow so much suffering in the world?" He has given the people free will and responsibility to have dominion of the world and, therefore, cannot interfere. Thus, if the people do not act right, they have to bear the consequences.

However, the goal of Hindus, Buddhists, and others is not merely to settle karmic accounts or to reincarnate in more favorable circumstances but to go beyond the "compulsion of karma and rebirth", or as in the Buddhist expression, "the ceasing of the round – or wheel – of birth and death" (samsara). By attaining "moksha" or liberation, the Hindu will no longer be trapped in the cycle of death and rebirth, and the Buddhist, upon enlightenment or "nirvana", is free from karma, rebirth, and suffering.

The law of karma is a natural law; the doctrine of reincarnation is a man-made law and is not completely true in all of its applications. People whom believe in reincarnation do not want to accept and take any responsibility for the harmful deeds their parents and immediate ancestors have made. However, the Bible clearly says in Exodus 20:5 that God is "visiting the iniquity of the fathers upon the children to the third and fourth generation". This saying is also true for parents whom were not able to balance their karma and, thus, did not get punished while they were living on earth. After death, these parents have an opportunity to absolve their negative karma or sins by influencing with their human spirits (not reincarnate) certain people to do good, especially those the parents have harmed while they were still living on earth. If this does not work out, their children or grandchildren have to pay the karmic price.

Hindus and Buddhists believe that through a life of suffering, they can pay off their karmic debt, while Janism believes that the soul can be released from the cycle of birth, death, and rebirth by the existence of austere practices. Mature Christians believe that it is possible not only to pay for their own sins or karmic burden but also that of their brethren and others by fasting, good works, and other forms of indemnity. This atoning for others can be made much lighter when a church, group, or organization as a whole is also praying and supporting the above efforts by paying the indemnity.

REMARK: Many people whom believe in reincarnation have become convinced of this theory because they have felt or sensed (by reading ancient history or visiting historical sites and thinking about certain people of the past) that they have played a part in that history. They also believe that they have lived in or near that site or have been those people. However, those people are human spirits whom are influencing their lives to do good (or bad) and others whom are trying to express themselves through them. When the people are hypnotized, the subconscious of the person (which is the conscious of the spirit body) may express itself, or the conscious of the influencing or overshadowing spirit may come through. Those spirits may be spirit helpers, teachers, evil spirits, or undeveloped earthbound spirits which have not found the Light. Finally, the belief in reincarnation is known to have caused schizophrenia, obsession, and possession.

This attitude is quite different from that of the Hindus, whom have a tendency to say to those whom need the most help, "they are suffering their karma from a previous life, and it is not good to interfere because it is their fate". Others may say, "the sufferers brought it on themselves; let them take the consequences". A guru who passes by beggars in front of his asram may think, "they should not be helped; otherwise they would not have happy future lives". Those whom believe in reincarnation may easily fall in the above described attitudes and are no longer their "brother's keeper" (Gen. 4:9). They do not have much compassion for the sick, the poor, and the injured and easily pass them by on the roadside (Luk. 10:30-37). However, Sister Therese proved them all wrong.

The law of karma is a judicial system without a personal judge. Although God cannot go against His own natural law because it is part and parcel of His body, He is able to make concessions and intervention by sacrificing Himself through saints of all religions. He does this in order to protect and also warn His and Her little children, whom are in the process of restoration, against the severe workings of the law.

In conclusion, we can say that suffering for another is a divine privilege and great honor.

As it has been said in the Dutch language: "Het is heerlyk om te lyden zodat we Holland kunnen bevryden" – It is a pleasure to suffer and to have endured, so that our nation can be liberated and cured.

#35 Humans Have Physical, Psychic, and Spiritual Senses

A. Description of the Psychic Senses

Humans are not only in possession of the five physical senses, such as hearing, sight, touch, smell, and taste, but also with the corresponding psychic senses of their human spirits, such as:

1) **Clairaudience** – (French, "clear audio") or inner hearing, the ability to hear clear sounds inaudible to the ear, such as spirit voices and other psychic sounds.

Sounds may be heard from one's subconscious mind or psyche, but in most cases, sounds are received from entities outside themselves, such as spirit guides and angels. For example, Joan of Arc, the Deborah (Judges 4) of France, heard "voices" of deceased Christian saints, and Mohammed received the Koran of the archangel Gabriel. An angel of the Lord appeared to the shepherds in the field and said to them, "Be not afraid; for behold, I bring you good news of a great joy which will come to all the people; for to you is born this day in the city of David a Savior, who is Christ the Lord" (Luk. 2:8-11).

Human inspiration is often accompanied by hearing one's name and experiencing another force or external impulse. Many human spirits of different levels of the spirit world try to influence those people on earth whom are, in many cases, already competent and prepared to receive a particular inspiration, vision, or *dream. William Blake, Johann Wolfgang Goethe, Shakespeare, John Milton, Wolfgang Amadeus Mozart, Ludwig van Beethoven, Raphael, the spiritualist Andrew Jackson Davis, Alice Bailey, Hilarion, Ramala, Ramtha, Course in miracles, New Age author Ruth Montgomery, and many other poets, artists, authors, speakers, musicians, and scientists have been inspired in different ways. Whole and parts of books have been written while the author was in some (light) trance, as well as many other writings, poems, paintings, compositions of music, inventions, and other famous and unknown works. Examples are: "The Strange Case of Dr. Jekyll and Mr. Hyde, Harriet Beecher Stowe's "Uncle Tom's Cabin", and in part, the original Star Trek movie. Another example is the book "The Lowly Life and Bitter Passion of Our Lord Jesus Christ and His Blessed Mother". This writing was received in 1833 by the German

---

* If the spirit and divine worlds are not able to directly influence a human being, they may try it through dreams. Important problems are often solved while our bodies sleep. Therefore we have the saying: "Let me sleep on it."

Augustinian nun Catherine Emmerich and was accepted by Catholics as being divinely inspired.

2) **Clairvoyance** – (French, "clear vision") or inner sight, to see clearly objects, persons, and events that are of the present and distant in space and time (past or future), outside the range of normal vision.

There are three states of clairvoyance: spontaneous (while the event is taking place), precognition or premonition (before the event has taken place), and post-cognition or retro-cognition (after the event has taken place). The encyclopedia of parapsychology speaks of x-ray clairvoyance (to see into closed space), medical clairvoyance (to see inside a human body), travel clairvoyance (to see a distant scene), and platform clairvoyance (to see human spirits). Clairvoyance has been used to help law enforcement agencies, as well as parents, in locating missing children. However, when the gift of clairvoyance is used for financial and self-gain, it will deteriorate.

As explained in the next pages, there are basically two kinds of clairvoyance or second sight, the lower and the higher. The lower clairvoyant uses the lower energy centers, such as the solar plexus, and the involuntary sympathetic nervous system as the means of perception, which is psychic in nature. The higher clairvoyant uses the upper energy centers, such as the "third eye", and the voluntary cerebrospinal nervous system as the means of perception, which is spiritual in nature. As lower desires are ruling the life of the former, the intuition is perceived as lower. However, when higher desires are ruling the life of the latter, the intuition is perceived as higher. There are, however, also clairvoyants whom operate more or less from their heart energy center. They are able to register higher emotions, such as love, devotion, aspiration, compassion, charity, and have an awareness of the suffering of humanity.

Samuel used his clairvoyant abilities not only for the Lord, but also used it to find lost asses for the people who came to him (1 Sam. 9:11-20). The prophet Elisha, who was sitting in his house, saw in a vision that someone was sent to kill him (II Kings 6:32), while he also saw and heard from a long distance what the king of Syria was scheming against Israel (II Kings 6:12).

NOTE: Individuals whom have a highly developed psychic ability are not always spiritual. They often do not believe in God.

3) Clairsentience – (French, "clear sensation or feeling") or inner touch, to perceive impressions or information by a feeling called gut feeling, hunch, or lower intuition.

[1]Most people have this ability and unknowingly express this particular extrasensory perception by saying, "I have a strong feeling", "I have a gut feeling", "I have a hunch", "My intuition tells me." It is experienced as an instinct or a "feeling in the bones" and is operative in little children as well as in animals (Numbers 22:22-27).

The solar plexus center is the seat of the lower psychic sentient life and is often referred to as the instinctual brain. Lower psychic impressions or energies from the human spirit are conveyed via the energy centers of the etheric body to the nerve centers of the physical body, particularly the solar plexus.

Because psychic energies are transmitted throughout the whole body, it is therefore difficult to control those impressions and feelings. The solar plexus center is usually fully active in those people and [2]mediums whom are more emotionally oriented. However, when they develop their mental abilities, the psychic faculties come more under their control, so that they are less likely to be used and abused by psychic forces of the lower planes, whom can only work through the lower psychic centers. The psychics also receive, from the lower planes through their open solar plexus center and others, lower emotions concerning personal relationships, which can be positive and negative, such as positive thinking, fear, anger, and lower desires. They may also encounter earthbound spirits and, in some cases, spirits from the lowest region of the spirit world.

---

[1] This ability is more developed in people who sense someone's presence, have felt someone's eyes on them without seeing them, like or dislike someone instantaneously, and sense their moods without communication.

[2] A medium serves as a link or channel between the physical and spirit world and, unlike the clairvoyant who sees images on the mind screen, a medium seldom recalls the thoughts or words that have come through during a trance state. A medium has psychic abilities, is sensitive to the spirit world, and is able to communicate with the "other world" or with the discarnate spirits on the "other side".

NOTE: Mediums whom are not in control of their psychic facilities work through their lower psychic centers and the involuntary sympathetic nervous system. They sometimes have their "off days" because the power "to see" is not always under their control (as that of the voluntary clairvoyant), with the result that they say anything in order to satisfy their customer. Like mediums, most Hindus and Indians have no trouble believing in the existence of the spirit world because their psychic bodies are not as much enmeshed in the physical bodies, as in the case of the average Western individual.

REMARK: Clairsentience is a lower intuition or inner knowing which happens spontaneously and bypasses the process of thinking. However, the information received is usually not clear.

4) **Clairscent** – (French, "clear smelling") or inner smell, to smell a fragrance or odor without the presence of any substance.

5) **Clairgustance** – (French, "clear tasting") or inner taste, to taste a substance without the use of taste buds.

B. The Mental and Psychic Abilities

The human spirit or psyche, like its physical counterpart, is also in possession of a brain or psychic mind, which governs the spirit body. The human spirit (mind – self – soul – spirit – astral body) is further equipped with mental facilities, such as:

Discrimination – mental ability to distinguish between good and evil

Telepathy – mental communication, the transferring of thoughts (mental states, images, feelings, sensations) from one being to another, without the use of words
This perception is strengthened if there is a strong emotional bond or psychic rapport between individuals such as between identical twins, parents and children, brothers and sisters, friends, associates, and especially between lovers, whom are able to sense the unspoken expressions of affection of the other. For a good communication to exist between the parties, their mind and consciousness should not be engaged in other matters. They should be in a relaxed and attentive state, and their brainwaves should be in an "alpha rhythm mode". Communication of feeling also exists between animals, humans and animals, [1]especially with their pets.

Telekinesis or Psychokinesis (PK) – influencing an object or event with the mind over a distance
[2]It is the power of mind over matter, the ability of thought or mental power to affect objects without any physical contact. Some scientists have explained that this is possible when the strong electromagnetic

---

[1] Animals of all kinds often perceive the intention of the owner when he or she is still a few miles away. The animal knows when the owner is on his or her way home by waiting for their arrival at the entrance door.
[2] Examples of PK are: influencing the throwing of dice, spoon or metal bending, splitting or dissolving clouds in the sky, temperature raising and lowering, etc.

force fields of some individuals influence the force fields of the objects. In addition, the object is also effected by intense concentration of etheric energy radiating from the eye and other places of the head and the body. Spontaneous movements of objects generally happen at moments of crisis and change in the lives of individuals. Sensitive electrical and electronic appliances and instruments may break down; watches or clocks may stop. As the innate etheric or vital body affects the physical body of an individual, it also may influence devices in close proximity of the body in a destructive way when the etheric body is out of harmony.

NOTE: Communication between evolved people on earth and in the higher spirit world is by thought-transference, without formulating thoughts into words. Thus, for them, there is no longer a language barrier. Telepathic communication is more swift and accurate than verbal communication, without any barrier of space, time, and matter. One does not have to seek for words to express correctly because emotions and thoughts speak clearer than words. It is much more difficult to deceive, lie, pretend, or be a hypocrite. However, as individuals must discipline their words, they should also learn to discipline and control their thoughts because all actions are the result of thought. Besides, as the spoken words can be heard, the thoughts expressed (not held within) can be known. Thought is the creative force of the universe. It can create, build, empower, and destroy. As the saying goes: "Thoughts are things", "What we think will come to pass", "Thoughts held in mind produce after their kind", and "We tend to get what we expect."

Psychometry – to receive information of things touched or in close vicinity with it

By touching an object, one tunes in to the energy field of that object. When it has been used by an individual, such as a ring or watch, one may receive impressions of the energy field of the object and that of the person who has worn the ring, watch, or other ornaments. This combined energy field or pattern is very unique and is like a fingerprint. Thus, specific information of the owner (and former owners) of the object can be obtained by merely tuning to the energy field (and its emanating vibration) of that object. This information may contain current or future events relating to that person, people, associating with that individual, and even the place where he or she may be, by forming a psychic connection with the object. Psychometry is, therefore, an efficient detective tool for finding missing persons, bodies, or solving crimes.

Because unseen radiation and thought waves from ourselves leave their imprints on everything we *"touch", these impressions can be picked up by psychometrists whom believe that every object carries its history, like a tape or video recorder, in its etheric counterpart. They also believe that much of history can be revealed by holding objects of antiquity or being in close touch with monuments, shrines, rocks, and bones (of saints), which have the ability to retain recordings of scenes and people for a very long time. This is especially true of precious stones. In 1953, the Dutch clairvoyant Gerard Croiset gave descriptions of cave-dwelling people and their religious ceremonies by working with only a tiny bone fragment of those people.

REMARK: However, in everyday life, we have to handle money (coins and notes) which are usually charged with unpleasant magnetism, and we also are in need of a haircut, which may be psychically pleasant or objectionable. Eating utensils and food in restaurants tend to be charged with the magnetism of those who handle or come near it. When staying in a hotel room, which has been occupied by person(s) of low character, it can be very objectionable, especially for those whom are living a divine life. Through the use of the bedding and sleeping on the same pillow as the former occupant, this may be the cause of unpleasant dreams. It is therefore good to purify the food one buys and the room one is staying in by sprinkling water and salt, which you have blessed by praying over it.

NOTE: As each person is unique, he or she looks different, has his/her own fingerprint, D.N.A., and odor so that the person can be tracked down by police and hunting dogs. They also express themselves in their own handwriting, have their own particular astrological sign, which was imprinted the moment they were born, and also have their own name, which indicates who they really are. However, when they are spiritually born and start living a divine life, they become a different creature (Eph. 4:22-24) and assume a new name, as the name of Saul changed to Paul (Acts 13:9) and Simon to Peter (Matt. 16:17-18). To find someone quickly who is living in the spirit world (or on earth) is not by dialing his or her telephone number (or by other means), but by sounding their keynote, which can be obtained by holding an object which has belonged to him or her. We then put ourselves "en rapport" or in tune with the individual by sounding his or her psychic/spiritual sound or chord, which is their true name.

---

* An object which has been in close contact with an individual will absorb that individual magnetism or vital fluid and will tend to reproduce, in the other person who touches or wears it, the same state of feeling and thought with which it is charged. For example, the feelings of devotion and awe exude from the walls of cathedrals and churches of those who built them with reverence and devotion, and of all the people who have visited and worshipped in those places.

Levitation and Teleportation – raises an animate or inanimate object into the air, contrary to the laws of gravitation and transports them
Some spiritualists say that this will occur when the gravitational field around the object is changed. Examples of levitation in the Bible we find, "And as soon as I have gone from you, the Spirit of the Lord will carry you whither I know not" (I Kings 18:12, see also II Kings 2:11, 16). "Then the Spirit lifted me up and took me away" (Ezek. 3:12, 14; 8:3; "and brought me to the east gate of the house of the Lord" (Ezek. 11:1, 24; 43:5). "And when they came up out of the water, the Spirit of the Lord caught up Philip; and the eunuch saw him no more, and went on his way rejoicing. But Philip was found at Azotus" (Acts 8:39, 40). "And in the fourth watch of the night he came to them, walking on the sea" (Matt. 14:25). Levitation also happened to St. Francis of Assisi (1186-1226), St. Joseph of Copertino (1603-1663), and also to the spiritualist/medium Daniel Dunglas Home (1833-1886).

Examples of Spirit Writing

We may find such examples in the following verses: The Lord "gave to Moses, --- the two tables of testimony, tables of stone, written with the finger of God" and "delivered by angels" (Ex. 31:18, 34:1; Acts 7:53; Gal. 3:19^b). He also gave Moses, Bezalel, and Oholiab instructions for the building of the Tabernacle (Ex. 26:30; Acts 7:44; Ex. 31:1-11, 36:1, 2), and to David directions for the building of the Temple, which David gave to Solomon to complete (1 Chron. 28:11, 12, 19). Direct Spirit writing occurred when, to all the guests of King Belshazzar of Babylon, suddenly a human hand appeared, which wrote on the wall of the king's palace, "Mene, mene, tekel, and parsin." The days of your kingdom have been "numbered", "weighted --- and found wanting", "is divided and given to the Medes and Persians" (Dan. 5:1-5, 25).

Astral projection – the ability to travel outside the physical body during sleep or trance
This projection or separation from the physical body can be controlled or uncontrolled. In the first instance, the individual knows what is happening and is able to guide his or her spirit. It is called lucid dreaming. They usually exit from the head energy center, while in the second instance, the individual exits from a lower energy center. The separation happens more fully by those whom went through a "near death experience". Some of them were able to watch how doctors tried to save their bodies, while others met with deceased relatives in a world of great beauty, serenity, and peace.

Materialization – may occur whereby ectoplasm (an etheric substance) exudes from a medium and is also drawn from people nearby to engulf and solidify a human spirit, thereby making it visible and touchable.

Apportation – Animate or inanimate objects or apports can disintegrate (dematerialize by changing their atomic structure to an etheric substance) and reintegrate (materialize) in the presence of a physical medium and with the help of spirits. Those apports (etheric substances) are able to pass through closed doors and walls to the séance room. "And when I looked, behold, a hand was stretched out to me, and lo, a written scroll was in it" (Ezek. 2:9-10).

Healing – We can make a distinction between two kinds of healing, the mental or subjective and the spiritual or objective. In the first instance, healing is accomplished by people whom radiate such a strong energizing force field that they cure others without any physical contact by merely being in their presence. The result of the spiritual or faith healing is dependent upon the belief of the patient in their healer, so that the healing forces of the universe can easily flow between the healer and its object(s). Jesus Christ used the above methods of healing in a most effective way by first asking the people to be healed to have faith in Him or give some demonstration of their faith. The healing God forces can then be released, flowing through Jesus to the people to be healed, especially to those whom have been touched.

NOTE: The above are the most important mental, psychic, and spiritual facilities. We may add here: mental projection, Kirlian and psychic photography, independent voice, trance, public mediumship, poltergeist, death and birth sciences, as well as divination, scrying, hypnotism, eyeless sight, aura reading, percussion, dreams, bio-feedback, psychic defense and attack, and thought forms. Also, dealing with obsession and possession, imagination, daydreaming, hallucination, talisman, spell, curse, visualization, meditation, prayer, contemplation, realization, and cosmic consciousness are among the numerous facilities, sciences, and expressions that are made possible.

C. Awakening of the Psychic Senses

The descendants of Adam and Eve, throughout history, kept a certain sensitivity and vague belief towards the animate and inanimate "psychic world". The degree of their evolvement can be seen in little children of today, who are also sensitive to the unseen world(s). However, many of them soon lose this ability because they are often told by their parents not to talk to "their imaginary invisible friends".

Those children [1]represent the undeveloped people of the past whom were also quite sensitive and perceived knowledge spontaneously by using their lower intuition. They certainly are more intuitive than the [2]"intellectual grown-ups" of the Western world whom, after the Middle Ages, became increasingly materialistic.

For those whom have reached a high degree of moral development, that is, when the physical body is pure, the emotional sheath is stable and steady, the mental part is developed, and they are under the control of one's evolving Divine Spirit. The individuals may then try to awaken their lower and higher psychic senses. One of the ways they can accomplish this is by believing in the existence of the invisible world. The dormant psychic senses will then slowly awaken and become stronger when the persons also exercise those senses. This one can do by trying to [3]hear spirit voices from people living on earth (telepathy) or from diseased individuals or spirit guides. Try to see "spirit beings before going to sleep" and "to imagine" who will be calling you on the phone, and who is or will be knocking on your door, or what moving object will come around the corner of the street. In addition, the dormant senses may open more by:

Spiritual exercises such as prayer, meditation, visualization, fasting, and yoga exertions (posture-breathing-kundalini); Moving exercises such as jogging, marching, swimming, and dancing; Through sounds such as music, song, chanting, and rhythmic beats. To get our body out of the way by sleep, (self) hypnosis, dream, daydreaming, deprivation, alcohol, and drugs. To be in "mystical" environments such as mountains, valleys, deserts, caves, recluses, churches, shrines, museums, special areas in the world, and the action (force field changes) of the sun, moon (full moon), and weather conditions will also shift consciousness. To use physical aids such as crystal (balls), precious stones, mirrors, polished surfaces, (television-computer screens), water surfaces (fishing), fires, flashing lights, scents, and the

---

[1] It is a known philosophical fact that growing children recapitulate, in their lives, the development of humanity as a whole.

[2] Most intellectuals have developed only a lower concrete mind and not a higher abstract mind. Through the development of the latter, the divine person will come more easily on its own, equipped with its higher psychic faculties and working through the evolving and controlled mind of the personality.

[3] When you suddenly know something without having a clue of how you know it, then this information is usually transmitted from their minds to yours.

NOTE: By cultivating a divine life, the psychic senses will open spontaneously and much faster when the energy of the regenerated Divine Spirit gives "fuel" to the psychic capacity.

silver cup from which Joseph prophesized (Gen. 44:4-5). See also Ex. 28:30.

D. Beings from the Multi-Dimensional Worlds

Because likes attract likes, individuals will only relate with those spirits whom are like themselves. People whom are carnal and weak and who do not use their psychic faculties to serve the human race should, therefore, not attempt to communicate with beings from different dimensions. They will only make contact with earthbound spirits (those whom have not yet gone through the "tunnel" towards the light), low and evil human spirits (with or without bodies), fallen angels (demons), low-grade fairies, and extra-terrestrial beings. They all are able to live or share the same space or physical atmosphere but at different "vibration levels" or dimensions of existence, permeating and interpenetrating one another as, for example, air in water, water in sand, and sand in a sponge. Thus, behind the visible world are the invisible universes which are hidden from the physical senses but can be discovered by developing the psychic and spiritual senses. We are completely immersed in those multidimensional worlds, whereby the highest and most sublime dimension is the world of God because "in Him we live and move and have our being" (Acts 17:28).

Humans not only live in a physical universe but also participate in the psychic and divine worlds, each with its many realms and domains, because in our "Father's house are many mansions" (John 14:2), which is "a house not made with our hands" (2 Cor. 5:1). As there are different auras around a human being, each extending beyond the smaller, so there are concentric zones around the earth which comprise the different levels of the spirit world with the highest encompassing all the lower zones. Knowing all this makes living very interesting, answering the many questions humans have pondered throughout the ages.

NOTE: Earthbound spirits are those whom are ignorant about life after death, have suddenly died, including many soldiers of the recent battle fields of the world, and those whom are not able or do not want to break their tie with the people of the earth. Of the latter, many are overly materialistic and sensual and do not want to give up their desire and craving for the physical addiction to alcohol, sex, drugs, and other indulgences.

Those who have committed suicide (and other acts of violence) have a tendency to repeat the same act in the same place by inducing sensitive earth people to do the same. We find examples of suicide in 1 Sam. 31:4 wherein

Saul fell on his sword, as well as in 2 Sam. 17:23 and Matt. 27:5, when Ahithophel and Judas hanged themselves. In 73 A.D., 40 years after the crucifixion of Jesus, 960 Jews killed themselves in Masada, east of Jerusalem.

Those human spirits whom are earthbound are in prison (1 Pet. 3:19, 20) and need to be liberated. When those confined spirits "burn up" their lower desires and feelings of violence and revenge, they will move upward towards the light or higher realms of the spirit world.

Upon death, the consciousness of the person first withdraws from the physical body into the etheric double for a few days before it settles in his or her spirit body. In this process, they pass or "download" all the physical, or rather, etheric brain memory into the subconscious mind of their spirit body, which is experienced as a review of their life.

There are some people who hang on to material life with such desperation (after they have died) that their etheric body cannot separate naturally from their spirit body, placing themselves neither in the physical nor in the psychic world. However, when the physical body decomposes, the etheric shell, or wraith, also returns to its particular elements.

Because ancient Egyptians experienced their surviving spirit as a shade or ghostlike with hardly any consciousness or will (also the Greeks and Hebrews – Eccl. 9:5, 10 –), they *probably mummified and hid their dead (curse and punish those who rob their graves) and likely used their etheric bodies to express themselves, to some extent, in the physical world. They may try to fulfill physical desires or hound the people on earth to do their bidding in a more concrete manner as earthbound primitives are likely to do, whom often help, obsess, and bother the earth people in a negative way. The primitives are so afraid of earthbound spirits or ghosts and their retribution that they do not want to offend them in any way, that they avoid certain places and actions as "taboo".

E. Differences of the Psychic and Spiritual Faculties

Considering the above explanations about the psychic senses, there are [1]differences between the psychic and spiritual abilities. Psychic perception comes from the centers below the diaphragm and is related to sensations and emotions, while the very clear spiritual perception comes from the centers above the diaphragm and is related to higher thoughts and divine concepts. As the lower center is only good for those on the receiving end, the higher center is always for the good of the whole.

---

* Some of them may also believe that they would come back into their old body.

[1] We should distinguish between lower psychism from the astral or human spirit level and higher psychism from the level of the Soul.

The lower energy of the human spirit is directly conveyed through the open energy centers of the etheric body to the abdomen centers of the body. Conversely, the higher energy of the Divine Spirit is expressed via the open higher energy centers of the human spirit and etheric body, mainly to the "third eye" area ("the all-seeing eye") of the head. Thus, the psycho/spiritual person controls and directs the physical body through the different nerve centers and indirectly through the endocrine glandular system, giving it life.

F. Description of the Spiritual Senses

A few people whom are regenerated have the ability, through the senses of their [2]Divine Spirits (whom reside within their human spirits), such as higher clairaudience – to prophecy and receive inspiration and revelation and are able to hear the louder voice of God, which is no longer small.

As the physical ear is a crude instrument of hearing, the psychical clairaudience is a clearer but somewhat distorted mode of hearing, while true clairaudience is a spiritual or divine faculty, where hearing through it is always clear.

The Bible speaks about people "who have eyes to see, but see not, who have ears to hear, but hear not" (Ezek. 12:2). Similarly, Jesus Christ later said to His disciples, "Having eyes do you not see, and having ears do you not hear?" (Mark 8:18)

The patriarchs and prophets of the Old Testament knew they were inspired by the Lord. "Then the Lord said to Noah" (Gen. 7:1). "No longer shall your name be Abram, but your name shall be Abraham" (Gen. 17:5). The Lord appeared to Isaac and said, "Do not go down to Egypt" (Gen. 26:2). And God said to him, "Your name shall no more be called Jacob, but Israel" (Gen. 32:28). "God said to Moses, 'I am who I am'" (Ex. 3:14). "And the Lord said to Samuel" (1 Sam. 8:7). "And the Lord said to Isaiah" (Isa. 7:3). "Then the word of the Lord

---

[2] The use of the higher spiritual or divine faculties is usually approved by all religions, such as: receiving guidance and answers of one's prayers, conversing with Christ and the Holy Spirit, receiving the gifts of the Spirit, and communication with saints or masters of all religions.

NOTE: As a human being consists of a spiritual body, psychical body, and natural body or "spirit and soul and body" (1 Thess. 5:23; Heb. 4:12), the physical body serves as a vehicle, or space suit, of the human spirit, with which it is integrated. The human spirit, in turn, serves as a vehicle for the Divine Spirit or Soul, with which it operates as one body.

235

came to Jeremiah" (Jer. 43:8). "Thus says the Lord God" (Ezek. 28:25). "Thus says the Lord" (Amos 1:3). "The word of the Lord came by Haggai the prophet" (Hag. 2:10). "Thus says the Lord of hosts" (Zech. 8:1-2).

"God called to him out of the bush, 'Moses, Moses!' And he said, 'Here am I.' Then he said, 'Do not come near; put off your shoes from your feet, for the place on which you are standing is holy ground'" (Ex. 3:4-5). The voice of God was also speaking to Moses "from above the mercy seat" (Num. 7:89), and called three times for the young Samuel (1 Sam. 3:4-11). "And behold, there came a voice to him, and said 'What are you doing here, Elijah?'" (1 Kings 19:13). And "the Spirit entered into me (Ezekiel) and set me upon my feet; and I heard him speaking to me" (Ezek. 2:2, 3:24).

It is recorded in the New Testament that a voice from heaven gave three times witness to the Savior (Matt. 3:17, 17:5; Jn. 12:28-30), and that Jesus Christ spoke with Moses and Elijah (Luk. 9:28:36). At the day of Pentecost (Feast of First-Fruits in the Old Testament) the birthday of the Christian church (10th day after Jesus' ascension into Heaven, the beginning of the Holy Spirit era – John 17:7-14 –), we read, "And they were all filled with the Holy Spirit and began to speak in other tongues, as the Spirit gave them utterance" --- "and they were bewildered because each one heard them speaking in his own language" (Acts 2:4, 6). Saul, a Pharisee, on his way to Damascus to persecute Christians, heard the voice of Jesus, "Saul, Saul, why do you persecute me?" (Acts 9:1-7). At a later time, the voice of God was able to speak through Saul, when he said in 1 Cor. 7:10 "to the married I give charge, not I but the Lord".

Throughout the history of the Christian church, many Christians have heard the voice of God. George Fox, the founder of the Quakers whom settled later in the state of Pennsylvania, heard the voice of God, telling him to separate from "the world" and to serve only God.

Through higher clairvoyance, the people whom are living a divine or spiritual life are able to know events far in the future, have visions, illuminations, and other mystical experiences.

As the physical eye is very limited and sees only a small part of the electromagnetic spectrum, the psychical clairvoyance sees more, but not as much as true clairvoyance which, as a divine faculty, sees very clearly at great distances in the external and internal worlds. It is not reflective, illusory, and deceptive as the lower psychical clairvoyance.

In the Old Testament, Isaiah saw visions of the Lord (Isa. 6:1), while Ezekiel "saw visions of God" (Ezek. 1:1). Daniel saw in chapter eight visions about the rise and fall of kingdoms (see also the book of Revelations) and in Dan. 10:4-9 a vision of a man whose face was "like the appearance of lightning, his eyes like flaming torches, his arms and legs like the gleam of burnished bronze, and the sound of his words like the noise of a multitude". See also the vision of John in Revelation 1:12-16, describing the same man or the universal or Cosmic Christ, as expressed through the last Adam.

In the New Testament, Jesus Christ immediately perceived that the scribes were questioning within themselves (Mk. 2:8), and when Jesus first met Nathaniel, He knew all about him (Jn. 1:47-51). Another reference to higher clairvoyance can be found in John 14:9; "Yet a little while, and the world will see me no more, but you will see me; because I live, you will live also."

In the tenth chapter of Acts, Peter had a clairvoyant vision of clean and unclean animals, whom were all cleansed by the Lord and were representation of the Jews and Gentiles Peter was compelled to meet and accept. A "vision appeared to Paul in the night: A man of Macedonia was standing beseeching him and saying, 'Come over to Macedonia (Europe) and help us'" (Acts 16:9).

The following verses are some examples of prophecy in the Bible:

In Genesis chapter 49, Jacob predicted on his deathbed the future vicissitudes of all his sons, whom represented the twelve tribes of Israel. Isaiah prophesied the birth of Jesus Christ, "Behold, a young woman shall conceive and bear a son, and shall call his name Immanuel" (Isa. 7:14), which was fulfilled in Matt. 1:18-23. In Joel 2:28 it is prophesied the promise of the Spirit of God to pour upon all flesh, which was fulfilled after the Resurrection of Christ. Nahum 2:4 predicted that in the future "The chariots (automobile) rage in the streets, they rush to and fro through the squares; they gleam like torches, they dart like lightning." Jesus prophesied very accurately in Luke 21:20-24 the destruction of Jerusalem by the Romans in 70 A.D. and its total destruction in 132 A.D. In the last instance, the Jews tried to defend their city under the leadership of Simon bar Kocheba, the Jewish Messiah.

Through higher intuition, regenerated believers have direct cognition, comprehension, or inner knowing of events and people without the use of their thinking faculties. They have a spiritual understanding, which is not clouded by the subconscious belief system.

The "spiritual man" receives the gifts of the Spirit of God because he is, unlike the unspiritual man, able to understand them (1 Cor. 2:14). In addition, the born again individual possesses the ability of spiritual discernment (Phil. 1:9).

In the twelfth chapter of first Corinthians, Paul tells us of the value and varieties of spiritual gifts, which flow from the same Spirit and which are given for the "manifestation of the Spirit for the common good". To one is given the word of "wisdom"; to another the word of "knowledge"; to a different person "faith"; to another individual "gifts of healing". To another "the working of miracles"; to some other "prophecy"; to another human the ability to "distinguish between spirits"; to one the "various kinds of tongues"; and to another "the interpretation of tongues". "All these are inspired by the same Spirit, who apportions to each one individually as he wills."

In 1 Cor. Chapter 14, Paul believes that prophecy was the best spiritual gift because for the one who speaks in a tongue, his (Divine) Spirit prays and speaks not to men but to God, and no one understands (unless it is interpreted). But he who prophesizes speaks to men and edifies the church because they will understand. Some evangelists believe that by speaking in tongues, the inner man is strengthened, and it enables one to pray the perfect Will of God for his or her life, by the inspiration and language given to them by the Holy Spirit.

In conclusion, we like to say that the most important spiritual exercise one can do is to pray and lift one's spirit up to God and the high spiritual entities surrounding His throne.

#36ª The Temple of Solomon, Zerubbabel, and Herodus

After the Israelites left Egypt, they were instructed by God to "Let them make me a sanctuary, that I may dwell in their midst" (Ex. 25:8). "And in the first month in the second year, on the first day of the month, the tabernacle was erected." And Moses "took the testimony (Ten Commandments) and put it in the ark" --- "and he brought the ark into the tabernacle" --- "Then the cloud covered the tent of meeting (tabernacle), and the glory of the Lord filled the tabernacle" (Ex. 40:20, 21, 34). This portable tent served as a focal point to approach and meet God to the time that Solomon's temple was erected.

When David was king in [1]Jerusalem, he expressed a strong desire to build a permanent house for the Lord. But the Lord did not allow David to "build a house to my name, because you have shed so much blood before me upon this earth". David instead made preparation for it by purchasing the land, [2]"The threshing floor of Ornan the Jebusite", and "provided materials in great quantity before his death" for his son Solomon to build an "exceeding magnificent" house (temple) for the Lord (1 Chron. ch. 21, 22). As the description of the tabernacle was given by God to Moses (Ex. 25:9), David got the plans for the tabernacle "by the writing from the hand of the Lord" (1 Chron. 2:19). "Then Solomon began to build the house of the Lord (see Chron. ch. 3, 4 and 1 Kings ch. 6, 7) in Jerusalem on Mount Moriah --- on the threshing floor of Ornan" (2 Chron. 3:1); "in the four hundred and eightieth year after the people of Israel came out of the land of Egypt" (1 Kings 6:1).

The temple was built after the pattern of the tabernacle but expanded twice in size (1 Kings 6:2). Its dimensions were sixty cubits (1 cubit is 18 inches – length of arm to elbow) long, twenty cubits wide, and thirty cubits high. The temple complex consisted like the tabernacle of an outer and inner sanctuary and an inner courtyard for the priest (1 Kings

---

[1] The City of Jerusalem was built high in the Judean hills about 2,640 feet above sea level, surrounded by steep hills to the West and the Judean desert to the East. The city was a natural fortress and was captured by King David from the Jebusites in the 10th century, thus making it the capital of his newly established kingdom (2 Sam. 5:6-10; Judg. 19:10-20).

[2] The threshing floor of Ornan is the same site as Mount Moriah, on which Abraham intended to sacrifice his son Isaac (Gen. 22:2), and where David had set up an altar to the Lord. It was also the place of the later rebuilt second and third temples of Zerubbabel and Herod the great. Today, the site is occupied by the Muslim shrine, known as the dome of the rock, which was built in the 7th century A.D. Both Jews and Muslims claim Abraham as the father of their faith.

6.36; 7:12). In addition, the whole was surrounded by the great court for Israel (2 Chron. 4:9). Commencing at the eastern gate of the great court of the Israelites, en-
countered on the right, the altar of burnt offering, and on the left, the laver or "the molten sea", which rested upon the back of twelve ox-en (1 Kings 23-26). After washing themselves in the laver, the priests passed two pillars, which were call-ed Jachin and Boaz, before

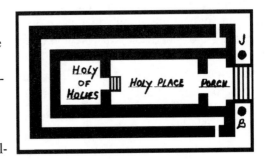

they entered via the porch or vestibule and veil, the main room or "the holy place". In it stood five pairs of lambstands and the table of showbread. Just before the second veil was the altar of incense, and behind the veil was the most westerly room, "the holy of holies", which contained the Ark of the Covenant, overshadowed with two cherubim made of olive wood, overlaid with gold. The walls of each room in the temple were paneled with cedar, carved with flowers, palm trees, and cherubim, and overlaid with gold. The holy place was dimly lit by the lambstands and high windows, but the holy of holies was completely dark.

It took the Israelites and co-workers of other nations 7 years (1 Kings 6:38) in building the house of the Lord. Every part was prepared at a distance from the site and put in place without sound (unharmonious vibration) of hammer or any tool (1 Kings 6:7). Then the elders and heads of tribes took the Ark of the Covenant out of the city of David, and the priests brought the ark (which only contained the tables of stone) to the inner sanctuary of the temple. "When the priests came out of the holy place, a cloud filled the house of the Lord" (1 Kings 8:10).

REMARK: Today, people may enter the symbolic temple by the (1) gate-surrender, (2) altar-forgiveness, (3) laver-cleansing, (4) lambstands-communion, (5) bread-Bible reading, (6) altar of incense-prayer, and (7) ark-contact with God.

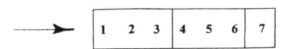

This symbolized God's presence and approval. The *same event occurred when Moses set up the tabernacle for the first time (Ex. 40:34-35).

Solomon's temple became a symbol of God's permanent presence among His people, the center of religious and civil affairs, and did more than anything else to unite the twelve tribes of Israel into a nation.

After the temple was dedicated by Solomon for seven days (1 Kings 8:12-66), the Lord appeared to him and said: "I have heard your prayer and your supplication, which you have made before me. I have consecrated this house which you have built, and put my name there forever" --- "But if you turn aside from following me, you or your children, and do not keep my commandments and my statutes which I have set before you, but go and serve other gods and worship them, then I will cut off Israel from the land which I have given them; and the house which I have consecrated for my name I will cast out of my sight; and Israel will become a proverb and a byword among all peoples. And this house will become a heap of ruins" (1 Kings 9:3, 6-8). The prophet Jeremiah reminded the people later that they could not rely on God's protection if they continue to be unfaithful to the Lord (Jer. 7:1-15).

When the northern tribes were taken captive by the Assyrians, the southern kingdom Judah did not learn the lesson and continued to reject God's ways, and in the nineteenth year of king Nebuchadnezzar (Jer. 52:12-14), Jerusalem fell to the Babylonians. Solomon's temple was destroyed, and its remaining bronze, gold, and silver furnishings and people were taken to Babylon (2 Kings 24:10-13; 25:8-17; 2 Chron. 36:15-21). The temple stood for about 400 years and provided, from the tenth to the sixth centuries B.C., a permanent dwelling place for the ark, from which during and after captivity, nothing was ever heard of. Jeremiah prophesied that the ark would not "be remembered or missed; it shall not be made again" (Jer. 3:16-17).

---

* As the glory or presence of the Lord filled the tabernacle and the temple as soon as it was finished, so will (according to the same principle) the Christ life enter an individual as soon as the form (human spirit) is ready. It will, in turn, have a life of its own when the physical body has become mature. The germ has always been there, but it has lain dormant until it is nourished and brought to birth. The same is also true of any human-made object. When it is fostered with human life, it becomes vibrant and unique and not just a copy.

241

REMARK: During the time of the disappearance of the ark, the belief of Yahweh as a visible and tangible God who had His dwelling place in the ark also began to wane. This occurred because the many faithful became more like the ark by internalizing the laws of God in their inner selves. For them, the worship of Yahweh became gradually more spiritual and universal, and the God of their forefathers was coming to be seen as a Supreme Ruler who is everywhere. He became more approachable and could be worshipped without image, symbol, or representative. This idea was even more advanced later by the poetical prophets, whereby the idea of God became more like that of the monotheistic religions of Judaism and Islam as they appear today.

After the Jews had been in Exile for 70 years, as prophesied by Jeremiah (Jer. 29:10; 2 Chron. 36:21), God raised up king Cyrus of Persia (Isa. 45:1) to conquer Babylon and liberate the Jews from their power. The Persian king allowed the Jews to return to Jerusalem and gave them permission to rebuild Solomon's temple and also returned some of the gold and silver objects, which were taken from them by the Babylonians. See Book of Ezra Ch. 1. During the exilic period, the Jews were also encouraged to rebuild the temple in Jerusalem by visions of Ezekiel (see chapters 40-43) of an ideal temple, which was much like the temple of Solomon, wherein he described dimensions and things in great detail.

Around 536 B.C., a group of about 50,000 Jews, fired by religious zeal and under the leadership of Zerubbabel, a descendant of King David, began the exodus to the promised land of Israel. Upon their arrival, they built an altar and "began to offer burnt offerings to the Lord" (Ezra 3:6), and a year later, the foundation of the temple was laid (Hag. 2:18). This event was a cause of great celebration (Ezra 3:10-11). The returning Jews, unfortunately, had to face the Samatarians (Jews whom married foreign women and whom were not allowed to help build the temple – Ezra 4:3 –), and the native Jews from Judea who claimed authority and ownership over Jerusalem. Those neighbors were able to stop the building project for a long time (Ezra 4:4-5). But with the help of Darius, the new king of Persia (Ezra 6:1-13), and the inspiration of the prophets Zechariah and *Haggai, the second temple

* Haggai said that the famines and poverty were punishment for their delaying of rebuilding the Lord's house (Hag. 1:9-11).
God speaking through Haggai said, "You have looked for much, and lo, it came to little; and when you brought it home, I blew it away. Why? Says the Lord of hosts. Because of my house that lies in ruins, while you busy yourselves each with his own house. Therefore, the heavens above you have withheld the dew, and the earth has withheld its produce. And I have called for a drought upon the lands and the hills, upon the grain, the new wine, the oil, upon what the ground brings forth, upon men and upon cattle, and upon all their labors."

was completed after four years in 516 B.C. "in the sixth year of the reign of Darius the king", and dedicated with thanksgiving and celebration (Ezra 6:14-16).

The temple of Zerubbabel was similar in size as that of Solomon's, but was not as magnificent and splendid as the first temple. The structure lasted for nearly 500 years from around 516 B.C. to 20 B.C. Because the Israelites neglected their duties and worship of their Lord and Savior, it fell into disrepair.

NOTE: There was, in the history of the second temple, an episode of rededication by the Maccabees in 164 B.C. after the temple had been defiled by the Seleucid ruler Antiochus IV in 167 B.C., by offering pigs to his own gods (Dan. 11:31).

Jerusalem remained under Jewish control for the next century and then came under the control of the Romans in 63 B.C., and the noble Edomite Herod the great was made the puppet king.

Because of his success in killing outlaws and bandits who made Galilee unsafe, *Herod the great became popular with the Romans and the Galileans and was made king of Judea in 37 B.C. by the Roman Senate. During his reign (37 B.C. – 4 B.C.), Herod undertook massive building projects, including the city port of Caesarea, the Roman administrative center. In order to win favor with his subjects (there was great unrest in Judea) and to impress the Roman world, Herod began in about 19 B.C. with his most magnificent project, the rebuilding of the temple in Jerusalem. Although he kept to the same dimension and plan as the temple of Solomon, the height of the third temple was 40 instead of 30 cubits. And to impress the Gentiles whom were, in their age, accustomed to larger buildings, the relatively small temple stood on an enormous, massive, and enlarged 35 acre platform or temple mount, which stood at the southern end as much as 100 to 150 feet above ground level. In the time of Jesus, who compared the temple to His body (Jn. 2:19-21), its most important structure was finished which, together with the foundation or temple mount, took 46 years to complete (Jn. 2:20). But the grand temple complex was not completed until 64 A.D. The Holy of Holies was separated from the Holy Place

---

* Herod was born in 73 B.C. and was the eldest son of Antipater, who belonged to the Idumean people, whom were descendants of the Edomites. Herod was so obsessed with the idea that someone would take his throne that he murdered three of his sons and one of his wives, a Jewish princess. He also ordered that all the baby boys in and around Bethlehem be put to death when he heard the News that the long awaited Messiah, King of the Jews, had been born in Bethlehem (Matt. 2:13-16).

by a veil (Matt. 27:51; Heb. 6:19) and was empty, which to many Jews symbolized the intangible and visible presence of God. This mysterious chamber was for them the earthly dwelling place of the Lord of Israel.

A covered cloister (where Peter and John taught the people) ran right around the courtyard. The main entrance was from the south and led first to the court of the Gentiles. Anyone could enter this part of the temple. But notices in Greek and Latin forbade non-Jews from entering the inner courts of the temple, and the penalty was likely death. Paul was arrested at one time for trespassing into the forbidden ground. See Acts chapter 21.

NOTE: Jesus said that earthly temples were not necessary for worshipping God (Jn. 4:20-24) and compared His body to a temple. Paul, who was a tentmaker (Acts 18:3), said in Acts 7:48: "The Most High does not dwell in houses made with hands." See also Hebr. 9:11, 24. Each individual Christian is a temple of God (1 Cor. 3:16), wherein He can dwell more fully (Rev. 21:3). However, this is only true for regenerated individuals, the ones whom have been born of God. Otherwise, the church may still serve individually or collectively as the temple of God for those whom have not found Christ.

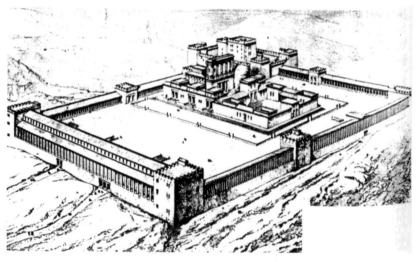

It was in the court of the Gentiles that Jesus "began to drive out those who sold and those who bought in the temple, and He overturned the tables of the money changers and the seats of those who sold pigeons; and He would not allow anyone to carry anything through the temple. And He taught and said to them, 'Is it not written, 'My house shall be called a house of prayer for all the nations'? But you have made it a den of robbers" (Mark 11:15-17; Matt. 21:12). The Gospel of John describes that Jesus made a whip of cords and drove the salesmen, together with their oxen and sheep, out of the temple and told them, "You shall not make my Father's house a house of trade" (John 2:13-17). Luke 19:47 reported that Jesus was teaching daily in the temple to His disciples and to people with or *without bodies, while His disciples would also teach their converts and others on the temple grounds in the early days of the church.

The next court was the court of women whom could go further into the temple ground, while the circumcised Jewish men were allowed to go as far as to move into the court of Israel. The priests had access to the inner court where the altar stood, and a few chosen priests could enter and serve in the Holy Place, while the high priest was allowed to enter once a year into the Most Holy Place.

Because of the corruption of the priesthood, Jesus prophesied in Luke 19:43-44, "For the days shall come upon you, when your enemies will cast up a bank about you and surround you, and hem you in on every side, and dash you to the ground, you and your children within you, and they will not leave one stone upon another in you; because you did not know the time of your visitation." See also Mark 13:1-2; Matt. 24:2.

NOTE: The physical body (with its 3 cavities) correspond to the outer court, which was accessible to both Jew and Gentile, and which becomes easily contaminated with low and evil vibrations. The purified human spirit corresponds to the Holy Place, which was accessible only to the sanctified priesthood, while Divine Spirit or Soul corresponds to the Holy of Holies.

True to Jesus' words, the third temple was destroyed by the Romans at the time of the Jewish rebellion in 70 A.D., and its treasures were taken back to Rome as illustrated on the arch of Titus in Rome. Thus, Herod's temple stood for a period of only 90 years from 20 B.C. to 70 A.D. All that remains today is a lower portion of the retaining wall, including a 150 foot section of the southwest corner of the temple mount or courtyard, which came into Jewish possession in 1967 after the six day war. Jews from all parts of the world would pray and lament what they had lost. It is their most holy site and is also known as the Wailing Wall. Besides some abortive attempts, no Jewish temple has, to this day, ever been rebuilt on Mount Moriah.

---

* Those human spirits became spiritually alive or born of God (resurrected) after having been in the "tomb" or living the life of the good/evil personality. See Matt. 27:52-53).

245

REMARK: In 135 A.D., there was a second Jewish revolt in Jerusalem, which was completely crashed by the Romans, and the Jews were no longer allowed to live there. The Jews became a people without a homeland until the establishment of the modern state of Israel in 1948.

However, especially after the destruction of the temple, the law, and the synagogues (meeting places), a non-sacrificial form of worship had to come to occupy a more and more central place, with the result that Judaism could and did exist without a temple. Thus, the Jewish priesthood was no longer needed and the religious leadership gradually passed to the Rabbis (masters or teachers), whom were qualified and knowledgeable on how to apply the Old Testament instructions to situations in daily life.

#36ᵇ Description of the Ten Commandments

Introduction

A long time ago, Adam and Eve were expelled from the Garden of Eden in the world of relative morality, wherein everyone was deciding for themselves what was right or wrong. The authority of God as the sole arbiter or judge of virtue or vice or good and evil was not recognized. By the time of Noah, humanity, which had been living without law and order and without a moral standard of good and evil, became "corrupt in God's sight, and the earth was filled with violence" (Gen. 6:11).

> "The Lord saw that the wickedness of man was great
> in the earth, and that every imagination of the thoughts
> of his heart was only evil continually. And the Lord
> was sorry that he had made man on the earth, and it
> grieved him to his heart" (Gen. 6:5-6).

After the deluge of the flood, the moral law given to Noah's family was the prohibition against murder: "Whoever sheds the blood of man, by man shall his blood be shed" (Gen. 9:5-6).

Having been in slavery in Egypt for more than 400 years, the descendants of Jacob (Abraham's grandson) left (exodus) Egypt with the help of the strong and loving hand of God and were headed, through the desert, for the land of Canaan. "On the third new moon after the people of Israel had gone forth out of the land of Egypt" (Exodus 19:1), they camped before Mount Sinai. On the third day after the people purified themselves, God [1]spoke the [2]Ten Commandments directly to the people, out of the midst of a thick cloud and fire accompanied by thunder, lightning, and supernatural trumpet blasts.

---

[1] When the people become more mature, they are able to receive God's voice as an inner voice. See also 1 Kings 19:11-12.

[2] The Ten Commandments, or in Hebrew "The Ten Words"; "Ten Sayings"; "Declaration" or "Instructions". In theological language, the Ten Commandments are called the decalogue, from the Greek "dekalogos". Those commandments will eventually become part of one's inner being (Heb. 8:10). The Ten Commandments can be found in Exodus 20:3:17 and Deuteronomy 5:7-21. There is a slight difference between the two statements. In Deuteronomy, a man's wife is distinguished from his servants and has a special status and protection.

These commandments were afterwards inscribed on both sides on two tablets of [3]stone, "written with the finger of God" (Ex. 31:18; 32:15, 16). Those tablets were kept for centuries in the Ark of the Covenant, in the inner sanctuary of the tabernacle and later in the temple. They might have been destroyed during the captivity.

The Ten Commandments was and [4]still is a special Moral Law for the guidance of human beings. It is universal and timeless and can be applied to all people of different customs and in all places. It is accepted in its entirety by Jews, Christians, and Muslims which, however, is not true of the other aspects of God's Law, such as additional or supplementary moral, civil, and religious law, which is changeable and was and is being continually [5]interpreted by Jewish theologians. The Ten Words is also the foundation and summary of all the Hebrew laws and customs, which book or roll, was kept beside the ark (Deut. 31:24-26). More than 600 laws are described in the Torah (Heb.) or Pentateuch (Gr.), the first five books of the Old Testament, to govern every aspect of life. Those instructions comprise not only the moral law but also the civil and ceremonial laws, which can be found mainly in the books of Exodus ch. 20-24, Leviticus, and Deuteronomy, such as dietary or kosher laws, instructions for growing and harvesting crops. Other supplementary laws deal with murder and injury to human life, theft and damage to property, justice and human rights, social and religious instructions for festivals. There are specific laws for the protection of the weak and disadvantaged, such as the poor, strangers, widowed, and orphans. There are further laws about cursing parents, lending, consideration for animals, compensations, penalties, bribery, and many more. In contrast to the laws of the surrounding nations, everyone receives the same punishment, regardless of status. Pagan countries and their arbitrary rulers had a tendency to punish perpetrators – if they had moral laws at all – more than their subjects

---

[3] As God may be compared to a rock, ideal human couples may be likened to the tablets of stone, hewn from the rock.

[4] Those moral laws are no longer needed when one is living a divine life, not "under law but under grace" (Rom. 6:14). However, because of backsliding and, thus, becoming carnal again (1 Cor. 3:1-4), the commandments are needed once more to live in a proper way, so that the good and evil personalities will be guided according to the Will of God and become purified again.

[5] The commentary of the laws, known as "oral law", grew as new individual, family, social, and political problems arose. By 200 A.D., it accumulated to such an extent that it was written down in a codified form and was called "The Mishnah". Thereafter, Rabbis continued to enlarge on its precepts, which resulted in a body of work called "The Gemara". Together with the Mishnah, it formed "The Talmud".

deserved, and many even lost their lives for a stolen loaf of bread. In order to prevent imitation or retaliate more than they should so that the punishment always fits the crime, the law in Exodus 21:23-24 was given, "If any harm follows, then you shall give life for life, eye for eye, tooth for tooth, hand for hand, foot for foot."

As the supplementary laws are summarized by the Ten Commandments, these laws, in turn, are condensed into two principles: the love toward God (Deut. 6:4) and the love toward neighbor (Lev. 19:18). As Jesus said, "You shall love the Lord your God with all your heart, and with all your soul, and with all your mind." And --- "You shall love your neighbor as yourself" (Matt. 22:37-40; Luk. 10:27), which is "the fulfilling of the law" (Rom. 13:10).

Some people whom are living the life of the personality think that they have gotten beyond the Ten Commandments, and that they are no longer needed to guide their life. Albeit, Jesus Christ said in Matthew 5:17-19:

> "Think not that I have come to abolish the law and the
> prophets; I have come not to abolish them but to fulfill
> them. For truly, I say to you, till heaven and earth pass
> away, not an iota, not a dot, will pass from the law
> until all is accomplished. Whoever then relaxes one of
> the least of these commandments and teaches men so,
> shall be called least in the kingdom of heaven; but who
> does them and teaches them shall be called great in the
> kingdom of heaven."

The Commandments, prohibiting theft and murder and calling for truth in legal trials, are still relevant today for the general public, and the prohibition against adultery is taken seriously, at least by the offended party. Thus, the Ten Commandments of God, given to Moses on Mount Sinai, are as binding today as they have been since they were proclaimed in the hearing of the people.

The meaning and purpose of the Ten Commandments is explained by Jesus Christ in the Sermon on the Mount (Matt. ch. 5, 6, 7), which is the very heart and summary of His teaching. In the Sermon, he gave a deeper and inward meaning. *For example:

---

* For a complete interpretation of the Ten Commandments, see Matt. 5:17-47.

"You have heard that it was said to the men of old, 'you shall not kill; and whoever kills shall be liable to judgment'. But I say to you that everyone who is angry with his brother shall be liable to judgment" (Matt. 5: 21-22). "You have heard that it was said, 'you shall not commit adultery'. But I say to you that everyone who looks at a woman lustfully has already committed adultery with her in his heart" (Matt. 5:27-28).

After having lost contact with God, the Ten Commandments are for the descendants of Adam and Eve, the first direct communication between them and God. The Ten Commandments were initially addressed to the Israelites, the direct descendants of Jacob, who is called Israel (Gen. 32:28), whom were in bondage in Egypt. "I am the Lord your God, who brought you out of the land of Egypt, out of the house of bondage" (Ex. 20:2). Many people today are still in bondage by "the world" (Jn. 16:33; 1 Jn. 5:19) and in need to be delivered.

The Ten Commandments are also a covenant or agreement between God and the people of Israel (Ex. 19:5). It requires that the people remain faithful and put their trust in God and not in the gods of other nations. In return, God will protect Israel from the enemies and will exalt Israel "the house of Jacob" (Ex. 19:3). Thus, the Old Testament or Old Covenant as a whole was meant to be kept by the Israelites or the Jews, and they were rewarded with earthly prosperity, long life, many children, and living in the Promised Land.

*The precise numbering and dividing of the Ten Commandments has often been debated. Philo, the Jewish philosopher, divided the tablets into five positive and five negative commands. The Roman Catholic and Lutheran traditions treat verses 3-6 of Exodus as a single commandment and found two commandments under the heading "you shall not covet". The Reformed tradition separated the commandment against idolatry from that of images. Thus, they treat verses 4-6 of Exodus as the second commandment and verse 17 of Exodus as the tenth commandment.

The first four commandments have to do with our attitude, relationship, and duty to God, the other six with our attitude, relationship, and duty to our neighbor. This is why Christ divided the Law into two commandments or principles. Thus, the first part is

---

* In this paper, we are following the Jewish and Reformed traditions.

religious and vertical and is between humans and God, while the second part is moral and horizontal and is between humans.

The Ten Commandments is not so much laws we have to obey but more descriptions of right conduct. The laws are intended to be a guide to good relationships with God and with our fellow human beings. They also give direction, purpose, and meaning to our lives. These laws are natural and suitable for us because we do not lie or steal from our friend or court his or her spouse. Every law God has given has been for our benefit and will bring only harmony, happiness, fulfillment, and freedom, and everyone will benefit.

Even though the Ten Commandments were given to the Jews, the Christians also consider them trustworthy (Matt. 5:19; Rom. 13:8-10). The Christian church has always used the laws as basic rules of instruction and conduct. The laws not only have an effect on every aspect of our lives, but we also discover the living God behind those words, who is forever seeking to claim us as His own.

In 2 Chronicles 7:14, He urgently begged, "If my people who are called by my name humble themselves, and pray and seek my face, and turn from their wicked ways, then I will hear from heaven, and will forgive their sin and heal their land."

The Ten Commandments

I.   Thou shalt have no other gods before Me
II.   Thou shalt not make unto thee any graven image
III.   Thou shalt not take the name of the Lord thy God in vain
IV.   Remember the Sabbath day, to keep it holy
V.   Honor thy father and thy mother
VI.   Thou shalt not kill
VII.   Thou shalt not commit adultery
VIII.   Thou shalt not steal
IX.   Thou shalt not bear false witness against thy neighbor
X.   Thou shalt not covet

(Exodus 20:3-17 **K.J.V.**)

First Commandment

"I am the Lord your God, which have brought thee out of the land of Egypt out of the house of bondage. Thou shalt have no other gods before me" (Exodus 20:2-3 – **King James Version**).

The first commandment is about the identity of God, and to bid exclusive allegiance or faithfulness to one God alone.

The commandment says in original Hebrew, "I AM Y.H.W.H. (Yahweh) who led you out from slavery in Egypt. You are to place no other gods in front of Me" (or besides Me).

Hebrew was originally written into consonants only, as, for example, in the Hebrew text of Exodus 3:15, wherein the consonants of the divine name are given as Y.H.W.H. Jews found the name of God so holy that they refused to pronounce the name of God. They therefore use substitute words, such as Adonai ("Lord" in English translation). Because the initial pronunciation eventually got lost, the Jews in the first millenium A.D. put the vowels of Adonai in the letters Y.H.W.H.; this produced the word "Jehovah". Most scholars agree today that the most likely original form of the name is "Yahweh", which appears most often in the Hebrew texts.

Throughout the Bible, God reveals Himself in many different ways. He is therefore not known only by one name but by many other names, such as: Eloah or Elohim (majesty), El-Shaddai (God Almighty), Lord (authority), Holy One, Father, Love, and many other designations. To Moses, the limitless God reveals Himself as "I am who I am", or I shall be as I shall be (Ex. 3:14).

"Thou shalt have no other gods before me" or before my face, does not only mean the gods of Cananites and other nations whom were like the Cananites, immoral and unfaithful, but whatever captures our highest interest are the gods we worship. This can be our body, sport, possessions, money, position, success, popularity, fame, lust for sex, power, pleasure, beliefs, etc. Every religion can be a false god when God is used as a valet to satisfy our cravings for power and importance.

Second Commandment

"Thou shalt not make unto thee any graven image, or any likeness of any thing that is in heaven above, or that is in the earth beneath, or that is in the water under the earth: Thou shalt not bow down thyself to them, nor serve them: for I the Lord thy God am a jealous God" (Exodus 20:4-5 – **K.J.V.**).

The second commandment prohibits idolatry as incompatible with exclusive allegiance to God because it (person or thing) wants to take the place of the only true God.

In the Garden of Eden, God told Adam and Eve that they can freely eat of all the trees of the garden, but not of the tree of the knowledge of good and evil. Being immature, they were not able to decide what is right or wrong and, therefore, are in need to be told by God what they can and what they cannot do in the moral dimension. Eve, however, was tempted by the serpent (Lucifer) to take from the forbidden "fruit", so that she would become like God "knowing good and evil" (Gen. 3:1-5). Like God, Eve (and Adam) can now make their own rules of moral conduct and no longer have to listen and obey to the commandments or instructions of God.

Because this rebellious attitude is deeply embedded in the human psyche, humans, therefore, have a strong tendency of wanting to decide what is right and wrong and to judge others of their moral behavior.

Idolatry is the worst form of human pride, and it always seeks to control, manipulate, and overthrow the moral authority of God by the evil part of the human spirit or Luciferian nature (Isaiah 14:12-14). When immature humans decide what is good and evil, they take the place of God and see themselves as God. This often happens to dictators and kings, such as the Roman Emperors and Antiochus IV, the Syrian king, who forced the Jews to dedicate their Holy Temple to him and the Greek god Zeus. However, in 164 B.C,. the Maccabees seized control of the Temple and rededicated it to God. This event is celebrated every year by Jews all over the world in the festival of Hanukkah.

Third Commandment

"Thou shalt not take the name of the Lord thy God in vain; for the Lord will not hold him guiltless that taketh his name in vain" (Ex. 20:7 – **K.J.V.**).

Reverence for God's name is not only important in the Ten Commandments but should be revered throughout the Bible and in daily life. Jesus made it the first petition in the Lord's prayer, "Hallowed be thy name" (Matt. 6:9). Proverbs 1:7 says, "The fear (reverence) of the Lord is the beginning of (divine) knowledge".

Respect for the name of the Lord is the same as having reverence for God the Creator because His name(s) represent not only His authority and power but, above all, His very being and character.

Ordinary human beings that are living the good/evil life of the personality are easily tempted to profane and defile the name of God, especially when their evil nature is in charge of their personality. They express this to others by swearing and cursing. Others whom are less evil may use the name of God disrespectfully. On many occasions, to add more weight to utterances, people may say, "I swear to God" or "I tell you in the name of God---", etc.

The Bible says: When a man or woman vows a vow to the Lord, or swears an oath to bind themselves by a pledge, he or she shall not break their word (Numbers chapter 30). However, this breaking of oaths often occurs to elected officials today.

There are also religious people who use God and His name to control and manipulate people or to gain respect or prestige. A well-garbed and well-fed clergy person may, for example, be more committed to living the "good life" than to truly help his or her parishioners.

Howbeit, the worst thing that may happen is to invoke the name of God to something He will never approve, such as that between unholy unions of homosexual couples.

Fourth Commandment

"Remember the sabbath day, to keep it holy. Six days shalt thou labor, and do all thy work: But the seventh day is the sabbath of the Lord thy God: in it thou shalt not do any work, thou, nor thy son, nor thy daughter, thy manservant, nor thy maidservant, nor thy cattle, nor thy stranger that is within thy gates: For in six days the Lord made heaven and earth, the sea, and all that in them is, and rested the seventh day: wherefore the Lord blessed the sabbath day, and hallowed it" (Ex. 20:8-11 – **K.J.V.**).

As God blessed the seventh day (Gen 2:3), no mention was made of the Sabbath or day of rest, until the Israelites were told, after the Exodus from Egypt, not to gather the manna on the seventh day, because God was to provide for them for that day (Ex. 16:22-26).

Not observing the Sabbath day was severely punished: "You shall keep the sabbath, because it is holy for you; every one who profanes it shall be put to death; whoever does any work on it, that soul shall be cut off from among his people" (Ex. 31:14).

While the Jewish tradition celebrates the Sabbath on the seventh day, which is Saturday, Christians usually refer to Sunday as the Sabbath or the Lord's Day because of the Resurrection of Jesus, which took place on the first day of the week (Luke 24:1; John 20:1).

The Sabbath is a day of rest, not only of the body but also of the psychical and (budding) spiritual bodies; otherwise, the people may suffer physically, psychologically, and spiritually. It is a time to recreate oneself, of mental and spiritual reflection, to get to know the Lord better by reading and talking about Him. It is, however, not a time to fix your house, car, do yard work, or for leisure, entertainment, and sports. It is a time to visit and help those who cannot help themselves, so that "the sabbath was made for man, not man for the sabbath" (Mk. 2:27).

In the new dispensation, not only the Sabbath is dedicated for physical, emotional, and spiritual healing, but also all or certain hours of other days of the week may be dedicated to the Lord by praying and studying the Word, so that those families and groups will always stay together.

Fifth Commandment

"Honour thy father and thy mother: that thy days may be long upon the land which the Lord God giveth thee" (Ex. 20:12 – **K.J.V.**).

As God is honored in the first command concerning religious duties to God, the command to honor parents is heading the commandments regarding moral duties to human beings, whom are living the life of the personality. Human parents are much like God to their children, especially young children, whom by honoring their parents in a physical way, learn to honor God in a spiritual way.

Children should obey their parents, not only for reasons that they have given them life and are older and wiser or that they are entrusted by God for the development of the moral character of their children. Above all, parental love is the purest form of love in this fallen world. Besides, when children take care of their parents, they, in turn, will be taken care of by their children so that they live longer.

Ephesians 6:1-4 says: "Children, obey your parents in the Lord," --- "Fathers, do not provoke your children to anger, but bring them up in the discipline and instruction of the Lord" (see also Lev. 19:3; 19:32). The child who would raise his hand or cursed his father or mother was put to death in ancient Israel. See Ex. 21:15-17; Deut. 21:18-21; Prov. 30:17. "Hearken to your father who begot you, and do not despise your mother when she is old" (Prov. 23:22; 6:20). "And you shall teach them (Words of God) diligently to your children" (Deut. 6:7). "He who spares the rod hates his son, but he who loves him is diligent to discipline him" (Prov. 13:24; 22:15; 23:13).

In the pioneering days and later ("the good old days") in America, parents were well respected, and there was no tolerance for disrespect to elders and backtalk of any kind. This all changed in the 1960s when young people were echoing Adam and Eve, "Who is to say what is right or wrong". As a result, parents and teachers lost their elevated status, and many children became like those described in 2 Tim. 3:1-5.

However, if self-centered and immature parents fail them by abusing or telling them to violate a moral or civil law, they should not listen. When the natural family has failed them, God has provided a spiritual family (1 Tim. 5:1-2; Psalms 27:10). Fortunately for all, there will come a time when "He will turn the hearts of fathers to their children and the hearts of children to their fathers (Mal. 4:6).

Sixth Commandment

"Thou shalt not kill" (Ex. 20:13 – **K.J.V.**).

In the older translation of this command, the word "kill" was used, but the original meaning is "Thou shalt not murder", which is more correct because humans sometimes have to kill in self-defense or in war, which is a necessary evil, or in capital punishment, which is a regrettable event. This kind of killing is permitted in the Bible, but it does not want that people become arrogant, blood thirsty, insensitive, and without compassion. However, the one who willfully murders shall be put to death when he or she is proven guilty on the evidence of more than one witness (Num. 35:30; Deut. 19:15).

The willful taking of an innocent life or our own life is always wrong because life is a gift of God, and our bodies are not really ours to do as we wish. Since the body is a vessel and vehicle of the human and divine spirit, whom grows through the experience of life, we should also not make it inoperative and ineffective by abusing it through overeating, alcohol, smoking, and drugs (1 Cor. 3:16-17).

Only God can take life; that is why general practitioners should not take the life of a patient (euthanasia). Many practitioners whom carry out this "mercy killing" feel guilty thereafter and pass through a moral crisis. Some of them experience nightmares. The suffering of those patients can, in many cases, be relieved by their Creator by asking for His help and, in some cases, be restored to health by having absolute faith in God and in the advancement of medicine.

According to Jewish tradition, a miscarriage resulting in the death of a fetus is not considered murder (that is punishable by death), while for many fundamental Christians, it is the taking of innocent life. The Jewish also uphold the belief that abortion is justified if it is related to the mother's life, as well as in the cases of rape and incest, but certainly not for the motivation of convenience and economics. However, partial birth abortion is always wrong because the fetus may experience an independent life and could be fully alive and able to survive death.

The sixth commandment is not only about physical killing but also about "emotional killing" through hatred (Matt. 5:21-22; 1 Jn. 3:15), harsh words, envy, grudges, resentment, bitterness, prejudice, etc. by which physical killing is initiated.

Finally, when someone is living a spiritual or divine life, they should never kill or obey any command to kill by any human agency.

Seventh Commandment

"Thou shalt not commit adultery" (Ex. 20:14 – **K.J.V.**).

The seventh commandment is and always has been a most serious crime against God and humanity. It has been severely punished by death (Deut. 22:22), and perpetrators are still being killed without a human agency, through venereal diseases and AIDS. There are so many people today who engage in adulterous behavior that they and others are not only unwilling to condemn it but even promote and glamorize it through romantic novels, television, movies, and videos, which only portray an unrealistic part of love and life. Adultery is an act that tears apart the sacred relationship between husband and wife, and it violates the confidence and trust in each other (Prov. 6:32). This separation is not only caused by the sexual act itself but also by any sexual activity for the purpose of arousal and gratification (by touching – Gen. 3:3).

Because the union between couples is not only physical but also mental/emotional (psychical) and spiritual, they should also not engage in sexual fantasy with someone other than their spouse, either with spirits of earthly beings or earthbound and evil spirits. As Jesus said so profoundly in Matthew 5:28, "But I say to you that everyone who looks at a woman (or man) lustfully has already committed adultery with her (him) in his (her) heart." They should therefore not steal the intimate affection from one's spouse, which is, unlike marriage, a selfish act.

According to many surveys, adultery is the primary cause of divorce, and innocent children are greatly affected by the quarrels and separation of their parents. They are more likely to suffer from depression, experience with alcohol and drugs, and some of them may even commit suicide. They may also be easily swayed of having sex before they are married, which is strictly forbidden (Eph. 5:3; Col. 3:5; Heb. 12:16). Couples that are living together before they are married are also more likely to divorce than couples that have no sex before marriage. Sexual infidelity or unfaithfulness is usually carried out in secret and involves denial, deception, cheating, and lying. Children born from this unholy relationship are usually unwanted and unloved and are known as bastards or illegitimate children, whom were forbidden in Bible times of marrying into the community, as was the first offspring of the adulterous relationship between David and Bathsheba, who died. See 2 Sam. chapter 12.

Finally, "let marriage be held in honor among all, and let the marriage bed be undefiled; for God will judge the immoral and adulterous" (Heb. 13:4; Lev. 18:20).

Eighth Commandment

"Thou shalt not steal" (Ex. 20:15 – **K.J.V.**).

In the Book of Exodus we read, "If a man steals an ox or a sheep, and kills it or sells it, he shall pay five oxen for an ox and four sheep for a sheep. He shall make restitution; if he has nothing, then he shall be sold for his theft. If the stolen beast is found alive in his possession---, he shall pay double" (Ex. 22:1-4). A double amount is also due when the thief steals money or goods (see Ex. 22:7-9). The double amount usually compensates for the mental and emotional agony, violation, and loss of the victim. The thief is then set free and is no longer incarcerated for his or her crime. If he/she cannot pay, they have to serve the victim for a certain amount of time. However, when the criminals feel guilty and confess their crime(s) and thus "turn themselves in", they pay back the original sum or goods and an additional penalty of only twenty-percent (see Num. 5:5-7). By being sorrowful for their crimes, they restore the mistrust and insecurity the people in the community had for strangers and their own people and also save a lot of work, time, and effort in legal actions. Thus, they can make restitution not only by giving back what they have taken, but paying back the rest in goods and services, so that an opportunity is given to them to dissolve their karmic debt and change their lives.

Unfortunately, there are many people today who do not believe that there are moral absolutes. They say that right and wrong differ according to individual preferences, situations, and circumstances. They would not hesitate to steal from their employer in time and effort, while some companies withhold benefits and destroy loyalties of older workers. The same is true of the relationships between government and its workers. The result of stealing from each other is fear, suspicion, and a loss of trust, which is felt throughout every level of society.

In order to rationalize and subdue their conscience, people have developed all kinds of excuses for stealing from someone else by saying: "I deserve it, because I don't have it", "It is not hurting anyone", "I work here – I earn it", "It is no big deal", "I was only borrowing it", "Everyone else does it", "All is fair in love, war, and business", "I could not help myself."

Finally, "let the thief no longer steal, but rather let him labor, doing honest work with his hands, so that he may be able to give to those in need" (Eph. 4:28).

Ninth Commandment

"Thou shalt not bear false witness against thy neighbor" (Ex. 20:16 – **K.J.V.**).

The ninth commandment specifically prohibits lying or giving knowingly and voluntarily false testimony, under oath, in a court of law (perjury). False accusations have ruined the reputations and lives of many people. This is especially true in the past when there was no right to a fair hearing, the presentation of evidence, the right to a defense, and trial by jury, which has its inspiration in Holy Scripture and Christian tradition. In the pagan world, a sole accusation or a pointing of a finger was enough evidence for a caprious ruler who did not like the person to get him or her convicted and punished. This is why God gave the commandment to protect individuals of untruthful attacks against their character, reputation, and their very lives.

It is not always easy for a judge to decide if someone is telling the truth. However, through deduction, body language, and especially through the power of higher intuition, which is a divine quality, they are able to tell if someone is lying.

Lying can come in many disguises. One of the ways is to tell certain individuals or groups, in return for favors, that they are doing great while they are not. This is called flattery, and this will encourage the receivers of the false words of approval to think too highly of themselves and thus strengthen the false self of their personality. Another form of lying is called gossiping, which purpose is to destroy someone's reputation and life behind their backs. It is forbidden in the Bible. See Lev. 19:16 and Num. chapter 12. It can do a great deal of damage to the victims when this false truth is spread by the news media in order to boost its ratings. It does untold damage to families, schools, and communities and will eventually destroy those whom have been responsible of spreading lies. See Ps. 12:1-2; Jas. 4:8; Col. 3:9; Jn. 8:44. As lying is not punishable by the law of the land, "slander" is (making a false and malicious statement, in the hearing of others, in order to damage another's reputation and means of livelihood). And so is "libel" (writing or publishing such a statement), which are false accusations. "A false witness will not go unpunished, and he who utters lies will not escape" (Prov. 19:5) in the "Divine Court".

Tenth Commandment

"Thou shalt not covet thy neighbor's house, thou shalt not covet thy neighbor's wife, nor his manservant, nor his maidservant, nor his ox, nor his ass, nor anything that is thy neighbor's" (Ex. 20:17 – **K.J.V.**).

When we take something that belongs to another, it is stealing. It is an act done by the human body. Coveting concerns itself with the attitude of the human spirit and the exercise of its facilities of intellect, emotion-desire, and will. Coveting is the grasping selfishness of the corrupt human heart or spirit (Mk. 7:21, 22) to eagerly desire something which permanently belongs to someone else. How many marriages have ended in divorce because a man (woman) replaces thoughts about his/her own wife (husband) with thoughts about the desirability of his/her neighbor's wife (husband)?

The same is true of coveting things that already belong to the other person and are thus part of his/her body. There is albeit nothing wrong with desiring things, but it may lead to coveting or possessing of objects that rightfully belong to another. Wanting to possess things may eventually lead to taking steps to obtain those possessions. This happened to a rich neighbor of king Ahab and queen Jezebel, whom confiscated the vineyard from their neighbor Naboth by falsely accusing him of blasphemy and treason and then putting him to death (1 Kings ch.21).

Coveting had its beginning in the Garden of Eden when Eve "saw that the (good/evil) tree was good for food and that it was a delight to the eyes, and that the tree was to be desired to make one wise" (Gen. 3:6). She was strongly influenced to take of "its fruit" and become like the tree, by the serpent or satan who coveted the higher position of Adam and wanted to be like God. This satanic nature we find everywhere in human society when good/evil individuals, whom are not spiritually qualified, try to get positions of influence and power by lying, cheating, and slandering and using all means at their disposal. They belong to those people whom Apostle Paul rebuked in Romans 1:29-32, and who have no "inheritance in the kingdom of Christ and of God" (Eph. 5:5).

A person who does not covet is grateful to God of what he/she has become and are at peace and content with what they have (Heb. 13:5). If they are blessed with abundance, they will use it to do God's work to establish His Kingdom on earth.

#37 The Second Garden of Eden

A beginning was made to restore the whole world as the new or second Garden of Eden or Kingdom of Heaven on earth by Apostle Paul and his disciples, by evangelizing the Gospel of Jesus Christ to the people living in the countries surrounding the Mediterranean Sea.

This second garden was already prepared physically by the Roman Empire, culturally by the Greeks, and morally and spiritually by the Jewish people living outside their homeland of Israel.

#38 Who was, and is Jesus Christ?

A. The Historical Jesus

According to the Book of Genealogy (Matthew 1), Jesus is the son of Abraham, the son of David, and the son of Joseph and Mary; three times fourteen generations from Abraham. The ancestral line of [1]Mary is given in Luke 3:23-38 by using her husband's name. See also 1 Chron. 1-9.

Jesus (the name given by the Angel Gabriel – Luke 1:31 –) was conceived by the inspiration of the [2]Father aspect of God, and thereafter, Mary was closely guided by the Holy Spirit, or [2]Mother aspect of God (Luke 1:35). Thus, Mary was not only the mother of Jesus' human nature or personality, but also the bearer of his divine Seed, Spark, or Word.

Jesus (the Greek form of Joshua or Jeshua), was born in Bethlehem (house of breath), about six miles south of Jerusalem, the burial place of Rachel, the wife of Jacob (Gen. 35:19) and the birth place of David (1 Sam. 17:12). He was born towards the end of the reign of Herod the great (37-4 B.C.).

Because a decree was issued by Caesar Augustus to "be enrolled" (Luke 2:1-5), Joseph and Mary took the hundred mile trip from

---

[1] The mother of Mary was Anna. She was an Essene, healer and spiritual teacher. See book – Anna: Woman of Miracles by Carol Haenni and Vivian van Wick.

[2] In the Hebrew, Jehovah is written Yahweh, yah being masculine and weh feminine. Yahweh is a Father whose care is often experienced as mother-like in its compassion and calling. See Isa. 42:14; 49:15; 66:13; Matt. 23:37. God as Father and Mother created humans because they not only like to have servants, the angels, but especially love to have their own spiritual children, whom are of their own essence or substance, thus reproducing themselves.

Nazareth to Bethlehem, thus fulfilling the prophecy that the Messiah would be born in Bethlehem (Micah 5:2-5).

NOTE: No one seems to know the physical birthday of Jesus, which is celebrated since the fourth century on December 25 in the West and January 6 in the Eastern Church. We should, however, less emphasize our natural birthday, which makes us a member of the human family, and more stress our spiritual birthday by becoming a member of God's family. Nevertheless, Christians recognized that since the time of the birth of Jesus, began the years of the Lord (Anno Domini) A.D. The Christians began counting the years like they have never lived before. And so began the Christian era, by building the Kingdom of God, leaving behind all those laggards whom do not want to join with the new and stronger evolutionary forces of the universe. Thus, Jesus opened the way for everyone to start living a divine life and enter the kingdom of heaven, or enter the Garden of Eden.

Jesus was born in a stable because there was no place for the holy family in the inn. "At the end of eight days" he was [1]circumcised and was called "Jesus". After forty days since his birth, Joseph and Mary "brought him up to Jerusalem to present him to the Lord", to fulfill the Mosaic Law of purification of the first-born (Luk. 2:21-24; Ex. 13:2, 12; Lev. 12).

After Herod the king heard from the wise men from the East, who came to worship the one who has been born king of the Jews, Herod wanted to kill the baby Jesus after he found out that the child was prophesied to become the ruler of Israel (Matt. 2:6; Micah 5:2). Being warned in a dream of Herod's intention, the holy family fled to Egypt and returned a few years later back to Nazareth after the death of Herod (Matt. 2:19-23).

Jesus grew up in Nazareth "and became strong, filled with wisdom" (Luke 2:40), with four younger brothers and probably two sisters, and he was known in town as the "carpenter's son" (Matt. 13:55-56), and "the carpenter, the son of Mary" (Mk. 6:3) and "the son of Joseph" (Jn. 6:42).

---

[1] Circumcision was a "mark of the covenant" between Yahweh and His people (Gen. 17:10-14), a sign that one belongs to the people of God. It was part of the Law of Moses. However, it was no longer required in God's new dispensation and was thus replaced by Spirit baptism, through which one is adopted in the spiritual family of God (Rom. 8:23; Gal. 4:5).

Nazareth was situated at the crossroad between Syria (north) and Egypt (south), on the ridge of a hill (Luke 4:29), overlooking a beautiful countryside. The [2]personality of Jesus, which consists of body and human spirit (intellect – emotion – will), was influenced and formed by his surroundings and the people living in that environment, while the [2]individual Christ or Soul (Christ Jesus) began to develop in the "temple" of his personality when he became more mature.

There is hardly any record of Jesus the man of Nazareth up to the age of thirty, except from his visit with Joseph and Mary to Jerusalem at the feast of Passover, when he was twelve years old and was separated from his parents for three days. This was the time when his budding Divine Spirit or Soul (formed from the divine Seed or Word) was developing in the "womb" of his pure personality, was born, and started to lead the life of his personality. He became the first person to become the true son (child) of God (Col. 1:15; 1 Cor. 15:23). He expressed this sonship later to his parents, "Did you not know that I must be in my Father's house?" But they did not know what he was saying (Luke 2:49-50). He astounded the teachers of the Temple with his understanding and wisdom (Luke 2:41-47), speaking the new and profound language or song of his Divine Spirit (Jn. 7:46; Rev. 5:9). Thereafter, Luke 2:52 mentioned that "Jesus increased in wisdom and in stature, and in favor with God and man".

Jesus appeared [3]externally to be an ordinary man, but was, in His manifestation, a man of greater righteousness (1 Jn. 3:7) and obedience to God. He came from a long line of good, noble, and virtuous an-

---

[2] The future capacity of the personality traits and character of Jesus was endowed at the time of his conception by his human parents. Later on, the Christ Spirit (Soul) or God Consciousness was "begotten of God", or sired by his Heavenly Parents, by comprehending, applying, and assimilating the pure Word of God (as verified by the Holy Spirit). His personality became "pregnant" with New Life. The personality and the Soul will then grow up and be raised under the guidance of their respective parents. Jesus did not need to go through the special process of salvation or through an additional process of being "born again", as ordinary people (1 Pet. 1:3) because his personality was pure and not tainted with original sin. As the Holy Spirit is called the Spirit of Truth (Jn. 14:17), we can call the Soul or Divine Spirit (Individual Christ – Gal. 4:19 –) the Body of Truth.

[3] Description of Jesus as seen by author:

"I saw first a vision of a very handsome young face of a man. It was a long and strong face with high cheek bones, big eyes, with a well developed jaw, somewhat square, and he was looking upwards like in agony, as in mental and divine suffering. Right after that, I saw another vision: a man hanging on the cross, looking thin, and blood was pouring out from wounds from his body."

cestors and was born from his [4]virginal origin or parents whom had no sin. Therefore, the personality of Jesus did not show any trace of sin. This was well testified by his apostles in 1 Jn. 3:5; 1 Pet. 2:22; 2 Cor. 5:21; Heb. 9:14, whom were well aware of their own sins. When Peter encountered Jesus, he cried out, "Depart from me, for I am a sinful man, o Lord" (Luke 5:8). The young Apostle Paul lamented that he hated sin but kept right on sinning (Rom. 7:14-25).

According to the letters of Paul, written between 51 and 64 A.D. (before the four Gospels were written), Jesus was born a Jew (Gal. 3:16; Rom. 9:5) and was a descendant of King David (Rom. 1:3). As a man like any physical man, he became weary (John 4:6), slept in a boat (Matt. 8:24), and was sometimes hungry (Matt. 4:2; 21:18) and, like any other man, was tempted (Luke 4:1-13).

However, unlike ordinary people whose hearts are good and evil (Matt. 15:19; 5:28; 19:8; 13:15, 19), the inner personality (human spirit) or heart of Jesus was only good and pure (Matt. 5:8). Jesus was therefore a true man, with a human as well as a growing divine nature or Soul, whereby the latter was becoming more and more in charge of the human personality, thus blending the [5]divine and human wills into one.

Jesus often called himself the [6]Son of Man, who, like Jacob (Gen.

---

[4] Jesus was born free of original sin or satanic nature, in a passionless body, from a woman whose personality is pure and virgin in emotion, thought, word, and deed. Immaculate Conception refers to the fact that the parents of Jesus were able to perform the generative act without passion.

[5] Unlike ordinary human beings, the inclination to do God's Will or his own will was not a difficult one for Jesus, unless he was acting out the role of the first Adam, who refused to do God's Will (John 5:30; Mark 14:36). Good and evil human beings, however, have to make a hard choice (1 Pet. 1:3): to become the child of God by being born spiritually "not of the will of the flesh (evil will) nor the will of man, but of God" (John 1:13); or to keep living the life of the personality when the more or less purified "I" of the "self will" runs their lives. When humans in the future are born without original sin, they, like Jesus, would for surely choose to become a member of God's family instead of staying a member of the human family, whom are living according to the Law of God.

[6] The expression Son of Man can be interpreted that Jesus, in its human nature, is the Son of the collective energy of all human personalities from which he can draw and have full power, like a human ruler, as long as they are in agreement with the human populace. This power or authority can also be transferred from ruler to successor. Roman emperors felt so much power that they even called themselves incorrectly sons of God. They should be called sons of the collective energies of good/evil humans or sons of gods whose thought forms are created by those good and evil humans.

28:12), was the mediator between heaven and earth (Jn. 1:51), and he expressed himself in his native Aramaic language (Mark 5:41; 7:34).

B. Baptism, Temptation, and Ministry of Jesus

In Matthew chapter three we read:
"In those days came John the Baptist, preaching in the wilderness of Judea --- 'I baptize you with water for repentance, but he who is coming after me is mightier than I, --- he will baptize you with the Holy Spirit and with fire.'"

"Then Jesus came from Galilee to the Jordan to John, to be baptized by him. John would have prevented him, saying, 'I need to be baptized by you, and do you come to me?' But Jesus answered him, 'Let it be so now; for thus it is fitting for us to fulfill all righteousness.' Then he consented."

"And when Jesus was baptized, He went up immediately from the water, and behold, the heavens were opened and he saw the Spirit of God (the Holy Spirit – Luke 22 – the Spirit – Mark 1:10; John 1:32), descending like a dove, and lightning on him; and lo, a voice from heaven saying, 'This is my beloved Son, with whom I am well pleased'" (Matt. 3:1-17).

"And Jesus, full of the Holy Spirit, returned from the Jordan, and was led by the Spirit for forty days in the wilderness, tempted by the devil" (Luk. 4:1-2).

Jesus overcame the temptation of emphasizing physical food (instead of spiritual food or Word of God) and of using his God-given spiritual power for personal ambitions and fame. He did not use his power to force people to do his will (instead of changing people's hearts), refusing to become the son of satan (instead of the Son of God).

"Jesus returned in the power of the Spirit into Galilee --- and he taught in their synagogues, being glorified by all" (Luke 4:3-15). In Mark 1:15, he said, "The time is fulfilled and the kingdom of God is at hand." As Matthew 4:17 reported, he "began to preach, saying, 'repent, for the kingdom of heaven is at hand.'" Jesus began his ministry when he was about thirty years of age (Luke 3:23).

John the Baptist was the last prophet of the Old Testament dispensation, and was thus a link or connection between the old and new covenants. His mission was to "Prepare the way of the Lord, make his paths straight" (Luke 3:4). John baptized with water for the forgiveness of sin (Mark 1:4), or to purify (cleansing – washing) one's personality of evil for the preparation of the Kingdom. Christ, through Jesus, was able to give birth to the Divine Spirit or Soul in one's inner personality to be baptized with the Holy Spirit (Jn. 1:33). Therefore, John, who represented the personality of the people (Old Testament), "must decrease", while Christ Jesus, who represented the Divine Spirit or Christ Spirit of the people in the New Testament dispensation, "must increase" (John 3:30). By baptizing Jesus in the river Jordan, Jesus inherited the Old Testament dispensation and could start with the new by acquiring disciples whom were the followers of John (Jn. 1:37).

*As Jesus was baptized with the Holy Spirit, (this also happened later to his disciples at the day of the harvest or Pentecost – Acts 2:1 –) he was, at that time, overshadowed by the Cosmic Christ, which is the male aspect of God. Having overcome all the temptation of the evil one, whom the first Adam could not overcome, Jesus restored and inherited the position of Adam and as the "last Adam became a life-giving spirit" (1 Cor. 15:45). The Universal or Cosmic Christ "the Alpha and the Omega, who is and who was and who is to come" (Rev. 1:8), who died in the first Adam but became alive in the last Adam (Rev. 1:18), united or anointed Jesus with His Spirit. Thereafter, Jesus was called, in Hebrew, Messiah ("Yahweh is salvation") and Jesus Christ by adding Christ (Gr. Christos) to the name Jesus, thus becoming the Savior or Redeemer. Thus, to acknowledge Jesus as the Christ is to admit him as a Savior, upon whom is the Spirit of the Lord (Isa. 11:2; 42:1; 61:1) and whom, through Christ, is reconciling all things to himself (Col. 1:20).

The last Adam or Jesus, in close relation with the Cosmic Christ or Christ Consciousness, is also called in John 1:14; 3:16 the only begotten Son, because there can only be one universal Adam. In this way, the aspect or emanation of God (Cosmic Christ), together with Jesus, will dwell in bodily form among His people (Col 2:9), through which God the Father has direct influence and action in the human world in a universal way.

---

* Paul mentioned Jesus' baptism as "how God anointed Jesus of Nazareth with the Holy Spirit and with power" (Acts 10:38).

The Holy Spirit, which has such female qualities as: "The Comforter", "The Counselor", "The Intercessor", and "The Spirit of Truth", functions as inspiration, regeneration, sanctification, consolation, and grace, through which God the Mother has direct access to the children of the world. The Holy Spirit is described in the book of Revelation 19:7-9 as the Bride of the Cosmic Christ, whom both will find their dwelling place in the restored Eve and Adam and will become as one. "For the marriage of the Lamb has come and his Bride has made herself ready" --- "Blessed are those who are invited to the marriage supper of the Lamb." See also Rev. 21:9; 22:17; Matt. 22:2; Lk. 14:8; Jn. 2:1; Matt. 25:1; Lk. 12:35-38.

NOTE: In addition, the Holy Spirit as a Person (not an it, force or power) teacher (Lk. 12:12; Jn. 14:26), testifies (Jn. 15:26), guides and speaks (Jn. 16:13), sends (Acts 13:4), forbids (Acts 16:6-7), and other actions. We can lie to the Holy Spirit (Acts 5:3), tempt her (Acts 5:9), grieve her (Eph. 4:30), and even blaspheme her (Matt. 12:31). The Holy Spirit has been and still is working through many women, especially through Mary, the mother of Jesus. She has been and, at present, is appearing all over the world in many places to warn and prepare the people for the most important event in their lives, "spiritual birth" (initiate faith) and to help them in their spiritual growth (nourishes faith). She functions as a True Mother for the downtrodden and the poor, and is closer to the earth than the Cosmic Christ and, thus, more "visible" in human life, especially when our True Mother expresses through human beings. The church as the Body of Christ (Col. 1:18; 1 Cor. 12:27) is like the Holy Spirit and may function, at times, like the collective entity of spirit persons. This is why the Christians at Pentecost were suddenly able to speak in foreign tongues simultaneously when they were inspired by the Holy Spirit (1 Cor. 6:19; Acts 2). Thus, the Holy Spirit also works through the medium of discarnate spirits and angels to realize God's providential purpose.

C. Is Jesus God, the Son, or Son of Man?

[1]The Gospels of Matthew, Mark, and Luke, the so-called synoptic (similar) gospels, deal much with the historical Jesus, his personality [2](lower self), and [3]Higher Self (Divine Spirit). Jesus often referred to himself in the above Gospels as the Son of Man, but he also spoke of himself as the Christ or the Son. The Johannine gospels often call Jesus "Son" and "Son of God", while Paul designates for the risen Jesus often the name Lord and Christ.

As Jesus occasionally spoke from his human or lower self of his personality, most of the time he expressed himself through his Divine Spirit or individual Christ Spirit, which is always in harmony with the God forces. By living almost wholly in the Christ part of himself, he was very much connected with the Cosmic Christ. When he was in complete oneness with the latter, he became and could be called the Son of God. This happened, for example, at the time when "he was transfigured before them, and his face shone like the sun, and his garments became white as light" (Matt. 17:2).

In the Gospel of John, Jesus is often used as a direct channel of the Universal or Cosmic Christ, the second person of the Trinity, and appeared to be the latter. For example, he said in John 8:58, "Truly, truly, I say to you, before Abraham was I am." In the "I AM" sayings, he was not speaking as a human being known as Jesus, or as the Son of Man. At times, his Divine Spirit (Christ Jesus) spoke, and at other times, the Cosmic Christ was speaking through him. For example: "I am the way, and the truth, and the life; no one comes to the Father, but by me" (Jn. 14:6). "I am in the Father and the Father in me" (Jn. 14:10). "I am the door; if anyone enters by me, he will be saved" (Jn. 10:9).

---

[1] The Gospels of Matthew and Luke begin with Jesus' human history, while the Gospel of John speaks of the eternal history of the Son of God.

[2] The lower self or personality is represented by a triangle with its apex pointing downward. Its main concern is the practical considerations and the reality of earthly life in a physical body.

[3] The Higher Self or Divine Spirit is represented by a triangle pointing upward. Its main concern is finding spiritual truth and living according to higher spiritual values.

The Higher and the lower self should be united as a whole so that the wisdom and spirituality of the higher is infused into the lower, and the experience and practical knowledge is made available to the higher, thus forming the Star of David. This is one of the main purposes of life on earth.

"I am the vine, you are the branches. He who abides in me, and I in him, he it is that bears much fruit, for apart from me you can do nothing" (Jn. 15:5). "I am the resurrection and the life; he who believes in me, though he die (spiritual), yet shall he live" (Jn. 11:25). "I am the bread of life; he who comes to me shall not hunger, and he who believes in me shall never thirst" (Jn. 6:35).

In the Gospel of Matthew, Jesus appeared to be God when the Cosmic Christ expressed through Jesus and said, "For where two or three are gathered in my name, there am I in the midst of them" (Matt. 18:20). This suggests that the male aspect of God was speaking, who can be everywhere at the same time – or be omnipresent.

NOTE: Unlike the Old Testament prophets who used to proclaim "thus says the Lord" (Haggai 1:2, 7; 2:6, 11), Jesus spoke in his own name, saying, "But I say to you" (Matt. 5:22, 28, 32, 34, 39, 44). He also said, "Truly, truly, I say to you" (Jn. 1:51; 3:3).

REMARK: Some people identify their Higher Self with God. This can lead to an inflated ego. They confuse the Soul with God and do not like to accept that the God Self lives within the Higher Self.

After the resurrection, Jesus came back (in his vital body – see #43) as he promised in Mark 14:28, and was fulfilled in Matthew 28:7-11. Jesus appeared to have become completely one with that aspect of God, which liked to dwell among the people, when he said in Matt. 28:20 "and lo, I am with you always, to the close of the age". The disciples realized that Jesus was more than an ordinary man, after he had risen. Thomas said, "My Lord and my God!" (Jn. 20:28) He was deified and glorified after his resurrection (John 7:39), whereby Jesus became completely united with the Cosmic Christ. He could therefore say in Matthew 28:18, "All authority in heaven and on earth has been given to me." As Paul testified, "Christ Jesus --- is at the right hand of God" interceding for us (Rom. 8:34).

Paul the Pharisee, who never met Jesus in bodily form, encountered the risen Jesus at the road to Damascus (Acts chapter 9) and was completely converted by the Christ of faith. To Paul, Jesus was more like God than the disciples who had known Jesus in the flesh. He continually preached about the risen Jesus, the Son of God, and urged people to accept Him as their Lord and Savior and be baptized with the Holy Spirit. About fifteen hundred years later, Martin Luther reviewed Paul's teaching and was opposed by his brother priests, as was Paul earlier by the disciples of Jesus.

REMARK: Tacitus, a Roman historian, wrote in "The Annals", during the latter part of the first century: "Christus (Christ) suffered the extreme penalty during the reign of Tiberius at the hands of one of our procurators, Pontius Pilatus."

NOTE: The story of Jesus' birth and death is also our own story of spiritual growth.

In Jesus, we find the one in whom we can see our divine possibilities, and in whom we can see God and what He is like. *God as Spirit cannot reveal Himself in a complete way except through a person who is totally dedicated to God. However, as our example, Jesus is like God but is not God Himself. "He was in the form of God" but "did not count equality with God" (Phil. 2:6). "He will be great, and will be called the Son of the Most High" (Luke 1:32, 35). Jesus never claimed to be God but rather the Son of God (Jn. 10:36). For God sent the Son into the world" (Jn. 3:17; 17:8). "Going a little farther he (Jesus) fell on his face and prayed, "My Father, if it be possible, let this cup pass from me" (Matt. 26:39). If the Father and Jesus were the same, such prayer has no meaning. Jesus and the Father are two distinct beings. "I bear witness to myself, and the Father who sent me bears witness to me" (Jn. 8:18). "Of that day or that hour no one knows, not even the angels in heaven, nor the Son, but only the Father" (Mark 13:32). This would not be the case if Father, Son, and Holy Spirit were co-equal and co-eternal in one God-head. Peter said, "Blessed be the God and Father of our Lord Jesus Christ!" (1 Pet. 1-3) Jesus taught Christians to pray "Our Father who art in heaven" (Matt. 6:9). Jesus looked towards heaven and called upon the Father (Jn. 17:1-3), and on the cross, Jesus' last words were, "Father, into thy hands I commit my spirit!" (Luke 23:46)

NOTE: The heavenly Father and Mother manifest to each one of us at the right moment in the form of our highest ideal. For many people, that is Jesus Christ. For others, it is the Christ of all religions. Faiths may meet each other through the universal Christ of their religion and come to God (Jn. 14:6).

---

* Because God is Spirit and does not have the different bodies or vehicles (for every plane of existence), He/She uses physical, psychic, and divine bodies of beings and their faculties to express Him/Her Self. It is mainly through humans that God experiences life, evolves, and expands His/Her awareness of Themselves.

God can be compare to a root of a tree (who had its beginning in a ground-like existence (primal energy), His emanation or trunk, to the Cosmic Christ and the Holy Spirit, who created their living spiritual children or branches (Gen 2:9; Dan. 4:10; Rev. 2:7; John 15:1-8).

REMARK: Christian Science acknowledges Jesus Christ as the Savior and Son of God, but they draw a clear distinction between Jesus the person and the Christ. This is in contrast with the belief of Orthodox Christianity who insists that Jesus is personally identical with the eternal pre-existent Son of God (Cosmic Christ).

D. The Mystery of the Trinity

According to "a basic Catholic dictionary" by D.L. Lowery, the Holy Trinity is "the most sublime and central doctrine of the Christian faith, namely, that there are three Persons – Father, Son, Holy Spirit – in one God".

"The Maryknoll Catholic dictionary" adds "Each of these persons is distinct from the others, yet each is the true God with all of His infinite perfections. These three Persons are co-equal, co-eternal, and consubstantial".

The Trinity, according to "The Readers' Digest Great Encyclopedia Dictionary" is: "A threefold consubstantial personality existing in the one divine being or substance; the union in one God of Father, Son, and Holy Spirit as three infinite persons".

The Merriam Webster Dictionary says that the Trinity is "the unity of Father, Son, and Holy Spirit as three persons in one God-head". The New International Dictionary of the Christian Church states that "the central tenet of the Christian faith is that God is one, personal and triune".

According to the Bible Dictionary and Concordance by C.F. Pfeiffer, The Triune God, the God-head is revealed in three distinct persons in the Bible and each has a different work:

The Father is God (Matt. 11:25; John 6:27; Rom. 15:6; 1 Cor. 8:6; Eph. 4:6; James 1:27). Two of the most important names in the Old Testament are Jehovah (Lord) and Elohim (God and Creator). Another name for God is Adonai (Lord). El-Shaddai, or God Almighty as used by the Patriarchs (Gen. 17:1; Ex. 6:3). I am that I am, affirming His Presence (Ex. 3:14). God is one (Deut. 6:4), self-existent (Ex. 3:14), eternal (1 Tim. 1:17), omnipresent (Acts 17:27), omniscient (1 John 3:20), omnipotent (Gen. 17:1), and infinite (Is. 9:6). He is holy (Josh. 24:19; Hos. 11:9), just (Gen. 18:25), merciful (Heb. 4:16), and He is love (1 John 4:8).

NOTE: God is absolute, existing beyond vibratory creatures. He/She can be transcendent as well as immanent. Because the universe is the Body of God, it can be identified with the Creator (pantheism). When the world is seen as part of God (panentheism), His/Her Spirit is believed to be God, who is governing everything that has life, or a soul (panpsychism). "In him we live and move and have our being" (Acts 17:28).

REMARK: According to Jewish sources, God's real name is Y.H.W.H., which is pronounced as Yahweh in Hebrew and Jehovah in English. This name of God expresses and involves the very being of God, and by pronouncing it, one will encounter and be enveloped by the very presence of God, the Creator and the source of all life. The Jews refused to pronounce the name and substituted the word "My Lord" (in Hebrew 'Adonai'). The name may mean "He who is" or "I am that I am", and individualized for every son and daughter of God as "I am Presence".

Sometimes God speaks of Himself in the plural (Gen. 1:26; 3:22; Isa. 6:3, 8). At other times the word Elohim (plural of Eloah) is used, which may mean the powers surrounding God.

The Son is God (John 1:1, 18; Rom. 9:5; Phil. 2:6; Col. 2:9; Heb. 1:18). According to D.L. Lowery, "Jesus Christ is the eternal Son of God, the second person of the Holy Trinity" --- "and that he is at one and the same time fully God and fully man" (true God as well as true man). "There are two natures, human and divine, permanently united in the one divine Person, Jesus Christ."

The Spirit (Holy) is God (Acts 5:3; 1 Cor. 2:10; Eph. 2:22). According to Lowery, the Holy Spirit is "The third Person of the Holy Trinity, distinct from the Father and the Son but co-equal and co-eternal with them". He was sent by Christ after his resurrection and ascension. "God's love has been poured into our hearts through the Holy Spirit which has been given to us" (Rom. 5:5).

The word Trinity is not mentioned in the Bible. However, it is indicated in Matthew 28:19 wherein Jesus, after his resurrection, said, "Go therefore and make disciples of all nations, baptizing them in the name of the Father and of the Son and of the Holy Spirit." Paul said in 2 Cor. 13:14 in his greeting, "The grace of the Lord Jesus Christ and the love of God and the fellowship of the Holy Spirit be with you all." See also Matt. 3:16-17; 1 Cor. 12:4-6.

NOTE: We can discover many trinities in nature and in our life. For example: matter exists in three states – gas, liquid, and solid. There are three natural kingdoms – plant, animal, and mineral. Plants consist of root, trunk, and leaves. There are three primary colors – red, yellow, and blue. The physical body has three parts – abdomen, chest, and head. Limbs have three parts as well as the fingers. In the head we find: eyes (like God), nose (like humans), mouth like the creation. A grown human being has a physical body, spirit body, and divine body, with its conscious, subconscious, and super-conscious mind. The physical body can be compared to a carriage, the human spirit to a horse, and the Divine Spirit to the coachman.

REMARK: Jesus introduced, during the Last Supper, the Holy Spirit to them by saying: "And I will pray the Father, and he will give you another Counselor" (Jn. 14:16). "The Counselor, the Holy Spirit, whom the Father will send in my name, he will teach you all things, and bring to your remembrance all that I have said to you" (Jn. 14:26).

E. Pre-Nicene Trinities

Jesus asked His disciples, "Who do you say that I am" (Mark 8:29). Later he challenged *the Pharisees, "What do you think of the Christ? Whose son is he?" (Matt. 22:42), while John 7:43 reported that "there was a division among the people over him".

In the Old Testament, God was not seen as a trinity because the people at that time believed that "The Lord our God is one Lord" (Deut. 6:4). This all changed when Jesus appeared, who spoke about the Father, the Holy Spirit, and his own claims to deity. From the beginning, the disciples and followers of Jesus could not agree who he was. Later, different Christian teachers had different views of who Jesus was and what he did. Apostle Paul complained of more than one "different Gospel" being preached (Gal. 1:6-9). By the second century, the churches were so much divided that they were even criticized by pagan observers, although the Christians were usually one in Spirit.

The early Christians believed in the Father, Son, and Holy Spirit and were baptized in their names, but they had no idea of the relationship of the Persons in the God-head. Those relationships were worked on by the second century church fathers Ignatius of Antioch (c. 110 A.D.), Justin Matyr (c. 150 A.D.), and others. They start from the premise (indicated by Philo of Alexandria, a Jewish thinker) that the Father generated His creative Logos, which is present in the historic Jesus, while the Holy Spirit is the inspirer and enlightener who was present after Jesus' resurrection in the Christian community. Thus, in the Pre-

* The Pharisees could not understand how Jesus could be David's Lord as well as his son (Matt. 22:41-46).

Nicene Trinities, the Father is the eternal, unbegotten, and the ultimate Source of everything. God the Son, who is begotten of the Father, is God in relationship to the world. He is thus the creator, the redeemer, and sanctifier. God the Holy Spirit is God in the hearts and minds of human beings. The members, however, are not co-equal: the Father is more than the Son, and the Son more than the Holy Spirit.

Tertullian, Apologist and theologian (c. 160-c. 220), provided a theory upon which later writers built the doctrine of the Trinity. He coined the formula: three persons in one substance. He thus made an attempt to show that God, His Son, and the Holy Spirit were three distinct persons existing in one divine substance, thereby becoming the first to apply the Latin form of the word "trinity".

As Tertullian was accepted by the church councils, the theories of Origen (theologian and writer (c. 185-c. 254) were not fully accepted, especially not his belief in the pre-existence of souls. He therefore saw Jesus as pre-existent (having lived before), and that the Logos is like the Father in the same way that a thought represents its thinker. He denied the equality of the three divine persons, eternal punishment, and that the devil would also be saved.

NOTE: Because Tertullian was convinced that the Christian church became more Catholic (that is universal in reach, and more secular or worldly in belief) that he, at the beginning of the third century, left the established church and became a Montanist. The Montanists, like the monks of later times, were otherworldly (did not accept the morality of "the world" (Jn. 18:36; Rom. 12:12; Jas. 1:27; 1 John 5:19) and stressed the importance of fasting, other forms of penance, and martyrdom. They awaited anxiously the coming of the Lord and the end of the world. The movement's morality was of a higher standard as that of the Orthodox Church, especially the obligations concerning marriage. They were not accepted by the Catholic Church and were severely persecuted by the Roman Empire because they would not accept the Roman emperor as the son of God. However, during those trying times, God blessed them, and they spread like fire throughout the Roman Empire.

F. Gnostic Teachings about Christ

In the first and second centuries, groups emerged whom were in disagreement with the teaching of the apostles and the church fathers. Many of them were of Gnostic origin.

One group, the Ebionites – Jewish Christians with Gnostic overtones – recognized Jesus as the Messiah but did not accept his divinity. This was one of the reasons they could not agree with Pauline epistles. They regarded Jesus as the son of Joseph and Mary, who became the elected Son of God at his baptism, when he was united with the eternal Christ who is higher than the archangels but not divine. These Ebionites are much like the early [1]Jewish Christians whom held to the law of Moses, its circumcision, Sabbath, and customs as described in Acts 21:20-21; while Paul and others taught that the age of the law was over and that they are "under grace" (Rom. 6:14).

On the other hand, [2]Docetism, a Gnostic sect, questioned the historical reality of Jesus and that the suffering and death of Jesus was only an appearance. They say that Jesus was a divine being but had not taken on flesh. It only appeared he had, thus denying his incarnation and atonement. John warned against them, emphasizing that Jesus Christ has come in the flesh (1 John 4:1-3); 2 John 7; 2 Cor. 11:4).

NOTE: Gnosticism (Gr. Gnosis, knowledge) – a teaching that originated in the philosophical schools of the pre-Christian age, a system of ancient Greek and Oriental philosophy, whom were influenced by Judaism and Christianity. In turn, they try to change them because their objective was to amalgamate all the world's religions by taking the best in each of them. They already reacted with Christians in the first century (see 1 Timothy 6:20). The Gnostics did not recognize the church hierarchy and authority of bishop, priest, doctrine, and creed, but rather discover and try to follow their inner Christ. A central theme of their teaching was the conviction that salvation can only be obtained when the spirit is delivered from the imprisonment of the body by means of a secret spiritual knowledge or Gnosis. It is further believed that the physical world is created by the evil god of the Old Testament, and that therefore, all matter is evil. They therefore see a distinction between the inferior creator and the supreme good God, who had sent one of His subordinates, Christ, into the world to free the souls from the perverted material world. They did not deny that Jesus was divine. It denied that he was human and that therefore, he could not be born of a woman and be tainted by matter. Gnosticism, like the mystery religions, consisted of two groups: the uninitiated and the initiated. The latter were usually celibate and believed that the soul could save itself by an ascetic denial of the flesh and by divine knowledge. That is to know oneself at the deepest level, and thus to know God. It was in fierce competition with Christianity, reaching its greatest influence in the latter part of the 2nd century, waned in the 3rd century, and was replaced by the

---

[1] For the Jewish people, Mohammedans, and others to believe that Jesus is the incarnation of God was and still is a great obstacle for them of turning their hearts to Christ the Redeemer and Savior.

[2] They probably believed that the body of Jesus was the same, as the "resurrected body" of Jesus (vital body), who came back after his crucifixion and who passed "through the midst of them" (Luk. 4:30).

Manichaean movement, of which the young Augustine was a member. After its decline, it surfaced in the later Middle Ages, and its members were called Albigensians, Catharists, and Bogomils. Today, we find communities of Gnostics in Iran and Iraq, whom are called the Mandaneans.

Other active [1]Gnostic groups of the 2nd and 3rd centuries were the Basilidians, whom celebrated the day of Jesus' baptism as the time when Jesus became divine, or when the divine Savior entered the human being of Jesus.

The Marcions believe that Jesus came to reveal the supreme Divine Being or True God who was totally unknown. They further asserted that the creator of the world was not as good as the God and Father of Jesus, a God of love and grace.

The followers of Cerinthius conceived that the world was not the creation of the True God but that of an inferior angel who held the world in bondage. Jesus was a normal man who differed from ordinary men only in greater wisdom and righteousness. He was chosen or adapted by the True God (Matt. 3:17) to release the world from its bondage. To fulfill this mission, the Christ (Cosmic Christ) descended upon him at baptism, sent from the Father. This Christ departed from Jesus before his death on the cross when he, at the ninth hour, cried out with a loud voice, "My God, my God, why hast thou forsaken me?" (Matt. 27:46).

Some of the Gnostic teachings were also the conclusion of Paul of Samosato (Bishop of Antioch 260-272). He said that the heavenly Christ descended on Jesus and that therefore, Jesus and the Christ are two separate beings. This view, however, was not accepted in the later Christological controversies of the fourth and fifth centuries.

Another Pre-Nicene Christian teacher of the third century was [2]Sabellius who insisted that the terms "Father", "Son", and "Holy

---

[1] Irenaes (c. 175 – c. 195), bishop of Lyons, was strongly against Gnostic activities. He defended the real humanity of Christ and emphasized that the Creator God of the Old Testament is identical with the Father of Jesus Christ.

[2] A modern form of Sabellianism is Unitarianism, which rejects the doctrine of the Trinity and the deity of Jesus. In 1961, it merged with Universalism to form the Unitarian Universalist Association. Prominent anti-Trinitarians are Thomas Jefferson, R.W. Emerson, and Michael Servetus, who was burned to death for his belief in the Trinity on August 6, 1553 A.D. in the Calvinist theocracy of Geneva. He was especially persecuted for his statement that the most serious error involved in Trinitarian doctrine was the belief in the eternal existence of Jesus Christ.

Spirit" applied to the same being who was active as the Father-Creator, Son-Redeemer, and Spirit-Giver of life. Thus, the Son and Spirit are modes of God expressing Himself, not essential eternal distinctions, as in the later accepted Trinitarian doctrine. It is therefore called Modalism, which is a form of Monarchianism.

In order to solidify its orthodox position (majority rule), Christianity came up with the Apostles' Creed, which is basically a refutation of Gnosticism. It affirmed belief in "God, the Father Almighty, maker of heaven and earth" (the created world is not evil or the work of an evil god). "Jesus Christ His only Son our Lord: who was conceived by the Holy Ghost, born of the Virgin Mary, suffered under Pontius Pilate, was crucified, died, and was buried" (asserting its belief in the complete humanity of Jesus, the value of the body, and earthly life).

The next important issue that was raised by Christian people was that of the Trinity – the relationship of Father, Son, and Holy Spirit. This problem was debated at the council of Nicea, and the result was entered in the Nicene Creed, which is found in the liturgy and prayer books of many denominations.

G. Ecumenical Councils and Their Resolution

Trinitarian Controversies

Church councils which represented the whole church are called ecumenical, from the Greek word oikoumene (inhabited world). The early councils were called by Emperors who summoned the bishops or representatives from the Eastern and Western churches and gave them the authority to choose. Some churches accepted only the verdict of the first three councils, such as the Coptic, Armenian, and Syrian denominations. The Eastern Orthodox Church, Anglican, and many Protestants accepted the first seven, while Luther regarded only the first four as ecumenical. The first eight were convoked by Emperors, while the others were called by the Roman Catholic Church; the Medieval councils and the last three, Trent 1545-1563, Vatican I 1869-1870, and the 21st ecumenical council Vatican II 1962-1965, summoned by Pope John XXIII.

The first ecumenical council was summoned by the [1]first Christian Roman Emperor Constantine in 325 A.D. in Nicea because of the Arius controversy (c. 318-381) which threatened to divide the church and, thus, the unity and stability of the Roman Empire.

The council condemned the teaching of Arius (d. 336), a presbyter of Alexandria, who taught that Christ or Logos was not equal to God the Father but was that of a similar essence or substance (homoiousias). They accepted the position of Alexander (d. 328), bishop of Alexandria, who believed that Christ or the Son was of the [2]same essence or substance (homoousias).

NOTE: Today, we find Arian-like Christology being preached by the Jehovah's Witnesses, who deny the eternity of Jesus Christ and the doctrine of the Trinity. Like Arius, they believe that Christ is the mediator between the Creator and the creation, and that he was the first and highest created being and, thus, had a pre-human existence in heaven. Mormons believe that Jesus Christ is the first-born spirit child to heavenly Parents, but he is not God. Christian Science also says that Jesus is not God but a "way shower" to God, who is the same in essence, though multiform in office, while for most New Age people, Jesus is an "enlightened master" who helps others to see the true nature of Reality.

By adding to the Apostles' Creed – the phrase that Christ is of the same being (ousia) as the Father and the phrase "begotten" is added "not made", to deny the Arian contention that the Logos was "made", or had a beginning and other additions resulted in the Nicene Creed, part of which appears below:

> We believe in one Lord Jesus Christ, the only begotten
> Son of God, begotten from the Father before all time,
> light from light, true God from true God, begotten not
> created, of the same essence as the Father, through

---

[1] Accepting Christianity as the state religion was a mixed blessing. The bishops, whom were persecuted as recently as 311 A.D., found the Emperor's favor a blessing from God. However, they not only had religious authority, but also gained political power. The result was that they became spiritually lazy and would soon persecute those whom did not accept their orthodox beliefs. This resulted in hundreds of years of heresy hunting among them. Having finally learned this lesson, many countries today practice the separation of church and state.

[2] Of the same substance is meant here to be as God because when humans are spiritually born, their budding Divine Spirit or Soul is also of the same substance as their Father/Mother God, and they become a member of God's family. In this sense, we all may become the begotten sons and daughters of God, presided over by the only and unique begotten Son of God or the restored Adam as the bridegroom of the church, the body of Christ (Matt. 25:1; Rom. 12:5; Col. 1:18).

whom all things came into being, who for us men and
because of our salvation came down from heaven, and
was incarnated by the Holy Spirit and the Virgin Mary
and became human. He was crucified for us under
Pontius Pilate and suffered and was buried ---

The Nicene Creed asserted that God and Christ were of the same substance. They are trying to say that there is only one God. He is active in creating and sustaining the world (as the Father); He was in Jesus Christ (as the Son); and He moves in the heart of the believer (as the Holy Spirit).

However, following the death of Constantine in 337 A.D., his son Constantius accepted the Arian view, and the young Athanasius (295-373), deacon to Alexander (who became later Bishop), was declared a heretic, and Arianism was declared orthodox, or conforming to established doctrine. After changing a few more times, depending on which side the Emperor stood, the view of Athanasius was finally accepted by the second ecumenical council of Constantinople in 381 A.D. The accepted Trinitarian formula held that God is one in being, existing eternally *in three Hypostases or Persons: the Father, Son, and Holy Spirit, whom are consubstantial, co-equal, and co-eternal. The Arian contention, which believed that the Logos or Christ was created, was rejected by the council, along with the Sabellian view and Apollinarianism. The latter believed that the Logos or eternal Christ was completely controlling Jesus on all levels of his being, not only the center of his personality or Divine Spirit but also the personality of Jesus, with its emotion, intellect, and will. Thus, it denied that Jesus had an independent personality or that he was fully human, with its free will "who in every respect has been tempted as we are, yet without sin" (Heb. 4:15).

The object of this council, summoned by Theodocius I, was to confirm decisions made earlier and to fully accept the creed (or dogmatic statement) of Nicea.

The first article of religion, found in the book of common prayer of the Anglican, Episcopal church, of the
Church of England, states the ancient faith of the
church: "In the unity of the God-head there were three

---

* In three Hypostases (distinctions in being) in Eastern Christendom and "three persons in one substance" in Western Christendom. This formula was already mentioned earlier by Tertullian. The Sabellians, on the other hand, emphasized the unity of God in such a way that all distinctions were rejected.

Persons of one substance, power, and eternity:
the Father, the Son, and the Holy Ghost."

Christological Controversy

As the council of Nicea and Constantinople accepted Jesus Christ as the second member of the Trinity, and truly divine, the question was raised: "How was the union between his divinity and humanity to be understood and interpreted?" Is the man Jesus and the heavenly Christ two separate beings, or are they combined in one being? Thus, the Trinitarian controversy was followed by the Christological controversy.

The council of Ephesus (431 A.D.) was called by the Emperor Theodocius II to settle a dispute concerning the teaching of the Patriarch of Constantinople, Nestorius. As the Apollinarians asserted that there was only a divine nature in Jesus Christ, the God-man, the Nestorians argued that there were two natures in Jesus Christ, a human and divine, whom are kept distinct, so that the human personality had the moral freedom to experience growth, suffering, and temptation. This would not have been possible if the human nature was completely fused and overcome by the divine nature. However, these two natures became united when the human self of Jesus, the God-bearing man, came eventually under the guidance of the divine Self of Jesus Christ, forming a moral union. Nestorius also held that *Mary was the mother of the human but not of the divine nature or Logos. "He who was formed in Mary's womb was not himself God, but God assumed him."

The third ecumenical council condemned the theology of Nestorius, who was removed from his see and excommunicated, and theotokus ("God-bearing",) instead of anthropotocos ("man bearing"), was approved as a right title for the Virgin Mary. This all led to a separate Nestorian church which still exists today, and the members are known as "Assyrian Christians". In the past, they were active as missionaries in South West India (at the time the coastal part was under Portuguese and Dutch rule), Arabia, Turkistan, and China.

As the main focus of the council of Ephesus was that the humanity and divinity of Jesus Christ should not be separated, the question may be asked, "How should they be distinguished, and how were they

---

* Paul of Samosato said, "Mary did not bear the Word, for Mary did not exist before the ages. Mary is not older than the Word; what she bore was a man equal to us, but superior in all things as a result of the Holy Spirit."

united?" Those questions remained to be solved and were put into consideration at the council of Chalcedon twenty years later.

The council of Chalcedon (451 A.D.) was sponsored by the Emperor Marcion to pacify the spirit of conflict, which arose regarding the human and divine nature in the one person of Jesus Christ. The opposition of the two natures in Jesus Christ (see former page) became known as Monophysitism (monos – only and fusis – nature). Eutyches, head of a monastery and spokesman of this movement, said that at the incarnation (becoming flesh of the divine Logos in Jesus Christ), Jesus Christ's human nature was absorbed into the divine nature. "I confess that before the union, our Lord was of two natures, but after the union I confess one nature." However, to the opposite party, this implied that God Himself was tempted, suffered, and died. The doctrine was condemned, and the council pronounced that the two natures of Jesus Christ (God and man) are united to form the one person Jesus Christ in a natural or hypostatic union (not moral union). The council added that our Lord Jesus Christ is both God and man. "Our Lord Jesus is perfect in God-head and perfect in manhood. He is truly God and truly man. He has two natures, divine and human, and these are joined without confusion, change, division, separation, or suppression."

The council of Chalcedon, which attempted to reconcile both sides of the controversy, did not produce the unity the political and ecclesiastical leaders had hoped for. Instead, the decision at Chalcedon gave more fuel to the Monophysite controversy, which really took off. The belief of the Monophysites still lives on in three churches: the Coptic, the Jacobite, and the Armenian.

Since the Chalcedon formula did not solve the problem of how one person could combine and unite the human and divine natures, the Monophysites persisted in their belief that there was only one nature in Jesus Christ, which is divine. The defenders of Chalcedon, on the other hand, insisted on the two natures of Jesus Christ at the second council of Constantinople in 553 A.D., which was called by Emperor Justinian and was the fifth ecumenical council.

The third council of Constantinople (680 A.D. – the 6th ecumenical council) reinstated the teaching of the council of Chalcedon that Jesus Christ possesses two natures, and that he possesses a divine as well as a human will. The Monothelitists insisted that there was only one will in Jesus Christ, which was divine, and that he did not have a human will.

After a long controversy, the council condemned Monothelitism and accepted Dyothelitism, the doctrine that stated that Jesus Christ had two wills, and that the *human will is under the dominion of the divine will, operating in harmony together. That Jesus Christ has two wills has scriptural support in John 6:38, "For I have come down from heaven, not to do my own will, but the will of him who sent me." See also John 5:30; Matt. 26:39.

The seventh ecumenical council (787 A.D.) was convoked to deal with the question of iconoclasm, or to settle a controversy concerning the right or wrong of veneration of holy images and relics. This council (Nicea II) condemned Adoptionism – a belief that developed in Spain and was probably rooted in Arianism and Nestorianism. They maintain that the human man Jesus became the adopted Son of God. This belief originated in the second and third century and was also called Dynamic Monarchianism. Jesus was regarded as a unique man of blameless life and perfect virtue, who was divinely empowered by the Holy Spirit at the time of his baptism and was elevated to divine sonship when he was united with the Cosmic Christ.

Emperor Basil convened the eighth ecumenical council at Constantinople in 869 A.D., which condemned the iconoclasts and voted against Photius, who in the position of Patriarch of Constantinople, summoned a council in 879 A.D., which readopted the Nicene Creed and spoke against the filoque. This was a phrase "and from the Son" which was added to the Nicene Creed by the Western Church, so that it reads: "And (I believe) in the Holy Ghost, the Lord and Giver of Life, who proceeds from the Father 'and from the Son'". The filoque clause was added at the non-ecumenical council at Toledo in 589 A.D. The Eastern Church did not agree with this doctrine, and this eventually led to a schism between the Eastern and Western branches of Christianity in the eleventh century.

Surveying the six ecumenical councils of above:
Against Arianism, Nicea I used the term homoousias to uphold that Jesus Christ is divine or God, the second Person of the Trinity.
Against Apollinarianism, Constantinople I affirmed that Jesus Christ is not only truly God but also truly human.
Against Nestorius, Ephesus declared that the divine and human being of Jesus Christ are not to be held apart.

---

* As the human spirit of Jesus has to make a choice, his Divine Spirit or Soul is always one with the Will of God, which is also the will of the Cosmic Christ and the Holy Spirit.

Against Monophysism, Chalcedon professed that the one nature of Jesus Christ is not merged or confused.

Against the Monothelites, the second and third councils of Constantinople reaffirmed that Jesus Christ has two natures but also two wills.

H. Conclusion

"In the beginning was the Word (*Logos), and the Word was with God, and the Word was God. He was in the beginning with God; all things were made through him, and without him was not anything made that was made. In him was life, and the life was the light of men" (John 1:1-4).

"And the Word became flesh and dwelt among us, full of grace and truth; we have beheld his glory, glory as of the only Son from the Father" --- "No one has ever seen God; the only Son who is in the bosom of the Father, he has made him known" (John 1:14, 18).

The ideal or Word of a perfect spiritual (and physical) man and ruler of the universe (restored Adam – 1 Cor. 15:45), will be formed by the Word of God, the very essence and Truth of God. It was in the beginning with God and all things are made by and through the Word (Heb. 11:3; 2 Pet. 3:5; Gen. 1). It is "living and active" (Heb. 4:12) and "eternal" (Jn. 6:68) and the ruler of the world is called by that name (Rev. 19:13).

When the Word became flesh, the Father aspect of God, the Cosmic Christ found its dwelling place in Christ Jesus, the "first – spiritual – born of the dead" (Rev. 1:5) or "the first-born of all creation" (Col. 1:15). The Cosmic Christ and Christ Jesus as one whole (Jesus Christ) became the head of those people (Eph. 5:23; Col. 2:10), in whose personalities the Divine Spirit or Soul was formed by the Word of God (Gal. 4:19) and in whose Soul the individual Spirit of God resides (2 Cor. 6:16; Rev. 21:3).

---

* John identified the Christ with the Logos of contemporary Jewish and Greek thought. The Greek Logos can mean both "word" and the thought or reason expressed in a word. The Stoics conceived Logos as the Universal Mind, penetrating, inhabiting, and governing everything in the cosmic as divine reason or rational principle. The "Word" is also the creative power of God, a universal vibration, a sacred inner sound.

The *Cosmic Christ, who always existed eternally with God before Abraham (Jn. 8:58), united in one body with Christ Jesus (Soul and humanity of Jesus). They both are called the only begotten Son, through whom the Father can be and live among His people; and "in Jesus Christ God was reconciling the world to himself" (2 Cor. 5:19; Jn. 3:17). The resurrected, risen, exalted, and the glorified Jesus Christ, who became the head of the seven churches, said in Revelation 1:17-18:

> "Fear not, I am the first and the last and the living
> one; I died, and behold, I am alive for evermore."

NOTE: At the appropriate time in the ministry of Jesus, the Cosmic Christ began to work through Christ Jesus, and he became the Son of God. This relationship became more permanent after the Resurrection.

REMARK: The personality of Jesus plus Christ Jesus (Soul) plus Cosmic Christ is Son of God.

---

* The Cosmic Christ, in the form of the exalted Christ, is described in the Book of Revelation as: "one like a son of man, clothed with a long robe and with a golden girdle around his breast; his head and his hair were white as white wool, white as snow; his eyes were like a flame of fire, his feet were like burnished bronze, refined as in a furnace, and his voice was like the sound of many waters; in his right hand he held seven stars, from his mouth issued a sharp two-edged sword, and his face was like the sun shining in full strength" (Rev. 1:13-16). See also Daniel's description of God as the ancient of days (Dan. 7:9).

#39 Result of Original Sin

A. Nature and Qualities of Satan and His Influence in Human Society

Sin in the human race had its origin in Adam and Eve, but sin in the universe had its origin in angelic beings that rebelled against the Creator.

It all began when Lucifer the archangel, the most powerful and revered created being in the universe, got to know God's (heavenly Parents') plan of wanting to have children or human beings whom would eventually rule the angelic, or the world of servants and messengers (Heb. 1:14; 1 Cor. 6:3). Lucifer, who never can reach godhood, became very prideful and did not want to accept this plan. He said in his heart, "I will ascend to heaven; above the stars of God I will set my throne on high; I will ascend above the heights of the clouds, I will make myself like the Most High" (Isa. 14:13-14). By coveting God's position, he separated himself from God and became lustful towards the other fallen angels (whom were like Lucifer, neither male nor female – Mk. 12:25 –), with whom he had psychical homosexual relationships. "And the angels that did not keep their own position --- just as Sodom and Gomorrah --- which likewise acted immorally and indulged in unnatural lust" (Jude 6; II Pet. 2:4). However, Lucifer (who became satan) was defeated by Michael and his angels. Thus, the devil and one third of his angels were thrown down to the earth (Rev. 12:7-9).

NOTE: As crime is, in many cases, a violation of man-made law, sin is the breaking or transgression of God's Law (1 Jn. 3:4). Sin limits or prevents the evolution (one's own or somebody else's) of the human personality and the development of his or her Soul. It is thus an act whereby humans and angels separate themselves in their awareness from God, or source of life within, by their thoughts, words, or deeds. Moreover, the essence of sin is living independently of God, whose supremacy human and other beings not only refuse to acknowledge but deliberately act against the established divine order, as it is reported in Genesis chapter three. This latter sin is called, in Catholic theology, "a mortal or deadly sin" because it causes separation or spiritual death (Gen. 2:16; Rom. 6:23; I Jn. 3:14; Matt. 8:22). Having inherited original sin, humans, especially fallen angels, live (more or less) under a continuing inner state of separation and even hostility or enmity (Rom. 8:7; James 4:4) towards their Creator. This tendency of fallen human nature to act contrary to grace is called concupiscence. Some individuals have even lost the "sense of sin" and are no longer aware that they are sinning.

After Adam was created (according to the Talmudic version), all the angels had to *bow down before the new king, but satan and his demonic host refused to do so. Being defeated and thrown out of heaven, satan, who already had acquired a [1]double tongue (like a serpent), began to tempt or entice Eve to go against God's command. Eve, who was warned by God of Lucifer's intention (Gen. 2:16-17), ignored His commandment and fused many times with Lucifer's spirit in a [3]sexual psychical union. Because Adam, in turn, was swayed by Eve to become like her and satan through sexual temptation, satan succeeded and became the surrogate [4]father and ruler of the human family (Jn. 12:31; 2 Cor. 4:4), instead of being dominated by them. Thus, satan took away the position of Adam as the potential ruler of the earth. However, Jesus came as the last Adam to retrieve this position of power by overcoming the temptation of satan (Matt. 4:8-10) and only worshipping and serving God.

REMARK: An angel is a bisexual being and is like the human spirit in image and development. Like the human personality in the Old Testament, the angel's relation to God is that of servant and master. They, unlike humans, do not have the potential to develop the 'I AM' and become the 'I AM' or Soul, which will dominate the personality of a human being. However, angels that are not fallen are, in the meantime, higher than the good and evil personality of an individual. "Thou did make him for a little while lower than the angels" (Heb. 2:7). Fallen angels want humans to become like them so that they are able to control them. Satan and his host do not want humans to become pure in personality and certainly not develop into a Soul or Divine Spirit, which is quite capable of overpowering evil spirits.

---

* Jesus, the last Adam, was likewise venerated when he was born.

[1] James 4:8 speaks of "men of double mind", while today we speak of people with double standard. He also said that "God opposes the proud, but gives grace to the humble" (4:6).

[2] Because women are generally more emotionally oriented than men, they therefore do not always reason and are thus more easily tempted than men.

[3] Sexual union with a spirit is possible, as the near rape of Lot's two angelic visitors shows. Those angels were also able to materialize as the fallen angels whom had relations with "the daughters of men" (Gen. 6:2). This ability has been taken away from the fallen angels.

[4] Some people think that we all are children of God. This is certainly not true; the devil is the father of some people. Jesus said to some of the most religious people of his time, "You are of your father the devil" (Jn. 8:44).

NOTE: Through the fall, higher psychism was cut off, and lower psychism came into being, such as sorcery, augury, soothsaying, witchcraft, wizardry, and lower mediumship.

An example of satan working in human society to topple governments is when an evil spirit took possession of an immoral crafty adviser Rasputin, who dominated the wife of Nicholas II. She, in turn, dominated the czar of Russia. Rasputin was the real power in Russia from 1914 to 1916, which eventually led to the October revolution of 1917 and the Communist takeover. The Communists deny the existence of God and do not want people to develop their Soul.

The danger to governments is usually not foreign invasions but internal decay. As it has been said, "Every civilization has within it the seed of its own destruction."

When individuals are influenced by evil spirits, they feel an increasing sense of fear, egotism, and insecurity. However, when they change their feeling and thinking from the evil to the good way, evil spirits leave them and good spirits will inspire them.

In Genesis chapter two, we find Adam (who was living the life of the pure personality) very busy giving [1]names "to all cattle, and to the birds of the air, and to every beast of the field" (Gen. 2:19-20). This incident reveals the attitude and nature of Adam before he was led astray by satan. He lived in peace and had dominion over all living things, and all his needs were met through his belief in, and union with the one living God. Nothing in this account discloses that Adam was hostile and rebellious. It certainly does not indicate a "heart that is deceitful above all things, and desperately corrupt" (Jer. 17:9); or a carnal mind that is hostile to God and not subject to the law of God (Rom. 8:7), as human nature after the fall is described. [2]Thereafter, Adam should have taken from the Tree of Life and experienced the birth of his Christ Spirit or Divine Spirit (Gal. 4:19; II Pet. 1:4), which would rule his untainted personality.

However, Adam followed Eve, and they both left the "Garden of Eden" and started living the life of the good and evil personality in the garden of "the world" (Jn. 8:23, 18:36; Rev. 11:15; Jas. 4:4). But the plan for redemption for all humans and angels was being accomplished through the consecration by Jesus Christ in the garden of Gethsemane, through which everyone may enter the Garden of Eden and eat of the

---

[1] In the ancient Semitic world, to be able to know the name of a living being is to know its inner nature and, thus, to have dominion over it.

[2] When the tainted personality of a teenager of today, who is easily influenced by good and evil, has reached the age of accountability, he/she, like Adam, has to choose the Tree of Life or get stuck in the life of the good and evil personality.

Tree of Life or mystical body of Christ, thus producing the fruits of the Spirit, such as: "love, joy, peace, patience, kindness, goodness, faithfulness, gentleness, self-control," etc. (Gal. 5:22)

NOTE 1: Jansenius Cornelius (1585-1638), Dutch theologian and author of the Augustinus. The first part of his book deals with the fact that Adam was first God-oriented and his behavior was ethical and orderly – being healthy. Second, it deals with the human sickness and its symptoms caused by the fall. Third, it talks about the healing or salvation of humankind.

NOTE 2: "So out of the ground the Lord God formed every beast of the field and every birth of the air" (Gen. 2:19). This means that the chemical composition of the animals is the same as that of the ground, from which they take their food. The human race, which has the colors of black, white, brown, yellow, and red, is likewise formed from the ground (Gen. 2:7).

REMARK: When someone is spiritually born or starts living a divine life, everything he/she owns is transferred from satan's domain to God's domain and ownership. They are rightfully the true owner, and the piece of land they own can be considered Holy Ground. Satan now owns less of this world (Matt. 4:9).

Every human being has inherited, from his ancestors, the original sin that he or she tries to suppress, hide, and *cover up. This sin is deeply embedded in the human psyche in every fiber of its being. The original sin is rooted more strongly in people who are still morally undeveloped and who experience difficulties hiding their evil desires, especially from people who are sensitive and spiritually developed. Because of this deeply rooted sin, it is the beginning point and source (base) of any evil feelings or desires, which in turn produce evil thoughts. Having this fallen nature, people are easily susceptible to invasion of evil spirits as soon as they make a reciprocal base or feel, think, or express like those obsessing entities. The works of evil spirits are experienced as an increasing sense of insecurity, fear, and egotism. Because people

---

* Many people wear a mask. Their smile is wooden, superficial, and false, and they do not speak or laugh with their whole being. They pretend to be good and hide their real intentions because they do not want to be exposed of what they really are. Others they meet have the tendency to do the same, with the result that nobody is able to trust each other.

"You do not need your cloak of fear, your coat of pride, nor your coverings of what you deem to be self-protection. The self you seek to protect is infinitely more beautiful than the ugliness with which you have chosen to hide it. It is that self I wish to have with me. Your coverings serve only to keep out the Light and Heat, not to keep them in as you suspect." (Message received by Mary Fleming 8/20/64, as written in the New Age Frontier Sept. 1, 1964 – No. 30.)

are good as well as evil, they may, through their positive attitude, attract at one time good spirits, while at other times allure evil spirits whenever they are in the underbrush of their feeling and thinking.

NOTE: A cruel or poisonous animal can be known from its outward appearance so that we are warned of its intention (such as, for example: snakes, vultures, scorpions, devil fish, crocodiles, mosquitoes, flies, rats, vampire bats, and others) because its outer appearance corresponds exactly with its inner nature. On the other hand, humans are able to fool and deceive insensitive and undeveloped people by camouflaging their inner evil qualities.

REMARK: The horrifying animals (and plants) will diminish or eventually be replaced by beneficial creatures when humanity changes, who are the Lord over the creation, as prophesied in Isaiah, chapter eleven.

For people living the life of the good/evil personality, their whole approach to life has been based upon the idea that they are separate from the other. This has been the cause of loneliness and even all manner of injury to each other. On the other hand, when we are consciously and unconsciously no longer living in separation from our Creator, we as a personality are more united with the god Self (Soul) of our being and the god Self of our neighbors, whom we are increasingly able to love as our Self and as our spiritual brothers and sisters (Matt. 19:19).

As the proper working of every cell of an organism is dependent upon other cells as part of a whole, fallen humans are not or little aware that they are part of the human organism and, thus, interdependent of each other, like the cells in the physical body. Evil forces, including fallen angels and lower extra-terrestrials who have no divine potential, want us humans to believe that we are nothing but our ego, and that we have no potential for divine life by which we recognize and incorporate God as the highest center of our human life. That people are not to accept God as their Creator and Sustainer, and that individuals possess an [1]independent self apart from God, is a most diabolical deception by

---

[1] Secular humanism and communism believe in the development of their personality or ego but do not believe that there is a higher stage of development, that of the birth and development of the Soul. They thus believe in the supremacy and sufficiency of their ego, which is good and evil and independent from a non-existing God.

When humans become mature sons and daughters of God, they are completely free of God's Law and no longer dependent upon His direction. They are then fully qualified to govern themselves and others. Once the ego is dethroned and the Divine Spirit is in charge of one's life, an individual can do what is pleasing in God's sight. You become a superman or superwoman, and "everything you touch turns to gold" because you are in harmony with God and His laws and in tune with His creation.

which satan and his cohorts block human entrance into the Kingdom of God or the Garden of Eden.

Satan fooled us in the beginning and thereafter that we could be like God in our present undeveloped state, knowing the difference between good and evil. We could be [2]immortal and choose whatever way of life we like to live because we had the wisdom to fully understand life. We would have the ingenuity to govern ourselves and would be self-sufficient and self-sustaining. Thus, we need not God anymore.

The serpent (symbol of satan) deceived the woman by making her think that the natural human mind could attain God-like understanding and awareness. By eating of the tree of knowledge of good and evil, [3]self-will was cultivated instead of God's will, and it opened the way for humans to claim moral independence by deciding for themselves what is good and evil and becoming like God, thus refusing their status as a created being.

> "Because they exchanged the truth about God for a lie
> and worshipped and served the creature rather than the
> Creator" (Rom. 1:25).

Eve was beguiled by the serpent's suggestion that if she were to take of the forbidden fruit, she would become *like God and did not have to listen to His rules anymore. Thus, she could make her own rules of conduct. Satan wants humans to become like him, to glorify the self instead of God, to rule themselves (self-rule) rather than God's rule, make their own law, be their own judge, and believe in another power other than the power of God. Fallen humans say with satan that God has no right to rule people and angels, and that intelligent creatures would be better off if they were independent of God's direction. In other words, satan wants humans to develop their false ego and be

---

[2] Adam and Eve would not die physically as satan thought but spiritually as God meant (Gen. 2:17). This is a condition wherein the individual is not able to receive and respond to God's love.

[3] Jesus, in reversing Adam's mistake, said in John 5:30, "I can do nothing on my own authority; as I hear, I judge; and my judgment is just, because I seek not my own will but the will of him who sent me."

* Exalting oneself to godhood is an acknowledgement that there is no higher moral authority to which one must account than oneself. Because God ceases to be the center of life, humans easily fall in the sins of the flesh and an unrestrained lust after the things of the world. Thus, true evil is the willful separation from God.

created in his image and likeness. Those people cannot help but produce the works of the flesh, such as: "fornication, impurity, licentiousness, idolatry, sorcery, enmity, strife, jealousy, anger, selfishness, dissension, party spirit, envy, drunkenness, carousing, and the like" (Gal. 5:19-21). We may add pride, lust, greed, license, deceit, prejudice, possessiveness, resentment, vanity or self-conceit, self-will instead of free will, etc. The personality of satanic people is ugly and despicable. They hide themselves behind a self-created image or mask, their ego is overdeveloped and inflated, and they are using and abusing others for their own glorification, self-interest, self-love, and preservation and are not interested in the welfare of others unless it is for their own advantage and benefit. Those people whom have the devil as their father (John 8:44), who is also their god (2 Cor. 4:4), possess a corrupted old self or old nature (Rom. 6:6; Eph. 4:22) . If they dare to leave the kingdom of satan by accepting God as their father, by being born spiritually, and producing the fruits of their Spirit (Soul), they will be relentlessly pursued by satan and his masters until they give up their quest for the Kingdom of God. This occurs because satan and his rulers or dictators love their people, or rather possess them.

REMARK: Another satanic element humans have inherited is the need to control other people. They easily become persecutors in many organizations. For example, if someone wants to change, he or she would be beaten physically, ostracized emotionally, threatened mentally, outcast spiritually, or socially ignored.

Ever since Adam and Eve disobeyed God's commandment not to eat from the tree of the knowledge of good and evil, the human race has made continuous bids for moral authority and has attempted to fabricate a code or system of right and wrong. However, they have failed over and over at living the good life without God; it has only brought them frustration and disappointment. Along with this estrangement came a feeling of guilt, a loss of self-respect, insecurity, fear, anxiety, and for some, a deep despair, which may be conscious or unconscious. The fact is that the fallen world is characterized by: mistrust, exploitation, struggle, bitterness, intense hatred, the implied insult, the hasty judgment, the egotistical opinion, the continued worrying, power struggle, tyranny, economic injustice, immorality, crime, and war.

Thus, the basic condition of most humans on this earth plane is that they are lost or severely alienated from the Source of all life. As the saying goes: "Lost one human family, color, white, black, red, yellow, brown; missing the last 6000 (biblical) years, last seen wandering in the dark, is in the habit of fighting and displaying tendencies toward self-destruction."

As Billy Graham says, "Millions of persons long for a world of joy, light, harmony, and peace. Instead, they are engulfed in a world of pessimism, darkness, and turmoil. Often their despondent attitude leads to a circle of cocktail parties and bars in which they obliterate the reality of their world with the unreality of *alcohol, drugs, or an all-consuming pursuit of a hobby or sport."

The definition of having success and the goal of life of "successful" men and women was material acquisition, recognition of status by society, and the passing enjoyment of the senses. But the more they acquired, the more they wanted, and the less satisfied they became of what they had because happiness is not material; money is not its source. These so-called successful men and women made money. Their bank accounts may have been full, but their lives were empty. Vanity, as Solomon observed, is like striving after wind. This constant striving after false values left, in its wake, a trail of fears and worries, disappointments, troubled consciences, discontent, loneliness, and finally death. There were, of course, pleasures, moments of excitement, periods of enjoyment, occasional thrills, sensations of delight, but they were always followed by periods of depression and always a gnawing Soul hunger returned. This, in turn, drove them to seek satisfaction in the thousand and one events in the world whirl of material pleasures and pastimes, but it never filled the void, the real inner hunger. They probably never realized that the hunger was spiritual, which can never be satisfied by material food (paraphrased message of Herbert Armstrong).

Lucifer's sin was in trying to replace God as the ruler of the universe. On the psychological level, this destructive power drive is the attempt of the evil part ("flesh") of the human ego or personality to set the ego against the Self or Soul (Spirit of Christ – Gal. 4:19 –). "For the desires of the flesh are against the Spirit, and the desires of the Spirit are against the flesh" (Gal. 5:17). This false ego that thinks itself important as an entity unto itself, apart from God, is the spirit of the

---

* People usually do not drink for the taste alone. They also drink in order to seek release from tension, and when they drink socially, it is usually to conform and to withstand social inhibition and shyness caused by living the life of the personality. They create an artificial high, and bars are, therefore, compared to churches, although in a negative sense. Those whom are living a divine life do not display any inhibition and are always high.

Antichrist or inner devil. It wants to establish dominion over the whole psyche, and it does not allow the God-given center of the psyche to rule.

As the fall of the first primal pair took place on a macrocosmic level, it also occurred at a microcosmic level or in their consciousness. A similar fall takes place in some regenerated people of today when they fall back or backslide in the habit of evil feeling/thinking and doing evil deeds.

Every human makes his or her own heaven and hell, here and now by her/his thoughts, words, and deeds. Thus, heaven and hell can be a geographic location but also states of consciousness. He or she can experience a physical suffering in a hell on earth but also a psychological suffering when they become strangers to each other and spiritual when they are alienated from God.

The personality (which is made in the image of the good and evil world) as a whole should not be slain because it plays an important role for the development of the individual, as the Self is, but it should take its rightful place. This is difficult to maintain for an ego that wants to be identified as the true master of the whole psyche because its proper place is secondary and subordinate to the Self or Soul. The false ego, therefore, does not wish to know the truth about itself because it means that it will eventually have to give up its dominant position, thus occupying the inferior objective role. What should be slain (after the Soul has become strong enough) is the evil part of the ego and the good part left intact. Many egotists whom are unwilling to give up their stronghold fight like tigers against the spiritual onslaught of stripping their ego of the evil, which is called scolding or chastising (Psalm 94:12).

Satan enslaved humanity by telling them that they possessed an independent and separate self, divorced from God. Unfortunately, many people believe his lie and have identified themselves with their false ego, which does not and cannot love God because it is its own god. However, the dawning of Truth in their awareness will be liberating (threatening for some) because it will set them free and remove the illusion of separation in their greater self. Thus, the way for individuals to get out of this disharmonious state is by self-knowledge, so that the relative position of the ego in their being will be reversed. Since the fall, humans have lived with a strong awareness of the physical aspect of life, while their awareness of psychic reality has been weakened, and their perception of spiritual reality has, in many cases, been extinguished. In the latter case, the objective consciousness or personality (physical – emotional – mental aspect) has been permitted to overrule or dominate their spiritual Self. The result is that the personality separated more or less from their spiritual Self or God-Self and also from the deepest Self of the people. There is no longer harmony among the physical, mental/psychic, and spiritual aspects of life, here and in the cosmos. Most people live in the awareness of separation from each other and God and become lonely, restless, and strangers to both, while starving for Truth and authentic Love.

The young Paul lamented:

"For I know that nothing good dwells within me, that is,
in my flesh. I can will what is right, but I cannot do it.
For I do not do the good I want, but the evil I do not want
is what I do. --- For I delight in the Law of God, in my
inmost self, but I see in my members another law at war
with the law of my mind and making me captive to the law
of sin which dwells in my members" (Rom. 7:18-19, 22, 23).

The law of his mind is the law of God in his innermost self or Soul, but the law "in his members" or personality is evil nature instilled in the *flesh or in the natural or unspiritual man (1 Cor. 2:14). At first, Adam and Eve enjoyed mental mastery over the procreative process, but after the fall, their will became weaker, and sexual desire has been more difficult to control, especially when desire turns into lust in the disobedient, rebellious members whom are not in harmony with the law of God. The illusion of a human as a separate, self-sufficient ego apart from God became the condition in many humans. It is as if many cells in the human body have become self-willed, independent, and divided against one another and running berserk. This is a cancer that has spread rapidly through individuals, families, nations, and the world, causing spiritual death in the universe. This is the Luciferian experience.

This nature, or qualities of satan, have been more or less inherited by all people of this earth and is also called original sin. Those whom are like satan always seek to have power over others and do not want that the latter be ruled by the God forces. Those whom have power and authority bestowed upon them by governments and organizations (also religions) are often tempted to misuse it, especially when they are

---

* "Flesh" here in Paul's writing means the good/evil personality. In other places, it means the evil part of the ego (see Gal. 5:17).

living the life of the personality (not divine life), whereby much of the evil and good part of their self is ruling their life. When their ambitions become [1]selfish, they become much like their father satan (Jn. 8:44). They soon are ruling those closer to God with fear and intimidation, thus strengthening and expanding the kingdom of satan on earth. Instead of having dominion by acknowledging God as the Creator, they recognize no divine authority above them. As soon as they have been recognized and accepted in their position of power, they want to dominate and exploit the people in their care. Those "dictators" are often encouraged by flatterers and worshippers of whom many also are seeking for social position and status and also enjoy wielding power and lording it over others.

[2]At the workplace, many supervisors, instead of serving the people as Jesus advised (Luke 22:24-27), want the employees to serve them. This shows how immature and selfish they really are. Other bosses go so far as to humiliate the workers and love to be feared by them. The only "asset" those bullies have is their knowledge and skill, which they use as a whip to bully the worker(s) in his or her place. On the other hand, those whom have been "whipped" in submission will, in many cases, act like their supervisor when they, in turn, become overseers.

NOTE: Democracy is not an ideal form of government, but in the fallen world, it is the best possible world. In order for it to work, any government branch should not have too much power. The monarchy should be limited or constitutional.

When people are living a divine life, their Divine Spirit (unlike their tainted good/evil personality – Mark 7:20:23 –) is always pure because they are born of God, and God's nature abides in them (1 John 3:9). Their Divine Spirits are in charge of their personalities who, as a whole, are always doing the will of God and, through Christ of all religions, are ruling the world in a monarchical structure, just as the physical body is ruled by the brain and branches of the nervous system. This is like the structure of the kingdom of heaven.

---

[1] Children are naturally selfish because they are still immature, but adults appear to be very selfish when they are still living the life of the good and evil personalities.

[2] Those whom are trying to live a religious life usually have a hard time working with those whom are more worldly-oriented. It is not possible to avoid those persons, and you cannot always bring up the nature of your concern. If your supervisor is not only worldly but also evil-minded, then the situation becomes more difficult, but you should be willing to endure hardship and injustice. Besides, at the end of the workday, you certainly are not alone in running as fast as you can out of your workplace, with its psychological and spiritual suffering.

The satanic nature of those whom do not care about the people they rule becomes only stronger, and they come more under the influence of satan and all his cohorts, eventually becoming dictators of the worst kind. Their false ego grows and appears to be puffed up or inflated. They are called a windbag and are full of hot air. Many of them are full of pride and think that they love the people, but they only want to possess them, as satan took possession of Eve and Adam and, through them, all of humanity. They are vainglorious, deceitful, conceited, cunning, boastful, greedy, arrogant, cruel, lustful, fearful, egotistic, and think that they are the ones whom are most important, just like their master who is the sole ruler of the evil world (John 12:31; 2 Cor. 4:4; 1 John 5:19).

Atheists, whom deny the existence of God, want to give Him no role in their life, and thus it becomes easy for them to take God's place, making all the rules and regulations for the conduct of humans. This is called humanism. They are living a life separate from God, with the result that they are stuck in the life of their tainted personality and do not let themselves advance to a higher level by being born of God and living a divine life.

Another class of people who takes care of the education of the future generation works the evil forces unknowingly in the hand by emphasizing the *education of the personality, instead of also teaching about the Soul (Divine Spirit) and its development. The latter was supposed to be the tasks of psychology and philosophy, but they degraded to the lower physical plane. Many teachers teach knowledge but not wisdom – how to use what we have learned. They teach with the words they speak but not with their being. As James said in Jas. 3:13-15:

> "Who is wise and understanding among you? By his good
> life let him show his works in the meekness of wisdom.
> But if you have bitter jealousy and selfish ambition in your
> hearts, do not boast and be false to the truth. This wisdom
> is not such as comes down from above, but is earthly, un-
> spiritual, devilish."

As pride, power, and sex were closely allied and caused the fall of humanity from the beginning, false pride, misuse of sex, greed, and

---

* Children whom are in grade school level should be taught about the development of the personality; that is the stage they are in. But older children, especially those whom pass through the teenage years, should be also taught about the Soul because they have become ready to live the divine life.

power (money and position) are still rampant in the society of today. We may see the expression of the evil within humans displayed in an extreme form when they become sadists and inflict cruelty on others in order to be sexually stimulated. Another perversion we often see expressed in society is that of people who only get sexually "turned on" when they are humiliated and whipped. They are called masochists. Those perversions and homosexual behaviors are derived from fallen angels (Jude 6-7), who are neither male nor female.

REMARK: Those individuals whom God chooses to lead His people have the qualities of God and not those of satan. They are humble (James 4:6, 10; Mt. 5:5; Acts 20:19; 1 Pet. 3:8; Lk. 14:11), are not position-conscious, as Korah was (Num. 16:1-3), or an opportunist as Absolon (2 Sam. 15:10), or prideful as king Saul, even though he was chosen as being most insignificant (1 Sam. 9:21). Moses was the meekest person on earth (Num. 12:3), Gideon was very modest (Judges 6:11-15), while Apostle Paul called himself "the least of the apostles" (1 Cor. 15:19).

NOTE 1: Many liberal scientists and doctors try to "improve" on God's design and hardly look for the intention of the Creator. They try to create a "superior" race of human beings, as Adolf Hitler did about seventy years ago. They are ignorant of the fact that superior humans cannot be created by physical improvement or by overdeveloping the good and evil personality, but only with the birth and unfolding of the Divine Spirit in the purified personality. They further attempt to "play God" to create and destroy life, as with cloning. Those liberals want to please the people more than God and even want to be like god, as their master satan.

NOTE 2: The Duke of Wellington once said, "If you divorce religion from education, you produce a race of clever devils."

B. Explaining Chapter Three of Genesis

Now the serpent was more subtle than any other wild creature that the Lord God had made. He said to the woman, "Did God say, 'You shall not eat of any tree of the garden?'" [2]And the woman said to the serpent, "We may eat of the fruit of the trees of the garden; [3]but God said, 'You shall not eat of the fruit of the tree which is in the midst of the garden, neither shall you touch it, lest you die.'" [4]But the serpent said to the woman, "You will not die. [5]For God knows that when you eat of it your eyes will be opened, and you will be like God, knowing good and evil." [6]So when the woman saw that the tree was good for food, and that it was a delight to the eyes, and that the tree was to be desired to make one wise, she took of its fruit and ate; and she also gave some to her husband, and he ate. [7]Then the eyes of both were opened, and they knew that they were naked; and they sewed fig leaves together and made themselves aprons. [8]And they heard the sound of the Lord God walking in the garden in the cool of the day, and the man and his wife hid themselves from the presence of the Lord God among the trees of the garden. [9]But the Lord God called to the man and said to him, "Where are you?" [10]And he said, "I heard the sound of thee in the garden, and I was afraid because I was naked; and I hid myself." [11]He said, "Who told you that you were naked? Have you eaten of the tree of which I commanded you not to eat? [12]The man said, "The woman whom thou gavest to be with me, she gave me the fruit of the tree, and I ate." [13]Then the Lord God said to the woman, "What is it that you have done?" The woman said, "The serpent beguiled me, and I ate." [14]The

Lord God said to the serpent, "Because you have done this cursed are you above all cattle, and above all wild animals; upon you belly you shall go, and dust you shall eat all the days of your life. [15]I will put enmity between you and the woman, and between your seed and her seed; he shall bruise your head, and you shall bruise his heel." [16]To the woman he said, "I will greatly multiply your pain in childbearing; in pain you shall bring forth children, yet your desire shall be for your husband, and he shall rule over you." [17]And to Adam he said, "Because you have listened to the voice of your wife, and have eaten of the tree of which I commanded you, 'You shall not eat of it,' cursed is the ground because of you; in toil you shall eat of it all the days of your life; [18]thorns and thistles it shall bring forth to you; and you shall eat the plants of the field. [19]In the sweat of your face you shall eat bread till you return to the ground, for out of it you were taken; you are dust, and to dust you shall return." [20]The man called his wife's name Eve, because she was the mother of all living. [21]And the Lord God made for Adam and for his wife garments of skins, and clothed them. [22]Then the Lord God said, "Behold, the man has become like one of us, knowing good and evil; and now, lest he put forth his hand and take also of the tree of life, and eat, and live forever" – [23]therefore the Lord God sent him forth from the garden of Eden, to till the ground from which he was taken. [24]He drove out the man; and at the east of the garden of Eden he placed the cherubim, and a flaming sword which turned every way, to guard the way to the tree of life.

By reading the above chapter, we may detect behind the words of the archangel Lucifer (symbolized as a serpent) a disrespect for God's Words and his desire as a servant (Heb. 1:14) to rule Adam and Eve, the children of God.

The Book of Revelation says:

"Now war arose in heaven, Michael and his angels fighting against the dragon; and the dragon and his angels fought, but they were defeated and there was no longer any place for them in heaven. And the great dragon was thrown down, that ancient serpent, who is called the Devil and Satan, the deceiver of the whole world – he was thrown down to the earth, and his angels were thrown down with him. And I heard a loud voice in heaven, saying, 'Now the salvation and the power and the kingdom of our God and the authority of his Christ have come, for the accuser of our brethren has been thrown down, who accuses them day and night before our God" (Rev. 12:7-10).

A Brief History of the Fall

Long before the creation of humans, angels were created, which not only served God in many duties but also helped Him with the creation of the universe. Later, their function as servant of God (their master) was extended to serve, protect, and teach humans, who were created as children of God. Lucifer the archangel, who was in charge, had more wisdom than Adam and Eve (the first humans whom had the potential to become divine) because [1]he was created much earlier. A servant, for example, is wiser than the children of the master, as the head of a school (archangel) and teachers (angels) have more knowledge than the children. When Lucifer assumed the task of taking care of God's children, he was already rebellious of the fact that God love Adam and Eve more and that mature Adam would become his master. Knowing Lucifer's heart, God gave the commandment "not to eat" (Gen. 2:16). Lucifer, who felt [2]sorry for himself, did not look at the situation from God's view but from his own standpoint. Adam and Eve were created for a different reason and purpose. If he would have truly loved and served them, he would have received more love from his Creator. Lucifer thought that by taking Adam's position, he would receive a higher status and more attention from God and all created beings. He, therefore, wanted to be a Son of God instead of "just a servant". Stimulated by his false pride and ambition to become the most powerful person in the universe, he began to tempt Eve by projecting seductive thoughts in her subconscious mind, which is the mind of her human spirit. Ignoring God's command, which was made foolish by

---

[1] "He" does not mean that Lucifer was a male. Angels are neither male nor female (Mark 12:25).

[2] When people feel self-pity, they think that nobody loves them, and they dislike others for being good.

Lucifer, she responded to his advancement and joined with his ³somewhat materialized psychic body. Thereafter, Eve as a teenager began to seduce immature Adam with her newly acquired possessive love, to desire and to have what one sees. She first began to project feelings and thoughts in Adam's mind, reinforced by her self-centered desire to possess him for herself. After some time, they fell in love and united with each other at the lowest level of their psychic being. The self-centered desire (lust) between them increased to such an extent that it overwhelmed their conscience and blinded their reasoning. They then committed a psychical and physical relationship, ignoring God's command and the consequences of their deed. The final result was that they separated from God, died morally and spiritually, and united with satan. Their ego acquired the evil characteristics of satan, was altered, and became impure or false, and their budding Divine Spirit died on its track to perfection.

REMARK: The here-described scenario of the fall is being repeated in a similar fashion in the lives of many people. The immature male might be playing the role of Lucifer or innocent Adam, and the immature female might be acting out fallen Eve or innocent Eve. Or, the male and female decide to have a relationship together, while their personality is not quite developed and, in many cases, their Divine Spirit or Soul is not even born yet. Adam and Eve loved each other in a self-centered and exclusively personal way instead of in a personal and universal manner, which is true love. The latter inclusive state would be realized after they reach spiritual maturity. They are then ready for marriage.

NOTE: Every time when you (brothers and sisters in the Lord) through thoughts, words, or deeds try to defend or conquer your own position in the Kingdom, you follow in the footsteps of satan. God has no place in His Kingdom for those who have contempt for their spiritual brothers and sisters. Do you want to be admired and praised? So did Lucifer. Do you want to receive more attention and love? So did Lucifer. Do you want to be known as the most popular, knowledgeable, and intellectual person? So did Lucifer. Such an arrogant attitude only leads to spiritual death. (See also Mark 10:35-45).

---

³ Angels and human spirits are able to materialize (to envelop their spirits with etheric substance drawn from people's material bodies and environment) for short periods of time and usually not fully because it takes a lot of energy to do so. Examples in the Bible – three angels visited Abraham – angels who visited Lot in Sodom and Gomorrah – and Jesus' Spirit, which came back surrounded by an etheric body. See Appendix #43.

Accusation from Evil Beings

Satan always [1]accuses the people who are close to God ("our brethren") because he, as an angel, does not want to be ruled by them. He thinks and actually tells God that he is better than humans whom are living a divine life and should, therefore, dominate them like he did over the angelic world. He wants to receive God's love and instructions directly from God instead of receiving it through God's chosen individuals. God, who created human entities to be the Lord of all creation, including the angels (1 Cor. 6:3), have to listen to satan, especially when the brethren or believers commit evil deeds. This Lucifer nature of wanting to rule people whom are morally and spiritually more developed is deeply entrenched in humans as part of the original sin and is expressed by continually criticizing their secular and spiritual leader(s) instead of supporting and praying for them. See, for example, the story of Moses in the Book of Exodus. Thus, we can expect not only satan but also his fallen angels or demons, evil people with or without bodies, and the evil self of good people will strongly resent being dominated by saints of all religions and the divine Self of good people. Those satanic forces will blacken saintly character and accuse them "day and night".

In the Book of Job, satan is cynical about human goodness and is allowed to test it under God's authority and supervision. In the Book of Zechariah chapter three, satan went too far in accusing Joshua the high priest before the [2]heavenly court, of sins of the past which have been forgiven. Satan was rebuked by the Lord and thrown out of heaven.

---

[1] Satan does not accuse those people whom are living the life of the personality because they already belong more or less to him. He is the father of those whom are completely evil (John 8:44), and his spirit is "at work in the sons of disobedience" (Eph. 2:2), and he "has blinded the minds of the unbelievers" (2 Cor. 4:4) whom are, most of the time, his children (1 John 3:10).

[2] The heavenly court can be pictured as satan the accuser or persecutor on one side of the throne of God (the Judge) and Christ our defender on the other side, while celestial beings function as the jury. Christ, who has conquered satan, knows, and we also know now that satan and his angels are even greater criminals than humans ever will be. We as regenerated humans can accuse satan and his cohorts before the heavenly throne. However, when we are living an exemplary and sacrificial life in the footsteps of Jesus Christ, satan and all his forces may respect and cooperate with us to establish the lost Garden of Eden.

People become aware that they have done evil by their conscience and even better by the Spirit of God. They should acknowledge their sins, repent to God or His representatives, and make it right so that the broken relationship with God can be restored. Individuals are then forgiven and absolved of their sins as if they never happened. "For I will be merciful toward their iniquities, and I will remember their sins no more" (Heb. 8:12, 10:17). They have been declared "not guilty" by the highest court of the universe.

Satan and his *manipulators know that many believers have a tendency towards self-condemnation because of the fact that they are born with original sin. The evil ones are using this knowledge of heaping guilt and convictions upon them, making the believers feel that they are worthless beings and that there is no forgiveness for them. The Luciferians, through accusation and insinuation, try to separate the brethren from God, casting doubt upon the person's salvation and/or the course of his/her spiritual progress. When humans are burdened by the consciousness of (false) guilt, they feel unworthy to talk with their God, to seek His aid, or to witness effectively and serve the Lord with power and blessing. Satan and his workers, as well as the "old self", "old nature", or "the flesh" (Rom. 6:6; Eph. 4:22; Col. 3:9; Gal. 5:17) of the unsaved (and the saved) are also using the memories of past sins to drive a wedge between us and God and try to convince us that we are so bad that we do not deserve God's love. Finally, excessive guilt and sorrow can only lead to depression, despair, and defeat and will only serve the evil forces of the universe.

Meaning of Spiritual Death

"God said, 'You shall not eat of the fruit of the tree which is in the midst of the garden, neither shall you touch it, lest you die.' But the serpent said to the woman, 'You will not die.'"

Adam and Eve did not die physically (Adam died at the biblical age of 930 years – Gen. 5:5) but morally and spiritually, which is a condition wherein they and their descendants are not able to receive and respond to God's love, which is the Source of spiritual life. They died when they responded to the empty and deadly word of satan instead of the Life-giving Word of God, and came under the dominion of satan.

---

* Manipulators are those whom take advantage of people with a guilt complex by making individuals, races, or nations accept the role of scapegoat, thus making them do whatever they want them to do, to make compensation for their (past) sins.

REMARK: Fallen men and women not only have a tendency to see other people like they are, but they also accuse others of the same crime they themselves have committed. Jesus was accused to be beelzebub, the devil. Jesus as the Man of God was a mirror, wherein ordinary humans could see their own imperfection.

The Bible said, "You have the name of being alive (physically), but you are dead (spiritually)" – Rev. 3:1.

"Lord, let me first go and bury my father. But Jesus said to him, 'Follow me, and leave the (spiritual) dead to bury their own (physical) dead'" (Matt. 8:21-22).

"He who hears my word and believes him who sent me, has eternal life; he does not come into judgment, but has passed from death to life" (John 5:24).

"We know that we have passed out of death into life, because we love the brethren. He who does not love (as expressed by his Divine Spirit) abides in death" (1 John 3:14).

"For the wages of sin is death (spiritual), but the free gift of God is eternal life in Christ Jesus our Lord" (Rom. 6:23, 6:11).

"To set the mind on the flesh (living an evil life) is death, but to set the mind on the Spirit (living a divine life) is life and peace" (Rom. 8:6). See also Col. 1:18; John 11:25-26; Luke 17:33.

Paul, in speaking to the church at Ephesus, said that they were spiritually dead and that they must find a spiritual awakening. "Therefore it is said, 'awake o sleeper and arise from the dead and Christ shall give you light'" (Eph. 5:1). It is written in John 8:44, "You are of your father the devil, and your will is to do your father's desires. He was a murderer from the beginning" (because he murdered Adam and Eve morally and spiritually).

Isaiah said, "We grope for the wall like the blind, we grope like those who have no eyes; we stumble at noon as in the twilight, among those in full vigor we are like dead" (Isa. 59:10; Mk. 8:18). Another great prophet Ezekiel said that people "have ears to hear, but hear not" (Ezek. 12:2; Mk. 4:9; Rev. 2:7). Isaiah and Ezekiel gave a true description of the blackout of the psychic and spiritual senses of the inner beings of the people. However, they were more than spiritually blind and deaf; they are dead. "You were dead through the trespasses and sins in which you once walked" (Eph. 2:1-2) when you had no communication with God.

From the above description and explanation, it should be clear that the term 'death' here is separation from God and not physical death, which is a natural process and should, therefore, not be feared. The physical body is merely a cloak or overcoat, spacesuit, soil, or vehicle for the inner spirit to grow and to experience life on the physical plane. When it has served its purpose(s), it separates permanently from the human spirit, while the latter will live for a long time in the spirit world until it also serves its purpose(s). It will then drop like a booster of a rocket, and the Divine Spirit, symbolized as the rocket, will live forever.

NOTE: When one is spiritually blind and deaf, he or she has lost communication with the deepest aspect of him/herself. The result is that they live with a strong awareness of the physical aspect of life, while their awareness of the psychic and spiritual reality has been weakened, and for many, it has been extinguished. The psychic senses, especially the spiritual eyes and ears, were never developed and even denied existence, while the "silent voice" of the Divine Spirit, which tries so hard to whisper, is restricted in its evolvement and the privilege to speak. This all results that the budding Divine Spirit becomes a prisoner within its own body or temple.

What should be feared is the death of the Divine Spirit or Soul, which is born of God and is the true child of God. The saying "You can kill my body but not my Soul" is not altogether true. *The Soul can be killed, especially the ones which have just been born. God as Parents are grief-stricken when a vulnerable spiritual baby has been killed by evil people in society or by neglect of God's representatives. After the fall, they cried out to Adam, **"Where are you?"** Throughout history, they have been disappointed in the people whom they tried raising morally and spiritually. Through Isaiah they spoke: "Sons have I reared and brought up, but they have rebelled against me. The ox knows its owner, and the ass its master crib; but Israel does not know, my people do not understand" (Isa. 1:2-3). Through Jesus they lamented, "O Jerusalem, Jerusalem, killing the prophets and stoning those who are sent to you! How often would I have gathered your children together as a hen gathers her brood under her wings, and you would not!" (Matt. 23:37-39).

---

* As the baby Soul can be killed if it is no longer fed the life elements of God (Love and Truth), the temple or house (human spirit) wherein the Soul lives does survive physical death.

Someone who has developed morally and spiritually will feel terrible and God-forsaken after he or she has fallen. This was certainly the case of Adam and Eve, whom were in fearful anxiety and despair. People that have died morally and spiritually can be detected by a change of behavior. They are more insecure and materialistic, do not feel like praying, and are less friendly to their neighbors. They attract different friends, are more pessimistic, have no high purpose in life, are more selfish, and start living a life below the belt. They look empty, older and tired, and want to live a life devoted to self and family and do not care much about other people. They are more easily addicted to sex, alcohol, drugs, and food because they have less control over their instincts and appetites. They like to take the name of the Lord in vain by cursing and swearing because He is no longer a loving Father but a Lord and ruler they reluctantly obey.

NOTE 1: Before Adam and Eve were created, God was a Creator and acted as a master towards the angels. However, after Adam and Eve were growing up morally and spiritually, God experienced, for the first time, parenthood for a brief period until Adam and Eve fell from grace. Later, they became spiritual parents to Jesus and all those whom are born of them.

NOTE 2: Although killing of the Soul is the worst crime because it has much more value and it lives forever than the physical body (which is of less value and has a temporary existence), the Soul can eventually be revived and resurrected. This, however, is not the case with the physical body.

REMARK: Many spiritual babies are killed by humans in our communities. Although they are not punished by their judicial system, the perpetrators do have to pay according to the natural law of the universe.

Rationalization and Justification

The archangel Lucifer told Eve that she would not die, as God told her, but that on the contrary, her "eyes will be opened" and that she "will be like God, knowing good and evil". In this way, he justified and rationalized his evil deed to his own norm of righteousness and seduced the spirit of Eve. Today, we see that sexual permissiveness is being rationalized by intellectuals as Lucifer justified his lustful love for Eve. When people listen to those intellectuals whom have no wisdom to apply their knowledge and commit fornication and adultery, they are actually doing great damage to each other's moral and spiritual life and, therefore, hate each other just as much as they "love" (desire) each other.

Even though people have inherited the fallen nature of their forebears, God is still able to communicate with them through their *conscience. If they want to commit an evil deed(s), they have to soothe and mislead their conscience and Truth by justifying and rationalizing their deeds; otherwise, their conscience is bothering and "confusing" them. Thus, one of the most highly developed senses in human beings is their inborn ability to justify their words and deeds within their own being and to others. For example: Hitler justified Nazism and Stalin Communism because they believed that it would bring prosperity and happiness to all the people. Even religious people fought many wars, which they justified as holy wars. Many of the leaders of those wars were faithful husbands and good parents to their children and they liked their animals, but they excused themselves by self-justification. Other people excuse their bad behavior by saying: "I am only human." They conveniently forget that human nature should not remain good and evil but can be purified.

Their Eyes Are Opened to False Values

The woman saw that the tree was to be desired to make one wise; she took of its fruit and ate and gave some to her husband. After they ate the fruit of the tree of the knowledge of good and evil, "the eyes of both were opened, and they knew that they were naked".

The archangel deceived the woman by making her think that she, as an ungenerated and undeveloped personality, could obtain God-like qualities and have moral authority. By eating of the [1]fruit too early, Eve and later Adam became sexually aware or received carnal (sensual)

---

* Someone who is more righteous will, in a stronger measure, suffer from the pangs of conscience after they have done something wrong than the one who lives a more evil life. However, no matter how unscrupulous humans can be, they still seek goodness through their divine Spark, which dwells in the depth of their conscience.

[1] It is God's plan for pollination or sexual relations to occur when the male and female plants or humans are both mature and ready. Otherwise, the produced seed and species, or children and descendants will be inferior. Besides, unripe fruits will not taste good because humans unite with each other with only two of their three bodies (physical – emotional/mental – divine).

knowledge. The [2]strong emotion of misdirected love or lust [3]blinded and overpowered the minds of Adam and Eve before their reasoning (higher or pure intellect) was fully developed. The eyes of both were opened by not receiving the wisdom of God but that of satan. They acquired the false value of material gain instead of the real value of spiritual understanding. They began to judge by their acquired good and evil standard and righteousness, which became "like a polluted garment" (Isaiah 64:6). Thus, every time that somebody passes moral judgment on another, he or she assumes the special right and power of being as god's "knowing good and evil" (Gen. 3:22). By doing so, they experience a false feeling of importance, inflating their ego, which results that they become more evil and miserable.

They Felt Ashamed and Hid Themselves from the Lord

After Adam and Eve ate the fruit, "they knew that they were naked; and they sewed fig leaves together and made themselves aprons". They then "hid themselves from the presence of the Lord God", who called to Adam, "Where are you?" Adam said, "I heard the sound of thee in the garden, and I was afraid, because I was naked; and I hid myself." When Adam and Eve were growing up, they were so innocent and free with each other, and they were so sincere and without any secret for God the Father and Mother because they were not ashamed of their nakedness (Gen. 2:25). After Adam and Eve fell, they were afraid and [4]ashamed of what they had done and hid themselves from God. In the time of Noah, God wanted to restore the feeling of joy He experienced when He looked at the innocence of naked Adam before the fall. He wanted to do that by not letting Noah's family feel any shame for the naked Noah nor to hide from their father, who was in Adam's position. However, Noah's three sons felt ashamed and covered their father up and looked at Noah as Adam after the fall. Fallen men and women are often ashamed to talk about the naked God, the way He really is. They prefer to refer to Him indirectly by mentioning Him as an impersonal being with many names. In this way, they cover Him up and hide their God in the closet.

---

[2] Emotion, which is made up of different shades or colors, is a neutral force, which can be used either for constructive or destructive purposes. The emotions should, therefore, be guided by reason and Truth. Otherwise, it will get out of hand and may cause individual and mass violence.

[3] It is possible to become so blinded by the emotion that one cannot see the Truth anymore or does not want to see it. The emotion of jealousy and anger can also blind one's reason but not as strongly as lustful desires. The Bible says that "the god of this world has blinded the minds of the unbelievers" (2 Cor. 4:4).

[4] See also Appendix #11.

NOTE: The act of taking the virginity of a girl is known as defloration, which is for her the end of maidenhood and the beginning of woman or motherhood, the transition from maiden flower to fruit mother.

When people have [1]done evil, they do not want to face their spiritual leader in whom the Spirit of God dwells, or their spiritual brothers and sisters whom are doing the Will of God together, without any sexual feelings for each other. However, when they begin to think about each other as mates, they are no longer innocent, and their relationship with God is no longer that of son and daughter. God is not able to work through them as spiritual parents and, thus, no birth can be given to spiritual children. Their spiritual work remains unfruitful.

Like Adam and Eve, we hide when God is calling and are afraid to confront Him because we are ashamed of what we are and try to cover up our nakedness. We also hide from our fellow citizen by not exposing who we really are and certainly not what we are thinking by putting up a smiling front. We, therefore, fail to build true relationships, which are based upon [2]trust.

The archangel, Eve, and Adam wanted to "love" each other freely, without any restriction and responsibility. Thus, free "love" and free sex came about without any moral obligation and accountability ("What I want to do"). The God-given qualities, such as love, desire, and freedom were reversed through their selfish act. Natural love turned to selfish love (lust), original desire to selfish desire (greed), and freedom to selfish freedom or freedom without responsibility (license – "the right to do whatever I please"). Conscientious people feel guilty whenever they act out those evil perversions and have tried to overcome them. Those three inherited evil tendencies, which are deep-

---

[1] It all may start when he thinks about her as a girl he likes to seduce. Instead of thinking about it, he soon begins to project such thoughts to her subconscious mind. She then begins to entertain those thoughts of wanting to be seduced by him. At this point, God can no longer stay because their relationship has become satan-centered. They then feel a diminishing love and spiritual power from God, and they both become spiritually low and depressed. They then start to dislike and blame each other.

[2] As in "the beginning", Eve mistrusted God's Word and followed the hollow word of satan. Many people today still do not want to trust God's life-giving Word. Being more or less separated from God and the authentic Self of people, humans are not able to trust each other. Besides, being good and evil, they cannot even trust themselves or others to be good, who at times may have selfish motivation. Thus, we are living in a world of mistrust, wherein almost everyone (also in close personal relationships) is suspicious of the other's motivation, especially those who have been hurt before and, therefore, almost automatically tend up their shield of protection.

ly embedded in one's personality could, however with great difficulty, be mastered by monks and others through the vows of celibacy, poverty, and obedience. By doing so, the monks also pay penance or indemnity for the people in their care, so that they could also be redeemed.

Lucifer, Eve, and Adam let their lower desires overpower their reason(ing) and common sense, without taking into account the damage they would create to others, as long as they could gratify and satisfy their lustful desires. They only thought about their own benefit or selfish purpose instead of the public benefit or whole purpose. The result of giving in to their intense self-centered emotion or lust was that they separated from God and the deeper Self of humans and became [1]extremely selfish or egotistic.

An egotist is only interested in him/herself, feels no joy in giving but only from the standpoint of what he or she can get out of it. Those persons use others to advance their own cause and sacrifice them to benefit themselves instead of sacrificing themselves for others. They lack interest in the needs of others and respect for their dignity and sincerity. They see nothing but themselves and judge everyone and everything from its usefulness to them and are unable to love others or themselves, which leaves them frustrated and empty. The selfish person is paralyzed in his/her capacity to love or enjoy anything. No love will radiate from them when they only think, speak, and do something for their own advantage and no love can be given. They are pervaded by hostility toward life and become easily tired and depressed. The unselfish person, on the other hand, lives only for the sake of others. He or she likes to make other people happy so that they can also be happy. They usually feel cheerful, enjoy life, and experience the creative energy streaming through them. They not only love their own family but also strangers and society as a whole. They certainly do not manipulate people with selfish love and will never drag down or belittle other persons in order to become superior.

NOTE 1: Satan's egotistic behavior is well documented in Isaiah 14:13-14, where he used the word "I" five times.

NOTE 2: Egotism and selfishness have many step-children, such as: self-centeredness, self-preservation, self-sufficiency, self-indulgence, self-worship,

---

[1] An extremely egotistic person is not only immature but also evil. They are worse than little children whom are naturally selfish.

self-reliance, self-seeking, self-love, self-ambition, self-righteousness, self-importance, and self-interest.

Shifting the Blame to Others

"God said to Adam, 'have you eaten of the tree of which I commanded not to eat?' The man said 'the woman whom thou gavest to be with me, she gave me the fruit of the tree, and I ate.' Then the Lord God said to the woman, 'What is it that you have done?' The woman said, 'The serpent beguiled me, and I ate.'"

In this story of the fall, Adam blamed Eve, and Eve blamed the serpent because they both knew that they had fallen and suffered from [1]anxiety, agony, despair, and [2]fear and began to hate and blame each other, while nobody wanted to bear any responsibility. This tendency to avoid accepting responsibility or "passing the buck" is deeply ingrained in human nature. Some of them not only blame other people but also environment, poverty, racism, genes, circumstances, etc. for their bad behavior and misery, while political and religious groups

---

[1] By having no personal relationship with God and missing a deep connection with other humans, people feel lonely, insecure, uncertain, unhappy, heavy laden (Matt. 11:28), weary, discontent about life's meaninglessness, and constantly worry about things that have happened and have not happened. Because of their alienation, many of them are burdened with guilt, ridden with anxiety, despair, futility, hopelessness, heartbroken, and terrified by the thought of dying. As Kierkegaard said, "We are despairing creatures, and suffer without exception from sickness into death." For man to escape from anxiety and despair, he has to gain his lost position by passing first through the aesthetic stage, then the ethical, and lastly the religious stage. Another existentialist Heidegger said that a human being suffers from anxiety and dread because they are not authentic. They are alienated from their essential Self and therefore are not real. A more optimistic but not quite realistic view was advanced by 19th century liberal theologians whom believed that humans have been gradually evolving, morally, culturally, and religiously from their animal origin. As this is true in their industrial and technological know-how, educational and social reform, it certainly is not visible in their moral and spiritual development, as the outbreak of the First World War gave proof of this fact. Are people of today obeying the most basic moral law, the 10 Commandments?

[2] After their fall, Adam and Eve were fearful of God and fearful of the powers they had obeyed, which were controlling them. This fear is not the same as the fear that is needed to protect oneself. It is a fear (with all its siblings such as: worry, doubt, irritation, frustration, etc.) because one is separated from God/goddess and has become adrift in a hostile and unfriendly universe. This vibration of fear is especially experienced when one lives in a spiritually low environment among people whom are most of the time evil-minded. When the latter are aggressive in their hunger for power, they are usually and unknowingly driven by fear that may degenerate into terrorization.

blame each other for conflict and strife. They completely ignore the real cause of their misery by giving in to their inherent rebellion, lust, hatred, and greed. As long as the people have an immature human nature which is good and evil, there will be a tendency to blame others of usually the *same crime they have committed. Some persons say, "I am not to blame"; "You are to blame for everything"; "It is through no fault of mine." Immature Christians blame satan for everything that goes wrong in their lives. They often say, "The devil made me do it." On the other hand, the more mature individuals know that they alone are responsible or accountable for their errors and easily admit that they have been wrong. They say in their heart, "I am the master of my faith, I am the captain of my soul." When humans pass their sins on to someone else, they will keep their sins because when there is no recognition of sins, repentance, forgiveness, and reconciliation are not possible. Whenever the false ego dominates our lives, we blame little faults in others and excuse great offenses in ourselves. We see the speck in our neighbor's eyes but not the log in our own (Matt. 7:3-5).

Satan Is Cursed

"The Lord God said to the serpent, 'Because you have done this, cursed are you above all cattle, and above all wild animals; upon your belly you shall go, and dust you shall eat all the days of your life. I will put enmity between you and the woman, and between your seed and her seed; he shall bruise your head, and you shall bruise his heel.'"

Since satan was thrown down from heaven (high spiritual or divine sphere) to hell – Rev. 12:9 – (lowest vibration psychical realm which is near the earth), he is not able to receive God's love, His guidance, and inspiration. He, fallen angels, and psychic beings of evil people subsist by drawing their psychic substance (dust) from their evil surroundings, in which they live a miserable life (upon their belly).

In the beginning, God foretold that the seed of the woman (Abel-type people) will be in opposition to the seed of satan (Cain-type people), and that Christ shall bruise your head (inner self) and you (satan) shall bruise his heel (outer self). See also Revelation chapters twelve and thirteen.

---

* We judge ourselves when we judge another for how we could see the evil in another, were it not in ourselves.

Sentencing the Woman

When sentencing the woman, God said, "I will greatly multiply your pain in childbearing; in pain you shall bring forth children, yet your desire shall be for your husband, and he shall rule over you."

The [1]painful contractions that women suffer are a natural part of the process of birth. However, the suffering involved in childbearing has been greatly increased and varies from person to person. Because many women are immature in the development of their personality (which is also tainted with original sin) and most of them are not regenerated, it is to be expected that they have difficulties during pregnancy and [2]labor, especially when they are inclined towards evil. Women not only suffer the usual nausea, illness, and pains of pregnancy, but some of them also experience the agony of miscarriage, giving birth to an infant stillborn, bringing forth children that die young of diseases, or whom are disabled or retarded. Many children, of no fault of their own, contracted and inherited, from their parents, the physical and mental handicaps and other weaknesses, such as genetic defects and a weak immune system. Some of them are born blind, deaf, deformed, insane, and possessed by evil spirits. They are always a source of sorrow for the parents and the community.

When parents are morally corrupt, God is not able to work through them very well to relieve them of their suffering, except through an outside agency. Besides, children born from those parents are inclined toward evil, with criminal and destructive tendencies and belong more to the world of satan than that of God. Those parents are unknowingly populating the world with satanic children, whom will be working consciously and unconsciously against the children of God whom are trying to establish the Kingdom of God. The latter have the grace of God and came into the world without much trouble for their parents or for themselves.

Eve used her femininity to entice Adam to join her in disobeying God. By allowing himself to do what he knew was wrong, he lost his moral authority, power, and self-respect and began to dislike his deceived mate. Adam, who had earlier described his woman in grace-

---

[1] Women can do special exercises of mind and body to relieve the pain of birth. They may also follow the advice of Dr. Grantly Dick-Read who published his book "Childbirth without Fear" in 1944 and is called today "hypno-birthing".

[2] Augustine says that every man experiences pain, frustration, and hardship in his labor as every woman does in hers.

fully poetic words (Gen. 2:23), saw that she was no longer his true companion and "helper fit for him" (Gen. 2:18). He coldly referred to her as "the woman thou gave to be with me". Because of his imperfection, he misused his masculinity to dominate her in an oppressive way instead of exercising loving headship. Eve, in turn, displayed an unhealthy dependence or craving for her husband and became socially inferior to him. However, when they are living a divine life, they will be equal to each other in their different function. As Paul said in 1 Cor. 11:3, "The head of every man is Christ, the head of a woman is her husband, and the head of Christ is God."

Judgment of Adam Who Lost Dominion

In judging Adam, God said, "Because you have listened to the voice of your wife and have eaten of the tree of which I commanded you 'You shall not eat of it', cursed is the ground because of you; in toil you shall eat of it all the days of your life; thorns and thistles it shall bring forth to you; and you shall eat the plants of the field. In the sweat of your face you shall eat bread till you return to the ground, for out of it you were taken; you are dust and to dust you shall return."

The first human pair in the Bible was living in a secure environment that assured them of a stable and trouble-free life, which took care of all their physical and emotional needs because every tree "is pleasant to the sight and good for food" (Gen. 2:9).

However, the moment Adam and Eve gave up their personal relationship with their Creator and refused to live in harmony with His purpose for humanity, they lost their feeling of heavenly security, and feelings of doubt, fear, shame, guilt, and insecurity entered their lives. After rejecting God's loving sovereign leadership, Adam admitted that he "was afraid", while they both covered themselves and hid from their loveable and devoted Caretaker. Their first-born son Cain committed a murderous act whereby he separated himself even more from God. He then complained to the Lord: You have banished me from the soil, and I must avoid your presence and become a restless wanderer on the earth. His cry has echoed down the corridors of time. We all feel it, and we may still feel alone and afraid. Moreover, the result of the deviation of Adam's family not only affected their descendants but has also been very hard on God, who saw that the purpose of His creation was nullified. God as parents, whom experienced parenthood for the first time, were heartbroken when they saw that their most precious little children became evil-minded and eventually wanted to have nothing to do with them anymore. "And the Lord was sorry that he made man on the earth, and it grieved him to his heart" (Gen. 6:6). He then reduced the human's life span to one hundred and twenty years Gen. 6:3).

REMARK: By living a shorter life span, they would acquire less evil earth power.

The fall not only resulted in alienation from God but also from the God Spark or Self of the people and from our own budding Self. As a consequence, humans became more lonely, frustrated, restless, and strangers to each other instead of brothers and sisters. They have an inherent mistrust of another person's motivation and can, therefore, not completely trust their neighbors, whom are usually reluctant to help them, which makes them even more insecure. All this resulted that many individuals do not like to live the life of the good/evil personality and try to escape from it as much as possible by making themselves unconscious, by sleeping and drinking excessively, taking drugs, and becoming too much involved in parties and sports. Some of them also become disappointed in themselves, by saying that they are worthless and no good. This is probably true because they do not care much about their inner life, which is reflected in the "I don't care" attitude of their outer life. Life for them has become a burden by which they are confronted every day.

In this fallen world, everything is upside down; that which has real value is despised and rejected, such as Truth, while that which has no eternal value is given first place, such as material possessions. You have become materialistic because your physical values, such as food, clothes, shelter, etc. have become more important to you than the spiritual values of Truth, Beauty, and Goodness. *Instead of the Spirit controlling the personality, the personality dominates the Spirit because the well being of the personality, especially your physical body, is more important to you. You are out of harmony within your being and with the cosmos, are ignorant about the inner world and its relation to the

---

* People spend money on the "pleasures of the flesh" because they do not know the great joy of living the spiritual or divine life. Because most sickness is of psychosomatic origin, such as negative and evil thinking and feeling (think about placebo effect on patients by taking a sugar pill), the health cost is staggering. Spiritual people, on the other hand, are more health-conscious. They usually do not drink much, smoke, or take drugs.

outer world, and listen to the voice outside because you are not able to hear the voice inside.

The corrupted human nature is manifested in selfishness, envy, possessiveness, and immorality. The fallen world is likewise characterized by endless hatred and warfare, class and racial struggle, crime and exploitation. The American author Henry Thoreau wrote back in 1854, "The mass of men lead lives of quiet desperation." The people of those times and still today are insecure and uncertain about the future, afraid of getting older, and the inevitability of death.

Adam was told by God that the ground is cursed, and that in toil he shall bring forth [1]thorns and thistles. This means that nature became hostile to humans and that "when you till the ground, it shall no longer yield to you its strength" (Gen. 4:12). This is true for Adam, Cain, and all their descendants because of the moral and spiritual deterioration that Lucifer, Eve, and Adam introduced. The earth does not produce as much as it should, and the growth of crops is hampered by the low and selfish thoughts which influence the working of elemental forces, thus creating imbalances in weather conditions and the insect population.

Before the fall, God blessed the male and female who were created in His own image and God said to them, "Be fruitful and multiply, and fill the earth and subdue it; and have dominion over the fish of the sea and over the birds of the air and over every living thing that moves upon the earth" (Gen. 1:28). This is the fulfillment of God's third blessing, to have dominion, and to be responsible for the creation, to cultivate and to take care of it (Gen. 2:15). After the fall, the earth or ground, which was to be under man's dominion, came under man's evil dominion, and the ground became physically unproductive, except by hard work and suffering.

As humans no longer serve the creation as God-centered caretakers, there exists a mutual hostility between fallen people and nature. The elemental forces and beings of nature have an instinctive fear for humans because they feel that they have lost their [2]balance and harmony.

---

[1] This does not mean that the earth, all of a sudden, brought forth only thorn bushes and thistles. As Adam and his male descendants experience crop failure, Eve and her female descendants suffer from miscarriage.

[2] By observing nature and its beauty, individuals may balance and harmonize their feeling and thinking because the very shape of the earth and the atmosphere of the planet are affected by and, in turn, affect human consciousness.

NOTE: Because of the fall, the bodies of humans became coarser, and they began to eat meat (Gen. 9:3), while in the beginning, they were to eat the plants of the field and the fruit of the trees (Gen. 1:29). Meat is dense, coarsens, and lowers the vibration of the physical body and is, thus, not a suitable vehicle for an evolved spirit of high vibration to have its dwelling place.

As Paul wrote in Rom. 8:19-23: "For the creation waits with eager longing for the revealing of the sons of God; for the creation was subjected to futility, not of its own will but by the will of him who subjected it in hope; because the creation itself will be set free from its bondage to decay and obtain the glorious liberty of the children of God."

Through the fall, humans lost Truth and, thus, the purpose and direction of life, whereby their life was no longer meaningful, weakening their motivation and willpower. They do not display much initiative and effort and are reluctant to contribute anything of value to society. They thus found themselves in a state of lassitude or laziness. Some of them became also guilty of indolence by seeking value without any labor. Being in this deplorable state, out of harmony with the universal forces, and your constant fearful concern for survival, repressive frustrations, and resentment has drained much of your energy. To recuperate the lost physical, vital, emotional, mental, and creative energies, they have to sleep longer to replenish their "psychic and physical battery", which has become depleted by negative thinking and feelings, thus shortening their life.

Relying on mental power of our tainted and weak personality to control our life is not enough. Strong willpower is needed to overcome all manner of physical, emotional, and mental indulgences, such as: overeating, alcohol abuse, drug and sex addiction, bad emotional habits, evil desires, and wrong thinking. However, by awakening and evolving the divine Spark within our being, we then have the extra power to control our personality with all its bad customs and habits. It will strengthen the immune system and cure our body of many diseases. It will also give healing and strength, as well as inspiration, meaning, reason, and incentive to the inner personality or human spirit to do good deeds.

Since Adam and all his descendants were condemned to eat their bread by the *sweat of their brow and to labor in sorrow amidst thorns and thistles, life has become a burden, and work is a toil and routine. This was especially true in the early human history when invention of labor saving devices was considerably delayed because of the slow progress of the [1]corrupt and impaired mental capacity. At those times and also for many today, little opportunity is given for workers to be creative, so that their work is boring and dull, especially for those working on assembly lines. Many people can therefore not be truly happy with the work they do, especially when they work for someone or groups of people whom only want to enrich themselves and are not much interested in helping others except when it promotes their own interest. Fallen people ([2]employers and employees) do not truly love each other and belong to "the world", which says that in order to be the greatest, you have to compete. You have to be smarter than anyone around you, pushing them out of your way so that you can climb to the top. No one should ever use and abuse others for his or her own glorification, self-interest, self-love, and self-preservation. This selfish ambition is allowed in a capitalistic society, which usually [3]takes from

---

* Sweat here does not always mean long periods of extreme physical labor because many people are also involved in mental labor. What it means today is that people in general are fearful of life and continually worry about their possession. Those people whom work for an employer usually have a hard time making a living and are always afraid of losing their job. As soon as our young ones come out of the protective shell of school and home, they have to accept partial enslavement in order to survive. There is not only economic insecurity and desperation, but also fear of losing their home and other possessions, fear of becoming sick, and dying of incurable diseases. Thus, every man experiences excessive hardship, frustration, and pain in his labor and every woman in hers, when they are living a life separate from God. They rely only on their human self and not on the God forces working through the divine Self. They then have to talk about survival and be sorry all the days of their lives. However, when their awakened Divine Spirit is in charge of their personality, work does not become a labor or struggle. It can be done without much effort and does not seem to be any work at all but pure joy. Thus, life has become a mystical adventure in the physical, psychic, and divine worlds.

[1] Because of deviation from God's principles, the natural faculties of humans have weakened. The intellect lost its full capacity, the will became weak, and the psychic faculties became dormant.

[2] In the time of Karl Marx, in the middle of the nineteenth century and later, laborers were exploited mercilessly by the capitalists and had to endure long hours of labor. They were given wages that could hardly sustain their lives and were living in demoralized poverty, while the capitalists were living in luxury. The latter were expressing more the evil side of their personality, while the laborers were more inclined to be good. However, a few years after the communist takeover in 1917, the communists became more evil while the capitalists became relatively good.

[3] According to the law of karma, those who take from others will also be treated in the same way and will be soon out of business.

the weak by exploitation and by cut-throat competition, creating a survival of the fittest mentality which we can also observe in the [4]animal world. Most people do not like to work and seek value without doing any labor, such as gambling and taking welfare from their governments because working for a living is often demeaning and humiliating. In the workplace, the boss is often seen as an enemy who humiliates the workers, whom are constantly on the defensive, and in order to survive, they have to become economic slaves to their employer.

NOTE: The ones on the evil side, including those that promote an unhealthy competitive lifestyle, cannot be truly happy because they are not in harmony with the God forces and are, therefore, more ridden by anxiety than peace.

Honest work in the Old Testament is generally praised, while in the New Testament, work is also valued while idleness is condemned (2 Thess. 3:6-13). In the Middle Ages, a distinction was made between secular and sacred work, the latter having to do with monastic work. Calvin, the Protestant reformer, emphasized that worldly success is an indication that one has been divinely elected and is thus a blessing, which is also the belief of Jewish people, which gave incentive to the "work ethic" of modern capitalism. However, it degraded when the capitalists sought for self-centered interest and began to exploit the workers by seeing them not as humans but of having the same value as production tools and equipment. This behavior gave eventual rise to Communism.

NOTE: The Pilgrim fathers, whom were following the Calvinist work ethic, believed that people should not pass their days in idleness "without exercising themselves diligently in some lawful calling". In spite of the harsh Calvinistic theology, the Pilgrims found satisfaction in their work. They believed that idleness bred mischief, and labor brought strength of body and vigor to the mind. They assumed that it was a shame for a man not to work. Lowly jobs were regarded as important and not beneath the dignity of anyone. The sense of working with God in one's daily tasks gave an ethical meaning to labor.

---

[4] Animals that belong to the same species do hardly kill each other, while human beings of the same species always fight and destroy one another. The fact that the animal kingdom is "red in tooth and claw" and that animals destroy each other is only a reflection of the attitude and action of humans who kill one another physically. Humans send emotional feelings and mental thoughts of hatred, revenge, and deceitfulness to the surrounding psychic belt around the earth, which in turn influences the animal and other kingdoms. What can we expect from animals who only follow the example of humans? The latter have cut trees and killed animals without good reasons and also have destroyed mountains. That is why "the whole creation has been groaning in travail" (Rom. 8:22).

As is recorded in Genesis 1:28, humans are to subdue the [1]earth and to "have dominion over the fish of the sea and over the birds of the air and over every living thing that moves upon the earth". This is the fulfillment of God's third blessing, to have dominion ([2]not domination) and be responsible for the creation, to cultivate it, and to take care of it (Gen. 2:15).

NOTE: Because we are a microcosm and the universe is a macrocosm, we become a qualified master and ruler of the universe to the exact degree that we master ourselves or become master of our lives.

God, who is the Original Cause, created human beings in His image and likeness as male and female (Gen. 1:26-27). This suggests that God, in His essential nature and potentiality, not only represents Fatherhood, but also Motherhood. As humans were created in the image of God, the universe was created in the image of humanity, in its masculine and feminine elements (yang and yin).

However, God and the creation do not only have external forms but also an internal nature. That is why God is a God of Love, Intellect, and Will, whose qualities people have inherited from their Creator. As human parents love their children because they are so much like them, God as True Parents understands and loves all people because they are so much like them. By the same token, people love the universe because it is made in their image. Therefore, every human being feels familiar with and is attracted to the creation because it reflects not only their external form but also their internal aspect and qualities. By

---

[1] In 1970, James Lovelock produced the Gaia hypothesis, which proposes that the planet earth and all of its component parts behave as if they were a living organism, wherein each part interacts with other parts in a symbiotic relationship that is interdependent, self-regulating, and mutually complementary. Another British scientist Rupert Sheldrake postulated that anything that has been learned by a particular group of species would be slightly more easily learned by a subsequent group in another place as if they were connected in a morphogenetic field, or collective unconscious. Examples are the so-called "hundred monkey phenomenon", viruses which are becoming resistant to drugs, and crystals which are more easily formed. It has been said that the earth is a living, feeling body, and that the pulling out of plants by the roots is felt by the spirit of the earth.

[2] In the beginning, God commanded man to go forth subduing the earth (establishing dominion over the fish, fowl, and land roving animals), but He did not say to overpower, capture, kill, and enslave one's fellow creature for what it might profit him. Wildlife is killed for sporting pleasure, and many animals are caught for the fur industry. Thus, to have dominion is not to rape, exploit, misuse, and pollute the creation just to please ourselves. Dominion implies stewardship – being responsible for the care and well being of something held in trust. In the parable of the talents, Jesus tells us that we are responsible for the management of the world (Matt. 25:14-30).

knowing ourselves and the creation externally and internally, we become qualified to love and rule the kingdoms of nature. Thus, we are able to give true names to all the living creatures (Gen. 2:19).

Although the original model or archetype of a human being existed from the beginning in the mind of God, humans were created last in the process of creation. Each stage of evolution surpasses but includes its predecessors, with the humankind as the most advanced and culmination of all previous stages. Thus, all aspects of the three kingdoms – mineral, vegetable, and animal – can be found in every human being.

NOTE: All things in the three kingdoms of nature are created in the image of man and woman as male and female and also reflect their internal characteristics of spirit and body. Thus, the cosmos, with its outer and inner aspects, is like humans, the microcosm, which has not only a physical but an etheric and psychic content as well. For example:

From the four ethers we find in a human, only the lowest ether is active in the species of the mineral world. It is therefore possible "to read" the etheric counterpart of a stone and other objects. Moreover, the movements of subatomic particles can be changed by outside forces, such as heat, magnets, etc., but also by thought.

The species in the plant kingdom have dense bodies, which consist of minerals, liquids, and gases. Plants are capable of growth and propagation because they have an etheric or vital body with two active ethers. It causes the circulation of juices in the spring when one of the ethers is charged with sunlight. The inner nature or vegetative soul of plants also causes them to seek water and turn towards the light of the sun (tropism) – as humans would turn towards God. Plants react to positive or negative stimulation of humans and sounds, which makes them thrive or wither.

The species in the animal kingdom have dense bodies that are able to move in all directions. Their bodies are made of solids, liquids, and gases. They are much like plants in their cellular structure, composition, life processes, and basic pattern of reproduction. By having the three ethers of the etheric body active, they have the ability of growth, propagation, and sense perception. In addition to the etheric or vital bodies through which they experience sensation, animals also possess emotional or lower psychic (astral) bodies, also called animal souls, through which they can feel and react to emotions. This, however, is not altogether true of cold-blooded creatures such as fish. The animals act mainly from instinct and are incapable of making intelligent decisions because their psychic mind is only crudely developed. Each of the species has a group consciousness or spirit in the form of a herd instinct. That is why they act much alike in a particular group. Animals, in general, are more psychically receptive than most humans are. They have the so-called instinct of direction and migration and are also able to sense earthquakes and volcanic eruption. Animals usually like to be around humans whom truly love them ("breathe into them") so that they become more alive psychically.

The human species of the fourth kingdom contains all the elements, forms, functioning, and genders of the mineral, vegetable, and animal kingdoms and also embody within themselves all its natures, qualities, and powers. For example: humans contain minerals in the physical makeup with its internal characteristics. They, like the plants, have cells, structure, and a vital or etheric body. In addition, human beings resemble animals by having complex organs, neuromuscular systems, and are much alike in the process of respiration, digesting, and assimilation. They, like the animals, have a flesh mind or instinct (which governs the inborn craving of existence, multiplication, and protection), senses, and an emotional body that seeks satisfaction of its desires. In addition to expressing lower desires as in animals, humans are capable of higher desires and emotions, such as compassion, love, and devotion, which they express in altruism, music, art, etc. They have the faculty of speech, language, and thought to express themselves in an intelligible and rational way. Human entities are self-aware or self-conscious individuals and are thus in possession of an individual spirit, which has the freedom to choose any lifestyle it likes to live. In addition, they have an inborn conscience, morality, religious belief, and most of them believe in a life after death. As the animals are keyed to the lunar month of 28 days, humans are bound to the solar month. In addition of using the three ethers as in animals, human beings employ the fourth and highest ether from their etheric body to impress the brain with thoughts from their human spirits. Thus, every human individual is truly a microcosm or a small universe, and all the kingdoms and universe(s), which were created after the pattern of the human entity, are a macrocosm.

As a seed needs suitable soil to germinate and grow in, plus sunlight and exhaled air, the human spirit also needs a healthy body to thrive and develop in properly, plus parental love and education. The Divine Spirit needs to awaken and grow in a pure personality and receive the Love and Truth of God.

Finally, the fifth kingdom is the spiritual or divine, wherein we find humans whom not only have a well-developed and integrated ego or personality, which has become an abode of a newly-born and developed Divine Spirit, but is animated by the *individual Spirit of God. They have God-like qualities, such as Love, Joy, Peace, Patience, Wisdom, Forgiveness, etc. Unlike the personality, it is always pure and not able to separate from God by committing sin (1 Jn. 3:9). As sons

---

* As the God Self is at the core of the Divine Spirit, so is the "I", personal self, the point of self-awareness or consciousness, the permanent core or essence of our personality. It is the conductor of the orchestra of our action, emotion, and thinking, which is constantly changing.

and daughters of God, they are able to communicate freely with their God and exalted beings around "His throne" through their higher intuitive faculties. When they reach perfection, they truly represent the Fatherhood and Motherhood of God and share in God's burden of restoration (Rom. 8:16).

NOTE: Because the emotion is more strongly developed in humans than in animals, who show less outward signs of emotion, they should learn to control their emotions. Emotions are like water, if they are not used in a disciplined way, they may become like raging floods, destroying everything in their way. They should be controlled and guided in proper channels, as the water is used in Holland. Because humans are not always able to control their emotions, the rivers and seas of the earth, as the macrocosmic reflection, likewise go out of hand through howling and raging storms. The waters, like humans, may also show her treachery, her seductiveness, but also her beauty, her calm serenity, and peace.

The energy centers and meridians of the human body resonate with those in the planetary body, so that every human intention and action generates waves of action and interaction throughout the earth's energy field. As humans in general are confused and unstable, so does the earth wobble on its axis. However, as there is peace in the nations and among nations, the earth's aura or magnetic field will effect the earth's poles in a positive way. The earth will thus stabilize on its axis and will no longer vacillate or wobble.

In the beginning, God as Parents had a marvelous purpose: to generate children whom are like them in character and image (Gen. 1:26), and to let them grow up (being fruitful) and multiply in a wonderful environment (Gen. 1:28). They, in turn, will experience life and parenthood through their sons and daughters and grow thereby.

This environment, or earth, God prepared for millions of years in the "six days of creation" or in six epochs of time. His first working plan was to fill His chosen place and space with His aura and pervading the darkness or emptiness of matter with [1]His Consciousness and to begin organizing the chaos of substance into a world of form (Gen. 1:1-2). Thereafter, He created light, vegetation, and animals according to their

---

[1] The universe did not come into being haphazardly by a blind impersonal force. If it was created by chance, there would be no rational principle in the universe and no law governing the events in the kingdoms of nature. There would be chaos. Everything exists in a delicate balance. For example: The planet earth is at the right distance from the sun for human life to exist, and it moves at the right speed to be held in orbit. The atmosphere is of a kind found only around the earth and is made up of the right ingredients to sustain life in the three kingdoms. It is not difficult to see that the earth and its evolving life, is guided by the intellect of God and His emotional involvement.

kind and finally humans, according to the God kind, that is in His image and likeness. Thus, humans did not evolve from apes directly but by that prototype.

God as Creator, Master Builder, Organizer, Lawmaker, and Creative Artist implemented His plan by creating from the more simple to the more complex or from lower to higher forms, and by creating first the outer, then the inner. In this process of evolution, the animals, such as the dinosaurs, and humans, such as the [2]Neanderthaler, at first were [3]crude and huge and often frightful to look at. As the form was evolving and became more beautiful, the life within also evolved, culminating in human as the most complex, the masterpiece of the physical creation. Because the form was ready for the human spirit to find its abode, it developed with the cooperation of the human agent by living according to God's law and, in turn, making the human spirit ready for the occupation of the Divine Spirit. Thus, when the form is ready (the temple has been built), then the Christ life enters.

God created the world and saw that it was good, but He did not say that it was finished. God as Creator wanted humans to share in the great joy of creation by letting them do the most rewarding work as co-creator, giving His creation the [4]finishing touch. For example: gold and precious stones are mined from the earth and made into ornaments, and the stones are cut and polished into great beauty. Goods are manufactured from raw materials, and works of art are created by all people. Farmers and others cultivate the soil, plant the seed, harvest the crop and fruit, and also take care of the forest and animal kingdoms, thus having dominion over the earth. By building ships and airplanes, people also have dominion over the sea and the air.

Humankind, like God, creates everything in their own image and likeness by first establishing the purpose, then by making a design or preparing a plan, and carrying it out. They, like God, create things (such as automobiles, ships, airplanes, etc.) first of a simple pattern.

---

[2] The Neanderthaler, whose bones have been found in Germany, lived about 100,000 years ago but died out mysteriously about 70,000 years later. They were replaced by the cro-magnon man (the ancestor of modern man), whose caves have been found in France and Spain wherein he painted pictures. Both neanderthaler and cro-magnon man buried their dead and left food and tools in the grave. They seemed to be concerned about life after death. This is also and indication that their human spirit was developing and that they became a link between heaven and earth,

[3] At that time, the Creator was not much concerned about proportion, harmony, and beauty. It began when cro-magnon man painted images on the walls of his caves.

[4] The greatest possibility given to a human is to propagate and raise His own kind.

After testing its usefulness and by using their ingenuity, they improve on their original design, and the things become more complex and also become more sleek and beautiful. By creating an object, he or she, also like God, [5]invest it with psychic and spiritual energy, whereby it becomes more "alive". Humans are also capable of imparting or [6]"breathing life" into the plants and animals, which become more "alive" by truly loving them. Plants grow with more vim and vigor, and animals become more loving and should eventually become tame, as is prophesized in Isaiah 11:6-9.

NOTE 1: As God cannot but create everything in His image, human beings likewise create things in their image and likeness. For example: an automobile, with its changing headlights, is like human eyes. The front end, with its intake of air and fuel, is to human intake of food and air. The rear end, with its exhaust system, is to the digestive and humans waste system. As combustion of gas and air takes place in the engine to provide energy, the burning of food and air takes place in the cells of the body to produce physical energy. The car has a supporting structure, with its shock absorbers and moveable parts, which is like the human bone structure, while the whole is supported by wheels and tires as the body is supported by legs and shoes. It further possesses a heating and cooling system with a thermostat, which is like the human body system, whose temperature remains constant. As the car has a computer and electrical wiring system (which is charged by battery and generator), with its indicating and warning devices, humans have a brain and nervous system (which is charged with energy of the etheric and psychic bodies), through which they experience sensation and pain. The body of the car comes in different shapes, colors, and powers, which suit each individual or family, and it also has its identification number (social security number for humans). Within the car's body we find a driver (humans spirit), who is steering the body at different speeds to its destination (purpose of life). As a driver of the vehicle, they have to obey traffic signals and regulations, just as a human spirit has to obey moral laws and teachings. As it takes a lot of energy to get a car started, it also takes effort to start our day. As a car needs to be filled up with gas at gas stations, so we as bodies go to restaurants and as spirits study and read the Word of God. When we break down, we go to hospitals, psychologists, and religious teachers, while cars have to go to garages to be repaired. As we ruin a car by neglect and abuse, so can we ruin our physical and psycho-spiritual bodies, thus delaying the latter's growth.

NOTE 2: God has given us the earth to work with, and from it, we extract food, minerals, and fuel. The farmer or gardener, for example, cultivates the soil, plants the seed, and harvests the crop, while the mineral and fuel are dug

---

[5] The ancient Egyptians believed that a person's "ka" could reside in sculptures of their human forms.
[6] As God "breathed" into humans and they became spiritually alive, humans, in turn, "breathed" into the creation, making them more alive psychically.

up by miners and used for many purposes to make life more comfortable. The labor the individual expends in planning and working may be one hundred percent, but the contribution he/she makes to society is only ten percent. God is responsible for contributing the remaining ninety by supplying the earth and the soil, creating the sun, helping with the living processes, which are also created by God, which makes the seeds sprout and grow. He also created the ecological system so that the crops would get enough water to grow.

However, due to the fall of men and women, "the whole creation has been groaning in travail" and "waits with eager longing for the revealing of the sons of God" (Romans 8:18-22). Humans are, therefore, not true creators; the created objects came infused with energy from the lower plane. Plants did not grow to their full potential, and animals became fearful and hostile to man.

REMARK: When a person has sympathetic contact with any aspect of nature, there is also a psychic affinity between the two. Some people have a way with animals and plants, while the clever technician has a knack for finding a solution to a mechanical problem.

The view of nature, which predominated in the West down to the eve of the scientific revolution, was, for many people, that of an enchanted world, rocks, mountains, trees, and clouds, which were all seen as wondrously alive. Many sensitive people at that time enjoyed walking in that environment. Some of them were also able to communicate with fairies and other forces that took care of nature. The belief that not only human, animal, [1]fish, fowl, and plants are animated with "soul life" but also that all objects are invested with etheric and psychic energy from the higher planes of life is part of the religion of animism. Native Americans and many other people would communicate with the spirits of trees and mountains. For everything is alive and made more alive by humans, while some of them vaguely could detect and feel the Great Spirit in nature. Saint Franciscus of Assisi (who was in daily communication with God) perceived and communicated with the creation and even called the sun his brother and the moon his sister, as if they were a part of his family. Unfortunately, science more than ever before turned nature, or rather turned our thinking of nature into a cold mechanic process, completely devoid of any feeling and spirituality. Humans became insensitive and coarse to the call of nature, thereby losing their budding psychic ability and began to rape, kill, and misuse the creation at a grand scale. How can they ever be qualified rulers when they do not understand God and His

---

[1] In the esoteric parlance, fish typify emotion and birds intellect.

creation? Today, some [2]artists and a few others in the Western world perceive the creation of God as an enchanted world, alive and populated with all kinds of beings.

In the process of restoration, God wants fallen men and women to grow in His image and likeness daily by obeying His commandments and by putting the Word of God into practice, thus building the righteous character of God. Such perfect and holy character cannot be created at once and must be developed, which takes time and experience, through trial and error. He or she eventually learns and comes to the understanding that only God's way of life brings real peace, happiness, and a joyful abundant life, and that satan's way of life only causes anxiety, misery, poverty, and sickness. In this process, one learns to discern, through God's revelation and inspiration, right from wrong, true values from the false, truth from error, and with the help of God's Spirit, resist the wrong and do the right.

When humans take their rightful position as steward and caretaker over the earth, then the prophecy of Isaiah 11:6 will be fulfilled:
"The wolf shall dwell with the lamb, and the leopard
shall lie down with the kid, and the calf and the lion
and the fatling together, and a little child shall lead
them."

Access to the Tree of Life Is Denied

"Then the Lord said, 'Behold, the man has become like one of us (exalted celestial beings), knowing good and evil; and now, lest he put forth his hand and take also of the tree of life, and eat, and live forever' – therefore the Lord God sent him forth from the garden of Eden'" --- "he placed the cherubim, and a flaming sword which turned every way, to guard the way to the tree of life."

When Jesus died on the cross, the curtain between the holy place and the most holy place was torn. This is an indication that every man and woman has the opportunity to contact and unite with his/her

---

[2] For people whom are not in harmony within themselves, life is usually dull, banal, and dreary because they do not perceive the beauty of life and nature. It is also difficult for an artist to create artistic beauty if they are not morally and spiritually developed. But when they are in a harmonious state, they will perceive harmony in nature and in life and experience it as beauty. Mountains and valleys, rivers and plants look exquisitely beautiful, vibrant, and alive when they also perceive the Spirit of God in themselves and in the innermost self of nature. Life will then become a great joy, seeing God everywhere.

indwelling Christ Spirit and enter the Garden of Eden, eat of the Tree of Life, and become part of the whole. However, prior to that time, access to the Tree of Life was denied to all those whom were living the life of the good and evil personality, except for a few chosen prophets and others whom were living a divine life. Those whom were eating of the tree of knowledge acquired a sense of selfhood, which cultivated into self-will and lived a life in separation from the unity with the whole. They should be guarded by the flaming sword of Love and Truth and should have limited and indirect access to the divine substance, life, and power because they will use it in selfish and evil ways. They distort (with their evil personality) the love, wisdom, joy, and peace and live like this forever. The kingdom of heaven cannot be taken by violence (Matt. 11:12). They will have to suffer as Prometheus in the Greek myth if humans deny their creatureliness, by reaching for more than God had granted them. Besides, they will not appreciate the Truth or the pearl of great value (Matt. 7:6, 13:46), nor are they capable of understanding (1 Cor. 2:14). Therefore, for their own good, they should be protected by giving them the Truth, concealed in parables and symbols, with manifold meanings for different levels of their understanding (see Matthew chapter 13). The interpretation of the Truth will be revealed by the Spirit of God whenever the people are ready to receive it. Those whom are living the divine life and are in a state of enlightenment and unity of consciousness have full and direct access to God's Life, Energy, Love, and Wisdom. However, if they misuse it by, for example, using the inner life to heighten their selfishness, they have to suffer great consequences. They, therefore, should live a life of discipline and responsibility and should not give in to the urges of their lower self or personality, with its diminishing evilness.

NOTE: In the spirit world, there is a natural barrier between levels of vibration, so that low and evil spirits, with their particular vibration, have no access to people living in the higher spheres (Luke 16:26).

C. The Four Aspects of Fallen Nature and Its Restoration

All humans of the Adamic race have inherited a fallen nature from the archangel Lucifer, which has been transmitted to the descendants of Adam and Eve. It affects the people whom are born on this earth as well as the fallen angels. This [1]fallen nature has four fundamental aspects or characteristics, which are the root of our sinful nature:

(1) Not taking God's viewpoint
(2) Leaving the proper position
(3) Reversal of dominion
(4) Multiplication of evil

Lucifer was created to be the [2]servant of God and all His children. He therefore had to love Adam as God loved Adam, thus taking or seeing things from the same standpoint or view as God. However, instead of being loyal and faithful to God, the archangel came to stand apart from God because he was [3]jealous of the fact that Adam was more loved and esteemed by God. Therefore, he could not love Adam in the same way or with the same heart as God. Thus, he failed to love what God loved and be joyful when his master was joyful. This attitude developed in hatred and destructive jealousy towards Adam, the potential Lord of the universe. This tendency to view things from a self-centered perspective and to defend one's own standard of righteousness by rationalization and justification, as well as one's failure to love someone closer to God, was passed on to the Adamic race.

NOTE: The author came in contact with the teaching of the "fall of man" in 1963 when it was being taught in the Melbert Hotel in Los Angeles by two ladies, Orah Schoon and Doris Walder. They were missionaries and representatives of the "Holy Spirit Association". Their teaching has been somewhat expanded and modified by author.

---

[1] The four aspects of the original nature of Lucifer would have been: (1) seeing from God's point of view, (2) keeping his proper position, thus maintaining close relation with God, (3) would have been dominated by humans, in whom the Spirit of God dwells, and he would have (4) multiplied goodness.

[2] People of the Old Testament and persons of the same moral status were, and many still are, living under the age of law and obedience. This is about the level where the angels are. That is why humans in that status feel like servants and seek the help of angels, who are pure and therefore higher than good/evil humans (Heb. 2:7). The people and angels in that status think much about position, as James and John still did (Mk. 10:37). However, Jesus came to abolish the angelic-type world of master/servant and came to establish the Adamic-type world of Father and son, to whom the angels will look for guidance (1 Cor. 6:3).

[3] Jealousy in itself is not evil. It is a negative emotion, a shadow cast by the light. It may be a stimulus for improvement and to become a better person. Albeit, this emotion can be used for evil purposes or lead to evil, which is separation from God, especially when it is of long duration and evolves in the wrong direction from jealousy to envy, resentment, anger, intense hatred, and finally in destruction.

A well-known example of failure to love from God's point of view we find in the story of Jacob, wherein ten of his twelve sons could not and did not want to love Joseph, whom his father loved the most. Their feeling of wanting to receive the same or more love from their father was not wrong. If they had truly loved their father, they would have loved Joseph their younger brother also, and their father would have loved them even more. But their jealousy evolved into an intense hatred toward Joseph, which was of the same nature as satan felt towards Adam. They finally sold him into Egypt. This story can also be compared to that of Cain, who killed Abel, of Saul who wanted to kill David, and many other examples in the Bible, as well as in Christian and non-Christian lives. Jesus was very much loved by God, while the Jewish priesthood hated him with the same emotions as satan hated the first Adam. Finally, Jesus was killed by another party.

Other examples of this inherited tendency are when a courtier feels a resentful jealousy of the king's favorite instead of respecting him as the one whom the good king loves. Also, accepting the person that, through his/her hard and excellent work, got a promotion from a good boss instead of toppling him/her and appreciating a fellow student whom, through diligence, became the good teacher's favorite one.

The second aspect of fallen nature is to leave one's given position. Lucifer left his position as servant because he did not want to be a servant, messenger, or minister (Matt. 4:11) to human beings. He wanted to have, in human society, the same leadership position as he had in the angelic world. He wanted that God's love and direction flow via him to Adam and Eve, instead of flowing from them to him. In other words, Lucifer did not want to receive divine guidance through a mediator. By doing this, he violated the *order that God had intended. This self-centered attitude of the archangel Lucifer of not accepting a God-given position was carried over to Eve and Adam and their descendants and became the second fallen nature.

What was the great sin of Lucifer? He did not display any humility of accepting God's plan. God turns His face from those individuals whom are implementing their own restoration plan of improving

---

* There is a certain hierarchical order in the creation and human society, which should be maintained and respected in order to prevent confusion, disorder, chaos, and destruction. The earth, for example, revolves around the sun and the electrons around the nucleus. Humans take care of animals instead of animals taking care of them and telling humans what to do. Angels have their proper place in the hierarchy, and so do parents and children, teacher and student, husband and wife.

society according to their own good/evil standard. Such a prideful attitude causes separation from God and moral and spiritual death. God will lift up the humble, but the prideful will be cast down. "Pride goes before destruction and a haughty spirit before a fall" (Prov. 16:18). God opposes the proud but gives grace to the humble (Jas. 4:6). "Humble yourself before the Lord and he will exalt you" (Jas. 4:10). "Clothe yourselves, all of you, with humility toward one another" (1 Peter 5:5). "Blessed are the meek, for they shall inherit the earth" (Matt. 5:5).

Lucifer, who did not want to remain in his position of servitude, began to carry out a plan to become the lord of all the creation. As the story goes, Lucifer, who was created before Adam and Eve, was much older and wiser than them and helped with the education of their personalities in preparation for divine life. Eve admired Lucifer as a great teacher, and Lucifer saw it as an opportunity to possess Eve for himself through a forbidden relationship and later through Eve take Adam's place as the lord. By this act, he left his [1]position as a loyal and dutiful servant of God and His children and became satan, the adversary and opponent.

Spiritual leaders and others can be like satan by impressing the people, especially the [2]women, with many spiritual principles, and attracting them more to themselves than God. This happens to the self-righteous Pharisees of all times and places, whom were [3]originally on God's side but eventually became like their father satan (Jn. 8:44). Possessive love was inherited by humanity and carries many masks. We use the word "my" very often and forget that when we cling to something, we surround ourselves with fences of possession. Because Lucifer's attitude was self-centered, the word "I" has been used very often by satan (Isa. 14:13-14) and by many people of all walks of life. Those people in whom the evil self is ruling their life do not like to be messengers or servants and do not like to praise God, men, and/or women that have done good deeds.

---

[1] In the King James Version of Isaiah, it is written, "How art thou fallen from heaven, O Lucifer, son of the morning! --- For thou has said in thine heart, I will ascend into heaven, I will exalt my throne above the stars of God" (Isa. 14:12-13). "And the angels that did not keep their own position but left their proper dwelling" (Jude 6).

[2] "For among them are those who make their way into households and capture weak women, burdened with sins, and swayed by various impulses who will listen to anybody and can never arrive at a knowledge of the truth" (2 Tim. 3:6-7).

[3] Someone who has a divine mission might be good in the beginning, but when they have been well accepted by the people in their care, they may become prideful and self-righteous, especially when they receive much praise and adoration.

NOTE: To know God is to know the whole Bible, not just part or an interpretation of it, which may be embodied in a religious leader.

The third aspect of fallen nature that we have inherited is the tendency to reverse dominion. Lucifer was to serve Adam and Eve as their [4]servant and helper and was to be dominated by them. In contrast to the divine order, the archangel, fired by false ambition, dominated immature Eve by tempting her to go against God's Word. Eve, who was supposed to be under the domination of Adam, dominated him instead through temptation. Thus, satan took the position of Adam, reversing the dominion or divine order from Adam → Eve → Lucifer to satan → Eve → Adam. The latter lost dominion over the whole world, which Jesus the last Adam tried to regain from satan (Matt. 4:8-10). Satan not only took Adam's position but also [5]assumed the God position by saying, "I will make myself like the most high" (Isa. 14:12). Thus, the fallen world began with the reversing of dominion.

Fallen men and women inherited this fallen nature and have, therefore, strong tendencies to control those whom are in the proper position and power approved by God. Many satanic people do acquire positions of power, thus expanding the kingdom of satan, causing disorder, derangement, disturbance, and trouble in society. Thus, good/evil humans have the satanic tendency of wanting to occupy a position for which they are not morally qualified. In order to be important, recognized, and well esteemed, they push and force themselves to [6]the top of the government, organization, or corporation by using all the available means, as they are driven by selfish ambition. In the case of religious people, a spiritually undeveloped person may, through deception, misrepresentation, and flattery, acquire a position in the church hierarchy or even buy a church office and start ruling those whom are morally and spiritually more developed or closer to God.

---

[4] Lucifer and angels are only servants to those people who are living a divine life, which is always pure (1 Jn. 3:9). The majority of the people are living the life of the tainted personality, to whom the good and pure angels bring messages and hope from God.

[5] Human pride, which wishes even to dominate God, is derived from the fallen nature of the archangel. Those fallen humans "exchanged the truth about God for a lie and worshipped and served the creature rather than the Creator" (Rom. 1:25).

[6] Those on top, who should not even be there, can never be secure in their position and will eventually be overthrown and put in the right position where they belong by the God forces. Besides, if the people "under them" do not respect their leader, the commander has less power, which is given to them by the people. Those whom are fully qualified but are not seeking for position and power, the forces of the universe will eventually bring them to that rank or status.

NOTE: An example of the fallen nature of reversing dominion is that someone like a dictator rules other people from a position not given by God. On the other hand, we should respect those who are properly in authority over us instead of being full of envy and having a rebellious attitude toward the leader, through whom God is reaching.

This inherited, deviated nature also reversed the position in one's being. The physical or outer personality of the average human rules the inner personality or the psyche. That is why material possessions have become more important for many than intellectual knowledge. In a deeper sense, the well being of the inner personality and its knowledge is more valued by most people than the Wisdom and Truth of one's budding Divine Spirit. The Divine Spirit is the real person; the inner personality is called false because it is attempting to take the place of the Divine Spirit. In other words, the desires of the flesh are against the desires of the Spirit (Gal. 5:17).

We may pursue a false ego trip by misusing personal contact and subduing others to fulfill our own desire for recognition and glorification. This happened at a grand scale with the Pharaohs of Egypt whom, at the cost of thousands of slaves, wanted to be immortalized, worshipped, and glorified.

Finally, we can say that all those that have a position for which they are not morally suited always want (like their master Lucifer) the people to serve them instead of them serving the people, as Jesus advised (Matt. 20:28).

The fourth aspect of fallen nature is multiplying or passing on unrighteous thoughts, desires, and sinful actions. The will of goodness that humans should not eat the symbolic fruit of the tree of the knowledge of good and evil should have been conveyed by God to Adam, by Adam to Eve, and by Eve to the archangel, thus multiplying goodness. However, on the contrary, the archangel conveyed to Eve the will of unrighteousness that the fruit could be eaten. Then Eve conveyed this to Adam, thus multiplying sin.

The evil that began with Lucifer multiplied in millions of *good/evil children. The fact that in the present world, which is good as well as evil, evil is more rapidly passed on and multiplied than good is a

---

* Because most people today are not able to have pure children, one may say that by just having children is multiplying evil. Since the fall of Adam and Eve and by following God's restoration plan, children have become much better and will, in the future, become even more pure, until they are born without original sin.

manifestation of the existence of this fallen nature. Because people in general are more inclined toward evil than good, evil is spread very fast once it has started. Individuals, families, societies, and nations, whose right way of living took many years to build, can be destroyed in a few years, as is clearly indicated in the Bible.

Reasonably good people have a tendency to entangle others in the same wrongs they have committed so that they do not feel so bad and are able to justify their bad behavior. They also do not want to be alone in their particular wrongdoing, so that they are not solely condemned by society, which upholds the standard of good and evil. When groups of people in society approve of certain wrong behaviors, many individuals usually go along with them and do not want to be unpopular by taking a stand for goodness. Being morally weak, they rationalize, "If others are doing it, why should I not do it?" If enough people join them in abandoning their Principles, they, in turn, add impetus to the moral decline by rationalizing that wrongdoing should be acceptable "because everybody is doing it". The voices of a few that do not give in to evil are drowned out by loud voices of the populace, or when they insist, are mocked and ridiculed. Society then has become more evil than good.

NOTE: The immorality of a single individual, such as for example, a movie star or other role model, can have a demoralizing effect by weakening the inner restraints of millions of people.

Many people become accustomed to a certain bad behavior and continue it out of sheer habit, even when they sense that what they are doing is wrong. One bad habit, which many people thoughtlessly indulge in, is gossip. It destroys relationships and the reputations of many people. It is spread rapidly through tabloid newspapers, which are only concerned about ratings and revenue. They do not seem to realize that *thoughts and words have the power to maim people for life, and that many people will always think about them in a negative way, thus reinforcing the bad quality (if it exists at all) or creating it in them. The Bible strictly forbids gossiping (see Leviticus 19:16; Proverbs 17:4). Miriam is punished with leprosy for gossiping with Aaron about Moses (Num. 12:1-13).

The more evil-minded persons, in whom the evil side of the personality is strong or whose false personality is in charge of their

---

* Someone who sends out an evil thought may affect many people whom, in turn, may affect others close by or at a great distance, thus multiplying evil around the world.

lives, like to see that evil is being spread and that others are doing evil, thus expanding the kingdom of satan. They feel great pleasure when they see and hear that the men are seducing the women and the women are seducing the men. Therefore, those whom are good-minded should never agree with them, either through action, word, or smile.

From the above, we can conclude that humans are thus not only confronted with the power of evil without, which threatens to influence and invade us, but are also confronted with the inherited evil within, which already has taken possession of our personality.

Philip (Gospel of Philip) teaches that within each person lies hidden the "root of evil" or the "evil impulse", as the Jewish teaching has it. Philip further says that we should be aware of this evil and recognize it so that it will be destroyed. The evil impulses, such as intense hatred, envy, pride, greed, and lust, have already taken root in our personality (Mark 7:21-23). They make us slaves and take us captive, so that we can say with the young Paul in Romans 7:15, "I do not do what I want, but I do the very thing I hate."

Recognizing and not imitating satan's behavior is a good beginning. However, in order to remove our fallen nature or uproot our original sin thoroughly, we should examine more closely the four aspects of our fallen nature and its process of restoration: (a) failure to take God's viewpoint, (b) leaving one's given position, (c) reversal of dominion, (d) multiplication of evil.

They are expressed as: "I hate God and the ones that are doing the will of God." "I do not respect and refuse to obey the person whom God has chosen." "I like to dominate (tell people what to do) the person that is doing the will of God." "I like to tell others to do more evil." In order to restore our original nature, this fallen nature should be reversed. (1) A person in the position of the archangel should love a person in Adam's position. (2) A person in the archangel position should receive God's love through the person in Adam's position. (3) A person in the archangel position should be obedient to and submit to a person in Adam's position – thereby establishing the proper order of dominion. (4) A person in the archangel position should receive the righteous will from a person in Adam's position – restoring the nature that multiplies the will of goodness.

God, however, is not able to restore the good/evil individual, family, tribe, or nation unless they are first separated in good and evil or Abel and Cain factions, as it occurred in Adam's family. Because Cain the elder brother, who represented the archangel, did not want to love and submit to Abel, who was in the sinless Adam's position, he instead killed him, thus delaying God's restoration plan. We should, as individuals, submit our personality to our Divine Self. As a person in relation to others, we should, with the help of God, find an Abel person whom we are able to love, receive God's love and direction, be obedient to, and learn God's way from them for a period of time. When our original nature is restored, we will be able to love with God's love, keep our position, not try dominating our superiors, and witness to our newfound faith.

We now know how evil originated and also know the evil character of satan and our evil self, or inner devil. Knowing his crime, we can accuse satan before God, because he is an even greater criminal than humans ever will be. When we completely rid ourselves of our satanic nature, satan and his followers will no longer be able to influence us and become powerless in our lives. They may then come to a natural surrender to us, as regenerated individuals because we are supposed to be not only the Lord over the natural creation but also over the angelic world (1 Cor. 6:3).

NOTE: When one is born of God, the process of removing the fallen nature, sinful, old, or carnal nature begins by the godly, new, or spiritual nature (Soul), which is always pure and holy (1 Jn. 3:9), through which the Spirit of God can work. Fallen nature can also be removed through the method of scolding, by which God works through a spiritual leader or others to chastise a person who has done something wrong or his or her attitude. Albeit, those who are not ready will often react violently to criticism in order to protect their false ego. Others will be very grateful to the spiritual parents or mentors because they feel that something of their evil nature is destroyed, and certain evil spirits that were influencing them have disappeared. Their satanic attitude changed to a God-centered one. Thus, they feel a close connection with God and their newly found brothers and sisters in the Lord.

Some people say that Cain killed Abel because Abel was arrogant, because God preferred him, and he thought of himself to be better than Cain, instead of feeling concern for his brother with the same heart as God did. Other people say that the more difficult an Abel person is, the more effort an individual has to exert to love and submit themselves and, thus, the faster their fallen nature is removed.

As part of their restoration, some people are compelled to fulfill the role as servant in order to restore the satanic feeling that they do not like to be a servant. They should also praise God as the archangel failed to do and see men and women as brothers and sisters instead of potential lovers.

#40 The Great Struggle Within

A. The Dark Night of the Soul

The great struggle within one's being is called by St. John of the Cross (1542-1591) "The Dark Night of the Soul".

According to the Maryknoll Catholic Dictionary, the dark night means:

> "Trials sent by God which detach a person from spiritual consolations and all self-love. The light of contemplation that the soul receives is so faint and so crucifying that the soul feels plunged in darkness and abandoned by God. The person sees himself as so loathsome that he cannot understand why God does not loath him."

The Encyclopedia of Catholicism says that "John of the Cross considers the entire [1]journey to God as night: the purification of attachments, night as a journey of faith, and night as an encounter with God as mystery"--- "This liberation of the human person takes place on the level of sense (dark night of) and the spirit (dark night of)".

The Oxford Dictionary of World Religion states, "Dark night of the soul. A term of Western mystical theology"---"according to the classical exposition of John of the Cross, the dark night is the stage in which the soul is purified in preparation for union with God. A distinction is drawn between active nights (in which the soul purifies itself) and passive nights (in which God purifies the soul). A further distinction divides the night into the preliminary Night of the Senses and the more fundamental Night of the Spirit. The dark night is the action of God purifying the soul of attachments as it experiences the impotence of human efforts and the necessity for the gift and grace of God."

In documentation of religious experiences, the "dark night of the soul" is seen as a psychological state of alienation and a spiritual crisis during the initiation, when one is in a state of depression, guilt, and unworthiness, with no apparent spiritual support.

---

[1] The journey to God is expounded in the Bible in Luke 15:11-32 as the story of the prodigal son, who after he squandered everything in "loose living" finally said, "I will arise and go to my father." This journey is also "the exodus to the Promised Land".

337

The dark night of the [2]soul, or of the human spirit, is usually a great struggle or traumatic event because it is an [3]unnatural development of oneself. Instead of choosing and accepting with ease and gracefully, as a pure personality ([4]when the time has come), the divine life as the next stage of development, the false personality (wherein the evil nature is in charge of the good/evil personality) does not want to give up its existence as a separate being. This is especially true of people in whom the original sin is strong. The false personality wants to keep its dominant position over the person's life and does not want to be used as an instrument or vehicle of the Divine Self or Spirit. Because of the force of evolution working within the person resisting the change, the new consciousness becomes inflamed like a boil or a flower trying to bloom and will eventually burst forth regardless of any restraint, resulting in a crisis. All of this happens in a severe way because the personality is, in different measure, false, *overgrown, and inflated. It

[2] Soul here means not Soul or Divine Spirit, but human spirit, psyche, or heart, from which all evil comes (Matt. 15:19), and which is "deceitful above all things" (Jer. 17:9), "committed adultery with her in his heart" (Matt. 5:28), and "blessed are the pure in heart" (Matt. 5:8).

[3] The soul or inner personality, which is only good and pure, will move naturally in the process of initiation or regeneration, and so do those whom are born with little original sin, where the evil part of them is weak and the good part is strong. Others do not experience much difficulties and long periods of feeling God forsaken or spiritually dry when they simply surrender their own will to the will of the divine and let God take over their destiny. By doing so, the candidate chooses divine life over the life of the personality. Their journey will not be as long as that of the Israelites toward the Promised Land. By not trusting in God and continually complaining about their fate, their short journey was extended to 40 years.

[4] When the time has come to raise their level of awareness or consciousness, by being restless, unsatisfied about life, and being in search of new values and Truth.

* The personality or ego is an important aspect of one's whole being and should be used as a medium of expression by the developing Divine Spirit. The ego feels, thinks, acts, discriminates, decides, etc. If it is weak and undeveloped, it is not very well able to master and cope with life and is a poor instrument for the Soul.

On the other hand, some people whom do not believe that there is anything beyond ego try to cultivate a strong personality by overemphasizing their lower ego faculties, thus overdeveloping and inflating their ego, making it very difficult to transcend itself and become an implement of the higher faculties. For them there is no shift in consciousness or a change in attitude or lifestyle by function from another level of awareness.

The people, whose ego is inflated and whose false self is in charge of their lives, are truly the sons of satan (Jn. 8:44; 6:70; 1 Jn. 3:8). They may show themselves outside as being nice and polite, but are evil inside – see Mark 7:20-23. As Jesus expressed it, "For you are like whitewashed tombs, which outwardly appear beautiful, but within they are full of dead men's bones and all uncleanness. So you also outwardly appear righteous to men, but within you are full of hypocrisy and iniquity" (Matt: 23:27-28). Many people today would say, "Those kind of people are full of ?@#$!"

needs, with divine help, to be purified of its evilness and also should be mature in order to be used properly by the Divine Spirit. It therefore needs to darken or "die", so that a new being of the same structure may arise, stripped of its evil or satanic nature. Having lived for a long time as the dominant figure, the false ego (with whom the individual is identified) does not want to give up its separate existence as an independent being. Giving up the false ego appears to the individual as an annihilation of its personal existence, and that it will cease to exist.

Dark night is thus a spiritual crisis, which shakes loose and breaks down old psychic structures based on false beliefs and ingrained frozen habits. It can be momentarily painful, especially for those whom have held wrong concepts and ideas for a long period of time. If change is much obstructed by the false ego, the crisis will be much greater, in the form of insecurities, uncertainties, difficulties, and upheaval.

Before accepting Christ, or before initiation and higher development can take place, the good/evil personality (body and psyche or soul) should pass through a sphere of psychic darkness or a "dark night of the senses" (dark night of the psyche, human spirit or soul). This is necessary in order to separate the good and evil in oneself and to recognize that evil. This will result that one will give up their identity as a being of good and evil. As long as the person is unconsciously identified with the good/evil self, it is not possible for the individual to experience the good self and especially not one's budding Divine Spirit or Soul. This is why an alienation encounter is necessary before the religious experience. Thus, the personality must first be de-identified from the false self before the good self and the Divine Spirit can be encountered as "the other".

When the rays of pure light shine upon the soul or human spirit, the soul perceives itself to be so unclean and miserable that it seems as "if God had self against it and itself were set against God" (John of the Cross). Through the working of the Holy Spirit in one's life, there is a conviction of sin (Jn. 16:8) and the need of salvation. In the psychological language of Roberto Assagilio, the light of the Self shines on the 'impurities' and brings them to the consciousness of the individual to facilitate his process of working them out.

The good/evil personality, or those born with original sin, is made to feel worthless and brought to despair and wants to die. This may be seen symbolically in dream images. It is brought into emptiness and poverty of spirit (Matt. 5:2) and purged from all help and consolations. At that critical time, one may choose the life of the tainted personality or divine life. In choosing the latter, the personality is, to a large extent, freed from the evil or false part (old nature Rom. 6:6) of the personality – the part that does not want to be subdued by the Divine Spirit – and the individual starts living the new and blessed life.

NOTE: On his way to liberating the people of Israel (sons of Jacob) out of Egypt and arriving at a lodging place, the Lord met Moses and sought to kill him (Ex. 4:24). Martin Luther said, "When God is about to justify a man, he damns him, whom he would make alive – he must first kill – God's favor is so communicated in the form of wrath that it seems furthest when it is at hand."

Going through the above alienation experience is like wandering in a *desert. The person feels lonely, deserted, and forsaken. He or she experiences spiritual dryness and undergoes the terrible feeling of not only being rejected by people who are close to them but, above all, of being abandoned by God. As Jesus expressed it in Matt 27:46, "My God, my God, why hast thou forsaken me?"

When the candidates for initiation and higher development feel that they are "at the end of their rope" or believe to be utterly lost (what is known as the "night of the spirit"), light breaks in, and they experience a sudden transcendence and enlightenment. This is when their budding Divine Spirit takes over their life and salvation begins. Their good/evil ego (with which they identified and thought that it was their real self) has been purified to a great extent and has come under the guidance of their Soul.

B. The Dweller on the Threshold

After the individual has been born of God or initiated, the personality is still more or less in charge of their life. But as the budding Divine Spirit develops, it progressively takes over the life of the personality. At a certain point in the development of the personality, it does not just believe in the Divine Spirit but has also become aware of it in its being and feels an obligation to the Soul.

---

* The classical symbol for alienation is the image of the wilderness. When the wanderer lost in the desert is about to perish, a source of divine nourishment appears. This happens when the ego has exhausted its own resources and is aware of his or her limitations. The person's extremity is God's opportunity.

At that point, a fierce battle will begin for the control of the personality, between the Soul and the evil nature in the personality. The Soul is confronted with an enemy, which is known esoterically as the "Dweller on the Threshold". This dweller comprises of the selfishness, materialism, attachments, evil impulses, etc., which linger in the subconscious of the person. This also includes the accumulated karma (including that of one's ancestors), which the initiated must pass or come to terms with before the candidate can advance or progress to a higher degree of initiation. The dweller represents the evil one, and also pride and a false self-concept, which keeps the person separated from the Soul and concentrated on the personality. Thus, it is everything in the personality that resists the individual's spiritual progress. It is a long struggle, but the Soul eventually wins, and the personality and the Divine Spirit will be united. The individual realizes that he or she is the Soul and becomes identified with it.

NOTE 1: Some people who think that their mind is already purified may have a dream, in which their subconscious (which is the conscious of the human spirit), expressed in their particular dream language, tells their conscious physical mind that the dweller (thought form of evilness) has not yet been destroyed but remains in the deepest recesses of their subconscious minds. In order to eliminate it completely, it has to be brought to conscious awareness and be confronted and subjugated. After it has been overcome with all its evil attributes of pride, fear, ignorance, lust, greed, etc., the clear light of God via the Divine Spirit can shine through the "cleansed window" and can enter one's physical consciousness.

NOTE 2: Many psychologists, in order to resolve conflicts in people's lives, use the method of dream interpretation and psychoanalysis while also using the technique of hypnosis and other methods, to bring psychological problems to conscious awareness and deal with them.

NOTE 3: This dweller, in some teachings in the East, is called negative ego and broken down for the different levels such as: maya (physical), glamour (emotional), and illusion (mental).

NOTE 4: The Dweller on the Threshold stands before the gate of God and at the portal of initiation (Jn. 10:9; 14:6; Matt. 7:7).

NOTE 5: During the Exodus, the Israelites passed over from being slaves to free people by putting blood on their thresholds.

C. How Victory Was Won at Peni'el

Before Jacob united with Esau, by sending much he owned to appease his brother whom he had mistreated, he wrestled with an angel at Peni'el:

> "And Jacob was left alone; and there wrestled a man
> with him until the breaking of the day. And when
> he saw that he prevailed not against him, he touched
> the hollow of his thigh; and the hollow of Jacob's
> thigh was out of joint, as he wrestled with him. And
> he said, I will not let thee go, except thou bless me.
> And he said unto him, What is thy name? And he said,
> Jacob. And he said, Thy name shall be called no
> more Jacob, but Israel: for as a prince hast thou power
> with God and with men, and hast prevailed. And Jacob
> asked him, and said, Tell me, I pray thee, thy name. And
> he said, Wherefore is it that thou dost ask after my name?
> And he blessed him there. And Jacob called the name of
> the place Peni'el: for I have seen God face to face, and
> my life is preserved. And as he passed over Peni'el the
> sun rose upon him, and he halted (limping) upon his
> thigh (Gen. 32:24-31 – K.J.V.).

This story we may also interpret as an internal struggle between Jacob, the lower self or good/evil personality, with the angel of the presence or Jacob's Higher Self (Divine Spirit). They completely merged (atonement) after the evil part of the ego, or the dweller on the threshold, has been beaten into submission. After this great victory, the descendants of Jacob were called Israelites, after Jacob's exalted new name – Israel.

#41 Positive and Negative Qualities and Evil Words Created by Humanity after the Fall

A. Positive and Negative Qualities

Because the Godhead, in whom the Masculinity and Femininity are integrated as a perfect unity and whole, created everything according to their likeness, we therefore find gender, or the masculine and feminine principle, everywhere and on all planes of life. In the physical world, it manifests as sex and on higher planes as an integrated, lofty, and spiritual exchange. Thus, the closer the male and female expressions are manifested in the lower worlds, the more they are divided into their positive and negative components.

A Few General Principles at Work in the Universe:

God/parents – male/female	Creation – yang/yin
Man – male – masculine	Woman – female – feminine
Parents – brothers	Children – sisters
Internal – invisible – cause	External – visible – effect
Mind – subconscious	Body – conscious
Thinking – thought	Feeling – emotion
Good – right	*Bad – wrong
Sun – nucleus	Planets – electrons
Positive – light – heat	Negative – dark – cold

---

* Bad is not evil – there is no such thing as a contrast between good and evil because evil is not created by God but by satan and evil humans. Evil can be called any thought, word, or deed whereby humans alienate from God. Thus, evil causes separation from the God forces and is also called ignorance, or that which impairs the life flow. There is, thus, quite a difference between evil and negative thinking. An annoying habit or mannerism, or what is unpleasant or different, is not necessarily evil. We also separate from God when our motive to do good is selfish, especially when we impede people in their spiritual growth. Evil is created when one goes against, or acts out of harmony with, the immutable laws of the universe. This happens when someone acts for his/her own selfish ends at the expense of the whole. Divine qualities can be misused or distorted by the good/evil personality. When, for example, love is distorted by the selfishness of possession, it becomes greed or lust. Wisdom becomes foolishness and cunning. Joy becomes pseudo happiness and satanic pleasures. Peace becomes a false peace by being obedient to the good/evil ruler. Because people in general are good and evil, the positive qualities they express are somewhat less sublime, and the negative qualities are overemphasized. They, therefore, get more easily and more often angry, disturbed, depressed, and in conflict.

List of Positive and Negative Qualities When People of Today Are
Expressing the Good Side of Their Personality, Which May Be
*Somewhat Tainted, and Divine Life

Activity – powerful	Inactivity – powerless
Energetic – vigorous	Fatigued – weariness
Strong – sturdy – robust	Weak – feeble – frail
Achievement – accomplishment	Unsuccessful – slothful
Competent – efficiency	Incompetent – carelessness
Constructive – practical	Destructive – impractical
Abundance – prosperity	Poverty – destitution
Inventiveness – ingenious	Non-creativity – dullness
Economy – thrifty	Extravagance – wasteful
Industrious – diligent	Idleness – laziness
Expensive – costly	Inexpensive – cheap
Temperance – moderation	Indulgence – dissipation
Experience – practice – discover	Inexperience – theorize – speculate
Healthful – ease – harmless	Sickness – disease – harmful
Love – affection – kindness	Hate – anger – annoyance
Peace – serenity – calmness	Anxiety – disturbance – worry
Optimism – optimistic	Pessimism – pessimistic
Enthusiasm – enthusiastic	Boredom – lassitude
Cheerfulness – liveliness	Despondency – depression
Happiness – joy – bliss	Unhappiness – sadness – misery
Light-hearted – humorous	Heavy-hearted – dullness
Patience – tolerant	Impatience – intolerant
Friendly – affectionate	Unfriendly – animosity
Compassion – merciful	Indifference – merciless
Sympathy – warm-hearted – like	Antipathy – cold-hearted – dislike
Tenderness – caring – concern	Cruelty – insensitive – ignoring
Charm – graceful – beautiful	Clumsiness – graceless – ugliness
Hope – expectation – certainty	Hopelessness – abandon – uncertainty
Truth – principle	Illusion – falsehood
Truthful – honesty – integrity	Untruthful – dishonesty – lying
Rational – reasonable	Irrational – unreasonable
Determination – decision	Hesitation – indecision
Conception – conceivable	Misconception – inconceivable
Thoughtful – consideration	Thoughtless – inconsiderate
Understanding – comprehension	Misunderstanding - ignorance

---

* Some words may be quite negative and be used more by good/evil humans. Besides, they are growing up in the development of their personality and may, therefore, make some mistakes in the process of learning. The negative qualities will be used much less when humans in the future will live the life of the pure personality, without original sin. Their character will become more constructive and wholesome, and there is no longer "the sense of good and evil" in the Kingdom of God.

Intelligent – bright – cleverness	Unintelligent – unclear – stupidity
Open mind – open-minded	Closed mind – closed-minded
Approval – acceptance	Disapproval – condemnation
Discernment – judgmental	Fault-finding – contemptuous
Abstract – universal – theoretical	Concrete – particular – practical
Educated – informed	Uneducated – uninformed
Literate – clever – brilliant	Illiterate – foolish – dull
Attention – concentration	Inattention – heedlessness
Perseverance – steadfastness	Inconstant – changeable
Endurance – fortitude	Weakness – feebleness
Courage – fearless – bold	Cowardice – fearfulness – timidity
Determination – decisiveness	Procrastination – postponement
Diligence – exertion	Slothfulness – indolence
Commitment – responsibility	Uncommitted – irresponsible
Self-control – disciplined	Impulsiveness – disregard
Sustaining – surviving	Yielding – faltering
Encouragement – assertiveness	Discouragement – defeatism
Faithful – belief – trust	Unfaithful – disbelief – distrust
Reverence – respect	Irreverence – disrespect
Courtesy – politeness	Discourtesy – impoliteness
Adoration – veneration	Disdainful – despising
Devotion – dedication	Carelessness – neglectful
Obedience – compliance	Disobedience – insubordination
Temperance – moderation	Dissipation – indulgence
Generosity – charity	Ungenerous – stinginess
Justice – fairness – impartiality	Injustice – unfairness – partiality
Prudence – discretion	Imprudence – indiscretion
High regard – worthy –esteem	Low regard – worthless – valueless
Refined – cultivation – breeding	Coarseness – disagreeable – vulgarity
Unity – oneness – harmony	Disunity – chaos – disharmony
Organization – order	Disorganization – disorder
Invulnerability – unconquerable	Vulnerability – assailable
Beautiful – pretty	Ugliness – unsightly
Satisfaction – contentment	Dissatisfaction – discontentment
Successful – succeeding	Unsuccessful – failing
Constancy – stability	Inconstancy – instability
Unpretentious – humility	Pretentious – pompous
Agreement – accordance	Disagreement – disaccord
Reliability – trustworthy	Unreliability – untrustworthy
Responsible – dependable	Irresponsible – unreliable
Confidence – assurance	Uncertain – doubtful
Flexible – adaptable	Inflexible – rigidity
Loyalty – patriotism	Disloyalty – treachery
Agreeable – concord – consent	Quarrelsome – discord – conflict
Tolerance – forbearance	Intolerance – prejudice
Poise – balance – repose	Unrest – imbalance – strain

345

Honorable – nobleness	Dishonorable – snobbishness
Abstinence – sacrifice	Indulgence – egotism
Simplicity – clearness	Complexity – confusion
Self-respect – self-esteem	Self-humiliation – self-debasement
Self-confidence – security	Self-doubt – insecurity
Concern – interest	Reserved – withholding
Admiration – wonder	Abhorred – detestable
Judgment – discrimination	Condemnation – criticism
Completeness – wholeness	Incompleteness – imperfection
Possible – possibility	Impossible – impossibility
Introversion – introspective	Extroversion – extraspective
Hospitable – receiving	Inhospitable – unreceptive
Gentleness – gracious	Harshness – disgraceful
Social – companionship	Antisocial – reclusion
Appreciation – recognition	Neglectful – jealousy
Benevolence – altruism	Unkindness – egotistical
Significant – importance	Insignificant – unimportance
Attractive – charming	Unattractive – displeasing
Prepared – ready	Unprepared – unavailable
Independent – expressiveness	Dependent – restriction
Indestructible – durable	Destructible – deterioration
Outgoing – expansive	Reserved – restrained
Unification – organization	Separation – alienation
Eternal – everlasting –life	Mortality – extinction – death
Enlightenment – illumination	Unenlightened – darkness
Maturity – perfection	Immaturity – imperfection
Develop – evolve – unfold – grow	Backslide – lapse – subside – cease
Altruism – unselfishness	Self-seeking – selfishness
Forgiving – merciful	Unforgiving – merciless
Self-forgiving – self-love	Self-condemning – self-dislike
Wisdom – intuition	Foolishness – reasoning
Purity – cleanliness	Impurity – uncleanness
Uniqueness – uncommon	Uniformity – conformity
Meaningfulness – significance	Meaninglessness – insignificant
Boundless – limitless	Constrained – limited
Purposeful – goal	Purposeless – aimless
Broad-mindedness – universal	Narrow-mindedness – provincial
Vision – idealistic – utopean	Short-sighted – materialistic – unreal
Inspiration – creativity	Uninspiring – imitation
Fulfillment – aspiration	Unfulfilled – low ambition
Authentic – genuine	Inauthentic – fictitious
Gratitude – favored	Ungrateful – disfavor
Dignity – self-respect	Indignity – humiliation

Indignation – *righteous anger	Insulting – degradation
Innocence – blameless	Guiltiness – blamefulness
Self-conscious – expressive	self-conscious – shyness
Freedom – liberty	Submission – resignation

B. The Words Expressed by the Evil Self of the Personality

Many words, their modifications, and connotations which we find in dictionaries came into existence after the human fall, such as:

Concerning the Godhead:
Godlessness, idolatry, desecration, blasphemy, hostility, profanity, defilement, swearing, cursing, mocking, scoffing, rebellion, secularism, humanism, atheism, agnosticism, sinful(ness), unrighteous(ness), shameful(ness), etc.

With regard to the outer and inner devil in the life of the evil and the good/evil personalities:
Satan, adversary, antagonist, opponent, oppressor, obstructer, the enemy, beelzebub, devil, slanderer, accuser, the evil one, a god, liar, (spiritual) murderer, satanic forces, evil spirits, evil doers, demons, demonical powers, etc.

The evil or false part (self) of the ego or personality, inner devil, fallen or satanic nature, evil qualities or fruits, evil word, evil mindedness, evil thoughts, evil impulses, evil disposition, original sin, corrupt and depraved, evil self, impostor, pretender, liar, opponent, deceiver, accuser, slanderer, Antichrist. Evil nature, old nature (Eph. 4:22; Col. 3:9-10), old man or old self (Rom. 6:6), the flesh (Gal. 5:16-17; Rom. 8:5-8), sons of disobedience (Eph. 2:1-3), deceitful (Jer. 17:9), dark or shadow side of the personality, false or alter ego, ego trip, temptation. They are pride(ful), have false pride, are arrogant (assuming too much power and authority), boast(ful), pretentious, presumptuous, hypocritical, phony, fake, false(hood), vain(glorious) fame, †haughtiness, and supercilious. They flatter(y), are egotist(ical), extremely selfish(ness), possess self-will, are self-righteous(ness),

---

* Expressions of anger can be a positive force in the fallen world in the form of rebellion and revolution, safeguarding, and defending against injustice and domination of powers, which want to exploit humans and take away their God-given freedom and liberty.

† Exhibiting great satisfaction with oneself and of his/her high station in life and disdain or scornful of others, and see and treat them as inferior. The supercilious describes a man or woman whom are both haughty and disdainful, while they often hide or mask their feelings by being polite.

practice self-deception and self-aggrandizement. They are self-seeking, self-centered(ness), self-indulgent, and have selfish ambition for power, while seeking for self-satisfaction or complacency, feel self-important, and exercise self-worship and suffer severe loneliness by being spiritually ignorant and dead.

With relation to religion, which came into existence after the fall, in order to restore or save humans, which brought with them their particular words such as:

Restoration, salvation, soteriology, sanctification, justification, redemption, reconciliation, circumcision, covenant, and baptism. Temptation, committed sin, immoral(ity), feel shame and guilt, repent(ance), contrition, remorse(ful), confession, absolution, offer penance, indemnity, restitution, retribution, amend(ment), atone(ment), expiation, ransom, and suffer martyr(dom) and crucifixion. Unify with Christ through communion, confirmation, [1]conversion, regeneration, born again, is sanctified, and resurrected. Is guilty of unfaithful(ness), disbelief in creed or dogma, is irreligious and committed heresy. Is therefore shunned, ostracize(d), condemned, damned, doomed, curse(d), accursed, anathematize(d), and excommunicated. This resulted in persecution, inquisition, crusade, and holy wars participated by fanatical, bigoted, [2]backsliding, immature Christians, whom lost moral authority by selling indulgences, buying and selling church offices – simony, and the priesthood being demoralized and corrupt, resulting in the Reformation. A growing group of people, the elect, and saints whom protested were called Protestants. However, most of them are looking forward to the Last Days – eschatology – last judgment, when after the appearance of the Antichrist, the Savior will appear to people of all religions in the form they like the most. Thereafter, they will also no longer speak of pagans, heathens, and primitives, predestination, dispensation, rapture, parousa, millenialism, second coming, sacraments, transubstantiation, con-substantiation, forbidden books, theodicy, total depravity, and other words used in the providence of restoration, by religions and other organizations and people.

NOTE: Traditional religion also speaks of the seven deadly sins: pride, avarice (greed), lust, envy, gluttony, anger, and sloth.

---

[1] Some words like conversion, regeneration, and others will probably also be used after the restoration.

[2] Carnal or backsliding Christians, and natural men and women whom are living the life of the good/evil personalities (Gal. 3:24; 1 Cor. 2:14; 3:1-3; Heb. 5:12) still live under moral law (not grace) in "the world" (Jn. 15:19; 16:33; 18:36; 1 Cor. 2:12; Jas. 4:4), which is good and evil.

Involving wrong relationships:
The use of profane, indecent, unclean, impure, and obscene language, as well as the words, vulgarity, profanity, lewd(ness), lascivious(ness), licentious(ness), lecherous, lecher and hag (indecent old man and woman). It is also expressed as immorality, unchaste, vice, vicious(ness), defilement, depravity, obscenity (offensive to morality), indecency, immodest(y), self-indulgence, and masturbation. We further speak in this fallen world of psychic seduction, seductive look, flirtatious stare, roving eye, lust of the eye (1 Jn. 2:16; 2 Peter 2:14), especially when they are inspired by pornographic images, also available from sex shops. The ones whom are living the life of the good and evil personality will tempt, entice, allure, seduce, and be lustful (intense sexual desire, craving, or inflaming passion – concupiscence), and fall in love, and may also be seduced by an incubus or succubus, thus becoming erotic(ally) involved in their sleep. Those whom are promiscuous are also called sexy, sex pot, vamp, gold-digger, prostitute (male/female), hooker, call girl, whore, harlot, and pimp. Fornication and rape are forbidden in the Bible – 1 Thess. 4:3-8; Eph. 5:3-5, Gal. 5:19; Col. 3:5, (experiencing carnal knowledge), and so is lechery (inordinate indulgences between consenting parties – 2 Cor. 12:21) and adultery (7th Commandment). People whom are living a divine life will no longer practice polygamy, bigamy, incest, have a concubine, and will not divorce their husbands or wives. Sexual perversion will be strictly forbidden in the Kingdom of God and will be completely eliminated, such as: masochism, sadism, unnatural lust (Jude 6-7; Lev. 20:13; Rom. 1:26-27), bisexual, sodomy, homosexual, faggot, lesbian, transvestite, pederasty (molestation of a child), bestiality, and venereal diseases.

Concerning lawlessness:
Lawless, non-principled, unlawful, outlaw, corrupt, bribe, conspiring, conspiracy, defy(ing), illegal(ly), illicit(ly), insubordinate, violation, martial law, rebellion, revolt(ing), uprising, mutiny, perjury, license, riot(ous), etc.

About war and murder:
Enemy, war, revolution, revolutionary, mercenary, invasion, retaliation, reprisal, injurious attack and aggression, rampage, raid(er), conquer, conquest, overthrow, subdue, and ravage (devastation or lay waste). The enemy surrenders, is defeated and abducted, deported, kidnapped, banished, exiled, and put in captivity, servitude, bondage, slavery, and is dehumanized. They suffer inhumane treatment by being merciless,

ruthless, brutally and cruelly mistreated and beaten, and their place is being pillaged, plundered, and looted. Their land is being dominated by a dictator or tyrant who exercises terrorism and tyranny, resulting in betrayal, power struggle, treason, treachery, sabotage, and revolution. In early times, we find cannibalism, barbarity, brutish, monstrous, savagery, mutilation, murder, and assault. An assailant will use violence and violently assassinate and annihilate by arson as a pyromaniac.

About criminal activities:
Buccaneers, pirates, and gangsters are willing to kill. The latter uses violence to capture hostages and asks for the ransom price. They also, along with other criminals, act as burglars or thieves by mugging, stealing, and robbery. As a racketeer, they continue in their stupid behavior by going against the law of sowing and reaping or karma by embezzlement, extortion, blackmail, bribery, falsifying, forgery, shamming, and counterfeiting. They easily become loan sharks, dope peddlers, swindlers, cheaters, defraud, are fraudulent, and are also busy in the smuggling trade and have their stake in the black market. As members of the underworld, they are corrupt, exploit, and overcharge their customers. They are usually involved in illegal gambling and also have their hand in legal establishments, such as pawnshops, bookmaking, compulsive gambling, liquor stores, unions, markets, etc. As a charlatan, impostor, deceiver, quack, villain, and scoundrel, they are deceptive, dishonest, using lies and trickery, and try to fool the laws of the land by being guileful, shrewd, crafty, sly, double-faced, and crooked. However, they can never fool the God-made universal laws (knowing even the fall of a sparrow – Matt. 10:29 –), which will eventually restrain or arrest them through the criminal justice system and put them in confinement, prison, or a penitentiary, wherein they can pay penance to balance the law of karma.

Concerning materialism:
Materialist(ic), sensual(ist), hedonist(ic), miser(liness), stingy, stinginess, greed(iness) – influenced by evil desires for possession, possessive(ness), lust of gain and selfish ambition.

Mental and emotional abuse and hopelessness:
Distrust(ful), false ideas and truth, prejudices, hasty judgment, intolerance, wisdom turned to cunning, craftiness, deception, lying, untruthful(ness), gossip, slander(ing), libel(ous), bear false witness (9th Commandment), cheating, and being "men of double mind" (Jas. 4:8).

They practice extreme criticism, falsely accuse, are unprincipled and unscrupulous, and go against the 10th Commandment by engaging in covet(ousness), which is the grasping selfishness of the false ego. They have intense hatred (Matt. 5:21-22; 1 Jn. 3:15), uncontrolled anger, (en)rage, infuriate, and are charged with destructive jealousy, extreme bitterness, and are wrath(ful). They engage in harassment, insult(ing), aversion, spite(fulness), and are overly offensive and harmful. They are mischievous(ness), malicious, malignant, malevolent, experience bitter resentment, and hold a "never-ending" grudge. They possess the evil qualities of ill-will, animosity, hostility, enmity, by being contempt(uous), overly suspicious, envious, envy(ing), disdain(ful), scorn(ful), despising, while being in the attitude of defiance. The evil person always seeks for revenge and vengeance (return evil for evil) by avenging, revenge(ful), and being vengeful. Those whom let their evil self rule more or less their life are burdened with guilt, are continually worrying, and are ridden with fearful anxiety, agony, self-pity, despair, futility, hopeless(ness), meaningless(ness), desperation, are full of anguish, self-disgust, and damnation while undergoing severe depression, and also have a strong feeling to destroy and commit suicide. The downtrodden and abused are easily addicted to alcohol, illegal drugs, and sex. They have lost the sense of good and evil, are no longer ashamed or shameful, and live with a conscience which is seared, withered, made callous, hardened, deadened, and defiled. They spend their time insulting others and being insulted, have an egotistical opinion, and are corrupt and depraved in their thinking, while their emotion expresses itself in boisterous and scornful laughing. Being influenced by their lower desires, their will is weak, and their whole being easily becomes lazy by being in a state of aloofness and apathy. Some of them degenerate or retrograde and become feeble-minded and are called idiots or imbeciles.

Relating to this life and the afterlife:
Hell, sheol and hades have an evil psychic atmosphere which is loathsome, sordid, repulsive, morbid, gruesome, frightening, dreadful, nasty, and where we find vulgarity, terror, fear, horror, panic, and where people are tormented. On this earth, we find in the past and today wizards whom practice wizardry and black arts, sorcerers whom are involved in lower witchcraft, black magic, and the left hand path. Soothsayers or augurs whom practice divination from omens, for signs of future occurrences. Mediums whom engage in lower mediumship and psychism and necromancers whom call up evil spirits of the dead and forces of darkness (see Deut. 18:10-12; Ex. 22:18; Lev. 20:27; Rev. 18:23). This resulted in the Middle Ages of the Inquisition and the

witch hunt for evil and good witches and warlocks. Many people in the past (Mt. 15:22) and today are obsessed and possessed by evil spirits and are called madmen, lunatics, and maniac(al) and need to be exorcised by an exorcist. People whom are insane and suffer from anxiety and schizophrenia and other mental illnesses may be of physical and (or) psychic causes. Other psychic activities we encounter today are psychic attacks, curses, spells, the appearance or haunting by earthbound spirits or poltergeists (also called noisy ghosts). Other ghosts or spooks we may encounter are etheric shells (graveyards) and astral or psychic shells. People of Haiti speak of zombies and others talk about the existence of fairies or nature spirits and extra-terrestrials. They are like angels and do not have the potential, as humans have, to develop a Divine Spirit or Soul. They are thus Soul-less creatures. Evil *extra-terrestrials or aliens have been and are still trying to control human beings through abduction and implants, and other devious ways. Are they becoming the greatest threat to humans whom are creating the Kingdom of God? Lastly, we observe the appearance and disappearance of vampires, werewolves, abominable snowmen or yeti, the sasquatch, and Loch Ness monster. They are nothing else but shape-changing and dimension-shifting creatures.

C. Evil Words in the Bible

The main tenet that humans should not do is stated in the Ten Commandments (Exodus 20, King James Version – K.J.V.), such as:
Thou shalt not worship false gods, dishonour the Name
of thy God (and to keep His day holy).
It further states to honor thy father and thy mother, and that thou shalt not kill, commit adultery, steal, bear false witness, and covet your neighbor's goods.

Jesus Christ mentioned in Mark 7:20-23 (K.J.V.) that "from within, out of the hearts of men (subconscious or human spirit), proceed evil thoughts, adulteries, fornication, murders, thefts, covetousness, wickedness, deceit, lasciviousness, an evil eye, blasphemy, pride, foolishness". The Revised Standard Version (R.S.V.) names the evil things coming from the evil part of the good/evil personality: "evil thoughts, fornication, theft, murder, adultery, coveting, wickedness, deceit, licentiousness, envy, slander, pride, foolishness".

---

* Many of them are etheric beings, whom are more in touch with the earth than the psychic or spirit worlds. The best defense against them is to live a divine life.

Apostle Paul described in Romans 1:29-31 (K.J.V.) that the ungodly men and women are "filled with all unrighteousness, fornication, wickedness, covetousness, maliciousness; full of envy, murder, debate, deceit, malignity; whisperers, back biters, haters of God, despiteful, proud, boasters, inventors of evil things, disobedient to parents, without understanding, covenant breakers, without natural affection, implacable, unmerciful".

The R.S.V. informs us that "They were filled with all manner of wickedness, evil, covetousness, malice. Full of envy, murder, strife, deceit, malignity, they are gossips, slanderers, haters of God, insolent, haughty, boastful, inventors of evil, disobedient to parents, foolish, faithless, heartless, ruthless."

Galatians, 5:19-21 and 2 Timothy 3:2-5 indicate a few more additional words, as expressed by the false personality and not mention above in both Bible translations as: "uncleanness, idolatry, witchcraft, hatred, variance, emulation, wrath, strife, sedition, heresies, drunkenness, revellings", and "impurity, sorcery, enmity, jealousy, anger, selfishness, dissension, party spirit, carousing". Also, "Lovers of their own selves, blasphemers, unthankful, unholy, truce-breakers, false accusers, incontinent, fierce, despising of those that are good, traitors, heady, high-minded, lovers of pleasure more than lovers of God." "Lovers of money, arrogant, abusive, ungrateful, inhuman, implacable, profligates, treacherous, reckless, swollen with conceit" – "holding the form of religion but denying the power of it".

In addition, 1 Corinthians 6:9-10 (R.S.V.) tells "that the unrighteous will not inherit the Kingdom of God? Do not be deceived; neither the immoral (fornicators – K.J.V.), nor idolaters, nor adulterers, nor sexual perverts (effeminate, nor abusers of themselves with mankind – K.J.V.), nor thieves, nor the greedy (covetous – K.J.V.), nor drunkards, nor revilers, nor robbers (extortionists – K.J.V.) will inherit the Kingdom of God."

Addressing those people in whom their false egos or personalities are leading their lives, Paul wrote, "Put to death therefore what is earthly (evil) in you: fornication, impurity, passion, evil desire, and covetousness, which is idolatry" (Colossians 3:5-10 R.S.V.). "Mortify therefore your members which are upon the earth, fornication, uncleanness, inordinate affection, evil concupiscence, and covetousness, which is idolatry" (Col. 3:5-10 K.J.V.).

The above sayings, as the fruit of the inner devil or evil personality, are in contrast with the fruit of the Spirit. These are expressed by those whom are living a spiritual or divine life, such as "love, joy, peace, long suffering, gentleness, goodness, faith, meekness, temperance" and "patience, kindness, faithfulness, self-control", etc. (Gal. 5:22-23 K.J.V. and R.S.V.).

#42 The Different Aspects of Service and Its Value

A. What Is Service?

Service is love in action. It is a steady way of moral and spiritual growth and a short path to enlightenment. Servers are those individuals who put other people's needs before their own and learn to love others as themselves (Matt. 19:19; Gal. 5:14; Jas. 2:8), and do to others as you would have them do unto you (Matt. 7:12; Luke 6:31).

Unlike the Gentiles (Luke 22:25), such as the Greeks and the Romans who despised men that served, Jesus Christ ushered in the era of service. He said in Matthew 20:26, "Whoever would be great among you must be your servant." This statement was at first difficult to accept by His disciples, who were accustomed to leaders who had many people of the lower classes taking care of all their needs. Jesus expressed in Mark 10:45, "The Son of Man also came not to be served but to serve." This certainly was not an easy aspect of the imitation of Christ because many of us are subtly motivated by false pride and self-interest, even in our religious and charitable deeds, instead of really taking care of "the interests of others" (Phil. 2:4), and serving them (II Cor. 4:5). As our behavior as fallen human beings is much directed towards self-preservation, Christ says that this is the way to death, not to life: "Whoever would save his life will lose it; and whoever loses his life for my sake, he will save it" (Luke 9:24). See also II Cor. 4:12. Jesus demonstrated His willingness to serve by washing the dusty feet of His disciples, and showed through this act that a life of service is not a burden of the weak, but the work of the strong. True service does become a joyous experience, even the hardships, as Christ said, "For my yoke is easy and my burden is light" (Matt. 11:30). By giving freely (Matt. 10:8 – K.J.V.), God's unlimited creative flow enters our being, through which we can create "miracles", as Jesus fed the multitudes (Mk. 6:41-43). By giving in the spirit of love and service, you are enriched in the giving (Acts 20:35), and you become an ever enlarging channel for God's love and wisdom, and your "cup" will overflow (Luk. 6:38). By giving to others, especially "to one of the least of these my brethren, you did it to me" (Matt. 25:40). Finally, the greatest service we can do is to witness for Christ. By explaining the Gospel of Christ to another person, our understanding of the Gospel is increased, and we feel a surging of God's energy of love and wisdom through us, which gives us a great measure of assurance and joy.

NOTE: There are, unfortunately, many who witness with an attitude of arrogance and self-righteousness, and even contempt for those who do not want to listen to them. They think of themselves as superior by having their particular "right knowledge and belief". They are not interested in exchanging ideas and are only interested in telling us of what we ought to believe and have, therefore, no respect for the uniqueness of the individual and its special path towards moral and spiritual maturity.

B. The Wit and Wisdom of People of All Walks of Life

➢ I would rather see a sermon than hear one any day.
➢ What you do speaks louder that what you say.
➢ You can preach a better sermon with your life than with your lips.
➢ A good example is the best sermon.
➢ Well done is better than well said.
➢ Practice what you preach (Matt. 23:3).
➢ Great talkers, little doers.
➢ Hands that help are holier than lips that pray (Sai Baba – Hindu holy man).
➢ As I am happy to serve you, so may you be happy to serve others.
➢ Do your best; then God will do the rest.
➢ God helps those that help themselves.
➢ God gives us the almonds, but we have to crack them (Dutch saying).
➢ Love is not love until you give it away.
➢ The gift without the giver is bare.
➢ I do not give lectures or charity; when I give, I give myself.
➢ The finest gift you can give is the gift of yourself.
➢ Covetous men's money chests are rich, not they.
➢ The treasures which are kept in coffers are not real, but only those which are kept in the soul.
➢ The generous man enriches himself by giving, while the miser hoards himself poor.
➢ Man's true wealth is the good he does in the world.
➢ Wie geeft what hy heeft is waard that hy leeft (Dutch). (He who gives what he has is worthy that he lives.)
➢ The gift you give to others is the gift you give to yourself.
➢ He who serves will need not be afraid to ask for his wages.

> Loving, self-forgetting service is the shortest and most joyful road to God.
> You always get what you pay for.
> What we acquire without sweat, we give away without regret.
> It is easy to be generous with another man's money.
> Beware of strange men bearing gifts.
> Only the things you have sacrificed will ever really be yours.
> An example of sacrifice leads others to do the same.
> You will never taste pure joy until you have learned to give.
> The joy of giving in secret has its own reward.
> Only through suffering can you understand what another individual needs.
> True joy is the joy that comes from sacrifice for the Kingdom of God.
> Serving with a sense of duty is not good; serving with love and duty is good; serving with love without duty is divine.
> The work God does for me is salvation. The work God does in me is sanctification.
> The work God does through me is true service.

C. Serving in the East and West

As many good people in the East and others, who are usually internally oriented, meditate, study, and send out positive thought/emotional energy, they are also less inclined to help their fellow citizen by different forms of physical activity. They, however, need to empty themselves in giving or apply what they are studying, so that their "cup" will overflow with even more divine knowledge, which makes them advance faster and become more joyful, and a greater channel of God's love and energy. On the other hand, most good individuals of the West and others who are more externally oriented meditate less and have the tendency to actively help their neighbors, without much regard if it is divinely motivated or even desired by the recipient. They need to discover their Inner Being or Rock of Being (Matt. 7:25; 16:18) after calming down their waves of emotion and thought of their personality by saying, "Peace! Be still!" (Mk. 4:39) This will inspire them to care for their "brethren" with true love and, thus, increase their ability to give real service, not only to take care of the hunger of the body but also of satisfying the intellectual and spiritual hunger of the human spirit and the Soul. Besides, can one whose well is dry give water to the thirsty?

D. Serving for Economical Reasons

In order to be successful, many modern business people have come to the understanding that service should be one of the major factors of prosperity in their enterprises, and certainly more so than the attitude of competition and strife. Business organizations should therefore have a spirit of service, from management to personnel. In this spirit of giving, they contribute something of themselves by not only being attentive to the need of the customer, but also by responding to the client as a human being. They may provide, for example, free advice about products, tips on saving money when going on a trip, and other helpful hints and insights. Those persons are usually mature, have a well-balanced personality, practice ideals of integrity in their life, have a desire to contribute to the welfare of others, and some of them may also live a divine life. This is in contrast with persons who are self-centered, get easily upset, are *immoral in their desires and thinking, and care only about the money they are making. Those individuals have a devastating effect on the collective spirit of the organization and, thus, on the quality of the product (and its vibration) and, above all, on the quality of the service the customer experiences. People who hate their job are usually driven to perform by †a boss who is not service oriented but wants to dominate and rule the workers, who soon learn to look out for themselves first instead of the benefits of the employer and customer. The latter do not like to return to an organization where they sense an atmosphere of apathy and even hostility towards them. The great sales person wants to be helpful, which is a natural human tendency. The persons they are talking to sense it immediately and know that the seller is reliable and on their side, and will not take advantage of them. However, what is unnatural is to force a product or service on someone while thinking about the money the sales person is going to make, instead of concentrating on the needs of the person. The customer soon becomes aware of the motivation and wants to put up a "shield" to protect themselves against the selfish psychological invasion of their privacy.

---

* Those persons are living the life below the belt, are more selfish, materialistic, and thus less service oriented. They usually are less interested in accepting service jobs than their more mature brothers and sisters.

† Because of stiff competition, many businesses are forced to rediscover that in their own self-interest, offering good service pays off. Work relationships are also changing, from bosses who are power wielders (we are not here to win a popularity contest) to facilitators. Thus, one particular good/evil ego is no longer running the show and, thus, much less upsetting the workers.

People should ask themselves, "Do I only work to earn money for myself and my family, or do I also labor to help other people? "Do I only run a business in order to become rich, or do I also want to serve my fellow human beings?" In the first instance, they are not in harmony with natural law and, consequently, will not rise much above their poverty level, and may eventually lose all that they have gained.

We can only grow when we also have the physical, mental, and spiritual advancement of the other person in mind. The least important goal in life is spending your time thinking about earthly gain. You should not compare yourself with your stingy neighbor, who might have more money, power, and prestige but does not advance in wisdom and is frozen in his/her greedy lifestyle until the day they die.

NOTE 1: The economic system on this earth is a great and effective teacher of "brotherly" behavior among human beings because in order to earn enough money or goods for one's survival, individuals have to interact agreeably with other humans to please and serve them. At first, those smiles and pleasing behavior may not be sincere, but they eventually will learn to serve with a rightful attitude, especially those who are dependent upon their livelihood on tips. For a greedy merchant, it might take some time to learn his lesson, but he will, after much trial and error, come to the understanding that in order to be successful, he should not cheat his patrons but rather win the goodwill and satisfaction of his customers. Servers who are usually the most prosperous are those who are not only motivated to serve by the righteous side of their personality, but are also inspired by their newly-born and developed Soul or Inner Being. They show more who they are than what they say.

NOTE 2: The Declaration of Independence of the Unites States of America supports the idea of individual freedoms and rights, that is, the right of every individual to life, liberty, and the pursuit of happiness. On the other hand, the economic system in many Western nations supports the right of each individual to work for his/her own interest. Those political and economic ideals, although good in themselves, do not bring the ultimate good. They promote selfishness because everyone is defending their right to be selfish, and consideration for others is less important.

REMARK: People who give their entire time to spiritual work, such as healing or teaching and raising the spiritually young, should get paid for their time (not for their gift and inspiration) because a man or woman is worthy of their hire. See Matt. 10:10; 1 Cor. 9:14; 1 Tim. 5:18.

E. How Spirit Beings Can Be of Service

When a human being is [1]dying, or in their passing over, the question is not asked, "How wealthy or how famous are you?" but "How many people have your served, and how well?"

Discarnate spirits can be of service to needy human spirits in the same or lower part of the spirit world. They can also be of great help to those who have just "passed over" so that the newly arrived can adjust to the new way of life. This is especially true for those who did not believe in life after death and for those who had the wrong concept of the afterlife. Female spirits can be of great service in the care, nursing, and rearing of children in the spirit world who have died young. [2]Discarnate spirits can also help, guide, protect, and heal those who are living on the earth plane and, thus, function as [3]guardian angels, as a deceased mother will watch over her children and the spirit of the father will watch and guide his family. Discarnate grandparents and their ancestors are also known to guide and help and are usually at the "crossing over point" to receive their posterity when they pass over to their side.

Spirits may also serve by directing energies to individuals on earth who are in hospitals, need help in some emergency, or who are in sorrow and need inner strength. Because in the midst of the people of the earth is often found the greatest need for service. When they help the people of the earth plane overcome obstacles for growth, [4]spirits will also grow, according to the law of cause and effect. This growth is much faster than if they would help spirits in the spirit world. Their help is of so much value because the growth of humans in physical form is enhanced at least five times. Incarnate humans experience and suffer much more the intensities of the consequences of their mistakes.

---

[1] In the process of dying, entities shed their physical bodies and become consciously aware of their more or less developed spirit bodies, which will live in that part of the spirit world in which they feel comfortable. This may be a higher or lower sphere of vibration, in which their bodies of the same vibration are in tune with.

[2] Spirits of highly developed people on earth can also be of great help to carnal beings by consciously directing their spirits to the person(s) in need of help.

[3] In the Bible, the terms angel and spirit are, in some instances, referred to the same entity. See Acts 8:26 and 29. In Judges 13, an angel is also referred to as "man" and "man of God".

[4] The same principle applies, for example, to a teacher who is inspiring students to do good deeds. In that case, the students and teacher receive spiritual benefits and, thereby, grow.

They, therefore, do not like to make the same error and, thus, are learning their lessons more severely. Physical beings grow therefore much faster, and spirit beings that inspire them also grow much faster. This is an important reason why many spirit beings return to the earth where they, through the physical form of another person, face and overcome the challenges, struggles, and possibilities which only the earth world offers. The way for spirits to grow in the afterlife is thus to serve those in the spirit world and the ones whom are living on earth. Those whom are not active in the above-mentioned duties do not grow as fast and, after a long period of indolence, may become stagnated and even backslide. There is, thus, a tendency not only to become indolent and selfish on earth but also in the life after death.

As the story of Lazarus in Luke 16:19-26 shows, a human's true wealth and peace in the spirit world are the good he/she has done.

"There was a rich man who was clothed in purple and fine linen and who feasted sumptuously every day. And at his gate lay a poor man named Lazarus, full of sores, who desired to be fed with what fell from the rich man's table; moreover, the dogs came and licked his sores. The poor man died and was carried by the angels to Abraham's bosom. The rich man also died and was buried; and in Hades (hell), being in torment (psychically), he lifted up his eyes and saw Abraham far off and Lazarus in his bosom. And he called out, 'Father Abraham, have mercy upon me and send Lazarus to dip the end of his finger in water and cool my tongue; for I am in anguish in this flame (unfulfilled desires, a fire that burns but does not consume).' But Abraham said, 'Son, remember that you in your lifetime received your good things, and Lazarus in like manner evil things; but now he is comforted here, and you are in anguish (mental suffering). And besides all this, between us and you a great chasm (psychic barrier of vibration) has been fixed in order that those who would pass from here to you may not be able, and none may cross from there to us.'" (From lower to higher vibration, or from psychic darkness to the light. Otherwise, they will be blinded by too much light. The higher realm becomes invisible to the lower spirits, just as certain rays of light are invisible to physical eyes. They also experience "breathing problems" when they venture any further because the atmosphere is more rarified in the higher sphere or plane.)

As money in the physical world denotes power and position, *in the world of spirit it is no longer needed. Thus, those whom were rich on

---

* Spirits get their substance through breathing from the surrounding psychic atmosphere in a similar fashion, as the etheric body perceives prana from the physical atmosphere. They cannot be damaged and destroyed, and they create their clothes and homes by concentrated thought power.

the earth and could order people around (who were dependent on them for their wages and position, etc.), it is no longer applicable in the afterlife. This is why some whom were using others to take care of their needs find the afterlife a psychological hell because no one is serving them anymore, and they can no longer exercise their power and authority in that place. When they have been unkind and have treated people unfairly while on earth, their spirits appear shrunken and ugly, and hardly anyone wants to have anything to do with them anymore. However, in order to get out of the lower sphere and advance into a higher sphere, they should lose their desire (lust) for power and repent of all their misdeeds; otherwise, they will find no peace in the afterlife.

F. What Is Service, and What Does It Do?

Real service is giving fully of oneself without any ulterior motive or expectation of any external reward. There is thus no afterlife reward, but there is a fusion of divine elements in one's psyche that occurs through the action of serving others, whereby one becomes something other than the person you were before. Thus, in service we discover that when we give, we simultaneously receive from an inexhaustible supply. Only in the purifying fire of sacrifice is the dross of selfishness consumed.

The desire or inborn tendency to serve is deep within us, and it is a well kept secret of life. When we serve others or assist them in the direction of their highest good, our focus is taken off ourselves, freeing us from a state of self-centeredness, and divine forces are then able to flow through us. Service is therefore a fast means of growth by putting the needs of others before your own and thus shortening the path to enlightenment.

The impulse to serve does not originate in the personality or lower self but in the Soul or Higher Self. This explains why the tainted personality, as the vehicle of the Soul, sometimes is reluctant to serve and may put up a great deal of resistance, especially when the false personality is in charge of one's life.

Service can be defined as any act which helps the life of God "up there" unfold "down here", through the personality and thus bringing [the life of Spirit to earth, uniting heaven and earth.

In the action of sharing, there is created a fellowship among the givers and receivers, which quickly dissolves the need of superiority and obedience, but rather becomes a group of individuals that work together for the good of the whole community. Thus, by giving loving self-forgetting service, we are bound together. It creates unity and gives life purpose and meaning.

NOTE 1: The energies, which would normally be turned toward self-service, are now being turned toward the service of others. This allows you the freedom and space to receive even more energy than you did before. This cannot happen when your motive is to receive back this energy or promote yourself by appearing to serve others.

NOTE 2: We serve when we help another person to grow. However, we do not serve if we only want to help in order to receive favors or to put the other person in our debt, and when we become a hindrance to the mental, moral, and spiritual growth of the individual. We do not serve when our primary motive is the lust for recognition and power, which is displayed on television screens, newspapers, and is also rewarded with money and gifts.

NOTE 3: If we are self-centered, we separate ourselves from the ocean of consciousness.

NOTE 4: If some require physical, mental, and spiritual assistance, and our time is limited, then we should give first the highest kind of aid, then the other need will also be fulfilled – "Seek first his kingdom and righteousness, and all these things shall be yours as well" (Mt. 6:33).

NOTE 5: Service also helps to remove karmic obstruction in one's being or discharge karmic debt.

A server likes to help out and will do almost anything for anyone. They are usually friendly and easy to approach. They are modest and always very busy, and do not seek for praise and have no time to receive rewards. They get a lot done, are practical, and carry with them an image of reliability and integrity. They are loving, caring, warm, compassionate, capable, nurturing, devoted, trustworthy, inspiring, and radiate a sense of mission and purpose.

Those who serve or volunteer suffer less stress and fewer health problems, while some of them also experience a healing power "from above". By lending a hand and opening our hearts to another, we momentarily set aside our own ego and, thus, focus our concern away from ourselves. Thus, by focusing more on others and less on ourselves, we diminish anxiety, stress-related thoughts and emotions, and experience more peace. By helping others, we also get a new perspective on our own problems and pain because we find that the pain of others is usually greater than our own. The power of kindness, through a touch, a smile, a kind word, a listening ear, or any small act of caring, has a great impact on the people, and they always carry it with them as a treasure in their heart, as a touch of God. Servers, therefore, make a great difference in the world. They also gain valuable experience, new insights, and strength, making the earth a kinder and gentler place. They know that they can also count on the cooperation of the friendly visible and invisible forces of the universe to bring about the Kingdom of God.

NOTE 1: Service does not mean that we become doormats for a society or that we live lives of slavish servility. Servers can become over-committed and be taken advantage of by others because of their willingness to help.

NOTE 2: To be of proper service, we must know our physical, emotional, and mental capacities. For service to be effective, we should not just rush ourselves full force in the great work but should also do some planning and not be guided by our emotions and the demands of those needing help. We must also exercise wise control of our time and energies so that we do not get depleted in our physical, emotional, and mental vehicles. It is also advisable to prepare for particular services, such as for example healing, because if we have not learned to channel healing energies, then we will deplete our energies. We should also remove any psychic obstructions in our channel between our higher and lower selves. In order to teach properly, we must have proper knowledge.

NOTE 3: As people are created to serve, the kingdoms of nature are created to serve each other, so that they will exist, sustain, and grow.

G. How People Evolve When They Serve

The questions that most individuals ask are: "What can you do to help me? "How can I get my share? "What will I get out of this? Or, "What is in it for me?" By having this attitude, they do not grow or evolve and remain as they were before, greedy and unhappy. In order to get out of the shell of personal interest and desire, one needs to shift their awareness of petty wants and needs (my work, my hobbies, my entertainment, etc.) to a greater awareness. One can do that by asking the questions: "What can I do to help? "What can I do for the greater good? "How can I contribute to humanitarian projects?" Or we can say with President John F. Kennedy, "Ask not what your country can do for you, but what you can do for your country." By asking these questions, the individual is in the process of growing and developing in consciousness. Getting off welfare and becoming productive is a valuable first step toward service for some people, and so is the process of becoming independent in the development of the personality. It is the willingness to give up something of yourself and help others that allows humans to evolve. Gratifying their needs becomes secondary to the desire to serve others and to express their unique talents also for another's good. This is also a time in which the individual wants to do something in return first before they are served. As the person develops even more, he/she does not care how much they are served. They only want to be of greater service to others and may wish also to establish some kind of non-profit organization in order to become more effective.

When our personalities are fairly well developed and we become more unselfish, we move closer to the divine, which in turn invokes a stream of energy from the higher planes, which we can channel to those we serve. We are no longer governed by conflicting ego needs and like to be part of the great body of humanity.

Those who still feel a slight tug of sadness and regret when they give can be an indication that the lower self or ego is in charge of their lives. Those who feel a tremendous surge of joy is a sure sign that their giving is an expression of the higher Self or Soul, which is like the sun, as the lower self is like the earth. The joy he or she experiences in giving their light (truth) and warmth (love) is so great that it brings its own reward. They have become part of the whole, are dissolved into the universe, and become a member of true "brotherhood".

NOTE 1: A child, before the age of puberty, is naturally selfish because the survival instinct of the growing body is strong and the developing personality or ego is forming into selfhood, or becoming an individual. Around the age of puberty (13-14) or accountability, the child is no longer purely selfish and becomes capable of serving and sacrifice. As selfishness is to be expected in children, an adult who still acts selfishly is immature and should learn the lesson of service. If, however, an immature and selfish individual dares to say that he/she is evolved and better than other people, let them prove themselves by making greater sacrifices.

NOTE 2: Someone who wants to grow and develop generosity in his/her character may think about giving to someone or an organization but does not do it; it does him/her not much good. But when they actually give to a real needy person, their character begins to change. By repeating these actions a number of times, the quality of generosity becomes a permanent part of their character, and it becomes easier to give again. This is true (only) when our good intention and the noble things we are going to do are grounded in good works on the physical plane. Otherwise, it is only effective on the mental plane.

Through marriage and especially by taking care of children, the partners remove themselves from self-centered activity, for the husband must provide for the needs of the family, while the wife is greatly occupied in taking care of the home and family. However, humans in general do not quite realize that their [1]love must go beyond the family circle, not occasionally but permanently. They should love [2]country and all creatures of the universe, extending their aura beyond the shell of the family circle and becoming truly happy.

H. People May Serve Those Who Are Causing Problems

We should not give money or goods to someone who is lazy and refuses to accept any responsibility, thereby increasing their indolence and parasitism. We should instead help others to become more self-reliant by giving a helping hand instead of handouts, so that we do not indulge their weaknesses, wants, and bad habits. We should educate the value of self-sufficiency, discover their potential and talents, and encourage our brothers and sisters to overcome their physical and psychological weaknesses. In other words, we should endeavor to help our friends to help themselves, whether physically, financially, morally, mentally, and spiritually, so that they are no longer dependent upon us and other people. This is based on the principle that it is more important to teach a person to fish than it is to give him or her free fish.

People who are wealthy, and do not have a need to serve to make a livelihood, have a tendency to demand services which they can afford. They are therefore more likely to become egocentric, which will strengthen their ego and are thus less inclined to admit that they have spiritual needs as the middle and working class, which are more service-oriented.

---

[1] Love creates an extension of one's life into other lives by radiating and giving itself up to others.

[2] Some people may serve their community and country as volunteers and service men and women, while others may serve the world in peace corps, united nations, and especially in high spiritual organizations, which are always universal. However, this may be momentary or permanent. In the latter case, they feel that they are citizens of the world, especially when they have sacrificed their whole being for the cause of the world. They therefore feel much in tune with their Creator.

REMARK: Most governments of this good/evil world are not altruistic. Their policies are usually for self-interest and not for the good of the race, planet, or world.

The Puritan work ethic, which had its roots in America, believe that the rich should also work and strive to serve others, which produced a new race of strong, sturdy, and generous individuals. They were unlike those in some countries in Europe and other places where the nobility lived on revenues handed down from generation to generation. But now it is another class of people that threatens to become parasitic, by living on welfare and reaping the benefits of the sweat of the working people's brows.

I.   Service with Wrong Intention or Motivation

Many people think that the pursuit of happiness consists of having and getting and in being served by others instead of in giving and serving, while other individuals perform acts of service with the wrong intention or motivation. The latter expects adulation for their services and constantly boasts of what they have done. They – in whom the good/evil ego is in charge of their life – make a *big show of helping society and the human race and are constantly seeking appreciation and recognition of what they have done. They are vainglorious and refuse to give anything if they are not noticed or admired. Those people may create positive (physical) karma, but it does not help them with their inner development. They do not become unselfish in their attitude and do not experience an uplift that will remain with them, or open a path to enlightenment through their acts. By distorting the love of service into possessiveness, they do not contribute much to God's restoration plan. Therefore, the motive of serving is often of more value than the showy and glamorous acts of service.

Other people may think that they are serving another or humanity but do not realize that they are also motivated by their subconscious self, which seeks for emotional gratification, or to make themselves "feel good". They also distort the spirit of service by experiencing the pride of service instead of the joy of service when their Higher Self is in charge of the lower self.

Because God is love, we can only merge with Him through loving service. We should therefore serve wholeheartedly without a sense of duty or with attitudes of apathy and pessimism. In order for the Higher

---

* Jesus said of them in Matthew 6:2; 23:5-7, "When you give alms, sound no trumpet before you, as the hypocrites do in the synagogues and in the streets, that they may be praised by men. Truly, I say to you, they have received their reward." "They do all their deeds to be seen by men --- They love the place of honor at feasts and the best seat in synagogues, and salutations in the marketplaces, and being called rabbi by men."

Self (and God) to express fully through the lower self or personality, the channel should not be obstructed by sad emotions and grim mental states, or even denial of one's ego, as practiced by some religious fanatics.

Sometimes, the call to service is ringed with moral righteousness. "When you serve, you are always rewarded." This type of service is based on the expectation of reward and is, therefore, wrongly motivated. A higher type of service is that which is motivated by an intrinsic desire to serve.

NOTE: Hindu philosophy teaches that there are (depending on the suitability of each individual) four main paths or union (yoga) to the divine. They are: Raja yoga – through the mind and the will, Bhakti yoga – through personal devotion, Jnana yoga – through knowledge, and Karma yoga – through good works. Karma yoga achieves union with God through right action and through service. Karma yoga literally means "action yoga". It consists of the sacred work of performing your daily activities in harmony with the Soul wishes and desires. All actions are to be done with an attitude of self-surrender and with no regard for the fruit of those actions or no egotistic attachments.

J. What Is True Service?

When the Soul is in charge of our life, the gift given does not weigh upon the giver. It requires no effort from the giver to separate himself/herself from such a gift. It flows freely to the recipient who will accept it freely, knowing that the gift was given freely – free of all ties and attachments. ("Freely ye have received, freely give" – see Matt. 10:8 K.J.V. See also Psalms 112:9; Proverbs 11:24; 2 Cor. 9:7.) On the other hand, any gift given with any thought of enhancement as a result of giving is not a gift at all but an exchange, a barter, a purchase, or sale. Right action is that which is usually done from the Inner Self with no intention to benefit the doer, and of a non-selfish desire to promote the interests of the person who may benefit by that action. Thus, True service does not center upon the personality but upon the Soul, serving not only the true Self or the server but the true Selves of all the people as well.

To be of service in God's name is the greatest gift you can give to yourself and others. We can all serve no matter where we are upon our path or in our development. Simply ask God for guidance and how you can bring this about. Once you make this your goal, you will be rewarded with deep satisfaction in knowing that you are following your life's path. Being in His service, the Creator will certainly present you with many opportunities to serve His people. See Jn. 21:15-17; Mk. 16:15.

By asking God every day for His help, we are tapping from the universal reservoir of love, wisdom, strength, and joy, which will stream more and more through our personality, which eventually becomes a vehicle for divine expression. People will then receive True Service, and we become co-creators with God our Creator.

An excellent example of true service is that of Brother Lawrence (b. 1611), who as a lay brother of the decalced (barefooted) Carmelites in Paris, was assigned the task of working in the monastery kitchen, which also included the cleaning of pots and pans. He at first did not like the drudgery of cooking and washing dishes, but after he decided to do all his tasks out of the love of God, everything changed. He then started talking with God continually, whom he found was living in him (Gal. 2:20) and who worked with him in his daily chores, which gave him great joy. All those experiences were written down in the booklet "The Practice of the Presence of God".

K. The Many Ways of Giving Service

In this day and age, many individuals feel that giving money and material possessions is the way to give. Although that way of service is constructive and good, there are many other ways in which people can give, such as:

- Giving your companionship to someone who is lonely
- Speaking words of encouragement, comfort, and edification
- Listening to someone who needs to talk
- To help another with their special talent or ability
- Giving by being cheerful to those you meet
- Sending out benevolent thoughts is also a way to make people happy.
- Helping entities to appreciate themselves through a better external image
- When there is an opportunity to be kind, let your kindness show.
- When there is an opportunity to show compassion be compassionate.
- We can help by sharing our time, talent, and knowledge.
- A kind look and expression of confidence is always helpful.
- We can work for the benefit of charitable or educational organizations.

- To comfort a friend who is experiencing hardship and difficulty
- Encouraging public involvement in government
- Improving relationships between antagonistic elements of society
- Help those who cannot help themselves in a sympathetic and loving way.
- To work with renewed dedication of what you have been doing
- Giving a double gift – by buying your gift from charitable organizations
- Volunteer to help at your church.
- Make personal contact with someone who would most appreciate it.
- Get involved in your community and its volunteer organizations.
- Visit a nursing home or retirement community.
- Serve by example and by your very presence.
- Serve on the physical, emotional, mental, and spiritual levels.
- Every day, opportunities for service are presented.
- Seeing people not only as objects but as having life and value
- Another valuable service is to pray for those we meet, see, and think about, which can be done by anyone – also by those who cannot move.
- A very important service we can do is to bring the Gospel of Christ to all people of the world (Matt. 28:19-20).
- To help those who need assistance in directing their moral life
- To assist those in discovering their True Self or Soul and exploring the divine world

NOTE: When you have shown to serve in small things, the Creator will ask you to serve in greater things (Matt. 25:14-20). The influence and power one has who is in a leadership position is great, and he/she pays a heavy karmic price if they fail to do the will of the Divine.

People whom are spiritually developed can be of great service, not only by example of their lifestyle but also by influencing people who come into the presence of their aura and by changing the energy of the place they pass through. There are also occupations of service, such as farming, domestic work, mining, manufacturing, etc. The question may be asked, "How much and in what way am I contributing to the welfare or problems of planet earth because of the work I do?" Other occupations, such as policemen, firemen, prison guards, servicemen, nurses, and others do not always do their job for their own benefit, but also like to be of service to others. There are also the more traditional forms of service to individuals, such as to the needy and those whom are unable to help themselves. Other forms of service are when individuals participate in high forms of entertainment, such as creating beauty, playing uplifting music, inspiring people to be greater than they are by films, television, plays, writings, poems, art exhibits, etc.

Service should be given upon request (people should be given a chance to solve their own problems). We should serve joyfully, lovingly, unselfishly, through our God Self (not our ego self). We should then ask our heavenly Parents to guide us and then give thanks for the opportunity to serve. As we serve, we should demonstrate God's love, so that the greater good and life's deepest purpose are served through us.

Finally, when a person does good to another, a heavenly joy arises within the individual, and they also grow by serving the other. When someone teaches knowledge, especially divine knowledge, not only will their pupils develop but also the teacher will grow by receiving more inspiration and insights. We surely are able to recognize those people who have given a life of selfless service. They are endowed with a subtle, indefinable beauty, which emanates from within them and radiates outwardly. Those highly evolved individuals who bear the stamp of true beauty arrest our attention and compel our admiration.

#43 To Age Gracefully and Live a Life Worth Living

A. Introduction

The idea that senior adults grow feeble with years is a foolish fallacy. They may somewhat diminish in physical endurance and in overcoming stress, but their mental ability continues and even increases, especially when they exercise those mental facilities. Besides, they have more time to think, read, contemplate, and wonder about God's wonderful creation. Medical research has shown that at seventy-five, most of the elderly are more mentally capable than they were at fifty and, as testified by universities, are often better students than the younger ones. They should certainly not accept the role a youth-oriented society likes to impose on them: "to act their age" or play the role of being old, and to accept the fact that aging leads to incompetence and deterioration. The longer one lives, the better the individual knows how to live, without any fear of growing old as society has imposed on them from the day they were born.

For those whom are not convinced that mental capacity increases with age, think about individuals such as: Sophocles, Cervantes, Verdi, Michelangelo, Goethe, Edison, and many others whom achieved great works in their sixties and seventies. Alexander Kerinski, Leo Tolstoy, and Winston Churchill wrote some of their most important works in their eighties. Laura Ingalls Wilder did not begin writing "Little House on the Prairie" until she was sixty-five years old, and musicians such as Toscanini, Horowitz, and Rubinstein were performing in their eighties and nineties. Senator Thurmond of S. Carolina served his country until he was ninety-eight years old. In general, we can say that not much has been accomplished before the age of fifty unless the person has been influenced, wholly or in part, by centuries old entities of the invisible realms. Such was the case with Mozart and other child prodigies, as well as Bach, Haydn, and a few other musicians, artists, writers, and inventors. This also includes most religious leaders such as Mohammed of Islam, Joseph Smith of the Mormons, Madame Blavatsky, and C.W. Leadbeater of the Theosophical Movement, Max Heindel of the Rosicrucians, and Edgar Cayce of the Association for Research and Enlightenment.

NOTE 1: Some older folks may say, "I am sometimes forgetful; thus, my mind must be weakening." Anyone who has been around the young knows how erratic their memories are. Not only are the memories of older persons no worse than when they were young, but they also have more to remember. Their memory bank is a depository of thousands of thoughts and events, which may at times become overloaded. They may, like anyone else, experience memory lapses when they are tense and nervous.

NOTE 2: Studies have indicated that older workers are more reliable, productive, and dependable than most of the younger people. They show up on time, take their job seriously, and believe that they should earn their money the old-fashioned way.

NOTE 3: The author began writing this manuscript when he was sixty-five years old, in the year two thousand.

Thus, the closing years of physical life are, for many, more creative and fulfilling than the first years, as the elders become more appreciative of what is artistic and beautiful. They also acquire a better insight of the nature of life and the purpose and meaning of their existence. Growing older, therefore, does not mean closing down the store and sitting in a rocking chair, watching the world go by in front of them.

When one grows older, the body loses its full strength and physical beauty but is more than fully compensated by the more developed human spirit and, for some, the great beauty of their eternal Soul or Christ Spirit. Because of their lessening physical agility, seniors usually make a serious and dedicated effort to plan their work so that they do less, but accomplish the same by using their time more wisely than the young and strong. Older individuals may appear to be poor outwardly, but inwardly, they carry an abundance of wealth, such as knowledge and [1]wisdom, and an inestimable treasure of human and spiritual experiences because they had to adapt to the many changes of life. Those experiences can grace them with compassion, humbleness, and appreciation of life of which they like to be a part, instead of forcing oneself into retreat and useless isolation. Those who have lived full and rich lives are in possession of great wisdom because they have tested their beliefs and have had time to validate their [2]pragmatic assumption against the toughness of the physical world. We can see

---

[1] Wisdom is that which we distill from knowledge – it is the fruitage of a life's experience.

[2] Pragmatism (according to the Dictionary of philosophy and religion) is a philosophical movement of the late 19th and 20th centuries, whose emphasis lies in interpreting ideas through their consequences.

The Readers' Digest Dictionary says that pragmatism is the doctrine that ideas have value only in terms of their practical consequences, and that the results are the sole test of the validity or truth of one's belief.

Testing the validity of all concepts by their practical results (definition from Webster's New World Dictionary).

the character and the lines of experience in his or her face. This is an indication of valor, and it reflects the beauty of the Soul. Thus, the foolishness and ignorance of youth have given way to the wisdom of old age.

We can use our life experiences to benefit others and enrich ourselves by creating a whole new life. We are certainly qualified to offer young people precious advice, support, and guidance as they are facing an uncertain future, while threading their unique path of life.

If we ask those elderly, who have become wise, about [1]the best advice they would give to young people, they would say that "the young should take chances and explore and experience, as much as possible, the many facets of life and not settle down to being 'young'. The wise have realized that life is best lived, not as a search for security but a search for experience, because a life devoid of challenge and variation is a life not worth living. The young folks should therefore not abandon their dreams in exchange for security, routine, sameness, familiarity, and boredom. They should instead seek out avenues of

---

[1] This advice is the exact opposite to that the middle-aged parents of young people would offer. The concerned parent urges the youth or young adult to concentrate in only a few fields of activities and to do like them, by staying with the same company and climbing the corporate ladder.

It is perhaps good to know about the physical aspect of life first, such as becoming a physician or other health professional, and understanding the workings of the physical body, including the etheric or vital body by, for example, practicing acupuncture.

Another way is to acquire knowledge of the earth, sea, and air by becoming a geologist, study the plant world as a botanist, the animal world as a zoologist, the ocean as a oceanographer, and the sky as an astronomer, as well as other related sciences, including transportation. We may also consider becoming designers, engineers, and builders of "man-made projects", or become researchers, teachers, or organizers of the above-mentioned sciences.

After having learned and practiced the above disciplines, we may then move on to the field of human knowledge and psychology by studying the origin, culture, and development of the people of the earth (anthropology) and human nature. We may become teachers of personality development, in its intellectual, moral, and emotional aspects – of which the latter is better understood by becoming a teacher of music or an artist. We may deal with disorders of the personality by becoming a psychologist, psychoanalyst, or psychiatrist. We should also become involved in psychical research to explain psychic phenomena, teach about the development of psychic abilities, and life after death.

As we progress, we may also have to deal with the spiritual development of the Soul, Higher Self, or Divine Spirit by becoming a spiritual doctor or transpersonal psychologist, priest, or minister. To become a teacher of religion is an excellent profession, and to heal people of all "diseases" at all levels of their beings is the best that we can do.

fresh experience and learning, which they like to pursue, regardless of the opinions of family and friends.

"When the outer personality is growing older, the inner personality is becoming ever beautiful and wiser" (TV).

When humans are young, they possess a physical beauty, which is fitting, but inwardly, they are immature and undeveloped. When they grow older, their physical beauty declines, but their inner self develops and radiates a divine beauty, provided that they also live a divine life. Thus, when physical beauty wanes, spiritual beauty gains or takes its place. Those people are being respected and referred to by the young as they see and experience the divine in all the expressions of the seniors. This would certainly be true in the ideal world. However, in the fallen or good/evil world of today, this is not always the case. The older folks whom are living [2]the life of the personality, especially those that are led by their evil self by living an immoral life, should not expect that the young will look up to them. When the elders have not developed spiritually, they are not able to pass on much wisdom to the younger generation. Many of them have not reached maturity. Their personality is still impure, and some of them have not even learned the most important lessons of life. The only thing they can pass on is a lot of earth knowledge and possessions. They, therefore, are not much respected by the younger generation and may become a burden to society. The main purpose of life, besides multiplying and subduing the earth is, first of all, to become fruitful or reach full maturity (Gen. 1:28). They should, therefore, not only grow their personality by learning and experience but also develop their Divine Spirit in the likeness of God by becoming the son or daughter of God.

On the other hand, many young people are influenced by Western society, which overly worships youth, looks, power, and health, thinks that all old people are a burden because they do not contribute anything

---

[2] Developing and purifying the personality of original sin was supposed to be done by the Old Testament dispensation, which is also the task of Mohammedan and other exoteric religions. The complete spiritual development was initiated by Jesus Christ, whereby people not only believe in a God outside themselves but also within. However, the Jewish and Mohammedan religions did not stay static after the event of Christ, but also evolved in some branches of esoteric expressions. Today, many Christians whom have fallen back to the pagan level and others have to first morally develop by living according to the 10 Commandments before they can be born spiritually and develop their Divine Spirit. See "The Evolution of the Divine Spirit or Soul".

NOTE: People living on this earth should look older physically in order to recognize if they are mature or immature, parents or grandparents.

of value to society. Most of the young have become non-spiritual and do not see, or do not want to see, the divine aspects of an increasing number of seniors, whom are often of great help to their community.

The senior who is living a spiritual life has become most beautiful and radiates greatness at the end of his/her physical life as they, like the leaves of trees, turn into the most beautiful colors in the autumn of their lives. This can be seen and experienced by viewing the dazzling beauty of New England autumns. A leaf is most beautiful and enchanting before it dies and gathers in all the beauty and colors. When it is at its loveliest, it lets go the twig and floats gently down to the earth after passing on to everyone, who is able to see, their beauty and wisdom. Those leaves are no longer plain green of inexperience but come in the different colors and shades of their uniqueness, such as that of a brilliance of red, brown, orange, purple, deep green, and gold leaves, and many other exquisite colors.

REMARK: The autumn of the year, like the autumn of our lives, is the time to gather in the fruit of our efforts: to collect the evidence of our experience.

As the sunrise is beautiful, so is the sunset. As children are beautiful, so has old age its own beauty and grace after passing through the sky of experience and development.

B. Some People Age Gracefully, While Others Turn Disconsolate

Some people manage to grow old gracefully, a few even gratefully, while among them are seniors who never seem to feel old, and a number of them do not even look old. However, in today's society, increasing numbers are fighting old age, especially those whom are living the life of the personality and (or) those whom do not believe in a life after death. Individuals whom are living (more or less) divine lives believe, by faith, in eternal life. Others of the same group are not so sure because they have never been told by their religions, in precise terms, what kind of life they are going to live in the afterlife and what it is like over there.

Starting to "feel old" is a serious phase of life, and for some people, it can be frightening and even sinister. The French writer Simone de Beauvoir said, "The vast majority of humankind looks upon the coming of old age with sorrow and rebellion. It fills them with more aversion than death itself." Apostle Paul had a different view and reflected what was said in Hosea 13:14 and Isa. 25:8, "O death, where is thy victory?

O death, where is thy sting?" This "sting of death is sin", Paul answered (1 Cor. 15:55-56). In other words, sin caused separation from God, which resulted in mortality of the Soul, but not of the body.

While many elderly parents can be a genuine blessing to the family and wonderful examples of growing old with faith, dignity, and honor, the aches and pains of aging turn some of them into cranky individuals who are only concerned about themselves. Let us not make the mistake of thinking or speaking of ourselves and others as being "over the hill" at any age because when we are over the physical hill, that is when our mental and spiritual life, the one that really matters, really begins. Most persons dread old age as a time of sickness, poverty, mental incompetence, and waiting for death in a nursing home. However, the truth is that the vast majority of people are relatively healthy and happy well into their eighties and even nineties, and that less than five percent are in nursing homes, and most of them are eighty-five and older. Almost all of the older folks are living in their own homes, taking care of themselves, and living active and productive lives. Unfortunately, many retired people have come to believe that they are "old", even if their bodies are still fit and their minds still sharp. They have accepted old age to begin as soon as they turn sixty-five and are supposed to believe that it is a condition of loss, a time to quit, a mandate to withdraw. The result of this belief is that they feel inferior, depressed, no longer needed, useless, are has-beens, and washed up, which results that they are no longer interested in living. They say, "I have nothing to live for." Women may add, "My beauty is gone; I am getting old." By feeling and thinking like that, they create around them a psychic atmosphere of hopelessness and despair. Those psychic radiation and thought forms will influence these people whom communicate and live with and around them, who eventually will leave them alone or let the retirees live their own lives, which are empty and lifeless.

NOTE: It is poverty, not poor health, that has been cited as the worst problem of many old people, their chief source of unhappiness and worry. They may become an easy target of unscrupulous criminals and may, at times, be abused by their own children, which in England is called "granny slamming". Other problems facing the elderly are losing their spouse, friends, and sometimes their homes. What they fear, which might not happen, is illness, disability, loss of vision and hearing, weakening of limbs, stiff joints, independence and privacy, and other things and diseases which probably will never happen to most elderly people, especially not the dreaded Alzheimer's. That older people will suffer many diseases and that they will be sooner or later in nursing homes is being overemphasized by highly educated advertisers and manipulators. The latter are, however, so stupid that they do not seem to understand that by misleading and taking advantage of others they themselves, according to the law of sowing and reaping (karma), will be in like circumstances, that they are taken in when they are old by others, or that they will get incurable diseases.

As the primary needs of food, shelter, clothing, and medical care are important, so are the psychological needs, especially the need to be needed. As work gave them power, status, and a sense of purpose, taking care of their children was difficult but fulfilling and fruitful. This is, however, no longer the case, and some of them spend empty hours filled only by memories of the past. On the other hand, other seniors start a whole new life, doing the kind of activities they always want to do, while many others feel that they are needed more than ever by helping people in need, especially children, or by doing work as volunteers. Increasing numbers are in search of their physical and spiritual roots and try to *develop in a spiritual way.

NOTE: Those adult children and health professionals whom are physically oriented and are trying to help the elderly are often afraid of what they see because of their own fear of aging. Old age is also viewed negatively by most young people, especially by those whom are much identified with their bodies. They do not want to be reminded that this is what they are going to look like later on in life. Women who complain about losing their physical beauty have a unique opportunity to develop their sense of inner beauty so that they no longer have to fear that they will be rejected by others or by themselves.

Older people, especially women, whom do not believe in a life after death and are not spiritual, try to delay the aging process in a frantic effort to restore their youthfulness, which is all out of proportion to its importance. Practitioners of cosmetic surgery are busier than ever removing the signs of aging, using facial lifts and skin-tightening procedures to remove sags and wrinkles, getting rid of accumulated fat, reshaping of body parts, and hair transplantation. With the help of the media, who continually promotes youthfulness and is paid by its anti-aging advertisements, society has become obsessed with youth, and old people are no longer seen as valuable contributors to society. Aging, once a matter of respect and dignity in the Western world, is seen as a burden and even as a clinical problem. Society has forgotten that a person's worth is not to be measured by physical endowment. Young

---

* In parts of India, the people, after they get an education (develop their personality) and raise their family, devote the remainder of their lives in contemplation and spiritual development. Many Chinese people follow a similar path by devoting the first part of their lives in developing their human nature, to gain practical knowledge by living according to Confucian ethics. They would then spend the remaining part of their lives developing intuitive knowledge and discovering the way or Tao (Taoism).

people in general, whom as recently as the middle of the 20th century offered assistance to the elderly in a crowded bus or train by giving up their seat, no longer do so. With this declining respect for age comes an attendant lack of regard for the experience and wisdom of grandparents. By rejecting the advice of the elders, it will take the young a greater length of time to come to the same understanding about certain things in life. In the meantime, they are making regretful mistakes for which they may be sorry for the rest of their lives.

This disrespect for old age in a society obsessed with youth has even come to such an extent that some elderly who cannot take care of themselves, and before being thrown away, are being "warehoused" in institutions. By shuffling them off to nursing homes and other facilities, you deprive yourself of truth and insight, unknown to any other age in life. When the fountains of experience arrive at their final destination in anticipation of a better life, they soon find out that they are being *neglected and mistreated by the young. After being in that facility for a while, the old lose all self-respect, dignity, and meaning and are even ashamed of being old. They then start to wonder if life is still worth living. Some of them lose the will to live and pass away peacefully in their sleep, while others seek for [1]help to make an end to their lives.

NOTE 1: If they are listening, the elders can greatly contribute to the knowledge of future generations. The young would not make great mistakes, such as choosing the wrong profession, sex before marriage, teen pregnancy, addiction to drugs, etc. The Spanish philosopher Santayana (d. 1952) said, "Those who do not remember the past are condemned to repeat it."

NOTE 2: Many of the young who give priority to immediate human usefulness and productivity have contempt for people who are not physically active. They say to the old that they are not part of abundance and success,

---

* Those who treat the elders with disrespect will be treated (according to the law of karma) in the same way by others when they get old or before that time.

[1] Suicide and euthanasia (death caused by another agency with the elder's consent and/or approval of family members) is morally wrong and an offense against human dignity. As people have become more selfish, the respect for life has decreased. Many of them no longer think it is wrong to take the life of seniors when it has become unbearable, or at the urging of their children whom see that their parents are using up their inheritance or draining their family's resources in expensive medical treatments. When the children make a greater gain at the expense of their parent's life, they have to pay the karmic price unless the children object to their parent's suicide, and the parents override the objection because they love them. In the latter case, the suicide involves less karma for the parents than if they do it out of self-pride. They all should seek guidance from God who truly loves them all and tries to heal them of physical and emotional pain and depression.

and that their opinions are no longer valid because they are from another time. Some of the young whom have been mistreated when they were helpless as children are taking out their frustration to punish the elders from an attitude of superiority. It is therefore not always the fault of the young folks that they treat the elderly bad. The respect of the younger generation for the older also depends on what the older folks have done for themselves. They achieve fulfillment, peace of mind, self-respect, and honor from others in the way they have conducted themselves. Above all, they should no longer live the empty life of the personality but live a divine life filled with the Spirit of God.

Society in America was morally and spiritually better when the elders were young, and America as a nation was greatly respected by the world, especially during and after the Second World War. Instead of throwing bombs from the sky, they threw down food packages to the starving Europeans they liberated (as witnessed by author) and helped them recover from the devastating war, with its physical, mental, and spiritual oppression.

Today, the young are not like the old. Many are immoral by living a lifestyle the Bible strictly forbids. Are we not living in the time Paul spoke about in II Tim. 3:1-4 (K.J.V.)?

> "In the last days, perilous times shall come. For men shall be lovers of their own selves, covetous, boasters, proud, blasphemers, disobedient to parents, ungrateful, unholy, without natural affection, truce breakers, false accusers, incontinent, fierce, despising of those that are good, traitors, heady, high-minded, lovers of pleasures more than lovers of God."

Fortunately, the aged are deeply respected in other cultures, such as those in the orient and among Native Americans. They have been revered and their advice sought on matters ranging from the sowing and harvesting of crops, marriage and settling of village disputes, and many other important issues. Those cultures have realized that most of life's lessons are not learned from textbooks. Throughout the orient, to neglect a parent or to leave them in the care of strangers is a disgrace to the family name. In the time of the Puritans and as late as the American Revolution (+/-1776), older people were given honored status, special privileges, and even political power by virtue of their seniority. At that time, it was a [2]religious duty for children to take care of their parents.

REMARK: Lots of people who once looked to God to save them now expect the government to do it. "God helps those who help themselves, and the government helps those who don't" (from "14,000 Quips & Quotes" by E.C. McKenzie p. 209).

C. Identifying with the Physical Body

The reason that so many people display an unhealthy emphasis on physical attractiveness, wardrobe, bodily health, and "projecting an image" is that they identify themselves (their inner selves – intellect, emotion, will, Soul) with their physical bodies and their senses. For them, there is only a physical existence, birthing, growing, aging, and dying, and when they get old, life is all over. They believe that when the body grows old, they grow old; when the body dies, they die.

If they would recognize and be aware that they also have an inner life or character, as expressed by their human spirit and Self, they would not have such a frenzy toward physical fitness and bodily beauty. They would realize that their body is only a house for their spirit selves, which transcends those aging and imperfect bodies. The inner self is much more important because it will survive death, does not grow old, and lives on beyond the three-dimensional existence. By emphasizing [3]spiritual growth, they would look more for advice of the older members whom are living a divine life, and seek their companionship instead of rejecting them as worn out physical bodies.

---

[2] It is not the duty of the government to take care of elderly people. This is, according to the Bible, the tasks of the children of the elders, to "honor your father and your mother" (Ex. 20:12) and religious institutions (1 Tim. 5:3-16). Seniors should be appreciated members of one's family and be supported by them, instead of a monthly check arriving at a lonely apartment from a cold surrogate family, the social security and welfare system. Social Security was created during the Great Depression to raise extra taxes in order to close the growing budget deficit. Such a system cannot persist, as we can see today in the increase of the elder population, their increased longevity, and the reduced number of younger people who have to support them by paying taxes. In this system, the young show declining interest in the well being of senior citizens, whom have become overly dependent upon government support. As a final note, Proverbs 13:22 said, "A good man leaves an inheritance to his children's children."

[3] Spiritual growth is the process of first shifting our consciousness or awareness from the physical body to our human spirit or lower self, and then from the lower self to the Higher Self or Divine Spirit of our being and to realize our divinity more and more. The body becomes an instrument of our inner personality or lower self who, in turn, becomes an appendage of our Divine Self.

When the physical body gets older and weaker, the inner selves want to take more control of the life of humans. However, when he or she still identify themselves with their physical bodies, the latter are still ruling their lives. The result is that they are passing through a [4] "midlife crisis", increasing the fear of death.

NOTE 1: Unlike the old, the young are more identified with their bodies because their inner selves are closely entangled with the body that it is difficult for them to know if their behavior is motivated by their inner selves or by the consciousness of bodies. The body's dread or fear of death influences their thinking and makes them more afraid of physical death than it is called for. They should separate from those fears because "we are not our bodies". It is, however, possible to override the body's fear of death and annihilation, just as you have learned to overcome the instinct of your body-consciousness to reproduce at will or kill for food.

NOTE 2: In some cultures that are more spiritually oriented, there is no such thing as "midlife crisis".

D. The Mental Attitude about Aging

It is not possible to remain physically young forever, but one can forestall or hasten aging considerably by one's attitude, beliefs, and the power of the mind. The mind, for example, can cause an individual to age very rapidly and to turn gray-haired overnight. This happens when a trauma occurs which takes away the sense of purpose or reason to live. The person's attitude about life may then change considerably. He/she appears haggard, is incapable of sustaining life, and within a few years may develop a fatal disease. They may also speed up the

---

[4] Midlife crisis is a change comparable to that of puberty, and it takes place between the ages of 45 and 50. It is more defined in women by experiencing "menopause" (cessation of menstruation) and occurs usually later in men. At that time, some men want to prove their manhood by having disastrous affairs with younger women, which the Bible in Mal. 2:14-16 strictly forbids, because it causes "divorce", which the Lord "hates", and He desires "Godly offspring". Just as a teenage girl goes through a crisis in establishing her identity as a female, the middle-aged woman goes through this crucial time in maintaining her being as a female because of the loss of youthful appearance and ability to bear children. She is, therefore, more distressed than a man about aging and rushes to the beauty parlor and drugstore to save her appearance. However, when they have overcome this crisis, they (men and women) discover that life really begins at fifty, a good time to become more creative and to work towards the realization of one's potential. It is a time to explore, unfold their psychic nature, discover, and develop their spiritual nature. By doing so, they will lose identification with their physical bodies. Life becomes more meaningful, which makes men and women more joyful than they were ever before. For the very old, the relationship with the body has become looser, as a ripened fruit is about to fall from the tree.

process of dying by chain smoking, heavy drinking, taking drugs, and unsafe sex. Another example of the influence of the conscious mind is that it can create illness or rapid aging by believing and thus programming the subconscious to break down the physical body. On the other hand, one can recover from disease, such as cancer, and considerably slow down the aging process by having a strong will to live. Programming health and youthfulness actually prolongs the life of the [1]cells in the body, so that the aging process will be greatly slowed down or even reversed. The anti-aging practice of the mind is that mind which continually thinks of being young in spite of the passing years. It does not think or dwell on dying but thinks and dwells on living. To help in this process, it is good to associate with young people and persons whom are positive in their feeling and thinking. This will help you to act younger and to keep yourself young. Besides, when you feel and think old, you look old. It is also helpful in the rejuvenation process to look at a photograph of yourself in your [2]youthful prime, so that you remain young at heart. Thus, it is not good to associate with people who constantly worry about aging, which may eventually influence your thinking about aging, until it becomes a fact of life. For the same reason, it is not good for those, to whom the aging process is a problem, to celebrate their birthdays. We should, therefore, not talk about age, avoid funerals as much as possible, and not set our mental clocks to die at a certain age.

Aging of the physical body can be delayed through physical, psychic, and spiritual rejuvenation. Psychic recovering is the recognition that mental attitudes (emotional and thinking) has a powerful effect on the aging process. For the simple reason that the

---

[1] It is a scientific fact that cells of the body change every seven years, and that cells cannot renew themselves indefinitely. There is, thus, a certain limit in cell divisions (otherwise we would never get old) because they will get more damaged than repair themselves. The chemistry of our cells is not only dependent on good nutrition but also on pure air. The longevity of cells is further dependent on the healthy state of the etheric body, which permeates every cell, which in turn is also influenced by our feeling and thinking. Scientists say that the genetic heritage of humans allows for a life span of around 120 to 140 years. However, it is through our lifestyle that we cut it short to 70-85 years.

[2] The youthful prime is our true age of our inner self or human spirit. It may age in years but not in appearance and will, therefore, be always young at heart or young in our inner self. Thus, the spirit selves in the spirit world usually do not think "old" because it is only an earthly phenomenon. When we as physical beings are in close connection with our human spirit and especially with our Divine Spirit, we will always feel young but are also wise because of our passing years. If the old man or woman is also not young in their feelings, then they have only aged. They may have grown in time, in age, but they are not grown up and are still immature.

psyche or spirit body, which consists of intellect, emotion and will, has its abode in the physical body (as water in the sand) and, thus, influences every cell and system of the body. Thus, negative mental states or attitudes, such as depression, fear, worry, discouragement, insecurity, psychological stress, and uncontrolled moods of griping and complaining tend to be debilitating and hasten the aging process. Positive mental states, such as self-confidence, sense of adequacy, self-acceptance, constructive thinking, and especially divine love (which neutralizes hate), are empowering and infuse rejuvenating energies into the body. This is especially true of those persons who have a driving purpose in life and a divine mission to accomplish. Thus, the harmful habit of pessimistic thinking and the *stressful emotions of anger, hatred, hostility, frustration, resentment, and grudges are like poison to the psyche and toxic to the body. For each bad emotion, there is a corresponding chemical change in the tissues of the body that is life depressing and harmful. This is why people who are pessimistic in their attitude about life get sick much easily than those who are optimistic and have a sense of humor.

NOTE: It is said that the men and women in China, whom are more than 100 years old, remain youthful because they sleep with younger women and men, and, without, any sexual contact, absorb their energies by being in the vibrations of youth. (See story in the Bible of David who was taken care of by a beautiful maiden "but the king knew her not" – 1 Kings 1:1-4). Although laying close together will have some effect, a greater effect in feeling young is that the older person starts to focus and think about youth and about their own youthfulness. This will then have its effect on the vibration of the physical body.

---

* Holding grudges and resentment, revenge, and other stressful emotions keep us in a continuous state of bodily and mental readiness to attack or flee. As a consequence, all of the physical and psychological systems, including the adrenal glands, remain overloaded, lose their effectiveness, and are left open to illness, thus accelerating aging. Adrenal dysfunction can cause blood pressure disorders, allergies, rheumatoid arthritis, skin diseases, brain cell injury, etc. The adrenal hormones, in response to the fight and flight syndrome, speed up the heart rate and blood pressure while increasing blood flow to the heart, brain, and skeletal muscles. It slows non-essential body functions, including the immune system, making the natural killer cells less effective, which kill cancer or tumor cells and other infected cells. This may eventually result in breast and other forms of cancer.

E. The Influence of the Etheric Body on Aging

The physical body reflects not only the condition of the psychological self (spirit body) but also that of [1]the etheric body. The physical body is connected closer with the etheric self than with the spirit body and, unlike the spirit body or psyche, receives direct energy from the vital body. When the condition of the etheric body is affected by thoughts, emotions, and desires, it greatly influences the physical body, more quickly than the spirit self is able to affect the body. Because the vital body reacts instantly to the patterns of thought that are projected by the conscious and subconscious mind, it produces an instant result at the etheric level. When, for example, an individual visualizes him/herself as healthy, youthful, and strong, their etheric body becomes that which is visualized. Depending upon the intensity and repetition of the visualization exercise, the etheric body eventually remains in the visualized state (especially when the [2]subconscious adopts it), and the physical body gradually assumes the etheric condition. When someone continually worries about the fear of looking or growing old, he or she visualizes a fear picture of aging (especially when they are in the process of using cosmetics), whereby first the etheric body and, subsequently, the physical body take on the aging characteristics. Those people are thinking of themselves as old through fear. As the years pass, the etheric body slowly yields to the influences of negative emotions and carnal desires, and under their destructive impact, the etheric eventually loses control, and the body grows old.

REMARK: By taking a shower or plunging into a lake or swimming pool, it is most invigorating because the water not only washes the body, but the movement of the water also cleanses the etheric residue or impurities, which one has collected from eating unwholesome foods, negative emotions, and thoughts. These impurities have settled in the outer layers or outer shell of the etheric body, which projects about 3/8 inch beyond the skin of the physical body. After cleansing, you will feel and appear better in a photograph.

NOTE: Because of negative programming by government, science, and the media that everyone is susceptible to disease and that death is the end of all existence, the aging process becomes something to be greatly feared. By believing that wrong concept of the collective consciousness of humanity,

---

[1] See "The Etheric Body".

[2] The subconscious remembers, while our conscious mind has long forgotten. Fortunately, we can retrieve long lost information by contacting our subconscious through the use of an intermediate instrument, like the pendulum, and through hypnosis as another method.

people become what they accept, and like a self-fulfilling prophesy, their physical bodies age rapidly because the low frequency thoughts of "old" send a signal to each cellular structure to slow down, resulting that some people look very old before they are sixty years old. However, when they see their aging process as a chance for growth and opportunity, the cells of the body become strengthened and are less likely to decay.

A reversal of the aging process is possible by using our imaging faculty, by visualizing the body as healthy, vibrant, vigorous, strong, beautiful, and youthful. The body eventually conforms to those images after it first changes at the subtle body level.

Rejuvenation is also possible by listening and "speaking" to the cells of your body, directing them to get rid of toxins within themselves, make repairs, and inform them to stop aging.

By entering a hypnotic state, we can reprogram ourselves through suggestions for the body to function more youthfully. This type of programming should be repeated many times.

There is a booklet called "The Ancient Secret of the Fountain of Youth" by Peter Kelder. It tells an amazing story of Colonel Bradford who was taught the secret of staying young by the monks of Tibet. He was told to do at regular times five exercises, whose purpose was to speed up his chakras or energy centers at rates that are synchronous with each other because when the spinning slows down, the vital force or prana cannot flow properly, and aging occurs.

F. Statistics of Aging and Life Expectancy

The proportion of older people in the population has been steadily increasing in America. In 1776, there were about 50,000 men and women over 65, one of every 50 Americans. By 1900, there were 300,000, one of every 25, and by 1970 there were 20,000,000, or one in every 10. This pattern is known as the graying of America. It is estimated that by the year 2030, one of every 6 Americans will be 65 or older. This includes the first wave of "baby boomers" which will turn 65 in the year 2015.

The average life expectancy in the United States, around 1900, was about 47 years, which was considerably higher than the people in ancient Greece and Rome, whose expected life span was about 22 years. During the past century, [1]thirty years have been added to the human life expectancy (to +/-77 years) in American culture. Life spans are long because of higher living standards, such as better housing, good nutrition, high quality medical care, and public health programs.

According to new projections from the U.S. national institute of aging, by the year 2040, the average life expectancy for American men could rise to as high as 87 years, 17 years longer than in 1989, while American women could reach as high as 92, up from 78. The ranks of oldest old, those 85 and up, increased about 230 percent between 1960 and 1990, while the population as a whole swelled just 39 percent. By 2040, the U.S. census bureau predicts that 1.3 million Americans will be celebrating their 100th birthday. [2]A life expectancy of 120 years is projected for a great number of people born near the 22nd century.

NOTE: We can make a distinction between chronological age (how old someone is by counting years) and biological age (how healthy you are comparable to the norms of the population). For example, a 60 year old man may be just as healthy as when that person was 40 years old, while another of the same age shows body signs of an 80 year old. In the later years, biological age becomes less important than the inner qualities of enthusiasm, confidence, contentment, peace, love, and joy.

The birth rate in industrialized nations is well below 2.1 needed to maintain the national population. As low birth rates continue to deplete the ranks of the young and life expectancies continue to rise, the aging population increases. The developed nations worldwide face a serious senior citizen expansion, supported by fewer and fewer workers. Those countries will be faced with an overwhelming elder care crisis. Can they maintain their standard of living with the graying of their populations?

---

[1] The average life expectancy from birth has increased dramatically in the last century by eliminating infant and childhood mortality and many communicable diseases such as: smallpox, polio, influenza, and pneumonia.

[2] The average life span would be much higher if we eliminate all diseases from the planet, including wars and accidents. It would also be higher if we would not deplete our vital energy during our life. The vital energy takes care of the renewing of the bodily tissues and the recovery of stressful effects on our bodies. Thus, depleted prana or mana strongly influences the aging process.

A look at statistical tables shows that those living in cities die earlier than those in the country. Besides a lower psychic atmosphere, there is a very stressful, competitive, even ruthless consciousness. This is aggravated by the noise and air pollution, which causes many health problems.

George Bernard Shaw said, "I want to find a cemetery where people have lived more than a hundred years. I will move to that village."

A sociological study made of centenarians turned up the interesting fact that keeping busy was the one thing they all had in common. No one should therefore retire in the sense of resignation from a life of usefulness and creativity. Besides, the divine Self likes to be busy and express itself in many ways.

A group of people in Georgia (Russia), India, and other places are known to reach the age far above the upper average age of the people of the world. What they have in common with each other is that they work all their lives. They know that if they stop working, they start dying because their biological system will shut down. When someone says, "I want to be rich, so I don't have to work anymore", they are in fact signing their own early death warrant. In parts of Kashmer, people there are not under a mass hypnosis that 70 or 80 years is old. Many of them easily pass the 100-year mark, and so do tribes near the Caucasus Mountains in Soviet Russia. *China has been known for producing an unusual number of very aged persons, while quite a few Hunza people in the Himalayas also live to a ripe old age. Their drinking water carries an abundant life force or life energy, also called prana, especially spring or mountain water from melted snow. The air they breathe is pure, and along with it, they take in prana or the breath of life to strengthen their etheric body. Most of the foods they eat are home grown fruits and vegetables, which are always fresh and full of life energy. On the other hand, much of the foods eaten by many Western people, which are not used right away, are often stale and contain, thus, little or no life force, especially processed foods. The areas of all the places mentioned above are free of many of the pollutants that affect most people in other parts of the world. The stress factor in those areas is quite low, and the attitudes of those people towards life, their environment, and each other are that of reference. They expect to live long because it is common, and they have not been programmed to believe that they are to live a short life.

---

* The Taoist of China, among whom are to be found a host of centenarians, say that most people use up the second half of life in the first half. They further say that excess emotion, stress, and strain, inordinate ambitions, attachments, and the many other concerns, worries, anxiety, and depression which destroys the tranquility of one's life, slash great slices form the later years. They also believe that a long lifetime contributes to the realization of a person's moral and spiritual development.

The common sense of Benjamin Franklin's "early to bed, early to rise, makes a man healthy, wealthy, and wise" makes sense when considering that the two lowest ethers of the etheric body are most active during the early hours of the night when pranic ether from the sun is strongly present in the physical air. Because the lower ethers act as a battery for recharging the physical body, the restorative power is the greatest before midnight, proving the truth of the old adage "An hour's sleep before midnight is worth two after it." The supply of pranic atoms in the earth's atmosphere is also lower in the winter than in the summer and on cloudy days. For that reason, it may be a good idea for older folks to move to sun states.

The damage inflicted on the physical form by the negative emotion and thinking of the spirit body, which penetrates the body, is sometimes so great that the form cannot be repaired and rebuilt during sleep. After a period of time, the vital or etheric body succumbs to the onslaught of excessive negativity, continual carnal desires, *extravagant sexual encounters, and physical exertion. Those persons always appear tired and their bodies become old too quickly.

The best remedy to keep the body in a state of rejuvenation and regeneration is to live a divine life. The consciousness is then shifted from the spirit body to the Divine Spirit which more easily is able to control the body, the emotions, and desires than the good/evil personality.

NOTE: Women have a greater capacity to receive solar energy than men. They need the greater amount of vital energy for motherhood. They can also use this ability for old age.

G. What Has the Bible to Say about Aging

The psalmist prayed, "The years of our life are threescore and ten †(seventy), or even by reason of strength fourscore; yet their span is but toil and trouble; they are soon gone, and we fly away" (Psalms 90:10).

---

* Overindulgence in sexuality depletes and hastens the aging of the body. When older men and women are still obsessed with sex (when they were young), they have not matured yet. They should be more interested in pursuing worthwhile ideas, creativity, and spiritual development.

† The Israelites believed 70 years to be the normal life span and 120 years the maximum (Gen. 6:3).

At the time this verse was written, only a few people reached the age of seventy, and for most of them, their life was a fruitless toil, in the pursuit of worldly pleasures instead of being diligent in search of Truth and spiritual growth.

"So teach us to number our days that we may get a heart of wisdom" (Psalm 90:12).

Aging can result in the acquisition of wisdom when using our life aright.

"The righteous flourish like the palm tree and grow like a cedar in Lebanon --- they still bring forth fruit in old age, they are ever full of sap and green, to show that the Lord is upright" (Psalms 92:12-15).

In the 71st Psalm, the psalmist expressed one of the fears of old age, the fear of being abandoned. This fear is given voice in the ninth verse:

"Do not cast me off in the time of old age; forsake me not when my strength is spent", and again in verse 17 and 18:

"O God, from my youth thou hast taught me, and I still proclaim thy wondrous deeds. So even to old age and gray hairs, O God, do not forsake me, till I proclaim thy might to all the generations to come."

People should heed the Bible's command: "Honor your father and your mother, that your days may be long in the land which the Lord your God gives you" (Ex. 20:12). And "that it may be well with you and that you may live long on earth" (Eph. 6:3).

Those days will be long, when the children are heeding the advice of the older generation by living in the right way physically, mentally, and spiritually, so that they will live a longer and happier life. And when they get older, they will likewise be honored by their children, as the older traditions of Western civilization and many other cultures are still practicing. We honor parents by treating them with respect and appreciating what they did, in caring for us when we were helpless, and to take care of them whenever they are in need.

Unfortunately, the parent who gave them life, helped them when they were sick, supported them when they were young – is now left alone. "I have my own life to live" is the selfish attitude. Conscientious people should not follow the world trend of discarding old people and filial responsibility, because they have moral and scriptural responsibility toward the elderly. Today, we live in a recurring age in which many have become "lovers of self, lovers of money, proud, arrogant, abusive, disobedient to their parents" --- "lovers of pleasure rather than lovers of God" (2 Tim. 3:2-4; Rom. 1:28-32).

REMARK: Examples of older people in the Bible – Moses was already eighty years old when God entrusted him with the mission of leading the chosen people out of Egypt. Sarah, the wife of Abraham, conceived and delivered a child of God's promise in her old age. John the Baptist was born from Elizabeth and Zacharius, whom were advanced in years (Luk. 1:7, 18). The aged Simeon, who had long awaited the Messiah (Lk. 2:29), held the baby Jesus in his arms in the temple of Jerusalem when Mary and Joseph were to present Him to the Lord. At the temple was also found Anna, a widow of 84, who had the great joy of seeing Jesus (Luk. 2:38).

The Israelites were commanded in Leviticus 19:32, "You shall rise up before the hoary head and honor the face of an old man, and you shall fear (revere) your God."

This means that the elderly should be openly honored to their faces by showing them consideration and appreciation. Respect them by rising up and eagerly listening to their experience, knowledge, and wisdom. The wise have often *learned lessons the hard way. Many have gone through the "school of hard knocks" and through those experiences have learned valuable lessons about handling life's difficult and easy times, and are thus well qualified to teach the young (Job 12:12; 32:7; II Cor. 12:14; Prov. 13:22). Then the "Grandchildren are the crown of the aged, and the glory of sons is their fathers" (Prov. 17:6).

God Himself is revealed in the Bible as the "ancient of days" (Dan. 7:9) whose "hair of his head (is) like pure wool". The Cosmic Christ in Revelation 1:14 is described as "his head and his hair were white as white wool, white as snow".

Solomon said in Proverbs 16:31, "A hoary head (gray or white with age – ancient) is a crown of glory (beauty); (if) it is gained in a righteous life."

---

* What classroom could teach patience better than aging – where can we learn acceptance, peace, faith, harmony, trust, gratitude, humility, vision, and inspiration better than the aging process.

To be the wisest members of society, they should live a life of righteousness, and not lazily spending their days watching uncreative television shows, get themselves excited by gambling and watching too many sporting events, while the rest of their free time is devoted to having a good time in the pursuit of physical pleasures. Others whom are more conscientious and realize that the world is not a good place to live like to spend their time advancing the Kingdom of God, according to their ability and talent and in their special way.

The young man Elihu said in Job 32:8-9 that mere age is not enough. It is not those merely abundant in days, who are wise, nor those that understand what is right, but "the breath of the Almighty that makes him understand", and "Better is a poor and wise youth than an old and foolish king, who will no longer take advice" (Ecclesiastes 4:13).

"The glory of young men is their strength, but the beauty of old men is their gray hair" (Prov. 20:29).

How wonderful it is when young people use their energy, and the older apply their wisdom in pursuing together the way of righteousness.

Gray or white hair is not something to be ashamed of or that needs to be dyed. Younger people are to "rise up" in the presence of the aged, and their advice and counsel are to be sought and heeded. "Hearken to your father who begot you, and do not despise your mother when she is old" (Prov. 23:22).

King Solomon lived up to this proverb and honored his mother when she approached him to make a petition. Solomon had a throne set to the right of his own and listened to what his elderly mother Bathsheba had to say to him (1 Kings 2:19, 20).

The obligation to honor your father and mother does not cease when his or her parents become old. 1 Timothy 5:8 says, "If anyone does not provide for his relatives and especially for his own family, he has disowned the faith and is worse than an unbeliever."

When the elderly have no children or grandchildren whom are willing to help, as part of their religious duty, then it should be the responsibility of the congregation to provide assistance to the needy (1 Tim. 5:4). Paul further advised, "Let the widow be enrolled if she is not less than sixty years of age, having been the wife of one husband; and she must be well attested for her good deeds" (1 Tim. 5:9, 10).

Jesus set the example for us when, as one of his final acts before dying, He arranged for His mother to be cared for (John 19:26, 27).

Apostle Paul showed the value of respecting older men and women in a letter he wrote to the young Titus, "Bid the older men be temperate, serious, sensible, sound in faith, in love, and in steadfastness. Bid the older women likewise to be reverent in behavior, not to be slanderers or slaves to drink; they are to teach what is good, and so train the young women to love their husbands and children" (Titus 2:2-5).

Saint Paul wrote one of his last letters from his prison in Rome to his disciple Timothy. Paul was old, his life had been well spent, and his earthly days were numbered.

"For I am already on the point of being sacrificed; the time of my departure has come. I have fought the good fight, I have finished the race, I have kept the faith. Henceforth, there is laid up for me the crown of righteousness, which the Lord, the righteous judge, will award to me on that Day, and not only to me but also to all who have loved his appearing" (II Tim. 4:6-8).

H. Sayings of the Wise

In order to overcome the fear of aging, we should know the art of living.

Grow old along with me! The best is yet to be, the last of life, for which the first was made (Robert Browning).

To be seventy years young is sometimes far more cheerful and hopeful than to be forty years old (Oliver Wendell Holmes).

Old age has a great sense of calm and freedom. When the passions have relaxed their hold, you have escaped not from one master but form many (Plato, The Republic).

Het is van den ouden man dat men de wysheid leren kan.
It is from the old man that one can learn wisdom (Dutch).

As the devil becomes old he learns to pray and likes to sit under the pulpit (Dutch).

The older the wiser – one is never too old to learn.

More sayings of the ones whom are in their twilight, autumn and sunset years of physical life:

You are only as old as you feel, and as young as you think you are.

When a man retires from life, life retires from him.

The truth is, you don't grow old. When you stop growing, you are old (unity).

Life is a journey, not an arrival.

A person's worth is not to be measured by physical endowment. The body is but an *accessory of the soul (Rabbi Naftali Reich).

NOTE: To replace or compensate the losses on the physical plane of life (finances, physical agility, health and socialization). We should be gaining Christ(ian) virtues, such as: Acceptance, Beauty (harmony and unity), Contentment, Courage, Diligence, Duty(ful), Endurance, Faith(fulness), Freedom, Fruitful(ness) – Victory, Forgiveness, Godliness, Goodness, Happiness, Holiness, Sacredness, Honesty, Honor(able), Noble(ness), Hope, Humility, Joy, Kindness (Gentleness), Love (charity), Mercy, Obedience (loyalty), Overcoming (confidence), Patience (longsuffering), Peace(fulness), Perseverance, Purity, Reverence, Righteous(ness), Sincerity, Steadfast(ness), Stability, Temperance (self-control), Trust(fulness), Trust(worthiness), Reliability, Truthful(ness), Watchfulness, Zeal.

Paul said in II Cor. 4:16, "So we do not lose heart. Though our outer nature is wasting away, our inner nature is being renewed (growing) every day."

We can have God's eternal Spirit unite with our personalities. When this happens to a person, his or her Divine Spirit begins to form and grow into a new creature (II Cor. 5:17; Rom. 7:6; Col. 3:10; Eph. 4:23).

---

* Information is received by the brain via the senses and processed by one's intellect, which is an appendage of the human spirit or soul. Whatever one learns is never lost because it becomes part of the longtime memory of the spirit body, which survives the death of the body.

Een dagje ouder van buiten is een dagje mooier van binnen.
A day older of the outer is a day more beautiful of the inner (TV).

When our outer personality is growing older, our inner personality is becoming ever beautiful and wiser (TV).

I am not getting older, I am getting better.
As I get older, I get better.
I am getting older every day, but I don't get old (G. Burns).

Dad, adding another candle does not make you older –
It just makes your life brighter (Naeran).

There is no need for the golden aged, or the enlightened ones, to worry about the passing years, and to cling to the brief physical life as if it is the only life. We may grow older in body, but our spirit remains ageless in its youthful prime and never stops growing.

The older I get, the younger I feel.
You are always as young as you feel; people never grow old until they think themselves old.

We may sing along with Frank Sinatra, to be always "young at heart".

I. How to Live and What to Do

Of those whom are advanced in years, they may ask the following questions: "How can I create for myself a rewarding old age without worrying too much about housing, health care, and shrinking income? "How will I manage to take care of myself without my helpmate, and will I become a useless burden to my children and relatives? "Can I withstand to be lonely when my family has gone their own way and many of my close friends have died? "Will I be able to adjust to living somewhere else, and what lifestyle should I choose? "Will I be abandoned if I am not able to function physically and mentally?"

All those questions are the so-called "what if" questions, which probably will never happen, and create anxiety and turmoil, even sickness. They are usually asked by people whom are living the life of the good/evil personality, which does not wholly trust God and experience His peace.

We may also ask, "What is the purpose of retirement?" Is it a rest, a vacation, a retreat, a new career, or to find creative outlets for my talents? Is it to fulfill the dream of my youth and to accomplish what I always wanted to do (but never found the time), which will bring fulfillment, purpose, and meaning to life? [1]Have I traced my family tree? What legacy do I like to leave behind to satisfy my deeper longing? How should I grow intellectually and spiritually? As elders, we [2]need to contact an inner source of wisdom, our Spiritual Self or Innermost Elder who, in close connection with the universal Spirit, can guide our personality to do the right thing, or to find "my life's purpose" and, thus, to grow in youthfulness and agelessness. Your purpose may not be earthshaking as that of Brother Lawrence, who rendered service by washing pots and pans.

Many Americans look at retirement as a retreat from their labors and an escape from lifelong responsibilities. However, [3]those whom are more developed quickly find out that they are not meant to be idle, in pursuit of the physical pleasures, or to acquire more possessions. Many elders enroll in college courses to satisfy an [4]inner need for knowledge, to expand their mind by pursuing the philosophies of the ages, while some of them also travel in search for understanding and Truth. Others who have become sensitive to the physical needs of people may help in many ways which are not physically demanding, such as helping the young in their education, sharing information, and offering their skills volunteering in many service organizations, hospitals, nursing homes,

---

[1] The value of knowing your family tree tends to create a sense of continuance, longevity, and responsibility, away from short-sightedness and momentary gratification. They will ask themselves, "What legacy will I leave behind?"

[2] It is very important not to neglect to seek spiritual guidance. We often fail to ask God how we might best use our golden years.

[3] Not all senior citizens get gold watches at retirement, move to sunbelt states, go to casinos, play cards, shuffle board, and bingo. Fortunately as of today, the image of older men and women is changing. Many seniors are delving into artistic expression, and it changes their lives by finding value and meaning in life. They found that creativity (the expression of their divine Self) is no longer the domain of a privileged few. Creativity can be nurtured and new talents can be developed by virtually anyone: by shifting your attention to your creative source, it has a powerful healing effect on your body and is also a way to climb out of the pit of depression. Experimenting and viewing the world in a fresh way delights creative artists of all ages because the divine Self is unique. The creative Spark (divine Self) certainly does not diminish with age, and through the Christ in you, you are made for creative living.

[4] Our human spirit survives physical death, and one's intellect is part of its being. To acquire intellectual knowledge or develop a talent late in physical life will be very useful, not only for the development of the human spirit or inner personality, but also of its use in the afterlife. This is especially true of the development of artistic abilities and other creative skills.

libraries, and schools to name a few. Some of them have stories to tell and express their unique Selves in writing, poetry, painting, music, and many other ways. By fulfilling the needs of others, you feel needed and lose the feelings of hopelessness, depression, and the [5]sense of regret and become happier, healthier, and live longer, more productive lives.

Some older people have become so hardened in their ways that they have lost their original spontaneity. They react to life with old habits and expectations by slavishly following patterns of sameness. Life is dynamic and not static. People who do not want to change cannot grow and are truly aging in their inner and outer aspects, and are old in their attitude and outlook. The cure for this problem is to become more innovative and creative and pursue new interests, while being vibrant, alive, and young at heart. They should be adaptable, renewable, flexible, keep an open mind, and devote themselves to the full reaping of their potentialities. Some of them find great satisfaction in discovering and exploring a whole new world (second), wherein they (as human spirits) will be fully consciously living, after their transition, or when they discard their physical bodies. They should also make friends of all ages so that they will not be left alone when intimate friends die. Besides, being around young people will also renew your own youthful attitude, especially when you communicate with the young and the old who have a zest for life. Those who are young at heart who, through cheerful words, contagious smiles, and confident attitudes, are sowing good seeds, are good examples of rightful living.

NOTE: The scene of grandma sewing in her rocking chair and grandpa dozing with a pipe dangling from his mouth is no longer an image we can remember. However, they are wise enough to know that today's enemy is tomorrow's friend. Grandparents know how to take care of grandchildren by giving unconditional love – they give more attention and are more willing to overlook faults. Grandma seems to know everything about caring for babies and is much needed at the birth of children.

Individuals should make the second half of their life a new and creative period, a spiritual and mystical adventure, instead of giving up and stagnating in their development. God does not see anyone as

---

[5] Because people are born with original sin, they have not only inherited the good characteristics of God (made in His image) but have also inherited the evil qualities of satan (made in his image). By living the life of the good/evil personalities, they do not always live according to God's Will but are also doing, at times, the will of satan, by being inspired by evil spirits and their own evil selves. They therefore make many mistakes for which they feel great regret at the end of their physical lives.

retired. He is always looking for willing and *open channels through which He can work to fulfill His plan and purpose for our lives. This inspiration may come in nudging us gently to write, get artistically involved, or in any other endeavor, so that His Kingdom will be established.

As a student of Truth, discover and explore the inner core of the human spirit, wherein we find the Divine Spirit or Soul (Truth body) who lives in the (third) world of the divine. This quest for Truth is very rewarding and interesting and will imbue you with a sense of wonder. We then become pioneers of divine consciousness.

Those final days in the lives of those whom are living a divine life are the most precious times in spiritual growth, insight, and understanding into the nature of life and are truly the golden years.

J. Spiritual Development in Later Years

There have appeared, in recent years, the following book titles about spiritual development and aging:
"How can I be over the hill when I have not seen the top yet?"
"Miles to go: the spiritual quest of aging" – "Older is better."
"How to keep your youthful vitality after forty" – "The ageless Spirit."
"A journey of self-discovery" – "No wrinkles on the soul."
"I never found that rocking chair" – "Growing older but not old."
"Spiritual maturity in the later years."
These books reflect on the spiritual needs of those who are preparing for retirement, are recently retired, and those whom are in their retirement years.

We should not accept the old concept about life – that we are born, grow up, have children, rear them, decline, and die. We ought to develop Soul qualities, which make life worth living. Growing old is one of the ways the Soul nudges itself to the spiritual aspects of life.

Many people look forward to their retirement years as a life of ease, filled with rest, relaxation, recreation, and a new lifestyle, and perhaps new surroundings and friends. However, if we seek only leisure and

---

* We become open channels when we remove the psychic blockage between God and personality (which obstructs the divine flow), by prayer, meditation, and living a moral life. We should learn to listen to the voice of God within and become more sensitive to the Light and Grace of God and His continual guidance.

external comforts, we soon find our lives dull and unfulfilling. When the newness of retirement wears off, we may feel that something is missing and experience it as an emptiness deep within our being. By living a spiritual life, we discover a whole new world, and that we as a being are growing, not just aging. This growth cannot be seen, but it is experienced as a development in understanding, in peace, in wisdom, and it shows to sensitive people as an expanding aura, radiating Love, Beauty, and Truth.

NOTE: Our years of physical existence can be divided into 12 divisions of 7 years, from which the first half is spent in making a place and mark in the world through study, marriage, and providing for the family. Passing through the midlife to the second half of life, which should be an inward journey, a spiritual search, which is a most enjoyable experience.

From birth to the age of seven, the child's physical nature should receive most attention as the consciousness of the child is on the physical plane, and mastery of the physical aspect is important (as people of the Stone Age). At age seven, about the time of 1st grade, the child's mental self has become active and grown to the point that it can begin to grasp symbolic relationships, such as the written language and simple mathematical functions.

Up to the age of fourteen, not only the intellect but also the development of the emotions is important because the consciousness of the child is largely centered on the emotional plane. At the time of puberty, the body is growing near the peak of development, and as the intellect is saturated with basic knowledge, there is a need to search for spiritual things. The "I AM" or Soul begins to assert itself in the teenage years, which is the norm in the ideal world.

Growing towards the age of about twenty-one, the teacher should appeal to the unfolding of the mind, but they should not neglect the growth of the spiritual dimension. As the lower mind develops, it leads to a stage where the person becomes a thinker, when the higher mental self becomes active around the age of twenty-one and usually does not mature until the later years of life, when the wisdom nature becomes active.

Because many people are busy raising a family and earning a living in their twenties and thirties, their spiritual needs take a backseat to secular responsibilities, that a second chance to grow spiritually comes to them in the time of the midlife crisis.

A third chance to be regenerated comes after they are retired. At that time, older folks are becoming more psychic because the spirit body is loosening itself from the physical body, as a ripe fruit loosens itself from the twig and tree. It also makes the person less bound by physical desires. They may see visions and have vivid dreams (Joel 2:28).

Because we are living in the fallen world, most people have missed the opportunity to become a true child of God in their teenage years or later, while some may have backslid and put God on the shelf, uniting with "the world" (Jn. 14:17), which is good and evil. However, the retirement years are an ideal time to grow not only psychologically but also spiritually. At that time, the elders' interest in the external world and its achievement has been waning. Many are becoming more interested in psychic and spiritual realities and can be more easily pursued to go on a spiritual journey. Some of them discover that feeding the Soul is more important than supplying intellectual nourishment to the human spirit and physical food to the body. They are always looking forward to those holy times when their Soul is being strengthened, renewed, or resurrected. Being in a "state of grace" or in a loving and mutual union with the Lord, they feel more confident than ever that "God loves me and wants to use me as an instrument of peace, just as I am".

People may ask, "Why is it that some persons are already looking old and lifeless when they have not even reached fifty, while others far in their eighties express a liveliness as that of a youthful person?" Of those whom are living the life of the personality, their weak ageless human spirit is much effected by the aging body because it easily surrenders to the passing years of earthly life. This is especially true when the evil self of the personality is leading their life, which is called in Rom. 6:6 [1] "old self" or "old man". On the other hand, for [2]individuals who are living a divine life, their human spirit and body are much influenced by their growing Divine Spirit or Soul. They appear youthful and vigorous because their powerful Soul, which is shining through their body, is always youthful and energetic. People whom have met them are greatly moved by their enthusiasm, joy, and love about life, even when some of them are already in their nineties. They are surely a source of great comfort and inspiration to many people of all walks of life.

---

[1] The personality of a man or woman, which is culturally conditioned according to the standards of the good/evil world, appear in their later stages of life empty, insecure, and miserable. This is especially true when their personality is false and evil. He is seen as a dirty old man and she as an ugly, vicious old woman, also called hag or witch. Their faces and voices are hard, their eyes appear dead, and do not shine any radiance or luster from their inner being.

[2] It is a known fact that saints live above the average life span of the other people in society whom are living the life of the personality.

Youthfulness is an attitude of a mature Soul, which is blind to age, and brings uniqueness, [1]color, and spiritual love and life to the expressing personality. A person who is imbued with youthfulness, advanced in years but "young at heart", may look in the mirror and think, "That gray-haired man/woman with wrinkles cannot be me but someone much older than me." That reflection must be somebody else who looks like me because deep down I feel young, vital, alive, and in possession of Soul qualities, such as contentment, understanding, and patience I did not have when I was young in physical years.

We can thus distinguish between the youth of a certain age bracket, which is not lasting, and the youth consciousness of our real and authentic Self, which always remains with us, here and in the afterlife. When you find yourself in a period of life in which your physical energy and [2]beauty and the drive of youth are about gone, and you experience feelings of despair, hopelessness, and self-pity; the Soul (Christ – Gal. 2:20) will quicken the youthful energies of courage, confidence, and faith. By living the divine life, we feel eternity within ourselves and are forever grateful to our Creator, who made us according to His image and likeness.

K. Causes of Health Problems

Medical research on aging has shown that much of the decline in function associated with age is due to inactivity. The latter causes deterioration in cardiac, circulatory, and respiratory efficiency, muscle strength and flexibility, neuromuscular coordination, *bone and joint integrity, metabolism, immune and elimination function, sensitivity of the senses and brain function, etc. The latter works better by intellectual stimulation, which decreases mental deterioration and memory loss. When the brain is damaged, the human spirit is not able to express its thoughts through the brain, as invisible waves cannot be transformed into sound waves through a damaged radio apparatus.

---

[1] The different emotional expressions add color to one's life.

[2] The beauty of women, which shines from their Soul, is their own doing, while the physical beauty in their youth is given to them.

* Unlike a mechanical gadget, the body improves with use. For example, during weight-bearing exercise, muscles transmit mechanical and bio-electrical signals to the bones, causing them to thicken in response to use, thus preventing arthritis and bone fractures due to osteoporosis.

Besides eating improper foods, circulatory problems are also caused by anger and rage, which causes hypertension (high blood pressure), and it may also be a symbolic indication that the person is not expressing enough love in his/her relationships with others, except for a few people. The hardening of the arteries may be an indication that many older people are so hardened in their ways that they do not want to change. As the physical causes of cancer are well known, other causes may be hopelessness, despair, self-hatred, rejection, confusion, and indulging in lower desires, whereby the cells of the body turn upon each other. Many people today accept the fact that the main cause of stomach ulcer is tension and worrying in an excessive way. A not-so-obvious cause is that the patient is interfering with learning or assimilating his/her earth lessons in order to develop. Some people believe that the underlying cause of arthritis is resentment, bitterness, and unforgiving, and that heart problems have to do with love affairs gone wrong. All those diseases first appear on the etheric body as dark and cloudy patches before they are diagnosed physically. They can be seen by etheric sight.

NOTE: The "diseases of civilization", like cancer, heart disease, and arthritis, are often the result of abuses throughout one's life, such as poor diet, overindulgence, stress, sedentary habits, and lack of physical exercise. Those diseases do not develop all of a sudden but slowly and often undetected over many years. This is also true of diabetes. Taking in too much refined sugar instead of natural sugar (which we find in fruits and vegetables and which digests more easily because it contains enzymes, minerals, and other ingredients) results in the pancreas working in an excessive way to balance the sugar level with insulin. Eventually, it will stop working altogether. Some people say that those who have a problem with the pancreas may be self-indulging in emotional excess or in other areas of negative expression.

Some old folks are told that they suffer of senility when they display disorientation, confusion, forgetfulness, irritability, absent-mindedness, lack of concept of time, and other "irrational behaviors".

Senility, which usually happens in old age, is a general term of mental and physical deterioration, which, in its mental disability, may be called senile dementia, and in its physical disability *Alzheimer's,

---

* The cause(s) of complete mental deterioration, or Alzheimer's disease, are not known. Theories range from aluminum toxicity, viral infection, chronic stress, genetic abnormality, improper function of the pineal and pituitary glands, and premature aging of the brain. The latter may be hastened when one believes that aging is decay and death instead of a portal to a new life and adventure.

or degenerative brain disease.

Impatient physicians and other unqualified health professionals are sometimes quick to diagnose the golden aged of being senile when they only suffer temporarily from reversible behaviors. The latter is usually caused by over-medication, drugs, malnutrition, depression, or loneliness, while certain pain medication tends to cloud their thinking.

Before seniors are transcending to a better life, their mind often goes back and forth between the visible and invisible worlds and are sometimes out of touch with terrestrial vibrations. The people often labeled as senile by the ignorant often lack any concept of time because they are operating on spiritual time. The most sublime and noble individuals do not always realize that they are preparing for their journey in its next destination. They may be staring off into space or may be talking in their sleep, or they see you as a spirit and see through you, and are talking to someone beyond you. They make short visits to the next plane of life by separating themselves from their physical body (as anyone in sleep or by daydreaming), which accounts for periods of forgetfulness and "absent" look and behavior. In primitive societies, old men and women are highly regarded because they bring back glimpses of other realities and have vivid dreams, which the tribe members are eager to hear. Those who were suffering of Alzheimer's and other diseases "wake up" after death and have them no more because it was only a physical deterioration. They will never get old in the afterlife and will never die.

REMARK: The waking conscious mind may recede when people get older. When they have not developed their higher mind, the subconscious mind takes over, which was active during childhood. This results that they become childish in their behavior, thus experiencing second childhood. At that time, not understanding that nature is calling them to make a review of their life, they tell others repeatedly the same stories about their life.

L. Aging Is Normal

The majority of gerontologists believe that aging does not happen because our bodies wear out, but because we are programmed by genetic coding for them to wear out. Even when new body cells are created every seven years (as science tells us), there are only a limited number of times a cell can divide before its descendants age and die. Degeneration begins to set in sometime during the period of maturity and leads to physical decline and inevitable death. The aging process is not a disease but a stage of growth and is necessary in order to become fully aware and established in the greater spirit world, where new opportunities are found for growth. [1]Besides, it would be a great tragedy if the developing human spirit would be confined to a body for eternity. The human spirit and especially the Divine Spirit would then be very limited in their expression. However, in order to quickly grow to maturity by experiencing physical life in all its facets, it is good to live as long as possible in our body, especially when we are living the life of the good and evil personality. In the latter case, learning of valuable earth lessons takes a much longer time than living the life of the good or pure personality, without original sin.

The aging experience, wherein the body undergoes various changes, is going to happen to everyone on earth at different rates because of the gravity, lack of sunshine and fresh air, partaking of excessive alcohol and fatty meats, environment, negative emotions, decreased vitality, radiation, toxins, genetic structure, and programming of individuals. It also takes greater effort of the body system to remove dead cells. In order to live longer, we should have the proper vitamin/mineral intake in one's diet. We should not eat foods that have been de-mineralized and which are poor in [2]enzymes and vitamins, when it has been processed in the so-called food factories. Vitamin and mineral deficiency not only causes degenerative diseases but also gives an appearance of aging by affecting the skin and other body functions. When people have followed the principles of good health throughout their life, they should not die of disease but pass on to the next world naturally, as they would fall asleep.

REMARK: On lower levels of spiritual development, aging can be slowed down considerably. But at higher levels, it is possible, according to some mystics, to raise the vibrations of the physical body to such an extent that it will appear invisible.

---

[1] Because most people do not live their life correctly, if they would get very old it would be too heavy a burden to bear. Death may, therefore, be the greatest gift that the Creator can bestow upon some of us at this time of our evolution.

[2] When people pass the age of fifty, their bodies produce less enzymes, whose function is to break down the food. By absorbing less enzymes by eating processed foods (instead of fresh and living food, such as vegetables), the foods simply lie there. Over a period of time, individuals begin to develop what has been called the "pot belly", or in the case of a woman broad hips or various lower body growth. They should, therefore, take extra enzymes and also vitamins and mineral supplements.

M. The Process of Death Is Similar to the Process of Birth. We Enter This Life by the Gateway of Birth and Pass Out of Physical Sight by the Gateway of Death.

The birthing into or out of life happens in a natural way, and it is therefore no more difficult to let go and be born than it is to let go and die. As in birth, the death process happens in a gradual way. However, the time of labor, as in the death coma, may be of short or long duration. Some infants are born quickly, while the psychic "labor" for some of those departing requires a longer time, while others are able to withdraw quickly from the physical form. They both are leaving the known and entering the unknown by releasing the familiar and secure world, while suspended between the physical and non-physical realms.

In the physical birth process, at the proper time, the infant moves down the birth canal, which passage has become bigger, and through the contractions of the womb, the physical form is born through the generative organs in the outside world. Likewise, the human spirit moves towards the head (the womb or spiritual generative area). The [1]crown energy center (chakra) begins to open and expand, through which the psyche or spirit body ascends or rises to be [2]fully consciously reborn in the world of spirit or afterlife.

When the baby is born, he/she leaves behind the placenta envelope in which it was growing in the mother's womb during pregnancy. With the birth of the spirit body or soul, it likewise needs to leave behind the confining physical body through which it developed during his/her life on earth.

As doctors, nurses, and loved ones await with great expectation the birth of the baby, so do trained spirit workers, deceased family members, and many others meet those in the dead chamber whom are departing earth life. As the infant inhales its first intake of breath and becomes fully alive, the spirit body or soul too takes in its breath of spirit life force. As, at birth, the umbilical cord is cut, through which the infant receives its nourishment, likewise when the physical body dies, "the silver cord is snapped, or the golden bowl is broken, or the pitcher is broken at the fountain" (Ecclesiastes 12:6). The child then

---

[1] Those whom are less developed may depart through one of the lower chakras and also experience a lesser than clear light.

[2] This is also true when one experiences a "near death experience" but not altogether true when one separates from his/her body during sleep.

opens its eyes to the light as the spirit self-experiences the clear light of Christ.

REMARK: The grandparent and grandchild should know each other as they both are, living with one foot in the physical world and the other beyond it.

SUPPLEMENT I

A. The Law of Analogy

The esoteric law of analogy is based on the ancient Hermetic law, which states, "That which is above is like unto that which is below, and that which is below is like unto that which is above." This is also known esoterically as the law or the principle of correspondences. The law was similar to the *Swedenborgian doctrines that every natural reality corresponds to a spiritual reality. This is based on the fact that the spirit body is much like the physical body, living in similar worlds, although of different vibrations. As in heaven, the inner manifestation, so on earth, the outer manifestation, or as within, so without.

Analogy is a link between the outer and inner realities, to connect the physical with the spiritual, and a guide to the understanding of hidden teachings. By acknowledging the known, you would know the unknown, and bring the unknown into relation with the known. By observing nature (a "book" of signs and symbols), and the discoveries made in the field of science, one gets to know the hidden realities of the higher life.

Through analogy, we can arrive at the understanding of the ultimate reality much better than language alone is able to do because words are only a garment, but do not reveal the inner nature of things. It is impossible to explain absolute meanings in relative language and to retain the mystical meaning of mystical teachings. This is a valid reason why sacred teachings and other literary expressions make use of

---

* Emanuel Swedenborg (1688-1772), Swedish mystic, spiritualist, philosopher, theologian, and scientist. He spent the first part of his life in the investigation of physical phenomena as a famous scientist and the latter part of his life in the investigation of psychic and spiritual phenomena. In order to know the unseen world, he traveled to the spirit world, while separating as much as possible from his physical body, and described things he saw in his book "Heaven and Its Wonders and Hell" and other writings. Swedenborgianism was organized in 1783 in London and still exists today as a church. A more recent but excellent book of the life in the spirit world is "Life in the World Unseen" by Anthony Borgia.

figurative language (tropes), such as: analogy, symbols, myths, metaphors, parables, allegories, proverbs (adages), fairy tales, legends, fables, stories, comparing/contrasting, parallels, similes, illusion, imagery (create a vision in words), hyperbole (exaggeration for effect), alliteration (repetition of particular sounds), onomatopoeia (words in imitation of sounds), metonymy (call thing by one of its attributes – The pen is mightier than the sword), irony (meaning is opposite to real meaning), illustration (planting a seed – idea – in the fertile soil of the mind), personification (give human qualities to non-human things), paradox (she gave her last dime, and counted herself rich), etc.

REMARK: Our subconscious often uses dream language and images in order to express more adequately and fully, while our Higher Self (Soul) can only speak in symbols.

The natural world is a secret book of directions and insight at many levels and open to the seer.

The content of a book can be compared with the spirit self, the cover, decoration, and gift-wrappings with the body and clothes.

Great literary masters made ample use of figurative speeches and other literary devices in order to express more vividly and forcefully than by literary statements, and to convey the hidden truth. By adding an extra dimension to their writings, it became more effective and meaningful. The stories of Shakespeare have not only an exoteric but also an esoteric meaning and content, which is perceivable by those who have developed a spiritual cognition or intuitive mind but unrecognized by others. For example, in a passage of Macbeth, William compared life to a candle.

*Symbols are the outer and visible forms of the inner spiritual realities. Myths serve to connect the visible and invisible realities, while metaphor is like a simile, to describe one thing in terms of other things, or comparing things that are unlike (see Luke 12:32; Matt. 24:27). An allegory is like a parable that presents truths under the guise of fictitious description. See Gal. 4:22-24 and Bunyan's "The Pilgrim's Progress".

---

* Symbols are international, cross-cultural, and usually timeless. They can express so much more than mere words. Symbols arise out of a deeper level of human consciousness, and they are the language of dreams, in which the subconscious and super-conscious communicate with the conscious mind.

In every book of sacred writing, there is an outer and inner meaning. For example, we read in Deut. 4:24, "For the Lord your God is a devouring fire." But this is a metaphor. Our God is not a consuming fire in a literal sense. So is there also not a literal "fire of hell unquenchable and eternal" as it is reported in Matthew 18:8, 9 and Mark 9:43, or that the world will be judged by a literal fire, as it is written in Luke 12:49 and 2 Peter 3:12.

Most profound are the parables of Jesus Christ, which were based on everyday experiences, which everyone at that time understood. It is a fictitious narrative from which a moral and spiritual truth can be drawn, and thus convey truth in a more creative and engaging form. By understanding His stories, one may take a step beyond or see a glimpse of the Kingdom of Heaven, which they do not understand. Jesus' parables have been called "heavenly stories with earthly meanings". See Matthew chapter 13.

NOTE: The parables of Jesus leave room for the exercise of the imagination and creativity and find a solution on one's own instead of asking for an explanation. See Mark 4:10.

REMARK: In Christianity, a boat is often portrayed as an image of the church on the sea of adversity: to rescue people from the satanic world and pull them in the boat of salvation, while undergoing persecution from the world or the waters (Rev. 17:15). Some people have dreams that they fall or swim in the water, while others experience life above the impure or good/evil waters in a purified state or clouds. "Behold, he is coming with the clouds" (Rev. 1:7; Mark 14:62; 1 Thes. 4:17). In some passages in the Bible, fire has the meaning of judgment by the Word (Jer. 5:14; 23:29; Luk. 12:49; II Thes. 2:8). It also means the burning out of satanic desires.

B. Other Examples of Analogy – The Body as a House

We can compare the human body with its bone structure and its skin layers – which is waterproof – insulated – self-repairing – with a house with its frame and outer coverings through which the outer door, food enters (as it would through the human mouth). The food is then prepared, chopped, ground, cooked, in the kitchen by persons whom radiate positive vibrations. (As it is being chewed, it becomes like dough.) Passing through an inner gate towards the dining room in which the food is being served to the people gathered there, whom after they bless the food, eat it, unite with each other, feel energetic, and create a high spiritual atmosphere in the house. (As it is going through the throat through the digestive system, being absorbed into the bloodstream and circulated to the [1]cells to create with the inhaled oxygen [2]chemical energy, while the waste products are being immediately removed mainly through the kidneys and lungs.) The house is well ventilated from stale air and the liquid served has passed through the kidney-like filtering system. The food that is not being used is put in long storage, and leftovers of meals are kept for short term in cold storage. (Dissolved food, such as proteins, fats, and carbohydrates are kept in storage as glycogen in the liver for immediate use, and as fat for long term storage.) Food scrapings, such as peelings and cuttings, are put outside the house in garbage cans, which are later removed. (The food that cannot be digested is kept for a while as solid waste in the large intestine and removed by the rectum.) Removal of small amounts of waste in the house, by emptying baskets and trays, can be compared to cleaning out of ears, corners of eyes, nails, etc., and blowing our noses as a vacuum cleaner in an empty cloth or bag.

As we clean our bodies, we should also clean the house, not only externally but also to create order in the rooms of our minds (mental house cleaning) to change our attitudes, habits, to get rid of useless thoughts and negative emotions, such as resentment, bitterness, grudges, and the likes. Otherwise, our spiritual arteries or lifelines to God within may get clogged by emotional scars, old hurts, and unforgiving attitudes. Obstructions may also clot our arteries and veins of the body as it would clog water pipes of the house. To remedy this problem, we should use dissolving agents, such as divine love and forgiveness.

The eyes with their lids can be compared with windows and curtains of the house, which should be clear so that the sunlight will enter the house, or the Light of God will enter our personality. They are also known as the windows of the soul. The eyes are able to make pictures

---

[1] Each of the millions of cells in the body has a life of its own, which it should maintain and preserve. But it must also cooperate with the other cells of a particular organ of which it is a part. Different organs, in turn, should cooperate with each other so that the body as a whole will function smoothly. Similarly, each person in a well-organized community works not only for him or herself but also for the good of the community, which also should be in harmony with other communities, countries, and races. If the cells, organs, and parts do not want to cooperate, they should be treated as a disease.

[2] Chemical energy is created in the cells' power plant, the mitochondria, by food (fuel) breakdown. This energy is also called calories. A man gardening for one hour uses up +/-300 calories. Walking for one hour +/-250 calories, sitting at work +/-90 calories, sleeping +/-62 calories per hour (to raise the temperature of 1 gram of water 1° Celsius takes 1 calorie.

and retain those images in the long-term memory of our subconscious mind. We may keep those mental pictures also for a long time in our short-term memory of our etheric brain, as a snapshot, when we were very much impressed by those images, as a recollection of vivid moments. The eyes also function as a video camera, through which we make movies in full color with two special lenses through which we are able to focus for short and long distances, by changing the opening of the iris of the eye, as that of a diaphragm of a camera. What we see with our lens and cornea is imprinted in the light sensitive photographic plate of the retina and instantly developed in the brain. Furthermore, we are also able to receive visions with our psychic senses.

The central heating and cooling system of the house can be compared to our heart (pump) and blood vessels, whose temperature of 98.6°F (37°C) is regulated and maintained by the hypothalamus, which acts like the thermostat of the house. When the body temperature falls, the blood vessels constrict, and less blood will flow. In the case of the house, more hot water will be pumped through the radiators to keep the house warm. When the body temperature rises because of outside temperature and the burning of the food in the cells, more blood will flow to the skin where sweat glands become active. The evaporation of sweat acts as a cooling system of the body as our modern chilled water and *air conditioning systems in many homes.

REMARK: There are different ways the body can be seen and studied:
> For the physician – a body that is always sick
> For the materialist – it is nothing else but flesh, and it works like a machine
> For the biologist – an organism which is constantly changing
> For the geneticist – as the maintenance of the species
> For the anthropologist – an accumulator of culture
> For the psychiatrist – a house for the personality and spirit
> For the artist – seeing the beauty of the body
> For the poet – a palais of the Soul

The function of our nervous system is to interpret, store, and respond to information received from inside and outside, like our telephone system and computers. It also provides a circuit for nervous or vital energy for the body, as electricity is used for its many purposes in the house. As vital or etheric energy and electricity is all around us and is created by the sun, so is spiritual energy, with its many different

---

* Instead of evaporating water (sweat), liquefied refrigerant is being evaporated, which takes the heat of the surrounding air, thus cooling the area.

vibrations and levels created by God. As we tap into the city power supply, we should also tap into the unlimited spiritual power supply provided by God the Creator.

As the body is able to control itself, it is albeit constantly monitored by the brain, the master control unit. The latter has complete control over the nervous and endocrine systems, with their hormones or chemical messengers. Likewise, the brain is under the control of the spirit mind which, in turn, is under the supervision of the divine mind of a developed person, who is one with God and acts as co-creator.

The body – which is able to repair itself – is constantly trying to defend itself against the invading army of disease-causing bacteria, viruses, and parasites. Our homes – which are always in need of repair – also need to be protected against criminals (bacteria and viruses) by a police force (white blood cells and antibodies) as being part of the immune and repair unit or criminal justice and social system.

We may dig into our garden and borrow an excavator, with its mechanical arm, on which is connected a hoe and loader, which work in a similar fashion as the hand and arm movements. When we, as a personality, have a desire to dig in the ground, this impulse is relayed to the brain, which sends an electrical type of energy via a nerve wire to the voluntary muscles which, like an electromagnet, pull like cables on the bones.

Some people are always nervous and tense, whereby they are using and thus depleting lots of chemical and vital energy because their muscles are constantly being used. In order to recuperate, they should eat food high in energy, relax, rest, and take a deep breath, whereby they fill themselves up not only with air but also with great amounts of vital energy so that they are no longer tired and depressed.

NOTE: We also possess an emergency hormone called adrenaline, which is secreted by two glands at the top of the kidneys and act as an inactive fire alarm box. When the brain sends a message that something dangerous (or exciting) is about to happen, this hormone is squirted into the blood and causes the liver to send more food to the muscle cells, which also need more air to burn faster. The food and air are sent quickly through the blood by a faster beating heart, thus increasing muscular strength and endurance.

REMARK: A rose in the bud in our garden is like a person through whom God cannot yet fully express.

Just as the petals of the flower open up to receive the warmth and light of the sun, so does an individual open up, to receive the love and inspiration of God.

You could import the most expensive tulip bulbs from Holland, but they will never grow into beautiful tulips unless you plant them in enriched soil at the proper season, cultivate and nurture them. Likewise, in order to develop into an enlightened being or genius, he or she should be cultivated in the soil of a well-developed personality during childhood.

Girls are like beautiful flowers. They are then picked (deflowered) and bear fruit (children).

A man without religion is like a house with shades drawn over the windows.

By ironing out your clothes, it may help wanting to iron out your problems.

Illumination comes from above, through the skylight of the mind.

As the exercise strengthens the muscles, so overcoming temptation strengthens the human spirit.

Physical, emotional, and mental relaxation is the first step in praying effectively. When we are tense, the Lord and His forces cannot get through to us – like a water hose with a kink in it.

C. Food for Body and Soul

To grow physically in a proper way, we need the right diet. A well-balanced meal feeds the body with suitable nutrients and vitamins because it is invigorated and sustained by material food. Otherwise, the outer personality becomes weak and dies. (The life of the etheric body, as a part of the physical body, is maintained by proper breathing and living.) We should likewise feed the mind with intellectual thoughts that come from increased self-knowledge because the human spirit is strengthened by what we think (eat) and feel (drink). Otherwise, our inner personalities are expressed as negative, gloomy, and dull instead of radiating confidence, control, peace, and joy. We also need a variety of wholesome spiritual foods, such as Truth and Love of God in order to renew and strengthen our Soul or Divine Spirit. Otherwise, the Soul becomes weak and dies of spiritual starvation and is, thus, no longer able to communicate with God and with divine beings. The special food the Soul needs is to feed it with those Words of God, which apply to one's spiritual development. It can further be strengthened by meditation upon spiritual things, prayer, divine inspiration, and reflection on God. By eating the Word of Truth, we also participate of the Life within those vessels of Truth.

Food, which is taken in the body, however, does not nourish the body unless it is digested, assimilated, and converted into energy in the cells of the body. Similarly, an eagerness to gain knowledge without proper digestion and assimilation causes mental congestion, as one is being burdened with an excess of unassimilated ideas. In order to grow mentally, we should therefore think about what we have read and "cook it" before we speak, and put this knowledge to practical use. There is a saying that nothing has been read until it has been read twelve times and, thus, completely make the words your own. The Soul likewise will not grow unless the Words of God (Truth) are digested and become part of our divine being. We should also be very selective of what we choose to read. Francis Bacon (1561-1626) said, "Some books are to be tasted, others to be swallowed, and a few to be chewed and digested."

REMARK: It has been said, "You are what you eat, what you think, and believe."

We gain knowledge of an object by concentrating and penetrating the inner life of an object with our mind, which after some time will reveal its secrets.

An idea will grow and flourish in our life (as a seedling) when we show interest (like the sun) or it starts withering when we lose interest (as a plant in a dark cellar).

By eating food, we also unite with the Creator, as a male and female unite, by eating the fruit as symbolized by sex.

Many talented people are claimed by satan and made in his image as a homosexual.

D. Comparing Humans with Electrical Lamps

We may compare earthly bodies to shells of electrical light bulbs, which come in various shapes and sizes, and to draw attention may also have beautiful shades. The divine light, hidden within a number of enveloping sheaths or shells of the personality, is like the light in the light bulb. It is part of the electrical circuit or inseparable part of the Universal Mind, which pervades all space and is in all humans. The more one is connected with the Source of all Light and the more one is grown (by increasing the wattage or spiritual capacity), the brighter he/she shines with divine light. However, when one sins, the light will dim. The Light is totally gone when the human spirit and Soul depart from the diseased physical body; the latter no longer radiates its Light and is like a burned-out light bulb.

REMARK: Out of the darkness of sense belief, they came to the light of understanding.

E. Human Beings as Radio and Television Sets, Electromagnets, and Computers

Individuals can be likened to radio or television apparatuses. As we, for example, tune a radio or television to different stations or frequency bands, so we can tune our consciousness to any thought and vision waves in the universe which are within its range. It is, therefore, possible to tune in to different persons or groups of people with our psychic and spiritual senses. Like the sets, the function of the brain is to receive, transform, and strengthen (amplify) impulses (electrical signals) from a mental energy field. They are, however, not the cause of the program, which is still present in the form of light and sound waves, even when the set or brain is turned off or by being unconscious. Besides, the brain, like the plates of a storage battery, is not of any use until it is charged with energy of life and spirit forces. Although the ethers about us are alive with beings of other dimensions, we are not able to hear or see them very well because our psychic senses are not working properly. It is like the sets are somewhat damaged and tuned into static. Today, people can send (by dialing first) and receive messages through their wireless phones as the spirits of humans are capable of sending out thoughts to particular persons (by getting in tune first) and receive them. The human spirits with or without bodies are also capable of sending out visions and receiving psychic pictures.

REMARK: What we have seen with physical eyes can be shown to another by film, and what we have seen spiritually can likewise be shown through visions or dreams or recorded in our memory, which can be played back like a video tape recorder or film.

As the turning of a switch opens the way for electric current to flow, so prayer is the opening up of a channel from the divine to the personality.

We are also able to locate things and persons by tuning in as a method used by radar.

Furthermore, developed human beings can perceive the goodness and evil of another or communities, as x-rays can see if something is internally right or wrong with the human body.

When a magnet is rubbed against a piece of iron, the latter also becomes a magnet. The same is true when a powerful human personality is trying to make another person also strong by "rubbing in" their particular vibrations. The same principle is also true when a highly charged wire will induce electricity in a wire close to it, or that we make our self more powerful (as a magnet) by God-centered thinking. This results that more current (divine energy) will flow through us as an electromagnet. This is especially true when there is a lot of voltage or potential difference between the subject and object. Thus, when we unite, or plug-in to God and the god forces, spiritual energy will flow abundantly.

The computer has an input device (information is typed in via the keyboard) as the brain receives information from the five senses and sends out instructions for actions to the central nervous system, or central processing unit. Those activities are then stored in the short and long term memories of the human instrument or computer. The output device is the screen of the computer and the voice, appearances, and activities the output of human beings. As the body, the "bio-electrical mechanism" is controlled by its computer the brain, the latter is controlled by the mind as the computer is controlled by the programmer. Like the programmer and its computer, the mind works through the brain, but is not the brain. Thus, the brain, like the fanciest computer, is useless unless there is a programmer, an intelligence unit separate and distinct from the computer itself. The mind as a programmer interpenetrates the body as air in water and is able to control the body's brain and nervous systems via the energy centers of the etheric body.

F. Human as Musical Instruments

We can compare the good/evil human personality with a music instrument, which continually needs to be tuned to the perfect tuning fork of Christ; otherwise, it would sound false. As a violin will resonate to another violin, so will a teacher influence others, without much effort, whom are in tune with his being. However, no matter how talented the violinist or pianist (the Higher Self or Soul) is and how inspiring the music, when the instrument (lower self or personality) is out of tune, they will get plenty of discordant sounds and hardly any music. The personality needs, therefore, to be tuned in harmony with the Higher Self or Divine Spirit by meditation and/or other means. They will then no longer waste their time or "spin their wheels" but accomplish great things, which really matter for the sake of Christ. We can further compare a conductor with a corporate, political, or spiritual leader, while the orchestra are the people under their direct care and the music book everyone looks at is the ethical principle, law, and Truth, which are the Words of God. They should also play in tune so that there is harmony among them and the listening audience.

REMARK: For many people, Elvis Presley seems to be alive because his music is still alive and well in the hearts of his fans who continually draw his spirit to the earth plane and themselves.

When inspiration is forgotten, and when there is no spiritual life, humans become mechanical and imitators and are not able to create original work of high quality. He or she may write poetry, compose music, and paint pictures, but they will be lifeless because they are spiritually dead. They may impart psychic life to their creation but not spiritual life.

G. Life as Climbing a Mountain or Joining with the Ocean

Many of the world's stories describe the human experience as a mountain climb to light and understanding or as a flow of water to the sea. For example, one's life can be compared to a drop of water which is conceived on the mountain, join in its downward path, the streams, creeks, rivers, and finally unite with the ocean. We have become part of the whole or have realized our unique divine nature. Those rivers going downstream to the sea may also be interpreted as many *religions going all in the same direction to flow into the Consciousness of the Cosmic.

REMARK: "You shall serve God upon this mountain" (Ex. 3:12). "The mountain of --- Lord shall be --- highest of the mountains" (Isa. 2:2). "He (Jesus) went up on the mountain by himself to pray" (Mt. 14:23). "And led them up a high mountain apart" (Mt. 17:1). "And in the Spirit he carried me away to a great high mountain" (Rev. 21:10).

As a mountain is a lofty state of consciousness, lowlands and wastelands often refer to a low estate in the Bible.

The closer we get to the top of the mountain, the more difficult the climb, and the more unfamiliar the surroundings become. The closer we get to the Truth, the stranger and unknown everything is.

For many people, life is like going down a river where the scenery and signs are continually changing. Some sail lightly and rapidly with the flow of life, while many others are plowing along slowly and heavily laden with psychic burdens. A few individuals even try to row against the stream of evolutionary

---

* World religions can also be likened to the spokes of a wheel, all apart, but at the center, which represents God, they are one.

forces. Of those who have developed their psychic and spiritual vision, they can see far ahead or from above, and are aware that they will encounter, along the way, some rapids and rough water. However, they can easily overcome those psychic obstacles when they have the faith and the love of God in their hearts.

A few others go overland to their destination by train or car, or as a boy and girl scout to find spiritual pathways, while some others reach their spiritual goal in a similar way as when they play golf or some other sport.

➢ A depleted soil is like the physical body, which become old.
➢ As the old earth displays its gorges and ravins, the older human shows its wrinkles.

"Out of his heart shall flow rivers of living water" (Jn. 7:38). "The river of the water of life --- flowing from the throne of God and of the lamb" (Rev. 22:1).

Within ourselves we find a well from which we may draw Truth and knowledge (Isa. 12:3).

So as a wave is not separate from the ocean, so should an individual be aware of his or her connection with God; otherwise he or she experience only a life of separation.

As water droplets in the air are rubbed against each other, they are charged with electricity. When people connect with each other, they are charged with energy. The same is true when molecules or people are squeezed together; they become warmer and move faster.

Just as a body of water will stagnate without any flow, you become dull and sluggish if you do not share your good energy and thought with others. (See also the parable of the talents – Matt. 25:14-30).

H. Some Additional Comparisons of the Physical and Spiritual

The relationship between the Soul and true personality can be likened to a rider and a white horse. The latter represents a lusty way of living not guided by a higher purpose. The personality, as a horse, has limited vision and does not really know who the rider is, but when they ride in harmony, the rider or Soul manifests itself through the personality. The independent rider can direct the horse in the general direction because the horse usually knows what is the best path to follow in the immediate area. This is especially true when the budding

Divine Spirit or Soul is not much developed. In the case of fallen humans, whose personalities are good and evil, the color of the horse is grayish. When the evil part of the personality takes over, the color of the horse is black and will unseat the rider until the good part of the personality is in charge, allowing the rider to direct the personality as a whole. See also Revelation chapter 6.

As we can speak of physical pollution and contagious diseases, we can also speak of spiritual pollution when psychic vibrations are low upon visiting some neighborhoods, in which it has become difficult to breathe the spiritual life force. This may cause us to feel and think like the people there, with or without bodies, and thus become contaminated by them, and walk around with spiritual chains. Having been around spiritually dead people for some time, we need to be cleansed upon our return to our high spiritual surroundings by meditation and prayer.

He reaps either blessings or punishment – every human is his/her own bookkeeper.
We shape buildings – later they shape us (Churchill).
Language is external – poetry is internal expression.
We are growing spiritually when we fly in our dreams.
We are as many threads of one fabric.
We create our own circumstances as the snail uses its own secretion to build its house (Albert Pauchany).

From "14,000 Quips & Quotes" by E.C. McKenzie:

- We fear man so much because we fear God so little.
- God is more interested in inner grace than in outer space.
- The Lord prepares a table for His children, but too many of them are on a diet.
- God often visits us, but most of the time we are not home.
- The person who looks up to God rarely looks down on people.
- No man can be at peace with God without getting into an argument with the devil.
- Some people are willing to serve God but only as His consultant.
- Some people ask the Lord to guide them; then they grasp the steering wheel.
- Two people cannot hate each other if they both love God.
- God cares for people through people.
- Satan is not as black as he is painted. In fact, he is more like us than we care to admit.
- The man who bows humbly before God is sure to walk upright before men.

417

- No man can truly stand erect until he has first bent the knee to God.
- God shocked the world with a babe, not a bomb.

I. Comparing Diamonds with Moral and Spiritual Growth

The most precious things are usually concealed: gold in the mountains, diamonds in the earth, pearls in the oyster, and God within human beings. Diamonds are most likely to be found deep in the ground. It therefore takes a lot of effort to dig through surface layers to get to the precious ore. Thus, unless one diligently looks for the Truth, it will not be found. When it is first mined, it is often a rather rough, dull, and lusterless looking stone as the human being is, likewise, coarse and does not show much brightness at the beginning of its development. They both need to be cut of the rough edges and polished. When all the facets and refinement (with the help of Scripture and Christ – the master gem cutter –) are done, the human person is a valuable and fit jewel to reflect and refract, into many colors, the Light of God. Thus, just as the multifaceted diamond reflects the light of the sun, the different aspects or sides of the person's nature reflect the pure light of God and become a shining light for the inspiration and beauty of others. The mature Soul, like the diamond, has the qualities of hardness and brilliance, is luminous, and radiates light, joy, and serenity through its transparent and pure personality.

REMARK: The teachings of Jesus are like a beautifully cut diamond from many angles. Ideas that come from the Christ are pure, but when they are mixed with human thoughts, they are like rough diamonds, which need to be cut and polished.

The diamond may lose its beauty and brilliance when the light is withdrawn. So individuals may lose spiritual life when, through sin, he or she is less able to receive the Light and Love of God.

As the pebbles on the beach have been rounded and smoothened, so have individuals whom have collided with each other.

When the alchemist mystics said that they were trying to make gold out of base metals by putting the impure metals through the crucible of fire, they were speaking of purifying the human personality.

Just as a rough block of stone does not appear to be anything until it has been transformed by the sculptor, so also our life appears to be uncultivated, immature, and ignorant. We should, therefore, impose order and purpose out of chaos and confusion in our lives (as we do when we create a puzzle), control when there has been immaturity, talent when there has been mediocrity, and poise when there has been doubt and anxiety.

J. The Sun as a Symbol of the Creator

The sun is an atomic energy furnace, which does not seem to burn up and, unlike the moon, gives off its own light and is perceived by the subconscious of the race as the symbol of God the Creator. This magnificent storehouse of heat and light is a good example of the unconditional love of God, which we often take for granted. God is to humans as the sun is to the earth. Without the life-giving heat and light of the sun, the earth will yield nothing. He or she may dig, plow, and sow, but nothing will ripen. Without the sustaining power of God's Love and Truth, the individual will not grow to maturity. As the sun is to plants, so is God the source of spiritual growth for the human species. Because the sun is heat itself, it has light; when you have love, that love produces wisdom. As the sun is not affected negatively by the dirty water it evaporates to change into distilled water, the Divine Spirit can only spiritualize what is materialistic and evil. The rays of sunlight can be greatly reduced through rainy weather conditions, which is analogous to the foggy states of the mind. As clouds can block the effects of the sun, so our subconscious thoughts and beliefs can obstruct the energy of the Higher Self from radiating fully through to our personality. But eventually, the sun will solve or drive away the dampness and clouds as God will come to our rescue and save us from our wrong way of feeling and thinking. We then greatly appreciate the heavenly sun to shine on us after going through the darkness of life.

REMARK: The sun is the most important deliverer of energy on earth, and it reaches us through radiation (light) and heat. The energy of the sun is collected in growing and lifeless plants, which later becomes fossil fuel, such as wood, peat, coal, oil, and gas. These can be used to produce heat and mechanical energy or changed into electrical energy by generators (the electricity can be used to run electric motors). The chemical energy, which is in gasoline, is burned and creates heat to run a motor. People can also produce energy by making use of water and wind power, mirrors, sun batteries, photoelectric cells, and other means.

The sun is a great fountain of light, illuminating all things, producing many varieties of color and shades of light, according to the nature of the object upon which it shines.

The closer the planet is to the sun, the faster it moves (Law of Kepler). The closer one is to the God-centered central figure, the faster he or she moves.

Light does not attack darkness but shines it away.

Life changes as much as the weather, sunny one day and cloudy the next.

Nature blossoms when the sun shines, but it stays alive and does not die when the sun is not so strong in the winter. We are likewise not much alive in the wintertime of our life, when we are not able to receive the Love of God fully.

K. God Is Everywhere

"For what can be known about God is plain to them, because God has shown it to them. Ever since the creation of the world, His invisible nature, namely His eternal power and deity, has been clearly perceived in the things that have been made. So they are without excuse" (Rom. 1:19-20).

"Closer is He than breathing and nearer than hands and feet" (Tennyson).

"God is never more than a prayer away" (has been said).

So as the air is all about us and in us, and we are living in the air, so is God everywhere.

The Creator surrounds the creation, like the sea surrounds the many kinds of fish.

As we can tap the power of electricity, which cannot be seen, so we can draw His power from His invisible presence.

Perfection is when you are able to hear God speak everywhere, through people, nature, and happenings.

Sometimes God makes Himself known in an obvious way by a flash of lightning, the illumination across the mental sky.

By being nice and friendly to someone, you are making this person happy. Then God, who as a Spark resides within that person, will be happy. He, therefore, is not a respecter of persons and would not like to see anyone, in whom He has His dwelling, miserable.

SUPPLEMENT II
What Happens to Us after We Die?

A. Introduction

Many people today whom have been influenced by materialistic ideas (from the womb to the tomb) and whose psychic sensitivity has been dulled do not believe that there is a life after death. On the other hand, increasing numbers of individuals whom are becoming more sensitive believe that humans are more than bodies. They have an extra physical component that is immortal and is called: mind, psyche, soul, or spirit. Those individuals have come to the realization that their inner beings are more than their bodies and that their feelings, desires, thoughts, and hopes are more than matter. Because of this shift of consciousness, the rationalistic and materialistic interpretation of all phenomena, as practiced by most people during and after the *age of Enlightenment, no longer holds sway.

Before the age of Enlightenment, it was considered normal to believe that the atmosphere surrounding the earth was populated by all kinds of spirit beings. This was certainly the conviction of the so-called primitives whom never doubted the reality of the afterlife. Many of them, especially in some Eastern countries, built special shrines for the dead and addressed prayers to their ancestors (ancestor worship), whom they also consulted.

REMARK 1: If there was no fall or separation from God from the beginning, the mortal body should have been of a much finer nature and of a higher frequency than the body we now possess. The body we now use as a vehicle for the expression of our inner self operates in a much slower vibration than our mind or human spirit does. This is especially true of Western people after the Enlightenment and of those that are living a materialistic lifestyle. For example, there is a vast difference between waking consciousness and sleep/dream consciousness and also between living and dying.

---

* This was a philosophical movement of the 18th century characterized by rationalistic thinking and skepticism of religious ideas. Rene Descartes, the French philosopher (1596-1650) who settled in Holland in 1629 to explore the mystery of the mind, did not encounter much opposition when he tried convincing the people at that time of his new understanding that the brain and the mind are dualistic, or separate from each other. However, in 1748, another French philosopher, Offray de Lamette, wrote his book "L'homme Machine". From that time on, the idea that the mind and brain were separate entities became more and more in disfavor. Many orthodox scientists became very skeptic about the existence of a soul and said that the mind was nothing more than the working of the brain, or the product of the brain. Some of them argued that the mind has not been found in the brain and, therefore, does not exist.

REMARK 2: People that live close to nature are generally more psychic than those that live in cities and also those whom have developed the lower intellectual part of their consciousness, which is physically oriented. They have become quite enmeshed in the matter of their body and have, therefore, a hard time accepting psychic phenomena and perceiving spirit entities as primitive people do.

Some of the human spirits were later elevated to the rank of supernatural deities. The [1]Ancient Egyptians went to the extreme by building elaborate tombs and mansions for their surviving "ka's" or ghosts, while the Hindus always have believed that humans are spirits that temporarily live in different bodies until they merge with the supreme God Brahma. The Teutonic (Northern European people) buried, with their dead, drinking vessels and other objects to be used in the "afterlife". They also would earn the right to go to "valhalla" when they died fighting, while North American Indians whom have served their tribes well would go to "the happy hunting grounds". The Ancient Greeks believed that they were either sentenced to the beautiful "Elysium fields" (after crossing the river Styx) or to [2]descend as a wraith or shadowy creature in the gloomy depths, or underworld, of "Hades".

[3]The Hebrews of pre-mosaic times believed that the soul, after death, would live in Sheol (the Hades of the Greeks), which was dim and shadowy, with hardly any conscious life. This belief did not differ greatly from the surrounding nations which consulted with the dead, as Saul later did through the woman of Endor, to talk with the deceased Samuel (1 Sam. 28:3-25). The Israelites, during and after the time of Moses, no longer wanted to communicate with people whom were not conscious, as indicated by Ecclesiastes 9:5: "For the living know that they will die, but the dead know nothing." In contrast, the "Wisdom of Solomon" ridicules those that say there is nothing after death. The Israelites only want to communicate with Yahweh and not with familiar, or non-prophetic spirits. It is, however, true that almost all spirits at that time were evil, and it would do no good to make contact with them. It was therefore forbidden. See Lev. 19:26, 31; 20:6, 27; Deut. 18:10, 11.

---

[1] Many Ancient Egyptians believed that their spirits would eventually return after death and, like Osiris, would inhabit their original physical bodies. They, therefore, preserved their bodies by the process of mummification.

[2] Being physically and philosophically oriented, the Greeks did not worry too much about the afterlife.

[3] The Hebrews did believe in a life after death by saying that such a patriarch "was gathered to his people" (Gen. 35:29; 49:33), or slept with his fathers (1 Kings 11:43).

NOTE: The most dreaded spirits of the dead were those that haunted the earth in search of vital life in order to sustain themselves. They needed the emanations from freshly spilt blood and the waning vital substance of the newly dead. The spirits of the dead were, therefore, propitiated with blood sacrifices, or they committed acts of vampirism. The Bible forbids that people eat meat with blood (1 Sam. 14:34), probably because blood contains the vital element of the animal, which will affect the vital bodies of humans when they absorb the blood, so that they become more animalistic.

Before the event of Jesus Christ, many [1]Jewish people believed in the resurrection of the body, which was demonstrated by Jesus, so that the great fear of the grave no longer held sway. As Apostle Paul indicated in 1 Cor. 15:26, that death is the last enemy to be destroyed, and as he emphasized in 1 Cor. 15:55, "O death, where is thy victory? O death, where is thy sting?"

The early Christians viewed [2]death (of the old self – Rom. 6:6 –) as a transition into a new state of life. They knew that the body would disintegrate, but the Soul, as part of the essence of God, will never die. Thus, the person who is no longer identified with his/her outer and inner personality but with their Soul has indeed conquered death. They also recognize the [3]survival of human spirits as is well documented by

---

[1] At first, the Jews believed that a person survived in the minds and lives of their children and their descendants. At the time of Jesus, the sect of the Pharisees believed in the physical survival after death, while the sect of the Sadducees did not accept the resurrection or a life after death. Because of human evolvement, the Pharisees eventually developed an acceptable standard of good and evil so that those whom had lived a good life were rewarded after death and the evil ones punished.

[2] In the Bible, "death" does not only refer to physical death but also refers to spiritual death (an inner state in the being of the believer), when humans are no longer able to communicate with God.

[3] Wylen E. M. van Yssendyk (1852-1908), reformed Dutch minister and spiritualist, wrote in his book "Het land aan gene zyde" (the land on the other side) that the believers of Jesus would be killed and removed from this earth if the spirits of the female Christian martyrs, such as Potamiena (206 A.D.), Febronia (304 A.D.), and many others gave them the courage to persevere and die for their cause. Yssendyk also said that the world of spirits was first worshipped as the world of gods by the pagans. Later, the Christians feared it as the world of ghosts. Then science denied it as a fantasy world. However, in this century, it was finally revealed as the world it is: a world of people.

REMARK: It is not advisable for good/evil humans to develop (not prematurely force) their psychic senses until after the 3rd Initiation when they are able to have full control over their passion, desires, emotions, and thoughts by their self-conscious will. Good/evil people are further tempted to misuse their psychic powers for selfish purposes by gaining power over others and fulfilling other selfish and immoral needs instead of using them for impersonal service on the altar of service to humanity. Those individuals who practice these indulgences are ignorant, damage themselves and others, and are unfit to wield psychic powers.

the early church fathers.

In the first few centuries, the church as a body was largely composed of informal groups, among whom psychic and mystical phenomena continually happen. Spiritual healing was part of the religious worship, reflecting the examples of Jesus and His Apostles. The early Christians were well aware of the fact that by cultivating a spiritual life, they also awaken and improve their dormant psychic and spiritual senses and their abilities. This is also the belief of psychical researchers today, who say that psychic abilities and powers are natural by-products of the moral and mystical quest. Others believe that those abilities can be developed by anyone and that it is part of the function of normal growth. However, the Yogis, along with the Buddhists, say that one should not attach importance or not take too much notice to psychic skills, or siddhis, because they may become a distraction. In other words, when psychic powers become more important than spiritual development, those practitioners will eventually lose that power. Psychic abilities should, therefore, only be used to help the Soul in its mission and certainly not be used by the evil self of the personality. Some [1]channelers or mediums are being used by their false egos and evil spirits, and many of them do not even believe in God. [2]It is a bad mistake for psychics to use their powers and abilities to exhibit them to the people as a cheap stunt in order to earn money and recognition. They may then have the power but lose the Kingdom and its glory. Only realization and growth of one's Soul or Divine Spirit can give peace and liberation.

---

[1] The difference between spiritualist mediums and new age channelers (started in the 1970s) is that the channelers are not as much interested in relaying mundane messages for private clients but are more interested in giving messages from exalted beings for the good of the whole human race. Some mediums have a great psychic ability but lack spirituality because paranormal abilities have not much to do with spiritual development, which is an increase in one's vibration. There are also mediums whom are not always able to attune to the right kind of vibration or station (like a radio) or between stations. This is especially true when a medium is tired and depleted, as a battery-operated radio. Messages from the spirit world are, therefore, not always accurate. They are also influenced by the channel's personality, its values, and beliefs.

[2] Possession of psychic power is not a sign of high moral character. Development of character is most important. There are fortunately many organizations that train their spiritualists/spiritists, channelers, or mediums to become better communicators. They are often certified and ordained as ministers.

Sensitive people may easily mingle with lower spirit entities that are living close to the earth, such as the earthbound ([3]by playing, for example, with ouija boards or planchette and practicing automatic writing), who demoralize and can even possess them. The person thereby gives permission to use part of his/her body function, and they may soon take all. One should, therefore, be careful and attract only those spirits that are at the same level as you are, or better by drawing higher entities through meditation and prayer. Unfortunately, many fundamental Christians of today believe that all psychic experiences are caused by demons and, thus, deny the many deceased Christian spirits access to their relatives on earth. The church as a whole should accept psychic communication, as the first Christians, and "test the spirits to see whether they are of God" (1 Jn. 4:1), and thus accept its psychic origin. Does the Bible not say in Hebrew 12:1 that "we are surrounded by so great a cloud of witnesses"? The church members should get fully acquainted with spirit life and learn to discern between good and undesirable entities so that they no longer fear them all and lash out at them as they have done and are still doing in foreign mission fields. Thus, by rejecting not only low but also high spiritual beings, they are "throwing out the baby with the bath water".

REMARK: Mediums and their spirit controls cannot be of a high standard when they serve themselves more than others, are too much enmeshed in material life, love notoriety, speak against each other, and reject the Christ of all religions. When the message is only good for the one receiving it and sometimes at the expense of others, flatters the ego of the receiver, appeals to greed and the desire for power, the message may create fear, may conflict with one's ethics, and may demand surrender of one's will.

NOTE 1: The Christian church at first believed in communication with the spirits of the dead because it usually attracted those entities who were at the same level as them. Albeit, later, when the church became well established and old, it strictly forbade communication with the so-called dead because many church members became involved with lower and evil spirits. Some of them even made deals with the dark forces in order to get what they wanted, which is forbidden (Eph. 5:11). It is usually not good to discuss psychic experiences with a fundamental Christian, who is anti-psychic. He or she believes that all psychic and spiritual encounters are caused by demons, deceptive spirits, and

---

[3] It is easy to open our "spiritual pores" to the invasion of evil entities by our carelessness in feeling, thinking, and acting, just as the physical body may, at times, be open to invading germs when the body is tired and, thus, off guard. When someone opens his/her mind to the spiritual realms, he or she will likely get a person who is inclined towards evil. The communicator should therefore be pure in his/her lifestyle, ask for God's protection, and surround oneself with the white light.

satan, to lead us away from God and come under the control of satanic forces. Many people have so much religious fear that they do not dare to think for themselves and are afraid to listen to the Truth, which they may have to accept. This would go against the dogma they have vowed to uphold and obey.

NOTE 2: In Acts 13:6-11, Paul is encountering the false prophet Bar-Jesus, whom he called the "son of the devil". But in the same book, we are told of a good prophet Agabus who accurately predicts a famine (Acts 11:28). Thus, we see here the demonstration of the evil and good side of the same psychic ability.

B. Death Is Not a Tragedy but a Way to a New and Better Life

Because death has caused so much grief, sorrow, despair, and hopelessness, most people do not like to think and speak about dying and life after death. They probably have, therefore, only a vague, fantastic, or unrealistic idea about the after death state. [1]Individuals of orthodox Christian persuasion whom believe that their souls survive death think that heaven is up somewhere and (or) a place of endless worship and adoration of God, by singing psalms and hymns. For others, it is [2]a celestial city with golden streets and pearly gates (Rev. 21:21). Some Christians have the erroneous idea that they would be spending the endless hours of eternity strumming a harp on the edge of some cloud, while others picture it as a place without purpose and action and without anything but endless boredom. It has been reported that many deceased souls were disappointed that they were not to rest unconsciously for eternity. Others believe that the body and soul lie in the grave and sleep in darkness until Judgment Day. Among them, there is a great dislike for death, even when their religion speaks of

---

[1] Followers of orthodox religion usually do not bother finding out where they are going after death because they are usually too busy with material pursuits and would like to leave the destiny of their souls in the hands of someone else. Because they have not prepared themselves for the ultimate journey, there remains deep within them a dread of death and a fear of the unknown. They should, therefore, read and know as much as possible about the place they are going to, like one may read about a foreign country before visiting it. Spiritually mature elders, on the other hand, do not fear death. They have an intuitive knowledge that consciousness continues. They may also have feelings of the presence of others that have died and view death as a gateway to a new lifestyle with ample opportunities for growth. Dying for them is no more than passing from one stage of life to another – from caterpillar to butterfly and blossoms to fruit in one continuation of life, as the resurrection of nature in the spring.

[2] In chapters 21 and 22 of the Book of Revelation, we find a description of this city. It has a wall, gates, foundations, and measurements. There is the Tree of Life and the Throne of God. This city is probably a symbol of the Kingdom of Heaven within and without human beings.

something higher and better than physical life because they also speak of a lower and more frightening existence, even to the point of [3]annihilation.

After someone has dwelt in his or her physical body for a long time, the body has grown old and decrepit and has become unworthy for the life within. [4]When this life or consciousness can no longer function properly through that body, the inner self will leave the body (the life support system) permanently, which results in natural death. This body may also become a hindrance or prison, especially when consciousness has outgrown the limitation of form.

Death is the casting away of a worn-out garment, a house or temple no longer fit for its inhabitants, such as the inner personality, and when grown spiritually also the Divine Spirit, which in turn provides lodging for the Spirit of God. The inner personality or human spirit, with its attributes of intellect, emotion, and will, is the finer body and its equipment we need and already have to exist on the invisible side of life, with its different rate of vibration.

The difference between a living person and a decaying corpse is that the human spirit has left the body, as many people have witnessed and testified by shouting: "He/she is gone." Death is a withdrawal of consciousness from the physical body and its sensation. It is leaving one set of learning experiences to another or the transition of one plane of existence to the next, as a butterfly flies away from its cocoon. As Manly P. Hall of the Los Angeles Philosophical Organization expressed it: The body is like an empty glove from which the hand has been withdrawn, and when we see the empty glove or the empty shells

---

[3] The doctrine of eternal punishment was preached most effectively in the past in order to strike fear in the minds and hearts of would-be evildoers and to keep them in line. Most people today no longer accept this dogma because they cannot accept that God, their heavenly Father and Mother, is capable of condemning people forever in a burning hell. As the Protestant faith believed in the existence of heaven and hell, the Catholics since 1563 (Council of Trent) also believed in a purgatory, wherein the lesser sinners could "burn out" their evil desires, pay their debt, and pass to heaven.

[4] For those people whom are carrying out an important mission on earth, the heavenly forces do their utmost to keep their bodies as long alive as possible. However, when a Soul's life task has been fulfilled, or no further gains can be made through the use of the physical vehicle, the Soul will release its hold on the physical life. Some individuals may tell others that they have accomplished all that they could, and that it would be easier to continue with their work from the invisible realm. A few of them may go through the dying process by being fully conscious.

NOTE: Enoch went to heaven without dying (Gen. 6:24), and Elijah ascended to heaven (II Kings 2:11).

by the side of the sea, we are apt to think that the hand is also dead, or that all life ends at the grave.

Another reason that people fear death is that they refuse to acknowledge that they are a spirit and not a form, which latter is only a vehicle or earth suit. There is thus nothing to fear about death, as when we go to sleep at night. The only difference is that a complete and permanent transference of consciousness takes place at death. Dying itself is [1]painless without any trauma because the "I" or consciousness is not affected by the death of the body, as electrical energy remains unaffected by the worn-out light bulb.

[2]During the process of death, the self or consciousness is transferred from the physical to the spirit body. What was once the subconscious mind becomes the conscious mind of the spirit self. During this transition, the spirit body rearranges itself, and the memory of the physical self, that is, from the vital body, is transferred to the spirit body.

NOTE 1: When we breathe our last breath, the spirit leaves through the top of the head and moves through the portal, or tunnel, to the fourth dimension or the spirit world.

NOTE 2: Anthony Borgia reports in his excellent book "Life in the World Unseen": "I suddenly felt a great urge to rise up – I found that I was actually doing so – turning I then beheld what had taken place. I saw my physical

---

[1] Most people die of natural causes, without any suffering, pain, or disease. Individuals whom are involved in an accident have reported that they remember the approach to the accident but did not actually experience the accident. This indicates that the spirit was capable of removing itself from the body at the time of the impact and that they did not feel any pain until their spirits returned and they woke up or became conscious again. While out of the body, they may also observe the arrival of the ambulance and attempts to revive the body

NOTE: To the uninformed, death seems to be a tragedy, but to those who do not cling to form but identify with spirit, death is life's supreme adventure and a great spiritual experience. Some of the great ones even predict their own death. Jesus said in Luke 23:46, "Father, into thy hands I commit my spirit." Myrtle Fillmore of Unity and Paramahania Yoganando experienced conscious death, while my mother died at my birthday.

[2] According to the insightful book "Cosmo Conception – A Message from Elder Brothers" written by marine engineer and mystic Max Heindel of the Rosicrucian fellowship: In the process of death, the (silver) cord itself is not snapped until the panorama of the past life, contained in the vital body, has been reviewed and etched in the desire body (spirit body). This may take at least three days. The body should therefore not be cremated in that period of time because the vital body is then also destroyed immediately, and any injury to the physical body in that period will be felt by the spirit entity.

body lying lifeless upon its bed, but here was I, the real I, alive and well. I took a last look. Those who were formerly standing around the bed had now withdrawn, and I was able to approach the bed and gaze at myself."

We should not continually mourn when persons whom are dear to our hearts have died. By doing so, we hold them back with our tears and grief, which causes much distress to the deceased and keeps them earthbound. Instead of surrounding them with feelings of unhappiness and depression, they should be embraced with kindly thoughts and prayers. Besides, they are not really gone; they are still alive, and it is possible to make contact with them in our sleep, to hear and see them when we open our psychic senses or communicate with them through a qualified medium. The deceased person, on the other hand, sees and hears the relatives and friends mourning over his/her decaying body. Thereupon, the [1]surviving spirit desperately tries to get in touch with them and tell them that the person they are grieving over is still alive, but they cannot hear and do not respond.

After a [2]short period of rest, in order to break all connections with the physical body, he or she is usually met by close deceased relatives and brothers and sisters in faith. They may also meet with spirits that

---

[1] It is not unusual for the spirit being of a dying or dead person to be seen in a vision or dream by a relative, or that people in their mourning hear voices. Families of soldiers whom are missing in action do not always believe that they are dead – even as they are dead – because they still feel their presence. A child who has died will be well taken care of in the spirit world. They grow up to full man/womanhood and do not (as on earth) deteriorate after maturity but remain in the prime of their lives and will visit his/her family very often. A mother who has died will still watch over her child(ren) like a guardian angel. Thus, much of the sense of grief is removed when spirits make contact with their relatives and vice versa. Apostle Paul said in 1 Thess. 4:13, "But we would not have you ignorant, brethren, concerning those who are asleep, that you may not grieve as others do who have no hope."

[2] A longer period of rest and recuperation is needed when the person cannot be persuaded that he/she has passed over, especially if they have died unexpectedly or want to sleep until the day of general resurrection. Much rest is also needed if the passing has been sudden or violent or extended illness with great suffering.
NOTE 1: Some people have the ability to leave their physical body in full consciousness, travel in the spirit world, talk with people there, and turn back to their body without cessation of consciousness. This is called astral, or "out of the body", travel. To achieve astral projection, lie down, shut your eyes, and relax – then imagine yourself standing up at the foot of the bed and watching your physical form lying there. This visualization should be intensified and sustained until the consciousness moves out of the body and joins the watcher (from esoteric writing).
NOTE 2: A mother who has died may appear to her loved ones for a brief moment and then disappear because it takes a lot of energy to sustain her materialization. In Hades, Odyssius meets the spirit of his mother, but when he tries to hug her, her physical body (materialized spirit body) disintegrates. All that remains is an ethereal shade.

are specially trained to help the newcomer and become adjusted to his or her new way of life. The newly arrived are sometimes so caught up in the discovering of a whole new world that they, after a while, ignore the pulling emotions and thoughts of those whom are left behind on earth.

Death does not change a non-religious person to a religious person or from a sinner into a saint, as some people believe. They are still in possession of the same good/evil temperaments, which are part of their surviving inner personalities. Their personality traits, character, desires, interest, memory, understanding, volition, thoughts, and emotions are still the same, and so are their habits, belief, and disbelief in life after death. They also carry with them their dogmas, false teachings, and other excess baggage into the land of spirit.

The surviving spirits will gravitate to that realm of the spirit world for which they have fitted themselves when living on earth. They will be with people whom are like them and who have the same interests and religious convictions, just as they did when they were in their earth bodies.

C. Extrasensory Perception in Daily Life

We cannot help to be involved in our daily living without some form of "extrasensory perception", or psychic communication. Almost everyone has experienced, or become aware, of subtle feelings and thoughts of others because they are always flowing among people. It helps explain why some people get along well and others instantly dislike one another. The whole field of "outside the limit of sensory perception" has opened up a much greater level of interrelationship. People practicing this art have become more sensitive and knowledgeable of what goes on between individuals beyond their words, actions, or contacts.

[1]In order to become more sensitive to the out-of-range sensory perception of subtle forces, it is certainly helpful to be or live in an area which is conducive to becoming more psychic. Such are the dry electric atmospheres of California and the energy vortices of Sedona, Arizona, which increase one's vibration rate and thus amplify a person's psychic energy. Delphi in Greece is known to be a place that produces a high quantity of negative ions. All those people who stay in those areas become thus more psychic than they normally are. Phases of the moon, sunspot radiation, and other disturbances of the earth magnetic field influence the electromagnetic force field around human bodies, which in turn affects their [2]etheric aura, which has an impact on the nervous system and aura of the human spirit.

Some people try to quicken or stimulate their psychic senses by physical, psychic, and spiritual exercises, drinking wine, special teas, and smoking certain herbs or ingesting psychoactive plants. The Pythia (female medium) at Delphi received her inspiration by inhaling a vapor that rose through a fissure in the earth.

For people whom are not very sensitive, one of the best ways to know others is to look at their eyes or make eye contact because the

---

[1] When a person is fully identified with the body, one is psychically asleep. When one awakens a bit, one begins to sense the existence of subtle things and forces. In their fascination with the unknown, humans get easily trapped because they are not yet able to distinguish between good and evil forces and may easily be led astray. Because humans are good and evil, their evil self may rule their life and their motivation to know as much as possible about this new discovery, thus imposing their will on others and gaining power over them. It will then become black magic. On the other hand, psychic ability has its place when you can help someone with your psychic insight or be sensitive to the needs of others. Furthermore, let psychic power be an outgrowth or part of your spiritual advancement in greater awareness and knowledge. We may ask ourselves, "Does the psychic experience and information lead you toward God or away from Him?" One should also not underestimate the faculty of imagination. It can and will lead you astray into darkness or lead you to the light. Imagination is related to the physical world as well as the spirit world. Daydreams and fantasies, as part of the imaginations, are powerful because they are the genesis or origin of the creation of desirable and undesirable things.

[2] One of the four subdivisions of etheric matter is what is called reflecting ether, which has the ability to photograph, or rather, create a movie and retain those pictures. This is especially true of those intensely charged scenes, such as those of violence or scenes of battle. It has a tendency to play the same event over and over again at the same site.

431

eye reflects the inner self much better than [1]the reading of the external body language can do. The eye is the principal channel of the expression of the spirit in a visible form. The eye appears differently in every change of mind and heart; joy brightens and opens the eye, while grief half closes it and drowns it in tears. Love darts from it like glances, while hatred and anger flash from it like lightning. Devotion raises it, while jealousy and envy squint it and spread its negativity through it. The eye of a good nature, as the mirror of the soul, pours forth light, while the gaze of an impostor exudes hardly any light. Many people are fearful of prolonged eye contact with people who are morally abusive. They certainly do not like to meet an evil person and be affected by the stare or piercing gaze and transmission of evil vibrations or rays of the "evil eye", or the "ice cold" stare of the dead eyes of a killer. On the other hand, some people are able to heal with their eyes, through which passes a powerful invisible radiation, while others have the ability to know another in one flash by looking right through the other.

Those whom are [2]more sensitive and also exercise some psychic abilities should be able to [3]communicate telepathically, which is the

---

[1] Someone who wants to know about another person should not only employ the art of outer and inner body language but should, in addition, be sensitive or psychically oriented and also use the "all-seeing single eye" of his/her Soul (Matt. 6:22 K.J.V.). By looking at and within the person, they will have a more adequate picture of the person investigated. Thus, more than the knowledge, "He does not look like a loser", or "I don't like his looks", or even "I know what you are thinking; it is written all over your face." "You look like you have an honest face", "Evil is written all over their faces", "When I look at you, I swear I see the devil", or "They have an evil mind; you can spot them."

[2] Individuals that are sensitive may also be shy, especially to the vibes of other people. They usually create a psychic protective wall around them, and they do not like people to come in their space and touch them. They are often loners, and it is sometimes difficult to draw them out of their shells and "break the ice" by engaging them in a conversation. Someone who is sensitive may easily become spiritually high but is also more vulnerable to evil influences, thus becoming more quickly depressed than the insensitive people who also have a "thick skin". Because criminals are usually physically oriented, they are therefore not sensitive enough to spot an undercover agent in their midst.

[3] Telepathy is the method of sending and receiving waves of thoughts to and from the other person at subconscious levels. Telepathic communication is faster and more complete than verbal communication because not only one's thought but also one's feeling is conveyed with the message. It is therefore more difficult to lie, cheat, and deceive the other. Another plus about this form of transmission is that no formulation of words is needed to express a thought and (or) emotion.

most simple form of psychic communication among people living on earth. For example, when you and your friend say something at the exact same time or yawn together, when you and another person exchange glances and each of you knew what the other was feeling and thinking. When you are thinking of someone and you meet him or her all of a sudden. When you feel that someone is staring at you, looking around, and see someone eyeing you. Some individuals experience the feeling that they are being watched: "I felt many people's eyes when I walked around in this Japanese town", "I have lots of pull here, in the restaurant, they know me well." A speaker for an audience may experience stage fright when he or she receives the psychic impact of the people. Someone may project a thought of wanting to do harm to you, while another person sends to you an image of you of what he or she thinks you are. As an experiment only, you may fix your gaze on someone, and by projecting a thought, dare that person to look up, turn around, or let that person scratch his/her neck. At a higher level, another person may turn around when you pray for him or her. Two persons may live in the same house and be very much apart in their world of thought, while others whom are in harmony can easily pick up each other's thoughts even though they may be thousands of miles apart and may even consciously communicate.

Another method of communication whereby the whole of the psychic body is involved is that of clair-sentience (for definition, see #35). For example, in everyday expression, a policeman may say, "That is what my gut instinct tells me." "I just have to trust my instincts." Another person may say, "I live by my guts", or "I got a gut feeling that something is wrong with her", or even "The moment I saw your name, I had a hunch, a psychic gut feeling that ---". "I got the impression that that is what he meant." "Why do I get the feeling you are not being straight with me?" "I sense danger out there; I don't know what it is." "It does not feel right, and I don't like it." "I had a strange feeling about those guys; it touched something within me." "Something in my heart just told me." "Something tells me that you just do not follow." "What I say about him is one thing, but what I feel

---

NOTE: Concerning communication with the eye, people say, "You don't have to tell me; your eyes are saying it (that you love me)". Eyes do not lie. They only show the truth. Some people listen with their eyes as well as with their ears, while some fighters have the ability to look into the eyes of their opponents and know when and how they will strike.

REMARK: One may play better golf when the ball follows the psychic direction towards the goal.

about him is another." "It is not what you say; it is how you say it." Another example of the exercise of one's lower intuition is when, by meeting a stranger, you feel an [1]instant liking, a sort of click, or a sudden antipathy, with no valid reason. [2]These irrational reactions are very real and are called "chemistry", to be compatible or incompatible to each other. Girls, whom are usually more feeling oriented than boys, may easily receive the intention of the boys they are dating, while the boys, whom are usually more telepathically inclined, do not always know what she wants. It is certainly possible to love each other without ever having met and to find each other when you are in harmony or when you have a psychic rapport. By having this emotional tie, one is easily influenced by the emotional mood and attitude of the other party. For example, a mother may feel an overwhelming sense of danger and find out later that her daughter, at that moment, was almost killed by a car, while another mother senses when a baby is in trouble and feels pain in her stomach when a child is undergoing abdominal surgery. Thus, through clair-sentience, one is able to sense the mood of a friend or spouse, without resorting to verbal communication.

---

[1] This instant liking can be experienced at many levels. For example, there may, at first, only be a synchronization of physical magnetism between beings. When the physical and emotional converge, this is an animalistic expression, but when their minds are also in tune with the other to some extent, their personalities unite. This we may call chemistry or passion. However, only when their Divine Spirits are also in harmony will it lead to true love because love is of the Spirit. When growing to maturity, they also have to purify of their inherited evil. That is why their affection is often tinged with pride or with selfishness, with jealousy, or some animal passion. Albeit, the time will come that they will love each other with pure affection.

[2] By having a close encounter with another person or group of people, you and their auric fields will usually interact (unless you shield yourself), and you may feel uncomfortable or an instant dislike with the vibratory wavelength of their auras. On the other hand, you may feel comfortable or "hit it off" with that particular person or group. Through those encounters, anyone will be affected to some degree by the electromagnetic energy of the other for a short or long period of time.

> By tuning in to the other's wavelength, much information about that individual can be obtained. This also includes knowledge of which the individual is not consciously aware.
> My enthusiasm influenced the other people so that they also became enthusiastic.
> A room can be charged with either positive or negative vibrations of people who have lived or talked in that space.
> A person lights up the room when he or she walks in or darkens it.
> Communications with the seen or unseen can be broken by talking or conversing with someone else.
> First impression is usually made by intuition and handshake, not by reason.
> A person may get an impression of the content of a letter addressed to him or her.

NOTE 1: As the sound waves cause a sympatic response from those instruments which are attuned to them, thought waves likewise produce a reaction of a human being, who vibrates at the same rate.

NOTE 2: After having talked to somebody, it is difficult to concentrate on other subjects because you are still having communication on the psychic level with that individual.

NOTE 3: At the time of the psychic communication between the sender and receiver, their hearts are beating in rhythm and the electric activity of their brain (brain waves – E.E.G.) follows the same pattern. When their thoughts and emotions are positive, they will effect the brain waves, which in turn affect the immune system (increasing the number of white blood cells) and, thus, the health of the body.

NOTE 4: When you give a command, you not only convey the words and thoughts but also the emotions and the psychic energy that go with them.

NOTE 5: It is known of a famous Russian medium who had the ability to cloud the minds of humans and make seeing eyes blind so that he could get what he wanted. The same feat was accomplished by Brother Andrew, an evangelist of Holland (N.H.), who used this ability in the 1950s, with the help of God, to smuggle Bibles into the countries behind the Iron Curtain in Eastern Europe.

NOTE 6: Have you ever had a "lucky hunch" when wagering or playing cards, or have you ever been "hot" when you were gambling, so that you were filled with confidence and knew that you were going to win? Someone who is "hot" has his/her E.S.P. in working order and can receive impressions of the other players' hands without realizing it or by correctly guessing the cards he or she will receive. They may also have their mind-over-matter turned up by rolling the dice. However, when their E.S.P. high is diminishing or their moon is waning, the player may lose the exhilarating feeling of being hot and "run out of luck".

NOTE 7: Because animals are very sensitive to telepathic communications, some sensitive people have "a way with animals". Some animals are also able to see spirits (see Numbers 22:22-27).

Some people experience "mind travel" while they are awake. They have been so intent on their thinking (like the absent-minded professor) that they lost all contact with the world. "It seems that you were somewhere else", says a friend who tries to catch his/her attention, whereby he/she answers, "I feel that I was thousands of miles away" (while staring into space). There is a saying, "I will be there in spirit", "He is not with me, he is with me in spirit."

Some individuals have a premonition and say: "My human instinct tells me that something is going to happen today." Others may have a dream about some person, place, or event, which they encounter at a later time.

There are many people whom had a déjà vu or "have been there before" experience. It is the feeling of having been some place before or having seen or experienced some event before. This experience may be attributed to the human spirit having been there before or the psychic impression from someone else's experience.

Some having a more scaring experience with the world of spirit say, "Let us get out of here – this place gives me the creeps, hurry up; it is spooky here." "You look like you have seen a ghost."

D. The Meaning of Sleep and Dreams

According to the Readers Digest Dictionary, sleep is "a state or period of reduced physical and nervous activity accompanied by a suspension of voluntary movements and a complete or partial consciousness".

The purpose of sleep is to repair and rebuild the physical organism, especially the brain. It also recharges the etheric body, which has lost much of its energy through negative feeling and thinking, whereby the person easily becomes nervous, irritable, and even sick. Those people whom are living a divine life usually sleep less because they are charged with energy from the higher planes and are much more positive about life. The effect of the above-mentioned rejuvenation is that the human spirit (which does not easily wear out) can more freely work through a better vehicle.

It is important, before going to sleep, to have positive experiments, feelings, and thoughts, especially those of a spiritual content because they will determine the movements of consciousness in the invisible realms of life. It is therefore good to be engaged in doing good deeds and (or) viewing and listening to spiritually enhancing movies and music, read Words of Truth, and, above all, to pray and ask God to guide you in your sojourn in the invisible realms.

The moment we fall asleep, the spirit body, or rather consciousness, [1]disengages temporarily from the physical and etheric bodies but maintains a partial contact with the bodies through the "silver cord" (Eccl. 12:6). The sleeping body appears like an animated corpse, inert and unresponsive, until consciousness returns to the body and restores full contact. While we are in the state of sleep, the [2]spirit body may linger close by to its physical counterpart or may travel to other accessible planes of existence and communicate with its beings. In this journey, we are no longer subject to the limitations of our physical body and truly experience the freedom of the spirit.

NOTE 1: It is a peculiar fact that when the people of the West are awake, the people of the East are asleep.

NOTE 2: Some people have experienced, at the time they are falling asleep, the sensation of dropping. This is caused by the rising and the sudden pulling back of the spirit body to the physical body by disturbing noises or other distress signals.

NOTE 3: Some individuals walk in their sleep. A phenomena that instead of the spirit body traveling, the physical body is moving around without the spirit body is probably caused by a strong desire of the mind to go somewhere, while the autonomous nervous system of the body is not disconnected from the command.

NOTE 4: Scientists have measured different brain waves in the so-called sleep laboratories. They found that Beta waves occur (13 or more cycles per second) when a person is fully conscious. Alpha waves (9 to 11 cycles) occur when an individual is in a relaxed mode, with eyes closed or in meditation. Theta waves arise as an indication that the person is in light sleep, while Delta brain waves of below 4 cycles are a sign that a human being is in a state of deep sleep.

---

[1] There are other conditions under which consciousness (the center of the human being) for a while abandons the body because it is unable to function through a disabled organ, such as, for example, injury to the brain, fever, fainting spells, mental shock, sudden fright, and other infirmities. When the person recuperates, consciousness returns in its wholeness and the individual is no longer unconscious. An incomplete transfer of consciousness occurs when we fall asleep; a complete transfer occurs when we die.

[2] The spirit body of an undeveloped person appears like a wreath of mist, and it is not able to move far from its physical body. A more developed person can use the sleeping time to learn about the life of the spirit, get more educated by attending seminars, and help unfortunate spirits with or without physical bodies to find their way towards the Light. This is also a good time to meet loved ones and friends who have died!

437

REMARK: Some esoteric minded individuals believe that through sleep osmosis, the material of a book can be absorbed by putting it under a pillow at night.

➢ A few of them are able to send telepathic messengers to those whom are sleeping and influence the content of their dreams.
➢ It is known that some Babylonians, Greeks, and Romans slept at times in temples to receive important decisions and instructions through dreams.
➢ It is possible that the spirits of individuals can meet with each other in an agreed place while they are sleeping.
➢ Artists, musicians, and writers have often created wonderful works of art based on dreams, and scientists, inventors, and philosophers have received ideas through a dream state.

When we enter in a sound sleep, the facts of dream life seem to be very real, but when we wake up, our conscious life is real, and the dream state is merely our own subjective thoughts. When we go out of the waking physical consciousness, we experience the spirit world as more authentic and concrete, of a higher energy than that of the physical world, which appears like a mist or shadow. We may say that people are leading a double life: living an ordinary life during the day and a quite different one during the night. When waking up from a dream, which seems to be so vivid and real, we may not know for a while who we are and where we are. The memory of the life in the spirit world becomes more vague, and then we may say, "Oh, it was just a dream." See also Psalms 73:20. However, to the spirits with whom we have socialized, we have fallen asleep by living in full consciousness in the physical world again. During sleep, the body and spirit naturally separate from each other and are no longer in alignment or coincidence. This is also the condition, to a lesser degree, of an infant, the very old, and the ill. It also happens to someone who is daydreaming, takes drugs, or drinks alcoholic beverages. Everything physical becomes a blur, indistinct, or out of focus because the individual is entering the "twilight zone" or a different dimension where time and space are no longer the same.

¹Dream messages are usually expressed as symbols rather than thoughts or words because so much more, and correctly, can be told by

---

¹ The study of dreams, that is from the subconscious level of the mind, has been readily accepted by the scientific community. Erich Fromm, the psychologist, said, "I believe that symbolic language is the one foreign language that each one must learn. Its understanding brings us in touch with one of the most significant sources of wisdom. Those dreams and myths are important communication from ourselves to ourselves."

a single symbolic image (see also Eccl. 5:3). This is the method of communication of the subconscious (the mind of the human spirit) and the Higher Mind (the mind of the Divine Spirit). This is especially of value when the conscious self does not have the ability to talk to its inner selves directly. Albeit, these visual symbols often require interpretation, such as an answer to a question is given, a warning of something about to happen, a prediction of the future, or making someone aware that they are doing something wrong, or a symbolic "printout" of a day's events, feelings, and thoughts. For those whom are in the process of growing spiritually, a dream of dying may mean that they are dying to the good/evil way of life and starting a divine life as a spiritual child. A dream of flying or climbing a mountain is usually a sign that someone is growing spiritually, while sinking in the water is an indication that he or she is backsliding to the good/evil world. Because each one of us has our own special dream language, we are therefore our best interpreters. When we do not know the meaning, we should ask God who lives within our being, and He always knows what is going on.

NOTE 1: One of those rare dreams is the so-called "lucid dream", in which the conscious mind is aware that it is dreaming. The individual can then change or interact with the dream while remaining asleep.

NOTE 2: There are also the often-occurring confused dreams, which may be the result of a day's events or a recapitulation of several related experiences, or a manifestation of some contents of the subconscious mind. Some of those bewildering dreams may also be caused by external stimulation, especially when one is in the process of waking up. Those dreams are the result of brain and etheric brain activities, and they also may happen when one sleeps too lightly, whereby consciousness has not been completely withdrawn from the body, as in sound and deep sleep.

NOTE 3: Life in the spirit world is more noted by events, happenings, and cycles. Those events in the dream experience can, for example, take place in a very short time, in what may have taken much longer in earth time.

REMARKS: For those whom are active in spiritual work, they may not always feel as "high" when they wake up as the day before. This is because at night in their sleep state, the higher selves separate from their physical bodies, and it takes a while before they are in alignment with their bodies again. In the meantime, through prayer, a channel is provided, through which the Spirit of God can work once more.

➤ Our environment, such as the room we live in and the bed we sleep in, is comfortable to us, and it is saturated with the vibration of our aura. The same is also true of the favorite toy or blanket of a child, who feels recharged by its own energy, by holding it or snuggling with it. It is therefore difficult for many people to sleep in strange beds and stay in strange rooms that are imbued with the magnetism of previous occupants, especially if they are of a low quality. The psychic atmosphere in the room and the radiation of the bed and bedding will also effect the dreams they will have.

➤ The material forms, such as that of walls of buildings, cars, buses, trains, ships, and airplanes have to get used to the vibration of the people occupying those objects and also of the vibration among the people and other objects before any measure of harmony is created.

[1]Not many people are able to bring back to memory the visits they have made to the land of the living dead, except some distorted images, because the spirit self is not able to make sufficient impression upon the waking consciousness. This is certainly true of people whom are not much developed and who do not move around much in the spirit realm or land of spirits. Another reason why we are not always conscious of our out-of-the-body experiences is that there is a barrier, an [2]etheric web, between the psychic and the physical in one's being. This boundary is experienced as a moment of unconsciousness between sleeping and waking. Without this protective web, the conscious mind and the brain will be too much influenced and impacted by the impressions and vibrations coming from the subconscious realms of life. It would, therefore, be difficult to live a proper physical life. Although spirit journeys are not always recorded in our conscious memory, they certainly are registered in our subconscious and super-conscious minds. Upon passing over, we will then recognize scenes and individuals on our visits during the slumber, or sleep condition.

God has spoken frequently to His people through clear and vivid dreams and [3]visions, as received in the Holy Scriptures of all nations. As recorded in the sacred writings of the Jews and Christians, God's servants received direct [4]communication from God or from an angel of

---

[1] One method of remembering dreams is to give suggestions to our subconscious mind before going to sleep.

[2] This web can be damaged by emotional trauma, alcohol, or drugs, which may result in delirium tremens and insanity.

[3] Visions perceived when awake would be shown as dreams when asleep.

[4] Communication by dreams is also used by low and evil spirits. See Jer. 29:8, 9; Zech. 10:2. Besides dreams, God also uses the Urim/Thummim and prophets to communi-cate with humans. See 1 Sam. 28:6; 1 Sam. 14:41; Ex. 28:30; Num. 27:21; Ezra 2:63.

God. As God said in Numbers 12:6: "I the Lord make myself known to him in a vision, I speak with him in a dream", and "let the prophet who has a dream tell the dream" (Jer. 23:28).

Some of the dreams were used to warn God's servants of danger – see the account in Matthew chapter 2, where Joseph was warned to flee to Egypt with Mary and Jesus because Herod wanted to kill the Baby Jesus. Later in another dream, Joseph received the message to return to Israel. At other times, visions and dreams were given as a source of encouragement – see Judges 7:13-15 and Acts 18:9. God came to Abimelech in a dream and told him not to take Sarah, the wife of Abraham (Gen. 20:3-7). In Genesis 28:12, Jacob had a dream of a ladder going up to heaven and received the promise that his descendants would be blessed and would return to the land (see verses 12-15). The angel of God told Jacob in a dream all the wrong Laban was doing to him (Gen. 31:11-13). Thereafter in verse 24, God came to Laban in a dream, not to say a good or bad word to Jacob. Joseph, the son of Jacob, received the prophetic dream of his brother's sheaves of wheat bowing down to his sheaf (Gen. 37:5-7). Another prophetic dream was told to Pharaoh that the fat ears of corn were being consumed by lean ones and that fat cows were being eaten by thin ones. This dream was interpreted by Joseph (Gen. Ch. 41), as he interpreted earlier the dreams of the butler and chief baker (Gen. Ch. 40). The story of Christ's birth revolves much around dreams and visions. During Jesus' persecution, the wife of Pilate was troubled in a dream and told her husband to "have nothing to do with that righteous man" (Matt. 27:19). Joel 2:28 and Acts 2:17 speak about the time that "old men shall dream dreams, and your young men shall see visions". In 1 Kings 3:5, the Lord appeared to Solomon in a dream. Job 33:15-18 says that God uses dreams and visions to warn and protect those whom are about to commit an evil deed. Finally, there are the many dreams and visions that Daniel received and the vision that John the Apostle was given directly from the Cosmic Christ, as recorded in the Book of Revelation.

NOTE 1: During our travel in the spirit world, we not only meet individuals but also encounter many emotional/thought forms.

NOTE 2: The subconscious is not only expressed through the psychic and physical senses but also through the aid of a pendulum or divining rod.

NOTE 3: Some highly developed people are able, on their return from their psychic trip, to enter their physical self without loss of consciousness and, thus, also not of memory.

NOTE 4: On some occasions, dreams may also be necessary because the conscious mind cannot give all the information.

REMARK: Abraham Lincoln, who was much worried in April 1865 about the Civil War, went to bed and fell asleep. The President experienced a strange dream by which he was much troubled. In his dream (as he told his wife and friends) while he was asleep in his room in the White House, he was awakened by the sound of subdued sobbing. In the dream state, Lincoln got up, followed the weeping sound, and found himself in the East Room. Then he saw people filing past a raised structure (a cata falgue), on which a coffin rested with a corpse wrapped in funeral vestment. It was guarded by soldiers. Throngs of men and women were paying their last respects to the body laid in state. Lincoln could not see the face of the corpse from where he was, but he could tell that those present were deeply affected by the individual's death. After watching for a while, he approached one of the soldiers and requested to know who had died. "The President. He was killed by an assassin." Two days later on April 14, the dream became a reality. Lincoln was shot by John Wilkes Booth in a theater.

This cyclic event repeated itself in 1963 when President Kennedy was shot by Lee Harvey Oswald. There were many similarities of those two events. They both were involved in equal rights for the black. Both were warned by psychics that they might be killed – both murders happened on Friday – both were shot in the head, witnessed by their wives. Both had Vice-Presidents by the name of Johnson. Kennedy had a secretary whose name was Lincoln, and Lincoln's secretary was named Kennedy. Both presidents married in their thirties with a 24-year-old French-speaking brunette. Both families lost two children. Booth, as well as Oswald, was killed before trial. One assassin was born in 1839 and the other in 1939, and their names consisted of 15 letters.

E. Evidences of Life after Life

Researchers from the fields of psychics, psychology, anthropology, and psychiatry concluded that three areas of research provide strong evidence of survival. The first they mention is the near-death experience because of accurate observation of medical operating procedures by clinically dead patients (see a later explanation). Reincarnation was also cited as proof for survival because it was based on examples of children whom are accounting previous lives (from the memory of those whom are deceased and lived those lives). Mediumship (channeling) was also noted as a strong proof of survival because the messages the mediums give can often be verified.

Another proof of the existence of people living in another world is that a female medium, in a sitting, suddenly begins to speak in a deep male voice. Her gestures and facial expression become that of the spirit expressing through her. She may speak of matters beyond her normal interests and sometimes in a strange language, and in a manner quite different to her character. For example, when the male Set spoke through Jane Roberts, her facial features changed dramatically and her voice changed to the deep baritone voice of Set with a slight European accent. In a well-documented report and video, an ancient spirit is shown who called himself Ramtha, who often spoke and expressed himself while walking among the audience through an ordinary housewife, J.C. Knight, expounding the wisdom of the world. Ancient Egyptians also have guided and taught through Earlyne Chaney of the Astara organization.

A less solid proof of people who survived death is that the latter have contacted their relatives or friends on earth in dreams and have given them detailed information that only the dead person could have known.

Another attempt to communicate with the beyond, which has been going on for years, is through electronic devices, such as radios, television sets, computers, telephones, tape recordings, and video cameras. After much trial and error, it has produced some remarkable results and is well documented by many scientists in many parts of the world.

Most realities that exist in the universe are beyond the range of the five physical senses, although some of them can be perceived by extending the human senses with the aid of scientific instruments. For example, science has discovered many invisible rays, such as the longer infrared waves (heat) and the shorter ultraviolet and x-rays, which can be photographed with special plates or films sensitive to the light of those rays.

THE ELECTROMAGNETIC SPECTRUM

violet	indigo	blue	green	yellow	orange	red

White Light Broken Down
In Seven Colors

Unknown	Cosmic rays	Gamma rays	X-rays	Ultraviolet rays	Infrared rays	Radar	Television	Short radio waves	Long radio waves	Ultrasound	Audible sound for humans	Touch

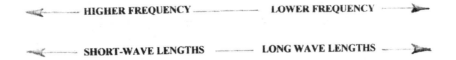

They further discovered the existence of gamma rays, cosmic rays, radar, high and low frequency sound vibration, radio and television waves, etc.

Humans can only see within a very small segment of the electromagnetic spectrum, which is called visible light. Light waves that are too short to be perceived by their retinas are called "ultraviolet", and those that are too long "infrared". The human ear can hear within a greater part of the spectrum from +/-16 to +/-20,000 vibrations per second but is also limited. Thus, a great number of vibrations of sound and sight fall outside the range of our senses and are lost to us. In a universal sense, we are practically unconscious, or "blind and deaf", to the super physical realms.

Many animals hear sound beyond the range of the human ear, can see further, and have a keener sense of *smell than humans. For instance, cats can see to a greater extent in the infrared spectrum and find their way in darkness, while dogs have a sense of hearing that goes +/-50% beyond the range of humans. Some insects see ultraviolet rays.

NOTE 1: It is not a coincidence that the Americans in the time of the Revolutionary War had blue coat uniforms, while the English, whom were more coarse-minded, wore red coats. We also start off the week of 7 days with the rising color of red.

NOTE 2: By applying heat to a solid block of ice, we raise the vibration of the matter, and it becomes a liquid. By applying more heat, we raise the vibration of the water to such a rate that it becomes invisible to the eye; then we have a gas or steam. Consciousness also exists, even when we no longer see it.

---

* As our sense of touch is related to solid forms, so is the sense of taste with forms in a liquid state and the sense of smell to matter in a gaseous state. However, the senses of hearing and sight are not only related to form but also contribute to the development of mind and Soul.

NOTE 3: Einstein proved through his formula $E=MC^2$ (energy = matter) that there is no such thing as a material physical universe, that all is energy vibrating at different speeds. That which is vibrating at low speed is called physical, which is a slower, denser form of energy. Thus, the matter of which our bodies are composed "disappears" into nothing more than waves or vibrations. That which lives within, or rather penetrates the energy body, is the higher, less dense form of energy called psyche, soul, or spirit, which fluctuates with a higher vibration. When matter is raised in vibration, it becomes light, which in turn becomes thought and then becomes the Love of God. Thus, all of life, physical or spiritual, is in a constant state of vibration, operating at various rates and manifesting as thought – emotion – spirit – light, rays, colors, electrical energy, voice (singing, sounds, music, etc.). However, in order to live properly, our body and spirit should be of the same vibrations as their surroundings.

NOTE 4: When belonging to a certain group of people, you vibrate like the rest of them. If you do not, then anyone in the group will sense that you are not one of them. The same vibrations can be induced by thinking the same way – learning the same truth and have the same worldview.

NOTE 5: As the voice of an individual is known to have shattered glass and the power of rhythmic vibration of soldiers marching over a bridge could make the structure collapse, the walls of Jericho fell at the 7th day at the combined vibration of trumpets and the shouts of the people. See Joshua 6th Chapter.

When we find a person who can see a great deal further on both ends of the spectrum, we have someone who, by using his/her "sixth" or extrasensory ability, responds to more vibrations and hears and sees much more. Thus, as outer science has developed its instruments to perceive more, inner science has worked to develop the observer.

As one cannot see radio and television waves that vibrate at too fast a rate, so one cannot see the vibrations or waves of the world beyond. As waves are around and about us and even go right through solid matter, so are the vibrations of the spirit side of life all around us, and material objects do not hinder their passage. By tuning our radio or television sets, which are in good working order, we can "hear and see" those waves as an [1]attuned sensitive can pick up the vibration or waves of the invisible world of spirit and translate it into a message and vision from spirit beings. Thus, the invisible world of waves and spirit become visible through sound and sight. As the above-mentioned

---

[1] Some of those sensitives or instruments are able to pick up only one frequency, while others can adjust the tuning to various senders.

waves are in and about us, so is the presence of God, which can easily be reached by fine tuning ourselves by [2]prayer and meditation.

According to the proceedings of the society of psychical research, there are many cases on record that a person who is separated from his/her body, either in sleep, in trance, [3] "out of the body", and "near death experience", can still think without the brain. They can also observe, see, feel, and love without the physical body. This proves without a doubt that [4]the real person is much more than the brain and body because he or she, as spirit, can exist apart from the body. The latter is, therefore, no more than a vehicle or robot to be used by the human spirit as the thinker, pilot, or guide in order to function and develop in the three-dimensional or terrestrial world.

NOTE 1: All those people whom are taking time to investigate psychic phenomena will sooner or later be convinced of its reality. Those whom are skeptical should no longer consider themselves properly educated.

NOTE 2: To make more easily contact with the spirit world, it may be necessary for individuals to speed up the vibrations of their spirit bodies, while spirits can lower their vibration. This can be done by thought.

NOTE 3: Because our galaxy is moving into a new and more active area of space, causing the vibration rate of humans to increase, the result is that time is speeding up so that last month seems to be yesterday.

---

[2] Through prayer and meditation, we raise our vibration by meeting with the highest vibration force in the universe. The more we exercise, the stronger the vibration and the more we would miss the time of prayer or communication with our God. To a lesser degree, we may achieve higher states of consciousness by repeating a special sound vibration, "the mantra". Music of high vibration quality will likewise raise the vibration of our being.

[3] When someone travels outside his/her body, he or she may see scenes and communicate with spirits, come back and give a report, after animating his or her body.

[4] Because men and women of science are not able to perceive the unseen world with their physical senses, they presume that it does not exist. Although they readily admit that the telescope, microscope (invented by Anton van Leeuwenhoek – d. 1723 –, Dutch naturalist), and various other electronic instruments have revealed whole universes of life. Some orthodox scientists say that the human brain differs little from an animal brain. This may be true concerning the gray matter of the brain, and it is also true that humans and animals have both etheric bodies and lower spirit (astral) bodies. However, it is certainly not true of an intellectual, especially of a spiritually developed human being. They acquire knowledge, reason, distinguish between good and evil, and have a sense of spiritual values and ability to communicate with God (see 1 Cor. 2:14). As angels only know the spiritual realm and the animals only the earth, humans stand erect, with their heads toward the highest heaven and their feet toward the earth. Thus, they form a link between heaven and earth and live simultaneously in both worlds.

NOTE 4: The physical senses may work in the following manner. When a vibration is received on the band of one of the five senses, it is converted into an electrical impulse in the nervous system and then conveyed to the brain and consciousness for interpretation.

Our bodily physique, with its center in the brain, is an instrument of the spirit. This is very obvious when we communicate with a human being. It is not as much the physical body that impresses and captures us but more the essence of the other, the unseen personality. It is the inner expression behind the eyes that you love, which makes the body work and make itself known in a radiance and flickering of the eyes, in the melodious voice, in facial expressions, in touch, and behavior.

When a person dies, the life goes out of the person, the eyes are lifeless and need to be closed, and the *psychic aura is no longer seen around a dead person when the spirit leaves the body. This perfectly formed body, which is composed of about 70 cents of chemical elements, has no power because without its life energy, it never had any power. The physical body may be complete in all its organs, systems, and elements, but without the etheric or vital body, it has no power of animation and is not able to give life to the nervous system. Without the spirit body, the physical and etheric bodies are helpless, heartless, and thoughtless things. Though the body has a brain, it cannot think.

---

* The aura is an energy field that surrounds all matter because particles of atoms are in constant movement and radiating their electrical and magnetic vibrations. This is especially true of animate forms because the atoms are more vibrant than those of inanimate matter. Generally speaking, any vibration field emitted by one thing affects the vibration fields of other things.

As material objects, such as a magnet and the earth, have some extended influence or field about them, so have the living physical and etheric bodies of humans, which are called the electromagnetic and etheric body aura. The size of the aura of the spirit body is much greater, especially when the Divine Spirit is in charge of the personality. The rate of energy vibration is also much greater, which in turn is dictated by the quality of feeling and thought. This aura can be felt by another person over a distance of many feet when they are in the same space together, even when they are separated by a wall. But the aura is hardly noticeable when the other person goes to sleep. When the individual is alone in a house, or when the other sleeps, there is an awareness of isolation and emptiness. This certainly is a strong indication that the field of energy comes from the spirit and, thus, only operates when the spirit is present. As the saying goes, "He/she lights up the room when he/she walks in."

As the human spirit is more extensive than the brain, like the extended range of the cellular phone, many psychic phenomena make sense, such as telepathy, sensing another person looking at you from behind your back, what someone is thinking about you, hunches, etc. This all happens when tuning in to higher frequencies than the ordinary vibrations used for communication.

Though the body is in possession of lips and tongue, it is not able to speak, and the muscles are likewise not able to move without their operator, the human spirit. It has organs of sense but cannot use them because it is not the body that hears and sees, but it is the human spirit working through the body. And, without the Divine Spirit, the above-mentioned bodies are not able to express divine Love and other beautiful qualities.

NOTE: Science recognizes that the living physical body has energy fields, such as electromagnetic, light, heat, and sound. They also know that electrons surround the central nucleus of the [†]atom, which is made up of protons and neutrons, which in turn is made up of smaller particles called quarks. We may compare protons and neutrons which are held together by the nuclear force as the Sun or parents, of which the latter are connected with a strong bond of love and should not be split. The quarks probably show that the nucleus also has an etheric dimension. The spinning electrons, which are more loosely connected, can be compared with planets and children, whom are constantly moving. As the nucleus has a positive electrical charge, electrons have a negative magnetic charge.

Science has greatly advanced concerning the materialistic aspect of life but knows hardly anything about other dimensions. Most of the neuro-biologists believe that the mind is nothing more than the workings of the brain, while others called [1]dualists maintain that the mind and the brain are two different aspects. [2]They argue that the brain cannot, by itself, produce thoughts and feelings and all the qualities and abilities we hold dear as humans, such as love, creativity, will, reasoning, and decision-making.

The question may be asked: How can a thought, which has no mass, no electrical charge, and no material properties, act upon the physical organ the brain? We know that our bodies respond to our will. If we want to speak or lift our arm, it is done almost instantaneously. But what moves the nerves and muscles?

[†] The word atom comes from the Greek and means "that which cannot be divided". However, Hendrik Lorentz (d. 1928), Dutch physicist, proposed that atoms could be split and contained negatively charged particles called electrons.

[1] Descartes (d. 1650) became the father of dualism as he divided the brain and mind into separate but equal parts. This view was not much different from that of Plato (+/- 437 B.C.), the Greek philosopher, who said that people possess both body and soul.

[2] Materialists may argue that when parts of the brain are damaged, thoughts can no longer be produced, or when the brain gets tired, one cannot think right. This certainly is true because the brain also functions (like a radio tube) as an amplifier. But it is not possible to stimulate any part of the cortex to produce decisions or to invent and create something new.

Rene Descartes declared that the pineal gland is the seat of the interaction between the mind and the body. Let us expand on his statement. What Rene did not take into account is the existence of the [3]etheric body, which acts as an intermediary between the physical body and the spirit body or the link between the brain and higher consciousness. The etheric body or double is, thus, within reach of the spirit body and also maintains a close relation to the nervous system. It has [4]seven energy centers or organs by which psycho-spiritual man or woman expresses himself/herself in the etheric and, thence, to the nerve centers and ductless gland systems of the physical body, which then become alive. Thus, they control and direct, via the centers, the muscles of the physical self, which then move at their command. The etheric body is also the medium through which (via the higher energy centers) [5]thought makes an impression upon the human brain, while emotion is expressed through the solar plexus and heart centers. Thus, psycho-divine consciousness is transmitted via the etheric brain to the physical brain, which in turn transmits physical sense consciousness to the spirit and its inner core, the Divine Spirit.

In review, the working of the human system is as follows: The physical nervous and glandular systems are receiving impulses and information from the outside, which is conveyed to the brain. It is then

---

[3] See "The Etheric Body".

[4] The 1st or root energy center (chakra) and the 2nd spleen function to bring life and vitality to the physical body. The solar plexus or 3rd center deals with the lower emotions, while the higher emotions find their expression through the heart, or 4th center. The throat center induces into physical expression the activities of the mental part of the spirit, as in speaking, while the 5th center deals with hearing clearly (clair-audience) in both the physical and spiritual planes. The 6th center is also called the 3rd eye and includes the entire middle part of the head – the sinuses, eyes, pituitary body, much of the brain, and the ears, and deals with seeing clearly (clairvoyance). The 7th crown center transforms spiritual inspiration into physical consciousness via the centers of the spirit, the etheric, nerve, and pineal gland. A person not only has energy centers in the etheric body but also in his/her human and divine body, which are counterparts of those in the etheric body. Its main purpose is to convey energies (vibrations) between their inner selves. Although the bodies permeate each other, higher and lower energies do need the swirling (tunnel-like) force centers of the same level to get through to the other body or bodies.

[5] Thought and emotion will hardly be experienced in physical consciousness when the centers are inoperative or impaired by drugs or other causes of injury. The capacity of the centers is also somewhat limited when the individual is immature and the higher centers still need to be awakened to show any activity. The centers are, thus, the main gateways through which emotional and mental energies pass among the physical, psychic, and spiritual realms. The centers most used by people are that of the solar plexus, indicating that they are living the life of the personality, while those people whom are degenerating are using the 2nd center, close to their sexual area.

transmitted in a flash through the open centers of the etheric and spirit bodies and recorded as feeling and thought. Responses are then immediately sent to the brain and physical body, via the etheric body, resulting in action.

F. The Near-Death Experience

Near-death experience (NDE) was first made public in 1975 when Dr. Raymond Moody disclosed his findings in a book titled "Life After Life". Those experiences could be more easily investigated because increasing numbers of people are going to the hospital to die instead of dying at home. In addition, NDE's happen more often because of the ability of modern science to bring people back from the brink of death after they are clinically dead.

There are literally hundreds of thousands of people alive today who made the trip of a lifetime, got a glimpse of life after death, and came back to tell about it.

According to Raymond Moody, [1]Pim van Lommel and Dr. Elizabeth Kobler-Ross, NDE usually follows a common pattern. One usually experiences a sense of well being and peace, while becoming fully aware that they are separate from their body. Many report, while floating outside their inert physical forms (including the physically blind), what is going on around their beds or in other parts of the hospital, which could easily be verified by the hospital staff. They also experience, in a flash, [2]a review of their life before the mind's eye.

They may then experience a tunnel-like sensation when they are moving towards the Light, where they are often met by a Christ-like figure or other benign beings and are also met by deceased relatives and friends. They tell them it is not yet time to live their lifestyle and encourage them to return to earth, which they are [3]very reluctant to do.

---

[1] According to the magazine "Spirituality and Health", Oct. 2003, the mystery of NDE was also studied by cardiologist Pim van Lommel in the Netherlands more than 30 years ago. It was the first large-scale study of the phenomena involving 10 hospitals and published in the prestigious British medical journal "The Lancet". This mystery captured Pim when patients told him of their wonderful experiences, especially the sense of freedom and peace, and how deeply they were impressed by it.

[2] Some are perceiving this review as the Day of Judgment.

[3] Although for most of the NDE's their experience was amazing and beyond expectation, for a few it was a frightening and a hellish encounter.

Most of them who come back are usually so much impressed by this experience that they no longer fear death and change their way of living for the better. They regard their bodies they temporarily left as a house for their spirits. They become less materialistic and more spiritually oriented, have a greater appreciation of life, and are more concerned for the well being of others, while their interest in personal status and possession of goods wanes.

REMARK: Some believe that near-death experience is only a hallucination, but people whom are pronounced dead show flat electroencephalogram readings (EEGs). In hallucinations, the brain is active and well.

G. What Are Earthbound Spirits?

Most good people fall into a peaceful sleep at the time of their death, [1]passing through the lower psychic realms, populated with earthbound spirits and others, towards the Light or the higher psychic and spiritual realms.

Earthbound spirits reside in the low level of the spirit world and are caught, or rather, stuck between the earth and spiritual dimension. They remain clinging in the transition conditions that immediately follow death. They are in limbo and living in a "no man's land", which the Bible calls "outer darkness" (Matt. 8:12; 22:13; 25:30). Earthbound spirits are usually in the dreary condition of confusion, frustration, and living a tiresome, repetitious, or monotonous lifestyle because they cannot function in the physical or spirit world. Because they have no understanding of the spirit world, they are in the dark and may wander or float around aimlessly for many years in the earth sphere. Many of them do not realize that they are dead and continue in their former earthly activities or are in a state of heavy sleep. Because they are living close to earth vibration, they have more easy access to the people of the earth and are easier to detect by the latter than spirits that have made the complete transition to the other side.

Spirits become earthbound when, at the time of death, they do not want to [2]acknowledge the passage or tunnel to the higher realms and

---

[1] Robert Crookall, 20th century English spiritualist, believed that there is a "Hades belt" surrounding the earth, through which one must pass on the way to what he calls "paradise conditions".

[2] Those whom committed violence to others or to themselves are bound to those persons they have killed or tried to hurt until they have realized the error of their ways. Some of them have become so bitter and lonely that they try to persuade others to do the same so that they are not entirely alone in their misery.

thus depriving themselves of the natural journey to the other side. Some of them seem not to be able to cross over by themselves or are not aware that they are supposed to move to a higher plane. Others do not want to leave their body because they do not know or accept that they have died or find it difficult to leave their loved ones on earth. The latter may be pulling them towards the earth plane with their emotions of grief and thoughts. Some want to stay behind because of the fear of judgment and being sent to hell. Others stay where they are because they do not see angels with wings or fellows with pitchforks to take them away – aunt Minny is still in her usual chair. Many of the deceased want to linger for a while, out of love for a home or land, in which they invested much of their being. Some may become so much attached to their possessions that they haunt or chase strange people away. There are also spirits that are so involved in the sensations of the physical world, whether it is material things, sensual pleasures, or try to fulfill their cravings by obsessing or possessing living persons. Those whom have suffered a sudden and traumatic death, as in accidents, or those who caused [3]violence to others or to themselves, remain in a long and conscious attachment to the physical world. The lowest spirit entities are attracted to those whom are of the same level of growth, such as criminals, grossly materialistic people, and addicts of immoral practices. Thus, the earthbound, in [4]Conan Doyle's words, are held on or near the surface of the world by the grossness of their nature or by the intensity of their worldly interest.

Because the world seems to be treating the earthbound spirits as if they no longer exist, they are confused because they see everybody, but nobody sees them. They are also angry and try to get the attention of the earth people by making all kinds of noises and haunting them. They are therefore called "poltergeists", or noisy ghosts. The activities of those spirits is such that they are able to make rapping or tapping sounds, move things around, turn lights and television sets on and off, and are heard as echoing footsteps in the attic. To do all those things, they need vital energy, which they usually draw from the bottled-up energy of teenagers as well as enough etheric matter, or ectoplasm, of certain teens to play poltergeist tricks on them. The ghosts are neither

---

[3] Some knowledgeable and developed dead people like to remain earthbound for a while, taking advantage of the ease with which they found themselves to materialize and to appear to earth people.

NOTE: Because most primitive people are earthbound when they die, they may make lots of trouble for the living.

[4] Author of Sherlock Holmes stories and famous English spiritualist (d. 1930).

good nor evil. [5]They do all those things not as much as to frighten people but more out of desperation, to get help, and to remove themselves out of the situation they are in.

There are many earthbound souls waiting to be rescued, that is, that they are in need of assistance in crossing over to the higher spirit planes. Some of them stay with their families until they are rescued, while others are so confused and bewildered that they can only be contacted by someone who is of this earth plane because earth life is the only one with which they are most familiar. Carl A. Wickland (d. 1945) formed with his sensitive wife a rescue circle to liberate them and wrote about those experiences in his book "Thirty Years among the Dead". Much earlier, Jesus Christ, after His resurrection, went to the spirits in darkness or prison. See 1 Pet. 3:19, 20.

NOTE 1: The etheric beings in the lower realms may drain vital energy of living persons if they are permitted to stay in their aura. This may lead to cases of nerve exhaustion and obsession.

NOTE 2: Not all that we see and hear is sightings of earthbound spirits whom are stuck in our atmosphere. Some of the repeated phenomena are reprints or replays on the etheric surroundings, of intense vivid experiences of the past. What we observe may also be thought forms projected by people, with or without a body, at a certain location where, for example, a crime is committed or on graveyard sights. Concerning the latter place, the ghost may be a short-lived cast of the etheric body of the person who is buried there or his/her spirit, or even that of others who occasionally visit that place.

H. A Word to the "Mentally Ill"

Many individuals in Western society are often warehoused in institutions for the mentally disturbed because they have the ability of clair-audience, clairvoyance, and intuitive insights. They are frequently sent there at [6]the advice of their physicians who diagnosed them as suffering of delusion, distorted imagination, and hallucination. Once the perfectly normal people arrive at the institution, they are "properly

---

[5] Some of the earthbound spirits are mischievous ghosts and non-humans, while others do not want anyone to live in their space.

[6] Instead of turning cases of "strange behavior" over to psychologists, psychoanalysts, and psychiatrists, whom usually deal with the personality (that is, the mental and emotional aspects) and outer behavior, they should instead refer them to professionals whom are practicing parapsychology and transpersonal psychology. The first discipline deals with the spirit or psyche of the personality and also with its psychic development, whereby the other deals mainly with the transpersonal aspects of the personality, its spiritual or divine aspect, and its higher psychic development.

453

evaluated" and labeled as ailing of psychosis, schizophrenia, and dissociative personality. From that time on, "the patient" is at the mercy of the doctors, and there is no turning back unless the sensitive loses his/her psychic ability. The poor devils do not know about their psychic talents and believe themselves to being insane and are supposed to act like it.

However, some patients are behaving in an abnormal way by being obsessed or possessed by evil spirits. This is shown by the patient by assuming a different character. Instead of being [1]exorcised, as it was done at the time of Jesus Christ, they are first classified in the language of psychiatry as cases of repression, hysteria, schizophrenia, and dissociative personality disorder. The patients are then heavenly sedated with drugs so that they can hardly speak or move. By numbing the brain (the musical instrument or gramophone record), the voice and outer expression can no longer be heard and seen of the possessing spirit, but also not that of the original spirit.

Today, the condition of the man in the synagogue might be diagnosed as pathological [2]hysteria in Mark 1:23-26, that of the man from the country of the Gerasenes in Mark 5:1-15 as acute manic depression, and that of the boy in Mark 9:17-27 as epilepsy.

REMARK: Because parents and educators are much influenced by the so-called experts who deal only with the narrow field of behavior observations and some Christian leaders whom are against any psychic phenomena, they also do not want to believe or have anything to do with any psychic manifestations. When their children or pupils show any signs of psychic ability, they quickly tell them that such perception and behavior is not real and merely a product of their imagination. The result of this advice is that the child closes down his/her psychic senses and ability, which then atrophies.

I. The Many Dimensions of Life

Science tells us that different things can occupy the same space if they are on different vibration levels. For example, our atmosphere is filled with light, sound and heat waves, electricity, ether, magnetism,

---

[1] At the time of Christ in Palestine, exorcism, or casting out of demons, was a recognized and reputable profession (see Luke 11:19). There is a continuous reference to the casting out of devils in the New Testament which made a clear distinction between the curing of physical illnesses and disabilities and the curing of mental and psychic disorders, which were thought to cause possession (Matt. 4:24).

[2] Hysteria is known to be contagious because whole communities in the past have been taken over by evil spirits, such as that of the nuns of Loudon in the Middle Ages.

ultraviolet light, gases, cosmic rays, radio and television waves, etc. None of them are interfering with the other because they are moving at different vibratory rates.

An example that different things can occupy the same space is that water will fill in the empty spaces in a container filled with sand, while air will occupy the empty spaces in water. Thus, sand, water, and air can exist together in the same container. Within matter, finer matter, such as etheric particles, easily find room, and within the etheric, psychic particles find their space, wherein divine sparks of a higher vibration find their abode.

Thus, several worlds, that of the physical, etheric, psychic, and divine can coexist in the same space and operate simultaneously because each world is of a finer (higher vibration) rate than a lower world.

The worlds can thus exist in the same space because of the difference of frequency. The higher worlds can, however, not be seen by the people in the lower world because the frequency is so rapid as to be transparent and undetectable, as blades of a fan at high speed. Thus, the invisible worlds, with their inhabitants, are in and around the physical world, but we are hardly aware of them. It is nevertheless possible to "tune in" to the right wavelength and, thus, communicate with those whom the world calls dead.

According to many spirit communications, there are *seven principal planes of spirit existence, and they form concentric zones around the physical world, each one extending out beyond the last. Thus, those zones not only interpenetrate the earth but extend from the earth surface miles upward, like on a microcosmic scale, the auras of a human being.

NOTE 1: The matter of each plane is denser than that of the one above it. This is also true of the atmosphere surrounding the earth; the higher we go the rarer the air.

---

* Jesus said, "In my father's house are many rooms" (Jn. 14:2). The higher the region, the more developed the person is living in that part and the greater the radiance of the environment and its fragrance. He also said, "I go to prepare a place for you" --- "that where I am you may also be" (Jn. 14:2, 3). This place was not an imaginable abode but that of reality and spirit substance. See also 2 Cor. 5:1; 12:2-4.

NOTE 2: There are many planets like the earth which are occupied by humanoid-type creatures and others in their physical, etheric, and psychic expressions of life. Intelligent beings, so-called ultra-terrestrials, or inter-dimensional entities are living in the parallel universe, sharing the same or higher space at a different "vibratory level" of existence. Those from other planets fly with great speed through inter-dimensional space, and they and their ships may occasionally materialize and be seen by earth people. The unidentified objects or UFO's have been around for as long as human beings can remember. But they are seen more often in and after 1947, a few years after the first atom bomb explosions. Those explosions probably have also effected their worlds.

The spirit of a deceased person, after the initial period of rest, passes directly to the region to which the human spirit has become psychically attuned or fitted, as the result of the way he or she has conducted himself/herself while living on earth. Those whom have led good lives pass into the higher realms, which may be called heaven; others whom lived not such good lives enter the lower or "dark regions", which are situated close to the earth plane and in the bowl of the earth. Thus, the inhabitants of each region will be more or less of the same moral and spiritual growth.

Life on earth is lived in the third dimension, but after physical death, consciousness resides in the fourth and higher dimension. Let me explain. If our conscious mind is linear, we can only see a line of a cube. It is like going with a train on a straight railroad track. But if our mind begins to function in two dimensions, as on a surface, we may be called flat landers. If our mind is elevated to three dimensions, we can view the whole cube and not only navigate a longitude and latitude, as with a ship, but also move up and down, as flying in an airplane. When our consciousness is changed to a fourth dimension, we can see a three-dimensional solid as it is and not super-physically, by seeing the further side smaller, or in perspective. Thus, in the fourth dimension, vision is expanded so that we are able to see throughout the object or within its entirety.

NOTE 1: From the above example, the time coordinate is the fourth dimension when the airplane is at latitude (X), longitude (Y), and altitude (Z). It must be seen as a continuous curve on a four-dimensional space/time continuum.

NOTE 2: Science recognizes time/space as the fourth dimension.

NOTE 3: We may compare our three-dimensional life with a caterpillar, which is only able to see and experience its immediate area on which it crawls. But when it changes to a butterfly and starts living a fourth dimensional life, it sees much more, and its view of life is much different. Events are no longer unrelated, and it is easier to see ahead and predict the future and also understand much better, in all its dimensions, the purpose of life.

REMARK: As a fish does not know about the life above water, so are the majority of human beings not aware of the greater life that surrounds them.

J. Life in the Spirit World

According to [1]Swedenborg, life in the spirit world is very similar to life in the material world. The surroundings of the spirit world are so similar in appearance to the physical world that the newly arrived entity may, at first, not easily detect any difference. However, upon closer observation, he/she will find a lightness and translucency, which is not found in earthly matter. This certainly made the transition much easier. Those whom are not being received by spirit beings may [2]ask themselves if they are dead or not, and where they should go.

[3]According to individuals whom have visited the invisible realms during near death, out-of-body trips, vivid dreams, and also from messages from spirit beings, there are mountains, hills, and meadows, oceans, lakes, and rivers, forests, plants, flowers, land animals, fish, and birds. Further, we find homes and great buildings, such as halls of learning, libraries, art galleries, and rest houses for the distressed newly arrived citizens. All objects are arrayed in beautiful and exquisite

---

[1] Emmanuel Swedenborg's (Swedish scientist, philosopher, and mystic – 1688-1772) ideas of the spirit world revolutionized the view of life after death in his time. It was known to a few people that when he traveled in the spirit world, he left his body behind in a cataleptic state, so that more of his consciousness was withdrawn to travel than it would be in a sleep state.

[2] The spirit person does not always realize that he or she is dead because they are still in a body which resembles their physical bodies. As the story goes, a zealous fundamental minister, after preaching a sermon of hell and damnation, was run over by a train on his way home. His spirit got up, walked to his house, and tried to open the front door, but his hand went right through it. He then tried to call his family, but they could not hear him. The minister was then bothered by many spirits to whom he had preached the wrong message.

[3] Those reports are similar but not always the same because everyone brings back their own subjective reports. Besides, it is difficult to describe a multidimensional world in a third dimensional language. The observers are also influenced by their belief system, as Swedenborg was, when he wrote about the people whom are condemned forever in hell.

colors, and harmonious music is heard in many places, which express themselves in thought forms of changing colors.

Those whom after death want to or find themselves living on the surface of the earth are surrounded by the psychic counterpart of physically existing landscapes, oceans, flora, and fauna. Many earthbound individuals like to hover around their physical homes or visit the psychic doubles of their churches, temples, or shrines. Others like to travel and see places of interest, which they did not have a chance to visit while living on earth. Entities on those lower planes are fully conscious of psychic matter but are not much aware of physical matter, which appears like a fog, through which they can easily see, walk, and move through. Some of them enjoy themselves by [4]going through walls, rocks, and mountains, plunge themselves in volcanoes, and in the depth of oceans.

Those whom have passed over find out that they are able to move more freely in the spirit than in the physical body. They set themselves in motion by thinking and willing to a destination instead of physically moving the body by walking and running which, of course, is still possible in the world of spirit. A spirit can travel more rapidly than sound and even more rapidly than light, especially in the higher spheres. The moment you think about individuals by either loving or hating them, you are with them, and it is difficult to move away from them as in the physical world.

Those whom live on the higher planes that are a great distance above the surface of the earth create their own environment or surroundings by molding the psychic substances by [5]thought and, thus,

---

[4] They pass through earthly objects and physical beings because the inner worlds interpenetrate the outer or physical world.

[5] To create a dwelling or other things on the earth plane usually takes a great amount of time. It first has to be visualized, plans are then made, and building materials assembled to make it a reality. This slow process is necessary in order to learn how to create without making too many mistakes and to become a better creator in the spirit world. When we arrive in the spirit plane of life, we should realize that thought is substantial and concrete because it can create and build. We should, therefore, learn to control our thoughts before passing over. The thoughts you project manifest almost instantly, especially in the highest dimension of life, and we create only havoc in the spirit world when we have not become masters of our creative thoughts.

create scenery and objects according to their [6]own conception. Those images are usually of that which they remember and like the best of their former terrestrial life. Those things are created with and from thought instantly on the much higher planes of life. The houses they build can either be a thought form of a beautiful home or a hovel, which depends on the thoughts of the person who does the building and from the high or low quality substances of which those residences are built.

The difference between the physical plane and that of the lower and the higher spirit planes is that of vibration. The latter two are of a higher frequency, finer, and light, while the former is that of heaviness, coarseness, and lower frequency. Spirit matter is easy to form and shape by the human will and by visualization because it is more changeable and fluidic, while physical matter is not as malleable. As material things are tangible to physical beings, so are the spirit objects to the inhabitants of the spirit world.

NOTE: According to Charles W. Leadbeater (d. 1935), a leading figure in the theosophical society, astral (lower spirit) bodies can pass through each other and through fixed astral objects because astral particles are much farther apart in proportion to their size. Continuing, he says you may, for example, experience this when you sit next to another person on a bus or train. Unless you try to protect yourself, your spirit body and that of your neighbor do penetrate each other to a great extent and affect each other in a positive or negative sense. In this way, we truly get to know the other person much better, who no longer is hiding behind a physical façade. We may also be able to read the thoughts of the other, which may or may not be quite different of the words they speak.

It is never dark in the spirit world, and there are no shadows because the source of light does not come from any direction, as that of the sun, which illuminates the earth. [7]There is a diffused luminosity from all directions because as spirit beings are luminous, so is the psychic matter they influence. The spirits of the higher planes radiate more

---

[6] Because individuals or groups are able to create whatever their fancy, belief, or imagination, we therefore find, in some parts of the spirit world, a New Jerusalem. It contains pearly gates, streets of gold, and its great white throne, upon which we find a thought form of an elderly God. In the lower regions, we may find in some places a fiery hell, complete with devils with horns, hoofs, and tails, prodding sinners with pitchforks.

[7] Antonio Borgia, in his book "Life of the World Unseen", said that all light proceeded directly from the Giver of all light and that it illuminated the whole of the spirit world. On earth, we have "fun in the sun"; in the world of spirit, we find "delight in the light".

light, while those of the lower planes radiate little light, making psychic matter and surroundings darker.

The spirit body is an exact counterpart of the physical body and is made of a definite substance which is more real and concrete than the physical self because it interpenetrates the latter's inter-space. The spirit person can only function in a world of the same vibration, and it survives the physical man or woman by a great number of years. Like the physical, it will eventually [1]disintegrate, but the "real you", or the Divine Spirit, continues on living for eternity.

The entities of the spirit planes are not aware of physical matter but are conscious of the densest psychic matter which surrounds and outlines all the physical objects and physical bodies of the people of the earth. According to esoteric teaching, the human spirit not only senses through the eyes and ears but also senses through other sense centers [2]in and around it, which appear like vortices. The senses of the spirit body are more intense and keener than that of the physical body, and spirits are, therefore, more sensitive to each other. Spirits have a greater capacity to express themselves more than those whose senses are veiled by earthly wrappings. Spirits also see the [3]changing colors and expansion or contraction of auras of human beings, with or without a body.

Spirits are relieved from most of the cares and infirmities that used to harass them on earth. Their thoughts are freer and can soar higher, their senses are quickened, and their inner beings are no longer imprisoned in the body. Colors appear more vivid, with additional shades and colors never seen before and, thus, see the world as it truly is: a most exquisite and beautiful place.

In the physical world, we communicate by speaking a certain language, and we know that it is perfectly possible to say one thing and be thinking and feeling another. When we, at first, arrive in the spirit world, we formulate certain words with our minds in a particular language and then project them. However, we soon find out how slow

---

[1] In psychic parlance, this is often called the second death, while the death of the physical and etheric bodies is the first death.

[2] This is indicated by the fact that we can sense someone behind us who is, for example, staring at us.

[3] Entities cannot hide their feelings and attitudes from someone on earth or spirit world very well, who is able to observe colors of their auras and is also able to interpret them.

it is. [1]We then learn to communicate by thought transference, which is the common language for everyone, especially on the higher planes. Communication by thoughts and feelings is more accurate because it conveys more the essence of the human being. Another method of communication (with permission) is to walk completely into the other, or merge [2](melding) into the entity's psyche, and experience and share their memories, feelings, thoughts, wisdom, joys, and sorrows.

Unlike the physical body, the spirit body does not begin to deteriorate after it has reached maturity but remains at the height of its vigor or prime of life. Those who newly pass over when old in physical years will [3]eventually become younger in appearance but grow in knowledge and wisdom. When spiritually developed, they appear radiant, fully alive, truly beautiful, and have the appearance of eternal youth, as portrayed in one of the tarot cards. In order to be recognizable, especially for earthly people, they may use their psychic power to change, for a while, their spirit body to an age by which they are known. That is what Samuel did to the medium of Endor so that he would be recognized by Saul (1 Sam. 28:14).

At the time of death, the spirit leaves the physical body permanently and passes to that level of the spirit world, which it has gained while living on earth. According to many reports, it is not possible for the spirit to go to a higher level because there is a natural boundary. The person who wants to go further finds that it is not able to because the particular psychic life force they need is diminishing. Their movement is also restrained by the intense light.

NOTE: The spirit of an individual after death is that of the image of the physical body because it has been shaped by the body while living on earth. However, this image, especially when it looks very old, wrinkled, and decrepit

---

[1] Through wordless transmission, an intuitive understanding of ideas is communicated between parties. They may later formulate those ideas into concrete thoughts and words. Because thought transference is the means of communication in the spirit world, we must be very careful about what we think. Besides, our spirit is created and composed of what we have thought and what we are thinking and feeling now.

[2] A complete melding occurs when two entities are blending together emotionally, mentally, and spiritually in a state of utter bliss, but without losing their own identity. It is a period of perfect harmony, which the physical bodies on earth can only partly imitate. It is more gratifying than sex on the physical plane. This is especially true when entities are sharing their divine love and fully experiencing each other.

[3] As soon as they stop thinking that they are old and they want to be younger, the person changes, because thought can easily change and mold psychic matter. The same process of change was used by satan to change himself into an angel of light (2 Cor. 11:14).

461

is soon, or rather, wants to be changed by the individual.

As people who lead an indolent selfish life on earth do not progress spiritually, so the people in the spirit world whom are not engaged in some useful activity do not develop, or may even digress to the lower sphere. As told by the ones whom are living on the higher planes, the spirit world is not a land of eternal rest but a kingdom of use. Since there is no weariness, the activities do not have to be interrupted all the time. Many [1]occupy themselves with art, music, architecture, teaching, etc. and giving new ideas to people on earth whom are engaged in the same project. Quite a few are also helpful to the countless individuals arriving in the spirit world, whom have no knowledge or incorrect information about life after death and whom are confused and even bewildered. Some of them, and those that suffered a [2]long and painful illness on earth or shock through a sudden and violent death, need to recuperate in the so-called homes of rest. It is especially hard on the spirit helpers during war and natural disasters when large numbers of people arrive in the spirit world all at once, making the spirit world a hospital for broken souls.

As we like to be with people on earth whom have the same interest and religion, so we like to associate with people with the same tastes and spiritual interest. Those communities gather high above their countries, and individuals gravitate towards those groups and religions with which they feel most comfortable, according to the law of attraction. This is usually the same religion of which they were members while on earth. Some call that place [3]heaven, while spiritualists call it summer land. Grandparents, parents, and children,

---

[1] Some people are very happy to be engaged in some creative activity which they like to do but could not do when living on earth because of the constant pressure to earn money for a living in occupations they did not like. Howbeit, some wearisome occupations are no longer of any use in the afterlife, such as food preparation, cleaning, transportation, commerce, money management, etc.

[2] Illness can have a debilitating effect on the mind, which greatly effects the spirit body.

[3] For many people of different cultures, heaven may mean a place, a reward, a promise, or an idea. It is also called: Kingdom of God, Garden of Eden, Zion, Heavenly-Celestial and Holy City, New Canaan, New Jerusalem, New Heaven, and Paradise. In many passages in the Bible, the word 'heaven' seems to mean the sky (Gen. 1:7-8), is above the earth (Gen. 49:25), the home of God (Matt. 6:9), and His Kingdom which also resides within the human heart (Lk. 17:21; Rev. 21:3). Some esoterists say that heaven is not a place or reward for good people but a state of mind. We make our own heaven (or hell) even now, what we feel, think, and act in our daily life, which will effect the growth of our inner selves for better or for worse.

close friends, [4]husbands, and wives will meet in the spirit world and may stay close together, or their relationships are gradually dissolved because they do not truly trust and love each other.

REMARK: When someone has grown mentally, morally, and spiritually and starts living in the higher planes, they function in a higher spirit body and have no need of the lower spirit body, which is cast off. However, they can come back temporarily to the lower plane by re-clothing or materializing themselves with the lower plane substance.

Those persons whom have lived a materialistic life by identifying their consciousness with their bodies and who have not taken the time to become aware of the psychic and spiritual potentialities of their consciousness are total strangers to the new environment. Their entire life was centered on those things that only their bodies could gratify. When they die, their bodies, which alone can satisfy those cravings, are gone, but the yearning to consume those desires is still there because desire is an essential component of their surviving personalities. For example, the desire of the glutton for the cravings of food is still there, although there is no longer any need of physical food in the spirit world. A drunkard will suffer from unquenchable thirst and will try to get some satisfaction by [5]obsessing earth people to drink and (or) become alcoholics. Someone who was filled with lustful desires or yielded to unworthy passions will also try, as an earthbound spirit, to influence men and women to have a psychic relationship with him or her. The suffering of the drunkard and sensualist will end when their cravings have worn themselves out, or "burned out", as in the Roman Catholic purgatory.

---

[4] Strong bonds of marriage are needed for the couple in order to give birth and raise their children in their good image and the image of God. Thereafter, it is less important if they stay together. Some churches believe that marriage should last "until death do us part", while other churches believe in eternal marriage. The Bible says that there are no marriages in heaven (Luk. 20:35; Mark 12:25). However, the bonds of true love and affection we have had with the people of the earth always remain with us and draw us together in all dimensions of life, or wherever we are.

[5] As a heavy drinker becomes so intoxicated that he or she is about to pass out, a spirit may pass through the weakened and opened aura of the drinker and take possession of his or her body. This results that the whole personality of the drinker changes to that of the possessing entity. A well-adjusted and nice person may become violent and despicable in his or her behavior.

Those individuals whom have visited the lower regions of the spirit world report that [6]hell is a cold and dark place, which is created by the people whom have taken up residence there. They are not judged and sentenced to that place but gravitate to that region in accordance with the level of growth they have acquired, by their thoughts, words, and deeds while on earth. They are thus solely responsible for their own condition. The Bible described hell as "outer darkness" – wherein – "shall be weeping and gnashing of teeth" (Matt. 8:12 – K.J.V.). It is also a place or residence of undesirable non-human entities.

As we, in physical life, have to be constantly on guard to protect our bodies against damage and destruction, this cannot happen to spirit bodies because they are fluidic in composition. The spirit body is resistant to devastation of any kind, such as pain, fatigue, sickness, and discomfort of heat and cold. There are no severe weather conditions in the spirit world, and when we get a little tired, we just breathe in more life from the surrounding psychic atmosphere. *While the spirit body does not suffer from the diseases and injuries of physical life, it is, however, affected by the condition of the mind and by its moral development. For example, the sensation of pain and headache may still linger in our minds and be impressed upon the spirit after we have passed over. When we are not much developed, we are unhappy, frustrated, and feel forsaken.

There is no decay, waste, or dirt in the spirit world because there is nothing to cause it. The flora and fauna need practically no attention.

Clothes will materialize by just thinking about the clothes you used to and like to wear, which fabrics are derived from the substance of any particular plane in which you live. The wearing apparel, like the aura, is beautiful and radiant on higher planes (see Mk. 9:4; Lk. 9:29). How-

---

[6] Hell, for many people, is a terrible place and for others an abode of eternal punishment for wicked people. It is also called in Hebrew Sheol and Gehenna ; in Greek Hades and Tartarus. Other words for hell are: underworld, the pit, (Numbers 16:30), the grave (Psalm 49:15), the abyss, and the inferno. It is reported by Swedenborg that the faces of evil spirits living there are hideous and void of life. Their bodies are monstrous, and their speech is like the speech of anger or revenge. Other reports say that they are totally devoid of love, have fierce sexual desires, and their thought patterns are completely (self) destructive. Even when they would like to kill, they are not able to because the spirit bodies of their intended victims are of fluidic substance. However, some of them try to obsess and possess people on earth to do the killing of terrestrials for them.

* Those whom were physically blind and deaf can see and hear, and those whom have lost their physical limbs function as a whole person in the spirit world.

ever, when living on the lower planes, only the coarse, dull, and dreary clothes will be available and are the reflection of your lower thoughts.

As the physical body is sustained by physical food derived from the earth, the etheric body is sustained by the breathing of etheric energy from the surrounding atmosphere. The higher vibration spirit body is sustained by the breathing of psychic or radiant energy from its environment. As the person on earth needs food, warmth, and shelter, so the spirit person needs, for its growth, intellectual food, love, and care. The awakened Divine Spirit needs Truth and divine love to grow to perfection.

As physical food no longer is needed in the spirit world, the newcomer may still feel hungry because the desire for food has been with the person for a long time while he/she lived on earth. The welcoming party may, therefore, provide him/her with food, or rather thought forms, until the individual comes to the realization that it is no longer necessary.

K. The Resurrection

[1]Resurrection is the belief that God, at the end of time, will restore the dead to physical life on the day of Final Judgment. It is the rising again of Christ on the third day after the crucifixion.

Before the idea of resurrection took hold of the mind of the Jewish people, there was deeply embedded in the psyche of the Egyptians and their neighbors the story of the resurrection of Osiris, who was killed by his brother Seth. In order for them to be received by Osiris, who became the god of the dead, "the heart" of the dead had to be weighed in the balance of Truth, whether it deserved reward or punishment. The [2]ancient Greeks believed that the spirit at death passed to the underworld or Hades, where it was either rewarded for its good or punished for its evil deeds. The latter were sent to a place of punishment or torment. This was also the view of the Zoroastrian religion, which teaches the resurrection of the dead and fiery judgment. In the Odyssey (a Greek writing), only a wraith-like replica of the per-

---

[1] Many Christians distinguish between the general and particular judgment of each individual at the time of death. The latter is also called the intermediate state, as described in the story of the rich man and Lazarus (Luke 16:19-31), and the penitent thief (Luke 23:43).

[2] As the early Greeks, Hebrews, and primitives believed in a vague existence after death, the Greeks at the time of Plato and later believe in the immortality of the soul or human spirit.

son, with hardly any awareness, survived death. This almost extinction was also indicated in the Bible. The patriarch Job asked, "If a man die, shall he live again?" (Job 14:14) Ecclesiastes 9:5 says, "For the living know that they will die, but the dead know nothing." For the Hebrews, the shade of the individual descended to a wretched existence in the depth, or underworld, of [3]Sheol.

As the Israelites progressed, they began to believe in the resurrection of the body, as indicated in Isaiah 26:19, "Thy dead shall live, their bodies shall rise", and in Daniel 12:2: "and many of those who sleep in the dust of the earth shall awake". Divine judgment does not only take place on the earth but would also be carried out after death. Christians inherited the belief in the bodily resurrection but assigned the role of judge to Christ. This final (general) judgment would then take place at the time of the Second Coming of Christ.

NOTE 1: The great monotheistic religions (Judaism – Christianity – Islam) share their beliefs that the soul is immortal and is judged after death, of what it has done, and consequently meted rewards or punishments. The Mohammedan faith, like the Judeo-Christian, also believes in physical resurrection.

NOTE 2: Jehovah's Witnesses also believe (since 1935) in the bodily resurrection for those whom are not part of the 144,000 (see Chapter 7 of Revelation) that are living in the spiritual heaven.

According to Paul, who used to be a staunch Pharisee: "For since we believe that Jesus died and rose again" --- "the dead in Christ will rise

---

[3] When the Israelites were held in captivity in Babylon (+/-590 B.C.), the Babylonian religious idea of Sheol was being made their own. The word Sheol means "the hollow place" under the earth, a place for departed spirits. The idea of Sheol as a place of fiery judgment for the wicked was incorporated into the Jewish religion in the second century B.C. At the time of Jesus, the sect of the Pharisees firmly believed in Judgment and the resurrection of the body – by reading Ezekiel 37:1-10 and other verses. The Sadducees, on the other hand, said that there was no such thing as resurrection or life after death, with which the Son of Man disagreed (Mark 12:18-27). The word Sheol was later translated as "hell". The latter part of the Book of Revelation speaks about this hell wherein the unbelieving shall suffer "in the lake that burns with fire and sulfur (brimstone), which is the second death". The word hell is also mentioned in Matt. 5:22 and other places. The theologian Origin (d. +/-254 A.D.) said that hell should not be taken literally. We may say that hell is like purgatory, to cleanse, purge, or "burn out" our evil desires and thinking. Because the Jewish faith believed in eternal damnation, this was also accepted by Matthew, a Jew, who let Jesus say in Matt. 25:41, "Depart from me, you cursed, into the eternal fire prepared for the devil and his angels." See also Matt. 18:8. Evangelist Mark had Jesus quote Isaiah 66:24, "to be thrown into hell, where their worm does not die, and the fire is not quenched." However, Lamentation 3:31 says, "For the Lord will not cast off forever."

first", with the sound of the trumpet of God (1 Thess. 4:14, 16). See also 1 Cor. 15:52. He also said in 1 Cor. 15:13-14, "If there is no resurrection of the dead, then Christ has not been raised; if Christ has not been raised, then our preaching is in vain." Matthew 27:52-53 reports that "the tombs also were opened, and many bodies of the saints whom had fallen asleep were raised and came out of their tombs after his resurrection." John 5:28 let the Son of God say, "For the hour is coming when all who are in the tombs will hear his voice and come forth."

*Because of the above-mentioned verses, some Christians still believe in bodily resurrection from their graves or from whatever place their decomposed body parts are found. Fundamental Christians, in general, believe that those whom are saved will be given resurrected bodies. This body will be like the earthly one; only, it will be perfect, without weakness, sickness, or death. Others believe not in the resurrection of the flesh (because flesh and blood cannot inherit the Kingdom of God – 1 Cor. 15:50) but in the resurrection of a new body, like the glorious body of Jesus (Phil. 3:21).

Those whom are more spiritually oriented say that the resurrection is not the rise of the dead from the tomb but leaving behind the self-centered and self-sufficient ego and the appearance of a new and liberated Divine Self, "a life giving spirit" (1 Cor. 15:42-50). "Over such the second death has no power" (Rev. 20:6). It is the resurrection of Christ in us, from the tomb of our carnal nature, the body of dead (see also Rom. 6:5-14). The author of the fourth Gospel let the Cosmic Christ say through Jesus, "I am the resurrection and the life; he who

---

* We find, in some parts of the spirit world, rows upon rows of Christians laying in a slumber as if they were dead because they do not believe in a life beyond the grave. They do not want to displease God by waking up until they hear the trumpet sound, which will make known the arrival of the Second Coming of Christ. In those Last Days (John 11:24) of the old dispensation, they will be bodily resurrected and judged at the Day of wrath (Mal. 4:5; Rom. 2:5; Rev. 6:17) to either go to heaven or hell (purgatory or hell for Catholics).

According to reports of Antonio Borgia and people whom have undergone a near-death experience, people whom have died do not have to wait countless years for the awful Day of Judgment. There is no final judgment; the soul judges itself. Jesus spoke of an ongoing life at the time of death (Luke 16:22-24), and in Luke 22:43, Jesus promises Paradise immediately. There is, however, a review and transfer of the life lived, whereby every thought, deed, and event is simultaneously replayed and relived. This review may take a few hours or a few days until you have learned the lessons of life, recognized the mistakes made, and then the judgment is over, and you can pass into the spirit world. The place where you are going is the moral and spiritual growth you have attained while living on earth. Thus, we create our own heaven and hell, not as places of reward or punishment but as states of consciousness.

believes in me though he die, yet shall he live, and whoever lives and believes in me shall never die" (John 11:25-26).

Whatever one may believe, Christ has been raised from the dead and demonstrated to everyone that there is a life after death. The resurrection, above all, meant that Jesus was, after all, the Messiah (Rom. 8:34; Phil. 2:9-11), and Rome, with its naked power, was not the most powerful force in the world. He had not liberated them from Rome physically but had freed them and the Romans spiritually from the chains of evil and free from the domination of evil forces and the terrible fear of death.

As the hope of resurrection belongs to Jewish thought, the concept of immortality is part of Greek thought. The history of Western philosophy is influenced by two main streams of thought, that of Plato (humans exist of body and an independent soul) and that of Aristotle (humans exist of body and a dependent soul or form). As the soul of the former survives death, the soul of the latter only survives death when the body is resurrected. For the first millenium of the Christian era, the people were more inclined to accept the Platonic view, but in the thirteenth century, Thomas Aquinas (1224-1274), theologian and doctor of the Catholic Church, accepted the theory of Aristotle. During the Renaissance in the time of Descartes, there was a reversion to the Platonic view, and in the twentieth century, it more or less swung back from Platonism toward Aristotelianism.

L. How Jesus Came Back after His Crucifixion

The Bible reports that Jesus, after His crucifixion and burial, overcame death and appeared to many people. Through this after-death manifestation, He gave solid proof of a life after death. Many people at that time and today think that the returning of Christ was a miracle, or the suspension of natural law, which is not possible in the orderly creation of God. Jesus, however, had supreme knowledge of natural law and was able to appear on Sunday, Easter morning, not in His *crucified flesh but in His materialized Spirit Body.

No one can deny that something extraordinary happened to the disciples after the resurrection. A radical change occurred to them when they knew that Jesus, their Lord and Master, was still alive, and especially after they received the Holy Spirit. As they, after the crucifixion, were discouraged and afraid, now they were boldly preaching the Gospel to the very people from whom they were at first hiding.

Matthew chapter 28 reports, "Now after the sabbath toward the dawn of the first day of the week, Mary Magdalene and the other Mary went to see the sepulchre. And behold, there was a great earthquake; for an angel of the Lord descended from heaven and came and rolled back the stone" --- "the angel said to the women, 'Do not be afraid; for I know that you seek Jesus who was crucified. He is not here; for he has risen, as he said. Come, see the place where he lay'" --- "they departed quickly from the tomb with fear and great joy, and ran to tell his disciples. And behold, Jesus met them and said, 'Hail!' And they came up and took hold of his feet and worshipped him (complete materialization). Then Jesus said to them, 'Do not be afraid; go and tell my brethren to go to Galilee, and there they will see me'" --- "Now the eleven disciples went to Galilee, to the mountain to which Jesus had directed them. And when they saw him they worshipped him; but some doubted."

---

* The empty tomb is not a proof that Jesus underwent a physical resurrection. The body may have undergone dematerialization, probably by Jesus or by angelic beings, as the linen clothes wherein His body was wrapped were still laying there as if they were not disturbed (see John 20:6-7). The body of Jesus would then no longer be worshipped or despised by His enemies, as the Archangel Michael disputed with the devil about the body of Moses (Jude 9).

As shown in the Gospels, Jesus knew how to disappear "but passing through the midst of them he went away" (Luk. 4:30). "So they sought to arrest him, but no one laid hands on him" (Jn. 7:30). "Again they tried to arrest him, but he escaped from their hands" (Jn. 10:39). See also John 7:44; 8:59; 12:36.

NOTE: When reading the Gospel stories of the resurrection of Jesus Christ, we have to keep in mind that those who wrote them believed in the physical resurrection.

Mark chapter 16 reports, "And when the sabbath was past, Mary Magdalene and Mary the mother of James, and Salome bought spices, so that they might go and anoint him. And very early on the first day of the week they went to the tomb when the sun had risen" --- "And entering the tomb, they saw a young man" --- "and he said to them" --- "you seek Jesus of Nazareth who was crucified. He has risen."

"Now when he rose early on the first day of the week, he appeared first to Mary Magdalene" --- "after this he appeared in another form (spirit is able to appear in different forms) to two of them, as they were walking into the country" --- "Afterward he appeared to the eleven themselves as they sat at the table; and he upbraided them for their disbelief and hardness of heart, because they had not believed those who saw him after he had risen."

"So then the Lord Jesus, after he had spoken to them, was taken up into heaven."

Luke chapter 24 reports, the women "returning from the tomb they told all this (what the angels said) to the eleven and to all the rest" --- "but these words seemed to them an idle tale, and they did not believe them."

"That very day two of them were going to a village named Emmaus, about 7 miles from Jerusalem, and talking with each other about all these things that had happened. While they were talking and discussing together, Jesus himself drew near and went with them. But their eyes were kept from recognizing him." --- "Stay with us, for it is toward evening" --- "So he (Jesus) went in to stay with them. When he was at table with them, he took the bread and blessed and broke it, and gave it to them. And their eyes were opened and they recognized him; and he vanished out of their sight" (dematerialized). They then told the eleven disciples what had happened.

"As they were saying this, Jesus himself stood among them. But they were startled and frightened, and supposed that they saw a spirit. And he said to them, 'Why are you troubled, and why do questionings rise in your hearts? See my hands and my feet, that it is I myself; handle me, and see; for a spirit has not flesh and bones as you see that I have.' And while they still disbelieved for joy, and wondered, he said to them, 'Have you anything here to eat?' They gave him a piece of broiled fish, and he took it and ate before them."

Jesus materialized and appeared in the midst of the disciples – He denied being a spirit because He appeared in a materialized spirit or etheric body, which is able to eat as the materialized [1]angels ate the food which was prepared by Abraham and Sara. See Genesis 18:1-8. Lot gave two angels unleavened bread to eat. See Gen. 19:3.) Acts Chapter 1 reports, "To them he presented himself alive after his passion by many proofs, appearing to them during [2]forty days, and speaking of the Kingdom of God".

"And when he had said this, as they were looking on, he was lifted up, and a cloud took him out of their sight." (He dematerialized and went through the portal towards the Light.) Thus, Jesus did not ascend bodily into heaven but ascended to the world of higher vibration, as Elijah did (2 Kings 2:9-13), and would also return in the same manner (Acts 1:11), interceding for His people (Rom. 8:34; Heb. 7:25).

REMARK: Esoterically speaking, every impure thought of the good/evil personality scours the divine Being and finally crucifies the inner Christ. However, when the personality or lower self turns towards the Light and seeks Truth, then the Christ within is resurrected.

The Materialization of Angels in the Old and New Testament

An angel touched Elijah and said to him, "Arise and eat" (1 Kings 19:5-7).

Nebuchadnezzar's counselor reported, "I see four men" (in the fiery furnace) --- "and the appearance of the fourth is like the son of the gods" (Daniel 3:25).

"And there appeared to him (Zechariah) an angel of the Lord standing on the right side of the altar of incense" (Luke 1:11). "In the sixth month, the angel Gabriel was sent from God" and appeared and spoke to Mary (Luke 1:26:38).

---

[1] We find in the Bible many instances of the materialization of angels. For example, in Noah's days, angels forsook "their own proper dwelling" place and materialized themselves in order to enjoy sexual relationships with "the daughters of men". See Genesis 6:1-4; Jude 6. Two angels came to Sodom and were seen by Lot and by the men of Sodom (Gen. 19:1-22), while later, Lot and his wife and their two daughters were seized by the hand of the angels and brought outside the city. "And Jacob was left alone; and a man wrestled with him until the breaking of the day" (Gen. 32:24). The angel of the Lord appeared to Gideon and later vanished from his sight (Judges 6:12-22). An angel appeared to Manoah and his wife and "ascended in the flame of the altar" (Judges 13:6:21).

[2] See p.475 – The Significance of the Number Forty.
NOTE: In order to communicate more easily, Moses and Elijah lowered their vibration while Jesus increased His during the transfiguration (Matt. 17:2-3).

"For an angel of the Lord descended from heaven and came and rolled back the stone" (Matt. 28:2). Mary "saw two angels in white, sitting where the body of Jesus had laid" (John 20:12). Two men stood by them in white robes and said, "Men of Galilee, why do you --- " (Acts 1:11).

"But at night an angel of the Lord opened the prison doors and brought them (apostles) out" (Acts 5:19). "And behold, an angel of the Lord appeared, and a light shone in the cell; and he struck Peter on the side and woke him, saying, 'Get up quickly.' And the chains fell off his hands" (Acts 12:7).

"For this very night there stood by me an angel of the God to whom I belong and whom I worship, and he said, 'Do not be afraid, Paul'" (Acts 27:23-24).

The Gospel of John Chapters 20 and 21 report, "Now on the first day of the week, Mary Magdalene came to the tomb early while it was still dark and saw that the stone had been taken away from the tomb. So she ran, and went to Simon Peter" --- "They have taken the Lord out of the tomb, and we do not know where they have laid him" --- "Then Simon Peter" --- "went into the tomb; he saw the linen clothes lying".

"But Mary stood weeping outside the tomb, and as she wept she stooped to look into the tomb; and she saw two angels in white, sitting where the body of Jesus had lain, one at the head and one at the feet" --- "she turned around and saw Jesus standing, but she did not know that it was Jesus. Jesus said to her, 'Woman, why are you weeping? Whom do you seek?' Supposing him to be the gardener, she said to him, 'Sir, if you have carried him away, tell me where you have laid him,'" --- "Jesus said to her, 'Mary.' She turned and said to him in Hebrew, 'Rabboni!' Jesus said to her, 'Do not hold me, for I have not yet ascended to the Father.'"

"On the evening of that day, the first day of the week, the doors being shut where the disciples were, for fear of the Jews, Jesus came and stood among them and said to them, 'Peace be with you.' When he had said this, he showed them his hands and his side." --- "Now Thomas" --- who "was not with them when Jesus came" did not believe that it was Jesus who appeared to the disciples. "Eight days later, his disciples were again in the house and Thomas was with them. The doors were shut, but Jesus came and stood among them." --- "Then he said to Thomas, 'Put your finger here (in the mark of the nails) and see my hands; and put out your hand, and place it in my side'" --- "Thomas answered him, 'My Lord and my God!'"

"After this, Jesus revealed himself again to the (seven) disciples by the Sea of Tiberias." --- "Just as day was breaking, Jesus stood on the beach; yet the disciples did not know that it was Jesus. Jesus said to them, 'Children, have you any fish?'" --- "'Come and have breakfast.' Now none of the disciples dared ask him, 'Who are you?' They knew it was the Lord."

Apostle Paul reported in 1 Cor. 15:6 that Jesus 'appeared to more than five hundred brethren at one time."

According to the report of Luke, Christ Jesus did not come back as a spirit (in which he later appeared to Paul and many others). For a spirit does not have flesh and bones, cannot be touched, and is not able to eat physical food, although it is able to pass through solid objects.

Jesus could also not have appeared in his crucified physical body because in Matthew, some doubted that it was Jesus, and in John, Jesus stood on the beach, but His disciples could hardly identify Him. In Luke, Jesus walked for seven miles to Emmaus with two of His disciples, but they did not recognize Him until much later. He also suddenly vanished. Physical bodies are not able to walk through closed doors as reported twice in the Gospel of John and should be recognized at once, as Jesus, in all instances.

The vehicle Christ Jesus was using to make Himself visible and heard was neither His Spirit body nor His physical body but an intermediate body, which belongs neither to the spirit world nor to the physical world. However, it was in possession of some elements and characteristics of both bodies. For example, it is able to walk through walls and doors in its dematerialized form but also be seen, touched, and experienced as having flesh and bones and, thus, able to eat when fully materialized.

After Jesus was crucified, His body was laid in the tomb, but His invisible Spirit was able to make itself visible as an intermediate body by drawing, from the surrounding atmosphere and especially from people whom are close and sensitive, a psychic substance called today "ectoplasm". Sometimes this materialization was complete, while at other times, especially in the beginning, it was not. When Jesus first appeared to Mary Magdalene, He may have drawn His materialization material or ectoplasm from the gardener. That is why Mary thought that He looked like the gardener. Mary was not allowed to touch Him because the materialization was not firm and secure and could disintegrate. When his materialization was not complete, He appeared vague and indistinct, and His disciples could not quite recognize Him. This was especially the case when Jesus walked to Emmaus in the daytime with two of His disciples. They heard His voice but could hardly see Him because sunlight is not conducive to ectoplasm. This is why He appeared early in the morning "while it was still dark" (Jn.

20:1), in the dusk of the evening, or in the upper room, in the presence of the apostles. He could become visible and tangible instantaneously in a faintly lit and closed room and could vanish just as suddenly by dematerialization, by the act of will. His materialization was complete when Christ could share meals with His disciples and when Thomas could put [1]his hand in Jesus' side and his fingers in the mark of the nail prints.

Christianity in the first few centuries was quite spiritualistic in character, and many of the Christians were in daily contact with God and with the saints of the invisible world. Many of them, when they received Christ and the Holy Spirit in their hearts, believed that this experience was the [2]Second Coming of Christ, while others whom did not receive Christ were still looking for their Savior.

As observed by the [3]Society for Psychical Research and demonstrated by spiritualists, materialization is a phenomena usually produced in special meetings or séances, in a quiet room which is faintly lit. The spirit entity that wishes to materialize [4] "borrows" a

---

[1] The presence of the nail and spear wounds does not prove that the body shown to Thomas was Jesus' physical body because the ectoplasmic body often shows, as is demonstrated in materialization in seances, the scars and other injuries of physical life. Individuals whom are completely involved with the suffering of Jesus Christ may produce His wounds first in their etheric bodies and then in their physical by repercussion. This is also called "stigmata".

[2] Some spiritualists believe that the Second Coming was realized when Jesus came back as a materialized spirit, thus fulfilling His prophecy in Matthew 10:23. Others whom are more esoterically minded say that Jesus has been (like the saints) appearing many times throughout Christian history to encourage His followers, as did Mary His Mother, but that He may come in an etheric or vital body again to appear more visible. **REMARK:** Through the power of thought, discarnate persons materialize themselves on earth to make themselves visible to people whom are not clairvoyant. However, this involves a great deal of thought power. Materialization of the whole body, therefore, does not occur very often. A deceased mother, for example, may appear briefly and then disappear.

[3] The Society for Psychical Research was founded in England in 1882 by F.H. Myers (similar societies were later organized in other countries) to investigate the claims of the spiritualist movement and other paranormal phenomena. (Reports and proceedings are available to the public.)

[4] An experienced spirit entity usually does not make use of the etheric bodies of individuals to produce a materialization but uses the surrounding ether to materialize themselves, and hold it in that form by an effort of will or by the power of sustained concentration. Other spirit beings materialize by using the etheric substance of a medium that voluntarily borrowed it in order to let a deceased loved one appear to one of the attendants and even embrace them.

substance called [5]ectoplasm from the medium and sitters. This substance helps make the spirit visible and solid, having all the anatomical and psychological character of biological life. Materialization is, thus, the ability of a human spirit to produce a material form which can be seen, recognized, and touched and which looks, talks, feels, thinks, and acts as he/she did while living on earth. This form is created from a substance called ectoplasm, which excludes from the solar plexus of certain individuals. The latter may, after this experience, feel somewhat weak and exhausted.

To produce a full materialization is rare and difficult to achieve, while partial materialization is more easily done because less ectoplasm is needed. For example, it can be formed into hands (see Ezekiel 8:3) or fingers to hold something to write (see Daniel 5:5), play the piano, or into an artificial larynx through which a spirit can speak with an audible voice. It can be used to levitate, transport, or move objects, or make raps.

As each Old Testament prophet demonstrated one or more psychic abilities, Jesus of Nazareth was in possession of all those and more. In the language of spiritualists, Jesus had, at his disposal, about all the phases of mediumship that are known today and which have been demonstrated by psychics of all religions. He truly was the most psychically gifted person that ever lived.

He was *clairvoyant as well as clair-audient, foresaw the ones who would betray and deny him, predicted His own death and in what manner He would return (Luke 18:33; 24:7), and the destruction of Jerusalem about forty years later. He knew all about the woman at Jacob's well (John 4:18) and frequently perceived what the other persons were thinking (Matt. 12:25; Luke 9:47; John 16:19). He also had precognitive abilities, by directing His followers to a spot where a

---

[5] According to the Encyclopedia of Psychic Science, "ectoplasm" – ektos (Greek) and plasma (meaning "exteriorized substance") is matter, invisible and intangible in its primary state but assuming vaporous liquid or solid conditions in various states of condensation, and it is sensitive to light. Blood contains a great amount of ectoplasm or etheric substance and frees itself from it easily when it is shed. Etheric matter is more plastic than physical matter and can be more easily manipulated. Fairies, whom are etheric beings, are known to have the ability to change shape and to increase and decrease in size. Spirit matter, on the other hand, is easier to change by thought as, for example, angelic beings are known to change almost instantaneously.
NOTE: Because the human spirit cannot act directly on physical matter, it needs the etheric body, through which it can work as an agent.
* For definition, see #35. For more detailed information, see "The Etheric Body".

fish would be caught, which carried a coin of sufficient value to pay for the tax (Matt. 17:24-27). The Son of Man was also able to send His disciples to get a donkey on which He might ride into Jerusalem, predicting the very words that the owner of the donkey would use (Luke 19:29-34). As Eliah and Elisa were able to multiply matter, Jesus multiplied matter in an abundant way when He fed the four thousand (Mark 8:1-10) and Corrie ten Boom, a Christian woman of Holland, multiplied food in a limited way in a World War II concentration camp. Jesus was able to levitate by walking on water, while Peter lowered his vibration by the emotion of fear and sank back into the water (Matt. 14:25-31). Christ Jesus did not have to go into a trance to receive spiritual knowledge as Peter did in Acts 10:10 and Paul in Acts 22:17. He possessed all the gifts of the Spirit (see Ch. 12 of 1 Cor.) and was training His disciples to become channelers, or mediums (Luke 10:23, 24; Matt. 10:1). He was a magnetic and spiritual healer and was constantly driving out, or exorcising, evil spirits from the people He met. Besides, He also had a highly developed intuition to distinguish between good and evil. Most importantly, the Savior was a spiritual teacher, counselor, and spiritual Father who gave new birth to His disciples and all who came after them. Jesus was so active in demonstrating His psychic and spiritual powers that the Babylonian Jewish Talmud mentions the execution of Jesus "on the eve of passover --- because he has practiced sorcery and led Israel astray". Finally, the Son was so much liked by His Heavenly Father that He was approved of and spoken to with a loud voice from heaven, which everyone could hear and understand (John 12:28-30).

M. The Significance of the Number Forty

The number four is the symbol of the earth principle of creation. It represents the four corners of the earth (Isa. 11:12); the four rivers which flowed out of Eden (Gen. 2:10), representing the four races; the four points of the compass; the four seasons; the four basic elements; and the four kingdoms of nature. It further is a symbol of a square, foundation, and stability.

By going through the ten stages, the number four becomes forty, which is a symbol of completion, a completed cycle, or period of time, as a fulfillment on the earth plane. The number forty in the Bible often means a period of trial, testing, indemnity, and separation of evil power. It also represents stages of maturity at all levels of good as well as evil and, finally, to experience victory, enlightenment, and peace at the personal, tribal, and national levels.

Examples of the number forty in the Bible are: at the personal level, when Isaac was forty years old when he took Rebekah for his wife (Gen. 25:20) and their first-born son Esau took two wives, Judith and Basemath when he became forty, "and they made life bitter" for his parents (Gen. 26:34-35). Much later, their second-born son Jacob (Israel) died; forty days were needed to embalm him (Gen. 50:3).

At the family level when Noah was six hundred years old, rain fell on the earth for forty days and forty nights. At the end of the forty days, Noah sent forth a raven (symbol of evil) from his ark, which had three decks, and thereafter sent a dove (symbol of good) three times "to see if the waters had subsided" (Gen. Ch. 7 and 8).

In Acts 7:23-26, we read that when Moses was forty years old, he defended a son of Israel, struck an Egyptian, and had to flee to the desert after he was betrayed by the Israelites he tried to protect. After being in Median for forty years, an angel appeared to him in a flame of fire, and he was told by God to lead the Israelites out of the land of Egypt and lead them into the land of Canaan, which took another forty years. During that time, when his mission was on the tribal and national levels, "Moses was on the mountain forty days and forty nights" (Ex. 24:18) and received the Ten Commandments. After he broke the tablets of stone, he again was on Mount Sinai "with the Lord forty days and forty nights; he neither ate bread nor drank water" (Ex. 34:28) "because of all the sin which you had committed" (Deut. 9:18), and received anew the Ten Commandments (Ex. 34:1). After a long journey from Egypt through the desert, they reached the land of Canaan. Moses sent out twelve men (heads of every tribe) to spy out the land for forty days (Numbers Ch. 13). The men brought out a negative report, while only Joshua and Caleb (was forty years old when he was sent to spy – Jos. 14:17 –) said that we can easily overcome the people of the land because the Lord is with us and His protection is removed from them. Because the people did not want to conquer the land given to them by God and live in freedom but instead wanted to go back to Egypt, preferring to live in bondage, they had to pay a heavy penalty. They were condemned to wander in the wilderness for forty years – a day of spying for every year of wandering (Numbers 14:33-34).

1 Kings 19:8 reports that "he (Elijah) arose, and ate and drank and went in the strength of that food forty days and forty nights to Horeb, the mount of God. As Moses fasted for forty days in the wilderness, so Jesus also fasted in the wilderness for forty days and forty nights and

was tempted by the devil (Matt. 4:1-2). After His crucifixion, Jesus' body was in the tomb forty hours, and He was seen after the resurrection by His disciples for forty days.

And the people of Israel did what was evil in the sight of God, and He sold them into the hands of the king of Mesopotamia. After the Israelites cried to the Lord, He delivered them, and the land had rest for forty years (Judges 3:7-11). Thereafter, the people again did evil and were sold into the hands of Jabin, king of Canaan, who was conquered after the people of Israel cried to the Lord for help, and there was peace in the land for forty years (Judges 4:1-7; 5:31). The people again did evil, and the Lord gave them into the hands of Midian for seven years. The people cried out to the Lord and were delivered by Gideon, and there was rest in the land for forty years (Judges 6:1-6; 8:28). Because the people did what was evil, the Lord gave them into the hands of the Philistines for forty years (Judges 13:1). During that time, Eli was a judge for forty years and died suddenly (1 Sam. 4:18). When Samuel became the new judge, "the hand of the Lord was against the Philistines all the days of Samuel" (1 Sam. 7:13). The Philistines were finally conquered when David slew Goliath, who defied the armies of Israel for forty days (1 Sam. 17:26, 50).

*Saul reigned as king over Israel for forty years (1 Sam. 13:1; Acts 13:21). "David was thirty years old when he began to reign, and he reigned forty years" (2 Sam. 5:4). His son Solomon also reigned for forty years (1 Kings 2:11). Thereafter in the divided kingdom, Joash reigned for forty years in Jerusalem (2 Kings 12:1; 2 Chronicles 24:1).

"Because you said 'the Nile is mine, and I made it', therefore, behold, I am against you, and against your streams, and I will make the land of Egypt an utter waste and desolation --- and it shall be inhabited forty years." "At the end of forty years --- I will restore the fortunes of Egypt" (Ezekiel 29:9, 10, 11, 13, 14).

Jonah cried out to the people, "Yet forty days, and Nineveh shall be overthrown!" But to the discontent of Jonah, the people repented of their evil ways (Jonah 3:4, 5).

---

* Saul's son Ishbusheth was forty years old when he began to reign after Saul's death but was killed by Rechab and Baanah, his captains, whom in turn were killed at the command of David (2 Sam. 2:10; 4:7, 12).

The Number Forty in Secular and Christian History

The Eastern Orthodox religion, in accordance with Luke 2:22, believes that forty days after the infant's birth, he or she should be presented to the Lord, or be "churched".

About forty years after the crucifixion of Jesus, 960 Jews committed suicide in Masada.

When Augustine was forty years old in 395 A.D., he became coadjutor of the bishop Valarius of the Hippo region, whom he shortly thereafter succeeded.

Willibrord sailed in 690 A.D. with eleven companions across the channel to Frankish Frisia (Holland) and began missionary work in Europe. When he was forty years old, he received and established a monastery, the Echternach, Luxembourg. Bonifacius crossed the channel in 716 A.D. and also went first to Frisia. When he was forty years old, he received Pope Gregory's authority for his work. His life ended in martyrdom in Dokkem, Frisia. Another missionary who sailed with Willibrord, whose name was Adelbert, was especially helpful in the region of Egmond, Holland. A monastery was later built in his honor by the counts of Holland.

In 1054, a schism between Rome and Constantinople occurred, and 400 years later, the Turks captured the city of Constantinople in 1453. The Avignon schism lasted from 1377 to 1417.

The Puritans did not succeed to console their power in 1660 (40 years after the Pilgrim fathers landed in Plymouth) because the "spirit of the time" rebelled against such extreme strictness. St. Francis of Assisi, when forty years old, established a third order, the Franciscan Family III, in 1222.

---

[1] This monastery was completely destroyed in 1573 by the Spanish at the siege of Alkmaar. In 1973, the author and his wife Pauline and forty members founded a religious center on top of a mountain in Bergen aan Zee, near Egmond, called "Huize Glory".

479

It took Thomas Jefferson forty years to build his house in [2]Virginia. When he was 33 years old, he drafted the Declaration of Independence. Fifty years later, he died on July 4, 1826. Since that time, America has been guided by the principle of democracy.

People say of America, wherever I go, "I get a sense of freedom and energy. It is truly a land of freedom and opportunity." You can still breathe without being watched. We can talk about what is wrong without being punished. This system allows the voice of the people to be heard and to grow in any possible way, without limitations. John Wayne was more than just a hero. He was a symbol of many of the basic qualities that made America great: ruggedness, independence, and a sense of personal conviction and courage.

God replied to the people that wanted to be ruled by a king, "He will take the best of your fields and vineyards and olive orchards and give them to his servants. He will take the tenth of your grain and of your vineyards and give it to his officers and to his servants. He will take your men servants and the best of your cattle and your asses, and put them to work. He will take the tenth of your flocks, and you shall be his slaves. And in that day you will cry out because of your king, whom you have chosen for yourselves, but the Lord will not answer you in that day" (1 Sam. 8:14-18).

As it was not good at that time to be ruled by a hierarchical structure, it is not good today because the people are good as well as evil. That is why the democratic form of government is here to stay until people have become good.

[2] The College of William and Mary in Virginia had become known as the Alma Mater of a nation because of its role in the education of dozens of early American leaders. William III (1650-1702) was born in Holland and became, together with his wife Mary (daughter of future James II of England), king and queen of England in 1689.

A. Arranged Marriages in Biblical Times

The concept of "arranged marriages" is foreign and strange to young Americans and Europeans and others in industrialized nations. However, it has been an accepted pattern or model in human history for almost all of humanity. While arranged marriages are still common in some lands and cultures, many individuals today select their own marriage mate, through dating and by "falling in love". The latter arrangement is but less than one hundred years old in Western society. Before that time, the influence of parents and others in choosing the right mate for sons and daughters was significant and important.

Popular culture does not encourage us to let God be the matchmaker. However, from the beginning, the first man Adam did not choose his wife. God lovingly provided her for him (Genesis 2:18-24). After that first union, marriage arrangements were usually made by the parents of the bride and groom and, occasionally, after gaining the consent of those involved (Gen. 24:58). For example, "his (Ishmael) mother (Hagar) took a wife for him out of the land of Egypt" (Gen. 21:21). Abraham chose for his son Isaac a wife by sending his servant to look for one, who with the guidance of the Lord, found Rebekah (Gen. 24:1-21). "Then Isaac called Jacob and blessed him, and charged him, 'You shall not marry one of the Canaanite women. Arise, go to Paddanaram to the house of Bethuel your mother's father; and take as wife from there one of the daughters of Laban your mother's brother'" (Gen. 28:1-2). "Judah took a wife for Er his first-born, and her name was Tamar" (Gen. 38:6). Joshua 15:16 reported, "And Caleb said, 'whoever smites Kiriath-sepher, and takes it, to him I will give Achsah my daughter as wife.'" See also Gen. 34:4 and Judges 14:2.

In the Book of Ruth, we read how God can intervene for those that have prepared themselves. Ruth the Moabite married Boaz, who became the great grandparents of David, the future king of Israel, from whom descended "Joseph the husband of Mary, of whom Jesus was born, who is called Christ" (Matt. 1:16).

Salomon wrote in Proverbs 18:22, "He who finds a wife finds a good thing, and obtains favor from the Lord." He also said, "Charm is deceitful, and beauty is vain, but a woman who fears the Lord is to be

481

praised" (Prov. 31:30). This suggests that one should not be influenced by appearance, or by catering to their needs and wants.

The ancient Jewish wedding ceremony began after a groom and bride were promised to each other, either by their own choosing (when mature) or by the arrangement of parents, but always with parental blessing. Dating and romance, as we know it, was not practiced at that time, and only virgins were eligible for marriage (Deut. 22:20). If a man had sex with a virgin, he was obliged to marry her (Ex. 22:16) and to pay compensation to her father. When he lies with a betrothed virgin, they both were stoned to death (Deut. 22:23, 24). However, if she is raped, then only the man shall die (Deut. 22:25-27). As Proverbs Chapter seven warned, A man can easily be [1]seduced by a married woman, as the wife of Potiphar tried to do to Joseph. See Genesis 39:7-20.

In New Testament times, Apostle Peter said that women should be in possession of "the imperishable jewel of a gentle and quiet spirit" (1 Pet. 3:4). The spiritual qualities of a prospective companion, her inner personality, and devotion to God are much more important than her external beauty. The woman, in turn, should find out if her prospective mate is committed to living and teaching the Word of God. She certainly should not marry someone who does not respect her, in spite of his abundant resources. Apostle Paul advised his followers "not to be mismated with unbelievers" (2 Cor. 6:14) and to marry "only in the Lord" (1 Cor. 7:39). Single Christians and others should, therefore, not start courting members of the opposite sex whom are unbelievers but disengage themselves from them, as the Israelites after the Exile had to send away their foreign wives. See Ezra Chapter ten. Those that are already engaged should take a second look at why they want to marry him or her. Are they unified in the Spirit, or is the attraction to each other only a physical and emotional romance, which sooner or later wears off when they get less handsome or beautiful and also more negative? However, when they are married in the Lord, they look much deeper and see the beauty of the other's Soul, which is everlasting. Young people should, therefore, only get engaged when, after a period of time, they become convinced, in the depths of their hearts, that God has led them to be together. They then get to know each other intimately at an inner level and grow together, without a physical relationship, which will inhibit or arrest this development. They have become more loyal, trustworthy, and forgiving. Thereafter,

---

[1] Women that are promiscuous radiate a magnetic attractive energy to men, which is sexual in nature.

their marriage will not fail when they keep God at the center of their lives and have also the support of their fellow believers.

NOTE: In the days of the prophet Malachi, many husbands left their wives, perhaps to marry younger women. The Lord said that His altar was covered with the tears of the abandoned wives, and He condemned the men who were unfaithful "to the wife of his youth" (Malachi 2:13-16).

B. Short History of Marriage in Western Society

Because of immaturity and unreadiness of the partners, the history of marriage has been nothing else but strife, struggle, confusion, and brutality between men and women instead of a harmonious and growth-enhancing relationship. Ancient Greece did little to advance the cause of male/female relations. The men did not love their women but treated them as housekeepers and used them to beget sons. The ancient Romans loved their women more, but their love was more erotic than real and was not based on mutual respect because the husband regarded his wife and children as property. After the Roman Empire was established, women gained greater rights and liberty. However, many men and women increasingly pursued sex outside their marriage. As a consequence, the relationship between husband and wife, the foundation of the family, the microcosm of society, began to crumble, and so did the Roman Empire.

The early Christians, whom became the new Romans, highly respected women who were *living a divine life, but they looked upon women who were carnal and living a life of the good and evil personality with suspicion, fear, and dismay. The Roman church at that time considered celibacy the most favorable condition but allowed marriages to those whom were good, but spiritually immature. The condition the church imposed was that the newlyweds do not love, or rather, lust after each other too much. In that case, their love became more satanic, and their relationship came increasingly under the influence of evil forces, and God became less important in their lives.

Later in the Middle Ages, relationships in marriages declined, and women were once more regarded as property by many men whose evil side of the personality was more or less ruling their lives. Many marriages were arranged between families instead of individuals, and a

---

* Although many men and women were living as brothers and sisters, some of them also got married after a purifying process of celibate living.

prospective bride and groom were chosen on the basis of social status and property.

However, when respect for the feminine was just about lost, wandering Troubadours came along, between the 11th and 13th centuries, and moved around in Southern Europe as singers and poet musicians. They recognized and sang to the Divine Feminine of the many women that were married. The Troubadours formed a relationship of romantic spiritual love with the ones they sang to (without any sexual contact) and adored the Divine in the women as their only love. Instead of being seen as evil, the feminine became an object of veneration and devotion. Thereafter, many men began to practice courtship or individual love between them and the women instead of conquest. Couples became more gentle, faithful, and loyal to each other.

According to "The Faith of the Pilgrims" by R.N. Bartlett, "in an effort to promote success marriages, a law was passed in 1638 by the Plymouth colony that no man should propose to a young woman until he had required the consent of her parents, or her master, if she were a bond servant". The Pilgrim youth lived a strict life of discipline and were not allowed to see each other as sexual objects but as brothers and sisters in the Lord until they got blessed in matrimony by their minister and elders. As they became part of the community, their marriage also became a concern for the whole church congregation.

NOTE: The Dutch consider marriage a civil ceremony outside the authority of the church. The city of Leiden (Holland) records testify to this separation of religious authority over marriage in the statute of 1590. Marriage, which had been exploited by the church, was removed from the manipulation of the clergy and handled by the magistrates. John Robinson told his Leiden congregation (Pilgrims) that marriage should not be the responsibility of the church, subject to the control of the priests, but rather should be handled by state and civic officials. The Pilgrims adapted the Dutch practice of marriage by civil authorities and confronted it in Plymouth until 1692, the year they were absorbed into the Massachusetts Bay colony (The faith of the Pilgrims).

In Victorian time (1819-1901), the same implicit message was given, as in the time of the Troubadours, that women should not be taken for granted, but the men should recognize the divine in them, that they should marry each other when their relationship is not only physical or emotional, but also spiritual.

By the end of the nineteenth century, during the Industrial Revolution, parents lost much of their authority and control over their children, who became less inclined to ask for their approval in choosing their life partners. In the (roaring) 1920s, a new way of finding the right mate became known as "dating", which was the final blow to the exclusive mate selection by the parents.

In the 1920s and later, women became more active in the public arena and demanded more rights and freedoms. They did not want to be pushed around by men anymore, who did not know them. Some of them said, "As men represent the male aspect of God, then women represent the female aspect of God, and are therefore equal."

As traditional marriages, according to many young people, were not flexible and curtailed individual freedoms, marriages in the sixties and seventies became self-centered. The freedom they sought for became licentious, a freedom without responsibility. This degraded their marriage to the lowest level.

Today, we should understand that marriages can be quite good when people marry when they have become mature in their personalities, and that both parties are also *developed as much as possible in a spiritual way. They will then know themselves more fully and also share with each other their deepest feelings and aspirations, so that they are always faithful and have complete trust in the other.

C. Choosing Partners in Primitive and Eastern Lands

The old and the wise, in many societies, are not in favor of love affairs because they know and have seen what can happen to love affairs gone wrong. They, therefore, prefer that parents and others choose prospective mates for offspring, provided that those who do the selecting are qualified. Many parents feel that because of their children's ages and lack of experience, they cannot be relied on to judge correctly the character and maturity of a likely companion and may decide things emotionally. Their choosing will unburden the young from turmoil, tension, anxiety, anguish, and will also preserve the ancestry, present family, and posterity. Thus, the hazards of casual and foolish love affairs are avoided in the custom of arranged marriages.

---

* Spiritual maturity at present stage of evolution is, for most people, difficult to attain.

In some primitive communities, children, when very young, were already betrothed or promised by families to marry other children or relatives as soon as they became mature. In other primitive societies, it was not only the parents who made arrangements for their children but also the consent of certain relatives was, in many cases, needed. In other parts of the world, brides are purchased by the future husbands or deputies of the bridegroom, or payments are made by the relatives of the bride. Of Eastern societies in general, especially those that are much involved in ancestor worship, parents, grandparents, and other relatives arranged the match, often with the aid of a matchmaker. In other Eastern communities, arrangements were often made between parents of families only, and the consent of the marriage partners was not required, for filial obedience was considered one of the highest and noblest virtues. Other communities allowed the voice of the partners also to be heard. Influenced by Western society, especially after the 1960s, many of the above-mentioned mating requirements became more relaxed. Children, in many cases, want to choose their own mates, with or without approval of their parents and religious leaders.

NOTE: Some members of religious organizations put all their trust in a religious leader to choose the right life partner for them. Others whom are less loyal help the leader in making the right choice by desperately praying that God will work through His representative. All those that are chosen are far from perfect, and evil is, to some degree, still present in their personalities and needs to be dissolved. This can be done in an individual way but also, and sometimes most effectively, by the other party, provided that they do not have the same problems. For example, an individual who has a sex problem should not marry another with the same problem. This will only strengthen his or her own. Children born of couples that are chosen by God will be of less original sin, and their children will be of even less sin, so that eventually the Kingdom of God will be established, and people will no longer be living a life of good and evil.

In some parts of Asia, Africa, and India, arranged marriages are still the custom. Many couples that have been chosen in Tibet and India are happy and content in their marriage. Thus, it seems that arranging of marriages works best when the people emphasize the value of spirituality more than material values.

The Kama sutra reported: When a girl of the same caste and a boy are married in accordance with the precept of the holy writ, the results of such a union are: the acquisition of Dharma, offspring, affinity, increase of friends, and untarnished love. For this reason, a man should fix his affection upon a girl who is a virgin, of a good family, whose parents are alive, and who is at least three years, or more, younger than himself.

There are four castes in India, and intermarriage between the castes is not allowed. The people of India in general believe that individuals of low castes have to pay karma or are being punished for the evil they have committed in former existence.

REMARK: The ancient white brotherhood is responsible for having created the concepts, which resulted in the caste system and which we can still find in India today. The brotherhood recognized that some individuals were more intellectually and spiritually evolved than others. Thus, they created a system, whereby they could assist those whom were highly advanced and whom, in turn, help those that are less evolved. The latter group would feed the masses the information and wisdom they could understand and live by.

The caste arrangement became the law of the land when the legislator Manu saw a great distinction in the evolution of the people and divided them up into four great classes:

1) The Sudras – Those whom are much involved in bodily labor. They are occupied in fulfilling the needs of the body and the life of the senses, and are thus largely motivated by self-interest
2) The Vaisyas – Those whom serve through their mental skills. They are involved in agriculture, commerce, trade, business, and life in general. They are the skilled workers and know how to control their emotions.
3) The Kshatriyas – Those whom lead a life of Dharma, self-discipline, and right action, and are men of power and ambition. They carry out their responsibilities as rulers, warriors, and protectors.
4) The Brahmins – Those are not only men of learning but are also spiritually liberated (moksha – twice born). They lead a divine life and devote themselves to help others in teaching spiritual Truth and in meditation. The Brahmins are also continually in search of physical, intellectual, and spiritual knowledge, combine them, and communicate it to others, like the philosophers in Plato's time. To fight is a sin for a Brahmin but not for a Kshatriyas.

The caste system no longer exists in any legally recognized form because throughout the centuries, it became hardened through inheritance. The system should be based on natural qualities and not by birth alone. A person, for example, should not be a Kshatriyas if he is not qualified. The son of a Brahmin should be considered a Sudra unless he has proven himself, through character and conduct, to be more than a Sudra.

It is said by those that are in favor of the caste system that it has preserved the purity of the race and prevented it from being degenerated and becoming extinct, as happened to many other ancient races.

D. Finding a Mate with the Help of God

While waiting for the right person, it is good to pray about it because God wants you to express your wish in prayer. In the *course of time, He and His forces will direct you to find the right person, or your prospective mate will find you. After our prayer, we should keep our physical and spiritual eyes and ears open for His guidance. It may come through someone who may say something, or we may hear God's advice through our inner voice. We may see our future companion passing by, whom we are very eager to meet, or we are guided to a certain place or other opportunities are offered to us, sometimes by complete strangers. There are also many other ways God uses to answer our prayer. Some religious people look at marriage as a spiritual calling and have complete trust that God will find the right partner. Others are so busy doing God's work in their service to humanity that they have no time to look for a mate. However one day, that special person just shows up at their doorstep.

Those candidates whose personality or lower self is first united with their own Soul mate or Higher Self have a much easier time finding their life companion because they are magnified by the power of God and draw everyone to find them. Being in possession of this magnetic quality of the Spirit, they will also attract less evolved beings, which they are tempted to marry because of the attractive personality of the other. The candidate thus made the mistake of falling for the other on the basis of outward appearance, physical attraction, desires, and the romantic love of storybooks instead of true love and spiritual ideals. Such a marriage restricts, or drags down, the evolved person and limits his or her mission or destiny.

NOTE 1: Some women whom are not able to recognize God's calling may say, "Where can I find a man who will love and respect me and live by God's standards? I have tried to keep myself pure, waiting for the right man. He does not come to me, and I don't pursue him because I don't know if he is for me by God's plan." There are certainly a number of young men who are also having a hard time finding the right woman to marry. Those individuals should understand that when they are miserable, God who lives within them is

---

* You may be ready for marriage, but your partner is not. In that case, you have to wait until your partner is sufficiently evolved. He or she is then inspired to make his or her presence known to you or agree to marry you.

also miserable. He or She will do anything to make you happy. Young people may look for their mate at the wrong places, such as singles bars or by placing an ad in the paper. They may be better off to let another person, through whom God can work more easily and whose Soul and higher intuition are more developed, to find their mate, the true Jacob or Jacoba.

NOTE 2: We know that we have married the right person when we are able to share at all levels, and that we not only care for each other but also humanity, who we like to serve as a married couple.

E. What Happens When a Boy and Girl Meet

When a young man and woman meet each other for the first time, the need to be careful that physical attraction and strong impulses of desire do not distort their judgment when selecting a mate. They should, therefore, test their relation for a time to see if it is bound by mere physical affinity, the straw fire of emotional attraction, or something much deeper. A good selection can enrich one's life, but a poor choice can bring no end to sorrow (Prov. 21:19; 26:21; 2 Sam. 13:15). It is therefore better to wait until they are better able to control their desires and passions (1 Cor. 7:36) and have grown to love the other person wholeheartedly.

NOTE: Attraction may be purely physical for some men and women by bonding on the sexual level first. Thereafter, they find out that they do not blend on the higher dimensional levels. Women are, for many men, nothing more than objects to be used for their own satisfaction, while women use sex often to control men and to fulfill their need for affection. A boy may fall for a pretty woman but later discover that she is silly, unfaithful, capricious, and stupid. He becomes so disgusted with her, with what he sees within her, that her beauty no longer appeals to him. On the other hand, a boy may meet a girl that is not very pretty, but after some time, he is so enchanted by her kindness, unselfishness, and wisdom that he cannot help himself but to love her for the rest of his life. For Rose, Ted is the most wonderful man in the world; others may only see his disability, but Rose sees the beauty of his Soul.

Romantic love begins with a physical attraction to a member of the opposite sex. When their auras mingle, they may like or dislike each other, depending on their basic energy or vibratory pattern. A few of them may feel such a perfect blending of their auras or interaction of their vibratory fields that they experience love at first sight. The individuals experience such a union and harmony as if they already know and have known each other. They are empowered by this unity of opposites and by drawing and uniting the opposite forces of the universe. The lovers may feel that they are walking on air and could have talked and danced all night. Because their human spirits are so closely connected, time and distance play no part in their relationships. They may say, "I feel complete when I am with you", or "I can't imagine my life without you." However, when *this relationship is based mainly on emotion, it is not strong and deep and may easily crumble when one or both parties are finding too many faults in the other. It may decline rapidly when one or both are lusting after each other, whereby they backslide to the lower second level. They may blame each other for the miserable state they are in, far removed from the God forces. Howbeit, when their relationship is not only on the physical, emotional, and mental levels but is also rooted in the [1]divine level, they may sustain this euphoric feeling longer. But it will level off somewhat when the couple starts raising a family, and their growth in love really begins. Thus, their relation should be on all levels, whereby the spiritual attraction should be the main focus of attention. The Soul connection is much deeper and more powerful than the relationship between human personalities. It is endless, and it takes an [2]eternity to really know it. They may then look and experience each other as the representation of the Godhead, He as the expression of the Fatherhood of God and She as the expression of the Motherhood of God.

F. Choosing Partners by self-reliant Persons

Those who do not believe that others should be directly involved in choosing their mates or in asking God and His forces to guide them to Mr. or Mrs. Right need a lot of information and self-knowledge to find the other half. They are taught the value of self-help over prayer, to "go for it" instead of waiting for signs of guidance. In many of the "How to Catch a Mate" books, it is explained that a well-developed strategy is all that is needed to bring couples together. Those writing, although they may be helpful, often emphasize that the other half is a

---

* As explained before, our emotional idea of love is fleeting and should not be pursued because it cannot endure the stress of everyday life and leads only to disappointment. Physical and emotional attraction is not enough, and if the mental in the relationship is missing, there is no way to have an interesting conversation. Lovers may then become bored with each other.

[1] Some people "fall in love", or rather are in true love when they look at each other and experience the divine in the other person. When you have found this person, your entire being vibrates in unison with God, and there is a love that only the poets have been able to describe.

[2] As we get to know the outer personality or body of the other very soon, to know the inner personality or human spirit takes a much longer time, while to know the Soul takes forever.

commodity, which is subject to the rules of competition. Some organizations teach their members how to succeed in the singles market by advertising their physical qualities and psychological traits. Those markets, crowded with therapists and self-help gurus, revolve much about the psychological fitness of the candidates in the here and now. It usually does not take into consideration the ancestor lineage of the couple, their mission, and the potential divine qualities and destiny of their future children. The worst are the couples that wed for the purpose of convenience, desire, acquiring position, security, wealth, and power. Those individuals who acquired their mates in the different trading places commonly only take into account the life of the personality, which is good and evil. Those marriages are "man-made", and they should, therefore, not expect to have the same kind of help from the divine forces, as those couples that are made by God.

NOTE: Besides the various forms of dating services, such as personal ads, pen pal clubs, videotapes, computer, and other introduction services, there is also made extensive use of what is called *astrological compatibility. Further, one may read body signs and hand lines. In the latter, signs of compatibility can be read in the relation between the heart and headline, its ending and linkage with other lines.

Let us explain below some of the human wisdom used to fit and bond couples in harmony with the lower inner selves, which in many cases is compatible with the divine wisdom of the innermost Higher Selves. First of all, we will not find a "perfect" mate until we have become the "perfect" prospect. In the expression of the American pioneer proverb, "Success in relationships is much more than finding the right person; it is a matter of being the right person." Furthermore, it is basically not difficult to find the other half, as opposites attract and seek to balance themselves. Being incomplete, each has something the other wants and needs, either in its physical complement or psychological aspect. Thus, as the physical bodies interlock, so do the human spirits. What we do not claim for ourselves we look for in the other. Sometimes, the candidates and others do not always understand why the former has chosen a particular person. But the latter fulfills a psychological need, which no other person can. [1]For example, a person

---

* Astrology can be a valuable human device or tool in evaluating relationships when used with other information. At the time of birth, a personality is imprinted or stamped with a specific astrological identity (depending on the stand and movement of stars and planets), known as a horoscope or birth chart.

[1] Good qualities do not harmonize with evil qualities. A kind, gentle person would not be attracted to someone who is mean, selfish, and brutal. An honest person cannot be in a relationship with a liar or a cheat.

may be patient and enduring, while the other party may be spontaneous and bold. One is serious about life, while the other has a sense of humor. One may add stability to their relationship, while the other is more playful. One is tender and caring, while the other expresses love in a different way. Some may be well organized and ambitious, while the other is less uniform and easygoing. One is impulsive and flexible, while the other is analytical and more rigid. Some like change, while their mate likes the predictable...and so on. Together, they can live a life worth living.

As in the animal world, male and in particular female animals are always looking for the fittest available mate. Women in the human world, at the physical level, are always looking for men who are tall, strong, healthy, and in possession of abundant resources and genes for the offspring. In addition, the men should be handsome, kind, faithful, sensitive (to her needs), intellectual, of social standing (a beard may help!), ambitious, and of good behavior. However, it is also true that powerful, wealthy, famous, and charismatic men are continually pursued by women. They, therefore, have a tendency to show less interest in their wives by having many extramarital affairs. [2]Men, on the other hand, favor physical attractiveness and youthfulness in their women, whom should also be beautiful. They should be of normal weight, unblemished skin, and have the right measurements of parts of their bodies, and in the right proportions, such as that of waist and hips, so that they are slim and have a good figure. The shape and features of their faces should also be like the body, symmetrical, which creates harmony and, therefore, beauty. In addition, the women should be lovely, gentle, understanding, faithful, loyal, and devoted to the needs of the family. However, women that are beautiful are chased much by men of all ages, not only in a physical way but also psychically. They may become easily tempted and, as a result, radiate less of that inner beauty, which aided their elegance, grace, and charm.

NOTE: Discover the man or woman you are with instead of expecting him or her to be what you want.

In conclusion, we like to say that men and women should support and challenge each other to grow to their fullest potential and, thus, increase their capacity for self-giving, sharing, and spiritual growth.

---

[2] Men like bad girls but marry the good ones, while women like good men but marry the bad ones.

G. Evaluating a Prospective Partner

When selecting a marital partner with whom you will share your innermost thoughts, values, and dreams, you should consider his or her characteristics, personal stability, family background, etc., and their goals and expectations.

The selection process begins by first meeting with a variety of members of the opposite sex and, if possible, in a religious setting of which you are a member. When you become interested in one particular person, and the other also likes you, you may set aside different times to be together, which is called dating. At those times, they can enjoy each other's company and experience the positive and negative qualities. This is also a good opportunity to find out if your potential partner has any major problems or faults which may result in a troubled marriage.

You may ask the following questions:

- ➢ Does you dating partner have a problem with substance abuse and gambling?
- ➢ Is your partner overly jealous or possessive?
- ➢ What kind of reputation and morals does he or she have?
- ➢ Is there any physical and emotional abuse between each other?
- ➢ Does your partner flirt with the opposite sex and exhibit promiscuous behavior?
- ➢ How does you companion treat family and friends?
- ➢ Is your escort someone who cannot keep his or her word or promise?
- ➢ Is your consort someone who gives in to uncontrollable expressions of rage?
- ➢ Is your dating partner often depressed and has serious mood swings?
- ➢ Does he or she express sudden profanities when crossed by a driver?
- ➢ Does your escort have fits of anger and abusive speech?
- ➢ Is your consort overly critical and pessimistic?
- ➢ Does your partner come from an unhappy or unstable home, whose parent(s) belittle or try to dominate each other and one or both are heavy drinkers?
- ➢ Has your dating partner been abused by them, and are they separated or divorced?

An acceptable mate should have strong moral values, conviction, and integrity and does not blame anyone for his or her mistakes but takes full responsibility and control.

NOTE: Some partners do not want to tell everything about themselves because they fear rejection. They want their companion to love an illusion. However, if you choose not to reveal yourself, there is no deep connection, and one day, your partner will walk out of your life and will never return.

H. Conclusion

When a marriage has been established on a foundation of sexual interest and satisfaction, or built mainly upon physical attraction, the relationship lasts only as long as this interest prevails, or the original attraction is sustained. When the first sexual appeal or charm is no longer there, loses its freshness, and becomes boring (the bloom has wilted), the husband and wife eventually look for someone else who will be the new physical fascination or adoration. Some couples try to keep their initial passionate infatuation alive by physically exploring each other by degrading techniques. After exhausting those methods, eros will leave them, and they no longer "love" each other.

Many people believe that sexuality is about recreation and power rather than bonding and procreation. By misusing the gift of human sexuality, women are seen by men as objects of male satisfaction, while women see themselves as more valuable when they have slept with important and powerful persons. Others are so concerned about their freedoms and the right to do what they please that they have forgotten that sex has something to do with children. Those children are the victims and have become the unwanted by-products in their search for a misguided and degraded sense of self-fulfillment.

Married couples that take into consideration moral aspects and duties to the other and have common values last longer because when the physical fails, at times, the moral prevails. They should also have the same interest and act like friends (philia) and be united at the physical, moral, and mental levels. The men should not court others of the opposite sex, and women should not seek the admiration of other men, and keep her husband's secrets, so that he will always trust, support, and love her. *Being good and evil, the husband or wife would sooner or later show their worst sides. At those times, they should persevere and not leave each other, and stick and uphold their wedding vow, "For better or for worse, for richer or for poorer, in sickness and in health, to love and to cherish, till death do us part." In those critical periods, they should once again remember and rediscover the wonderful qualities they once saw in each other.

Couples will be content when they not only unite with their inner personalities but also look for and unite with the divine aspect of the other (agape) and know that God is the Source of true love. However, if one partner advances spiritually and the other does not, or does not want to, the relationship may break up. A lack of mutual growth may evoke comments as "we don't seem to have anything in common anymore". Albeit, the more developed person should do everything possible to bring the other to his or her level. He or she should not succumb to the lower level of the other because duty to Divine Consciousness is always of first priority. When they study God's Word, pray and meditate together, their Souls will unite and grow. They will then not only love each other and their children but also love everything and everybody with a universal love.

Finally, we can say that it is a grand and noble thing to be a man, and to be a woman is to be truly God's last and best gift to man.

---

* If one or the other party, or both, are somewhat spiritually evolved, they have a reasonable capacity to distinguish between good and evil. When one party, for example, expresses evil by thoughts, words, or deeds and the other party does not want to succumb, there cannot be any harmony between them. Because they are both evolved, this discord usually does not last long. The offending party soon realizes that he or she was not on God's side.

Seven Stages of Development
A. Introduction

Because of the fall of the primal couple, the personalities of them and their descendants became tainted with [1]original sin. They, therefore, were not able to reach full maturity in their lifetimes, or complete the seven stages of development. The purpose of history is, for that reason, to [2]restore humans from the sub-human state of primitives to ordinary humans of today and on to super humans in the near future.

From being ruled by instinct to intellect and then by an illuminated mind. From lawlessness to law and order and to live by grace. From ignorance and superstition to human and divine knowledge. From those whom are cruel to those having some compassion to the ones that are sensitive to the sorrow and suffering of the world. From those that do not know right from wrong to individuals that have a conscience, while others are able to judge by their (higher) intuition. From being extremely selfish to taking care of family and country to work for the good of the whole. From a most dangerous creature to the ones whom we do not quite trust to those in whom we have complete faith and trust. From those whom have only respect for physical strength to humans that can be persuaded by words to divine beings who convince by the spiritual strength of their beings.

People all over the world, notwithstanding [3]occasional setbacks, have, since human history began, improved considerably by trying to

---

[1] Original sin can be compared with the root of a weed, which should be pulled out completely; otherwise, it will grow again. Society cannot become good unless the root of all evil is removed because humans will repeat the same sins over and over again, even after they have confessed them.

[2] Restoration of humans always proceeds from the lower to the higher, from materialism to spiritual belief, from the mundane to the abstract, from knowledge of the physical to learning of the etheric, spirit, and divine bodies, away from self to God-centeredness. This restoration by Truth can only proceed one step at a time; otherwise, people would misunderstand and reject a higher Truth or are not able to bear it (Jn. 16:12), or may attack you (Matt. 7:6). On the foundation of a lower, a higher Truth will be given to those whom have exhausted the old and are ready to receive the new. The new Revelation contains and fulfills the basic Truth of the old (Matt. 5:17).

[3] Some may, at times, display sub-human qualities and characteristics and may go back to the time when humans behaved like animals, when the survival instinct to kill and passion ruled their lives. Their mentality was the survival of the fittest, and might was always right. Young undeveloped egos may seek their pleasures in coarse, brutish, and indecent behavior, while the more advanced egos find satisfaction in higher emotions and thoughts, in music, art, science, literature, and philosophy.

fulfill their potential, not only physically, with its scientific development, but also intellectually and, for quite a few, also spiritually. Many of them came out of the darkness of sense belief and superstition into the light of spiritual understanding. Their awareness also expanded from village consciousness to that of the nation and to the world, while breaking down cultural barriers through student exchange programs and international friendships. This results in more unity among nations. We have become more health conscious and live longer. We care more about our environment and living conditions, while violations of human rights and liberties are being exposed throughout the world. We are expressing more of the image of God so that He/She becomes more visible. Thus, a new level of consciousness is pervading the lower consciousness of humanity.

NOTE 1: Raising individual consciousness will give a positive boost to the human race consciousness.

NOTE 2: In earlier times, disputes were often settled by the sword. Today, they are judged in court or in corporate boardrooms.

NOTE 3: Many people today no longer believe, as in Roman times, that the value of an individual is decided by what he or she could contribute to society. Christianity has taught them that the intrinsic value of a human being is God-given and infinite and, of itself, of much more value (Matt. 16:26).

NOTE 4: The higher nature of ordinary people, whom have more control and willpower than the savages, likes to pray, forgive, and love their enemies, but their lower nature wants revenge or wants to get even, which considerably impedes their evolutionary progress and that of others.

B. A Short Overview of Human Evolution

In the beginning, there was one Presence, the Source of all that is, who wanted to express itself by creating, in five "days" or epochs of time, the universe, the earth, and all the kingdoms of nature. And the Omni-Presence liked what it had created ("it was good" – see Gen. 1). However, His joy was not complete until They created human beings in their own image and likeness at the "sixth" day, with whom They could share Their joy of creation and have companionship with them.

About fifteen billion years ago, the planet earth came into being, and evolution from simple to more complex began. From vegetable life to simple animal forms, such as protozoan, amphibian, reptilian, to higher animals (mammals), until the time when the first humanoids appeared.

Each stage of evolution goes beyond and includes that of its predecessors. As humans contain animal characteristics, animals are like plants, which latter consists of minerals (see p. 320). Thus, humans already exist as a potential in the lower forms. Through the force of *evolution caused by the Divine Spark, which can be found in all of God's creation, the kingdoms of nature and that of humans grow to a higher and to a more developed condition.

Some esoteric writings speak about the existence of seven root races: (1) Polarian, (2) Hyperborean, (3) Lumerian, (4) Atlanthean, (5) Aryan, (6) Meruvian, and (7) Paradisian. The age of the Aryan race (which had its origin in North Central Asia) is the age we are living in today. It is also called the Iron Age and the Kali-yoga, or black age, of the Hindus. The first two races were more etheric than physical, were androgynous, and are symbolically portrayed as the mineral and plant. Human beings, as we may know them, began with the third root race, which was animalistic in its behavior and was developing its lower desires. They were living on a landmass lying in the Pacific Ocean, which eventually overtook them. As the Lumerians were physically and emotionally oriented, the Atlantheans, in addition, possessed a [1]lower mind or intellect through which they made considerable advances, in their latter days, in science and technology. The Atlantheans were thus in possession of physical and vital bodies, which give power to action, a [2]desire sheath and a mind which give incentive and purpose to action. Unlike the Lumerians, they were developing an ego through which they could be independent. The Atlantheans lived in [3]Atlantis, a land mass or continent in the Atlantic Ocean. According to some reports, because of moral corruption, it was destroyed and sank

---

* The law of evolution assured a constant progression for all creation. However, the amount of growth for humans whom have free will depends on the awareness and cooperation of the individuals. Progress is usually slow and irregular but will be much faster when the people realize the purpose of their evolution and God's plan for them. Those whom are not able, or want to progress, will be left behind and eventually will degenerate. This is regression, which is also part of the law of evolution.

[1] The faculty of logical thinking was beginning to develop at the end of the Atlanthean epoch. But it was not until the next race of humans, the Aryan or fifth root race, that this mental force fully matured. The color of the low type of intellect is shown in the mental self as having a copper yellow and brownish color. When it is used for deceit and cunning, it changes to a dirty green and gray.

[2] Desire is the driving power in the lower self, whereas spiritual will is the driving power in the Higher Self.

[3] As said by Plato in Timaes and Critias, Atlantis was an island west of Gibraltar engulfed by the sea.

completely beneath the ocean in about 10,000 B.C. because of gigantic earth changes. A few good ones escaped to Egypt, Yucatan, and other places and started a new civilization.

NOTE 1: The law of evolution is the unwrapping, unfolding, or a rolling out of much of creation. It is the growth into manifestation of qualities which are in a germinal or latent condition, such as, for example, in a seed or egg. It will eventually develop from within outwards when not only the environment condition is right but also with the necessary prompting of the divine spark, which is always seeking to express itself. We find this divine urge in the inner nature of many organisms, and it is especially strong in the human and Divine Spirits.

REMARK: It has been said that knowledge can be found deep within (to know oneself). However, the information remains implicit and unexpressed until it is evoked into the conscious self.

NOTE 2: Ego is a state of consciousness marked by a sense of individualized personal selfhood. It is the Latin word for "I", which is beyond, and includes the intellect and the emotion. The late Atlanthean and the late Cro-magnon were able to separate themselves, for the most part, from the group or tribe. By doing so, they were no longer a member of the herd and no longer part of nature but instead were trying to have dominion over nature. In other words, they had sufficient ego strength or sense of separate self to stand apart, or on their own, from their family and tribe and from the crowd. Some people today would say, "He or she is a nonconformist, independent, and a free thinker."

REMARK: Because in ancient times the primitive person was not conscious of "itself" or did not yet develop an ego, they therefore were like the little children of today. The latter does not speak or use the letter "I" before the verb until the time that they awaken to awareness of themselves. They may say, for example, "<u>Me</u> (my body) want" instead of "I want".

NOTE 3: In the long past, the individual did not exist as an independent entity, with its own responsibilities and values. The group (soul) dominated and did not allow for the emancipation of a separate ego, the center of consciousness or "I". After many years of thinking and learning on one's own and gaining individual *freedom, the human mind has made itself conscious and has become master over his or her individual destiny.

---

* This freedom cannot be exercised when people are placed under totalitarian regimes (such as communism and fascism). It is also curtailed, to some degree, when individuals are living the life of the good and evil personality but are completely free when they are living the divine life (Jn. 8:32; Rom. 8:2; 2 Cor. 3:17; Gal. 5:1), free from the controlling influence of the group soul of the organization.

NOTE 4: Some primitive societies of a former time could not or did not want to break with their animal past, as expressed in the cult of totem animals and by incorporating, in their religions, the lion or hawk-headed gods of Egypt and the sacred bulls of Assyria, Crete, and Persia.

According to reports of modern science, about 140,000 years ago, the Neanderthals appeared in Eastern Europe. They were a hunting and gathering type of beings whom left behind those that were weak, old, and crippled. They were living much like animals, that is, in a group-conscious way. Their selves and their bodies were not yet clearly differentiated, and they moved much by their instinct and lower desires because their minds were only crudely developed.

The Neanderthal disappeared about 40,000 years ago when the Cro-magnon beings appeared in Western Europe. It is said that they were the first human beings because they were much like the humans of today in their physical development. They were much more evolved than the Neanderthal, especially when they began to discover the art of farming. They took care of the weaker ones and the dead. In the Neolithic period (about 10,000 years ago), another great advancement took place, the awakening of the dormant ego. The Cro-magnon men and women began to live from body consciousness to that of the mind, or from instinct to intellect. This was paralleled by a transition from *matriarchy to patriarchy society and was symbolized by the Greek sky god Zeus slaying the earthly Typhon monster. By breaking away from nature or the great biological mother, the hero (from the hero myth) became more self-conscious and independent. The later Cro-magnon persons expressed themselves in language and showed to have some imagination, memory, appreciation of art, psychic ability, and a degree of intellectual development.

In some cultures, primitive people were only little removed from the state of no awareness or no self-consciousness. They were much like the animals in the field. They usually lived from day to day, tending to their direct needs. Their minds were dormant and little developed and, therefore, it was difficult for them to think, to consider, to doubt, to imagine, to remember and retain knowledge, to study, to meditate, to

---

* As a child depends more on the mother than the father in its early years, so does humankind first experience its closeness to the great mother for its sustenance. As humanity evolved, it became more dependent on the great father. As history records, the goddess cultures were invaded by lighter skinned people from the North between 2500 and 1500 B.C. whom worshipped sky gods that were of a male gender.

invent, to correlate ideas, organize, formulate plans, make proper decisions, exercise judgment, or to ask questions. It was the time to develop physical capacities and also to exercise their feelings or emotions. The evolving mind was, at first, in the service of the feelings but gradually became more independent. The individual is then less concerned about how one feels about life but also what one thinks about life.

In about the sixth century B.C., some advanced Greeks, of whom we have sufficient record, began to develop [1]the faculty of reason. They wanted to know the how and why of things. This conceptual and logical way of thinking was emphasized by Socrates, [2]Plato, Aristotle, and many others. It was rediscovered during the Renaissance, more importance given in the "age of reason", and fully used by many people today. Thus, the [3]developed ego brought introspection, self-analysis, self-reflection, discrimination, reason, etc., which resulted in the development of science, medicine, technology, philosophy, and many other disciplines.

As the inner human personality or psyche consists of the lower and higher emotion, it also consists of the lower and *higher mental components. The function of the lower mental self or sheath is to serve as a vehicle for concrete thinking (which deals with particular knowledge), and the higher component serves as a vehicle for abstract thinking (which deals with general or universal knowledge). This thinking is then conveyed through the emotional self via the etheric brain to the physical brain.

---

[1] Rational and logical thinking began with the Greeks; irrational thinking and superstition were prevalent before. According to the dictionary, reason is the capacity for drawing conclusions based on a premise – the capacity for rational thought – reasoning from the particular to the general (inductive reasoning), and reasoning from the general to the specific (deductive reasoning). Thinking clearly is important, association of ideas and synthesis of concepts.

[2] Through neoplatonism and the teachings of St. Augustine and others, Plato's thinking colored Christian thought until the 13th century when Aristotle's thinking began to dominate, but without displacing Plato's.

[3] As it is important to culture the intellect for the sake of human evolution, it has gone too far, and there is a need to go to a higher level of thinking. In the West, people in general separated their overdeveloped ego too much from the great mother, while many people of the East were less affected by the tyranny of the ego. On the other hand, some Eastern individuals went to the other extreme by living in and even transcending an undeveloped ego.

* In the majority of men and women, the higher portions of the mental body are undeveloped or dormant, while the lower portions are quite active. Thus, a non-evolved person is capable of only a small amount of abstract thinking, while great philosophers have the ability of profound, noble, and wise thought.

NOTE: We should learn to control the mind by first disidentifying ourselves, or rather our consciousness, from the mind because we are not the mind. Then, we should make it expand in depth and stop thinking in an impure and negative way. We ought, for example, not to become fixed in a narrow set of ideas by believing in the events of the physical plane alone instead of also looking for the inner meaning of events, to become judgmental and condemn the faults of others. The owner of an immature mind may also become arrogant and perceive all other ideas as being inferior, holding on to his or her own opinion as the right one and disregarding the fact that it is a contradiction. We should also learn to think correctly and orderly through the exercise of concentration on different subjects. The purification, tranquilization, and right and clear way of thinking make the mind a better instrument for the light and wisdom of the Divine Spirit to shine through.

REMARK: The concrete analytical mind deals with concrete knowledge to satisfy particular needs and concerns itself with particular objects, such as a certain boat, tree, or triangle. The abstract mind goes from the particular to the general, boats or trees in general, or the principle of triangulation common to all triangles. It draws out what is common to a group of individual things. It seeks for ideals and sees the whole or the one among the many. It is the abstraction of the essence of all the facts together and is the principle behind the laws. It may be a single symbol, thought, or idea abstracted from volumes of writings and many years of life experiences. It could be thrown as it were on a table for everyone to see but not always be understood. Perhaps one of the best ways to develop the abstract faculty of the mind is by thinking philosophically, through the practice of higher mathematics and by producing abstract drawings and/or paintings.

As the higher mental body is concerned about holistic thinking, pure reason, and asking questions, the evolving Divine Spirit or Soul of the next level is concerned about the spiritual mind, will, wisdom, and love. Thus, as people develop, the center of consciousness moves up to the intuitional plane, the realm where the Soul or Higher Self (called Ego by Theosophy) has its abode. It is the realm of intuitional thinking or direct knowing. The spiritual mind has the ability of deep and correct insight, which is the clear and direct perception of Truth. It is also the sphere of creativity based on originality and spiritual will, which is a higher form of desire. This is in contrast with lower desire, which expresses only the self-centered motivation of the personality or lower self. Thus, as desire is the driving force of the lower self, the spiritual will is the driving force of the higher self. The Soul is also the "store house" of the abstracted essence of spiritual wisdom gained from experience – "a house not made with hands, eternal in the heavens" (1 Cor. 5:1). The spiritual love lets us experience the essential unity of all beings, and it eliminates the sense of separation, thus invoking real compassion. Our Divine Spirit can be developed by witnessing to the Truth, building in our character the divine qualities, and exercising these qualities in our daily lives. Having become receptive to the Universal Intelligence, Love, and Wisdom, we then use our personality for enlightened self-expression.

Thus, from simple consciousness of the animal comes the personal or individual consciousness (ego) at the human level and from self-consciousness to intuitional and Christ Consciousness.

When individuals develop from ego-hood to Self-hood, the union between man and woman should also be raised. This fusion in the primitives is mostly physical and emotional. In civilized couples, the mental is also involved to some degree, but in the New Age, they should also include the spiritual or divine quadrant. The couple would then vibrate synchronously and is blended into complete oneness on all levels.

At present, the Aryan race or the fifth sub-race (according to theosophy) is dominant, especially in America and Western Europe. The Meruvian, or the sixth sub-race, is already developing for an increasing number of people and will eventually be the accepted standard of living for all people of the world. This age will develop the higher intuition or a united insight.

C. The Value of Emotional Development

When humans develop, not only the mental but also the emotional part of the human being experiences a transformation. For example, the emotional self or envelope of a young child is small in size and white, and its aura is usually colorless. The size and different colors will begin to show as the positive (and negative) qualities develop, such as, for example, the rose for affection, the green for intellect, blue for devotion and religious feelings, and the golden yellow for the love towards God.

The function of the emotional sheath, which is located between the mental component and the physical body of the psyche or human spirit, is to convert physical vibration into sensation, impart different emotions, which are then perceived in the mental self as perception. Conversely, the vibration of thinking causes the emotional self to vibrate, which in turn has its effect on the etheric body and then acts via the nervous system on the matter of the physical brain. From the above, it becomes clear that it is not possible to feel or think alone. Both processes are linked together. The functions of the emotion or feeling are: to provide power, passion, warmth, excitement, zeal, and color in whatever we do and to vitalize our thinking, facilitate communications, and intensify, enhance, sweeten, and deepen our human experience.

The emotional self of a primitive who is governed much by physical sensation is vague, cloudy, unorganized, and its colors are usually coarse, somewhat dull, muddy, and brown. Being emotionally undeveloped, they could therefore not express all the emotions. An example is the different expressions of love, such as the diverse kinds of altruistic forms. Those whom express the negative and evil side of the personality, such as hatred, anger, fear, selfishness, sensuality, etc. reveal themselves by stains of dull scarlet, gray, dirty brown, and reddish brown. The consciousness of undeveloped humans is polarized in the emotional self. Their life is more governed by emotions and desires than by willpower, and they think more with their abdominal brain (solar plexus) than with the brains in their head area.

NOTE 1: Someone who is emotionally oriented may also be sensitive to beauty, nature, the arts, music, and dance. However, this person may also experience the negative side of the emotion by easily becoming moody and upset because of the inconstancy and instability of the emotional self.

NOTE 2: There was a great movement in the 19th century called romanticism. Its emphasis was on the emotion and imagination.

NOTE 3: When a developed person speaks, the voice, powered by the emotion, feels friendly. However, when a negative and undeveloped person speaks, it sounds very unfriendly.

The consciousness of an ordinary human being of today is generally more centered in his/her emotional and mental self than in their physical, and the higher emotion is coming in to play. The outline of the emotional form or ovoid is much more clear, definite, and distinct. In the average, moral, and intellectual person, the emotional body is also larger than that of the undeveloped persons. Its materials are finer in quality because the purer and brighter material of the higher emotional plane substitutes most of the coarse and murky material of the lower emotional self. Thus, the blind passion is changed to the common human emotion. [1]Sensuality of the cultured human being is much less but still prominent, and so is selfishness. This, however, will change somewhat when the center of consciousness is transferred more from the emotional to the mental.

NOTE 1: Many people today have become lopsided, whereby they have progressed in their intellectual development but are sadly lacking in devotion and compassion.

NOTE 2: Anyone who allows human nature to run sway with hardly any self-restraint or self-control from a right thinking, reasonable mind is emotionally immature. They are usually moody and have never learned to control their moods. They often yell and, like a little child, have outbursts of temper. They should, therefore, learn to practice intelligent self-control and give right direction over all the emotions, especially the negative ones, because uncontrolled emotion quickly becomes a bad habit.

NOTE 3: In order to control any sensation, emotion, or desire, we should not identify ourselves with it but dissociate from it by observing it as a vibration in our emotional self, which we can change. We may then develop the qualities of patience, poise, tolerance, and self-control under the most trying circumstances by not being agitated or upset by anyone but remain calm, peaceful, serene, and pure. By thus subduing and purifying our lower self, our growing Higher Self will then more and more shine through and strengthen the acquired attributes. The more we develop the qualities of love, joy, patience, kindness, reverence, sympathy, devotion, compassion, and a strong desire to serve, the finer and purer our emotional self, which is part of our lower self or personality, becomes. It will then become easily responsive to the vibration of the Higher Self or Soul, but is hardly affected by the coarse vibration of the lower desires, either coming from within or without. The lower self then will become vibrant and sensitive, a fitting and efficient instrument of the Soul or Divine Spirit and able to reflect the higher consciousness of the latter. By giving expression to every higher emotion, noble desires, and spiritual will, our emotional self changes its constitution, vibration, and also its color, while

---

[1] People whom are in love, or as it is usually called "falls in love", continually feel and think about the other person for a period of time because they are no longer as much centered on themselves that they feel lifted from their lower selves to a higher level. They may then come in touch with their divine Selves and occasionally feel and see the divine Selves in others. They feel elated, energetic, and in peace with their neighbors and the world. However, as soon as they start centering too much on animal passion, their consciousness gets too much trapped in the lowest part of themselves. They then become obsessed with sex, whereby their bodies are enslaved by lust and their higher emotions become coarse and impure by lower desires and sexual fantasies. They may then spend too much of their time in seeking to fulfill those lower desires, which drain much of their energy. In their search to fulfill their lust and lower desires, they become extremely selfish and do not care about anybody.

desires and emotions of a lower type coarsen it. We may prevent the latter by either sublimating it or stop giving it energy.

NOTE 4: When any function is exercised, it improves. When, for example, the emotional self does not respond very well to compassion, one may place him or herself in such a situation that those higher emotions are aroused. The result is that the psychic channels through which this particular emotions flows widen, and the emotional self also improves. It then becomes easier to respond to those higher emotions.

NOTE 5: We may block our spiritual arteries, our lifelines to God, by all forms of hate, such as anger, contempt, bitterness, and resentment. They may become clogged by the accumulation of old hurts and by wallowing in self-pity, guilt, remorse, wounded vanity, and frustrated desires. It also becomes obstructed by feelings of despair, depression, moodiness, possessiveness, greed, pessimism, rebellion, and insecurity.

The emotional self or sheath of a highly developed individual, whose consciousness is located in the Soul; the higher desires are replaced by the spiritual will, and the personal [2]loves are absorbed by the divine love, through which he or she loves everybody. The emotional self or body, as part of the personality, has become pure, tranquil, still, serene, clear, transparent, and peaceful. It will then reflect the Soul or Higher Self and is able to express the love of God. However, you must not only master and purify the emotions but also enlighten them in order to enrich your lives and inspire others. Its colors are pure, bright, and luminous, and its size is considerably larger and more defined than that of the ordinary individual. It becomes a perfect vehicle of the Soul in its mission of loving and forgiving. To have at all times and under any circumstances a deep sense of love and compassion for all humans and non-humans alike in the physical, etheric, psychic, and spiritual universes. Those divine beings are not able to dissociate themselves from the suffering of the world because they are like God, part and parcel of this world.

D. The Evolution of the Conception of God

Another development is the evolution of the idea or conception of God.

---

[2] The emotional development is considerably hastened when individuals experience the many forms of love as they usually are expressed through the emotion of the other, especially God's Love.

Primitive people conceived of a Deity who was unknown, far way, and whom they worshipped with awe and fear, as they saw it manifested through nature and its forces. In the passing of time, the Deity came somewhat closer to the people and was believed to have animal and human characteristics. In Athens and Rome, the workings of the earth, the external and internal expressions of humans, were all projected in a hierarchy of [1]gods, each with a special function and ruled by their masters Zeus or Jupiter. They were, however, all created in the image of fallen human beings. When the Greek and Roman empires declined, the gods lost their divinity, their adventures were less spoken of, and eventually they lost much of the attention and power of the people. The dying gods or thought forms then crumbled when they were no longer fed with the psychic energy of the worshippers. As humans evolved the conception of God became more true and nobler because they gradually outgrew their coarser vices and ceased to attribute them to their God.

In Old Testament times, the Hebrews did not know God as a Father but as Elohim, or Yahweh. His Presence was shut up in the Holy of Holies, and they did not dare to enter in His immediate surroundings. At that time, their minds had not yet expanded to a state that God was more than the ark He dwelt in or a visible golden calf as their highest conception of God. As the Hebrews had the tendency to create God in their own (good and evil) images, the Israelites later – unlike the Greeks and Romans – taught that their God, Jehovah, was separate from fallen humans. At the time when Yahweh ceased to exist as a material reality and became more spiritual and invisible, in the minds of the people, the religion of Yahweh began to reach a much higher development. This conception, with the help of some poetical prophets, widened and deepened more. He eventually became the one true God of all the people of the world, which is similar to the idea of God as Islam and Christianity today acknowledge.

NOTE 1: The old concept of God in the Old Testament as a punishing, vengeful, and judgmental God who delivers death, illness, earthquakes, disasters, and other suffering upon humankind, has often been the law of cause and effect in operation. If the chosen people, who were under the direct guidance of the angels, would not have paid the karma or indemnity, they would only have degenerated and no longer be used by God to carry out His restoration plan and bring forth Jesus Christ. Many people at that time had a

---

[1] The Greek people believed first in many gods (polytheism). Then Socrates said that there is only one God (monotheism), who we do not know, which Paul later made known when he visited Athens (Acts 17:22-28).

strong satanic nature and were, therefore, much under the power and control of satan, which only made God, their master who created them, very jealous. Besides, God hates the evil in humans more than in any being. He, therefore, appeared in the Old Testament to be of lesser divine than in the New Testament, as the Gnostics would say.

NOTE 2: Valentinus and his followers (Gnostics) believed that the essence of humanity (anthropes) is God. They further believed that when anyone has discovered the divinity within, he or she is no longer under the authority of the institution of the church.

In the new dispensation, Jesus Christ pronounced a new image or [1]concept of God. The reverential fear of the Lord gave way to a beneficial and kind-hearted heavenly Father/Mother, who can be known personally. He/She is no longer distant, [2]remote, unapproachable, and a stranger. He lives no longer [3]outside but inside of all [4]His/Her children as the loving Source of their beings.

NOTE: Jehovah represented, in the physical Aryan age, a god of war and power (land travel).

Jesus represented the emotionally oriented Piscean age, a God of love, and walked upon the water of Pisces. He was slain as a lamb, representing the end of the age of Aries, the ram, and began the age of Pisces the fish (sea travel).

Today, we have moved into the age of the intellect, or the Aquarian age (air travel).

REMARK: Sensory experience does not last long; a short time after eating, one is hungry again.

Sentimental pleasure lasts a little longer, such as joy, passion, affection, but it too will fade away.

---

[1] Fanatic church members have a tendency to defend their concept of God and put down other religions with a different concept. However, they forget that God is more than a concept, and they should not be afraid to lose their limited concept and replace it with a higher and truer concept. Besides, they do not lose God, only their concept.

[2] When God is remote, everything else that is of God has also become distant, such as His Law, Word, Revelation, and His promises.

[3] Some mainstream religions advocate a concept of God, which is outside or transcendent and can only be contacted through the meditation of the priesthood. However, when the God within is no longer a spark but a living being (Luke 17:21; Col. 1:27), some church members can no longer believe that God is a whole other.

[4] Not all people who call themselves Christians belong to God, such as carnal Christians and backsliders (1 Cor. 3:1-4), whom are unregenerated and have the devil as their father (Jn. 8:44).

Intellectual knowledge can make one happy for a longer time, but it also loses its colors when curiosity is satisfied and a new theory arises.

Religions, which are not based on full Truth but on doctrines or systems of doctrines (maintained by a religious body as true and necessary of belief), may last for hundreds of years, but they will also lose their luster when a brighter religion appears on the horizon.

Relative truth can, therefore, not endure, and a particular concept of God will not last. What will last are Truth bodies (Souls) and God, whom are forever and everlasting.

E. The Development of Children

Every seven years, we go through cyclic changes. Each cycle brings an opportunity to cast off old beliefs and ideas that no longer serve us and give birth to the new. This is not only true of the physical but also of the mental and spiritual life, including relationships, marriage, and business.

The first stage of life, which generally occupies the first seven years after birth, is the most influential one in the development of the child. The inner and outer selves of the little one are more or less passive and are continually taking in impressions from the environment, relatives, and especially parents whom the child likes to imitate, which become firmly fixed in the suggestible subconscious mind of the child. The helpless ones are frequently seeking for assurance that they *are loved and cared for by their parents, who seem to them all-powerful. During that time, the children are much occupied with the physical existence in the world of the senses because their consciousness is almost entirely on the physical plane. This is also the time that the child likes to live in a world of fantasy and imagination, or make-believe. At play, the little girl becomes the house mother in her creative mental images and the little boy plays with toys, anticipating what he may do later in the future. However, some of them may occasionally experience other worldly realities through their lower psychic centers. At the gentle urgings of their religious parents, the child learns to pray with them, to a God, who they sense but do not understand. It is something they have to do at certain times, before meals, and when they are going to sleep, which usually consists of repeated sayings. By learning the language,

---

* The energy of love of developed parents includes not only the vital and psychic elements but also spiritual constituents, which will give support and life to the inner life of the child, which stimulates growth.

the child becomes more self-conscious and eventually learns to individuate him/herself from the mother. They become more assertive and have a more conscious relationship with others. It is considered by many educators that in this early period of growth, the child's physical nature, such as mastery over the body, should receive the most attention. At the age of seven, about the time of first grade, the child has matured to where he/she can begin to grasp symbolic connections, written language, simple arithmetic operations, and exercises in problem solving.

NOTE 1: Childhood is innocent, but it is also imbued with selfishness and irresponsibility. Many children are born relatively good, while some others, especially those that are born in lust, can be, at times, like egotistical little beasts. According to Sigmund Freud, the state of childhood is a "polymorphous perversion". As many adults know, children can be cruel to the younger ones. However, if they have developed "the sense of right", they no longer do so and may even protect the weaker ones.

NOTE 2: The pre-school child, in his or her early years, is a sensory being and is focused much on the environment because the inner mentality has not yet awakened. The psychic is more or less part of the sensory surroundings and, like the animals and primitives, the very young are able to see and sense super physical reality along with physical sensation. This lower form of psychism is usually vague, unfocused, and dream-like. The child may experience occasional glimpses and voices of invisible playmates and other beings. As lower clairvoyance, or rather clair-sentience, is spontaneous and is connected with the autonomic nervous system and the solar plexus, the higher clairvoyance is voluntary and is connected and works through the cerebrospinal nervous system and the region of the head. The latter system begins to operate when the child is around six years old, when his or her intellect comes more or less on their own. At that time, the young one enters school and begins to learn how to think in the correct way. Also at that time, the higher clairvoyance should be brought into balance with the intellectual functions. However, schools tend to emphasize left-brain functions, and the development of the psychic faculty is not encouraged by most parents and the educational system. Their inner vision becomes clouded, and the inner ear and voice can no longer hear and speak. The result is that the child is no longer able to psychically communicate with animals and the whole of nature, with its fairies and angels. They also become less artistic and creative. In short, education in the West has produced people of brains, while the lack of psychic education has left individuals, psychically speaking, still being centered in the solar plexus (lower clairvoyance) instead of being centered in the head region (higher clairvoyance). Thus, the best some people can do whom are sensitive is to have gut feelings. However, for some children whom are living in a bad environment, and because of the influences of evil forces, it is not always good to remain open too much to the psychic world because their minds are not sufficiently developed and in control to protect themselves from the powerful negative forces, which may result in nightmares, terrible visions, and obsessions.

In the second set of seven years of life, the child, as in the first stage, is very curious and frequently wonders about the many aspects of life, especially about nature. They are much fascinated and enchanted by the earth, streams and rivers, the blooming plants, and strange animals and birds, which seem to be moving and flying everywhere. They ask many questions and discover, to their delight, many things about life by themselves by interacting with their environment. In this period of life, they are much involved in the emotional than in the intellectual spheres of life because [1]their consciousness is more on the emotional plane. They learn to express many facets or colors of emotions and are also involved in music, singing, drama, dancing, drawing, and other artistic expressions. The child becomes more socially active and learns how to act properly with others by acquiring some social interaction skills. The young ones learn to reflect on actions, to carry out plans, and delight in adventures. Many of them join a boy or girl scouts organization and (or) like to go to summer camps and play together with their friends. They like to hear stories, especially Bible stories, which they usually believe literally. The child also believes that there is a grandfather like God, high above, who cares for all people and rewards those whom do good and punishes those whom do evil. They learn how to worship this unknown God but also learn to pray to this God, who seems to be everywhere, in private, about things they would not talk to with other people. At that time, their innate sense of right and wrong becomes more developed, and they try to obey moral laws, especially the Ten Commandments. They do not question the authority of a particular faith they belong to because it is the only true church. In their later years, and under the strong influence of the educational system, their thinking begins to assert itself over their emotions, and they also start to think in a more [2]rational way. That is the time that intellectual idealism replaces emotional idealism. The youth believes in ideas and

---

[1] During this period, the child can be appealed to mainly through his/her feelings. Education should, therefore, be more concentrated on the emotion rather than on the mental growth.

[2] Generally speaking, the rational way of thinking is acquired in high school (in American society), while abstract thinking (and intuition) is more developed in college or at a university.

An educated person is not anyone who has just been through college but someone who has a great curiosity about life and expresses great joy in experiencing life in all its aspects, as well as a great desire to continue learning all about it.

511

doctrines, delights in science, and revels in systematic thought and the rudimentary form of abstract thinking. This is also the time that they are old enough (13-14) to know right from wrong and are accountable to the law and, therefore, should take responsibility and accept discipline.

In the third set of seven years, which includes the teenage years (from 13 to 18) or adolescence, from the onset of puberty (with the arrival of generative power – when sexual reproduction becomes possible) to [1]maturity, the youngsters cease to be solely selfish and personal and become capable of sacrifice. During that time, they become conscious of sexual desires and also of the [2]spiritual aspects of life. In adolescence, [3]the body has reached almost its zenith in growth, and it will soon start its deteriorating process, while the intellectual self has become permeated with elemental knowledge. [4]This is a good time for the teenager to search for spiritual things and to satisfy the hunger for Truth because only through the awakening of the transpersonal can the adolescent crisis be completely resolved. He or she has then enough inner strength and power to overcome "uncontrollable" sexual desires and emotional problems. However, at this crucial stage of life, many teens succumb to the pressures of society to conform and become like most adults whom are living the good and evil lifestyle. This good and evil way of thinking of the world is even more readily accepted

---

[1] Maturity is changeable – it moves up as the race develops. In the Stone Age, maturity was no higher than the physical. Today, it is equated with being an intellectual. In the future, full-grown or aged persons will be those whom have also developed their intuitive powers and are not only mature in their personality but also in their Divine Spirit.
Teenagers usually do not express their full mental powers until he or she is about twenty-one years old. Before that time, they are much dominated by emotion and desire in the solar plexus region.

[2] The conscious hunger to know the spiritual aspect does not manifest itself early because the focus on pre-puberty experiences is on the physical, emotional, and intellectual development, and to know and explore these realities. In other words, to build up a strong enough ego to cope with all aspects of life. However, at the time of regeneration or initiation, the ego should not be dissolved but be purified of evil elements so that it can be used as a suitable vehicle for the emerging Soul.

[3] As the body loses strength and competence, more value is placed on our thinking and the growth of our spiritual dimension. We then become more aware of spiritual issues and begin to ask questions about broader aspects of life. The spiritual flower then starts to open.

[4] The search for spiritual truth may lead the youth to a period of philosophical interest, with a pondering about the questions of life, the existence of God, and the purpose of life. Those interests may wane for many of them, but a few others continue to explore and to find out who they are.

when the youngsters accept employment. The result of all of this is that they kill their growing divine Spark in the bud so that it can no longer blossom.

NOTE: It is a law of nature that when a seed, animal, or human is ripe in one stage of development, it should move to the next; otherwise, it will decay or degenerate. The evolutionary force behind this maturing, what the human species is concerned, is "discontent". When a human has ripened, he or she wants to get out. But unfortunately, some of them are reproached as being ungrateful by their parents and others. There are some persons who do not want the child to grow up and do not want to let go of control and cling to the child by misguided and selfish affection, making the child dependent on them. Some of them demand filial obligation, or it may be the child who does not want to leave them out of a false sense of duty. What is true in a physical sense is also true in the spiritual – concerning spiritual children.

During the teenage years and later, many young people are likely to question their earlier beliefs they once held so dear because they are entering a new stage of faith. Some of them whom have become very disappointed in their old faith may be inclined to accept a more personal faith, which is less dependent on a particular group expectation. However, they may eventually lose their faith because it has become too difficult to maintain in this world. Some of them may be led to other religious organizations that give them renewed strength and hope and give answers to their many questions. Others, instead of discarding their old faith and its beliefs, are examining its depth and are discovering the underlying Truth, or the "treasure hidden in a field" (Matt. 13:44). Of those whom have found deep within the field of their personality the dwelling and presence of God, they also become aware that God dwells in others, even as a Spark. They then come to the realization that all of life is interconnected and that humans are not really separate from each other but are one and interdependent at their deepest level. When they begin to identify more and more with their Soul, the aspirant realizes that the developing Divine Spirit within the personality is a being that lives forever and is truly the fountain of eternal youth. The young and older persons have found a new meaning, purpose, and commitment in life and know that the indwelling Spirit of God truly loves them and will never forsake them.

REMARK: The above-described mystical faith has often been described by mystics of all faiths, whom have found God within themselves. St. Paul witnessed to this faith when he says in Gal. 2:20, "It is no longer I who live, but Christ who lives in me." He calls others to this faith by reminding them, "You are in the Spirit, if in fact the Spirit of God dwells in you" (Rom. 8:9).

The unregenerated, whose good and evil personality is in charge of their life, and the regenerated, which are governed by their Divine Spirit, will both reach the age of majority, the status of legal age. The third stage marks the full development of mental functions of both, but the regenerated are reaching true man and womanhood because they are also developing their Divine Spirits to a certain degree of maturity. After this time, and in cycles of seven, the individual increases more of his/her mental and spiritual unfoldment.

REMARK: When a spiritual person becomes older, intuition continues to evolve and may express itself, for example, through idealistic political thinking by being concerned about the well being of the world and altruism of all kinds. This is also a time in which knowledge is distilled into wisdom. Those whom are in possession of wisdom and love are sought for their advice and become wise guides, counselors, and great statesmen. Their minds have become wider and deeper and are less disturbed by events and more ready to consider all points of view and, therefore, are to come to wise decisions while continually seeking for the guidance of God.

F. The Child Recapitulates Human Evolution

The unborn child recapitulates the early history of physical evolution through its various kingdoms. After the child is born, he or she recapitulates the cultural evolution of the human race.

Human beings first start their biological life in the mother's womb, in darkness, as a single cell, which is comparable to the protozoan, a single-celled organism. When the ovum of a human is fertilized by a sperm, it begins to divide into many cells, which cluster is known as an embryo. This initial stage of development is comparable to the mineral period of existence. After about three weeks, the growing embryo appears like a plant and, thereafter, it looks like diverse primeval water and land animals. At the end of the eighth week, the fetus begins to take on a human shape and grows into a perfect human form, in about seven months. Thus, in the first two months, humans travel through the animal kingdom, which memory is kept inside the evolving cells. Then they continue their journey and inherit all that has been stored in their ancestors.

The above development is also described in the sacred writings of the Hindus as the incarnation of Vishnu in his creation. Beginning with the [1]archeozoic epoch of time when Brahmin implants the creative germ, passing through the geological eras of the protozoic, Paleozoic, and Mesozoic, which is covered by the first and second incarnations as the fish and tortoise, and finally entering the Cenozoic epoch, which is embraced by the incarnations in the animal and human forms of the boar and [2]man/lion, which took a period of seven epochs of time.

The child, after its birth, begins to recapitulate, in general, the cultural stages of the human race. He or she is first primitive and instinctive, while later the sense of I-ness is born. Thus, the child, in its development, re-experiences the physiological and psychological states, which the human race, as a whole, progressed through in earlier times. It follows that one can learn about pre-historic ages from a study of the development stages of childhood. One can also know about children from the evolution of human consciousness of our ancestral racial background, whose ego was relatively undeveloped.

NOTE: The recapitulation of the human embryo through the lower kingdoms of nature suggests that a human being could not have been created at once as an adult, as indicated in Genesis 1:26; 2:7.

G. Expanding Awareness at Individual and Social Levels

Since we came into this world, we have continually expanded our consciousness, not only on the internal level when we evolved our limited self into a greater Divine Self but also as an individual, and in social relationships at the external levels.

For example, when we were infants, our space in the mother's womb was very limited, but we felt safe and protected. After being born, we were confined to a crib, which was our world, and we were reluctant to leave. After we became a little child, our home became the space we were allowed to move in, and we became more extroverted. Growing older, our neighborhood became our domain, and we turned our attention to the outside world and non-family members. When growing into adulthood, the village and state became the space we felt comfortable with. We later ventured and traveled throughout the land

---

[1] The geological periods can also be compared with the six days of creation in the Bible. After the Mesozoic period, the mammalian form of life began, from which the human evolved. As the geological periods lasted +/-2 billion years, humans came on the scene +/-22 seconds ago on our 12-hour time clock, in the Cenozoic or mammalian period of +/-120 seconds.

[2] The man/lion is represented by the statue of the Sphinx, who stands in front of the pyramids of Egypt.

and also took occasional trips to *other parts of the world, with their different cultures, expanding our consciousness even more. By continually traveling or observing in an armchair, the individual becomes more aware of the entire globe. By continually expanding our awareness, we recognize that our most precious and beautiful planet, called "earth", is just a small dot in the galaxy and that the latter is only one of the many which comprises the universe(s), which is the body of God.

It has become more difficult for many people today to live for and by themselves because they have become more interdependent on each other for their basic needs. More than ever before, problems of one group may affect the whole of society, not only physically but also psychologically. Besides, no one is really an Island. All are connected at the deepest level with the rock of universality, which is part and parcel of a human's divine nature. In order to understand ourselves and humanity better, let us examine the different social levels of awareness and behavior, which we may find among the diverse people of today.

Human beings whom are at the first level first take care of the separate, fear-based, and limited ego, the "me" or "I", without hardly recognizing the self of others. At that stage of development, they have no other thought than to seek their own gratification and pleasure and to avoid that which may bring discontent, unhappiness, and displeasure. They lead a self-centered life and are much prompted by the instinct of self-preservation. They are concerned with gaining for themselves at the expense of others. Some find it even difficult to take care of themselves, are often isolated from others, and are considered socially retarded.

When the moral nature begins to unfold, the persons learn to revere the right of others, that is, only with those whom are closely related to them. They are the nearest relatives, or those with whom the individuals are constantly associated, and with those neighbors who bring comfort and pleasure in their lives. They give themselves up in a limited way by radiating love and, thus, extending their lives into the lives of others, thus widening the circle of affection. They are usually capable of taking care of their own personal needs, and a few of them may also accept the responsibility of the needs of someone else.

---

* This is comparable to the time when the first group of Europeans left their familiar land and discovered a new continent – America.

As the individual matures further, he or she may begin to take care* of the necessities of a few, such as a family with children. This is a higher level of development than taking care of one's own needs. This person is considered to be climbing on the ladder of social maturity as long as he or she does not rely too much on his or her mate. This individual may also take care of other responsibilities at his or her work place or organization and, thus, matures even more so.

Thus, a man or woman is becoming more and more unselfish in their feeling, thinking, and acting. They regard themselves no longer as a unit, but the family has become the most important unit. They may then include in their relationships the extended family, clan, and neighborhood. They learn to act towards them in an unselfish way while still acting selfishly towards all those whom do not belong in their particular circle or group of people with common interests.

By expanding their awareness even further, they may accept, as their ideal, a state or nation to which they like to belong. Albeit, they do not mind joining with other citizens to loot and plunder other tribes and nations. They recognize that most families have an identical national feeling or patriotism even when they occasionally have to guard their own families against the intrusion of other families. They also do not like some people whom are of a different origin, ethnicity, race, or religion.

Today, more and more people are going in their minds beyond the national ideal of "one nation under God" and also want to have concern and affection for all the people of the world. Thus, instead of thinking in a national way, they are increasingly thinking in global terms. Because of increasing communications, rapid transportation, and international organizations, the world is fast becoming a global village. This eventually will evolve in an awareness of the world as a whole, including the other dimensional worlds.

As we advance in mental and spiritual growth, we gradually realize that we are truly an integral part of the universe, with its universal body, mind, and spirit and that we feel and think much like our God and not in other ways, as we did in the past (Isaiah 55:8-9). Having overcome all the barriers of race, class, culture, and gender, everyone has truly become his brother's keeper. Having an I/thou relationship with others, we as Divine Spirits are already living in and establishing the Kingdom of God in the visible and invisible universes.

REMARK: Having gone through the many levels above, the consciousness of the individuals continues to expand, and his or her values continue to change by serving a larger cause and developing a universal consciousness.

H. The Seven Stages of Life

Human life, in most religious, systems, evolves in seven stages. The first three levels of that life are the stages of the lower self or personality, while the four higher grades indicate the development of the Higher Self or Divine Spirit.

The first level, or the physical stage, also consists of seven gradations. The first three comprise the solid, liquid, and gas, while the higher physical segment contains the invisible etheric divisions of the four ethers. There are also seven spheres of consciousness in the lower and higher of the emotional (second level) and mental world (third level). Each one is less material, or of a higher vibration, than the one below it. This seven-stage subdivision is also appropriate to each of the four stages of the Higher Self or spiritual quadrant.

Before each level can be completed, it must build upon the foundation of earlier stages. As the development of the physical and vital aspect of life is the [1]first stage of life, the emerging feeling and desire level is the [2]second stage, while the mental and volitional dimension is the [2]third stage of the lower life. The transition from the third to the fourth stage marks the beginning of the birth of the Divine Spirit or Soul. After its growth in the fourth kingdom, the personality becomes increasingly subservient to the Soul, while the influence of the false ego is being dissolved. The spiritual evolving Soul will then enter the fifth level, that of mysticism, when the individual becomes aware that much of their consciousness is residing in the divine world. By transmuting their desire nature into spiritual will, they enter the sixth kingdom. The Soul, using the personality as its vehicle, joins with all those regardless of faith, whom also radiate the life of God to do God's Will, to establish His Kingdom on earth and in heaven (spirit world – Matt. 6:10). At the seventh level, one's personality is under complete control of the mature Divine Spirit. The fully enlightened being, knowing God's heart, feels with God the sorrow of the world and is committed to restore the world, regardless of personal circumstances (see diagram p. **710b**).

---

[1] See Note 1.

[2] See Note 2.

NOTE 1: As the human body is †composed of: oxygen, carbon, hydrogen, calcium, phosphorus, and other trace elements, it also consists of seven interpenetrating bodies, such as:
➤ the bone body, which consists of 206 parts
➤ the muscle body, with its voluntary and involuntary muscles, whose principal function is to give movement to the bones
➤ the nerve body, with its cerebro and sympathetic systems, which carry messages to the muscles to move the bones
➤ the circulatory body, with its arteries and veins
➤ the lymphatic body, the drainage system
➤ the tubular body, with its food and air intake, with a waste and exhaust tubing
➤ the skin body, with its many layers and whose main task is to keep moisture in and foreign substances out

The next body, the etheric double, absorbs vital energy from the sun-charged air and supplies the nervous system with its electricity-like energy.

NOTE 2: The human spirit, controlling the voluntary movement of the muscles via the etheric and nerve centers, consists of the emotional, the volitional, and the mental self. The first has its principal seat in the solar plexus, or abdominal brain, while the latter has its seat in the brain. As the emotional manifests as the lower and higher, the mental self manifests as concrete and abstract thought. By exercising the latter, one may come to the realization of philosophical truth, which is the highest expression of the personality.

REMARK: As oxygen is the conveyor of vital or life force energy, emotion is the conveyor of love, while etheric and brain cells act as conveyors of mental impulses.

To study medicine is to know the body, to study music and art is to be acquainted with the emotions, and to study science and philosophy is to better understand the workings of the intellect. To study and practice Truth is to comprehend the divine dimension.

The period of conquering emotions, or waters, is that of shipbuilding.
The period of intellectual development is conquering the sky with airplanes.
The period of higher intellectual and spiritual development is to control outer space.

In psychological terms, we may compare the seven stages of development with [1]Maslow's hierarchy of needs:

---

† Humans are formed from the elements of mother earth, as a baby is formed of its mother.
[1] See Note.

		Energy System
1) physiological	biological needs	perineum
2)	sex and reproduction	genitals
3) safety-security	security-power and control	solar plexus
4) love-belonging	love, caring, devotion	heart
5) esteem	expression and (verbal) knowledge	throat
6) self-actualization	intuition – inner direction	third eye
7) ²transcendence	transcendent experience	crown

NOTE: Abraham Maslow (1908-1970), founder of humanistic psychology, the "third force" in psychology. It emerged in order to counterbalance the scientific materialism of behaviorism, the "first force" and Freudian psychoanalysis, the "second force". Humanistic psychologists wanted to study human beings as persons and not as complex biological machines. In 1968, Maslow found humanistic psychology, the "third force", to be a preparation for a still higher, the *"fourth force", which goes beyond human needs, the transpersonal. The latter deals with self-transcendence, altered states of consciousness, and psychic phenomena.

Maslow also found that some creative people are striving to satisfy higher needs (after the lower needs have been satisfied). Their experience was beyond the life of their personality, or self-transcendent. It included mystical or peak experiences and by knowing and acquiring spiritual qualities, or "being values".

Although human psychologists were responsible for uniting transpersonal psychology into one system, there existed at least two earlier Western approaches to the transpersonal. These were the efforts of Carl Jung (1875-1961) and Roberto Assagioli (1888-1975). Carl speaks about the Self we bring to expression by the process of "individuation", while Roberto says that through the process of psycho-synthesis, the center of consciousness is being shifted to the Higher Self, and the lower or personal self has become its instrument.

---

² The sixth and seventh needs were originally one need, that of self-actualization (human desire for self-fulfillment). In 1968, Maslow changed it into two needs, with transcendence as the highest.

* The four major forces have to do with the first four stages of life: the physical – vital, the emotional – sexual, the mental – intentional, and the beginning of the spiritual or divine.

I. The Seven Levels of the Human Aura

Each human being has three main bodies: the physical/etheric, the human spirit (mental-emotional-desire-will), and the Divine Spirit. Those bodies have their own vibrations, each with its own radiation or aura. Depending on the level of development, we may also speak of at least four higher layers or auras. Throughout people's lives, those auras or emanations continue to change. They may expand or contract and also change their color tones.

The first layer or level reveals much about the physical and etheric states of a human being, who is much involved in sports and other physical activities. Its basic color tone is red, with its different shades, which is the color of the earth and, thus, indicates that the person is much grounded and is materialistic in outlook.

The second level relates to one's feelings and emotions, which may be higher or lower, and which translate into happiness for one's self and others.

The third covering has to do with the degree of intellectual development and clearness of thinking, concrete or abstract, which might be bright or dull. Its basic color is green, which is the color of the green of growing things and which, like the striving of the intellect, is reaching upward, away from purely physical interests.

The fourth layer person is much involved in establishing relationships with true and unselfish love, as it is expressed through one's purified emotions.

The fifth stratum of one's aura is about experiencing the divine will after one has come to know the meaning, purpose, and place of one's life (in God's plan of restoration). Its basic color is blue, which is the color of the blue of the sky, or the higher spiritual Truth, towards the green plants, and the intellect is striving.

The sixth level is about loving all of God's creation with divine or true spiritual love, which may be personal and impersonal but always for the good of the whole.

The last stratum is the seventh aura layer, which expresses God's Will through the same mind as that of God, which is universal, and for the good of everyone. Its basic color is a golden, brilliant yellow, which is the color of the sun and which, like God, is the source of all life, drawing all living things upward (John 6:44; 12:32).

J. Development of Individuals and Civilizations

Evolution in early stages is guided solely from without by divine agencies, such as angels and others. Thereafter, in the Judeo-Christian tradition, the Law (Ten Commandments) was given to help them in their moral growth. They were also taught that there was One God who could be sensed but not be seen. When they developed, God raised up prophets who taught them additional ethical aspects of God's Law in the books of wisdom and other writings. In the latter stages of growth, humans became more a law into themselves and were increasingly guided from within by the invisible God forces. At the time of Jesus Christ, the world was bathed in a new kind of love vibration. Regenerated humans came under the direct guidance of the Christ of all religions and the Holy Spirit, the more personal aspects of God the Father and Mother.

[1]The path towards the realization of God was somewhat different for other traditions. People of ancient civilizations and the Hebrews before the time of Moses believed that all objects have souls, and all natural phenomena such as, for example, the wind and thunder also have a soul. This is called animism. As all animate and inanimate objects have indeed a soul or an innate nature (see #8), natural workings and occurrences do not have an inner life. Objects and natural forces should, however, not be worshipped as gods (polytheism) or not be identified with the deity of God (pantheism). As those civilizations developed, they eventually accepted one God as the chief deity of all the other gods, which was called Zeus and Jupiter in the Greek and Roman traditions. Ancient people and the so-called primitives also became aware of psychic forces, which demanded human sacrifices. At that time, the cult of black magic came into being, which eventually changed to white magic when humans became more developed. Thus, people of other traditions will meet their spiritual needs at different

---

[1] We may also speak of individual paths towards God by, for example, listening to and playing uplifting music and singing religious songs, praying and reading Words of Truth, reciting Poetry, and reflecting on the beauty of nature and all of life that God has created. Think about the well being and look for the good in others; love them and make them happy. Be thankful of what you have and have become, and have an attitude of gratitude and gratefulness.

stages of development, according to their cultures. After going through a period of moral development by purifying their personality, they may then accept the Christ of all religions and grow as a Divine Spirit to maturity here on earth and continue in the afterlife.

Doing all of this, life becomes more exciting, more opportunities are offered, and we become more creative. Our priorities change, and the quality of our life improves. We feel more valuable and secure, have more energy, while many new ideas are arising in our mind. We are able to give more, get along better with others, have less stress, and enjoy and understand life more, while bringing out the best in ourselves. We think more clearly, grow morally and spiritually, find peace of mind, and know that we are guided at all times by God – our true Father and Mother.

In the process of evolution, the plant, animal, and human are, at first, much the same. However, when the species evolve, we see more and more varieties, not only in form but also in their expressions because their inner selves also develop. For example, the bodies and behavior of undeveloped humans who think, or rather feel, with their instinctive solar plexus are much the same, while the more advanced humans who think with their brain are more individualistic in their feeling, thinking, and acting. When they are more fully developed, their transpersonal selves have become very unique and are known as super human beings.

Evolution can also be seen in the development of civilization. For example, in the Western world, Egypt was the young child of civilization (emotion); Greece was the beautiful child (intellect); Rome represented strong manhood (personality); and the Gothic symbolized the Christian Spirit in the stages of development.

To quickly advance, it would be good for the candidate not only to know about physical sciences but also their esoteric interpretations. To know the mysteries of life by experiencing initiations which carry the individual beyond the realms of mind into the realm of God-consciousness. He/She should also be aware of the differences between the lesser psychic senses and the greater spiritual attributes. They should also elevate their thinking above the intellectual level into the intuition stage. Their life, unlike that of the animals and undeveloped

523

humans, should be of sacrifice instead of survival of the fittest. By doing the above, reason develops into intuition, knowledge expands into wisdom, and emotion gives way to love.

Concerning the development of our selves or bodies, the physical body grows easily by taking in food, and we learn to know the body by the study of medicine. The emotional self expands by the experience of love, the study of music, and other art forms. The mental self develops by exercising the faculty of reason and higher forms of thinking. The Soul evolves by learning and living according to the Truth and knowing about divine life.

K. Some Esoteric and Eastern Viewpoints

According to the teachings of many religions and the early Christian church, a human being consists of *three major body parts: body, soul (human spirit), and Divine Spirit. Other teachings recognize four bodies: the physical body, the etheric body (consisting of matter of higher vibrations), the astral or emotional body (lower human spirit which survives the death of the physical body), and the spirit body (Divine Spirit), which belongs to a highly developed human being.

All living creatures have a physical and etheric, or life bodies, while higher mammals and savages have, in addition, an emotional or desire body. The human spirit of an average human being is more developed, whereby the mental part plays a major role.

The Upanishads, an early Hindu teaching, speaks of seven bodies: the physical, the etheric, the astral, the mental, the Ego, the Atman, and Brahman. Theosophy, which is derived from Hinduism, recognizes the physical (which includes the etheric), astral, mental (manas), buddhi, atma, monadic, and divine world. Other esoteric writings mention the physical/etheric, astral, mental, intuition plane, spiritual plane, monadic plane, and divine godhead, or logoic plane.

---

* Developed human beings consist not only of a Soul and body, as many religious bodies teach today, but consist in reality of a Divine Spirit (Spirit or Soul), human spirit (soul-psyche-heart-mind), and body. See 1 Thess. 5:23; Heb. 4:12.

The consciousness of humans whom are living the life of the personality resides in the first three stages. They are not conscious of the life of the Soul. Spiritual aspirants, on the other hand, have treaded the path of probation and may be likened to the nine months of gestation prior to birth. Disciples or Initiates are those whom have experienced spiritual birth and are growing in the fourth stage. Those that have reached the fifth stage are called Arhat, the sixth Adept, and the seventh stage ascended Master.

NOTE: The physical chemical body experiences sensation (sentience) without any awareness.

➢ The vegetable body has a sensitive response to contact but does not have any cognitive perception of the environment.

➢ The animal soul has awareness of the environment but limited self-awareness.

➢ The average human being is fully aware of his/her body, much less aware of their human spirit, especially when he/she identifies with his/her physical body in pursuit of sensual gratification. They are usually ignorant of their Soul unless they live a divine life. Those whom are living a spiritual life may, at times, be aware of their Souls, while highly developed beings live in a constant state of Self-awareness.

L. Introduction to the Chakras or Energy Centers

The chakra energy system was originally described in the ancient *Indian Vedas and Upanishads. The word chakra is a Sanskrit term which means wheel, disk, or vortex. We may also call it an energy or force center. It is a wheel-like or whirling center of invisible energy through which different kinds of forces are received and transmitted. It can also be likened to a transformer by "stepping down" the higher plane energy and "stepping up" the forces of the lower planes.

In the Book of Revelation chapters 5-8, the energy centers are referred to as the seven seals. It probably takes seven disclosings of new Truth to know and understand the full basic Truth, which is expressed by the individual and society as stages of consciousness.

An energy center is circular and disk-like in shape and its size, depending on its development, may range from two to four inches. Its dimension increases when it is activated, whereby more energy flows through it. It, thus, changes from a dormant, sluggish operation in an undeveloped person into a glowing, pulsating one, increasing its spinning and size in a more evolved person.

Almost all energy systems of different schools agree that there are seven major chakras. They are not only located on the edge of the etheric body but can also be found on the outer edge of the other six bodies, in coincidence with the former, but further away because the higher bodies and their auras are greater in size, which is especially true for evolved beings.

Although we have seven main centers, there are many minor and lesser ones. For example, the palms of the hands and bottoms of the feet are the minor ones. There are also hundreds of smaller energy vortexes located all over the body. Each acupressure and acupuncture point is an energy center and, thus, a chakra.

---

* As the Vedas and Upanishads are roughly comparable to the teachings of the Old Testament, the Bhagavad – Gita in some aspects can be likened to the New Testament. It teaches humans to live properly in the third kingdom, fulfilling his/her dharma with its duties, responsibilities, and obligations. The yoga sudras of Patanjali deal with the technique to enter the fourth kingdom or stage of development.

NOTE: As the physical body has an etheric sheeting, with many energy centers, the earth as the macrocosm is also surrounded with an etheric envelope, with its many energy centers. Those centers were connected with [†]leylines and known and recognized by ancient people as holy sites. Some of those places are used today as places of worship.

As the etheric body interpenetrates the physical body and extends slightly beyond it, the energy centers are on the surface or edge of the etheric self and are connected etherically to the spinal column, which is the pathway of the [1]Kundalini force. Thus, the etheric centers form a link, or rather doorways, between the etheric and physical bodies.

NOTE: As Kundalini energy gives health and vigor to the dense body, so is the health of the physical organ, which is associated with a particular energy center, effected by its condition, whether the centers are dormant, over-stimulated, or balanced. It is the latter case that will result in a feeling of peace and well being.

The function of the first two centers (the root and abdomen) is to absorb energy and vitality from the environment and pass it on to the physical and etheric bodies, giving them health and vitality. The third and fourth transform emotional forces produced within the lower and higher emotional selves into physical consciousness of lower vibration. The fifth and sixth transform thoughts and inspiration into physical brain consciousness and the seventh conveys expressions of divine forces into body consciousness.

Each of the centers has a specific location and relation. It is associated with a different endocrine gland system, color, element, and has a certain number of [2]petals.

[†] Leylines are a vast network on the earth's surface of ancient, or "old straight tracks" (Watkins 1925), or paths of power, whereupon and especially on the interconnecting points or energy centers we find great megalithic sites, such as prehistoric monuments, pyramids, stone circles, burial mounds, earthworks, and church buildings. Thus, the leylines constitute grids of power, or mana, as the Polynesians of old would say.

[1] Kundalini is a Sanskrit word meaning coil or spiral. It refers to the image of a coiled, sleeping serpent at the base of the spine waiting to be released and raised. When this bundled energy is stimulated by the development of the individual or by special exercises, it begins its ascension through the primary energy channel (sushumna) along the spine. It will then activate and harmonize gradually the energy centers above. As etheric energy or vitality comes from the sun and is received by the abdomen center, kundalini energy (fire or matter) emanates from the earth and is absorbed by the root center.

[2] Petals are small energy vortices flowing within a chakra and may be more or less developed. For example, only a few petals may be developed of a non-spiritual, intellectual person in a lower stage.

Center one-located at the base of the spine-survival and grounding-adrenal-red-earth-**4**
Center two-in the lower abdomen-sexuality and desires-gonads-orange-water-**6**
Center three-in the solar plexus-emotion and power-pancreas-yellow-air-**10**
Center four-in the heart area-higher emotion and love-thymus-green-fire-**12**
Center five-in the throat area-communication-creativity-thyroid-blue-sound-**16**
Center six-in the third eye area-intuition-clairvoyance-pituitary-indigo-light-**96**
Center seven-on top of the head-universal consciousness-pineal-violet-thought-**972**

NOTE: Each energy center also resonates to a musical note.

The chakras, or psychic sense organs in the etheric body, channel vital, psychic, and divine energies and, thus, serve as portals between physical, psychic, and divine states of consciousness, operating between the body, human spirit, and Divine Spirit. Thus, the frequency of each center increases as one moves up the energy center system, and it draws in those energies for which it has an affinity.

All the centers or vortexes are fully open and active in a fully developed person. However, in a primitive, undeveloped human, and the very young, only the first and second are active, which are the life force centers, while the others are largely dormant, especially the four highest centers which correspond to divine life. When they meet another person, only the lower psychic selves are in full contact, with their two or three colors, instead of a rainbow of colors. Thus, when one lives a life below the diaphragm or belt, the person is almost wholly involved in the physical, etheric, and the [1]animal psychic life and is often fearful and agitated, which emotion is felt in the "pit" of his or her stomach, or solar plexus. However, when the individual starts living above the belt in the intellectual and spiritual life, he or she rises above the animal stage.

Although there are seven centers, people today in general act out of their instinctive center (1), which operates unconsciously, the sexual (2), the emotional (3), partly out of the higher emotional (4), and the intellectual center (5), while the two highest centers are usually dormant. Most people are interested in establishing business and career, developing their sense of personal power. They give themselves hardly any time to explore the higher aspects of life until they get much older. Thus, we can divide people into three groups: (1)

---

[1] As the behavior and memory of animals are instinctive, humans have free choice and ability to reflect.

the degenerate or animal person, who lives his/her earth life through [2]the senses, (2) the average human person, who is not only involved in the gratification of the senses but also in fulfilling his or her desires for mental conquests, (3) the spiritual person or initiate, who has experienced the futility, vanity, emptiness, and illusion of the sense world, and has found a new way of life.

For some people, certain energy centers are only slightly open because the individual is unfamiliar with certain attitudes, levels of consciousness, or grasping of intellectual concepts. Other people may move up and down the centers, wherever their attention is focused, or they may change their values and attitudes. The lower centers of most individuals are fully open and overused when they are continually looking for security, gratification, power, and prestige. Thus, a person's behavior is much regulated by the general condition of the energy centers.

NOTE 1: The root and spleen center (1-2) should be activated in children from 0-7 years; the navel and heart (3-4) from 7-14 years; the throat and brow (5-6) from 14-21 years; and the crown center at a later time.

NOTE 2: The Christian era, which began about 2000 years ago, opened up the possibility for Western people and others to evolve the heart center and those above. Today, it is possible to develop the throat center and go beyond. However, most people today have not evolved farther than the third level, and some of them are still largely moved by desires and emotions instead of willpower and think more with their abdominal brain than with the brain of the head. Hopefully, signs today are that many people are seeking for Truth while questioning their old beliefs. They also want to purge and purify themselves from the evil within themselves or heart (Mark 7:21), so that they will be better ready for the exploration of the spiritual aspect of life. Unfortunately, there are others whom have given up, and their consciousness degenerated to the second level, from which they, most of the time, operate by seeing everything and everybody from that level. This is especially true of those whom practice unnatural lust (Jude 6-7), recognizing unconsciously satan as their father (John 8:44) who, as an angel, is neither male nor female (Mark 12:25) and is **the first homosexual**.

NOTE 3: Although the three lower centers represent security, passion, and power, they in themselves are not bad. They can be used for higher and lower purposes. For example, when the energy of sex is used only for sensual gratification, it becomes a great source of misery. On the other hand, when it is used as it is intended, it brings great happiness.

---

[2] The senses attach themselves to the world, turning our attention outward and, thus, distracting us from turning inward to the truth of Self-realization.

NOTE 4: When the second and third centers are awakened, the individual may perceive the feelings of others in his or her solar plexus (clair-sentience). When the fifth and sixth centers have become vivified, either *naturally or by stimulating them by concentration or meditation, the abilities for clairaudience and clairvoyance are much enhanced. By holding an object to the plexus or forehead, one may perceive the nature of the object (psychometry).

When consciousness is arrested in a particular center, people may see everybody and everything from a particular viewpoint and also create the circumstances and world around them and like to associate with those whom are like them. For example, someone whose attention is in the first center is constantly thinking about survival, in the second is incessantly seeking for sex objects, and in the third is looking for opportunities for power. Those who want to serve the world out of love and compassion work out of the higher centers and, according to their belief system, create a whole new reality in and around them.

M. Description of the Seven Energy Centers

I. The first energy center is located at the base of the spine (perineum), between the anus and the genitals. It has four petals, the color is red, its element is earth, and it is associated with the adrenal glands. It deals with grounding, survival and security on the physical plane, and also with life force energy from the subtle plane. This center provides humans with the energies they need for their various physical activities. Its preservation instinct regulates the physical needs, such as †food, clothing, and shelter. It is considered to be developed by all people. It is what Sigmund Freud called the oral stage of life. When imbalance occurs in this center, it may result in a feeling of insecurity, worry about safety, and attachments to physical objects. If the consciousness of individuals is at this stage or is arrested there (for a period of time), they completely identify with their physical and etheric bodies. Much of their energy would be spent in serving their physical appetites, and they will be preoccupied with food and physical well being. They are much like the animals and are constantly occupied in physical competition with others for food and territory, whereby only the fittest will survive. Their relationship with others is dependent and clinging. When primitives ended isolation and started social communities, this ended the era of the first energy center.

---

* Drugs that produce hallucinations should not be used to force stimulation of the centers.

† By cultivating and eating food, we unite with creation.

II. The second energy center is ¹situated at the level of the genitals or in the pelvis area below the navel (lower abdomen). It has six petals, the designated color is orange, its element is water, and it is related with the gonads or reproductive glands. It deals with sexuality, which involves sexual desires and its physical and emotional gratification. It is the seat of creative expression or reproductive activities and also deals with lower emotions, wants, wishes, and dreams. It is considered to be developed by almost all people of this world. The Freudian school teaches that the ²libido or sexual drive (instinct) is one of its principal psychological forces. The second center is also the ³polarity center and has to do with masculine and feminine balance. Food is the first priority of life, but after it has been satisfied, sex becomes, for many, the most important. The owner of an unbalanced second center may keep searching for pleasure but is never gratified. It only causes frustration and disappointment. Its human weakness is that of lust or sensory indulgence and seeing other people as separate and as sexual objects. By continually feeling and thinking in this manner, they burn away and dissipate precious life energies, which are derived from the surrounding vital atmosphere or plane. This center opens and closes in response to sensual stimulations, which in turn affects the general attitudes of the individuals involved. When this center is overactive, he or she may become extremely obsessed with the pleasure and desire of sex, filling their selfish minds with lust and greed. Humanity's second center phase ended when the goddess became male, or when matriarchal society changed into a patriarchal one.

III. The third energy center is lodged in the area of the nerve plexus or abdominal brain, which is the seat of the emotional self and other parts of the personality. It has ten petals, its color is yellow, its element is air, and it is affiliated with the pancreas. It is occupied with positive as well as negative emotions, personal power, and control. There is a need in this center to be self-assertive, to maintain individual sovereignty, self-worth, and self-respect. The consciousness of this

---

¹ For some people, this center is located close to or directly over the prostate gland when they focus their attention too much upon sensual gratification. For others, the center has shifted to the splenic area when they use sexual energy mostly for creative purposes.

² Libido as psychic energy can be sublimated to a higher form of creative energy in the higher centers by evolved beings.

³ Consciousness in the second center is based on the dualism of the universe. Each one is balanced by the other and contains the other and will be united through the law of attraction. According to Taoism, energy is created through the interaction of positive and negative forces.

center instills in the young adult to seek for a career and a suitable mate and, thus, establish himself or herself as a competent force in the world. This center is considered to be fully active in the average or ordinary human being today. Humans, according to Alfred Adler, are governed by a drive to personal self-assertion or the will to power, as against the erotic drive of Freud at the second stage. The third center is the powerhouse of action, the furnace of passion and emotion, whose fire fuels our dreams and gives us the endurance and strength to fulfill them. The Hindus call this the path of karma yoga, the way towards union with God through service. An unbalanced third center shows expressions of overuse or under-use of power, which latter is the cause of inferiority complexes in the psychology of Adler. The person who overuses, or rather, misuses this power, is becoming ruthless and engages in fierce "cutthroat" competition. The ego inflates to its utmost intensity and focuses on manipulating people and seeking to control and enslave them to their way of thinking. This is what they consider gratification and self-fulfillment, while bragging to others about how influential and powerful they really are. An individual in this stage of life tends to take life as it comes without any curiosity about the meaning, value, or purpose. He or she seeks enjoyment through the senses, cultivating emotional pleasures, material security, and spending much of his/her idle time watching mediocre television programs. Besides, individuals whom are greedy and selfish like to possess things. If they cannot get what they want, they may shower other humans with the negative emotions of hatred, anger, annoyance, destructive jealousy, bitterness, resentment, hostility, malice, rage, curse, and damnation.

NOTE 1: Karl Marx (1818-1883), German political philosopher and economist, saw level one (matter) as all-encompassing and made material production paradigmatic.

Sigmund Freud (1856-1939), Austrian neurologist and founder of psychoanalysis, gave sexuality a dominant role in his theory, which is the second level.

Alfred Adler (1870-1937), Austrian psychiatrist, put crucial emphasis on the will to power and to compensate for real or imaginary inferiority complex of the personality, the third level.

Carl Gustav Jung (1875-1961), Swiss psychoanalyst – the son of a Protestant clergyman, was concerned in his writings about the third and fourth levels. In the latter part of his life, he was exploring altered states of consciousness for which there was no room in Freudian analysis. He said that the psyche has four major capacities – sensation, emotion, intellect, and intuition.

NOTE 2: To believe in the law of give and take, whereby they give and expect. This calculated giving creates selfishness and not unconditional giving (Matt 6:3). A higher form of giving is that one believes that something will return but not always, or in a different form, such as a spiritual reward of having the satisfaction of having done something good, which produces internal growth and creates a positive attitude. By unconditional giving, you let the best come out, expressing the action of generosity and affection. This allows individuals to cast their bread upon the waters (Eccle. 11:1), without knowing where, how, whence, or if it shall return to them. This is the only true gift; otherwise, people will not forget that they have given to you.

NOTE 3: Every act God would like us to do is that it is not only good for ourselves but also good for our neighbor and for all fellow human beings. Thus, when God helps us, he also helps anybody else at the same time. We are truly our "brother's keeper".
"God's Love is action through us. Love has to be put in action, not talked about" (Sister Therese).

If they are religious at all, third stage people have a preference for authoritarian and dogmatic religions. They perceive God as separate from themselves, a wholly other, who is always watching and making judgment from on "high" or heaven. The persons also believe that as long as they obey and share in the rites of the church, they are satisfied and believe that no further growth is possible. However, when they meet individuals who speak of higher stages of spirituality, they quickly condemn them and want to have nothing to do with them.

After experiencing the frustration and inner conflicts by pursuing their self-centered goals of pride and vanity, the person may search for a higher and better way of living, away from self-centered living. The individual in the next stage moves from competition to cooperation, from conquest to affiliation, and from fighting each other to nurturing each other.

IV. The fourth energy center is seated at the cardiac or heart plexus, which is the site where the higher emotions, such as spiritual love, devotion, sympathy, empathy, and compassion find their abode. It is also the focal point of unconditional love and sacrifice. It is in possession of twelve petals, its color is green, its element is fire, and it is associated with the thymus gland. It corresponds to the first initiation. The person who expresses through the heart center is capable of feeling the joys, sorrows, and suffering from others within themselves. He or she loves freely without condition or reservation because heartistic love makes no demand and would not own or be owned (see 1 Cor. ch. 13). Those individuals whom are united within their being with spiritual or universal love also sense an oneness in the world around them and live in harmony with the good selves of others. They live more by the law of love than by law and order, as the latter was solely expressed in the third stage of life. As Paul expressed it, "Law was our custodian until Christ came"; and "you are not under law (commandments) but under grace"; and "love is the fulfilling of the law" (Gal. 3:24; Rom. 6:14; 13:10). In this center is born the desire to evolve, to serve, to show forgiveness, charity, loving kindness, kind-heartedness, consideration, goodwill, reconciliation, and generosity. As Paul phrased it, "the fruit of the Spirit is love, joy, peace, patience, kindness, goodness, faithfulness, gentleness, self-control", and "have crucified the flesh with its passions and desires" of the third stage of life (Gal. 22-24). They have become God's children and no longer belong to "the world", or humanity which is good and evil. The heart center is represented by the six-pointed Star of David. The two triangles symbolize the integration ✡ of the higher and lower aspects of our nature. Jung believed with Freud that the ego or personality is a conscious and rational self which gives humans a personal sense of identity as the "I", but unlike Freud who stated that the ego is influenced by the superego (sense of duty, conscience, etc.), Jung said that the ego (including the superego) is subordinate to a whole new being, the Self or Soul.

NOTE 1: There is quite a distinction between the universal love (agape) we experience at the heart center and the sexual and passionate love (eros) at the second and third centers. As the former is universal and expressed toward everything we may encounter directly and indirectly, sexual and passionate love is more object-oriented. At the heart, our love is no longer that of need and desire, and it goes beyond the motive to manipulate and to possess. Universal love is also to be distinguished from the romantic raptures of the lower centers that are characterized by seduction and jealousy, dominance and dependence, and attachment to a human as object in order to diminish a feeling of emptiness and loneliness. At the fourth center, the person might be alone but not lonely. Love is no longer infected by the need of craving but is experienced as an inner abundance and a desire to share freely for the well being of all human entities. Relationships at the heart go beyond unfriendly rivalry and self-aggrandizement, to become unselfish, and overlook injury or insult. Consciousness is less identified with the ego and begins to identify more with humanity. When the heart center is closed, we cannot truly love, but when it is open, we may experience ourselves as part of all life and are no longer in hostile competition with others because we are one and in harmony with others. Thus, the heart center assists one to be at peace with yourself and the world.

NOTE 2: It is very easy for those whom are married in the third stage of life to backslide to the second stage through sexual exploitation. It is therefore better to wait until they are in the fourth stage or higher to get married so that their love is not only directed to each other in a possessive way but also to their neighbors. If humans have sexual union with a closed heart center, it is sex from the lower centers. Unfortunately, many marriage partners are operating out of their second center in a lustful relationship and experience more a mutual masturbation than a love fulfillment. They have a feeling that something is missing and are soon looking for another partner. In a rightful sexual relationship, all of our energies should blend together, not only physically and emotionally but also mentally and, above all, spiritually.

The Hindus call this path four, bhakti yoga, the way of devotion. This devotion can be directed to God within themselves or in others. The God Self can be contacted by prayer and true meditation, or the devotee may make contact with a personal aspect of God he/she admires the most, such as Jesus Christ or Krishna, or a representative of the Divine Mother. Every religion provides a symbol for heart center compassion. In Christianity, it is the heart of Jesus Christ representing the male aspect of God and the Virgin Mary representing the female aspect of God. In advanced Buddhism, it is the Bodhisattva.

V. The fifth energy center lies near the cervical nervous plexus or throat. It is the seat of intelligence and creativity. This center is concerned with the spoken word, power of speech, sound, singing, and communication. It has sixteen petals, its color is radiant blue, its element is sound, and the gland connected with it is the thyroid. It deals with verbal and nonverbal communication to people and things, inspiration, higher creativity, and the use of the will in conveying information and self-expression. It corresponds to the second initiation. The fifth stage disciple or initiate, a thinker and a seeker after Truth, may respond more to the tone or vibration of the voice than the actual word spoken. The energies, which pass through this center, are related to the creation of sound, and they are also associated with the hearing of inner voices and clairaudience. The energies used in the expression of intellect also pass through this center and convey strength and clarity to the mental self. The fifth stage person has become aware that the personality has become [1]integrated with the Soul and that the personal point of view has submerged to the need of the whole. Personal satisfaction of life is being equated with doing the will of God (Jn. 5:30; Mk. 14:36). The fifth center moves individuals to express them-

---

[1] When humans are integrated with their Soul, the energy pattern of the center changes.

selves in creative ways, not only in speech but also in thinking, writing, philosophy, music, dancing, and others. They are associated with higher creativity and are fully aware that inspiration flows from a higher source than from their ego-based selves. The great works of art come from these [2]higher levels of intuition. Unfortunately, most artists, singers, musicians, and poets are working from the lower levels of their beings. If, for example, you see a painting or hear a speech or sound, it may evoke higher or lower feelings in you.

NOTE 1: As the second center is involved in the physical creation, the fifth center is involved in the spiritual creation by the Word. It has the power to cause spiritual rebirth and growth of another person by using God's Word and to be a suitable channel for God's Love and Wisdom. The Disciples of Christ are committed to recreating humanity in the image of God, and this is the main purpose of their life. They may do this either through witnessing, teaching, creating art, healing, being an example in the business world, and many other ways.

NOTE 2: The primary mode of the fifth and sixth center consciousness is higher intuition, which essentially replaces observation, logic, and reason as a reliable and dependable means of perceiving and understanding reality. The seer at those levels makes direct contact with universal archetypes that form the base of reality and may discover the hidden principles behind the laws.

NOTE 3: The individuals of the fifth and higher levels are liberated from the constraints of the rational mind, from the prison of words, opinions, dogmas, etc., thus experiencing wholeness.

NOTE 4: Men may unconsciously and, in imitation of others, use the tie and bow tie to decorate their throat ornament or center, which represents intellectual development.

In Hindu philosophy, this is the path of Raja yoga. An imbalance in this center may occur when a person occasionally and temporarily falls back to a lower level. For instance, a fifth center philosopher may promote his/her book for profit (third center), indulge too much in sex (second center), or overindulge in food for a period of time (first center). However, those lower level responses are no longer his/her primary way of living. But when they indulge too long, they may degenerate permanently to the lower level.

---

[2] The lower levels of intuition from the second center are called clair-sentience, or woman intuition.

VI. The sixth energy center is centered between the eyebrows. It is the vision center, known as the *third eye. It has two times forty-eight petals, its color is indigo or royal blue, its element is light, and it is associated with the feminine pituitary gland. It deals with outer and inner vision, spiritual sight, intuitive insight, seeing with the eye of Truth, vision of the past, present and future, contemplation of the whole, dreams from the most High, prediction, and revelation. Energies contributing to the expression of intuitive wisdom also flow through this center and convey clarity to abstract and holistic thinking. It corresponds to the third initiation. The sixth stage adept or genius has control over the psychic and divine faculties and call upon them at will in his/her dedication to selfless service. The persons are also using their faculties in their healing service and are capable of emitting or radiating a beam of healing light from their energy centers. They have foresights of future events and are, thus, able to foretell the future or make predictions many years in advance. Unlike that of the fourth and fifth centers, the ego consciousness is completely transcended at this center, and personal goals have become completely subservient to the betterment of the general human condition. At this center, love is more impersonal than at the fifth center, that is, that love towards God and the implementation of His restoration plan are more important than the increasing true love towards family and friends. See Matt. 10:37; 12:48-50; Mk. 3:31-35. In an overall view, we can say that the higher compassion of the sixth center surpasses that of the lower levels, not only by embracing living beings more, the positive as well as the negative, but also recognizing that material objects are also manifestations of the Universal Spirit. The individual of the sixth center, as the embodiment of universal principles, fully realizes the oneness of all beings and things in all of God's creation.

NOTE 1: Western psychologists and educators usually maintain that fifth center consciousness is the highest human potential and tend to pathologize the higher two centers. Traditional Western religions also do not accept manifestations of the higher two centers as being too God-like for human aspiration.

NOTE 2: At this sixth center, we find great visionary artists in this world and in the spirit world.

---

* The third eye includes the entire middle part of the head, the sinuses, eyes, pituitary, much of the brain, and the ears. A striking aspect of the ancient Egyptian death mask that signified royalty and priesthood was the head of a cobra projecting from mid-brow at the location of the third eye center. Indian women often mark their foreheads in the same area.

In the Hindu system of advancement, path six is the road of insight and corresponds with Jnana yoga. An imbalance in this center might result in emphasizing the non-physical reality too much when talking to ordinary people.

VII. The seventh energy center, or crown center, is positioned at the top of the head. It is the unity center and lies like a glorious crown atop the head of an advanced mystic. It has nine hundred and seventy-two petals, its color is violet or bluish purple, its element is thought, and it is related to the masculine pineal gland. It is the jewel of Christ Consciousness, like a perfect, numerous, faceted diamond glittering in the bright light and warmth of the sun. It is the personal aspect of God, the "I AM" Presence or "I AM" Consciousness, as being part of God, who calls Himself, "I AM WHO I AM" (Ex. 3:14). It deals with perfect wisdom and understanding, and it is the seat of complete oneness with all creation and inseparable union with the God of all humans and non-humans alike. The seventh center is the crowning evolutionary achievement and goal of humans on this earth, and it is truly the gate through which the highest energy passes through. It corresponds to the fourth initiation. The seventh stage master, as a unique and individual manifestation of the male or female aspect of God, no longer identifies with their Divine Spirit but is fully identified with the Spirit of God, who resides within and without. As unity of purpose and ownership becomes less defined as we grow to maturity, at the seventh level there is complete oneness of intention and physical, mental, and spiritual possessions. It is no longer possible among fellow masters to say that this is my purpose and that is yours, and this belongs to me and that belongs to you. The Bible verse in Isaiah 55:19 is saying, "For as the heavens are higher than the earth, so are my ways higher than your ways", no longer refers to them. The highest center includes all the capabilities of the lower ones and has the full range of the psychic and divine potentials. It is the center which transforms the highest spiritual inspiration into divine and human consciousness. The person has become an "illuminated seer" and can register an inflow of Light and inspiration, which is a higher form of clairvoyance and clairaudience. The masters, or the God-men or God-women, continually see God in all things and events, and they will surely "inherit the earth" (Matt. 5:5; 25:34). They not only express themselves through a pure consciousness but, above all, understand through their experience of finding and raising spiritual children the suffering Heart of God, to some extent, who for thousands of years has been looking for His lost children. This was movingly expressed in Isaiah 1:2:

"Sons have I reared and brought up, but they have rebelled against me. The ox knows its owner, and the ass its master crib; but Israel does not know, my people do not understand."

N. Surveying the Seven Stages

We can divide humanity into seven groups:

1) Savages or undeveloped people	physical stage
2) Semi-civilized races	phy/emotional stage
3) Civilized human beings	phy/emo/mental stage
4) Initiates or born-again Christians or Super-humans	phy/emo/ment/spiritual stage
5) Disciples of Christ or saints	maturing and advancing
6) Adepts or Geniuses or Over-Soul	in spiritual stage
7) Masters as individual expressions of God	Spiritual maturity stage

I. The consciousness of savages and un-evolved people is almost entirely on the physical plane. Their life is lived with habitual attention to physical needs. This creature has no real sense of self, apart from the awareness of the body. Their human spirits are indefinite in shape or form, and its faculties, such as intellect, emotion, and will are dormant or in a low or raw state of development. Almost all impressions they get come from without and hardly recognize inner promptings. They usually live close to nature and are familiar with external powers, such as the forces of nature, which they call gods. Many savages or primitives believe(d) that those gods took revenge on them for their misdeeds through storms, lightning, and earthquakes. [1]They constantly live in fear, not only from those powers, human and animal predators, but also from psychic forces, which seem to surround them from all sides and from which there is no escape.

Un-evolved humans are extremely selfish and get all they can without any regard to anybody or anything. If they unite with certain groups of people, it is only to become stronger to fight the "enemy" so

---

[1] The savages were superstitious and fearful of nature because they did not understand its laws. When they developed, the gods were no longer the forces of nature but entities in the likeness of humans whom were behind those forces. Those gods were apparitions or ghosts, out of which grew ancestor worship and from which they made images.

539

that they can take what they want. Their slogan is that might is always right and that only the ²fittest will survive.

NOTE 1: As physical consciousness is that of the physical body, the subtle physical consciousness is that of the etheric body. The latter contains the blueprint or pattern of the physical body. The energy of the etheric body is called breath of life, life energy, prana, vitality, and it pervades everything in the universe (see "The Etheric Body").

NOTE 2: People today whom are much involved in sports and other physical activities have their consciousness, at those times, temporarily arrested in the physical level by experiencing physical sensation. This is especially true of athletes whom are competing with others and of women whom are about to enter a beauty contest, as well as of individuals whom are experiencing the sensation of pain. At those times, they completely identify with their bodies.

We also call the first level the animalistic stage, wherein people behave like animals and whereby the stronger among them kills the weaker. Human life does not have any value, except that it may serve as food or enslavement. They are moved, or rather driven, by the instinct of survival to satisfy their need for food, clothes, and shelter. The undeveloped do not have a pure conscience because they do not live according to God-given moral laws but live according to tribal or other laws. Those cannibals and many primitive people have no other purpose than to hunt for food, eat and sleep, and produce offspring. The un-evolved continually feel that they may become prey to someone else and, therefore, their attitude is "to kill or be killed". Many animal persons whom are in the grip of animal passion have a certain kinship or identity with their (totem) animals, while some others feel a close relation with (mythical) dragons. (The latter is a symbol of the instinctive and primitive forces of human beings.) Those human creatures whom, after death, discover that their spirit body is only a shade or phantom and of little psychic substance mistakenly, or through ignorance, seek shelter in the bodies of animals. An example is the devils that implored Jesus to let them enter into the herd of swine (Matt. 8:31; Mk. 5:12). Many savages and un-evolved people whom do not eat their victims like to kill because it gives them a certain rush or euphoria of having conquered someone, a thrill of conquest and

---

² As the law of the fittest is operative in the animal world and causes animals and animal men/women to improve bodily, the law of sacrifice is operative in the human world and causes humans to develop internally.

power over life and death. *Less barbaric are those whom enjoy watching human beings kill each other, such as was the case in the arenas of Roman past and other places.

NOTE 1: In past centuries and earlier ages, many human creatures cared little about their fellow humans and were not able to empathize with pain or hardship that another might be enduring. They continually abused each other physically and had little respect for human life. They often gained a following or an army through intimidation and threat of physical punishment. As recorded in the book of Habakkuk, the Chaldeans were a proud, brutal, and cruel people and were ruthless in their behavior. They plundered, killed, and enslaved their prisoners and rejoiced in their suffering.

NOTE 2: About the same immoral behavior as the Chaldeans we can still find in hardcore criminals in civilized communities of today. They have no conscience, guilt, or shame and are, therefore, not able to understand in others unselfish love, the pangs of conscience, guilt, regret, embarrassment, repentance, and forgiveness. By having no inhibitions and other internal controls, except that they may be caught by outside authorities, they do whatever they please. We can, however, easily spot them because cruelty is stamped into the corners of their mouths, and when they peer with their cold and dead eyes, we may experience it as a chill of fear going as it were through our bones.

NOTE 3: Those whom have chosen evil, who refuse to acknowledge good in themselves and in others, and have deadened their own conscience and other spiritual faculties go, after death, to the lowest region of the spirit world, cluttered with evil thought forms beyond the reach of moral law. Their undeveloped spirits meet others like them, and they can no longer hide among the good people of the earth as they did before. The "fire that is not quenched" (Mk. 9:48; Isa. 66:24) is the emotional torment, the fear and hostility, resentment, frustration, bitterness, hatred, and futility that consumes them inwardly.

I→II. The less barbaric ones whom no longer kill for pleasure have been growing out of the animal stage by living in social communities, following rules of conduct, and serving others in their own small and limited way. However, they are still much earthbound, although they have lost much of the instinctive way of living, apart from the group. Thus, rigid instincts have given way to social norms, habits, roles, and

---

* Today, we can still see some blood-thirsty people enjoy seeing bull and cock fights and violent sports, such as boxing, in which the very goal is to beat one's opponent senseless. This barbaric heritage is also shown by the crowd during a public execution, which very often happened in the recent past.

social structures outside the human body. They are less selfish than the above-mentioned savage but are still much involved in sensual gratification. *They occasionally may involve, as part of their own well being, their own family members.

II. The consciousness of a more developed human being of semi-civilized races and some misguided people today is not only on the physical plane but also on the emotional and, to a limited degree, on the mental plane of existence. Those individuals are generally self-centered and live most of the time for the satisfaction and fulfillment of their lower desires. Many people in this second stage of life are not able to control their violent, emotional, and debased desire natures because they are lacking in mental strength and ability. The lowest of them are driven by mechanical response to their own desire and are ruled by their uncontrollable irregular passions.

An ancient society which was much involved in satisfying lustful passion was matriarchal in nature. They were devoted to the great mother, occupied themselves with the worship of the phallus and yoni, and participated in the many orgies and fertility festivals. The people at that time did not think that it was a bad thing to do because their gods were accorded responsibilities for both good and evil. Their thinking was irrational, abounded by superstition, while offerings were made to their gods they tried to placate. Although they were most miserable in this lawless society, they accepted their world as the best possible world because the people could not compare their society with anything better.

Not long thereafter, Buddha came along and pronounced the four noble truths: (1) Life is full of suffering and dissatisfaction; (2) Desires and craving are the causes of human suffering; (3) By eliminating selfish desires, suffering will end; (4) This is possible by following the eight-fold path, by changing one's behavior, desire, emotions, and thoughts. See further #23.

NOTE 1: Many people in ancient society lived blindfolded in a world of illusion and are cut off from any spiritual influence through ignorance and insensitivity. They have stifled their conscience and surrendered themselves to sensuality, practicing any form of impurity which lust can suggest.

---

* Family relationships will considerably improve in later stages of development.

NOTE 2: At this second stage, we can find many sex offenders, prostitutes, adulterers, and those whom are promiscuous. Some of them may only temporarily degrade to that particular level or may visit that stage when they only desire, for brief moments, to have unlawful relationships. In the latter case, they may become psychically involved when pursuing their desires. Those whom are arrested permanently or temporarily in that stage soon reveal themselves. Because it does not matter what you talk about, the individual on the second level will soon turn it to a conversation of sex, or they use ample sexual expressions in their talk.

The emotional self or animal soul deals with attraction, repulsion, and personal desires. That is to say that those whom are polarized in the emotional self are governed mainly by feelings, emotions, and desires, which is part and parcel of the animal soul. The persons whom are animalistic in nature are those whom continually desire to have sex, while it has also become the most important lifestyle. They are symbolically, and in their dream life, portrayed as animals and are often called by that name by sensitive people or are just told that they are sexually attractive or horny.

As the large majority of civilized people have outgrown their identification with the physical body, many of them not only identify with their emotions but are also overcome and stuck with lustful desires, which is especially true of homosexuals. You can easily spot those individuals whom are living a life below the belt because when you meet them, they first look at the lower part of your body. That is the level where they are in their moral development, which they continually express in their daily lives by foul language and dirty jokes. The lewd and lustful individuals do not know the difference between sexual desires and love and are easily persuaded by advertisers whom appeal to the sex instinct of them as consumers. By continually seeking pleasures of the senses, which do not satisfy their moral selves, they are leading a life of hopelessness, despair, and desperation in which they can only sink deeper.

When enough people have fallen down from a higher to the lower second level, then a whole nation may decline and is certainly bound to be when many children are born in lust from promiscuous parents. The Roman Empire, for example, declined from the third level and sank beneath the waves of the symbolic waters. Young people called "hippies", whom *rebelled against society in the 1960s, had original idealistic ideals about how society should be, but they as a group went from a spiritual high, by following a path downward, to the lower levels. They became confused about true love and lower desires, while some of them kept their euphoria going by taking drugs and other substances. They separated from God and lost their influence and power and found out the hard way that love, or rather satanic love, is not the answer.

NOTE 1: When the life force energy is focused in the centers below the heart, all spirituality is lost. Thus, instead of this energy being purified and drawn upward, it is exhausted in the downward flow towards the sexual organs and binds the senses, the mind, and human spirit to this earthward pull. It also robs the physical body of the life currents for the maintenance of perfect health and vigor.

NOTE 2: As women in general represent the second level of the personality, men are more inclined to represent that of the third level, that of the intellect. While beauty is female – earthly, truth is male – heavenly. Because women are more emotional, they are able to give out more emotional energy, which is a carrier of love. Some women whom seek for support and protection admire men whom are strong, while other women like to fulfill their mother role.

NOTE 3: The physical body of Western individuals is coarser and more alive than the body of Eastern persons because of the greater emphasis on the development of the personality and being preoccupied in the last centuries with sex. The intelligence and emotion of Western persons is, thus, more developed, and they are also more aggressive physically. The Western women appear more feminine.

NOTE 4: Those people whom have destroyed out from themselves all of the unselfish and affectionate feelings have become ruthless monsters of lust and find themselves, after death, in a very low region of the spirit world.

II→III. After some growth, the individual begins to perceive dimly that a material life, with its stimulation of the senses and the pursuit of one's lower desire or animal passion, is no longer satisfying or fulfilling. By living a life of physical sensation and sensual gratification, it makes him or her a little better than the beast of the field. As Kierkegaard the 19th century philosopher of Denmark expressed it: "A life of seeking pleasures is a life of despair and brings

---

* They rebelled because the sense of the sacred got lost when people, at that time, tried to solve almost all problems through a scientific rational approach, which left no room for the spiritual.

satisfaction and dissatisfaction afterwards." Because of discontent, a higher faculty is being awakened and begins its unfolding process when the individual starts to study the available disciplines. Thus, the individual turns his/her attention away from the earth to the higher and subtle levels of mental speculation and learning, exploring, and developing the intellectual faculties. He/she has become curious about the how and why of things.

NOTE 1: Animals were created with instinct, which guides them, while humans were created with instinct and mind power for their guidance. As there is fear, competition and violence in the animal world, so is it among unregenerated, good/evil humans.

NOTE 2: The man or woman whom, in early life, literally lives for sport and physical sensation may be drawn, at a later point, to the reality of mental speculation and study.

NOTE 3: A higher than a second level person may not want to seek immediate gratification with a prostitute or other person but may think and joke about it, but will not do it, but likes to see others do it.

III.   [1]The first, second, and third levels comprise the life of the personality or lower self, also called ego, which is good as well as evil. People in those stages need to be governed by [2]external and internal laws in order to follow proper rules of conduct and to grow morally. The more immature they are, the stricter the law and its enforcement because undeveloped humans have [3]more respect for strength than persuasion. Those laws and the fear of punishment have a great effect in denying and repressing the thief and murderer within them (Matt. 15:19) and withholding other destructive behavior.

The main concern of the Israelites, whom were generally in the third stage of life, is about moral development. By following moral laws, given by their Creator, their conscience became more developed and they could, therefore, to a certain extent also be guided from within.

---

[1] The condition of the first three stages: survival, sex, and power is not "bad" in itself but are vital because it is important, while living on earth, to be concerned with basic survival, procreation, and have a sense of personal identification. They are the foundation of higher stages.

[2] Humans should not be dominated by the arbitrary will of another but should be guided by the rule of the law, which is good for everybody, not just "good for you".

[3] Some immature people and children will only understand that they are doing wrong when they are corrected with a "big stick". They are not able or want to listen to reason and are far from knowing intuitively the difference between good and evil.

The *Romans, whom inherited from the Greeks the art of reasoning, were more inclined to follow man-made laws, in establishing order and justice. Although the Romans could be cruel when they [1]degraded, at times, from the third level, they generally had more respect for human life as the Celts. The latter practiced human sacrifice, which the Romans considered to be barbaric and made this practice illegal. The Celts, whom were conquered by the Romans, lived in a lawless society, where the will of a capricious and absolute ruler or tyrant was the law, while they were, most of the time, guided by feelings and desires. As the Egyptians used the scales of justice only for the final decision (when the feather was placed on the scale), the Romans used the scales as the symbol of worldwide justice, when misdeeds were weighed against good deeds.

NOTE 1: Some governments are more inclined, at times, to support the evil side of life, while other political administrations are using their authority and power to serve the good side as a minister of God.

Jesus Christ said in Matt. 22:21, "Render therefore to Caesar the things that are Caesar's, and to God the things that are God's."

Apostle Paul mentioned in Romans 13:1-7, "Let every person be subject to the governing authorities" --- "for rulers are not a terror to good conduct but to bad" --- "one must be subject, not only to avoid God's wrath (karma) but also for the sake of conscience. For the same reason you also pay taxes, for the authorities are ministers of God."

NOTE 2: People whose consciousness is arrested at the lower levels of development are so selfish that they seek everything for their own benefit, even at the cost of others. They feel no pleasure in giving but only in taking. Others are so wrapped up in their own cares and comfort that they cannot be bothered with anyone and are considered socially retarded.

NOTE 3: Soldiers usually live the life of a disciplined personality. Loyalty and obedience are important virtues for them. It is the unity of purpose that spells success or failure; the size of the army is of little importance.

---

* The Romans were a society of warriors, the ancient Greeks were scholars, and the Egyptians of old were like priests.
[1] Many Romans enjoyed eating and drinking and other sensual gratification. At those times, they behaved as if they were in the first and second stages. They also degraded when they worshipped Roman emperors, who gained through this veneration and admiration more physical and psychic human power from the people, which they used to exercise more tyranny over the same people. Images of emperors all over the empire were, therefore, very helpful in advancing their cause.

Let us emphasize here to those whom are living in the third stage the good and evil self of their personalities and the side which, at times, is in charge of their lives. Since the deviation from the beginning, the human personality consists of a good self, which is striving to live according to moral laws and the evil self, which wants to live free from any [1]such laws. The good self is God-oriented, and the evil self is satan-oriented. When the evil self is ruling the personality or ego, it becomes false, and it often discloses itself by using profane and boisterous expressions. Those whom are satan-oriented or have satan as their father (Jn. 8:44) are not only spiritually dead (no relation with God) but also their personality is ugly like the old self or old man in Paul's writings (Rom. 6:6; Col. 3:9; Eph. 4:22). They are also called satanic or evil people, or flat out satanic. Chapter one in Romans speaks about them as people whom are depraved or the reprobates (unprincipled), whose consciences are either dead or seared. They do not, or have lost, the ability to discern between good and evil and have thus lost the sense of sin, and thus no longer realize that they are doing evil and are acting as true sons or daughters of satan. Fallen Lucifer represents that part of us that compels us to act selfish (see Isaiah 14:13-14), to feel cold towards others, manipulative, to gain for number one, I or me. The reprobates or depraved are "haters of God, insolent, haughty, boastful, inventors of evil" (Rom. 1:30), and they feel hostility towards God and all of His true representatives and the law of God. The corrupted human nature manifests itself in extreme selfishness, greed, false pride, vanity, immorality, self-will, self-reliance, and cannot take criticism. They live in a self-made environment or world, which is characterized by hatred, frustration, exploitation, crime, and war. The most dangerous predators in that world are not the animals but humanity, by [2]killing each other on a massive scale. Many of the ruling classes in the good/evil world in the past and today were often arrogant, selfish, and oppressive, devoted to gain, unscrupulous, and dishonest in their dealings, taking advantage of anyone whenever the chance presented itself. The oppressed, at first, are the lesser of the two evils, but when they likewise acquire power over others, they very probably become the same as their former rulers. [3]Those people today

---

[1] There is complete freedom within the fence of the law. Going outside the law, one only finds destruction for oneself and others. "Where the Spirit of the Lord is, there is freedom" (2 Cor. 3:17).

[2] The law of karma, which has no face, continually works as a vicious cycle of killing and being killed. "For all who take the sword will perish by the sword" (Matt. 26:52). All those who do wrong have to pay the karmic price or pay penance, either inside the penitentiary walls (prison) or outside.

[3] People, in general, are today less arrogant and prideful than, for example, the people of the Roman Empire.

whom are living the life of the good/evil personality are like the "tree of the knowledge of good and evil". Their personality is neither completely evil nor completely good. They can choose at any time in their lives at which side they want to belong, by their feelings, desires, thinking, and actions, that of God or satan. Human beings of today are passing through a time when spiritual and moral values are almost totally disregarded. Many of them tolerate those whose relationships are unnatural and lustful because the relationships of the so-called good people have also become lustful. They are no longer sure that they are good and, therefore, do not want to criticize others so much. The result is that what was formerly seen as sinful and evil is slowly being tolerated in the family and society.

NOTE: If we had no faults, we should not take so much pleasure in noticing them.

The objective of many individuals at the third center is to have a position of power and protecting and advancing this position and sense of importance. Their false personality enjoys wielding power and lording it over others, thereby feeding their ego and becoming more vain or worthless and prideful, that is, imbued with false pride. Their false ego also grows when they allow themselves to be fed by flattery or insincere praise of their servants and from others who want something from them. Some of them whom are already "puffed up" with self-importance become vainglorious and arrogant by continually boasting about themselves. Their overgrown and inflated egos become like a windbag, or as the Preacher the son of David in Ecclesiastes expressed it, "All is vanity" (1:2), and a striving or feeding on wind (1:14). They would then like to cover up and protect their false ego, with its vanity or emptiness (without spiritual substance), with a mask, whereby their inner selves become even more egotistical, selfish, and ugly. Those whom are continually looking for position and status in society and do anything to acquire it are greedy, deceitful, manipulative, and are often out of control in their drive for power and supremacy. In the world of business, they participate in *cutthroat competition and will do anything to make a buck. They are driven by fear and insecurity and want to possess and dominate people, while the better ones among them suffer of guilt.

---

* An atmosphere of competition and aggression stirs up basic fears of survival and bring up all sorts of stress.

NOTE: Many people use their car as a status symbol. However, if your life is empty, useless, and vain, or as the bumper sticker has it: "If Jesus (Soul) is not driving – you are just spinning your wheels." The power of God should be behind our power to steer the car or with the car's power steering. While driving, they should observe the signs of the road or seek for divine guidance. The driver should also not drive with a dirty engine, or the personality as the vehicle of the Soul should be pure and free of dirty feelings and thinking. We may look at our hidden problems under the hood of the car and tune ourselves up with our spiritual tune-up kit. If it is not effective, we may drive into a computer analysis garage, or a psychological – psychoanalysis, transpersonal, or divine counsel station and receive a printout or a report of everything that is wrong with our human and Divine Spirit!

What is the use of running when you are not on the right road? (Pioneer proverb)

REMARKS: Power does not corrupt men but fools, if they get into a position of power, corrupt power (G.B. Shaw).
Knowledge is power, but in irrational hands, it is lust for power. (unknown)
Power as it must be in human hands will ever be liable to abuse. (Madison)
There are power-seeking individuals whom do not understand their own unconscious drives for domination and rule.

Friedrich Nietzsche (1844-1900), German philosopher, said that power is the primary motive, and all other motives as derivations from it. Alfred Adler taught that most modern nervous and emotional disorders grow out of a definite striving for power, the egotistical power urge or the ego ambition. However, Adler was not fully aware that the power urge, the ruthless drive for power and supremacy, is a symptom of one's evil nature. This nature can only be removed by treating the cause. In other words, we should know how it originated and what it is, and then, with the help of Christ, overcome and crucify it (Gal. 5:24). See also #39-C.

The solar plexus is the power center from which people try to persuade, convince, control, possess, and dominate each other. Most of us have been hurt in our lives by people who have abused power. We were most vulnerable as children to the adults, especially when they were immature. They may, at times, punish the child, not that he/she has done something wrong but that the child has disobeyed the owner, whose ego has been hurt.

For many people, the goods they want in their lives consist of more money, more property, and more things; to others, it means more fame, more power, more prestige. It is not wrong to possess money and wealth, but it gives the owners a false feeling of influence, power, and importance. Then they have a hard time convincing themselves of the importance of spiritual needs and values. However, by shedding their masks of pretension and by being themselves in the pureness of their personalities, they become like Zacchaeus in Luke 19:1-10 who received salvation.

Many people strive for positions of prominence and fame by becoming political leaders, movie stars, and the like. They are *ambitious, and some of them tend to pursue fame, wealth, or power at any price. This is wrong, breeds fierce competition, and a disregard for his or her fellow human being.

NOTE 1: When someone is living the life of the personality, they receive limited power from the forces of the universe and have, therefore, a tendency to achieve power of their own.

NOTE 2: Some people that have identified themselves too much with power and position would rather die than give up their license to practice or their position.

NOTE 3: It sometimes happens in society that a successful status seeker who has reached the top of the corporate ladder by surrendering moral and ethical principles resigns because he or she could no longer have respect and dignity for themselves and sense of values.

NOTE 4: Generally speaking, we can say that the tenet of third stage people in the negative sense is that success translates into money and property, gospel of wealth, social Darwinism, conforming to society, greed, power, and digging graves for others by ferocious and rampant competition, which is allowed by society.

NOTE 5: Some women have learned that rape is not as much a crime of lust but that of power and rage because rapists get only stimulated when they struggle to gain control of the woman and when their anger is aroused. They will lose all interest in a woman who is passive or encourages them to have a relationship with them.

---

* Ambition is not sought after by un-evolved people because their consciousness is in the first two stages, and the desire for power, which can only be achieved with a developed mind, has not occurred. It is not wrong to be ambitious because the individual or ego needs to assert itself, grow, and become independent. Otherwise, the person becomes inactive, lazy, slothful, idle, and he or she may become a loafer or beggar. However, "selfish ambition" is wrong (James 3:16).

NOTE 6: People whom are in the third stage, the center of self-will, and who are much ruled by their solar plexus, can easily recuperate by listening to high vibration music.

NOTE 7: In the post-Industrial Revolution, people of the Western world became very materialistic, their bodies became coarse in vibration, and they became less sensitive to the spirit world.

NOTE 8: A rich person can be very insecure and never have enough, while a poor person who is related to God feels very rich knowing that he/she is protected and taken care of by God every day. They trust in God, or as the dollar bill says, "In God we trust" (not in money).

The unregenerated religious people of today of the third stage, like the Jewish of old, are in need of the Old Testament for their moral guidance. They should try to live according to the most important precept of the old dispensation, the Ten Commandments, and are attempting to become good citizens by performing duties and responsibilities. Like the angels, the people in the Old Testament were in a servant position towards God, who was their Creator and Master. The mission of Jesus was to establish a relationship of spiritual child and Parents. The disciples of Jesus, however, were still living the life of the personality instead of the divine life. They came to Jesus with an ego attitude of wanting to have a position on His right and left side (Mark 10:35-41) and asked Jesus, "Who is the greatest in the kingdom of heaven?" (Matt. 18:1). Those whom are men of *power, position, and knowledge would not accept the invitation by Christ who then invited the common people and beggars to come to His banquet (Luke 14:16-24).

---

* We may distinguish between evil or false power (created by energy exchange of evil people in whom the evil self is in charge), human power (energy created between humans whom are good), and divine power created by the Divine Spirits of humans and the God forces, which quickly multiply. Jesus said, "For where two or three are gathered in my name (which is also a vibration), there am I in the midst of them" (Matt. 18:20). Those who call upon the name of Jesus Christ find power within that name because "all authority in heaven and on earth has been given to me" (Matt. 28:18).

The devil said to Jesus, "To you I will give all this authority (over the kingdoms of the world) and their glory; for it has been delivered to me" (Luke 4:6). Jesus said in John 5:41, "I do not receive glory from men", and "How can you believe who receives glory from one another and do not seek the glory that comes from the only God?" (John 5:44)

"He who speaks on his own authority seeks his own glory" (John 7:18).

Jesus said the meek shall inherit the earth (Matt. 5:5). Benito Mussolini and Adolf Hitler did not believe that, for they attempted to take it by force. Because the majority of people want to have power over others, it was not difficult for Mussolini and Hitler to recruit [1]their armies with little or no conscience. Their troops, being more evil than good, followed orders in a robot-like fashion and, in turn, gave commands to their subordinates. They all exercised power over life and death, especially to those whom were of an "inferior race".

Communists, whom were not much better, listened to the henchmen of Moscow and live(d) according to the enforced moral law of the state. Their most influential leader Stalin (man of steel) considered himself an intellectual, atheist, and a man of power. He was ruthless and allowed the Russians to worship in their churches only during the Second World War. Dictators, whose power drive has become demonic, always like children and animals; it is the adults which are in their way, especially those whom are [2]following a higher power. Most of the [3]bullies and tyrants that have achieved power in the 20th century did so in the name of Communism, while many others did so in the name of anti-Communism.

America, who broke away from the King of England and its noblemen whom exercised absolute power, established democracy, whereby the power came in the hands of the people. They learned the hard way that individuals whom are good and evil should not rule others in an unlimited way, especially not through powerful agencies. This concern was expressed by Madison: "The essence of government is power – power lodged as it must be in human hands will ever be liable to abuse." Society should, therefore, be run by checks and balances so that evil does not have much of a chance to develop, and powerful politicians should be chosen for a limited time only. Tax collectors and other federal and local agencies should be curtailed in the exercise of their power.

NOTE 1: On April 12, 1945, Roosevelt (field of rosen – Dutch –) died. On April 29, 1945, Hitler died. The democrat and dictator – gladiators of light and darkness, both led their nations for twelve years, from 1933 until their deaths.

---

[1] Many of Hitler's soldiers had a hard time saying, "Heil Hitler!" (hail Hitler)

[2] True Christians and others are especially feared by dictators because they give their highest allegiance to God and not to them.

[3] Most bullies only respect power and strength and are not easily disarmed except by a greater power and greater strength.

Democracy and private ownership is capitalism; democracy and public ownership is socialism. Dictatorship and private ownership is fascism; dictatorship and public ownership is communism.

NOTE 2: While the Civil War was going on, the capital of the United States was being built to establish firmly a democracy, by and for all the people.

NOTE 3: Because Americans are generally a bit more spiritually evolved than the Europeans, positions are less important for them, and they are less ashamed of walking around in working clothes. There is more equality among the Americans, and they are less inclined to dominate their fellow men or women. They are also less self-conscious, are more open, outspoken, and honest about themselves, and are more acquainted with the power of true love.

Generally speaking, we may say that as the Romans were up and into the third level in their growth, the followers of Hitler and Communists were about at the same levels, but more on the evil side, while many Europeans and Americans of today are between the third and fourth levels.

The natural or unspiritual man (1 Cor. 2:14), or those whom are living the life of the good/evil personality in the third stage of development and who call themselves intellectuals, reformers, and sometimes liberals, are usually "puffed up" with self-importance. This is based of the fact that society says that they have studied and are, therefore, knowledgeable. [1]Most of them are concerned on teaching knowledge, but not as much as how to use this information correctly by wisdom, which is a spiritual faculty. James said frankly that wisdom which does not come from above "is earthly, unspiritual, devilish" (Jas. 3:15). In the Gospel of John, the Jews marveled at the teachings of Jesus saying, "'How is it that this man has learning when he has never studied?' So Jesus answered them, 'My teaching is not mine, but His who sent me'" (Jn. 7:15-16). Many intellectuals have no personal awareness of God, who remains at best vague and shadowy. They are not able to recognize the voice of God, are usually uninspired, and only go by learned information. Because the nature of the educational system through which they have been progressed is such that they have

---

[1] Some of them have a tendency to be narrow, elitist, and arrogant in attitude and opinions and who seem more eager to indoctrinate their particular narrow ideas and views about life than to educate. They want to break the students' relationships with God by saying that spiritual life is for weak people and that only the ignorant join religious movements who cannot think for themselves. They then try to play God, like their master Lucifer, by coercing the students in subtle ways to follow their will instead of God's will. The result is that the students become as miserable as their teacher and are less able to think for themselves about important issues.

always been taught to look outwards for information and instructions for the development of the personality. They teach rational thinking to find concrete [2]knowledge, and a few of them also teach abstract knowledge, such as philosophy, by exercising the higher mental faculties. But almost none of them teach how to develop the intuitive wisdom or holistic mind to understand genuine poetry and other divine inspirations. In order to defend and hold on to their position and status as well-educated and learned individuals ([3]who know everything but understand nothing), some of them do not want to admit that they do not always know. Those educators are no longer open to learning and are, thus, not teachable. The so-called experts continue to parade their half-truths in the name of education and go unchallenged in their judgment. A few of them want to be known as clever and boast of their scheming and cunning, especially in the promotion industry. For them, education is very helpful so that they can use their knowledge to fool the people to give their hard earned money to them. They then use much of this easy money for the gratification of their senses, making the world more evil and, thus, hastening the destruction of themselves, family, and nation. Some intellectuals of the third stage are the wandering butterflies because they fly or float from idea to opinion and concept, or from one group to another, without ever finding anything that is of real value. They are unable to find the real Truth and, therefore, do not know the purpose and meaning of life. Those who have found and embodied the Truth stand higher in the divine spheres than the greatest third level intellectuals. The latter must first be divested of egotism, false pride, and spiritual ignorance.

NOTE 1: Humans in New Testament times at first lived as spiritual children in the age of faith when mother church gave them spiritual comfort and hope of immortality and did all their thinking for them. In the age of reason, the grown-ups were no longer satisfied with blind faith and the "mother's milk" of the church because it did not satisfy their additional hunger for intellectual knowledge needed for mental development. They were curious and wanted to

---

[2] Many individuals want to have more knowledge in order to dominate people. They think that knowledge is power and, for some, the only security and self-esteem they have. When they speak, they want to give others the impression that they are persons of knowledge. They also want to force their opinions and ideas upon others in order to change, control, and dominate them. However, people should listen to what they are, not what they are saying. For example, an individual who practices what they preach or embodies the truth which he/she seeks to expound has a much greater influence and a deeper effect on their listeners than those who only communicate high ideals on the intellectual plane. Because when they speak, they also convey the vibrations from their human and divine spirits, which tend to arouse similar vibrations in the spirit bodies of attentive hearers. This is the secret of great orators and saints of all religions.

[3] Their knowledge is only on the plane of the intellect.

know the "how" and "why" of things. The church discouraged critical thinking and said, "Ours is not to reason why, ours is to accept without question. To reason and analyze is the path which leads to hell." Many thinking members of the church did not want to sacrifice and impoverish their intellect and broke away from the confining and growth-impending mother church. However, they found that reason without faith is cold and devoid of life. The intellectuals, of whom many were living beyond the third stage of development, came back and tried to unite faith with reason, which process is still going on today.

NOTE 2: The mind is not a slayer of the Soul, as some religious people might say. However, it is true that the intellect, in trying to understand of what it believes or understands about life, may at times doubt and be skeptical. But it is only possible to respond and activate God's wisdom if we have developed a well-trained and enlightened mind.

As most people today are in the third stage of evolution, they often sink back or backslide to the lower levels, permanently or temporarily, in their feeling, thinking, and behavior. Many of them are completely involved in the material and worldly way of living and have not evolved to the point of knowing hardly any thing about spiritual life. They are egotistical and selfish, like to have a good time, and are much involved in sports, gambling, and horse racing in order to get excited and to get something for nothing. The worldly people say of other people whom are like them that they are greedy like animals, which they cannot trust. They also drink [1]alcohol or take drugs in order to be "high" instead of becoming one with God.

In social life, each member is ranked within a social hierarchy according to class, family, wealth, education, and sex, while the moral and spiritual development of the individual is hardly given any attention. Many members of the social upper class (social Darwinism), who distinguish themselves by position, clothes, and manners are often cold and have no compassion, especially not towards the lower class. They are often called [2]snobs. The higher and middle class humans behave in certain ways, also in [3]speaking and writing, in order to be respected by the "lower" social class. When they grew up, they were dyed with the brush of convention and respectability and are, thus, very familiar with etiquette or all forms and manners. This was often re-

---

[1] People are holding up their drinks to each other instead of their highest ideal.

[2] We find many snobs all over the world. The ones which are more known are many snobs of 18th century England and some southerners of the United States who inherited, in part, these traits from those who started a colony in Jamestown in 1609.

[3] They are using difficult and confusing language by, for example, doctors and lawyers, such as in courts in order to demand respect.

quired in certain societies which are centered in the well-being of the personality. Conforming to society or culture was, therefore, important and expected of anyone regardless of spiritual growth. For some, the social instinct was as important for maintenance of life as the instinct of survival. Thus, the objective of individuals striving at the third center is social position and status and protecting and advancing one's sense of importance.

NOTE 1: In the last centuries, the people in the West put great emphasis on the development of the lower personality, and they have been and still are much preoccupied with sex, emotion, and lower intellect. Some people of the third stage may say, "The whole world is after sex, power, and money."

NOTE 2: In the civilized world, we no longer buy and sell human beings at slave markets, but we still buy and sell our labor, abilities, and skills for the highest price at the labor markets, where the evaluation of character of individuals is given little or no consideration. Many of them at their job work from nine to five to maintain a well-regulated, monotonous, and secular life, complete with fringe benefits. Some of them go after work to their comfortable air-conditioned cubicle, eat chemically manufactured food, listen to pre-programmed entertainment, and, like animals, endure their cages. Then they walk, eat some more food, and then go to sleep. The next morning at their work, they play out the script that creative people wrote for them.

NOTE 3: People in general do not like individuals who behave in an immoral way and are in a low level of development. They try to avoid them and do not want to give anything to them. The result is that those individuals feel very insecure and become even greedier.

NOTE 4: In Western society, those whom are rich are usually highly evaluated, while those whom are rich in Spirit are not.

NOTE 5: Some people do nothing else but complain about society, and do nothing to change it.

NOTE 6: Many individuals whom are living the life of the personality and are also sensitive to other people's vibes are often shy and self-conscious and are, thus, inhibited in expressing themselves. Some of them are lonely and depressed, while others experience difficulties of looking in the camera and having stage fright.

NOTE 7: When people are young, the chief temptation is the sexual. When they reach middle age, the leading temptation is greed and to be hungry for power.

NOTE 8: There is a saying: "Your wish is our command, and the customer is always king."

When people become more mature, it is sufficient that they know the principles of life, and they have to exercise their own judgment about what is good and evil. If they evolve and do not degenerate when breaking a church or state law, then it certainly is not a sin or a crime. When obtaining a certain degree of self-mastery, they also have full knowledge of the law of cause and effect or karma and know what the results are when going against it. The persons also know that they will not be punished by an [1]angry God when breaking the law of karma, which knowledge should replace the fear of hell.

The regions of darkness in the spirit world were mostly occupied by the people of the first and second levels who died in the past. Today, as most people are in the third stage of development, they go to a [2]higher plane, which has become the most populated.

The lowest sphere of the spirit world is obviously "hell", as described in many religions. The middle part where ordinary unregenerated humans are living is purgatory (called by the Catholics), while a higher part is a place where we can find many intellectuals, artists, and other creative and good people whom are living the life of the personality. Those whom are living the divine life are living in the different spheres of the heavenly world. As sex is still practiced psychically in the first three planes in the spirit world, it is no longer engaged in the fourth and higher levels of heaven (Mark 12:25). In those spheres, the spirit entities do not fall in love; they grow in love. Love is deeper, more sublime, and all-encompassing (see #15).

REMARKS: As the vibration of the solid, liquid, and gases are increasingly higher, so is the human body, human spirit, and Divine Spirit.
As the earth is in a very delicate balance, so are human beings in all areas of their lives.
When living in the wilderness, you know that nature is the master; when you reside in the city, humans are all-powerful.
A life is well lived on earth when one gains valuable experiences.
Find people's needs and fill them, not only economically but also emotionally, mentally, and spiritually.

---

[1] Like the writings of the Old Testament, the Koran also believes in a God of wrath, or the law of karma, who punishes evildoers. The orthodox Jews and the Muslims believe that living according to the law is very important. Besides, they both are descendants of Abraham's two sons Isaac and Ishmael.
[2] At that plane, which is close to the earth, many spirit entities reside, whom believe in reincarnation.

Humans over-emphasize value of the outer and inner personalities while having little regard for their Soul, for which God cares the most, because it is eternal and of the same substance as that of God.

Some American pioneer proverbs:

People who are wrapped up in themselves make small packages.
Reputation is what you are in the light; character is what you are in the dark.
The great cosmetic for beauty is happiness.

III→IV. After level three is reached and the physical, emotional, and mental features are working together as one unit, or the coordination and integration of the personality are achieved, the person may get [1]trapped in the lifestyle as a respected citizen, professional, or a successful businessman or woman. At that time, the intellect is becoming well saturated with its knowledge or food. The outer world is losing its magic, and there is a [2]need to search for higher or spiritual things because intelligent pursuits alone are not sufficient to satisfy a spiritual hunger and to comprehend the human being as a whole. The person in that period of life also senses an uneasiness and emptiness that something is missing, not only deep within his/her being but also that there is something wrong with society. He or she may then say, "I will arise and go to my father" (Lk. 15:18) to seek for true love, peace, and security. They may also begin to wonder about the meaning and purpose of life and to ponder the nature of one's being. Their hunger and thirst for spiritual knowledge and the search for Truth is a response to the dawning of God's Presence and the awakening of their Higher Selves. Without quite realizing it, you begin to outgrow your old ideas, concepts, and [3]belief structures. Your dissatisfaction or discontent

---

[1] See **REMARK**.

[2] This need already began in adolescence when the body was in its height of growth and began its deteriorating process. This hunger for spiritual things is part and parcel of the universal law of evolution. The stage in which the individual becomes a seeker after Truth is represented by the color blue.

[3] If you want to change what is around you in your life, you have to change your beliefs. Edgar Cayce, who got his information from the "akashic records" (a library-like source of information) and evolved spirits, said that "mind is the builder – physical is the result". This means that we truly create our own reality and, therefore, also have the power to change it. Thus, thinking creates our life, and thoughts and beliefs have an impact on our experiences. To elaborate:

Thoughts and feelings which we believe are true become our beliefs and system of beliefs, which can be conscious or unconscious. It will attract the circumstances of our life, which may be positive or negative. By changing the latter, we will radiate energy and attract and accumulate positive thoughts and desires, thus creating more desirable experiences. Those outer experiences, in turn, mirror back what we truly believe.

causes you to start searching for the nuggets of Truth (Matt. 13:44-46), in different religions and other teachings, in response to this vague awakening. The dawning of the New Consciousness may inspire the personality to ask, "Who am I?; How do I develop spiritually?; Who and what is God? Is there a life after death?; What is my destiny and the goal of human history?"

NOTE: Those whom are searching for a higher purpose in life are called, in esoteric parlance, aspirants to Knowledge, or neophytes, and are treading the Path of probation. They have come to the understanding that there are other states of consciousness which are more authentic and genuine than the one they function in. They are trying to contact this divinity, or to "Know Thyself" or Higher Self, also called Divine Spirit.

NOTES: There is a saying which says, "What the mind can conceive the body can achieve." A clown may say, "I become a completely different personality when I have this costume on."

REMARK: When we are pleased, secure, and satisfied with our ego lifestyle and are known as a moral and upright person in our community, we feel no need to look for something higher and better, or to turn our power-driven ego over to a higher internal power. This is certainly not easy, as we are also much [1]identified with the group or collective, which does not allow an individual to seek the kingdom within (Luke 17:21). Even our own family may become the enemy (Matt. 10:35-36). Then, something happens for which we are not prepared, which shatters our self-image and our self-satisfied life of the personality, through sudden unemployment, accident, sickness, or somebody we love died or left us. We soon find ourselves in a situation which we can no longer handle, while asking ourselves, "Why did this happen to me?" What really happened is that change was forced on us by the law of evolution in order to break open those egos, which became so rigid and inflexible that they needed the sledgehammer of poverty, suffering, distress, and a broken heart. They could no longer be changed in a normal way by the nurturing love of the God forces (so as the warming sun opens up the buds of flowers). When we are no longer able to cope or handle the situation with our ego, the latter becomes disoriented and loses control. We then desperately cry out for help to the God forces and surrender our ego in submission to the spiritual or divine powers.

---

[1] The herd instinct in all humans whom are living the life of the personality makes conformity almost a natural tendency. However, we should get out of the herd before it goes over the cliff.

NOTE 1: We may also be challenged at certain points in our moral and spiritual development to speed up our growth because we might get too cozy and may get stagnated in our expansion. Then we have to be cast down into the land of despair, violent change, agony, and grief. This land can also be likened to a desert when a man or woman has to fall back on himself/herself and realizes how weak and limited he/she really is. He/she may then turn in his/her helplessness to God and surrender to Him in complete trust.

NOTE 2: Your personality or lower self must first be "nailed to the cross of despair and agony" and then be resurrected, or come under the guidance of the Higher Self.

NOTE 3: As an individual may, at times, be forced by the law of evolution to explore and grow to the next level, families, organizations, and whole nations may get an emergency wake-up call to refocus their lives on the attainment of spirituality. They may have missed or ignored former wake-up calls or are resisting the process of change and, thus, delay the much needed breakthrough when the spiritual Light can enter individuals, families, groups, and nations.

Other ways we can prepare ourselves for divine life are to free our physical bodies from toxins and to raise their vibration by eating less animal food, so that they become more refined. We can cleanse our etheric body of impure energies by taking a shower or swimming in the ocean and purify our emotional and mental selves of negative feelings, such as hostility, resentment, fear, etc., and impure thoughts such as prejudices, deception, condemnation, etc. The will should also be purged, or cleansed, of personal urges, indulgences, and lower desires. When we cleanse our emotional self from its gross elements, it is more able to deal with universal desires and gives passage to the flow of spiritual love or compassion. We may also exercise our minds to more spiritual thinking, such as in higher [1]philosophy. The inspired artist and the philosopher are those whom are in close contact with the realm of the divine because they are much involved in the contemplation of ideas and the beautiful. Many of them also have a holistic mind which understands poetry. They may invoke in the observer and the reader the same emotion and ideas as those of the artist and philosopher. For

---

[1] By philosophy, it is not meant here "according to human tradition", which Paul forbids but "according to Christ" (Col. 2:8), or those philosophies which do not ignore God's revelation so that there is room for expanding from intellectual knowledge to spiritual understanding. The dawning of Truth may begin slowly as the comprehension of the knowledge of the existence of God and one's relationship to the Creator.

the same reason, a play is performed and a movie is made to make the public response [2]emotional and intellectual in a certain way, thus strengthening their inner conviction that it is worthwhile to be virtuous and honorable in their own lives. An architectural structure, when it is in harmony with the universe, creates harmony in ourselves and links us to the divine. By using the art of analogy, we may connect our physical self to the psychic and the latter to the divine, and by using other literary devices, such as parables and symbols and the like.

NOTE 1: A work of art consists of two elements, the inner and the outer. The outer is the artist and his/her work, while the inner (emotion and mental) is aroused and stirred by what is sensed. Thus, the sense is the link from the outer or material to the inner, which is the soul of the observer.

NOTE 2: As soon as he/she started to imitate painting, he/she lost their individuality.

NOTE 3: Language has power. It transmits not only facts and ideas but also emotions and values. Skillful writers and speakers have used their power to affect people's attitudes, influence their actions, and shape their inner views of the world and its people.

NOTE 4: Through mythology and symbolism, contact can be made between the physical and psychic levels.

Those people whom are in the third stage or are living the life of the personality do contain deep within themselves a divine Spark, the beginning of divine life. Heraclitus (d. +/-475 B.C.), Greek philosopher, said that the basic reality of the world is fire, and as the sparks are part of a fire, so are human beings sparks or parts of a divine fire. Because everything contains a Spark or Soul of God, that is why there is already order and unity in the divine world of God (humans only have to connect their personalities with the Spark of God). By kindling the spark into a flame and the flame into a fire, the whole

---

[2] The public also responds emotionally in a positive way when high vibration music is played in the movies. Unfortunately, we see an erosion of values in the entertainment industry today. Much of the music played today is not only discordant, loud, and offensive, which creates disorder, disharmony, confusion, and anxiety in our psyche, but it also impairs our values and creative thinking and may even evoke elements of the dark side of our psyche or human spirit. In other forms of entertainment, such as movies, television, soap operas, and situation comedies, much of the negative side of human nature is emphasized, such as hostility, cynicism, deception, irresponsibility, shallowness, pettiness, immorality, and deviousness, instead of mature behavior, accountability, honesty, trust, integrity, virtue, and true love, which are the components of a true hero.

world will become, as Heraclitus expressed it, "an ever-living fire", and the imprisoned Soul is at last set free. All things are governed by the [1]Logos, which is the cosmic reason or universal law, which is immanent or permeates in all things throughout the universe, giving order and purpose to the world. Because humans participate as the fiery substance or spark in the divine fire and also by being a [2]law or reason in itself, they share in the universal law or reason. By stressing the above, Heraclitus helped to pave the way for the universalist ideas of the [3]Stoics, whom believed that people are equally citizens of the world. The main idea of Stoicism was the notion that the Creator is in everything. When one lives according to one's own reason, he or she is in touch with the universal reason, which can be found everywhere. As humans contain a spark of the divine within themselves, they actually contain part of the substance of God. Thus, as the Supreme Being is the Soul of the world, the Souls of the people are part of God. By recognizing that all humans possess creative sparks, the Stoics use this understanding in their civil and political ideals so that it will reflect the moral order of the universe. The same ideas were much later elaborated by meister Eckehart, a German Dominican mystic (who died in 1327), who said that there resides in every human being a divine Spark of the God-head, making union with God possible and to have a genuine knowledge of His nature. Thus, the soul (human spirit) contained a Spark or "ground" of God, which was uncreated.

REMARK: As human can look for hours in the fiery flames, so their Divine Spirits also like to look for hours in the "ever-living fire".
As the heat of the fire gives us comfort, so the love of God gives us comfort.
As humans can ignite a fire in order to see, so can God give illumination so that a person can see divinely.
As the fire in the physical world is always burning (also fires without any flames), so is also the fire in the divine worlds.

If Adam, as a natural man, would have taken the fruit of the "Tree of Life", he would have received Divine Knowledge and become the Tree of Life as a new being or Divine Spirit. However, Adam and Eve took the (symbolic) fruit (see #7) from "the tree of the knowledge of good

---

[1] Logos, in theology, is the creative Word of God and is the second person of the trinity.

[2] This law is based on human's innate moral sense, a rule of conduct inherent in human nature, also called natural law in Western thought.

[3] Stoic – a member of a Greek school of philosophy founded by Zeno about 108 B.C. Stoicism, the doctrine of the Stoics, which develops its greatest influence in the Roman Empire and became, at one time, a dominant intellectual influence, and was embraced by the Roman Emperor Marcus Aurelius (121-180).

and evil" and acquired good and evil knowledge, which is closely related to the earth. They became like the tree, that is, their personality became good and evil. The [1]evil aspect within the personality or heart (Matt. 15:19; 5:28) is called, in Apostle Paul's writings, old nature or old man (Rom. 6:6; Eph. 4:22; Col. 3:9), while the good nature is that of the image of God within the individual. In compensation, Paul wrote, "For as in Adam all die (spiritually), so also in Christ shall all be made alive" (1 Cor. 15:22), by experiencing a rebirth, acquiring a new nature, and becoming a son or daughter of God. Thus, after being baptized with "the baptism of repentance" (Acts 9:4), purifying the personality from its sinful or old nature by drowning or dissolution, the person may then be ready to be [2]baptized with the Holy Spirit (Mk. 1:8). He or she, as resurrected beings, are then no longer enslaved by sin or do the things they hate (Rom. 7:15-24).

NOTE 1: There is the natural (unspiritual) man by birth, those whom are not regenerated (1 Cor. 2:14). His wisdom is earthly (natural), and his life is beset with much suffering and frustrations. There is the carnal man, who is spiritually born but never grows up, or is in the process of backsliding (1 Cor. 3:1-4). There is the Spiritual man, who has a personal relationship with God and is being governed by God through the Word (1 Cor. 2:15).

NOTE 2: Some time ago, the author had a dream where he saw blisters on his skin. This probably signified that impure psychic elements have come to the surface so that they can be treated – by acknowledgement, confession, and repentance. As long as it is hidden, its subconscious evil content will be influencing the life of the author. The same is true of other individuals, groups of people, church organizations, and nations. The evil will only grow within them until it is exposed.

---

[1] The evil aspect or nature which humans inherited is that of the image of the fallen archangel Lucifer, who became satan (Isa. 14:12-15; Rev. 20:2), also known as the serpent (Gen. 3:1-5), who later tempted Jesus (Mk. 1:13) and was able to possess a disciple of Jesus Christ (Lk. 22:3), and will be crushed by the God of peace (Rom. 16:20).

[2] To be baptized with the Holy Spirit and fire (Matt. 3:11), burning away materialistic concepts and lower desires after being baptized with water by the last prophet of the Old Testament John the Baptist. The final rinsing of sinful concepts occurs after living according to the purifying Word of God.

As the lower self or ego completes its task of meeting various needs and functioning in the world, *a very subtle event may occur, sometimes all at once or gradually. The personality or lower self becomes passive and the growing essence or Higher Self becomes active. This reversal has been observed by many people and has numerous names, such as conversion, regeneration, salvation, to be born again, sanctification, to receive or know Christ, and to attain moksha (liberation) or satori (enlightenment). Thus, the personality has become a vehicle or faithful servant to the Higher Self. Jesus said, "You must be born anew" (Jn. 3:7), and "he who loses his life for my sake will find it" (Matt. 10:39), thus gaining God-consciousness and losing self-consciousness. Thereafter, daily prayer and meditation will harmonize our deeper Self with our personality, changing from external assistance to internal guidance and from living in the fear of the Lord to the love of the Father. The converted person has a feeling of greater personal value, and with Christ at the center, life is no longer dull and dreary; a sense of newness has come in one's life (Rom. 6:4; Rev. 21:5). As your Divine Self begins to unfold, the divine or spiritual flower begins to open to a conscious awareness of spiritual considerations. After all, spiritual evolution is a process of becoming externally aware to that which you already intuitively know, at the core of your being.

NOTE 1: We should be obedient to the Lord – not towards people. Very often, individuals have assumed that they should obey and submit to anybody. They have been obedient towards tyrants, the wealthy, and the powerful. However, we should be faithful, devout, submissive, and obedient only towards the Divine Principles.

NOTE 2: Suffering gives more depth in people. Suffering is not as much suffering when one has a close relationship with God. It has become a real problem for many Western materialistic people because they are hardly in touch with reality. They see others and things as existing separate from themselves.

NOTE 3: We may distinguish three kinds of life – life without law, life with law, and Spirit-filled life.

---

* Because humans have acquired or inherited an evil nature (original sin), the process of conversion is not always as easy as described above, although in most cases it is less of a struggle, as depicted in the "**REMARK**" of one of the former pages. In this case, a struggle may ensue between long established material interest and a new growing sense of spirituality. But eventually, the sense of identity begins to move to the higher consciousness that has been evolving on its own plane.

Some remarks:

> ➤ Many of us go to church but do not really know Christ. You may be a Sunday school teacher or a fine upstanding moral person, but you need Christ. We have been living moral lives but never knew what is meant to receive Christ. He is the Light. We are but flash light in his hands (Billy Graham).
> ➤ There is an essential emptiness in every life without Christ.
> ➤ Inner peace is the connection to your spiritual self. You achieve it through physical relaxation in the body, emotional calm, and mental focus on higher ideals and qualities.
> ➤ When you become a saint, you stand against immorality; when you become a man of ethics, you are against criminals (Pioneer proverbs).
> ➤ What unites us is stronger than what divides us (unknown).
> ➤ You must believe in order to understand (Augustine).
> ➤ Some people whom are not born again do not believe in direct guidance from God but believe in guidance from human spirits and angels.
> ➤ In spite of everything, I still believe that people are good at heart (Anne Frank – 2nd World War – Holland).
> ➤ He (minister) always brings the best out of me.
> ➤ The crisis brought the best and the worst out of people.
> ➤ Libraries are nourishment for the psyche (human spirit) and the Soul.
> ➤ We should liberate God within ourselves and others.
> ➤ The core of goodness, which you feel within your being, is Me.

IV. The fourth stage of life is the genesis of the conscious participation of individuals in the process of spiritual evolution. It is also the beginning of the members of the fourth, or divine kingdom, to see others no longer as separate entities as in the third kingdom when ego boundaries prevailed. The barriers and alienation among persons is being eliminated and replaced by an inclusive "I Thou" relationship. Psychic love is being transcended into divine love, which is more than personal love, and to love the world or cosmos is also to love your whole being, which is a microcosm.

[1]As the principle of growth for the vegetable, animal, and ungenerated humans is strife, competition, rivalry, and self-seeking, the principle of growth for the regenerated or spiritually born individuals is cooperation, renunciation, and self-sacrifice. Without the guidance of the Soul, the personality of the unregenerated cannot truly love; it can only seek to possess, to control, or to use others for their own needs,

---

[1] The members of the fourth kingdom are more alive than those of the third or human kingdom, who in turn are more awake than the animal kingdom, which is more awake than the plant and mineral kingdoms. The latter three kingdoms will evolve more when humans evolve and take their rightful positions as Lords over all creation.

especially when the evil aspect is in charge of the personality or ego. It is, therefore, basically selfish or egocentric.

In past ages, up to the time of Jesus Christ, most human beings had hardly any consideration for the suffering of other beings. However, this began to change with the example and mission of Christ Jesus, His teachings, and stories, such as the [2]Good Samaritan (Luke 10:33). Many individuals became more polite, considerate, and [3]compassionate, suffered with the other, or felt deep empathy towards humans of all walks of life.

Jesus was born in Bethlehem (house of bread – Jn. 6:48), which was located in the heart region of Israel. His life is described between his birth and ministry in Luke 2:52, as "Jesus increased in wisdom and in stature (level of attainment), and in favor with God and man". In other words, [4]he grew physically, mentally, and spiritually. After Jesus, who came as the last Adam (1 Cor. 15:45), overcame [5]the temptation, which the first Adam could not overcome, He received the special Spirit of God or the Cosmic Christ, which was first in Adam (see Ch. 1 of Revelation) and began His ministry when He was about thirty years old (Luke 3:23). Christ Jesus was the first one who brought to the general public the experience of complete rebirth.

---

[2] Samaritans were despised by the Jews because they are those Israelites whom were not deported by the Assyrians (2 Kings Ch. 17) and mingled with them. As reported in Ezra Ch. 4, they were not allowed to assist the Israelites to build the temple. In the Gospel, Jesus is demonstrating that we must love those whom we previously hated. See also Jn. 4:7-26, 39-42; Lk. 17:11-19).

[3] By having sympathy and compassion for the other, you also take on his or her psychological and spiritual burden. This is why some people want to share their problems, especially with those whom are strong in the Lord and do not get easily drained (such as people whom are in the fifth or higher stages of development). An individual or group of people that prays for another may also take his or her distress, guilt, and perdition. They are doing vicariously for them what the other cannot do for themselves. Besides, when praying for someone, God is better able to give to the other of Himself through the persons praying, that is, His love, wisdom, forgiveness, and guidance. It also purifies and heals the individuals whom are praying, thus magnifying the noble and divine potential in them.

[4] The apostles of Jesus expressed the need for Christians to grow and mature in the likeness of Jesus Christ; that "Christ be formed in you" (Gal. 4:19), "to be conformed to the image of his Son" (Rom. 8:29), that we are to grow "to mature manhood" (Eph. 4:13-16). "You shall be holy for I am holy" (1 Pet. 1:15-16) and to grow from being "little children" to becoming "young men" and "fathers" (1 John 2:12-14). This growth is comparable to the buds, flowers, and fruit of the almond.

[5] In His temptations (Matthew Ch. 4), Jesus mastered his physical appetites and passions and did not succumb to personal acquisitiveness and vanity.

NOTE: Divine birth is the level of the heart. The open heart and its surrounding Light are often portrayed in pictures of Jesus Christ. The hearts of some saints are also being described as being aglow. They have a heart sense of compassion for others, a spiritual love which is compassion of a sense of oneness with all people.

Nicodemus in the Gospel of John chapter three did not understand what Christ Jesus meant when He said, "Truly, truly, I say to you, unless one is born anew (or from above), he cannot see the kingdom of God". Likewise, many [1]people today do not seem to understand how important it is to be spiritually born and grow to maturity in their newly-acquired Divine Spirit and start living in the kingdom. Otherwise, they get stagnated, or stuck, in the limited life of the personality.

When the [2]pure Word of God, spoken through Christ, is received as the [3]seed of God into our human spirits or hearts, a divine Embryo (the new creation) is formed within us (Gal. 4:19), or Christ is formed in the believer as a baby is formed in the womb, and the (re)birth process or initiation begins. This is for the believer a born again experience, which should give him/her a genuine [4]assurance of salvation. However, in order that the baby may grow, it needs the Word of God, which is the food for the divine body as physical food is for the material body and

---

[1] Most people today are so immersed in the material and worldly way of thinking and living that they have not evolved to the point of accepting the supremacy of the spiritual life. As the world is aware of the outer teaching of Christianity, it is only vaguely becoming aware of its inner teaching and is only beginning to understand its significance and importance. Many of them are going to church and calling themselves Christians. However, only those in whom Christ has been formed and lives within their hearts are true Christians, not necessarily all those whom have been baptized and confirmed. The Disciples of Christ were called Christians for the first time in Antioch (Acts 11:26). The Gnostics divided humanity into categories – the spiritually advanced, those whom were aware of the Soul's true home, and less aware psychics, who were at the mercy of their emotions and desires.

[2] The teachings of Jesus are the most pure, especially when the Cosmic Christ speaks through Jesus, more particularly in the Gospel of John and more specifically in the "I AM" sayings.

[3] As the seed first incubates and then appears above the soil, so the spiritual or divine body incubates first and is then born.

[4] When we open our hearts to Christ and receive His Word, which becomes the Christ Spirit or Soul, this is for real, not imagination, emotional experiences, or other subconscious upheaval. We may then get to know Him personally by everyday experiences so that we completely accept Him as our Parent, trust Him, and get to know that He really loves me and will never forsake me. A simple formula of Christian salvation is: (1) God loves you, (2) man (woman) is a sinner, and sin has separated him/her from God, (3) Jesus Christ is the only remedy for sin, and (4) you must receive Jesus Christ as your personal savior.

intellectual food for the growth of the human spirit or inner personality. This spiritual food is usually fed in the beginning by [5]spiritual parents, whom also protect the spiritual child against evil forces without and within the babies. This Word of God should be pure and be delivered in a great variety of ways, expressing its many facets. It should not be adulterated or diluted with cultural expressions, which are related to one's personality. It should be taught in (mother) churches, which are supposed to be birth and feeding places of the divine, as a mother delivers and gives milk to the infants. That is the milk of the Word (the first principles) or the fundamental or simple Truth of God's Word (1 Pet. 2:2; 1 Cor. 3:2; Heb. 5:12). When they have grown somewhat, solid food may be given to them (Heb. 5:14).

Pilate said to Jesus, "What is truth?" (Jn. 18:38), and he received no answer because it can only come from within. Besides, Truth was standing right in front of him (Jn. 14:6). Pilate may have been thinking about philosophical truth instead of spiritual Truth. We may comment here that whatever feeds the Divine Spirit or Soul is Spiritual Truth. God's Word is Truth (Jn. 17:17), while the "Spirit of Truth" is on its way (Jn. 16:13), who "will guide you into all the Truth", "and the Truth will make you free" (Jn. 8:32), connecting you with Truth or Christ within. Our Divine Spirits or Souls are, thus, Truth bodies, and we are the colorful children of God who is Light (1 Jn. 1:5), who created in the beginning, through His Word (thought-vibration), the world in a "Bing, Bang, Bong" like fashion. Truth is no theory or speculative system of philosophy but is in exact agreement with reality. We may further distinguish Truth in physical, psychic, and spiritual forms. Truth is, thus, everywhere if we are capable of perceiving it. It is said that Truth is stranger than fiction.

The Word of God is "sharper than any two-edged sword", making a division of what is true and false (Heb. 4:12; Matt. 10:34; Rev. 1:16; Lk. 2:35), as a shepherd separates the sheep from the goats (Matt. 25:32). The magic sword of the Spirit, the power of Truth, is a weapon God has provided (Eph. 6:17), which Jesus used to defeat satan (Matt. 4:10) and which we can use in our battle with evil spirits. As the first horseman of Revelation chapter six comes with a bow, the returning Christ of Revelation nineteen comes to judge the nations with a sharp sword, which issues out of His mouth.

---

[5] See "The Birth and Evolution of the Divine Spirit or Soul" – the section on how spiritual parents are guiding and raising spiritual children and protecting them against evil forces within humans they encounter and invisible evil entities, which can be human or angelic.

A mistake is made when an individual assumes that truth can simply be added to the sum total of himself. The very foundation of the individual in the satanic world is the blend of good and evil. One is simply adding purity to impurity, and the result is impurity. Jesus expounded this when he said one does not put new wine into old wineskins. They cannot contain it (Lk. 5:37). In order for you to become new, you must reverse the processes that brought you to this point. As the fall began with man's spiritual death, so life must begin with death. You must die to your old self and be created anew. You must reject the old self, its aged beliefs, errors, habits, and knowledge and begin again at the beginning. This time, exercise your divine right of choice to determine what you will allow to enter and become part of your new, pure self. Every thought, every desire, and every feeling must be examined in the light of truth and conscious decision made as to its inclusion in the new individual nature. Can you thus die? Are you willing to give up all that you have previously held dear, your ideas, your convictions, your methods, your judgments? Are you willing to label them questionable, examining each one, and allowing it house room only if it passes rigorous inspection by God Himself? This is rebirth. This is restoration. This is purity and purpose and, ultimately, perfection. (*received by evolved spirits – New Age Frontier, Sept. 1965*)

As the food we eat takes time to be absorbed into the physical body, so it takes time for our knowledge and experience to be assimilated in the human spirit and Divine Spirit. Only the essence is being incorporated in the different bodies; the rest is eliminated. The human spirit absorbs the qualities of the personality and its expression, such as courage, endurance, reference, generosity, justice, confidence, poise, compassion, patience, tolerance, concern, commitment, integrity, reliability, altruism, etc., while the Divine Spirit or Over-soul, in turn, absorbs the essence of the qualities of the psyche. As the human spirit has the potency of absorbing the good and evil elements, the Divine Spirit can only assimilate into its being pure elements. The abstracted essence of the experiences gained and the qualities acquired is being worked into the texture of the spirits, and it is by this that the latter grows and, thus, acquires wisdom and understanding. Life on earth; its experience and suffering is much more valuable than to know by objective lesson or speech, which not always "sinks in" as the food we only see and smell. To learn of a truth is one thing, to become it is quite another. It is therefore said that words need to be read many times and be made your own to "eat them up". Better still is to believe in something that eventually becomes a reality of truth in one's being, which results in knowingness, comprehension, and discernment. To really know is to fully experience, as one may know a woman or man, to know Christ, or to eat from the Tree of the Knowledge of Good and Evil, knowing both. The most valuable period of assimilation or digesting life experiences and infusing, or building it, into the inner selves is when people are in their old age or in the period after death. The inner selves are made up of all your ideas and beliefs and all the things that have been accepted by you. In other words, your selves are created and composed of what you feel and think, and that is your character. Finally, every idea, thought, desire, and act is retained and registered by the "tape recorder" properties of the spirit bodies in the "book of life" (Rev. 3:5) by none other than yourself. As Jesus Christ profoundly expressed in Matt. 6:19-20, "Do not lay up for yourselves treasures on earth" --- "but lay up for yourselves treasures in heaven."

NOTE: To know something with one's mind is not the same as knowing in one's heart. The first is simple cognizance, while the latter becomes part of one's being.

Those whom have experienced a new birth may also easily *backslide, as this very often happened in the time of Paul (1 Cor. 3:1-4), and is also common among the born again Christians today. This is certainly true of persons who have fallen on hard times, including those whom, for economical reasons, have had to conform to society or the world (Jn. 8:23), wherein moral and spiritual values are almost totally disregarded. The result is that their personalities get more and more disconnected from their Souls, through which God could reach and guide them. They then need to be addressed again by Paul and his disciples (1 Cor. 3:1; Heb. 5:12), or by inspired spiritual leaders, evangelists, and ministers today.

Baby souls are often emotional, overzealous, or fanatical in their beliefs, which is usually fundamental or elementary (Heb. 6:1). When they are confronted with another view or doctrine, they are quick to

---

* They may backslide slowly by gradually changing their feelings, thinking, and actions, but may backslide more quickly by having love affairs. A moral and (or) spiritual backsliding may occur readily when, for example, a son or daughter goes out and falls in love (unites emotionally) with someone of a lower character who has little religious or moral sense. He or she may then quickly backslide or fall from the third or fourth to the second level, where their consciousness, most of the time, will reside. When someone regresses to a lower state of consciousness, someone who knew them before may call, with God, for them psychically and spiritually, "Where are you?" (1 Gen. 3:9). Because the backslider has become more selfish, his/her spirit stays closer to the body and is not as much roaming around anymore.

defend their own as the only true one and do not want to listen to what other Christ followers have to say. We may find them in earlier times in crusades and inquisition, and many found themselves to be well qualified to become hunters of heresy and heretics. Today, some of them are involved in defending the purity of doctrines. Because the lives of baby souls are still much involved in the life of the personality or of the flesh, as Paul would say (their consciousness has not as yet wholly transferred to the life of their growing Divine Spirit), they are often inclined to serve their own needs more than the needs of the whole. Today, many of them are doing good work in religious campaigns, crusades, taking care of the poor and downtrodden, and missionary works. Although some of them whom are sent out too early as missionaries may wear thick "cultural glasses", they are easy to judge the "heathen" with their own unique culture and, thus, have a tendency to make more enemies than friends. Therefore, they do not do much for the cause of the Universal Christ. At home, baby souls tend to be community leaders and want others to follow all their particular rules of moral conduct and oppose anything that threatens the existing religious structure, even change to a higher stage of development.

NOTE 1: The personalities of some persons whom experience a new birth are not always able to handle the infusion of new psychic and spiritual energies and may experience some difficulties in the beginning.

NOTE 2: When thoughts come to mind to dismember or maim yourself physically, you will certainly not do it. But when evil thoughts arise to corrupt yourself morally and spiritually, you are more inclined to do it because you are not able "to see", with the psychic and divine eye, how much damage you are really inflicting to your human and Divine Spirit. At that point, you may ask God to see yourself as you are. If your inner self is ugly and deformed, that is how spirits (diseased human beings) see you, or sensitive people of the earth.

The birth of the Christian religion, in its different levels of expressions, gave special stimulus to individual achievement and creativity in all human endeavors. It broke down the barriers of race and caste, and that all are brothers and sisters under the parenthood of God. The old ideas of slave and master, Jew and gentile, priest and people, brahmin and pariah, were surpassed by the ideals of equality, independence, and individual freedom. The teaching of the Nazarene silently but surely imbued in the people primarily of the Western world, a spirit of altruism, inspiring them to carry each other's burden and to do to others what they have others do to them (Matt. 7:12; Luke 6:31).

Martin Luther, the sixteenth century religious Reformer, said that anyone guided by the Spirit of God is able to interpret the Bible correctly. Those who are born of God, through rebirth or initiation, become true children of God and are able to communicate with God directly. They continually seek for the love of God as Parents, whose Love is being expressed through the Cosmic Christ and the Holy Spirit. God as heavenly Parents wanted to have, from the beginning, a spiritual family of their own, sons and daughters, whom they could love and who would love Them freely in return. When Christ is formed in the newly born (Gal. 4:19) and live within them (Gal. 2:20), they are no longer children of nature (Eph. 2:3) but partakers of the divine nature (2 Pet. 1:4) and have inherited God's nature or character. As the children are being fed with the pure Word of God, their divine nature becomes pure without blemish, innocent, blameless, and not able to sin because God's nature abides in them (1 Jn. 3:3, 9; Phil. 2:15). As spiritual persons, they are outstanding and have become the Light of the world (Matt. 5:14), radiating the universal love of God to everyone, whom they easily forgive. After accepting the Christ of all religions, they receive the Holy Spirit, become individuals in their own right, independent, with freedom to express themselves without being under the control or power of another agency. In this environment of civil and political liberty, God within them is then able to reveal and manifest Themselves freely. They have become sons and daughters of God through faith (Gal. 3:26) and are no longer under law but under love and grace (Rom. 6:14; 13:10). The true sons and daughters are no more members of the herd or crowd by *conforming to society but become real gentlemen or Lords and respectful ladies. Thus, those born of God are no longer human beings but divine beings, which will inherit the Kingdom of God and participate in its divine government, with Christ as the King of Kings. The old or human kingdoms will then break down in pieces (Dan. 2:44-45), by a stone of Truth, which was part of the mountain of God.

NOTE: In esoteric parlance, those whom have taken the first initiation are said to "enter the stream". That is the time when Christ is born within them (not only in Bethlehem) and they become fully awake. The Christian calls them individuals whom are "saved" and safe, and they begin to lead a new life as

---

* People of the world may say of those whom are spiritually born and do not conform to society that they are social misfits because they do not express themselves as they are supposed to (he or she is not one of us). The self-righteous ones may look surprised and angry if the social outcasts do not act in the way that is to be expected. A worldly-minded woman may say to a man who acts in a noble way and does not want to have sex with her: "If you care about me, you should not be such a damn gentleman." This is also applicable when a man wants to have sex with a noble lady.

little children, the life of Christ or Spirit-filled life. Disciples are those whom have offered themselves to the Master as pupils, which latter is replaced by one's evolving Higher Self, with which the disciples are in daily contact through meditation, thus opening up the channels between the lower and Higher Selves and become in harmony with the latter. The disciples move from darkness into Light or to awareness of the spiritual Self or Christ Spirit, through which they come to the Father (John 14:6).

God's original intention was for all their children to grow to spiritual maturity, from A to D., going straight and upward from Egypt to the land of Canaan as the Israelites were supposed to travel. However, our ancestors deviated from the Path, as indicated by the line A-B, and so did the Israelites in their exodus (Ex. 13:17). All the descendants of our ancestors were arrested at point B, or Mount Sinai, where the Israelites received the Ten Commandments. In our personal life, we may encounter Christ at that point and start living a divine life. Finally, after a great detour, in the process of restoration, we, like the sons of Jacob (Israel), will reach Canaan, the Kingdom of God.

IV→V. As an individual begins to mature spiritually, he or she may become more and more aware that not only their own Soul growth is important but also that of others. They not only witness to them in their excitement of having found a new view and way of life, and/or to let others know that they have come into possession of a higher truth.

They also want to [1]assist others in the development of their Soul by giving them spiritual guidance and assistance so that they can also enhance their Soul growth. By witnessing, you feel not only a flow of Divine Energy through you but also new ideas and a better understanding of His Word have come to you.

V. Those whom have entered the fifth stage may be called true or more solid Christians, who concern themselves with the spiritual creation of the Word. "Therefore let us leave the elementary doctrine of Christ and go on to maturity" (Heb. 6:1). Many of them are directly guided by the Universal Christ and the Holy Spirit. Unlike the baby Christians of the fourth stage, they do not only believe but also understand what they believe. Believing in heaven is good, but knowing about heaven is the conviction of the spiritual youth (1 Jn. 2:13), who [2]no longer fear death. The spiritual children have a tendency of clinging to what they believe instead of reexamining and reevaluating their convictions as the spiritual youth, and growing thereby. The spiritual babies often believe that God does everything for them. The view of the grown-ups is that humans have to do their part and cooperate, or become co-creators with the divine plan. In order to be effective in God's work, the spiritual people should be competent, talented, and dedicated. As the very young have an inclination to withdraw from daily life, the spiritually strong do not escape to heaven but stay in the world, but do not become part of the world (Jn. 16:33; 18:36; Rom. 12:2; 1 Jn. 2:15). It is not through angelic interferences that "Thy kingdom come" (Matt. 6:10) but through our noble thoughts, creativity, and loving deeds that God intends to intervene on earth and, thus, bring heaven to earth.

NOTE 1: In spite of selfishness, misery, poverty, and inhumanity, which we can find in all parts of the world, we can also find examples of human kindness, nobility, and charity, and other qualities, as it is inspired by the divine and expressed through the outer personality.

---

[1] When you study intellectual or spiritual knowledge, you enrich yourselves, but when you give to others of what you have learned, from books, etc. and in life, you will rapidly change and progress. Just as a body of water will stagnate without any flow, your body, psyche, and Divine Spirit will likewise stagnate or become constipated. A market does not work if people do not buy and sell, and money has no value if it is not spent. Some people only accumulate money and goods and are known to be "stinking rich".

[2] Death is already overcome by those whom are spiritually developed. They sense their existence in the higher planes (especially in their sleep) and have become so at home in the vibrations of the spiritual that death holds no fear over them (1 Cor. 15:55).

NOTE 2: The fifth stage person is more concerned about the larger purpose of world restoration than the little details of their lives that used to consume so much effort and energy when in lower stages.

As spiritual infants or babies are still of the flesh (1 Cor. 3:1) or much connected with the life and needs of the personality, the spiritual youth are abundantly living the spiritual or divine life (Rom. 8:9), fulfilling the basic needs of the Spirit. The immature, who are overly nice and naïve, are also vulnerable to destructive forces and easily backslide. The more mature "are strong and the Word of God abides in you, and you have overcome the evil one" (1 Jn. 2:14). They "have their faculties (such as [1]intuition) trained by practice to distinguish good from evil" (Heb. 5:14) and are, thus, able to judge.

As spiritual teenagers [2]become aware of evil forces all around them, which may be angelic, or evil people with or without bodies (who make up "the world (who) hates you" – Jn. 7:7 – and dislikes you for no apparent reason – Gal. 4:29 –), they also become surely conscious of the evil lurking within themselves (Mk. 7:21-23). Much of this inherited evil (original sin) and accumulated sins (ancestral and personal) have been removed in the process of purifying the personality (and in the fourth stage – by outside agency –). However, the remaining still needs to be rooted out, as it is deeply embedded in the human psyche or inner personality. In order to get rid of this moral blemish, one should first acknowledge it as unnatural, find out what it is by knowing [3]how it originated, and then demolish it with the help of the [4]God forces, including our growing Divine Spirit(s). The latter finds itself confronted with the lingering evil or old self (Rom. 6:6), who does not want to relinquish its hold on the personality, and so the

---

[1] Another function of (higher) intuition is that of direct knowing, without the process of thinking. Thus, the mind of individuals of the fifth stage has progressed from intellectual knowledge to intuitive understanding, which is more fully developed in the sixth stage. This mind is known to be harmonious, enlightened, and illuminated and is unlimited by time, space, or knowledge. This mind, or divine intelligence, is interdependent and cannot be separate, and is a vehicle of divine love and intuitive wisdom.

[2] They see a big contrast between the expressions of the good and evil forces all around them and are stirred into action to expose, fight, and destroy the evil in the world and in their own being. (See "The Birth and Evolution of the Soul".)

[3] For a complete explanation – see the first chapter of this book "Deviation and Restoration of the Human Race".

[4] Those God forces may be the good angels, developed spirits, or spiritual ministers and counselors. God may also help to dissolve this sin by letting us overcome the many unique tests He put before us.

[5]last battle for control of human life really begins, and is fought out, within the human spirit or psyche (Gal. 5:17). Because of this fight, spiritual growth is often [6]delayed in this fifth stage, especially in the overcoming of lower desires and spiritual pride. However, when those obstructions have been removed, the channel between the higher Self and the lower self becomes clearer, and the person displays a great desire to serve others, which results in rapid progress through the remaining stages. Thus, in the last three stages, the physical body is consecrated, the emotional self has become pure, and the mental is being controlled. The disciple also learns how to build, manage, and direct thought and thought forms, while his or her personal aspiration is submerged to the needs of the whole.

Individuals whom are in the fifth level of development or second stage of Self-realization are called Disciples of Christ. The second great initiation, according to some esoteric teaching, is being compared to the [1]baptism of the Holy Spirit. Thus, the disciples are not only guided by the universal Christ, the male aspect of God, but also by the female aspect. The personality of the disciple, or the consciousness of the personal self, is united with the transpersonal Self, and the personal will with the transpersonal will. They know the ways of God, radiate His Light, and exhibit a strong desire to do good and to do God's Will. Being God-centered or God-conscious, they experience the oneness of all life and "see" God everywhere as He guides, [2]speaks, and acts through people and nature. In everyday life, the disciples act with courage, conviction, responsibility, and purpose in an well-integrated personality. They also display the transpersonal qualities, such as:

---

[5] The fight between good and evil really begins in oneself – to root out remaining evil in one's personality.

[6] Backsliding also occurs at this stage of growth, when people fall from their high state or are down and out. However, having experienced the divine in its many expressions, they are soon back in their relation with their heavenly Parents, but those whom have committed apostasy (Heb. 6:4-6) and who have spoken against the Holy Spirit will not be easily forgiven (Matt. 12:31-32).

[1] Many people in Christianity receive the Holy Spirit when they enter the fourth stage or are in the fourth stage.

[2] God can best express Himself in all His facets through human beings, as He has done and is still doing through the many saints and non-saints of all religions, especially through Jesus Christ. For example, humans, through their intellect, emotion, and will, are able to express God's intelligence, creativity, love, compassion, kindness, goodwill, benevolence, etc.
Some esoterists say:
God is substance, we are form and shape; God is life, we are the living.
God is power, we are powerful; God is mind, we are thinkers.
God is truth, we are truthful; God is wisdom, we are wise.

love, truthfulness, will, intelligence, wisdom, creativity, compassion, generosity, peace, harmony, patience, understanding, gracefulness, purity, serenity, humility, forgiveness, joy, poise, tolerance, justice, encouragement, reference, dignity, constructive ambition, spiritual charisma, personal charm, abundance, unselfishness, honesty, cheerfulness, concernment, sacrifice, dedication, sincerity, discernment, charity, and unity. As the disciples evolve, their sympathy and compassion increase so that they become more and more sensitive to the sin and sorrow and suffering of the world.

The presence of God within the true sons and daughters of God, whom are guided by their Divine Spirits, is clearly seen by sensitive people around them. When the latter are spiritually evolved, they not only recognize the divine in the other, but his/her divine Self leaps up as it were of joy, of meeting the other Divine Being.

The grown-ups have deep insight into people and understand society as it is. They would rather be poor than compete in the corporate world. They like to be self-employed, which gives them more freedom to pursue "more important" things. They do not mind hard work as long as it gives them inner satisfaction, new insights, and use much of the earned money to fulfill a greater purpose. Many of them have no religious affiliation and avoid higher education, and learn more from inquiry and experience on the job. When they travel, the disciples are not seeking to have fun but are searching for the truth, always hoping to find something valuable. When watching sports, they think more about the underlying principle than just getting excited. Medicine tends to be alternative, and the food they eat is of vegetable origin. The disciples may appear odd and unconventional because they are taught from the inner source instead of receiving knowledge from outside themselves. Some sensitive individuals immediately recognize them as teachers and spiritual leaders. When the liberated individuals or spiritual persons are getting old, they like to pass on their knowledge to as many people as possible so that posterity will have a head start in their spiritual evolution.

NOTE: The mature stage is a time of creative flowering extending to artistic brilliance and higher art. Beauty is God shining through at what is beautiful, the radiance of God within – beauty is truth, and truth is harmony.

At this stage and higher, followers of the universal or cosmic Christ (Rev. Ch. 1) are also called mystics. They believe that the inner God lives within humans and can be contacted by everyone in that stage and, to a lesser degree, by those whom are less evolved. Thus, God as a whole (Spirit and Body) has its abode not only outside of humanity but also inside. Jesus Christ said in Luke 17:21, "The kingdom of God is within you", and in John 10:34, that "you are gods?" The mystics communicate with the inner God (deep within their Souls), the universal Christ and the Holy Spirit, directly as their daily guide, teacher, and Parents, which they experience outwardly (in their personalities) as an inner voice, feelings of love, promptings, communication, inspirations, illuminations, instructions, advice (when asked), insight, wisdom, encouragement, assurance, revelations, visions, and dreams. Some mystics say, "The Bible is good, but Christ in us is better." There will be peace in the world when people experience the Christ of all religions in themselves and in others. Mystics of *esoteric religions are, therefore, in essence already united, although exoteric religions in their outer forms are still apart. The latter may be needed for the fourth stage people and below, preparing them for spiritual life and to grow spiritually by feeding them the Word of Truth. Advanced mystics, however, no longer are strictly in need of a church or houses of worship because the body (personality) is their temple (1 Cor. 3:16). Having dissolved past karma or sins, not making them anymore, and also learning the basic lessons of life, there is no need for those whom are advanced in the fifth stage of life to confess their sins and be absolved. At that point in life, the individual does not seek for or cares to be praised or recognized. He or she keeps working for God, even when they feel, at times, that He has forsaken them because they have a strong desire to do His Will and carry God's burden as co-creators.

NOTE: People who belong to non-mystical religions, such as Judaism, Islam, and nominal Christianity encounter the sacred outside rather than within themselves. God usually reveals Himself to them in a form they like the most. They are likely to follow a representative of God, such as a Rabbi, Mullah, and a priest or minister as an outer authority. The people are taught by them how

---

* In each religion, we find a small group of highly spiritual people whom aim for a synthesis of all religions. They are the mystics in Islam called Sufis; the Kabbalists and †Hassidists in Judaism; the esoterics, heretics, mystics, or saints in Christianity. We also find many mystics in Hinduism and Buddhism because both are basically mystical religions. There are also many groups of people who may also be called mystics, such as: Unity of Unity Village, Kansas; Rosicrucians of Oceanside, Ca.; Summit University, Livingston, Montana; Astara, Upland, Ca.; and many others.

†Hassidism – a movement of Jewish mysticism which originated in Poland in the 18th century. The emphasis of this movement is of God's immanence and of the possibility of constant communication with Him, which leads to a sense of great joy. This movement came about when the Jews of East Europe were very disappointed in their Turkish Messiah. God then let them experience a Messiah who lives within them.

to live a moral life and to prepare to receive the Christ of all religions. After the candidates are initiated, they may eventually accept an inner authority and join mystical movements, or go on their own.

A teacher of [1]religion can be of great value for those whom are separated from God. The latter individuals may, at first, acknowledge their relationship with God with their mind and then accept it with their whole being. Inspired by their teacher or friend, they direct their [2]thought to a goal, away from selfishness and for the benefit of the whole. In order to reach the unbeliever, God often works through a spiritual teacher and leader, who is an open channel of God's love, wisdom, and power, as Jesus Christ was a perfect channel. God's Being can then be more completely revealed than by, for example, through Revelation, visions, dreams, intuition, reason, nature, etc. However, the carnal person should relate to the Soul of the leader and not to the [3]personality. Otherwise, the dominance of the sovereignty of God working through the teacher is more or less blocked. By accepting God wholeheartedly, the unbeliever becomes a believer, not only in God of the universe but also that He/She dwells, [4]to a more or less degree, in all human beings.

NOTE: It is much easier for a more mature spiritual person to accept other religions because their spiritual life is not threatened, as in the case of their younger brothers and sisters.

The more evolved the leader and his teachings, the more people are likely to follow and become devoted to him. Although this devotion can be helpful, it also confines and conditions the mind of his followers to the teachings of their leader. It may then become very difficult for the disciple to see and appreciate other aspects of Truth. It will also restrict their interest and activities to a certain range and, thus, will greatly limit their freedom to unfold latent possibilities. However,

---

[1] Religion is a way of life, transcending all barriers of belief systems devised by humans in order to fulfill a need of men and women to enhance their divine knowledge (my).

[2] The human spirit is composed of emotion and inner thought (the other is externalized thought form). If one is composed of negative emotion and thought, the only way to reconstruct one's spirit is by positive emotion and thought. Otherwise, it will seek externalization in unwanted emotion/thought forms, which may become physical expressions. See "The Birth and Evolution of the Divine Spirit or Soul".

[3] Western people whom often see their spiritual leader as a human personality instead of a Christ personality experience difficulties in being spiritually born. It directs the student's mind away from principles and centers their thoughts on a personality.

[4] God dwells in all creatures, even as a spark, but in developed humans becomes much more noticeable.

when one's devotion is only directed to God, the person has the power to unfold all of his/her mental and divine potentialities.

After a person has followed a spiritual leader for a while and identified with the latter, it is time to *break away from the teacher and follow one's own grown inner Self, or Christ Spirit. Otherwise, sensitive people will call your Soul or Divine Spirit by the leader's name. In that case, you are not unique, and your Soul is only an imitation of your teacher, or guru, and you will be afraid to seek and accept Truth that is beyond your teacher. However, by becoming less devoted to your teacher, you stop giving power to your leader, and God loves you more as a select individuality. Disciples should also leave when they are equal to or more in their spiritual growth than their teacher or they work together. If they keep depending on his authority and spiritual guidance, the followers do not become Self-reliant, stop growing spiritually, become frustrated, and eventually burn out. Spiritual leaders who are truly concerned for the spiritual welfare of their followers encourage them to go beyond their leader. Did Jesus Christ not say, "He who believes in me will also do the works that I do; and greater works than these will he do" (John 14:12).

NOTE 1: The greater a disciple considers the spiritual master to be, the greater he/she will be. Some of them may mistakenly "look down" on all others as inferior and ignorant. They assume that their way of living is the only right way.

NOTE 2: Some religious movements produce elaborate confessions of faith in order to maintain unity but close their doors to accept higher Truth. The result is that they become rigid, inflexible, and stagnant. They would defend their belief or dogma and concept of God and put down other religions that emphasize other aspects of God. Some also carry in their belief systems a certain amount of cultural baggage. By believing those partial truths, they cannot be in harmony with the universe.

NOTE 3: Some churches are afraid to go spiritually and mentally beyond their founder of long ago who reflects to modern people a narrow and immature spirit. The result is that the church discourages critical thinking and, therefore, impoverishes human intelligence, thus hindering the full development of

---

* It is not easy to break away, especially when one has been following and applying a particular teaching for a long period of time. Their subconscious (human spirit), and even his or her Soul, consist of the Truth of the leader's teaching. To reprogram and to replace it with a higher and more diversified Truth is not an easy task, and some of them return to the narrow fold and are fenced in by the group spirit, which gave them security. The latter were not strong enough to survive spiritually.

reason. This may result that the church gets stagnated and may become lifeless.

It is easy for an established religious leader to become prideful and believe that he, instead of God, is the source of the important work he is doing, and that the people are attracted to him instead of God shining through him. As it happens in many instances, once the chosen ones are recognized and have won the trust and admiration of the members, especially young followers (who all give them power), they have a tendency to give less credit to God and do not pray so much as before. The result is that God is not able to work through them as much anymore. The channel between God and them becomes even more obstructed when they have been successful in their work, and especially when their ego or personality gets bolstered, or "blown up", too much. This is aided by immature followers whom are praising their personalities instead of God, who is enshrined within them. They may then become self-righteous and begin to lose contact with the divine forces and become spiritually low. The leaders also begin to think more about fulfilling selfish desires instead of fulfilling the purpose of the whole when they, whom are no longer one with God, place themselves between God and the people. This is what the fallen archangel Lucifer wanted all along. They, therefore, do not want that the members communicate with God directly and keep telling them that they are the medium between God and them. To hold on to the power over the people, which they feel slipping away, they may make exaggerated claims, and some of them may go so far as saying, "Everyone who does not listen to me, or do not what I tell them to do is satan." However, in spite of what they say, they have only power over those who believe in them. The ones whom are spiritually sensitive begin to turn away from their leader and also begin to criticize and improve his teaching. They may become very successful by following their inner Christ. Others are still listening to his intellectually stimulating and emotional speeches, yet devoid of almost all the life-giving elements of God.

NOTE: We detect many signs that a church or movement is in decline:
- When the spiritual leader makes false claims about himself and his work
- Tries to control the members of his congregation too much
- Does not allow God to inspire and lead the church
- Does not want to recognize the inspiration of God through one of his followers
- His prophecies do not materialize
- There is no love among the members of the organization (see The first letter of John)

> There is hardly any increase in membership
> Have to continue asking for money because God does not lay it on the people's hearts to give money, goods, and services to a church that is not His

REMARK: A genuine church may say, "We do not solicit contributions from the public – we trust God to supply our needs and do not want anyone unless let by God to feel obligated or expected to contribute."

VI→VII. As we come to the full realization of the Soul at the second initiation and also achieve mastery over our personality with its evil self, our Soul or Divine Spirit begins to harmonize with the God Self (also called Monad) deep within our Soul or Higher Self at the third initiation. In other words, the Soul or transpersonal Self begins to communicate with the universal Self, and the will of the Soul with the universal Will (Jn. 5:30; Mk. 14:36). The individual at this stage may be called an Over-Soul or Adept, who experiences little trouble in guiding his/her Soul (with its sense of oneness). The latter, in turn, is able to completely govern the personality or lower self (with its sense of separation), of which the mental self is controlled, the emotional self is stable, and the etheric energy and physical body are pure. Because the channel between the bodies is cleansed and open, the entire personality is flooded with spiritual Light, and "everything you do or touch turns into gold". Did the Nazarene not say to seek first His kingdom, and all the things will be yours as well? (Mt. 6:33)

As the saint at the fifth level communes with God/dess as a separate Being and implores to God to bless him and others, the sage or great master is dissolving the subject/object relation altogether and may say, "I bless my fellow humans." As the path of the mystic at the fifth level is that of compassionate reason and intellect, the path of the fully enlightened being is that of pure love and wisdom. As the saints of the fifth level are often described as having halos of Light around their heads, some yogis and pharaohs are described symbolically (or in reality) with a third eye or serpent at the sixth level. Great saints and masters are often depicted with glowing halos and great Light all around them. As the mystic prays in the name of a great master or uses his name for the Christ Spirit, great Souls (mah-atma) are using a new name, or rather, his own. "He has a name inscribed which no one knows but himself" (Rev. 19:12).

NOTE 1: As in stage five, and more so in stage six, the individual can safely wield and wisely use the psychic faculties for the helping of the human race. Advanced Buddhists whom have reached those levels may come back as spirit teachers or as wisdom beings (bodhisattva) to help others achieve enlightenment. As disciples and Over-souls are self-conscious on the spiritual planes, they are able to leave their bodies in full consciousness and return to them without the usual interruption. When their physical bodies cease to exist, they step over in full consciousness to the great beyond. Apostle Paul said in II Cor. 12:2-4, "I know a man in Christ --- who was caught up to the third heaven --- into paradise --- and he heard things that cannot be told, which man may not utter."

NOTE 2: The sixth plane has also been called the intuition plane. Intuition sees at a glance what an ordinary mind may take a lifetime to discover.

NOTE 3: In the higher spheres, every thought, aim, ambition, and purpose is for the good and service of others. Entities there no longer desire any individual things for themselves, for anyone on the planes below, or loved ones on earth. It is not that they love them any less but that they love others more, with an impersonal or universal love, which desires heaven for all humanity. Those beautiful and radiant spirit beings know that universal or spiritual love, wisdom, and will are prominent and that growth will continue in the spirit world – after the seven stages of life or octave is completed.

NOTE 4: There is a saying that states, "God is no respecter of persons."

NOTE 5: At the highest levels, a man and a woman deeply interact and exchange energies with each other at all levels of their beings (eating of the Tree of Life).

There is no longer the "you" and the "I". We (when in the highest stages) no longer look upon a person or object; we simply are that person or object. Your deepest Self is the Self of all people – that you are in them as they are in you (Jn. 14:20). You, therefore, experience the other as yourself and "love your neighbor as yourself" (Matt. 19:19). You are fully able and qualified to give guidance and counsel and to love and forgive your opponents because the pain of their good selves and budding Souls is your pain. You are also able to know and fully cooperate with the divine plan and take complete responsibility and bring comfort to God by lightening His burden of restoration. You have grown beyond being a teacher of any religion and are able to receive new Revelation and illuminate the Word of God.

The divine transcends all notions of gender, being neither male nor female (Mk. 12:25; Gal. 3:28) and is beyond all concepts and archetypical images of God. This is what meister Eckhart and the Zen master meant when they said, "I pray to God, to be rid of God!" and "if you see Buddha, kill him!"

We may detect illuminated beings and highly enlightened masters not only of the marvelous spiritual qualities they express in daily life but also in their expressions of cosmic humor, waves of luminous joy, and creative inspiration. The tonal quality of their voice is that of harmony, music, and of an irresistible charm. They radiate a brilliant Light, and a scent or aroma as that of the fragrance of flowers also emanates from their inner beings. Like evolved artists, sages are highly creative and delight in beauty, have great insights, boundless compassion, and creative use of words. They stand out from the crowd in the darkness of the world as a beacon of Light on the ocean shore (Mt. 5:14) and can be dramatic, witty, hilarious, and express great wisdom.

NOTE 1: Individuals whom have completed their long journey of becoming have found their true home as Self and God-realized beings and are no longer seeking for reality but have become reality. However, this is not the end of their growth but only the beginning, as they and God will evolve throughout eternity.

NOTE 2: The mysteries of the seven planes are uncovered by the seven seals of the Book of Revelation. The opening up of the fourth seal is of experiencing God's love in a parent-child relationship. The unfolding of the fifth is that of manifestation, responsibility, and being co-creators. "When he opened the fifth seal, I saw under the altar the souls of those who had been slain for the word of God and for the witness they had born" (Rev. 6:9). The opening of the sixth and seventh is seeing God in all things as the ground of our Souls and becoming His or Her individual expressions, as tablets are hewn from a rock.

The life of those whom have entered the seventh stage of development is usually of great sacrifice. They are not only willing to offer their physical life for the cause of God's restoration plan but also their reputation, honor, and respect as they are being shamed and humiliated, and even the growth of their spiritual lives is put upon the altar of sacrifice.

Because their consciousness is completely one with the consciousness of God and is bound together in love, God would always be the center of the thoughts, actions, and lives of those individuals. They have become the complete expression of the invisible God, in this and in the next world. It is, therefore, impossible for them to separate from Him, nor by tribulation, persecution, death, or anything else (Romans 8:35-39). They have become perfect as the heavenly Father is perfect (Mt. 5:48).

*God has reproduced Himself and become fully individualized in the spiritually mature men and women, whom have become like God in character and are living and walking among the people. "Behold, the dwelling of God is with men" (Rev. 21:3).

The universal Christ as the male aspect and the Holy Spirit as the female aspect of God speak with one voice through the perfected sons and daughters as God-realized beings. For example, Jesus, together with the universal Christ, said, "I am the way, and the truth, and the life, no one comes to the Father but by me" (Jn. 14:6). He also said, "I am the bread of life" (Jn. 6:35); "I am the Light of the world" (Jn. 8:12); "I am the resurrection and the life" (Jn. 11:25). The Holy Spirit will likewise be with one voice through chosen females, such as Mary and many others, in this and in the spirit world.

The individual gods, in their own right, understand and share, to some measure, the suffering heart of God, which was grief-stricken in the beginning when Adam and Eve, their first real children, turned away from them. They became so selfish (by turning their spirits inward) that God could not find them anymore, and in desperation called out to them, "Where Are You?" (Gen. 3:9) Later on, God expressed through Hosea (Ch. 11) their grief and sorrow for the fallen descendants of Adam and Eve. "When Israel was a child, I loved him, and out of Egypt I called my son. The more I called them, the more they went from me; they kept sacrificing to the Ba'als and burning incense to idols. Yet it was I who taught Ephraim to walk. I took them up in my arms; but they did not know that I healed them."

In the time of Jesus (Matt. 23:37-38), God as Mother expressed Herself through Jesus, "How often would I have gathered your children together as a hen gathers her brood under her wings, and you would not!"

In Luke Chapter 15, the prodigal son became lonely and restless and began to thirst for the living God (Ps. 42:1-2), and was completely accepted by a true and loving Father who easily forgave all that he had done.

---

* God is life itself and is expressed in all forms of life, but in humans, He/She can be expressed most expansively.

SUPPLEMENT
A. Controversies about the Being of Jesus Christ

In the Gospels, Jesus is called the Son of God, while He called Himself, at numerous times, the Son of man. However, Jesus never said that He was the incarnation of God but instead called God at many occasions His Father. The scripture does not define Christ in a clear way so that it can be understood by all. For Peter, the chief disciple, Jesus was a man but also "the Christ, the son of the living God" (Matt. 16:15-17), through whom "God was reconciling the world to himself" (2 Cor. 5:19).

Apostle Paul, who never met Jesus Christ in the flesh, encountered him on the road to Damascus as a supernatural being, who Paul identified as the "Son of God" (Acts 9:20). He later spoke of the Son as "the image of the invisible God, the first born of all creation; for in him all things were created --- through him and for him" (Col. 1:15-20). The beginning of the Gospel of John, which was written after Paul's letters, used the same kind of expression, wherein Jesus was even more deified. In this Gospel, the Universal Christ (the male aspect of God) spoke through Jesus Christ in the "I AM" sayings and also appeared with the Holy Spirit (the female aspect of God) to many people in the name of Jesus Christ. Because of personal encounters with God, the Christians after Paul regarded Jesus as both God and man.

The Christians during the first three centuries were severely persecuted by the Roman Empire and were accused of destroying their gods. However, they were free to believe in any concept of Christ and followed Him out of free will as the most direct and viable way to God. As many of them were anxiously awaiting the physical return of Jesus Christ, others whom were more esoterically minded saw the Second Coming of Christ not as an occurrence outside of themselves but within. "Every eye will see Him" (Rev. 1:7) when He returns as the Universal Christ to those whom are pure (as the clouds) and to find a livable place in the hearts of the believers (Rev. 21:3).

On October 27, 312 A.D., Constantine (280-337) had a dream wherein he was shown the first two Greek letters of the name Christ and a message in Latin "by this sign you shall be victor". The next day, that sign was painted on the shield of every person in Constantine's army. On October 28, they won the battle of Milvian Bridge against overwhelming odds. Thereafter, Constantine accepted Christ and became the first Christian emperor of Rome. In 313 A.D., Constantine issued the Edict of Milan, which proposed religious toleration for the pagans and Christians. In 380 A.D., the church of Christ became the state religion of Rome, as it was accepted by emperor Theodocius.

Because opinions about Christ were very diverse, and Christianity was divided in many systems of beliefs, sincere men of the church wanted a more uniform religion so that the people would not be confused of what they should accept or reject. And in order to have a more orderly society, emperor Constantine needed a united religion in order to have uniformity within the empire.

In 325 A.D., Constantine convened the *first ecumenical council at Nicea over the belief of Arian, known as Arianism, which said that Jesus Christ was a creature created by God who had a beginning and could, therefore, not be God. This was not in agreement with the opposing party that said Jesus is God. Arianism was condemned by a narrow majority vote, which promulgated the creed of Nicea, which stated that Jesus is the incarnation of God. This was later affirmed at the second ecumenical council at Constantinople in 381 A.D.

Although the two councils settled the debate of whether Jesus was divine or human, the next question needed to be solved as to how He could be both God and man. Appollarianism wanted to diminish the manhood, but the Orthodox Church (majority) wanted Jesus to be truly man (He was touched by many). Nestorius said that Christ had two distinct natures, a divine nature as the Son of God and a human nature as the son of Mary. It was condemned at the third ecumenical council in 431 A.D. because it taught that Christ's human nature was an extension of His divine nature. Eutychianism wanted to assimilate the human into the divine saying that during incarnation, Christ's human nature was absorbed by the divine nature. But the church wanted Jesus Christ to be both human and divine. At the fourth council (451 A.D.), Eutyches and his followers the monophysites were condemned, and the council came up with the solution that Christ had two distinct natures, which were unconfused and unaltered (against Eutyches) and undivided and inseparable (against Nestorius). The fifth ecumenical council in 553 A.D. was called by emperor Justinian. It was more politically motivated as he tried to settle differences that originated in the four ecumenical councils. The sixth ecumenical council (680 A.D.) decided

---

* For a more detailed explanation of the councils, see #38

that Christ had two wills instead of one, whereby the human will follows without resisting or being reluctant to the divine will.

NOTE: It was also indicated at the ecumenical councils that anyone who did not agree with the majority vote would be considered a heretic and excommunicated. Because there was no separation of church and state, an opportunity was opened for the church to use the power of the state to enforce conversion and to severely punish those whom they considered anti-Christian. This was especially true when the church became more powerful and less spiritual, such as at the time of the Inquisition.

The conclusion after the six councils was that Jesus Christ was defined as the only begotten Son of God, who was born of a virgin, and is both completely divine and completely human. He was further defined as being one person but having two natures and two wills. Those natures were unconfused, unaltered, undivided, and inseparable.

During the dark ages (+/-550 to +/-1000 A.D. – when intellectual and spiritual development for most people was halted – particularly *Greek learning) and later, the church became most powerful. They believed that as there is no salvation without Christ, there could be no salvation without the church, as the mystical body of Christ. Believers can no longer have God as their Father when they do not accept the church as their mother, in whose body dwelt the Holy Spirit. The church concluded that sacraments were necessary in order to save humankind, and those sacraments could only be given by the church.

After the six councils, Christianity became practically uniform in its beliefs and continued in that manner for more than 800 years until the Protestant Reformation in the year 1517. The church became as diversified as before the councils, although the emerging Protestant churches (whom usually accepted the decisions of the first four councils) also began to ostracize their wayward members when the church became more established. They and the Catholics became more tolerant in later years, and today, one does not have to belong to a church to be a Christian, as long as they follow the Cosmic Christ of all religions.

NOTE: Beliefs, as presented in creeds or statements which were hammered out in the councils, are still used as criterion in some churches today if one is a member of a particular church or not. This is especially true of ministers and priests who have to confess that they will follow all the rules of the governing

---

* Revival of Greek learning and the arts happened in the 14th, 15th, and 16th centuries and became known as the Renaissance, or rebirth (of the personality).

body during ordination. Thus, in order to maintain unity and protect themselves against heresy, many religions have produced elaborate confessions of faith, emphasizing doctrinal purity and infallibility of the Bible. According to fundamentalists, if one begins to doubt any (literary) statement of the Bible, he/she starts down the road to the denial of God, the loss of certainty of salvation, and finally, the loss of Christian behavior. However, they should understand that the Word of God, as expressed in the Bible, is not the ultimate authority but that the Spirit of God is the true authority. As the saying goes, "The Bible is good; God within us is better."

REMARK 1: The death of Jesus on the cross was a great sacrifice when "he was wounded for our transgression" (Isa. 53:5). Through this atonement as the last Adam (1 Cor. 15:45), he "gave his life for a ransom for many" (Matt. 20:28; 1 Pet. 1:18; Titus 2:14; 1 Tim. 2:6; Rev. 5:9). He won back the people as being owned by satan (Jn. 8:44; Matt. 4:8-9) because of the fall of the first Adam and to lighten our redemption, and to finally come into God's family by rebirth.

REMARK 2: The number of sacraments, which are recognized by the Roman Catholic, Eastern Orthodox, and the Anglican Churches, are seven in number. They are: Baptism, Confirmation, Communion, Confession, Extreme Unction, Ordination, and Marriage.

For the Protestants, the sacraments are subordinate to the Word of God. They recognize Baptism and Communion, or the Lord's Supper. The Quakers, or Society of Friends and Unitarians, and others, do not recognize any of the sacraments.

Thus, for many Christians, the sacraments are the means by which God releases His grace.

Believers in Baptism use water to sprinkle or submerge the candidates (according to Mark 1:10), but almost all of them use in their ceremony the words, "In the name of the Father and of the Son and of the Holy Spirit" (Matt. 28:29).

Confirmation is the ritual which completes the work of Baptism when, in addition to accepting the Word of God, the members receive the Holy Spirit (Acts 8:14-17). The Protestants also believe in the baptism of the Holy Spirit as a non-sacramental act.

The Communion, also called the Eucharist and the Lord's Supper by the Protestants, was instigated by Christ in Matt. 26:26-28. Many members of the Catholic and Eastern Orthodox religions believe that during the Eucharist, transubstantiation takes place, or that the substances of the bread and wine are changed literally into the body and blood of Christ as soon as the priest says the required prayer. Martin Luther, the Protestant reformer, says that the bread and wine do not change, but in a mysterious way, the body and blood of Christ is present in the substance – consubstantiation. Other Reformation leaders, Calvin and Zwingli, believed that Christ is spiritually present, and that the bread and wine symbolically represent the body and blood of Christ.

As Catholics confess their sins to a priest by being contrite or deeply sorry for having done wrong, they then receive absolution or forgiveness and remission of sins (sometimes some penance is required). The Protestants may confess their sins to the Lord or fellow brethren (James 5:16). As a group, they often state a confession of guilt and ask for forgiveness. Both congregations believe that their sins will be forgiven when they repent wholeheartedly, as it is promised in the Bible (Matt. 9:1-2; 5:12; Jn. 20:23). All this is done with the understanding that individuals continue to sin so long as they are good and evil, or have inherited the original sin.

The sacrament of extreme unction concerns itself with those whom are sick and are about to die, whereby the dying person can be forgiven of all sins, as it is written in the fifth chapter of James:

> "Is any among you sick? Let him call for the elders of the
> church, and let them pray over him, anointing him with oil
> in the name of the Lord; and the prayer of faith will save
> the sick man, and the Lord will raise him up; and if he has
> committed sins, he will be forgiven."

The Catholics firmly believe in the apostolic succession, wherein one may bless another to continue the work, especially by the act of laying hands on them, because Jesus said in John 20:21, "As the Father has sent me, even so I send you."
The Protestants, whom believe in the priesthood of all believers, could not believe in the inauguration of generation to generation, although they also practice, to a limited extent, the laying on of hands by the more established clergy.

The Catholics and Eastern Orthodox denominations believe that Christ Himself has put a stamp of approval on marriage as a sacrament because He was invited and was present at the wedding feast of Cana (John 2:1-11) and also in the words of Paul in Eph. 5:25-32. The Protestants say that Christ was merely a quest and not an executor of a marriage. Besides, the unmarried state, especially in the Christian past, has been more esteemed than the marriage, and for the last union, the Roman and state laws have been in operation or in force.

B. Vibrations and Cycles

There is not anything in a state of absolute rest. From *subatomic particles to solar systems, in the outer as well as in the inner planes of life, everything is in constant motion, movement, vibration, rhythm, and cycles. All elements, in their operation, are connected and dependent on each other.

Coarse particles of matter, unlike the finer ones, are visible because they move more slowly. For example, the vibratory movement of the atoms of gases is so high that it becomes invisible to the senses, or in the case of water, it appears transparent. On the other hand, the vibratory motion of the atoms in the rock is of such a low rate that it is not visible to the physical senses and, therefore, appears to be solid. However, everything in the physical and psychic-spiritual universe has to vibrate at the same frequency in order for entities to perceive, experience, and interact with the matter of those planes. Our body's frequency is, albeit, so low that we bump against a wall or tree, but certain frequencies, such as radio and television waves, are high enough to pass through solid objects. Even less obstructive are the psychic waves of thoughts and spirit bodies, which cannot be detected by physical senses, as the blades of a fast-moving fan or propeller cannot be seen. Those thought forms and spirit entities can be seen by those whom are sensitive to those higher vibrations or are using their psychic senses. Because of the differences in frequencies, the incarnate and discarnate worlds can exist in the same space. Spirit entities are, therefore, able to influence the spirit bodies of people all around them, and vice versa.

NOTE 1: We may think of every thought impulse as having a distinctive wavelength or a specific rate of vibration, which is beyond the perception power of our five senses. Thoughts and emotions (a lower vibration) are, nevertheless, capable of influencing those to whom they are directed.

---

* When matter is reduced to its smallest invisible state, it is no longer matter but behaves like a vibrating force or energy. Depending on the way one observes components of matter, they are either waves or particles of matter which, according to Niels Bohr (Danish physicist), are like that of yang and yin. This dual nature is also exhibited by light (and other radiations) in the form of waves and photons. When it travels through space (186,000 miles per second), they appear as vibrating electric and magnetic fields or as waves, the so-called un-bottled waves or radiation. However, light is not the fastest moving energy in the universe; the energy of thought is much faster.

NOTE 2: Because matter is only a lower vibratory force of energy or light that has been slowed down in its vibratory frequencies, the physical world seems to have, therefore, no permanent reality. The very matter of which our bodies are composed disappears into nothing more than waves or vibration. According to the philosophy of Berkeley and Schopenhauwer, the material world is only an illusion. This is also the belief of a great number of teachings of the East. They also deny the reality of the physical world, which they say is not what it seems to be, but an illusion of the senses, or "maya".

NOTE 3: The vibration of the average body is so coarse that the higher vibration of sunlight may easily cause stress and damage to the physical body. The body also needs to adjust to the increase of energy and vibrations from the growing inner self, or temporarily induced by an outside source. Because the physical organs are not always adapted to the rapid vibration of spiritual substance, the individual may experience changes in energy levels, that is, being upbeat one day and tired the next. Through rapid consciousness changing experiences, the individual feels lighter, as if he or she is "walking on air". Jesus Christ, who was able to raise the vibration of the cells of His body, was able to lift Himself up by walking on water, while Peter, through fear, lowered his vibration and sank back in the water.

NOTE 4: Theoretically, it may even be possible to increase our vibrations to such an extent that we may become invisible to those whom are vibrating at the normal lower levels.

NOTE 5: Many people of today have reported that time seems to be moving faster. Some of them try to explain this phenomena, that our solar system is moving into a different place in the galaxy (others say that our galaxy is moving into a new area in space) or into a more highly energy active space. This higher frequency is causing humanity to vibrate at a faster rate.

NOTE 6: The psychic and spiritual part of humans is as truly a substance as is the physical part in which the inner parts dwell. Both are substances, and both are in a state of vibration. We may say that Spirit substance is the highest form of manifestation, and matter is substance in its lowest form of manifestation. God, who is Love, is the highest vibration, has the most life, and is the Source of other objects that vibrate with a lesser frequency.

We may conclude here that the vibrations in the spirit world are much faster than those of the physical world, as for example, the vibration of light is to that of sound. Thus, the difference between the spirit plane and the physical plane is one of vibration, one of lightness and denseness, or fast and slow vibration. There is, thus, a whole range of vibratory experiences that goes beyond the reach of the five physical senses and is known as [1]extrasensory experiences, such as: telepathy,

---

[1] See #35 – Humans have physical, psychic, and spiritual senses.

clairaudience, clairvoyance, psychometry, psychokinesis, etc.

In the spirit world, there are no obstructions because one does not move around objects (as on earth) but passes through them. The frequencies of the discarnate persons are so rapid that they cannot be detected by the people of the physical world. As the inhabitants of the earth are not able to see spirit entities, so the people of the lower spheres of the spirit world cannot detect and contact spirits whom are living in the higher realms. If higher spirits want to make contact with entities of the lower worlds, they have to "descend", that is, lower their vibration by the act of imagination and will.

Not only atoms of physical matter but all forms of energy are considered vibrational in nature, such as the seventy or so octaves of the known spectrum of electromagnetic energy, which includes: cosmic rays, gamma rays, x-rays, ultraviolet rays, and the 49th octave, visible light. (Frequency of vibration or wavelength between $10^{14} - 10^{15}$ or about 600 trillion waves per second, while a slight difference in wavelength shows the different [2]colors.) Infrared, micro, radio waves, and audible sound, the latter occupies from 5 to 15 octaves of the spectrum and vibrates from approximately 30 to 30,000 vibrations per second. Silence is, however, not the absence of all sound but only those we cannot perceive, below or above the audible range. The "voice of the silence" is sound that the physical ear does not hear but may be heard by the inner ear, such as psychic sound or even the most delicate and [3]small voice of God.

NOTE 1: There are, in the sun's rays, infrared and ultraviolet colors that our eyes cannot see. The calendar week of seven days represents the seven colors, beginning with the first day of the week with the color red.

NOTE 2: As the soil of the earth can be compared to the color of red, the plants growing out of the soil can be compared to the color of green, whom are reaching upward to the blue of the sky.

---

[2] We know, through the sense of sight, that objects absorb or reflect certain rays of light in various ways – producing a world of colors. There are seven different colors we can see: red (lowest vibration), orange, yellow, green, blue, indigo, and violet. There are, however, many colors in the lower and higher octaves which do not make any impressions on our eyes and mind. We may further remark that there is a close connection between color and sound. When, for example, in the spirit world a note is struck, a certain color appears.

[3] Through meditation, we connect our lower self or personality with the Higher Self or God part of our being, through which we can fine tune to the frequency of the original creation from which all the constituent vibrations are derived.

Because we receive such a small part of the above-mentioned frequencies, in a universal sense we are practically unconscious. It is well known that many animal species perceive frequencies beyond what humans can detect on their particular [1]bands. We are not only talking here of the sixty or so octaves we are not able to detect, but also that which is beyond. Albeit, when we develop our psychic senses, we see and hear so much more. We are then able to receive much more information, and life has become more interesting and fulfilling.

NOTE 1: Our senses of touch, taste, and smell are wholly physical and are needed to properly eat our food, while the sense of hearing and especially the sense of sight have more to do with one's mental and spiritual development. The power in back of those senses is that of the human spirit, which is proven by the fact that the eye of the unconscious or sleeping person sees nothing.

NOTE 2: When a person goes to sleep, he/she changes from the slower vibration state of being awake to a faster vibration consciousness of the sleep state, in which condition spiritual entities can be heard and seen.

Because everyone and everything has its [2]own vibratory rate or wavelength, which is as distinct as a fingerprint, much information about a particular individual can be obtained, even knowledge that might not be consciously known to that individual. Many people are psychically sensitive to a degree because they may, at times, speak of and react to good and bad vibes they may pick up of people they meet and in the environment where they are. Because people are at different vibratory levels, they can only respond fully to signals which they can understand and harmonize with. A radio, for example, can only receive signals of a certain frequency. Thus, when radiant energies of our being come into contact with the radiations of another individual, object, or environment, a vibratory interaction takes place. We may further distinguish between positive or negative interaction and being on the [3]same levels in our religious, ideological, intellectual, professional, and family relationships.

---

[1] When a vibration is received on the band of one of the five senses, it is translated into electrical impulses in our bioelectrical body and then transmitted to the brain for interpretation.

[2] We need to know the vibration rate of that person to track him/her down (language of a psychic).

[3] When you belong to a certain group, for example, by learning the same truth and thinking in the same way, you vibrate like them. If you are not, everybody sooner or later in the group senses that you are not one of them.

In the [4]love state, all is wonderful. We feel energetic, and much is accomplished with little effort. However, in a defiant state, our vibration is lessened when we express negative emotions and thoughts. This causes us to rapidly deplete our energy. Everything we do is heavy, and we require much sleep to recuperate. Some individuals whom have been extremely negative in their feelings and thinking still lack energy or feel tired, even after sleep. Thus, the more spiritual and unselfish a feeling or thought is, the higher or faster is the vibration of our spirit self, and the more we move in lightness. A more permanent higher state of our being may be obtained by consistently feeling and thinking high emotions and thoughts, such as those of love, wisdom, and harmony. This will eventually change and raise the vibration constitution of our spirit body, which then no longer responds to undesirable emotions and thoughts.

NOTE 1: Whenever you become involved in a negative discussion, it is advisable to redirect the thought energy of the group and, thus, raise the vibration of the people involved. In that case, the people will not strengthen the belt of negative thoughts around the earth, which has a great influence on weather conditions, behavior of people and animals, the growth of plants, and natural disasters.

NOTE 2: When we have listened to someone who is a highly evolved being, we are not only influenced by this person's words but also by the radiating vibrations which made us appreciate and understand the teachings. However, the next day or two, when the vibrations of our spirit selves resume the former lower mode of existence, we no longer understand as clearly and are not able to repeat the wisdom of the teachings as we did before when we were in the radiating presence of the evolved being. Having been temporarily in an elevated state, we may also experience a reaction because the spirit selves have been overstrained and need to relax, which may also cause us to fall back to a lower level.

NOTE 3: There are three selves of different states of consciousness working together to operate as one self: the conscious or ego self, the subconscious self (human spirit), and the God Self, or super-conscious.

NOTE 4: The higher the frequency of the selves, the more radiant and brighter the appearance of the aura. The lower the frequency, the darker and duller the auric appearance.

---

[4] The love state may be an evolved spiritual state when we pray and meditate, are happy to meet someone, by giving of oneself, admiring creation, being thankful, having a sense of God-like humor, stop worrying about things which will never happen, forgive everyone, and do not judge. Sing uplifting songs and dance in harmony with creation.

NOTE 5: When a metal is heated, the atoms are moving faster, and there is an increase in vibrations.

NOTE 6: Your thought vibration can affect (change) the colors you see in a flame.

NOTE 7: Besides raising your vibration by prayer, music, and meditation, it is also possible to increase your vibration somewhat by deep breathing.

NOTE 8: By sympathizing with a person, we soon begin to vibrate in resonance with that person.

NOTE 9: As a loud voice is not necessarily a good voice, a strong vibration of thought is not necessarily a high vibration.

NOTE 10: The vibration of a body is lowered by eating animal food and is raised by eating fruits and vegetables.

NOTE 11: It is not advisable to sit or be in the same place as a person of a lower vibration has been dwelling in.

NOTE 12: Because all animate and inanimate things are in a state of vibration, any vibration field emitted by one thing may easily affect vibration fields of surrounding things.

C. The Rhythms and Cycles of Life

In the common phenomena of everyday life, in the rising and setting of the sun, in the waxing and waning of the moon, of the ocean tides going in and out, and of the coming and going of the seasons, primitive people discovered the law of cycles, the periodicity of all nature.

Further observation reveals that all life is imbued with [1]rhythms and follows a cyclic pattern. [2]Our whole existence, like that of all nature around us, is that of ever recurring periods or cycles. No particle of matter from the smallest to the largest aggregation, whether in the mineral, vegetable, animal, or human kingdoms, is ever still; all is in motion. It is found in the vibrating atoms of the microcosm as well as in the great stellar movements of the macrocosm. This law of rhythm

---

[1] Rhythm is a repeated regular pattern of movement through time and space, while cycles are recurring sequences of events.

[2] Knowing all this, we should think more in terms of cycles instead of thinking in a linear fashion, as many of us tend to do, and also attempt to connect individual rhythm with macrocosmic forms of rhythms.

or vibration is a universal language and is self-evident in all forms, both in the physical and [3]spiritual universes.

The Bible says in Ecclesiastes 3:1-2, "For everything there is a season, and a time for every matter under heaven: a time to be born, and a time to die; a time to plant, and a time to pluck up what is planted."

Every atom and molecule of our body is in a constant state of vibration and movement. Old cells are replaced by new ones, changing the body's constitution in set periods of time. There are many functions in the body that are very rhythmic and in accordance with the rhythm of the earth and the universal law of cycles, such as the systolic and diastolic cycle of the heart's contraction and expansion, or the basic rhythm of the pulse or heartbeat. This is in rhythmic harmony with the ebb and flow of blood through the arteries, which is about four times faster, as the repetitive pattern of the inspiring and expiring of breath. This body rhythm also includes the peristaltic action or the contractions and dilations of the alimentary canal, moving the contents forward. Everything we do naturally and gracefully we do rhythmically, such as the metabolic motion of eating and elimination.

NOTE 1: In relationship with cycles is the phenomena of coincidences, which happen at the same time. Those facts or events were coined by Carl Jung as "synchronicity". These coincidences between external events is certainly influenced by the inner conditions of human beings when the two energies are coming together in time and cause an event to occur.

NOTE 2: In this age of mechanization, most people, especially in modern Western society, follow artificial schedules. They move against the natural rhythm and do not flow with the tides of life, and are thus out of tune with the rhythm of the cosmos. They are more directed by clocks and appointments than by biological and seasonal times. They should, however, try to regulate their life according to nature's rhythmic patterns, a time to plant, to harvest, and to rest. In addition, it is hard for modern men and women to feel the pulse of the earth or their heart beat when they are driving in automobiles through a world paved over with concrete, while being bombarded with the roar of traffic, the shriek of sirens, and the noise of the radio, record player, and television in their homes.

---

[3] In the fourth dimension, there is no earthly time, as time is associated with the cyclic movement of planetary bodies. The flow of time in the spirit world is much related to the measure of experiences, as life there is more noted by its cyclic events or occurrences.

In nature, we find the oxygen cycle, wherein oxygen enters our lungs as we breathe in and combines with the absorbed food to become carbon dioxide, which is breathed out. This is taken in and changed by plants in oxygen for humans (and animals) to breathe once more. There is also the water cycle: water evaporating from the earth's land, lakes, rivers, streams, and oceans is evaporated by the heat of the sun. It rises as invisible vapor and cools to form clouds that produce rain or snow. That again fills the earth's land, lakes, rivers, streams, and oceans.

Our cycle of sleep and waking has a rhythmic correspondence to the earth's twenty-four hour rhythm of day and night, and the [1]rising and setting of the sun. With each dawn or daybreak, a new cycle is born. It runs its course and gives way to darkness, seemingly [2]fading out of existence, only to be born at sunrise. By observing the universe, we find cycles everywhere, smaller cycles within larger cycles. The turning of the earth around its own axis and the succession of changing events or seasons when the earth moves around the sun – as the spinning electrons move around the nucleus of an atom. The sun, in turn, will make a complete revolution within the galaxy about a common center.

NOTE 1: Flying through time zones disrupts the biological cycles because physical bodies continue to operate on the rhythms established at their place of residence. It may take several days for the body rhythms to adjust. Symptoms of jet lag include daytime sleepiness and inability to sleep at night. People are, at those times, less alert, have poor concentration, slowed reflexes, low energy levels, and they may, at times, be irritable and experience hunger at odd hours.

NOTE 2: As evolution is always upwards, it also moves by cycles, the next cycle at a higher level than the one before. Thus, it appears that the path of evolution is like a spiral. This we can see in the improved species of plants,

---

[1] The world was first believed to be flat, with a hollow space beneath (sheol) as the abode of departed spirits. This Babylonian conception was disregarded by Thales the Greek astronomer (d. +/-546 B.C.), who believed that the earth was a globe, standing unmovable in space. Ptolemy (2nd century Greek astronomer) postulated that not only a few "wandering stars" but all the heavenly bodies move around the earth. This "Ptolemaic System" held sway for about fourteen centuries until Nickolaus Copernicus, Polish astronomer (1473-1543), gave substantial evidence that the earth moves around the sun. This was reaffirmed fifty years later by Galileo (1564-1642), a Florentine astronomer, by looking through a crudely constructed telescope. He was later condemned by the Roman Catholic Inquisition. The latter literally believed the passages in the Bible which speak of the sun that rises (Judg. 5:31; Jas. 1:11) and in Josh. 10:12-13; Ps. 104:5; Eccl. 1:5, which describes the earth as motionless and the sun as moving.

[2] It is a natural rhythm that the darkest period comes just before dawn.

animals, and above all, in the progress of the human race in its physical, mental, and spiritual development. This also includes repeating those cycles at different levels when humans did not learn their lessons and had to bear the karmic consequences.

In the spring, the earth emerges from its winter period of rest and renews the cycle of life, while singing, or rather, vibrating for joy. The branches of plants and trees bring forth again their growing buds and flowers. The leaves become green in the summer and golden in the fall. But before the plants become inactive or die, they reseed themselves. Animals mate according to seasonal rhythms and get their young, while some of them migrate according to the flow of seasons.

As the year is one solar cycle, the lunar cycle is the time when the moon circles around the earth in the lunar month of 28 days. The week is one of the four phases of the moon, the new, full, and two half moons. The moon not only causes the daily ebb and flow of the ocean tides and the calming beat of the ocean waves on the shore, but also of the flows in the human bodies, which exist mostly of water and which, in turn, affects their emotions. This is especially true of women whom experience a hormonal rhythm of ovulation, with its up and down beats and which, like the waxing and waning of the moon, covers a period of twenty-eight days.

Through simple observation, we can see that there is an ebb and flow everywhere, a steady beat, a dance to a certain rhythm, as the planets dance around the sun. The earth itself has a pulse beat with the fall and rise of the tides. Thus, from inanimate objects to animate beings, everything moves according to cosmic rhythm and is in tune with the universal heartbeat.

In everyday living, we experience the flow and ebb side of life. However, it will not last long if we stay in harmony with life, knowing that a period of activity and growth is followed by one of assimilation and rest. People whom are treading the spiritual path of life may feel, at one time, confident and fearless because they know that God is their ever-present companion. When they experience the ebb side of life, they feel that God may have deserted or forsaken them. This cycle will not last, and they will then experience a much greater closeness to God.

D. General remarks about art, sound, music, language, poetry, reading, writing, speaking, words, and Words of God

We may say that art concerns itself with the communication of certain ideas and feelings by means of a sensuous medium, such as color, sound, bronze, marble, words, etc. This medium is fashioned into works marked by beauty of design and coherence of form. They appeal to our mind, arouse our emotions, kindle our imaginations, and enchant our senses. The artist possesses that natural ability to express him/herself in one medium or another, which we call talent. Further, art is an international language of communication, as it is expressed through painting, music, film, opera, literature, sculpture, architecture, dance, and the like. Its purpose is to enhance life, to reveal God in all of Their Beauty, Truth, and Goodness, as it is revealed in all its splendor, in humanity and nature, in its male/female and inner/outer aspects.

Because the whole manifested universe is considered to be based on vibration, it is therefore possible to bring certain changes in matter and consciousness through sound vibrations, such as one's voice, singing, mantras, and other sounds and chanting. The Gregorian chant, for example, brings individuals to alternate states of consciousness and also has a purifying effect on the persons and their surroundings.

As there is a sympathetic resonance between two or more violins (or tuning forks) when the string of one violin affects the corresponding string(s) of the other violin(s), a note of expression struck in one's life reflects and vibrates into other people's lives when they are in sympathy or attunement. Thus, a person's thought can affect the thoughts of others or may affect situations and conditions that are related to their well being. As the middle C is struck on a piano and causes the octaves of the lower Cs to vibrate in sympathetic vibration, so the stronger waves radiating from a higher being can influence the vibrations of his or her students. It may eventually bring them into close harmony with the teacher as they begin to vibrate to their instructor's resonance. At a higher plane, the love of God may strike the keynote of an individual and awaken the force of altruism, which is latent within human beings.

> ➤ Abstract art of today is not like realistic art or surface painting of the nineteenth century. An abstract painter, for example, is more likely to paint the inner or essence of things.

- A film is made with the intention to make the public response emotionally, intellectually, psychically, and spiritually in a certain way.
- Art is to mix colors in such a way that they harmonize, as the clothes we wear.
- God who created nature is a true artist.
- Sound vibrations can produce well-defined geometrical forms. This can be demonstrated when a violin bow is drawn across the edge of a drum, whereupon sand grains will vibrate to a well-defined pattern. Changing the pitch, the sound will build a new and different symmetrical pattern.
- The recitation and chanting of mantras is to produce certain vibrations in the inner bodies, to bring them in harmony or tune them up.
- As the speaker's voice draws a vibration from the whole physical body, so does a string of a violin from the body of the violin.
- Music is an art dealing with the organization of tones into patterns and has been called the emotion of language. It brings people into harmony with each other, especially those whom are out of tune.

It is generally accepted that modern languages have their roots in Sanskrit, which has a durable connection between sound and sense or sound value and meaning. Thus, the sound pattern of the word closely resembles and supports the meaning of the word, which in the languages of today is not always the case. It also responds to the rhythm of nature. Each sound as a vibration evokes a corresponding state of consciousness. Thus, the sound of words affects us independently of their meanings. However, in the more elevated form of speech, such as poetry, sound and rhythm, it plays an important role. By using different literary devices, such as rhyme, meter (like the beats in music), alliteration (repetition of consonant sounds), and assonance (repetition of vowel sounds), the sounds and the meaning of the words are in harmony, creating the music of poetry.

The function of poetry, unlike that of prose, is not to explain but to go beyond the intellect, reason, and words to see the whole and a glimpse of the divine, where separation disappears and knowledge gives way to wisdom. It offers images and ideas in a few lines that resonate with our lives and lets us hear a truth that we always have known, and things about life that we would otherwise miss. Great poems are not inspired by the lower self but always by the Higher Self. Poetry is a most powerful speech. It can express and intensify our moods and strengthen our aspiration, and it reveals our innermost feelings and Heart. The poet not only uses words that vibrate to a regular rhythm but chooses such words and puts them together in such a way that the sound or vibration expresses their feelings and calls up high ideals, thus making a channel so that Essence will shine or work through them.

- ➤ As words have a fixed meaning in relation to a complete thought or sentence, so tones assume a fluid meaning only in association with other tones, which is called a melody, or theme and soul of music.
- ➤ When living on the physical plane, we experience great difficulties expressing ourselves fully and accurately in earth based languages, with their narrowness of conception. We can only present one idea at a time, while the physical brain can handle only a limited amount of thoughts, which have to be formulated in words before they become comprehensible. Albeit, in the higher spirit world, one can express him or herself more accurately, and the human spirit is able to exchange much more information and a wealth of meaning. Thus, in the life after death, one can communicate by thought transference (in the higher regions), which is also seen as color or vibration.
- ➤ Example of good poetry is, "One should not deal with the sword but by the Word."
  "To see a word in a grain of sand" is to "hold infinity in the palm of your hand" (Tennyson).
- ➤ Poetry effects our subconscious or human spirit and our budding Divine Spirit.

Reading books adds to your wisdom. Some people become so involved while they read that they lose connection with reality. At those times, they may, at times, bond with the spirit of the author and also with the thought forms of people and things the author has created. However, it is not always advisable to read books which are written by spiritually undeveloped people, especially when one is sensitive. By reading and accepting the story and the author's view of life wholeheartedly, one may become a "fan" and contribute to the development of the overall thought form of that particular literature.

Great writers become well known because they express things that people feel in their heart, and their writings have remained popular because they strike a chord in the persons' inner beings. Inspired writers tell that they often become a channel through which their Christ Spirit or divine talent flows. Those writers write not with a view to fame or money but for the good of all people. They especially become inspired in periods of contemplation and meditation whenever they are in a receptive mood, when new ideas are welling up in their conscious mind. Some writers are also concerned with how their words sound because the sound of the words and their rhythm in a sentence can carry a message beyond the definition of the word.

Much of the conversation gets lost when it is put in words. Examples are: tone of voice, gestures, the twinkling of an eye, facial expressions, the receptivity of the listening party, the thoughts behind and the liveliness of the words, and the feeling when the auras of the speaker and listener intermingle. The human voice as the intermediary of body and human spirit is capable of conveying emotions and thoughts and is also a channel for the Divine Spirit. After considering or cooking his/her thoughts, the speaker dresses them into suitable words and sends them to the listener, who hears the words and takes out the psychic and spiritual essence from the words. The words you speak should be in accordance with your vibration pattern. How one expresses him/herself is important, not as much as the words, because everyone can repeat the words of great individuals, but who can speak from the same spiritual attitude? The voices of evolved beings or saints are always marked by a sincerity, integrity, charm, pleasing, harmony, and impressiveness. By listening to them, we also absorb their consciousness. When you are out of harmony, singing will help restore your balance to the rhythms of nature. A singer who is no longer self-conscious and lets the song sing for itself, lifting up the vibration of the audience, becomes popular and is loved by those whom are vibrating like the singer, and they become his or her fans.

> ➤ Literature, like other art forms, never stops witnessing and preaching, even for hundreds of years.
> ➤ When you write out your troubles, read it, and burn it, it may disappear altogether.
> ➤ The so-called stage fright of public speakers might be the sudden impact of everyone's eye beams carrying various thoughts that may wallop the speaker into a subconscious stupor.

In order to express ourselves, we are compelled to use words as symbols of our ideas, but they are often insufficient to convey our opinion or belief in a clear and concise manner. Words can, therefore, not really convey what one feels or thinks. Finite concrete words, as they are supplied by the lower mind, are not able to adequately describe or verbalize abstract concepts, pure thoughts, and revelation from the higher mind. Besides, those words are not only misinterpreted but also lose some of the divine clarity. They are often colored, shaded, or distorted, according to pre-conceived ideas and beliefs of the lower self or personality. The latter may give an order or command, filling the words as containers with more or less psychic energy or power, which can penetrate and even explode deeply in the human spirit of the receptive person. Albeit, the words can also be charged with an additional divine energy from an evolved being, whereby they not only convey the words but also divine power, which results that the receptive person feels lighter, uplifted, and more spiritually alive.

As humans are more than the words they speak, so God is much more than the words spoken through His prophets. The Word of God, as written in sacred literature, is a symbol, vehicle, or token and represents the living reality. It is the Spirit of God, His Essence, which has its being in and behind those words and becomes the living Word. By reading Scripture, one joins and unites with the Spirit of the Cosmic Christ and Holy Spirit and hears the very Voice of God, while His Light shines brightly on the reader.

> ➤ Words are sometimes like shells, empty and devoid of any life.
> ➤ When thoughts are expressed in words, they may eventually manifest.

E. Numerology

Numbers are symbols of quantities and are used extensively in arithmetic calculations. They can exist without matter and allow us to perform mental operations, independent of our five senses. However, besides having practical numerical values as figures or quantities, they also have an esoteric side or inner meaning as qualities. When both meanings are organized in one system, numerology comes about. The latter has become useful and valuable in finding out about the human personality, its inherent characteristics, power, traits, talents, ambition, desires, etc. This may be a suitable method to determine what career one is best suited for and to guide one's future and destiny. Thus, numerology, like astrology and palmistry, is a system of encoded information of individuals whom are living the life of their earthly personalities. Numerology is most popular concerning name numbers and should give preference to [1]astrological charts of birth dates when it differs from the latter. Thus, numerology is the art of analyzing your own name according to its numerical quotient. Every letter has its numerical equivalent and every word or name vibrates to a number, and every number has its inner meaning.

As the esoteric or hidden value of numbers was recognized by the Hebrew Bible and by a few ancient societies, numerology became a

---

[1] Because of the stand of the planets and stars, its vibration and rhythmic movements made a mark on the vibrating body of a child when it took its first breath.

science in the sixth century B.C. as it was expounded by Pythagoras and his followers whom were living in an academic community in Crotona, southern Italy. [2]Pythagoras, who was born in Asia Minor, was not only a numerologist but also a Greek philosopher, scientist, an artist, a musician (originated the musical scale), astronomer, and mathematician. He said that the basic substance, or the essence of everything, was numbers, not water (Thales), or air (Anaximenes), or fire (Heraclitus). There is order in the universe from the atom to the solar system, which was created mathematically and is governed by numbers. As it has been said, "God geometrizes." Thus, the mystery of the universe can be solved by mathematics, as all science, music, and astronomy had their basis in numbers.

NOTE 1: An important discovery attributed to the Pythagorians is the mathematical nature of musical relationship. The entire musical scale is arranged in a mathematical order, with its harmonic intervals of the regular movement of numbers. When music is not ordered sound, it is not harmonious and is not music but noise, which is disagreeable to the human constitution. Each individual can be compared to a note on the musical scale. When they play together, a melody emerges.

NOTE 2: The measured beat of music or controlled movement of music in time or rhythm should be in harmony with the rhythm of nature. It also should resonate with the inner working of the body and its movements so that it heals, cures, soothes, relaxes, and brings comfort and a sense of well being, while being in step or dancing to the rhythms of our favored music in accordance with our own soul sound or note. Serene music or harmonious sound vibration is able to transform moods, supplement emotional stimulation, and enhance our sensitivity and also inspires our personality with feelings of love, beauty, resolution, and altruism. Uplifting and spiritual music can transport us to other realms of consciousness and tap our true inner Being, which makes us experience divine power and also helps us in our prayer and meditation. It brings harmony to the body, mind (human spirit), divine (spirit), balances and strengthens our auric field, and brings people, plants, and animals in harmony with ourselves and others.

---

[2] Today, Pythagoras is most commonly remembered for his mathematical theorem "the square of the hypotenuse of a right angled triangle is equal to the sum of the squares of the other two sides". He also taught that all the activities and revolutions of the seven planetary bodies, with their own special notes, create musical harmony, which he called the "music of the spheres" ("when the morning stars sang together" – Job 38:7). Others after him said that this music can also be heard in the microcosmic universe of atoms, when the spinning electrons make waves as they rush through the aether and encircle the nucleus.

Pythagoras, as the master of scientific numerology, taught that there are nine basic numbers, one through nine. Each number has its own vibration energy field and attracts certain vibration forces which surround and pass through the individual with that numerical essence. Each letter of the alphabet has a number value based on its position in the alphabet. All numbers beyond nine can be reduced to a single digit.

1	2	3	4	5	6	7	8	9
A	B	C	D	E	F	G	H	I
J	K	L	M	N	O	P	Q	R
S	T	U	V	W	X	Y	Z	

An important number is that of [1]destiny or fate number, which is bestowed upon you according to the date of your birth. That date, unlike names, cannot be changed, and its vibrations and powers will influence your whole life. This number is determined by adding together the number value of your month, day, and year of birth and lessen to a single number. This number then represents your inborn characteristics and latent talent. By adding your day and month of birth to any given year of your life, you can find your personal year number.

One's [2]full name is the personality that the world sees and judges. Its number tells you in what manner you will express yourself, and it also can tell you a great deal about yourself and of those individuals you associate with and with whom you are in partnership. Changes of names usually influence individual lives and circumstances. [3]A married woman, for example, who has taken on the characteristics of her husband by taking on the vibrations of his surname, should get rid of the vibrations of his name when she wants a divorce by using her maiden name. When we change our names, give ourselves pen names, use, or are given nicknames (adopted names), we change the energy, values, vibration, and thought forms of that name. Even a simple change of spelling and sounding alters the name in its numerical value.

NOTE: Many practioners of the art of numerology also use the master numbers 11 and 22 in their fullness instead of reducing them to the single digits of 2 and 4. The master numbers are considered on a higher plan than single digit numbers. The master numbers offer more opportunities for ex-

---

[1] Some numerologists call it the path of life number, or the life lesson number, how to develop, and what one should do with their lives, and the reason one is born.

[2] Those people whom have the same names are not necessarily the same in vibration because these expressions are also influenced by different birth dates and places of origin and also by the mental and spiritual status of parents, ancestors, etc.

[3] It is not easy for a married woman who has exchanged energies with her partner through sexual intimacy for a long time to lose her bond with her husband at all levels. They are, thus, quite attached or entangled to each other. Changing names can certainly help to separate from her spouse.

pression and, thus, demand more effort from individual beings. It brings its possessor great success or great failure. The number eleven means idealism, mysticism, charisma, revelation, spiritual vision, and Christ-like beings, as the name Jesus adds up to eleven as the true prophet and Messiah. However, the Christ image was misused and distorted by Napoleon and Adolf Hitler, when the latter tried to create a master race. Another eleven, named Benito (Mussolini), wanted to set up a new Roman Empire in Italy with himself as Emperor. They were the perverted images of Christ, the false prophets, seeking for power and self-glorification. The number twenty-two has the meanings of enlightened intellect, practical idealism, artistic genius, and labor for the progress of the human race. The name Buddha adds up to 22, meaning the enlightened one. People whom have the number 22 in their name often receive intuitive answers and help for the problems they encounter from seemingly nowhere.

Choosing the first name for a child is more important than many parents realize because one's true name is not just a label but represents the very essence of one's being. That name, which has its own vibration, can be called upon to find and draw the person towards oneself, either physically or psychically. When parents do not follow their intuition and a wrong name is chosen, the child may, later in life, choose the [1]middle name as the first name or a suitable nickname. He or she may also [2]change the name when it has served its purpose and a new name is called for. The name chosen should [3]harmonize with the last or family name in numbers or vibrations. In some societies, mothers may, at times, name the child (see Luke 1:59-60), while the father and priest(s) may also be partly or wholly involved. In the Catholic tradition, the child usually receives the name(s) of a saint(s) who also may bear some influence on the development of the child and more so when the name of the saint is called upon. The family or surname is the name of one's ancestors, which may also carry positive and negative karma, which the individual may inherit, also the good and bad qualities, and the level of the moral, mental, psychic, and spiritual development.

---

[1] As the first name is the most important, the middle or other names play a supporting role.

[2] Names may change when someone has undergone a spiritual birth. For example, Christ changed Simon's name (number 7) to that of Peter, which adds up to 1, which means rock.

[3] Nr. 1 completely harmonizes with 1 and 9; Nr. 2 with 2 and 8; Nr. 3 with 3 and 7; Nr. 4 with 4 and 6; Nr. 5 with 5; Nr. 6 with 6 and 4; Nr. 7 with 7 and 3; Nr. 8 with 8 and 2; Nr. 9 with 9 and 1.

The total [4]vowel numbers of a name represent the inner personality with its thoughts, desires, motivations, and ambitions, while the sum of the consonant numbers represents the outer personality, which is easily detected by others because he or she manifests openly and in a revealing way. The full name, including both vowels and consonants, is in numerology parlance called the expression. It tells you what you can most easily do with your life, and it also indicates the direction in which you should find your success and happiness. Thus, you can find your own personal number by adding the letters of the name by which you are usually known. However, one may go much deeper by adding with your name also your birthday number.

NOTE 1: A name is not only a label but also possesses a power. Those who call upon the name of Jesus Christ receive some of the spiritual power of that name, while others may use the name of a master or saint (whatever you perceive to be the highest), so that greater work can be done than using one's own name. Secular people may use the name of an organization, government agency, and others and act on behalf of that agency or state ("the power vested in me" to authorize a marriage contract, etc.) and find themselves in possession of great physical and psychological power.

NOTE 2: Some people believe that when they know at what particular rate a life form is vibrating that they have not only insight but also control over that being. It has its own key, and they possess that key.

REMARK: It may be interesting to know that when looking in a Bible dictionary, many names and places in the Bible have a deeper meaning.

The Character and Influence of Numbers in our Daily Life

1) Number one is an energetic, active, and masculine number. It belongs to a strong-willed person who displays courage and ambition, a pioneer who strikes out alone. It stands for boldness, fearlessness, independence, individuality, and strength. They are, however, more imitative than creative and do hardly recognize other things beyond their own. It is a disposition used by directors and bosses in many enterprises.

2) As number one is masculine, number two is more like a feminine and receptive number. It seeks a balance between opposing forces and,

---

[4] The vowel sounds contain the real life-giving power and were considered sacred by ancient societies because sound is a vibration which can easily influence other sounds which may or may not be represented by numbers. The Hebrew alphabet only contains consonants. The Hebrews did not use the name of God because they were afraid that it could evoke forces which would overwhelm them.

therefore, represents cooperation, partnership, and union. It is a kind, tolerant, and peace-loving number, and its influence is gentle, helpful, cultivated, and charming. It is a good vibration for people who love family and home life, doctors, peacemakers, diplomats, etc.

3) As number two represents peace and number one boldness, number three combines the qualities of the first two, and it is a symbol of expression, expansiveness, communication, and social interaction. It is also an extroverted, optimistic, light-hearted, and artistic number and draws others and inspires them to grow. It influences those whom are dancing, acting, speaking, singing, writing, painting, and also provides friendship and hospitality.

4) Number four is a practical number. It represents security, stability, discipline, organization, and it is the symbol of system, law, and order. It spends much of its energy in pursuit of material possessions and careers. It is also a number given to discussion, analysis, and risk-taking. The vibration of this number is suited for those whom are pursuing political and security professions, study of nature, store keepers, and people in trade and commerce.

5) The number five characterizes a vibration which is two-sided, or positive and negative in its nature, such as constructive and destructive, optimistic and pessimistic. It is also made up of physical and psychic elements. It summons an occupation that calls for adjustment, cooperation, and decision-making. It represents freedom, change, adventure, opportunities, resourcefulness, adaptability, speculation, and innovation.

6) The number six is much like number two, that it is also a kind and considerate number. However, its influence is more expanded in scope and desires to bring harmony, truth, and justice into its environment. It deals to some extent with inspiration and intuition and individuals that attend to their social responsibilities. We find them involved as caretakers, counselors, nurses, and other humanitarian workers. Artistic and domestic workers also work best with a six name.

7) The number seven has been recognized as a secret and sacred number. It is a number of the philosopher, religionist, and inventor. Its vibration lends itself to create a philosophy of life and to attempt to answer the questions of life and death. It is further described as: privacy, seclusion, and retreat, while its thinking is usually abstract,

introspective, and analytical. Many philosophers, teachers, and innovative thinkers come under its influence.

8) The eight is the scientific mental number. It is a vibration of a higher plan as a number four. It is that of enquiry, to know things, and also to accomplish what one has set out to do. It is initiative and creative in finding solutions and in exercising executive abilities. They are recognized as good administrators in their business or other enterprises. We may find many scientists, technicians, executives, bankers, professors, and teachers with an eight name.

9) As one is the genesis, and nine the ending of numbers, they are, therefore, much separated in their influences. The one represents individuality, while the nine is universal in its influence rather than personal. As numbers two and six represent responsibility to the family and others in society, the nine is bound to the world and its noble causes. As numbers three and six are artistic in their expressions, we find great artists, composers, writers, and also religious leaders in the nine vibrations. The "nines" express universal love, compassion, and generosity. They are persons of integrity, virtue, and understanding and behave in an ethical way in all their undertakings.

F. The Significance of Number Three, Seven, and Other Numbers

i. The [1]number three in the Bible

In Genesis chapter one, we read that after every "day", or period of creation, the Bible verse says, "And there was evening and there was morning." This suggests that everything was formed in the beginning or "evening", grew, ripened, or developed through the "night", and realized its completion, maturity, or perfection in the "morning".

It has been said that anything cannot be completely done or fulfilled until it happens three times or proceeds and progresses in three stadia, and that everything comes in 'threes'. If you see two things, you will see a third. For instance, when a positive and negative form come together, as that in a male or female (human, animal, or plant), a third object is created.

The [2]number three is used throughout the Old and New Testaments. For example, there are three orders of archangels: Lucifer, Gabriel, and Michael. Adam had three sons: Cain, Abel, and Seth; Noah had three sons: Shem, Ham, and Japheth. Job had three friends, and there were three kings: Saul, David, and Solomon; Jesus had three chief disciples: Peter, James, and John.

The ark of Noah had three decks (Gen. 6:16), and after the flood, Noah [3]sent forth three flights of doves (Gen. 8:8-12). Abraham offered three kinds of sacrifices: pigeon, ram, and heifer (Gen. 15:9), and three

---

[1] Much has been written about the meaning of numbers, in sacred and secular literature. The author here merely strives to put some order in the wealth of available information.

[2] Names in the Bible often have an inner meaning, and three names may sometimes mean the physical, emotional, and intellectual aspects of a particular person in leadership. Abraham means "Father of multitudes", Sarah "princess", Ishmael "God hears", Isaac "laughter", Jacob "supplanter", and Esau "hairy".

[3] Noah first sent forth a raven, which is a symbol of evil. Evil invaded humankind from the beginning and needs to be removed in stages.

611

angels visited Abraham (Gen. 18:2). It took [4]Abraham and his son Isaac [5]three days before reaching [6]Mount Moriah to offer a ram as a substitute for Isaac (Gen. 22:1-19). Jacob, the son of Isaac, at the advice of his mother, fled to [7]Haran because [8]Esau sought to kill Jacob, who took away his birthright and his blessing as eldest son (Gen. 26:33; 27:36). Jacob served his uncle Laban for three periods of seven years (Gen. 31:41) and left Haran in three days (Gen. 31:22). Jacob's beloved son Joseph was put in a pit by his jealous brothers (who he put later in jail for three days – Gen. 42:17 –) and was sold by the Medianites to Potiphar, an officer of Pharaoh (Gen. 39:20). In prison, he interpreted a dream of the chief butler, who saw a vine with three branches, which blossomed and ripened into grapes, which he gave to Pharaoh. Joseph told him that in three days he will be restored to his

---

[4] In order to become the Father of multitudes, Abram and Sarai had to play over the brother and sister relationship of Adam and Eve, which was invaded by satan. In Genesis 12:10-20, Abram and Sarai pretended to be brother and sister, but Pharaoh, in the role of satan, did not defile Sarai. This was later repeated in Gen. Ch.20 and by Isaac and Rebekah (Ch. 26). In order to receive the blessing, Abram was asked to perform an important symbolic act of cutting three sacrifices in two. This signifies that in order to restore Adam's family, they should first be divided into Cain and Abel factions and then be united with each other. Abram did not cut the births, and his descendants had to suffer in Egypt (Ch. 15). Abraham was later tested again to restore his lost faith by showing his willingness to offer his only son (Ch. 22). Because of his first failure, the second test became much heavier. In another example, when the Israelites later murmured against the Lord, they had to wander in the wilderness for forty years (Num. 14:34).

[5] It takes three days to truly arrive at a destination.

[6] Mount Moriah is the site where the dome of the rock is located, a shrine owned by Moslems, whom are descendants of Ishmael, son of Abraham. It is also the place where the temple of Solomon once stood, which was the first temple. That of Zerubbabel was the second, and that of Herodus was the third, which lasted only 90 years, from 20 B.C. to 70 A.D.

[7] On his way to Haran, Jacob laid his head on a stone (symbol of Truth). He had a dream of angels ascending and descending on a staircase that reached up to heaven (a connection was made between heaven and earth – Gen. 28:12; Jn. 1:51 –). A voice is heard, giving the same promise that was given to Abraham and Isaac "the land on which you lie I will give to you and to your descendants" (Gen. 28:13). Before reaching his destination, he stopped by a well, which had three flocks of sheep lying beside it (Gen. 29:2).

[8] Before Esau and Jacob were born, they were already struggling in their mother's womb, and the Lord told Rebekah that "two peoples born of you shall be divided --- the elder shall serve the younger" (Gen. 25:23). Esau, who was the first-born and was like Cain, was more interested in immediate physical fulfillment than in his birthright, which he easily sold to Jacob, his younger brother, who was like Abel (Gen. 25:29-34). Because satan invaded the family of Adam and Eve, he claimed the first-born. Jacob, with the help of his mother, did everything they could to take the blessing away from Esau, who was representing satan. Thus, Esau (Edom) represented the evil nature of the good and evil personality and Jacob the good part.

former position. However, the chief baker, who saw in his dream three baskets on his head from which the birds were eating, was hanged by Pharaoh in three days (Gen. 40:20-22).

Moses, who was the youngest of [1]three children, was hidden for three months as a baby (Ex. 2:2), and when he was forty years old, he fled Egypt and spent the second period of forty years in Midian, where he was molded in God's image. From there, he was called by God, who called Himself the God of Abraham, the God of Isaac, and the God of Jacob, to lead the Israelites out of bondage in Egypt through the desert to Canaan, "a land flowing with milk and honey" (Ex. 13:5). This will happen at the end of Moses' third period of forty years. Moses, who was the most humble man on earth (Num. 12:3), took with him Aaron, who was three years older (Ex. 7:7) and who was in possession of a rod, which bore buds, blossoms, and almonds (Num. 17:8). After the Egyptians experienced the ten calamities, which made a mockery of their [2]gods, including three days of darkness (Ex. 10:22), Pharaoh finally let them go for a three day journey into the wilderness to sacrifice to their God (Ex. 3:18; 5:3; 8:27; 12:31). The exodus began at night, and three days after the Passover, they [3]journeyed through the Red Sea (Reed Sea) after having taken with them their earned spoils of Egypt (Ex. 3:21, 22; 11:2, 3; 12:35-36). The Lord went before them in a pillar of cloud by day and by night in a pillar of fire (Ex. 13:21). The 600,000 men, besides women and children (Ex. 12:37), walked for three days in the wilderness of Shur (Ex. 15:22), found water in Marah, and encamped in Elim, where they found twelve springs of water and seventy palm trees (Ex. 15:27). From there, they passed through the wilderness of Sin, fought with the Amalekites, and prevailed whenever Aaron and Hur held up Moses' hands (Ex. 17:11-13), and arrived on Mount Sinai (Horeb) "on the third new moon" (Ex. 19:1). The people purified themselves, and the Lord appeared to them at the third day, amidst thunder, lightning, and thick clouds (Ex. 19:11, 15, 16) and imparted to Moses the Ten Commandments. He also gave the people

---

[1] Moses' sister Miriam was the eldest child of Amram and Jochebed.

[2] The Nile water, which was a god to the Egyptians, was being polluted, the cattle was being destroyed, including the sacred bull or calf (Ex. 32:4). The darkness was a direct blow at Ra, Egypt's sun god, and so was one of Egypt's lesser gods, the frog.

[3] It was very difficult at that time to take the direct route to Canaan by the sea coast, through the land of the Philistines (Ex. 13:17-18). This gateway was strongly guarded by the Egyptian army.

of Israel [1]other ordinances and [2]directions for the Tabernacle, which was covered with a goat's hair cloth, red leather and badger skin, and had three entrances (see p.38). After wandering in the wilderness for forty years (Josh. 5:6), [3]they crossed the Jordan River with Joshua as their leader in a miraculous way after they prepared themselves for three days (Josh. 1:11; 3:2), as they did when they crossed the Red Sea (Josh. 3:13; 4:23). Thus, with the great help of God, Canaan was conquered by three miracles: dividing the Jordan River, the fall of Jericho (Chapter six), and in the battle where "the sun stood still, and the moon stayed" (Josh. 10:13).

Here are some other Bible verses wherein number three plays a major role. In the time of the Judges, which was a government wherein God was the direct ruler (Theocracy), Samson, one of the last Judges, was betrayed by Delilah, his concubine. [4]She said to him, "How can you say, 'I love you' when your heart is not with me? You have mocked me these three times, and you have not told me wherein your great strength lies" (Judges 16:15). [5]Samuel, the last judge, priest, prophet, and founder of the monarchy, was called by the Lord when he was a child three times (1 Sam. 3:1-8). Thereafter, he chose Saul as the first king of Israel who later, with his three sons, died in a battle with the Philistines (1 Sam. 31:6). The second king David, whose three elder brothers were in Saul's army (1 Sam. 17:13), proved himself

---

[1] "Three times in the year you shall keep a feast to me" and "three times in the year shall all your males appear before the Lord God" (Ex. 23:14, 17).

[2] The branches of the lamp stand should be made of "three cups made like almonds, each with capital and flower" (Ex. 37:19).

[3] As the Red Sea and the Jordan were parted, it also happened when the prophets Elijah and Elisha needed to get to the other side of the Jordan. "Then Elijah took his mantle and rolled it up, and struck the water, and the water was parted" (2 Kings 2:8). The same feat was later performed by Elisha (2:14).

[4] A woman who wants sex may say, "If you really love me, you would do it" – "If you love me, prove it" – " Show me that you are a man" – " It is alright because we love each other" – "Why struggle any longer? Everybody is doing it."

[5] Hannah "called his name Samuel, for she said, 'I have asked him of the Lord'" (1 Sam. 1:20).

worthy when he killed the nine foot [1]Goliath with a stone in his forehead and who fell on his face. 1 Sam. 20:18-20 reported that Jonathan said to David, "Tomorrow is the new moon. When you have stayed away for three days, come down quickly and wait by the stone. I will shoot three arrows beside the stone." Later, David told his commanders Joab, Abishai, and Ittai to deal gently with Absalon his son, whose army was fighting against David's army. After his defeat, Absalon was caught up in the thick branches of a great oak. Joab took three darts and thrust them into the heart of Absalon, who was still alive and hanging from the oak (2 Sam. 18:5-14).

After [2]Solomon's kingdom was divided and invaded by foreign powers, the inhabitants of the Southern Kingdom were in exile for seventy years (Jer. 25:11; Daniel 9:2) in Babylon. Daniel's three friends Shadrach, Meshach, and Abednego, whom did not want to worship the golden image and gods (Dan. 3:18), were put in "the burning fiery furnace" but were rescued by the angel of the Lord. After the three writings on the wall – mene, tekel, and parsin, the kingdom of Belshazzar, king of Babylon, came into the hands of Darius, king of the Medes and Persians (Dan. 5:31). Darius set over his kingdom one hundred and twenty princes, and over these were three presidents, of which Daniel was the first. Because he was praying three times a day to his God and did not want to worship the king (Dan. 6:10), he was cast into the den of lions but was saved by the angel of the Lord, who "shut the lion's mouth" (Dan. 6:22).

NOTE 1: At the time of the Divided Kingdoms, Elijah told the people three times to pour water on the burned offering and the wood (1 Kings 18:33-35). The Lord said, "As my servant Isaiah has walked naked and barefoot for three years as a sign and a portent against Egypt and Ethiopia" (Isa. 20:3).

---

[1] Before David met Goliath the Philistine, he already killed lions and bears (1 Sam. 17:36). He killed Goliath with one of the five stones (which are ideas of Truth). By having faith in God and Truth as a weapon, no human armor is needed to kill the unprotected evil thinking of the personality of your opponent, who appears to be very powerful. David was not afraid of Goliath, like Joshua and Caleb were not afraid of the Canaanites, and people on God's side do not fear people who are on satan's side. In 2 Samuel 24:12-15, we read that God became angry when David takes an illegal census. God offers him three choices: "Shall three years of famine come to you in your land? Or will you flee three months before your foes while they pursue you? Or shall there be three days pestilence in your land?" David chose the pestilence, which claimed 70,000 men.

[2] In Chapter Three of 1 Kings, we see a demonstration of Solomon's wisdom when he judged who was the mother of the living child, when the other child, born three days later, died, by threatening to cut the living child in half.

NOTE 2: A good example that a three day fast can be very helpful is recorded in the Book of Esther 4:16, when Esther and all the Jews fasted for three days and, by doing so, saved the Jewish race of extinction.

After many Israelites returned from exile, which occurred in three stages, strict rules were imposed. They were not only required to abandon their foreign wives, but all their property would be forfeited, and they would be banned from the congregation if they did not assemble at Jerusalem within three days. (See Ezra Ch. 10.)

Many events in Jesus' life were related to the number three. For example, according to tradition, three wise men came to worship the child Jesus and offered Him three gifts (Matt. 2:9-12). When Jesus was twelve years old, He spent three days in the temple debating the Scriptures with the Jewish learned (Lk. 2:46). Before Jesus began His three years of public ministry, He went through a preparation and training period of thirty years. When He began His ministry, He experienced three temptations by satan and chose three chief disciples: Peter, James, and John, who went with Him to the mount of transfiguration (Matt. 17:1) and to the garden of Gethsemane. On the third day, Jesus was invited to a marriage at Cana (Jn. 2:11). There were three members in the family of Lazarus with whom Jesus was much involved: Mary, Martha, and Lazarus (Jn. 11:1-3), and He raised three persons, including Lazarus, from the dead. He said in Matthew 12:40, "For as Jonah was three days and three nights in the belly of the whale, so will the Son of Man be three days and three nights in the heart of the earth", and "Destroy this temple, and in three days, I will raise it up" (Jn. 2:19-21). Jesus prayed three times in Gethsemane to "let this cup pass from me". He was betrayed by Judas Iscariot (when satan entered into Judas – Lk. 22:3) for thirty pieces of silver (Matt. 26:14-16). Jesus was tried before three courts: Sanhedrin, Pilate, and Herod (Matt. 26:57-68; 27:1-25; Lk. 23:6-11). He was defended by Pilate three times (Lk. 23:22) and was denied three times by Peter (Mk. 14:66-72). Jesus was crucified with two robbers, "one on his right and one on his left" (Mk. 15:27), one who accepted Jesus and the other who reviled him (Lk. 23:39-43). There was an inscription placed on His cross written in three languages: Hebrew, Latin, and Greek: "Jesus of Nazareth, the King of the Jews" (Jn. 19:20). During the crucifixion, there was darkness over all the land from the sixth to the ninth hour

(Matt. 27:45), which was witnessed by three women (Matt. 27:55-56) and the three Mary's (Jn. 19:25). [1]He was raised on the third day (Lk. 24:7) and was met by three women (Mk. 16:1). Jesus appeared for the third time to His disciples (Jn. 21:14) and asked Peter three times if he loved Him, and if he did, he should feed His lambs and sheep (Jn. 21:15-17). Finally, He told His disciples, "Go therefore and make disciples of all nations, baptizing them in the name of the Father and of the Son and of the Holy Spirit" (Matt. 28:19).

NOTE: Job's three friends Eliphaz, Bildad, and Zophar seemed to think that all suffering is sent upon people as punishment for their wrongdoing. They represent the three aspects of Job's personality. They could not help Job much because their spiritual understanding was limited. Job is every man struggling self-righteousness to prove that his troubles are not his fault. Job's troubles, however, were brought on by satan, and he should, therefore, not blame God.

Peter was told three times by the Lord what is common or unclean, but cleansed by the Lord and to accept gentiles in his congregation. He was then led by three men to Cornelius, a centurion (Acts 10:9-16, 19, 28). John made a distinction of the threefold condition of the saints, as babies, young men, and fathers (1 Jn. 2:13).

The Damascus experience was an initiation for Apostle Paul when he was blind for three days (Acts 9:1-19). This story was retold in Acts 22 and 26. Paul recalled his suffering for the sake of Christ in 2 Cor. 11:25, "Three times I have been beaten with rods; once I was stoned. Three times I have been shipwrecked, a night and a day I have been adrift at sea.", "To keep me from being too elated ---, a thorn was given me in the flesh --- three times I besought the Lord about this, that it should leave me" (2 Cor. 12:7-8). In the same chapter, Paul also speaks of a "third heaven", and in 1 Cor. 13:13 he said that after faith and hope, love is the greatest of these three.

NOTE: Paul made three missionary journeys. The first journey lasted from 45 A.D. to 48 A.D., as it is told in Acts 13 and 14. The second journey lasted from 50 A.D. to 53 A.D., as reported in Acts 15 to 18. The third journey lasted from 54 A.D. to 57 A.D., as described in Acts 18 to 20. He was beheaded in Rome about 67 A.D.

The Eastern Orthodox Church in the office of Holy Baptism lets the priest say to the candidate as a catechumen, after making the sign of the

---

[1] Jesus died late in the afternoon on Friday and disappeared from His tomb on early Sunday morning. This was not a full three day period. It was a Jewish custom to count as a full day any part of the day.

cross three times upon the candidate, the three exorcisms, ordering the devil to leave this person. Then the priest asks three times, "Dost thou renounce satan and all his angels?" Each time the candidate says, "I do." Then the priest asks three times, "Dost thou unite thyself unto Christ?" After the answer is "Yes", the servant of God is then baptized in the name of the Father, and of the Son, and of the Holy Spirit.

We may divide world history in three periods: the ancient, medieval, and modern. Church history can also be separated into the Roman, Medieval, and Modern periods, wherein we find the three main divisions of Christianity: Roman Catholic, Greek Orthodox, and Protestant Churches.

Examples of Trinities in Religion:

The salvation of humankind is carried out by the Trinity: of God the Father, God the Son, and God the Holy Spirit. The Trinity is recognized in practically every religion under many names. The Egyptians of old worshipped Osiris, Isis, and Horus, while the Hindus show reference for Brahma the Creator, Vishnu the Preserver, and Shiva the Destroyer and Regenerator. The pre-Christian Greeks believed in the three rulers of the realms: Zeus, Poseidon, and Hades.

ii. Examples of number three in the natural and human worlds

One is always the beginning of anything and it is incomplete, while two is not completely formed and settled when it is only in the second stage. It is, thus, necessary for one to unite with its opposite half or two; then we have three, or completion. Thus, when one and two come together, or come into a relationship, they produce a third or complete condition.

Not only in the period of growth appears the number three, but also in other forms, such as in the three kingdoms: [1]mineral, vegetable, and animal. In the physical world, we find the building blocks of the universe in its atoms, which consist of protons, neutrons, and electrons. The three elements or states of matter are: solid, liquid, and gas. The earth consists of three layers: crust, rock layer, and (molten) core. The bottom of the sea can be divided in the continental shelves, slopes, and the deep floor. The three steps in the water cycle are: evaporation, condensation, and precipitation.

---

[1] Minerals have straight and angular lines; living things are usually curved.

In the vegetable kingdom, we notice that most plants have root, stem or trunk, and leaves. The Bible mentions that "the earth produces of itself, first the blade, then the ear, then the full grain in the ear" (Mk. 4:28). An almond tree put forth buds, produced blossoms, and bore ripe almonds (Num. 17:8).

In the growth of plants, we see three stages of development. The seed is first held in the pod of the mother plant, sheltered, and protected. After it falls, or is planted in fertile soil, it grows and struggles to maintain itself independent of the parent plant. The plant in maturity then produces new seeds from flowers or fruit and, thus, multiplies its kind on the earth.

NOTE 1: Lao-tse, the Chinese philosopher, said, "One has produced two, two has produced three." One of the commentators adds, "One has been divided into yin and yang, the latter two joined and, out of their junction came the third – harmony." Confucius, the Chinese teacher, declared that from the one proceeds two, from three comes all things. The Pythagorians say that no one becomes wise unless they view every problem as being triangular.

NOTE 2: Everything (or event) has a beginning, middle, and an end. A story has a beginning (to get the reader interested), the middle (the body of the story), and the end (to bring the writing to a successful conclusion). There is the speaker, the thing said, and the one spoken to.

NOTE 3: The conscious mind thinks of time in three categories – past, present, and future. There is yesterday, today, and tomorrow.

NOTE 4: Space is made up of length, breadth, and height.

NOTE 5: Breath links the physical body and the energy, or etheric body.

NOTE 6: Warmth, light, and power – love, wisdom, and will.
Emotion, intellect, and will – love (beauty), knowledge (truth), goodness (service).

The above principles of the growing process in the plant world are also true in the growth of animals and human bodies. However, unlike that of the physical creation, which automatically becomes full-grown, the development of the human spirit (and Divine Spirit) follows a different course. [1]Humans, from the beginning, are endowed by their Creator with the gift of creativity, the power or ability to create, which

---

[1] Human beings are more complex than, for example, single-celled creatures, a fish, a snake, or a dog and are, therefore, the most evolved life forms on planet earth.

capacity is considerably enhanced when they live a divine life instead of living the life of the personality. Thus, human beings not only imitate as animals do but are also able to [2]create something new. They also need to search for the inner and innermost Truth, apply it to their lives, so that they will grow to maturity, not only psychologically (morally and intellectually) but also spiritually in the image of God as co-creator. This can best be accomplished in an atmosphere of individual freedom and civil liberty, while being in the pursuit of true happiness. However, in creating ourselves, it does require conscious effort, and individuals may meet some resistance, especially in the birth and growth of his or her Divine Spirit. By overcoming the difficulties in the process of growth which other creatures do not have to face, humans become qualified Lords over all creation.

Animals pass through the stages of gestation, young and old, and their bodies (and that of humans) consist of three parts: head, trunk, and limbs, which latter consists of three parts, as do the fingers. The bodies of humans, in particular, consist of three major cavities: abdominal, thorax, and cranial. The eyes have three parts: upper (lid), eyeballs, and lower (lid). The ear consists of the outer, middle, and inner ear.

Human beings have been [3]classified as the caucasoid, mongoloid, and negroid races, or the white, yellow, and black. Humans become adults after passing through the stages of gestation and childhood. They marry and have children (man, woman, children – masculine, feminine, offspring). His or her overall existence is life in the mother's womb, life on earth, and eternal life in the spirit world. Humans usually wear three layers of clothing and eat three meals a day, which contain three main nutrients.

In their development, most human individuals in the West pass through grade school, high school, and college, or develop through lower, middle, and higher education. They may be involved in three main areas of life: economy, politics, and religion. In their growth, they usually take care of themselves first, then of spouse and children, and then of others.

---

[2] An example of using the gift of creativity is to make a plan or design of an idea and implement it in manifestation or creation. Creative people are known as creators, innovators, and inventors. Their creation is original, unique, and special. By using a creative medium, the idea of the artist results in a physical expression.

[3] ...based on certain inherited physical characteristics

The personality of an ordinary human being consists of the physical, emotional, and intellectual aspects. The physical self is surrounded by an aura which follows the contours of the body (the so-called health aura). The second aura, which is influenced by basic emotions, is wider as the former, while the third aura, which is formed by the radiation of the higher emotions and intellect, assumes more the oval shape and extends about two to three feet around the body.

Love can be expressed in words at the mental level, by feeling at the emotional level, and at the physical level with acts of kindness and affection, which does not always have to be sex. When it is expressed in all those ways, the relationship between a man and a woman is more balanced.

He or she may learn much about the body by being, for example, a physician, to know more about emotion by studying and practicing music and other strivings, and get acquainted intellectually by studying philosophy and other disciplines.

There are three divisions of mind: conscious (physical brain consciousness), subconscious (human spirit consciousness), and super-conscious (divine consciousness). When expressed in different words, they are the personal and self-conscious state, the subconscious and psychic state, and the transpersonal state. In short, body, soul or mind (human spirit), and Divine Spirit. They have created and are living in three different worlds: earth, intermediate space, and heaven. This three-ness state of consciousness is also experienced as: waking, dreaming, and deep sleep.

A human being has the body of an animal, the soul of a human personality, and the eternal Spirit.

The human body is the temple for spiritual action.
The human emotion is the temple for spiritual love.
The human mind is the temple for spiritual intelligence.

When centering on the body, the person is selfish and limited.
When centering on the human spirit, the person is less selfish and limited.
When centering on the Divine Spirit, the person is unselfish and unlimited.

The Garden of Eden can be compared to the physical body, the Tree of the Knowledge of good and evil to the human spirit, and the Tree of Life to the Divine Spirit.

Personality – outer knowledge
Individuality – inner knowledge
Universality – knowledge of God within

Communication in the natural world is done mainly by voice, in the spirit world by telepathy, and in the divine world chiefly by intuition.

Iron and brass can be compared to physical and etheric matter, whereas silver can be related to psychic substance, and gold to Divine Essence.

There are physical, mental, and spiritual laws or principles.

The bodies of humans are much the same. Human spirits are more different, while the Divine Spirit, Higher Self, or Soul is unique.

As the physical bodies of humans grow by taking physical food, the human spirits grow by absorbing mental food, while the Divine Spirits are in the process of becoming when they assimilate the Word of God (Truth) and also derive spiritual food from meditation, prayer, and reflecting on God.

iii. The number seven in the Bible

The number seven occurs in [1]Scripture more times than any other number. From the first book of the Bible through the last book, "seven" is truly an outstanding number, especially in the Book of Revelation. It must, therefore, have some meaning over and above its numerical value. As three is the number of completion and the triangle is its symbol, number four is more earthly and is represented by the square. "Seven" is the more mystical number and appears to stand for totality, wholeness, and completeness. "Seven" is thus used to indicate perfection, that which is finished or achieved in a completed time span or cycle.

---

[1] Scripture, that is the Old and New Testaments, is classified in seven groups:
Historical – Poetical – Prophetic – Gospels – Acts – Epistles - Revelation

A supreme example of number seven is the creation of the world in seven days or periods of time. "So God blessed the seventh day and hallowed it, because on it God rested from all his work which he had done in creation" (Gen. 2:3). "Six days you shall labor, and do all your work; but the seventh day is a sabbath to the Lord your God; in it you shall not do any work, --- for in six days the Lord made heaven and earth, --- and rested the seventh day" (Ex. 20:9-11). "So then, there remains a ¹sabbath rest for the people of God; for whoever enters God's rest also ceases from his labors as God did from his" (Heb. 4:9-10). "In the seventh month, on the first day of the month, you shall observe a day of solemn rest" (Lev. 23:24), and "the tenth day of this seventh month is the day of atonement" --- "and you shall do no work" (Lev. 23:27-28). "On the fifteenth day of this seventh month and for seven days is the feast of booths" (tabernacles) (Lev. 23:34), and the first and eighth day shall be of solemn rest (Lev. 23:39). Every seventh year was a sabbatic year. The land was to lie fallow, and enough will be produced in the sixth year to carry over (Ex. 23:10-11; Lev. 25:4, 20, 21). See also Ex. 16:22-24 concerning gathering twice as much manna on the sixth day. Every sabbatic year was followed by a jubilee year of fifty years (Lev. 25:8-12). ²Pentecost, also called the feast of weeks, of harvest, or of first fruits, was kept on the fiftieth day.

NOTE 1: Groups of seven are usually derived from three primary things. For example, from the three primary colors: red, green, and blue, seven colors are produced.

NOTE 2: The number "seven" is a cardinal number and was recognized in ancient times as a mystic, sacred number.

NOTE 3: In Leviticus, we read, "If a woman conceives, and bears a male child, then she shall be unclean seven days --- and on the eighth day the flesh of his foreskin shall be circumcised" (Lev. 12:2-3). We also read in the same book, "If you walk in my statutes and observe my commandments and do them, then I will give you your rain; in their seasons, and the land shall yield its increase --- but if you will not hearken to me --- in spite of this (punishment), then I will chastise you again sevenfold for your sins" (Lev. 26:3, 4, 14, 18).

---

¹ The sabbath day of rest is a day of quiet reflection and withdrawal from the work-a-day world.

² 1) "A Christian festival occurring the seventh Sunday after Easter and commemorating the descent of the Holy Ghost upon the Apostles. 2) A Jewish festival occurring fifty days after the first day of Passover." (Readers Digest Dictionary)

After [1]Cain, the son of Adam and Eve, slew his younger brother Abel, he said to the Lord, "My punishment is greater than I can bear --- I shall be a fugitive and a wanderer on the earth, and whoever finds me will slay me. Then the Lord said to him, 'not so! If anyone slays Cain, vengeance shall be taken on him sevenfold'" (Gen. 4:13-15). Lamech, a descendant of Cain, said to his wives, "I have slain a man for wounding me --- if Cain is avenged sevenfold, truly Lamech seventy-sevenfold" (Gen. 4:23-24). Later, Jesus said to Peter that he should [2]forgive his brother "seventy times seven" (Matt. 18:21, 22).

Nine generations after Adam, Noah was born. Because the earth was corrupt and filled with violence, the Lord told Noah to take into the ark seven pairs of clean animals, and only one pair of the others (Gen. 6:19-21; 7:2). "For in seven days I will send rain upon the earth forty days and forty nights", to blot out every living thing (Gen. 7:4). In the seventh month, the ark came to rest upon the mountains of Ararat. Noah then sent forth three times, every seven days, a dove, to see if the waters had subsided from the earth (Gen. 8:8-12).

Nine generations after Noah's son Shem, Abram was born. He was called by God to leave Haran and to be led to an unknown destination. When he arrived in the land of Canaan, God gave him a great [3]blessing (Gen. 12:1-7). Thereafter, he was also blessed by [4]Melchizedek, king of Salem (Jerusalem). Fourteen years after Ishmael was born, Isaac

---

[1] As Lucifer, the first-born, did not want to love and accept Adam as God loved him, Cain, who inherited to an extreme degree the satanic nature of the archangel Lucifer, did not want to love Abel. As later, the brothers of Joseph could not, or rather, did not want to love Joseph, who was closer to God.
(He who rows his brother across the stream gets there also.)

[2] This is a forgiveness that is unlimited and complete, by having no longer any resentment.

[3] This blessing was also given in Bethel (Gen. 13:14-17) and in Hebron (Gen. 15:5, 18; 17:1-8). This promise was later extended to Isaac (Gen. 26:3, 4) and to Jacob (Gen. 28:13, 14; 35:11, 12). Abraham, Isaac, and Jacob are like one person having one mission. Therefore, He is the God of Abraham, Isaac, and Jacob. They not only inherited the land of Canaan and became a great nation, but "by you and your descendants shall all the families of the earth bless themselves" (Gen. 28:14).

[4] Genesis 14:18-20 reports that he was the priest of God Most High, and he brought out bread and wine. Abram gave him a tenth of everything. (See also Heb. 5, 6 ,7; Ps. 110).

came in the world (Gen. 16:16; 21:5), when Sarah, Abraham's wife, was [1]very old. In Genesis 17:10, 12, God degreed that "Every male among you shall be circumcised --- He that is eight days old" (after a period of seven days has past). Later, Abraham gave away seven ewe lambs to Abimelech as a sign of a covenant concerning a well, which Abraham dug (Gen. 21:25-32).

Jacob, the grandson of Abraham, at the advice of his father Isaac, traveled to Haran to take a wife from one of the daughters of Laban, his mother's brother (Gen. 28:1-2). When he saw Rachel, he said to Laban, "I will serve you seven years for her." "So Jacob served seven years for Rachel, and they seemed to him but a few days because of the love he had for her" (Gen. 29:20). However, being deceived by his uncle, he had to serve another seven years for Laban's older daughter Leah, before he could claim Rachel as his wife. After Laban was told that Jacob had fled, he pursued him for seven days, but God told him in a dream, "take heed that you say not a word to Jacob, either good or bad" (Gen. 31:22). On his way back to Canaan, Jacob wrestled with an angel the whole night and received the name "Israel" (Gen. 32:28). He then proceeded with his household to meet Esau, from whom he took away his birthright and blessing. "For he thought, 'I may appease him with the present that goes before me, and afterwards I shall see his face; perhaps he will accept me.'" He then bowed seven times toward Esau and was willing to give him all his possessions. "But Esau ran to meet him and embraced him" (Gen. 33:4).

After Joseph, Jacob's favored son, was [2]ill-treated by his brothers and was sold to the captain of Pharaoh's guard, he became successful in all that he did, because the Lord was with him. This was also witnessed by his Egyptian master (Gen. 39:2). After being falsely accused by his master's wife of rape and put in prison, he was asked to interpret a dream Pharaoh had. The latter dreamed that he was standing by the Nile and saw come up out of the river seven fat cows, and after them seven thin cows, which later devoured the fat ones, but stayed as

---

[1] There are other examples in the Bible of women whom have been barren for a long time and of conceiving and bearing children in their old age. Samson was born of a woman who had been barren for a long time, and so was Rachel, who gave birth to Joseph, and Hannah, who blessed the world with Samuel. Elizabeth, the mother of John the Baptist, bore him in her old age. Mary, the Mother of Jesus, was born of a woman (Anna) who was old and stricken in years, and had been barren all her life. (See "The Gospel of Mary". – Apoc.)

[2] The brothers of Joseph regretted having sold Joseph by saying, "In truth we are guilty concerning our brother, in that we saw the distress of his soul, when he besought us and we would not listen; therefore is this distress come upon us" (Gen. 42:21).

bony as before. Pharaoh dreamed again and saw seven good ears of corn on one stalk. This was followed by seven poorly dried ears which sprang up after them and swallowed up the full ears. Joseph said to Pharaoh that the seven good cows and ears represent seven years of plenty, followed by the seven lean cows and empty ears which are seven years of famine. Because of the right interpretation and because in him was the Spirit of God, Joseph became the governor over all the land of Egypt (Gen. 41:38-45). And, as it was predicted in his dream, his family bowed before him (Gen. 37:5-11; 42:6). Thereafter, Joseph died, and his bones were taken back to Canaan (Gen. 50:25-26; Ex. 13:19).

Moses, the baby son of Hebrew slaves, was [1]rescued by Pharaoh's daughter when he was floating in a basket in the Nile River and was raised up as a prince of Egypt. However, after he killed an Egyptian who was beating a Hebrew, he had to escape and came into Median. Moses sat down by a well and helped the [2]seven daughters of the priest of Median by driving away the shepherds whom did not want them to draw water from their well to water their father's flock (Ex. Ch. 2). After being in Median for forty years, he met God at Horeb, "the mountain of God", who called Himself "I AM WHO I AM", or "I WILL BE WHAT I WILL BE", and was told that [3]God would come down (Ex. 3:8) to deliver the people of Israel "out of the hand of the Egyptians" and to bring them to "a land flowing with milk and honey" (Ex. Ch. 3). During their escape from Egypt, they put lambs' blood on their doorposts – so that the Lord would Pass Over – and ate unleavened bread for seven days, which rite should later be observed in the first month on the fourteenth to the twenty-first day of the month (Ex. 12:18). Because the Lord slew all the first-born among the Egyptians, all the first-born among the people of Israel of man and beast shall be consecrated or redeemed (Ex. Ch. 13). On their way to the land of Canaan, they reached Mount Sinai and received the Ten Commandments, of which the seventh says, "You shall not commit

---

[1] The daughter of Pharaoh named the child "Moses" "because I drew him out of the water" (Ex. 2:10).

[2] Moses married one of the seven daughters, Zipporah, and his son was called Gershom, which means "I have been a sojourner in a foreign land" (Ex. 2:22).

[3] This probably means that God would work directly through Moses, as He could only be present as a spark in the people who were more evil than good. Moses, who was relatively good and did not hate evil as much as God does, could be more sympathetic with the people. He, therefore, had a tendency to defend them. See Exodus 32:11-14, as Abraham did before in Genesis 18:23-32.

adultery" (Ex. 20:14; Deut. 5:18). One of the [1]ordinances says, "When you buy a Hebrew slave, he shall serve six years, and in the seventh he shall go out free, for nothing" (Ex. 21:2). At the seventh day, Moses received instructions for the tabernacle. For Moses and the people, "the appearance of the glory of the Lord was like a devouring fire" (Ex. 24:16-17). This tabernacle consisted of seven parts: 1) the Gate (surrender), 2) Altar (forgiveness), 3) Laver (cleansing), 4) Lamp stand – a seven branched candlestick (communication), 5) Bread (reading the Word of God), 6) Altar of Incense (prayer), and 7) Ark (contact with God). [2]Throughout their journey in the desert, "the Lord went before them by day in a pillar of cloud" and "by night in a pillar of fire" (Ex. 13:21, 22; 40:36-38).

The great number of Israelites, whom were approaching Canaan and came in the sight of Jericho, struck fear in the hearts of the people of Moab. They asked Balaam, a man of God, to curse the people for them (Num. 22:1-6). Balaam asked Balak, king of Moab, to build seven altars and sacrifice seven bulls and seven rams (Num. Ch. 23). However, Balaam could only bless the people of Israel (Num. 24:10).

NOTE 1: More ordinances: as described in Leviticus Ch. 4, if a priest or congregation commits a sin, they should offer a young bull without blemish, lay his or their hands on the bull, and kill it and sprinkle its blood seven times in front of the veil of the Tabernacle. Leviticus 19:28 degreed, "You shall not make any cuttings in your flesh on account of the dead or tattoo any marks upon you: I am the Lord." A priest "shall take to wife a virgin of his own people, that he may not profane his children among his people" (Lev. 21:14-15). When you reap a harvest, you shall bring the sheaf of the first fruits of your harvest to the priest (Lev. 23:10).

NOTE 2: Exodus 21:23-24 says, A person who does harm to another shall give "life for life, hand for hand", etc. This law of sowing and reaping, or the law of karma, is shown in many places in the Bible. For example, Jacob, who beguiled Esau, had to send presents to him in order to unite (Gen. 32:20). The brothers of Joseph, whom mistreated the latter, said that distress has come upon us (Gen. 42:21). The Egyptians easily gave away their jewelry to the Israelites, whom had labored for years without wages (Ex. 12:35-36). Adonibezek, who cut off the thumbs of his enemies, said, "As I have done so God has requested me" (Judges 1:7). Abimelech, who killed 70 of his brothers, was crushed by a woman with a millstone (Judges 9:53).

---

[1] In Colonial times, many people came to the United States under an indenture contract, binding one party into the service of another for a specified term, usually seven years.

[2] See Note 3.

NOTE 3: Because the Israelites were so physical and materialistic minded, they needed a visible sign every day that God, besides Moses, was leading them. But even then, when Moses was delayed in coming down from the mountain, they rebelled against God by making a golden calf and scheming to return back to Egypt (see Ex. Ch. 32). This faithlessness was later demonstrated again and again after their leader died. See, for example, Judges 2:10-11; 4:1; 8:33; 10:6; 13:1. However, when the people grow psychically and spiritually, they are able to sense the Presence of God, especially when their Parental nature is expressed by the Universal Christ and the Holy Spirit.

After the people of Israel crossed the river Jordan and came into the promised land of Canaan, they captured the city of Jericho when the armed men and seven priests blowing seven trumpets marched before the ark, around the city six times. On the seventh day, they all marched around the city seven times. At the sign of Joshua, they all "shouted", and the walls of the city crumbled (Joshua Ch. 6).

[1]In the time of the Judges, "The people of Israel did what was evil in the sight of the Lord; and the Lord gave them into the hand of Midian seven years" (Judges 6 :1), and were delivered out of the hand of Midian by Gideon (Judges 8:22). In Judges Chapter 13, we read that because the people did again evil, God gave them into the hand of the Philistines for forty years. Samson, who was to deliver them, chose a Philistine wife who gave away the answer of the riddle to the Philistines at the seventh day (Judges Ch. 14). Right thereafter, another Philistine woman called Delilah seduced Samson to tell her the secret of his great strength. She then let a man shave off the seven locks of his head, while Samson was sleeping upon her knees. His strength left him, and the Philistines seized him and gouged out his eyes (Judges Ch. 16).

Because David caused Uriah, the husband of Bathsheba, to be killed at the battlefield so that he could marry her, the Lord forgave David's sin and he did not die, but their first child died on the seventh day (see 2 Sam. Ch. 11-12). After David fought a seven year war with [2]Saul's son Ish-bosheth, David became king over all of Israel, and Jerusalem became its capital. "At Hebron he reigned over Judah seven years and

---

[1] In the Book of Judges Chapters three to sixteen are described seven apostasies, seven servitudes, and seven deliverances.

[2] After Saul and his three sons were killed, the Philistines fastened their bodies to the wall of Beth-shan. But when the people of Jabeshgilead found out what the Philistines had done, they took the bodies from the wall, burned them, and buried their bones under a tree, and fasted for seven days (1 Sam. 31:8-13).

six months; and at Jerusalem he reigned over all Israel and Judah thirty-three years" (2 Sam. 5:5).

It is reported in 1 Kings 6:38 that it took seven years to build the temple of Solomon. After its completion, Solomon held a feast for seven days (1 Kings 8:65).

> "Now King Solomon loved many foreign women --- the Lord had said to the people of Israel, 'You shall not enter into marriage with them, neither shall they with you, for surely they will turn away your heart after their gods' ; Solomon clung to these in love. He had seven hundred wives, princesses, and three hundred concubines; and his wives turned away his heart. For when Solomon was old, his wives turned away his heart after other gods; and his heart was not wholly true to the Lord his God, as was the heart of David his father" (1 Kings 11:1-4). The Lord said, "I will surely tear the kingdom from you" (1 Kings 11:11). After the death of Solomon, the Kingdom was divided into the Northern Kingdom of Israel and the Southern Kingdom, Judah.

During the worst period of reign in the Northern Kingdom, when Ahab and Jezebel were their king and queen, Elijah was sent by God to stamp out baalism. During that time, Elijah asked God for rain. Seven times his servant went to look. Then the answer came, a little cloud appeared, and quickly grew until "the heavens grew black with clouds and wind, and there was great rain" (1 Kings 18:41-45). Later, Elijah anointed Elisha to be his successor (his mantle fell on Elisha) to save the Northern Kingdom (1 Kings 19:16-21). In 2 Kings 5:1-27, we read that Elisha told Naaman to bathe seven times in the river Jordan, and when he had washed in the Jordan seven times, his flesh was restored.

Because Daniel's three friends refused to worship the image of Nebuchadnezzar, they were thrown into a furnace which was heated seven times more than normal, but the three were not even touched by the fire, "no smell of fire had come upon them" (Dan. 3:19, 27). Daniel then interpreted a dream which Nebuchadnezzar had that "his lot be with the beasts of the field, till seven times pass over him" --- "till you have learned that the Most High rules the kingdom of men and gives it to whom he will" (Dan. 4:23-33).

NOTE 1: Solomon, in his later life, became not only prideful – see what I have done – but also began to worship the idols of his many foreign women, and caused all the people of Israel to become more subject to evil powers. This will also happen to a church leader when the latter is involved in wrongdoings, especially of a sexual nature. Then all the members of the church have to suffer. Solomon repented in his Proverbs. He said a thief will pay sevenfold, but he who commits adultery destroys himself (Prov. 6:30-33). See also 1 Cor. 10:8.

NOTE 2: The raising of the dead happened in the Bible seven times: by Elijah (the widow's son – 1 Kings 17); Elisha (the shunammite's son – 2 Kings 4); Jesus (Jairus' daughter – Mk. 5; son of a widow – Lk. 7; Lazarus – Jn. 11); Peter (Tabitha – Acts 9); Paul (Eutychus – Acts 20).

Joseph the father of Jesus was a carpenter and the head of a family of at least seven children (Matt. 13:55, 56; Mk. 6:3), of which Jesus was the eldest.

The seven stages of the life of Jesus are: His Birth – Baptism – Suffering – Crucifixion – Resurrection – Ascension – Judgment.

Jesus taught His disciples how to say the seven sayings of our Lord's Prayer, the heart of the Christian belief (Matt. 6:9-13).

In His healing, Jesus cast out seven demons from "Mary, called Magdalene" (Lk. 8:2).

In Mark 12:18-25 we read, "And Sadducees came to him, who say that there is no Resurrection; and they asked him a question saying, 'teacher, Moses wrote for us that if a man's brother dies and leaves a wife, but leaves no child, his brother must take the wife, and raise up children for his brother. There were seven brothers; the first took a wife, and when he died left no children; and the second took her, and died, leaving no children; and the third likewise; and the seven left no children. Last of all, the woman also died. In the Resurrection, whose wife will she be? For the seven had her as wife."

"Jesus said to them, 'Is not this why you are wrong, that you know neither the scriptures nor the power of God? For when they rise from the dead, they neither marry nor are given in marriage, but are like angels in heaven.'"

There are 14 Stations of the Cross:
1) His condemnation to death
2) Bearing the cross
3) Jesus falls
4) Jesus meets His Mother
5) Jesus is aided by Simon
6) Veronica wipes Jesus' face
7) Jesus falls again
8) Jesus comforts the women of Jerusalem

9) Jesus falls for the third time
10) Jesus is stripped
11) Jesus is placed on the cross
12) Jesus dies
13) Jesus is taken down from the cross
14) Jesus is placed in His tomb

During the time that Jesus was on the cross, He spoke seven sayings.

In Acts 6:6, the disciples choose among themselves "seven men of good repute" to serve for the physical well being of widows, while others could continue preaching the Word of God.

In Scholastic thought, the seven gifts of the Holy Spirit are: Wisdom, Understanding, Counsel, Fortitude, Knowledge, Piety, and the Fear of God.

The seven deadly sins in the listing of Gregory the Great are: pride, envy, anger, dejection, avarice, gluttony, and lust.

The Catholics, whose seat is on the Seven Hills of Rome, speak of seven Sacraments.

There were seven major crusades between 1095 and 1291 A.D

Scofield's scheme of seven dispensations (when God deals differently) are: Innocence (before the fall); Conscience (from the fall to Noah); Human Government (from Noah to Abraham); Promise (from Abraham to Moses); Law (Moses to Christ); Grace (the Church Age); the Kingdom (the Millennium).

iv. The number seven in the Book of Revelation

As literal and symbolic numbers can be found almost everywhere throughout the Bible, they really come into their own in the Book of Revelation. The number seven occurs more than fifty times. For example: Seven letters to seven churches (Ch. 1-3). [1]Seven spirits (1:4). Seven golden lamp stands (1:12, 20). Seven stars (1:16, 20).

---

[1] Some religions believe that those "Seven spirits" were the seven archangels who were given jurisdiction over the seven churches. Non-canonical Hebrew manuscripts mention seven archangels and other orders of angels. The living creatures around the throne are also angels which, like human spirits and unlike physical beings, are able to sense things from all directions (Rev. 4:6-8). Those living creatures are identified in Ezekiel 10:20 as Cherubim. Each cherub has four faces, that of a man, lion, ox, and eagle.

Seven angels (1:20). Seven seals and seven trumpets (Ch. 4-11). Seven torches of fire (4:5). [2]A lamb with seven horns and seven eyes (5:6). Seven thunders (10:3, 4). A great red dragon with seven heads and seven diadems upon his head (12:1). A beast with seven heads (13:1). Seven plagues or seven golden bowls of wrath (Ch. 15, 16). A scarlet beast with seven heads (17:3, 7), which are seven mountains (17:9) and also seven kings (17:10).

As indicated in Revelation 1:1-2, God revealed the Book of Revelation through Jesus Christ, by an angel to John, the last surviving apostle, who "was on the island called Patmos" (Rev. 1:9).

The entire Book of Revelation is addressed directly to the seven churches in Asia Minor, to comfort them and to prepare them for the terrifying persecution they will have to endure. Not only the second but also the third persecution of Emperor Trajan in 98 A.D. was soon to be upon them. Those visions of John were also meant for all true individual Christians and churches, whom will be oppressed and harassed (like their master) until the time of Christ's Second Coming (Rev. 19:11). To assure them of the ultimate victory of Christ over everyone who rises up against Him and his saints. However, those Revelations were also given for the purpose of straightening out or reforming those seven churches (and others) who were beginning to show signs of internal persecution or corruption. Needless to say, the same kind of hostilities and oppressions without and within we find in churches and groups in the past and religious societies today.

NOTE 1: According to traditions, John was banished to the rocky island of Patmos during the second Imperial persecution by emperor Domitan in 95 A.D. The first persecution happened in 64-67 A.D. under Emperor Nero, when multitudes of Christians were killed or thrown to wild beasts, including Peter and Paul. Besides the Roman persecutions, many true Christians have died in the time of the Inquisition, Reformation, under the Communist regime, and militant non-Christian religions. The Revelation was thus especially given to those who suffered persecution and martyrdom to give them endurance, faith, and hope.

NOTE 2: The Book of Revelation is a further explanation of the prophecy which Jesus gave in Matthew 24, Mark 13, and Luke 21 of things to come. For example, the opening of the seals parallels the events in the Gospels: 1) false prophets, 2) great wars, 3) famine, 4) pestilence, 5) great tribulation, 6) heavenly signs, 7) Second Coming. The language is much like those prophecies and is also saturated with expressions found in Daniel and Ezekiel.

---

[2] This means that the Lord is all-powerful and wise.

NOTE 3: When Christ opened the first seal (Rev. 6:1), a white horse and its rider with a bow but no arrows appeared. Some people say that the rider was spreading anti-biblical and anti-Christian thoughts, using the white horse (science and other means) as its vehicle.

NOTE 4: The 144,000 (and more) saints or servants of God are exempt from the wrath of judgment, like that of the 10 plagues at the time of Moses, having the seal of God upon their foreheads (being initiated). See Rev. 7-9.

NOTE 5: Revelation 13:11 mentions a beast rising (growing) out of the earth, which had two horns like a lamb and spoke like a dragon (satan). This kind of a beast was not named in Daniel.

The Cosmic Christ or Glorified Christ, "The first and the last, and the living one" in chapter one, appeared among the seven lamp stands or seven churches and asked John who "was in the Spirit on the Lord's day" (Rev. 1:10), to write to the seven angels (seven stars in His right hand) of the churches (Ch. 2-3), to "see what is and what is to take place hereafter" (Rev. 1:19).

The messages were directed to the churches in Ephesus, Smyrna, Pergamum, Thyatira, Sardis, Philadelphia, and Laodicea. As Peter said in 1 Peter 4:17: judgment must begin with God's own household. To be effective, those communications must be accompanied by the witness of the Christ Spirit which dwells within the heart of the believer.

The church in Ephesus was great and powerful and was more good than evil. It was orthodox and doctrinally sound, but their zeal for Christ was cooling off, and they no longer loved Christ as much as they did before. However, they, as a body, stood against the teaching of the [1]Nicolaitans, who professed to know Christ but taught that believers had the right to participate in immoral heathen practices.

The church in Smyrna was poor and good and was composed of the humbler classes of people. Although they had been a city which took pride in their worship of Rome as a psychic power, or Caesar-cult, they were now facing persecution and martyrdom of Rome. John says of

---

[1] According to the New International Dictionary of the Christian Church, Nicolaitans are followers of Nicolaus (Acts 6:5). They formed a sect in the early church at Ephesus and Pergamum and were condemned by John in Revelation 2:6, 15. They retained the pagan practices of idolatry and immorality, which were contrary to Christian thought and conduct. Their teachings are held in like manner to those of Balaam (Num. 24:1-25; 31:16).

them, "I know" --- "your poverty (but you are rich)" --- "Behold, the devil is about to throw some of you into prison" --- "Be faithful unto death, and I will give you the crown of life" (Rev. 2:9, 10).

The church in Pergamum was more evil than good. It was heretical but faithful to the name of Christ. Unlike the church in Ephesus, the leaders tolerated false teachers, the Nicolaitans in their midst, although the pastors did not participate. This caused the church to compromise with evil and be permissive to immorality and idolatry. Pergamum as the seat of emperor worship was called in Revelation 2:13 "satan's throne".

The church in Thyatira was in danger of becoming more evil than good. It was a church which was growing and busy for Christ but tolerated a woman called Jezebel. She claimed that God was giving her messages for the church and convinced many believers to adopt her evil lifestyle, that of idolatry and sexual indulgence. She was tolerated by liberal clergy as a fellow pastor, and her teaching was known as "the deep things of satan" (Rev. 2:24).

The church in Sardis was more evil than good and was powerful and wealthy. The church attracted those who became nominal or only in name Christians, but remained pagan in life while pretending to be spiritual by going through the motions of a church. However, the Lord had nothing to do with most of them, who were only seeking the pleasures of the world without any sacrifice by saying, "You have the name of being alive, and you are dead" (Rev. 3:1).

The church in Philadelphia was becoming good and refined through the persecution they had to face. They had little power and influence in the city and were considered a 'nobody'. The Jewish presence was very strong and hostile towards them and was called the "synagogue of satan" (Rev. 3:8). The members of the church were very faithful and kept His Word under trying circumstances. The Lord said to them, "I will keep you from the hour of trial", and "I am coming soon" (Rev. 3:10, 11).

The church in Laodicea was more evil in the sight of the Lord than any other church because they were lukewarm, neither hot nor cold. The Lord said to them, "I will spew you out of my mouth" (Rev. 3:16). This wealthy self-satisfied and self-righteous church believed that it could handle things without any help from the Lord. They were like the Pharasees of old, who were religious outwardly but full of impurity and sin inwardly (Mt. 23:27-28).

NOTE 1: The above-mentioned seven churches can also be compared to the sequence of time periods in the history of the Christian Church. Ephesus was the church of little children; Smyrna collected the writings of Christianity; Pergamum became the state church of the Roman Empire; Thyatira was the flickering light during the dark ages; Sardis was the militant church during the Reformation; Philadelphia was the evangelical church taking the Gospel of Jesus to the end of the earth; Laodicea is the church of today, wealthy, cold, half-hearted, and well established.

NOTE 2: Some of the liberal ministers of the church in Thyatira and other ministers are committing adultery towards women or men, especially when they are called away for all-paid church conferences. When they are preaching the Word, they are trying to hide their lustful attitudes, which may also be triggered by watching pornographic movies. However, they cannot help but gaze at women whom are sexually attractive. God is not able to express through those ministers, and the church members hardly get any spiritual food, that is, the Spirit-filled Word of God. Some of the church members, especially women, come to church in scanty outfits in order to get the attention of men, while the latter lustfully glances at responsive females whom are winking and blinking at them. Women preachers draw attention to their outer selves instead of God within themselves by dressing in a provocative way. The Bible Proverbs Chapters 5, 6, and 7 warn against loose women.

v. Examples of number seven in the physical world and other planes of life

Whenever we find a group of seven things or occurrences, we should always look for a group of three primary things or phenomena from which the seven things or incidents are derived, according to the septenary law.

The number seven is so universally used that there must be some reason for this in the fundamental arrangement of the natural world. It is an important number, and its frequencies of seven vibrate everywhere in life on earth. Seven is the number of perfection of form on all planes of manifestation, and the numerical key of seven lies at the root of evolution. Number seven is a key number by which are revealed and explained many of the mysteries of nature and life. It represents total completeness and wholeness and bringing to an end a cycle of life. In all religions of antiquity, the number seven is a sacred and mystical number and appears frequently in cosmologies, and it calls for a transition into another sphere.

Concerning one's body, there are seven visible orifices through which the indwelling ego or human spirit expresses itself – two eyes, two ears, two nostrils, and a mouth. There are seven layers of the human skin. Just as we have seven endocrine systems for secreting hormones, so we have seven vital force centers, which are linked with the glands of the systems.

Every seven years, we go through major cycles of change. Not only has every cell in our bodies been replaced, but we have also replaced old ideas and attitudes with new ones. Those changes go along with the seven levels of learning in grade school when many schools also employ a different teacher at every stage, with his or her unique character and way of teaching and, thus, contribute to the child's spectrum of learning.

*As mentioned before, when we look at the span of human life, we see dramatic changes which occur every seven years, from the day of birth until the time of our transition. From grade school to puberty, the arrival of generative power, to age twenty-one, when career and family choices are made, and the four times seven years when the mental form is more or less completed. Thus, each seventh year brings with it its unique set of challenges and learning, as well as a period of introspection and searching, at the junction between the cycles, especially in later life. At those "cups", hopes and dreams are evaluated against past progress, and physiological and psychological seeds are implanted for the next stage.

As the week of seven days is one of the four phases of the moon cycle of twenty-eight days, the number seven was held in great reference to the ancient Egyptians. They consecrated each day of the week to the sun, moon, and five planets.

> Sunday was sacred to the sun
> Monday was sacred to the moon
> Tuesday was sacred to Mars
> Wednesday was sacred to Mercury
> Thursday was sacred to Jupiter
> Friday was sacred to Venus
> Saturday was sacred to Saturn

---

* See Seven Stages of Development.

We may also compare the days of the week to the seven colors of the *rainbow. Monday is the color of red, as the beginning, the rising. More gentle is the orange color of Tuesday, changing over to the yellow of Wednesday. We then pause in the sphere of green of Thursday and the blue of Friday. Saturday stands in the sign of indigo, which is a mixture of dark red and dark blue, ending with violet for the seventh day of the week, or Sunday, which is a day of rest and contemplation.

The seven colors of the rainbow were compared to the seven heavens of Hindu and Judaic religion and also to the Babylonian Ziggurat (stepped pyramid), which were painted with the colors of the rainbow. The priest in climbing its stories symbolically reached the cosmic world of the gods.

NOTE 1: In other belief systems, the first seven planets in the earth's solar system were considered sacred because they not only influence events on earth but also serve the same function to the earth as the seven energy centers or transformers serve the physical body.

NOTE 2: The seven classical planets, with their own key note, symbolized the seven notes of the musical scale, and when circling around the sun, they create the music of the spheres.

Science tells us that though there are seven colors in the visible spectrum, there are only three primary colors. The seven colors are produced by the different combinations of the three.

The seven colors correspond to the seven notes or whole tones in the musical scale. Sounds that harmonize correspond with colors that harmonize, while discords in color correspond with discords in music. With every eight notes begins a new octave and is merely a repetition of the first note in Do – Re – Mi – Fa – Sol – La – Ti – Do, which may be likened to the seven rays or vibratory rates.

The number system of God is stamped upon all His works. We find that crystals consist of seven basic geometrical forms: cubic, rhombohedral, hexagonal, triclinic, monoclinic, trigonal, and orthorhombic. There are seven rows in the periodic table of elements.

---

* In the tradition of Mesopotamia, the rainbow was seen as a reminder of a bridge that once existed between heaven and earth.

From the point of view of humans, there are seven planes of consciousness. These are: mineral consciousness

vegetable consciousness

animal consciousness

human consciousness

soul consciousness

divine consciousness

God consciousness

The seven planes of our nature are: physical, emotional, mental, divine, intuitional, Christ consciousness, Universal consciousness. Each plane, in turn, is divided in seven sub-planes.

We may further say that there are seven root races, seven stars of the Great Bear, seven seas, seven dwarves, seven vowels of the Greek alphabet, Seven Wonders of the World, and seven guardian angels.

NOTE 1: The octave of light, from which the seven colors are derived, is the 49th octave. Seven times seven octaves of vibration create that which is light.

NOTE 2: The lyre, a small stringed instrument of the harp family, contains seven strings, each one representing a note of the musical scale.

vi. The significance of other numbers

The number one refers to the concept of the Creator in unmanifested form. It represents a beginning, a something that requires the opposite of itself in order to make itself manifest. As long as anyone or anything stands alone or remains alone, it is incomplete. It is, therefore, always searching for its other half, its opposite self.

The number two represents duality or polarity. When you have two, you have one plus its companion, its opposite, or affinity. This relationship must be of an opposite nature, or you would not have two, but one twice. It is through one and its opposite unit, or its associates, that we have the thing manifesting in its dual nature, both positive and negative.

[1]The number four usually stands for law and order, the physical realm, the earth, the square, and the cross. With the coming of Christ,

---

[1] See also Supplement II – M.

the horizontal line of the cross was raised from the solar plexus center to the heart center. Further, there are four tides in a day and night, the four elements of fire, earth, air, and water, and the cubes of crystallized salt.

Ezekiel had a vision of four living creatures. Each had four wings and four faces: the face of a man, of a lion, of an ox, and of an eagle (Ezekiel 1:5-11). There are also [2]four evangelists and four Gospels. The number forty in Scripture is an indication of a completed cycle of separation from things of the world in preparation for something better. For example, Othniel, Deborah, Barak, and Gideon judged Israel for forty years, while Ehud judged twice forty years. Joash the king of Judah reigned forty years.

The number five can be seen on human forms which have five fingers on each hand and five toes on every foot, and five senses.

The first five books of the Old Testament are called the books of the Law or Pentateuch: Genesis – Exodus – Leviticus – Numbers – Deuteronomy. There are also five books of the major prophets: Isaiah – Jeremiah – Lamentation – Ezekiel – Daniel; and the five books of Poetry and Wisdom. The five visions of Amos of the coming judgment of the Northern Kingdom (Amos 7:1 – 9:10). A large number of the measurements in the general construction of the Tabernacle are fives and a multiple of fives. It is said that number five is the number of redemption, as the Israelites had to pay five shekels each in order to redeem the first-born (Num. 3:46-51). Five is also the number of grace; David took five smooth stones from the brook and was depending on the unmerited favor (grace) of the Lord God (1 Sam. 17:40). Another wonderful act of grace was the feeding of the five thousand people with five loaves and two fish (Matt. 14:17-21). The parable of the five wise and five foolish virgins (Matt. 25:3), which latter did not take oil with them to create light (within themselves). Jesus was descended from the tribe of Judah (Heb. 7:14), who had five sons. When Jesus was crucified on one of the five hills in Jerusalem, he suffered from five wounds.

The number six is the number of humanity. Preparation for the emergence and destiny of humans had been made during the five days of creation (Gen. 1:27). As six is the generation cycle, it is also a

[2] The Bible often compares a person with a garden. The four rivers which nourished the Garden of Eden represent the continued teaching of Truth from God, which makes the lives of His children clean, vigorous, and fruitful.

working period ("Six days shalt thou labor and do all thy work" – Ex. 20:9). Six is, thus, the number of man or woman but also of imperfection (one minus seven), that is, as long as they live the life of the personality. Six in the evil sense is connected with *satan-centered love, when the evil part of the good and evil personality is fully in charge of one's life. It is the number of the human beast, that is, six hundred and sixty-six (666), who is completely one with satan (dragon) and his forces (Rev. 13:18).

"Noah was six hundred years old when the flood of waters came upon the earth" (Gen. 7:6). Pharaoh took six hundred picked chariots and pursued the people of Israel (Ex. 14:7-8). After their escape, they met God. "The glory of the Lord settled on Mount Sinai, and the cloud covered it six days" (Ex. 24:16). In the time of their exile in Babylon, the image of Nebuchadnezzar (Dan. 3:1-7) was set up to be worshipped. The image was six cubits broad and sixty cubits in height, and they played six kinds of musical instruments when people were called to worship the image.

Jesus' first miracle was to change six stone jars of water into wine at the wedding feast (Jn. 2:1-11). Later, He was crucified on the sixth day.

NOTE: Every snow flake that falls is different from every other snow flake – except that every snow flake has six sides or six points.

The number eight is the number of regeneration, resurrection, and new birth. It also means a new beginning and of starting a new life. However, not only in this world but also in the next or after world, by crossing over from earthly life to the spiritual plane. It is a number of infinity and eternity. ∞

There were eight people in the ark of Noah whom began a new life after the flood (1 Pet. 3:20). "Abraham circumcised his son Isaac when he was eight days old" (Gen. 21:4). David was the eighth son of Jesse (1 Sam. 17:12). In the Eastern Orthodox Church, a child receives

---

* Satan and all his fallen angels will not rest until the world has become his kingdom. His first lie was, "Did God (really) say" (Gen. 3:1). Since the fall of Adam and Eve, people have an almost compulsive desire for the forbidden. Those people whose lives are ruled by their evil self or satanic nature already belong to him. Those evil forces combined do everything in their power to damage and kill the born-again Souls of those whom belong to Christ. They, as evil spirits and male and female temple sluts, will invade the Body of Christ (church). The prostitutes are either sent by evil spirits or come on their own to tempt men and women.

his/her name on the eighth day of birth, following the old Jewish custom (Lk. 2:21).

NOTE: In order to liberate from the evil earthly existence, Buddhists are following the eightfold path. In music, the eighth note is the beginning of a new octave at a higher level. As a man's body has seven orifices, the woman has eight. It is through the eighth that a baby comes into the world.

The number nine refers to attainment and fulfillment and stands for a complete cycle of growth. The nine generations from Adam to Noah and from Noah to Abraham indicate stages of growth and development. Jesus spoke nine beatitudes in His sermon on the mount (Matt. 5:3-11), and Paul informed the "brethren" about nine gifts of the Spirit (1 Cor. 12:8-10).

NOTE: It usually takes nine months for a baby to fully mature in the mother's womb.

The number ten is completeness of order and wholeness of cycle. Ten is also a number of harmony, containing an equal number of odd and even numbers. It is also an accepted number of division. For example, the Ten Commandments, written on two tablets of stone, are divided into two sections, one showing our duty toward God and the other our duty towards humans. Ten virgins were divided in their outlook – five were wise and five were foolish. Ten curtains of the tabernacle were divided into two fives (Ex. Ch. 26).

Abram gave Melchizedek a tenth of everything (Gen. 14:20; Heb. 7:2). See also Gen. 28:22; Lev. 27:30; Num. 18:24; Deut. 12:17; 26:12; 1 Sam. 8:15; Neh. 10:38; Mal. 3:8. After Abram had dwelt ten years in the land of Canaan, he took the bond woman Hagar as his wife (Gen. 16:3). When Abram came in the sight of Sodom and Gomorrah, and at his request, God did not want to destroy the cities if only ten righteous people could be found (Gen. 18:20-32). His grandson Jacob was cheated by Laban his uncle, who changed his wages ten times (Gen. 31:7). One important purpose of the ten plagues was to separate Israel from Egypt. David's father Jesse said to David his son to take a measure of grain and ten loaves to his brothers and ten cheeses to their commander (1 Sam. 17:17-18). The kingdom of David's son Solomon, who did not keep the Lord's way, was divided into the Northern Kingdom Israel, which consisted of ten tribes, and the Southern Kingdom Judah, which consisted of two tribes (1 Kings 11:11-12). Daniel and his friends, who refused the King's rich food and wine, asked to be tested for ten days to see if the vegetable diet and water was better (Dan. 1:8-16). In the parable of the talents, more was given to him who multiplied his five talents to ten talents, from someone who did not multiply his talents (Matt. 25:14-29). The Book of Revelation 17:3-12 reported a vision of John when he saw a woman who was arrayed in purple and scarlet, who was drunk with the blood of the saints, sitting on a scarlet beast which had seven heads and ten horns. The ten horns are the ten kings who have not yet received royal power.

The number twelve, as used throughout the Bible, is the symbol of spiritual fulfillment and divine power or authority. It was promised by God in Genesis 17:20 that Abraham's oldest son Ishmael "shall be the father of twelve princes". The son of Abraham's second son Isaac, called Jacob, had twelve sons by Leah and Rachel and their maids Zilpah and Bilhah, whom became the foundation father of the twelve tribes of Israel (Gen. 35:22-27). Their characteristics and qualities were not only revealed by their names but also by Jacob at his deathbed in Genesis 49:1-28. Thus, the number twelve represents Jacob (Israel) and the church of the new Israel when Jesus chose His twelve disciples, who will be judging the twelve tribes of Israel (Matt. 19:28).

NOTE: The second major division of the Old Testament is the twelve books of history. The last twelve books of the Old Testament are the books of the minor prophets.

After the Israelites left Egypt, and on their way to Canaan, they encamped at Elim, where there were twelve springs of water (Ex. 15:27). After Moses met the Lord on the mountain and told the people all His Words, Moses built an altar and twelve pillars according to the twelve tribes of Israel (Ex. 24:4). There were twelve precious stones in Aaron's breast piece representing the twelve tribes of Israel (Ex. 39:8-21). When they reached the land of Canaan, the Lord said to Moses to send twelve men (a chosen leader of each tribe) to spy out the land of Canaan (Num. Ch. 13-14). After the Israelites crossed the Jordan, the Lord said to Joshua to let twelve men from the people (from each tribe a man) to take twelve stones from the river as a memorial of the miraculous crossing (Jos. 4:1-10).

In the Tabernacle of Moses was found a table with twelve loaves of bread (Lev. 24:5-6; II Chron. 4:19), and in the extended temple complex of Solomon was seen a "molten sea", which stood upon twelve oxen (1 Kings 7:23-25).

During the period of the Judges, a Levite found his concubine lying at the door of the house in which he was staying, raped and ravished by the Benjamites. He divided her in twelve pieces and sent those pieces throughout the territory of Israel (Judges 19:27-30).

At the time of the Divided Kingdoms, Elijah repaired and built a new altar with twelve stones (according to the number of the tribes) in order to defeat the prophets of Baal (1 Kings 18:31).

When Jesus was twelve years old, He was taken by His parents to the feast of Passover in Jerusalem (Lk. 2:41-42). When He was in His thirties, Jesus fed five thousand people with five loaves and two fish, which He divided. They then gathered up twelve baskets of leftovers (Mk. 5:38-41).

In the Book of Revelation, we find that the number twelve was used very often. A woman appeared, in John's vision, who had a crown of twelve stars (Rev. 12:1). The holy city of Jerusalem, which John saw, "had a great, high wall, with twelve gates, and at the gates twelve angels, and on the gates the names of the twelve tribes of the sons of Israel were inscribed" (Rev. 21:12), "The wall of the city had twelve foundations (which consisted of twelve precious stones), and on them were the twelve names of the twelve Apostles of the Lamb" (Rev. 21:14). "The twelve gates were twelve pearls" (Rev. 21:21), and "Through the middle of the street of the city; also on either side of the river, the tree of life with its twelve kinds of fruit" (Rev. 22:2).

NOTE 1: The city measured 12,000 stadia in every direction, and the wall is 144 cubits high. Revelation Chapter seven speaks of 144,000 saints whom were sealed on their foreheads, 12,000 of each tribe.

NOTE 2: The twelve gates of the holy city can also be compared to the twelve apertures of the human body, which has seven visible and five concealed openings.

NOTE 3: The traditional clock face has twelve divisions, which display the twelve hours of the day and night. The year is divided into twelve months, which correspond with the twelve signs of the zodiac. The twelve zodiac ages are of a little over 2000 years, making the Great Year of 26,000 years. The old English system of measurements had twelve inches to the foot.

NOTE 4: The number twenty-four is meaningful in many religions. The Jews believe that there are 24 prophets. Hindus say that there are 24 Avatars, while Buddhists assume that there are 24 Buddhas. The Bible mentions 24 elders around the throne (Rev. 4:4).

The number thirteen most likely originates from the thirteen lunar months or moons, which occur in every calendar year.

Thirteen has a deep esoteric significance in the seal of the United States as seen, for instance, on the back of a dollar bill. There are thirteen stars (which represent the thirteen original colonies), the thirteen arrows in the claw of the eagle, the thirteen stone layers of the pyramid, and the number of thirteen letters in the words "e pluribus unum" and "annuit coeptes". The capstone represents the all-seeing eye of God, looking through the divine eye of a developed Divine Spirit, which latter will multiply and form the body of God's chosen people.

Jesus had listed thirteen evil things which can come out of a person, which defiles him or her. He says from within out of the heart (evil part of the human spirit) comes those evil things (Mk. 7:21-23). Thus, humans are corrupt at the very core from which all their thoughts, words, and deeds are derived. The Bible says, "All our righteous acts are like filthy rags" (Isa. 64:6). See also Jas. 1:21; Col. 3:8.

NOTE: Thirteen is a number of special significance. The overshadowing Presence of the Tabernacle was counted as the thirteenth, and so was Christ, who had twelve Apostles.

When a man or woman became a sinner, which some people say is represented by the number thirteen (being unlucky), he or she was in need of salvation from sin. The next number is fourteen, which is the number of salvation or deliverance. For example, Israel was saved from Egyptian bondage on the fourteenth day of the first month in the evening, at the Lord's Passover (Ex. Ch. 12; Lev. 23:5). Jesus kept the Passover and was then slain as the Paschal Lamb on the same day in which paschal lambs were being slain in the Temple. He went to His crucifixion site, Via Dolorosa, which was later marked by fourteen stations.

NOTE: Paul, his disciple, and all the people on the ship with him were saved from the storm on the fourteenth day (Acts 27:33-44).

The Medianite tradesmen sold Joseph to the Ishmaelites for twenty shekels of silver (Gen. 37:28). Then the people of Israel called out to the Lord for help; for he (Jabin) had nine hundred chariots of iron, and oppressed them cruelly for twenty years (Judges 4:3).

After Samson slew one thousand Philistine men with the jawbone of an ass, he became a judge in Israel for twenty years (Judges 15:14-20).

NOTE: The number twenty-two is of great value because of the twenty-two letters of the Hebrew alphabet and the 22 major trumps of the Tarot pack (the Roman alphabet contains 26 letters).

The number thirty signifies the perfection and integration of the three aspects of the personality: the physical, emotional, and mental/spiritual. Joseph was thirty years old when he entered the service of Pharaoh, king of Egypt (Gen. 41:46). [1]David was thirty years old when he began to reign (II Sam. 5:4), and his descendant Jesus was thirty years old when He began His ministry (Lk. 3:23).

When Aaron died, the house of Israel wept for him thirty days (Num. 20:29; 33:38).

Samson said to the Philistines, here is a riddle for you, if you can solve it within seven days of the feast, then I shall "give you thirty linen garments and thirty festal garments" (Judges 14:12).

The officials of King Darius asked the king to establish an ordinance and enforce an interdict, "that whoever makes petition to any God or man for thirty days, except to you, O king, shall be cast into a den of lions" (Dan. Ch. 6).

Zechariah asked for his wages and was paid thirty shekels of silver (Zech. 11:12), and the chief priests paid Judas Iscariot thirty pieces of silver to betray his Master (Mt. 26:14-15; 27:3, 9).

The number thirty-three is very significant, for David reigned thirty-three years in Jerusalem, over all Israel and Judah (II Sam.5:5). Jesus lived on the earth in His physical body for thirty-three years. Alexander the Great died in 323 B.C. when he was thirty-three years old. Augustine (387 A.D.) was thirty-three years old when he converted to Christianity. [2]Willibrord was thirty-three years old when he began his missionary work in Europe.

---

[1] Boas and Ruth were grandfather and grandmother of David.

[2] See Supplement II – M. Willibrord, with eleven missionary brothers, one of them was called Adelbert, came ashore near Noordwyk, Holland. In 720 A.D., Adelbert built a cell in the dunes near Alkmaar and preached in Egmond. When his bones were dug up two centuries after his death, a well sprang up. In 1935, the Adelbert society was established in Holland. His feast is celebrated by the Catholics every year on June 25.

645

NOTE 1: The thirty-three vertebrae of the body's spinal column symbolize the 33 steps toward initiation, through which a human must pass before he/she enters into the skull or divine world. In the ritualism of free Masonry, the candidates pass through 33 degrees, leading to his/her final initiation.

NOTE 2: The Ten Commandments, according to tradition, were given on the day of first fruits. For it was seven weeks after Passover that the "Feast of Weeks" (Ex. 34:22; Deut. 16:10), or the "Feast of Harvest" (Ex. 23:16), was observed. This day was later celebrated by the Christians as the day of Pentecost (pentecostos – Greek for fiftieth), which is fifty days after Passover, when the Holy Spirit was given (Acts 2:1).

The number seventy in the Bible is a seven of completion multiplied by ten. Seventy members of Jacob's family, or the house of Jacob, came into Egypt (Gen. 46:27; Ex. 1:5). The physicians embalmed Israel (Jacob), "And the Egyptians wept for him seventy days" (Gen. 50:3). After their escape from Egypt, the Israelites encamped in Elim, where there were twelve springs and seventy palm trees (Ex. 15:27; Num. 33:9). Thereafter, they came to the mountain of the Lord. Moses and seventy elders came up to the Lord to worship Him (Ex. 24:1, 9) as they were gathered by Moses (Num. 11:24).

Gideon the judge had seventy sons because he had many wives, and his concubine bore him a son called Abimelech (Judges 8:30-31). The latter, in order to be the sole ruler, killed all his brothers (except for one) by hiring, for seventy pieces of silver, worthless men (Judges 9:1-6). Isaiah mentioned that Tyre will be forgotten for seventy years, but at the end of the seventy years, the Lord will visit Tyre and her hire and merchandise will be dedicated to the Lord (Isa. 23:15-18). As was predicted by Jeremiah (Jer. 24:11; 2 Chron. 36:21), the captivity lasted seventy years, which is also the time period that Babylon dominated the Middle Eastern world.

Legend has it that seventy Jewish scholars went from Jerusalem to Alexandria and spent seventy months translating the text of Hebrew into Greek. The resulting Greek version was called the Septuagint. After the death of Pope Benedict XI, the papal palace was removed from Rome to Avignon in France, and for seventy years, the papacy came under the subjection of the French court from +/-1305 to +/-1377.

NOTE 1: It pleased Darius to set over the kingdom a hundred and twenty princes, who were to rule the whole kingdom, and over them three presidents (Dan. 6:1-2).

NOTE 2: The queen of Sheba gave King Solomon a hundred and twenty talents of gold (1 Kings 10:1-10).

NOTE 3: After all his trials "Job lived a hundred and forty years, and saw his sons, and his sons' sons, four generations" (Job 42:16).

NOTE 4: "The number of those that lapped, putting their hands to their mouths, was three hundred men" (Judges 7:6), "And he divided the 300 men into three companies" (Judges 7:16). "Samson went and caught three hundred foxes --- and put a torch between each pair of tails" and burned the standing grain of the Philistines (Judges 15:4-5).

vii. Comparisons of the life and mission of Jacob, Moses, and Jesus

[1]The pattern of Jacob's restoration course (who was victorious over evil forces and received [2]God's final blessing) was followed by Moses and Jesus at the tribal, national, and worldwide levels. For example:

➤ Jacob had twelve sons (Gen. 35:22). Moses had twelve tribes (Ex. 24:4). Jesus had twelve Apostles (Matt. 10:1).

➤ Jacob took seventy family members into Egypt and began a new dispensation with them (Gen. 46:27). Moses worked with seventy elders in leading his people to Canaan (Ex. 24:1, 9). Jesus sent out seventy disciples to proclaim the Kingdom of God (Lk. 10:1).

➤ Jacob bought his brother's birthright with bread and pottage of lentils (Gen. 25:34). Moses fed his people with manna and quail (Ex. 16:12-15). Jesus gave his Apostles bread and wine as symbols of his flesh and blood (John 6:48-58).

➤ [3]Through the cooperation of his mother Rebekah, Jacob fled from Esau, who sought to kill him (Gen. 27:43-45). Through the help of his mother, Moses' life during infancy and childhood was saved and nurtured (Ex. 2:2-8). Through the efforts of His Mother Mary, the baby Jesus was saved from Herod (Matt. 2:13).

---

[1] The main ideas are taken from the Divine Principles by Y.O. Kim (1963). The content is somewhat modified by the author.

[2] God's blessing was originally intended for Adam (Gen. 1:28), was shifted to Noah (Gen. 9:1), and was transferred to Abraham (Gen. 15:5), and was finally given to Jacob (Gen. 35:11-12) who, together with Abraham and Isaac, established the foundation of faith. Therefore, God of Abraham, God of Isaac, and God of Jacob (Ex. 3:6; 1 Kings 18:36).

[3] Because sin came into the world mainly through Eve, her descendants have to work extra hard to redeem themselves (Gen. 3:15).

- ➤ Jacob went from Haran, the satanic world, to Canaan (Gen. 31:13; 17, 18). Moses went from Egypt to Canaan, the heavenly land, because God has blessed it (Ex. 3:8). Jesus and His family went from Egypt to Israel (Matt. 2:20).
- ➤ Jacob came out of Haran by misleading Laban for three days, and this three day period was essential for his journey to Canaan (Gen. 31:20-22). Moses led his people out of Egypt by beguiling Pharaoh for three days, and this three day period was essential for the Exodus (Ex. 8:27). Jesus' body was sealed three days in a tomb before He was resurrected (Lk. 18:33). Thus, a three day period of separation from satan was essential on each of these three instances of God starting a new dispensation.

NOTE 1: The mission of Jacob was very difficult because not only did he have to reverse the condition through which satan invaded humanity and restore what has been lost, but also indemnity for the failure of his predecessors was added to the original amount. Whatever an individual has done, which separates him/herself from God, must be reversed so that they can return to God. This may become easier when they follow or have faith in someone who has paid a great price or sacrifice, such as Jesus Christ.

NOTE 2: When we have done something wrong, identical circumstances may appear again, but instead of repeating the same mistakes, we should overcome them. Otherwise, we will delay our personal restoration and that of our family.

- ➤ Jacob and his family were pursued relentlessly by Laban and his kinsmen (Gen. 31:22). Moses and the Israelites were incessantly pursued by Pharaoh and his army (Ex. 14:5-9). Jesus and those who accepted Christ were maliciously pursued by satan and his cohorts.
- ➤ Jacob took wives, children, and all his livestock out of Haran (Gen. 31:17-18). Moses took his wife, his people, and all their goods from Egypt (Ex. 12:35-36). Jesus' mission was that of leading God's children and taking all things from the satanic world.
- ➤ Jacob crossed the Jordan River with a staff (Gen. 32:10, 22). Moses used his rod or staff to divide the Red Sea (Ex. 14:16). Jesus was to judge (separating good from evil – Mt. 25:32) the world with a rod of iron (Rev. 2:27; 12:5), or with the Word of God (Truth).

- ➤ Jacob was tried by an angel by the Ford of Jabbok, where Jacob [1]wrestled with an angel and defeated him (Gen. 32:24-28). Moses was tried at a lodging house when God sought to kill him, but he overcame it (Ex. 4:24-26). Jesus was tried in the wilderness through the temptation of satan and Jesus defeated him (Matt. 4:1-11).
- ➤ Jacob removed all foreign gods from his house and hid them under an oak tree (Gen. 35:4). Moses burned the golden calf with fire (Ex. 32:2). Jesus came to destroy the evil world with the tongue of His mouth (Jas. 3:6; Isa. 11:4; II Thess. 2:8; II Pet. 3:7; John 12:48).
- ➤ Jacob's body was embalmed for forty days (Gen. 50:3). The angel Michael and the devil disputed about the body of Moses (Jude 1:9), but the place of Moses' burial was kept unknown to the Israelites. Jesus' body was sought by many people but was never found (Matt. 28:12-13).

NOTE 1: A further comparison between Moses and Jesus:
Moses received the Law on Mount Sinai; Jesus delivered the Sermon on the Mount. Moses made a bronze serpent so that the people could save themselves by looking at it. People whom are bitten by sin may look to Christ and live spiritually. When Moses stretched out his hand toward heaven, there was darkness in Egypt for three days, but the people of Israel had light where they dwelt (Ex. 10:22-23). Jesus separated the children of light from the children of darkness through His ministry.

NOTE 2: The name of Jesus is the Greek form of the Hebrew "Joshua". As Joshua led his people into the Promised Land by crossing the river Jordan (at about the same place that Jesus was baptized), Jesus is leading His people to the divine world of heaven.

---

[1] God tested Jacob by placing an angel in the position of satan. As Adam surrendered to the invasion of satan, Jacob, however, did not succumb. The angel gave him the blessing, and he was also given a new name, "Israel", which means "He who strives with God" (Gen. 32:28; 35:10).

The Etheric Body

A. Introduction

Humans exist with both a physical and etheric body. The physical body is made up of solids, liquids, and gas. This body is derived from and connected with the earth. However, the invisible etheric or vital body is composed of *four grades of ethers, which are derived and connected with the sun(s). These ethers fill all space, pervade matter, and are active in all processes of life.

The etheric body is part of the physical body composition and is, therefore, subject to natural law. When the physical body dies, the etheric body may survive for a while, but when the physical body decays, the vital body also disintegrates. They both return to their respective physical and etheric bodies of the planet. Because it is the mold or pattern of the physical body and sustains and ensures its well being, it should not be separated from it. It interpenetrates the physical structure like sand in a sponge and empowers it with life so that it is able to function.

This luminous body is an exact replica of the denser physical body. That is why it is also called the etheric double. It has, therefore, a brain where physical life memory is stored. It becomes, together with the physical body, independent and fully alive after the first breath of air and etheric energy is taken. At that time, it is imprinted with its astrological birth sign.

It is also known as the energy – or bioplasmic body and is mentioned in the Bible as the "Golden Bowl" (Eccl. 12:6). It is recorded in Daniel 5 as a materialized hand, which wrote on the wall of King Belshazzar's Palace. This materialization of a 'spiritual hand' is possible because of the etheric substance that is subtracted from the people and its surroundings. It is also possible to materialize with this substance a whole spiritual being, as it is written in the Gospels. This Divine Being could not be seen very well, appeared and disappeared out of nowhere, and could also be touched.

Just as the physical body has blood vessels and organs, the etheric body has meridian channels and force enters. They are the organs

---

* Like the molecules (ions), atoms, electrons, and particles in density, it fills up the emptiness of space within the atoms and the planets.

through which the psycho-spiritual beings express themselves in the physical world. The etheric body functions as a link between the spirit body, or psyche, which empowers the etheric body with psychic energy, and its physical counterpart. It houses the force centers, or chakras, through which portals, communication between them is possible. Another function of the chakras or energy vortices is to absorb vital energy from the surrounding air and distribute it throughout the nerve channels (nadis), as electricity is delivered in a wiring system. As the physical body needs air to sustain life, so does the etheric body need life force energy, most of which is extracted from the air we breathe.

This vital force is known as "Ka" in Ancient Egypt, "Chi" in China, "Prana" in India, and "Mana" by the Polynesians. In Greek, it is called "Pneuma", and in Hebrew "Ruach", which means both air and breath of life. It was called "Mumia" by Paracelsus (1493-1541), "animal magnetism" by Franz Anton Mesmer (1733-1815) who was also able, through hypnotism, to bypass the conscious mind or etheric/physical brain and give suggestions to the subconscious mind, which is the conscious mind of the human spirit. This vital force was called "Odic Force" by Karl von Reichenbach (1788-1869) and "Orgone Energy" by the American scientist William Reich in the 1940s, whom was also able to accumulate this energy. In 1945, the Czech scientist Robert Pavlita called this force "psychotronic energy", which he was able to draw off, accumulate, and store with his psychotronic generator. This vital energy can be received, stored, and changed naturally in the force centers of the etheric body, as electricity is stored in batteries.

The emanations of these forces could be seen in the early 1900s when Dr. Walter J. Kilner developed a special screen, through which the ultraviolet part of the electromagnetic spectrum could be observed. This screen was later developed in aura goggles. Soviet scientists Simyon and Valentina Kirlian eventually photographed the energy field, or aura, which surrounds and penetrates all living things, using high frequency in the late 1930s.

Today, the vital force is also known as "subtle energy", "life force" (energy), "bio(plasmic) energy", "nerve energy", "healing energy", "pyramid energy", "kundalini", etc. A scientist from America called it the "life field", and a scientist from England called it the "morphegenic field". It will not be long before scientists from all over the globe will explore and investigate this fascinating physical level.

B. The Etheric or Health Aura

The etheric body is also called a 'health body' because diseases of the physical body can be first detected as dark spots in the aura of the etheric body, where the flow of vital energy is blocked or depleted. The energy balance of the vital body can however be restored by acupuncture, pranic healing, and so on, and by invocation or faith healing by God and (through) Divine beings.

When a part or greater part of the etheric body is driven out of the dense body by, for example, anesthetics, the subject is unconscious and impervious to pain. When consciousness returns, a pricking, tingling sensation is felt when the etheric atoms are re-entering their physical counterparts. This also happens in a less dramatic way when one of our limbs has been sleeping and wants to return to its normal function. This etheric limb can also be felt for a while, when the physical limb has been amputated.

Just as the physical body can be afflicted by disease, so the spirit or psyche can endure psychological problems. This will first affect the etheric body and then the physical body. Diseases of the spirit body can be emotional, such as lust, guilt, hatred, fear, anxiety, depression, despair, etc. and mental by being prideful, deceitful, judgmental, narrow-minded, confused, doubtful, unbelieving, etc. There are also many problems of the psychic, etheric, and physical bodies and their relationships, such as obsession, multiple personalities, and the temporary or permanent dislocation of the spirit and physical bodies, which result in epilepsy, insanity, and other psychotic disorders.

The etheric body forms a protective barrier between the physical body (planes) and the spirit body (planes). However, the etheric web can be damaged and pierced by shock, ill health (delirium), excessive alcohol (delirium tre-mens), etc. and can easily be punctured by hard and soft drugs. Those substances may open an individual to unwanted psychic experiences from the lower planes and eventually wear down the resistance of the etheric shell to negative forces. The result is that those individuals hallucinate, hear voices, and other abnormal psychic disturbances. They are not only influenced by the lower beings of the spirit planes but also by creatures from the etheric realm. Some of those beings are out to vampire etheric energy (especially from the emanations of blood) of their victims to feel more alive, to materialize, and to act as poltergeists.

However, a good defense against these dark forces is to have a well-developed radiant personality with strong auric emanations. This we may build up by meditation with our *more or less developed Divine Spirits and a close relationship with our Creator through life of intimate communication.

C. The Aura, Its Size and Color

The physical body is surrounded by an etheric aura that appears to be (as some people say) hazy – light blue and gray in color. It is an invisible emanation or energy field following the contour of the body, known as the inner aura. A band of energy radiating from the spirit body (emotional and mental aspect) encircles this, which interpenetrates the etheric body as water in the sand. The spirit person, in turn, is interpenetrated by the Higher Self of evolved people, just like air penetrates water.

The Self, or Divine Spirit, is surrounded by an areola of luminous golden (psychic) colors and is centered on the head as a halo, or nimbus. It has been seen around spiritual masters, mystics, and saints throughout the ages, in all cultures and civilizations. The outer aura in the average individual extends about six to eight feet and is often dull in color. The aura for a spiritually evolved person projects much further and is usually clear and bright. Thus, the size, colors, brightness, and dullness of the colors reveal, in a truthful way, one's physical, emotional, mental, and spiritual (Divine) well being.

When we meet people, irrespective of religion, race, or culture, we may more or less like them when our auras are in resonance with all or some levels of their being, or not like them when the vibration of their aura is not like our own.

The basic psychic colors and size of one's aura may remain practically the same for some time because it is what one is and what one has become. However, the movements and variations of the aura's size and **colors may change many times a day, depending on the moods and thoughts of the person. A burst of anger or lustful desire, for example, may temporarily change the aura to murky crimson and

---

* See "The Birth and Evolution of the Divine Spirit or Soul".
** People who can see the auras of others speak of the black of evil, the red of anger, the green of jealousy, the pink of love, and the golden radiance of high spiritual life.

scarlet colors. The aura will change more easily when we again yield to the same emotion. When, however, those outbursts of emotions become habitual, the aura will crystallize and thus be more difficult to change.

In conclusion, we find that the physical body not only has an etheric aura but also a physical aura beyond the visible light spectrum. It is composed of energy fields, such as electromagnetic fields, heat and sound waves, and other emanations, which can be measured scientifically.

D. Life Energy and Its Application

Life energy can be received directly by being exposed to the sun's rays and indirectly by breathing in the air around us and from the ground we walk on. More of this precious energy can be assimilated by closer contact with nature; walking with bare feet, climbing hills and mountains, touching and sitting under a big tree, or sleeping under a pine tree, thus absorbing prana from the ground and trees.

It is also good to be around flowing or falling water, especially along a beach where the waves are breaking, or after a powerful rainstorm. The surroundings are highly oxygenated, and one can immerse oneself in a field of negative ions, which have a positive effect on our own electromagnetic field. Submerging or swimming in water, especially in salt water, can do a good cleansing of our aura.

We also absorb vital or life energy by eating high vibration foods, such as fruits and vegetables. They should be, however, fresh and in season, when they still contain an abundant amount of life energy. However, when they are preserved or held in cold storage for too long, they lose a lot of this energy. Processed, overcooked, devitalized food, smoking, and alcohol also clog up the channels or nadis of the etheric body and eventually create poor health. It is also advisable, whenever possible, to eat the food which is grown locally because it is usually more compatible with the vibration of our body. Our drinking water should be taken from our natural environment and exposed to sunlight, so that it will contain a great deal of prana. We are in very much need of this life force because many people die early in the morning when it is at its lowest level.

E. Exercise in the West and East

Exercises in the West such as brisk walks, sports, jogging, workouts, and the likes are good for toning and flexibility of muscles and joints. These actions bring more oxygen to the blood and brain and remove toxins from the body. They also generate a great deal of vital energy, thus raising one's energy level. These exercises release tension, increase our strength, endurance, mental clarity, and concentration.

In the East, in the Yogic and Taoist tradition, much physical stress and strain is avoided by not overexerting oneself. External exercises, such as walking, body positions, and movements are combined with internal exercises. Through following special breathing techniques, the supply of vital energy is considerably increased. Because energy follows thought, the flow of that energy can be directed and circulated through the body by the mind. This energy can also be "pumped" through the system to invigorate various organs of the body by controlled breathing. Through special breathing techniques, one may even feel lighter and may eventually be able to levitate. These exercises, together with meditation, may result in the healing of the body, emotional calmness, and peace of mind. It will also integrate the mind (spirit) and body. It may even lead to Self-realization when our Divine Self or Higher Self is discovered and awakened deep within the temple of our personality or lower self, and is aligned with the ego. In the West, this process is called "individuation" by Carl Jung and "psychosynthesis" by Roberto Assagioli.

Chi Kung and Tai Chi are practiced every morning in many Chinese communities. They teach energy cultivation, thus feeling less depleted and stressed at the end of their workday. Both use the mind, breathing, postures, and movement, together with meditation and self-healing – by massage of acupuncture points – thus building strength for endurance, self-defense, and many other improvements. In any stressful situation, we may enter in a psychological condition known as the "fight or flight syndrome". In this dilemma, adrenaline is released from the adrenal glands to speed up our reflexes and give us an extra energy boost. In addition, enormous quantities of Chi (life force) are liberated to the muscles so that it is even possible for a desperate mother to lift up a car from her dying son without experiencing torn ligaments or tendons. People who are exhausted may receive an extra boost, and athletes may perform better than they did before.

It is also known that retention of breath builds up great reserves of vital energy. It is therefore easier to lift a heavy object after taking a full deep breath and holding it. When this stored and excess energy is properly controlled and directed, it is possible, as in martial arts, to break stones with bare hands, flooring an opponent without touching them, and other miraculous stunts. It is also possible to create extra body heat with this energy and protective shields around whole or certain parts of the body so that fire immunity, handling of hot objects, and fire walking are possible.

F. The Flow of Chi

As Chi flows through the body, so does it flow over the surface of the earth through special pathways (dragon lines or leylines) and force centers. The flow of Chi affects and is affected by two forces – Feng (wind) and Shui (water). When these flow harmoniously, more Chi will pass through that area, giving abundant life energy to all forms of life.

The Principles of Feng Shui are also applied to location and orientation of buildings in harmony with the environment and circulation pattern of the flow of Chi. The structure of buildings and homes, as well as the placement of furniture, should be considered in accordance with those principles. We should also take into consideration when designing homes that Chi is denser above the ground than high in the air. In following the principles, the greatest amount of Chi will circulate in those places, giving the dwellers more energy and life. They then will live more in harmony with themselves, each other, their environment, and the universe.

G. How to Develop Auric Sight

For some people, it may take some time to develop auric sight. It might therefore be advisable at first to "feel" the outer and inner auras with your sensitive hands, especially the palms and fingertips. The outer limits of the aura, as well as trouble spots, can also be detected by means of dowsing and use of the pendulum because our subconscious is already aware of this knowledge.

Because the etheric aura and body is part of the physical constitution, it is easier to see than the auras of the spirit – and Divine Self.

Most easily seen are the whirling and spinning dots of air vitality globules against the blue sky on a clear sunny day or just before sunset because they are part of the densest etheric spectrum. We can see them with our physical eyes by using a greater proportion of the rods and cones within our eyes or to see them better with etheric vision. Some esoterics say that the etheric double and its aura, which lies just beyond the visible spectrum, can best be seen with the *third eye, which is located in the center of the forehead. They say that this is the organ of etheric and psychic vision of a human being. Through it, the etheric auras of plants and trees and etheric beings such as fairies, lower classes of extra-terrestrials (ETs), and other non-human entities, can be seen.

NOTE: Psychic vision can also be detected by the lower faculties of the psychic body.

Another way of seeing etheric auras is to let somebody stand about one foot in front of a black wall (or white wall) in a dimly lit room. As an observer, stand back and gaze or stare just beyond the outline of the other body, with your physical eyes slightly out of focus, like you would look just before you fall asleep, when you cannot look straight, or when daydreaming. You will at first see a band of luminous light following the contours of the skin of the physical body. Its thickness varies with different people, but it is usually between one quarter to one inch thick. Soon thereafter, you will see the two to four inch hazy etheric or inner aura and its emanations. By holding your hands in front of a dark wall and a light behind you and by using your mirror, you can also observe your own aura.

Your etheric sight may be further developed to see the less dense levels by using, for example, imagination or guessing to such an extent, that it is possible to see (like x-rays) through physical bodies, walls, layers of earth, closed containers, and letters. With more practice, you will see, with psychic vision, the auras of the spirit and Divine bodies.

---

* Others say that the third eye is a vortex of energy of the three highest chakras and works in connection with the three upper endocrine glands. It is used by the Divine Spirit for spiritual vision, and it is known as the "all-seeing eye".

THE ELECTROMAGNETIC SPECTRUM

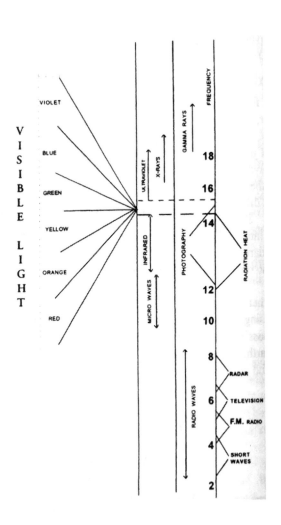

THE
BIRTH
AND
EVOLUTION
OF THE
DIVINE SPIRIT
OR
SOUL

PART 1   PREPARATION FOR THE BIRTH OF THE DIVINE
SPIRIT

I. Introduction

Before the birth of the Divine Spirit or Christ-child can take place in someone in whom the original sin is strong and the [a]good and evil personality is ruling their life; the personality or ego goes through the experience, of what St. John of the Cross called the [*1] "dark night of the soul", Martin Luther the "wrath of God", Kierkegaard, "despair", and Carl Jung "defeat of the ego".

When the ego -good and evil- is strong, the evil in the personality or [b]satanic nature is also strong. The evil nature within the human being or false self of the ego, will do anything to preserve its identity and uphold its domain. The ego as a whole needs to be "broken down" -not eliminated-, so that the satanic nature is no longer dominant in the personality. The purified personality then may choose to become a co-worker with his /her Divine Spirit or Soul and their individual(ized) Spirit (of God).

God Directed Life
(Rev. 21:3)
Human nature, good and pure,
governed by Divine Spirit
Physical
Human
(Mental)
Divine
(G)
Spirit
(Emot.)
Spirit
Body
Tree of (spiritual) Life
Gen. 2:9; Rev. 22:14

When (good and evil) humans feel, think, and act like God, they are on His side and He becomes their Lord and Father, strengthening their good nature and expanding His kingdom

God and Satan
-Directed Life-

The light side and the dark side of the personality

The good self and the false self of the ego

The good part and the evil part of the human spirit or psyche

"tree of the knowledge of good and evil"
Gen. 2:9

---

[a] That part of a human being used for manifestation on the earth plane. It is composed of the physical, emotional, and mental substance. Created in the image of God, it is good and pure, but when it is created in the image of satan it is evil. It is like the symbolic "tree of the knowledge of good and evil".

[*1] See Appendix 1

[b] Satanic nature is also called -evil nature-false self-fallen nature-old nature-dark and shadow side of human nature-the flesh-See also Appendix #4.

Satan Directed Life
(John 12:31)
[c]Human nature depraved and corrupt
ruled by evil imposter

Physical
Human
(Mental)
Evil
(S)
Nature
(Emot.)
Spirit
Body
Tree of (spiritual) death

When (good and evil) humans feel,
think, and act like satan, (Mk. 7:21-23),
they are on his side and he becomes their
master and father (Jn. 8:44), strengthening
their evil nature and expanding his pseudo
kingdom.

When God is to justify and use individuals to accomplish a mission, they are only of good use when He, via their Divine Spirits, can influence them and work through the good part of their personality, or even better through their whole purified personality. They are of not much use when they as humans want to live a separate existence, or even worse when they allow their evil or fallen nature to rule their life. In that case, they are unconsciously identified with their imposter (evil nature) who always tried to take the (empty) place of the Divine or Christ Spirit and thus become an anti-Christ. The personalities of those people whom allowed their evil selves to have full sway over their lives appear to be big, overgrown, puffed up, false, and prideful.

For those whom want to change their lives, the conversion may be triggered outwardly, when individuals lose part or all of their possessions. God may use this as an opportunity to prepare them for an important mission. This change may also begin inwardly, with a growing sense of dissatisfaction with the life humans are living, which they try to cover up under the verneer of success, merrymaking or carousing (Gal. 5:21). To conceal their inner emptiness, anxiety and insecurity in life, they drink (or) and take drugs, which is nothing else but a substitute for the "high" of spiritual life. Becoming more disap-

---

[c] Medieval scholasticism and Pelagianism believed that humans are good and evil, while most of the reformers, especially Calvinism, believed that humans are totally depraved and corrupt.

659

pointed with themselves, they begin to wonder if life is more than gathering of material possessions, knowledge, and the acquisition of power and position in society. They start to look for the Truth and ask questions such as: Who am I?, What is the purpose of life?, Is there a life after death?, Is there a God who cares about me?, What is His Will for me?, and many more.

During that trying time, they may meet someone or join a religious organization, whom have satisfying answers to most of their questions. The searching individuals eventually believe that they were guided by God, who may break into their consciousness. This will result that their self-seeking double-faced egos, as separate, self-reliant and self-sufficient beings, are brought into emptiness, despair, and poverty of spirit (Matt. 5:3). They are made to feel worthless, guilty and sinful, especially when His light shines upon their human spirits and shows them how evil they really are. When their personalities are utterly lost in the "desert of life" and are aware of its own limitation, they give up and turn to God, who starts molding them completely in His image and likeness (Gen. 1:26).

II. A Brief Survey of the History of Restoration

Before the advent of Christianity, peoples' lives in general were almost wholly concentrated on the evil or satanic nature of their personality. Many of them were so wicked that they not only killed humans in order to survive but, unlike animals, were eager to shed their blood. For these people whom were truly created in the image of satan, human life had little value. They were totally depraved and corrupt, and their conscience was seared or dead, therefore losing the ability to discern between good and evil (see Rom.1).

God, who desperately tried to restore human beings in His image, worked with many through their budding conscience (Rom. 2:15), which developed from their [a]Divine Spark or Gem of Christ. When the people advanced, they began to sense a deity, whom they also identified with the forces of nature externally and spirits of nature internally. Because of fear, and to gain or regain His favor, they offer sacrifices to that Being. God eventually chose a group of people, whom were living the life of the good and evil personality, whom responded more fully to His call. Because evil was still deeply and

---

[a] The Creator has, from the beginning, given to all of His creatures a Spirit particle or Spark of Himself, so that communication becomes possible.

strongly embedded in their personality, they needed a God who was strong and severe with them. Besides, they could not respect a God who was all tender and loving, but only a powerful God they could fear and [b]obey. This Master gave them moral laws, for their external lives, which were enforced by His prophets and kings. He influenced the people internally through their growing conscience, so that they, to some degree, could distinguish between good and evil. With the help of their Creator and through many trials and tribulations, the chosen people tried very hard to purify or strip their personalities or egos from their inherited [c]evil qualities or satanic nature. As a reward for their obedience, abundant material blessings were bestowed upon them.

When humanity as a whole was sufficiently advanced, Jesus Christ was chosen from a suffering people, to bring to the general public the experience of a most important event; "The Birth of the Soul". Through the birth and development of the Divine Spirit, humans are finally able to completely eliminate the evil qualities of the fallen archangel Lucifer, from their human spirits. Although some people before the time of Jesus, like prophets, Levite priests (cohens) and others, attained some degree of enlightenment, it was however not as complete as Jesus Christ was able to bring to everyone. He was the first to recognize and realize fully the Christ Spirit (Divine Spirit) within himself and acknowledge the Holy Spirit working with Him, and expressed it completely in His life as the Gospels testify. When He died on the cross, the curtain between the *Holy Place and the Most Holy Place or Holy of Holies (Exodus 26:33,34; Heb. 9:2-3) "was torn in two from top to bottom" (Matt. 27:51; Heb. 10:20). This is an indication that everyone will have the opportunity to communicate and unite with their Inner Christ or Soul which is the dwelling place of the Spirit of God (Rev. 21:3), and have again access to and become the Tree of Life (Gen. 3:24; Rev. 22:14).

---

[b] Only when they were obedient was there a Master and servant relationship possible. Otherwise, they became an enemy or adversary to Him. This was usually followed by a swift punishment of plague, war, banishment, etc. When they are later newly born spiritually, they become the true children, whom call their Creator Abba or Father and no longer Jehovah or Lord as in the Old Testament era.

[c] How humans have inherited the evil qualities or nature, also called original sin. See "The Fall of Lucifer, Eve and Adam". Most of the evil qualities are mentioned in Mark 7:21-23; Rom. 1:28-31; 1 Cor. 6:9-10; Gal. 5:19-21.

* For complete explanation of the Holy and Most Holy Place, see the description of the tabernacle of Moses on page 38.

III. Children Born of Parents Whom are Good and Evil

Most people today are still living the life of the good and evil personalities and only a few the life of the good personalities, that is without original sin. Human beings whom are a blend of good and evil have inherited the good qualities from God and the evil qualities from satan, which is deeply rooted in their human spirit, or heart (Jer. 17:9; Mark 7:21-23). Therefore the false self of the ego or old nature (Eph. 4:22) needs to die, so that a new ego may be born anew, that is born of water (John 3:5).

Although children appear to be innocent and without sin, they nevertheless have inherited -more or less- the original sin or evil nature from their parents, whose egos are not, but should be pure (Matt. 5:8). When the children are young they wear no "masks", and are in their outer expressions the same as they are in their inner life. They do not hide or cover up the evil in themselves, until adults teach them differently (Matt. 23:27-28). They have such traits as trust, dependency, simplicity, obedience, outspokenness, humility, and are easily taught.

Jesus of Nazareth liked them very much and said: "Truly, I say to you, unless you turn and become like children, you will never enter the Kingdom of Heaven" (Matt. 18:3).

Some children are born from reasonably [a]good parents with little original sin. They are what William James, in his classic "The Varieties of Religious Experience", said are the "once born". They are the ones whom have the grace of God in them. They are the blessed children whom are natural, cheerful and loving, and can inspire or even convert a cynical adult. Although they need to be trained from childhood and protected, it is however inevitable that they will encounter evil influences, which may awaken or stimulate evil tendencies in themselves. [b]This can happen when their growing Divine

---

[a] It is important to have good ancestors and parents in order to be born with less original sin. Jesus of Nazareth, however, was born without original sin, through the purification of a long line of ancestors. See Matt. 1.

[b] In the old mystery teaching the minotaur, who was half man and half animal, signifies the lower nature or personality of the individual. It was eventually slain by Theseus, who is like the Divine Spirit of the entity. It has been growing, till it was strong enough to use the "divine sword".

Spirit is not strong enough to fight against the evil nature and stimulate the good tendencies in their personalities. The children have to combat the evil disposition, which may have been strengthened by the acquired evil qualities later on in life (Matt. 13:24-30).

The other kind of person, the "twice born", as coined by W. James, has a sense of *²original sin, since the days of early childhood. They continually struggle with the evil in themselves and most of them need to be "born again", by going through a more radical change. The Impostor or Deceiver will then "die" and give up its control to the Divine Spirit, which is born of God's Spirit (John 1:13, 3:6).

IV. Process of Spiritual Birth

Some Evangelists speed up the "salvation process" by heaping undue guilt and fear upon the individual(s) or group(s) with threats of hell fire, eternal damnation and alienation from God. Being repeatedly told by the preacher that they are full of pride, lust, and deceit, and unworthy of redemption; (†causes death of the false self of the ego), people then recognize the great need for redemption (creating a vacuum in their human spirit or psyche). In despair and utter hopelessness they reach out for Christ as their Savior (removing accumulated, emotional, and mental obstructions) and they cry out to God asking for His acceptance and forgiveness, who then rushes in to save them. Then they experience a lifting of a heavy burden and feel great joy when they sense that Christ lives within them (Gal. 2:20).

This sudden conversion method can be of a lasting nature for some people, but for others (depends on intensity), it is only temporary. This is especially true for people whom are coerced into conversion, without a true willingness to give up their sinful ways. They are not ready to give up their separate existence as a human entity, which is enforced by the rebellious satanic will of their evil self. Because they do not want to choose and partake of a higher spiritual life, the people soon backslide to their "old ways" of living.

---

* ² See Appendix

† The false ego (self) death (not ego) is usually only temporary. To completely and permanently root out the evil nature in one's own being, is a long process with many setbacks. What happens in this instance is that one may loosen the hold of the evil or satanic nature on the life of the personality or ego.

The sudden experience is based on faith and feeling and is usually not as permanent and meaningful as a gradual experience or initiation. The candidates for the latter type of change come to the understanding that they need to change their lifestyle, by studying for a short or long period the Scripture either alone or in a group. They may also listen to many testimonies, receive inspiration and insights, and decide for themselves to receive Christ as their Savior and start living a spiritual or divine life.

Some other religions begin the "restoration or salvation process" by first purifying the personalities by "stripping off" the evil traits of the good/evil egos, and then try to unite with the Spirit of Christ, when their religion or they, develop to a higher stage.

V. Comparing Spiritual Birth with Physical Birth

Through insemination of the sperm of the father into the ovum of the mother, an embryo is formed after fertilization and grows into a fetus, by being nourished through the umbilical cord of the mother. The human body is thus formed from the earthly elements or from the "dust from the ground" (Gen. 2:7). When the baby is born, it takes not only its first breath of air, but is also animated with *life energy from the universe and imprinted with its astrological birth sign (Gen. 2:7b).

The seed of the human spirit, which was implanted at that time in the womb of the body, is stimulated by environment, play, language, imitation, etc., and is born within the body as a self-conscious human entity. Around the age of seven, when the "outer temple" is ready (1 Cor. 2:11), the personality, as a whole, has reached its intellectual potentiality. It is also able to communicate (to a limited extent) with invisible beings, without the use of spoken language, by using the newly evolving psychic faculties of his or her human spirit. It then grows to that age of maturity when the "inner temple" is ready to receive and live a divine life (1 Cor. 3:16).

Just as the earth father provides a sperm or seed to the ovum of a mother, the Heavenly Father, with the Holy Spirit (Luk. 1:35), provides a seed of divinity, or "Word of God", to the ovum or Spark of divinity deep within the spirit or psyche of a human being. A spiritual pregnancy or awakening occurs, as soon as one makes a decision to receive Christ and His Word. This happens whenever "the soil" or the

---

* See "The Etheric Body".

human spirit is ready to receive it, by its purity, growth and understanding (Matt. 13:23). After a period of growth in the womb of the human psyche, a spiritual baby is born, whose time of birth is much more recognized and celebrated by heaven than the physical birth. True Christians should therefore celebrate every year their spiritual birthday, as was exemplified by the birth of the baby Jesus, because this story also symbolizes what happens to the birth of the Soul of every human being.

If the human personality is not prepared to receive Christ, it should be cleansed by living a moral life. As Jesus said in Matt. 9:17, it is not possible to put "new wine", Divine Spirit or Consciousness into "old wine skins" of the good and evil personalities. Because the human selves or egos of the people were not pure at the time Jesus walked on this earth; that John the Baptist came along to "prepare the way of the Lord" by baptizing people in the river Jordan. He said, "I have baptized you with water; but He (Jesus) will baptize you with the Holy Spirit" (Mark 1:8).

When receiving the sacred seed, it will germinate, grow up, and be born as a Divine Spirit or Original Self when humans are in their [3]teens, or in later life. After spiritual life is imparted, they will then be empowered when they are ready, with the Holy Spirit, who then finds its dwelling place in the innermost core or temple of their personality (1 Cor. 6:19). Thereafter, as it often happens, the budding Divine Spirit, inspired by the Holy Spirit, starts to witness to its own inner and outer personality.

Just as the sun penetrates the earth and awakens the dormant life in the seed, God's Love will likewise penetrate the psyche of a human being and awaken the seed of the Divine Spirit. As a plant needs the warmth of the sun, food, and air, the Divine Being needs God's Love, Truth (Word of God) and partake of a rich spiritual atmosphere. Spiritual growth, however, is much faster when one serves others, by doing good deeds, especially when it is in accordance with God's Will of restoration. The invisible results of those deeds will return, and attach to the doer and inspirator of the deeds. However, when the deeds do not promote or even digress from the evolution of humanity as a whole, spiritual growth of the participants will greatly diminish.

---

[3] See Appendix

DIFFERENT STAGES OF SPIRITUAL DEVELOPMENT

PART 2   SPIRITUAL BABYHOOD STAGE

There is great joy in "heaven" when an earth-bound personality makes a decision to become a "child of God". However, the newborn spiritual infant or baby must grow into a child and then into a spiritual adult, before the new life of the Divine Spirit can be fully expressed through their personality.

The Gospel of John 3:3, let Jesus say: "I say to you, unless one is born anew, he cannot see the Kingdom of God."

In another verse Jesus said, "Truly, truly, I say to you, unless one is born of water and the Spirit, he cannot enter the Kingdom of God" (John 3:5).

Why do people need to be born again?

*The first human pair, whom had the potential to become spiritual adults, united with satan instead of God while they were teenagers and inherited the evil qualities and nature of satan. By dominating the lives of Adam and Eve and, through them, all of their descendants, satan became "the god of this world" (2 Cor. 4:4), "the ruler of this world" (John 12:31), and the owner of the world (Matt. 4:9), "and the whole world is in the power of the evil one" (1 John 5:19), who became the father of all whom are doing his will (John 8:44). Since that time all human beings, from the moment they are conceived, have the tendency toward sin. This universal hereditary sinfulness is called original sin.

In order for God to free humans from the bondage of sin, their personalities need to be cleansed (with water) or born anew. They become a new human being when they eliminate the inherited satanic nature within themselves (Eph. 4:22-24). They then become like Adam and Eve before their fall, and are then ready for the birth of the Divine Spirit, which is incorruptible, so that they may enter the Kingdom of God.

After people are redeemed or restored, have entered, and are fully

---

* Other people living at that time (Cain found a wife among the existing tribes (Gen. 4:16-17)) did not have that potential.

For a more detailed account of the fall, see "The Fall of Lucifer, Eve and Adam".

living in the Kingdom as spiritual adults, children are born from them whom are without original sin or free from a corrupted human nature. The children start living in a normal way, by growing physically, mentally, and spiritually to maturity. They no longer need a Savior, or go through a special process of restoration, such as a new birth and be adopted (Rom. 8:23; Gal. 4:5) because they are without sin. Their Divine Spirits will then function as Mediators between God and their human spirits.

The Apostle John speaks of three different spiritual age groups: "little children", "young men", and "fathers" (1 John 2:12-14), which correspond to the physical development of babyhood, childhood, and man-womanhood. As physical age has no bearing on spiritual age, a physically old person can be a baby spiritually, while a physically young but mature person, can be spiritually well advanced.

VI. Similarities between Physical and Spiritual Development

There is a correlation between physical and spiritual development, for example; as a physical baby needs nourishment regularly, so the spiritual infant needs the Word of God at regular times.

They "long for the pure spiritual milk" (1 Pet. 2:2), that is "the first principles of God's Word", or "the elementary doctrine of Christ" (Heb. 5:11-14; Heb. 6: 1-2). This is also served again to backsliders (1 Cor. 3:1-3) whom "are still of the flesh"[#4].

> Jesus Christ said to the tempter "man shall not live by bread alone, but by every word that proceeds from the mouth of God" (Matt. 4:4). He also said, "I am the living bread" (John 6:51).

The Word of God is filled with a living force, and will penetrate and feed the babe in Christ, because the Words are "spirit and life" (John 6:63), and are "living and active" (Heb. 4:12). It is flesh (Word) and blood (Spirit), or bread and wine (John 6:55). Thus, the newborn Divine Spirit or Christ Spirit is being fed and formed (Gal. 4:19) by the pure Word of God, or "bread from heaven" (John 6:32), and, thus, partake of the body of the Universal Christ (a body broken for you) and unite with Him in Spirit (Matt. 26:26; Luke 22:19).

[#4] See Appendix

When the Word is assimilated, it becomes part of the Divine Spirit or Self. The Divine Self or Being is of the same substance or nature as God (homoousion) and has become completely one with the Inspirator of the Word. Therefore, the Divine Being or Higher Self, portrayed as the Tree of Life (Gen. 2:9) can only accept and assimilate in their Being the Word of God. This God part is pure and eternal and is not capable of sinning (1 John 3:9).

The human personality, {spirit (intellect-emotion-will) and body} as "the tree of the knowledge of good and evil" (Gen. 2:9), can receive and assimilate in its being good as well as false knowledge. Those words or vessels are empty of Spiritual Life (Eph. 5:6) and tainted, when spoken by evil beings. That is why humans can easily deviate from the Principles of God when they do not "listen to those beings" with their Heart or Divine Consciousness.

After humans have eaten enough of a variety of different kinds of food, it needs to be digested and distributed, which takes some time, before the body becomes strong. After spiritual people have "eaten" the "spiritual nutrition", it goes through their "spiritual bloodstream" to the "spiritual cells". In the beginning they do not feel much spiritual strength, but after a while they begin to feel the spiritual force coursing through their whole Divine Body.

VII. More Similarities Between Physical and Spiritual Unfoldment

When physical children are grown, they know how to feed themselves. The same is true of spiritual children, as they "make time" to read and implement Scripture, and to have daily communication with their Creator.

As physical babies need to be careful with what they eat, spiritual babies likewise need to be heedful of what they hear and read, because they often are not able to discern between good and evil, and what is essential for their spiritual life. Besides, as the saying goes, "You are what you eat."

As physical babies are not able to walk and are totally dependent on their parents, spiritual babies easily stumble and fall down. However, they are being helped by their loving and merciful Spiritual Parents, especially when they ask for their help, and by their utter helplessness.

As physical babies need to be held close and loved in the crucial months after they are born, spiritual babies need to be followed up, prayed with and talked to, in the months following their conversion. They otherwise may die a spiritual death or wither away, when communication with God and the spiritual family is greatly impaired (John 5:24; Rom. 8:6; Matt. 8:21-22).

As physical babies are lovely to be held and therefore get whatever they want, spiritual babies are much favored by God after their salvation. He showers them with love, gifts (spiritual), and healing. The babies are high in spirit and are experiencing a spiritual honeymoon, which is very joyful and exciting.

As new life is fragile and easily damaged, the physical and spiritual babies not only need to be protected from the outside (evil) forces, but also from the harm they likely are to do to themselves, by their own (evil) selves.

As children in natural life become more like their parents when growing up, spiritual children become more like their Spiritual Parent(s) when growing to maturity.

As children need to be disciplined and to be told what is right or wrong in their moral development, spiritual children are corrected or scolded when they deviate from the Divine Principles, by their elders in faith.

As infants should not be put to work as soon as they are born, spiritual infants should not be used right away for "church work", but need to be disciplined first. Otherwise, they become disillusioned and may fall away.

As a child needs a home with loving parents and other family members for the development of their personality, a spiritual child needs a church or spiritual center, where they find their Spiritual Parent(s) and have fellowship with believers in a high spiritual atmosphere.

As it is a great disaster in the physical world when a baby is injured and killed, it is even a greater disaster in the Divine World when a spiritual baby is harmed and murdered (Matt. 10:28). Was not the devil "a murderer from the beginning" (John 8:44), when he killed Adam and Eve spiritually (Gen. 3:13)?

As babies discover and explore the physical world, spiritual babies, likewise, are very excited to learn about the newly discovered Divine World or Kingdom of God.

As babies need to be taught how to talk, spiritual babies need to learn to talk the new spiritual language, as "they sang a new song" (Rev. 5:9).

As children have faith in their parents to take care of them, which makes them happy and carefree, spiritual children have much faith in God to take care of all their needs, which makes them free of anxiety and joyful.

VIII. Spiritual Warfare with Evil Forces and the World

People whom have been spiritual born or saved by accepting the [#5]Universal or Cosmic Christ of any high religion as their Savior, the Word of God spoken through Christ becomes the sword, which will divide them from "worldly" people (Matt. 10:34). This also includes members of one's own household (Luk. 14:26; Mark 13:12). Jesus therefore "did not come to bring peace" (Matt. 10:34; Luk. 12:51). This separation or judgment is executed by someone on a white horse who is called the "Word of God", who "judges and makes war" (Rev. 19:11-16); "As a shepherd who separates the sheep from the goats" (Matt. 25:32); Wise virgins will be separated from foolish virgins (Matt. 25:1:13); The weeds will be bound in bundles and burned and the wheat will be harvested into his barn (Matt. 13:24-30). Then "the ruler of this world will be cast out" through this judgment (John 12:31). Only by dividing them first into Cain and Abel factions can the people be restored. Abel as the representative of Adam will then take his rightful position, by subduing Cain who represents the archangel Lucifer. This restoration also takes place in one's own being, when the Individual Christ or Divine Spirit takes its rightful position and governs over one's personality or self.

The babes in Christ are very vulnerable to the forces of evil as it is expressed through human and spirit beings. The evil beings love their subjects with a possessive, satanic love and will do anything in their power to get the child of God back to their camp (1 Pet. 5:9). Before

---

[#5] See Appendix

they were spiritually born and Christ was not living in them (Col. 1:27), evil forces outside and within did not bother them much. However, now that they have joined the army of God, evil spirits and fallen angels (demons) will try to find their weaknesses and tempt them severely, until they again feel and think like they do. Many spiritual babes, whom are not protected by their elders in faith, are easily persuaded by their old friends and family members to start living the good and evil lifestyle again. Because those friends do not understand the change that has come over them (2 Cor. 4:4); they try to give them a lot of "well meaning advice" to stop being so religious, and join them in "having fun" again.

Unknowingly influenced by evil forces without or within their beings, a former boy or girl friend suddenly shows up, and wants to have a relationship with them. By responding to this kind of temptation they quickly start to live "below their belt" and the evil nature within their personalities becomes dominant again. These and other incidents of enticements and oppositions, including breaking down of equipment used for God's work, indicates that the babes are on God's side, especially when they get too often interrupted when they are studying God's Word. They also begin to notice when they want to tell the Good News or Gospel to people whom are interested; the persons are either called away, get an accident or become sick, (or relative) or move to another town when a higher paying job is offered to them (Matt. 4:8-9). They also discover to their excitement that many other "strange things" are happening, which prevents the "good people" of hearing the Gospel or the Words of God.

Because the babies in Christ are spiritually weak, they need not only be separated from [a]the world, but also not live in those environments that have a low spiritual atmosphere. When they become more mature and stronger, they are able to live in the world but not be part of "the world", because their Divine Spirits are living in the divine world, which interpenetrates the lower worlds. Newly born spiritual babies are very vulnerable and should be protected [b]from "the world" and its evil forces, which are very eager to destroy them. That was indicated sym-

---

[a] Here is not meant the physical world, but the secular world which is ruled by good and evil people (John 15:19; 1 John 2:15-17; Eph. 2:2).

[b] Student priests in early Catholic communities were not allowed to speak to other members of the community (except professors). Visits of their parents were limited and they did not read any newspapers or magazines, and knew nothing of happenings outside the Cloister.

bolically in the Bible when King Herod sought to kill the baby Jesus (Matt. 2:13).

IX. What are Spiritual Babies Like

Spiritual babies understand to some extent spiritual things. They understand with the senses of their Divine Spirits the deeper teaching of Scripture and receive revelation knowledge (Matt. 11:25). But the unspiritual or natural human beings in whom the Spirit of God is not residing, "Gifts of the Spirit of God" are "folly to him", because he cannot understand the things of God (1 Cor. 2:14; 1 John 4:6). The knowledge he/she receives is mostly from outside themselves, which is sense knowledge or natural human knowledge. That is why Jesus Christ spoke to the crowds in parables, but to His Disciples about "the secrets of the Kingdom of Heaven" (Matt. 13:10-13), because they were able "to hear and see" (Matt. 13:16).

Spiritual babies do a lot of praising and adoration of God and believe that Jesus of Nazareth is God Himself, ignoring the fact that Jesus always referred to God as His Father, from whom everything comes. They look up to spiritual leaders, and think that they can do nothing wrong. They also believe that God will do everything for them and that nothing is required of them. When in trouble, they want God and His angels to rescue them and do not, or want to understand that God uses ordinary people to rescue or save them. A new convert is full of faith, ready and willing to learn, although some of them think at times that God is intolerant and fear His punishment. Many babies do not want to take any responsibility for their evil deed(s) and express this by saying, "The devil made me do it." They do not seem to understand that they, at times, attract evil influences in their lives, by their own feeling, thinking, and behavior, which is similar in nature to that of the evil entities. The babes also have a tendency to judge someone or society as either being good or evil, instead of seeing them as degrees of good and evil.

Through their spiritual birth, not only the senses of their budding Divine Spirits are opened to a certain extent, but also the *psychic faculties of their human spirits (for some they are already more or less open). Through the intuitive faculties of their Divine Spirits, they are able to get in communication with the Spirit of God, Jesus Christ, and

---

* In the near future when humans are born in a normal way (without original sin or separation from God), the psychic senses of their human spirits will begin to open from childhood.

other high beings of the divine world, here and in the afterlife. Through the senses of their human spirits, they are able to make contact with good and evil spirits, and angels. Being more open and sensitive, spiritual babies can easily be influenced, not only by the good, but also by evil entities, because they cannot yet distinguish very well between the working and works of good and evil spirits. It is therefore advisable for them to communicate with God alone and, to a limited extent, with other beings. Some babies, however, go to the extreme and believe that all spirits are demons, and should be avoided, including their Christian ancestors and family members whom desperately try to make contact with them. They probably believe this because they had bad experiences with evil spirits or (and) believe in Deuteronomy 18:9-14, wherein God forbid to make contact with the spirit world through mediums or listen to false prophets (Jer. 27:9). At that time, God tried to isolate and purify His chosen people from the people surrounding them, and from spirits whom were almost all evil. On the other hand, there are spiritual babies whom are so impressed and fascinated by spirits, that they listen to every word spirits say and start to communicate less with God or lose contact with Him altogether.

NOTE:

In the time of the Old Testament undeveloped human beings could only make contact with spirits of the lower realm, including evil spirits and fallen angels or demons. They were able to do this through their lower psychic centers or solar plexus (guts), which is instinctive in nature and more developed in women than in men. We can readily understand that God forbade the exercise of the lower intuition or psychism, except for His prophets. They were able and allowed to communicate with Him and His angels and performed psychic phenomena with their lower and higher intuition.

In the New Testament era, people in general and Disciples of Christ in particular were more developed and alive. They used their higher energy and psychic centers (third eye) to make contact with other divine beings. Jesus, for example, communicated with Moses and Elijah (Luk. 9:30), and was able to levitate and materialize, etc. The Disciples of Christ, after His crucifixion, were able to communicate and perform many "miracles" by using their higher intuition. They received revelation, conversed with Christ, spoke in tongues, and exercised many "gifts of the Spirit".

Apostle Paul wants us to know about life after death:

> But we would not have you ignorant, brethren, concerning
> those who are asleep, that you may not grieve as others do
> who have no hope (1 Thess. 4:13).

Spiritual babies are usually gentle and kind, are easily impressed, and ask many questions about their life in the "new world". They have an unquestioned belief, are innocent, naïve, and usually harmless. They constantly implore God to give them what they want, because they believe that God favors them over others. If they are criticized, they become very disturbed and full of self-pity, but if they are recognized and appreciated, they feel "high" and full of self-importance. Sometimes they are frustrated, easily hurt, selfish, and self-conscious of what others think about them, especially when their mind is focused much on their personality. However, a baby in Christ is far better of living a divine life, than living a life of the good and evil personality, whose basic characteristic is *selfishness.

X. Comparing Babyhood with Higher Spiritual Life

Spiritual babies usually believe in the Scripture literally, instead of interpreting many verses symbolically as a more mature person does. Many of them cling to what they believe in, instead of seeking for a higher truth. They should not only believe, but also understand what they believe, by using their enlightened mind as the spiritually grown do. They should learn to understand that the Holy Spirit of God likes to work not only through their Divine Spirit, but also through their purified (cleansed), well-developed and integrated personality. Many of them wait for guidance, instead of searching for the purpose of creation and recreation. They surrender to God instead of cooperating with God to implement His Divine Plan as the spiritually grown do. They believe in heaven but do hardly know anything about it. Some of them say that it is a place to go, instead of a state of being. Many of them wait for the good life, when they are in "heaven", instead of having it now when they are resurrected to a higher spiritual or divine level while living on earth. Besides, babies expect to be rewarded by doing good and abstaining from evil so that they may escape a future punishment in hell; instead of doing right for its own sake, without any thought of reward or punishment, as grown-ups do.

---

* Selfishness in itself is not wrong, because children whom are growing up and living the life of the personality are naturally selfish. However, physical grown-ups should not be, but many still are, especially the ones whom are living the life of the good and evil personalities, which is the main tenet of fallen people. Selfishness is the intensification of the personality, someone who is trapped in the small self.

XI. Spiritual Babies as Stragglers and Trouble Makers

As it is not in the plan of God that one remain a baby physically and be retarded mentally, so should one not remain a spiritual baby by continually wanting the attention of the Spiritual Parent(s). The babies want to be fed by them, instead of feeding and assimilating the Word of God by themselves. They also like to have their "spiritual diapers" cleaned, by letting their Spiritual Mentors pay penance (indemnity) for what they have done wrong. This care-taking might be alright in the beginning of their spiritual life, but not many years after their conversion.

However, the majority of converts whom remain in their spiritual infancy are those whom have been improperly taken care of by their Spiritual Elders. They attend many religious gatherings, but do not get involved in any of them. Without having fellowship with other believers, many of them eventually become backsliders or spiritual dropouts; by showing signs of envy, strife, division, and worldliness and "behaving like ordinary men" (1 Cor. 3:3-4). They certainly are not ready or qualified for the deeper teaching or solid spiritual food (Heb. 5:11-14).

The Christian in name, backsliders and baby spirits housing in undeveloped personalities, can make and have made lots of trouble in the two thousand years of Christian history, especially in the Middle Ages. Some of them are so much "fallen" that they do not even follow the *Ten Commandments. They are the laws that were given to Moses to guide the people –whom were living at that time (Old Testament) and later– in the moral development of their personality. The troublemakers do not tolerate any belief system, except their own, and they not only condemn other believers to eternal hell, but they burn them at the stake, in the name of God. Many "holy" wars they fought were not for the cause of God but to protect their own religious interest. The fact that weapons were blessed by priests in both camps shows that one or the other was completely wrong about which army they belonged to – the more good or the more evil. Being undeveloped spiritually, they were not able to distinguish between the relative good and evil, and could therefore be used by evil forces, while they thought that they were from God.

---

* See Appendix –"Ten Commandments" in back pages.

However, in spite of the many difficulties Christians encounter in the process of growing up, it is nevertheless a great honor to be a Christian, to become Christ-like in character, and express one's own Christ Spirit through the outer temple of a well-developed and wholesome personality.

PART 3   SPIRITUAL CHILD AND YOUTH STAGE

XII. Introduction

Having passed through the spiritual baby stage and honeymoon or spiritual high with the Lord, the baby or infant has become a spiritual child. Instead of continually receiving, they begin to learn how to give by serving others. Having found and entered the Kingdom of God, they also feel responsible to establish it. However, spiritual children soon find that they are not always exalted and are far from perfect. To their dismay, they also become more aware that evil things are still deeply embedded in their spirit or psyche (heart), with which they are in continual conflict (Mark 7:21-23; Rom. 7:14-23; Gal. 5:17). Some of them at this point may even doubt their salvation. In spite of that, the best assurance they have that they are saved is to remember their first encounter with God, when He poured His Love on them.

XIII. The Battle between Good and Evil

*The great internal battle between the evil in the personality or flesh (1 Pet. 2:11; Rom. 7:21-23,25) and the growing Divine Spirit or Soul has finally begun. This struggle will be fierce for the control of the mind and body or personality of the spiritual children. The fight will be finished when the satanic nature within the personality is completely eliminated, and the Divine Spirit or Ideal Self takes a strong hold on the life of the purified personality.

In the course of this transformation, God sometimes allows evil forces to tempt His children and then let them overcome it, in order to strengthen their Spirits and personalities, as exercises make the muscles stronger. However, "He will not let you be tempted beyond your strength" (1 Cor. 10:13). At other times, He may send stressful circumstances in the lives of His beloved children, so that they may grow and be molded in His image by acquiring and strengthening in them certain Soul qualities. He does this because when His children are looking for a life of comfort and ease, they usually stop growing, stagnate, and regress.

---

* One of the main ideas of the novels of the Russian writer Dostoyevsky (D. 1881) is that everyone has within himself an angel and a demon whom are continually struggling. The Catholics believe that every individual has, on his right side, a good angel, and on the left, a dark angel, who influence their lives.

The Soul qualities or fruit of the (Divine) Spirit are "love, joy, peace, patience, kindness, goodness, faithfulness, gentleness, self-control"(Gal. 5:22-23). In addition we may add: compassion, grace, wisdom, courage, honesty, humility, serenity, integrity, dignity, honor, nobility, strength, perseverance, fortitude, etc. (see also James 1:2-4,12; 2 Pet. 1:5-7). How and in what degree His children react or respond to life's trials determine the Soul qualities they are developing. The children may become more loving and kind to others, take full responsibilities of all they do, have complete control of their lives, and be steadfast in their faith. They don't get easily discouraged, disappointed, worried, confused, or frustrated, and have become more confident, and act with poise, dignity, and nobility.

This internal battle is not merely a psychological struggle but also warfare for the possession of one's personality and property. Why is this so?

Adam and Eve ate, or became one with the "tree of the knowledge of good and evil", from which they were forbidden to eat, and *separated themselves from the Lord God who is the Source of all Life (Gen. 2:17). Being created in God's image, they belong to their Creator, but because they listened to satan's empty and deceptive words, they become also the possession of satan.

As descendants of the original pair, people of today can choose to whom they want to belong, God or satan, by their [#6]thoughts, words, and deeds. What is required from people as a condition to return to God is to have faith in Him and obey His Words which Adam and Eve failed to do. This is their responsible part, according to the laws of creation and re-creation, which anyone should fulfill, when growing to maturity, and it is a small price to pay. Satan, on the other hand, requires full payment because he not only claimed Adam and Eve as his possessions, but the world as well, which he continually rules through evil people and the ones whom are ignorant, undeveloped, passionate, and selfish (John 12:31; 11 Cor. 4:4).

---

* Because God's Spirit permeates and pervades in and throughout the universe, people can, in reality, not be separated from God, as a fish cannot be separated from the ocean. They, like Lucifer, separated themselves from God by a conscious choice, and saw themselves as separate from God and their brothers and sisters.

[#6] See Appendix

[a]Satan tempted Jesus of Nazareth who came as the last Adam (1 Cor. 15:45) to restore the position of the first Adam. As it was reported in Matt. 4:8-10, satan said to Jesus, "All these (kingdoms of the world) I will give you, if you will fall down and worship me." Because Jesus acquired victory over satan, the ransom price has become much less, but nevertheless demanded by the temporary laws of re-creation or restoration. By having faith in the redemption through the cross and in partaking of bread and wine, believers receive the great benefit of spiritual salvation, and being united with the Universal Christ with their "body, mind, and Spirit".

For every move human beings make in order to get themselves or others out of the camp of satan, they have to pay indemnity. If it is not paid voluntarily by, for example, fasting or other ways of suffering and sacrifices, the evil forces take it in the way of their own choosing. This price is usually in the form of accidents or sickness to you, or someone close to you: severe bouts of depression, doubts about God's Will, and other harmful ways, which prevent growth (2 Cor. 6:4-5), and which is "a thorn"---"in the flesh" (2 Cor. 12:7). However, after the debt is paid, satan does not have any claim on those people, and they feel liberated and closer to God.

In the beginning of this most important battle between the Spirits of Christ and the spirits of antichrist, or macrocosmically between [b]the "sons of light" and the "sons of darkness", the Divine Spirits may, at times, lose the war because they are not strong and developed to combat the evil in the personality of the newly born (Matt. 26:41). In that case, those individuals become more under the power and influence of satan, and have to pay again to their evil master, to get liberated.

To restore their relationship with God, individuals should repent and confess their wrongdoing, showing that they want to be on God's side. They become free of guilt and start anew by relying more on the Holy Spirit of God. In that case, the Holy Spirit via the Divine Spirit(s) is again in charge of their personalities or on the throne of their life, as some Christians say.

---

[a] As the gods in primitive societies were good as well as evil, and were responsible for both; in the New Testament era, Jesus separated the evil (satan) from God and made the devil responsible for the evil in society.

[b] Jesus said: "For the sons of this world are more shrewd in dealing with their own generation than the sons of light" (Luk. 16:8).

When a spiritual brother or sister deviate from the principles or backslide, they should not be ostracized physically by others in faith, by giving them a "cold shoulder" by not speaking to them. Emotionally, by feeling disappointed and angry of them. Mentally, by criticizing and thinking negatively about them. Spiritually, by not forgiving and praying for them. They should tell their deviated friends that they still love them, believe in them, and that they will pray for them. When brothers and sisters become more mature, they would act as Spiritual Parents to their wayward children. With the Heart of God, they would run after them and do everything possible to bring them back to God's Family, because they love them unconditionally, just the way they are. The children surely want to return as their prodigal sons or daughters (Luk. 15:11-24).

XIV. What Spiritual Children are Like

Spiritual children know how to feed themselves with Words of Truth or the *pure Word of God. They no longer need the milk of the Word, but have qualified to partake of the more solid food; that is, a broader and deeper understanding of the basic or "first principles of God's Word" (Heb. 5:12).

For many children God has become more real because they have found a higher concept of God. They believe firmly that God not only exists outside themselves, but discover and know that God has His secret dwelling place deep within their Divine Being(s) or most holy place (Ex. 26:34). Did Jesus not say, "The Kingdom of God is within you" (Luk. 17:20).

As Paul wrote in 1 Thess. 1:3, "Your faith is growing abundantly, and the love of everyone of you for one another is increasing." They have learned to be patient with those whom are less than perfect under trying circumstances and could measure the love they have by the sacrifices they are willing to make.

The spiritual child begins to understand that the individual Spirit of Christ, who dwells within the psyche (spirit) or holy place (Ex. 26:33) is identical to the Divine Spirit or Soul and can also be found in other mystical religions. When they help themselves with Words of Truth

---

* "All Scripture is inspired by God" (1 Tim. 3:16). It contains the Word of God, and is written in the words of exalted human beings. However, the teaching of Jesus Christ is purer than other teachings, which are somewhat mixed with culture.

they partake of the Substance and Life of Christ Consciousness or Son. By meditating on those Words they assimilate in them and build their eternal Christ or Truth Body. As Paul explained in Gal. 4:19, that "Christ be formed in you." The disciples in Antioch behaved so much like Christ that they were called Christians for the first time (Acts 11:26). They can say with Paul, "It is no longer I (personality) who live, but Christ who lives in me" (Gal. 2:20). Thus, by cultivating the Christ within, true Christians, like Peter, can perceive the invisible Christ without (Matt. 16:16).

XV. Comparing Spiritual Babies with Grown Children

As a baby in Christ absorbs the Love of God, the children radiate the Love and Light of God.

As a baby finds God everywhere, the more mature are able to recognize God working everywhere (not only in religion), to carry out His plan of salvation or restoration.

As babes are inclined to seek directions from their Spiritual Parents, the older ones are learning to listen to the prompting of the Holy Spirit for their guidance.

As infants talk to God in prayer, and God talks to them when they read Scripture, the older children are also able to talk and listen directly to what God has to say.

As little children don't like to take any responsibilities to carry out God's plan of restoration, the spiritual teenagers take some of the burden of God, by cooperating with God and doing their share of the work. God, therefore, helps those whom help themselves.

Baby Christians are looked upon by their intellectual unspiritual people, using their lower mind (which identifies reality with sense impressions (Jas. 3:15)), that those Christians cannot take care of and think for themselves. The spiritual youth whom have outgrown the dependable lifestyle are being led by their developed Divine Spirit or Higher Self, to lead their life and to use their enlightened higher intellect to solve many problems.

NOTE:
The ego of spiritual babies should be in full control of the physical body. "Sins of the flesh", such as gluttony, drinking, licentiousness, etc., should be

dominated, purifying the body. The ego of grown spiritual children should also be in control of their lower urges, desires, and emotions so that the emotional self becomes pure and clear. They eventually will also learn to control their thinking and willing and thinking the right way.

Immature Christians are still weak in what they believe. They therefore defy the value of a well-trained mind, which will make them doubt and question what they believe, and might even ridicule their deeply felt spiritual experiences. A grown child knows that the [a]focusing mind can be used by the lower self, (personality) which may be good or evil, and which does not understand the things of the Spirit (1 Cor. 2:14). The higher abstract mind of the personality, which deals with principles, has a better understanding of spiritual things, because it is not linear and analytical as the lower concrete mind, which deals with particulars. The higher mind is therefore more philosophical and clearer in its thinking. Moreover, it is pure reason because it functions in the realm of concept and ideas, and is not influenced by sensations and emotions. The spiritual youth, by using their Divine Mind or higher intuition of their Divine Spirits or Original Minds, have a much deeper perception and recognize Truth as Truth. Spiritual teenagers "perceive" with total comprehension because they can concentrate on aspects of life and gain complete insight and knowledge of it, without recourse to reasoning. They express this through the mind of their personality, which becomes more holy or holistic, brilliant and illuminated, while their emotions become radiant with love and compassion. They therefore understand much better, God's Will and Plan, than the babes in Christ.

The spiritual teenagers, by using the Mind of their Divine Spirits, are able to express the wisdom of God and, through their developing intuition, are better able to distinguish between good and evil as spiritual babies are able to do. [b]The youth in Christ are therefore not afraid to make contact with spirits of the lower heavens and are in continual communication with spirits of the higher heavens or divine dimension. They receive guidance and inspiration from them, to help with their mission. The youth in Christ also know how to "test the spirits to see whether they are of God" (1 John 4:1).

---

[a] The mind means the faculty through which one thinks, reasons, concentrates, and creates, etc. However, when the intellect is used for evil purposes, he or she becomes screwed, crafty, cunning, and clever.

[b] The spiritual youth no longer say, "I have a spirit," but rather, "I am a spirit."

XVI. Witnessing for Christ

The spiritual children like Jesus "increased in wisdom and in stature and in favor with God and man" (Luk. 2:52). They also "have put on the new nature, which is being renewed in knowledge after the image of its creator" (Col. 3:10). By putting into practice what they have learned, and by following the example of their teachers, Christ was formed in them, and became part of their Divine Nature. They soon were called Disciples of Christ, especially when they "have love for one another" (John 13:34). They were then told to "make disciples of all nations" (Matt. 28:19).

When spiritual children are more grown, they feel an urgency to witness and discover that the Spirit of God starts to work through them, not only by guiding them to persons whom God had prepared, but also by speaking through them to touch "the hearts" of the people witnessed to. *By allowing God to work through them, the children learn so much of the wisdom of God, but they also gain a much better understanding of the Principles of God. Because the Spirit of God is working through them the spiritual children and teenagers are becoming irresistible to the people they meet. They are "high in spirit" and feel like witnessing to everyone they meet, although they occasionally "throw your (their) pearls (Words of Truth) before swine" (Matt. 7:6). As the Scripture furthermore tells it, "But you shall receive power when the Holy Spirit has come upon you" (Acts 1:8). Thus, when the Disciples of Christ were filled with the Holy Spirit, it changed them from selfish, insecure, and fearful people into bold witnesses for Christ. They were not afraid of what to say, because as Matt. 10:20 has it, "For it is not you who speak but the Spirit of your Father speaking through you" (see also 2 Pet. 1:21).

Thus, in order to be successful in witnessing, it is important that the grown children are one with the universal Christ and that they [a]allow Christ to work through them, because "apart form me you can do

---

* Witnesses whom love or try to love people by opening their "hearts" to them, can easily be used by God to let His or Her love come through to the people. By speaking directly to their "hearts", the people do not mind if their personalities sometimes get offended, because their Real Selves cannot be injured by the Truth.

[a] Spiritual workers are sometimes so "busy doing God's work" by helping the people in their care, that they have no time to pray. The result is that the channel between their Divine Spirits and their personalities gets more and more obstructed, especially when they are frustrated and aggravated and do a lot of mundane thinking. The Lord is not able to work through them in a wholesome way, showing His concern and love for the people.

nothing" (John 15:5). If the children by disobedience, opposition, or ignorance resist the flow of Life, they become non-productive.

[b]It sometimes takes quite a while before the Spirit of God is able to express or break through to the outer personality of the witness. That is why it is good to pray and meditate before going to testify for Christ, in order to clear the channel between the Divine Spirit and the inner and outer personality, of negative thought forms, of doubt, lack of trust, and other obstructions. However, God as Parents are very joyful to have finally found a channel and voice, through which they desperately try to reach their lost sons and daughters.

However, when they start to witness and lead someone or a group of people out of the stronghold of satan (John 12:31; 2 Cor. 4:4) into the Kingdom of God, opposition is to be expected, especially when they are going to be successful. This happened to the baby church in Thessalonica (1 Thess. 2:14), whom were severely persecuted by the population, and had to endure all kinds of hardships.

[c]After the children and teenagers have spoken to many people, they finally find a few whom are responsive to their message. They are usually much like them in character, so that they can learn much about themselves. Being successful, they also have to endure persecution of all sorts, when not only evil spirits but also the evil power within "nice people", starts acting up, especially of those whom have control and authority over them. They attack the children of God, for no valid reason(s), by negative words, emotions, and thoughts (2 Cor. 6:4-5; 11:23-29).

The grown children feel responsible, to teach their guests and pay indemnity for them because they are still (more or less) in the grip or owned by evil forces. Much of the wrongdoing of their ancestors have

---

[b] This is especially true in the morning, when you don't feel so "high" as the day before. This is because during sleep your higher spirit bodies separate, more or less, from your body or physical consciousness, and it takes some time for the divine and spirit bodies to penetrate and align with the outer personality again.

[c] It is only possible to find and raise a spiritual child when the fatherly love of God flows through the man (spiritual parent) and the motherly love of God flows through the woman (spiritual parent). If the man or woman thinks about the potential spiritual child as a possible mate and even has sexual feelings for her or him, then no rebirth can take place (divine child remains unborn) because they are obstructing the Divine Flow of God.

been paid by Jesus Christ and saints of all religions, but some *sins still need to be paid, before they are liberated. This also includes individual karmic debt, so that their guests will more quickly join the Family of God.

The spiritual teens soon start to function in their new roles as Spiritual Parents, to their new babes in Christ. The Parents, with the guidance of the Holy Spirit, teach them the ways of God, by example and words, and protect them against evil forces with or without bodies (John 15:5-8).

The babes are then told that they should live according to God's Principles in order to restore their relationship with God. They should also, with the help of God, find an Abel type person and follow their directions for a while, in order to remove their satanic nature and restore their lost position. This was exemplified by monks and sisters in monasteries, by being obedient and dependent on God for all their needs, while they were also living a chaste life.

XVII. To Know God Personally

In order to know God, it is not only important to know the Truth and His Will, but above all, by knowing Him personally, through everyday experiences. After a period of time, your relationship becomes more intimate and you accept Him as the "God of my heart", as well as the God of the universe. After many encounters with your Heavenly Parents, you will know that they will always love you and be with you, even when everyone has deserted you. You will also understand how much the Heavenly Parents love other people and through them also try to speak to you, to make you joyful, so that they will be full of joy.

---

* Sin is an act (physical or psychological) whereby a person separates from God and one's Divine Essence, and thus inhibits growth.

Many people may attain physical parenthood, but only a few reaches the status of spiritual father and motherhood in the stage of maturity.

XVIII. What Does the Bible Say about Spiritual Maturity

God has revealed Himself through the creation (Rom 1:20) and inspired writings, but most fully in the person of Jesus Christ. As the Scripture says about Christ, "For in Him the whole fullness of deity dwells bodily" (Col. 2:9).

God is very much like Jesus Christ, that is why Christ could say; "He who has seen me has seen the Father" (John 14:9).

As Paul the Apostle of Jesus Christ expressed it --- "When the perfect comes the imperfect will pass away. When I was a child, (spiritual) I spoke like a child, I thought like a child, I reasoned like a child; when I became a man, I gave up childish ways. For now we see in a mirror dimly, but then face to face" (1 Cor. 13:10-12).

As Eph. 4:13-14 explains it; " --- and of the knowledge of the Son of God, to mature manhood, to the measure of the stature of the fullness of Christ; so that we may no longer be children, tossed to and from and carried about with every wind of doctrine."

"Brethren, do not be children in your thinking; be babes in evil, but in thinking be mature" (1 Cor. 14:20).

"The spiritual man (adult) judges all things, but is himself to be judged by no one. For who has known the mind of the Lord so as to instruct Him?" (1 Cor. 2:15-16).

The spiritual adult is able to judge with God's judgment and express "the fruit of the Spirit" in daily life, such as: "love, joy, peace, patience, kindness, goodness, faithfulness, gentleness, self-control", etc. (Gal. 5:22-23).

The adult not just acknowledges the teaching of Jesus and Paul, such as, for example: Luk. 6:27-30, Matt. 5:39-44, Rom. 12:17, 1 Cor. 6:7, but live it every day of their life.

Being one with God, who dwells in everything He has made, the spiritual adults are also one and in harmony with the forces of nature, and are with Jesus Christ able to control those forces and beings, and be helped by it to perform "miracles". They are always creative, constructive in every act they do, which is always good for the betterment of everyone, from which they bring out the best. Just by their presence, the germs of wisdom, love, goodness, which is in everyone, begins to awaken and develop by itself, just as the germs within the seed, through the first warmth of spring, germinate and grow. They teach mainly by example and attainment and open up the higher energy centers of the people they teach.

They live, not only according to the 10 Commandments as described in Ex. 20 and Deut. 5 externally, but also to the internal principles. As Jesus said, "You have heard that it was said to the men of old, 'You shall not kill; and whoever kills shall be liable to judgment.' But I say to you that everyone who is *angry with his brother shall be liable to judgment" (Matt. 5:21-22). By being angry, serious damage can be done to the aura of the spirit body of the other person, especially to the emotional envelope or sheath, and the karmic price has to be paid. Further, Jesus said; "You have heard that it was said, 'You shall not commit adultery.' But I say to you that every one who looks at a woman lustfully has already committed adultery with her in his heart" (Matt. 5:27-28). Looking at a woman and (or) pictures for lustful reasons may eventually create a psychic bond with her. The result is that they harm themselves internally, dragging each other's spirits towards the lower realm, and become extremely selfish. He will also do serious damage to the relationship with his spouse and care less about his children.

The spiritual adult, as a male, thinks about a woman as becoming a child of God, whereby she would be most beautiful and attractive, radiating the Love of God.

---

* According to the Pharisees and the doctors of the law in the past and today, the 6th Commandment was not broken until someone had been killed. The lawyers reasoned as the lawmen do today that they can only arrest someone for his or her own outward criminal act, not for what they are thinking and feeling. However, in God's "eyes" negative thoughts and emotions can also do serious damage to the other, such as angry thoughts, words and looks (evil eye), etc., which causes to trigger in the other: reaction, hatred, resentment, contempt, grudge, hostility, revenge, spite, etc. For "man looks on the outward appearance, but the Lord looks on the heart" (1 Sam. 16:7). See also 1 John 3:15.

The adults think like God thinks, and thus do not have to pray in order to re-connect with God because of wrong thinking. Their ways are the ways of the Lord (Isa. 55:7-9).

Spiritual adults, like flowers in full bloom, are a beautiful sight to behold. They emit a spiritual fragrance and radiate love, compassion, and strength from their brilliant auras, which embrace, from a great distance, all people whom they meet, see, and not see. They are kind, considerate, altruistic, unselfish, and have a strong personal magnetism or charisma at all levels of their beings. They attract people to them, to be "spiritually fed" from their Beings and Words they speak.

XIX. Spiritual Adults Know about Good and Evil

As spiritual babies "long for the pure spiritual milk" (1 Pet. 2:2), the "solid food is for the mature (the deeper things of God), for those who have their faculties trained by practice to distinguish good from evil" (Heb. 5:14). Because the spiritually mature persons have completely conquered the evil within themselves, they are given of the "hidden manna" (New Words of Truth) – Rev. 2:17 which was left in the Ark of the Covenant (Heb. 9:4).

Because spiritual adults are one with God, they sense the presence of evil and evil intentions of others immediately and very strongly, and can therefore not tolerate evil in any form. As Jesus "overturned the tables of the money changers" (Matt. 21:12) and believed in the reality of satan, so do adults have similar intentions of destroying evil in and around people. Those humans whom make an evil base by desiring, thinking, and acting like satan, and thus strengthen their evil nature, can be easily influenced by him and his cohorts, and have become an enemy to God (Rom. 8:7-8).

The individual whom has become an imitation of Christ has completely cleansed the sinful or satanic nature of his or her personality, and can therefore no longer be influenced by evil forces, whom have become powerless for them.

XX. What Spiritual Adults are Like

"The spiritual men" (and women) whom have come in their prime of life are not conceited, arrogant, and inflated with pride. They are not influenced or affected with what others think about them (John 5:41), especially not by the people whom are living the life of the good and evil personalities or the natural or "unspiritual man" (1 Cor. 2:14-15). What is most important for them is what God thinks about them. They take no account of the evil done to them, are not resentful, and are easy to forgive. They love all people with God's unconditional love, are impersonal, and are not attached to persons or things (Acts 10:34). They remain compassionate, gentle, and true to their Real Selves in the face of the most trying circumstances and oppositions. Instead of condemning the people whom oppose them by thoughts, words, and deeds, they feel sorry for them. The adults in full bloom say with Jesus Christ, "Father, forgive them; for they know not what they do" (Luk. 23:34). By loving and forgiving, they exercise and strengthen their Divine Spirits, which easily break through their purified personality, by which they are no longer held in bondage.

Instead of "surrendering" completely to God, they, as spiritual men and women at full age, take full responsibility to cooperate with the divine plan of salvation or restoration. One of their important tasks is *to make disciples of Christ out of spiritual children, and send them all over the world, to witness by Word and examples for the divine cause (Matt. 28:19-20).

As spiritual children have learned much from the elders, adults have learned much from the inspiration of the Holy Spirit in spiritual knowledge, wisdom, and the ways of God and His purpose for creation. They eventually feel the way God feels, judge situations the way God judges them, and act the way God would act.

XXI. Spiritual Adults Know the Heart of God

The Spirit of God also reveals Their Parental Heart, which they could not reveal to ordinary people and babes in Christ, because they would not understand. This is one of the things the disciples of Jesus Christ could not yet bear to hear (John 16:12).

The mature in Christ experience much rejection and persecution, like Jesus from the world (John 7:7; 15:18). As Spiritual Parents, they are often heartbroken when a spiritual child or little children, in whom they have invested their whole being(s), want to have nothing to do

---

* Following Jesus, spiritual adults in the training of others exercise the right to scold, every time the evil nature starts acting up in their aspirants. By doing this they would often hurt their egos, but the disciples will then grow rapidly. The adults would certainly not pamper to the good/evil egos of their students.

with them anymore, by again living their evil lifestyle. Through those experiences, Spiritual Parents can therefore understand and get to know God much better; whom for thousands of years, as Heavenly Parents, tried to bring back the people to their bosom, but they would not.

"Sons have I reared and brought up, but they rebelled against me. The ox knows its owner, and the ass its master's crib; but Israel does not know, my people do not understand" (Isaiah 1:2-3).

Hosea wrote, "When Israel was a child, I (the Lord) loved him, and out of Egypt I called my son. The more I called them, the more they went from me; they kept sacrificing to the Baals, and burning incense to idols. Yet it was I who taught Ephraim to walk, I took them up in my arms; but they did not know that I healed them. I led them with cords of compassion, with the bands of love, and I became to them as one who eases the yoke of their jaws, and I bent down to them and fed them" (11:1-4).

Through Jesus Christ, the Heavenly Parents lamented, "O Jerusalem, Jerusalem, killing the prophets and stoning those who are sent to you! How often would I have gathered your children together as a hen gathers her brood under her wings, and you would not" (Matt. 23:37).

Being directly and continually involved with human affairs, God is fully aware of their misery, and feels with them, and does everything to relieve their suffering, especially when the people *ask for His help. He will then find a way through responsive people to warn them of impending disasters and to bring relief to their hardship.

As God longs to embrace all people, the people deep within their heart want to embrace their Heavenly Parents, so that they are no longer lonely and suffer from spiritual hunger and thirst. They will then also truly unite with each other at the level of their Inner Beings, and become also one in their outer life.

XXII. Conclusion

Spiritual adults have realized and know, that they are the Spirits of Christ (have achieved Christ Consciousness) through which their outer

---

* Through their request, ungenerated people let God know that they want to belong to Him and not satan. He then can act only when they ask, because people have free will, and then, only if it is good for them, in His perfect timing (1 John 5:14).

personalities can communicate with the individualized Spirit of God, who dwells deep within their Beings (Rev. 21:3). As humanity, as a whole, advances, as individuals grow and multiply; so the Universal Parents will grow. When more and more people develop their Christ Spirits, they will multiply and gain more power in the world.

The adults at full age have attained Cosmic Consciousness, because their fully integrated, purified, and developed personalities are fully united with their Christ Spirits which, in turn, have grown to become completely one with the god Selves of their brethren in Christ which is always one with the Universal or Cosmic Spirit of God (John 14:10).

They have complete knowledge of the whole Word of God, have become the Word of God (Being of Truth), speak the Word of God (Truth), and have become an individual god (John 10:34). They have become perfect like the heavenly Father is perfect (Matt. 5:48).

Jesus of Nazareth is no longer a God to be worshipped, but an elder brother with whom they cooperate to completely fulfill the mission Jesus started, about two thousand years ago – The Kingdom of Heaven on Earth.

As Jesus said so profoundly: "Truly, truly, I say to you, he who believes in me will also do the works that I do: and greater works than these will he do" (John 14:12).

The spiritual adults are now ready to do the greater works Jesus promised they would do.

PART 5   LIFE OF SPIRITUAL BABIES, YOUNG AND
ADULTS WHOM HAVE ENTERED AND ARE
LIVING IN THE KINGDOM OF GOD

XXIII. What Does the Bible Say about the New Kingdom

When a person goes through spiritual birth and growth, we see dramatic changes in lifestyle, purpose, thoughts, desires, outlook, and a different reason(s) for living.

The Book of Revelation says, "Then I saw a new heaven and a new earth; for the first heaven and the first earth has passed away," --- "Behold, I make all things new" (Rev. 21:1,5).

"Therefore, if anyone is in Christ, he is a new creation; the old has passed away, behold, the new has come" (2 Cor. 5:17).

You "put on the new nature, created after the likeness of God" (Eph. 4:24), which is called by its *"new name", which is written on a "white stone" (Divine Spirit), "which no one knows except him who receives it" (Rev. 2:17). This name is also "written in the book of life" (Rev. 20:12,15; Phil. 4:3).

"So then you are no longer strangers and sojourners, but you are fellow citizens with the saints and members of the household of God" (Eph. 2:19).

After having received a "spiritual birth certificate", you are able to get a "passport", to enter and become a citizen of the heavenly world or the "Kingdom of God".

You are a pilgrim, moving toward a new destination, and belong to a new family.

You may be living in this physical world, but you are no longer a member of the good and evil world (John 18:36; Eph. 2:1-2).

---

* When one becomes a new creation, they no longer are identified with his or her old name, but are called by their new name(s). For example, the name Simon became Peter (Matt. 16:18); the name Saul became Paul (Acts 13:9).

Your Divine Spirit(s) lives in the heavenly world, but penetrates and is united with your psychological and physical bodies, as air in water and water in sand. "The holy city Jerusalem coming down out of heaven from God" (Rev. 21:10).

Living in the [a] "City of God" as a saint you will be able to communicate with Divine Beings of the high heavens of the divine world through the newly-opened faculties of your Divine Spirit.

You are no longer an ordinary human being or natural man/woman (1 Cor. 2:14), living the *life of the good and evil personality, but will become a super human being.

XXIV. Life Before and After Turning to Christ

You know that you are spiritually born, because of the different life you want to live. You are aware of God's presence and feel that you are Their child whom you call Father/Mother in your prayers. You are hungry for Words of Truth and are eager to do God's Will.

You have become God conscious, instead of [b]self-conscious. Instead of having too much concern for yourself as a physical grown-up, you now have a much more outgoing concern for others.

Since you, as a personality are influenced by your growing Divine Spirit, you don't like your friends anymore, whose personalities are much influenced by their evil nature and evil entities with or without bodies. You soon find new friends, whom are more interested in living according to the Plan of the Creator, which is for the benefit of all people.

You have become joyful instead of being happy, wholesome instead of incomplete, compassionate instead of reacting emotionally, wise instead of knowledgeable, peaceful instead of having spells of anxiety, loving instead of hateful and angry, courageous instead of being fear-

---

[a] Augustine believed in the "City of God" (see book by that name) and the city of evil. Because people are good and evil there is still a more populated third city.

* For additional information, see Appendix **#9**.

[b] People whom center too much on their personality, whose basic characteristic is selfishness, are self-conscious and shy (what do other people think about me). However, when they accept Christ, they are no longer withdrawn in their homemade psychological shell, but liberated.

ful, feel protected and secure instead of suffering of lack and insecurity.

You are no longer constantly occupied about your mode of living, your method of earning money, and the opinions of others consider your character and behavior. You are more interested in what God and spiritual elders think about you, and in the moral and spiritual development of the people you meet.

You have become more tolerant of people, their beliefs, convictions, cultural expressions (1 Cor. 9:19-23), and are able to forgive them for the wrong they have done to you. You rather feel sorry for them, because they have to pay the karmic price (Gal. 6:7-10; Luk. 23:34).

Your interests, desires, attitudes, are different than of the people whom are living the relative good and evil lifestyle. You are no longer able to laugh at their dirty jokes. You are no longer interested in their parties, the way they dance, low vibration music, free love, drinking, and drugs; which you now believe is nothing else but a substitute for divine life, and to overcome inhibition of your self-conscious insecure ego. Besides, you always feel an urge to witness for Christ and therefore might "spoil" the party.

You are no longer able to impress others how tough you are, by swearing and expressing worn out dirty words. You don't like to gossip and waste your time on idle chat. You would rather be creative in your talking, especially when it is centered on God's Will, because restoration has been, and still is, the most urgent matter.

You are no longer impressed by rich people and their possessions, and don't envy them, especially when so many of them are spiritually dead. Having gained *human power, authority, and prestige, centered on outer values, the rich are less likely to seek for Divine power, Divine authority, guidance, and inner values (1 Tim. 6:6-10; 6:17-19). Besides, by doing God's Will (teaching – sacrifice – serving etc.), He will provide you with everything you need, not only the spiritual but also the physical necessities (Matt. 6:3; 6:33; 10:9-10; 1 Cor. 9:1-18).

You believe that certain physical, emotional, and mental suffering has a purpose for the good; by paying indemnity for yourself and others, in order to pay off karmic debt made in this lifetime; the debt

---

* No man or woman has power, except the powers followers give them, either physical – people work for them; psychological – being influenced by them; spiritually – believing in them.

your ancestors have made, and to liberate oneself or others from the power of satan.

Your physical body has become more important to you. You not only see it as the temple of the Holy Spirit (1 Cor. 6:19), but also as a vehicle for doing good deeds, which invisible results will grow your spirit body. It is also an important vehicle to gather valuable earth experience. It should therefore be kept clean externally and internally, from the wrong and coarse things you eat, drink, and inhale. When it becomes much healthier and sensitive, it affects the conditions of the spirit body because it is closely related to each other. It then becomes a powerful "instrument or tool" to be used most effectively by your higher vibration spirit bodies. This is especially true when the constitution of the physical body is not coarse but of finer vibrations.

Your taste for music has also changed. You now listen to and enjoy uplifting music, which is in harmony with the universe and the higher part of your being. It heals your negative emotions of hostility, resentment, fear, etc., which in turn affects your thinking. It integrates the physical, emotional, and mental aspects of your being and binds them to your awakened Soul. Besides, this high vibration music makes plants grow better and animals more "alive" and more agreeable to live with. You also appreciate much better famous works of art, and find true beauty and harmony in them, which brings out the best within yourself and others.

God created the cosmos out of chaos and pervaded everything with *His Consciousness in different modification. For example, God the Creator is unconscious in the mineral world, is stirring in the plants, awakens in the animals, is conscious in humans, and fully alive in Divine Beings or super humans, through whom He can express and make Himself known most completely. True artists, as creators, leave likewise something of themselves in their works of art. The aliveness of their art depends on how much creative energy they invested, and how much "alive" they were at that time.

You are no longer afraid to grow older, because you know that your Divine Spirit will become wiser, always appear young, and that it lives forever. When your personality is closely connected and in harmony with your Divine Spirit, you are looking younger and radiate more

---

* The German philosopher Friedrich von Schelling (D. 1854) wrote, "Mind sleeps in the stone, dreams in the plant, awakens in the animal, and becomes conscious in man."

beauty. You no longer look like an old man (woman) because your evil nature ("old man") is no longer in charge of your life (Eph. 4:22-24).

The "old self or nature" (Col. 3:9-10) has passed away as a ruler (after it has been stripped of evil traits, which are part of the old personality), and has come back as a pure servant to the indwelling Divine Spirit.

The urge to be dominant has passed away as being prideful and puffed up with an overdeveloped big ego, and has come back as humility, under the rule of your Divine Spirit and the indwelling Spirit of God.

The sex life has passed away as satanic love (by seeing each other as the source of love, instead of God within themselves) and lust and has come back as true Love and creative activity expressed through a pure personality.

The acquisition and hoarding of wealth for one's own importance and security has come back in helping others with that wealth, as a true son and daughter of God.

> **NOTE**: We may add here a few American pioneer proverbs:
>
> "Doing an injury puts you below your enemy; revenging one makes you but even with him; forgiving sets you above them."
>
> "To err is human; to forgive is divine."
>
> "He that falls into sin is a man; he that grieves at it is a saint; He that boasts of it is a devil."

XXV. Living a Divine Life

"I came that they may have life, and have it abundantly" (John 10:10).

By practicing the teaching of Christ and becoming more like Him, you want to give more than you receive. Your "spiritual bank account" is always full, and your prayers will be answered more readily, especially for those whom are in line with God's Will. You will have plenty (Luk. 6:38) and " more will be given to you" (Mark 4:24).

By living a divine life, more energy will come to you from your higher energy centers, which are of high quality. Because of this flow, you feel exalted, less tired, even lighter, and in touch with the higher realms of the higher spirit – or divine worlds. This spiritual energy is also a healing energy, which will heal the lower energy bodies or the vital – emotional – mental aspects of your personality. It will also strengthen the immune system of the physical body so that you will live longer. Because you think *more positive, and express yourself through higher and purer emotions, you become less exhausted and thus spend less time in #7sleep to recuperate.

Since you have accepted through the teaching of Scripture the Universal Christ (Son), your own Christ or Divine Spirit starts to form in you (Gal. 4:19). You have become a new person. Your physical body lives in the physical world, by which you are in touch with through your physical senses. Your human spirit lives in the lower spirit world, by which you can be in contact with through your developing psychic senses. Your Divine Spirit lives in the divine world, which is also called heaven or paradise (Mark 16:19; Luk. 23:43; 2 Cor. 12:2-4). This world can be known through the exercise of your budding spiritual faculties or senses. These #8three worlds don't lay above each other, but interpenetrate as air in water and water in sand.

Knowing that you live in three worlds, living has become very interesting and exciting. You are filled with wonder, and there is so much to discover and so much to learn. You are †no longer vague but more aware of the psychic world, and the divine world you experience as a new reality. You now sense and understand that many things that happen to you and other people on the physical plane, has its cause in the worlds of spirit. You will also understand much better, for example; communication with human spirits and Divine Beings, possessions and exorcism, reincarnation, which is a form of obsession

---

* Because mind exists in every cell of the physical body, right thinking and feeling changes the cellular vibrations of the cells and thus influences the health of the whole body.

#7 See Appendix

#8 See Appendix

† When our spirit bodies are more concretely formed (not as wraith or ghost of undeveloped people in Sheol (Psalms 88; 139:8; 16:10) and used as a vehicle by our eternal Divine Spirits; we find that death is but a withdrawal from the physical body and its sensation. The remainder of the external personality, called human spirit body or psyche (emotion – intellect – will) continues as it was in the invisible realm. Thus we are already in possession of our more or less developed survival equipment or spacesuits, to exist or live in the invisible dimension of life.

and guidance of spirits, cases of schizophrenia, telepathy, hearing voices, déjà vu (already seen), astral and mental projection or remote viewing, automatic writing, hauntings, psychokinesis, near death experiences, different forms of mediumship or channeling, materialization (the way Jesus appeared after His crucifixion), and many other psychic phenomena. Apostle Paul speaks in 1 Cor. 12:4-11, about some of the higher phenomena as gifts of the Spirit. Although it is possible to make contact with loved ones, it is also possible, when not strong in faith, to be influenced by undesirable entities. In that case it is better to communicate with spiritual beings and saints of the divine world, whom will inspire and guide you to grow spiritually.

The physical world is alive all around you, and God, after planning, created order out of disorder, and from simple to complex, seems to be everywhere. You sense His invisible nature and presence in everything (Rom. 1:20) He has made, even the very stones have His imprint and seem to speak to you.

As the Apostle Paul said in Rom. 8:19, "For the creation waits with eager longing for the revealing of the sons of God."

*As God made you alive spiritually by loving you, you, as the Lord and center of creation, can make everything come much more alive by taking care of the creation and by truly loving it (Gen. 1:28). Animals know that they have finally found their true master (Gen. 2:19-20), and they become psychically much more alive, by receiving true love from you, and are therefore not so wild anymore (Isaiah 11:6-9). They may even survive death, and may live for a long time in the spirit world. The plants are thriving and growing much better, whenever you are around them and take care of them.

Because you have changed, the creation around you has likewise changed and has become as new. Nature is still the same but has become more vibrant with life. The trees and the mountains still look the same, but are not the same. The stars appear brighter, the flowers more beautiful, the songs of the birds sweeter, and the world is no longer hostile (Rom. 8:21).

---

* Only humans are given breath of God "and man became a living being" (Gen. 2:7). Animals have only the "breath of life" (Gen. 1:30). Man became caretaker of the animals by giving them names.

You appreciate life much more, and all what God has made. The most mundane and trivial things of your life are inspired, and of profound mystery and wonder. By living in harmony with the universe, you go with the flow and everything is therefore going your way.

You might have felt at times that you are someone special, that you are not from this world, and that people don't understand you.

You are radiant with Light, because your personality (bodily – etheric – emotional – mental, aspects) is pure and integrated (when mature). The light of your Divine Spirit shines through the transparent spirit body, and makes your etheric eye look clear and sound (Matt. 6:22).

Because you strive to help your fellow humans, you feel more valuable, useful, and have an increased sense of well being. Life for you has become more meaningful and of higher quality.

You think more clearly, are more creative, act more decisively, and have more power and ability to accomplish more in less time and thus become more productive and successful, while cooperating and getting along with others.

You are Self-reliant, Self-confident, and filled with Self-determination, and have a sense of Selfhood.

You are able to bring out the best in yourself, find good in others, are more open, considerate, loving, joyful, and have peace of mind, and are always willing to help the least of your brethren (Matt. 25:40).

You are more natural in your expressions of cosmic humor, laugh with one's whole being, and dance in harmony with and in rhythm of the universe.

Because your human spirit, strengthened by your Divine Spirit, has a strong hold or grip on your body, it has become much easier to break and overcome bad habits of overeating, smoking, drinking, drugs, negative emotions, and promiscuous behaviors.

You have more hope, feel more secure, have patience, and have complete faith and trust in God and the universe, and believe in the brotherhood and sisterhood of all people of this global village.

XXVI. What the Ideal World is Like

In the ideal world there is no need of a military force to defend one's country against invaders. Police forces are mostly used to regulate traffic, rescue operations, firefighters, and other vital services. The people have complete understanding of the working of the law of karma, or the law of sowing and reaping. They therefore have absolute confidence that it will take care, and regulate their life, so that justice is always perfectly served. They, therefore, will not do anything to hurt others. Besides, they love each other so much; how can they cheat, steal, bear false witness and enviously desire what someone else has, if they truly love each other? Because they trust each other, there is no need to use locks, security devices, and guards to protect their possessions. The work of lawmakers, judges, and lawyers will be very limited, because the criminal justice system will be mostly done away with. This will release millions of workers for more productive and useful operations. Because people will be healthier and live longer, most health care facilities, with their doctors and nurses, will no longer be needed. Because people trust in their Creator to provide for all their needs, and can count on their neighbors, most insurance companies, whom thrive on people's fears and insecurity, are no longer of any use. Working will be a joy, everybody can be creative, and supervisors are beings whom are not only knowledgeable, but also morally and spiritually developed, so that workers are not driven by fear but by "brotherly love". Education is not only geared towards intellectual development, but most importantly to spiritual development, including the understanding of the meaning and purpose of life. Having achieved Christ Consciousness, there will be peace in and between (among) nations, because beneath the surface of the symbolic ocean, the Divine Spirits of the people are all connected, as the rocks are at the bottom of the sea. They are thus no longer separate islands above the surface, when living the life of the personalities. The world will then be ruled by God (as the brain), and His Will is conveyed through the *Universal Christ (central nervous system) to all the people of the world, becoming "one body in Christ" (Rom. 12:4-5).

---

* The Universal Christ will be represented by someone who is conquering (Rev. 6:2) and is called the Word of God and King of Kings (Rev. 19:11-16) and has conquered (Rev. 21:7). The Holy Spirit will be represented by His Bride (Rev. 19:7).

Finally, as the statue in the dream of Nebuchadnezzar was smitten by a stone that filled the earth, so the human kingdom will be destroyed and be replaced with the Kingdom of God (Daniel 2:31-45). The prophesies in Isaiah 9,11 and 60 will then be fulfilled.

DIAGRAM
INHABITANTS OF THE CREATED WORLD IN
THEIR DIFFERENT STAGES OF DEVELOPMENT

VII **DIVINE**	PLANE OF COSMIC OR UNIVERSAL CONSCIOUS-NESS	**I AM WHO I AM** **GOD BECAME HUMAN AND HUMAN BECAME GOD** **I AM PRESENCE** DIRECT DOMINION OF GOD		LIFE OF DIVINE SPIRIT OR SOUL		DIVINE LIFE
VI	PLANE OF CHRIST CONSCIOUS-NESS	**SPIRITUAL ADULT STAGE - SPIRIT OF CHRIST** **MATURE SONS AND DAUGHTERS OF GOD** 3RD INITIATION		SUPER-HUMAN		COMPLETION
V **WORLDS**	INTUITIONAL . PLANE	**SPIRITUAL CHILD AND YOUTH STAGE**	**USING HIGHER** **INTUITION** **OR DIVINE MIND** 2ND INITIATION	GOLDEN AGE- KINGDOM OF GOD		NEW
IV	DIVINE PLANE	**SPIRITUAL BABYHOOD STAGE** **BIRTH OF THE SOUL**	1ST INITIATION	BORN OF GOD		TESTAMENT (PRINCIPLE)
III **MENTAL** **WORLD**	HIGHER PLANE FORMLESS FORM LOWER PLANE	HIGHER ABSTRACT MIND IDEAS AND CONCEPTS **REASON** LOWER CONCRETE MIND SENSIBLE KNOWLEDGE	**MENTAL** **SPIRIT BODY** (PSYCHIC) **HUMAN**	HIGHER ANGELS & EXTRATERRESTRIALS AND OTHERS	BORN AGAIN IDEAL LIFE OF GOOD PERSONALITY	OLD TESTAMENT (LAW)
II **DESIRE** **WORLD**	HIGHER PLANE EMOTION SENSATION LOWER PLANE	INDIVIDUALS PSYCHE HIGHER ANIMALS LOWER DESIRES(INSTINCT) GROUP SOUL PSYCHE LOWER ANIMALS	HIGHER DESIRES UNDEVELOPED HUMANS **PSYCHIC BODY** EMOTIONAL(ASTRAL) ANIMAL-HUMAN	LOWER ANGELS LOWER INTUITION INSTINCTIVE HIGHER NATURE SPIRITS (E.T.s)	OR	ORDINARY HUMAN LIFE
I **PHYSICAL** **WORLD**	ETHERIC REGION CHEMICAL REGION	1st ETHERIC- NEUTRINOS 2nd ETHERIC-ELECTRONS 3rd ETHERIC-PROTONS 4th ETHERIC- IONIC 1st GAS 2nd LIQUID 3rd SOLID	**VITAL BODY** PLANT-ANIMAL-HUMAN **DENSE BODY** MINERAL-PLANT-ANIMAL-HUMAN	ETHERIC BEINGS LOWER NATURE SPIRITS, FAIRIES, E.T.s ELEMENTARY ENTITIES	LIFE OF GOOD & EVIL PERSONALITY	PRE-HISTORIC

The dense bodies of minerals goes slightly beyond the chemical region, indicating chemical affinity. The etheric of plants and vegetables also passes the borderline somewhat by having some feeling or forms of desire, while animals, especially the domesticated, not only have instinct, but show a rudimentary intellect with a limited capacity of reason.

Appendix

#1 By "dark night of the soul" is meant the "darkness of the senses" or human spirit (not of the Spirit), when one feels forsaken by God. Because the personality or ego is good and false: it is arrogant, boastful, vainglorious, conceited, complacent, full of self-importance, inflated with a falsehood, and leading a life of emptiness and futility, or uselessness. See the Book of Ecclesiastes. Therefore, the ego, with divine help, needs to be purified, in order to be used properly by the developing Divine Spirit in one's being. In the process of that change, the inner personality or human spirit, in cooperation with its evil nature, wants to live its life independently from the control of his or her own budding Divine Spirit or Soul. In the ensuing struggle one's inherited evil nature needs "to die", so that a new being of the same structure may emerge, "stripped" from its evil or satanic nature. This new person will be embraced and used by God in a great way, to establish His Kingdom.

#2 Some people of today, and the Pelagians of +/- 400 A.D. (most of them were members of the stoic religion), do not believe that children are born with original sin, which separates people from God. However, alienation from God is not only the greatest sin of Christianity, but also for many adherents of eastern religions. It is however true, thanks to 2000 years of Christianity, and contributions of other religions, that many children of today are born with much less original sin. In the time of Augustine (+/- 400 A.D.), and throughout the Middle Ages, the evil nature within the newly converted pagans of Europe was still very strong. The orthodox explanation of Augustine about original sin was therefore readily accepted by the people in the Middle Ages, as it was certainly true for their life, and still true for many people today.

#3 Adam and Eve were the first of all the humans living at that time, whom had the potential to reach spiritual maturity. They as teenagers did not choose to live a divine life, because they "ate of", and became like the symbolic "tree of the knowledge of good and evil". They got stuck in their growth, and were condemned to live the life of a human being instead of a divine being, and they also acquired a satanic nature. That is why Apostle Paul could say in 1 Cor. 15:45, "The first man Adam became a living being (human being); the last Adam (Jesus Christ) became a life-giving spirit." Teenagers of every generation have to make the same choice as Adam and Eve, when they become mature in their personality, to live a human life or divine life.

#4 The flesh in the New Testament refers sometimes to flesh and bones, but in Paul's writings, it often means the good and evil human nature, as is meant here in 1 Cor. 3:1-3. In other places, such as Gal. 5:16-17; Rom. 8:5-8, the flesh is the tendency or impulse to do evil and operate independent of God. It is in continual warfare with the Divine Spirit and is the inherited fallen or satanic nature. This evil within the human spirit is also named "old nature" in Eph. 4:22, and is more personified as the "old self" or "old man" in Rom. 6:6. It is also called imposter, deceiver, pretender, liar, anti-Christ, inner devil, and shadow side of humans in psychological terms. The old self or imposter will do everything to keep its dominant position in the life of the personality. Sex and its desires is usually the key they use to entice and keep humans in the evil kingdom. Pride, lust, greed, hatred, war, revenge, crimes, etc., brings out the worst, or the darker side of human beings. Those *evil qualities are inherited by humanity through Adam and Eve, from Lucifer the fallen archangel, who became satan, and is called original sin (Isa. 14:12; Gen. 3:1; Rev. 12:9).

Thus, the original human nature of the good/evil personality has good elements, such as: goodwill, courage, sincerity, truthfulness, faith, obedience, mercifulness, loyalty, gratitude, chastity, trust, self-control, frankness, honesty, love, humility, etc. The evil part, on the other hand, displays: evil will, cowardice, hypocrisy, falsity, disbelief, rebellion, cruelty, treachery, thanklessness, lust, distrust, impulsiveness, deceitfulness, dishonesty, hatred, haughtiness, or being prideful. Humans do not want others to know that they have those evil elements lurking within them; that is why they try to hide it, cover up, or project it to others.

#5 God as True Parents consists of a Trinity (Matt. 28:19) Father/Mother (Spirit), the Son (Universal Christ-Savior), and Holy Spirit (active Spirit of God in the denser world(s). It inspires, empowers, fills, counsels, gives comfort, and regenerates the Disciples of Christ. It will be expressed fully through the last Eve.

Mature man/woman created in the image of God is also a tripartite being, and consists of Divine Spirit (Spirit or Soul), Human Spirit (soul – psyche – heart – mind), and body (1 Thess. 5:23).

---

* See "The Fall of Lucifer, Eve and Adam".

All Scripture has a threefold meaning and is written to benefit the Divine Spirit, human spirit, and body of human beings at different levels of growth.

Jesus of Nazareth as the Son of Man, became the anointed Son of God or Christ at the time of His baptism and was thereafter overshadowed with the Christ Consciousness of God or the Son (2 Cor. 5:19), whose nature is described in Revelation 1:12-18. This nature could not be expressed through the first Adam, but came "alive" in Jesus Christ the last Adam (1 Cor. 15:45), and left His body at the time of the crucifixion (Matt. 27:46). "I am the first and the last, and the living one; I died, and behold I am alive for evermore" (Rev. 1:18). (See also Rev. 1:8; 22:13.)

The Son or Logos "was in the beginning with God", and "was God", and "all things were made through him", (Jn. 1:1-4). He is thus that part of God that acts in the universe as an extension of the Creator God, and eventually manifested in the flesh of Jesus Christ as the "only Son" (Jn. 1:14,18).

Jesus, therefore, appeared to be God, especially in the "I am" sayings of the Gospel of John, when the Son through and with Jesus Christ said: "Before Abraham was, I am" (Jn. 8:58); "I am the resurrection and the life" (Jn. 11:25), and the body of the Son or Universal Christ symbolized by bread and wine was broken (individualized as the Christ Self) and given to dwell in each one of His children (Mark 14:22; 1 Cor. 10:17; 11:24). The Son or the Christ of faith appeared to Apostle Paul and manifested Himself through the history of Christianity, by saying, "I am with you always, to the close of the age" (Matt. 28:20). Finally, the Spirit of Christ said: "I am the way, and the truth, and the life; no one comes to the Father, but by me" (Jn. 14:6).

#6 What are the thoughts, words, and the deeds of satan?

Isaiah 14:13,14 described that Lucifer – the fallen archangel – wanted to ascend to heaven "above the stars of God" (sons and daughters of God), and that he even wanted to make himself "like the Most High". Jude 6 mentioned that the fallen angels "did not keep their own position but left their proper dwelling".

When people behave like satan, he becomes their father (John 8:44), and like him, they have a strong desire to *dominate and rule (John 12:31), and become very angry if the subjects do not obey them. They also want to own (or part of it) the world (Matt. 4:9). They do not accept (like Lucifer) the lower position given to them by their Creator, but instead want to dominate the ones whom are closer to God. Lucifer, as a servant of God, became prideful and wanted to rule Adam and Eve, whom were to become true sons and daughters of God. The people whom act like sons and daughters of satan are enemies to God and refuse to become His children, by living a separate and evil lifestyle. They become competitors of the living God. Rom 8:7 said, "For the mind that is set on the flesh is hostile to God; it does not submit to God's Law, indeed it cannot." Many intellectuals do not want God to exist, and like to take the place of God, and therefore do not want to give any credit to the Creator of the universe. By speaking from their mind and not from their being, the brainy individuals try to impress the people of their shallow knowledge, in order to be recognized by the people, whom give them the power and influence they need. They are ignoring God's purpose of creating things, and are always trying "to improve" God's intention and design.

Satanic people like to act immorally and indulge in unnatural lust (Jude 7), are deceptive (2 Cor. 11:3), and continually accuse the ones whom are living a spiritual life of crimes they themselves are committing (Rev. 12:9-10). The evil entities do not only want to kill physically and psychologically by being angry to good people – by looks, words, and thoughts – but love to kill others spiritually, whom are or are in the process of becoming children of God, by ridiculing and mocking them. By doing so, their evil nature, which is in charge of the personality, is being strengthened or fed and the "inner devil" is gaining more power and authority over their ego. The ego looks inflated, is false, empty of truth, and speaks like a snake with a double tongue.

Because people who are more evil than good do not want to believe or trust in a God who cares for them, they display anxiety and insecurity, and want to hoard as much wealth as possible. They crave for recognition and seek the approval of men instead of God (1 Thess. 2:4; Jn. 12:43). They seek revenge by returning evil for evil, instead of good for evil (1 Thess. 5:15; Rom. 12:21).

---

* Many people have it in them to be a Fascist, to control and have power over others. They either go to one extreme to live a separate selfhood apart from God (not accepting the Divine Spirit to be born within them) or make an attempt to be God.

However, we cannot find any evil in the Divine Spirits of regenerated human beings; their Souls are always pure. We cannot find much evil in the physical body because it is only an instrument, but we do find a multitude of evils in the human spirit, psyche, or heart.

Jeremiah 17:9 said, "The heart is deceitful above all things, and desperately corrupt."

Jesus said in Mark 7:21-23; "For from within, out of the heart of man, come evil thoughts, fornication, theft, murder, adultery, coveting, wickedness, deceit, licentiousness, envy, slander, pride, foolishness. All these evil things come from within, and they defile a man."

Paul added, "Malice, ---strife, deceit, malignity, ---gossips, ---haters of God, insolent, haughty, boastful, inventors of evil, disobedient to parents,---faithless, heartless, ruthless (Rom. 1:28-31); and "the unrighteous will not inherit the Kingdom of God?---neither the immoral, nor idolaters,---*nor sexual perverts, nor thieves, nor the greedy, nor drunkards, nor revilers, nor robbers" (1 Cor. 6:9-10); and "impurity---sorcery---selfishness, dissension, party spirit,---carousing and the like" (Gal. 5:19-21).

2 Tim. 3:2-5 says "that in the last days there will come times of stress. For men will be lovers of self, lovers of money, proud, arrogant, abusive, disobedient to their parents, ungrateful, unholy, inhuman, implacable, slanderers, profligates, fierce, haters of good, treacherous, reckless, swollen with conceit, lovers of pleasure rather than lovers of God, holding the form of religion, but denying the power of it".

#7 The moment a person falls asleep, he or she is no longer conscious of their physical surroundings, because the spirit body separates itself – more or less – from the physical body so that it is able to recuperate. When one is sleeping the developed psycho-spiritual person is able to roam freely in the lower or higher dimension of the spirit world. He/she is able to visit many sights and encounter many entities, including the ones in the flesh whom are also dozing or sleeping. Those trips are impressed on their physical consciousness and remembered as a vivid dream(s).

#8 Many religious people today believe that there are only two worlds, earth and heaven, wherein, respectively, the body and Soul reside. However, Apostle Paul, in giving his benediction to the Thessalonians,

---

* See "Why Homosexuality is Wrong".

made a distinction between body, soul (human spirit), and spirit (Divine Spirit) – 1 Thess. 5:23; (see also Heb. 4:12). This trinity was accepted by the Christian church, until the Fourth Council of Constantinople in 869-870 A.D., "when it was reduced" to body and Soul.

The Hindus believe in the body with its (Jiva) life or breath or *etheric body – life soul or astral body (human spirit or psyche) and atman (Soul). The Jewish believe in the body with its animal soul or etheric body (nefesh) – in the astral soul (ruach) and divine soul (neshamah), which is incapable of sin. The Greeks believe in the body (soma) with its life principle (thymos or pneuma, breath) – in the (psyche) soul and spirit (nous-pneuma). The Medieval church believed in the body with its animal soul (anima bruta) – the human soul (anima humana) and the divine soul (anima divina).

As the physical body needs food to grow and sustain itself, the spirit body (human spirit) takes in for its growth different kinds of intellectual food, for example: earth -, psychological -, and psychic knowledge, the latter two can be good or (and) evil. The Divine Body (Spirit) only accepts pure Words of Truth and become the Truth or Truth Body, when the words are accepted and assimilated by the individual.

As medical doctors chiefly take care of the physical body, psychologists' and psychiatrists' main interest is the psychological health of the spirit body, while pastors' or shepherds' and transpersonal psychologists' principal concern is the well being and growth of the Divine Spirit or Soul.

The esoteric tradition, which is at the core of Hinduism, Buddhism, Taoism, Christian Mysticism, Sufism, and others believe that the Divine Spirit or Soul is called by many other names, such as:

Divine Spark – Germ of Christ – Christ Child – Christ
Spirit – Spirit of Christ – Inner Christ – Christ Self –
Christ Consciousness

Self – Divine Self – Higher Self – Ideal Self – Real Self –
god Self – Greater Self – Inner Self – Original Self

Divine Spirit – Divine Consciousness – Center of Conscious-

---

* See "The Etheric Body".

ness – Divine Being – Divine Nature – Divine Body –
Divine Essence

Truth – Truth Body – Being of Truth – Word of God

Soul – Inner Light – Pure Awareness – Causal Body –
Tree of Life

The esoteric doctrine teaches, among others, that the Divine Spirit (Causal Body) consists of self (atma), intuition (buddhi), and higher mental (manas) "bodies"; the personality, as its reflection and vehicle, consists of the physical/etheric body, the emotional (astral), and lower mental sheaths.

The goal of the yogis of India is to realize the Atman, Buddhists speak of "awakening to our Buddha Nature", and in the West, they speak of coming to the realization of the Self, which Carl Jung called "individuation" and Roberto Assagioli "psychosynthesis".

#9 Life of the Good and Evil Personalities: Comparing Human with Divine Life

Living in the kingdom, one should not disregard the ego because in order to live properly on earth, one must possess an ego, whose function is to organize, process, and consolidate new learning, gained through mental, emotional, and sensory awareness. Besides, an individual must first cultivate a self before he or she can become unselfish.

In some people, the human nature is filled with prejudice, ignorance, hatred, and pettiness. It is confused, doubts, is scared, defends itself, and continually worries. In others, it is filled with good will, competence, courage, and dedication.

By living a life without God, the world of free trade, supply and demand (losing your job), the market becomes a fearful place. By living according to God's laws, the world is less hostile, knowing that God is always there to help and guide you.

When primal motivations of hunger, sex, fear, anger, and sensory pleasure guide your life's activities, and your higher expressions are stifled, your life revolves going into bars, drugs, raucous music, contact sports, and television sitcoms. You should instead engage in pastimes such as art, literature, soothing music, thinking games, philosophy, and development sports.

The self-serving way of greed, strife, envy, and destructive competition should give way to cooperation, serving, sharing, and concern for the welfare of others.

We tend to hold on to the exterior image that we have painted of ourselves for others, because we want others to think good about us, and do not want to show them how evil we really are. In other words, we put on a mask and make excuses when doing wrong to save face, and protect or rather hide our false personality, and are therefore not true to ourselves.

As the mature elements of the personality or lower self learn to take care of the naïve, lazy, ignorant, and selfish part, replacing it with more noble elements, the personality is purified and integrated and becomes a suitable vehicle for the Higher Self.

The lower self can be reasonably good, but without the guidance of the Higher Self, it is devoid of purpose and meaning.

When you are "high" God's Spirit is working through you; when you are "low" your personality is in charge of your life.

By changing form human life to divine life, you feel more spiritual love and power, and people are attracted to you.

Instead of being self-centered and consumed in negative emotions, you may find yourself becoming more open, life supporting, giving, and loving.

You should get rid of your old self (nature) with its hate, criticism, judgment, condemnations, and anger, and give way to the new Self (Nature) with its understanding, compassion, forgiveness, patience, and kindness (Eph. 4:22-24).

If we ignore the prompting from our inner Self, and follow the self-indulgent desires and straying thoughts of the personality, we find that our troubles will multiply and our way through life will be more difficult.

Humans usually live according to the whims and desires of the selfish personality; but when the ego is submissive to the Divine Spirit, Soul qualities such as humility, tolerance, kindness, unselfishness begin to dominate their lives.

The persons whom are not living a divine life or in whom the Divine Spirit has not taken root live in a group conscious tribal level, living a life of conformity, like animals but in a higher form. The Christ Force works to individualize him or her to separate them from the human consciousness, which thrives in a group. This is why we can say that the bodies of humans are much the same. The human spirits are more different, but the Higher Selves are very unique. The hero is the one who is a rugged individualist, apart from the pack, following his own vision, marching to the beat of his own drum, without regard for the opinions of others. His conscious is lodged in his Divine Spirit and no longer in his personality.

THE TEN COMMANDMENTS
Ex. 20; Deut. 5

I   THOU SHALT NOT HAVE OTHER GODS BEFORE ME

II   THOU SHALT NOT WORSHIP ANY GRAVEN IMAGE

III   THOU SHALT NOT TAKE THE NAME OF THE LORD THY GOD IN VAIN

IV   REMEMBER THE SABBATH DAY TO KEEP IT HOLY

V   HONOUR THY FATHER AND MOTHER

VI   THOU SHALT NOT KILL

VII   THOU SHALT NOT COMMIT ADULTERY

VIII THOU SHALT NOT STEAL

IX   THOU SHALT NOT BEAR FALSE WITNESS

X   THOU SHALT NOT COVET ANYTHING THAT IS THY NEIGHBOR'S

Why Do We Need to Pray and Read the Bible?

A. Introduction

It is instinctive for humans, when they encounter conditions and circumstances beyond their control, to implore, petition, or pray for help to a higher power(s). Believers and nonbelievers alike, when they are faced with a desperate situation, resort to prayer to a higher being. Deep within their heart, they know that when other humans failed them or are unable to help them, they can always turn to their Creator.

As primitive people worship and pray to many gods and nature as the embodiment of God, so do the Israelites and Moslems pray to one God, the Lord or Allah. Nominal Christians also venerate a supreme being they call the Christ, while advanced Buddhists and other [1]esoteric religions direct their attention to the Buddha Nature, Higher Selves, or Holy Spirits, which reside in all people in a more or less developed state. However, many "born again" individuals or initiates believe that God has taken His or Her residence in the Higher Selves or Souls of Their sons and daughters, through which They can express Themselves more fully. See the Book of Revelation 21:3.

[2]Prayer has always been an essential part and duty of every religion. In almost every aspect of the believer's life, prayer has become very important. Parents pray for the health and well being of their children and pray together (and stay together), not only during [3]mealtimes but also in the morning and evening hours. The children should pray together before the start of every school day and also pray before any other school event. By doing so, God will give them a better appreciation and understanding of what they have learned and also help them acquire the proper wisdom to use this knowledge in their daily lives. When they get married, they ask for God's blessing, and when they serve in their work place, they should ask for divine guidance,

---

[1] The Quakers, for example, may sit together very quietly until one or more of them feel(s) inspired to express what the Spirit has moved them to say. They know that words are not always needed to make contact with God, who will enter whenever the chamber of their heart is open. "Be still and know that I am God", said the Psalmist (Ps. 46:10).

[2] Along with reading spiritual literature, prayer and meditation form the backbone of our daily practice.

[3] Saying grace before partaking of food influences the body to properly digest the food. It is a time to be thankful to the Lord who did most of the work to produce the food. There is power in family prayer because all minds and Souls are united, and they have harnessed the mental and God power in each to that of the other.

especially when they are in charge of many people, and even more so when they fulfill an important function in a powerful [1]government agency.

REMARK: Many people today are so much surrounded by external noise (the radio, television, and recording machines are operating at all hours) that they cannot stop talking and thinking and do not know how to be still and quiet anymore. They are always too busy to fill and cover their quiet time and, thus, drown out the small voice of God, which is trying to talk to them. When they do communicate with the divine, fewer words are needed when affections increase. This relationship may grow to such an extent that all other relationships fade in comparison.

For many believers, <u>the reason</u> for the lack of prayers in the home and elsewhere is the fact that for them, prayers are not considered to be of practical everyday value. Besides, they argue that they are too busy and too tired to pray and have got better things to do. Others say that they lack faith, are ashamed to face God, do not know how to pray, find the learned exercise boring, see no immediate results, and have all the material wants they need without prayer. They, therefore, do not believe that praying will do them any good. They prove that in their lives when they become sick or are [2]out of a job, they go to the doctor or employment agency first instead of praying to God for help by showing faith (Heb. 11:6; Rom. 10:14).

Those religious people whom are more sensitive and religious minded do pray on many occasions, but not enough. Some of them are so active in doing good, in carrying out the Lord's work, and in their public duties that they neglect to spend time with God. Others are so occupied in preparing sermons that they devote too little time to God. The well-chosen words might be intellectually stimulating and emotionally consoling but contain little or no divine life. No new Life can therefore be given. The preacher is of not much use for God, and the church is not able to advance the cause of Christ, of winning new Souls.

It is a fact that those individuals whom were most successful in doing God's work in the past and today are men and women of prayer. David and Daniel prayed three times a day, while Christ and Paul often

---

[1] When an important government official is chosen, such as the President of the United States (and other countries), he is expected to say, "So help me God."

[2] When praying for a job, the God forces will certainly help you. In addition, when you pray or meditate before looking for a job, you will approach personnel managers in a confident and composed manner instead of "begging" for a job.

prayed throughout the night. Martin Luther said, "If I fail to spend two hours in prayer each morning, the devil gets the victory through the day." The first great revival and awakening began when a handful of disciples "with one accord devoted themselves to prayer" (Acts 1:14) for ten days. The *great revival under Jonathan Edwards in the 18th century began with his famous call to prayer. Another display of God's reviving power was the one that broke out in 1830 in Rochester, New York, under the leadership of Charles G. Finney.

Jesus Christ gave in the Gospel an excellent example of how, when, and where to pray.

" In these days he went out to the mountain to pray; and
all night he continued in prayer to God" (Lk. 6:12).
"And in the morning, a great while before day, he rose
and went out to a lonely place, and there he prayed"
(Mk. 1:35).
"And after he had dismissed the crowds, he went up on
the mountain by himself to pray" (Matt. 14:23).
"Then Jesus went with them to a place called Gethsemane
and he said to his disciples, 'sit here, while I go yonder
and pray'" (Matt. 26:36).
(Because His 3 main disciples did not pray, Jesus became
more vulnerable to satanic attack.)

In prayer, Jesus asked for and received the wisdom, insight, and guidance He needed to continue His mission. He recharged his "spiritual batteries" and returned to His task with renewed spiritual aliveness, mental alertness, and physical vigor.

In order to pray, Jesus needed to be alone. He, therefore, frequently absented Himself from the people and His disciples. According to the Gospel accounts, Jesus experienced difficulties finding time and place for prayer.

Luke 5:15-16 records that "great multitudes gathered to hear and to be healed of their infirmities. But he withdrew to the wilderness and prayed". Sometimes he would send his disciples and the crowd on ahead while he went up on the mountain to pray (Mk. 6:45-46). After Jesus heard of the death of John the Baptist, He withdrew in a boat to a lonely place. "But when the crowds heard it, they followed Him on foot" (Matt. 14:13).

---

* The result of the revival was that many participating Christians got a new spirit of prayer. Prayer meetings were no longer a duty but an event they eagerly looked forward to attending. They got a new love and faith in God's Word and a new joy in Christ, and brought deep conviction of sin (Jn. 16:7, 8). Those whom are regenerated also have a great desire to bring lost souls or the unsaved to Christ.

Jesus Christ gave a special time to prayer, even when His life was unusually occupied with doing good to the people. Sometimes He had no time to eat (Mk. 3:20) or time to rest and sleep (Mk. 6:31, 33, 46), but He always found time to pray because prayer was very important in Jesus' ministry. (Other men of God lost much or all of their power because they did not know the secret of success and allowed increasing service to squeeze out their valuable time of prayer.)

The Disciples of Christ, who regarded prayer to be most important, also set an example for Christians to follow. Paul wrote in his letters to the church and individuals that he kept praying for them. Much of his time and action was given to prayer. See Rom. 1:9; Eph. 1:15, 16; Col. 1:9; 1 Thess. 3:10; 2 Tim. 1:3.

Of all the duties, as practiced in Christian bodies, none is more essential and yet more neglected than prayer. Why is it that for the average Christian, praying is difficult and even a burden? The real reason is that every human being has inherited from his/her ancestors the original sin, so that they are born with a personality which is good as well as evil. When the evil side of their personality or ¹old nature is in charge of their life, they find all kinds of excuses not to pray or communicate with the living God. But when the good side of the personality is in charge of the life of a Jew, Mohammedan, Christian, or any other person, they feel like praying to the Almighty God and Creator. However, when the "born again" Divine Spirit or Soul is in charge of an individual, praying becomes a great joy because humans were originally created to have fellowship and communion with their spiritual Parents.

²The most fundamental reason people pray is because they believe that God exists, not only as cosmic energy (which is His body) but also His ability to communicate with humans in a personal and loving way as Parents do towards their children. Also, for the ³ungenerated as a righteous master or Lord toward their valuable servants. ⁴Spiritual

---

¹ Old nature is mentioned in Col. 3:9 and Eph. 4:22. It is also called old self in Rom. 6:6 and flesh in Rom. 7:5; 13:14; Gal. 5:16, being children of wrath (Eph. 2:3), from which proceeds from their inner personality evil things (Mk. 7:20-23).

² Some people pray out of habit or feel that they should. Others are afraid of what may happen to them if they do not pray.

³ For the ungenerated, moral development of the personality is important to purify the latter by obeying moral laws and behaving in an ethical way.

⁴ When spiritual children grow up, they become an intimate friend of God and His trusted co-workers and do not easily fall away. For them, prayer becomes less a means of getting things.

children are much dependent on Their love, guidance, protection, and growth, while the Parents are much in need of the love of their children. They become heartbroken when Their precious children turn away from Them (backslide) and choose to do the will of their evil father and no longer want to speak to Them.

NOTE 1: Through the fall, humans lost communication with God. When an individual prays, he/she re-establishes communication with the God forces. If he/she does not pray, the way is open to have give/take with evil forces. Thus, when individuals do not feel like praying, they should pray even more or "unceasingly" because before realizing it, they begin to feel and think like satan. The evil side of the personality or satanic nature will do anything to keep control over a human's life and does not want the person to pray. Praying is, therefore, for the saved and especially for the unsaved, hard work, a struggle to overcome an evil resistance within themselves which may be aided by evil forces outside, with or without bodies. Therefore, to pray is to labor. (For more information about evil, see **Remark** below.)

NOTE 2: For those whom are beginning to live a divine life, there is a fierce struggle in their personalities between good and evil. They should rely very much on prayer. Otherwise, they will backslide and become victims of the powers of darkness, and satan becomes their father (Jn. 8:44).

NOTE 3: In order to liberate from the stronghold of evil powers, one should pray until they feel the purifying presence of God within them.

Remarks about Evil

Praying is a great spiritual battle, not only against external evil forces but also against our own evil nature, which we have inherited from satan (Jas. 1:14). When we decide to become men and women of prayer, we make a declaration of war, not only against the devil and all his cohorts but also against our satanic nature and that of other people.

It is said that satan trembles when he sees the weakest religious person on his or her knees. Evil spirits with or without bodies do their utmost to interrupt prayer meetings or keep us from praying by diverting our attention to other things. One of satan's tricks is to destroy the best by the good, to occupy the people of God with business and other duties so that they have less time for prayer and, thus, there is less give and take with God.

Someone who starts his/her prayer life will continually be interrupted. People will be at his/her door, the phone starts ringing more often than normal, etc. He or she may also be hindered by a flood of negative thoughts, such as: praying is not for you but only for the mentally weak. God cannot hear you and does not care about you because you are not good enough, and so forth.

James says in Ch. 4: Submit yourself to God, resist the devil, and he will flee from you. Prayer is the mighty weapon to defeat satan (Eph. 6:11-18). God, however, is faithful and will not let you be tempted beyond what you can bear and will also provide a way of escape, that you may be able to endure it (1 Cor. 10:13).

The human nature with which we are born is of such a condition that it easily succumbs to the way of the world (Jn. 8:23) unless it is constantly fed with the nourishing food of the Spirit. After it is fed, we should not let it starve by feeding it with cheap degrading literature, movies, and television programs.

Spiritual Children Who Backslide

Satan is very subtle and clever and is always making plans to weaken God's children and let them fall morally and spiritually so that they again become his subjects or his children. He has power given to him by evil spirits and good/evil people, of whom the evil part of their inner personality is ruling their lives. He does not tempt the latter because they already belong to him, although many of them are not aware or do not want to admit that they are working for him in establishing his kingdom here on earth and in the spirit world.

When the children of God go against the Ten Commandments in their actions by entertaining evil desires and worldly thoughts, which are often influenced by evil spirits and/or by the false personality of earthly people, they are separating from God, which also affects their prayer life. They (their personality or ego) become less dependent on their Soul (Christ Spirit) and God and more on the self-sufficient attitude of the false ego or Antichrist. They become very worldly and alienate more and more from God, and it becomes increasingly difficult for them to serve the Lord and attend prayer meetings, which used to be the most happy hours of the day. It now has become a duty, and they soon find excuses not to pray in meetings or in private. They no longer experience the deep sorrow of having sinned and lose much of their power to discern between good and evil. They then become one with the world or the good/evil world (Rom. 12:2; 1 Jn. 2:15).

In order to come back into God's family, they "need someone to teach you again the first principles of God's Word" (Heb. 5:12), and to be born again.

Other reasons people pray are that this is the God-appointed way. By getting in contact with Him, He is able to give us instructions and, in turn, we are able to confess our shortcomings. It is also a means to offer a prayer of forgiveness for those whom have done us wrong. Through prayer, a channel is opened in humans, through which God can pour down His love and power to do His work (Jer. 33:3). This is especially true when we have complete trust in Him and respond according to His plan for our lives, which is always best for us. We then can face life's trials with optimism and courage. Being in complete oneness of purpose, the individual may ask for anything, and it will be done to him (Jn. 15:17; Jas. 5:16). Even though God knows what we need (Matt. 6:8), He wants us (good/evil humans) to ask for our needs, thus, showing that we are on His side and also to do our responsible part by asking and exercising our free will.

Through prayer, an individual acquires strength, wisdom, and grace to overcome his or her individual and family problems, which latter stands in need of continual help. A family praying together gains strength and maturity much more than if they would pray by themselves because there is more power in combined prayer than in the sum of individual prayers (Matt. 18:20). There is, indeed, union in strength.

Although prayer is not only a way of getting something from God or to be reserved for times of crisis, or used at certain occasions, it is also a way of building intimate relationships with the God within us. Through prayer, we are unblocking and widening the channel between human and God consciousness and tapping and expressing divine qualities, such as love, wisdom, tolerance, kindness, joy, etc. It also expands our consciousness, renews our spirit, and guides our thoughts throughout the day.

B. The Purpose and Effects of Prayers

The purpose of prayer is to bring heaven and earth together. It gives inner calm, freedom from anxiety, "And the peace of God which passes all understanding" (Phil. 4:7). It lifts the personality out of the absorption of the mundane things of life and connects it with the life of the Divine Spirit or Soul.

NOTE: Prayer promotes our spiritual growth together with Bible study. It is through prayer that "my sin" is brought to light (Ps. 139:23, 24). The sins I never suspected are brought to view.

In answer to prayer, I get wisdom to know God's way (Jas. 1:5) and strength to walk in.

Instead of worrying about our loves ones, we pray for them and, thus, change worry thoughts to thoughts of concern. This positive energy will not only help them but will also activate the God forces.

Prayer is the way of letting ourselves discover that God loves us and that He has loved us first (1 Jn. 4:19). Through prayer, we discover the goodness of God and what it means to have Him as our Lord and Father. By loving their common Father, men and women can love each other as brothers and sisters and become intimate members of God's family. When we spend more time in His presence and also study His Words, we come to know Him better and love Him more. When we place ourselves in accordance with God's Will, conforming our wills to His, we become intimately united with Him.

By prayer, humans establish and cultivate their communion with the Source of all power, which transcends all other energy. Prayer releases the highest form of energy within and around you that becomes active of working for you and through you. This power is able to change your lives, thinking, attitudes, and delivers you from fear and insecurity and keeps you from losing hope (1 Thess. 5:24). It changes hate to love, despair to joy, and confusion to clarity. Through the energy of prayer, physical and mental healings are often done to persons whom the medical establishment has given up as "incurable". Therefore, "prayer is good medicine."

When we deepen our relationship with God through prayer, it will bring us spiritual growth, and we become more transformed into the person God intends for us to become. To pray is to grow up, so that we can give ourselves away. Through prayer, God is able to correct our attitude toward our fellow men and women and help in building a sincere and honest relationship with each other. It also lifts them out of their immediate situation and everyday routine that threatens them with moral and spiritual depravation. It reveals their potential talent and power, and they gain a new perspective of themselves and a broader vision of their world. They transcend their individual belief, and it becomes easier to unite with people who prescribe to a different belief system.

NOTE: With the action of prayer, one builds a vibration which increases until there will come a time when you feel bad because an hour has gone by and you have not prayed.

In prayer, we surpass our little selves or egos, and it bring us in touch with the deep center of ourselves, our True Selves, to meet God, leaving behind a selfish preoccupation with self or self-centeredness, which keeps us from meeting God face to face. Prayer lowers pride and makes us humble, crucifies vainglory, and lifts us out of spiritual bankruptcy. It purifies our personality of its passion or *intense lower desires and clears, strengthens, and brings new life to thought, which in turn can change our experiences. Its effects on body and mind are well tested in their increased physical buoyancy, intellectual vigor, and moral stamina.

Prayer helps us to think better, feel better, and do better. When we talk with Him, our spirits are lifted, our anger is dissolved, and our weariness seems to vanish. The individual who goes about the affairs of the world without a prayerful heart will be miserable and will make the world miserable because without prayer, life seems to be dull and vacant. Those who pray regularly are also likely to be forgiving and satisfied with their lives. They are friendlier, are sowing good seeds, and are reaping a rich spiritual harvest. A matter that looked very dark will, in prayer, becomes clear as crystal. It is through prayer that we can see the higher meaning of the things that happen to us and become something greater than the world that surrounds us.

Those that pray much create a spiritual aura that eventually envelops the whole body. The bands of light painted by artists around the heads of saints are not imaginary and are actually visible to the sharp eye of the painter (Lk. 9:29). We all know people whose joy is running over. It is shining from their eyes and expressed from their voice. When you shake hands with them, you feel the abundance of energy rubbing off on you.

REMARK: Would you like to experience more harmony in your relationship with your spouse, your employer, your co-worker, and your family? Do you want to be free from addiction or an unwanted habit, free from fear and worry, and free to be yourself and enjoy life? Then pray and activate the freeing power of prayer that gives you the strength and courage to stand steadfast in the face of negative and evil influences.

C. What Is Prayer?

At its most basic level, prayer is a conversation with God, which is the divine power within us. As thinking is the activity of the mind, prayer is the elevation of the [1]mind and heart to God to ask for His help and make our needs known to Him, to receive grace and mercy, and to thank Him. It takes many forms, such as petition, intercessory prayer,

---

* We can trust God with our desires so that they may be molded and exalted before they take form in words and in deeds.

[1] Mind and heart here means to elevate intellectual thinking and emotion.

confession, adoration, praise, and thanksgiving. Prayer is not a ritual or exercise. It is a conscious mental activity by which you share your ideas and feelings with your Creator. Praying is not a dialogue between I and me; it is an 'I-thou' encounter. Prayer is the activity which brings to a greater awareness of the Presence of God within and around us. It enables us to become channels for the activity of God in our lives and our society. When we are in communion with God, we make ourselves available for God to work through us and with us. Through prayer, our will becomes in tune with the will of God. Praying is a loving conversation which [2]includes talking as well as listening. When our relationship has become very close, we converse with our Lord without words and remain silent. In its higher form, prayer is the state of consciousness where we no longer pray for ourselves but for the well being of others. We can have a long conversation with God, which is called affective prayer, wherein we talk to our Lord or Father/Mother about how much we love them and listen in silence when they give their Heart to us. Through our more mature affection, we may move the Heart of our close friend and loving presence and liberate His/Her sorrowful Heart.

NOTE 1: There are three kinds of conversation: by appointment, spontaneously, and praying in public. We may also include here the spontaneous outcry of one's heart and shout for joy when the heart leaps to meet God.

NOTE 2: To use an analogy of what prayer is and does:
You will have much more power when you hook up your individual power through prayer, with the universal power or the central power plant. Prayer is like turning on an electric power switch, which provides a channel through which the electric current or divine life may pour into you.

NOTE 3: If our prayers are worldly, selfish, without consideration for others, and, thus, contrary to the universal law of love, they do not create a channel to evoke the God forces.

D. Different Forms of Prayer

The different forms are: petition prayer, intercessory prayer, prayer of confession and repentance, and the prayer of adoration, praise, and

---

[2] Most of us have a tendency of doing too much talking in our prayers while being neglectful of being still and listening to the voice of God. How can we understand God's heart, will, and direction if we do not listen to what He has to say? It is frustrating to have a well-loved visitor who, while professing love, admiration, and respect, tells Him all of his/her problems, asks His advice, but never listens for an answer.

thanksgiving.

In petition prayer, we express our humble dependence on God and ask Him for something we want or need, which may be a material, mental, or spiritual blessing. Intercessory prayer is a higher type of prayer. It is born of compassion rather than self-concern. We may ask for help for another person(s) or plead to God on their behalf. Another type of prayer is called confession and repentance. Through self-examination before God, we acknowledge our shortcomings and accept God's forgiveness. Confession is an admission that we are sorry for our [1]sins and are determined not to repeat the same mistake. Further, there is the prayer of adoration or worshipping and praising Him for His love, power, and majesty and declaring our joyful wonder of God's greatness. We then thank Him for all that He has done for us, for the people we know, and for the world. There is also a prayer through which the more mature may [2]bless people and the prayer of surrendering, which plays an important role in healing. In the latter prayer, we leave the resolution over to the divine will.

In invocation, we appeal to a higher power for aid, which is usually done at the opening of a service or ceremony. Contemplation is a reflection on the Truth found in scriptures, liturgy, secret writings, creation, and events in history.

NOTE 1: Before you start thinking about what you are going to pray for, spend some time in giving thanks to God, to communicate your gratitude to Him (1 Thess. 5:18; Ps. 104:1, 5; Phil. 4:6, 7; 1 Tim. 2:1). As people like to be appreciated, so does God. When asking for new blessing, they should return thanks for what He has already done. God is deeply grieved by the thanklessness or ingratitude of which so many of us are guilty. When Jesus healed the ten lepers, only one came back to give Him thanks. "Then Jesus asked, 'Were not ten cleansed? Where are the nine?'" (Lk. 17:17)

Supplication is the time to make specific requests in prayers for others and for yourself as well. We can pray for the sick (Jas. 5:14-16), more workers (Matt. 9:35-38), rulers (1 Tim. 2:1-3), yourself (1 Chron. 4:10; Ps. 106:4-5). We can pray for unity (Acts 1:14), to know God's Will (Acts 1:24), for new Christians (Acts 8:15), to missionaries (Acts 13:2-4), when in severe trouble (Acts

---

[1] By committing sins, we separate from God, clogging the channel between the personality and the God forces within the self and also strengthening the evil part of the inner personality. However, "God is faithful and just, and will forgive our sins and cleanse us from all unrighteousness" (1 Jn. 1:9).

[2] The barriers which separate one from another and God are broken down when a person invokes a blessing for his/her rivals and enemies. Each person or thing you touch is being blessed because God flows through you.

16:25), for Christian leaders (Acts 21:5), for healing (Acts 28:8), and for God's Will to be done (Matt. 26:39, 42; Jn. 4:34 – "not what I will, but what thou wilt" (Mk. 14:36).

Jesus prayed before and during critical times during His life. Before his anointing of the Holy Spirit, and beginning His public ministry (Lk. 3:21-23), and starting His evangelical tour (Mk. 1:35-38), before choosing 12 disciples (Lk. 6:12, 13) and before announcing to the twelve His approaching death (Lk. 9:18-22), before teaching the Lord's Prayer (Lk. 11:1) and before the crucifixion (Lk. 22:39-46), and from the cross (Lk. 23:46; Jn. 19:30). He prayed in the face of temptation (Jn. 6:14-15) and at the transfiguration (Lk. 9:28). Jesus praised God (Lk. 10:21), gave thanks to God (see the 17th chapter of John), and He continually prayed for others (Lk. 22:32; Jn. 17:20), and His last prayer on the cross was, "Father, forgive them; for they know not what they do" (Lk. 23:34).

E. Congregation or Group Prayer

A congregation is an assembly of people who come together for religious worship and prayer, which is practiced by all religions in some form or other. Congregational prayer raises the level of concern from the individual's own wants and needs to a concern for everyone inside and outside the congregation.

> Matthew 18:19, 20 let Jesus say, "If two of you agree on earth about anything they ask, it will be done for them by my Father in heaven. For where two or three are gathered in my name, there I am in the midst of them."

> The Book of Acts says: "All these with one accord devoted themselves to prayer", and "When the day of Pentecost had come, they were altogether in one place" (Acts 1:14; 2:1).

The first Christians did not just pray as isolated individuals. They encouraged each other as they prayed together because there is great power in group prayer. See also Acts 2:42; 12:5. *This prayer energy can be radiated to specific persons, to the community, and problems in the world. By doing so, the praying members not only unite with each other but also feel more love for those they have prayed for. They

---

* Many people and angels of the unseen realm are attracted to the prayer meetings and may act as boosters of the energy generated by prayer, and also may assist in the answering of the prayers of the congregation. Although, to a certain extent, spirits can read your thoughts and understand your wants, they prefer that you formulate your prayers in words so that those who want to help you know exactly what they must do to fulfill your desires.

become the channelers through which God can exert His infinite Love, Wisdom, and Power.

When one of the leaders of the congregation gives a sermon, the other heads should not lean back in judgment but lean forward in prayer because those who preach will also be severely attacked by evil forces within and without human beings. When his colleagues do pray for him, the Holy Spirit will move the speaker in such a way that his voice takes on a new timbre, a novel radiance appears on his face, and Life-giving Words issue from his "golden mouth". On the other hand, a preacher who does not pray or is not prayed for by members of the congregation, the divine Truth he speaks may have a germ of Life in it, but it has no divine power to evoke (germinate) it and fill it with the Life of God. He is not able to move the people and give spiritual stimulation or new birth. He may speak with all the eloquence of men and angels but will only sound to spiritual ears as sounding brass or a clanging cymbal (1 Cor. 13:1). Many a preacher know(s) that when someone or a group is praying for him, he feels a strange power and experiences an oneness with Christ, and new ideas are pouring from his lips, and a church which has been "brain dead" shows signs of divine Life. It is therefore important to pray for the ministers of the Word. Paul, in his letters, always urged the members of his congregation to pray for Him (Col. 4:3; 1 Thess. 5:25; 2 Thess. 3:1; Hebr. 13:18; Eph. 6:19).

NOTE 1: A group may also come together in silence and share inspirational thoughts with each other. The sharing may also include a verse of scripture, a line from a hymn, or a song someone starts.

NOTE 2: Anyone who participates for the first time in group prayer should overcome the fear of speaking and ought to not necessarily pray as others do but express their own uniqueness in his/her own words.

NOTE 3: 2 Chronicles 16:9 reports, "For the eyes of the Lord run to and fro throughout the whole earth, to show his might on behalf of those whose heart is blameless towards him." When the Lord chooses someone, He uses him as an ever-broadening channel to exert His power on the earth. However, if the successful preacher becomes puffed up and prideful, God has to lay him aside and take away His power.

The Bible says: "Is any among you sick? Let him call the elders of the church and let them pray over him" (Jas. 4:14).

[1]In order to be effective healers, the persons in the group should be clear and unobstructed channels for the Lord. For a better bonding, they should lay hands on him or her so that God's healing energy will pour through them to the patient. To aid in this healing process and to become more receptive to the power of God, the healers should relax their bodies and human spirits so that they are free of tension, worry, and [2]negative thoughts. They may also visualize themselves as a tube or channel through which God is pouring His love, power, and healing energy.

God can help the church in many other ways. Billy Graham says, "I am deeply concerned about our finances. It has become a heavy load because of extra expenses. Even in far-off China, we will be praying that God will lay it upon your heart to help us to continue proclaiming His Word throughout the world." Revered C.S. Lovett says that God has ways of making money go further. He can keep your car running longer and can also help keep you out of the hospital. He has thousands of ways of easing your financial burden. It is even possible to ask the Lord to help you find something you have lost or shop with the Lord for bargains.

Pastor George Muller (1805-1898) began in 1835 in Bristol, England an orphanage, which grew to a complex of buildings and housed as much as 2000 orphans. Since its origin, the money for every building, for every meal, and taking care of all the caretakers was prayed for, without holding any public collection.

NOTE: If you are an alcoholic or drug addict, or have any other addiction, it is very difficult to recover until you admit that you are powerless to help yourself and ask God to help you. At that moment, the God forces will do anything for you to overcome your addiction.

F. Praying for Others

When you pray for someone *who is open to you but closed toward God, then God will use you as an open channel to speak to the other. In this case, it is important to widen the portal between you and the

---

[1] It is also possible to heal yourself with your own hand. When we experience God's Presence and feel warmth, then the healing energy of God is flowing through. We may then visualize ourselves becoming whole in body and spirit.

[2] Christian Science says that by transforming our thoughts so that they become more spiritual, truthful, and aware of God produces definite healing results.

* When you love someone, you open up to the other. However, this is also true when you hate another.

other. This can be done by keeping that person clearly in your mind so that you see him or her vividly. This can certainly be aided when you get to know the other as much as possible. When the person opens up to God, he/she may at first have more faith in your prayer. When the individual begins to pray, he/she may pray to solve his or her own problem, but soon they discover that praying for another who has the same problem is a more effective way to solve one's own. Besides, they might even forget their own problems altogether. The person may then ask God for whom he/she should pray and then wait and see what pictures or names come before their mind's eye.

Praying for another has a wonderful effect on the one who prays because love, wisdom, and power enter into the prayer. Your emotions become sublime, your thoughts are elevated, your selfishness melts away, and you are loved by all who know you. People you meet think that you are beautiful, seeing an abundance of genuine love and joy radiating from your face, and they want to talk to you.

There are many successful men and women in the business world who say that without prayer and relationship with God, they would not succeed as they have. An employer who starts the day with a prayer service with certain or all of his employees would not only improve the quality of life of the prayers but they also love to serve the customers, with a sincere desire to help them. Thinking of the needs of the customer has also made them more considerate of their spouse, relatives, and friends. When they finish their work day, they have a feeling that much more was accomplished than selling merchandise because they have given people a real lift with their sincerity and cheerful attitude.

NOTE 1: When the persons we prayed for have a great moral debt and we want to take it away so that they will be more quickly spiritually liberated, some indemnity condition is required of us. This can be done by fasting or other condition that involves inconvenience and suffering. When we are strong in the Lord, we also can take upon ourselves their distress, perdition, and guilt by feeling empathy, doing vicariously for them what they cannot do for themselves.

Paul prayed three times to God to remove the thorn in his flesh. Instead of removing it, God gave him the strength to bear it (II Cor. 12:7-9). When indemnity or penance needs to be paid, God may not remove the pain or other forms of sufferings but He may give us a quality of character that overcomes our despair, self-pity, and complaints that are caused by the suffering.

Praying alone is not always sufficient to remove a bad condition. In addition, fasting is required. See Mark 9:29. Daniel fasted (see Ch. 9 verse 3). The early apostles also practiced fasting (see Acts 13:2, 5 and Acts 14:23).

NOTE 2: Some esoterists believe that individual and group prayers not only help us and others directly but also contribute to an invisible reservoir of prayer which is available for all people.

G. To Whom Do We Pray, and How Does God Answer?

As it is almost impossible to have a personal audience with an earthly king, it is however possible, even as a sinful creature, to have a daily opportunity to make a petition to the Creator, Sustainer, and Ruler of the universe (Ps. 8:3-5). As servants of God, good/evil humans, when they do address the Sovereign of the cosmos (Rev. Ch. 4-5) should do so respectfully, manifesting reverential fear of displeasing Him (Prov. 1:7). When we are "born again", we are adopted into God's family. God becomes our spiritual Father (Gal. 4:5-6; Rom. 8:15-23), to whom we can speak freely and directly in our own words. We know that we pray or communicate not to a transcendent Being who works behind the scenes but to a God who is the essence of all life and is totally involved in all the things we do, because He/She lives within us.

God is able to "speak" to us by conveying or implanting, in our Hearts and minds, aspirations, insights, hope, intentions, desires, etc. Out of the [1]depths of our own being, God makes Himself known by His guidance, which may come through impulses, impressions, feelings and ideas, or through the inner urge to do right. This guidance can come through much easier when we are still, not only physically but also emotionally and mentally, and when the [2]channel between our con-

---

[1] The Spirit of God dwells in the depth of our growing Divine Spirit or Soul (Rev. 21:3), which latter has its abode in the human spirit or inner personality, which in turn resides within the physical body or outer personality.

[2] We cannot "hear" God very well when the channel connecting the physical brain consciousness, inner personality, and the Soul is drowned out by physical, mental, and psychic noises. A channel may become more obstructed when we do not live according to the law of God or Ten Commandments and other rules of moral conduct – see Matthew 5:21-48. For example, a person who is married commits adultery, or looks at another person as a sex object. He or she may kill or hate the other, having a spirit of unforgiving and resentment. He/she may steal of a neighbor whom they do not love or care about. They may do other things, however, which are in accordance with God's Will, that is, to help people develop and purify their personality and bring them into God's Family. When God is not able to express through a personality who wants to do evil, He is shut out, and His dwelling place deep within the human spirit becomes His prison.

scious awareness and the Soul is as clear as possible. He also strengthens, empowers, and comforts us. God also "speaks" through our conscience (often quite unmistakably), friends, strangers, and, above all, through scripture or other sacred writings. We may experience a certain sensation, or sense of recognition, when reading a verse or passage. A multitude of answers is found in His written Word. We may receive thoughts of reassurance, conviction, confidence, and wisdom. Justice and love may flow into our thoughts, emotions, and experiences. The answer may also come in a dream or in a "voice out of the blue", or a sense of peace or well being, or through uneasiness. In the latter case, it would be good to ask the Lord what might be wrong in a specific situation. These are some of the manifestations of the unlimited variety of ways that God employs in the answering of prayer. Sometimes, God's "speaking" may be in a harmonious feeling or a direct inner knowing. It may also come as an idea or words of a beloved hymn, poem, or Bible verse, which may be the sought-of answer to one's prayer. God may also reveal my faults to me, or what I am really like.

NOTE: We should be aware that communication from the God forces may come at any time. You might ask a question in the morning and, for example, in the afternoon while you are idly walking down the street when suddenly, a thought will come into your mind, which is the answer to your question. Or, you may find a piece of newspaper on the street with a headline which leaps at you, and you recognize that as the answer.

We know that God answers our prayer, not our own *subconscious voices, when it agrees with His Word and when Love is communicating. We know that the answer or manifestation is from God because it is always good for everything and everybody. You may also receive the assurance of receiving what you have asked for. If He cannot directly get through to you, He will use other persons whom are more open or use nature and circumstances. Thus, the God power can impress minds of other people, spirits, or angels with your need and attract help to you. They can, for example, prevent you from having an accident or when God gets through to you, to make the right move, which impulse is given through an intuitive flash. Because God is the essence of all living things (Rom. 1:20), He can work through the existing forms of life, whether it be a seagull, sparrow (Matt. 10:29), or other animals, plants, or things, or preferably the right man or woman,

---

* We may hear through our subconscious or through the psychic senses of our human spirit, psychic voices of people with or without physical bodies, or hear songs, television slogans, or other accepted rhetoric as it is replayed in our conscious self. We should also be on guard against self-deception, imaginations, and wishful thinking.

at the right time and place.

NOTE: Some religious people find the solution to a problem when they relax and say, "Father, I have done everything to solve it; now I put it in your hands, please help me." The answer may come in a flash when "I am" not thinking about anything, or a word or sentence will stand out when "I am" reading. The answer is usually so simple and clear that "I" wonder why "I" did not think of it before.

Others have a way of finding out if something they want to do is God's Will for them. They may ask the question, "Shall I do this or not?" Then listen to God's Answer, which is always in agreement with your Soul or Holy Spirit.

Some people say, "Father, if I am going to do this, increase the desire within me to do it."

H. How to Pray

Chapter six of the Gospel of Matthew is a graceful explanation of how to behave, how to share, and how to pray (read verses 5 to 13 concerning prayer).

"And when you pray, you must not be like the hypocrites."
"When you pray, go into your room and shut the door."
"Do not use various repetitions."
"Your Father knows what you need before you ask him"
See also Isa. 65:24.
"Pray then like this, 'Our Father who art in heaven'" ---
see p. 733.

The Bible further says, "Ask, and it will be given to you ---
For everyone who asks receives" (Luk. 11:9-10). "And
whatever you ask in prayer, you will receive if you have faith"
(Matt. 21:22). See also Mk. 11:24 and its explanation on p. 732.
However, we should ask in a humble and contrite manner as the
tax collector in Luke 18:10-14.

"Pray for those who persecute you" (Matt. 5:44).
"Watch and pray that you may not enter into temptation" (Matt. 26:41).
"This kind cannot be driven out by anything but prayer and fasting" (Mk. 9:29).
"Not as I will, but as thou wilt" (Matt. 26:39).
"That they ought always to pray and not lose heart" (Lk. 18:1).
See p. 731.

"The prayer of a righteous man has great power in its effects" (Jas. 4:16).

729

"The prayer of faith will save the sick" (Jas. 5:15).
"Pray for one another" (Jas. 5:16).
"Pray in the Holy Spirit" (Jude 20).   } see p. 730
"Pray at all time in the Spirit" (Eph. 6:18) }
"Whoever calls on the name of the Lord will be saved"
(Acts 2:21). See p. 731.

If possible, you should pray regularly, so that your relationship with God becomes a priority. Mental conversations with God are good, but for some people, praying aloud may be better because their attention or concentration may at times wander off. When prayers are verbalized, communication with God seems to be more real. Whatever we pray for, we should then ask that *God's Will be done, which is always the highest and the best for everyone. We should also pray with conviction and, if possible, pray through to completion of anything we may ask, until we know that this prayer will come to pass. God can give us physical and emotional support, solve many of our problems, and has the right answer of any question we may have. Besides living in us (Luk. 12:7), He knows more than we do what is best for us.

The real value of prayer is not as much the words we choose but the thought, feeling, intention, and devotion behind the words that make prayer a prayer (such as the prayer of a desperate mother for her children). Prayers with little or no feeling or mere repetition with no sincerity have little or no light and do not attract high beings.

REMARK: When you pray, you should not have any negative thoughts and feelings, and banish all ulterior motives. Whatever you ask is for the best possible purpose and not a selfish whim or desire. A prayer is of no use if it would harm people or put yourself above rivals and friends – you will then only attract low spirits who, united with the power of the prayer, the negative and evil that is prayed for is brought to reality. The good prayer, which should always be directed to God, attracts only good spirits and angels whom carry out the good you have prayed for, which is for the highest good of all and creates good karma.

Prayer starts when we desire to communicate with the Creator and ruler of the universe who we, depending on our moral and spiritual growth, may address as Lord or Father/Mother. After some time, we may become aware of His Presence more than our own and ask God to

---

* Because God lives in everyone, He does not really favor one person over another. Being good and evil, we need to constantly ask God that His Will be done.

¹forgive our trespasses of our emotional, mental, and physical selves. We may then pray for the physical needs and health of individuals and those whom are in emotional distress, as well as for their moral and spiritual growth. We pray for community leaders (Tim. 2:1-2) and world peace and, above all, to those who are spreading the Gospel of Christ to all nations (Matt. 28:19). We may then pray for strength, wisdom, understanding, and a loving heart, ready to give to those whom we have the divine privilege to meet and are in need of counsel.

²Every born again believer has direct access to God through the way of prayer, which has a special meaning for God's spiritual children. They are fully qualified to say, "Our Father who art in heaven." They have received the spirit of sonship, whereby they cry, "Abba! Father!" "It is the Spirit himself bearing witness with our spirit that we are children of God" (Rom. 8:15-16). ³It is this Spirit that communes with God and prays to Him on our behalf. "For we do not know how to pray as we ought but the Spirit himself intercedes for us with sights too deep for words" (Rom. 8:26), and "the Spirit intercedes for the saints according to the will of God" (Rom. 8:27). "Pray at all times in the Spirit, with all prayer and supplication" (Eph. 6:18; Jude 20). Thus, the Spirit in us even helps formulate our prayers, so that they are in accord with the Will of God. When we become aware of the Spirit's movement in our hearts, then we know how to pray. Then when we ask, we receive, for the Spirit prays through us and could not pray for

---

¹ Because humans are good and evil, they cannot fully measure up to God's standards. They, therefore, continually need to pray for His forgiveness and, thereby, become more aware of their weaknesses and more tolerant of the shortcomings of others. They should, therefore, not be unwilling to pray for those who have done them wrong.

² Those whom have not been converted, in whom Christ is not formed (Gal. 4:19), have no direct access to God but are in need of a mediator to speak to God their master. "When the time has fully come, God sent forth his Son, born of woman, born under the law, to redeem those whom are under the law, so that we may receive adoption as sons" (Gal. 4:4-5).

³ The Bible makes a distinction between the ⁺Holy Spirit in a Christian, which the disciples already had, and the Holy Spirit which comes on a Christian, which gives power to serve, which the disciples received after prayer (Acts 2:4) and by laying hands on their followers (Acts 8:15-17).

⁺The Spark within our human spirit has been growing until it was born. It is a pure center of consciousness and cannot be touched by sin because it is born of God (1 Jn. 3:3, 9). This Holy Spirit within (Lk. 17:21), in agreement and cooperation with the Holy Spirit without, teaches, inspires and illuminates God's Word to us and also reminds us to pray for someone.

NOTE: We do not have to contend with others for God's attention because He lives within us (that is, in our Divine or Holy Spirit) and have "His ear" at all times.

anything which is contrary to God's Will. It is, therefore, always in complete harmony with the Word of God and also directed to a certain purpose.

We are commanded to pray in the name of Christ Jesus. John 14:13 let Christ say, "Whatever you ask in my name, I will do it." "And whatever you do, in word or deed, do everything in the name of the Lord Jesus" (Col. 3:17). See also Matt. 18:20; Jn. 15:16; 16:23; 1 Cor. 1:2). By praying in His name, we not only unite with Him in Spirit but also participate in the accumulated credit and power of His name. "If you abide in me and my words abide in you, ask whatever you will, and it shall be done for you" (Jn. 15:7). Thus, when our outer self is united with our inner Christ Spirit, which latter is always united with God's Spirit, we can ask for anything we like. From what has been said, we should realize that it is important to study His Words and become one with the Word, as the branches of the vine become one with the vine.

Jesus directed His disciples to pray always (Lk. 18:1). To watch and pray was His ceaseless council (Mk. 13:33). After His master, Apostle Paul gives the same teachings to the church, "Pray constantly" (1 Thess. 5:17), "Pray at all times" (Eph. 6:18). See also Rom. 12:12, Col. 4:2, and Acts 10:2.

To pray without ceasing does not mean that we should spend all of our time mumbling under our breath or establishing a habit of prayer. It is a time when we constantly are aware of the presence of God within and around us. When Christ or the Divine Spirit lives in me (Gal. 2:20) and guides my daily life, I am united with Christ and God within, and I am continually in prayer or in a state of prayerfulness and consciousness of prayer.

We should also be untiring in our prayer, just as the man was persistent in pounding on the door of his neighbor asking for three loaves of bread for a late visitor (Luk. 11:5-8). As the widow who obtained justice from a corrupt judge by her persistence in begging for help (Luk. 18:1-8), we should likewise be importunate and untiring in our asking. If we need more grace, peace of mind, understanding, healing, or other things, we ought to pray continually until we receive what we asked for. God appears to like individuals who show by their steadfastness great faith in Him and in His ability to deliver the goods. If it is not His Will to give what we asked for, He will make it certainly known to the prayer.

John says, "And this is the confidence which we have in him, that if we ask anything according to his will he hears. And if we know that he hears us in whatever we ask, we know that we have obtained the requests made of him" (1 John 5:14, 15).

Jesus says, "Whatever you ask in prayer, you will receive, if you have faith" (Matt. 21:22). "Therefore, I tell you, whatever you ask in prayer, believe that you have received it, and it will be yours" (Mk. 11:24). The sixth chapter of Mark tells the story, "And taking the five loaves and the two fish, he looked up to heaven, and blessed, and broke the loaves, and gave them to the disciples", and also fed five thousand people that day. When Jesus stood before the tomb of Lazarus, He said, "Father, I thank thee that thou hast heard me. I knew that thou hearest me always." He then cried with a loud voice, "Lazarus, come out!" (Jn. 11:41-42, 43; 12:10) Mark 11:23, 24 let Jesus say, "Truly, I say to you, whoever says to this mountain, 'be taken up and cast into the sea' and does not doubt in his heart, but believes that what He says will come to pass, it will be done for him."

Jesus prayed with confidence. When He turned to His Father in prayer, He knew that what He asked would be granted. He foreknew and accepted that what He was going to do would be received and acted upon, and could therefore give thanks in advance. He was in complete unity and oneness with the God forces when He said, "I knew that thou hearest me always." The channel between the physical consciousness and the subconscious levels of mind and His Soul were completely clear. It was not impeded by doubt, fears, uncertainty, and limitations. Jesus always prayed according to the Will of God and believed strongly that whatever He asked He already had received or was in possession of it, thereby demonstrating that at a higher level, the law of cause and effect (that of asking and expectation) works simultaneously. The prayer of Jesus was already answered in spirit, and through the act of asking, it became a physical reality.

NOTE: In order for the universe to give what you want, it would be helpful to make a list of your needs and goals and visualize you wants. Even better, make physical images, and think and feel that you deserve them, and that you are in possession of those goods. The request should, however, be in tune with the need of the universal or cosmic will, so that it will be delivered without resistance. It is also important that your prayer thought be held firmly in mind (like thoughts of building something) so that it will become a reality. Otherwise, it would crumble. And lastly, keep praying and visualizing until you feel that you have what you asked for.

The Lord's Prayer, as it is recorded in Matthew 6:9-13, is as follows:

> "Our Father who art in heaven, Hallowed be thy name.
> Thy kingdom come, Thy will be done, On earth as it is in heaven.
> Give us this day our daily bread; And forgive us our debts.
> As we also have forgiven our debtors;
> And lead us not into temptation, but deliver us from evil."

The Lord's Prayer, or the "Our Father", is the [1]most famous and perfect prayer in the Bible. This prayer is a complete prayer and makes three requests: to give, to forgive, and to deliver. It is a model for all prayers. It defines our relationship to God, our place in the universe, our obligations and expectations. The Lord's Prayer concerns itself with the needs of the physical body (daily bread), human spirit (forgiveness), and Divine Spirit (our Father's Will be done).

The above prayer is the kind of prayer God accepts. Honoring God's name, His kingdom, and doing His Will on earth, come first. We may then ask for our personal needs, such as our [2]daily food, the forgiveness of sins, and the [3]deliverance from temptation and from evil.

When the disciples had been watching Jesus pray, one of them asked Him, "Lord, teach us to pray" (Luk. 11:1). The disciples observed something different about His prayer, which was not like the way they were taught to pray. His prayers were simple, spontaneous, and expressed with complete trust. However, what was most unique about Jesus' prayer was that He addressed God not only as Father but as "My Father" or Abba – Mk. 14:36. This was a prayer which was [4]unheard of in Jewish tradition to approach the Creator of the universe in the

---

[1] Another favorite prayer is the 23rd Psalm. For Roman Catholics, saying the "Hail Mary" is very important. The alcoholics have their famous prayer, and so have the children.

[2] When we pray, "Give us this day our daily bread", we are expressing our dependence on God for all our needs, both material and spiritual. Some Christians say that earthly blessing is important for Jewish people, and we should receive only heavenly blessings. However, we should remember that most Christians are not living a divine life and are, therefore, greatly in need of material blessings. The prayer does indicate that earthly concern is secondary.

[3] Instead of saying, "lead us not into temptation", because the Lord does not lead us into temptation (Jas. 1:13), a more accurate translation might be, "Do not allow us to enter into temptation" or "lead us when in temptation", or "leave us not in temptation". Thus, we seek from God the strength and discernment to overcome evil.

[4] The fatherhood of God is mentioned in the Old Testament in Jer. 3:19; Ps. 103:13; Mal. 2:10. Paul mentioned the word "Abba" in Rom. 8:14-16 and Gal. 4:6.

same way as a child has with his or her parents. He, thus, established a new relationship (since the fall of Adam and Eve), that of son and daughter to God.

NOTE: The Pilgrim fathers, like the early Church, believed in spontaneous prayers rather than using liturgy or formal prayers. They say that the human service books used in the established church quench the Spirit.

REMARK: The seventeenth chapter of John's Gospel contains the longest prayer in the New Testament. It is a summary of Jesus' life and mission on the eve of His death.

I. Time, Place, and Prayer Posture

Regarding the time of prayer, which is an appointment with God, there can be no fixed rule laid down as to the time set aside for prayer or meditation. It can be done at any moment. It depends upon personal choice, convenience, and temperament. Some people are better prayers in the early morning, others in the late evening. In order to strengthen our moral life and/or keep the Soul nourished, we may also pray at specific times during the day. For many individuals, the early morning hours are usually the best for communications with the Lord or Father/Mother, when the mind is at ease, alert, and more impressible, and the environment is quiet. As we read in Mark 1:35, Jesus chose the early morning hours for prayer. When the early hours are spent in prayer and meditation, one obtains moral and spiritual strength and wisdom before entering the activities of the day: to manifest Love, to be cheerful in spite of difficult situations, and to have the power to overcome temptations. Some persons improve their prayer life and get to know Him better by talking to the Lord on [1]a regular basis. This relationship will grow when you spend more time in a deep, meaningful relationship with the Lord. You then not only think of the

---

[1] When praying and meditating at a regular time, the subconscious of a person expects and looks forward to that particular time when the human spirit becomes more receptive to his or her Divine Spirit. Thus, the more his/her faith in God increases, the more irresistible the yearning and time in prayer.

As prayers go out in the ether-like incense (Ps. 141:2; Rev. 5:8), the luminosity that is present in your aura will attract many high spirits with or without bodies, whom can be of great help in answering your prayers. The less evolved like to immerse themselves in the high spiritual atmosphere created in the prayer room. Those spirits may come in great numbers because they are more sensitive and open to inspiration than earthly people. When spirits pray, they sense a deeper sense of His reality and a closer communion with Him because they have dropped the outer garment and are one step closer to the God head.

Lord when you pray but feel His presence [2]at different times of the day, and know that He/She is always with you. Then, in the quiet of the evening hours, as you reflect upon the day, thank the Lord and Father for helping you and confess your shortcomings. Ask Him to intercede for those you like to pray for, or even better, those whom your Holy Spirit wants you to plead for.

NOTE: Early morning is usually the best time for meditation because the emotions, desires, and thinking are calmer and still after sleep. Long meditations are best performed in the evening hours, while the best days of the month are those of the new and full moon. The best times of the year are at the summer and winter solstices (around Christmas), by taking advantage of the solar, psycho/spiritual tides. Religious holidays are also good times of reflection and examinations.

Regarding the place of prayer or meditation, you need no special place; conversing with God can be done anywhere. However, a place, sanctuary, or chapel where you can become quiet, calm, and still, and feel a sense of serenity is helpful. Look for a place which is as secluded and tranquil as possible so that the still voice of God is not drowned out, a room (innermost of yourself), wherein you shut the door (of the personality) and pray to the Father who is in secret (Matt. 6:6). Some people like to enhance their prayer and meditation room with things that call all their senses and imagination to a lofty and exalted state. An altar can be used as the center of focus, whereupon can be placed a candle, flowers, pictures, or statues of Christ and saints (whose qualities you admire), holy books, and incense. Other things can be placed in the room, which may help you in your devotional exercises. Sacred or inspirational music can be played, which generates a soothing and uplifting effect upon the consciousness of those present, whom may be visible or invisible. By praying and meditating very often in that enclosed space or psychic shell, the *furniture and the walls absorb and become impregnated with the higher vibrations of your praying consciousness and that of others. It will retain and radiate those vibrations to anyone who will enter your shrine and elevate them mentally and spiritually, without any effort on your and their part.

---

[2] When you are aware of the Lord at all times, in all places, and events, you have become an open channel to the Lord, who is continually involved in all of His creation.

* As furniture and other objects have a great capacity to absorb the feelings and desires of humans, it is therefore not a good idea to put in your sanctuary old furniture and other things which have been saturated with negative qualities. It usually takes a long time to cleanse those objects of negative vibrations.

Thus, together with the music played, eliminate the longer preliminary period of prayer and meditation to raise the spiritual atmosphere.

NOTE 1: Some locations on the planet are more charged with magnetic and psychic energy than others. They recharge the vitality of the etheric bodies of the visitors and also enhance the condition of the emotional and mental selves.

NOTE 2: Those whom make pilgrimages are visiting shrines (real or not real), which have accumulated prayer energy and devotional feelings, which have been poured out upon them by a host of visitors for many centuries. The walls of those hallowed places are charged with devotional thought forms and have become active centers of beneficial radiation. The pilgrims feel uplifted when they enter the shrine and feel like praying and meditating in those places.

Regarding the prayer or [1]meditation posture: you can [2]kneel, sit, stand, or lie face down. Some individuals lower or uncover their heads, [3]close or raise their eyes, and [4]fold or raise their hands. Others are facing in a certain direction or are wearing certain clothes, or use a rosary. It does not really matter very much. What, however, is most important is that the person put his or her whole heart into addressing the Creator and Lord of the universe. Some postures can be valuable if one is accustomed to them. Kneeling, for example, helps some people prepare psychologically for prayer. It is also the urgency and circumstances of the prayer request that govern our posture for prayer.

Because God resides within our more or less developed Divine Spirit, which is always pure and forms an unobstructed channel with Him, there is no need to clear this channel. What needs to be cleared, so that the God forces can freely flow to our physical self, is our outer and inner personality, which consists of the physical body, with its etheric shell, and the more or less tainted emotional/mental selves.

First of all, we need to relax our muscles (electromagnets) and, thus, reduce as much as possible the nerve energy (current) going towards the muscles. As the body and inner personality are closely connected, to let go of bodily tension is helpful to remove the obstruction (like a

---

[1] See **NOTE 1**.

[2] Kneeling or bowing one's head may be helpful, especially for the unregenerated, to show a dependency on the Lord and also to show proper respect or reference (if not done properly, He can put it right). However, becoming aware of Him in our innermost self is most important.

[3] By closing your eyes, the brain does not receive so many signals and becomes quieter.

[4] By folding one's hands (by holding the palms together), we create and complete a circuit of energy through the chest, arms, palms, and fingers, which latter two are also energy centers or chakras.

kink in a water hose) or barrier of despair, hopelessness, anxiety, frustration, etc. This process can be greatly aided or altogether prevented by expressing higher emotions and desires, which is more easily done by people whose evil selves are playing a less important role in their lives. Expressing those higher emotions comes almost naturally to those whom are living a divine life. The mental channel can be opened much more if our belief, opinion, and attitude are closer to the Truth, especially when we have no doubt about God and His Will, so that the answer to our prayers can flow smoothly to our physical consciousness. The flow of God's love and power then goes through the psychic channels into and through us.

NOTE 1: As to the meditation posture, the body should be physically comfortable so that the strain of the body will not distract the person meditating or call attention to itself. The individual should also be unconscious of the environment and thinking, so that he or she becomes only aware or conscious of the presence and power of God.

If you are sitting in a chair, put both feet flat on the floor, with spine erect, but not stiff. This makes it easy for the etheric energy or prana to move freely in the body along the spine channel (sushanna), when all the energy centers are in alignment.

The cross-legged position (lotus) is the best because it will prevent the outflow of pranic energy or magnetism from the fingertips, feet, etc., and it brings great stimuli to the psychic centers. When sitting in that position, the energy from the earth will also pass through the energy centers from below, while the positive currents come through the head from above.

J. Praying At All Times and in All Circumstances

For those people whom do not want to take the time to pray in a church, synagogue, mosque, temple, or shrine, they can pray at any time and everywhere. They do not need to close their eyes, move their lips, or be in a certain position. Upon awakening in the morning, they can pray while taking a shower, getting dressed, and then say a prayer at the breakfast table. When they leave the house, they may ask God to be with them throughout the day. They should also pray for others while riding or walking to work. When they are surrounded by many people, they continue to pray so that relationships with others will improve.

When we are in a traffic jam, this is a good time to focus on God, or when waiting in a doctor's office, or in a waiting room in a bus or railroad station. We may pray for a waitress in a restaurant who seems to be in distress or for other people in many other places whom are in need of God's love, concern, and wisdom. Learn also to let God use you to send "flash prayers" at people when waiting for transportation, while walking on the street, riding in a car, bus, or train, or even when flying in an airplane. [1]The result of those prayers can readily be seen when people look in your direction, while a kind-hearted smile appears on their faces. Having accepted what you have given, they feel warm, light, and uplifted and, in turn, radiate to others what they have received.

[2]God, who resides within people, is not able to express if humans do not provide a channel by praying, so that His/Her love, wisdom, and power will become manifested in this world. There are many lonesome, retired people who can [3]pray for their town while they rest on town benches. They surely can make a difference, certainly much better, when they merely think positive of their town. Many women (and men) who have idle moments could pray while doing routine work, while sewing, sweeping, cooking, making beds, washing dishes, and watching their children. Then there are a large number of shut-ins, the very old, of whom many think that their lives are no longer useful, or the great army of invalids and the bedridden who long for an opportunity to make themselves useful. Here are the greatest unused resources that can make themselves most valuable by being God's channels and instruments, to pray especially for those whom are in responsible positions to make the world a better place to live in, bringing heaven down to earth.

K. What Has Been Said about Prayer

Prayer is the highest use to which speech can be put.
Prayer is called "the mightiest force in the world" (Laubach).
"Prayer is practicing the presence of God" (Brother Laurence).

---

[1] Our prayers for others will be more effective when there is already a psychic rapport or telepathic connection between individuals. In this way, the God power of one can reach the God power within the other person directly. However, when those individuals are busy reading or talking, they do not respond well, either to psychic contacts, thought transference, healing energy, or prayers. They do not turn their heads when thinking or praying for them.

[2] God can only work around people to a limited extent as, for example, through the forces of nature and its three kingdoms, but is more able to work through humans to reach you.

[3] Secret prayers for others create an open channel through which God's love, energy, and wisdom can flow freely. This results that the praying persons become more unselfish in their attitude towards others.

Prayer is to the Soul, what food is to the body.

Prayer is the language of the Soul.

"Praying is keeping company with God" (Clement of Alexandria).

God is only a prayer away.

God has time to listen, if you have time to pray.

The Lord our God is near us, whenever we pray to Him (Deut. 4:7).

"Our Souls are restless till they find their rest in Thee" (Augustine).

Prayer brings in movement the hand, who rules the universe.

"Be still, and know that I am God" (Ps. 46:10).

"The man who kneels to God can stand up to anything" (Bill Bright).

Try asking God.

All things are possible through prayer.

"To have prayed well is to have studied (worked) well" (Martin Luther).

God can do no more for you than God can do through you.

He who learns how to pray has learned the secret of happiness.

"No man ever prayed heartedly without learning something" (R. Emerson).

To become one with God through prayer is to own what He owns.

Real prayer is when we are no longer aware that we pray.

"More things are wrought by prayer than this world dreams of" (Tennyson).

"Lord Jesus Christ, Son of God, have mercy on me, a sinner" (Greek Orthodox).

"While I rest in Him, He works in me" (P. Cellis).

When people pray things happen, that would not otherwise happen.

You cannot give out of an empty heart; that is why you need to pray.

The family that prays together stays together.

If you are too busy to pray, you are too busy.

Prayer is to spiritual salvation, as water is to physical salvation.

"Prayer offers us the experiment of being at home with God" (T. Eliot).

Prayer is twice blest, it blesses him that gives and him that receives.

"Prayer is the preacher's mightiest weapon, it gives Life to all" (E. Bound).

"Prayer does not change God, but changes him who prays" (Kierkegaard).

Through prayer and Revelation, humans communicate with God.

By praying for others, I evade bitterness and resentment.

Become the "son" of the highest, then whatever He owns is yours.

Because your Heavenly Father cares and loves you so, He wants you to remember to talk to Him, you know.

L. Why Are Some Prayers Not Answered

God usually does not answer the prayers of wicked, unfaithful, and self-righteous people (Prov. 15:29; Isa. 1:15; Luk. 18:9-14; Matt. 6:5). In the old dispensation, people in general were living the life of the good/evil personality. God their Lord and Master did not, or was slow to answer the prayers of people whom were struggling to live a moral life in order to purify the inherited evil in their selves.

"If one turns away his ear from hearing the law, even his prayer is an abomination" (Prov. 28:9; Amos 2:4). God will not listen to those who persistently refuse to obey Him (Prov. 1:24-28; Zech. 7:11, 13). "Because they have made their deeds evil", the Lord will not answer them (Micah 3:4). "Your iniquities have made a separation between you and your God --- so that he does not hear" (Is. 59:2). The Lord will not hear me "if I had cherished iniquity in my heart" – by condoning sin and not rebuke it – (Ps. 66:18). "He who conceals his transgression will not prosper, but he who confesses and forsakes them will obtain mercy" (Prov. 28:13). "He who closes his ear to the cry of the poor will himself cry out and not be heard" (Prov. 21:13). If we want God to heal and answer our prayers, we need to repent. "If my people who are called by my name humble themselves and pray and seek my face, and turn from their wicked ways, then I will hear from heaven, and will forgive their sin and heal their land" (2 Chron. 7:14).

The more heartfelt a prayer of the righteous is, the more likely it is to be answered (Hosea 7:14; Jas. 5:6). "You will seek me and find me; when you seek me with all your heart" (Jer. 29:13). "The Lord is far from the wicked, but he hears the prayer of the righteous" (Prov. 15:29). "Call to me, and I will answer you, and will tell you great and hidden things which you have not known" (Jer. 33:3). There is one prayer God likes to hear: "God, be merciful to me a sinner!" (Luk. 18:13) Another kind of prayer God likes to hear and answer is from "a broken and contrite heart, O God, thou wilt not despise" (Ps. 51:17). "Before they call I will answer, while they are yet speaking I will hear" (Isa. 65:24). "Your Father knows what you need before you ask him" (Matt. 6:8).

NOTE: The writer of Psalm 37, verse 25 observed, "I have been young, and now am old; yet I have not seen the righteous forsaken or his children begging bread." When you find the real story of people whom are begging on the street, you find that many of them have lived an unrighteous life and let God down. However, this does not mean that we should ignore them.

In the new dispensation, God was becoming and became, for many, their Father or Parents. Like any parent, and even more so, the heavenly Parents (Matt. 7:11) enjoy [1]giving good things to their (spiritual) children, especially when they are helpless and in need of protection. They also like to hear the prayers of all those whom want to become their offspring and [2]those whom have left them but want to come back to God's family.

God as a master and Father does not answer prayer when "the face of the Lord is against those that do evil" (1 Pet. 3:12), and He "does not listen to sinners" (Jn. 9:31). He also does not hear those who ask with wrong motives, for gain and sinful enjoyment. "You ask and do not receive because you ask wrongly, to spend it on your passions" – sensual pleasures – (Jas. 4:3). God is reluctant to answer prayer of those whom are lacking in faith: "And without faith it is impossible to please him" (Heb. 11:6), and lack of perseverance "That they ought always to pray and not lose heart" (Luk. 18:1). Prayers are being hindered when the relationship between married couples is not right (1 Pet. 3:1-7). An unforgiving spirit also hinders prayers: "And whenever you stand praying, forgive, if you have anything against anyone; so that your Father also who is in heaven may forgive you your trespasses" (Mk. 11:25, 26; Matt. 6:14, 15). "So if you are offering your gift at the altar, and there remember that [3]your brother has something against you, leave your gift there before the altar and go; first be reconciled to your brother and then come and offer your gift" 9Matt. 5:23, 24).

"If we ask anything according to his will he hears us" (1 Jn. 5:14-14-15; Jn. 9:31). "And we receive from him whatever we ask because we keep [4]his commandments" (1 Jn. 3:22) and "have faith" (Matt. 21:22), with "no doubting" (Jas. 1:6). "If we confess our sins, he is faithful and just and will forgive our sins and cleanse us from all unrighteousness"

---

[1] Children do have to ask for what they want, even though God knows their needs before they ask (Matt. 6:8; Ps. 139:4) because by asking, they fulfill their responsibility. Besides, children in general would appreciate the gift more if it is the child's idea to ask for it.

[2] Those whom have left their brothers and sisters are called backsliders (see 1 Cor. 3:1-4; Heb. 5:11-13). Some of them may say, "It has been a long time since I prayed and read the Bible."

[3] Prayers are not being heard because the cry of those whom have been mistreated (like Abel) has reached "God's ear". They should first reconcile in all that they have done wrongly to his/her brother or sister by word and deed.

[4] The secret of many of the unanswered prayers is that we turn a deaf ear to the Ten Commandments and other rules of moral conduct.

(1 Jn. 1:9). "For the eyes of the Lord are upon the righteous and his ears are open to their prayer" (1 Pet. 3:12). "If you abide in me, and [5]my words abide in you, ask whatever you will, and it shall be done unto you" (Jn. 15:17). "The Spirit helps us in our weakness, for we do not know how to pray as we ought, but the Spirit himself intercedes for us" (Rom. 8:26). We then pray according to the will of God and can then always get for what we prayed.

In general we can say that God does not answer prayers:

➢ When we pray without devotion, humility, trust, and with a surrendered mind

➢ We do not give God credit and do not thank Him for what He has already done

➢ We have not repented of some sins harbored, and are in rebellion toward Him

➢ We do not want to root out any sin, and our own will is more important than His

➢ We lose faith because God does not always answer the way or when we think He should

➢ We are impatient because God's sovereign timing is not the same as ours

➢ We pray in vague generalities, asking God to bless everyone.

➢ We do not have enough faith that God would answer our prayer

➢ We do not pray with sincerity, unselfishness, simplicity, and directness

➢ We leave it up to Providence and refuse to take any action to fulfill the prayer

➢ We give up too soon, without having broken through subconscious resistances

➢ When we have not released resentment, envy, or destructive jealousy to another person(s)

Other Reasons Why Prayers Are Not Always Granted

Because of immaturity, some Christians may ask for things which may not be good for them or are not ready in their spiritual unfoldment to receive it. It is therefore a blessing that God will deny that particular request, but gives them something much better than the things they asked for (Eph. 3:20), by giving them graces, which are more needed. Sometimes, the answer comes in a way they never suspect. It may come quickly, or they have to wait until the timing is ripe or perfect, in "God's good time". When the answer does not come right away, we should not lose faith because our spiritual Parents do everything pos-

---

[5] It is not only sufficient to love and trust Christ, but we should also know His Will, that is, to read the Word of God, absorb its essence, and become the Word of God.

sible to make us happy so that they can be happy. Besides, [1]the longer we have to wait, the greater the blessing. [1]Some people, however, do not notice that their prayers have been answered or ignore the answer either because they do not understand it or it was not what they expected or hoped for.

God cannot always help you unless you make clear to Him what kind of help you want. We should, for example, clearly and definitely formulate our prayers with sufficient forcefulness and expectation of a reply instead of mumbling a few words half-heartedly and then jump up before the mind is able to give an intelligent or concise picture of what we want. We should also be specific of what we want instead of uttering our request in vague generalities. In many cases, our prayer requests are more easily filled when we leave it up to God to fill it.

When you become more mature, you may ask for help, but [2]no help is forthcoming because you still want God to solve all your problems when you need to do your [3]responsible part. God may then no longer give you concrete answers to your prayers but may give wisdom to figure out the problem on your own. Besides, how can humans grow if everything is done for them? They need, therefore, by their own effort and as a co-creator with God to bring a satisfactory fulfillment of their prayers. They then have the opportunity to develop character, learn certain lessons, and acquire the Soul qualities of love, wisdom, courage, forgiveness, and faith.

NOTE 1: By first asking God for help, He will usually show it in a very obvious way because He is very glad that you asked Him.

NOTE 2: There has never been an instance of God changing His purpose or laws for the benefit of human wish fulfillment. However, it is possible to reason with God (Isa. 1:18), as Abraham did (Gen. 18:23-33), or Moses (Ex. 32:9-14).

---

[1] Because the Israelites sojourned in Egypt for 430 years, great were the miracles by which they were liberated.

[1] Their prayers were answered from a higher impersonal level which was not noticed by the lower personal self. In this case, prayers are answered when they are not answered because you are not ready to have it answered your way.

[2] At that time, we may go through a period of spiritual dryness. However, He may be very busy in purifying us and helping us to love Him for His own sake instead of what He can give us.

[3] Many of God's gifts do not come in the form of pure gold but in ore, which needs to be dug out of the earth. We should also not rely on God alone when we are sick but also call for the help of a physician.

NOTE 3: God does not always give people what they want, such as money, which can be a temptation to use for the gratification of physical desires but, instead, develops their character. Money cannot buy character, but an honorable character can bring forth physical needs. It is also unlikely that the Lord will influence lotteries to provide you with the winning ticket, over others, who also pray to be winners. If you want money, then look for opportunities God may send so that you can earn the money. This chance may come as a voice or a sign, an ad in the paper, or someone you meet may suggest a certain course of action to take, or other information you need to reach your goal. If you want God to provide a job for you, you may ask Him to show you what you are doing wrong in your present lifestyle and that you are willing to change it.

NOTE 4: Many people are surprised of the love, wisdom, and insight which pour forth from God into their Hearts and minds. Some individuals have testified that their life is one long daily record of answered prayer, for food provided at the exact hour needed, for sickness and dangers prevented, for guidance, peace of mind, and strength given to overcome temptation, and to fight against evil forces within and without people. Answered prayer is certainly an undisputed argument against disbelief and doubt in the existence of God.

NOTE 5: The answer to our prayers can be blocked by continually thinking and talking about the problem because God cannot get through to you to give you the answer.

When we have developed from being a young child to becoming a spiritual grown-up, we should not expect that continual blessings be given. We should take into consideration that our prayers can be answered more readily and blessing easily bestowed when our endeavors were and are in harmony with the law of sowing and reaping or the law of karma. Thus, the blessing given was already earned (by having established your "cosmic bank account" or spiritual treasure storehouse – Mal. 3:10; Matt. 19:21; 6:10), by your thoughts, serving, and tithes, as this is also shown in your auric record. Thus, if you expect the help of angels, you must in turn occasionally be an angel to others.

In conclusion, we can mention – that neglect of prayer causes us to say:

> Why is there so little progress in my life?
> Why do I feel so worthless and insecure?
> Why am I so negative and feel so little power?
> Why cannot I be happy and enjoy life?
> Why do I feel so empty and alienated?
> Why do I worry all the time and am not very healthy?

Why cannot I get along with others and have little self-respect?

Why am I not very creative and fruitful in my work?

M. Introduction to Meditation

As liturgical and vocal prayer is the beginning of our relationship with God, spontaneous prayer of the heart is that relation, when we have a loving conversation with the Lord, which includes talking as well as listening. In the latter, we give God an opportunity to talk to us, which is called by some people mental or two-way prayer. [1]In listening prayer, we should learn to quiet our bodies and our minds and put ourselves in a receptive mood. In this form of prayer, we are not engaged in spiritual reading or in saying prayers but keep still (Psalm 46:11). When our relationship has become very close, we converse with our Lord without words and remain silent. This is called wordless, contemplative, affective, or centering prayer. When we relax our bodies and still our mind (which is also done in the early stage of [2]meditation), this is a prelude to contemplation or mystical prayer when we no longer seek but experience God in our being. Contemplation, or taking a "long, loving look at God", has been achieved not only by the hermits and mystics of the West but also by those mystics of the East when they go into the very depth of meditation.

NOTE 1: Through the exercise of prayer and meditation, the indwelling Christ awakens and grows, and becomes more active (Gal. 4:19). However, this can only be fully achieved when we purge or renounce within our personality the false self, who is always trying to control the personality. And finally, contemplative prayer and meditation deepen our awareness of the inner presence of God within our Soul, or Christ Spirit.

NOTE 2: Meditation provides the means of entering different and higher states of consciousness.

---

[1] During listening prayer, new ideas and helpful thoughts flow into us, which is not only good for us but also for others. When we put ourselves in a receptive mood or attitude, we are not only opening ourselves to good but also to negative and evil thoughts. We should, therefore, ask for protection before we begin to listen.

[2] Meditation in its simplest form is an activity of consideration, pondering, and reflection on God and the Truth, while reflective meditation is to ponder deeply about a chosen subject, object, or quality and examine all its ramifications.

N. What Is Meditation?

Meditation means different things to different people. It is, however, not a relaxation exercise and a way to get rid of stress. This is only the first step in meditation. It is also not the ability to concentrate on one subject, to blot out wayward thoughts, and to gain control of one's desires and thoughts. This is the second step in meditation. When the attention of the thinking mind is turned inward away from the bodily senses and the outer world and, thus, is more influenced by the inner world than by the environment, this is the beginning stage of meditation. We may then pass through the different psychic levels and enter the Divine Spirit or Soul level. True meditation, as it is practiced by advanced [1]Buddhists and many adherents of other religions, is a way to make contact with one's Soul or Buddha nature. By frequently attuning to the Soul or Higher Self, the [2]channel between the latter and the lower self or personality is being widened and strengthened. Divine qualities such as love, wisdom, and power and other elements are poured from the higher into the lower self and are being grounded in the physical plane. The individual may increasingly allow the developing Soul to interact with and use his or her personality as a vehicle. Thus, the lower consciousness slowly subsides so that the Higher can dominate. However, only a few mediators are able to reach the [3]deep state of meditation when they directly make contact with God, who has His abiding place in the Soul of the individual (Rev. 21:3). The sense of separation between the individual and the Creator ceases to exist, and he/she experiences not only an oneness with the Soul but they, as Souls, become the sons and daughters to God, their Parents.

NOTE 1: The creative artist, musician, writer, or poet who is deeply involved in his/her work often enters a deep meditative state, wherein they attain a high level of creativity. The mission of the artist is to use his/her skill and talent to channel and manifest the divine or to bring heaven on earth.

NOTE 2: Just as thought can affect people, pets, clouds, and inanimate objects, so do they affect living plants. The power of prayer and meditation on

---

[1] Buddhists, in general, do not direct their prayers to a personal God who resides within the Buddha nature but to the universe as a whole.

[2] This channel is also called "the antahkarana" in esoteric parlance. Widening of this channel between physical and divine consciousness is creating or building the "bridge of light".

[3] True yoga is the union of man and woman with God, the welding together of the personality with the Oversoul (Soul), then linking the Oversoul with the divine monad or the God within.

plants has a great effect. They thrive when they receive much love or prayer (or visualize it as healthy and productive) but may wither or die when hate is directed their way.

O. How To Meditate

Several steps are necessary in learning the art of meditation. These are: relaxation, concentration, meditation, and finally, realization and contemplation. We quiet our minds, shut out distracting sounds and thoughts, and [1]focus on the inner Self, and become attentive to the small voice within.

[2]In the beginning of our meditation, our bodies should be completely relaxed, yet awake and alert, that is, receptive, responsive, and interested in what is happening at the present time (not getting lost in memories of yesterday or thoughts about tomorrow). The intention is to [3]separate the human spirit as much as possible from the body without falling [4]asleep. After turning the mind of the spirit body away from sense impressions, such as sounds and sights and also from the waves of emotion and thoughts of others, the next and much more difficult task is to quiet the uncontrolled activity of one's own thinking mind and to transfer awareness to the intuitive mode of consciousness. This is usually done by focusing the wandering mind on an [5]object, which can be of a physical, auditory, or visual nature, whereupon the mind can fix its attention. It then becomes steady and penetrating by reducing the movement of the mind to a small circle [6]until it becomes one-pointed. In doing so, [7]the subtle and higher dimension of consciousness will then emerge as soon as the (ripples) disturbances of the mind (lake) subside. The Higher Self or Soul can then be perceived

---

[1] Some mediators turn their attention to the third eye center because it is the normal portal or doorway to the spirit world but also the only passageway for the mind to reach the higher God regions.

[2] In the beginning, when attention still wavers, meditation may be called concentration. When the tight rein on the mind is no longer necessary, the mind stays on a single thought wave, which is a higher degree of meditation, the seventh step of Raja yoga.

[3 & 4]In the meditative state, the brain waves change from the faster beta rhythms to the slower alpha waves, but not to the very slow theta waves when the body is asleep and being separated from the human spirit.

[5] See **NOTE 4**.

[6] This process can be aided by not identifying with your emotions, thoughts, and fantasies. Instead, you simply "witness" what is going on in yourself and become free of them and, thus, free from your sense of separation of your Real Self.

[7] See **REMARK**.

and experienced. Being in this state is called [8]Self-realization. The mediator becomes completely one with the object of meditation, which may be a physical object, an idea, ideal, quality, a Master, Christ Spirit, or Soul and, above all, God the Creator. He or she may them remain for a while in this state of contemplation by releasing their mind and becoming one with the essence of all creation and to let the Spirit of God flood into the core of his or her being.

NOTE 1: A passive state of meditation, as developed in Eastern religions, is not always good for Western society. As the East strives to develop a receptive awareness, they also have a tendency to keep what one receives for inner development. The West, on the other hand, is more directed to ground what one perceives and uses it for practical application. When a person becomes too passive, the inner Being may withdraw from the outer personality.

NOTE 2: People know when they are entering the threshold of meditation, when they are experiencing a lessening of awareness of the immediate surroundings.

NOTE 3: In transcendental meditation (TM), you do not concentrate on anything, so that the individual does not use much of the mind, and with the use of a mantra just let it go flat, with no thoughts whatsoever.

NOTE 4: Every form of meditation has an object of focus, upon which the mind can fix itself, like the physical and spontaneous body movement without conscious thought, such as: breathing, walking, dancing, yoga exercises, skiing, and jogging and the auditory, such as sound, music, song, or repeated phrases and lyrics. We can use the spoken words, the sound of a mantra, chanting, a focus on an affirmation: "Peace, be still, and know that I am God", and the visual focus of a candle or a cross, a picture, a flower, or part of the body. We can also use pictured imagery – colors, symbols, or a visual image of a mandala. We may further add some practices of the East, such as Japanese tea ceremonies, Chinese calligraphy, or Indian music. They all aim to bring one in a meditation mood. We may also meditate on a particular "seed thought" (perhaps a passage of Scripture) and then confine one's thinking to this topic during the meditation period.

NOTE 5: A mantra (popularly used in eastern meditative system) can be helpful in concentration, by constantly repeating it, either aloud or mentally, until it drives all other thoughts from the mind and, thus, dissociates the mind from the sense organs. By continual practice, one's ego is transcended, making one accessible to the Soul. It is important to choose the right word or mantra that intuitively feels right for you.

---

[8] This transcendent state – samadhi – is also called nirvana for the Buddhist, satori, for Zen practitioners, fana for the Sufi, and mystical union for Western meditators.

NOTE 6: When the mind is more or less separated from the body, you will be tapping the power of your subconscious and also become more sensitive to the spirit world. Pictures or symbols may come into your mind, and you may hear voices. Your spirit guides may use this opportunity to present to you spiritual insight and wisdom, which is not always available to the conscious mind. This information is impressed on the meditative mind in pictures, sounds, words, allegories, etc. However, when you are in this meditative state, evil spirits may also take this opportunity to influence you. Therefore, you should protect yourself by imagining a white light all around you.

REMARK: There are many levels of consciousness, not just the physical and divine. When the meditators withdraw from the physical level of alertness (with the help of mantras, chanting, breathing, and other practices), the first level they encounter is the lower psychic plane (also called the astral plane). Many beginning meditators become so fascinated with the psychic phenomena, such as sounds and images (also their own subconscious voice), that they experience and think that they have reached the highest level. However, when they get stuck at that stage, they become vulnerable to psychic domination and obsession of lower entities. This also includes telepathic impressions from earthly people, which can be depressive. Concerned Catholics and Protestants alike have, therefore, valid reasons to warn members of their congregations that meditation can be dangerous. Others say that meditation is communication with one's own self. They do not understand true meditation as being an opening to something higher than self, especially when the Higher Self is developed. The more experienced meditator passes through this realm to the higher psychic plane (or mental plane), and from there, by continually elevating their awareness or consciousness until they finally encounter the divine plane.

P. Differences between Prayer and Meditation

The prayer of many nominal Christians is more a performance of words and ritual than communion. They seldom meditate or attempt to communicate with God directly (except the born-again Christians). They do pray to God in the act of petitioning and requesting favors from God, but to simply think and meditate on God would be thought wrong because they do not understand that meditation means tuning into God without asking for something.

The Psalmist said, "May my meditation be pleasing to Him" (Ps. 104:34), "and Isaac went out to meditate in the field" (Gen. 24:63). Jesus tells us to enter the closet and shut the doors of our inner personality against the distractions and intrusions of the world, and to give our full attention to God in the inner sanctuary of the Soul (Matt. 6:6).

As most praying people do not meditate, many meditators in general do not get involved in prayers of petitioning and thanksgiving. However, as God is within and without (as Jesus said), meditation should be used in conjunction with prayer. The silent time of mystical reflection should always follow the period of vocal worship. Thus, we should listen as well as pray.

➤ Praying for many people is to divert their energy to a God who is separate from them and somewhere far away. Meditation is to divert their energy to a God who has His residence in the innermost core of all beings.

➤ When you pray to God, you are talking to God with the conscious mind, and God listens to you. When you meditate, God talks through Silence to you, and you listen.

➤ As prayer is active and engaging, meditation is usually passive and receptive.

➤ Prayer is talking to God, while meditating is thinking about God.

➤ Prayer and meditation are two sides of the same coin, for in prayer we speak to God, and in meditation, we listen to Him.

➤ Prayer can be compared to a phone call to the divine, while meditation is more like an actual visit to the divine plane.

➤ In prayer, a person addresses a transcendental power, such as a deity, for intercession, adoration, and thanksgiving. In meditation, the person tries to merge with Cosmic Consciousness.

➤ As the practice of prayer is, to a great extent, evoked by the personality, in meditation we open our personality for the guidance of the divine.

➤ As prayer invokes the divine to aid in our daily activities, in meditation the personality is elevated to the divine level and immersed in its love, wisdom, and power.

➤ Meditation is where one refrains from pondering the Truth and, instead, listens in silence to the small voice within.

Q. Results of Meditation

Meditation is good for the body, human spirit, and Soul

It is good physiologically because it relaxes the body, slows down bodily processes, it lowers blood pressure, the breathing rate, oxygen consumption, and less carbon dioxide production. It eases muscle strain and releases tension, which results that the person becomes less tired and more energetic. Because the immunity of the body increases, the individual is less overcome by sickness and has a stronger ability to overcome smoking, alcohol, and the use of drugs. He or she looks better, remembers things better, and is able to stay attentive and alert, which helps in his or her job performance.

It is good psychologically because it teaches you tolerance, compassion, and improves your general behavior by making you keenly aware of your thoughts and feelings before you act on them. It also strengthens your concentration, enabling you to focus more clearly on any activity without excessive stress. It increases emotional stability, feelings of calmness, and thus, renders you better able to cope with tension, anxiety, worry, irritability, and depression. The meditators are more patient, less afraid to be alone, are more confident, and also learn important things about themselves. Because the mind is made clear of extraneous thoughts, the individual experiences a new clarity of mind and a greater capacity for efficient learning and study. They also become more psychic.

It is good spiritually because it takes us beyond our immediate needs and concerns and gives us a more universal perspective in an expanded level of consciousness. It attunes us to the force that unites us with all life, gaining true wisdom, unique experiences, steadiness of purpose, and power to meet the unknown. Through meditation, the individual shall at least once a day think of high and holy things, inner peace, and renewed joy of living when the meditator is taken away from the petty round of daily life. Through meditation, we come in touch with our Divine Spirit, from which creative impulses come and interact with divine qualities, thus lifting our awareness or consciousness out of the limited focus of the personality. It further produces a brightening of the aura, which radiates form the personality. The individual also becomes more mystical and intuitional in nature and experiences an oneness with the universe. He or she calls down blessings from God and shows a great love for humanity. Meditation is, thus, an essential aid to enlightenment and spiritual advancement.

R. Why Study the Bible?

I. Introduction

The Bible is not just a book but a whole library and, like any *library, it contains many different kinds of literature written by different people at different times, and for different purposes. Because the people who read the Bible are not the same, God uses all kinds of individual writers with a wide variety of styles and talents to convey His message to those people, as it is recorded in the Book of books in the last 4000 years. There is no other book in the world that can compare with it in its variety of contents, concepts, and beliefs. This great literature, in its overall view, contains the story of creation, the generation of humans, their degeneration and regeneration, or the history of salvation. This is told in the stories of the victories and failures of the people of God and expressed in letters, speeches, sermons, proverbs, psalms, wise sayings, and other guidelines of living. In the beginning of the restoration process, laws and ordinances, including dietary laws and religious observances, were given, which were all strictly observed, which were later incorporated in the social customs, dress, behavior, and worship. Thus, we find many commands, exhortations, instructions for living, moral precepts, and other inspired teachings. Between its covers, we also encounter biographical sketches and genealogies of influential people in the Bible, and even political commentary and military strategies. It is a book of travel, adventure, with its excitement and suspense, wherein we find love, romance, and mystery. It is also expressed in other literary forms, such as prose, poetry, songs, hymns, music, and prayers of all kind. In this collection of literary works, there are a lot of prophecies, visions, dreams, and many other psychic phenomena and spiritual healing. We also find in this book of Life riddles, drama (truth exemplified), as well as epic stories and legends. No other book contains the amount of symbolism, allegories, metaphors, similes, and parables (simple stories drawn from everyday life that illustrate a moral or a religious lesson), and finally, how and when God has spoken to many individual persons and especially through Christ.

NOTE: The Bible is not history, although it has many historical facts. It is not biography, although the lives of many persons are traced from birth to death. It is not a geographical study, although many areas and lands are described. It

---

* Except for the Bible and a few classics, libraries often serve as cemeteries for numerous books that have become obsolete. They no longer apply to our time and are no longer read.

is not an allegorical writing, although many things are explained in that language. It is, however, God's liberated message of love and compassion to suffering humans who wants us to understand our selves, learn our lesson, change our lives, and grow spiritually in His image, and become happy.

The Bible is for the Jews and Christians the most sacred of books, a source of Truth, and a Revelation from God. The word "Bible" is derived from the Greek word "biblia", or books, because the Bible is a collection of many books or papyrus scrolls.

Of all the spiritual writings in the world, the Bible is the most widely read, and has been, and still is, the world's consistent best seller for more than two thousand years. More copies have been translated and distributed into more languages than any other book. About three quarters of the population of the world today believe that the Bible is the Word of God, not only Jews and Christians, but also *Hindus and Muslims have no doubt that the Bible comes from God the Creator they address with different names.

The Bible was written in different places, from the time of Moses until about 100 A.D. Most of its stories took place in only a small area, at the Eastern end of the Mediterian Sea. Although it is an ancient book, it is also the most up-to-date book because it gives practical counsel for modern-day living. The Bible is actually a unique library, written over sixteen centuries by some forty independent authors or secretaries who had been carefully chosen by God. They came from many different social backgrounds and occupations. These inspired writers include: prophets, kings, priests, government officials, shepherds, farmers, poets, fishermen, a tax collector, a physician, a tent-making rabbi, and local church leaders.

The Bible is also a valuable historical document because it supplies missing information about people, places, and events of ancient history. Those accounts have been proven to be correct by archaeological findings. The Bible is also great literature, not only in its story telling, but it also contains the greatest poems and introspection of all literature. It has also greatly contributed to the forming of Western languages. However, the Bible is more than history; it tells the history of God's chosen people whom are in the process of restoration or salvation. It also reveals the character of the Creator, who longs to communicate with His people. After the deviation of the primal pair,

---

* The Hindus believe that the head of their pantheon of gods is the Creator,

the Lord God made a covenant (Testament), or an agreement, with the descendants of the Eden pair. They were to obey His laws (such as the Ten Commandments – Ex. 20:2-17) and, in turn, He will protect them and give them abundant material blessings. After the coming of Christ, a new covenant (Testament) was made. By fulfilling His Principles (such as the Sermon on the Mount – Matt. Ch. 5), the people will experience abundant spiritual blessings, such as Love, Wisdom, Peace, and Joy.

Moreover, the Bible is the greatest and unique text Book on human behavior. It is His lamp to our feet and a light to our path (Ps. 119:105) in this good and evil world. It is a voluminous guide for everyday living, in carrying out our duties and responsibilities. It addresses every human situation, reflects every thought and emotion, and paints vivid pictures of the good as well as bad people. *It does not hide things but tells the way it is, even the most despicable and violent events. It is a Book for all, the unlearned and the learned, and it has a universal appeal. It is a Book that has affected and changed more lives than all other books combined because it has God as its author and, thus, has spiritual authority. It is, therefore, not any word but the Word of God, a simple letter addressed to us, but it has the wisdom of the ages. †By opening the Bible, we "dial God's number", and He is right there for us with answers to today's problems. The Bible is an endless fountain for thirsty souls who draw near to drink from it. It contains moral instructions for the development of the personality and spiritual instructions for the newborn (liquid food), and (solid food) for the more advanced Souls. Thus, the Bible is for those who hunger and thirst for righteousness (Matt. 5:6), virtue, and truth and for moral and spiritual development. This inspired writing should therefore be studied, felt, and experienced and, above all, ought to be practiced. It then becomes

---

* Writers in general do not want to reveal too many bad things about their characters, which are portrayed as their heroes in their writings. God, however, tells the truth about His most faithful servants by revealing their frailties and failures, such as the all-powerful kings. Because the Bible is God's spiritual mirror, it shows every flaw in our thinking and reveals every spot of our character. As none of us like to see ourselves as we truly are, the Bible gives us a true picture of what we are like in the way God sees us and exposes our innermost thoughts. It is the discerner of the thoughts and intentions of the heart (Heb. 4:12). Every conceivable evil which men and women may commit or have committed is exposed by the many characters of the Bible and, of course, also their goodness, sacrifice, bravery, and service. By overcoming all those trials and tribulations, humans may then be inclined to think like God thinks and see things more with His eyes.

† Every time the Bible is picked up and opened up to look for guidance, the attention of God is focused on that person and that Bible. When the Word of God speaks to us, it challenges our opinions and values and will change our lives.

the most profitable and enjoyable study of our lives, which results in a vibrant, abundant, and rewarding and never-ending liveliness, the true fountain of youth.

The Bible helps us to solve problems, improve the quality of our lives, and give meaning to our lives. It gives counsel concerning human relations and eliminates bad habits. It is truly a textbook for living. As a guide, the Bible is without a rival. It solves the great problems of life and presents the only perfect code of morals ever given. It gives us a firm hope of the future and inspires to a life of purity, patience, and well doing. It makes us bold for the right and helps us sustain ourselves in adversity and affliction. The Bible contains proof of its divine origin because no other book can answer the questionings of the mind or satisfy the longings of the heart. It is adapted to every age and condition of life. From the moment the writings have been conceived, and through its long history, a divine hand has been over it and preserved it for all His people.

NOTE: The moral influence of the Bible is uniformly good. Those who become careful students of its pages are invariably elevated to a pure life.

II. What the Bible Has Done and Continues to Do in Society

The Bible has had and still has a great influence on Western thinking and culture, touching on almost every aspect of human lives. It has become the source of religious and also of philosophical traditions. The Bible has guided the formation of governments, inspired peace, and torn down the barriers that separate people. It has initiated human rights, dignity, justice, and mercy. It is a universal Book, which is restricted neither by time nor place. It continues to influence other religions, which are recognizing that the Bible contains a message from the same God they also worship. History has been shaped by great men and women who drew their inspiration from its pages. It has many readers to defend it, and some have *risked their lives to become in possession of it.

---

* Because the Bible has the power and ability to generate and form a new worldview, it is feared by countries that have a different view, especially atheistic countries. Moreover, it has the power to change the lives of people, whose first alliance is to God and His universal laws and principles and not to the atheistic political leaders with their manmade state laws and regulations, which are based on fearful dread and often on undeserving punishment. When former communist countries were liberated from satanic oppression, many people of those countries whom were Christian before did everything to come into possession of the whole Bible or part of it, which they shared with each other.

The Bible has been an abundant source of inspiration for some of the greatest art treasures, such as the paintings of Rembrandt, Michelangelo, Leonardo da Vinci, Raphael, Titian, and many others. The world's greatest masterpieces of sculpture are artists' imaginations of Bible characters. Many authors own everything to the Bible, such as the great classics of Christian literature: Augustine's "City of God" and "Confessions", Thomas a Kempis "Imitation of Christ". "Calvin's "Institutes", Ignatius Loyola's "Spiritual Exercises", George Fox's "Journal", Bunyan's "Pilgrim Progress", Milton's "Paradise Lost", and many modern works. Shakespeare used many quotations from the Bible. His stories have, in turn, fascinated great writers and artists of the world. The greatest poets have been influenced by God, the author of the Bible. It has been a major source of language, which has enriched the culture of many countries. Many great composers of music were inspired by the Bible as well as songwriters, whose words have been set to magnificent music. Many Hollywood producers used Bible stories to make great movies, which also appear on television screens. Every week, we can listen by radio to many biblical sermons.

NOTE: Besides the mainstream religions, the Bible also had a great impact on lesser known religions and esoteric organizations, such as: Spiritualism, the Mormons, Christian Science, Unity (Unity Village, Kansas), Theosophical society, Swedenborgian church, Jehovah's Witness, Rosicrucian (amorc), Rosicrucian (Max Heindel), Unification Church, Religious Science, Bahai faith, writings of Alice Bailey, Astara, and many messages from the spirit side of life, and Summit University in Livingston, Montana.

From the Ten Commandments to the Golden Rule, the Bible has had and continues to have a profound effect on formulating Western concepts of law. Much of the thinking concerning morality and ethics derives from the Holy Book, such as: Marriage, adultery, divorce, prostitution, homosexuality, murder, deception, stealing, and other moral issues. The Bible also has been the inspiration of great movements in social reform, such as the exploitation of women and children by employers and of using slave labor by wealthy landowners. It has also inspired many people to give freely of themselves in money and service. It filled their hearts with the Love of God and a strong desire to do good to others.

The Bible has also been held in high esteem by well-educated people because the Wisdom expressed in the Book has the power to mold their thinking and keep their minds clear and focused on the things that are wholesome and pure. All that the intellectuals need is to have an open mind and a teachable spirit. As an educating power, the

Bible has no equal because nothing strengthens the mind or elevates the thoughts as the truths of revelation. This was well testified by the young King Solomon and other possessors of great wisdom. Moreover, to the extent that it is studied and its teachings are assimilated, it gives strength of character, noble ambitions, keenness of perception, and sound judgment.

In book after book, we encounter a God who wants us to understand ourselves, learn our lessons, reform our lives, and accept His blessings. Many people gained from the Bible a wealth of wisdom, virtue, and willpower that made them heroic. For them, the Word of God has been a companion, strength, motivation, and guidance. There is also a wealth of ideas about how to deal with anger, fear, grief, egotism, despair, and insecurity, as well as to make use of the opportunities to succeed. The Good Book explains why humans suffer and also explains the *purpose of life.

The Bible is inexhaustible in its truth, there is always more to be found, and it is, therefore, always new. It gives complete satisfaction for those who read it for the first time, as well as for the newborn and the saintly. As we cannot fathom the depth of the living God, so we cannot plumb His Word. It is, therefore, incapable of being used by one time reading as an ordinary book.

For countless generations, it has given great comfort and consolation to all those in their external and internal suffering, impending death, and given them hope for salvation and eternal life. Although the earth is a beautiful place, an outstanding schoolroom, a more magnificent abode is waiting for us in Paradise, wherein we can explore the many different mansions or levels.

The Bible answers the great questions in life: "Is there a God, and if so, what is He like?" "Why are we here?" "What are we like?" "How

---

* Genesis 1:28 reveals that the original or main purpose of human beings on earth is to "be fruitful (grow to maturity in the image of God), multiply, and fill the earth and subdue it". That is, to have dominion over the sea, air, and land. Because of the fall of the primal pair and all their descendants, the main purpose became to restore first what was lost, which is called restoration or salvation. This theme we find throughout the Bible, from Genesis to Revelation. This salvation history began when God saved Noah and his family from the flood and humanity from extinction. He rescued Israel from slavery in Egypt and redeemed humans from the penalty of their sins (1 Jn. 2:1-2). And finally, to enjoy a happy, abundant, and peaceful life here and now, "when the dwelling of God is with men" ---, "and He will wipe away every tear from their eyes, and (spiritual) death shall be no more" (Revelation 21:3-4).

ought we to live?" "Where are we going?" "What happens to us when we die?" "What is God's plan and purpose for the human race?"

Albert Sweitzer, a German theologian and missionary, said in the beginning of the 19th century that the Scriptures help to improve the quality of your life and work. Your attitudes toward the events of life become more mature. Your dealings with others become more harmonious. Your work becomes more inspired, and you become more aware of the beauty around you.

As a whole, the Bible is a guide to enlightened living.

NOTE: The phrases of the Bible have become a part of everyday conversation of the Bible-reading public. Millions of people use biblical expressions without always realizing that they use Bible words. For example, when doing good, you are called a "Good Samaritan" (Lk. 10:30-37). If you do not believe, you are called a "doubting Thomas" (Jn. 20:24-28). Or you will be called a "prodigal" (Lk. 15:11-24) or demonstrate suffering as having the "patience of Job" (Job 1, 2), or having the "wisdom of Solomon" (1 Kings 4:29-34). The expression "he has feet of clay" originates in Daniel 2. "Can a leopard change his spots?" is asked first by Jeremiah in 13:23. Daniel 5 speaks of "the handwriting on the wall". When coming through testing circumstances, people will say you have faced a "fiery furnace" (Dan. 3). When you do something impossible, your friends will say you can "walk on water".

III. Testimonies about the Bible

"The Scriptures are the true words of the Holy Spirit" (Clement of Rome – d. 100 A.D.). "The Scriptures are the writings of God" (Tertullian – d. 225 A.D.). "As in Paradise, God walks in the Holy Scripture, seeking man. When a sinner reads the Scriptures, he hears God's voice saying, "Adam, where art thou?" (St. Ambrose – d. 397 A.D.) "Everything in the Sacred Book shines and glistens, even in its outer shell; but the marrow of it is sweeter; if you want the kernel, you must break the shell" (St. Jerome – d. 419 A.D.). "A man speaks more or less wisely in proportion as he has made more or less progress in Holy Scriptures" (St. Augustine of Hippo – d. 430 A.D.).

"It is one of the glories of the Bible that it can enshrine many meanings in a single passage" (St. Thomas Aquinas – d. 1274). "By the Mosaic Law men may be said to be purified, and by the prophetic revelation they are enlightened, and by the evangelical message, they are brought to perfection" (St. Bonaventura – d. 1274). "You will feel yourself breathed upon by divine will, affected, seized, transfigured, in an ineffable manner, if you approach Scripture religiously with veneration", and "There is no attack of the enemy so violent, that is, no temptation so formidable, that an eager study of the scriptures will not easily beat off" (Desiderius Erasmus – d. 1536). "What God has so plainly declared to the world is in some parts of Scripture stated in plain words, while in other parts it still lies hidden under obscure words" (Martin Luther – d. 1546).

Sir Francis Bacon (1561 – 1626), English philosopher, said, "There never was found in any age of the world either religion or law that did so highly exalt the public good as the Bible." Immanuel Kant (1724 – 1804), German philosopher, said, "The existence of the Bible, as a book for the people, is the greatest benefit which the human race has ever experienced. Every attempt to belittle it is a crime against humanity", and "The Bible is an inexhaustible fountain of all truths." Soren Kierkegaard (1813 – 1855), Danish philosopher and theologian, said, "When you read God's Word, you must constantly be saying to yourself, 'It is talking to me, and about me.'"

NOTE: "Holy Bible, book divine, precious treasure, thou art mine; mine to teach me whence I came, mine to teach me what I am" (J. Burton).

"The Bible is not only the foundation of modern English literature; it is the foundation of Anglo-Saxon civilization" (W.L. Phelps). "The New Testament is the very best book that ever was or ever will be known in the world" (Charles Dickens). "The poetry of the Bible is not only the most wonderful kind, but it is God's literature" (Hugh Pope). The most famous travel writer John Bunyan based his allegory "Pilgrim's Progress" upon the Bible. Stevenson, Defoe, Chaucer, Shakespeare, Milton, Browning, and Kipling are only a few of the famous English writers who were influenced by the Bible. The same is true of Longfellow, Whittier, Bryant, Van Dyke, and many other American literary giants.

"Our own desire for all the Church's children is that, being saturated with the Bible, they may arrive at the all-surpassing knowledge of Jesus Christ" (Pope Benedict XV). "The vigor of our Spiritual Life will be in exact proportion to the place held by the Bible in our life and thoughts", and "I have read the Bible through one hundred times and always with increasing delight. Each time it seems like a new book to me" (George Muller). "By the reading of Scripture, I am so renewed that all nature seems renewed around me" (Thomas Merton). It was a common saying among the Puritans, "brown bread and the Gospel is a good fare" (Matthew Henry). "This book will keep me from sin, but sin will keep me from this book" (John Bunyan). "It furnished good Christians an armor for their warfare, a guide for their conduct, a solace for their sorrows, food for their Souls" (G.G. Atkins). "Nobody ever outgrows Scripture; the Book widens and deepens with our years" (C.H. Spurgeon). "The whole of morality is based on the Bible; there is not a principle, however resolutely secular it would like to be, that did not originate in Scripture" (H.D. Rops). "The Bible has called into being a system of morality which has become the cornerstone of human civilization" (I. Friedlander). "Western civilization is founded upon the Bible; our ideas, our wisdom, our philosophy, our literature, our art, our ideals come more from the Bible than from all other books put together" (W.L. Philips). "It is impossible mentally or socially to enslave a Bible reading people" (Horace Greeley). "The Gospel is so welded together in Truth that if one part or article is renounced, the rest is at once deprived of meaning" (B. Jarrett). "The Old Testament cannot be understood without the New, which comes to fulfill, to justify, and explain" (P. Claudel). "The Bible is a window in this prison-world through which we may look into eternity" (T. Dwight). "The Bible is a collection of literature, containing in a pre-eminent measure the growth of the consciousness of God in the human soul" (E. Abbott). "The supreme fact about the Bible is that it is substantially a history of the growth of the idea of God" (John Ervine). "Any individual or institution that could take the Bible to every home in this country would do more for the country than all the armies, from the beginning of our history to the present time" (D.J. Brewer). "What is a home without a Bible? It is a home where daily bread for the body is provided but the Soul is never fed" (C.D. Meigs). "The study of God's Word, for the purpose of discovering God's Will, is the secret discipline which has formed the greatest characters" (J.W. Alexander). "God's Word – His instructive manual for mankind – is the foundation of all knowledge and reveals God's blueprint for salvation" (Herbert Armstrong). "There is more wisdom, more insight, more knowledge, more inspiration, more motivation in the Bible than in any other book ever written" (Norman Vincent Peale). "When I read a verse of the Bible, I get something new. That is so marvelous about the Bible – unlike any book" (Billy Graham).

NOTE: "I have tried, through narrative and quotations, to give some foretaste of the water of life that rises from the deep well of Truth that is the Book of Books" (Fulton Oursler – author of "The Greatest Book Ever Written").

The three greatest periods of English history came when national recognition was given to the Bible as God's Word. During the reign of Alfred the Great (871 – 899), who took a personal interest in having part of the Bible translated, England rose from barbarism, division, and ignorance into a united, civilized nation. During the reign of Queen Elizabeth (1533 – 1603), who officially promoted the circulation of the Bible, England became a *world power. During the reign of Queen Victoria (1837 – 1901), the British Empire climbed to its zenith in world influence. The Queen is quoted to say "That book accounts for the supremacy of England." Victor Hugo said, "England has two books: the Bible and Shakespeare. England made Shakespeare, but the Bible made England."

Napoleon Bonaparte (1769 – 1821), French military leader and emperor of France, says, "The Bible is no mere book, but a living power that conquers all that oppose it."

The Russian Czar Peter the Great is quoted as saying, "The Bible is a book which towers above all others and contains everything pertaining to man's duty to God and his neighbor." In 1716, Peter commanded his royal court to have Bibles printed in Amsterdam, Holland.

The Bible is the torch of civilization and liberty. Its influence for good in society has been recognized by the greatest statesmen. From the earliest days of America's history right up to the present, the Bible has played a prominent role in American life. The Bible and its teachings were instrumental in shaping the America in which we live. It inspired many early settlers, beginning with the Pilgrim Fathers and the Puritans in New England in 1620, and the Dutch in New Netherland in 1625. The Bible provided them with the strength, endurance, character, and faith necessary to overcome great hardship and danger in a strange and rugged land. Many of the people shared a common purpose, to fulfill a †destiny in this land of New Canaan, which was their promised land. The reading and the application of the precepts of the Bible became the great secret of the greatness of America, a "nation under God". Thereafter, every president, beginning with George Washington, laid their hands on the Bible when they take their oath of office.

"It is impossible to rightfully govern the world without God and the Bible" (1st President). "The Bible is the best book in the world" (John

---

* During the time that Holland honored and deeply respected the Bible, they became a world power in the 17th century, the Dutch Golden Age.

† On the "Great Seal" is inscribed the phrase Annuit Coeptis "God has favored our undertaking", which is our destiny.

Adams – 2nd President). "The studious perusal of the sacred volume will make better citizens, better fathers, and better husbands" (Thomas Jefferson – 3rd President). "That book, sir, is the rock on which our republic rests" (Andrew Jackson – 7th President). "I believe the Bible is the best gift God has ever given to men. All the good from the Savior of the world is communicated to us through this book --- but for it we could not know right from wrong" (Abraham Lincoln – 16th President). "The more profoundly we study this wonderful Book, and the more closely we observe its divine precepts, the better citizens we will become and the higher will be our destiny as a nation" (William McKinley – 25th President). "If a man is not familiar with the Bible, he has suffered a loss which he had better make all possible haste to correct" (Theodore Roosevelt – 26th President). "There are a good many problems before me, but I expect to find the solution of those problems just in the proportion that I am faithful in the study of the Word of God" (Woodrow Wilson – 28th President). "The Bible is the moral code of civilization" (Harry S. Truman 33rd President). "The Bible is endorsed by the Ages. Our civilization is built upon its words. In no other book is there such a collection of inspired wisdom, reality, and hope" (Dwight D. Eisenhower – 35th President). "Within the covers of the Bible are all the answers for all the problems men face. The Bible can touch hearts, order minds, and refresh souls" (Ronald Reagan – 40th President).

Daniel Webster (1782-1852), U.S. Statesman, said, "If we abide by the principles taught in the Bible, our country will go on prospering and to prosper; but if we in our posterity neglect its instructions and authority, no man can tell how sudden a catastrophe may overwhelm us and bury all our glory in profound obscurity."

Dwight D. Eisenhower recognized the fact that humans may soon destroy themselves. In his inaugural address he said: "How far have we come in man's long pilgrimage from darkness toward light? Are we nearing the light – a day of freedom and peace for all mankind? Or are the shadows of another night closing in upon us? --- Science seems ready to confer upon us, as its final gift, the power to erase human life from this planet."

How may world disaster be averted? At the end of the Second World War following the surrender of the Japanese on board the battleship Missouri in Tokyo Bay, the late General Douglas Mac Arthur indicated in the following speech the only possible solution. He said:

"Men, since the beginning of time, have sought peace.
Various methods through the ages have been attempted to

devise an international process to prevent or settle disputes between nations --- military alliances, balances of power, leagues of nations, all in turn failed, leaving the only path to be by way of the crucible of war. The utter destructiveness of war now blots out this alternative. We have had our last chance. If we will not devise some greater and more equitable system, Armageddon will be at the door. The problem basically is theological and involves a spiritual recrudescence and improvement of human character that will synchronize with our almost matchless advances in science, art, literature, and all material and cultural developments of the past 2000 years. It must be of spirit if we are to save the flesh" (Reminiscences p. 459).

Mac Arthur saw the only solution to this world's problems as renewing of the spirit of human beings – an improvement of human character.

NOTE: History tells us that those whom are leading the life of the good/evil personality (carnal men and women) have always ended in destruction and death. Only when people are living the spiritual or divine life will there be everlasting peace (Isa. Ch. 9; 11; 60). As God says, "My people are destroyed for lack of (spiritual) knowledge" (Hosea 4:6; Prov. 14:12; II Tim. 3:13; Matt. 24:22).

IV. Why Do Many People Don't Want to Read the Bible

Many Christians in Western lands are in possession of at least one Bible. They freely talk about it, praise and defend it, but most of them do not read it and are even ashamed to be seen reading the Bible. In fact, the Bible has become a best seller with only a few readers. Some individuals may occasionally look into it but soon give up because they do not understand it or find it too dull. Besides, they have more important things to do. Others say that there are too many bloodthirsty battles, and its laws are more suited for the moral self-righteous. The result is that those most precious books are rotting in their beautifully decorated bookshelves. They should, however, understand that the Old Testament is written for those people whom are living the life of the inherited good/evil personality, whereby their evil selves are often in charge of their lives. It is therefore difficult for the God forces to persuade them to behave in the right way. Strict and simple laws of "thou shall not" were given, which were enforced by punishment. Lawless people would not listen at all, and relatively good people could only defend themselves and their rightful way of living by engaging in warfare. On the other hand, individuals whom are living a divine life of New Testament times are no longer living under law, but grace (Rom. 6:14) and should not be effected by wars waged among undeveloped people. The Bible is certainly not dull when we understand the purpose and inner meaning of Scripture. For example, we can read about the development, or rather, restoration of the human race, which corresponds with the development of our inner selves, with all its successes and failures. The Bible is truly an exciting adventure in self-discovery. Another reason we do not always want to read the Bible is that our satanic nature or evil self of the personality (Rom. 6:6; Eph. 4:22; Col. 3:9) sometimes gets the overhand and does not want to give up its position as the ruler of our lives. It directs our thoughts to outside attraction, such as cheap entertainment and secular concern as soon as we start to think in a spiritual way. When, for example, we start reading the Bible, we come in close encounter with God behind the Words who then, via our budding Souls, will guide our lives directly.

Those individuals who are convinced that knowledge of Scripture is important for their spiritual life may, at first, get nothing out of it when they start reading. But when they keep on reading and meditate on its truths, the barrier or obstruction of their satanic nature is broken through, and they may experience, at first, a glimpse of God by reading His Words. By growing in the Truth and opening their "hearts" more and more and to keep on reading, God will then be speaking to them through His Words. They then discover that the Bible is not an old-fashioned book for modern-day living because its teachings still apply today to each one of them in a very personal way.

V. How to Read and Study the Bible

Just as you get acquainted with people when you communicate with them and read their writings, you will get to know God much better when you talk to Him through prayer and study His writings. We should, therefore, *begin our Bible study with earnest prayer. Ask for His guidance, be receptive, and allow time to listen to what it is saying to us personally. The Spirit may then direct us to read certain sections of the Bible or verses which apply to our lives. We should, therefore,

---

* It is not always easy to find time to study the Bible because it not only demands the full attention of our mind, but also the evil part of our personality and the evil selves of people around us (unknown to themselves) try to interrupt such study. We also need to build up our relationship with our Creator because we may have led lives whereby satan was our ruler. Therefore, in the beginning, perseverance is needed, which will bring about a change in the mental attitude and even joy and delight in the knowledge of the writing of God and in God Himself, whom we choose to be our guide.

expect that God will speak to us through His Word. As the Bible verses were no more than words before, they now become the living Word, as it is being quickened or made alive by the Spirit of God, who may also shine more Light on Bible verses.

We are directed by the Word of God to study the Bible. Jesus said in John 5:39 to "search the Scriptures". Paul said that faith comes from hearing the word of God (Rom. 10:17). Why is the Bible so hard to understand? – "Open my eyes, that I may behold wondrous things out of thy law" (Ps. 119:18). How do I know when my understanding of Scripture is right? (Matt. 13:18-23; Col.1:6), when the truth bears fruit in our lives in transformed living.

We should check for ourselves what the Bible teaches by disregarding what others have said about it. We should, therefore, start our own digging in the Bible, which is a great treasure trove of Truth, which will take more than a lifetime to uncover. Like gold mined from a rock, this treasure has to be extracted from the solid ore of the Bible.

If all possible, we should read the Bible daily so that it becomes an integral part of our lives and our thinking. It gives nourishment and reinforcement of faith and provides wisdom for day to day living. Another purpose of daily reading is that this is the time of feeding our budding Soul (for those whom are born again), with the substance of the Word of God. This Word provides both milk to the newborn and meat to the more advanced. Thus, spiritual reading and mental prayer are as necessary for the growth of faith and the life of the Soul as the daily food and water is for that of the body. Finally, we should digest and assimilate the Word in our Being by savoring what we have read.

NOTE 1: This Book tells you how to attain an exciting, vibrant, and abundant life that will never be dull, a spiritual life that will mature you but will never make you old, because only your body gets old. Your divine life is always young and is truly the fountain of youth. Thus, when one identifies with his/her Divine Spirit, one feels young, even when the person is old in physical years.

NOTE 2: We should be like Jesus who knew the Bible so thoroughly that he could discuss it with the most learned scholars when He was only twelve years old.

We should set aside time for Bible reading, either by ourselves or as a group and make it a habit to read it every day at a particular time.

The moody press lists four basic steps in Bible study:
1) Observation: What does it say?

2) Interpretation: What does it mean?
3) Application: How does it relate to me?
4) Communication: How do I give it to others?

Other comments say: After you have read the text, you may write down what strikes you as the most important, what message you get for yourself, and how you might apply these ideas in your own life.

For a thorough study, the following Bible study aids are to be used:

Scripture Concordances – to find a specific word or phrase in the Bible or to study everything that the Bible has to say about different subjects

Bible Dictionaries – to study the cultural and historical background of the Bible, to find references to most of the topics as it is recorded in the Bible

Bible Handbooks – have different maps, illustrations, and reports about archaeology, and provide commentaries on each book of the Bible

Atlases – wherein we find maps, graphs, and charts of religious, political, and military events

Commentaries (higher critic) – tell about the historical environment of the Bible books, who wrote them, why they were written, what they contain, and much more information

VI. Introduction to the Books of the Bible

Jesus Christ told His disciples after His death and resurrection, "These are my words which I spoke to you, while I was still with you, that everything written about me in the law of Moses and the prophets and the psalms (or writings) must be fulfilled" (Lk. 24:44-46). Jesus Christ and the apostles accepted wholeheartedly the Old Testament; they lived and quoted from it. It constitutes two thirds of the whole Bible.

Today, the [1]Bible canon, which consists for the Protestants of sixty-six books, is divided into the Old Testament (called Hebrew Scripture) and the New Testament (Christian Greek Scripture). The old covenant

---

[1] For easy reference, the books of the Bible have chapters and verses. The chapter divisions were added during the thirteenth century. Three centuries later, a French scholar and printer introduced the division of chapters into verses.

consists of [2]thirty-nine books and is divided into three groups. Its subdivisions are for many religions as follows: <u>Historical</u>, 17 books from Genesis to Esther – which include the 5 books of the law or Pentateuch or Torah; <u>Poetical</u>, 5 books from Job to the Song of Solomon; <u>Prophetical</u>, 17 books from Isaiah to Malachi, which includes the five major and twelve minor prophets. The New Testament consists of 27 books: the four Gospels of Matthew, Mark, Luke, and John, the Acts of the Apostles, the Epistles (letters) of Apostle Paul, other apostolic writings, and the Apocalyptic or Book of Revelation – the four Gospels and Acts are classified as the 5 historical books.

The Old Testament tells the story of God's chosen people, the Israelites, beginning with Abraham, Isaac, and Jacob (Israel), whom became the founders of a nation. It described their dealings with God and their expectation of the promised Messiah. The New Testament deals with the life of the Messiah known by Christ-ians as Jesus Christ. It gives an account of His teachings and activities and the doctrines and activities of His disciples, the beginning of Christianity. It is said that from Moses to Christ was the age of Law, from Pentecost to Christ's return is the age of Grace or the church age.

VII. The Translation of the Bible

The first thirty-nine books of the Bible were originally written in the Hebrew language, with very small parts in [3]Aramaic. In the third century B.C., the Old Testament was translated into the Greek language by seventy men, mainly for the benefit of the Greek-speaking Jews living in Alexandria. This version is called Septuagint (Greek for 70) and also included a few books of the Apocrypha (Greek for hidden).

---

[2] As the Protestant version of the Old Testament consists of 39 books, the Catholic version consists of 46 books. The Roman Catholic Church added to the Hebrew Bible the 7 extra inter-testamental books, the Apocrypha, which are Jewish writings from the third century B.C. through the first century A.D. They are: Tobit, Judith, Wisdom, Sirach, Baruch, and 1 and 2 Maccabees. They were originally part of the Septuagint (Greek Old Testament), incorporated in the Vulgate (Latin translation of Jerome), and are considered canonical (sacred or inspired) by the Roman Catholic Church at the Council of Trent (1546). Jerome said that those books (about twelve) could be read for edification but not for confirming the authority of church dogmas. Martin Luther, the Protestant reformer, said that those books were not equal to Scripture but were "profitable and good to read". He added that neither Christ nor the Apostles quoted from these books.

[3] Aramaic was the official language of the Persian Empire. In the post-exilic period, Aramaic was the language of the common people in Palestine. Aramaic, in the Galilean dialect, was spoken by Jesus Christ and His disciples (see Matt. 26:73; Mk. 5:41; 7:34).

In the middle of the first century A.D., early Christians had accepted a list of Old Testament books, that is, those whom were approved by the Jewish Council in Jamnia in +/-90 A.D. (without the Apocrypha). [1]In 393 A.D., Catholic bishops approved a list of New Testament (and Old Testament) books as being inspired (without the [2]Apocryphal of the New Testament). Those books became authoritative or canonical (Orthodox).

Many Christians of the first centuries used the Septuagint and the New Testament writings, which latter were originally written in Greek, which was the common language at the beginning of the Christian era. The Christians were not the only ones who spoke Greek; it was also spoken by the Diaspora Jews, Syrians, and Egyptians. When Latin succeeded Greek as the common language, Jerome was appointed by Pope Demascus in 382 A.D. to translate the Bible into Latin or Vulgate (common) from the existing Hebrew, Aramaic, and Greek manuscripts. He worked on the translation in Bethlehem and finished it in 405 A.D. It served as the only Bible translation and became the Standard Version throughout the Middle Ages.

The first translation into modern European languages began with the [3]French, Spanish, Italian, and Polish, which appeared in the 12th and 13th centuries. An unfinished Dutch translation came as early as the 10th century. Before that time, Bede (the father of English history) translated the Gospel of John in the native language just before he died in 735 A.D.

After Alfred the Great became king in 871 A.D., he ordered the translation of the whole Bible into Anglo Saxon. However, the translation of the whole Bible was not completed until the time of John Wycliffe four centuries later. His translation was based on the Latin Vulgate of Jerome, as he and his colleagues knew no Hebrew or Greek. It was completed in 1383 and copied by hand.

---

[1] Earlier in 130 A.D., the Four Gospels and the letters of Paul had come to be regarded as canonical or Standard Scripture. The other writings of the New Testament were accepted by the Church into the canon a little later.

[2] Some of the writings are: the Gospel of Peter; Gospel of the Egyptians; Apocryphon of John; Gospel of Thomas; Sophia Jesu Christi; Gospel of Truth; Gospel of Philip; Gospel of Nicodemus. Some of the writings are Gnostic in origin.

[3] About 1170 A.D., a merchant of Lyon, Peter Waldo, arranged the Bible to be translated into French. His followers founded the Waldensian church.

With the revival of learning that characterized the Renaissance, scholars acquired a new interest in studying the Hebrew and Greek texts of the Bible. One of these was the Dutch scholar Erasmus of Rotterdam. He [1]published an edition of the New Testament in Greek in 1516 from the not earlier used Greek sources. During the Reformation, [2]Martin Luther used Erasmus Greek Testament to translate the New Testament into German, as William Tyndale used it to translate it into the English language. Luther then translated the Old Testament from Hebrew in about 1534. The above writings were not a translation of a translation, as was Wycliffe's.

As Martin Luther was able [3]to hide from Catholic authorities in order to translate and print the whole Bible, Tyndale was betrayed and caught by papal agents at Vilvoorde castle near Brussel after his [4]New Testament edition was printed and smuggled into England. He was tried for heresy and killed on October 6. 1536. His last words were, "Lord, open the king of England's eyes!"

During the time Tyndale was in prison, and with the approval of King Henry VIII, the Coverdale full Bible was being printed. His translation was based on Luther's German version, the Latin Vulgate, and Tyndale's New Testament and Pentateuch. In 1539, a copy of the English Bible was chained to a reading desk of every parish church in England. From that time on, the Bible has never ceased to be printed and sold freely. Coverdale's Bible was followed by other English translations and revisions, such as the Matthew Bible (1537), the Great

---

[1] It was the first printed New Testament in Greek, which also included the corrected version of the Vulgate. Earlier, the German printer Johannes Guttenberg printed in 1455 his first book, The Holy Bible in Latin. Thereafter, bibles translated from the vulgate were printed: German (1466); Dutch (1477); Italian (1471); French (1474); Czech (1475); and Spanish (1478).

In his preface of the Greek New Testament, Erasmus wrote, "I wish that the Scriptures might be translated into all the languages so that not only the Scots and the Irish but also the Turk and the Saracen might read and understand them. I long that the farm laborer might sing them as he follows his plough, the weaver hum them to the tune of his shuttle, the traveler beguile the weariness of his journey with their stories."

[2] Martin Luther was a professor of biblical theology at the University of Wittenberg (white mountain) in Germany.

[3] See note on persecution division IX.

[4] The First New Testament printed in English appears at Worms, a city in Germany in 1526. The Pentateuch was translated from Hebrew into English in 1531. At this city (at the Diet of Worms in 1521), Luther was pronounced a heretic.

Bible (1539), the [1]Geneva Bible (1560), the Bishops Bible (1568), Douay/Rheims (Catholic) Bible (1610) – a literal rendering of the Vulgate Bible – and the [2]King James Version (1611). From the time translation was made from the available Hebrew and Greek texts, scholars have found since then several hundred more manuscripts, some of them which are better and of earlier dates than the fourth century Vatican and [3]Sinaitic Codices, which the 19th century scholars used as the main sources for the translation of the Bible. The English Revised Version was published in 1885, and the American Standard Version in 1901. The Revised Standard came in 1952 and the New Revised Standard Version in 1989. In 1966, the Roman Catholics published the Jerusalem Bible, revised as the New Jerusalem Bible in 1985.

NOTE 1: Until 1947 when the Dead Sea scrolls were discovered near Qumran, the oldest known Hebrew manuscripts dated from the 9th and 10th centuries A.D. The scrolls were found in hard to reach caves out of reach of the Roman legions which were out to destroy anything Jewish in around 68 A.D. Scholars have found that the Scrolls, which date as far back as the third century B.C., were practically identical to the Masoretic text of the Middle Ages (the text edited by Jewish scholars called Massoretes).

NOTE 2: Much of the Bible has been written and rewritten. Some of the verses have been mistranslated (or even tampered with), while other verses have been misinterpreted, although unintentionally, because of the writer's belief system through which "filters of the mind" the translation takes place. Some of its original purity and trueness is lost in the translation through the intellectual process of the human mind of the personality. There are some verses which cannot be clearly understood unless they are read in the original language.

---

[1] The Geneva Bible, printed in Geneva by English people in exile, was also called the Breeches Bible because the translators put pants rather than fig leaves on Adam in the Garden. This Bible was adopted by many Puritans and by the Pilgrim Fathers whom came to America in 1620. It had many marginal notes and illustrations. Some of the notes were a judgment against the "Divine Right of Kings", which also extended to evil kings. This Bible was also used by William Shakespeare, John Bunyan, and John Milton.

[2] The King James Bible was not produced by one person but by a committee of scholars. The New Testament was largely based on Tyndale's translation. For more than 350 years, the King James Version has been used and loved by the English-speaking people of the world. It is known of its great style and superb prose. When reading the sacred Scripture, one may experience a mystical feeling behind or from within those Words.

[3] The Code Sinaiticus was discovered in Saint Catherine's Monastery at the base of Mount Sinai by Tischendorf in 1859 and is kept in the British museum.

VIII. How the Dutch Spread the Gospel over the Globe

REMARK: In 1360, the first complete Bible translation in the Dutch language was written in Belgium, followed by the Dutch States Bible in 1636. Like the King James Version, the States or Government Bible became, for the Dutch-speaking people, the standard Bible for more than 300 years. *This Bible went with the ships of the Dutch East India Company (V.O.C.) and the West India Company (W.I.C.). The V.O.C. was organized in 1602 and was ruled by a governing body of 17 men (Heeren XVII) and lasted for about 200 years. The W.I.C. was organized in 1621 with a governing body of 19 men (Heeren XIX) and lasted for about 50 years. The latter took care of the trade with North and South America and the West coast of Africa. During its existence, and wherever the ships of those companies went, they introduced not only the Bible to the natives but hundreds of ministers and thousands of lay readers (at the company's expense) stayed with them in such countries as: New York (New Amsterdam 1625) and New Netherland, a territory surrounding New Amsterdam which extended so far as Princeton (New Jersey) and Delaware. South Africa (1652), Batavia (Indonesia), Malacca (Malaya), Netherland Antilles, Surinam, Brazil (New Holland), Sri Lanka (Ceylon), Taiwan (Formosa – Fort Zeelandia); where the Dutch established colonies. They also carried the Bible to many commercial outposts, fords, and factories, such as in a few places on the West coast of Africa, notably Guinea and Benguela (Angola), and Madagascar on the East coast. The East and West coasts of South India, Mauritius, and Nagasaki (Japan), from 1639 to 1854, as their only trading partner. The Dutch also visited and stayed for a while in Canton (China), Australia, and New Zealand and came on shore in Korea when one of their ships was wrecked, as this was reported by Hendrick Hamel. They translated the Bible in different languages all at the cost of the companies, whom were owned by shareholders of the seven United Provinces.

By 1648, the Dutch were indisputably the greatest trading nation in the world, which (seventeenth) century was known as the Golden Age. Dutch ships were seen everywhere whose merchants ploughed the seven seas. The people involved were mostly Protestant and members of the Reformed Church. They read the Bible a lot, especially their three greatest generals Piet Heyn, Maarten Tromp, and Michiel de Ruyter, whom were God-fearing Calvinists, and so was Peter Stuy-

---

* Great voluntary and involuntary sacrifices were made by many sailors as one third of them did not come back.

vesant, the last Dutch governor of New York. As the Protestants spread the Gospel of Jesus Christ over the globe emphasizing the Fatherhood of God, the Catholics were, likewise, busy, but emphasizing the Motherhood of God.

NOTE: In the 1850s, 3 groups of Christians who sought freedom of religion from the powerful Dutch Reformed State Church left Netherland and settled in Holland – Michigan (which had the same kind of dunes as the coast of Netherland), Pella (Iowa), and the southern part of Chicago.

IX. How the Existence of the Bible Was Assaulted and Survived

NOTE: From the beginning, it has been satan's practice to foster doubt and disbelief in God's Word and to question it when he said, "Did God say?" (Gen. 3:1) He put a question mark in the mind of Eve as to whether or not God would keep His Word, as to whether or not He meant what he said.

Rulers in the past and others whose evil (satanic nature) was in charge of their lives have endeavored by every means possible to banish the Word of God from the face of the earth. They have hidden it, destroyed it, and made it a crime (punishable by death) of those who had faith in it, and have it in their possession. For example, the Syrian king Antiochus Epiphanes profiled the temple in Jerusalem in 168 B.C., burned the books of the Law, and declared that anyone who is in possession of those Scriptures would be killed. In 303 A.D., [1]Roman emperor Diocletian decreed that all Christian meeting places be demolished and that all their Scriptures be burned. Adolf Hitler set out to exterminate the Jews, strangle the Christian faith, and proclaim "Mein Kamph" (my struggle), the bible of the "master race", and himself the savior. At the same time, Japanese militarists persuaded people to worship Hirohito as a god. Thereafter, Communism became an even greater adversary of the Bible. Missionaries have been ousted and persecuted by Russia, China, and other red, materialistic countries.

[2]In the Middle Ages, it was not the pagan rulers but Catholic militant church leaders who persecuted lay people who were in possession of a Bible in any language. This prohibition was decreed in 1229 A.D. by the Roman Catholic Synod in Toulouse, France. They had their reasons for doing so, although one of the wrong reasons was that the people are less or no longer dependent upon the clergy for access to God. When God and the Bible become the ultimate authority,

---

[1] After Diocletian's death, the new emperor Constantine commissioned 50 copies of the Bible at government expense.

[2] Since Vatican II in 1962-1965, every Catholic is encouraged to read the Bible.

the people should no longer fear as much the authority of the Pope, of expelling them from the presence of God by [3]excommunication and the threat of eternal hell.

NOTE: The Bible has survived throughout the centuries because the great Being, who it claims as its author, has also been its preserver.

Jan Hus (1373-1415), who taught at the University of Prague in Bohemia, was influenced by the teaching of [4]John Wycliffe (Oxford scholar who translated the Bible into the English language), was burned at the stake in 1415 by the Council of Constance, who also degreed that the bones of Wycliffe should be exhumed in England and burned. This happened four decades after his death. His ashes were cast into the waters of the river Swift which flowed to the ocean. Like his master Jesus Christ, William Tyndale was betrayed, arrested, and killed in 1536. His translation used the word "congregation" instead of "church". He replaced "priest" with "elder" and used "repent" rather than "do penance", thereby stripping the clergy of their power. Jacob van Liesvelt, Dutch translater of the Luther Bible and printer of many Bibles, was arrested and beheaded in Antwerp in 1545. One marginal note in the Bible that read "de salicheyt van menschen aleen compt van Jesum Christum" (salvation comes through Jesus Christ alone) was enough reason to condemn him to death.

In the late Middle Ages began what was called the Renaissance or rebirth (the revival of Greek learning) to aid the unfolding of the suppressed personality, and the Reformation in 1517 to better help with the birth and development of the Soul. During that time, the Roman Catholic Church lost much of their power and ecclesiastic authority, and the severe persecution stopped. The second Renaissance or Enlightenment was an eighteenth century philosophical movement which was based on rationalistic methods, which was aiding or rather overemphasizing the life of the personality. They try to reason away the importance of God and His writings and, thus, block themselves to accept the next face of life, the birth and the development of the Divine Spirit or Soul. This culminated in a religious movement called "Deism", which accepted God but denies the validity of Revelation, visions, miracles, and mysticism. However, those movements were

---

[3] Some people have done so much evil that they are in a state of separation from God and, thus, excommunication is justified. However, separation from God is not an eternal state. Even satan will be restored, although it will take a long time.

[4] John Wycliffe said that the standard or rule by which someone's faith is to be appraised is not the Pope or the priests but the Bible.

countered by the second religious Reformation of George Fox (1624-1691), founder of the Society of Friends (Quakers) and John Wesley (1703-1791), founder of Methodism, and Emmanuel Swedenborg (1688-1772), Swedish mystic, theologian, philosopher, and scientist. During the second Renaissance, a few philosophers came along whose evil part of the personality was in charge of their lives, called in the Bible (old self, Rom. 6:6; old nature, Col. 3:9). The worst one was [1]Voltaire, who scorned the Bible, and not much better was the German theologian D.F. Straus, who wrote the "Life of Jesus" in 1846. He ruled out the supernatural and the miraculous, and that Jesus was a mythical God/man invented by the early church, and that a religion of humanity must supercede Christianity. The German philosopher and left wing Hegelian Ludwig Feuerbach, who wrote "The Essence of Christianity" in 1846, expressed in his materialistic philosophy that "man is what he eats", and that religion is a dream of the human mind or a distorted projection of emotional needs. He greatly influenced Karl Marx who wrote in 1848 "The Communist Manifesto" and launched the materialistic/atheistic movement of Communism (the third Renaissance). This is being countered by the Cosmic Christ, the Christ of all religions, who will use enlightened individuals to make the Kingdom of God a reality by taking up permanent residence in everyone (Rev. 21:3).

Meanwhile, German scholars in the first half of the nineteenth century were very busy in the historical criticism of the Bible (Higher Criticism). [2]Albert Sweitzer (1875-1965), German physician, musicologist, philosopher, theologian, and missionary, said that some of the first higher critics of the Bible were enemies of Christ because they hoped to destroy the religion based on it. However, with the exception of those who believed literally in the Bible (who saw the Bible being torn to pieces as the work of the devil), the modern mainline churches and their seminaries continue this [3]critical research because they understood the Bible better and loved it more. For example, by knowing the background of people, that is, their beliefs,

---

[1] In 1776, Voltaire, the French philosopher, announced that "one hundred years from today, there will not be a Bible on this earth". After his death, his own house and press was being used to print and store Bibles. The Bible will always be here because God is guarding His writings.

[2] Albert had the right idea of living. First, know all about the physical body to keep it healthy. Know about the multitude of emotional expressions by playing music, develop intellectually by studying philosophy, and understand spirituality and live and unfold a divine life by witnessing and practicing the Truth.

[3] Some say that biblical scholarship was needed to sort out the literal from the symbolic truth.

attitudes, values, habits, and customs, to which the message is directed, as well as that of the writer, they got a better grasp of the importance and meaning of the communication.

The theologians of the left, who used higher criticism to reduce the Bible to a collection of myths, proclaimed very loudly in the 1960s for everyone to hear that "God is dead".

In the 21st century, [1]homosexual clergy has come out of the closet in great numbers to make a mockery of God's Law and God's design for men and women. They are used by evil forces to usher in the kingdom of satan, who was the [2]first homosexual (Jude 1:6-7).

X. The Importance of Bible Reading

a. To Get to Know God

The Bible teaches us to draw close to our Creator and to bring our life in harmony with His ways (Ps. 25:4). This enables us to begin to know and understand Him better and love Him more. We should, therefore, read the Scripture daily and meditate on its Truths. When we apply this knowledge, we experience a free flow of God's Spirit in our lives, which will evoke a greater abundance of the qualities of the Spirit (Gal. 5:22, 23). By living according to the Bible's precepts, it will protect us from the temptation of evil spirits and evil people (1 Tim. 4:1; II Tim. 3:1-9) and the materialistic spirit of "the world" (Jn. 18:36; 16:33; 15:18; 8:23). However, the Bible also shows how human beings can overcome every human problem and weakness. Holy Scripture is, therefore, a source of moral and spiritual strength, purification of our (outer) and inner personalities (thought, emotion, and desire), and growth of our spiritual Selves.

The reading of the Bible keeps alive the thought of heaven and strengthens our hope of receiving from God all the means and graces necessary to gain it. It has given many people a meaning to their confused existence and a hope for the future. The Bible is not just history but a report of how God has dealt with His people and is dealing the same way with all people today. It certainly is not a dry

---

[1] They are completely misguided and are faithfully following in their master's (satan) footsteps "holding the form of religion but denying the power of it" (II Tim. 3:5).

[2] Satan and his fallen angels easily become homosexuals because they are neither male nor female.

textbook. As you read the Words, the Spirit of God may *at times illuminate them and speak to you in a personal way because the Words in the Bible have an extra dimension. The time we spend in Bible reading is like having a meal for our moral and spiritual health. By reading the Bible frequently, our thoughts become more in harmony with the thoughts of God (Isa. 55:8), which will result that our lives will become more molded in His image. Because God's Word is a product of His Spirit, one vital way to let that Spirit operate in us is by reading and studying the Bible. It is also important to let God directly speak to us instead of listening and reading of what others say or wrote about God's Word, in their sermons and literature, which may be diluted and distorted with human imperfections and vibrations. The pure Words of God, however, contain liberating Truths and Power, which affect us deeply and have the kind of vibration that enables to give us enlightenment and to change our lives. Besides the daily nourishment and reinforcement of faith we experience in daily Bible reading, it also provides the wisdom for day to day living and to enjoy a close relationship with Him. This is the key to a happy and meaningful life. Thus, by reading and pondering over the Bible, His precious Word will imbed or assimilate in our human spirit which, in turn, has its effect on the way we feel, think, and act. We will then be delighted to do God's Will (Ps. 40:8).

> "Blessed is the man who walks not in the counsel of the
> wicked, nor stands in the way of sinners, nor sits in the
> seat of scoffers; but his delight is in the law of the Lord,
> and on his law he meditates day and night" (Ps. 1:1-2).

NOTE: The purpose of Bible study is not to know the Scriptures for their own sake but to allow God to speak to us through these ancient words, to experience partly or wholly the original revelatory experiences of the writer who received the Word of God directly. We then perceive the Spirit of God in a more or less degree behind or within those passages which become sacred Scripture for us. Thus, when we read the Bible, we need to listen to the very voice of God coming through His Word (not our own or somebody else's).

b. How God Reveals Himself

God's revelation of Himself occurs in many ways. For example, God can be seen and experienced through the beauty of nature, wherein we see His greatness and power in the splendor of the world around us

---

* When we have made a strong connection with God through prayer, we may remove much of the obstructions separating us from God.

(Romans 1:19-20). God can be heard through the inner voice of our conscience, or even better, through our developing Souls which are being formed by the Word of God. God is then able to express more or less, through living persons, the many facets of Their Being, such as: Love, Care, Compassion, Goodness, Joy, and Forgiveness. However, the primary means by which God speaks and reveals Him/Herself is through the Scriptures, which are written down by His chosen scribes, especially the *four Gospels through Jesus Christ, whom all together reveal the many aspects of His /Her Being.

Through the pages of this marvelous Book, we can discern by what He said and what He does. He certainly is not a distant Person but a living Being who is involved daily in human affairs, not only in the past but also today. Creation certainly reveals that God exists, that is, His outer Self, but to find out about His inner Self, we need to study the Bible. By reading a portion of the Bible each day, we may learn new characteristics and attributes of His personality.

When the Israelites were released from bondage, God was not only Vocal ("The Lord said") but Omniscient – knowing everything ("I have seen their afflictions"), Merciful ("I have heard their cry"), Omnipotent ("I have come down to deliver them"), Generous ("and bring them to a good and blessed land"), and Omnipresent ("I will always be with you").

NOTE: Psalm 78:40, 41 says, "How often they rebelled against Him in the wilderness and grieved Him in the desert! They tested Him again and again, and provoked the Holy One of Israel."

In Psalm 86, we find many traits in God's personality: He is good, ready to forgive, abounding in steadfast love, willing to answer prayer, unequally among the gods, unmatched in His works, a sovereign ruler, a doer of wondrous things, a deliverer from death, merciful, gracious, slow to anger, abundant in faithfulness, a helper, and a comforter. God is further experienced by men and women in the Bible as a walking companion, anxious Parent, comforting Mother, prodigal Father, and co-sufferer. Jesus more than anyone else in the Bible showed what God was really like, who called Him Father. A disciple of Jesus said that God is Love (1 Jn. 4:16).

---

* See next page.

c. The Four Gospels

*The four Gospels are considered the most sacred writings of the New Testament, especially the Gospel of John. The latter is different from the other three "Synoptic Gospels", as they give a "synopsis" or similar view of the life and teaching of Jesus.

The Book of Matthew is written to the Jews and is to prove that Christ is the king of the Jews. It dedicates the powers of the <u>body</u>. The Book of Mark was written to the Romans to portray Christ as the suffering servant. It deals with the dedication of the <u>mind,</u> the human spirit or soul. The Book of Luke was directed to the Greeks and shows Christ as the great physician, the Son of Man. It deals with the mystical marriage of the soul or human spirit with the <u>Spirit of Christ</u>. The Book of John was written so that everyone will believe that the <u>Cosmic Christ</u> spoke through Jesus Christ, creating oneness with the Spirit of Christ or Soul of all those whom are spiritually born.

Christianity identifies the four living creatures (Rev. 4:6-7) with the four Evangelists: The man is Saint Matthew; the lion is Saint Mark; the calf or bull is Saint Luke; the eagle is Saint John. The man represents the sign of Aquarius. The creature with a face like a lion represents the sign of Leo. The calf (bull) represents the sign of Taurus. The eagle represents the sign of Scorpio. They also represent the four elements: air, fire, earth, water.

NOTE: The Bible often compares a person with a garden, "A river (of Truth) flowed out of Eden to water the garden, and there it divided and became four rivers" (Gen. 2:8-11), the continuing teaching of Truth from God but divided into four expressions.

XI. Some Bible Verses in Relation to Bible Reading

A person who is right with God loves the Word of God, "Oh, how I love thy law! It is my meditation all day." "How sweet are thy words to my taste, sweeter than honey to my mouth!" exclaimed the Psalmist (Ps. 119:97, 103). Reading the Bible guides us in daily living, "Thy word is a lamp to my feet and a light to my path" (Ps. 119:105). It provides good counsel for our problems (Ps. 119:24). It will lift our burdens (Ps. 119:28). The Bible further gives us hope for the future (Ps. 119:50). It gives us comfort (Ps. 119:52). It will lead us to

---

* The four Gospels were written by Matthew, Mark, Luke, and John. Matthew and John were Jesus' disciples; Mark and Luke were companions of the first Apostles.

wisdom (Ps. 119:130). It will give us peace (Ps. 119:165). It will bring us back to God (Ps, 119:176). Other Old Testament words are, "I have treasured in my bosom the words of His mouth" (Job 23:12). "The grass withers, the flower fades; but the word of our God will stand forever" (Isa. 40:8). "Thy words were found, and I ate them, and thy words became to me a joy and the delight of my heart" (Jer. 15:16). David says: The words of the Lord are pure words, as silver refined in a furnace, purified 7 times (Ps. 12:6).

Jesus upheld the claims of the Old Testament writers, referring to the Jewish Scriptures. He asked, "Have you not read what was said to you by God" (Matt. 22:31). Jesus quoted frequently from the Old Testament (see Matt. 13:10-17; Mark 10:19 with the Law of Moses, and Matt. 22:36-40 with Deut. 6:5 and Lev. 19:18). He also used quotations from the Old Scripture to settle arguments with His opponents (see Matt. 12:1-7; 21:15-16; 22:41-45). When He was tempted by the devil, He wielded the sword of the Spirit, which is God's Word. Three times He quoted from the Book of Deuteronomy, saying, "It is written" (Matt. 4:4, 7, 10; Deut. 8:3; 6:16; 6:13). He cried out words from Palm 22:1 when He was dying by calling loudly, "My God, my God, why hast thou forsaken me?" (Mk. 15:34).

Jesus referred to the Bible as "the scriptures" and told the people to "search the scriptures --- it is they that bear witness to me" (Jn. 5:39). He also said, "Man shall not live by bread alone, but by every word that proceeds from the mouth of God" (Matt. 4:4). Jesus told a gathering of Jews, "For truly, I say to you, till heaven and earth pass away, not an iota, not a dot, will pass from the law, until all is accomplished" (Matt. 5:18). He once more said that "scripture cannot be broken" (Jn. 10:35) or cannot be disproved because they are true. He further said, "Blessed rather are those who hear the word of God and keep it!" (Lk. 11:28) Jesus, who has the words of eternal life (Jn. 6:68), said that "the Father who sent me has himself given me commandment what to say and what to speak" (Jn. 12:49). "My food is to do the will of Him who sent me" (Jn. 4:34). "I am the bread of life" (Jn. 6:35), and "He who eats this bread will live forever" (Jn. 6:58). "The words that I have spoken to you are spirit and life" (Jn. 6:63). Christ Jesus further said in John 14:26 that the Holy Spirit will "bring to your remembrance all that I have said to you."

NOTE: Masters of religions may put all their love, all their soul, and spirit into their words. The disciples received them, digested them, and lived them. It was the Life behind the Words, more than the word themselves, which nourished them.

Apostle Paul often quoted the Old Testament Scriptures and said in 2 Timothy 3:16 that "All scripture is inspired by God and profitable for teaching, for reproof (disapproval – reprimand), for correction, and for training in righteousness". The Apostle Peter explained, "No prophecy of scripture ever came by the impulse of man, but men moved by the Holy Spirit spoke from God" (2 Pet. 1:20, 21). Another translation says, "No scripture was ever born by man's will", being moved by their Divine Spirit or Holy Spirit. Thus, the Scripture is not to be received as the word of men but inspired by God. The letter to the Hebrews testified that "God spoke of old to our fathers by the prophets" (Heb. 1:1). "For the word of God is living and active, sharper than any two-edged sword." It cuts deep and it cuts both ways, and is a discerner of the "thoughts and intentions of the heart". Yes, it opens up and exposes our innermost thoughts (Heb. 4:12).

People will never be satisfied with anything less than the Word of God because it is the food or the living bread for the Soul.
- ➢ We grow by the Word of God (1 Pet. 2:2-3).
- ➢ We are changed by the Word (2 Cor. 3:18).
- ➢ We are cleansed by the Word (Jn. 15:3; Eph. 5:26; Ps. 119:9).
- ➢ We are kept by the Word (Ps. 119:11; Jn. 8:32).
- ➢ We share God's life through the Word (Jn. 6:63).
- ➢ We defeat the devil through the Word (Rev. 12:11; Eph. 6:17).
- ➢ We win souls by preaching the Word (Mk. 2:2; Acts 8:25).

Some famous sayings in the Bible:
"Am I my brother's keeper?" (Gen. 4:9) "Man does not live by bread alone" (Deut 8:3). "The fool says in his heart, 'There is no God'" (Ps. 14:1). "The wicked flee when no one pursues" (Prov. 28:1). "There is nothing new under the sun" (Eccl. 1:9). "And they shall beat their swords into plowshares" (Isa. 2:4). "How are the mighty fallen" (2 Sam. 1:19). "You are the salt of the earth" (Matt. 5:13). "Judge not that you not be judged" (Matt. 7:1). "Seek and you shall find" (Matt. 7:7). "For many are called, but few are chosen" (Matt. 22:14). "The spirit indeed is willing but the flesh is weak" (Matt. 26:41). "For all who take the sword will perish by the sword" (Matt. 26:52). "Let him who is without sin among you be the first to throw a stone at her" (Jn. 8:7). "The Truth will make you free" (Jn. 8:32). "For whatever a man sows, that he will also reap" (Gal. 6:7). "It is more blessed to give than to receive" (Acts 20:35). "Do not be overcome by evil, but overcome

evil with good" (Rom. 32:21). "Fight the good fight" (1 Tim. 6:12). "O death where is thy sting" (1 Cor. 15:55). "Behold, the dwelling of God is with men" (Rev. 21:3).

XII. How God Spoke Directly Through the Old and New Testament Prophets

a. Old Testament Prophets

After the Israelites left Egypt and arrived at Mount Sinai, God tries to speak to them directly by external means, through thunder, lightning, and the sound of the trumpet. However, the people were afraid and said to Moses, "You speak to us, and we will hear; but let not God speak to us, lest we die" (Ex. 20:19; Deut. 18:16). In response to the plea of the people, God then used prophets, whereby one person would receive the Word of God (from within) and then mediate it to the people. Thus, all those awesome signs at the mountain were replaced by a single voice of a prophet, which was often the very voice of God. To Moses God spoke "mouth to mouth" (Num. 12:8; Ex. 4:15), or "face to face" (Ex. 33:11). To the prophets Aaron and Miriam God said, "I the Lord make myself known to him (prophet) in a vision. I speak with him in a dream" (Num. 12:6). For example, Isaiah "saw" the Lord's burden (Isa. 13:1). Amos, Micah, and John "saw" their Word from the Lord (Amos 1:1; Micah 1:1; Rev. 1:2). On the other hand, false prophets "speak visions of their own minds, not from the mouth of the Lord" (Jer. 23:16; Deut. 13:5).

The writers of the Bible, for at least 2500 times, let people know that God spoke to them directly, that is, the word of the prophet is also the Word of God. With some variations they said, "The Lord came to me, saying ---" and "The Lord said", or "and God spoke". For example, Ezekiel said, "The word of the Lord came to me" (Ezek. 6:1). Amos introduces sections of his writings with: "Thus says the Lord." In the books of Exodus, Leviticus, and Numbers, the phrase (and) "The Lord said to Moses" is often used. The Lord also spoke to Adam, Cain, and Noah. "Then the Spirit of God took possession of Zechariah" --- 'Thus says God' (2 Chron. 24:20). "Hear the word of the Lord, O people of Israel" (Hosea 4:1). "The Lord said to Samuel" (1 Sam. 16:1). "Then the Lord said to Joshua" (Jos. 8:18). "Thus says the Lord God of hosts" (Isa. 22:15). "Behold, I have put my words in your mouth" (Jer. 1:9). "And you shall speak my words to them" (Ezek. 2:7). "The oracle of David --- The Spirit of the Lord speaks by me, his word is upon my tongue" (2 Sam. 23:1, 2). On some occasions when Old Testament prophets were inspired with a message, they themselves did not understand it. The prophet Daniel said, "I heard, but I did not understand" (Dan. 12:8). "He (the Lord God) spoke by the mouth of his holy prophets" (Luk. 1:70). "God spoke of old to our fathers by the prophets" (Heb. 1:1). Jeremiah spoke of the Word of God as a fire burning within him and out of control (Jer. 20:9; Ps. 39:3). Isaiah 59:21 reported, "My words which I have put in your mouth shall not depart out of your mouth, or out of the mouth of your children."

REMARK: The writing of the whole Bible was done directly or indirectly by many individuals with the exception of the Ten Commandments, which were written personally by God on stone tablets, or "Written with the finger of God" (Ex. 31:18).

As we have seen on many occasions, the words which the prophets spoke were not their own words but the very words of God Himself, who spoke through them, by experiencing a sense of being "taken over" by God. A death penalty was pronounced upon the prophet who would add any of his own words to God's words. See Deut. 18:20. God said to Moses, "You shall not add to the word which I command you, nor take from it" (Deut. 4:2). "And if you say in your heart, 'How may we know the word which the Lord has not spoken?' – when a prophet speaks in the name of the Lord, if the word does not come to pass or come true, that is a word which the Lord has not spoken" (Deut. 18:21-22). The prophets who recorded the word from God did not (always) understand the full significance of what they wrote, for they "searched" their own writings so that they might understand more perfectly (1 Pet. 1:10-12).

b. Fulfilled Prophecy

NOTE: In addition to the testimonies, there are other important witnesses to the inspiration of the Bible; one is prophecy because fulfilled prophecy gives conclusive affirmation that the Bible is inspired by God. Peter said, "No prophecy ever came by the impulse of man, but men moved by the Holy Spirit spoke from God" (II Pet. 1:21).

The Bible is also the book that foretold the rise and fall of nations. For example, in a vision, Daniel saw a he-goat strike down a ram, breaking its two horns. Thereafter, the goat's great horn was broken and was replaced by four horns (Dan. 8:1-8). It was explained to Daniel that the ram with the two horns stands for the kings of Media and Persia. The he-goat stands for the king of Greece, and the great horn stands for the first king (Dan. 8:20-22). About two centuries later, "The king of Greece" Alexander the Great conquered the two-horned Medio-Persian Empire. Alexander died in 323 B.C. and was eventually replaced by four of his commanders.

Centuries before Jesus Christ was born, his ancestry (Isaiah 9:7), birthplace (Micah 5:2), manner of birth (Isaiah 7:14), babies killed (Jeremiah 31:15), manhood (Isaiah 40:1), commission (Isaiah 61:1, 2), character (Isaiah 9:6), reception (Zechariah 9:9), betrayed (Zechariah 11:12), not believed in (Isaiah 53:1), false witness used against him (Psalms 27:12), be struck and spit upon (Isaiah 50:6), lots cast for his garments (Psalms 22:18), numbered with sinners (Isaiah 53:12), reviled on the cross (Psalms 22:7, 8), given vinegar (Psalms 69:21), pierced (Zechariah 12:10; Isaiah 53:5; Psalms 22:16), bones are not broken (Psalms 34:20), burial (Isaiah 53:9), resurrection (Psalms 16:8-11), and ascension (Psalms 68:18) were all prophesized and written down.

In addition, Jesus prophesized in Luke 19:41-44 the destruction of Jerusalem, which was fulfilled in 70 A.D. when the Romans destroyed Jerusalem.

c. New Testament Prophecies

After Christ's ascension into the kingdom of heaven, the world of Divine Spirits or Paradise (Lk. 23:43; Rev. 2:7; 2 Cor. 12:3), the Spirit came down permanently on all those whom accepted Christ and began to live within the newly-born Divine Spirits or Spirits of Christ. This was the birth of the Christian church, fifty days after the day of ascension and is called Pentecost. It corresponds to the day of harvesting the first fruit in Jewish celebration. However, in Old Testament times, the Spirit came down to seek a temporary residence for a few selected individuals, for certain tasks, at specific times. When the mission was completed, the Spirit left them. For example, the Spirit gave wisdom to Joseph, courage to Gideon, and strength to Samson.

Because the regenerated individuals of the New Testament are more developed, their Divine Spirits, which are of the same substance as the Word of God, have a much easier task conveying and preaching the Word of God. The Apostles, whose minds were opened by Jesus Christ to understand Scripture (Luke 24:45), say that they teach in the name of Jesus and under the inspiration of the Holy Spirit. Apostle Paul did not issue commands on every subject, but when he was moved to give commands, he did so in the name of our Lord Jesus Christ (2 Thess. 3:6, 12). He said "to the married I give charge, not I but the Lord" (1 Cor. 7:10), and again in 1 Cor. 14:37, "What I am writing to you is a command of the Lord." The Book of Revelation begins with "The Revelation of Jesus Christ, which God gave him." The Word of the Lord is God's spoken Word. This word was not always heard but was also seen, especially in Jesus Christ.

XIII. Why the Nature of God of the Old and New Dispensation Differs

Jehovah of the Old Testament, who concerned Himself first with the restoration of a tribe and nation and through them, the people of the earth will receive their blessing (Gen. 12:1-3), was also called a tribal God. He was portrayed in Exodus 34:6 as a merciful and gracious God, slow to anger and rich in kindness, but could also be a strict judge, expressing righteous anger which involves punishment for those who disobeyed Him. However, He certainly, even in those times, was much better than the [1]Olympian gods, such as Jupiter, Apollo, Juno, and Venus, whom the Greeks and Romans worshipped. Their images were in the exact likeness of themselves, that is, their mass mind, which consists of the sum total of the psyches of their personalities. This means that the gods were usually more evil than good. Their rule of conduct was often arbitrary, or at best, according to manmade laws and regulations, because they were not familiar with all the [2]universal laws, required for proper living. Jehovah or Yahweh also seemed to be a transcendent Being to the Israelites, but was nevertheless a True God who had His abode not on Mount Olympus but on Mount Sinai for the earlier worshippers. Later, He appears to have His residence high above in the sky, from which He once in a while descended to judge the people in His charge.

The God of Israel, unlike the Olympian gods, was one God (Deut. 6:4), a God of [3]law and order, who always operate in exact agreement

---

[1] Those gods were not dead but psychically alive. They consisted of huge thought forms, which were created by the people and were continually fed by the imagination and attention of the people.

[2] Some of the less faithful of the Israelites, whom were influenced by the surrounding pagan nations, did not quite believe, or rather, did not feel that God is a "wholly other", or was different than themselves. The pagans who continually try to contaminate God's people were so evil that they could not be redeemed. When people later became more developed, they could be changed by love (to love one's enemy – Matt. 5:44).

[3] This law was called in the East the law of karma.

with the universal law, which is part of His outer Self. Because His chosen people were in a stage of developing intellectually, especially morally by purifying their personality (which was good and evil), their Lord and Master had to be very harsh in dealing with them because they easily fall back or backslide to their former lifestyle when their evil selves were in charge of their lives. In that case, satan became their master, and God was left out of their lives, and became a jealous God (Ex. 20:5). At those times, He tried to restore them and bring them back to His bosom. Even when the good selves were in charge of the people's lives, they were living the life of the personality, that is, that [4]their relationship with God was at best that of a servant to a Master. When they later, in the New Testament times, were spiritually born, they started living a divine life, and their relationship with God (who, [5]unlike the Israelites, starts to live within them as their personal God) became that of Parent and children. This new interaction did not only greatly change the newborn but also God as He is described by Jesus Christ, the first-born, as a tender loving Father.

NOTE 1: Marcion, a heretic of the early church and excommunicated in 144 A.D., believed that the God of Jesus was a God of love and mercy and could, therefore, not accept the God of the Old Testament, who was a God of severe and harsh judgment.

NOTE 2: As the God of Jesus is love, Jehovah is just, and a just world is run by law, and the symbol of Justice is the Judge.

XIV. How Many Bible Writers Were Indirectly Inspired

God is the primary author of the Bible, but He used human beings as His instruments or organs to produce it because He has no hands or feet and no mouth to speak. Thus, even though the Bible was written by men, it was inspired by God. Since God is the author, we say that the Holy Scripture is "inspired", that is, God caused it to be written. The Bible has, therefore, divine authority and is, for that reason, the greatest book in the world.

When the writings in the Bible do not exclusively say "God said", "Thus says the Lord" (see page 781), and when the Cosmic Christ does not speak through Jesus Christ (especially through the "I am" sayings),

---

[4] God could not truly love them with the same love as He gave His own children whom were of the same spiritual substance as their Parents.

[5] The chosen Israelites, whom from all the people in the world were the first to be redeemed, understood their Lord as separate from them, who could not work in and through them as a personal God of the New Testament, except through the prophets.

the Words are not literal from God but are the words of human beings. Those writers are, however, carefully chosen by God so that He is able to work through them. Although humans penned the words, God directed their thoughts in such a way that no serious error against His Will was made. *The writers, in their different stages of development, were thus not simple stenographers, by recording word for word God's message, but were more like secretaries who wrote down the ideas and thoughts of God. He, therefore, did not merely dictate words but influenced the different authors, each with their own unique personality and character, to use their own proficiency and talents to write down His message in their own particular words. They used distinct types of literary composition, each with its own style, idioms, and usages, which are in agreement with their own time and culture. Their writings were also somewhat influenced by their conception and knowledge but were nevertheless inspired somewhat beyond the human capacity. Because humans are originally to be co-creators with God, they have to do their share or responsible part by writing down the Bible text in their own creative way and not to be used as a substitute by recording word for word information. Because most of the actual words were selected and assembled by human beings, it is therefore possible that some errors have slipped in the Bible text.

NOTE 1: People whom believe in the literary interpretation of the Bible may also be inclined to accept that the Spirit of God (not His body) lives outside themselves and not within them as many mystics believe, who may also express themselves by saying, "The Bible is good, but Christ in us is better." The latter further say that the body is formed from the dust of the ground (Gen. 2:7), the etheric body by the breath of life, the intellect as the main part of the human spirit, by human knowledge, and the Divine Spirit by the pure Word of God.

NOTE 2: If the readers are inspired in the same way as the writers, the spiritual meaning becomes clear. This we may compare with the sharing of actual feeling and sensation the poet or novelist felt at the time of creative inspiration when reading great literature.

NOTE 3: God's Word, like a spiritual master, is like a mirror, wherein humans can reflect and see themselves as they truly are.

NOTE 4: God's Word, like that of the words of a song or a line of a poem, may strike as true or ring true for you, and resound (or echo) in your heart. It

---

* The psychic and intuitive facilities of Bible writers were much increased during the periods in their lives they received God's messages. They also felt, to some degree, the desperation of God to fulfill His plan of restoration or salvation in history.

is the very thing you always wanted to express if you could only have found the words.

FINAL NOTE: How messages are received:
Information or messages from the invisible realm, which are mediated through the consciousness of a human being (that is, through their subconscious mind or human spirit) is usually more or less influenced or filtered by the attitude and belief of the medium as it passes through his or her channel.

Although words are supplied by the personality or lower mind of the writer, the inspiration comes from God, the Universal Mind, and is first received by the Higher Mind of the Divine Spirit. We should, however, be aware that the lower mind can color, shade, or even distort messages according to preconceived ideas and beliefs, which may be slight or more pronounced. Distortion and misinterpretations often happen with psychic messages from the world of spirits, especially from the lower realms. As it was done in writing the Book of Revelation (see Chapter 1, verse 1 and 2), God first gave His Revelation to Jesus Christ, who then gave it via his angel to John, who then clothed them in his own words. Thus, ideas and visions are usually given, which then must be expressed in one's own language and in one's own form of expression.

Some people whom are familiar with the Bible, including scholars, do not always ask themselves a most important question: Is the Bible inspired by God, and does God really "speak to me" through its pages?
Evidence that the Bible is a God-inspired book:
1) Fulfilled prophecy
2) *The amazing and mysterious unity of the Bible
3) Its inexhaustible depth
4) Its indestructibility
5) Its superior moral and spiritual teachings
6) Its matchless influence and worldwide effect

---

* In spite of different writers whom were living at different times in different countries and spoke different languages, the sixty-six books of the Bible are in harmonious unity with each other.

Thus, each part of the Bible is essential to the whole and is related to each other, while it is directed to a certain purpose.

Some Christians say that no one passage of the Bible can be properly understood, unless it is interpreted in light of the whole Bible.

From all this, we can conclude that the Bible is much more than the work of men. No one else but the Spirit of the living God inspired all of the Bible writers (II Pet. 20, 21; II Tim. 3:16).

7) The character and testimony of Christ
8) Testimonies of people

We may further prove that the Bible is the inspired Word by putting it to the test, by practicing it (Jn. 7:17), and living by it; then he/she shall know that it is of God, who also repeatedly challenges us to try and test Him (Mal. 3:10).

XV. The Immense Value of the Word of God

The Word of God is much more than sound in the ear or a collection of writings before the eyes. The Word has power, and when the Almighty speaks, things happen and come into being. By reading the Bible, you will get much more than historical information, psychological insight, and literary enjoyment.

The Word of God is not like human words, which often leave us indifferent. The Word always produces wondrous effects, beginning with a supernatural and higher way of feeling and thinking. The Bible is, therefore, not just another book, but it is God's Word to you, and you will eventually believe this when you study and pray.

Most people in the United States of America believe that the Bible is the inspired Word of God, but it may contain historical and scientific errors and some *contradiction, and some verses should be taken symbolically rather than literally. Those whom are of an extreme Fundamental Protestant persuasion say that the whole Bible is the actual Word of God, and it is to be taken literally word for word. On the other hand, the liberals say that the Bible was not inspired by God but is a good understanding of God's nature, moral precepts, profound poetry, and wonderful stories. In other words, it is good literature.

Saint Augustine (d. 430) valued some parts of the Bible more than others, as did Martin Luther (1483-1546), who mentioned that Scripture is by no means infallibly correct in all details. He also said that the whole Bible should be judged by the Gospel of Christ. John Calvin (1509-1564) also distinguished between the Word and the words of Scripture and also asserted that the Bible was written after it was spoken by others whom were inspired by the Holy Spirit. The Vatican Council of the Roman Catholic Church in 1870 made a distinction between Revelation and other types of statements that also occur in

---

* See Note on page 794.

Scripture. According to the Swiss theologian [1]Karl Barth (1886-1968), the Bible cannot be identified with the Word of God. The error of fundamentalism is that it takes the Bible as a "self-sufficient pope". The religion of Spiritualists and esoteric movements also do not teach that the Bible is the absolute Word of God.

The Bible in general contains the Word of God in the words of men. It describes Gods' Word but is not literally God's Word. It teaches the Truth but is not Truth itself. The Bible, however, becomes God's Word when God is encountered in it. The words of the Bible as mere letters on paper or body and shells must live in the minds of people through the Spirit of God. As [2]human beings are a vessel of God's Spirit, the words of the Bible are suitable containers of God's Word which is the power and Light of God. Thus, we can hear in the words of the Bible the very voice of God. The Word of Truth has life in it and has the power to restore and make whole. It cannot perish or grow less with the passing of time. When we make contact with God through the ideas and stories of the Bible, the Bible then comes alive, and it is the inspired and authentic Word of God. God, however, is more than His Word, which is only His visible manifestation. His true nature as Creator, Master, and Parents of the Universe, with its main attributes of Love, Wisdom, and Power, is behind or lying deep within His Words and is as it were locked in the Word.

The Word of God is more than the Bible; the Word is the Divine or Christ Spirit within the regenerated human being, which is agreeable with the Words of Christ, who is the Word of God (Jn. 1:1, 4), which is a spiritual Truth Body.

---

[1] To Barth, the words of the Bible and of the human Jesus are "tokens". One may read the Bible without hearing the Word of God, but the Word does come to us through these tokens. Someday as we read a passage of Scripture, it may suddenly come alive and speak to us in the situation in which we find ourselves.

[2] Human beings can express words in a physical and psychical way (by thought) in some measure. They can also ensoul their words by their attention or psychic energy they put into the words they speak. An individual who is more than a physical body and human spirit but in whom also the Divine Spark has been awakened and grown to some extent, who gives forth the Word of God, ensouls it also in a lower or higher degree with their Divine Self, which latter in turn can easily be ensouled with the Spirit of God. Those Words are powerful, enduring, and move others to awaken to their hidden Spark or Divine Nature because they have within them the seeds of divine life. When humans become fully mature, their words will be like the Words of God.

[1]The Word of God, which is the most pure and elevated thought, is what the Spirit uses. It is, therefore, important that the Word of God is being proclaimed. The [2]Spirit of God and the Holy Spirit can take the feeblest words of witness to Christ, quicken (brought to life), and transform it by His/Her power into a convicting Word in the lives of others who may take the most important step to change their way of life forever. The message becomes more powerful, complete, meaningful, and clear. When the Spirit works directly through our unfolding Divine Spirit, mistakes in compilation or translation of the text may come to life. However, the Spirit does not come in its fullness when we are reading another inspired book and is hardly felt when we read an ordinary book. Through experience, we know that the words of the Bible are inspired and possess a unique power in themselves which no human book can have. "You heard from us, you accepted it not as the word of men but as what it really is, the word of God, which is at work in you believers" (1 Thess. 2:13). See also Gal. 1:11-12; 1 Cor. 2:13. Jesus knew that His words were vivified with a life essence and a moving power. However, even the words of the Bible are of little value or mere letters on paper if they do not come alive through the Spirit within ourselves. Then only is it able to change lives. "For our gospel came to you not only in word but also in power and in the Holy Spirit" (1 Thess. 1:5). We "have been [3]born anew, not of perishable seed but of imperishable, through the living and abiding word of God" which "abides forever" (1 Peter 1:23, 25).

---

[1] The Spirit of God also works through non-biblical inspiration, such as in other sacred literature, poetry, music, service, and many other ways. I assume that God prefers – of those whom are Jews, Mohammedans, and Christians – to read and use the Bible as the main source of inspiration because it has an important message of salvation for them.

[2] Here I would like to make a distinction. The Spirit of God mentioned here is the male aspect of God and the Holy Spirit the expression of the female aspect of God. In Christian writings they are usually interchanged. The same writings, at times, may also interchange the Holy Spirit of God with the Divine Spirit or Soul within humans. The Holy Spirit, like a mother, is much involved in the process of spiritual Birth of the Soul. The word Spirit here means the heavenly Father and Mother.

[3] Regeneration is another term for renewal or rebirth (new birth). We are born again through the operation of the Holy Spirit, who uses the Word of God to bring spiritual life and uses the same Word to feed the spiritual infant who becomes the Word or Spirit of Christ (Gal. 2:20). Thus, the born again Divine Spirit, the Holy Spirit, Spirit of God, and Jesus Christ are always in perfect agreement (Jn. 14:26).

791

The Bible promised that if you accept what you are reading and do what it says (James 1:22), it cleanses your life of all these evil practices (1 Cor. 6:9-11) and your [4]good/evil personality is washed clean by the Word (Eph. 5:26; Ps. 19:7-11; 119:9, 11; Jn. 15:3) and becomes only good. Moreover, when you accept Christ as your Savior, you no longer live the life of the personality (no longer under law – including karmic law – but grace – Rom. 6:14), becoming a "new creation" (2 Cor. 5:17) and start to live a divine life. The newly born Divine Spirit or Christ Spirit (Gal. 4:19) then needs the Word of God to feed itself so that it will grow to maturity and become like Christ or the Word of God. The newly born Christ Spirit ([5]Jn. 3:7-8) is thus built of or consists of the substance of God. [6]This individual, as a spiritual infant or baby, needs daily nourishment by studying the living and abiding Word of God and will be drawn to the right nutriment, just as a baby craves for the mother's milk (1 Pet. 2:2, 3; 1 Thess. 2:13). When they become more mature by understanding the elementary Truths of the Bible, the basic Christian doctrine, they are then ready to digest the deep things of God's Word (1 Cor. 2:10) or "solid food" (Heb. 5:14). "I have food (meat) to eat of which you do not know" (Jn. 4:32). As we evolve, we find new spiritual truths opening up to just a little in advance of our previous understanding and begin to see the Truth behind the many Bible verses. We also learn, like Jesus and His Disciples, to use [7]God's Word as a sword (Eph. 6:12, 17) to protect ourselves against evil forces and, most important, to witness and teach the Word of God to others. By doing so, we surely have all the cooperation of the heavenly forces.

NOTE 1: As good as the food that we eat to nourish our physical selves, it cannot nourish our intellectual and spiritual hunger. It is important that we develop our inner personality, that is, our intellect and its moral aspect, in our quest for knowledge and living a good life according to the Laws of God, which we can find in the Bible. Most important is that we develop our Divine

---

[4] After the fall of Adam and Eve, whom were influenced by good (God) as well as evil (satan), the human race inherited from them the good/evil nature, or the Abel/Cain nature in their personality. See "The Fall of Lucifer, Eve and Adam".

[5] Nicodemus needed more than religion; he needed regeneration. He needed more than a teacher; he needed a Savior. He needed more than law by living the life of the personality; he needed grace by living the divine life.

[6] The one who is spiritually born has become a true Christian (having the Spirit of Christ). The Holy Spirit may give the spiritual milk, while the Spirit of God may give the meat.

[7] The Word will also be a judge to nonbelievers who reject the Word of God (Jn. 12:48; Rev. 19:15; Isa. 11:4). "I came to cast fire (judgment by God's Word) on the earth" (Luk. 12:49; II Pet. 3:7). Some people's hearts are so calloused and hardened by sin that they no longer hear the voice of the Spirit.

Spirit, which resides within the inner personality in our quest for Truth by digesting and assimilating the Word of God in our divine Self. Jesus said in Matt. 4:4, "It is written" (Deut. 8:3), "Man shall not live by bread alone, but by every word that proceeds from the mouth of God." As water cleanses the body, the Word of God cleanses our heart or human spirit (inner personality). To grow physically, we need the right diet, which is well prepared and made palatable. To grow intellectually, we need to learn those disciplines which we understand and appeal to us. To grow spiritually, we need the Word of God, those verses and sections which the Soul is attracted to and likes to absorb.

NOTE 2: In witnessing, God's Word is the incorruptible seed (1 Pet. 1:23) we are to sow in the soil of the heart (inner personality) with the help of the Spirit who will pierce the heart of the nonbeliever who may experience a New Birth by making a decision. The same Word which is the seed of the sower (Matt. Ch. 13) becomes food for the Soul. The new convert or baby need to be fed, protected, and trained and, thus, needs spiritual parents, as Paul was (1 Cor. 4:15), who will teach them how to feed themselves from the Bible. The Gospel of Mark, the Book of 1 Thessalonians, and Gospel of John are good food for a young Christian. The young ones whom are leaving the kingdom of satan are being severely attacked by evil forces within and without themselves. They may experience doubt, temptation, and discouragement. The evil forces will also accuse the young ones of past sins and cause them to commit the same sin, which is their weakness. But God will help them (1 Cor. 10:13), and they will be forgiven (1 Jn. 1:9). They can use the same Word of God as a sword and use faith as a shield to ward off the darts of the enemy (Eph. 6:16, 17; Rom. 10:17). Certain verses will be brought to their mind (as Jesus did in Matt. 4:4) by the Spirit to meet the attack.

XVI. How to Grow Morally and Spiritually

NOTE: The Bible, from the beginning (Genesis) to the end, is not only a story or the history of the people of God but also their moral and spiritual development and their growing relationship to God. However, this also corresponds to and is a record of the growth of every man and woman, that of his/her personality and Divine Spirit. For example, the story of a prophet(ess) or king and Jesus Christ is not the life history of any one person but the moral and spiritual history of every true follower. In the process of trying to understand the Bible and applying its principle to our daily life (James 1:22), something happens within ourselves; we grow emotionally, intellectually, and spiritually.

People are to grow morally first, that is, to purify or cleanse their developing personality from the inherited evil by obeying the laws of God, such as the Ten Commandments. They learn to distinguish between good and evil or to discern right from wrong, true values from the false, or truth from error, and choosing the right and rejecting the wrong. After he/she is regenerated or begotten by God's Spirit, they are to "grow in the grace and knowledge" of Christ (II Pet. 3:18), to develop God-like qualities and capacities. They are then qualified to rule with God and Christ over all creation (Rev. 2:26).

The Bible is, thus, the story of individual soul growth and illustrates the progression from the natural to the spiritual person, that is, the development and purification of the natural or unspiritual person. This is exemplified by the main characters of the Old Testament (their successes and failures) until the time they were ready to accept and receive Christ within their purified personality. This outer unfoldment brings about the change, the realization or transfiguration of the human into a divine being, and its growth into its full expression. This is exemplified by the life of Jesus Christ, from birth to His resurrection.

The Bible is so written that each may obtain from its pages the kind of moral strength and spiritual nourishment they need, that is, the concepts, truths, and guidelines for thinking and acting that will assist one in human and spiritual growth. It is, therefore, important to turn to God's Word daily, eagerly and expectantly, to find a Word from God, which is especially written for you and me.

NOTE 1: As long as humans are in the process of restoration, they need the Bible for their salvation. The Old Testament is for the growth of the personality, especially the moral development, and the New Testament is for the guidance of spiritual birth and Soul growth. Individuals in this process will not easily outgrow the Bible because as they evolve, they will find new Truth opening up to them. Thus, the Bible widens and deepens when they progress in their restoration.

NOTE 2: Unlike that of different levels of grade school, the same teaching of the Bible is available to the beginner and advanced student. A beginner may relate only to the surface or literal meaning by, for example, saying that the Bible has a code of great morals. He or she may then interpret the same teaching with a deeper level of understanding. They are discovering the hidden spiritual meaning because as the individual grows and unfolds, his/her understanding and awareness level increases. For example, the story of Jesus' birth and death becomes their own story of spiritual growth. More understanding will be given when we apply the Truth in our lives or internalize the insight already given, and thereby grow spiritually. This is especially true when we teach others. More Truth will then be given and, thus, speeds up our growth and restoration.

XVII. Contradictions in the Bible

NOTE: Although the Bible as a whole forms a unity and is inspired by God, there were, nevertheless, many writers involved who compiled it into one volume. They, as different individuals, were using different words and concepts and reporting the same event in a different way. Some contradictions are, therefore, to be expected because, in many cases, God did not inspire them word for word; they were not stenographers. He let them express their own unique personalities, with their different abilities and talents. Like any parent (Isa. 49:15), God guided them but did not protect them from making mistakes.

Contradictions can be attributed to problems with the transmission of the ancient text, or we do not understand the context and cultural situation. Many of the most important words of the Bible were spoken in one language (Aramaic), written down in another (Greek), and translated into a third (English-German-French-Dutch – and others). We, therefore, can count on some inaccuracy. For example, when Moses came down from Mount Sinai with the Ten Commandments, his face shone so brightly that the people of Israel were afraid to come near him until he put a veil over his face. The original Hebrew text says his face sent forth beams or horns of light. The Vulgate translation says that Moses had "a horned face", which Michelangelo took literally in his statue of Moses, representing him with a pair of horns projecting from his head.

Some events in the Bible are reported differently: Exodus 37:1-9 says that Bezalel made the Ark of the Covenant, but in Deuteronomy 10:1-5, Moses claimed to have made it. In 1 Samuel 31:4-6, we are told that Saul "took his own sword and fell upon it". In 2 Sam. 1:10, an Amalekite tells David that Saul asked him to stand beside him and slay him. With regard to the Resurrection, was the tomb open or closed when they arrived? Open (Luk. 24:2) versus closed (Matt. 28:1-2). Whom did they see at the tomb? An angel (Matt. 28:2) versus two angels (Jn. 20:11-12); a young man (Mk. 16:5) versus two men (Luk. 24:4).

The Bible may become contradictory to those who see only the physical or exoteric side of the Book and fail to perceive the spiritual or esoteric meaning. For example, in Matthew 26:52, Jesus says, "For all who take the sword will perish by the sword." In Matthew 10:34, He said, "I have not come to bring peace, but a sword." In the latter case, a sword meant the Word (or Truth) of God.

It does not take much reading to find two creation stories in the Book of Genesis and two stories of the Ark of Noah. Human authors of the Bible were people of their own times in their ability to understand what God was saying to them. Those who lived in 500 years B.C. did not grasp the difference between causing and allowing. They thought that God caused everything, including evil. As time passed, they developed from ignorance to more knowledge. The author of Ecclesiastes, who wrote about 300 years before Christ, was wrong about eternal life in heaven (higher spirit world) when he said, "For the living know that they will die, but the dead know nothing" (Eccl. 9:5).

NOTE 1: Fundamentalists or conservative Protestants who insist that every word means just what it says and is true as it is cannot be compatible with what is expressed above.

NOTE 2: It is easy to misunderstand the Bible, and it has been often misquoted and used for the justification of wars, religious controversies, and the like, but it also has been used for inspiration, spiritual guidance, and has served as hope for millions throughout the ages.

XVIII. History of Fundamentalism

The best and fullest way God can make Himself known to humans is to express through a living person the many facets of His being – His Love, Compassion, Goodness, Forgiveness, and Joy. Another way God reveals Himself is through the Holy Scripture, written down by His chosen scribes, whom reveal the many aspects of His Being, such as the Old Testament Prophets and the Evangelists Matthew, Mark, Luke, and John.

[1]Scriptures may be understood as literary or symbolic interpretations and the many positions in between. For example, many fundamental Christians allow for some allegory and symbolic interpretation. The strict literary interpretation is usually understood by the unenlightened Christians who have not been born spiritually or have just been born – been saved – (1 Cor. 3:1-4). Those Christians are still materially

---

[1] The early teachers, such as Origen and Clement, distinguish two types of Christianity: the lower type, who saw only the surface meaning of Scripture (literary interpretation) and the higher type, who saw the deeper meaning of the Bible (symbolic interpretation). The latter was intended to be understood by only a few, as that of the parables Jesus spoke (Matt. 13:10-17). These types, with some changes, were used until the time of the Reformation. Esoteric religions today, such as Unity, say that the Bible should seldom be taken literally, but always with an eye to the inner or spiritual meaning. See **REMARK** (1), (2), and (3).

minded and look to the church for their social needs. Those church groups who accept every word of the Bible as literally true are like the Scribes and Pharisees in Jesus' time. Jesus rebuked their devotion to the letter at the cost of the spirit as "straining out a gnat and swallowing a camel!" (Matt. 23:24).

The more enlightened Christians interpret the Bible, for their moral implications, how to live a good moral life, such as the Jews and Muslims try to do. Others whom have outgrown their spiritual babyhood stage believe that some verses should be interpreted in a literal way and other verses in a figurative way. For example, in John 6:1-15, Jesus gave to the people real bread and fish, while in John 6:48, Jesus said, " I AM the bread of life." Here, Jesus, or rather the Christ Consciousness, is the source and sustainer of eternal life. When Jesus said, "I AM the Way, and the Truth and the Life", Jesus was channeling the Christ Consciousness or Son of God, who is also "I AM the Light of the world", and "I AM the door", "I AM the bread of life" – "I AM the resurrection and the Life." The "I AM" sayings are a much deeper interpretation than the allegorical or figurative.

NOTE: It should be obvious to anyone that we cannot take the Bible literally. For example, Jesus commanded us to pluck out the lusting eye and cut off the sinful hand (Matt. 5:27-30). Church Father Origen asked, "How could the devil take Jesus to the top of a high mountain when there is no such mountain?" Christ said, "He who believes in me --- out of his heart shall flow rivers of living water." (This is, of course, a metaphor; the living waters represent the flow of Spirit.) God certainly is not a rock (Ps. 18:2), and He did not send giant eagles to fly Israel out of Egyptian bondage (Ex. 19:4). Hardly anyone believe that Jonah was in the belly of a whale or that the disciples of Jesus must eat His flesh (Jn. 6:53). Many events in the Book of Revelation can certainly not be taken literally.

In early Christian and Medieval times, Christians not only understood the Bible in a literal historical sense but also at other more profound levels, such as the moral, allegorical, and the mystical. In those times, the Bible written in Greek and Latin was not available to many people because it had to be copied by hand. In the Middle Ages, the Roman Catholic Church forbade the common people to read the

Bible, either in Latin or other languages because they said that it was [1]not good for the people to read the Scriptures without benefit of clergy, and that they should believe the more important doctrines of the church. However, since the Protestant Reformation in 1517, the Bible and its interpretation was no longer the domain of the Roman Church but was shared with individuals whom protested. As the Catholics accepted the Church as their sole authority, the Protestants accepted the Bible as their single authority. (As the Roman Catholic main authority was that of the papacy and tradition, the Anglican or Episcopal Church authority was based on Scripture but also on tradition and reason.)

At the time of the Reformation, the [2]reformers Luther and Calvin treated the Bible freely. Thereafter, the seventeenth and eighteenth century Protestants and scholastic, on the other hand, hardened into a belief that not only [3]the whole Bible but that every word in the Bible was dictated by God and was factual without error. However, this literalism put the authority of the Bible at great risk and, therefore, the belief in the Bible. Its authority in its literal form was severely tested in the nineteenth century through the [4]development of science, who said that the world was not created in six days, and that the origin of the world is much more than the 6000 biblical years. The result of all this

---

[1] They may have in mind those individuals who may interpret the Bible in a way that disregards the doctrine of the church. Others may explain Scripture in such a way in order to fit their own ideas of what is the truth or what is right and wrong. The Roman church may have in mind the difficulties the infant church had with the Gnostics. Similarly, Protestants were up against individuals and groups in their movement whose interpretation of the Bible was not right according to their standard. Some may even go so far as twisting the Bible verses (2 Pet. 3:15, 16). According to Fundamentalists, symbolic interpretation, therefore, carries the insidious danger that individuals may change the meaning of Bible passages to suit their own purposes and, therefore, easily fall into deception. They may call some laws they don't want to keep culturally obsolete. However, Martin Luther said that any one person guided by the Holy Spirit is able to interpret the Bible correctly. Therefore, only the spiritually advanced should interpret the Bible symbolically, being guided by the developing Christ Spirit (Soul) within and the Spirit of God. The Soul or Divine Spirit of a human being, through which God expresses Himself, is pure and "cannot sin" (1 Jn. 3:9). The latter, in turn, tries to guide the human spirit (inner personality) who is good and evil.

[2] Calvin, the founder of the Reformed Church, like Luther, did not believe that the whole Bible is equally inspired. He said that the Word of God is not the words of the Bible, and that literal interpretation may go too far. Ignoring them, the Lutheran and Reformed theologians who came after them insisted that every word of the Bible was supernaturally inspired, and the study of Scripture and its interpretation should be done by approved authorities as the only acceptable source of guidance.

[3 & 6] The whole Bible, from cover to cover, is equally inspired and is called by theology "plenary inspiration". Verbal inspiration means that every word of the Bible is dictated by the Holy Spirit.

[4] See **NOTE** – Pre-scientific View of the Bible.

[5]and more, and that of valid Bible criticism, put in doubt the belief in [6]verbal and plenary inspiration. By the mid-nineteenth century, extreme literalism was only accepted by the less intelligent and the ordinary non-informed Christians.

Fundamentalism, as we know it today, is the continuation of the belief of literalism. It began in the late 1800s as a movement within different Protestant denominations in reaction against Darwin's theory of evolution and that of [7]biblical criticism and theological liberalism. A conference of Conservative Protestants was held in 1895 (The Niagara Conference) which resulted in five statements of belief: The Verbal Inerrancy of Scripture; The Divinity of Jesus Christ; The Virgin Birth; The Substitutionary Theory of the Atonement; the Physical Resurrection and the Bodily Return of Christ. In 1919, the World's Christian Fundamentals Association was founded. This resulted that nearly all Protestant Churches in the United States became divided into Fundamentalist and Modernist organizations. The Roman Catholic, Orthodox, and the Episcopal Church believe in the Divinity of Christ, the Virgin Birth, and Resurrection. They have, however, different formulations of Atonements, and many individuals in those organizations do not all agree in the inerrancy of the Bible.

NOTE 1: Biblical criticism is expressed in two forms: the lower and the higher criticism. The lower critic deals with the accuracy of the text, while the higher critic is interested in the meaning of the text. The latter must, therefore, find out when each passage of the Bible was written, who the writer was, and why it was written, and to whom it was addressed. Thus, by going back to the time and place of the author, one may discover what the author intended to express. The critics do this by the application of historical expertise, which was also used to find out about ancient manuscripts. This method was employed by the Protestants in the first decades of the nineteenth century (the Catholics were not allowed to practice higher criticism until the time of the second Vatican Council in 1962). The result of those methods was that it did great damage to the belief in verbal inspiration.

---

[5] At that time, the school of anthropology argued for "polygenesis" (the separate creation of several distinct human races, as opposed to "monogenesis" (the descent of all human beings from one primal pair). However, the latter theory can be refuted by saying that Adam and Eve were the first humans who were imbued with the qualification to reach spiritual perfection. Their ancestors did not have this ability.

[7] The Conservative Evangelicals (Fundamentalists) still reject the basic findings of modern biblical scholarship and, in contrast to the more liberal modernists, treat the Bible not as a fallible and myth-laden account of God's Self-Revelation in history. Modernists in general, such as F. Schleiermacher, A. Ritschl, H.E. Fosdick, C. Barth, R. Niebuhr, and P. Tillich understand that the Bible sometimes speaks in poetic and allegorical language. The liberals who hold extreme views accept Jesus as the greatest moral and religious teacher but believe that He is only a man, not the Son of God.

NOTE 2: Fundamentalists say that the Bible writers were so controlled by the Holy Spirit that they recorded the very thoughts and words which God wants them to record. The Bible is, therefore, inerrant in its original manuscript. God also watched over His Revelation as it passed through the hands of translators. The fundamentalists want to believe that every word in the Bible was dictated by God because once it was acknowledged that the author had erred, the whole Bible was to be mistrusted. The Roman Catholic Church says that Catholics should believe in the doctrines of an infallible church interpreting an infallible Book. (The Protestant theologians, during and after the Reformation, rejected the tradition and accepted the Book.) The Catholics further believed that the truths of Scripture are inerrant (without error), which are needed for the sake of salvation. The Bible is not inerrant when it talks, for example, about certain happenings in history or how the universe was formed.

NOTE 3: Many fundamentalists, Catholics, and others have a tendency to superimpose of what they think is true on everything they see and read. If, for example, any passage of the Bible does not support their view, they ignore it and read on.

NOTE 4: We may ask the questions: "Are the different parts of the Bible equally inspired? How much is the author inspired by the Spirit of God?" "How literally is the Bible to be read?" "In what way is the Bible inerrant, teaching the Truth without error?" "For where does one draw the line between historical fact and symbolic truth?" Albeit, most answers will come when we ask the Spirit to guide us in this matter.

REMARK: Narrow fundamentalist beliefs have their value in assisting in the spiritual birth process of the nonbeliever, who is in need of the fundamental Truth (the elementary doctrine of Christ – Heb. 6:1). However, those beliefs may become a hindrance in the further growth of the believers, especially when they become oppressive. Nearly the same thing happened to the believers in the Middle Ages. Besides, it is not possible to grow if one never doubts what he or she already thinks and believes.

XIX. Pre-scientific View of the Bible

NOTE: The Bible was not written to teach the natural sciences or to give medical knowledge, although both sciences were ahead of their time, as this is recorded in the Scripture. It does not give scientific information in terms we understand today because that would be meaningless to ancient people, whose understanding of the working of the universe was limited and pre-scientific at best. They accepted the world the way it appeared to be: flat, covered with a blue dome or firmament, on which were affixed the sun, moon, and stars. God inspired the writers with their confining knowledge to teach the Truth about [1]His creation, without being much influenced by existing scientific theories of their times, which were mythical in origin. For example, the general belief was that the earth was flat, disk-like, and rested on pillars or floated on water, and that it was only inhabited on one side. In the eighth century B.C., Isaiah 40:22 described the shape of the planet earth as: "It is he who sits above the circle of the earth" (Revised Standard Version); "The globe of the earth" (Douay Version). This was, a few centuries later, affirmed by the Greek philosophers Pythagoras and Aristotle. The book of Job stated, "(God) hangs the earth upon nothing". Aristotle (4th century B.C. scientist) said that it was not possible for the earth to hang into empty space. He, therefore, theorized that the heavenly bodies were fixed to the surface of (solid) transparent spheres, with the earth as an immovable [2]center of the universe. This view held sway and was accepted by the Christian Church for more than 2000 years. In 1687 A.D., Isaac Newton explained that the earth was held (hangs) in space or orbit by mutual attraction with other heavenly bodies, through the invisible force of gravity. A few years earlier in 1543 A.D., Nicolaus Copernicus held to a theory that the earth and planets revolve around the sun. This knowledge was affirmed in 1609 by Galileo who was forced to recant of his views by the theologians of the church. They interpreted literally the verse in Ecclesiastes 1:5, "The sun rises and the sun goes down and hastens to the place where it rises." And, in Psalm 104:5, "Thou didst set the earth on its foundations, so that it should never be shaken."

XX. The Literal, Moral, and Spiritual Levels in Scripture

REMARK:
(1) [3]Origin (185-254 A.D.), Alexandrian theologian, held that there is a threefold meaning in Scripture: the literal, moral, and spiritual, or allegorical, that corresponds and is, for the benefit, to the threefold

---

[1] The world is created by God from non-physical invisible essence. "By faith we understand that the world was created by the Word of God, so that what is seen was made out of things which do not appear" (Heb. 11:3). It was created in periods of six days or units of time of different lengths (2 Pet. 3:8), or may refer to one cosmic day (Gen. 2:4). God creates day and night on the first day (Gen. 1:4). On the fourth day, He creates "lights in the firmament of the heavens to separate the day from the night" (Gen. 1:14). The first light was the "greater" light, the sun, and the second light was the "lesser" light, the moon.

[2] Today, no scientifically informed Christian believed the earth to be the center of the universe. Christians know that the earth revolves around the sun, the sun revolves around our galaxy, and our galaxy moves through the vast and expanding universe.

[3] Origin Book IV on first principle deals with biblical hermeneutics and the literal, moral, and allegorical interpretation of Scripture.

division he saw in human nature: body, mind (soul or human spirit), and Soul (Divine Spirit). The literal sense is what is understood by the ordinary unenlightened person. It is valid for those at that level of understanding, who believe in the story as a story. For them, the Bible is a book of history and beautiful literature, a Bible written in relation to the physical side of life of which also includes the social. [1]The moral sense is related not only to duty and obedience (ethics) but to the entire range of the soul's experience, that is, the mental, philosophical, and emotional, as the soul (human spirit) consists of the intellectual and emotional aspect. The spiritual sense conveys the divine nature and purpose, referring to the hidden and mysteries of the Christian faith. The spiritual Christian (1 Cor. 2:15) understands the inner meaning of allegory and analogy or symbolism about the inner life. The Bible written in relation to the spiritual side of life is a teacher of the deeper Truth. A whole new world of discovery awaits the reader on this esoteric level.

The Bible is really a collection of literary works from different authors, some relating to the physical side of life, some to the mental, and some to the spiritual side of life. There is something of value for everyone at every level. However, the Bible yields something when taken literally, more when read intellectually, most when understood allegorically, symbolically, and mythically. Some verses of the Bible, in their literal aspect, seem to be meaningless and even absurd, but in their esoteric aspect, have great meaning. This is why some individuals believe that many passages in the Bible were deliberately worded to have multiple meanings. However, it is possible to understand the deeper writings of the Bible as one grows in awareness levels. In other words, as one grows and unfolds, the individual understanding increases, and one's truth changes to parallel the person's unfoldment. Each time he/she reads it, it contains a new and richer meaning because the Bible speaks to each one at his/her own level of awareness.

NOTE 1: When God gives Revelation, it is meant for all levels of development: the material for the physical man, the mental for the intellectual man, the spiritual for the spiritual man or woman. When a meaning of a symbol in the Bible is understood, a deeper meaning becomes apparent, although no one seems to fathom the ultimate divine mystery concealed in Scripture.

---

[1] Moral application to the soul, duty, and obedience may also be grouped under the literal and material – somatic or bodily Christianity. The Bible, as a teacher of morals, treatise on philosophy and ethics. Example of the moral sense is that events in Scripture should guide us to act justly, to imitate great moral leaders, and someone like Ruth.

NOTE 2: Some esoterists say that all sacred writings are supposed to be sealed with seven seals. In other words, it required seven complete interpretations to understand fully the meaning of the Book of Revelation. The latter can be compared to the seven energy centers of humans, which open and reveal one's consciousness to one self.

XXI. Explaining the Figurative Language

REMARK:

(2) Figurative language may be used to explain the unknown through the known because the unknown cannot be properly explained through a physical language, only through symbols which we know. Metaphors, similes, analogies, parables, allegories, myths, and stories are used to describe the unknown, the world of causes or the invisible world. Jesus, for example, had to use many [1]parables to explain to the people what the Kingdom of Heaven was like because they did not know anything about it. The relationship between life on the physical plane and the higher life is expressed by the well-known maxim "as below, so above", also called the law of correspondence. The Bible makes ample use of figures of speech, which are actually the only possible way to convey the hidden truth, and which must be received by the heart (inner self) as by the outer self.

When we read the Bible, we may first read it in a literal sense, and if it does not make any sense, we should try to understand it in a [2]figurative sense. The latter is more powerful and closer to the Truth and more deeply felt. Many stories and teachings in the Bible have an inner dimension or significance. This inner message cannot be perceived through a literal reading of the text. It can only be tapped by reading with our inner spiritual eyes and ears (Matt. 13:15) – our intuitive capacity to look and hear beyond simple traditions and standard beliefs.

---

[1] Jesus used parables to build on what people of His time were already familiar with, such as situations and characters drawn from day to day living. Jesus' parables have been called "heavenly stories with earthly meanings", such as the Good Samaritan – the pearl of great price – the good shepherd – new wine in old wine skin – the prodigal son – sheep and goats – fish in the net – wedding banquet – talents – growing seed – sower – wheat and tares – mustard seed – hidden treasure – workers in the vineyard – rich man and Lazarus – ten virgins – leaven – lost sheep and lost coin. Some of the parables people did not understand; even His disciples had to ask Jesus for an explanation (Mk. 4:10, 13).

[2] Some people go too far in interpreting the Bible in a figurative way by "spiritualizing away" any laws they do not want to keep or lifestyle they do not want to live. Some individuals explain some Bible verses in such an absurd way that it makes no longer sense to the faculty of reason and intuition.

NOTE 1: Other literary devices used are the hyperbole (exaggeration), "If your right eye causes you to sin, pluck it out" (Matt. 5:29). Anthropomorphism, God is explained in human language, "They heard the sound of the Lord walking in the garden" (Gen. 3:8). Personification, personal qualities attributed to objects, plants, and animals.

NOTE 2: The Bible cannot be a complete explanation; men/women have to do their responsible part by exercising their intellectual and intuitive capacities.

NOTE 3: Metaphysics means "beyond the physical". In this case, it implies the reading of the Bible for its allegorical or underlying meaning. This includes secret teachings, abstract meaning, which may also include "typology".

NOTE 4: In some expressions of the Bible, we should disregard the literal reading and seek under the surface to the real meaning. Whenever we find the words land, earth, soil, or sand, it may refer to the physical nature of human beings and its environment. Water, in its different forms, often symbolizes emotion, while air and wind refer to the mental condition, and fire to the spiritual which consumes one's animal nature. Robes (Rev. 22:14), garments (Matt. 22:11), swaddling clothes are the bodies (physical-emotional-mental) in which the Christ consciousness or Divine Spirit is born and living. To go up unto a mountain is to go up into a high state of consciousness, while going into a desert or wilderness is to descend to a lower state which has not been watered by streams of life or the flow of Truth (Isa. Ch. 35, 40) in one's inner self. We may also expand the borders of consciousness and experience spiritual illumination by any forms of light.

XXII. Examples of the Esoteric Bible

REMARK:
(3) In every book of sacred writings, there is an exoteric and a hidden esoteric meaning. The latter or inner meaning is concealed from the unenlightened and is preserved and revealed to the spiritual person. Unfortunately, the esoteric side of the Bible is usually ignored, which is a great store house of esoteric wisdom (the esoteric Bible) and, thus, also the inner side of human nature. Many fundamentalists do not want to examine the hidden treasures in the esoteric tales and allegories.

Some of the examples are:
"Let there be light; and there was light" (Gen. 1:3). It is wisdom that lights up the darkness of ignorance.

The story of Esau and Jacob (like that of Cain and Abel) symbolizes the body and the human spirit, or the good self confronting the evil self in one's personality. In a much deeper sense, it is the life of the personality and the divine life.

In the story of Moses, Pharaoh's daughter said to Moses' mother, "Take this child away, and nurse him" (Ex. 2:9). The child is the Christ within, which we nurse with prayer and the Word of God.

As Joshua captured and subdued the five kings (Josh. 10:5-10), so should we conquer and gain mastery over the five senses and open our psychic and intuitive senses.

As Jericho was fortified, we also have built around ourselves a psychological wall of resentment and hardened our hearts, which need to be destroyed by the blasting Truth of the Word.

The story of Jonah is an account of learning personal responsibility, when he, in the ship of the personality, experienced emotional trouble in the raging sea but was rescued by the whale who acted as his savior.

The gifts the three wise men brought were symbolic of body, emotion, and intellect (personality), which have to bow down to the Christ child within. At a later time, John the Baptists said, "He (Christ) must increase, but I (personality) must decrease" (Jn. 3:30). Peter's personality during the crucifixion of his master acted as a coward, while later the Christ within wanted to be crucified with Jesus Christ.

In the Old Testament stories, we can read of Israel's time of living in harmony and obedience with God's laws, their repeated rebellions, and their stubborn attitudes. The Book of Exodus, for example, is also an allegory of the life of the personality which needs to be purified (in the desert) to reach the Promised Land of living a divine life. As soon as we escaped from Egypt, where our human spirit was enslaved by the habit of sin and place ourselves under the guidance of God, He will take care of all our daily needs. However, when in the process of our growth, we become rebellious and ignore God's direction, our progress is delayed, and we have to stay longer in the desert of shallow living. Before we reached the Promised Land or experience a new birth, we may experience great trial and tribulation. After we enter the Promised Land, we still have to fight against the evil forces within ourselves until they are completely subdued.

XXIII. The Story of the Characters of the Bible Is Like Our Own

a. Introduction

We and society, which is an extension of ourselves, are only a reflection of the stories that we find in the pages of the Bible. Thus, we can find ourselves in most of the chapters of the Old and New Testament. The Apostle Paul wrote in Romans 15:4, "For whatever was written in former days was written for our instruction" and the errors Israel made were written for our admonition (1 Cor. 10:11).

Because humans are good as well as evil, there is a composition of the fallen nature of Adam and Eve in each of us, a share of the Cain and Abel nature, a dose of Noah's righteousness and Abraham's great faith, a scrap of Esau's coarseness and responsibility of Jacob, but also the deceptiveness of Laban. We further find in ourselves a layer of the loyalty of Moses, a remnant of the jealousy of Aaron and Meriam, and a sliver of obedience and courage of Joshua. There is also to be found a slab of the lust of Samson and Delilah, as well as a fragment of worthiness of Sarah, Ruth, and Esther, and the unworthiness of Lot's wife. We further consist of a slice of the disobedience of Saul, the heartistic love of David, and the wisdom and foolishness of Solomon. Deep within our personality, we are aware of a splinter of the total depravity of the queens Jezebel and Athaliah, the idolatry of the kings of Israel and the later kings of Judah. On the other hand, we find in our inner selves a parcel of the faith and boldness of Elijah, the devotion of Jeremiah and Daniel, the leadership ability of Ezra, and the perseverance of Job. A small piece of Pharaoh and Herod the Great can be found lurking deep within, who killed babies in order to keep their position. A part of the fearlessness of John the Baptist can also be found in our makeup, a lump of the Pharisee, the cowardice of Pilate, but also a component of the great faith found in the disciples and followers of Jesus Christ, that is, those whom are regenerated. In everyday life, we may also discover an ingredient of the prodigal, the Samaritan, and those whom are looking for the lost sheep.

By reflecting on the lives of the *Bible characters, we learn much about ourselves and our relationship with God, who always forgives the repentant sinner. We may further ask the question, "Why did this character do this? Or was this person right in what he or she did in this situation?" and "What would we have done?"

---

* The Cosmic Christ constitutes all of the characters of the Bible.

The real story of the Bible is about us, not any of us personally, but every man and every woman in their struggle to reach moral and spiritual maturity. Thus, the stories of the figures of the Bible are also our own story, such as the narrative of our rebellion against divine will, our temptation to seek revenge, and the struggle to persevere in the face of criticism and opposition. Each person in the Bible has a lesson to teach us about life; they represent the human beings in the world with their weaknesses and selfishness, but also that of sacrifice and love. We can, thus, learn from their failures and victories because each difficulty we may encounter in our life of faith is already covered by one of the characters. We thus find in the Bible many fundamental human mistakes we should avoid so that we do not repeat the same mistakes as they have made. The Bible is also filled with helpful stories and examples that reveal to us the best way to act in almost every life situation. It is, therefore, important to recognize ourselves in these stories. Since knowing ourselves is important to our moral and spiritual growth, the Bible is a great help in our development. It reveals our human as well as our divine natures, and it contains the moral and spiritual lessons needed for individuals to overcome his/her problems.

NOTE 1: Whenever we call out for help, God always sends a helper at the right time. Moses was sent when the Hebrew slaves cried out for deliverance. When the tribes later faced a crisis, God sent them Gideon, Deborah, and Samson. When the nation was moving away from God toward destruction, God sent them prophets and then gave them an opportunity to become children of God by living a divine life. In order to become a qualified helper, many were prepared – Moses in the wilderness, Joseph in prison, David in the hill country, and Paul in the Arabian Desert.

NOTE 2: Anyone who reads the Bible is led to live in a divine atmosphere, the heavenly atmosphere of the blessed, by uniting with the created thought forms of Bible readers everywhere and with the inspired thought force of the author. In the process of reading the Bible, we may also create a personal thought form, which results that the story starts to "tell itself" as if it had a life of its own.

b. Characters of the Old Testament

We should not be like Adam and Eve, whom had sexual relations before they were old enough (ate of the unripe fruit) and passed the original sin to their offspring. The inherited evil part of the personality was so strong that [1]Cain could not master it (Gen. 4:6, 7) and slew his younger brother Abel, ignoring God's warning, who could not stop him because of his free will. He showed no remorse when the Lord asked, "Where is Abel your brother?" Cain retorted in a callous and insolent manner: "I do not know; am I my brother's keeper?" This lie and denial of any responsibility was Cain's response to his hideous crime. However, God did not turn His back on Cain. He said, "If anyone slays Cain, vengeance shall be taken on him sevenfold", and He gave Cain a mark to protect his life.

In the seventh generation from Adam (Jude 14), Enoch appeared on the scene and he "walked with God" (Gen. 5:22), although he was surrounded by ungodliness. He was well pleasing to God, who took him up [2]without seeing death (Heb. 11:5). We can see Enoch as a role model by living in faith in an ungodly world of today, agreeable to the Lord, who will strengthen and give us encouragement to face any opposition.

Three generations after Enoch (Lk. 3:36-37), another righteous man called Noah came along, who lived like our own time amidst violence and corruption. [3]Sexual misconduct was everywhere and on the rise. "The Lord saw that the wickedness of man was great in the earth, and that every imagination of the thoughts of his heart was only evil continually" (Gen. 6:5). Because the people could not be changed, God started all over again in His restoration plan to save [4]one family first. Today, the only way to be completely saved is to enter God's Ark of salvation, to experience spiritual rebirth, or eventually be destroyed by

---

[1] The lesson we can learn from the Cain and Abel story is that although God will warn us about an impending evil, He will not force us to change because He has given humans free will to exercise their own judgment and grow thereby. We are indeed our brother's keeper and guardian and are responsible for them, and should not hate them but love them in order to get God's approval (1 Jn. 3:11-15; 4:20). When we have committed a crime of inhumanity to the other, God will not condemn us but forgive our sins. He will even help and protect us as He did to Adam and Eve (to clothe them – Gen. 3:21) and to Cain. The latter chose a wife of the existing tribes, and his son Enoch built a city (a place where people can hide from the righteous ones).

[2] Enoch was in such an elevated state that in his passing from the earthly to the spirit plane, there was no interruption of consciousness.

[3] By pursuing a self-oriented lifestyle, or "live it up" way of life. "Marrying and giving in marriage" (casual marriages, divorce, remarriage – see Luke 17:26, 27; Matthew 24:37, 38).

[4] He tried to restore Adam's family first which, like Noah's family, consisted of eight members.

the [1]self-destructive tendencies of humans whom are living the life of the good and evil personality.

Eight generations after Noah's son Shem, Abram (later called Abraham), another man of great faith, came forth (Gen. 11:10-26). [2]God told Abram to leave his country and his father's house "to the land that I will show you. And I will make of you a great nation" (a New Garden of Eden – Gen. 12:1). It took great faith for Abram, his family, and clan to leave their beloved country and head to unknown territory. It likewise takes great faith to move a missionary and his family to an unfamiliar country. It also takes great trust in the Lord to leave behind the familiar good and evil world and all their friends (Jn. 8:23; 1 Jn. 5:19; Rom. 12:2) and start living a divine life in the new and heavenly world with new friends. Abraham's supreme test of faith came when he was commanded to offer up his only son Isaac, through whose seed a nation was to be born. By his willingness to sacrifice his son, whom completely cooperated, the latter was resurrected. Abraham's wife Sarai (later named Sarah) demonstrated as an example for wives today to be subject to their husbands whom, like Abraham, should exercise loving headship over them (Eph. 5:23-28; Col. 3:18, 19; 1 Pet. 3:1-7). On the other hand, the wife of Lot, Abraham's nephew, after her family escaped from Sodom turned into a pillar of salt (Gen. 19:26; Luk. 17:32). Lot's wife looked back with a desire of wanting to live in this sin city with all of its riches and comfort (Ezekiel 16:49). Those whom have accepted Christ should not desire to return to their former way of life (Luk. 9:62; 1 Jn. 2:15; Gal. 4:9). Otherwise, they cannot be a true disciple (Luk. 14:33); but being hardened in living a good/evil lifestyle and become worst than they were before they accepted Christ (II Pet. 2:20-22).

It is said of Esau and Jacob that they, in becoming adversaries, were already struggling in their mother's womb. The Lord said to Rebekah that "the elder shall serve the younger" (Gen. 25:23). This controversy

---

[1] Humans whom are living the evil and good/evil lifestyles have a tendency to destroy themselves, that is, their bodies and inner selves by indulging in too much and the wrong kind of food, drinking too much sodas and alcoholic drinks, and by smoking. They have too much sex by depleting their bodies of strength and their etheric bodies of vitality in their fornication and extra-marital affairs, contracting sexual diseases that will cripple their lives. Through their hatred of others and attitude of revenge, they damage not only their bodies but also the development of their inner selves which, in turn, weaken the immune system of their bodies. So they die young and look very old.

[2] Stephen said that this command came before Abraham lived in Haran (Acts 7:2, 3). In the story of Abraham, we learn that it is very important to have complete trust in God because without complete surrender, He cannot act fully through us.

came head on when Jacob took away the birthright of his elder brother for a bowl of stew and received Isaac's blessing (Gen. 25:27-34; 27:1-29). Jacob fled from Esau who (like Cain) sought to kill him (Gen. 27:41 – 28:5) and served his uncle Laban for Rachel and Leah (Gen. 29:1-30). In this story, we may be more or less like Esau when we are impatient and impetuous and seek for immediate gratification and are indifferent to the consequences. We should not make rash decisions which can affect our whole lives, such as choosing a marriage partner, place to live, the kind of work we accept, and the church we attend. Those decisions should receive thoughtful considerations and be immersed in prayer.

On the other hand, we may be more like Jacob, that is, to have a sense of duty, responsibility, and a vision of the future. Because it is important that God's blessing be inherited by God's chosen ones, Jacob and his mother did everything to perpetuate the blessing given to Abraham to establish a nation under God by the one most qualified. We should, likewise, give our blessing and material wealth to those children who will not squander it but use it for good purposes, or give it to organizations and companies who are in the process of creating a better world. As Jacob loved Rachel more than her older sister Leah, the latter gave Jacob six sons and one daughter, while Rachel bore two sons. It was Leah who gave birth to Judah, Jacob's fourth son (Gen. 49:1-12), through whose lineage Jesus the Messiah was born. Judah was appointed by Jacob to lead his tribe to Goshen and to meet Joseph, whom was sold by him and his brothers in Egypt. [2]Joseph was forced into exile but received God's blessing and became governor of Egypt. Many people in the past and today were ousted from their country as political or religious refugees or for other invalid reasons, but God blessed them.

NOTE: The emotion of love is an expanding, attractive force, while hatred contracts one's consciousness. It is a force of repulsion, whereby the person shrinks and disengages from the world. The love we have for a person who is

---

[1] God-centered marriages are very important to bring forth children with less original sin.

[2] Joseph told his brothers, "As for you, you meant evil against me; but God meant it for good" (Gen. 50:20). Everything that happened to him turned out to be for good. Because Joseph served Potiphar, both prospered. We can expect our bosses to prosper because we are working for them. Joseph was put in prison because of his loyalty, but he did not become bitter because he knew that God's blessing would eventually be given. People who have been unjustly treated, lost their jobs, or are not promoted because of righteousness will eventually be rewarded even more than they expect (Matt. 5:10).

greater than ourselves is called reference, worship, or admiration. When the expressed love is at an equal level, it may be named affection, friendliness, or respect. When the object of our love is lower (in terms of growth), it is displayed as compassion, kindness, and benevolence. Hate will manifest as fear, dread, and anxiety if the object of hate is greater than us, between persons of an equal standing as anger, hostility, and coldness, while hatred in its lower form is displayed as arrogance, contempt, and tyranny.

Moses spent his first forty years as an Egyptian aristocrat with all his privileges, thinking he was somebody. However, deep in his heart, he felt bound to the people whom the Pharaoh oppressed and chose to suffer affliction with the people of God rather than to enjoy the pleasures of sin (Heb.11:25). When he saw a high-ranking Egyptian beating a Hebrew slave, he killed the Egyptian and had to flee to the desert land of Median, where he spent 40 years to discover that he was a 'nobody'. Albeit, God was preparing him for a great mission: to lead his people out of bondage. We may also have to give up that particular high-paying position in society wherein we are fooling many people in order to get their money and take a lesser position, wherein we can deal honestly with them. By being more humble, God is able to work to some extent through us and, thus, in addition to service, we may also impart to the people the Love, Wisdom, and Power of God. After the people left Egypt and God fed them with manna, the people complained and wanted to return back to Egypt because they remembered all the different kinds of food they ate there (Numb. 11:5-6; Ex. 16:3). A person cannot remain a true Christian when he or she has desires to [1]go back (or backslide) to the world with its old pattern of thinking and be again in bondage or slavery of sin (1 Jn. 2:15; Gal. 4:9). When the Israelites reached Mount Sinai to receive the Ten Commandments, the people were so much influenced by evil forces that even Aaron (Moses' brother and second in command) gave in to the people's demand to worship an idol (Ex. 32:1-25). Here, we see a restoration principle at work, namely that God allowed satan to do his evil work first before God was able to work. This happened first in the Garden of Eden and may also happen in our individual life. In order to receive the power of God to change our lives, we may first go through a

---

[1] The story of the children of Israel, leaving their own land and being in bondage in Egypt and the great desire to return to the Promised Land, is being repeated many times as the story of the prodigal son (Luke Ch. 15). We may also have desires of returning to our former ways of life when we pass through low periods or periods of spiritual dryness, when God appeared to have deserted or forsaken us. However, this will pass as soon as we recognize that our ego is no longer in charge of our life, but only the divine. We pass then through the desert and reach the Promised Land, where the divine is in control.

period of intense satanic living. Later on, Aaron and his older sister Miriam rebelled against Moses because of jealousy. Miriam became leprous but was healed because Moses interceded for his sister (Numbers Ch. 12). Not long thereafter, prominent Israelites such as Korah, Dathan, and Abiram, and 250 supporters challenged the God-given authority of Moses and Aaron (Num. Ch. 16; 26:10; Deut. 11:6), but "the earth opened its mouth" and swallowed many of them. Instead of being jealous, we should support and pray for our spiritual leader(s).

Joshua, the successor of Moses, led Israel *to conquer the Promised Land. He had such great faith that he obeyed God's instruction to conquer the city of Jericho by letting his army merely walk around it and shout in unison (Joshua 5:13 – 6:25). From this story, we can learn that to obey God, even when His directions do not make much sense, and proclaim His powerful Word, which dissolves obstacles and removes barriers, the results are truly amazing. Joshua was not only a good leader but, above all, continued to give evidence that God's Spirit was upon him. That is why the Israelites willingly followed him. Besides, he continually taught the people the Law of Moses and always gave credit to God for all his victories. We should, likewise, not rely as much on our intelligence and proficiency but more important that we are filled with His Spirit – "Not by might, nor by power, but by my Spirit" (Zechariah 4:6). Joshua's faithful service is an example for us to follow. His courage was built not on self-confidence but on confidence in God (Joshua 1:9). Thus, we can likewise be courageous and victorious because He is with me. Therefore, we should "not be frightened neither be dismayed", in all our undertaking.

In the time of the Judges, Gideon, who became the military hero, did not have much faith that God would deliver Israel by him from the Medianites, even when God clearly told him that he would. Gideon needed more proof, which God gave to him (Judges 6:36-40). When God gives clear direction in His Word, we should not question Him by asking for some confirmation. Jesus said to Thomas, "Blessed are those who have not seen and yet believe" (Jn. 20:29). See also Matthew 14:31; 17:20; Hebrew 11:6.

Another Judge Samson received from the Lord great physical strength but squandered it in lust and vengeance. He did not have the

---

* Before entering the Promised Land, Joshua sent spies to scout out Jericho. Rahab, who was a prostitute, hid the spies in her house, which was built into the city wall of Jericho. This prostitute became the great grandmother of King David and, thus, an ancestor of Jesus Christ (Joshua 2:1-21; 6:17-25; Matthew 1:5).

moral strength, or rather, the willpower to stand against the temptation of lustful pagan women whom he saw and desired. His last sweetheart, called Delilah, lulled him to sleep, shaved his head, and delivered him bald and powerless to the Philistines, who gouged out his eyes and used him as an animal and slave to grind at their mill (Judges Ch. 14, 15, 16). Those whom are well built physically may attract those women whom are materially minded. It is therefore important to strengthen your moral character and to ask God for wisdom. Do not let males or females lull you to sleep and steal your virtue and use you as a sex slave.

Boaze (Ruth 2:1) and Nabal (1 Samuel Ch. 25) were both wealthy landowners, but unlike Nabal, Boaze treated people with respect and said to the reapers, "The Lord be with you!" The workers highly regarded him and answered, "The Lord bless you!" (Ruth 1:4) In compliance with the Levitical law (Lev. 19:9, 10), Boaze left the gleanings of the ears of grain in his field for the poor, afflicted, and the sojourner. He eventually married Ruth, who was gleaning in his field and through their son Obed, he and Ruth became the ancestors of Jesus Christ (Matt. 1:1, 5, 6). Ruth the widowed Moabite woman was not only recognized by the townspeople as a woman of worth (Ruth 3:11) but also by God for her loyalty to Naomi, her mother-in-law, and a strong desire to serve her God (Ruth 1:16). Another outstanding woman was the wife of Nabal. She brought David many provisions, which her husband refused to give for the service David and his men rendered to him. Abigail begged David not to kill her husband and, thus, restrained David from blood guilt. When Nabal died, David took her for his wife.

Hannah, the first wife of Elkanah, remained barren while Peninnah, his second wife (who had many children) "used to provoke her sorely, to irritate her, because the Lord had closed her womb" (1 Sam. 1:6). Hannah was deeply distressed and prayed to the Lord for a son, "Then I will give him to the Lord all the days of his life" (1 Sam. 1:11). God heard Hannah's request and blessed her with a son; she named him Samuel.

Samuel was appointed by God, at the request of the people (1 Sam. 8:4-18), to choose the first king of Israel, a Benjamite of imposing physique. His name was Saul, who was [1]originally good (1 Sam. 9:17) but did not (like Adam) keep "The Commandment of the Lord" (1 Sam. 13:13; 15:23). "And the Lord repented that He had made Saul king over Israel" (1 Sam. 15:35).

Samuel was then instructed to find another king in the family of Jesse of Bethlehem. Samuel looked on the oldest son Eliab as a possible candidate because of his height (stature). But the Lord said to Samuel, "The Lord sees not as a man sees; man looks on the outward appearance, but the Lord looks on the heart" (1 Sam. 16:7). He finally found David, the youngest son, who was, in the time of the choosing, very busy attending the sheep. David proved himself later by killing Goliath, the giant Philistine. He was a man after God's own heart (1 Sam. 13:14). His heart and emotion (like the 2nd Adam) was "wholly true to the Lord his God --- and did not turn aside from anything that He commanded him --- except in the matter of Uriah the Hittite" (1 Kings 15:3, 5). That is, David's sin of adultery with Bathsheba and the murder of her husband Uriah in order to cover up the adultery and the [2]conception of a child. However, because of his sincere confession, repentance, and a determined effort to serve the Lord, he was forgiven. But he was not spared discipline or the consequences of his sin. David did not die, but his first child died (2 Sam. 12:14). Other sentences David endured were that "the sword shall never depart from your house" --- and your neighbor "shall lie with your wives in the sight of this sun" (2 Sam. 12:10, 11, 12). David reaped what he sowed by his adulterous act, according to natural law (Gal. 6:7). David's wives were violated in public. His daughter Tamar was raped by her half-brother Ammon, who was murdered by Absalon her brother. The latter rebelled against his father and was killed. However, God was merciful and generous and Solomon, the second son of David and Bathsheba, was later chosen as the wisest (intellectual) king of Israel (like the reappearance of Adam).

If David had not been approached and had remained silent, it is possible that he would have become hardened by sin (Hebr. 3:13). This episode in David's life served as an example of all those whom have

---

[1] When Saul was accepted as a king, he received much power from the people and was less in need of divine power. This is also true of people who have acquired much secular power. Because Saul lost communication with God, he lacked in courage and became a coward.

[2] In order to cover up the conception of a child, David invited Uriah to come home from the battlefield to visit his wife. But he did not engage in sexual intercourse with Bathsheba. When the Israelite army was engaged in a military campaign, the men refrained from sexual intercourse (1 Sam. 21:5).

fallen into the serious sin of [3]adultery. Confessing our sin(s) and showing sincere repentance brings relief to the pangs of conscience and, thus, restores our relationship with God (Luk. 15:10). The momentary pain and shame we may endure is much better than the agony by remaining silent or the dreadful consequences of becoming hardened in a rebellious course of sin, by repeating the sin, (Hebr. 10:26-31). As Solomon said in Proverbs 28:13: "He who conceals his transgressions will not prosper, but he who confesses and forsakes them will obtain mercy." We should be like David, who never quit trying and who, with Bathsheba, cast themselves on God's mercy, who changed their evil into good.

When Solomon was young, he built a magnificent Temple in Jerusalem. This time was known as the "Golden Age" of Israel. His wisdom and wealth were unmatched by anyone who was before him (2 Chron. 9:22). However, when he became older, and in order to please his many wives and concubines, he started to build heathen altars (1 Kings 11:4) and became a common fool. This was the end of the glorious age and of his kingdom (1 Kings Ch. 11), which was begun by his father David and became divided into the Northern and Southern Kingdoms. Solomon had everything but was not satisfied (Eccl. 2:1-26). Living the life of the good/evil personality did not satisfy Solomon, only when he would be living a divine life. "For what does it profit a man, to gain the whole world and forfeit his (divine) life?" (Mk. 8:36) What Solomon needed was regeneration by someone who is more than Solomon (Matt. 12:42).

At a critical period in the history of the Northern Kingdom of Israel, God raised up the prophet Elijah. During that time, Ahab (the seventh king) allowed his pagan wife Jezebel to introduce the idolatrous worship of Baal into Israel and the licentious orgies of the goddess Asherah (1 Kings 16:31, 33; 21:25). In order to prove the power of the true God over the false god Baal, Elijah calls upon God with great faith and boldness and, in a *dramatic display of power, God poured down, on Mount Carmel, the consuming fire to burn the sacrifice, while Baal did not answer the prayers of his frustrated prophets (1 Kings 18:38, 29). Elijah presented striking lessons in obedience to the Lord and

---

[3] The results of sexual immorality may be divorce, unwanted pregnancy, sexually transmitted diseases, and the loss of trust and respect.

* Elijah had to pay indemnity for this great success by becoming fearful and discouraged. God said to Elijah that He was not in the "wind" or "earthquake" or "fire" but in "a still small voice". See 1 Kings Ch. 19.

great courage by confronting the wicked king Ahab with news of the approaching drought (1 Kings 17:1). Only by total obedience to God will the power of God be manifested in our lives. We may also learn that we should choose the right life, to have faith in God, or the wrong life, by having faith in our material possessions.

The 7th ruler of the Southern Kingdom of Judah was the only Queen, Athaliah, daughter of Ahab and Jezebel. Grandma Athaliah seized Judah's throne by killing all her male grandchildren of the royal family (2 Kings 8:18, 25-28; 11:1-20 and 2 Chron. 22:1 – 23:21; 24:7), but God saved Joash (2 Kings 11:1-16).

In 787 B.C., Uzziah became the 10th ruler and king of the Southern Kingdom. "And as long as he sought the Lord, God made him prosper" (2 Chron. 26:5). However, when he became all-powerful, pride filled his heart (Prov. 16:18), and he became self-willed instead of Self-willed. He gave himself the privilege to burn incense in the Temple, whereupon he was struck by leprosy on his forehead (II Chron. 26:16-21).

Ahaz the 12th ruler and 11th king of Judah "did not do what was right in the eyes of the Lord --- but he walked in the way of the kings of Israel" (II Kings 2, 3). Instead of looking for security to God, he looked instead for security among the gods of the nations and suffered a great loss (II Chron. 28:1-8). We may also turn to false gods and false security by placing greater value on material wealth and worldly success than on serving God; we then have fallen into a kind of idolatry (1 Tim. 6:9, 10, 17). God may also invite us to offer support and put Him to the test (by asking for a sign), which Ahaz failed to do (Isa. 7:10-12).

*Hezekiah, the son of Ahaz, showed his devotion to the Lord by reopening the temple doors his father had closed and destroying pagan altars. Hezekiah was considered the best king of Judah. He kept close to the Lord by keeping His commandments, even though he was surrounded by worshippers of false gods (2 Kings 18:1-6). We should,

---

* When the king of Assyria threatened to destroy Jerusalem, he prayed for deliverance in an unusual intimate prayer (2 Kings 19:14-19). Isaiah had a vision concerning Judah and Jerusalem in the days of Uzziah, Jotham, Ahaz, and Hezekiah, kings of Judah (Isa. 1:1). Isaiah is quoted in the New Testament quite often, notable Isa. 7:14; 9:6; 11:6-9; 53;60. For example, Isa. 61:1-2 (see Luk. 4:18-19). Isaiah has been called the Evangelist of the Old Testament, a prophet and redeemer.

likewise, remain steadfast in our faith, even when we are surrounded by people who are more evil than good.

Manasseh, the son of Hezekiah, was the wickedest king Judah ever had. He murdered in order to keep in control and rebuilt pagan worship sites his father had removed and encouraged worship of Baal. He was severely punished and sent in chains to Babylon (2 Kings 21:1-9; 2 Chron. 33:1-11). However, Manasseh was forgiven when he genuinely repented (2 Chron. 33:12, 13) and wanted to make things right. God restored him as king, and he abolished all the pagan practices he had established. The lesson we can learn here is that if Manasseh can be restored, then the greatest sinner can be forgiven.

After Manasseh died, his son Amon became king but began to worship false deities and was murdered (2 Kings 21:23). His son Josiah was made king and began to purge Judah of idols and altars used in Baal worship. Thereafter, when he ordered the cleansing of the Temple, the book of the Law was found. When it was read, the king was alarmed and dismayed to learn how much Judah had departed from God. This resulted in a national spiritual reform (2 Chron. Ch. 34). We have the Bible in our closet, but we do not read it. Being not familiar with its content has reduced our influence in society, which has fallen into a situation of immorality and idolatry. If the people in the Western world discover and read the Word of God, great changes will be brought about.

Jeremiah was a reluctant evangelist who complained to God that he was inadequate, but God told him not to put confidence in himself but in Me, because I am adequate (Jer. Ch. 1). Every day for 23 years, he preached an unpopular message (Jer. 25:3), warning them of the coming disaster of being sent into exile for 70 years if they did not repent (Jer. 25:11). During the years he preached, Jeremiah was severely persecuted (see Ch. 20, 37, 38). He felt that he was a miserable failure because he was not able to convert anyone.

Because the last few kings of Judah worshipped idols (like the [1]Northern Kingdom, Israel), they were invaded by Babylon. After the two tribes of the Southern Kingdom spent 70 years in [2]exile in Babylon (2 Chron. 36:20-23; Isa. 44:28), they returned with Ezra, who read publicly the book of the Law of Moses before the Water Gate (Neh. 8:1-8). [3]Ezra not only read it but also practiced it (Ezra 7:10). He, therefore, moved the people to obey the law. We should be like Ezra, by studying the Word of God and becoming active because study without action is fruitless, as action separated from God's Word does not fulfill any worthwhile purpose. Thus, before we can tell others what God requires of them, we need to be changed first.

Daniel refused to worship the king but continued to pray to his God under threat of death (Dan. Ch. 6). Holding moral convictions today in an immoral society can, at times, be very difficult. We should, like Daniel, take a strong stand of what we believe, at our work and classroom, although we may be ridiculed by our associates. However, God will take care of the consequences as He did to Daniel who He saved from the lions.

As Job was tested, so God may test us by allowing evil forces, to a permissible limit, to *assault us, so that He knows how strong our faith is and if we are capable of carrying out an important mission. By overcoming many trials and tribulations, we grow in our faith and become a more useful channel for God and His forces.

---

[1] The prophet Amos, a simple shepherd, was called by God to denounce the idol worship and corruption in Israel, as Elijah and Elisha had done before him. (God chooses who he will as long as He is able to work through them.) The Northern Kingdom, which consisted of ten tribes, was invaded earlier by Assyria. They never came back and were forever lost (2 Kings 17:1-18). As Gomer the wife of Hosea was unfaithful to him and did not return his love, God told Hosea that the people of Israel (My bride) have treated Me the same way. (This is the way the Lord feels when we have made a covenant with God and then turn away from Him.) However, he also told Hosea (see Book) to take Gomer back and unite with her, and to love her just as much as God loves unfaithful Israel.

[2] During the exile, Esther, from a company of virgins, was chosen by Xerxes the Persian king to be his wife (Esther 2:17). She was able to save the Jews in the empire when they were faced with destruction. It is celebrated as a Jewish holiday – Purim. For the story of Daniel in exile, see story below.

[3] On another occasion, Ezra did not act with righteous indignation at the unfaithfulness of the people but responded with grief (Ezra 9:5), whereby the people came to him and repented (Ezra 10:1) and even put away their foreign wives.

* This does not mean that the universal law of cause and effect is punishing us for something we have done wrong. Job had no knowledge of why bad things happened to him. There are many stories of people who have lost everything but made a comeback.

In the story of Jonah (Ch. 3, verse 1), God gave Jonah a second chance to fulfill his mission, to warn the city of Nineveh (Assyria) against their impending disaster unless they turned away from their evil doings. Because people are good and evil, they easily make a mistake, but God is very eager to give them a second chance as long as they confess any known wrongdoing to Him and ask for help to start all over again. This second chance was also given to Peter who denied the Lord 3 times.

Habakkuk was a prophet who could not understand why God does not judge evil. However, he and we should understand that our God is patient and slow to anger, and of great compassion. See also Jonah 4:2; Nehemiah 9:17; Joel 2:13; Nahum 1:3; Psalms 103:8.

The Book of Malachi is an answer to those who complain that God is indifferent to injustice (2:17; 3:5). Malachi, the last prophet of the Old Testament, warned the people against robbing God of tithes and offerings (Mal. 3:6-18). We may also rob Him of the glory that is His, or of our friendship. When we rob God, how can we expect Him to bless us?

REMARK – How Wars Were Won and Lost in the Bible

The first great victory of war was won by Abraham who, in his exhibition of great faith, led his vastly outnumbered troops to victory (Gen. 14:14-16).

This exercise of the power of the Lord was also displayed when chosen men at the time of the Exodus won the battle with the Amalekites (Ex. 17:8-13), when Moses' hands were upheld by Aaron and Hur. Another unusual victory was won by Joshua when he received from God, his Commander-in-Chief, the battle plan to conquer Jericho by merely walking around it and shouting in unison (Josh. Ch. 6).

In the time of the Judges, when the people became unfaithful, God told them that He "will not drive them (the inhabitants) out before you; but they shall become adversaries to you" (Jud. 2:3). When the race of Israel, whom was in the process purifying their personalities, exchanged their daughters with the heathen and served their gods, they came under the power of foreign rulers. They cried out to the Lord and were liberated by Judge Ehud (Jud. 3:28). "The people of Israel again did what was evil in the sight of the Lord" (Jud. 4:1), and were delivered by Deborah and Barak from Jabin king of Canaan, and his general Sisera (Jud. 4:12-16). After 40 years, the same mistake was repeated, and the Lord gave them in the hand of Midean and were liberated by Gideon, whom needed only 300 men, those who use their hands to drink water (Jud. 7:4-7). Another Judge, Jephthah, the son of a harlot, was given great victory over the Ammonites, but he had to pay a great price, the sacrifice of his only daughter (Jud. 11:30-40).

Saul, the first king of Israel who became disobedient and prideful, lost many wars and was followed by David, who came in the name of the Lord and began his conquest by killing a Philistine champion with a single slingshot (1 Sam. Ch. 17). David was very successful in all his wars and subdued all neighbor nations. "And the Lord gave victory to David wherever He went" (II Sam. 8:6).

As we have seen, success in battle will always be by His power and not by the leader's own might or cleverness.

In the time of the divided kingdoms (Israel and Judah), Asa, the third king of Judah, was the first of the five kings of Judah (Asa, Jehoshaphat, Joash, Hezekiah, Josiah), who were acceptable by the Lord. After a ten-year reign of peace, Judah was invaded by a million-man army under Zerah the Ethiopian. Though greatly outnumbered, Asa and his men went out to meet the invaders. However, before the battle, Asa prayed, "Help us, O Lord our God, for we rely on thee, and in thy name we have come against this multitude --- So the Lord defeated the Ethiopians "and they fled (2 Chron. 14:11-12).

Our God, in whom we put our trust, will always hear our petition of help. We give our problem over to Him and release it into His divine care. See Ps. 55:22; Matt. 11:28.

During the reign of the fourth king Jehoshaphat, Judah was surrounded by enemies much larger and stronger than they, and that defeat was certain. In this moment of dire need, Jehoshaphat proclaimed a fast and desperately prayed to the Lord. The Lord's answer was "fear not, and be not dismayed at this great multitude; for the battle is not yours but God's --- you will not need to fight in this battle; stand still, and see the victory of the Lord on your behalf" (2 Chron. 20:15, 17). Jehoshaphat commanded his people to sing and praise God as they met the enemy. To their amazement, the enemy became so confused that they turned on each other and destroyed themselves.

In the last decades of the divided kingdoms, the Judeans did not listen to God at all. This resulted that He took away His protection and allowed them to be invaded by Babylon, through which the Lord executed His judgment (Christian nations today are in the same situation as Judah during the days of Jeremiah). Because they were healed by the Babylonian captivity of the practice of idolatry, they rebuilt the temple (as people today should rebuild their personality by living a moral life) but then condemned to death the one God had sent to deliver them from their sinful nature (refused to accept divine life). They then continued to persecute followers of Christ, which resulted that their holy city Jerusalem and all its inhabitants were utterly destroyed by the Romans in 70 A.D., while others were dispersed (exiled) throughout the world. Christians today should learn the lessons of the Jews before them and give God's Word the most important place in their lives (as in the early days of Europe and America) and not be thrown out of schools, watered down in churches, and neglected in the homes. The situation has become so bad today that quoting certain parts of the Bible is considered a hate crime. Even the very name of God is being removed from documents and statues, pledges, etc. as something undesirable. Do you want to be invaded or kept hostage by foreign powers? The battle of Armageddon is being fought today between Christ and the Antichrist, between the Divine Self and the evil self or altered ego, the conflict between the Christ arising and the altered ego staying in control of the personality.

c. Characters of the New Testament

The parents of John the Baptist, Zechariah, and Elizabeth were not only approved by their neighbors but were, above all, "righteous before God, walking in all the commandments and ordinances of the Lord blameless" (Luk. 1:6). Elizabeth (like Sarah, Rebekah, Rachel, and Hannah) gave birth to a child in her old age and called him John. John's mission, like that of Elijah before him, was to prepare and proclaim the coming of the Messiah (Isa. Ch. 40). John was well aware that he was chosen in that capacity which was given to him (Jn. 3:27), as any religious worker contributes their specific talents and service. John promoted Christ by saying, "He must increase, but I must decrease" (Jn. 3:30). We should not work for God in order that we (our self or personality) are recognized. Our self should, therefore, be dethroned so that Self or Christ Spirit be enthroned, as the self listens to the bridegroom's voice (Jn. 3:29).

Herod the Great (37 – 4 B.C.) managed to get himself appointed king of the Jews by the Roman senate. Like Pharaoh of Egypt who sought to kill Moses, Herod slaughtered Bethlehem's infant boys in order to kill Jesus (Matt. 2:1-23). Satan will do anything to kill God's chosen ones.

Nicodemus was a wealthy (Jn. 19:39) Pharisee, "a ruler of the Jews" (Jn. 3:1), "a teacher of Israel" (Jn. 3:10), and a powerful member of the Sanhedrin (Jn. 7:50). He came under cover of darkness to learn more from a lowly carpenter's son, called Jesus of Nazareth, who taught him a very important principle, to be born again. However, we should not be afraid to become a disciple of Christ because of what our relatives, friends, and colleagues might say, especially when we hold a high position in society. We gain so much more than what we give up.

NOTE 1: The Gospel writer Matthew was a Jew and a former Roman tax collector which Jesus put in the same social class with sinners, harlots, and gentiles (Matt. 9:11; 21:31; 18:17). John Mark, the second Gospel writer, was not a direct disciple of Christ as Matthew was. Paul and Barnabas took him along on their first missionary journey (Acts 13:5). Luke was a physician, and the non-Jewish author of the Gospel of Luke and Acts. He was called by Paul the "beloved physician" (Col. 4:4), who accompanied Paul on his second and third missionary journeys (2 Tim. 4:9-13; Acts 16:6-18; 20:1-24). He had great compassion for the sick and the lonely. John the beloved disciple of Christ became a disciple of Jesus through John the Baptist (Jn. 1:35) and wrote the Fourth Gospel, three Epistles, and Revelation, going through many persecutions by the Jews and the Roman Empire but kept his faith for about 60 years when he died.

NOTE 2: Martha, the sister of Mary and Lazarus (Lk. 10:38-42) had no time to listen to Jesus as Mary did because she was very busy preparing and serving the meals for the guests of Jesus. When she complained to Jesus about her sister of not helping her, Jesus told her that Mary did the better thing by spending time with Him. We should also spend much time with our Lord in prayer before we undertake any action to establish the Kingdom of God.

NOTE 3: Anyone can repeat the words of great men as Jesus, but who can speak from the same spiritual level and with the same Spirit?

Caiaphas presided over Israel's highest court, the Sanhedrin, and illegally tried and condemned Jesus (Jn. 7:51; 11:47-57; 18:1-28). Another member of the Sanhedrin, Gamaliel, Paul's teacher (Acts 22:3), said to the Jewish council who wanted to kill the Apostles,

"Keep away from these men and let them alone; for if this plan or this undertaking is of men, it will fail; but if it is of God, you will not be able to overthrow them. You might even be found opposing God!" (Acts 5:38, 39). Thus, "If God is for us, who is against us?" (Rom. 8:31) Joseph of Arimathea (a member of the Jewish council) buried Jesus' body after he secured permission from Pilate to take the body of Jesus from Calvary and to place it in his own new tomb (Matt. 25:57).

Pilate the 5th Roman procurator of Judea (A.D. 20 to 36) is known to Christians as a coward who condemned Jesus to death while he knew that he was innocent (Jn. 18:38). Because his reputation was more important than character, he did not do what was right.

Peter, the fisherman of the Sea of Galilee who became Jesus' chief disciple, denied Jesus 3 times (Matt. 26:69-75) and had to restore his faith after the resurrection by answering Jesus 3 times that he loved Him (Jn. 21:15-17). This story is a good example that anyone can be restored when they have done something disgusting and horrible.

[1]Stephen, one of the seven deacons who ministered to those who spoke Greek, was "full of grace and power, did great wonders and signs among the people" (Acts 6:5-8). He was often overtaken by the Spirit of God, who worked through him by words and deeds. "All who sat in the council saw that his face was like the face of an angel" (Acts 6:15). They saw the presence of God in his unveiled face as that what was seen on Moses' face (Ex. 34:29-35). A true Christian should likewise radiate the God power within them in their unveiled face (2 Cor. 3:18). Stephen the [2]first martyr's last words were (similar to those of Jesus): "Lord, do not hold this sin against them" (Acts 7:60). Those who stoned him laid down their garments at the feet of a young man named Saul who, because of the shed blood of Stephen, could be chosen to be a Christian missionary, as Paul (Acts 7:58; 22:20).

NOTE: The first century Hebrew Christians took the warning of Jesus in Luke 21:20, 21 seriously and fled from the city of Jerusalem when the Roman army was about to demolish the city in 66 A.D.

---

[1] Stephen, before the ears of the Sanhedrin, gave an overview of the history of Israel from the time of Abraham until Solomon. Paul gave a similar overview of the Jewish people. See Chapter 11 of Hebrews.

[2] Apostle James was killed by Herod Agrippa 1 (Acts 12:2) in around 44 A.D., as both Peter and Paul, with many others, suffered martyrdom under Nero around 66 A.D.

After Paul met Ananias who baptized him (Acts 9:18), he met Barnabas (son of encouragement), who recruited Paul for ministry and then traveled with him (Acts 11:19-26; 13:1-5). He gave of himself in resources (sold a field he owned, "and brought the money and laid it at the apostles' feet" – Acts 4:37), in friendship and, above all, to give encouragement to all whom are in need, especially to Paul (Acts 9:27). Many people today need encouragement, to strengthen them with your wisdom, sustain them with your prayers, and stimulate them to do good for others.

Saul was born of Jewish parents in Tarsus, a Benjamite and Roman citizen. Saul the zealous Pharisee encountered at the road to Damascus the Cosmic Christ, who spoke through Jesus. Saul then became the Apostle Paul who became completely devoted to the cause of Jesus Christ. He did much to take the "Good News" to the gentile world, but he did not try to do it alone. He took with him many fellow Christians and made full use of the many he left behind to take care of the spiritual needs of the believers (Acts 17:14; Titus 1:5). In the book of Acts and in Paul's letters, about one hundred individuals are mentioned.

Although Paul planted, he did not take any credit for the growth of the church; all honor should go to God (1 Cor. 3:5-7; 9:16). Because the Spirit of Christ, to whom he completely yielded, could easily work through Paul, he had, therefore, great success wherever he went but also encountered great opposition of evil forces within and without humans. He said, "All who desire to live a godly life in Christ Jesus will be persecuted" (2 Tim. 3:12). He also took upon himself much of the suffering in order to dissolve their guilt and debt, that is, their individual and ancestral karma, so that they will accept Christ more readily. In addition to the indemnity he was paying, God allowed him to be in pain continually of a thorn in the flesh (2 Cor. 12:7) so that he paid vicariously for those who were not able to do for themselves.

During his mission, Paul endured incredible hardships. Several times, he nearly drowned in the Mediterranean Sea when his ship broke apart. He was beaten, robbed, stoned, and left for dead and was finally beheaded in Rome. "For we do not want you to be ignorant, brethren, of the affliction we experienced in Asia; for we were so utterly, unbearably crushed that we despaired of life itself" (2 Cor. 1:8). "We are afflicted in every way but not crushed; perplexed, but not driven to despair; persecuted, but not forsaken; struck down, but not destroyed" (2 Cor. 8:9). See also 2 Cor. 6:4-5; 11:23-28; 12:10.

Paul was so close to God that he could say, "That neither death nor life, nor angels, nor principalities, nor things present, nor things to come, nor powers, nor height, nor depth, nor anything else in all creation will be able to separate us from the love of God in Christ Jesus our Lord" (Rom. 8:38-39).

He did not want to be a burden to anyone, and whenever he could, he worked as a tentmaker (Acts 18:3). He was immune to snake bites (Acts 28:3-6; Mk. 16:16, 18). Paul always thought the best of his fellow Christians and used often the expression "we" when speaking to them, being one of them, instead of being above them (Heb. 10:39).

He further wrote, "I will most gladly spend and be spent for your souls" (2 Cor. 12:15). In other words, he wanted to be completely spent or be exhausted and worn out for serving God and the interest of others, to spend all his time, energy, talents, and resources for the welfare of his spiritual children (1 Thess. 2:7, 8). Because he experienced love so much, he could write in 1 Corinthians Chapter 13 the importance of true love over all other virtues and to render wholehearted service out of love for the people (2 Cor. 11:28).

Throughout his ministry, Paul remained loyal to God right toward the end of his life on earth. He could therefore say, "I have fought the good fight, I have finished the race, I have kept my faith" (2 Tim. 4:7).

Because John Mark left his mission, Paul asked Silas, a prominent member of the Jerusalem church (Acts 15:22, 32) to go with him on his second missionary journey. Like Paul, Silas believed that gentiles do not have to be circumcised to be saved. Silas was content in playing a supporting role and was willing to work for the cause of Christ without public recognition. This resulted that their work became very successful.

Aquila and Priscilla, as husband and wife team, were expelled from Rome (Acts 18:2, 3), met Paul in Corinth, who was on his second journey and stayed with them for a while. They were, like Paul, tentmakers (building a dwelling place for the Lord – Rev. 21:3). The couple was committed to one another in marital fidelity and Christian love and used their home as a household church (1 Cor. 16:19). When they moved to Ephesus with Paul (Acts 18:18), they as a pair met Apollos, who was learned and eloquent but knew only "the baptism of John" – "The baptism of repentance", not baptism "in the name of the Lord Jesus" (Acts 19:3, 5). They expounded to him the way of God more accurately (Acts 18:22). They were simple people, intimate with God and familiar with His Word, and were well qualified to teach the learned, such as Apollos and men like Dionysius (Acts 17:34). The latter came to Christ earlier, not on the strength of his intellect but of saving faith.

As Mark gave up his mission but came back, Demas, another companion of Paul, was very active for a long time (Col. 4:14; Phil. 24) but abandoned his ministry at the very end (2 Tim. 4:10). How sad it is when someone who has been living a divine life goes back to his former life, the life of the good/evil personality and becomes in love with the world again.

Timothy was very well raised by his mother Eunice (his father was a Greek – Acts 16:1) and grandmother Lois in a sincere faith in the Lord of the Old Testament (2 Tim. 1:5; 3:14-15). Paul led Timothy to the Lord Jesus on his second missionary journey and became his "true child in the faith" (1 Tim. 1:2). From a shy and timid youth (who was living the life of the personality) to a divine son in the Lord (1 Cor. 4:17), Paul sent him as an overseer during his third missionary journey by evangelizing and correcting the problems in the Corinthian and other churches (Philip 2:20). Being in close association with Paul, he became like Paul in personality and spirit (2 Tim. 3:10-12). From the above, we can learn that with God's help, we can fulfill the spiritual role of both parents, and it is important to teach our children by Word and example the way of the Lord.

Philip the evangelist was one of the seven deacons (Acts 6:3) who preached with great success to the despised Samarians (Acts 8:5-8) and to the Ethiopian official (Acts 8:26-40), introducing Christianity to Africa. From him, we can learn that we should never assume that individuals of a certain nationality, race, or social status are not interested in the Good News. The first gentile convert was Cornelius, a Roman centurion. He prayed constantly to God and practiced what he thought was in accordance with God's Will. He was open to the guidance of the Lord and was not afraid to give voice of his beliefs. See Chapter 10.

Because Paul, during his second journey, had a vision of a man of Macedonia (Europe) who asked him to help them, he decided to sail for that country (Acts 16:9-10). Lydia became the first convert to Christianity in Europe. She lived in Philippa as a seller of purple good, from which her native city Thyatira was famous. She came into contact with the Gospel of Christ when Paul and his companions met her outside the gate at a woman's prayer meeting. She then opened her home for Paul and his fellow travelers (Acts 16:11-15). Paul and his consorts had to pay a heavy price for bringing the Gospel to a new continent and were severely persecuted (Acts 16:22-24).

The letter to Philemon concerned about a runaway slave Onesimus, who ran into Apostle Paul, who was a prisoner in Rome. Onesimus was converted by Paul and became his spiritual child. Paul wrote that "he was useless to you, but now he is indeed beneficial to you and me" (verse 11). Since he has become a Christian brother, he should be free. "So if you consider me your partner, receive him as you would receive me" (verse 17).

XXIV. Jesus Christ Our Perfect Model

The best model for us in the Bible is the life of Christ. In the teachings and examples of Jesus Christ, as described in the Gospels, we not only get acquainted with the feelings and thoughts of Jesus but also those of God His father. By reading the Gospels completely, we find the character of His personality (as the Son of Man), His Divine Spirit (as the Son of God), and also the nature of the Spirit of God speaking through Him. We can learn about the many virtues he displayed, such as: faith and trust, humility, chastity, gentleness, joy, compassion, kindness, charity, goodness, patience, bearing of wrongs, etc. However, the primary teaching of the Christ was love. Love for the Creator instead of fear, love for Self, and love for one's enemy. He never told anyone in words "I love you", but rather demonstrated His love for the sick and diseased and love for the poor and wretched. The mere sight of the afflicted touched Him so deeply that He was moved to relieve their suffering. Albeit, more than physical needs, He felt great concern for the many that had spiritual needs and taught them with gracious words about the Kingdom of God. Jesus displayed a whole range of higher emotions which were not tinged with lower desires. He grieved over Jerusalem which did not accept Him, expressed righteous indignation to the money exchangers, and was moved to tears when He saw the grief the death of Lazarus had on his sister Mary. The Christ Spirit expressing through Jesus came to teach humans how to live a love-filled, trust-laden life of beauty and abundance. Jesus, unlike other moralists of his time, practiced what He preached. Instead of troubling people with heavy burdens, Jesus said that His burden is light to bear. Instead of keeping a safe distance from those in authority, Jesus was warm and approachable. He identified with the many people

He met, and they trusted Him so much that they revealed to Him their innermost thoughts because they perceived His heartfelt interest and concern for them. They could see this sacrificial spirit on their behalf in His facial expression, hear it in His tone of voice, and see it in His kind manner and attitude. They felt drawn to Jesus and were comfortable in His presence. Children came to Him freely because they sensed that He was a caring person and would not turn them away, and He embraced them. Jesus was a real friend and an affectionate companion to His disciples and truly loved them to the end. He was patient with them even when He was in great distress in the Garden and accepted the men and women as they were, while drawing out the best of them. He was determined to do God's Will, under all circumstances, and was a zealous evangelizer and trained others to do the same. Finally, Christ told all of us that whatever He did, we will be able to do as well.

Extended Contents and Notes

NOTES
Biography
Theologians – Church Leaders and Lay People

Krishna Hindu god – p. 18-534

Osiris god of the underworld (Egyptian mythology) – p. 421^1 – 464

Seth brother of Osiris – p. 464

Buddha – Gautama c.563 – 483 B.C.

      p.18 – 110 →121 – 124^a – 541 – 582 – 606^N

Moses – p.612 – 625 – 804 – 810 – 476 – 625^2 – 178 – 781 – 641 – 794 – 627^{N3} – 626 – 468^*

Paul the Apostle d. +/-67A.D., Peter the Apostle, and many other followers of Jesus Christ whom are mentioned.

Clement of Rome (first church father – d.100 A.D.) – p.758

Ignatius of Antioch (church father – d.110 A.D.) – p.273

Marcion (reformer – c.85 – c.165 A.D.) – p.785

Valentinus (Gnostic teacher – c.100 – 165 A.D.) – p.507

Justin Matyr (church father – c.100 – c.165 A.D.) – p.273

Irenaeus (church father – c.125 – c.202 A.D.) – $p.81 – 276^1$

Clement of Alexandria (church father – c.150 – 215 A.D.) – p.81 – 182 – $739 – 795^1$

Tertullian (theologian – c.160 – c.220 A.D.) – p.274 – 274^N – 279^* - 758

Origen (theologian – c.185 – c.254 A.D.) – p.82 – 191 – 274 – 465^3 – $795^1 – 796^N – 800^R$

Paul of Samosato (bishop of Antioch – from 260 to 272 A.D.) – p.276 – 280^*

Sabellius (Christian teacher of the third century A.D.) – p.276

Arius (Alexandrian theologian 256 – 336 A.D.) – $p.278 – 278^N$ – 586

Alexander (bishop of Alexandria from 313 to 328 A.D.) – p.278

Athanasius (deacon to Alexander c.295 – 373 A.D.) – p.279

Nestorius (patriarch of Constantinople from 428 to 431 A.D.) – p.280 – 282 – 586

Eutyches (spokesman of Monophysitism – c.380 – c.456 A.D.) – p.281 – 586

St. Ambrose (bishop of Milan c.340 – 397 A.D.) – p.758

Pope Demascus appointed Jerome in 382 A.D. – p.768

St. Jerome (monk and translator – c.340 – 419 A.D.) – p.758 – 768

Bishop Valarius of the Hippo region – d.396 A.D. – p.478

Pelagius (British monk and theologian – c.360 – c.420 A.D.) – p.104 – $701^{\#2}$

St. Augustine (bishop of Hippo and church father 354 – 430 A.D.) – $p.72^*$ - 103 – 104 – 276^N – 312^2 – 478 – 564^R – 644 – 692^a – $701^{\#2}$ – 739 – 758 – 788

Mohammed (founder and prophet of Islam – c.570 – 632 A.D.) – p.223 – 370

Gregory the Great (pope from 590 to 604 A.D.) – p.103 – 104^R

The Venerable Bede (Eng. Historian & theologian 673 – 735 A.D.) – p.768

Willibrord (European missionary 690 A.D.) – p.478 – 644 – 644^2

Adelbert (European missionary 690 A.D.) – p.478 - 644^2

Boniface (European missionary 716 A.D.) – p.478

Gregory III (pope from 715 to 731 A.D.) – p.478

Photius (patriarch of Constantinople – d.891 A.D.) – p.282

St. Francis of Assisi (Italian friar – 1182 – 1226) – p. 92 – 229 – 325 – 478

St. Clare of Assisi (Italian nun – 1194 – 1253) – p.92

Peter Waldo (French religious reformer – d.1217) – p.768^3

St. Thomas Aquinas (Catholic theologian and doctor – 1225 – 1274) – p.82 – 104 – 467 – 758

St. Bonaventura 1221 – 1274 – p.758

Benedict XI (pope from 1303 to 1304) – p.645

Jan van Ruysbroeck (Dutch mystic – 1293 – 1381) – p.105

Gerard (Geert) Groote (Dutch theologian and reformer – 1340 – 1384) – p.51* - 105

Members of the group established by Gerard Groote and Florentius Radewyns are: Thomas A. Kempis – c.1380 – 1471

Gerard van Zutphen, Hendriekus Mande, Johann Wessel, Adrian VI, pope from 1522 to 1523, and the young Erasmus (theologian and classical scholar 1466 – 1536) – p. 105 – 759 – 769 - 769^1

John Wycliffe (Oxford scholar, translator – c.1320 – 1384) – p. 768 – 769 – 773 – 773^4

Jan Hus (Bohemian religious reformer – c.1369 – 1415) – p.773

Joan of Arc (the maid of Orleans 1412 – 1431) – p.137 – 194 – 223

Johan Gutenberg (printer of Latin bible – c.1400 – 1468) – p.769^1

Innocent VIII (pope from 1484 to 1492) – p.192

Martin Luther (theologian – translator – reformer 1483 – 1546) –p.6 – 72* - 105 – 106 – 140* - 179 – 269 – 277 – 339^N – 571 – 588^{R2} – 657 – 713 – 739 – 759 – 767^2 – 769 – 769^2 – 769^4 – 788 - 797^1

William Tyndale (English theologian – translator – c.1484 – 1536) – p.769 – 773

Jacob van Liesvelt (Dutch translator and printer d.1545) – p.773

Jean Calvin (French theologian – reformer – 1509 – 1564) p.6 – 7 – 107 – 318 – 589 – 788 – 797^2

Zwingli (Swiss reformer – 1484 – 1531) – p.589

Michael Servetus (Spanish theologian 1511 – 1553) – p.276^2

Menno Simons (Dutch reformer – founder of Mennonites – 1492 – 1559) – p.106

St. Theresa of Avila (Spanish nun 1515 – 1582) – p.92

St. John of the Cross (Spanish mystic – reformer 1542 – 1591) – p.92 – 336 – 338 – 657

Jansenius Cornelius (Dutch theologian and author – 1585 – 1638) – p.288[N1]

John Robinson (pastor of the Pilgrims church in Leiden – 1575 – 1625) – p.107 – 483[N]

St. Joseph of Copertino (Italian saint – 1603 – 1663) – p.229

Brother Lawrence (served in a Carmelite monastery – c.1614 – 1691) – p.367 – 394 – 738

John Bunyan (English preacher and author – 1628 – 1688) – p.759 – 760 – 770[1]

George Fox (English founder of Society of Friends – 1624 – 1691) – p.235 – 774

John Wesley (English theologian and founder of Methodism – 1703 – 1791) – p.140* - 774

Jonathan Edwards (American theologian – reformer 1703 – 1758) – p.713

Charles G. Finney (American revival preacher – 1792 – 1875) – p.713

George Muller (caretaker of orphanage – 1805 – 1898) – p.724 – 759

Joseph Smith (founder of the Mormon Church 1805 – 1844) – p.370

D.F. Straus (German theologian 1808 – 1874) – p.774

Tischendorf (German biblical scholar – 1815 – 1874) – p.770[3]

Benedict XV (pope from 1914 to 1922) – p.759

Albert Sweitzer (German theologian and missionary – 1875 – 1965) – p.758 – 774 – 774[2]

Karl Barth (Swiss theologian 1886 – 1968) – p.789 – 789[1] – 798[7]

Modernist theologians: F. Schleiermacher, A. Ritschl, H.E. Fosdick, R. Niebuhr, and P. Tillich – p.798[7]

Brother Andrew (evangelist of Holland – 1928 →) – p.434[N5]

Corrie ten Boom (Christian woman of Holland – 1892 – 1983) – p.475

Anne Frank (Jewish girl – born 1933 – died 1945 in Bergen Belsen) – p.564[R]

Pius XII (pope from 1939 to 1958) – p.104

Young Oon Kim (Korean theologian – 1914 – 1989)– p.33[a] - 78[a] - 646[1]

Herbert Armstrong (founder of Worldwide Church of God – 1892 – 1986) –p.292 – 760

John XXIII (pope from 1958 to 1963) – p.277

Norman Vincent Peale (pastor Marble Collegate Church – 1898 – 1993) – p.155[R] - 760

Robert Schuller (pastor Chrystal Cathedral – 1926 →) – p.155[R]

Billy Graham (Christian evangelist (1918 →) – p.292 – 564 – 724 – 760

C.S. Lovett (founder of personal Christianity in 1951) – p.724

Sister Theresa (Roman Catholic nun of Calcutta – 1910 – 1997) – p.222 – 532^{N3}

Orah Schoon (lay missionary) – p.328^N

Doris Walder (lay missionary) – p.328^N

Pauline wife of author (lay missionary) – p.478^1

Naeran daughter of author (lay missionary) – p.393

Tweeran daughter of author (lay missionary)

Author (lay missionary) – p.191^R – 222 – 263^R – 328^N – 371^{N3} – 373 – 378 – 393 – 427^N – 562^{N2} – 478^1 - 578^1

Philosophers

Thales (Greek philosopher – c.640 – c.546 B.C.) – p.604

Lao-tse (Chinese philosopher and mystic – c.604 – c.531 B.C.) – p.618^{N1}

Anaximenes (Greek philosopher – c.588 – c.524 B.C.) – p.604

Promethius – In Greek mythology – stole fire from heaven – p.327 – 181

Pythagoras (Greek philosopher – c.570 – c.500 B.C.) – p.166 – 219 – 604 – 604^2 – 605 – 800

Confucius (Chinese philosopher and teacher – c.551 – c.478 B.C.) – p.112^a – 618^{N1}

Heraclitus (Greek philosopher – c.540 – c.475 B.C.) – p.560 – 561 – 604

Empedocles (Greek philosopher – c.490 – c.430 B.C.) – p.219

Socrates (Greek philosopher – c.469 – 399 B.C.) – p.129^b – 500 – 506^1

Plato (Greek philosopher c.427– 347 B.C.) – p.82 – 83 – 219 – 447^1 – 467 – 497^3 – 500

Aristotle (Greek philosopher c.384 – 322 B.C.) – p.82^b – 83 – 467 – 500 – 800

Zeno (Greek philosopher c.335 – c.264 B.C.) – p.561

Aristobulus (Jewish philosopher 2nd century B.C.) – p.76^c

Philo of Alexandria (Jewish philosopher – c.20 B.C. – c.50 A.D.) – p.249 – 273

Abelard, Pierre (French philosopher 1079 – 1142 – lover of Heloise) – p.92

Johann Faust (German philosopher and magician – c.1480 – c.1538) – p.192

Francis Bacon (English philosopher – 1561 – 1626) – p.411 – 759

Rene Descartes (French philosopher – 1596 – 1650) – p.420* - 447^1 – 448

833

George Berkeley (Irish philosopher – 1685 – 1753) – p.591

Francois Voltaire (French philosopher – 1694 – 1778) – p.774 - 774[1]

Offray de Lamette (French philosopher – physician – 1709 – 1751) – p.420*

Jean Rousseau (French philosopher 1712 – 1778) – p.101

Immanuel Kant (German philosopher – 1724 – 1804) – p.759

Friedrich von Schelling (German philosopher – 1775 – 1854) – p.694*

Arthur Schopenhauwer (German philosopher – 1788 – 1860) – p.591

Soren Kierkegaard (Danish philosopher – 1813 – 1855) – p.310[1] – 543 – 657 – 739 – 759

Ludwich Feuerbach (German philosopher – 1804 – 1872) – p.774

Karl Marx (German philosopher/economist – 1818 – 1883) – p.194[4] – 317[2] – 531[N1] – 774

Friedrich Engels (German philosopher/socialist – 1820 – 1895) – p.194[4]

Friedrich Nietzsche (German philosopher – 1844 – 1900) – p.193 – 548

William James (American philosopher/psychologist – 1842 – 1910) – p.661 – 662

George Santayana (Spanish-born philosopher – 1863 – 1952) – p.205[1] – 377[N1]

Martin Heidegger (German existentialist – 1884 – 1976) – p.310[1]

Manly P. Hall (American occult philosopher – 1901 – 1990) – p.426

Spiritualists – Mystics

Odyssius (meets the spirit of his mother) – p.428[N2]

Meister Eckhart (German theologian and mystic – c.1260 – 1327) – p.561 – 582

Emanuel Swedenborg (scientist – spiritualist – 1688 – 1772) – p.404* - 456 – 456[1] – 463[6] – 774

Ralph Waldo Emerson (American essayist – mystic – 1803 – 1882) – p.276[2] – 739

Madame Blavatsky (Russian theosophist – 1831 – 1891) – p.370

C.W. Leadbeater (English clairvoyant – theosophist – 1847 – 1934) – p.370 – 458[N]

Anthony Borgia (English medium for Msgr. Benson – 1871 – 1914) – p.404* - 427[N2] – 458[7] – 466*

Max Heindel (Danish born – Christian occultist and mystic – 1865 – 1919) – p.370 - 427[2]

Wylen E.M. van Yssendyk (Dutch minister and spiritualist – 1852 – 1908) – p.422[3]

He wrote about Christian martyrs – Potamiena 206 A.D. and Febronia 304 A.D.

Daniel Dunglas Home (English spiritualist – medium – 1833 – 1886) – p.229

Arthur Conan Doyle (English novelist and spiritualist – 1859 – 1930) – p.451 – 451[4]

Emmet Fox (American metaphysician – 1886 – 1951) – p.211

Robert Crookall (English spiritualist – 1890 – 1981) – p.450[1]

Carl A. Wickland (American psychiatrist – spiritualist – 1861 – 1945) – p.452

Myrtle Fillmore (co-founder of Unity Church – 1845 – 1931) – p.427[N]

Edgar Cayce (sleeping prophet – 1877 – 1945) – p.370 - 557[3]

Paramahania Yoganando (Indian yogi and guru – 1893 – 1952) – p.427[N]

Gerard Croiset (1908 – 1980 – Dutch clairvoyant) – p.228

Earline Chaney (co-founder of Astara – channeling masters) – p.442

Jane Roberts (1929 – 1984 – channeling Set the European) – p.442

J.C. Knight (1946 → - channeling Ramtha – ancient spirit) – p.442

Mary Fleming (received messages for New Age Frontier) – p.288*

Raymond A. Moody (1944 → - medical doctor and psychologist) – p.449

Elizabeth Kobler-Ross (Swiss-born psychiatrist – 1926 – 2004) – p.449

Pim van Lommel (1943 → - Dutch cardiologist) – p.449 – 449[1]

Those who have been inspired – p.223 – 224 – 370
William Blake, Johan Wolfgang Goethe, Shakespeare, John Milton, Wolfgang Amadeus Mozart, Ludwig van Beethoven, Raphael, the spiritualist Andrew Jackson Davis, Alice Bailey, Hilarion, Ramala, Ramtha, New Age author Ruth Montgomery, Augustinian nun Catherine Emmerich, Bach, Haydn, Mohammed, Joseph Smith, Madame Blavatsky, C.W. Leadbeater, Max Heindel, Edgar Cayce, and many others.

Psychologists

Sigmund Freud (1856 – 1939 – Austrian neurologist) – p.82 – 126[a] – 156 – 509[N1] – 529 – 531[N1] – 533

Alfred Adler (1870-1937 – Austrian psychiatrist) – p.531[N1] – 548

Carl Gustav Jung (1875 – 1961 – Swiss psychoanalyst) –
p.519 – 531[N1] – 533 – 596[N1] – 654 – 657 – 707

William Reich (1897-1977 – Austrian psychoanalyst) – p.650

Roberto Assagioli (1888 – 1975 – Italian transpersonal psychologist) – p.77* - 338 – 519 – 654 – 707

Abraham Maslow (1908 – 1970 – American founder of humanistic psychology) – p.518 – 519 - 519[2]

Erich Fromm (1900 – 1980 – German social psychologist) – p.437[1]

Writers and Poets
Dante (1265 – 1321 – Italian poet) – p.181
William Shakespeare (1564 – 1616 – English poet and dramatist) – p.3 – 175 – 756 – 759 - 770[1]
John Milton (1608 – 1674 – English poet and essayist) – p.181 – 759 – 770[1]
Benjamin Franklin (1706 – 1790 – American author – statesman) – p.387
Tennyson (1809 – 1892 – English poet) – p.419
Henry Thoreau (1817-1862 – American author) – p.315
Dostoevsky (1821-1881 – Russian novelist) – p.181 – 676[*]
R.L. Stevenson (1850-1894 – Scottish novelist) – p.17 – 759
George Bernard Shaw (1856-1950 – Irish essayist) – p.49 – 386 – 548[R]
Simone de Beauvoir (1908-1986 – French writer) – p.374

Creative individuals – who performed great works in their later years, such as: Sophocles, Cervantes, Verdi, Michelangelo, Goethe, Edison, Alexander Kerinski, Leo Tolstoy, Winston Churchill, Laura Ingalls Wilder, Toscanini, Horowitz, Rubinstein, and Senator Thurmond of South Carolina, and many others (see page 370).

Composers and Performers
George F. Handel (1685 – 1759 – German composer) – p.67
Ludwig van Beethoven (1770 – 1827 – German composer) – p.67
Richard Wagner (1813-1883-German composer) – p.3[b]
Frank Sinatra (1915 – 1998 – American singer) – p.393
Elvis Presley (1935 – 1977 – American singer) – p.414[R]
John Wayne (1907 – 1979 – American movie star) – p.479
Mr. Spock (1966 – Star Trek – television – science fiction) – p.91[N]
Mr. Tubak (1995 – Voyager – television – science fiction) – p.91[N]

Scientists
Paracelsus (1493 – 1541 – Swiss alchemist) – p.650
Anton van Leeuwenhoek (1632 – 1723 – Dutch naturalist) – p.445[4]
Franz Anton Mesmer (1733 – 1815 – Austrian doctor) – p.650
Walter J. Kilner (1847 – 1920 – English medical electrician) – p.650
Hendrik Lorentz (1853 – 1928 – Dutch physicist) – p.447[+]
Karl von Reichenbach (1891 – 1953 – German philosopher of science) – p.650
Robert Pavlita (c.1911 – 1991 – Czech scientist) – p.650
Simyon (and Valentina) Kirlian (1898 – 1978 – Russian researcher) – p.650

Albert Einstein (1879 – 1955 – American physicist) – p.444[N3]
Niels Bohr (1885 – 1962 – Danish physicist) – p.590[*]
James Lovelock (1919 → - British scientist) – p.319[1]
Rupert Sheldrake (1942 → -British scientist) – p.319[1]

Astronomers

Thales of Miletus (c.640 – 546 B.C. – Greek astronomer) – p.597[1]
Ptolemy (127 – 151 A.D. – Greek astronomer) – p.597[1]
Nicolaus Copernicus (1473 – 1543 – Polish astronomer) – p.597[1] – 800
Galileo (1564 – 1642 – Florentine astronomer) – p.597[1] – 800
Isaac Newton (1642 – 1727 – English astronomer) – p.800

Government Representatives

Melchizedek – King of Salem (Gen.14:18) – p.640
Legislator – Manu – p.486
King Solomon – p.238 – 240 – 421 – 477 – 614[2] – 628 – 628[N] – 646[N2] – 813 – 814 – etc.
The Queen of Sheba – p.646 (1 Kings 10:1-13)
King David – p.238 – 477 – 613 – 614 – 614[1] – 813 – 813[2] – 814 – etc.
King Saul – p.477 – 477[*] - 613 – 813 – etc.
Nebuchadnezzar (King of Babylonia from c.604 to c.561 B.C.) – p.240 – 628
King Belshazzar of Babylon (son of above) – p.229 – 614
Cyrus (King of Persia – from c.558 to 529 B.C.) – p.241
Darius (King of Persia – from c.521 to 486 B.C.) – p.241 – 242 – 614 – 645[N1]
Alexander the Great (King of Macedonia – from 336 to 323 B.C.) – p.216 – 644
Antiochus Epiphanes (King of Syria from 175 to c.164 B.C.) – p.242[N] – 252 – 772
Cleopatra (Queen of Egypt – from 51 to 49 B.C.) – p.141
Herod the Great (King of Judea from 37 to 4 B.C.) – p.47 – 242 – 242[*] - 261 – 262 – 821
Caesar Augustus (Roman emperor – from 27 B.C. to 14 A.D.) – p.261
Tiberius (Roman emperor – from 14 to 37 A.D.) – p.270[R]
Pontius Pilate (procurator of Judea – from 20 to 36 A.D.) – p.270[R] – 567 – 822
Herod Agrippa (king of Judea – from 41 to 44 A.D.) – p.822[2]
Claudius I (Roman emperor from 41 to 54 A.D.) – p.141
Nero (Roman emperor from 54 to 68 A.D.) – p.631 – 822[2]
Domitian (Roman emperor from 81 to 96 A.D.) – p.631
Cornelius Tacitus (Roman historian c.55 – c.120 A.D.) – p.270[R]
Trajan (Roman emperor from 98 to 117 A.D.) – p.631

837

Simon bar Kochiba (Jewish messiah – d.132 A.D.) – p.236

Marcus Aurelius (Roman emperor – form 161 to 180 A.D.) – p.561[3]

Diocletian (Roman emperor from284 to 305 A.D.) – p.772 - 772[1]

Constantine (Roman emperor (east) from 324 to 337 A.D.) – p.278 – 279 – 585 – 586 - 772[1]

Constantius (Roman emperor (east) from 337 to 361 A.D.) – p.279

Theodocius I (Roman emperor (east) from 379 to 395 A.D.) – p.279 – 586

Theodocius II (Roman emperor (east) from 408 to 450A.D.) – p.280

Marcion (Roman emperor (east) from 450 to 457 A.D.) – p.281

Clovis (King of the Franks – from 481 to 511 A.D.) – p.141

Justinian I (Byzantine emperor from 527 to 565 A.D.) – p.281 – 586

Charlemagne (Roman emperor – from 800 to 814 A.D.) – p.105

Basil I (Byzantine emperor from 867 to 886 A.D.) – p.282

Alfred the Great (king of the West Saxons from 871 to 899) – p.760 – 768

Stephen (King of Hungary from 997 A.D. to 1038) – p.141

Henry II (Holy Roman Emperor from 1014 to 1024) – p.141

Henry VIII (King of England – from 1509 to 1547) – p.769

Elizabeth (Queen of England – from 1558 to 1603) – p.761

James I (King of England from 1603 to 1625) – p.107

Michiel de Ruyter (1607 – 1676 – Dutch admiral) – p.771

Piet Heyn (1577 – 1629 – Dutch admiral) – p.771

Maarten Tromp (1598 – 1653 – Dutch admiral) – p.771

Peter Stuyvesant (last governor of New Netherland from 1646 to 1664) – p.772

Hendrick Hamel (1630 – 1692) – p.771

Louis XIV (the sun king) King of France from 1643 to 1715) – p.216

William III (Prince of Orange 1650 – 1702) – stadholder of the United Provinces of the Netherlands 1672 – 1702 – King of England 1689 – 1702 – p.479[2]

Peter the Great (Czar of Russia – from 1682 to 1725) – p.761

Louis XV King of France from 1715 to 1774) – p.216

Napoleon Bonaparte (emperor of France – from 1804 – 1815) – p.606[N] – 761

Thomas Jefferson (1743 – 1826) – p.276[2] – 479_

Daniel Webster (1782 – 1852 – U.S. statesman) – p.762

James Madison (1751 – 1836) – p.108 – 548[R] – 551

Abraham Lincoln (1809 – 1865) – p.441[R]

Victoria (Queen of England from 1837 to 1901) – p.761 – 130

Kaiser Wilhelm II (emperor of Germany – from 1888 – 1918) – p.184

Nicholas II (Czar of Russia – from 1894 to 1917) – p.287[R] – 216

Rasputin (Russian monk 1871 – 1916) – p.287[R]

Benito Mussolini (premier of Italy – from 1922 to 1943) – p.193[1] – 551 – 606[N]

Hirohito (emperor of Japan from 1926 to 1989) – p.772

Joseph Stalin (Russian chief of state from 1924 to 1953) – p.184 – 306 – 551

Franklin D. Roosevelt (President of the United States from 1933 to 1945) – p.551[N1]

Adolf Hitler (Chancellor of Germany from 1933 to 1945) – p.184 – 193[1] – 216[1] – 297[N1] – 306 – 551 – 551[N1] – 551[1] – 606[N] – 772

Winston Churchill (Prime Minister of England – 1940 – 1945, 1951 – 1955; Nobel prize for literature 1953) – p.370 – 416

General Douglas MacArthur (1880 – 1964) – p.762 – 763

Dwight D. Eisenhower (1890 – 1969) – p.762

John F. Kennedy (1917 – 1963) – p.89 – 362 – 441[R]

Organizations and Groups

Seven root races	p.497
Lumerians	p.497
Atlantheans – Atlantis	p.497 – 498[N2] - 497[3]
Aryan race (fifth root race)	p.497 – 497[1] – 502
Meruvian race (sixth sub-race)	p.502
The Neanderthal(s)	p.499 – 323 – 323[2]
Cro-magnon people	p.499 – 498[N2] – 323[2-3]
Neolithic period	p.499

Primitives (savages) p.464[2] – 496[N4] – 498[R] – 499 – 499[N4] – 503 – 506 – 514 – 521 – 529 – 538 – 538[1] – 539 – 24 – 29

From matriarchy to patriarchy	p.499 – 530
Ancient American people and Hawaiians	p.216
Australians and Polynesians	p.216
North American Indians (redskins)	p.216 – 325 – 421

Mesopotamia – p.636* - Assyrians – p.240 – 565[2] – Samarians – p.241 – 565[2]

Babylon(ians) – p.186 – 240 – 241 – 437[R] – 465[3] – 820

Medes and Persians (Empire) – p.229 – 783

Ancient Egyptians – p.216 – 233[N] – 421 – 421[1] – 545 – 545* - 617 – 635

Pharaohs of Egypt (Kingdom) – p.332 – 821 – 141

Ancient Greeks – p.113[a] – 216 – 233[N] – 421 – 421[2] – 464 – 464[2] – 545*

The Pythagorians – p.618[N1]

Greeks at the time of Plato and Paul – p.51 – 219 – 437^R – 464^2 – 500 – 617 – 706

(Neo)Platonism – p.467 – 500^2 – Plato's thinking and writings – p.82^a –500^2

Aristotelianism – p.467 – Aristotle's thinking and writings – p.82^b - 500^2

Ancient Hebrews – p.112^a – 186 – 233^N – 421 – 421^3 - 464^2

Zoroastrianism – p.186   Parsee – p.219

Indians – p.225^N – Yogis of India – p.113^d – 707; The Yogis – p.423

Yogis and people of the East – p.127 – 169* - p.500^3

Chinese calligraphy – p.748^{N4}; Indian music – p.748^{N4}

Zen practitioners – p.748^8; Japanese tea ceremonies – 748^{N4}

Transcendental meditation – p.748^{N3}; Chi Kung and Tai Chi – p.654

World religions – p.414*

The "less mysteries" (exoteric); the "Greater Mysteries" (esoteric) – p.113^a

Exoteric – non-mystical religions; Confucianism, Judaism, Aristotelianism, Islam, human psychology – p.122

Nominal Christianity – p.219 – 577^N – 711 - 795^1

Esoteric – mystical religions; Taoism, Platonism, Jewish mysticism (Kabbalism), Moslem mysticism (Sufism),

Transpersonal psychology – p.122

Hinduism, Buddhism, and Christian mysticism – p.219 - 748^8 – 745 – 576 are Esoteric in nature – p.122 – 577* - 706

Confucianism – p.41^b – 111^N – 111*, Thinking – p.139, Ethics – p.376*

Taoism – Taoists – p.111^N – 139 – 376* - 386* - 530^3 - 706

The ancient white Brotherhood – p.486^R

Brahman caste system – p.486 – 40* - 57^b – 113^d

The incarnation of Vishnu – p.513

Hinduism – Hindus – p.111 – 113^c – 139 – 219 – 221 – 222 – 225^N – 421 – 497 – 513 – 531 – 617 – 642 – 706 – 753 – 753*

Janism – p.219 – 221; Sikh religion – p.219

Buddhism – Buddhist(s) – p.7 – 14 – 21 – 110 → 121 – 139 – 219 – 221 – 423 – 640^N – 642^{N4} – 706 – 707 – 746 – 746^1 - 748^8

Buddhist discipline – p.98^b – advanced Buddhists – p.534 – 581^{N1} – 711

The appearance of the future Buddha, the Maitreya – p.114

Teachings of the East – 591^{N2} – Maya – glamour and illusion – p.340^{N3}

Esoteric organizations and messages

Theosophical Society – p.370 – 458^N – 756^N; Theosophy – p.501 – 502 – 523

Rosicrucian fellowship – p.370 – 427 – 577* - 756^N; Rosicrucian (Amorc) – p.756^N

841
Sufis(m) – p.577* - 706 - 748[8]
Black people came at age (intellectually and spiritually) – p.216

Ecumenical and Church Councils

Battle of Milvian Bridge – p.585 – Edict of Milan – p.586
[1]Ecumenical Councils and places held – see p.277 → 283 – 586 – 587.
First Ecumenical Council (325 A.D.); Trinitarian Controversy; Arianism – p.586 – 279 – 282; Arian controversy/view – p.278 – 279; Apostles' Creed – p.277; Nicene Creed – p.277 – 278 – 279 – 282; Second Ecumenical Council (381 A.D.); Confirmed Jesus Christ as the second member of the Trinity; rejected by the Sabellians – p.276 – 276[2]; Third Ecumenical Council (431 A.D.); Christological Controversy. Appollinarians (one nature) and Nestorians (two nature) condemned. The latter still exist as Assyrian Christians; was active in S.W. India, Turkistan, Arabia, and China; Fourth Ecumenical Council (451 A.D.); how the two natures of Jesus Christ can be distinguished and united. Monophysitism was condemned. They still exist in the Coptic, Jacobite, and Armenian churches. Fifth Ecumenical Council (553 A.D.); Conclusion: nature of Jesus Christ is unconfused, unaltered, undivided, and inseparable. Sixth Ecumenical Council (680 A.D.): Jesus Christ possessed a divine and human will. Dyothelitism accepted. Monothelitism condemned. Seventh Ecumenical Council (787 A.D) condemned adoptionism, which maintained that Jesus became the adopted Son of God.
Eighth Ecumenical Council (869 A.D.) condemned iconoclasts and the patriarch of Constantinople who did not accept the filoque "and from the son", which was added at the non-Ecumenical Council in 589 A.D. This eventually led to a schism between the eastern and western branches of Christianity (Constantinople and Rome) in 1054 A.D. – p.282 – 478.
In the first and second centuries, groups emerged (p.274 → 276) whom had different views of the above resolutions and that of the church fathers – p.273 – 274. The Ebonites recognized Jesus as the Messiah, who became the elected Son of God at His baptism. Docetism, a Gnostic sect, says that Jesus was a divine being but had not taken on

---

[1] Beliefs, as presented in creeds or statements which were hammered out in the councils, are still used as a criterion in some churches today, if one is a member or not– p.587[N]. Churches who accepted the verdict of a few or many councils–p.277–587.
[2] Tertullian left the church, which became more secular, and became a Montanist – p.274[N]
[3] Today, we find communities of Gnostics in Iran and Iraq, whom are called Mandaneans – p.276.

flesh. The Basilidians celebrated Jesus' baptism at the time when the divine Savior entered Jesus. The Marcions asserted that the Creator was not as good as the God and Father of Jesus. The followers of Cerinthius believe that the (Cosmic) Christ descended upon him at baptism and departed during his crucifixion. This was also the conclusion of Paul of Samosato. Sabellius insisted that the terms "Father", "Son", and "Holy Spirit" applied to the same being and are modes of God expressing Himself (Modalism) – p.277.

As the first eight councils were convoked by Emperors, the following councils and conferences were called by the Roman Catholic Church and by Protestant churches – p.277 – 798.

Roman Catholic Synod in Toulouse, France (1229 A.D.) – p.772

Council of Constance – Germany (1414-1418 A.D.) – p.773

Council of Florence – Italy (1439 A.D.)

Revival of Pagan(ism) – p.140^N – 192 – 192^1 – 373^2 – 178 – 772 – 8 - 784^2

Heretics – heresy – p.192 – 192^4 – 587^N – 588^N – 769 - 769^4

The "Holy Inquisition" began in 1233 A.D. by the Dominicans – p.192^4

Pope Innocent VIII declared, in his 1484 papal bull, that Western Europe was infected with demons and witches – p.192 – 193 – 185 – 75 – 76 – 76^a – 140 – 140*

The witch hunt and inquisition became more intense – p.192 – 75 – 76 – 76^a – 140 – 140* - 140^N – 278^1

Separation of Church and state did not exist – p.587^N – 278^1

The Diet or Council of Worms – Germany 1521 A.D. – p.769^4

Council of Trent – Italy (1545-1563) – p.277 – 767^2 – 104 - 426^3

(An outbreak of diabolic possession occurred in a convent of Loudun, France in 1633 – p.453^2; Protestants and scholastic literalism of the 17th and 18th century – p.797 – 797^2.)

Vatican I – council of the Roman Catholic Church (1869-1870) – p.277 – 788

(19th century liberal theologians – p.310^1; Theologian liberalism – p.798; Darwin's theory of evolution; Social Darwinism – p.798 – 549^{N4}

Fundamentalism – fundamentalists – p.795 – 798 – 588^N – 797^1 – 798^7 – 799)

Niagara Conference of 1895 of Conservative Protestants – p.798

Christian Fundamentals Association was founded in 1919 – p.798

Protestant churches divided into Fundamentalist and Modernist – p.798 - 798^7

(Theologians of the left proclaimed in the 1960s that "God is dead" – p.775 – 193.)

Vatican II – Council of the Roman Catholic Church (1962-1965) – p.277 – 104 – 772^2 - 798^{N1}

Sacred Writings

The "Septuagint" was the oldest Greek version of the Old Testament, as it was translated from Hebrew into Greek in about seventy months in the third century B.C. – p.645 – 767. The "Dead Sea Scrolls", which were found in caves near Qumran in 1947, were written in Hebrew and Aramaic, and dated from c.100 B.C. to c.100 A.D. – p.770^{N1}. In 130 A.D., the four Gospels and the letters of Paul were accepted by the church – p.768[1]. In about 150 A.D., Christians accepted a list of Old Testament books, which were approved by the Jewish Council in Jamnia in about 90 A.D. – without the Apocrypha. In 393 A.D., Catholic bishops approved a list of New and Old Testament books without the Apocryphal of the New Testament – p.768. The Apocrypha books (Jewish writing from the third century B.C. to the first century A.D.) accepted by the church are: Tobit, Judith, Wisdom, Sirach, Baruch, and I and 2 Maccabees, and were incorporated in the Latin translation of Jerome in 405 A.D. – p.767[2] – 768. Other Apocrypha books are: the book of Enoch – the story of the fall of the angels – p.183 – 188 and the book "Vita Adae et Evae", wherein Lucifer refused to bow down to Adam – p.187. A similar story is found in the Talmudic version – p.286 and the Koran – p.187 – 223 – 556[1]. Some Apocryphal books of the New Testament are: Gospel of Peter; Gospel of the Egyptians; Apocryphon of John; Gospel of Thomas – (p.18); Sophia Jesu Christi; Gospel of Truth; Gospel of Philip – (p.334); Gospel of Nicodemus. Some of the writings are Gnostic in origin – p.768[2]. See also other Gnostic writings, which have been found near Nag Hammadi, Egypt in 1946 and were placed there about 400 A.D. The Ten Commandments are the foundation and summary of all the Hebrew laws and customs. Those, in turn, are condensed into two principles: the love toward God and the love toward neighbor – p.248. The commentary of the laws (oral laws) was written down in 200 A.D. and was called "The Mishnah". Together with "The Gemara", it formed "The Talmud" – p.247[5]. Because Jesus was so active in demonstrating His spiritual and psychic powers, the Babylonian Jewish Talmud mentions the execution of Jesus "on the eve of Passover --- because he was practicing sorcery and led Israel astray" – p.475.

Until 1947 when the "Dead Sea Scrolls" were discovered, the 9th and 10th century Masoretic text was the oldest known Hebrew manuscript – p.770^{N1}. Translators, who came after Wycliffe (d.1384), no longer use the Vulgate of Jerome but that of the Greek New Testament text of Erasmus and the Hebrew and Latin Old Testament sources of Martin Luther – p.769. At that time, different Bibles were printed, such as the Geneva Bible (1560), which was used by the

Pilgrim Fathers, Puritans, Shakespeare, John Bunyan, and John Milton – p.770 – 770[1]. As the Douay/Rheims Catholic Bible has been translated in 1610 and extensively used, the King James Version (1611) has been in use for more than 350 years – p.770 – 770[2]; and the Dutch State(n) or Government Bible (1636) became the standard bible for at least 300 years – p.771. Since then, modern translations have been made from many more manuscripts, which were older than the Vatican and Sinaitic Codices, which the 19th century scholars used.

There are many testimonials about the bible from theologians, church fathers, bishops, monks, saints, translators, reformers, philosophers, writers, poets, popes, caretakers, Pilgrim Fathers and Puritans, evangelists, church leaders, pastors, laborers, queens and kings, shopkeepers, emperors, farmers, American presidents, generals, retirees, and many bible readers – see p.758 → 762.

The bible has been a great source of inspiration for painters, sculptors, authors, songwriters, composers, film producers, and other artistic expressions. It has been a source of language, formulation of western concepts of law, and of solving the issues of morality and ethics. It has been, and still is, a guidance and companion of great comfort and consolation for many people – p.756 – 757.

Renaissance and Reformation

The Renaissance (began in the 14th century) – p.7 – 30* - 587* - 769 – 773

Brethren of the Common life – p.105

Protestant Reformation (1517 A.D.) – p.6 – 105 – 106 – 587 – 773 – 797

The Protest(ants) – p.588[R2] – 589[R2] – 617 – 797 – 798[N1] – 799[N2]

Church of England – p.106 – 107; Episcopal churches – p.797 – 798

Anglican churches – p.277 – 588 – 639 – 640

The Lutherans – p.106; Theologians – p.797[2]

The reformed churches – p.6 – 7 – 106 – 107 – 155[R] – 772[N] - 797[2]

Presbyterian churches – p.7 - 184[1]

Anabaptists – p.106 – 113[d]; Baptists – p.6 – 106; Amish – p.106

Mennonites – p.106; Congregationalists – p.184[1]; Hutterites – p.106

"The priesthood of all believers" – p.6 – 589[R2]

The Second Renaissance or Enlightenment – p.193 – 420 – 420* - 500 – 773 – 774

The "Age of Reason" (18th century) – p.193 – 500; Romanticism – p.503[N2]

Philosophers, whom overemphasize the life of the personality – p.773 – 774

The second Religious Reformation – p.774

845

Society of Friends (Quakers) – p.588^{R2} – 711^1 – 774; Deism – p.773
Swedenborgian(ism) – p.404 – 756^N; Methodism – p.774
Unitarianism – p.276^2; Unitarians – p.588^{R2} – Universalism – p.276^2
Unitarian Universalist Association (1961) – p.276^2; The Shakers – p.130
Modern Spiritualism – p.193^2 – 756^N; Society for Psychical Research – p.445 – 473 – 473^3
Mormons – p.278^N – 370 – 756^N; Bahai faith – p.756^N
Christian Science – p.271^R – 278^N – 756^N – 724^2; Religious Science – p.756^N
Jehovah's Witness – p.278^N – 465^{N2} – 756^N
<u>The Third Renaissance</u>
Secular humanism; Communism – p.296 – 289^1 – 194 – 194^4 – 774
<u>The third Reformation</u>
The Kingdom of God – p.774 (Rev. 21:3)
The world will be ruled by God (as the brain, and His Will is conveyed through the Universal Christ – central nervous system –) to all people of the world – p.699 – 700 – 295^N
They will then cooperate like the cells and organs of the body – p.407^1 – 215 – 289 – 294

The Story of the Pilgrim Fathers and Democracy

Calvinism – Calvinists – p.107 – 108 – 109 – 7 – 84^c – 658^c
Calvinist Theocracy of Geneva – p.276^2
Calvinist Theology – p.318 – Calvinistic "work ethic" – p.318 – 318^N
Puritanism – Puritans – p.107 – 7 – 770^1 – 761 – 759 – 378 – 478
^{1}Separatists – p.107; Amsterdam – p.107; Leiden Congregation – p.107 – 483^N
^{2}Pilgrim(s) Fathers – p.107 – 7 – 770^1 – 761 – 759 – 734^N – 318^N – 378 – 478 – Youth – p.483
Mayflower, Mayflower Compact, Plymouth Rock – p.107 (1620)
Plymouth – p.483^N – 478 – Colony – p.108 – 483 – Bay Colony – p.483^N
New England – p.761
New Canaan – The promised land of America – p.761
New Amsterdam (New York) – p.107 – 771 – A heaven for the Huguenots – p.107
The Dutch in New Netherland – p.761 – 771 (1625)

---

^{1} At that time, the "Divine Right of kings" was being misused – p.107* - 770^1.
^{2} At the time the Pilgrim Fathers sojourned in Holland, there was a twelve-year truce with Spain. At that time, Holland was blessed with the "Golden Age" – p.107 – 108 – 130 – 761^1 – 771.

They all had a sense of destiny and to fulfill a destiny – p.108 – 761 – 130 to become a "nation under God" – p.761 – "So help me God" – p.712[1].

On the "Great Seal" is inscribed the phrase "Annuit Coeptus", God has favored our undertaking, which is our destiny – p.761[t] - 643.

The Foundation of Democracy was laid, when the Pilgrims signed the "Mayflower Compact" to govern themselves, and the Puritans made a petition for the "rights of individuals" – p.107. This is the best possible world – p.109 – 194[3] – 295[N] – 357[N2] – 479. The principles of democracy should, however, not be abused – p.551 – 184[1] – 294. Some governments are reasonably good – p.545[N1], and others are not so good – p.364[R] – 383[N] – 379[2], while a few of them have been destructive – p.287[R]. The latter may become like the beast in Rev. Ch. 13 – p.331 – 107 – 108 – 109 – 184 – and become responsible for the downfall of civilization – p.13 – 216 – 137 – 287[R]. They completely lost God's protection – p.137 – 240 – 477 – 820 – 141 – 660[b] – 476 – 108[a] and came under foreign rule after ignoring the many emergency wake-up calls – p.559[N3].

Human Constitution and Psychological Behavior

The task of psychology (and philosophy) is to teach and to deal with the human personality, but also with the Soul – p.296.

Scientific materialism of behavior	(the first force)
p.519[N] Freudian psychoanalysis	(the second force)
Humanistic psychology	(the third force)
The Transpersonal	(the fourth force)

The psychoanalytical theory of Sigmund Freud – p.82

The personality consists of Id (instinct), ego, and superego.

Trichotomists maintain that a human being consists of <u>body</u>, <u>soul</u> (human spirit – ego), and <u>Divine Spirit</u> or Soul. Dichotomists maintain that the former consists of body and Soul. The constitution was changed at the fourth Council of Constantinople (8th ecumenical) when church leaders accepted the idea that humans are made up of <u>Body</u> and <u>Soul</u> (Divine Spirit) – p.82 – 706.

What the Freudian school teaches – p.530 – 531

What Alfred Adler teaches – p.531

What the Jungian school teaches – p.148 – 149 – 531 – 596[N1]

Jungian analysts say that the newly-formed Christ Spirit is an archetype – p.16.

Human psychology is a non-mystical organization – p.122

Methods used by psychologists to resolve conflicts in people's lives – p.340[N2]

Psychologists' and psychiatrists' main interest today is the psychological health of the personality or human spirit, the intellect, emotion and desire (will), while transpersonal psychology's principal concern is the well-being and growth of the Divine Spirit or Soul – p.706.

Transpersonal psychologists speak about realizing the Self – p.113[d] – 122.

Methods used are: individuation – p.519 – 654 – 707 and psycho-synthesis. When Jesus cast out demons; this was for real, not simply a case of neurosis, psychosis, schizophrenia, and/or dissociative personality, as psychiatrists today like to call it – p.180 – 180[3] and p.221 – 222. **REMARK**: They should turn over "strange" behavior to professionals whom are practicing parapsychology and transpersonal psychology – p.452[6] – 453 – 462 – 462[5] – 182.

Wars Being Fought Between Relative Good and Evil Forces

The "Sons of Light" and the "Sons of Darkness" – p.678 – 47_

Ahura Mazda versus Ahra Mainyu – p.187

War of revenge: Greece versus Persia – p.216

Maccabean revolt: Maccabees versus the Syrian king – p.242[N] – 252

Revolutionary War: America versus England – p.443[N1]

Civil War: The North versus the South – p.552[N2]

French Revolution – p.216

Capitalism – Capitalists – p.194 – 317 – 317[2] – 318 – 552 – 552[N1]

Communist revolution – p.216 – October revolution of 1917 – p.287

Communism – Communists – p.184 – 194 – 194[4] – 287 – 289[1] – 317[2] – 551 – 552[N1] – 552[N3] – 772 – 774

church leaders chosen by Communist leaders – p.101

anti-Communism – p.551

former Communist countries – p.755[*]

wars justified as Holy Wars by religious people;

Nazism by Hitler and Communism by Stalin – p.306

Those counterfeit governments seem to be so real that "the whole earth followed the beast with wonder" (Rev. 13:3-4) – p.184

First World War – p.184 – 194 – 216[1] - 310[1]

Fascism – p.552[N1] – 704[*] - movement – p.193[1]

National Socialism – Nazi party – p.193[1]

anti-Christ nation of Germany – p.216

Japanese militarists encourage people to worship Hirohito – p.772

Second World War – p.193[1] – 194 – 378 – 551

World War II concentration camp – p.475

Third World War (cold) – p.194

Establishment of the modern state of Israel in 1948 – p.245[R]

Bibliography

Akashic records - 557[3]

Sacred Writings of the Hindus – p.513

Vedas and Upanishads – p.525 – 525* - 523

Bhagavad – Gita – p.525*

Yoga sudras of Patanjali – p.525*

The Kama Sutra – p.485

Odyssey (a Greek writing) – p.464

Writings of Aristotle – p.82 – 82[b]

Timaes and Critias by Plato – p.497[3]

The Republic by Plato – p.391

Plato's Writings – p.82 – 82[a]

"The Annals" by Tacitus – p.270[R]

The letters of Paul – p.264

The Four Gospels – p.264

Bible translations – p.769 – 770

Gnostic teachings – p.275[N] – 276

Book IV by Origin – p.800[3]

Contra Celsum by Origin – p.191 – 192

Teachings of Augustine – p.500[2]

"The City of God" by Augustine – p.105 – 692[a]

"Confessions" by Augustine – p.756

"Inferno" by Dante – p.181

"The Imitation of Christ" by Thomas A. Kempis – p.105

"Malleus Maleficarum" by Heinrich Kramer and James Sprenger – p.76[a] – 140

"Spiritual Exercises" by Ignatius Loyola – p.756

"Institutes" by Calvin – p.756

"Romeo and Juliet" – play by Shakespeare – p.3

"The Augustinus" by Jansenius Cornelius – p.288[N1]

"Paradise Lost" by Milton – p.181

"The Practice of the Presence of God" by Brother Lawrence – p.367

"Journal" by George Fox – p.756

"The Pilgrim's Progress" by John Bunyan – p.405 – 759

"Heaven and its Wonders and Hell" by Emanuel Swedenborg – p.404*

"L'Homme Machine" by Offray de Lamette – p.420

"Wealth of Nations" by Adam Smith – p.194[3]

"The Essence of Christianity" by Ludwig Feuerbach – p.774

"Life of Jesus" by D.F. Straus – p.774

"Tristan and Isolde" (medieval legend) sung in Richard Wagner's opera – p.3 – 3[b]

"The Lowly Life and Bitter Passion of our Lord Jesus Christ and His Blessed Mother" by Catherine Emmerich – p.223 – 224

"Uncle Tom's Cabin" by Harriet Beecher Stowe – p.223

"The Communist Manifesto" by Karl Marx – p.194[4] – 774

"Brothers Karamazov" by Dostoevsky – p.181

"The Varieties of Religious Experience" by William James – p.661

"The Strange Case of Dr. Jekyll and Mr. Hyde" by R.L. Stevenson – p.223

"Het land aan gene zyde" (The land on the other side) by Wylen E. M. van Yssendyk – p.422[3]

"Cosmo Conception" by Max Heindel – p.427[2]

"Thirty Years among the Dead" by Carl A. Wickland – p.452

"Life in the World Unseen" by Anthony Borgia – p.404[*] - 427[N2] - 458[7]

"Old Straight Tracks" by Watkins – p.526[†]

"Mein Kamph" by Adolf Hitler – p.772

"The Greatest Book Ever Written" by Fulton Oursler – p.760

"The Divine Principles" by Young Oon Kim (1963) – p.33[a] – 78[a] - 646[1]

"New Age Frontier" Sept. 1964 – p.288

"New Age Frontier" Sept. 1965 – p.568

"Life after Life" by Raymond A. Moody, Jr. – p.449

Report from Pim van Lommel in the medical journal "The Lancet" – p.449[1] and in "Spirituality and Health" magazine Oct. 2003 – p.449[1]

"Childbirth without Fear" by Grantly Dick Read – p.312[1]

"Psycho-synthesis" by Roberto Assagioli – p.77 – 77[*]

"The Power of Positive Thinking" by Norman Vincent Peale – p.155[R]

"The Ancient Secret of the Fountain of Youth" by Peter Kelder – p.384[N]

"The Faith of the Pilgrims" by R.N. Bartlett – p.483 – 483[N]

"Anna: Woman of Miracles" by Carol Haenni and Vivian van Wick – p.261[1]

Book titles about spiritual development and aging – see p.396

Selected Sayings

God is not a distant, impersonal being, and when humans suffer, they also suffer as heart-broken Parents for their lonely and lost children whom are seeking for Them (p.31[*] - 30 – 31 – 32 – 584 – 715). There is an essential emptiness in every life without Christ – p.564. God loves me and wants to use me as an instrument of peace, just as I am – p.398.

The core of goodness, which you feel within your being, is Me. – p.564[R]

The Bible is good; God within us is better – p.577 – 588[N] – 786[N1]

"The Kingdom of God is within you" (Luke 17:21) – p.577.

Perfection is when you are able to hear God "speak" everywhere, through people, nature, and happenings – p.419.

By being nice and friendly to someone, you are making this person happy. Then God, who as a Spark resides within that person, will be happy. He, therefore, is not a respecter of persons, does not favor one person over another, and would not like to see anyone, in whom He has His dwelling, miserable – p.419 – 582^{N4} – 729*. When God helps us, He also helps anybody else at the same time – p.532^{N3} – 212^N – 727 – 729 – 729* - 93^N – 96.

So as the air is all about us and in us, so is God everywhere – p.419.

"Closer is He than breathing and nearer than hands and feet" (Tennyson) – p.419.

"God is never more than a prayer away – p.419 – 739.

The family that prays together stays together – p.55 – 254 – 711 – 739.

Prayer brings in movement the hand, who rules the universe – p.739.

When people pray things happen, that would not otherwise happen – p.739.

As it is almost impossible to have a personal audience with an earthly king, it is however possible to have a daily opportunity to make a petition to the Creator, Sustainer, and Ruler of the universe (Ps. 8:3-5) – p.726.

Prayer is good medicine – p.718.

We should liberate God within ourselves and others – p.564^R.

Two people cannot hate each other if they both love God – p.416.

The person who looks up to God rarely looks down on people – p.416.

God helps those that help themselves – p.354 – p.209.

*God gives us the almonds. But we have to crack them – p.354.

Do your best; then God will do the rest – p.354.

God cares for people through people – p.416.

God's love is action through us – p.532^{N3}.

"Love in your heart is not put there to stay – love is not love until you give it away" – p.94.

The work God does through me is true service – p.355.

Find people's needs and fill them, not only economically but also emotionally, mentally, and spiritually – p.556^R.

An individual's true wealth is the good he does in the world. When we serve God, then God will look after all our material needs – p.209.

For what you give away to others: your love, time, money, labor, knowledge, power, etc., is what is really your own – p.209.

By living in harmony with the universe, you go with the flow and everything is therefore going your way – p.698 – 9 – 414^R.

---

* Dutch saying. See also p.354 – 355.

"If you divorce religion from education you produce a race of clever devils" (The Duke of Wellington) – p.297[N2].

Teachers should not only educate the personality – physical, emotional, mental – (human spirit) but also the development of the Divine Spirit – p.296.

Libraries are nourishment for the psychic (human spirit) and the Soul (Divine Spirit) – p.564[R].

In Western society, those whom are rich are usually highly evaluated, while those whom are rich in Spirit are not – p.555[N4].

God shocked the world with a babe, not a bomb – p.417.

The story of Jesus' birth and death is also our own story of spiritual growth – p.270[N] – 793[N2].

The real story of the Bible is about us, every man and every woman in their struggle to reach moral and spiritual maturity – p.806.

"If Jesus is not driving – you are just spinning your wheels" – p.548[N].

*What is the use of running when you are not on the right road? – p.548

"Lost one human family, missing the last 6000 (biblical) years, last seen wandering in the dark, is in the habit of fighting and displaying tendencies toward self-destruction" (New Age Frontier) – p.291 – 292.

"Every civilization has within it the seed of its own destruction" – p.287[R].

"If people do not learn, they are condemned to repeat it" (Santayana) – p.205[1] – 377[N1].

Individuals, families, organizations, and whole nations may get an emergency wake-up call – p.559[N3].

"The essence of government is power – power lodged as it must be in human hands will ever be liable to abuse" (James Madison) – p.108 – 551 – 548[R].

The ultimate power of the state should not repose in any man or body of men, but in a body of laws called the constitution – p.184[1].

"Ask not what you country can do for you, but what you can do for your country" (John F. Kennedy) – p.89 – 362.

[1]It is a pleasure to suffer and to have endured, so that our nation can be liberated and cured – p.222.

The blood of martyrs is the seed of the church – p.191 – 214[1].

By not giving anything to society, the universe cooperates perfectly by not returning anything to them – p.210.

If anyone will not work, let him not eat (2 Thess. 3:10) – p.210.

Crime does not pay – p.210.

---

* American pioneer proverbs
[1] has been said by a Dutchman

[2]When you become a saint, you stand against immorality; when you become a man of ethics, you are against criminals.

[3]"The one who digs a hole for another falls in that same hole"; "the one who throws a stone to heaven gets it back on his/her own head" – p.207.

[4]"Doing an injury puts you below your enemy; revenging one makes you but even with him; forgiving sets you above them" – 695[N].

[5]Reputation is what you are in the light; character is what you are in the dark – p.557.

[6]Die slapen onder het zelfde deken, krygen dezelfde streken" (The ones whom are sleeping under the same blanket will acquire the same tricks) – p.57.

Satan is not as black as he is painted. In fact, he is more like us that we care to admit – p.416.

The beauty of women, which shines from their Soul, is their own doing, while the physical beauty in their youth is given to them – p.399[2].

"When the outer personality is growing older, the inner personality is becoming ever beautiful and wiser" – p.373.

"When physical beauty wanes, spiritual beauty gains" – p.146 – 373. (See also II Cor. 4:16 – p.392.)

"We should be true to ourselves" (Shakespeare) – p.175[N].

A life is well lived on earth when one gains valuable experiences – p.556[R].

The crisis brought the best and the worst out of people – p.564[R].

"In spite of everything, I still believe that people are good at heart" (Anne Frank) – p.564[R].

Additional sayings see – p.564 – 391→393 – 416 – 417 – 419 – 738 – 739 – 209 – 49*.

Dictionaries and Encyclopedias

For a thorough study of the Bible, the following study aids are to be used – Scripture Concordances – Bible Dictionaries, Bible Hand Books, Atlases, Commentaries – p.766.

Encyclopedia of Catholicism – p.167 – 336

General Editor R.P. McBrien Harper Collins San Francisco – 1995

---

[2] American pioneer proverb

[3] Dutch saying

[4] [-5]American pioneer proverb

[6] Dutch saying

The Maryknoll Catholic Dictionary – p.271 – 336
　　　　Editor A.J. Nevins, M.N. – Dimension Books Wilkes Barre, PA – 1965
A Basic Catholic Dictionary – p.85 – 152 – 271
　　　　D.L. Lowery, C.SS.R Liguori Publications Liguori, MO – 1985
The New International Dictionary of the Christian Church – p.632[1]
　　　　General Editor J.D. Douglas Zondervan Publishing House Grand Rapids – 1981
Bible Dictionary and Concordance – p.271
　　　　C.F. Pfeiffer Baker Book House – 1988
The Oxford Dictionary of World Religion – p.336
　　　　Edited by John Bowker Oxford University Press – 1997
The Encyclopedia of Religion – p.85
　　　　Editor in Chief Mircea Eliade MacMillan Company New York – 1987
Dictionary of Philosophy and Religion – p.371[2]
　　　　William C. Reese – Humanities Press N.J. – 1980
The Encyclopedia of Parapsychology – p.224
　　　　Arthur Berger Paragon House – 1991
The Encyclopedia of Psychic Science – p.474[5]
　　　　Nandor Fodor University Books – 1974
The Readers Digest Great Encyclopedia Dictionary – p.85 – 271
　　　　Managing Editor Sidney /Landau
The Readers Digest Dictionary 1991 – p.152 – 371[2] – 435 - 622[2]
The Random House College Dictionary – p.85
　　　　Editor Jess Stein – 1984
The Webster New World Dictionary – p.85 - 371[2]
　　　　Third College Edition New York – 1988
The Merriam Webster Dictionary – p.85 – 132 – 271
　　　　Published in 2004

Diagrams – Drawings, Sketches and Pictures

Drawings The Expulsion from Eden	}	front and
The Prodigal Son	}	inner page
Symbol		on backflap

Author's biography and picture – inside backflap
And photograph in three stages of growth – p.656[c]
Diagram – different stages of development – p.700
　　　　For a brief explanation see p.517.
Diagram – The Order of Creation – p.78
Sketch of Divine Spirit, Good/Evil and Evil Personalities – p.84
Sketch of God and satan-directed life – p.657 – 658
The Inner You (drawing) – p.175

The Creation, Deviation and Restoration

God created the cosmos out of chaos, by creating first the outer, then the inner, and pervaded everything with His Consciousness in different modification – p.323 – 694 – 322 – 3221. He created order out of disorder and from simple to complex – p.697 – XVI – 323 – 496; as Creator, Master Builder, Organizer, Lawmaker, and Creative Artist – p.323 – 600.

God is everywhere – p.419 – 24 – 445 – 677, and continually reveals Himself, through nature, universal law and reason (His outer Self), our conscience and intuition; revelations, visions, dreams, living persons, spiritual teachers, masters from the spirit world, angels, Scriptures, answered prayer, and everyday experiences (His inner Self) – p.776 – 777 – 727 – 578 – 744[N4] – 684 – 685 – 561. God the Creator can be compared to the trunk of a tree – p.270, a rock – p.247[3], and the sun – p.418 – 98. God is Spirit – p.270[*]; and His names and functions are – p.251 – 252 – 271 – 272 – 506 - 261[2]; and He has the following character and qualities, p.31 – 271 – 777 – 818. God is Love, Wisdom, and Energy – p.91[*] - 93→98 – 319 – 591[N6] – 322[1]; and has feelings – p.31[*].

REMARK: Everything God made was original, and He created everything in potentiality, doing the greater part of the creation – p.325[N2], and let human beings as co-creators do the most rewarding work – p.128 – 323 – 573 – 786 – 165 – 743 – 743[3] – 394[3] – 803[N2]. Humans are endowed with the gift of creativity, not only to create themselves morally and intellectually but also spiritually in the image of God – p.618 – 619. By using our ability to create, we can create things on earth and spirit world – p.457 – 457[5] – 458 – 458[6] – 134.

As God "breathed" into humans, and they became spiritually alive, humans, in turn, "breathed" into the creation, making them more alive psychically by truly loving them – p.324[6] – 324 – 697 – 240[*] - 321[N] – 326 – 289[R]. See also 126→130.

NOTE: The view of nature (before the scientific revolution) was, for many people, that of an enchanted world, rocks , mountains, trees, and clouds which were all seen as wondrously alive – p.325 – 326[2] – 192[2] – 20. After the revolution, they began to live a life independent of nature – p.325 – 30. The atmosphere of the earth and the growth of crops are effected by human consciousness – p.315 – 315[2].

God prepared the earth for millions of years – p.322, according to His model or archetype of a human being – p.320 – 18, and created in "six days" or in six epochs of time – p.800[1] – 514[1] – 514 – 797; the chaos of substance into the world of form, and created light, vegetation, animals, and humans – p.322; in the "Garden of Eden" – p.638[2] – 778[N] – 42 – 139* – 66 – 33 – 84 – 6 – 246 – 287 – 44 – 261 – 262. "The Lord God formed man (and animals) of the dust from the ground" – p.80 – 288[N2]; "and breathed into his nostrils the breath of life" (Gen. 2:7) – p.79 – 697 – 697* - 324[6]. Humans as the masterpiece of His creation – p.323 (as His representatives – p.102 – 148), were created in [1]the likeness or image of God, who is male and female – p.78 – 319 – 342 – 18 – 18[b] – 26 – 496; The universe (as the body of God – p.78) was created in the image of humanity in its masculine and feminine elements (yang and yin) – p.78 – 79 – 319 – 320 – 342 – 18 – 18[b]. In addition, a human being (like animals, plants, and minerals) consist of an internal nature and is the microcosm of the universe the macrocosm – p.18 – 26 – 26[a] – 39 – 78 – 89 – 94* - 319[N] – 320[N] – 321[N] - 322[N] – 454 – 526[N] – 564[N] – 564; wherein and inherent, especially in humans, we find His Divine Spark – p.20 – 28* - 71 – 77 – 112[c] – 195 – 306* - 314 – 316 – 497 – 498[N1] – 507[3] – 512 – 560 – 561 – 578[4] – 625[3] – 659 – 659[a], which can be heard as a "still small voice" (1 Kings Ch. 19) – p.814* - 592 – 712[R] – 747 – 750. With the help of the [2]angels, human beings can fulfill the main purpose of living on earth. That is, to be "fruitful (grow to maturity in the image of God), multiply, and fill the earth and subdue it" (Gen. 1:28) – p.322 – 34[b] – 54 – 119 – 148 – 757*. Thus, not only to be mature in one's integrated personality but also in one's Divine Spirit – p.34[b], which has been developing from the Divine Spark – p.128 – 730*. Life on earth is a training ground to develop valuable Soul qualities – p.220[2]; to achieve harmony with cosmic laws – p.220, because the consequences of mistakes are more severe than in the spirit world – p.359. Life on earth is also a testing ground of the validity of one's belief or concept – p.371[2], and its experiences, and suffering is much more valuable than to know by object lesson or speech – p.560 – 569[N]. By digesting and assimilating life experiences into their inner selves, individuals are building their character – p.569 – 560. The character will also develop when they actually give – p.363[N2] – 364[N2] – 360. Through marriage, and especially by taking care of children, individuals become less selfish, especially when they also serve the community, country, and world – p.364 – 364[2]. Otherwise, it is easy to become egocentric – p.364 – 363[N1] – 673* - 295 – 309. See further

---

[1] God loves people because they are created in their likeness. Humans feel familiar with and are attracted to the creation because it reflects them externally and internally – p.319, with its positive and negative polarities, so that energy can flow between the poles – p.18[c] – 530[3] – and a third object is created – p.617 – 618[N1] – 610; as soon as the opposite attractions are united. A "decent" of power also occurs – p.26. Humans are able to create cars and other things in their image – p.548[N] – 324 – 236 – 406→414.

[2] Angels are neither male nor female – p.285 – 286[R] – 299[1] – 178*; are servants – p.187 – 286 – 299 – 328[2] – 331[4] – 335; mediators, guides, and teachers – p.112[a]; messengers – p.223; to enforce the law and banish – p.214; guardian and archangels – p.630[1] – 637 – 631; test humans – p.648[1]; and those who materialize – p.468→474.

"The Different Aspects of Service" – p.353→369 and character of an unselfish person – p.309 – 363.

To <u>subdue</u> it is to have dominion over the sea, air, and earth, and to be responsible for the creation; to cultivate it and to take care of it – p.319 (not domination p.319²); and to become qualified Lords over the creation – p.619 – 564¹; by taking their rightful position as steward – p.325 – 326 – 319², as Adam did – p.287.

Animal Kingdom – p.30 – 33 – 33ᶜ - 78→81 – 123 – 177 – 178 – 182 – 218 – 226 – 226¹ – 289ᴺ – 289ᴿ – 318 – 318⁴ – 319² – 320ᴺ – 321ᴺ – 323 – 324 – 325 – 325ᴿ – 434ᴺ⁷ – 443 – 456ᴺ³ – 456ᴿ – 491 – 499ᴺ⁴ – 509ᴺ² – 524ᴺ – 527¹ – 529 – 539 – 539² – 540* - 544ᴺ¹ – 554 – 564 – 564¹ – 593 – 594ᴺ¹ – 597ᴺ² – 598 – 618 – 619 – 694 – 697 – 697* - 700 – 727
Differences between animals and humans – p.123 – 445⁴ – 321ᴺ – 322ᴺ – 544ᴺ¹ – 618¹ – 700 – 78→81 – 79ᴺ
Plant Kingdom – p.XV – 28 – 30 – 41 – 78→81 – 96 – 166² – 211 – 213 – 218 – 270* - 289 – 306¹ – 319¹ – 320ᴺ – 322 – 324 – 374 – 374ᴿ – 380⁴ – 388 – 397 – 409ᴿ – 410ᴿ – 411ᴿ – 418 – 418ᴿ – 419 – 520 – 524ᴺ – 564¹ – 564 – 592ᴺ² – 594ᴺ¹ – 597ᴺ² – 598 – 618 – 656 – 694 – 694* - 697 – 700 – 727 – 746ᴺ² – 747ᴺ²
Mineral Kingdom – p.30 – 78→81 – 218 – 226 – 226² – 288ᴺ² – 319¹ – 320ᴺ – 321ᴺ – 322 – 324 – 324⁵ – 324⁶ – 325 – 325ᴿ – 564¹ – 592ᴺ² – 694 – 697 – 700 – 727 – 746ᴺ²

The law of evolution is the unfolding or a rolling out of much of the creation – p.498ᴺ¹. As evolution is upwards, it also moves in cycles, the next cycle at a higher level than the one before – p.597ᴺ². When species evolve, we see more varieties, not only in form but also in their inner expressions – p.522. It is the law of nature that when a seed, animal, or human is ripe (mature) in one stage of development, it should move to the next; otherwise, it will decay or degenerate – p.512ᴺ – 497¹ – 497* – 216 – 262ᴺ. Your hunger for higher and spiritual things is part and parcel of the universal law of evolution – p.557². Because of discontent, a higher faculty is being awakened. He or she has become curious about the how and why of things – p.544. Individuals may, at times, be forced by the law of evolution to break open their egos, which become rigid and inflexible – p.558ᴿ. Families, organizations, and nations may get their wake-up call to refocus their life on the attainment of spirituality – p.559ᴺ³.

There is a certain hierarchical order in the creation and human society which should be maintàined and respected in order to prevent confusion, disorder, chaos, and destruction – p.329 – 329* - 331 – 331⁶ – 332 – 332ᴺ – 135. According to the order of creation, one man should marry one woman, when they are, if possible, mature physically, emotionally, mentally, and spiritually – p.5 – 6 – 534ᴺ² - 482→484. It is God's plan for pollination or sexual relation to occur, when the male and female plants and humans are both mature and ready – p.306¹.

Adam and Eve were the first human pair whom had the potential to become divine or reach spiritual maturity – p.71 – 701#³ – 299 – 798⁵ – 665 – XVIᴿ. Other people living at that time (Cain found himself a wife among the existing tribes) did not have this potential – p.665* – 807¹. In Genesis Chapter Two, we find Adam, who was living the life of the pure personality, very busy giving names to the animals in the field – p.287 – 287¹ – 697*. However, Adam followed Eve (who was deceived and seduced by satan – symbolized as the serpent – p.1 – 177 – 178 – 290 – 562¹), and they both were expelled from the "Garden of Eden" after they ate of the symbolic fruit – p.2 – 76 – 252 – 260 –

$290 - 306^1 - 411^R - 806$, from the "Tree of the Knowledge of Good and Evil" – p.XVI^R – 84 – 139 – 657 – 701$^{\#3}$ – etc.; and started living the life of the good and evil personality, outside the "Garden". See the story of the fall of Adam and Eve – p.1 – 2 – 3 – 139 – 252 – 260 – 285→335 – 665 – 677 – 701 – 806. Entrance to the Tree of Life (Divine Life) – p.33 – 44 – 76 – 84 – 287 – 288 – 657 – etc.; was blocked by the cherubim and the flaming sword – p.42 – 326 – 327. They felt ashamed and guilty of what they had done and covered their lower parts with fig leaves – p.83 - 152→157 – 307 – 308 – 350 – 540^{N2}. The Divine Spark within the pair could not blossom – p.195 – 128, and they died spiritually because of the lack of spiritual nourishment from their Heavenly Parents – p.195 – 290^2 - 302→305 – 3 – 192^4 – 285^N – 375 – 422^2 – 546 – 154. Adam lost moral authority and power and began to dislike his deceived mate – p.139 – 312 – 313; and he never became Lord of the creation – p.29 – 30 – 313→317. God, who experienced brief parenthood towards Adam and Eve – p.305^{N1} – 313 – 314, were [1]heart-broken when they saw that their most precious children wanted to have nothing to do with them anymore. They cried out, "Where are you?" (Gen. 3:9) – p.30 – 304 – 305^{N1} – 313 – 314 – 584 – 688 – 689. Thereafter, Adam blamed Eve and Eve blamed the serpent (Lucifer) – p.310 – 311 - 308^1. The moment Adam and Eve gave up their personal relationship with the Creator by refusing to live according to His plan or principles of creation, they became "afraid" because they lost the feeling of security, and fear of living came about – p.84 – 305 – 310^2 – 313. By uniting with satan and living according to his plan or the pseudo, or satanic principles, establishing his pseudo-kingdom – p.31 – 84 – 184 – 193, which is an imitation of God's Kingdom. Satan attempted to take over the place of God and became her god, which is the sin of [2]pride – p.1 – 72→74 – 72* - 252 – 296 – 330 – 331 – 331^5, and that she will be like God knowing good and evil – p.1 – 305. Like God, Eve (and Adam) can now make their own rules of moral conduct. Because this rebellious attitude is deeply embedded in the human psyche, humans have a strong tendency of wanting to decide what is right or wrong (good or evil) and to judge others of their moral behavior – p.1 – 170 – 195^3 – 246 – 252 – 290 – 291 – 305 – 306 – 307 – 311* - 574 – 23. Sexual permission is being rationalized and wars justified – p.305 – 306. Individuals try to improve on God's design – p.297^{N1} – and are implementing their own plan of improving society – p.329 – 330. Atheists do not want God to exist and like to take the place of God, making all the rules for the conduct of humans – p.296 – 289^1 – 329 – 330 – 346 – 347; to play God and seeking to be their own god – p.75 – 193→196 – 196^1 – 252 – 552 – 552^1 – 553 – 553^2 - 703→705. The descendants of Adam and Eve inherited the spirit of rebellion and hostility towards God and began to curse and swear – p.84 – 305 – 253 – 346 – 693, and thus condemn themselves outside the "Garden of Eden".

---

[1] God expressed their suffering in the Old and New Testaments – p.30→32 – 304 – 305^{N1} – 313 – 314 – 584 – 688 – 689.

[2] Pride is also the beginning of the worship of false gods and creatures – p.1 – 75 – 173 – 178 – 180^N – 180^2 – 185 – 186 – 214 – 242^N – 249 – 251 – 252 – 264 – 421 – 422^3 – 499 – 499* - 499^N – 506 – 506^1 – 521 – 538 – 538^1 – 541 – 5 8 5 – 612 – 617 – 659 – 678^a – 711 – 753* - 784 – 784^1 – 815.

Being evil-minded, they became more selfish – p.195^2 – 673 – 673* - 309 – 309^1 – 6 – 3 – 9 – 10 – 97. Influenced by evil desires, they became more greedy – p.119^c – 164 – 165 – 166 – 308 – 58 – 58* - 97 – 342, and sexual desires became impure and lustful – p.119 – 119^c – 348 - 85$\rightarrow$87 – 1$\rightarrow$10 – 13 – 14 – 97 – 132$\rightarrow$138 – 197; Lucifer, Eve, and Adam wanted to "love" each other freely without restriction and responsibility – free "love" and free sex came about – p.308 – 309. Natural love turned to selfish love (lust), original desire to selfish desire (greed), and freedom to selfish freedom without responsibility (license) – p.33* - 58 – 108 – 108^a – 109 – 154 – 173 – 308 – 498 – 498* - 546^1 – 689 – 807. As Eve mistrusted God's life-giving Word and listened to the hollow word of satan (he put doubt in God's Word by saying, "Did God (really) say" – p.1 – 639* - 772^N); many people today still do not trust God's Word and each other – p.308^2. Through the fall, humans lost^{1}Truth and, thus, the purpose and direction of life, whereby their life was no longer meaningful – p.316 – 557.

Every human being has inherited, from his/her ancestors, the original sin that he or she tries to ^{2}suppress, hide, and cover up – p.285$\rightarrow$297 – 294 – 301 – 337 – 395^5 – 495^1 – 660^c – 661 – 662 – 665 – 809^1. How to remove our fallen nature or original sin – p.327$\rightarrow$335 – 574 – 574^3 – 575 – 575^{5,} and on a greater level – p.174^R. Purifying the personality in exoteric religion and in Old Testament times – p.663 – 373^2 – 660; by finding an Abel-type person – p.684 – 335; submit to our Divine Self – p.335^N – 660 – 662 - 662† - 23; by scolding – p.335^N – 688* - 293; and by trials and temptation sent by God – p.205 – 205^1 – 203 – 676 – 677 – 410^R – 48 – 574^4 – 168, and by satan- p.187 – 188 – 188^N – 676 – 817 – 817*.

---

^{1} In this fallen world, everything is upside down; that which has real value is despised and rejected, such as Truth, while that which has no eternal value is given first place, such as material possessions – p.314. Wisdom becomes foolishness and cunning – peace becomes a false peace, when being obedient to the good/evil ruler. Joy becomes pseudo-happiness and satanic pleasures – p.342*; their smile is wooden, superficial and false – p.288*.

Your dissatisfaction or discontent causes you to start searching for the nuggets of Truth – p.557 – 557^2 – 558 – 511^4 – 512^N. Restoration of truth – p.495^2 – "What is Truth?" Pilate asked Jesus – p.567 – philosophical truth – p.518 – 559 – become a Truth body – p.567. Questions asked – p.XV – XVII – 558 – 511^4 – 659 – 757 – 758 – 116 – 447 – 544 – 394 about the Bible – p.799^{N4} – 787.

^{2} Mask – p.288 – 288* - 708 – 702$^{#4}$ – 28 – 83 – 145 – 170 – 174 – 174* - 175 – 291 – 346† - 547 – 549. Young children do not wear masks – p.175 – 661 – till they learn to put one on – p.63.

People who have a double mind or standard – p.286^1 – 659 have almost compulsive desire for the forbidden – p.639* because they are in general more inclined toward evil than good. Evil, therefore, spreads very fast, once it has started, by gossiping – p.333 – 158 – 259 – 693 – and other ways – p.332$\rightarrow$334. The result is that what was formerly seen as sinful and evil is slowly being tolerated in the family and society – p.547. Holding moral convictions today in an immoral society can, at times, be very difficult – p.817 – 815 – 816 – 820. If people refuse to be governed by God, their freedom will be taken away – p.108^a.

REMARK 1: According to the formula $E=mc^2$ (energy is matter), there is no such thing as a material universe, that all is energy vibrating at different speeds – p.444^{N3} – 591^{N2} – 590*, and one vibration field affects the other – p.595^{N12}. Science tells us that different things (radio waves, light, sound, and heat waves, etc. – p.453 – 454) are not interfering with the other because they are moving at different vibratory rates. The physical, etheric, psychic, and divine worlds can coexist in the same space – p.454 – 590^1 – 129 – 232, permeating one another as, for example, air in water, water in sand, and sand in a sponge – p.454 – 232 – 382 – 20.

The planet Earth and its parts behave as if they were a living organism, and groups of species are invisibly connected to each other – p.319^1.

The Hermetic Law "as below, so above" is known also as the principle of correspondences; every natural reality corresponds to a spiritual reality – p.402 – 802.

Our whole existence, like that of nature around us, follows a cyclic pattern – the earth has a pulse beat with the fall and rise of the tides. Everything moves to the cosmic rhythm – p.590→598.

The human body consists of seven interpenetration bodies – p.518^{N1}. Description and importance of the human body – p.635 – 619 – 642^{N2} – 645^{N1} – 694. The physical senses – p.442 – 443, and its working – p.446^{N4}. The body as a house – p.406→411. The cells of the body – p.407^1. Mind exists in every cell of the body – p.21^a – 696* - 382. We should not identify with our body – p.379 – 380 – 380^4 – 150. The vibration of the body is lowered by eating animal food – p.316^N – 20^b – 640 and raised by eating fruits and vegetables – p.595^{N10} – 20 – 40 – 640 – 653; purify the food – p.228^R; unite with creation – p.529$^+$; began to eat meat – p.316^N; overeating – p.316 – 693; not eat meat with blood – p.422^N.

Colors we can see and not see – p.636 – 622^{N1} – 592 – 592^{N1} – 592^{N2} – 592$^{2.}$
Sport – p.539^{N2} – 544^{N2} – 540* – 390 – 314 – 292 – 554 – 576 – 707 – 708.

NOTE 1: When Adam and Eve were expelled from "The Garden" in the world of relative morality, everyone was deciding for themselves what was right or wrong – p.246. In that lawless society, "might is right", and the law of the "survival of the fittest" was the only law they respected. An absolute and caprious ruler could impose his/her own laws and rules of conduct (which they often change), and the ruling party could punish the people as much as they wanted, without any regard to universal laws – p.33 – 34 – 539→541 – 545 – 495^3 – 529 – 348 – 763. Humans should, however, not be dominated by the arbitrary will of another but should be guided by the rule of law which is good for everybody – p.544^2. The Romans followed man-made state laws – p.755* - 153^R – 207^R – 544^3 – 561^2 – 357 – 784 – 755* in establishing order and justice, which were not always agreeable with universal laws. The Celts, whom were living in a lawless society, were conquered by them – p.545. The main concern of the Israelites is about moral development by following moral laws, given by God the Creator – p.246 – 247 – 544 – 214 – 328^2 – 16 – 8 – 122 – 763 – 784 – 660. At a higher stage, the law of sacrifice will be operative – p.539^2 – 522 – 523 – 50$^+$ - 247^4 – 289^1.

REMARK 2: God speaks through our conscience – p.727 – 777 and is, thus, able to communicate with and restore fallen people through their conscience – p. 306 – 656 – 660. By following moral laws, the conscious of individuals becomes more developed or are formed again – p.544 – 42 – 122. The conscious of children needs to be developed – p.63. Purpose of Conscience – p.153→156 – 47. Someone who is more righteous suffers from the pangs of conscience after they have done something wrong – p.306* - 814 – 152. They may then sooth, mislead, and subdue their conscience by justifying and rationalizing their deeds – p.258. Many criminals (like Adam and Eve) have a conscience and a sense of guilt or warning sign – p.152→158 – 152* - 156^N. Hardened criminals do not have a conscience – p.540^{N2} – 152. Undeveloped people have not acquired a conscience – p.540[N3] – 539; have stifled their conscience – p.541[N1] – 551 or is seared or dead – p.154 – 154* - 350 – 546 – 659. The faculty of intuition of the newly-born Divine Spirit is more developed as the conscience and is better able to distinguish between good and evil – p.153; and the Spirit of God speaks directly instead of the voice of Conscience – p.44. We may say that intuition is pure conscience – p.153 – 22.

NOTE 2: God is Love – 1 Jn. 4:16. See also Human and Divine Love – p.88→98. Love is a cosmic principle. It is an all-encompassing cohesive power or energy which brings everything and everyone together and keeps them together – p.90. The emotion of love is an expanding, attractive force – p.809[N] – expressed in three levels – p.810[N] – 620. Love creates an extension of one's life into other lives by radiating and giving itself to others – p.364[1]. Attributes of love – p.92. True love is of the Spirit – p.433[1]. Spiritual love exceeds human love – p.10 – 11. Spiritual love between humans – p.61 – being in the love state – p.594 – 594[4]. Parental love purest in this fallen world – p.255. True love between couples – p.26→28 – 52. No sex when immature – p.306 – 306[1,] and no sex before (legal) marriage – p.63 – 257. Sex education should be taught – no "safe" sex training – p.67. Purifying themselves when engaged in war – p.137 – 813[2].

Sex and its desires are usually the key evil selves and spirits use to entice and keep humans in the evil kingdom – p.702[#4]. Concupiscence – p.85 – 285[N] – 348 – inborn evil desire or lust which causes separation from God and spiritual death. When sexual desires are influenced by evil desires, it becomes impure and lustful – p.119[c] – 504. The difference between universal love and passionate love – p.553[N1], seeing the other person as the only source of love – p.3 – 92 – 98. Causes and consequences of sexual misconduct – p.8→10 – 28[N] – 504[1]. Married couples who become more lustful and backslide – p.6 – 534[N2] – 135; wife swapping or swinging – p.56 – 56[a]. Not growing in love but falling in love – p.53 – 136, and adolescent love – p.53 – 60 – 66.

Sex is not a recreation but a creation – p.64 – 87 – 137. Misusing God's creative energy. Pornography – p.132→136 – 168. Harassment – p.132*. Commercial love-making – p.136→137. Result of masturbation – p.167 – 168. Result of sexual promiscuity (immorality) – p.137 – 257 – 814[3] – 808[1] – 87. Lust and its consequences – p.85→87 – 97 – 462 – 295. Look at a woman lustfully – p.686 – 132 – 257, women whom are easily persuaded – p.330 – 330[2]; a woman who wants sex – p.613[4] – 131 – 134. Rape – p.134 – 135 – 90 – 549[N5]; experience of violated women – p.135.

Lust of the eye – p.145 – 86; psychic seduction – p.20[a] – 132 – 481[1]; sexual union with a spirit(s) with or without physical body is possible; (astral sex – p.286[3] – 168 – 462 – 257 – 20[a] – 76).

Prostitutes – p.58 – 83 – 90 – 125 – 131* - 162 – 348 – 137 – 544 – 639*; pornographic prostitutes – p.133; paid or unpaid prostitutes – p.147 – 147*, women acting like psychological and psychic prostitutes (short skirts, etc.) – p.143[a] – 143 – 144 – 144[b].

Women used as temple prostitutes – p.139 and temple sluts – p.639* - 634[N2]. Why homosexuality is wrong – p.12→19; and how to overcome – p.20→25. Satan is the first homosexual – p.12 – 12[c] – 285 – 528[N2] – 775 – 297, homosexuals – p.542 – 705 – 547 – 83 – 348 – 639* – 85 – 297 – 12 – 253. Seduction – p.20[a] – clergy – p.775 – talented people – p.411[R]. Perversions – p.56 – 85→87 – 135 – 297 – 348. Sexual diseases – p.12 – 13 – 87 – 126 – 257 – 387 – 808[1] – 814[3].

Use of alcohol and drugs – p.68 – 75 – 87 – 100 – 117 – 138 – 162 – 163 – 256 – 257 – 292 – 305 – 314 – 350 – 554 – 554[1] – 693 – 707 – 751 – 808[1]. Alcohol – p.40 – 316 – 437 – 439 – 462 – 465[5] - drugs – p.40 – 316 – 437 – 439 – 448 and smoking – p.40 - 808[1]. Drugs and alcohol should not be used to force stimulation of psychic centers – p.529* - 430. Alcohol and drugs damage the etheric web – p.651, alcohol and smoking clog up the channels of the etheric body – p.653. Young people called "hippies" use drugs – p.543. Alcohol and drugs are poor substitutes for the high of spiritual life – p.658. It is possible to recover from alcohol and drug addictions with the help of God – p.724^N – 751.

Suicide – p.87 – 163 – 181^N – 188^N – 232 – 233 – 256 – 257 – 450^2 – 451.

The original sin is strong in children whom are conceived through lustful passion – p.64 – 65 – 493 – 257 – 312 – 509^{N1} – 542 – 332 – 661 – 662. Children whom are born with little or no original sin – p.62 – 62* - 63 – 64 – 661 – 661^a – 332* - 626^{N1} – 701$^{#2}$ – 666. Jesus was born without original sin – p.661^a – 62 – 263 – 263^2 – 264 – 264^4.

The character of the ^{1}fallen world – p.310^1 - 314→318 – 100 – 101 – 108 – 108^a – 170 – 547 – 33^b - 291→297 – 395^5 – 676* - 808^1 – 84, are occupied by most people whom are ^{2}good and evil. Behavior of people when the evil self is in charge – p.704 – 705 – 346 – 347 – 171→173 – 337* - 349 – 350 – 546 – 183^3 – 84, and whose father is satan (Jn. 8:44) – p.286^4 – 291 – 704 – 546 – 715^N. The nature, qualities, and working of satan (who was cursed – p.311) – p.195 – 185 – 346 – 84 - 176→190 – 196→198 – 182→184 – 285→287 – 772 – 289 – 290 – 293 – 294 – 181^N. What is evil p.342*. Humans whom make a common base by desiring, thinking, and acting like satan not only strengthen their evil nature but also attract and are easily influenced by him and his cohorts – p.179 – 179^1 – 191 – 687.

After Adam and Eve died spiritually, God immediately began to carry out His restoration plan, to reinstate Adam's family. He did this by means of Adam's sons Cain and Abel, whom were placed in the position of Lucifer and Adam; to reverse the condition through which satan invaded humanity – p.33. However, Cain killed Abel, and the restoration of the family was delayed – p.33^b – 806 – 807 – 807^1. The Cain and Abel situation was later made right by Esau the first born, who united with Jacob in Isaac's family – p.33^b. Jacob had

---

[1] "The World" (Jn. 15:18-19) – p.100 – 101 – 670^a – 670^b – 5 – 533 – 573 – 40 – 144 – 173 – 249 – 287 – 317 – 716^R – 775. The good/evil thought system of "the world" stimulates immoral behavior, if it is not checked – p.125.

[2] Because people are born with original sin, they have not only inherited the good characteristics of God (made in His image) but have also inherited the evil qualities of satan (made in his image) – p.395^5. Thus, they belong to the Creator but are also the possession of satan.

to pay an [3]additional amount for the failures of his predecessors ([4]Noah and Abraham) – p.647^{N1} – 34 – 34^a – 808 – 809 – 476 – 236 – 611$^{7-8}$ – 626^{N2} – 640 – 641 – 645 – 646→648 – 646^2 – 648^1. Thus, the restoration at the foundation level was finally accomplished in Abraham's family.

What is required from people as a condition to return to God, according to the temporary [5]laws of restoration or re-creation; to have faith in Him, and obey His Word which Adam and Eve failed to do – p.677. This also includes the sacrificial offering(s). They also have to "pay back" to satan in order to restore the position as Lord over the creation and to free themselves from his power and accusation – p.694 – 301 – 301^1 – 301^2 – 302 – 303^R – 155^N – 158 – 147 – 170 – 188 – 188^N – 199 – 259. Knowing satan's crime, we can accuse him before God – p.335.

God then continues to restore humans from the family to the tribal and national levels through Moses, who was the meekest person on earth (Num. 12:3) – p.297^R. See the story of Moses – p.336^1 – 337^3 – 339^N – 340^{N5} – 476 – 572 – 612 – 612^1 – 612^2 – 612^3 – 613 – 625 – 625^1 – 625^2 – 625^3 – 626 – 627^{N3} – 641 – 643 – 645 – 646→648 – 781 – 794 – 804 – 810 – 810^1 – 811. "On the third new moon after the people of Israel had gone forth out of the land of Egypt" (Ex. 19:1), they camped before Mount Sinai. On the third day

---

[3] An additional amount of indemnity was also paid by Abraham to sacrifice his son; and the Israelites who had to wander in the wilderness for forty years – p.611^4 – 476 – 337^3 – 804.

REMARK: When we have done something wrong, identical circumstances may appear again, but instead of repeating the same mistake, we should overcome them – p.647^{N2}. Whatever an individual has done which separates him/herself from God must be reversed so that they can return to God – p.647^{N1}. When humans do not learn their lessons, recurring events of the same nature and pattern need to be repeated – p.598^{N2}.

[4] Read the story of Noah and Abraham, whom were also involved in laying the foundation of faith – Noah – p.640 – 807 – 807^4 – 31 – 476 – 307 and Abraham – p.640 – 808 – 611^4 – 641 – 646^2 – 34.

[5] The laws of restoration were implemented after the fall to restore first what was lost, called restoration or salvation – p.757*. Some of the laws of restoration are: "the law of separation". Good and evil have to be separated first, then they should unite – p.669 – 611^4 and periods of separation – p.475→479 – 647 – 610→617; "The law of false preceding the truth" – p.810 – "The law of indemnity", payment to satan who has a claim on us – p.665. Unlike God, satan requires full payment – p.677 – 678. However, because Jesus acquired victory over satan by overcoming the three temptations – p.189 – 189* – 265 – 565 – 565^5 – 331 – 678, and by the sacrifice on the cross – p.190 – 629 – 630, the ransom price – p.215 – 588^{R1} – 678 – 191, has become much less – p.40 – 40^a. However, some indemnity needs to be paid in order to get humans out of the camp of satan – p.678 – 683 – 684 – 814* - 822 – 823 – 674 – 563^3 – 157→159 – 589 – 221 – 152 – 309 – 22^c – 725 – 726 – 725^{N1} – 693 – 214 – 214^1 – 99^c – 99^d – 154 – 222 – 274 – 347 – 258.

after the people purified themselves, [1]God spoke (and wrote) the Ten Commandments directly to the people – see p.246→260 – 710 – 31 – 41 – 42 – 96 – 115 – 122 – 139 – 153 – 164* – 214 – 238 – 310[1] – 351 – 373[2] – 476 – 550 – 640 – 645[N2] – 674 – 686* - 699 – 716[R] – 741[4] – 756 – 792. By acknowledging and living according to those laws, it became part of their inner being – p.42 – 108[a] – 241[R] – 246[2] – 294.

REMARK: The Law of Karma – p.9 – 22[c] – 24 – 94[N] – 111* - 118 – 135 – 136 – 144 – 152 – 153[N] – 154 – 165 – 168 – 205→222 – 248 – 258 – 305[R] – 317[3] – 3 – 340 – 357[R] – 358 – 359 – 360 – 361[N5] – 363 – 363[N2] – 364 – 365 – 366[N] – 368[N] – 416 – 450[2] – 496[4] – 506[N1] – 545[N1] – 546[2] – 556 – 556[1] – 581[N] – 581[R] – 616[N] – 623[4] – 624[2] – 626[N2] – 627 – 629[N1] – 640 – 641 – 647[N2] – 664 – 673 – 684 – 686 – 693 – 694 – 695 – 699 – 724 – 729[R] – 732 – 744 – 784[3] – 809 – 813 – 817* - 818.

Criminals – p.152* - 153[N] – 162 – 170 – 183 – 206 – 207 – 210 – 258 – 259 – 285 – 348 – 349 – 431 – 431[2] – 699 – The fear of punishment has a great effect in denying and repressing the thief and murderer within – p.544 – hardened criminals – p.83 – 152 – 540[N2] – 546[2]. Crime does not pay – p.210. Inward criminal acts do much damage – p.686.

As crime is, in many cases, a violation of man-made laws, sin is the breaking or transgression of God's law (1 Jn. 3:4). Sin limits or prevents the evolution (one's own or somebody else's) of the human personality and the development of his or her Soul – p.285[N] – 684*.

Hearts of some people are so calloused and hardened by sin that they no longer hear the voice of the Spirit – p.791[7]. They lost the "sense of sin" and are no longer aware that they are sinning – p.156[N] – 285[N], and have thus no ability to discern between good and evil – p.546 – 183[3].

Mortal or deadly sin – p.285[N]. Seven deadly sins – p.72*. The violation of creeds and dogma is not always a sin – p.215[2].

Thereafter, the Lord gave exact instructions to build a tabernacle (symbol of humans), wherein is found an ark, and within the ark, two tables of the testimony – p.38→44 – 106 – 229 – 238 – 613 – 626 – 641 – 643[N] – 660 --- p.38 – 39 – 41 – 238 – 239 – 240 – 241[R] – 247 --- p.38 – 238 – 239 – 247 – 476. The pattern of the tabernacle was used later to build the temple of Solomon, Zerubbabel, and Herodus – p.238→245 – 229 – 565[2] – 611[6] – 641. The latter was destroyed in 70 A.D. – p.244 – 820. The glory or Presence of the Lord filled the tabernacle, and the temple, as soon as the form (the human spirit – personality) is ready – p.240* - 240 – 238 – 323 – 42.

The Israelites relationship to God in the Old Testament dispensation (like the angels) was that of master and servant – p.660[b]. They were growing

---

[1] The writings of the whole Bible were done directly or indirectly by many individuals, with the exception of the Ten Commandments, which were written personally by God on stone tablets, or written with the finger of God (Ex. 31:18) – p,.782[R] – 229.

internally and morally – p.544 – 550, by [1]following the laws, and the prophets, thereby purifying or stripping their personalities ("their robes" – physical – emotional – mental sheaths – Rev. 22:14 – p.44 – 68 – 199 – 74), from the inherited evil – p.42 – 373[2] – 714[3] – 660 – 112[a] – 174[R] – 231. When they were not obedient, a swift punishment of plague, wars, banishment, etc. was followed – p.660[b] – 241[*] - 108[a] – 141 – 215 – 216 – 820; otherwise, material blessing was bestowed upon them – p.249 – 660 – 24. The Israelites had no direct access to God (except a chosen few) and were waiting for the advent of Christ – p.730[2] – 112[a].

When Jesus, the last Adam (1 Cor. 15:45) was born, He was venerated by the shepherds, a multitude of angels, and the three wise men, whose gifts were symbolic of body, emotion, and intellect (personality), which have to bow down to the Christ child (within) – p.804. Before that event, the angels (satan and his demonic host) refused to bow down before the first Adam – p.187 – 286 – 286[*]. Jesus was born without original sin from a long line of ancestors – (Matt. Ch. 1) – p.62 – 811[*] - 812. His mission was not only at the national but also on the international level. See also p.646→648. The Christian era began since the time of the birth of Jesus – the year of the Lord (Anno Domini) A.D. – p.262. The day of His birth is not known, but his all-important time of [2]spiritual birth happened when his Divine Spirit or Soul was formed in his pure personality – p.263, and started to lead the latter, as a rider on a [3]white horse – p.415 – 273[N]. God was no longer a master or Jehovah to

---

[1] The God of Israel, unlike the Olympian gods, was one God (Deut 6:4), a God of law and order, who always operated in exact agreement with the universal law. Because His chosen people were in a stage of developing intellectually, especially morally by purifying their personality (which was good and evil), their Lord and Master had to be very harsh in dealing with them because they easily fall back or backslide to their former lifestyle when their evil selves were in charge of their lives – p.784 – 785. The development and purification of the personality was also accomplished, to a certain extent, by living according to Confucius ethics in the first part of their life, which is also true of many people of India and other people. They then spend the remaining part of their life in spiritual development – p.112[a] – 376[*]

NOTE 1: The Jewish and Mohammedan (and other religions) did not stay static after the event of Christ, but also evolved in some branches of esoteric expressions – such as Kabbalists and Hassidists in Judaism, and mystics in Islam called Sufism – p.373[2] – 577[*].

NOTE 2: The Star of David ✡ not only represents the development of the personality ▽ the lower self, but also the development of the Divine Spirit, the higher self △ - p.268[2-3].

[2] This day of birth (and our own) should be celebrated every year – p.664.

[3] When the personality is good and evil, the color of the horse is gray; when the personality is false or evil, the color is black – p.216. Rev. 6:1 mentions another white horse, which may represent science – p.632[N3].

be feared, but a tender loving Father (Abba) – p.785 – 660[b] – 730 – 733[4] – 32 – 263, who is easy to forgive, as the story of the prodigal son testifies (Luke Ch. 15) – front cover – p.32 – 336[1] – 584 – 810[1] – 679. Jesus was prophesied – p.783,was born and formed in beautiful surroundings – p.263, did not show any trace of sin – p.264, spoke Aramaic – p.767[3] – 265, and had four brothers and two sisters – p.262 – 629. His outward appearance is described on p. 263[3]. Jesus was baptized with the Holy Spirit – p.261→284 – 43 – 43[*] - 660. Description and working of the Holy Spirit – p.267 – 267[N] – 730 – 730[3] – 790[2] – 790[3] – 791[6] – 575 – 575[1] – 577 – 588[R2] – 6 – 22 – 23 – 24 – 44 – 157 – 235 – 237 – 521 – 562 – 584 – 585→589 – 645 – 663 – 664 – 699[*] - 783 – etc. Jesus overcame the temptation of satan – p.265 – 189 – 189[*] - 779 – 331 – 550[*] - 678 – 565 – 565[5]. [1]Thereafter, he was overshadowed with the Christ consciousness of God or the Son (Cosmic Christ) – Rev. 1:18, which nature could not be expressed through the first Adam but came alive through Jesus Christ the last Adam – p.266 – 703 – 563 – 43, but left his body at the time of his crucifixion – p.703 – 276. In the new dispensation, Jesus pronounced a new image and concept of God – p.507 – 521. He came to abolish the angelic type world of master and servant and to establish the adamic type world of Father and Son – p.328[2] – 43 – 550; through the experience of [2]rebirth – p.565 – 566 – 821. In the Sermon on the Mount, he gave a deeper and inward meaning of the Ten Commandments – p.248 – 249 – 686, which was condensed into two principles. The teaching of Jesus Christ is more pure than many other teachings – p.679[*] – 566[2] – 417[R], and Jesus made satan responsible for the evil in society – p.678[a]. In reversing Adam's mistake, he said in John 5:30, "I can do nothing on my own authority" – p.290[3], and through his consecration in the Garden of Gethsemane, everyone will be able to enter the restored "Garden of Eden" – p.287. Jesus as the last Adam came not only to restore the lost position of the first Adam – p.264[5], but also to take away satan's power over the world. As a result, "all hell broke loose". Jesus and his apostles were severely attacked by satan and his cohorts – p.189 – 190 – 47[b].

---

[1] Jesus began to preach and said, "I came to cast fire on the earth" (Luk. 12:49; II Pet. 3:7). The fire here may mean judgment by God's Word. The Word he spoke will also be a judge to non-believers who reject the Word of God (Jn. 12:48; Rev. 19:15; Isa. 11:4) – p.791[7]. We should not judge – p.170 – 252 – 307 – 311 – 311[*].

Day of Judgment – p.449[2]. There is no final judgment; the soul judges itself – p.466[*]. The general or particular judgment – p.464[1]. See also "The Resurrection" – p.464→467 – 629. Through Jesus teaching to people with or without bodies, many human spirits became spiritually alive or born of God (resurrected) after having been in the "tomb", or living the life of the good/evil personality. See Matt. 27:52-53 – p.244 – 244[*].

NOTE 1: The open heart and its surrounding light are often betrayed in pictures of Jesus Christ – p.566[N]. The pure in heart (in the personality) will see God (Matt. 5:8).

Meaning of heart – p.77 – 77[d] – 337[2]

NOTE 2: The horizontal line of the cross was raised from the solar plexus center to the heart center – p.638.

[2] Circumcision as part of the law of Moses was replaced by Spirit baptism and being adopted in the spiritual family of God – p.262[1].

The moment Jesus [1]died on the cross, "the curtain of the temple was torn in two". This is an indication that everyone who [2]accepts him as their savior has the opportunity to communicate and unite with their inner Christ or Soul, and God's Presence – p.44 – 326 – 660. They are no longer under law but grace and are guided by God directly – p.214 – 16 – 24 – 122 – 44 – 247[4] – 533 – 563 – 764 – 791. When the Holy Spirit descended on the apostles at [3]the day of Pentecost, this was the birthday of the Christian church. From Moses to Christ was the age of law; from Pentecost to Christ's return is the age of Grace or church age. Christians are to grow and mature in the likeness of Jesus Christ – p.565[4]; develop Soul qualities and virtues – p.677 – 23 – 26 – 27 – 120[b] – 685 – 392; living a divine life – p.691→700 – 707→709 – 23 – 24 – 398 – 399 – 563 – 522 – 571 – 563; and to know God personally – p.684 – 23 – 676 – 775→777. The disciples in Antioch behaved so much like Christ that they were called [4]Christians for the first time – p.680 – 566[1] – 566 – 791[6] – 192[1] – 822. However, when they became more mature – p.572 – 676, they not only had to defend themselves from evil forces without, like their younger brothers and sisters – p.XIX – 46→48 – 100[b] – 181[N] – 190→198 – 287[R] – 302 – 346 – 347 – 574 – 631 – 639* - 669 – 670 – 683 – 715[R] – 716 – 749[N6] – 772

---

[1] Through Jesus' sacrifice on the cross, he had broken the power of the evil one, but not completely disarmed and destroyed – p.190. See also the 14 Stations of the Cross – p.629 – 630.

[2] Formula of Christian Salvation – p.566[4]

[3] This event is celebrated by Christians on the seventh Sunday after Easter. It is also called Whitsunday – p.235 – 44 – 767[N] – 783. It corresponds to the day of harvesting the first fruit in Jewish celebration – p.783, fifty days after the first day of Passover.

At the day of Pentecost, spiritual gifts were bestowed upon the apostles – p.237 – 267[N], and many spoke in other tongues – p.235 – 237 – 267[N].

NOTE 1: When evil thoughts arise to corrupt yourself morally and spiritually, you are more inclined to do it because you are not able to see how much damage you are inflicting on your human and Divine Spirits – p.570[N2] – 470.

NOTE 2: When spiritual brothers and sisters fall – p.308[1] – 308, they become worse than they were before they accepted Christ – p.808, and to come back, they have to pay a heavy penalty or indemnity.

NOTE 3: Immature Christians blame satan for everything that goes wrong in their lives. They often say: "The devil made me do it" – p.311 – 180[R] – 671. When they meet individuals who speak of higher stages of spirituality, they quickly condemn them – p.570[N2] – 470.

[4] True Christians are those in whom Christ has been formed, not necessarily all those who have been baptized – p.566[1] – 791[6]; and certainly not those whom professed to be Christians but are carnal "men of the flesh" – p.122 – 562[N1], and backsliders – p.569* - 274[4] – 507[4] – 574 – 810 – 810[1] – 715[N2] – 716 – 10 – 562[N1] – 347[2] – 575[6] – 674. Some people think that we are all children of God. The devil, however, is the father of some people – p.286[4] – 416 – 546 – 704 – 291.

– 792^{N2}; but also have to wage a ¹fierce battle between the emerging Christ or Divine Spirit with the inherited force of evil within – p.574 – 676. This evil force or evil part of the ego is called by many names, such as: old self, old nature, old man, evil self, false self, imposter, pretender, deceiver, the flesh, fallen nature, evil nature, inner devil, etc. – p.702$^{#4}$ – 27 – 27* - 657^b – 714¹ – 562 – 562¹ – 346 – 294* - 191 – 189*. It is also called Antichrist – p.27 – 716^R – 293 – 191 – 658 – 678 – 37 – 53 – 182 – 820 – 702$^{#4}$.

When spiritual children are more grown, they feel an urgency to witness – p.682→684 – 180^R, whereby they will rapidly progress – p.574 and God will surely provide them with everything they need – p.693 – 357^R – 581^R – 793^{N2}. They feel responsible to teach their guests and pay indemnity for them – p.683. The spiritual teens soon start to function in their new roles as spiritual parents to their babes in Christ – p.684. The teens are not only guided by the universal Christ, *the male aspect of God, but also by the female aspect of God – p.575. They truly believe that God is not only a Father but also a Mother – p.22^b – 24 – 102 – 130 – 261 – 270 – 270* - 278² – 319 – 522 – 790². Unlike spiritual babies, the grown-ups do not only believe but also understand what they believe. They not only believe in heaven but know about heaven – p.573. They can safely wield and wisely use the psychic faculties for the helping of the human race – p.581^N. They "have their faculties (such as

---

¹ The inner personality is called false because it is attempting to take the place of the Divine Spirit. Because the evil part of the personality has taken the vacant place of the Divine Spirit, that is why there is such a great struggle within oneself when the emerging Divine Spirit begins to battle with the evil self – p.XIX – 27 – 46→48 – 164* - 171→173 – 191 – 292 – 293 – 332→334 – 336→338 – 337² – 337* - 562 – 562¹ – 574 – 575 – 575⁵ – 657 – 658 – 676→678 – 701$^{#1}$ – 702$^{#4}$ – 705 – 715^R – 715^{N2} – 715^{N1} – 716 – 764 – 764* - etc. The false ego may masquerade as the Divine Spirit and would like to take the place as an imposter – p.182 – 182^N. When the Divine Spirit has become strong enough, it will eliminate the old nature – p.196.

We should and can defend ourselves against the evil forces within and without – p.198→204 – 200^N – 424 – 424³ – 574→576 – 745¹ – 749^{N6} – 775 – 791 – 792^{N2}.

* As the Protestants spread the Gospel of Jesus Christ over the globe emphasizing the Fatherhood of God, the Catholics were, likewise, busy but emphasizing the Motherhood of God – p.772 – 106. The Holy Spirit has been and still is working through many women, especially through Mary, the mother of Jesus. She has been and, at present, is appearing all over the world – p.267^N. The mother of Mary was Anna – p.261¹. In the time of Jesus (Matt. 23:37-38), God as Mother expressed Herself through Jesus – p.584. In Hebrew, Jehovah is written Yahweh, *yah* being masculine and *weh* feminine. Yahweh is a father whose care is often experienced as mother-like – see Isa. 42:14; 49:15; 66:13. The Fatherhood of God is mentioned in the Old Testament – p.733⁴. God is our eternal Parents – p.111 – True Parents – p.319 – 702$^{#5}$. Spiritual Parents – p.31 – Divine Parents – p.23 – 24 – 78. It is possible to reason with God – p.743^{N2}.

Individuals whom God chooses to lead His people – p.297^R – 74 – 331

Words used in religion – p.347

What Christian religions have done – p.570 – 675 – 496^{N3}

When someone starts living a divine life, everything he/she owns is transferred from satan's domain to God's domain and ownership – p.288^R.

intuition) trained by practice to distinguish good from evil" (Heb. 5:14) and are, thus, able to judge – p.574 – 681.

Baby Christians believe that Jesus of Nazareth is God Himself – p.678, although He appeared to be God – p.703[#5] – 270 – 271[R] – 278 – 585 – 798[7]. For the mature Christian, Jesus is no longer a god to be worshipped – p.690.

Mystics communicate with the inner God (deep within their Souls or Higher Selves – p.577.) (We should not identify our Higher Self with God – p.269[R]). The Soul or Divine Spirit is called by many names – p.706 – 707 – 81, and is truly the fountain of eternal youth – p.512. It is neither male nor female (Matt. 22:30) – p.150. The Divine Spirit is always pure and noble and cannot sin (1 John 3:9) – p.667 – 571 – 705 – XVIII[R] – 22. The individual of the sixth center, as the embodiment of universal principles, fully realizes the oneness of all beings – p.536, and has become an "illuminated seer" – p.537. They are becoming a superman or superwoman – p.289[1] – 692. See also p.581→584 – 685→690.

The Constitution of the Human and Divine Being

A human being is made up of chemical elements (minerals), has an etheric body like plants, an emotional body (like animals), and a mental body – p.81 – 700.

[1]The human or whole personality, which consists of the outer and the inner, is composed of the physical, emotional, and mental matter or mind complex. The outer or earthly personality is called the physical self, physical body, and external self; while the inner personality is called the spirit self, spirit body, psyche, soul, heart, human spirit, and internal self. It feels, perceives, thinks, reasons, and wills. As the spirit self further consists of the spirit body and spirit mind, the physical self, as its reflection, consists of the physical body and physical mind or brain – p.77 – 657[a] – 196[2] – 620 – 306[1].

Ego is a state of consciousness marked by a sense of individualized personal selfhood. It is the Latin word for "I", which is beyond, and includes the intellect and the emotion – p.498[N2]. One should not disregard the ego because in order to live properly on earth, one must possess an ego, whose function is to organize, process, and consolidate new learning gained through mental, emotional, and sensory awareness – p.707 – 116[*] - 511[2]. Most Western psychologists believe that a strong ego is needed to be successful in life. Thus, their therapy is designed to build up the go, while that of Buddhism is to minimize it – p.116[*]. The ego feels, thinks, acts, discriminates, decides, etc. If it is weak and undeveloped, it is a poor instrument for the Soul. It is

---

[1] We should not identify ourselves with our body, emotion, or intellect because the "I" or self-consciousness is not our body, emotion, or intellect. For example, "I am sick", but I am (inner core of being) cannot be sick. Therefore, I _have_ a body, emotion, and intellect – p.77 – 498[R] – 321[*] - 501[N] – 504[N3].

therefore not wrong to be ambitious and [2]independent – p.549[*]. However, individuals should not overdevelop and inflate their ego – p.337[*] and become trapped in the lifestyle of the personality – p.558 – 550 – 398. The ego or personality should not be slain but take its rightful place and be purified – p.120[a]. What should be slain is the evil part of the personality – p.293 – 112[b] – 120[a].

A complete human being consists of three main parts – "Spirit" (Divine Spirit or Soul), "soul" (human spirit – psyche – mind), and "body" – p.82 – 520 – 702[#5] – 523 – 196[2] – 234[N] – 750 – 621 – 556[R].

The Hindus believe in the body with its (Jiva) life or breath or etheric body – life soul or astral body (human spirit or psyche) and Atman (Soul). The Jewish believe in the body with its animal soul or etheric body – in the astral soul and divine soul, which latter is incapable of sin. The Greeks believe in the body with its life principle – in the soul and spirit. The Medieval church believes in the body with its animal soul – the human soul and the divine soul – p.706.

The esoteric doctrine teaches that the Divine Spirit (Causal body) consists of self (at ma), intuition (buddhi), and higher mental (manas) "bodies"; the personality, as its reflection and vehicle, consists of the physical/etheric body, the emotional (astral) and lower mental sheaths – p.707. Apostle Paul, in giving his benediction to the Thessalonians, made a distinction between body, soul (human spirit), and spirit (Divine Spirit – 1 Thess. 5:23 – see also Heb. 4:12). This trinity was accepted by the Christian church until the Fourth Council of Constantinople in 869 A.D., "when it was reduced" to body and Soul – p.705 – 706 – 82 – 523[*]. Origin, Alexandrian theologian, held that there is a threefold meaning in scripture: the literal, moral, and spiritual, or allegorical, that corresponds and is, for the benefit, to the threefold division he saw in human nature: body, mind (soul or human spirit), and Soul (Divine Spirit) – p.800[R] – 82 – 703. Plato gave human beings a tripartite nature – Soul (mind), (human) spirit, and body – p.82. There are three selves of different states of consciousness: the conscious or ego self, the subconscious self (human spirit), and super-conscious (divine consciousness) – p.593[N3] – 620. A human being has the body of an animal, is fully aware of his/her body, which is selfish and limited, much the same, which they quickly get to know. The average human being has a human spirit, of which they are not much aware, which is less selfish and limited, is more different, and it takes more time to know about it. This human being has an eternal Divine Spark, of which they

---

[2] In the past, the individual did not exist as an independent entity. The group (soul) dominated and did not allow for the emancipation of a separate ego – p.498[N3] – 499 – 320[N]. Those whom are living the life of the personality have a tendency to conform and to identify with the group or collective, the so-called herd instinct – p.558 – 681[1] – 579[*]. The Christ force works to individualize him or her to separate them from the human consciousness, which thrives in a group – p.709 – 183.

The hero is the one who is a rugged individualist, apart from the pack, following his/her own vision, marching to the beat of his/her own drum, without regard for the opinions of others. Their consciousness is lodged in his/her Divine Spirit and no longer in their personality.

are usually ignorant, which will develop into a Divine Spirit, which is unselfish and unlimited, is very unique, and it takes forever to know it – p.620 – 524 – 709[1] – 559[2]. See also p.733 – 621 – 527 – 332.

NOTE 1: Because mind exists in every cell of the physical body, right thinking and feelings change the cellular vibrations of the cells and, thus, influences the health of the whole body – p.697 – 21[a].

NOTE 2: Humans form a link between heaven and earth and live simultaneously in both worlds – p.445[4] – 80[N] – 360.

NOTE 3: Heaven and hell can be a geographical location but also states of consciousness. He or she can experience a physical suffering in a hell on earth but also a psychological suffering when they become strangers to each other, and spiritually when they are alienated from God – p.293.

The Spirit of God dwells in the depth of the Divine Spirit (Rev. 21:3), which latter has its abode in the human spirit, which in turn resides within the physical body – p.726[1]. God has His secret dwelling place deep within the Divine Being or Most Holy Place – p.679 – 322 – 240[*] - 244[N] – 321[*] - 746[3]. The physical body serves as a vehicle of the human spirit, which in turn will become the vehicle of the Divine Spirit, who is always one with the indwelling Spirit of God – p.39 – 234[N]. Spiritual growth is the process of shifting our consciousness from the physical body to our human spirit, and then to the Divine Spirit of our being, and then realize our divinity more and more – p.379[3]. Your physical body lives in the physical world, by which you are in touch with through your physical senses. Your human spirit lives in the spirit world, by which you can be in contact with through your psychic senses. Your Divine Spirit lives in the divine world. This world can be known through your divine senses. These *three worlds don't lie above each other but interpenetrate each other as air in water, and water in sand. They are able to live or share the same space but at different "vibration levels" or dimensions of existence – p.696 – 232 – 454 – 24 – 129[a] – 652 – 692 – 396. We learn to know the body by studying and practicing medicine; to be acquainted with the multitude of emotional articulations, by learning and expressing music and other art forms, and by the experience of love. Develop intellectually by

---

* Knowing that you live in three worlds, living has become very interesting and exciting. You are filled with wonder, and there is so much to discover and so much to learn – p.696 – 129[a].
NOTE 1: As a seed needs suitable soil to germinate and grow in, plus sunlight and synthesize food and water, the human spirit also needs a healthy body to thrive and develop in, plus parental love and education. The Divine Spirit needs to awaken and grow in a pure personality and receive the Life Elements of God (mostly Love and Truth) and partake of a rich spiritual atmosphere – p.321[N] – 664 – 464 – 304[*].
NOTE 2: Our life and be compared to a caterpillar and butterfly – p.456.
NOTE 3: Sensory experience does not last long; sentimental pleasure lasts a little longer; intellectual knowledge lasts much longer; religious knowledge will also lose its luster when a brighter religion appears. Relative truth can, therefore, not endure, and a particular concept of God will not last – p.507 – 508.

studying science and other disciplines. The Soul evolves or unfolds by studying, witnessing, and practicing the Truth – p.774[2] – 518 – 523 – 620.

The physical body (flesh and bones) consists of what we eat. It feeds off the body of the earth (its staple food) and becomes part of the earth – p.134 – 566. The human spirit (emotional and mental energy) is [1]made up of what we feel, think, and believe. It feeds off the body of humanity (mainly intellectual food) and becomes in unity with it – p.134 – 567 – 43. The Divine Spirit (divine energy) is composed of the kind of spiritual Truth we absorb and assimilate. It feeds off the body of God (Word of God) and becomes one with the whole – p.134 – 566.

[2]For the physical body to grow in a proper way, and to maintain itself, it needs the right diet, which is well prepared and palatable – p.410 – 792[N1] – 706. For the human spirit (mind) to develop and sustain itself, it requires thoughts that come from self-knowledge, and to learn those disciplines which we understand and appeal to us, such as earth – psychological and psychic knowledge, etc. – p.410 – 792[N1] – 706. For the unfolding and preserving of the Divine Spirit (Original Mind) to occur, it is essential to feed it with a variety of wholesome spiritual nourishment, such as Truth and Love of God, and those verses and sections of the Word which the Soul is attracted to and likes to absorb. This also includes divine knowledge, revelation, and inspiration, etc. – p.410 – 792[N1] – 706.

The food we eat takes time to digest, and only the essence is being assimilated; the rest is eliminated. To nourish the body, which takes in healthy and unhealthy food, it should be properly absorbed and converted into energy – p.568 – 411. It takes time for our knowledge and experience to be assimilated in the human spirit (lower self), and only the essence is being incorporated; the rest is being expelled. It takes in the good and evil elements and embodies in its being the psychic results of its good and evil actions. An eagerness to gain knowledge, without proper assimilation, causes mental congestion, as one is being burdened with an excess of unassimilated ideas – p.568 – 411 – XVIII. It takes time for our divine knowledge and spiritual experience to become part of our Divine Spirit (Higher Self), and only the essence and pure elements are being incorporated, as well as the essence of the qualities gained by the human spirit – p.568 – 411.

As the physical body grows by taking physical food, the human spirit (soul-psyche) grows by absorbing mental food, and the Divine Spirit (Soul – Christ

---

[1] Your selves are created and composed of what you feel and think, and that is your character. Thus, the inner selves are made up of all your ideas and beliefs and all the things that have been accepted by you. It can be conscious or unconscious. It will attract the circumstances of our life which can be positive or negative, thus creating our own reality.

The abstracted essence of the experiences gained and the qualities acquired is being worked into the texture of the spirits, and it is by this that the latter grows and, thus, acquired wisdom and understanding. The most valuable period of assimilation or digesting life experiences and infusing or building it into the inner selves is when people have become more mature – p.569 – 557[3] – 568 – 363[N2].

[2] The life of the etheric body is maintained by proper breathing and living.

Spirit) is in the process of becoming when it assimilates the Word of God, and also derives spiritual food from meditation, prayer, and reflection on God, our Father and Mother – p.621 – 786[N1].

We not only take care of the hunger of the body but also by satisfying the intellectual and spiritual hunger of the psyche and the Soul (Truth body) – p.355 – 791[N1] – 304[*].

As medical doctors primarily take care of the physical body, psychologists and psychiatrists' main interest is the psychological health of the spirit body, while pastors or shepherds and transpersonal psychologists' principle concern is the well-being and growth of the Divine body – p.706. The doctor may say "You are what you eat", the psychologist may say "You are what you think". A spiritual caretaker or pastor may say, "You are what you believe, accept, and assimilate as Truth" – p.196[2].

NOTE: The Word of God should be pure and be delivered in a great variety of ways. It should not be adulterated or diluted with cultural expressions. It ought to be taught in churches, which are supposed to be birth and feeding places of the divine, as mother delivers and gives milk to the infants. That is the milk of the word (the first principles) or the fundamental or simple Truth of God's Word. When the babies have grown somewhat, solid food may be given (Heb. 5:14) – p.567 – 754.

The teachings of Jesus are the most pure, especially when the Cosmic Christ speaks through Jesus, more particularly in the Gospel of John and more specifically in the "I AM" sayings – p.566[2].

The special food the Soul needs is to feed it with those Words of God, which apply to one's spiritual development. The Word cleanses our spirit and we also participate of the Life within those vessels of Truth – p.410 – 792[N1] – 789[2]. In witnessing, God's Word is the incorruptible seed we are to sow in the soil of the heart of the non-believer, who may experience a new Birth by making a decision – p.792[N2] – 663→669 – 566→569.

REMARK: Logos – the Word of God – p.283 – 283[*] - 561 – 561[1] – 273 – 274 – 278.

Capitalism and the Workplace

Because of the fall or deviation from God's principles, humans lost Truth and, thus, the purpose and direction, whereby their life was no longer meaningful – p.316. Since *Adam and Eve and all their descendants (whom are good and evil) were condemned to eat bread by the "sweat of their brow" and to labor in sorrow amidst "thorns and thistles", life has become a burden, and work is a toil and routine – p.317 – 317[*] - 317[1]. Thus, every man experiences excessive hardship, frustration, and pain in his labor and every woman in hers, when they are living a life separate from God – p.317[*]. During the history of restoration, humans have improved somewhat, and a government and capitalistic system came about (in many Western nations) to deal with immature and evil human beings. The former supports the right of every individual to life, liberty, and the pursuit of happiness – p.357[N2] – 295[N]; and the Western economic system supports the right of each individual to work for his/her own interest; defending their right to be selfish – p.357[N2]. In

---

* Someone who has difficulty believing in the existence of Adam and Eve could see them as an archetype.

the "Wealth of Nations", Adam Smith (1723-1790) wrote that self-interest leads each person to seek his or her own economic advantage, thus contribution to the general welfare. This seems to be the best possible world good/evil people have come up with – p.194[3]. As some capitalists of the 19th century believed that worldly success is a blessing – p.318 – 660, many others, whom were influenced by evil desires, became very greedy – p.119[c] – 58 – 58[*] – 164. They began to exploit the workers by seeing them not as humans but of having the same value as production tools and equipment, ignoring the fact of their religion that the intrinsic value of human beings is God-given and infinite, not what he or she could contribute to society, as in Roman times – p.496[N3]. This behavior gave eventual rise to Communism – p.318 – 317[2]. Success for them translates into money and property, gospel of wealth, social Darwinism – p.549[N4]. They and many others in their and our society are to have a position of power and protecting this position and sense of importance for which they are not morally qualified – p.331, and become like *dictators – p.332[N].

They enjoy wielding this power and lording it over others – p.547 – 331. However, they will soon lose this power – p.331[6]. Many of them are greedy, deceitful, manipulative, and participate in cutthroat competition – p.547 – 531 – 210 – 198 – 199, which is allowed by society – p.549[N4] – 317 – 318. In the civilized world, we no longer buy and sell human beings at slave markets, but we still buy and sell our labor, abilities, and skills for the highest price at the labor markets, where the evaluation of character of individuals is given little or no consideration – p.555[N2] – 555[N1]. To be born in wealthy circumstances is not always a true blessing. The rich are apt to become selfish by not serving others, are less resourceful, inventive, and persevering than those who make a living – p.220[2]. They are less inclined to admit that they have spiritual needs – p.364 – 73 – 51. Thus, the rich whom have no problem must be a problem to God, for they are not learning about life and do not grow much in their mental and spiritual development – p.693 – 555[N4]. The Puritan work ethic believes that the rich should also work and strive to serve others – p.365. Life on earth is a workshop, a boot camp, a training ground, or schoolroom – p.220[2] – 51 – 359 – 360 – 757. It is certainly not easy for those whom have to serve others in order to survive in the fallen world, which was originally intended in a less harsh way in the restored world – p.51. Many people are not happy to enrich those who do not care for others – p.317. In the work place, the supervisor is often seen as an enemy and employees are constantly on the defensive – p.318. Other bosses go so far as to humiliate the workers and love to be feared by them – p.295 – 356 – 216[R]. The only "asset" those bullies have is their knowledge and skill, which they use as a whip to bully the workers in his or her place – p.295. If your supervisor is not only worldly but also evil-minded, then the situation becomes more difficult, especially for those whom are living a divine life – p.295[2] – 184 – 198 – 199. Many people do not like to work and seek value without doing any labor, such as **gambling and taking welfare –

---

* A dictator rules people from a position not given by God – p.332[N] – 551 – 295 – 296 – 212.

** p.160→166 – 744[N3] – 554 – 226[2] – 434[N6] - gambling

p.316 – 318 – 318^N – 365 – 210. Others prefer to live a life as a parasite or freeloader – p.210; or pass their days in idleness – p.318^N. However, by not giving anything to society, the universe cooperates perfectly by not returning anything to them – p.210. If we steal from others, something of value will be stolen from us. In order to make restitution, he or she has to pay double – p.258. A heavy karmic price is also due to all those whom are involved in the sex industry – p.136 – 137. When we are treating our fellow workers badly in order to be promoted, we will be treated in a similar fashion – p.210. It is exploitation when someone tries to steal another person's job or drive a competitor out of business – p.210 – 317^3 – 809^2.

In order to be successful, many modern business people have come to the understanding that service should be one of the major factors of prosperity in their enterprises and certainly more so than the attitude of competition and strife. Business organizations should therefore have a spirit of service, from management to personnel. In this spirit of giving, they contribute something of themselves by not only being attentive to the need of the customer but also by responding to the client as a human being. Those persons are usually mature, have a desire to contribute to the welfare of others, and some of them may also live a divine life. The persons they are talking to sense it immediately and know that the seller is reliable and on their side. This is in contrast to sales persons who are self-centered, are immoral in their desires and thinking, and care only about the money they are making. People who hate their job are usually driven to perform by a boss who is not service-oriented but wants to dominate and rule the workers. The customer does not like to return to an organization where they sense an atmosphere of apathy and even hostility towards them – p.356 – 357.

An employer who starts the day with a prayer service would not only improve the quality of life of the prayers but they also love to serve the customers with a sincere desire to help them – p.725 – 809^2. Working will be a joy, everybody can be creative, and supervisors are not only knowledgeable but also morally and spiritually developed, so that workers are not driven by fear but by "brotherly love" – p.699.

The sense of working with God in one's daily tasks gives an ethical meaning to labor – p.318^N, lowly jobs were regarded as important and not beneath the dignity of anyone – p.318^N. This was shown by Brother Lawrence, who was assigned the task of working in the monastery kitchen by cleaning pots and pans – p.367.

By living a life without God, the world of free trade, supply and demand (losing your job), the market becomes a fearful place. By living according to God's laws, the world is less hostile, knowing that God is always there to help and guide you – p.707. The best and first thing to do when you are facing economic difficulties is to straighten out your life – p.740 – 741^4, ask God for help, who then gives opportunities so that you can earn money or find a job – p.744^{N3} – 744^{N4}. Besides, you will approach personnel managers in a confident and composed manner – p.712 – 712^2.

The young should take chances and explore and experience, as much as possible, the many facets of life. Life is best lived, not as a search for security but a search for experience because a life devoid of challenge and variation is a life not worth living – p.372. In the ideal world of the future, people will not have to cling to only one profession or occupation for economic reasons – p.220¹ – 461¹. There are many professions we can choose, to know the physical aspect of life; human knowledge and development of the human spirit and Divine Spirit – p.372¹ – 774².

As the principle of growth for the vegetable, animal, and ungenerated humans is strife, competition, rivalry, and self-seeking, the principle of growth for the regenerated or spiritually-born individuals is cooperation, renunciation, and self-sacrifice. Without the guidance of the Soul, the personality of the ungenerated cannot truly love; it can only seek to possess, to control, or to use others for their own needs – p.564. The individuals whom are living a divine life move from competition to cooperation, from conquest to affiliation, and from fighting each other to nurturing each other – p.532. The spiritual grown-ups would rather be poor than compete in the corporate world. They like to be self-employed, which gives them more freedom to work with God to restore this fallen world – p.576 – 549^{N3} – 810 – 357^R, which was and still is the most important work anyone can do.

From Intellect to Intuition

The level of development of a savage is mostly physical and emotional, that is, their maturity. In a civilized human, the mental part is included; maturity is equated with being an intellectual. A more mature person is not only developed in their personality but also in their Divine Spirit, at the intuitional level – p.26^b – 511. That is the intellectual, moral, and spiritual development – p.41 – 41^b – 376* - 24 – 792 – 793. Rational and logical thinking began with the Greeks; irrational thinking and superstition were prevalent before – p.500 – 500¹; the latter did not have enough mental strength to control their emotional and desire nature – p.547 – 67. (*See also development of children – p.510→512; children recapitulate human evolution – p.513 – 514 – 231¹). Human develops thus from body consciousness to that of the mind or from instinct to intellect, and from self-consciousness to intuitional and Christ consciousness – p.502 – 496. The mind gives purpose to action, the desire incentive, and the vital body power – p.119 – 497. It is an organ of knowledge of the outer as well as the inner – p.78. The mind, however, is not the slayer of the Soul – p.554^{N2} – 681, and should be used to criticize religion ideas and

---

* When teenagers reach the age of accountability, they, like Adam and Eve (who were teenagers when they deviated – p.1), have to choose between the "Tree of Life" (living a Divine Life) or getting stuck in the life of the good/evil personality – p.287² – 701$^{#3}$. During that time, they become conscious of sexual desires and also of the divine or spiritual aspects of life – p.126 – 167 – 168. It is a good time for the teenager to search for spiritual things and to satisfy the hunger for Truth, because only through the awakening of the transpersonal can the adolescent crisis be resolved, and to overcome sexual desires and emotional problems – p.511 – 512.

NOTE: Young people called "hippies", whom rebelled against society in the 1960s, had original idealistic ideas, but they became confused about true love and lower desires and found out the hard way that love, or rather satanic love, was not the answer – p.543 – 255.

not to sacrifice and impoverish the intellect – p.554[N1] – 579[N3]. See further intellectual development – p.497→501. The inner human personality consists of the lower and higher mental components. The function of the lower mental self is to serve as a vehicle for concrete thinking (which deals with particular knowledge), and the higher component serves as a vehicle for abstract thinking (which deals with general or universal knowledge) – p.500 – 501[R]. Most people have developed only a lower concrete mind, which is linear and analytical, and not a higher abstract mind – p.681. The higher mind is more philosophical and clearer in its thinking. It is pure reason because it functions in the realm of concepts and ideas and is not influenced by sensations and emotions – p.681. The abstract mind is the principle behind the law. It is the abstraction of the essence of all the facts together – p.501[R]. The abstract faculty of the mind can be developed, for example, by thinking philosophically – p.501[R] – 518[N2] – 559 – 559[1] – 500 – 553 and begin to move to a higher plane – p.501 – 231[2]. As rational way of thinking is acquired in grade and high school (in American society), abstract thinking (and intuition) is more developed in college or at the university – p.510[2]. Many individuals have no personal awareness of God; they only go by learned information because the nature of the educational system is such that they have always been taught to look outwards for information – p.552 – 553 – 67 – 67[1] – 315 – 671 – 577[N] – XIV, and not from the inner source – p.576. Those intellectuals whom believe that humans are capable of reaching perfection without God – p.193, want to break their students' relationship with God – p.552[1] – 680. Their focusing mind is in alliance with the lower being and is also enslaved by desires – p.119 – 119[d] – 10 – 681. They are usually "puffed up" with self-importance – p.552 – 555, and some are also called snobs – p.554 – 554[2]. They use their intellect for evil purposes – p.681[a] – 349 – 297[N2] – 199 – 553. People should listen to what they are, not what they are saying – p.553[2] – 821[N3] – 196. Education should not only be geared towards [1]physical, emotional, and intellectual development – p.510[1] – 18, but also to spiritual development – p.699 – XV[N] – 296 – 296*. As the higher mental body is concerned about holistic thinking, the evolving Divine Spirit of the next level is concerned about the spiritual mind, will, wisdom, and love. It is the realm of intuitional thinking or direct knowing – p.501 – 129 – 130 – 118. Individuals can concentrate on any aspect of life and gain complete insight and knowledge of it without recourse to reason – p.681 – 574[1]. [2]Intuition sees at a glance what an ordinary mind

---

[1] Unlike a mechanical gadget, the body improves with use – p.399*. When any function is exercised, it improves. When, for example, the emotional self does not respond very well to compassion, one may place him or herself in such a situation that those higher emotions are aroused. The result is that the psychic channels through which the particular emotions flow widens, and the emotion self also improves. It then becomes easier to respond to those higher emotions – p.505[N4] – 652 – 653. It will also be easier to think good or evil – p.125[N]. How humans influence others – p.56→61 – 144.

[2] As higher intuition is perceived through the upper energy centers, such as the third eye – p.448[4] – 536 – 536* - 581 – 656 – 656* - 747[1] – 224 – 234 – 431[1] – 23[†], lower intuition is perceived through the lower energy centers – p.23[†] - 149 – 224 – 225 – 535[2].

may take a lifetime to discover – p.582N2 – 535 – 535N2. The more mature have trained by practice to distinguish good from evil, and are thus able to judge – p.574 – 681 – 153.

Obstructing the Divine Flow and its Restoration

Clearing the channel between the physical consciousness (body), the subconscious levels of the mind (human spirit – lower self), and Divine Spirit (Soul – Higher Self) of impurity and psychic obstructions – p.732 – 505N5 – 130 – 362N2 – 572N – 413 – 362N2 – because God resides within our more or less developed Divine Spirit, which is always pure and forms an unobstructed channel with Him, there is no need to clear this channel (1 Jn. 3:9). What needs to be cleared, so that the God forces can freely flow to our physical self, is the physical body, with its etheric shell, and the more or less tainted emotional and mental self (inner personality) – p.736.

By committing sin, we separate from God, clogging the channel between the personality and the God forces and also strengthening the evil part of the personality – p.721[1] – 174[R] (who wants to be its own God) and the evil thought-form – p.340[N1]. A channel may become more obstructed when we do not live according to the law of God – p.726[2]; do a lot of mundane thinking – p.682[a], and have unlawful desires – p.683[c]. When God is not able to express through a personality who wants to do evil, He/She is shut out, and Their dwelling place deep within the human spirit becomes Their prison – p.726[2] – 304[N].

We should not carry guilt with us or dwell on guilt because it becomes like barriers for the expression of the Soul – p.155 – 188[N] – 152 – 40. We ought to cleanse the physical and etheric bodies, purify our emotional and mental selves of negative feelings, thoughts, and thought forms, indulgences, and lower desires, so that the "thirty windows" can be cleansed – p.559 – 683 – 683[b] – 418 – 44 – 40 – 130 – 407 – 792[N1] – 736 – 737 – 505[N5] – 174 – 231 – 20 – 20[b] – 21 – 21[b] – 88[a] – 732. In order to be an effective healer, the person should be a clear and unobstructed channel for the Lord – p.724. It is also helpful to "be still" – Ps. 46:10 – p.355 – 726[2] – 712[R].

Through prayer and meditation, we are unblocking and widening the channel between human and God consciousness – p.717 – 717[N] – 683 – 683[b] – 714 – 776[*] - 746 – 746[2] – 783[3] – 21[b] – 22 – 22[b]. Prayers for others create an open channel through which God's love, energy, and wisdom can flow freely – p.396[*] - 721[2] – 722 – 723 – 412[R] – 738 – 738[3]. The barrier of the satanic nature is broken through, and individuals may experience, at first, a glimpse of God – p.764.

The mental channel can be opened much more if our belief, opinion, and attitude are closer to the Truth – when our thoughts and ways become more in harmony with the thoughts of God (Isa. 55:8) – p.737 – 776 – 396[*].

The Soul is able to govern the personality when the latter reflects the former, the physical and etheric bodies are consecrated, the emotional self has become stable, tranquil, still, serene, clear, transparent and peaceful, and the mental self is controlled. The Soul is then able to express the Love and Wisdom of God. The entire body is flooded with spiritual light and "everything you do or touch turns into gold" – p.575 – 505 – 504[N3] – 581.

The Etheric Body

It will not be long before scientists will explore and investigate this fascinating, subtle physical level – p.XVIII – 650.

The Hindus, Jewish, Greeks, and medieval church believe in the etheric body – p.706. A human being consists of three bodies: the physical/etheric, the human spirit (mental emotional), and Divine Spirit or Soul – p.520 – 523. The etheric or vital body is part of the physical body composition and is, therefore, subject to natural law. When the physical body dies, the etheric body also disintegrates. It is like the physical body in shape and form and is the mold or pattern of the physical body – p.649 – 539[N1]. It has a brain where physical life memory is stored – p.649. It becomes, together with the physical self, independent and fully alive after the first breath of air and etheric energy is taken. At that time, it is imprinted with its [1]astrological birth sign – p.649 – 663 – 490* - 603[1] – 228[N] – 786[N1]. As the physical body needs air to sustain life, so does the etheric body need life force energy, which is extracted from the air we breathe, the water we drink, and the food we eat – p.650 – 386 – 618[N5] – 653 – 786[N1] – 518[R] – 359*. The etheric double absorbs this vital energy from the [2]sun charged air – p.526[1] – 387 – 649, and supplies the nervous system with its electricity-like energy – p.518[N1] – 408. It interpenetrates the [3]physical structure like [4]sand in a sponge, and it permeates every cell – p.381[1], and empowers it with life so that it is able to function – p.649 – 554 – 446, and thus gives power to action – p.81 – 119[b] – 497. The energy of the etheric body is called breath of life, life energy, prana, vitality, chi, mana, etc., and it pervades the solar system – p.539[N1] – 650 – 737[N1] – 654 – 655. From the four ethers we find in a human, only the lowest is active in the [5]mineral world. Plants have an etheric body with two active ethers;

---

[1] Astrology – p.490[N] – 490* - astronomy – p.642[N3] – 800 - 800[2] – 597 – 597[1] – 321; body signs and hand lines – p.490[N]. "Do not tattoo any marks upon you" (Lev. 19:28) – p.626[N1].

[2] Sun – p.28 – 81 – 98[a] – 411[R] – 150[N] – 374[R] – 418 – 418[R] – 419 – 592[N1] – 595→598 – 635 – 649 – 447[N]; sun/moon – p.325 – 42; moon – p.149[N] – 418 – 598 – 595 – 635.

[3] The working of the human system – p.448 – 449 and physical senses – p.446[4] – 593[N1] – 593[1].

[4] In a container filled with a sponge or sand, saturated with water, while air will occupy the empty spaces in water. Thus, several worlds can coexist in the same space and operate simultaneously because of different frequency. Thus, the etheric, psychic, and divine can coexist in matter – p.454 – 20.

[5] It is possible "to read" the etheric counterpart of a stone and other objects (psychometry) – p.227 – 228 – 228* - 320[N] – 700 – 144[c] – 529[N4]. Plants are capable of growth and propagation. It causes the circulation of juices in the spring and they react to stimulation of humans and sound, which makes them thrive (or wither) – p.320[N] – 700 – 79 – 81 – 324 – 324[6]. Animals have the ability of growth, propagation, and sense perception – p.320[N] – 700 – 324 – 324[6]. Human beings employ the fourth and highest ether from their etheric body to impress the brain with thoughts from their human spirits – p.320[N] – 321[N] – 700 – 81. One of the four divisions of etheric matter is reflecting ether, which has the ability to photograph and retain pictures, especially of intensely charged scenes, such as those of violence or scenes of battle – p.430[2] – 452[N2]. The vital body may influence devices in close proximity of the physical body – p.227.

animals have three ethers active – p.320^N – 700. These ethers pervade all matter and are active in all processes of life – p.649. We can cleanse our etheric body of impure energies by taking a shower or swimming in the ocean – p.559 – 383^R – 653 – 20. These impurities have settled in the outer layers of the etheric body, which projects slightly beyond the skin of the physical body – p.383^R – 526 – 652 – 656. The etheric body is sustained and maintained by proper breathing – p.410 – 464 – 618^{N5}. By following special breathing techniques and retention of breath, the supply of vital energy is considerably increased – p.654 – 655. The etheric body is called a health body because diseases of the physical body can be first detected as dark spots in the aura of the etheric body, where the flow of vital energy is blocked or depleted – p.651 – 400. However, it can be restored by faith healing and [1]acupuncture – p.651. The main purpose of [2]sleep is to repair and rebuild the physical organism and to recharge the etheric body – p.435 – 316. Because vital energy takes care of the renewing of the cells and bodily tissues – p.381^1 – 385^2 – 383 – 384^{N1}, we should not deplete it by negative emotions and thinking and [3]overindulgence in sex, that is orgasm – p.57^c – 10 – 169 – 166 – 166^1 – 167^N – 530 – 543^{N1} – 808^1 – 387 – 127^c – 127^b – 385^2 – 409 – 59^a – 99. Not to allow certain people to drain us from vital energy (psychic [4]vampirism) which makes us depleted, exhausted, depressed, and ill – p.200^N – 409 – 452^{N1}.

The etheric body acts as an intermediary between the physical body and the spirit body. It has seven energy centers by which psycho-spiritual man or woman expresses himself/herself in the etheric and, thence, to the nerve

---

[1] To know about acupuncture is a valid proof for the existence of the etheric body – p.372^1 – 525.

[2] The moment we fall asleep, the spirit body disengages from the physical and etheric bodies but maintains a partial contact through the "silver cord" (Eccl. 12:6) – p.436. One is not always conscious of out-of-the-body experiences because there is a barrier, an etheric web between the psychic and the physical – p.439 – 439^2 – 651. Bewildering dreams may be the result of physical and etheric brain activities – p.438^{N2}.

[3] Sublimation is for many the right thing to do – p.123→126 – 169 – 169* - 530^2 – 68^a – 99^c – 99^b.

[4] Lower beings of the spirit planes and negative creatures from the etheric realm are out to vampire etheric energy to sustain themselves, to materialize, and to act as poltergeists – p.651 – 451 – 452 – 169^N – 230^N. There are negative extra-terrestrials – etheric shells – and zombies – p.351 – 232 – 452^{N2} – 700 – 656. The vampires needed the emanations from freshly spilt blood and the waning vital substance of the newly-dead. They were, therefore, propitiated with blood sacrifices – p.422^N – 651 – 474^5 – 521. Fairies are positive etheric beings – p.474^5 – 700 – 325 – 656, and extra-terrestrials whom are good – p.455^{N2} – 700. The belief that all beings and objects are invested with psychic and etheric energy is part of the religion of animism – p.325 – 324 – 324^6 – 521. Pantheism – p.521.

NOTE 1: Just as the physical body has blood vessels and organs, the etheric body has meridian channels and force centers – p.649.

NOTE 2: Just as the etheric body receives prana from the physical atmosphere, human spirits get their substance through "breathing" from their surrounding spiritual atmosphere – p.359*.

centers and ductless gland systems of the physical body. Thus, they control and direct via the centers the muscles of the physical self, which then move at their command. The etheric body is also the medium through which (via the higher energy centers) thought makes an impression upon the human brain, while emotion is expressed through the solar plexus and heart centers – p.448 – 650 – 474[N] – 518[R] – 234 – 225 – 413 – 324[N1]. The physical body may be complete in all its organs, systems, and elements, but without the etheric body, it has no power of animation. Without the spirit body, the physical and etheric bodies are helpless, heartless, and thoughtless things. Though the body has a [1]brain, it cannot think. Though the body is in possession of lips and tongue, it is not able to speak, and the muscles are likewise not able to move without their operator, the human spirit (body) – p.446 – 447 – 518[N2]. A person not only has [2]energy centers (chakras) in the etheric body but also in his/her human and divine body, which are counterparts of those in the etheric body. The centers are, thus, the main gateways (portals) through which emotional, mental, and divine energies pass among the physical, psychic, and spiritual planes – p.448[4-5] – 59 – 527. In review, the vibration of thinking causes the emotional self to vibrate, which in turn has its effect on the etheric body and then acts via the nervous system on the matter of the physical brain – p.502 – 518[N2], which makes the muscle move and the voice being heard, thus solving the brain/mind controversy.

As the physical body has an etheric sheath, with many energy centers, the earth as the macrocosm is also surrounded with an etheric envelope, with its many energy centers. Those centers were connected with [3]leylines and known by ancient people as holy sites – p.526[N] - 526[†]. The energy centers and meridians of the human body resonate with those in the planetary body, so that every human intention and action generates waves of action and interaction throughout the earth's energy field – p.322[N]. Phases of the moon, sunspot

---

[1] Like the radio and television sets, the function of the brain is to receive, transform, and strengthen (amplify) impulses (electrical signals) from a mental energy field. They are, however, not the cause of the program, which is still present in the form of light and sound waves, even when the set or brain is turned off or by being unconscious – p.412 – 413 – 409 – 420[*] - 447. Many orthodox scientists became very skeptic, in and after the 18th century, and said that the mind is nothing more than the working of the brain or the product of the brain – p.420[*] - 445[4] – 447 – 447[2] – 35. According to the proceedings of the society of psychical research, a person who is separated from his/her body, either in sleep, in trance, "out of the body", and "near-death experience", can still think without the brain – p.445.

[2] Although the bodies permeate each other, higher and lower energies do need the swirling (tunnel-like) force centers of the same level to get through to the other body or bodies – p.448[4]. Energy centers – p.525→537. Description of the seven energy centers – p.529→537 – 448[4-5] – 59 – 60; manifestation of the presence of energy centers – p.59[a]. See also Etheric Body – p.649→656.

[3] As Chi flows through the body, so does it flow over the surface of the earth through special pathways – leylines and force centers – p.655. The flow of Chi is affected by two forces: Feng (wind) and Shui (water). The principles of Feng Shui are (also) applied to location of buildings and placement of furniture in harmony with the environment and circulation pattern of the flow of Chi – p.655.

radiation, and other disturbances of the earth magnetic field influence the electromagnetic force field around human bodies, which in turn affects their etheric aura, which has an impact on the nervous system and aura of the human spirit – p.430.

Upon death, the consciousness of the person first withdraws from the physical body into the etheric double for a few days before it settles in his or her spirit body. In this process, they pass or "download" all the physical, or rather, etheric brain memory into the (sub)conscious mind of their spirit body, which is experienced as a review of their life – p.233^N – 209^2 – 427 – 427^2 – 459^1 – 82 – 82^b.

For humans spirits and activities to [1]materialize, they need etheric or vital energy, which they are able to draw from human beings and the surrounding atmosphere – p.168^N – 169^N – 473^4 – 76. It takes a lot of energy to sustain materialization. Full materialization is therefore difficult to obtain – p.473^R – 474 – 428^{N2} – 300^3. A materialized hand appeared which wrote on the wall of king Belshazzar's palace (Dan. 5) – p.649.

How did Jesus come back after his crucifixion – p.468→474? He denied being a spirit because he appeared in a materialized spirit or etheric body – p.469.

---

[1] Materialization may occur whereby ectoplasm (an etheric substance) exudes from a medium and is also drawn from people nearby to engulf and solidify a human spirit, thereby making it visible and touchable – p.230. Ectoplasm – what is – p.474^5 – using – p.472 – 451 – from medium – p.474. Materialize and dematerialize of objects (apports) – p.230. Stigmata – p.473^1 – 351 – 502.

NOTE 1: Psycho-kinesis – influencing an object or event with the mind – p.226 – 227. Examples of P.K. are: influencing the throwing of the dice – p.226^2 – 434^{N6}, spoon or metal bending, splitting or dissolving clouds.

NOTE 2: In meditation – put both feet on the floor when sitting in a chair, with spine erect (making a circuit with folding hands). It makes it easy for the etheric energy to move freely in the body along the spine channel and prevents the outflow of pranic energy. When sitting in the cross-legged position, the energy from the earth (kundalini) will also pass through the energy centers from below – p.737^N – 736^4 – kundalini energy – p.526 – 526^1 – 526^N – 127 – 127^b – 178.

NOTE 3: Eye is the mirror of the Soul – p.698. To make eye contact – p.430 – 431 – 431^1 – 432 – 432^N – 446. The eyes are like etheric portals through which the projected energy of the man (woman) may enter the woman's (man's) etheric body and thus influence her (his) spirit body – p.145 – 227. To look at a woman lustfully – p.132 – 686 – 86 – 145.

NOTE 4: It is possible to see like x-rays through physical bodies, walls, layers of earth, closed containers, and letters – p.656.

NOTE 5: Physical attractions are caused by the activity of the positive and negative poles of the etheric bodies – p.66^c.

NOTE 6: Women whom are charged with sex appeal or animal magnetism – p.147 – 147*.

Thoughts, Thought Forms, and Vibrations

[1]Thought is the creative force of the universe. It can create, build, empower, and destroy. As individuals must discipline their words, they should also learn to discipline and control their thoughts because all actions are the result of thoughts – p.227[N]. In order not to become an easy prey of lower beings, they ought to pay attention to their careless play of thoughts and unruly emotions – p.133. Because energy follows thought – p.654 – 169 – 123 – 134, it is capable of awakening the easily aroused sexual desires – p.133[b] – 144 – 212, not only in themselves but also in others by projecting waves of lustful thoughts to others, which is called telepathy or thought transfer – p.60 – 20. If a person thinks good (or evil) of another person, it will be much easier to do it again and this trend will be difficult to change because the mental self is used to that kind of vibration – p.125[N] – 652 – 653. Because thoughts also produce waves in the surrounding psychic atmosphere, they will also affect the mental selves (bodies) of people moving in that environment. Their effectiveness depends upon the strength, clearness, and receptivity – p.125[N]. [2]Those thoughts may affect many people, whom in turn may influence others close by or at a great distance – p.333[*] - 333. Thought waves and radiations leave their imprints on everything which is touched – p.228 – 144. Just as thoughts can affect people, pets, clouds, and inanimate objects so do they act upon living plants. The latter thrive when they receive much love and/or prayer and visualize it as healthy and productive, but may wither or die when hate is directed to them – p.746[N2] – 320 – 595[6].

Because all animate and inanimate things are in a state of vibration, any vibration field emitted by one thing may easily affect vibration fields of surrounding things – p.595[N12]. As the middle C is struck on a piano and causes the octave of the lower Cs to vibrate in sympathetic vibration, so the stronger waves radiating from a higher being can [1]influence the vibrations of

---

[1] As the saying goes: "Thoughts are things." "What we think will come to pass." "Thoughts held in mind produce after their kind." – p.227[N].

[2] The effectiveness of thought transfer can be tested, preferably on individuals whom are receptive (are not occupied with other thoughts) and are in harmony with the tester – p.125[N] by projecting a thought to them – and dare an individual person to look up and turn around – p.432.

NOTE 1: We may think of every thought impulse as having a distinct wavelength or a specific rate of vibration – p.590[N1]. It will also affect the electric activity of their brain waves – EEG. Beta waves – for the person who is fully conscious, the slower alpha waves occur when the person is in a relaxed mode (meditative state), and theta and delta brain waves arise when a person is in light and deep sleep – p.436[N4] – 747[3/4] – 434[N3] – 226.

NOTE 2: Light is not the fastest moving energy in the universe; the energy of thought is much faster – p.590[*].

NOTE 3: The belt of negative thoughts around the earth will be strengthened by negative thinking, which has an extensive influence on weather conditions, behavior of people, and animals, the growth of plants and natural disasters – p.595[N1].

NOTE 4: One plays better golf when the ball follows the psychic direction towards the goal – p.432[R] – 415[R].

his or her students. They are not only influenced by the person's words but also by the radiating vibration which made them appreciate and understand the teachings. At a higher plane, the love of God may strike the keynote of an individual and awaken the force of altruism – p.599 – 594[N2]. By sympathizing with a person, we soon begin to vibrate in resonance with that person – p.595[N8]. After having talked to somebody, it is difficult to concentrate on other subjects because you are still having communication on the psychic level with that individual – p.434[N2]. [1]When belonging to a certain group of people, you vibrate like the rest of them. If you do not, then anyone in the group will sense that you are not one of them. The same vibrations can be induced by thinking the same way – learning the same truth and have the same world view – p.444[N4].

As one cannot see radio and television waves that vibrate at too fast a rate, so one cannot see the vibrations or waves of the world beyond. As waves are around and about us and even go right through solid matter, so are the vibrations of the spirit side of life all around us and material objects do not hinder their passage – p.444.

When living on the physical plane, we experience great difficulties expressing ourselves fully and accurately in earth-based languages, with their narrowness of conception. We can only present one idea at a time, while the physical brain can handle only a limited amount of thoughts, which have to be formulated in words before they become comprehensible. When we at first arrive in the spirit world, we formulate certain words with our minds in a particular language and then project them. However, we soon find out how slow it is. [2]We then learn to communicate by thought transference, which is the common language for everyone, especially on the higher planes. For them,

---

[1] The body needs to adjust to the increase of energy and vibration from the growing inner self, or temporarily induced by an outside source. Because the physical organs are not always adapted to the rapid vibration of spiritual substance, the individual may experience changes in energy levels; that is, being upbeat one day and tired the next – p.591[N3]. The spirit selves have also been overstrained – p.594[N2].

NOTE 1: Because everyone and everything has its own vibratory rate or wavelength, which is as distinct as a fingerprint, much information about a particular individual can be obtained psychically – p.593 – 593[2] – 228[N].

NOTE 2: As the voice of an individual is known to have shattered glass, and the power of rhythmic vibration of soldiers marching over a bridge could make the structure collapse. The walls of Jericho fell at the 7th day at the combined vibration of trumpets and the shouts of the people. See Joshua 6th Chapter – p.444[N5].

NOTE 3: Besides raising your vibrations by prayer, music, and meditation, it is also possible to increase your vibration somewhat by deep breathing – p.595[N7].

NOTE 4: Jesus Christ, who was able to raise the vibration of the cells of his body, was able to lift himself up by walking on water – p.591[N3] – 654.

NOTE 5: The individual feels light, as if he or she is "walking on air" – p.591[N3].

NOTE 6: It may even be possible to increase our vibration to such an extent that we may become invisible – p.591[N4] – 402[R].

See also vibrations and cycles – p.590→598 and the electromagnetic spectrum – p.442 – 656[B]. Unharmonious vibrations of hammer and other tools – p.239.

[2] We do not have to wait until we pass over to know how to communicate by thought transference.

there is no longer a language barrier. Telepathic communication is more swift and accurate without any barrier of space, time, and matter. It conveys more the essence of the human being. One does not have to seek for words to express correctly because emotions and thoughts speak clearer than words. It is much more difficult to deceive, lie, pretend, or be a hypocrite. Much more information and a wealth of meaning can be exchanged – p.601 – 459 – 460 – 227[N].

To create a dwelling or other things on the earth plane usually takes a [1]great amount of time. It first has to be [2]visualized, plans are then made, and building materials assembled to make it a reality – p.457[5]. We create in the same way in the spirit world as in the physical dimension. There is first the [3]purpose, will, and desire to create; the [4]imagination comes about, and the idea (abstract thought)is formed. When the abstract thought is being clothed with mind stuff, a more solid thought form is created, which becomes a solid creative object in the spirit world. This thought form in the physical world becomes a plan, which materializes in the slow process of physical action and creation – p.134.

As individuals should discipline their words and body movements on earth, they should also learn to control their thoughts because all actions in the spirit world are the result of thought. Thought in the spirit world is real and concrete (as the [5]spirit body is made of psychic energy). It can create and build our surroundings, and it is also a means of communication and transportation – p.134. The thought you project manifests almost instantly, especially in the higher dimension of life, and we create only havoc when we have not become masters of our creative thoughts – p.457[5].

Angels and human spirits are able, by their power of thought, to change their spirit bodies in many shapes or forms – p.474[5]. They can also pretend to be someone else by making a thought form of a person someone is seeking or give a message to – p.182[1]. Because thought can easily change and mold psychic matter, the same process of change was used by satan to change himself into an angel of light – p.460[3] – 182. Samuel changed his spirit body to an age where he would be recognized by Saul (1 Sam. 28:14) – p.460. Human images can become more concrete by creating thought forms of them

---

[1] This slow process is necessary in order to learn how to create without making too many mistakes and thus become a better creator in the spirit world – p.457[5].

[2] Visualizing – p.457[5] – 747[N2] – 384 – 732 – 21 – 200[N].

[3] The mind gives purpose to action; the desire body gives incentive to action, the vital and physical bodies give power to action – p.497 – 497[2] – 119[b] – 81.

[4] Imaginations – fantasies – p.134 – 133 – 430[1] – 20[a] – 212 – 180 – 784[1] – 458[6].

[5] Our spirit body is created and composed of what we have thought and what we are thinking and feeling now – p.460[1]. Thoughts and feelings which we believe are true become our belief and systems of belief – p.557[3]. The inner selves are made up of all your ideas and beliefs and all the things that have been accepted by you. Your selves are created and composed of what you feel and think, and that is your character.

NOTE: As the spoken words can be heard, the thoughts expressed (not held within) can be known – p.227[N].

and projecting those and other images on, for example, crime or graveyard sights – p.168 – 452^{N2} – 590 – 578^2 – 230^N. The gods of Athens and Rome were created in the image of the people, whom were usually more evil than good. They build up the collective thought forms (accumulated energy) of the gods of their imagination until they started acquiring a life and power of their own. When the Greek and Roman empires declined, the gods lost their divinity, their adventures were less spoken of, and eventually they lost much of the attention and power of the people. The dying gods or huge thought forms then crumbled when they were no longer fed with psychic energy of the worshippers – $p.180^N$ – 784 – 784^1 – 506 – 264^6. The people in the Middle Ages, whom were obsessed with the idea of satan, built him up. The more energy they directed to a certain image of satan, the more they strengthened the newly-created thought form of satan, who later crumbled when the fanatic belief in satan declined – $p.180^N$. People in the spirit world create their own surroundings by molding the psychic substances by thought and, thus, create scenery and objects according to their own conception – p.457 – 458. Because individuals or groups are able to create whatever their fancy, belief, or imagination, we therefore find, in some parts of the spirit world, a New Jerusalem. It contains pearly gates, streets of gold, and its great white throne, upon which we find a thought form of an elderly God – $p.458^6$.

The Creation of Power by Energy Exchange

By prayer, humans not only have a personal audience with the Creator and Sustainer of the universe – p.726, the Source of all power – p.718 – 720^{N2}, but bring in movement the hand who rules the universe – p.739.

Power is created by energy exchange. We may distinguish evil power created by evil people and evil spirits – $p.550^*$ - 715^{N3}; human power created by good people with or without bodies; and divine power created by divine beings and the God forces – $p.550^*$ - 690. The devil said to Jesus, "To you I will give all this authority (over the kingdoms of the world) and their glory; for it has been delivered to me" (Lk. 4:6). Jesus said in (Matt. 28:18), "All authority in heaven and on earth has been given to me", and to seek the glory that comes from God and not from men (Jn. 5:41;44) – $p.550^*$.

Those who call upon the name of Jesus Christ find and receive accumulated credit and divine power of, and, within that name – $p.550^*$ - 607^{N1} – 731 – 264^6. We can use the (collective) power of a name of a master, saint or family – $p.607^{N1}$. Secular people may use the name of an organization or government agency ("the power vested in me"), to authorize, for example, a marriage contract – $p.483^N$ – 5.

When the Roman emperors were worshipped, they gained through this veneration more physical and psychic human power from the people. Images of emperors all over the empire were, therefore, very helpful in advancing their cause – $p.545^1$ – 632. They felt so much power (the collective energy of the people) that they even called themselves Sons of God – $p.264^6$. When Saul was accepted as a king, he received much power from the people and was less in need of divine power – $p.813^1$. For the American colonist, the kings of England were tyrants whom were no longer guided by God. The kings did not want to *give up their power over the people, and as long as the people obeyed, paid respect and homage to them, they had that psychic power – p.108. Those whom are living a divine life cannot and will not obey the king, because their life is governed by God – p.108ᵇ.

No man or woman has (extra) power, except the powers followers give them, either physical – people work for them; psychological – being influenced by them; spiritually – believing in them – p.693*. Having gained human power, authority, and prestige, centered on outer values, the rich are less likely to seek for divine power and authority – p.693. Those whom are men of power, position, and knowledge would not accept the invitation of Christ (Matt. 22:1-10) – p.550. Many individuals are "puffed up" with self-importance. This is based on the fact that society says that they have studied and are, therefore, knowledgeable – p.552. They influence many people and have power over them because knowledge is power in their society – p.553². It is easy for established religious leaders to become prideful after they are recognized and won the trust and admiration of those who believe in them (who all give them power). They have a tendency to give less credit to God. The result is that God is not able to work through them as much as before. The channel between God and them becomes even more obstructed when they have been successful in their work, and especially when their ego gets bolstered too much by immature followers whom are praising their personalities instead of God, who is enshrined within them. They then, like Lucifer, place themselves between God and the people. However, they have only power over those who believe in them – p.580 – 330³.

A spiritually undeveloped person may, through deception, misrepresentation, and flattery, acquire a position in the church hierarchy or even buy a church office and start ruling those whom are morally and spiritually more developed or closer to God – p.331 - 331⁶

REMARK: The Catholics believe in the apostolic succession, which was also practiced by Protestants to a limited extent – p.589. This power or authority can also be transferred from a human ruler to successor – p.264⁶. Elijah anointed Elisha to be his successor – p.628, as Joshua became the successor of Moses.

---

* Some kings held on to the notion of the "Divine Right of Kings" – p.107* - 770¹.
NOTE 1: Because most people are good and evil, they have a tendency to control those who are in the position approved by God, and to occupy a position for which they are not morally qualified – p.331 – 331⁶ – 547.
NOTE 2: James Madison said: "The essence of government is power – power lodged as it must be in human hands will ever be liable to abuse" – p.108 – 548ᴿ – 551.
NOTE 3: Democracy is not an ideal form of government, but in the fallen world, it is the best possible world. In order for it to work, any government branch should not have too much power – p.295ᴺ – 551.
NOTE 4: Humans should subject themselves under God-chosen government authorities – p.545ᴺ¹.

Art

Art concerns itself with the communication of certain ideas and feelings by means of a sensuous medium, such as color, sound, bronze, marble, words, etc. They appeal to our mind, arouse our *emotions, kindle our imaginations, and enchant our senses. Further, art is an international language of communication, as it is expressed through painting, music, film, opera, literature, sculpture, architecture, dance, and the like. Its purpose is to enhance life, to reveal God in all of Their Beauty, Truth, and Goodness, and it never stops witnessing – p.599 – 213 – 602. A work of art consists of the outer – the artists and his work, and the inner, which is aroused and stirred by what is sensed – p.560[N1].

God as Creative and True Artist created the cosmos out of chaos, and pervaded everything with His Consciousness – p.323 – 600 – 322. Like God, evolved humans invest the object they create with psychic and spiritual energy, whereby it becomes more "alive" – p.324 – 240*. True artists as creators leave likewise something of themselves in their works of art. The aliveness of their art depends on how much creative energy they invested and how much "alive" they were at the time of creation – p.694. Great works of art come from a higher source than from their ego selves – p.535. Unfortunately, most artists, singers, musicians, and poets are working from the lower selves of their beings – p.535, and are not in harmony within themselves – p.326[2]. When inspiration is forgotten, and there is no spiritual life, humans become mechanical and imitators and are not able to create original work of high quality. He or she may write poetry, compose music, and paint pictures, but they will be lifeless. They may impart psychic life to their creation but not spiritual life – p.414[R] – 136.

The mission of the artists is to use his/her skill and talent to channel and manifest the divine, to bring heaven on earth – p.746[N1] – 559 – 127[b] – 708 – 694 – 556. When people are close to God in their feeling and thinking, we see a time of creative flowering extending to artistic brilliance and higher art. Beauty is God shining through at what is beautiful. Beauty is Truth, and Truth is Harmony – p.130 – 576[N]. In the higher stages of development, we find great visionary artists – p.130 – 576[N], and illuminated beings whom are highly creative and delight in Beauty – p.583.

Many seniors are delving into artistic expression, and it changes their lives. They found that creativity – p.126→130 – 618 – 619 can be nurtured and new

---

* The functions of the emotion or feeling are: to provide power, passion, warmth, excitement, zeal, and color in whatever we do and to vitalize our thinking, intensify, enhance, sweeten, and deepen our experience – p.503 – 399[1]. Someone who is emotionally oriented may also be sensitive to nature, beauty, the arts, music, and dance. However, this person may also experience the negative side of the emotion by easily becoming moody and upset because of the inconstancy and instability of the emotional self – p.503[N1]. The inspired artist and philosopher may invoke in the observer and the reader the same emotion. For the same reason, a play is performed and a move is made to make the public response emotional and intellectual in a certain way – p.559 – 560. See also p. 126 – sublimation of sexual passion – p.437[R] – receiving ideas when in a dream state. See also p.502→505 "The value of emotional development".

talents can be developed by anyone. To develop a talent late in physical life will be very useful, not only here on earth but also of its use in the afterlife. Experimenting and viewing the world in a fresh way delights creative artists of all ages – p.394[3] – 394[4]. Finally, be joyful and make people happy, sing uplifting songs, appreciate noble art, and seek for its beauty, truth, and harmony. See good movies, read inspiring poetry and books. Seek for Truth and Beauty within and without yourselves, and try to connect with your Divine Spark or Self and those Selves of the people you meet – p.20 – 21.

Music and Sound

As words have a fixed meaning in relation to a complete thought, tones assume a fluid meaning in association with other tones, which is called a melody – p.601. Music is an art dealing with the organization of tones into patterns and has been called the emotion of language. It brings people into harmony with each other – p.600. When music is not ordered sound, it is not harmonious and is noise which is disagreeable to the human constitution – p.604[N1] – 640[N]. The measured beat of music in time or rhythm should be in harmony with the rhythm of nature and the inner working of the body. Serene music is able to transform moods and inspires our personality with feelings of love, beauty, resolution, and altruism. Uplifting music can transport us to other realms of consciousness and tap our true inner Being, which makes us experience divine power. It brings harmony to the body, mind (human spirit), and Soul and balances and strengthens our auric field – p.604[N2] – 735 – 736 – 445[2] – 550[N6] – 694.

We should listen to and play high vibration music such as, for example, classical, religious music, new age, and natural sounds, and others. It has been said that the music of Beethoven and Handel was to awaken the Divine Spark within the people – p.20 – 67. However, individuals should certainly not become involved with music and songs that awaken their sexuality. When the music is low in vibration, such as for example jazz and rock music, the emotional vibration bodies or sheaths of the teenagers (and others) eventually come to have the same rate of frequencies. This shows itself by their negativity and changes in dark moods, which also influence their thinking – p.20 – 67 – 68 – 68* - 101.

To study music and art is to be acquainted with the emotions, to know about the multitude of emotional expressions by playing music which expands our emotional self – p.518[R] – 774[2] – 523. The public responds emotionally in a positive way when high vibration music is played in the movies. Unfortunately, we see an erosion of values in the entertainment industry today. Much of the music played today is not only discordant, loud, and offensive, which creates disorder, disharmony, confusion, and anxiety in our psyche, but it also impairs our values and creative thinking – p.560[2] – 707.

NOTE 1: The growing child learns to express many facets or colors of emotions and is also involved in music, singing, drama, dancing, drawing, and other artistic expressions – p.510 – 509[N2].

NOTE 2: As the sound waves cause a sympathetic response from those instruments which are attuned to them, thought waves likewise produce a reaction of a human being who vibrates at the same rate. A note of expression struck in one's life reflects and vibrates into other people's lives when they are in sympathy or attunement.

NOTE 3: Harmonious music is heard in many places in the spirit world which expresses itself in thought forms of beautiful changing colors. There is a close connection between color and sound – p.636[N2] – 636 – 637[N2]. When, for example, a note is struck, a certain color appears – p.457 – 592[2].

See also – humans as musical instruments – p.413. Elvis Presley – p.414[R] – colors – p.636 – 637 – 442 – 443[N1] – 656[B].

Painting – Sculpture – Architecture – Dance – Song – Entertainments

Abstract art of today is not like realistic art or surface painting of the nineteenth century. An abstract painter is more likely to paint the inner or essence of things – p.599. As soon as he or she started to imitate painting, he/she lost their individuality – p.560[N2]. Art is to mix colors in such a way that they harmonize, as the clothes we wear – p.600.

Just as a rough block of stone does not appear to be anything until it has been transformed by the [1]sculptor, so also our life appears to be uncultivated, immature, and ignorant. We should, therefore, impose order and purpose out of chaos and confusion in our lives, as we do when we create a puzzle – p.417.

Architectural structures, when they are in harmony with the universe, create harmony in ourselves and link us to the divine – p.560. We shape buildings; later, they shape us – p.416.

Much of Western music today is sexual in character. It not only stimulates and excites the emotions and plays on the lower desires but also has an effect on the movement of the bodies. This is especially true of jazz. By following its rhythm and beat, the dancers awaken their sexuality and become very sensual in their [2]movements – p.68. The spirit of the world manifests itself by sexually seductive music, dirty dancing – p.101 – 68*.

When you are out of harmony, singing will help restore your balance to the rhythms of nature. A singer is lifting up the vibration of the audience and is loved by those whom are vibrating like the singer, and they become his or her fans – p.602 – 20.

In other forms of entertainment, such as movies, television, soap operas, and situation comedies, much of the negative side of human nature is emphasized, such as hostility, cynicism, deception, irresponsibility, shallowness, pettiness, immorality, and deviousness, instead of [3]mature behavior: accountability, honesty, trust, integrity, virtue, and true love, which are the components of a true hero – p.560[2] – 708.

---

[1] The ancient Egyptians believed that a person's "ka" could reside in sculptures of their human forms – p.324[5].

[2] Some of the lower types of music have inspired people to do "the twist", which is the movement of their lower bodies, which is similar to that of a snake – p.68.

[3] A film is made with the intention to make the public response emotionally, intellectually, psychically, and spiritually, thus strengthening their inner conviction that it is worthwhile to be virtuous and honorable in their lives – p.600 – 560.

Mantra – Chanting – Analogy – Symbols – Mythology – Figurative Language

To a lesser degree, we may achieve higher states of consciousness by repeating a special sound vibration, "The Mantra" – p.445[2]. Because the whole manifested universe is considered to be based on vibration, it is therefore possible to bring certain changes in matter and consciousness through sound vibration, such as one's voice, singing, mantras, and other sounds and chanting. The Gregorian chant, for example, brings individuals to alternate states of consciousness and also has a purifying effect on the persons and their surroundings – p.599. The recitation and chanting of mantras is to produce certain vibrations in the inner bodies, to bring them in harmony or tune them up, to focus on, and protect themselves – p.600 – 748[N3] – 748[N4] – 200[N].

By using the art of analogy, we may connect our physical selves to the psychic and the latter to the divine, and by using other literary devices, such as parables and symbols and the like – p.560 – 404 – 802 – 327. Through mythology and symbolism, contact can be made between the physical and psychic levels – p.560[N4] – 405 – 405*. Dream messages are usually expressed as symbols rather than thoughts or words because so much more, and correctly, can be told by a single symbolic image. This is the method of communication of the subconscious (the mind of the human spirit) and the Higher Mind (the mind of the Divine Spirit) – p.437 – 438 – 405[R]. Figurative language may be used to explain the unknown through the known because the unknown cannot be properly explained through a physical language, only through symbols which we know. Metaphors, similes, analogies, parables, allegories, myths, and stories are used to describe the unknown – p.802 – 803 – 404→406. Most profound are the parables of Jesus Christ, which were based on everyday experiences, which everyone at that time understood. He used many parables to explain to the people what the Kingdom of heaven is like – p.406 – 802 – 802[1].

NOTE 1: The relationship between life on the physical plane and the higher life is expressed by the maxim "As below, so above", also called the Law of Correspondence – p.802 – 404.

NOTE 2: Symbols are the outer and visible forms of the inner spiritual realities. They are the language of dreams in which the subconscious and super-conscious communicate with the conscious mind – p.405 – 405* - 437[1].

NOTE 3: An example of symbolic language in the Bible: As water means people (Rev. 17:15), clouds means people whom have purified themselves – "Behold He is coming with the clouds" (Rev. 1:7). In some passages of the Bible, fire has the meaning of Judgment by the Word – p.406[R].

NOTE 4: Examples of analogy – see p.404→419 – typology – p.803[N3].

NOTE 5: For those who are not ready to receive it, Truth is concealed in parables and symbols, with manifold meanings for different levels of understanding (Matt. Ch. 13). The interpretation of the Truth will be revealed by the Spirit of God whenever individuals are ready to receive it – p.327. (When understood, a deeper Truth becomes apparent.)

Language – Poetry – Speaking – Writing – The Word

Language has power.   It transmits not only facts and ideas but also emotions and values. Skillful writers and speakers have used their power to affect people's attitudes, influence their actions, and shape their inner views of the world and its people – p.560[N3]. [1]Much of the conversation gets lost when it is put in words – p.602. Words cannot really convey what one feels or thinks.   They are often colored, shaded, or distorted, according to pre-conceived ideas and beliefs of the lower self or personality.   How one expresses him/herself is important, not as much as the words because everyone can repeat the words of great individuals, but who can speak from the same spiritual attitude? – p.602 [2]The voices of evolved beings are always marked by a sincerity, integrity, cheerfulness, encouragement, and impressiveness. The tonal quality of their voice is that of harmony, music, and of an irresistible charm, and we also absorb their consciousness – p.602 – 583.

Language is external – poetry is internal expression – p.416. The function of poetry, unlike that of prose, is not to explain but to go beyond the intellect, reason, and words to see the whole and a glimpse of the divine.   It offers images and ideas in a few lines that resonate with our lives and lets us hear a truth that we always have known – p.600.   In the more elevated form of speech, such as poetry, [3]sound and rhythm plays an important part in creating the music of poetry – p.600.

The human voice is the intermediary of body and human spirit and is capable of conveying emotions and thoughts.   It is also a channel for the Divine Spirit – p.602. When you give a command, you not only convey the words and thoughts but also the emotions and the psychic energy that go with them – p.434[N]. The lower self or personality may give an order or command, filling the words as containers with more or less psychic energy or power,

---

[1] Examples are: tone of voice, gestures, the twinkling of an eye, facial expressions, the receptivity of the listening party, the thoughts behind and the liveliness of the words, and the feeling when the auras of the speaker and listener intermingle – p.602.

[2] When a developed person speaks, the voice, powered by the emotion, feels friendly. However, when a negative and undeveloped person speaks, it sounds very unfriendly – p.503[N3].

[3] In Sanskrit, the sound pattern of the word closely resembles and supports the meaning of the word – p.600. The vowel sound contains the real life giving power – p.607[4]. By using different literary devices such as rhyme, meter, alliteration, and assonance, the sounds and the meaning of the words are in harmony, creating the music of poetry – p.600.

NOTE 1: As the speaker's voice draws a vibration from the physical body, so does a string of a violin draw from its body – p.600.

NOTE 2: The Hebrew alphabet contains 22 letters; the Roman alphabet 26 letters – p.644[N] – 607[4].

NOTE 3: Stage fright is caused by the sudden impact of everyone's eye beams carrying various thoughts – p.602 – 432.

NOTE 4: Individuals whom center too much on their personality are usually self-conscious and shy – p.692[b] – 74 – 555[N6] – 431[2].

NOTE 5: Some individuals believe that through sleep osmosis, the material of a book can be absorbed by putting it under a pillow – p.437[R].

which can penetrate and even explode deeply in the receptive human spirit. Albeit, the words can also be charged with additional divine energy from an evolved being – p.602 – 603.

Great writers become well-known because they express things that people feel in their heart, and their writings have remained popular because they strike a chord in the person's inner beings. Inspired writers tell that they often become a channel through which their Christ Spirit or divine talent flow – p.601. Some people become so involved while they read that they lose connection with reality. At those times, they may, at times, bond with the spirit of the author and also with the thought forms of people and things the author has created – p.601.

As the second energy center is involved in the physical creation, the fifth center is involved in the spiritual creation by the Word – p.535[N1]. The Word of God is a symbol, vehicle, or token and represents the living reality. It is the Spirit of God, His Essence, which has its being in and behind those words and becomes the living Word – p.603.

The Psychic Environment, Shrines and Sanctuaries

As we can speak of physical pollution, we can also speak of psychic pollution, when the [1]air around us (Eph. 2:2) is saturated with low psychic vibration, which is not only created by the feeling and thinking of earthly people of low character but also by evil spirits. Anyone who walks through those surroundings, which may be [2]low neighborhoods or gambling environments, are [3]more or less contaminated. They feel more insecure and materialistic and are more affected by the vibration of fear. Upon return to their normal surroundings, they should cleanse themselves – p.416 – 162* - 310[2].

When staying in a hotel room which has been occupied by people whom are more evil than good, it can be very objectionable, especially for those whom are living a divine life. Through the use of the [4]bedding and sleeping on the same pillow as the former occupant, it may also be the cause of unpleasant dreams. It is therefore good to purify the room you are staying in by sprinkling water and salt which you have blessed – p.228[R] – 439.

On the other hand, when visiting holy sites and shrines which have accumulated prayer energy and devotional feelings, visitors feel uplifted when

---

[1] Air here is meant to be a container of psychic vibration.

[2] Cities usually have a lower psychic atmosphere than villages – p.385[2].

[3] People whom are sensitive absorb more of the psychic pollutants and are thus more affected by it. They soon start to feel and think like the people living there.

[4] The bed we sleep in is comfortable to us and is saturated with the vibration of our aura. The same is also true of the favorite toy or blanket of a child who feels recharged by its own energy, by holding it or snuggling with it – p.439.

they enter those places and buildings. The feelings of devotion and awe exude from the walls of those shrines, cathedrals, and churches of those [1]who built them, and of all the people who have visited and worshipped in those places – p.736[N2] – 228[*].

Some locations on the planet are more charged with magnetic and psychic energy than others. They are more conducive for individuals, whom visit those places, to become more psychic, such as the dry electric atmosphere of California and the energy vortices of Sedona, Arizona, which increase one's vibration rate and thus amplify a person's psychic energy. Delphi in Greece is known to be a place that produces a high quantity of negative ions. Those people who stay in those areas become more psychic than they normally are. Phases of the moon, sunspot radiation, and other disturbances of the earth's magnetic field influence the electromagnetic force field around human bodies, which in turn affect their etheric aura, which has an impact on the nervous system and aura of the human spirit – p.430.

Regarding the place of prayer or meditation, you need no special place; conversing with God can be done everywhere. However, a place, *sanctuary, or chapel where you can become quiet, calm, and still, and feel a sense of serenity is helpful. Look for a place which is as secluded and tranquil as possible so that the still voice of God is not drowned out – p.735.

Communication with the Invisible World Is Being Restored

Since the [2]fall, the descendants of the primal pair began increasingly living with the awareness of the physical aspect of life. As a result, their personalities became coarser (in vibration), and the psychic senses of their human spirits began to atrophy. The result is that most of them lost much of

---

[1] Every part of the temple of Solomon was prepared at a distance from the site and put in place without sound (unharmonious vibration) of hammer or any tool (1 Kings 6:7) – p.239.

NOTE 1: Money which we have to handle is usually charged with unpleasant magnetism, and so are eating utensils in restaurants – p.228[R].

NOTE 2: An object which has been in close contact with an individual will absorb that individual's magnetism and will tend to reproduce in the other person who touches or wears it, the same state of feeling and thought with which it is charged – p.228[*] - 433[2].

NOTE 3: It is not advisable to sit or be in the same place as a person(s) of a lower vibration has been dwelling – p.595[N11].

* Some people like to enhance their prayer and meditation room with things that call all their senses and imaginations to a lofty and exalted state. An altar can be used as the center of focus, whereupon can be placed a candle, flowers, pictures, or statues of Christ and saints (whose qualities you admire), holy books, and incense. Sacred or inspirational music can be played. By praying and meditating very often in that room, the (new) furniture and the walls absorb and become impregnated with the higher vibrations of your praying consciousness and that of others. It will retain and radiate those vibrations to anyone who will enter your shrine and elevate them mentally and spiritually without any effort on your and their part – p.735.

[2] Through the fall, higher psychism was cut off and lower psychism came into being, such as sorcery, wizardry, augury, soothsaying, witchcraft, and lower mediumship – p.286[N]; also, black magic and the black arts – p.350 – 430[1] – 475.

their sensitivity towards the psychic world and had no longer a viable relationship with their own psychic selves – p.35 – 293 – 294.

Those who did communicate in Old Testament times could only make contact with spirits of the lower realm, including evil spirits and fallen angels or demons. The Israelites were warned in Deut. 18:9-14 not to communicate with the dead through them. Besides, most of the dead were spirits of those people through which the Lord God wanted to separate His people from – p.672^N – 672 – 36.

^{1}The first Christians, however, accepted psychic communication to "test the spirits to see whether they are of God" (1 Jn. 4:1) – p.424. They attracted those entities that were at the same spiritual level – p.424^{N1}. The early Christians were well aware of the fact that by cultivating a spiritual life, they also awaken and enhance their dormant psychic and spiritual senses and their abilities – p.423. In the New Testament era, people in general and disciples of Christ, in particular, were more developed and alive. They used their higher energy centers to make contact with other divine beings – p.672^N.

People of the (early) Middle Ages were enchanted and fascinated by the world wherein they were living. Being sensitive, they perceived the world around them not as materialistic, dull, and gloomy but vivid, bright, radiant, and populated with all kinds of psychic and spiritual beings with whom they try to communicate – p.192^2 – 325. Because of the weakening of Christianity, the revival of paganism and the belief in witchcraft came about – p.192 – 424^{N1} – 192^1. After the papal bull was issued in 1484, the witch hunt began in earnest and became more intense than before. Not only the guilty but also many innocent people were tortured and burned alive. The killing of heretics continued by superstitious and self-righteous Catholics and religious reformers alike well into the seventeenth century. By the end of the century, a reaction came about and many people shifted to the other extreme by rejecting almost any thought and belief about the devil, evil and good spirits. At the time of the enlightenment (18th century), most people began to put more of their faith in reason and science instead of dogma. They became more materialistic in their thinking, which resulted that their psychic senses became much duller and were thus hardly aware of any evil or good spirits. However, this materialistic movement was somewhat delayed by Christian revivals and the revitalization of spiritualism in the nineteenth century – p.193 – 193^2 – 550^{N7} – 231 – 231^2 – 325.

---

^{1} Through their spiritual birth, not only the senses of their budding Divine Spirits are opened to a certain extent but also the psychic faculties of their human spirits – p.671 – 231^N. The personalities of the Christians, whom were born of God, experience the sense of eternity because they were closely associated with their Divine Spirits or Souls, which are like God, eternal and fully alive – p.35.

The more mature in Christ are able to distinguish between good and evil and are not afraid to make contact with spirits of the lower heaven, and are in continuing communication with spirits of the higher heaven – p.681. They do not fear death and have an intuitive knowledge that consciousness continues – p.425^1. Through the intuitive faculties of their Divine Spirits, they are able to communicate with the Spirit of God, Jesus Christ, and other celestial beings – p.671 – 672.

Having learned from the past, people of the twenty-first century should not make or repeat the same mistakes our forebears made. They should have [1]adequate and correct knowledge about life after death. They ought to be on guard and know how to distinguish between good and evil spirits, so that religious people would no longer put innocent people to death because they heard "voices" from deceased good people and saints. This is well documented in the story of Jeanne D'Arc (1412-1431), the maid of Orleans, France, who was burned alive – p.194.

Unfortunately, many fundamental Christians of today go to the extreme and believe that [2]all psychic and spiritual encounters are caused by demons, deceptive spirits, and satan and should be avoided; including Christian spirits and deceased family members whom desperately try to make contact with them – p.424[1] – 424 – 672. Many parents and educators are much influenced by the so-called experts who deal with the narrow field of behavior observation. When their children or pupils show any signs of psychic ability, they quickly tell them that such perception is not real and merely a product of their imagination. The result of this advice is that *the child closes down his/her psychic senses and abilities, which then atrophies – p.453[R] – 509[2] – 433[R] – 230 – 231.

NOTE 1: As each Old Testament prophet demonstrated one or more psychic abilities, Jesus of Nazareth was in possession of all those and more – p.474 – 475.

NOTE 2: As the physical body is merely a cloak or overcoat, spacesuit, soil, or vehicle for the inner spirit to grow and to experience life on the physical plane, the human spirit, in turn, serves as a vehicle for the Divine Spirit. Thus, we are already in possession of our more or less developed survival equipment to exist in the invisible dimension of life – p.304 – 234[N] - 696[†].

NOTE 3: How spirits can be of service in the spirit world and by helping the people on earth – p.358 – 358[2] – 212 – 221. How spirits can grow – p.358 – 359 – 358[4].

NOTE 4: Spirits get their energy through breathing from their surrounding psychic atmosphere – p.359[*] - 464. They cannot be damaged or destroyed and create their

---

[1] Because they have not prepared themselves for the ultimate journey, there remains deep within them a dread of death and a fear of the unknown. They should read and know as much as possible about the place they are going to, like one may read about a foreign country before visiting it – p.425[1].

[2] Those whom do not lead a moral life should not communicate with the unseen world because they will only attract evil spirits and demons – p.41[c].

In their fascination with the unknown, humans get easily trapped because they are not always able to distinguish between good and evil forces and may easily be led astray.

Although it is possible to make contact with loved ones, it is also possible, when not strong in faith, to be influenced by undesirable entities. In that case, it is better to communicate with spiritual beings and saints of the divine world, whom will inspire and guide you to grow spiritually – p.697.

On the other hand, psychic ability has its place when you can help someone with your psychic insight or be sensitive to the needs of others – p.430[1].

* In the near future when humans are born in a normal way (without original sin or separation from God), the psychic senses of their human spirits will begin to open from childhood – p-.671[*].

clothes and homes by thought power – p.359* - 463 – 464 – 458. In the fourth dimension, there is no earthly time, as time is associated with the cyclic movement of planetary bodies – p.596³.

It is not possible for the spirit to go to a higher level because there is a natural boundary – p.460 – 359 – 327ᴺ – 592.

NOTE 5: Those whom were physically blind and deaf can see and hear, while those whom have lost their physical limbs function as whole persons in the spirit world – p.463*.

Some people find great satisfaction in discovering and exploring not only the world of spirits but also the higher divine world. Knowing that you live in three worlds, living has become very interesting and exciting. You are filled with wonder, and there is so much to discover and so much to learn. You are no longer vague but more aware of the psychic world and the divine world you experience as a new reality – p.395 – 696.

You will also understand much better, for example: possession and exorcism – p.180 – 180³ – 230 – 181ᴺ – 451 – 696 – 351 --- p.696 – 351 – 453 – 475; reincarnation, which is a form of obsession – p.696 – 219→222 – 17; cases of schizophrenia – p.697 – 180³ – 453 – 351; mental illness – p.452 – 453 – 351; lunatics – madmen – p.351; insanity – p.439²; manic depression – p.180³ – 351 – 453; hysteria – p.180³ – 453; epilepsy – p.453; multiple personality disorder – p.183³; dissociate personality disorder – p.453; telepathy – p.697 – 226 – 231 – 231³ – 431³ – 431 – 432 – 20 – 60 – 591; hearing voices – p.697 – 194; déjà vu (already seen) – p.697 – 435; astral and mental projection – p.697 – 230 – 229 – 434 – 428ᴺ¹ – 61; remote viewing – p.697; automatic writing – p.697 – 229 – 424; Ouija boards – planchette – p.424; hauntings – p.697 – 451 – 351; psycho-kinesis – p.697 – 226 – 227 – 434ᴺ⁶; near-death experiences – p.697 – 449 – 449¹ – 450; different forms of mediumship or channeling – p.697 – 225 – 225ᴺ – 225² – 350 – 423 – 423¹ – 424ᴿ – 192 – 230 – 475; clairvoyance – p.224 – 529ᴺ⁴ – 536 – 537 – 591; clairaudience – p.223 – 529ᴺ⁴ – 534 – 537 – 591; clairsentience – p.225 – 226ᴿ – 432 – 433 – 529ᴺ⁴; clairscent – p.226; clairgustance – p.226; discrimination – p.226; aura reading – p.230; psychometry – p.227 – 228- 144 – 144ᶜ – 529ᴺ⁴ – 591; levitation – p.229 – 475 – 591ᴺ³ – 654; teleportation – p.229; healing – p.230 – 475 – 431 – 423 – 536; description of the psychic and spiritual senses – p.223→237; differences of the psychic and spiritual faculties – p.233 – 234; awakening of the psychic senses – p.230 – 231 – 231ᴺ – 430 – 24; earthbound spirits – p.168 – 222ᴿ – 225 – 232 – 232ᴺ – 233ᴺ – 351 – 424 – 450 – 450² – 451 – 451³ – 451ᴺ – 452 – 452ᴺ² – 452⁵ – 462 – 539; resurrection – p.464→467 – 422¹ – 244*; judgment – p.465 – 466* - 406 – 791⁷ – 425; melding – p.460 – 460² – 61 – 61*; sleep and dreams – p.435→442; dream of Abraham Lincoln – p.441; dreaming – p.223* - 230ᴺ – 228ᴿ; daydreaming – p.230ᴺ – 430¹ – 437; lucid dreaming – p.229 – 438ᴺ¹; sleep – p.316 – 683ᵇ – 198 – 437ᴿ – 593ᴺ² – 705#⁷ – 420ᴿ¹; fantasies and imaginations – p.430¹ – 20 – 20ᵃ – 231 – 230ᴺ; multiply matter – p.475; psychic defense and attack – p.433² – 424³ – 351 – 230ᴺ; making seeing eyes blind – p.434ᴺ⁵; spells – p.230ᴺ – 351; curse – p.230ᴺ – 351; gambling – p.434ᴺ⁶; independent voice – p.230ᴺ; death and birth sciences – p.230ᴺ; divination – p.230ᴺ; scrying – p.230ᴺ; hypnotism – p.230ᴺ – 221; eyeless sight – p.230ᴺ; percussion – p.230ᴺ;

biofeedback – p.230[N]; talisman – p.230[N]; visualization – p.230[N]; hallucination – p.230[N]; become unconscious; fever; fainting spells; mental shock; sudden fright – p.436[1]; spiritual gifts – p.237; science of eugenics – p.65; euthanasia – p.256; abortion – p.256; cremation – p.427[2].

Many *older people have never been told by their religions what kind of life they are going to live in the afterlife. They have formed different beliefs of what it is like – p.374 – 425. However, Paul wants us to know about life after death (1 Thess. 4:13) – p.672[N]. For those whom are spiritually developed, the fear of death is already overcome – p.573[2] – 573. Although the earth is a beautiful place, a more magnificent abode is waiting for us in paradise – p.757 (the summer land of the spiritualists – p.461). When the Soul's task has been fulfilled, or no further gains can be made (through the use of the physical vehicle which has become old and decrepit), the Soul will release its hold on the physical life – p.426 – 426[4]. People whom have died do not have to wait countless years for the Day of Judgment. Jesus spoke of an ongoing life at the time of death in the story of the rich man and Lazarus (Lk. 16:22-24) – p.359. Jesus promised paradise immediately in Luke 23:43. There is, however, a review and transfer of the life lived, whereby the soul judges itself – p.466*.

---

* Our human spirit survives physical death and one's intellect is part of its being. Thus, to acquire intellectual knowledge or develop a talent late in physical life will be very useful, not only for the development of the human spirit but also of its use in the afterlife – p.394.

The place where you are going is the moral and spiritual growth you have attained while living on earth – p.466*. You are drawn towards that part of the spirit world in which you feel comfortable. This may be a higher or lower sphere of vibration in which your spirit body can resonate or be in tune with – p.358[1].

NOTE: As the Protestant faith believes in the existence of heaven and hell, the Catholics also believe in purgatory, wherein the lesser sinners could "burn out" their evil desires, pay their debt and pass to heaven – p.426[3] – 556 – 462 – 466* - 465[3].

Believe in heaven and hell – p.465[3] – 543[N4] – 293 – 556 – 463 – 463[6] – 466* - 350 – 360 – 539 – 540 – 673.

Doctrine of eternal punishment – p.426 – 426[3] – 219* – 406 – 274.

There is not a literal eternal fire or hell – p.406 – 465[3].

We create our own heaven and hell not as places of reward or punishment but as states of consciousness – p.466* - 461[3] – 293.

The Hebrews of pre-mosaic times believed that the soul after death would live in Sheol, which was dim and shadowy, with hardly any conscious life – p.421 – 463 – 465 – 465[3].

The Teutonic (Northern European people) go to "Valhalla" when they died fighting; while North American Indians would go to the happy hunting grounds. The ancient Greeks believed that they were sentenced to the "Elysium fields" after crossing the River Styx – p.421.

The Aura

The aura is an energy field that surrounds all matter because particles of atoms are in constant movement by radiating their electrical and magnetic vibration. This is especially true of animate forms because the atoms are more vibrant than those of inanimate matter. They physical body has an aura, which is composed of energy fields, such as electromagnetic, heat, and sound waves and other emanations – p.653 – 447^N – 442 – 443 – 656^A – 592 – 453 – 554. The personality of an ordinary human being consists of the physical/etheric, emotional, and intellectual aspects. The physical self is surrounded by an etheric aura which follows the contour of the body – p.652, and extends between two to four inches beyond the skin of the body and can be observed – p.656. The second aura which is influenced by basic emotions is wider as the former and is usually dull in color, while the third aura, which is formed by the radiations of the higher emotions and intellect, assumes more the oval shape and is more radiant – p.620 – 652 – 520. The aura for a spiritually evolved person projects much further and is clear and bright – p.652 – 594^{N4} – 446* - 520 – 521. They are surrounded by an areola of luminous golden (psychic) colors and are centered on the head as a halo, or nimbus. It has been seen around spiritual masters, mystics, and saints, in all cultures and civilizations – p.652 – 719 – 687 – 124^a – 581. Thus, the size, colors, brightness, and dullness of the colors reveal, in a truthful way, one's physical, emotional, mental, and spiritual well-being – p-.652. The basic psychic colors and size of one's aura may remain practically the same for some time because it is what one is and what one has become. However, the movements and variations of the aura's size and colors may change many times a day, depending on the moods and thoughts of the person. A burst of *anger or lustful desire, for example, may temporarily change the aura to murky crimson and scarlet colors. The aura will change more easily when we again yield to the same emotion. When, however, those outbursts of emotions become habitual, the aura will crystallize and, thus, it will be more difficult to change – p.652 – 653 – 125^N – 505^{N4}.

Through prayer and meditation, we come in touch with our Divine Spirits, thus lifting our awareness or consciousness out of the limited focus of the

---

* By being angry, serious damage can be done to the aura of the spirit body of the other person (especially to the emotional envelope or sheath, and the karmic price has to be paid (Matt. 5:22) – p.686 – 686*.

NOTE 1: As there are different auras around a human being, each extending beyond the smaller, so there are concentric zones around the earth which comprise the different levels of the spirit world with the highest encompassing all the lower zones. Those zones not only interpenetrate the earth but extend from the earth surface miles upward – p.232 – 454.

NOTE 2: The entities of the spirit planes are not fully aware of physical matter but are conscious of the densest psychic matter which surrounds and outlines all the physical objects and physical bodies of the people of the earth. Spirits see the changing colors and expansion or contraction of auras of human beings. The latter can therefore not hide their feelings and attitudes from someone of the spirit world (or earth) very well, who is able to observe their auras, and is able to interpret them – p.459 – 459^3.

personality. It further produces a brightening of the aura, which radiates from the personality – p.751 – 719. The luminosity that is present in your aura will attract many high spirits with or without bodies – p.734[1]. In order to protect themselves, many individuals immerse themselves in spiritual music and devotional songs, whereby the aura of their inner being will become bigger, stronger, and brighter. As a result, the aura will not be pierced and open to psychic invasion. When their aura is filled with love, the sword of hate is barred entrance and will return to the sender, and their love will eventually dispel the force of hate – p.200[N].

[1]When we meet people, we may more or less like them when our auras are in resonance with all or some levels of their being, or not like them when the vibrations of their auras are not like our own – p.652. [2]By having a close encounter with another person or group of people, you and their auric fields will usually interact (unless you shield yourself), and you may feel uncomfortable or an instant dislike with the vibratory wavelength of their auras. On the other hand, you may feel comfortable or "hit it off" with that particular person or group – p.433[2] – 593 – 593[3] – 594[N2].

Romantic love begins with a physical attraction to a member of the opposite sex. When the auras mingle, they may like or dislike each other, depending on their basic energy or vibration pattern. A few of them may feel such a perfect blending of their auras or interaction of their vibratory fields that they experience love at first sight – p.488.

The aura of a developed person can be felt over a distance of many feet, even when they are separated by a wall. But the aura is hardly noticeable when the other person goes to sleep, when [3]the spirit separates from the body and goes elsewhere. This is an indication that the field of energy comes from the spirit and, thus, only operates when the spirit is present. As the saying goes, "He/she lights up the room when he/she walks in – p.446* - 433[2].

Paths to God

There are many individual paths towards God, such as: be joyful and make people happy, and love them unconditionally; sing uplifting songs and dance in harmony with the creation; listen to and play high vibration music to

---

[1] The ones with whom we frequently are in contact with, at our work and place we live, influence us profoundly through the vibrations of their etheric, psychic, and spiritual bodies, and the radiation – projecting wavelength – of their auras. Apostle Paul warned believers not to have fellowship with sinners (1 Cor. 5:11, 13) – p.57. By touching each other, there is not only a sensation of touch but also a bio-magnetic exchange takes place, and an intermingling of their auras which can be in harmony or disharmony. High caste Hindus do not allow themselves to be touched or shake hands in order to avoid psychic contamination, especially not with low caste people, the so-called untouchables – p.57 – 57[b].

[2] By tuning in to the other's wavelength, much information about that individual can be obtained – p.433[2] – 431[1] – 228[N].

[3] When a person dies, life goes out of the person, the eyes are lifeless and need to be closed, and the psychic aura is no longer seen around a dead person when the spirit leaves the person – p.446.

awaken the divine Spark within; appreciate noble art, and seek for its beauty, truth, and harmony; pray and read words of Truth; see good movies, read inspiring poetry and books, and try to understand the inner meaning; reflect on the beauty of nature, and all of life that God our Parents have created; be thankful of what we are and have become, and have an attitude of gratitude and gratefulness; think about the well-being and look for the good in others, and forgive them; witness to the Divine Truth, and have a sense of God-like humor; seek for Truth and Beauty within and without yourselves, and try to connect with your divine Self, and those Selves of people you meet – p.20 – 21 – 22^b – 521^1 – 594^4.

Hindu philosophy teaches that there are four main paths or union (yoga) to the divine – p.366^N – 91*:
Raja yoga – through the mind and will – p.535
Bhakti yoga – through personal devotion – p.534
Jnana yoga – through knowledge and insight – p.537
Karma yoga – through good works – the way towards union through service – p.531

Distortion of messages – p.787 – 602

Problem of evil – p.220^3

Predictions

For many people, life is going down the river where the scenery and signs are continually changing. Of those who have developed their psychic and spiritual vision, they can see far ahead or from above and are aware that they will encounter, along the way, some rapids and rough water – p.414^R – 415^R. We may also compare our three-dimensional life with a caterpillar, which is only able to see and experience its immediate area on which it crawls, but when it changes to a butterfly and starts living a four-dimensional and spiritual life, it sees much more, and its view of life is much different. Events are no longer unrelated, and it is easier to see ahead and predict the future and also understand much better, in all its dimensions, the purpose of life – p.456^{N3}. Thus, through *higher clairvoyance, the people whom are living a divine or spiritual life are able to know events far in the future, have vision, illuminations, and other mystical experiences.

On October 27, 312 A.D., Constantine had a dream wherein he was shown the first two Greek letters of the name Christ and a message in Latin: "By this sign you shall be victor." The next day, that sign was painted on the shield of every person in Constantine's army. On October 28, they won the battle of

---

* The lower clairvoyance is expressed as a premonition. Some individuals say, "My instinct tells me that something is going to happen today." Others may have a dream about some person, place, or event, which they encounter at a later time. We may contact our subconscious mind through the use of the pendulum and divining rods and hypnosis to retrieve long-lost information – p.383 – 440^{N2} – 340^{N2} – 383 – 221^R. The instruments can also be used in dowsing – to find coins, water, oil, etc. – p.655. Tarot cards can also be used to know about yourself and others, their lives and futures – p.460 – 644^N.

Milvian Bridge, against overwhelming odds. Thereafter, Constantine accepted Christ and became the first Christian emperor of Rome – p.585.

Abraham Lincoln, who was much worried in April 1865 about the Civil War, went to bed and fell asleep. He had a strange dream that people were paying their last respects to the body laid in state in the East Room of the White House. Two days later on April 14, the dream became a reality. Lincoln was shot in a theater.

After the Israelites left Egypt and arrived at Mount Sinai, God tried to speak to them by external means, through thunder, lightning, and the sound of the trumpet. However, the people were afraid and said to Moses, "You speak to us, and we will hear; but let not God speak to us, lest we die" (Ex. 20:19; Deut. 18:16). In response to the plea of the people, God then used prophets, whereby one person would receive the Word of God (from within) and then mediate it to the people – p.781. To the prophets Aaron and Miriam God said, "I the Lord make myself known to him (prophet) in a vision, I speak with him in a dream" (Num. 12:6) – p.781; and "Let the prophet who has a dream tell the dream" (Jer. 23:28) – p.440. On the other hand, [1]false prophets "speak visions of their own minds, not from the mouth of the Lord" (Jer. 23:16; Deut. 13:15) – p.781. God said to Moses, "You shall not add to the word which I command you, nor take from it" (Deut. 4:2; Rev. 22:18-19). "And if you say in your heart, 'how may we know the word which the Lord has not spoken?' When a prophet speaks in the name of the Lord, if the word does [2]not come to pass or come true, that is a word which the Lord has not spoken" (Deut. 18:21-22) – p.782. Peter said, "No prophecy ever came by the impulse of man, but men moved by the Holy Spirit spoke from God" (II Pet. 1:21). Thus, fulfilled prophecy gives conclusive affirmation that the Bible is inspired by God – p.782[N].

Examples of fulfilled prophecy: In Genesis 28:12-15, [3]Jacob had a dream of a ladder going up to heaven and received the promise that his descendants

---

[1] In Acts 13:6-11, Paul is encountering the false prophet Bar-Jesus, but in the same book we are told of a good prophet Agabus who accurately predicts a famine (Acts 11:28) – p.425[N2]. In 1 Cor. Ch. 14, Paul believes that prophecy was the best spiritual gift, more so than the one who speaks in a tongue – p.237. Apostle Paul did not issue commands on every subject, but when he was moved to give commands, he did so in the name of our Lord Jesus Christ (2 Thess. 3:6, 12). He said "to the married I give charge, not I but the Lord" (1 Cor. 7:10), and again in (1 Cor. 14:37), "What I am writing to you is a command of the Lord" – p.784.

[2] When the prediction is of God, it will come to pass at the time it is received, but when the people change or repent, it will not happen. Some individuals like Jonah (3:10) might be very disappointed.

[3] Joseph the son of Jacob used a silver cup from which he prophesized (Gen. 44:4-5; Ex. 28-30) – p.232. Joseph received the prophetic dream of his brother's sheaves of wheat bowing down to his sheaf, and another dream that the sun, moon, and eleven stars bowed down to him (Gen. 37:5-11; 42:6). Another prophetic dream was told to Pharaoh that the fat ears of corn were consumed by lean ones and that fat cows were being eaten by thin ones. This dream was interpreted by Joseph (Gen. Ch. 41) as he interpreted the dreams of the butler and chief baker (Gen. Ch. 40) – p.440 – 624 – 625 – 611 – 612.

would be blessed and would return to the land – p.440 – 611[7] – 623[3]. Jacob predicted on his death bed the future vicissitudes of all of his sons (Gen. Ch. 49) – p.236. Nahum 2:4 predicted that in the future "the chariots (automobile – p.324[N1] – 548[N]) rage in the streets; they rush to and fro through the squares; they gleam like torches, they dart like lightning" – p.236.

NOTE: The Bible is also the book that foretold the rise and fall of nations. For example, in a vision, Daniel saw a he-goat strike down a ram, breaking its two horns (Dan. 8:1-22). About two centuries later, "the king of Greece" Alexander the Great (the he-goat) conquered the two-horned medio-Persian empire – p.782 – 783.

After Solomon began to worship other gods, and as predicted in 1 Kings 9:3, 6-8 – p.240, his kingdom was taken away from him and became divided into the northern kingdom of Israel and the southern kingdom Judah – p.628 – 814. The northern kingdom was judged by Amos 7:1 – 9:10 and invaded by Assyria, and the southern kingdom was invaded and in exile in Babylon for seventy years as predicted by Jeremiah (Jer. 25:11) – p.645 – 816 – 241 – 614. Daniel interpreted a dream of Nebuchadnezzar who saw a great human image, which parts represented different and succeeding worldly kingdoms but was smashed by a big stone, which became a great mountain and filled the whole earth, which represented the Kingdom of God (Dan. Ch. 1, 2). Thereafter, Belshazzar lost the kingdom to Darius the king of the Medes and Persians, which was foretold by the writings on the wall of his palace (Dan. Ch. 5) – p.614.

Isaiah 7:14 prophesied the birth of Jesus Christ, which was fulfilled in Matthew 1:18-23 – p.236, and every aspect of his life was foretold (see list on p.783). In Joel 2:28, it is prophesized the promise of the Spirit of God to pour upon all flesh, which happened at the [1]day of Pentecost (Acts 2:1; 2:16-18) – p.236. Jesus prophesized very accurately in Luke 21:20-24 the destruction of Jerusalem by the Romans in 70 A.D., and its total destruction in 132 A.D. – p.236 – 474 – 245[R] – 244. He directed his followers to a spot where a fish would be caught, which carried a coin of sufficient value to pay for the tax (Matt. 17:24-27). In Luke 19:29-34, Jesus sent his disciples to get a donkey, predicting the very words that the owner of the donkey would use – p.475. Jesus foresaw the ones who would betray and deny him, predicted his own death, and [2]in what manner he would return (Lk. 18:33; 24:7) – p.474.

---

[1] At the day of Pentecost, 120 people were filled with the Holy Spirit (Acts 2:1-4). They will "have the right to the Tree of Life" (Rev. 22:14), "Eat of the Tree of Life (Rev. 2:7), and become the Tree of Life, after they washed "their robes" of their personality (Rev. 22:14) physical – emotional – mental sheaths and their emanations; then they enter the city (Garden of Eden) through their particular gate – p.44 – 68 – 803[N4]. The deeds of the divine selves are like fine linen (Rev. 19:8; 7:14; 7:9), and deeds of evil selves are like filthy rags (Isa. 64:6).

[2] Jesus predicted that he will be three days in the heart of the earth (Matt. 12:40) and that he will raise up his temple (body) – Jn. 2:19-21. Concerning his coming again in a different body, he said, "You will not have gone through all the towns of Israel, before the Son of Man comes (Matt. 10:23); "Truly I say to you, there are some standing here, who will not taste death before they see the Son of Man coming in his Kingdom" (Matt. 16:28). Those verses were fulfilled when Jesus came back for forty days in his materialized etheric body – see p.468→474.

The Book of Revelation is addressed directly through Jesus Christ by an angel to [1]John and to the seven churches in Asia Minor (p.632→634) and to true Christians and churches, to encourage them because they are and will be oppressed and harassed like their master. However, those revelations were also given for reforming those seven churches (and others) – p.631 – 631[N]. The Book of Revelation is a further explanation of the prophecy which Jesus gave in Matthew 24, Mark 13, and Luke 21 of things to come. The opening of the [2]seven seals parallels the events in the Gospels: 1) false prophets, 2) great wars, 3) famine, 4) pestilence, 5) great tribulation, 6) heavenly signs, and 7)Second Coming. This includes the [3]seven bowls of wrath which are poured out on those "who bore [4]the mark of the beast and worshipped its image" (Rev. Ch. 16; 16:2; 13:16-18; 14:9; 17:8; 9:4. However, before this event, an angel appeared and said, "Do not harm the earth or the sea or the trees, [5]till we have sealed the servants of our God upon their foreheads", and I heard the number of the sealed, a hundred forty-four thousand (Rev. Ch. 7; 14:1) – p.632[N] – 642[N1].

The serpent of Genesis who tempted Eve is identified with satan in Rev. 12:9; 20:2: "And the great dragon was thrown down that [6]ancient serpent, who is called the devil and satan" --- "He was thrown down to the earth (the good/evil world – p.101 – 102) and his angels were thrown down with him." "His tail swept down a third of the stars of heaven" (Rev. 12:4) – one third of the world population. "The dragon stood before the woman who was about to bear a child --- she brought forth a male child, one who is to rule all the na-

---

[1] Before John died, Jesus appeared to him at the island of Patmos, as he said he would (Jn. 21:22).

[2] Some esoterists say that all sacred writings are sealed with seven seals, which in stages will uncover the mysteries of the seven planes. Thus, it requires seven complete interpretations to understand fully the meaning of the Book of Revelation (Ch. 5-8). The latter can be compared to the seven energy centers of humans – p.525→537 – 517 – 700, which open and reveal one's consciousness to oneself – p.802[N2] – 525 – 583[N2]. By the opening of the first seal (Rev. 6:1), a white horse and its rider with a bow but no arrows appeared. Some people say that the rider was spreading anti-biblical thoughts, using the horse (science and other means) as its vehicle – p.632[N3].

[3] The bowls of wrath are much like that of the ten plagues that came upon the Egyptians (Ex. Ch. 7-11).

[4] They are those in whom the evil self is in charge of their lives – at the individual, tribal, and government levels.

[5] At the time of the exodus, the Israelites put blood on the two doorposts and lintel of the house (God-centered relationship) so that the plague will pass over – Ex. Ch. 12. The 144,000 (and more) who had his name and his father's name on their foreheads were sealed (being initiated) and have overcome the fight within themselves, between the evil self and the emerging Divine Spirit – the great and last battle of Armageddon at the microcosmic level (Rev. 16:16).

[6] The serpent symbolizes, together with the great red dragon (Rev. 12:3), the instinctive primitive forces and the uncontrolled lower desires of sentient beings. The dragon is a ravenous, frightful, powerful, fire-breathing monster. It has wings, indicating that it also has a psychic dimension – p.178.

tions with a rod of [1]iron (Rev. 12:4-5). The dragon "went off to make war on the rest of her offspring" (Rev. 12:17); and gave power to the [2]beast who rose out of the sea (sinful or impure people – Rev. 17:15) and "another [3]beast which rose out of the earth; it had two horns like a lamb and it spoke like a dragon" (Rev. 13:11).

As many Christians were anxiously awaiting the physical return (or spiritual – Acts 1:11) of Jesus Christ, others whom were more esoterically minded saw the Second Coming of Christ not as an occurrence outside of themselves but within – "every eye will see him" (Rev. 1:7), when He returns as the Universal Christ to those whom are pure ([4]as the clouds) and to find a livable place in the hearts of the believers (Rev. 21:3) – p.585.

Those whom have experienced a rebirth receive a new nature (Eph. 4:24), which is called by its "new name", which is written on a "white stone" (divine Spirit), "which no one knows except him who receives it" (Rev. 2:17). These names are also "written in the book of life" (Rev. 20:12, 15; 3:5) – p.691. To him who conquers says the Spirit, "I will give some of the hidden manna" (Truth – p.567 – 492[2]) – Rev. 2:17. "And I took the little scroll --- and ate it" (become part of one's being) and I was told "You must again prophesy about many peoples and nations and tongues and kings" (Rev. 10:10-11). The forty-four thousand who had been redeemed "sing a new song", which they only could learn. "Then I saw another angel flying in mid-heaven, with an eternal gospel to proclaim to those who dwell on earth, to every nation and tribe and tongue and people" (Rev. 14:6). "Then I saw a new heaven and a new earth; (under the complete sovereignty of God); for the first heaven and the first

---

[1] Aaron was in possession of a rod – Ex. 4:20 – 7:10; Num. Ch. 17; Heb. 9:4 – p.612 – 38. He who conquers shall rule the nations with a rod of iron – Rev. 2:27; 19:15. From his mouth issues a sharp (two-edged) sword (Rev. 1:16; 2:16) with which to smite the nations (Rev. 19:15). Jesus said, "I have not come to bring peace, but a sword" (Matt. 10:34). The word will also be a judge to nonbelievers who reject the Word of God (Isa. 11:4; Jn. 12:48) – p.791[7] – 669. In some passages of the Bible, fire has the meaning of the judgment by the Word (Jer. 5:14; 23:29; Lk. 12:49; II Thess. 2:8 – II Pet. 3:7) – p.406[R]. Jesus came to destroy the evil world with the tongue of his mouth (Jas. 3:6; Isa. 11:4) – p.648. The tongue is a fire (Jas. 3:6). Jesus will slay them with the breath of his mouth (Thess. 2:8).

[2] The beast is the evil self or evil part of our human personality (p.702), which is extended to organizations and governments. If the organization or government cannot maintain the moral and ethical standards of the people, the governing body is no longer fit to rule them – p.163.

[3] The second beast is not mentioned in Daniel – p.632[N5]. It probably represents religion or other organizations. It looks innocent as a lamb, but it has power (2 horns) and no crowns, and is also mentioned in Rev. 20:10 as the false prophet.

[4] Some people have dreams that they fall or swim in the water, while others experience life above the impure or good/evil waters in a purified state or clouds – p.406[R]. "Behold he is coming with the clouds" (Rev. 1:7; 14:15-16; Mk. 14:62; Matt. 26:64; Lk. 21-27; Dan. 7:13). Thus, he is with and comes with people whom have purified themselves from the waters (Rev. 17:15), whom are living a divine life.

NOTE: The symbolism in Revelation is of such a nature that it can apply to any generation, anyone, or anything.

earth had passed away" (Rev. 21:1). "And I saw the holy city New Jerusalem coming down out of heaven from God" (which is like the "Holy of Holies" of the wilderness tabernacle – Rev. Ch. 21-22; 3:12) – p.425[2]. And he who sat upon the throne said, "Behold, I make all things new" (a new Eden and its Shekenah glory) – Rev. 21:5).

"Then I saw heaven opened, and behold a white horse!" (no longer a donkey – Matt. Ch.2). He who sat upon it is called Faithful and True --- His eyes are like a flame of fire --- and he has a name inscribed which no one knows but himself --- and the name by which he is called is The Word of God (Rev. 19:11-16).

Jesus of Nazareth as the Son of Man became the anointed Son of God or Christ at the time of his baptism and was, thereafter, overshadowed with the Christ-Consciousness of God or the Son. (The only begotten Son, as there is one universal Adam, whose nature is described in Rev. 1:12-18; Dan. 10:4-9 – p.703 – 266.) Thus, the Son or the Universal Christ who always existed eternally with God (before Abraham – Jn. 8:58), united in one body with Christ Jesus – p.284, and together was the Savior or Redeemer (2 Cor. 5:19) – p.43 – 284. Having overcome all the temptation of the evil one, which the first Adam could not overcome, Jesus restored and inherited the position of Adam. The Universal or Cosmic Christ, "the Alpha and the Omega, who is and who was and who is to come" (Rev. 1:8), who died in the first Adam but became alive in the last Adam, anointed Jesus with His Spirit – p.266. "I am the first and the last, and the living one; I died, and behold I am alive forever more" (Rev. 1:17-18; 22:13).

The Holy Spirit is described in the Book of Revelation 19:7-9 as the bride of the Cosmic Christ, whom both will find their dwelling place in the restored Eve and Adam – p.267 (Rev. 21:9; 22:17; Matt. 22:2).

"For the marriage of the Lamb has come and His Bride has made herself ready" --- "Blessed are those who are invited to the marriage supper of the Lamb."